TYPES OF MANKIND:

OR,

ETHNOLOGICAL RESEARCHES,

BASED UPON THE

ANCIENT MONUMENTS, PAINTINGS, SCULPTURES, AND CRANIA OF RACES,

AND UPON THEIR

NATURAL GEOGRAPHICAL, PHILOLOGICAL, AND BIBLICAL HISTORY

TYPES OF MANKIND:

OR,

ETHNOLOGICAL RESEARCHES,

BASED UPON THE

ANCIENT MONUMENTS, PAINTINGS, SCULPTURES, AND CRANIA OF RACES,

AND UPON THEIR

NATURAL GEOGRAPHICAL, PHILOLOGICAL, AND BIBLICAL HISTORY

SAMUEL GEORGE MORTON,
J. C. NOTT
AND
GEO. R. GLIDDON

GYAN

Published by

Gyan Publishing House
5, Ansari Road
Daryaganj, New Delhi-110002
Phone: 011-47034999, 9811692060
E-mail: books@gyanbooks.com

Distribution Network
gyanbooks.com
India, USA, Canada, UK, Australia

ISBN: 978-93-6780-246-5 (HB)

First Published, 1854

2nd Impression 2024

Printed at: Gyan Press, Delhi.

TYPES OF MANKIND

Author: SAMUEL GEORGE MORTON , J. C. NOTT AND GEO. R. GLIDDON

TYPES OF MANKIND.

Samuel George Morton

TYPES OF MANKIND:

OR,

Ethnological Researches,

BASED UPON THE

ANCIENT MONUMENTS, PAINTINGS, SCULPTURES,
AND CRANIA OF RACES,

AND UPON THEIR

NATURAL, GEOGRAPHICAL, PHILOLOGICAL,
AND BIBLICAL HISTORY:

ILLUSTRATED BY SELECTIONS FROM THE INEDITED PAPERS OF

SAMUEL GEORGE MORTON, M.D.,
(LATE PRESIDENT OF THE ACADEMY OF NATURAL SCIENCES AT PHILADELPHIA,)

AND BY ADDITIONAL CONTRIBUTIONS FROM

PROF. L. AGASSIZ, LL.D.; W. USHER, M.D.; AND PROF. H. S. PATTERSON, M.D.:

BY

J. C. NOTT, M.D., AND GEO. R. GLIDDON,
MOBILE, ALABAMA, FORMERLY U. S. CONSUL AT CAIRO.

—"Words are things; and a small drop of ink,
Falling, like dew upon a thought, produces
That which makes thousands, perhaps millions, think."—BYRON

PHILADELPHIA:
LIPPINCOTT, GRAMBO & CO.
1854.

TO THE

MEMORY

OF

MORTON.

ANNOUNCEMENT.

On publishing a work calculated to attract notice in the scientific and literary world, it is due to the Authors, the Subscribers, and ourselves, to invite comparison between the proposals set forth in the *First Prospectus* [New Orleans, Dec., 1852], and their realization in the greatly-enlarged form in which "Types of Mankind" now issues from our hands.

In the first place, that monument, which Dr. Nott and Mr. Gliddon proposed jointly to erect to the memory of Samuel Geo. Morton, has become augmented by the contributions of Prof. Agassiz, Dr. Patterson, and Dr. Usher.

Secondly, in lieu of a book projected to contain printed matter equivalent to Vol. I. of the Smithsonian Institution, we have the satisfaction of presenting our Subscribers with more than double the typographical amount originally promised. "Above 200 woodcuts" were guaranteed: the number, herein furnished, runs up to Fig. 362. No lithographic Plates were contemplated in the first announcement, and but one Map. Of the former we now include five, whereof one is a colored Tableau; of the latter two, and both are tinted: at the same time that the Tables, &c., are abundantly increased in number and variety. Nor in the general execution, quality of paper, and minor details, has labor or outlay been spared to exceed every promise made, by the Authors or ourselves, from the commencement of this undertaking.

The whole of these *addenda* are placed before Subscribers at the original price of *Five Dollars* per copy; and it is owing to the unexampled and liberal support they have given to our enterprise that we are thus enabled to serve them without stint or loss.

In conformity with the *First Prospectus* the work is supplied "stitched, with an appropriate cover," to the Subscribers whose names are printed in the Alphabetical List: all extra-expenditure having been bestowed upon the *contents* of this volume rather than upon its envelope. Non-subscribers who may desire copies of the present edition can be supplied with *bound* volumes alone, and at Seven dollars and a half each.

LIPPINCOTT, GRAMBO & CO.,
Publishers.

PHILADELPHIA, February, 1854.

PREFACE.

BY GEO. R. GLIDDON.

"The subject of *Ethnology* I deem it expedient to postpone. On this I have collected a mass of new materials, which I hope in time to produce; but until they have been submitted to the masterly analysis of my honored friend, SAMUEL GEORGE MORTON, M. D., Philadelphia, a synopsis from my hands would be premature." *

LITTLE did I expect, while penning the above note, that, ere four years had run their course, it would fall to the lot of Dr. NOTT and myself to "close ranks" and partially fill the gap left in American *Ethnology* when the death-shot struck down our friend and leader. To him the "new materials" were submitted: by him they were analyzed with his customary acuteness; and from him would the world have received a series of works superseding the necessity for the present volume, together with any public action of my colleague and myself in that science so indelibly marked by MORTON as his own. The 15th of May, 1851, arrested his hand, and left us, with all who knew him, to sorrow at his loss: nor, for eleven months, did the endeavor to raise a literary monument to his memory suggest itself either to Dr. Nott or to myself.

"Types of Mankind" owes its origin to the following incidents:—After a gratifying winter at New Orleans, I visited Mobile in April, 1852; partly to deliver a course of Lectures upon "Babylon, Nineveh, and Persepolis," but mainly to renew with Dr. Nott those interchanges of thought which amity had commenced during my preceding sojourn, in 1848, at one of the most agreeable of cities. MORTON and *Ethnology*, it may well be supposed, were exhaustless topics of conversation. Deploring that no one had stepped forward to make known the matured views of the father of our cis-Atlantic school of Anthropology, it occurred to us that we would write one or more articles, in some Review, básed upon the correspondence and

* *Hand-book to the Nile;* London, Madden, 1849; p. 18, note.

printed papers of Morton in our several possession. Before doing so, however, we conceived it to be due to Mrs. Morton and her home-circle, to inquire by letter, if such proceeding would obtain their sanction; and also whether, in Mrs. Morton's opinion, there were among the Doctor's manuscripts any that might be eligibly embodied in our proposed articles. The graceful readiness with which our proffer was met is best exemplified by the fact that Dr. Nott and myself received immediately, by express from Philadelphia, a mass of Dr. Morton's autographs on scientific themes, together with such books and papers as were deemed suitable for our purposes. On a subsequent visit to Philadelphia, I was permitted to select from the Doctor's shelves whatever was held to be appropriate to our studies; and, while this book has been passing through the press, the whole of Dr. Morton's correspondence with the scientific world was entrusted to Dr. Patterson and myself for mutual reference. But, the unbounded confidence with which we have been honored, whilst most precious to our feelings, enhances greatly our responsibility. Actuated, individually, by the sole desire to render justice to our beloved friend, each of us has executed his part of the task to the best of his ability: at the same time we can emphatically declare that, until the pages of our work were stereotyped, no member of Dr. Morton's family was cognizant of their verbal contents. Thus much it is my privilege to testify, in order that, if any of the writers have erred in their conceptions of Morton's scientific opinions, the *onus* of such inadvertence may fall upon themselves exclusively. Nevertheless, the singleness of purpose and harmony of method with which Dr. Nott, Dr. Patterson, and myself, have striven to fulfil our pledges, are guarantees that no erroneous interpretations, if any such exist, can have arisen intentionally. Throughout this volume, Morton speaks for himself.

The receipt at Mobile of such welcome accretions to our ethnographical stock prompted a change of plan. In lieu of ephemeral notices in a Review, Dr. Nott united with me in the projection of "Types of Mankind"; the scope of which has daily grown larger, in the ratio of the facilities with which we have been signally favored.

On the first printed announcement of our intention [New Orleans, December, 1852], the interest manifested among the friends of science was such, that, by March, I counted nearly 500 subscriptions in furtherance of the work.

Prof. Agassiz's very opportune visit to Mobile during April, 1853, led to a contribution from his own pen that bases the Natural History of mankind upon a principle heretofore unanticipated. Dr. Usher kindly volunteered a synopsis of the *geological* and *palæontological* features of human history; and Dr. Patterson, fellow-citizen, professional colleague, and admiring friend of Dr. Morton, undertook the biographical Memoir which justifies this volume's dedication. The frank concurrence of Messrs. Lippincott, Grambo & Co. has removed every obstacle to effective publication: and thus, through the liberality and thirst for information, so eminently characteristic of American republicanism, "Types of Mankind," invested with abundant signatures, issues into day as one among multitudinous witnesses how, in our own age and land, scientific works can be written and published without solicitation of patronage from Governments, Institutions, or Societies; but solely through the co-operative support of an educated and knowledge-seeking people.

The departments of our undertaking, respectively assumed by Dr. Nott and myself, having been already set forth (*infra*, Part III., Essay I., p. 626), repetition is here superfluous. But while, on my side, I was enabled to devote nearly twelve months of uninterrupted seclusion (in Baldwin county, Alabama) to my portion of the labor, it must not be forgotten, on the other, that my colleague at Mobile performed his task under the ceaseless pressure of the severest professional duties. In view, therefore, of the amount of Dr. Nott's achievements under such adverse circumstances, the reader who may be pleased to criticize the editorship of "Types of Mankind," whilst recognizing my colleague's hand in every line of Part I., and his frequent suggestions throughout Parts II. and III., as concerns the substance, will act but justly if, as regards modes of expression, he should direct any strictures towards myself; whose part it has been occasionally to connect the various sections of this work by reconstructed sentences, or through a few intercalated paragraphs, consequent upon the reception of new "copy" from Dr. Nott during the passage of these sheets through the press. Even at this later stage of our enterprise, owing to the distance between Mobile and Philadelphia, and to the dire havoc produced by a yellow fever simultaneously among our friends around Mobile Bay, I have not possessed the advantage of Dr. Nott's revision of "proof-sheets," nor had he the time to propose alterations.

The Preface to my *Otia Ægyptiaca* assigns sufficient reasons why any aspirations of mine towards excellence in English composition would be vain. With myself, style is ever subordinate to *matter;* but my valued friends, Mr. Redwood Fisher, Mr. Lloyd P. Smith, and Dr. Henry S. Patterson, have most obligingly looked over a large portion of the "revises" as they came from the hands of the stereotyper.

I indulge the hope that all those gentlemen who have directly promoted the scientific interests of our work, will find in it due acknowledgment of their courtesies. For the free use of the collection of Egyptological works — the best accessible to the public in this country — belonging to the Philadelphia Library Company, Dr. Morton's brother-in-law, Mr. John Jay Smith, will accept my sincere thanks.

The Publishers state, on another page, the endeavor made to furnish our Subscribers with counter-value for their subscriptions far in excess of my original promises; and with these brief expository remarks my pen would stop, did not personal gratitude claim expression.

Those acquainted with my earlier life (spent in the Levant until the age of thirty-two) may, perhaps, read some portions of this volume with feelings of surprise at the range of studies once so alien to my vocations, prospects, and ambition. By way of explanation let me state, that, whatever may have been the ground-work previously laid for the prosecution of self-culture, there was one obstacle to progress which would have been insurmountable, when (one among the million seeking freedom) I re-landed in the United States (1842), but for the friendship of a gentleman who — unlike Pharaoh's chief butler that did not "remember Joseph, but forgat him"—had known me *in illo tempore* at Memphis. The munificence of Mr. R. K. Haight of New York obviated all difficulty by placing the necessary materials for study at my disposal; and not content with facilitating the attainment of my desires by his encouraging acts at home, Mr. Haight, on two occasions, enabled me to seek instruction abroad, at the fountain-sources of Paris, London, and Berlin. The pulsations of a grateful heart, and the hope that some readers may deem favors so magnanimous not uselessly bestowed, are the only reciprocities that can at present be tendered to him by

G. R. G.

Philadelphia, 1st Jan., 1854.

POSTSCRIPTUM.

BY J. C. NOTT.

I have just received from Philadelphia *proof-sheets* of the above Preface, and hasten to add a few words.

Above three hundred and sixty wood-cuts, besides many lithographic plates, adorn this volume, and upon them, to some extent, depend its value and success. The reader can well imagine the immense labor and heavy expense required to prepare a series of illustrations of this kind, wherein minute accuracy is so indispensable, and where such accuracy can be attained only through long-continued and patient industry combined with high artistic skill. So great, indeed, were the difficulties to be overcome, that the authors could never for a moment have entertained the idea of publishing a work like "Types of Mankind," had it not been for the aid generously proffered by Mrs. GLIDDON, the accomplished lady of my colleague. To her amateur pencil are we indebted for the drawings of more than three hundred of our wood-cuts, together with those for the lithographed Berlin-effigies.

To say nothing of the outlay which these illustrations must otherwise have involved, it would have been impossible for us to obtain, here, an equal conformity to originals through hired artists. Mrs. Gliddon's hand was stimulated by no mercenary considerations; and we have enjoyed the incalculable advantage of having her near us at Mobile, for more than twelve months; laboring with us and for us: ever ready to alter or amend as our caprice, or necessity, might dictate. Although Mrs. Gliddon was unaccustomed to drawing on wood, and notwithstanding that the wood-engravers at Philadelphia (compelled, owing to the nature of the case, to carve from her drawings alone without recurrence to the originals), may here and there have slightly erred, I venture to assert that no scientific work in our language presents as long a series of illustrations more reliable for faithfulness to originals.

Many of the heads, however, are given in simple outline, and the majority have required reduction; but persons who are familiar with the great works of Rosellini, Champollion, Prisse, Lepsius, Botta, Flandin, Layard, Dumoutier, &c., from which these figures have been copied, will at once recognize a truthfulness in Mrs. Gliddon's designs (viewed ethnologically) which speaks more than the encomiums of an admiring friend.

Nor is it proper that I should close this *Postscript* without some acknowledgment to her husband. In the first place, it is mere justice to state, that Parts II. and III. are almost exclusively his own work: because, although not uninformed on the points therein treated, and agreeing in their scientific results, I wish to mention that the materials, conception, and execution of these portions of our volume are due to him. Of Part I., on the other hand, a fuller share of responsibility must fall upon myself. The special province, which I have attempted to explore, is the *Natural History proper* of mankind; and I have sought to illustrate it through the physical and linguistic history of primeval races, as deduced from the time-worn monuments of nations by the leading archæologists of our nineteenth century. This effort has also been much facilitated through the zeal and experience of my collaborator, Mr. GLIDDON.

It is with no small gratification I now feel assured that, through Dr. PATTERSON'S effective "Memoir," MORTON'S cherished fame will evermore preserve its rightful place among men of science; and, again, that those grand Truths, for which I have long "fought and bled," are at last established by the unanswerable "Sketch" of our chief naturalist, Prof. AGASSIZ; as well as triumphantly confirmed through the teachings of scholars who have investigated the records of antiquity in Egypt, China, Assyria, India, Palestine, and other Oriental countries.

J. C. N.

MOBILE, ALA., January 12th, 1854.

CONTENTS.

PART I.

PART II.

PART III.—*Supplement*—BY GEO. R. GLIDDON.

MEMOIR

OF

THE LIFE AND SCIENTIFIC LABORS

OF

SAMUEL GEORGE MORTON.

BY HENRY S. PATTERSON, M.D.,

EMERITUS PROFESSOR OF MATERIA MEDICA AND THERAPEUTICS IN THE MEDICAL DEPARTMENT OF PENNSYLVANIA COLLEGE; FELLOW OF THE COLLEGE OF PHYSICIANS; RECORDING SECRETARY OF THE MEDICAL SOCIETY OF THE STATE OF PENNSYLVANIA.

WHEN the authors of the present work, pressed with the labor of preparing for the printer their abundant materials, first suggested that I should assist them by furnishing a notice of the scientific life of our deceased friend and leader in Ethnology, I hesitated somewhat to undertake the task, feeling that the selection, dictated by their partial friendship, might by others be deemed inappropriate, and myself considered deficient in those relations which would warrant the assumption of the office. Subsequent reflection, however, convinced me that an acquaintance of fifteen years, approaching to intimacy,—frequent professional and social intercourse,—my position in the Medical Faculty, that was founded mainly by his labors,—devotion in a great degree to the same studies,—community of sentiment in regard to the topics of most interest to both,—that all these combined to constitute a sufficient reason why I should freely accept the duty assigned me. I do it cheerfully, for to me it is a grateful duty and a source of pleasure, thus to be allowed to bear testimony to the worth and services of the great and good man whom we all had so much cause to love and honor. His life I do not propose to write. There is but little in the quiet daily walk of any civilian, to furnish a theme for biographical narrative. That of Morton was eminently placid and regular; and all that can be said upon it has already been well and eloquently expressed in the able addresses of Professors

Meigs, Wood, and Grant.* To Dr. Wood also we are indebted for his exposition of Morton's eminent services to medical science, both as a teacher and writer; a point too frequently overlooked in regarding him in the more prominent light of a Naturalist. Passing over these topics, my object will be to consider mainly his contributions to Natural Science, and especially to Ethnology. As introductory to a work upon anthropological subjects, we desire to present Morton as the Anthropologist, and as virtually the founder of that school of Ethnology, of whose views this book may be regarded as an authentic exponent.

Let me be permitted, however, a few words in relation to the personal character and private worth of Morton. At the mention of his name there arise emotions which press for utterance, and which it would do violence to my feelings to leave unexpressed. If I have felt this affection for him, it is only what was shared by all who knew him well. What was most peculiar in him was that magnetic power by which he attracted and bound men to him, and made them glad to serve him. This influence was especially manifested, as I shall have occasion to observe again, in the collection of his Cabinet of Crania. In looking over his correspondence now, it is surprising to see the number of men, so different one from another in every respect, who in all quarters of the globe were laboring without expectation of reward to secure a cranium for Morton, and to read the reports of their varied successes and disappointments. In his whole deportment, there was an evident singleness of purpose and a candor, open as the day, which at once placed one at his ease. Combined with this was a most winning gentleness of manner, which drew one to him as with the cords of brotherly affection. He possessed, moreover, in a remarkable degree, the faculty of imparting to others his own enthusiasm, and filling them, for the time at least, with ardor for his own pursuit. Hence, in a measure, his success in enlisting the numerous collaborators, so necessary to him in his peculiar studies. It may be affirmed that no man ever came within the sphere of his influence without forming for him some degree of

* A memoir of Samuel George Morton, M. D., late President of the Academy of Natural Sciences of Philadelphia, by Charles D. Meigs, M. D. Read Nov. 6th, 1851, and published by direction of the Academy: Philada. 1851.

A Biographical Memoir of Samuel George Morton, M. D., prepared by appointment of the College of Physicians of Philadelphia, and read before that body Nov. 3d, 1852, by George B. Wood, M. D., President of the College: Philada. 1853.

Sketch of the Life and Character of Samuel George Morton, M. D. Lecture, introductory to a course of Anatomy and Physiology in the Medical Department of Pennsylvania College. Delivered Oct. 18th, 1851, by William R. Grant, M. D. Published by request of the Class: Philada. 1852 personal attachment. His circle of attached friends was therefore large, and the expression of regret for his untimely loss general and sincere.

It was in London, and while seated at the hospitable board of Dr. Thomas Hodgkin, (to whom I had been introduced by a letter from Morton,*) that I first heard the news of his decease. He was the subject of an animated and interesting conversation at the moment, (for Dr. H. and he had been classmates at Edinburgh,) when a gentleman entered with an American newspaper received by the morning's mail, and containing the sad intelligence. A cloud came over every countenance, and every voice was raised in an exclamation of sudden grief and regret; for he was more or less known to all present. My next appointment for that day was with Mr. S. Birch, of the Archæological department of the British Museum, who had been a correspondent of Morton, and could appreciate his great worth. During the day, Mr. Birch or myself mentioned the melancholy tidings to numerous gentlemen, in various departments of that great institution, and always with the same reply. All knew his name, and felt that in his decease the cause of science had suffered a serious deprivation.

And this seemed to me his true fame. Outside the walls of this noble Temple of Science rolled on the turmoil of the modern Babylon, with its world of business, of pleasure, and of care, to all which the name of Morton was unknown, and from which its mention could call up no response. Within these walls, however, and among a body of men whom a more than princely munificence enables to devote themselves to labor like his own, he was universally recognized and appreciated, and mourned as a leading spirit in their cosmopolite fraternity. But always there was this peculiarity to be noticed, that wherever a man had known Morton personally at all, he mourned not so much for the untimely extinction of an intellectual light, as for the loss of a beloved personal friend. Certainly the man who inspired others with this feeling, could himself have no cold or empty heart. On the contrary, he overflowed

* Among the letters with which Dr. Morton favored me, on my visit to Europe, was one to Dr. Alexander Hannay of Glasgow. This he particularly wished me to deliver, and to bring him a report of his old friend; for Dr. H. had been an intimate of his student days, although their correspondence had long been interrupted. The letter was written in a playful mood, and contained sportive allusions to their student life at Edinburgh, and a wish that they might meet again. On reaching Glasgow late in May, I sought Dr. H., and found that he had recently deceased. Morton himself, as I afterwards learned, had then also ceased to breathe. That letter, so full of genial vivacity and present life, was from the hand of one dead man addressed to another! And should they not meet again? Rather had they not already met where the darkness had become day! It is a beautiful and consolatory belief, and one that the subject of this notice could undoubtingly hold and rejoice in.

with all kindly and gentle affections. Quiet and unobtrusive in manners, and fond of the retirement of study, it was only in the privacy of the domestic circle that he could be rightly known; and those that were privileged to approach nearest the *Sanctum Sanctorum* of his happy home, could best see the full beauty of his character. That sacred veil cannot be raised to the public eye, but beneath its folds is preserved the pure memory of one who illustrated every relation of life with a new grace that was all his own, and who, in departing, has left behind him an impression on all hearts, which not the most exacting affection could wish in any respect other than it is.

The early training of Morton was in strict accordance with the principles of the Society of Friends, of which his mother was a member. His school education—whose deficiencies he always mentioned with regret, and remedied by sedulous labor in after years — was throughout of that character, and had all the consequent merits and demerits. It is a system which represses the imagination and sentiments, while it cultivates carefully the logical powers; and which strives to turn all the energies of the pupil's mind toward the useful arts, rather than what may be deemed merely ornamental accomplishments. When it carries him beyond the rudiments, it is usually into the higher mathematics and mechanical philosophy. Its aim is utility, even if necessary at the expense of beauty. It therefore does not generally encourage the study of the dead languages, with its incidental *belles-lettres* advantages, and free access to poets and rhetoricians. This plan of education I believe to be an unsuitable, and even an injurious one for a youth of cold temperament and dull sensibilities. When, however, the subject of its operation is one of opposite tendencies, so decided as to be the better for repression, it may become not only useful, but the best training for that particular case. Such I conceive to have been the fact in regard to Morton. Endowed by nature with a delicate and sensitive temperament, with warm affections, a keen sense of natural beauties, a fertile imagination, and that nice musical appreciation which made him delight in the accord of measured sounds, he had an early passion for poetical reading and composition. Even in boyhood he wrote very creditable verses; and his later productions, — for he continued to indulge the muse occasionally to the end of his life, although he would not publish, — often rose considerably above mediocrity.

The following lines may answer as an average specimen of his easy flow of versification, as well as of his youthful style of thought and feeling. They were written on the occasion of a visit to Kilcoleman Castle, county Cork, Ireland, where Spenser lived, and is believed to have written his immortal poem.

LINES

WRITTEN ON A BLANK LEAF OF SPENSER'S "FAERY QUEENE."

I.

Through many a winding maze in "Faery Lande"
O Spenser! I have followed thee along;
Aye, I have laughed and sigh'd at thy command,
And joy'd me in the magic of thy song:
Wild are thy numbers, but to them belong
The fire of Genius, and poetic skill;
'Tis thine to paint with inspiration strong,
The fate of knight, or dame more knightly still,
To sway the feeling heart, and rouse it at thy will.

II.

And musing still upon the fairy dream,
I sought the hall oft trod by thee before;
I bent me down by Mulla's gentle stream,
And, looking far beyond, gazed fondly o'er
Old Ballyhoura, where in days of yore
Thou watch'd thy flocks with all a shepherd's pride;
And fancy listened as to catch once more
Thy Harp's lov'd echo from the mountain side,—
But ah! no harp is heard in all that region wide!

III.

The flocks are fled, and in the enchanted hall
No voice replies to voice; but there ye see
The ivy clasp the sad and mould'ring wall,
As if to twine a votive wreath for thee:
All — all is desolate, — and if there be
A lonely sound, it is the raven's cry!
Let years roll on, let wasting ages flee,
Let earthly things delight, and hasten by,
But thy immortal name and song shall never die!

Had this inherent tendency been fostered, he would doubtless have taken a high rank among our American poets. Certainly he would have been another man than we have known him. Perhaps his nervous temperament, delicate fibre, acute feelings and ardent sympathies, might have been developed into the same super-sensitiveness we have seen in John Keats and other gifted minds of a constitution similar to his own. But the tendency was checked and repressed from the outset by his domestic influences, by his teachers, and subsequently by himself. When he devoted himself to a life of science, he was earnest to cultivate that style of thought and composition which accorded with his pursuits; for only by severe mental discipline, and long-continued effort, could he have acquired that caution and rigid accuracy of diction, which characterize his productions. His school appears to have been unsatisfactory to him, for he never had a fondness for the mathematics, the main topic of study. He was nevertheless of a studious turn, reading industriously, and with special interest, all the works on History to which he had access. It is probable that in these readings was laid the foundation of a taste for those anthropological studies which have since rendered him famous, and in the prosecution of which his extensive historical knowledge gave him eminent facilities.

At the same time probably he imbibed his first fondness for Natural Science. From his stepfather, (for his mother married again when he was thirteen years old,) he derived a taste for and knowledge of mineralogy and geology, the first branches to which he turned his attention.

Destined originally for mercantile pursuits, young Morton soon found the atmosphere of the counting-house uncongenial to him. He resolved to adopt the medical profession, which was indeed the only course open, to one of his tastes, and in his circumstances. The Society of Friends, by closing the Pulpit and the Bar against the able and aspiring among its youth, has given to Medicine many of its brightest ornaments, both in Great Britain and in this country. This fact will serve to explain the great success of so many physicians of that persuasion, as well as the preponderating influence of the medical profession in all Quaker neighborhoods. May not the eminence of Philadelphia in medicine be accounted for, in part at least, in the same way? Carlyle has said that to the ambitious fancy of the Scottish schoolboy "the highest style of man is the Christian, and the highest Christian the teacher of such." Hence his ultimate aspiration is for the clerical position. But to the aspiring youth among Friends there is but the one road to intellectual distinction,—that is through medicine and its cognate sciences. The medical preceptor of Morton was the late Dr. Joseph Parrish, then in the height of his popularity. Elevated to his prominent position against early obstacles, and solely by force of character, industry, and probity, he was extensively engaged in practice; and, although unconnected with any institution, his office overflowed with pupils. His mind was practical and thoroughly medical, and so entirely did his profession occupy it, that he seemed to me never to allow himself to think upon other topics, except religious ones, in which also he was deeply interested. A strict and conscientious Friend, he illustrated all the best points in that character. As the remarkable graces of his person proverbially gave a beauty to the otherwise ungainly garb of his sect, and rendered it attractive upon him, so the graces of his spirit, obliterating all that might otherwise have been harsh or angular, contributed to form a character gentle, kindly, lovely, that made him the light of the sick chamber, and a comforting presence at many a dying bed. To no member of our profession could the proud title of *Opifer* be more truly applied, for his very smile brought aid to the suffering, and courage to the despondent. The reader will pardon me this digression; but as the Highland clansman could not pass by without adding another stone to the monumental cairn where reposed his departed chief, so can I never pass by the mention of his name without offering some tribute, however humble, of reverence and respect, to the memory of my excellent old master. Such was the teacher from whom mainly Morton also received the knowledge of his profession; though, had the influence of Dr. Parrish alone controlled his mind, it would have been confined rigorously to the channels of purely medical study and investigation. But, in order to provide adequate tuition for his numerous pupils, Dr. Parrish had associated with himself several young physicians as instructors in the various branches. Among them was Dr. Richard Harlan, then enthusiastically devoted to the study of Natural History, between whom and the young student there was soon established a bond of sympathy in congeniality of pursuits. That the friendship thus originated was subsequently interrupted, was in no manner the fault of Morton, to whom it was always a subject of regret. Harlan has now been dead some years, and although by no means forgotten in the world of science, he has not been accorded the full measure of his merited distinction among American naturalists. An unfortunate infirmity of temper, which was not at all calculated to conciliate attachments, but rather the reverse, deprived him of the band of friends who should have watched over his fame, and so his memory has suffered by default. Yet at one period he was the leading authority on this side the Atlantic in certain departments of Zoology. By him Morton appears to have been introduced to the Academy of Natural Sciences, in whose proceedings he was afterwards to take such an important part. He attained his majority in January 1820, received his Diploma of Doctor of Medicine in March, and was elected a member of the Academy in April of the same year. He had probably taken an active interest in its affairs before this time, although not eligible to membership by reason of age; for in one of his later letters now before me, he speaks of it as an institution for which he had labored, "boy and man," now some thirty years.

Soon after this last event he sailed for Europe, on a visit to his uncle, James Morton, Esq., of Clonmel, Ireland, a gentleman for whom he always preserved a high regard and grateful affection. His transatlantic friends seem to have attached but little value to an

American diploma, and desired him to possess the honors of the University of Edinburgh, then but little passed beyond the zenith of its glory. After spending the summer at his uncle's house, he went to Edinburgh, where he heard the last course of lectures, delivered by the chaste and classical Gregory. The American schools not being recognized by the University as *ad eundem*, he found himself obliged to attend the full term of an under-graduate. This would have left him ample leisure as far as his mere college studies were concerned; for the youth who had graduated with approbation under the tuition of Wistar, Physick, and James, and their compeers, could not have fallen far short of the requisitions of any other Medical Faculty in Christendom. But his time was not spent in idleness. He sedulously cultivated his knowledge of the classical tongues, hitherto imperfect, and he devoted himself to the study of French and Italian, both of which languages he learned to read with facility. He also attended with great interest the lectures of Professor Jameson on Geology, thus confirming and reviving his early fondness for that branch of science. After his return to America, he presented to the Academy a series of the green-stone rocks of Scotland, and a section of Salisbury Craig near Edinburgh, collected by himself at this time. In October 1821, he visited Paris, and spent the winter there mainly in clinical study. The next summer was devoted to a tour in Italy and other portions of the continent, and in the fall he returned again to Edinburgh, where, after attendance upon another session, he received the honors of the doctorate. His printed thesis* may be taken as a fair exponent of his mental condition and calibre at this period. It is very like himself, and yet with a difference from him as we knew him later in life. It is quiet and indeed even simple in tone, without affectation and without any of the declamation in which young writers are so apt to indulge. Its style is clear and sufficiently concise, and as a piece of Latinity it is correct and graceful. It takes up the subject of bodily pain, and considers it in regard to its causes, its diagnostic value, and its effects, both physical and psychical, leaving very little more to be said with regard to it. But it is evident throughout that the essay is the production of one who is more ambitious of the reputation of the *littérateur* than of the *savant;* who writes,—and that probably marks the distinction,—with his face turned to his auditory rather than to his subject. The sentence marches sometimes with a didactic solemnity almost Johnsonian, while the frequency of the poetical references and quotations,—Latin and Italian as well as English,—and the facile fitness with which they glide into

* Tentamen Inaugurale de Corporis Dolore, etc.—Edinburgi, M.D.CCCXXIII.

the text, show how familiar they must have been to the mind of the author. Indeed Edinburgh was, at the period in question, the principal centre of taste and philosophy, as well as of science, in Great Britain; and it is not likely that one of Morton's literary turn and studious habits would miss the opportunity to pasture in either of these rich fields. The ethical tone of this production is also worthy of note. It is characteristic of the writer, and grew in a great measure out of his mental constitution, which, free from all violence of passion, was habitually cheerful, hopeful, and kindly. Hence comes that beautiful spirit of philosophical optimism, which, perceiving in all seeming evil only the means to a greater ultimate good, attains all that stoicism proposed to itself, by the shorter way of a cheerful and unquestioning resignation to the Divine Will, not because it is omnipotent and irresistible, but solely because it is the wisest and best. The following extracts will sufficiently explain my meaning:—

"Alma rerum Parens nil frustra fecit; ne dolor quidem absque suis usibus est; et semper cogimur eum agnoscere veluti fidelem quamvis ingratum monitorem, et quoque inter præsidia vitæ nonnunquam numerandum." —(p. 9.)

"Dolor enim nos nascentes aggreditur, per totam vitam insidiosus comitatur, et quasi nunquam satiandus; adest etiam morientibus, horamque supremam angoribus infestat. At ego tamen Dolorem, quanquam invisum, et ab omnibus, quantum fieri potest, ab ipsis semotum, non omnino inutilem depinxi, sed potius eum protuli, ad vitam conservandam necessarium, a Deo Optimo Maximo constitutum." — (p 37.)

This conviction animated Morton throughout his life, consoled him in suffering, cheered him in sickness, and gave to his deportment much of its calm and beautiful equanimity.*

---

* The subjoined graceful lines breathe the same spirit. They occur among his MSS. with the date of May 1828. I quote them as illustrative of the thought above indicated.

THE SPIRIT OF DESTINY.

Spirit of Light! Thou glance divine
  Of Heaven's immortal fire,
I kneel before thy hallowed shrine
  To worship and admire.
I cannot trace thy glorious flight
  Nor dream where thou dost dwell,
Yet canst thou guard my steps aright
  By thine unearthly spell.

I listen for thy voice in vain,
  E'en when I deem thee nigh;
Yet ere I venture to complain,
  Thou know'st the reason why;
And oft when, worldly cares forgot,
  I watch the vacant air,
I see thee not,—I hear thee not,—
  Yet *know* that thou art there.

In 1824, he returned to Philadelphia, and commenced his career as a practitioner of medicine. He seems immediately to have resumed his place and labors in the Academy of Natural Sciences, which, in the next year, was deprived of the active services of some of its most efficient members, by the removal of Messrs. Maclure, Say, Troost, Lesueur, and others, to New Harmony, whither they went to participate in the benevolent but ill-starred social experiment of Robert Owen. It was a pleasant dream of a good heart and a visionary brain, and has now faded away from every one but the originator, who holds it still in his extreme old age with the same fervor as in his ardent youth; but then it had many firm believers. So enthusiastic was Maclure especially in its advocacy, that he declined about this period to assist the Academy in the erection of a new Hall, from a conviction that, in the reorganization of society, living in cities would be abandoned, and their edifices thus left untenanted and useless. One cannot imagine a body of more simple-hearted, less worldly, and less practical men, than the Philadelphia naturalists who went to reconstitute the framework of society on the prairies of Indiana; and it is impossible to repress a smile at their Quixotism, even while one heaves a sigh for the bitterness of their disappointment.

They left in 1825, and the first papers of Morton were read in 1827. His main interest still seems to have been in Geology. In the year mentioned he published an *Analysis of Tabular Spar from Bucks County*, and the next year some *Geological Observations*, based upon the notes of his friend, Mr. Vanuxem. About this time his attention was turned to the special department of Palæontology, by an examination of the organic remains of the cretaceous formation of New Jersey and Delaware; and with this his active scientific life may be regarded as commencing.

Some few of the fossils of the New Jersey marl had been noticed by Mr. T. Say, and by Drs. Harlan and Dekay; but no thorough investigation of this interesting topic was attempted until Morton assumed the task. He labored in it industriously, being assisted in the collection of materials by his scientific friends. Three papers on the subject were published in 1828, and from this time the series was continued, either in Silliman's Journal or the Journal of the Aca-

---

And when with heedless step, too near
  I tempt destruction's brink,
Deep, deep, within my soul I hear
  Thy voice, and backward shrink.
The poisoned shaft, by thee controlled,
  Speeds swift and harmless by;
But, when the days of life are told,
  Thou smitest — and we die!

demy, until it closed with the fourteenth paper in 1846. In 1834, the results then obtained were collected and published in a volume illustrated with nineteen admirable plates.*

This book at once gave its author a reputation and status in the scientific world, and called forth the warm commendations of Mr. Mantell and other eminent Palæontologists. It traces the formation in question along the borders of the Atlantic and the Gulf of Mexico from New Jersey to Louisiana, following it by the identification of its organic remains. The great body of the work is original, scarcely any of the species enumerated having ever been noticed before. Subsequent researches enabled him to add considerably to this collection, and, among others, to describe a species of fossil crocodile (*C. clavirostris*) entirely new and differing considerably in structure from its congeners hitherto known. In regard to the fossils of the cretaceous series, he is still the principal authority.

Nor was he neglectful of the other branches of Natural Science, although too well aware of the value of concentrated effort to peril his own success, by a too wide diffusion of his labors. Still he maintained a constant interest in the operation of every department of the Academy, and watched its onward progress with solicitude and satisfaction. To the Geological and Mineralogical, and especially to the Palæontological collection, he was a liberal contributor. Among the papers read by him before the Academy was one in 1831 on "some Parasitic Worms," another in 1841, on "an Albino Racoon," and a third in 1844, on "a supposed new species of Hippopotamus." This animal, which has been called *H. minor vel Liberiensis*, was entirely unknown to Zoology until described by Morton, who received its skull from Dr. Goheen, of Liberia, and at once recognized its diversity from the known species.† Notwithstanding the published opinion of Cuvier, that the field of research was exhausted in regard to the Mammalia, our gifted townsman was enabled to add an important pachyderm to the catalogue of Mammalogy, and that too from the other hemisphere.

Let it not be supposed that, amid these absorbing topics of research, he relaxed for a moment his attention to his professional pursuits. On the contrary, he was constantly and largely engaged in practice, and, at his decease, was one of the leading practitioners of our city. Neither did he allow himself to fall behind his professional colleagues in the literature of medicine. He was among the first to introduce on this side the Atlantic the physical means of diagnosis in

* Synopsis of the Organic Remains of the Cretaceous Group of the United States. By Samuel George Morton. Philadelphia: Key and Biddle. 1834.

† The Academy has recently (January 1852) received a specimen of it.

thoracic affections. He was also one of the earliest investigators of the morbid anatomy of Phthisis Pulmonalis; and his volume on that subject, although superseded by the later and more extensive researches of the French pathologists, is a monument of his industry and accuracy, and a credit to American medicine.* He also edited Mackintosh's Practice of Physic, with notes, which add materially to its value to the American physician.† In 1849, he published a textbook of anatomy, remarkable for its clearness and succinctness, and the beauty of its illustrations.‡ He was early selected by Dr. Parrish as one of his associates in teaching, and lectured upon anatomy in that connexion for a number of years. He subsequently filled the chair of anatomy in the Medical Department of Pennsylvania College from 1839 to 1843. As a lecturer he was clear, calm, and self-possessed, moving through his topic with the easy regularity of one to whom it was entirely familiar. He served for several years as one of the physicians and clinical teachers of the Alms-house Hospital, and it was there that most of his researches on consumption were made. He was a Fellow of the College of Physicians, but did not take an active part in their proceedings, from the fact that their stated meetings occurred on the same evenings as those of the Academy, where he felt it his first duty to be. His only contribution to their printed Transactions is a biographical notice of his valued friend, Dr. George McClellan, prepared by request of the College.

We now come to a portion of his scientific labors, upon which I must be allowed to dwell at greater length. I refer of course to his researches in Anthropology, commencing with what may be designated Comparative Cranioscopy, and running on into general Ethnology. The object proposed primarily being the determination of ethnic resemblances and discrepancies by a comparison of crania, (thus perfecting what Blumenbach had left lamentably incomplete,) the work could not be commenced until the objects for comparison were brought together. The results of Blumenbach were invalidated by the small number of specimens generally relied upon by him; for in a case where allowance is to be made for individual peculiarities of form and stature, the conclusions gain infinitely in value by extension of the comparison over a sufficient series to neutralize this disturbing element. There was therefore necessary, first of all, a

* Illustrations of Pulmonary Consumption, its Anatomical Characters, Causes, Symptoms and Treatment. With twelve colored plates. Philadelphia: 1834.

† Principles of Pathology and Practice of Physic. By John Mackintosh, M. D., &c. First American from the fourth London edition. With notes and additions. In 2 vols. Philadelphia: 1835.

‡ An Illustrated System of Human Anatomy, Special, General, and Microscopic. Philadelphia: 1849.

collection of crania, and that not of a few specimens, but widely enough extended to give reliable results. The contemplation of these facts shows the magnitude and boldness of the plan, which would have sufficed to deter most men from the attempt. But Morton was not easily discouraged, and although he doubtless occupied a wider field in the end than he proposed to himself in the outset, it is evident that from the beginning he contemplated a full cabinet of universal Craniology, Human and Comparative. His own account of the commencement of the collection is as follows: "Having had occasion, in the summer of 1830, to deliver an introductory lecture to a course of Anatomy, I chose for my subject *The different forms of the skull as exhibited in the five races of men.* Strange to say, I could neither buy nor borrow a cranium of each of these races; and I finished my discourse without showing either the Mongolian or the Malay. Forcibly impressed with this great deficiency in a most important branch of science, I at once resolved to make a collection for myself."* Dr. Wood (*Memoir,* p. 13,) states that he engaged in this study soon after he commenced practice; and adds, "among the earliest recollections of my visits to his office is that of the skulls he had collected." The selection of the topic above-mentioned shows that he was already interested in it.

The increase was at first slow, but the work was persevered in with a constancy and energy that could know no failure. Every legitimate means was adopted, and every attainable influence brought to bear upon the one object. Time, labor, and money, were expended without stint. The enthusiasm he felt himself he imparted to others, and he thus enlisted a body of zealous collaborators who sought contributions for him in every part of the world. Many of them sympathized with him in his scientific ardor, and quite as many were actuated solely by a desire to serve and oblige the individual. A friend of the writer (without any particular scientific interest) exposed his life in robbing an Indian burial-place in Oregon, and carried his spoils for two weeks in his pack, in a highly unsavory condition, and when discovery would have involved danger, and probably death. Before his departure he had promised Morton to bring him some skulls, and he was resolved to do it at all hazards. This effort also involved, of course, a very extensive and laborious correspondence. He was in daily receipt of letters from all countries and from every variety of persons. It was mainly by the free contributions of these assistants that the collection eventually grew so rapidly. Among the

---

* Letter to J. R. Bartlett, Esq. Transactions of the American Ethnological Society, vol. ii. New York: 1848.

contributors I may mention William A. Foster, Esq., as presenting 135 specimens, Dr. J. C. Cisneros 53, and Dr. Ruschenberger 39. George R. Gliddon, Esq. presented 30, beside the 137 originally procured by his agency; William A. Gliddon, Esq., 19; M. Clot-Bey 15; and Professor Retzius 17, with 24 more received since the death of Dr. M. Over one hundred gentlemen are named in the catalogue as contributing more or less, sixty-seven of them having presented one skull each. It is not to be supposed, however, that even the portion thus given led to no outlay of means. The mere charges for freight from distant portions of the globe amounted to a considerable sum. Dr. Wood (*loc. cit.*) estimates the total cost of the collection to its proprietor from ten to fifteen thousand dollars. At this moment it is undoubtedly by far the most complete collection of crania extant. There is nothing in Europe comparable to it. I have recently seen a letter from an eminent British ethnologist, containing warm thanks for the privilege even of reading the catalogue of such a collection, and adding that he would visit it anywhere in Europe, although he cannot dare the ocean for it. At the time of Dr. Morton's death it consisted of 918 human crania, to which are to be added 51 received since, and which were then on their way. The collection also contains 278 crania of mammals, 271 of birds, and 88 of reptiles and fishes:—in all, 1656 skulls! I rejoice to state that this magnificent cabinet has been secured to our city by the contribution of liberal citizens, who have purchased it for $4,000, and presented it to the Academy.

Simultaneously with his accumulation of crania, and based upon them, he carried on his study of Ethnology, if I may use that term in reference to a period when the science, so called at present, could scarcely be said to exist. Indeed it is almost entirely a new science within a few years. While medical men occupied themselves exclusively with the intimate structure and function of the human frame, no investigator of nature seemed to turn his attention to the curious diversities of form, feature, complexion, &c., which characterize the different varieties of men. With a very thorough anatomy and physiology, our *descriptive history* of the human species was less accurate and extensive than that of most of the well-known animals. So true was this that Buffon pithily observed that "quelque interêt que nous ayons a nous connaitre nous mêmes, je ne sais si nous ne connaissons pas mieux tout ce qui n'est pas nous." But every branch of this interesting investigation has recently received a sudden and vigorous impulse, and there has grown up within a few years an Ethnology with numerous and devoted cultivators. That it still has much to accomplish will appear from the number of questions which the pages of this book show to be still *sub judice*. Indeed it is the widest and most attractive field open to the naturalist of to-day. To quote the admirable language of Jomard:

"Car il ne faut pas perdre de vue, maintenant que la connaissance extérieure du globe et de ses productions a fait d'immenses progrès, que la connaissance de l'homme est le but final des sciences géographiques. Une carrière non moins vaste que la première est ouverte au génie des voyages; il importe, il est urgent même, pour l'avenir de l'espèce humaine et pour le besoin de l'Europe surtout, de connaître à fond le degré de civilisation de toutes les races; de savoir exactement en quoi elles diffèrent ou se rapprochent; quelle est l'analogie ou la dissemblance entre leurs régimes, leurs mœurs, leurs religions, leurs langages, leurs arts, leurs industries, leurs constitutions physiques, afin de lier entre elles et nous des rapports plus sûrs et plus avantageux. Tel est l'objet de l'ethnologie, ce qui est la science même de la géographie vue dans son ensemble et dans toute sa haute généralité. Bien que cette matière ainsi envisagée soit presque toute nouvelle, nous ne pouvons trop, néanmoins, recommander les observations de cette espèce au zèle des voyageurs."*

The attempt to establish a rule of diversity among the races of men, according to cranial conformation, commenced in the last century with Camper, the originator of the *facial angle*. The subject was next taken up by Blumenbach, who has been until recently the controlling authority upon it. His *Decades Craniorum*, whose publication was begun in 1790, and continued until 1828, covers the period when Morton began this study. His method of comparing crania, (by the *norma verticalis*,) and his distribution of races, were then both undisputed. The mind of the medical profession in Great Britain and in this country had then, moreover, been recently attracted to the subject by the publication (in 1819) of the very able book of Mr. Lawrence,† avowedly based upon the researches of the great Professor of Göttingen. Dr. Prichard had published his Inaugural Dissertation, *De Hominum Varietatibus*, in 1808, and a translation of the same in 1812, under the title of *Researches on the Physical History of Man*, constituting the first of a series of publications, afterwards of great influence and value. Several treatises had also been published with the intention of proving that the color of the negro might arise from climatic influences, the principal work being that of President Smith, of Princeton College, New Jersey. Beyond this, nothing had been done for the science of Man up to Morton's return to this country in 1824. A new impetus had been given, however, to the speciality of Craniology by the promulgation of the views of Gall and Spurzheim, then creating their greatest excitement. These distinguished persons completed the publication of their great work at Paris in 1819, both

* Etudes Géographiques et Historiques sur l'Arabie, p. 403.

† Lectures on Physiology, Zoology, and the Natural History of Man, delivered at the Royal College of Surgeons, by W. Lawrence, F. R. S., &c.

1

before and after which time Spurzheim lectured in Great Britain, making many proselytes. The phrenologists of Edinburgh must have been in the very fervor of their first love during Morton's residence there, and they included in their number some men of eminent ability and eloquence. Collections of prepared crania, of casts and masks, became common; but they were brought together in the hope of illustrating character, not race, and were prized according as fanciful hypothesis could make their protuberances correspond with the distribution of intellectual faculties in a most crude and barren psychology. Morton's collection was ethnographic in its aim from the outset; nor can I find that he ever committed himself fully to the miscalled Phrenology — a system based upon principles indisputably true, but which it holds in common with the world of science at large, while all that is peculiar to itself is already fading into oblivion.* Attractive by its easy comprehensibility and facility of application, it acquired a sudden and wide-spread popularity, and so passed out of the hands of men of science, step by step, till it has now become the property of itinerant charlatans, describing characters for twenty-five cents a head. The very name is so degraded by these associations, that we are apt to forget that, thirty years ago, it was a scientific doctrine accepted by learned and thoughtful men. There can be no doubt that it had its effect (important though indirect) upon the mind of Morton, in arousing him to the importance of the Craniology about which everybody was talking, and leading him to make that application of it, which, although neglected by his professional brethren, was still the only one of any real and permanent value.

It is evident that the published matter for Morton's studies was very limited. A pioneer himself, he had to resort to the raw material, and obtain his data at the hand of nature. Fortunately for him he resided in a country where, if literary advantages are otherwise deficient, the inducement and opportunities for anthropological research are particularly abundant. There are reasons why Ethnology should be eminently a science for American culture. Here, three of the five races, into which Blumenbach divided mankind, are brought together to determine the problem of their destiny as they best may,

* The ensuing paragraph will show more clearly Morton's matured opinion on this subject. It is from an Introductory Lecture on "The Diversities of the Human Species," delivered before the Medical Class of Pennsylvania College in November 1842.

"It (Phrenology) further teaches us that the brain is the seat of the mind, and that it is a congeries of organs, each of which performs its own separate and peculiar function. These propositions appear to me to be physiological truths; but I allude to them on this occasion merely to put you on your guard against adopting too hastily those minute details of the localities and functions of supposed organs, which have of late found so many and such zealous advocates."

while Chinese immigration to California and the proposed importation of Coolie laborers threaten to bring us into equally intimate contact with a fourth. It is manifest that our relation to and management of these people must depend, in a great measure, upon their intrinsic race-character. While the contact of the white man seems fatal to the Red American, whose tribes fade away before the onward march of the frontier-man like the snow in spring (threatening ultimate extinction), the Negro thrives under the shadow of his white master, falls readily into the position assigned him, and exists and multiplies in increased physical well-being. To the American statesman and the philanthropist, as well as to the naturalist, the study thus becomes one of exceeding interest. Extraordinary facilities for observing minor sub-divisions among the families of the white race are also presented by the resort hither of immigrants from every part of Europe. Of all these advantages Morton availed himself freely, and soon became the acknowledged master of the topic. Extending his studies beyond what one may call the zoological, into the archæological, and, to some extent, into the philological department of Ethnography, his pre-eminence was speedily acknowledged at home, while the publication of his books elevated him to an equal distinction abroad. Professor Retzius of Stockholm, writing to him April 3d, 1847, says emphatically: "*You have done more for Ethnography than any living physiologist;* and I hope you will continue to cultivate this science, which is of so great interest."

The first task proposed to himself by Morton, was the examination and comparison of the crania of the Indian tribes of North and South America. His special object was to ascertain the average capacity and form of these skulls, as compared among themselves and with those of the other races of men, and to determine what ethnic distinctions, if any, might be inferred from them. The result of this labor was the *Crania Americana*, published in 1839. This work contains admirably executed lithographic plates of numerous crania, of natural size, and presenting a highly creditable specimen of American art. The letter-press includes accurate admeasurements of the crania, especially of their interior capacity; the latter being made by a plan peculiar to the author, and enabling him to estimate with precision the relative amount of brain in various races. The introduction is particularly interesting, as containing the author's general ethnological views so fár as matured up to that time. He adopts the quintuple division of Blumenbach, not as the best possible, but as sufficient for his purpose, and each of the five races he again divides into a certain number of characteristic families. His main conclusions concerning the American race are these:

"1st. That the American race differs essentially from all others, not excepting the Mongolian; nor do the feeble analogies of language, and the more obvious ones in civil and religious institutions and the arts, denote anything beyond casual or colonial communication with the Asiatic nations; and even those analogies may perhaps be accounted for, as Humboldt has suggested, in the mere coincidence arising from similar wants and impulses in nations inhabiting similar latitudes.

"2d. That the American nations, excepting the polar tribes, are of one race and one species, but of two great families, which resemble each other in physical, but differ in intellectual character.

"3d. That the cranial remains discovered in the mounds from Peru to Wisconsin, belong to the same race, and probably to the Toltecan family."

The publication of a work of such costly character, and necessarily addressed to a very limited number of readers, was a bold undertaking for a man of restricted means. It was published by himself at the risk of considerable pecuniary loss. The original subscription list fell short of paying the expense, but I am happy to say that the subsequent sale of copies liquidated the deficit. The reception of the book by the learned was all he could have desired. Everywhere it received the warmest commendations. The following extract from a notice in the London Medico-Chirurgical Review for October 1840, will show the tone of the British scientific press:

"Dr. Morton's method and illustrations in eliciting the elements of his magnificent Craniography, are admirably concise, without being the less instructively comprehensive. His work constitutes, and will ever be highly appreciated as constituting an exquisite treasury of facts, well adapted, in all respects, to establish permanent organic principles in the natural history of man."

"Here we finish our account of Dr. Morton's American Cranioscopy; and by its extent and copiousness, our article will show how highly we have appreciated his classical production. We have studied his views with attention, and examined his doctrines with fairness; and with perfect sincerity in rising from a task which has afforded unusual gratification, we rejoice in ranking his 'Crania Americana' in the highest class of transatlantic literature, foreseeing distinctly that the book will ensure for its author the well-earned meed of a Caucasian reputation."

From among the warmly eulogistic letters received from distinguished *savans*, I select but one, that of Baron Humboldt, who is himself a high authority on American subjects.

"Monsieur,—Les liens intimes d'interêt et d'affection qui m'attachent, Monsieur, depuis un démi-siècle à l'hemisphère que vous habitez et dont j'ai la vanité de me croire citoyen, ont ajouté à l'impression que m'ont fait presque à la fois vôtre grand ouvrage de physiologie philosophique et l'admirable histoire de la conquête du Mexique par M. William Prescott. Voilá de ces travaux qui étendent, par des moyens très differens, la sphère de nos connaissances et de nos vues, et ajoutent à la gloire nationale. Je ne puis vous exprimer assez vivement, Monsieur, la profonde reconnaissance que je vous dois. Américain bien plus que Sibérien d'après la couleur de mes opinions, je suis, à mon grand age, singulièrement flatté de l'interêt qu'on me conserve encore de l'autre coté de la grand vallée atlantique sur laquelle la vapeur a presque jeté un pont. Les richesses craniologiques que vous avez été assez heureux de réunir, ont trouvé en vous un digne interprète. Votre ouvrage, Monsieur, est également remarquable par la profondeur des vues anatomiques, par le détail numérique des rapports de conformation organique, par l'absence des rêveries poétiques qui sont les mythes de la Physiologie moderne, par les généralités dont votre "Introductory Essay" abonde. Rédigeant dans ce moment le plus important de mes ouvrages qui sera publié sous le titre imprudent de *Kosmos*, je saurai profiter de tants d'excellents apperçus sur la destribution des races humaines qui se trouvent épars dans votre beau volume. Que de sacrifices pécuniares n'avez vous pas dû faire, pour atteindre une si grande perfection artistique et produire un ouvrage qui rivalise avec tout ce que l'on a fait de plus beau en Angleterre et en France.

"Agréez, je vous supplie, Monsieur, l'hommage renouvellé de la haute consideration avec laquelle j'ai l'honneur d'être,

"Monsieur, votre très-humble et très-obeissant serviteur,

"ALEXANDRE HUMBOLDT.

"à Berlin, ce 17 Janvier, 1844."

The eminent success of this work determined definitely its author's ulterior scientific career. From this time forward he devoted his powers almost exclusively to Ethnology. He sought in every direction for the materials for his investigation, when circumstances led to his acquaintance with Mr. George R. Gliddon, whose contributions opened to him a new field of research, and gave him an unexpected triumph. Mr. G. first visited this country in 1837, being sent out by Mehemet Ali to obtain information, purchase machinery, &c., in reference to the promotion of the cotton-culture in Egypt. Morton, who never lost the opportunity of securing an useful correspondent, sought his acquaintance, but failing to meet him personally, wrote him at New York under date of Nov. 2d, 1837, inquiring his precise address, and soliciting permission to visit him in reference to business. Illness preventing this visit, he wrote again, Nov. 7th. The following extract is interesting, as displaying his mode of procedure in such cases, as well as the state of his opinions, at the date in question:—

"You will observe by the annexed Prospectus that I am engaged in a work of considerable novelty, and which, as regards the typography and illustrations at least, is designed to be equal to any publication hitherto issued in this country. You may be surprised that I should address you on the subject, but a moment's explanation may suffice to convey my views and wishes. The prefatory chapter will embrace a view of the *varieties of the Human Race*, embracing, among other topics, some remarks on the ancient Egyptians. The position I have always assumed is, that the present Copts are *not* the remains of the ancient Egyptians, and in order more fully to make my comparisons, it is very important that I should get a few *heads* of Egyptian mummies from Thebes, &c. I do not care to have them entirely perfect specimens of embalming, but perfect in the bony structure, and with the hair preserved, if possible. It has occurred to me that, as you will reside at Cairo, and with your perfect knowledge of affairs in Egypt, you would have it in your power to employ a confidential and well-qualified person for this trust, who would save you all personal trouble; and if twenty-five or thirty skulls, or even half that number can be obtained, (and I am assured by persons who have been there that no obstacles need be feared, but of this you know best,) I am ready to defray every expense, and to *advance* the money, or any part of it *now*, or to arrange for payment, both as to expenses and commissions, at any time or in any way you may designate. With the Egyptian heads, I should be very glad to have a skull of a Copt and a Fellah, and indeed of any other of the present tribes in or bordering on Egypt, and which could be probably obtained through any one of your medical friends in Cairo or Alexandria. I hope before you leave to be able to send you one of the lithographs for my work, to prove to you that it will be no discredit to the arts of this country. Sensible how infinitely you may serve me in a favorite though novel inquiry, I cannot but hope to interest your feelings and exertions on this occasion, and therefore beg an early answer."

To this letter Mr. G. responded freely and cordially, readily undertaking the commission, which resulted in supplying Morton with crania, which form the basis of his renowned *Crania Ægyptiaca.* Without the aid thus afforded, any attempt to elucidate Egyptian ethnology from this side the Atlantic would have been absurdly hopeless; with it, a difficult problem was solved, and the opinion of the scientific world rectified in an important particular. The correspondence thus originated led to a close intimacy between the parties, which essentially modified the history of both, and ended only with life; and which resulted in a warmth of attachment, on the part of the survivor, that even death cannot chill, as the dedication of this volume attests. With the prospect of obtaining these Egyptian crania, Morton was delighted. How much he anticipated appears from the following passage in the preface to his *Crania Americana:*—

"Nor can I close this preface without recording my sincere thanks to George R. Gliddon, Esq., United States Consul at Cairo, in Egypt, for the singular zeal with which he has promoted my wishes in this respect; the series of crania he has already obtained for my use, of many nations, both ancient and modern, is perhaps without a rival in any existing collection; and will enable me, when it reaches this country, to pursue my comparisons on an extended scale." (p. 5.)

The skulls came to hand in the fall of 1840, and Morton entered eagerly upon their examination, and upon the study of Nilotic Archæology in connection therewith. Mr. Gliddon arrived in January 1842, with the intention of delivering a course of lectures in this country upon hieroglyphical subjects; and the two friends could now prosecute their studies together. They had already been engaged in active correspondence, Morton detailing the considerations which were impelling him to adopt views diverse, in several points, from what were generally considered established opinions. I regret that I have not access to the letters of Morton of this period, but the following extract from a reply of Gliddon, dated London, Oct. 21st, 1841, will show the state of their minds in regard to Egyptian questions at that time:—

"With regard to your projected work, (*Crania Ægyptiaca,*) I will, with every deference, frankly state a few evanescent impressions, which, were I with you, could be more fully developed. I am hostile to the opinion of the *African* origin of the Egyptians. I mean of the *high caste*—kings, priests, and military. The idea that the monuments support such theory, or the conclusion that they *came down the Nile*, or that 'Merawe' is the Father of Egypt, is, I think, untenable, and might be refuted. Herodotus's authority, unless modified in the way you mention, *dark skinned* and *curly* haired, is in this, as in fifty other instances, quite insignificant. We, as hieroglyphists, know Egypt better *now*, than all the Greek authors or the Roman. On this ground, unless you are convinced from Comparative Anatomy, with which science I am totally unacquainted, and be backed by such evidence as is incontrovertible, I urge your pausing, and considering why the ancient Egyptians may not be of Asiatic, and perhaps of Arabic descent; an idea which, I fancy, from the tenor of your letters, is your present conclusion. At any rate, they are not, and never were, Africans, still less Negroes. Monumental evidence appears to overthrow the African theory. . . . . Look at the portraits of the kings of Egypt, in the plates of Prof. Rosellini's *Monumenti Storici*, and then read his 2d vol. text, at the end. They are facsimiles, and is there anything African in them, (excepting in the Amunoph family, where this cross is shown and explained,) until you come down to the Ethiopian dynasty? For 'Merawe' read Hoskins's Ethiopia — it is a valuable work, but I differ *in toto* from his chronology, or his connection between Egypt and 'Meroe' *down* the Nile.

"The Copts *may* be descendants of the ancient race, but so crossed and recrossed, as to have lost almost every vestige of their noble ancestry. I should think it would be difficult, with 100 skulls of Copts, to get at an exact criterion, they are so varied. Do not forget also the effect of wearing the turban on the Eastern races, except the Fellahs, who seldom can afford it, and wear a cap.

"It has been the fashion to quote the Sphinx, as an evidence of the Negro tendencies of ancient Egyptians. They take his *wig* for woolly hair — and as the nose is off, of course it is *flat*. But even if the face (which I fully admit) has a strong African cast, it is an almost solitary example, against 10,000 that *are not African*. We may presume from the *fact* that the tablet found on it bears the name of the 5th Thotmes—B. C. 1702—Rosellini, No. 106—that it represents some king, (and most probably Thotmes 5th himself,) who, by ancestral intermarriage, was of African blood. In fact, we find that Amunoph 1st—B. C. 1822 — and only five removes from this same Thotmes his successor, had an Ethiopian wife — a black queen — 'Aahmes Nofreari.' If the Sphinx were a female, I should at once say it stood for 'Nofreari,' who, as the wife of the expeller of the Hykshos, was much revered. The whole of the Thotmes and Amunoph branches had an African cast — *vide* Amunoph 3d — almost a Nubian: but this cast is expressly given in their portraits, in contradistinction to the aquiline-nosed and red Egyptians. Look at the Ramses family— their men are quite Caucasian — their women are white, or only yellowish, but I can see nothing African. I wish I were by your side with my notes and rambling ideas — they are crude, but under your direction could be licked into shape. The masses of facts are extraordinary, and known but to very, very few. Unless a man now-a-days is a hieroglyphist, and has studied the monuments, believe me, his authority is dangerous; and but few instances are there in which amongst the thousand-and-one volumes on Egypt, the work is not a mere repetition or copy of the errors of a preceding work — and this is but repeating what the Romans never comprehended, but copied from the Greeks, who made up for their ignorance then, as they do now, by *lies*. All were deplorably ignorant on Egyptian matters. Anything of the Champollion, Rosellini, and Wilkinson school for ancient subjects, is *safe* — for the modern, there is only Lane. I mention these subjects just to arrest your attention, before you take a leap; though I have no doubt you leave no stone unturned. Pardon my apparent officiousness, but I do this at the hazard of intruding, lest in your earnest comparisons of 'Crania,' you may not lay sufficient stress on the vast monumental evidences of days of yore, and mean this only as a 'caveat.'"

But they soon found themselves in want of books, especially of costly illustrated works. Not only was it essential to verify quotations by reference to the text, but the plates were absolutely indispensable.

The desired books did not exist in any library in the United States, and Morton had already gone as far as prudence permitted. In a letter now before me, Gliddon writes him from New York in despair, stating that, for his part, he could not move a step further without access to Rosellini, (*Monumenti*, &c.,) of which there was not a copy in the country. This serious difficulty was finally removed by the munificent liberality of Richard K. Haight, Esq., of New York, who, actuated solely by a generous desire to promote the interests of science, imported and placed at the disposal of our students the superb volumes in question.

Morton's study now was more than ever "a place of skulls." His correspondence, having been widely extended, was at last bearing its fruit. Contributions came dropping in from various quarters, not always accompanied with reliable information, and requiring careful deliberation before being assigned a place in his cabinet. Nothing short of positive certainty, however, would induce him to place a name upon a cranium. The ordeal of examination each had to undergo was rigid in the extreme. Accurate and repeated measurements of every part were carefully made. Where a case admitted of doubt, I have known him to keep the skull in his office for weeks, and, taking it down at every leisure moment, sit before it, and contemplate it fixedly in every position, noting every prominence and depression, estimating the extent and depth of every muscular or ligamentous attachment, until he could, as it were, build up the soft parts upon their bony substratum, and see the individual as in life. His quick artistic perception of minute resemblances or discrepancies of form and color, gave him great facilities in these pursuits. A single glance of his rapid eye was often enough to determine what, with others, would have been the subject of tedious examination. The drawings for the *Crania Ægyptiaca* were made by Messrs. Richard H. and Edward M. Kern,*

* Even while I write (Dec. 1st, 1853) the news has reached us of the brutal murder by Utah Indians of Richard H. Kern, with Lieut. Gunnison, and others of the party engaged in the survey of the proposed middle route for a Pacific Railroad. So young, and so full of hope and promise! to be cut off thus, too, just as his matured intellect began to command him position, and to realize the bright anticipations of his many friends! The relations of Mr Gliddon and myself to this new victim of savage ferocity were so intimate, that we may be excused if we pause here to give to his memory a sigh—one in which the subject of our memoir, were he still with us, would join in deepest sympathy. But the sorrow we feel is one that cannot be free from bitterness, while the bones of Dick Kern bleach unavenged upon the arid plains of Deseret. We have had too much of sentimentalism about the Red-man. It is time that cant was stopped now. Not all the cinnamon-colored vermin west of the Mississippi are worth one drop of that noble heart's-blood. The busy brain, the artist's eye, the fine taste, the hand so ready with either pen or pencil,—could these be restored to us again, they would be cheaply purchased back if it cost the extermination of every miserable Pah-Utah under heaven! He is the second member of

who were then also engaged in preparing the magnificent illustrations of Mr. Gliddon's hierological lectures; and these gentlemen have informed me that not the slightest departure from literal accuracy could escape the eye of Morton. This was true, not only of human figures, but equally of the minutest hieroglyphic details. Dr. Meigs, in his Memoir, relates an instance of his acumen, in which, while inspecting the ægis in the hand of a female divinity, he noticed the resemblance to the face of a certain queen, and at once referred it to that reign; which, on examining the text, proved correct. The two following anecdotes, for which I am indebted to Mr. Gliddon, resemble the well-known instances of scientific acuteness and perspicacity that are related of Cuvier.

In the summer of 1842, Mr. G. met in New York with Mr. John L. Stephens, then recently returned from his second visit to Yucatan. The conversation turning upon crania, Mr. S. regretted the destruction of all he had collected, in consequence of their extreme brittleness. One skeleton he had hoped to save, but on unpacking it, that morning, it was found so dilapidated that he had ordered it thrown away. Mr. G. begged to see it, and secured it, comminuted as it was. Its condition may be inferred from the fact that the entire skeleton was tied up in a small India handkerchief, and carried to Philadelphia in a hat-box. It was given to Morton, who at first deplored it as a hopeless wreck. The next day, however, Mr. G. found him, with a glue-pot beside him, engaged in an effort to reconstruct the skull. A small piece of the occiput served as a basis, upon which he put together all the posterior portion of the cranium, showing it by characteristic marks to be that of an adult Indian female. From the condition of another portion of the skeleton, he derived evidence of a pathological fact of considerable moment, in view of the antiquity of these remains. How much interest he was able to extract from this handful of apparent rubbish will appear from the following passages:—

"The purport of his opinion is as follows:—In the first place, the needle did not deceive the Indian who picked it up in the grave. The bones are those of a female. Her height did not exceed five feet, three or four inches. The teeth are perfect and not appreciably worn, while the *epiphyses*, those infallible indications of the growing state, have just become consolidated, and mark the completion of adult age. The bones of the hands and feet are remarkably small and delicately proportioned, which observation applies also to the entire

---

his family that has met this melancholy fate. His brother, Dr. Benjamin J. Kern—a pupil of Morton, and surgeon to the ill-fated expedition of Colonel Frémont in the winter of 1848–49—was cruelly massacred by Utahs in the spring of 1849, in the mountains near Taos. So long as our government allows cases of this kind to remain without severe retribution, so long, in savage logic, will impunity in crime be considered a free license to murder at will.

skeleton. The skull was crushed into many pieces, but, by a cautious manipulation, Dr. Morton succeeded in reconstructing the posterior and lateral portions. The occiput is remarkably flat and vertical, while the lateral or parietal diameter measures no less than five inches and eight-tenths.

"A chemical examination of some fragments of the bones proves them to be almost destitute of animal matter, which, in the perfect osseous structure, constitutes about thirty-three parts in the hundred. On the upper part of the left tibià there is a swelling of the bone, called in surgical language a *node*, an inch and a half in length, and more than half an inch above the natural surface. This morbid condition may have resulted from a variety of causes, but possesses greater interest on account of its extreme infrequency among the primitive Indian population of the country."*

Mr. Gliddon, while in Paris in 1845–6, presented a copy of the *Crania Ægyptiaca* to the celebrated orientalist, M. Fulgence Fresnel, (well known as the decipherer of the Himyaritic inscriptions, and now engaged in Ninevite explorations,) and endeavored to interest him in Morton's labors. More than a year afterwards, having returned to Philadelphia, he received there a box from R. K. Haight, Esq., then at Naples. The box contained a skull, but not a word of information concerning it. It was handed over to Morton, who at once perceived its dissimilarity to any in his possession. It was evidently very old, the animal matter having almost entirely disappeared. Day after day would Morton be found absorbed in its contemplation. At last he announced his conclusion. He had never seen a Phœnician skull, and he had no idea where this one came from; but it was what he conceived that a Phœnician skull should be, and it could be no other. Things remained thus until some six months afterwards, when Mr. Haight returned to America, and delivered to Mr. G. the letters and papers sent him by various persons. Among them was a slip in the hand-writing of Fresnel, containing the history of the skull in question.† He discovered it during his exploration of a *Phœnician* tomb at Malta, and had consigned it to Morton by Mr. H., whom he met at Naples. These anecdotes not only show the extraordinary acuteness of Morton, but they also prove the certainty of the anatomical marks upon which Craniologists rely.

The *Crania Ægyptiaca* was published in 1844, in the shape of a contribution to the Transactions of the American Philosophical Society. This apparent delay in its appearance arose from the author's extreme caution in forming his conclusions, especially in view of the fact that he found himself compelled to differ in opinion from the majority of scholars, in regard to certain points of primary importance. Most ethnologists, with the high authority of Prichard at their

* Stephens' Yucatan, vol. i. pp. 281–2.—Morton's Catalogue of Crania, 1849, No. 1050.

† Catalogue, No. 1352.

head, ascribed the Nilotic family to the African race; while the great body of Archæologists were disposed to consider the aborigines of Egypt as (probably black) Troglodytes, from the Upper Nile, whose first halting-place and seat of civilization was at Meroë. But Morton took counsel with none of those authorities of the day. *Optimi consultores mortui;* and these dead, but still eloquent witnesses of the past, taught him clearly the identity of cranial conformation in the ancient Egyptian and the modern white man. He established, beyond question, that the prevailing type of skull must come into the Caucasian category of Blumenbach. He pointed out the distinctions between this and the neighboring Semitic and Pelasgic types. The population of Egypt being always a very mixed one, he was able also to identify among his crania those displaying the Semitic, Pelasgic, Negro and Negroid forms. Turning next to the monuments, he adduced a multitude of facts to prove the same position. His historical deductions were advanced modestly and cautiously, but most of them have been triumphantly verified. While he, in his quiet study at Philadelphia, was inferentially denying the comparative antiquity of Meroë, Lepsius was upon the spot, doing the same thing beyond the possibility of further cavil. The book was written when it was still customary to seek a foreign origin for the inhabitants of every spot on earth except Mesopotamia; and the author, therefore, indicates, rather than asserts, an Asiatic origin for the Egyptians. But his *resumé* contains propositions so important, that I must claim space for them entire, taking the liberty of calling the attention of the reader, by Italics, particularly to the last.

1. The valley of the Nile, both in Egypt and in Nubia, was originally peopled by a branch of the Caucasian race.
2. These primeval people, since called Egyptians, were the Mizraimites of Scripture, the posterity of Ham, and directly associated with the Libyan family of nations.
3. In their physical character, the Egyptians were intermediate between the modern European and Semitic races.
4. The Austral-Egyptian or Meroite communities were an Indo-Arabian stock, engrafted on the primitive Libyan inhabitants.
5. Besides these exotic sources of population, the Egyptian race was at different periods modified by the influx of the Caucasian nations of Asia and Europe — Pelasgi or Hellenes, Scythians and Phœnicians.
6. Kings of Egypt appear to have been incidentally derived from each of the above nations.
7. The Copts, in part at least, are a mixture of the Caucasian and Negro, in extremely variable proportions.
8. Negroes were numerous in Egypt. Their social position, in ancient times, was the same that it is now; that of servants or slaves.
9. The natural characteristics of all these families of man were distinctly figured on the monuments, and all of them, excepting the Scythians and Phœnicians, have been identified in the catacombs.

10. The present Fellahs are the lineal and least mixed descendants of the ancient Egyptians; and the latter are collaterally represented by the Tuaricks, Kabyles, Siwahs, and other remains of the Libyan family of nations.
11. The modern Nubians, with few exceptions, are not the descendants of the monumental Ethiopians; but a variously mixed race of Arabians and Negroes.
12. Whatever may have been the size of the cartilaginous portion of the ear, the osseous structure conforms, in every instance, to the usual relative position.
13. The teeth differ in nothing from those of other Caucasian nations.
14. The hair of the Egyptians resembles in texture that of the fairest Europeans of the present day.
15. *The physical or organic characters which distinguish the several races of men are as old as the oldest records of our species.*

The sentiments here enunciated he subsequently modified in one essential particular. In his letter to Mr. Bartlett of Dec. 1st, 1846, (published in vol. 2d of the Transactions of the American Ethnological Society, p. 215,) after reiterating his conviction that the pure Egyptian of the remotest monumental period differed as much from the negro as does the white man of to-day, he continues:—

"My later investigations have confirmed me in the opinion, that the valley of the Nile was inhabited by an indigenous race, before the invasion of the Hamitic and other Asiatic nations; and that this primeval people, who occupied the whole of Northern Africa, bore much the same relation to the Berber or Berabra tribes of Nubia, that the Saracens of the middle ages bore to their wandering and untutored, yet cognate brethren, the Bedouins of the desert."

Further details on this point will be found on pp. 231 and 232 of the present work.

The reception of this book was even more flattering than had been that of its predecessor. To admiration was added a natural feeling of surprise, that light upon this interesting subject should have come from this remote quarter. Lepsius received it on the eve of departure on his expedition to Djébel-Barkal, and his letter acknowledging it was dated from the island of Philæ. One can imagine with what intense interest such a man, so situated, must have followed the lucid deductions of the clear-headed American, writing at the other side of the world. But probably the most gratifying notice of the book is that by Prichard, in the Appendix to his Natural History of Man, of which I extract a portion. He quotes Morton largely, and always with commendation, even where the conclusions of the latter are in conflict with his own previously published opinions.

"A most interesting and really important addition has lately been made to our knowledge of the physical character of the ancient Egyptians. This has been derived from a quarter where local probabilities would least of all have induced us to have looked for it. In France, where so many scientific men have been devoted, ever since the conquest of Egypt by Napoleon, for a long time under the patronage of government, to researches into this subject; in England, possessed of the immense advantage of wealth and commercial resources; in the academies of Italy and Germany, where the arts of Egypt have been studied in national museums, scarcely anything has been done since the time of Blumenbach to elucidate the physical history of the ancient Egyptian race. In none of these countries have any extensive collections been formed of the materials and resources which alone can afford a secure foundation for such attempts. It is in the United States of America that a remarkable advancement of this part of physical science has been at length achieved. 'The Transactions of the American Philosophical Society' contain a memoir by Dr. Morton of Philadelphia, in which that able and zealous writer, already distinguished by his admirable researches into the physical characters of the native American races, has brought forward a great mass of new information on the ancient Egyptians." (p. 57.)

This brings us at once to the consideration of Morton's opinion upon the much-vexed question of the unity or diversity of the various races of men, or rather of their origin from a single pair; for that alone practically has been the topic of discussion. It is a subject of too much importance, both to the cause of science and the memory of Morton, to be passed over slightly. Above all, there is necessary a clear and fair statement of his opinions, in order that there may be no mistake. His mind was progressive on this subject, as upon many others. He had to disabuse himself of erroneous notions, early acquired, as well as to discover the truth. It is therefore possible so to quote him as to misrepresent his real sentiments, or to make his assertions appear contradictory and confused. I propose to show the gradual growth of his convictions by the quotation, in their legitimate series, of his published expressions on the subject.

The unity and common origin of mankind have, until recently, been considered undisputed points of doctrine. They seem to have been regarded as propositions not scientifically established, so much as taken for granted, and let alone. All men were held to be descended from the single pair mentioned in Genesis; every tribe was thought to be historically traceable to the regions about Mesopotamia; and ordinary physical influences were believed sufficient to explain the remarkable diversities of color, &c. These opinions were thought to be the teachings of Scripture not impugned by science, and were therefore almost universally acquiesced in. By Blumenbach, Prichard, and others, the unity is assumed as an axiom not disputed. It is curious that the only attack made upon this dogma, until of late, was made from a theological, and not from a scientific stand-point. The celebrated book of Peyrerius on the pre-Adamites was written to solve certain difficulties in biblical exegesis, (such as Cain's wife, the city he builded, &c.,) for the writer was a mere scholastic theologian.* He met the fate of all who ventured to defy the hierarchy, at a day when they had the civil power at their back. Now they are confined to the calling of names, as *infidel* and the like, although mischief enough

* Præ-Adamitæ, sive exercitatio super versibus duodecimo, decimotertio et decimo quarto capitis quinti Epistolæ D. Pauli ad Romanos. Quibus inducuntur primi Homines ante Adamum conditi. Anno Salutis MDCLV.

can they thus do, inflicting a poisoned wound. Then they had their fagots in the Place de Grève, and as they could not catch Peyrerius, the Sorbonne ordered his book publicly burned by the common hangman. There is something ludicrously pathetic in the manner in which he addresses his essay to the then-persecuted Jews, with an *utinam ex vobis unus!* and adds, "Hoc mihi certe cum vobis commune est; quod vitam duco erraticam, quæque parum convenit cum otio meditantis et scribentis." The press fairly rained replies to this daring work, from both Catholic and Protestant writers, but not one of them based on scientific grounds, nor, indeed, in the defence of Genesis. Peyrerius would appear to have confessedly the advantage there. But it was asserted that the denial of mankind's universal descent from the loins of Adam, militated with the position of the latter as "federal head" of the race in the "scheme of redemption." The writer's offence was purely theological, and hence the charge of Socinianism and the vehemence with which even a phlegmatic Dutchman could be roused to hurl at his devoted head the anathema: *Perturbet te Dominus, quia perturbasti Israelem!* * This excitement over, the subject was heard of no more until the French writers of the last century again agitated it. Voltaire repeatedly and mercilessly ridicules the idea of a common origin. He says—"Il n'est permis qu'à un aveugle de douter que les blancs, les Nègres, les Albinos, les Hottentots, les Lappons, les Chinois, les Americains, soient des races entièrement différentes."† But Voltaire was not scientific, and his opinion upon such questions would go for nothing with men of science. Prichard therefore sums up his Natural History of Man, (*London*, 1845,) with the final emphatic declaration "that all human races are of one species and one family." The doctrine of the unity was indeed almost universally held even by those commonly rated as "Deistical" writers. D'Hancarville, and his fellow *dilettanti*, will certainly not be suspected of any proclivity to orthodoxy; yet, in his remarks upon the wide dissemination of Phallic and other religious emblems, he gives the ensuing forcible and eloquent statement of his conviction of the full historical evidence of unity:—

"Comme les coquillages et les débris des productions de la mer, qui sont déposés sans nombre et sans mesure sur toute la surface du globe, attestent qu'à des tems inconnus à toutes les histoires, il fût occupé et recouvert par les eaux; ainsi ces emblêmes singuliers, admis dans toutes les parties de l'ancien continent, attestent qu'à des tems antérieurs à tous ceux dont parlent les historiens, toutes les nations chez laquelle existérent ces emblêmes eurent un même culte, une même religion, une même théologie, et vraisemblablement une même langage."‡

---

* Non-ens Præ-Adamiticum. Sive confutatio vani et Socinizantis cujusdam Somnii, &c. Autore Antonio Hulsio. Lugd. Batav. MDCLVI.

† Essai sur les Mœurs, Introd.

‡ Recherches sur l'origine, l'esprit et les progrès des arts de la Grèce, London, 1785, L. 1. xiv.

Morton was educated in youth to regard this doctrine as a scriptural verity, and he found it accepted as the first proposition in the existing Ethnology. As such he received it implicitly, and only abandoned it when compelled by the force of an irresistible conviction. What he received in sincerity, he taught in good faith. There can be no doubt that in that early course of 1830, he inculcated the unity doctrine as strongly as ever did Prichard.

But this state of opinion could not continue undisturbed. The wide ethnic diversities which so forcibly impressed one who contemplated them merely as an historian and critic (as Voltaire), could not fail to engage the attention of naturalists. The difficulties of the popular doctrine became daily more numerous and apparent, and it owed its continued existence, less to any inherent strength, than to the forbearance of those who disliked to awaken controversy by assailing it. The ordinary exposition of Genesis it was impossible for naturalists longer to accept, but they postponed to the utmost the inevitable contest. The battle had been fought upon astronomy and gained; so that *Ma pur si muove* had become the watchword of the scientific world in its conflict with the *parti prêtre.* The Geologists were even then coming victorious out of the combat concerning the six days of Creation, and the universality of the Deluge. The Archæologists were at the moment beating down the old-fashioned short chronology. Now another exciting struggle was at hand. Unfortunately it seems out of the question to discuss topics which touch upon theology without rousing bad blood. "Religious subjects," says Payne Knight, "being beyond the reach of sense or reason, are always embraced or rejected with violence or heat. Men think they *know* because they are sure they *feel*, and are firmly convinced because strongly agitated."* But disagreeable as was the prospect of controversy, it could not be avoided. It is curious to read Lawrence now, and see how he piles up the objections to his own doctrine, until you doubt whether he believes it himself! The main difficulty concerns a single centre of creation. The dispersion of mankind from such a centre, somewhere on the alluvium of the Euphrates, might be admitted as possible; but the gathering of all animated nature at Eden to be named by Adam, the distribution thence to their respective remote and diversified habitats, their reassembling by pairs and sevens in the Ark, and their second distribution from the same centre — these conceptions are what Lawrence long ago pronounced them, simply "zoologically impossible." The error arises from mistaking the local traditions of a circumscribed community for universal history. As Peyrerius remarked two centuries ago, "peccatur non raro in lectione sacrorum

* R. Payne Knight. Letter to Sir Jos. Bankes and Sir Wm. Hamilton, p. 23.

codicum, quoties generalius accipitur, quod specialius debuit intelligi."* The most rigid criticism has demonstrated, beyond the possibility of disputation, that all the nations and tribes mentioned in the Pentateuch, are included strictly within the so-called Caucasian race, and that the writer probably never heard of (as he certainly never mentions) any other than white men. This discussion, even to the limited extent to which it has gone, has called forth much bitterness; not on the part of sincere students of the sacred text, but of that *prêtraille* which, arrogant in the direct ratio of its ignorance, substitutes clamor and denunciation for reason, and casts the dirt of opprobrious epithets when it has no arguments to offer. But already this advantage has arisen from the agitation:—that some preliminary points at least may be considered settled, and a certain amount of scholarship may be demanded of those who desire to enter the discussion; thus eliminating from it the majority of persons most ready to present themselves with noisy common-place, already ten times refuted. The men who, in the middle of the nineteenth century, can still find the ancestors of Mongolians and Americans among the sons of Japhet, or who talk about the curse of Canaan in connexion with Negroes,† are plainly without the pale of controversy, as they are beyond the reach of criticism. There is, even in some who have recently published books on the subject, such a helpless profundity of ignorance of the very first facts of the case, that one finds no fitting answer to them but—expressive silence! To endeavor to raise such to the dignity of Ethnologists, even by debate with them, is to pay them a compliment beyond their deserts. They have no right whatever to thrust themselves into the field,—the lists are opened for another class of combatants. Therefore they cannot be recognised. With Dante,

"Non ragionam di lor; ma guarda, e passa!"

It was impossible for Morton, in the prosecution of his labors, to avoid these exciting questions. We have his own assurance that he early felt the insuperable difficulties attending the hypothesis of a common origin of all races. He seems soon to have abandoned, if he ever entertained, the notion that ordinary physical influences will account for existing diversities, at least within the limits of the popular short chronology. There are two ways of escaping this difficulty—one by denying entirely the competency of physical causes to produce the effects alleged; and the other to grant them an indefinite period for their operation, as Prichard did in the end, with his "chiliads

* Op. cit., p. 163.

† The Doctrine of the Unity of the Human Race, examined on the Principles of Science, by John Bachman, D. D. Charleston: 1850. pp. 291–292.

of years," for man's existence upon earth. Morton inclined to the other view, mainly in consequence of the historical evidence he had accumulated, showing the unalterable permanency of the characteristics of race, within the limits of human records. But he was slow to hazard the publication of an opinion upon a question of so great moment. He preferred to wait, not only until his own conviction became certainty, but until he could adduce the mass of testimony necessary to convince others. This extreme caution characterized all his literary labors, and made his conclusions always reliable.* A true disciple of the inductive philosophy, he labored long and hard in the verification of his premises. With an inexhaustible patience he accumulated fact upon fact, and published observation upon observation, often apparently dislocated and objectless, but all intended for future use. Many of his minor papers are mere stores of disjointed data. More than once, when observing his untiring labor and its long postponed result, he has brought into my mind those magnificent lines of Shelley:

Hark! the rushing snow!
The sun-awakened avalanche! whose mass,
Thrice sifted by the storm, had gathered there
Flake after flake, in heaven-defying minds
As thought by thought is piled, till some great truth
Is loosened, and the nations echo round,
Shaken to their roots, as do the mountains now.†

In fact, he had an eye, in all his investigations, to the publication at some future period of a work on the *Elements of Ethnology*, which should contain the fully ripened fruits of so many years of toil. Of this project he speaks in some of his letters as "perhaps an idle dream," but one for whose realization he would make many sacrifices. For it he reserved the complete expression of his ethnological doctrines. This consideration, and his extreme dislike of controversy, made him particularly guarded in his statements. Constitutionally averse to all noisy debate and contention, he was well aware also that they are incompatible with the calmness essential to successful scientific inquiry. Nothing but an aggravated assault could have drawn from him a reply. That assault was made, and, as I conceive, most

* In a letter of Prof. O. W. Holmes to Dr. Morton, (dated Boston, Nov. 27th, 1849,) I find the following passage, so just in its appreciation of his scientific character, that I take the liberty of quoting it:—

"The more I read on these subjects, the more I am delighted with the severe and cautious character of your own most extended researches, which, from their very nature, are permanent data for all future students of Ethnology, whose leader on this side the Atlantic, to say the least, you have so happily constituted yourself by well-directed and long-continued efforts."

† Prometheus Unbound, Act II., Scene 3d.

fortunately for his reputation. Without it, he would probably have ceased from his labors without having published any such explicit and unmistakeable expression of opinion, on this important question, as his scientific friends would have desired. As it is, he has left no room for doubt or cavil as to his position in the very front of our onward progress in Anthropology.

The first published opinion of Morton in reference to this question is found in the *Crania Americana*. It will be perceived, that, recognizing the entire incompetency of ordinary climatic and similar influences to produce the alleged effects, he suggests, as an escape from the difficulty, that the marks of Race were impressed at once by Divine Power upon the immediate family of Adam.

"The recent discoveries in Egypt give additional force to the preceding statement, inasmuch as they show, beyond all question, that the Caucasian and Negro races were as perfectly distinct in that country, upwards of three thousand years ago, as they are now; whence it is evident, that if the Caucasian was derived from the Negro, or the Negro from the Caucasian, *by the action of external causes*, the change must have been effected in, at most, one thousand years; a theory which the subsequent evidence of thirty centuries proves to be a physical impossibility; and we have already ventured to insist that such a commutation could be effected by nothing short of a miracle." (p. 88.)

In his printed Introductory Lecture of 1842, the same views are repeated, and the insufficiency of external causes again insisted upon. In April of the same year, he read, before the Boston Society of Natural History, a paper which was republished in 1844, under the title of *An Inquiry into the Distinctive Characteristics of the Aboriginal Race of America*. From this paper I extract the following striking passage:

In fine, our own conclusion, long ago deduced from a patient examination of the facts thus briefly and inadequately stated, is, that the American race is essentially separate and peculiar, whether we regard it in its physical, moral, or its intellectual relations. To us there are no direct or obvious links between the people of the old world and the new; for even admitting the seeming analogies to which we have alluded, these are so few in number, and evidently so casual, as not to invalidate the main position; and even should it be hereafter shown that the arts, sciences, and religion of America can be traced to an exotic source, I maintain that the organic characters of the people themselves, through all their endless ramifications of tribes and nations, prove them to belong to one and the same race, and that this race is distinct from all others." (p. 35.)

His unequivocal assertion of the permanency of the distinctive marks of Race in the final proposition of his *resumé* of the *Crania Ægyptiaca* has already been given, (*supra*, p.xlii.) Two years afterwards he published this emphatic declaration:

"I can aver that sixteen years of almost daily comparisons have only confirmed me in the conclusions announced in my "Crania Americana," that all the American nations, excepting the Eskimaux, are of one race, and that this race is peculiar and distinct from all others."*

* Ethnography and Archæology of the American Aborigines. New Haven: 1846. (p. 9.)

The next citation is from the letter to Mr. Bartlett before mentioned:

"But it is necessary to explain what is here meant by the word race. I do not use it to imply that all its divisions are derived from a single pair; on the contrary, I believe they have originated from several, perhaps even from many pairs, which were adapted, from the beginning, to the varied localities they were designed to occupy; and the Fuegians, less migratory than the cognate tribes, will serve to illustrate this idea. In other words, I regard the American nations as the true autocthones, the primeval inhabitants of this vast continent; and when I speak of their being of one race or of one origin, I allude only to their indigenous relation to each other, as shown in all those attributes of mind and body which have been so amply illustrated by modern ethnography."*

In a note to a paper in Silliman's Journal for 1847, he says:—

"I may here observe, that whenever I have ventured an opinion on this question, it has been in favor of the doctrine of *primeval diversities* among men — an original adaptation of the several races to those varied circumstances of climate and locality, which, while congenial to the one, are destructive to the other; and subsequent investigations have confirmed me in these views."†

One would suppose that whoever had read the above publications could have no doubt as to Morton's sentiments; yet Dr. Bachman and others have affected to be suddenly surprised by the utterance of opinions which had been distinctly implied, and even openly published years before. To leave no further doubt upon the subject, he thus expresses himself in his letter to Dr. Bachman of March 30th, 1850:—

"I commenced the study of Ethnology about twenty years since; and among the first aphorisms taught me by all the books to which I then had access, was this — that all mankind were derived from a single pair; and that the diversities now so remarkable, originated solely from the operations of climate, locality, food, and other physical agents. In other words, that man was created a perfect and beautiful being in the first instance, and that chance, *chance* alone has caused all the physical disparity among men, from the noblest Caucasian form to the most degraded Australian and Hottentot. I approached the subject as one of great difficulty and delicacy; and my first convictions were, that these diversities are not acquired, but have existed *ab origine*. Such is the opinion expressed in my *Crania Americana;* but at that period, (twelve years ago,) I had not investigated Scriptural Ethnology, and was content to suppose that the distinctive characteristics of the several races had been marked upon the immediate family of Adam. Further investigation, however, in connection with zoological science, has led me to take a wider view of this question, of which an outline is given above."‡

In order to present still more fully and clearly the final conclusions of our revered friend on this topic, I append two of his letters. The first is addressed to Dr. Nott, under date of January 29th, 1850.

---

* Transactions of American Ethnological Society, vol. ii. New York: 1848. (p. 219.)

† Hybridity in animals and plants, considered in reference to the question of the Unity of the Human Species. New Haven: 1847. (p. 4.)

‡ Letter to the Rev. John Bachman, D. D., on the question of Hybridity in animals. Charleston: 1850. (p. 15.)

"I have read and re-read your *Two Lectures* with great pleasure and instruction. I am especially pleased with the triumphant manner in which you have treated the absurd postulate, that one race can be transmuted into another. The only illustrations that can be adduced by its advocates, as you justly observe, are certain diseased and abnormal organizations, that, by a wise law of nature, wear out in a few generations. Some of your aphorisms have delighted me. 'Man can *invent* nothing in science or religion but falsehood; and all the truths which he *discovers* are but facts or laws which have emanated from the Creator.' This is a noble sentiment admirably expressed. I am slowly preparing my memoir 'On the Size of the Brain in various Races and Families of Man; with Ethnological Remarks.' The latter clause will give me sufficient scope for the expression of my views on those sensitive points of Ethnology in which I entirely agree with you in opinion; leaving out all theological discussion, which I have carefully avoided. You will observe a note in my Essay on Hybridity, in which I avow my belief in a plurality of origins for the human species, and I have now extended those observations, and briefly illustrated them; but in so doing I find no difficulty with the text of Genesis, which is just as manageable in Ethnology as it has proved in Astronomy, Geology, and Chronology. When I took this ground four years ago, (and in the *Crania Americana* my position is the same, though more cautiously worded,) it was with some misgivings, not because I doubted the truth of my opinions, but because I feared they would lead to some controversy with the clergy. Nothing of the kind has happened; for I have avoided coming into collision with men who too often uphold a garbled text of Scripture, to defeat the progress of truth and science. I have had some letters from the clergy and from other piously-disposed persons, but the only one that had any spice of vehemence was from a friend, Dr. Bachman, of Charleston. A number of clergymen have called upon me for information on this subject, and I confess to you my surprise at the liberal tone of feeling they have expressed on this sensitive question; and I really believe that if they are not pressed too hard, they will finally concede all that can be asked of the mere question of diversity; for it can be far more readily reconciled to the Mosaic annals than some other points, Astronomy, &c., for example. As for Chronology, we all know it to be a *broken reed.* Look at the last page of Dr. Prichard's great work — the last page of his fifth and last volume — and he there gives it as his matured opinion that the human race has been 'chiliads of centuries' upon the earth! He had before found it necessary to prove the Deluge a partial phenomenon, and he also admits that no physical agents could ever have produced the existing diversities among men; and ascribes them to *accidental varieties* which have been careful to intermix only among themselves, and thereby perpetuated their race! Compared with this last inadequate hypothesis, how beautiful, how evidently and inherently truthful is the proposition — that our species had its origin, not in one, but in several or in many creations; and that these diverging from their primitive centres, met and amalgamated in the progress of time, and have thus given rise to these intermediate links of organization which now connect the extremes together. Here is the truth divested of mystery; a system that explains the otherwise unintelligible phenomena so remarkably stamped on the races of men."

The remaining letter is addressed to Mr. Gliddon, under date of Philadelphia, April 27th, 1851, little more than two weeks before its author ceased to breathe. I publish it *verbatim*, so that the reader may see that the concluding emphatic declaration stands unqualified by anything in the context.

"My dear Sir:—Have you Squier's pamphlets on California and New Mexico? Is it not in them that is contained a refutation of the old fable of *white Indians* on or near the Rio Gila? If so, please send me the above paper by mail as soon as you can. I must have them somewhere, but I am in an emergency for them, and they cannot be found. I am hard at work at my chapter for Schoolcraft's book, and am desirous to get it off my hands.

I send you a paragraph from the Ledger which will gratify you. There is no higher praise than this. It is all the better for being so aphorismally expressed. *The doctrine of the original diversity of mankind unfolds itself to me more and more with the distinctness of revelation.*

"With kindest remembrances to Mrs. G. and your fine boy, I am,

"Ever faithfully yours,

"S. G. MORTON."

These citations are sufficient for our purpose, I apprehend, especially the laconic emphasis of the last, which may be regarded as the *ethnological testament* of our lamented friend. I have been thus full upon this point, because I believe it but justice to his memory to show that he was among the very earliest to accept and give shape to the doctrine stated. As the mountain summits are gilded with the early dawn, while the plain below still sleeps in darkness, so it is the loftiest spirit among men that first receives and reflects the radiance of the coming truth. Morton has occupied that position among us, in relation to this important advance in scientific opinion. I have desired to put the evidence of it fairly upon record, and thus to claim and secure the distinction that is justly due him.

Many well-meaning, but uninformed persons have, however, raised an outcry of horror against the assertion of original human diversities, in which they have been joined by others who ought to know better. The attack is not made upon the doctrine itself, nor upon any direct logical consequence of it. The alleged grievance consists entirely in the loss of certain corollaries deducible from the opposite proposition. Thus it is asserted that our religious system and our doctrine of social and political rights, alike result from the hypothesis of human consanguinity and common origin, and stand or fall with it. To this effect we have constantly quoted to us the high authority of Humboldt, who says, "En maintenant l'unité de l'espèce humaine, nous rejetons par conséquence nécessaire, la distinction désolante de races supérieures et de races inférieures."*

In a note he again applies the term *désolante* to this doctrine. I have used the French translation, because it is the more forcible, and because it was that read by Morton, whose felicitous commentary upon it I am fortunately able to adduce, from a letter to Mr. Gliddon, of May 30th, 1846.

"Humboldt's word *désolante* is true in sentiment and in morals—but, as you observe, it is wholly inapplicable to the physical reality. Nothing so humbles, so crushes my spirit, as to look into a mad-house, and behold the drivelling, brutal idiocy so conspicuous in such places; it conveys a terrific idea of the disparity of human intelligences. But there is the

* Cosmos: traduit par H. Faye. Paris: 1846. I. p. 430. Also, note 42, p. 579. Otté translates by *depressing* in one place, and *cheerless* in another. Cosmos: New York, 1850. I. p. 358.

unyielding, insuperable reality. It is *désolante* indeed to think, to *know*, that many of these poor mortals were born, were created so! But it appears to me to make little difference in the *sentiment* of the question whether they came into the world without their wits, or whether they lost them afterwards. And so, I would add, it makes little difference whether the mental inferiority of the Negro, the Samoiyede, or the Indian, is natural or acquired; for, if they ever possessed equal intelligence with the Caucasian, they have lost it; and if they never had it, they had nothing to lose. One party would arraign Providence for creating them originally different, another for placing them in circumstances by which they inevitably became so. Let us search out the truth, and reconcile it afterwards."

Here are sound philosophy and plain common sense. As the facts are open to investigation, let us first examine them, and leave the inferences for future consideration. If the proposition prove true, we may safely trust all its legitimate deductions. There is no danger from the truth, neither will it conflict with any other truth. Our greater danger is from the cowardice that is afraid to look fact in the face, and, not daring to come in contact with reality, for fear of consequences, must rest content with error and half-belief. The question here is one of fact simply, and not of speculation nor of feeling. Humboldt may deny the existence of *unalterable* diversities, but that is another question, also to be settled only by a wider observation and longer experience. The ethical consequences he so eloquently deprecates, moreover, appear to me not to be fairly involved, unless he assumes that the solidarity and mutual moral relations of mankind originate solely in their relationship as descendants of a single pair. If so, he has built upon a sandy foundation, and one which every moralist of note will tell him is inadequate to the support of his superstructure. The inalienable right of man to equal liberty with his fellows depends, if it has any sanction, upon higher considerations than any mere physical fact of consanguinity, and remains the same whether the latter be proved or disproved. Ethical principles require a different order of evidence from material phenomena, and are to be regarded from another point of view. The scientific question should, therefore, be discussed on its own merits, and without reference to false issues of an exciting character, if we hope to reach the truth. I cannot forbear the conclusion that, in this matter, the Nestor of science has been betrayed into a little piece of popular declamation, unworthy of his pen, otherwise so consistently logical. But the acme of absurdity is reached by those clerical gentlemen at the south, who have been so eager to avail themselves of Humboldt's great authority in opposition to the doctrine of diversity, while they deny all his premises. Do they consider all doctrine necessarily *désolante*, because an argument in favor of slavery, true or false, may be based upon it? Humboldt does. And again, if the denial of a common paternity involves all the deplorable consequences indicated by the latter, does its assertion carry with it the contrary inferences? They say not. If, then, the doctrine of unity gives no essential guarantee of universal liberty and equality, why reproach the opposite doctrine with destroying what never existed? Thus, these gentlemen must stultify either themselves or their champion, while that which with him was merely a rhetorical flourish becomes, in their hands, a ridiculous *non sequitur.*

In the course of these discussions it became necessary to define, with greater precision, certain terms in constant use. This was especially the case with the word *species*, the loose employment of which occasioned much confusion. According to the prevalent zoological doctrine, the production of a prolific offspring is the highest evidence of specific identity, and *vice versâ.* The important results of the application of this law to the races of men are apparent. But other authorities deny the validity of the alleged law and its application. "Wir dürften," says Rudolphi, "also wohl deswegen auf Keine Einheit des Menschengeschlechts schliessen, weil die verschiedenen Menschenstämme sich fruchtbar mit einander begatten." The question of Hybridity, therefore, presented itself to Morton in a form that demanded attention and settlement before going farther. He seized the subject, not to speculate, and still less to declaim about it, but cautiously to gather and sift its facts. His first papers were read before the Academy of Natural Sciences in November, 1846, and published in Silliman's Journal the next year. They contain a large number of facts, from various authorities, together with the author's inferences. For these, and the entire discussion of the topic, I refer the reader to Chapter XII. (on Hybridity) in this work. But the controversy into which it led Morton forms too prominent a part of his scientific history to be passed over in silence. It was not of his seeking, but was forced upon him. A literary club at Charleston, S. C., being engaged in the discussion of the Origin of Man, the Rev. Dr. Bachman assumed the championship of the unitary hypothesis, taking ground upon the evidence afforded by an invariably prolific offspring. His opponents met him with Morton's papers on Hybridity. These he must, of course, examine; but he first addressed Morton a letter, of which the following is an extract:—

Charleston, Oct. 15th, 1849.

"We are both in the search of truth. I do not think that these scientific investigations affect the scripture question either way. The Author of Revelation is also the Author of Nature, and I have no fear that when we are able to read intelligibly, we will discover that both harmonize. We can then investigate these matters without the fear of an *auto-da-fe* from men of sense. In the meantime all must go with respect and good feeling towards each other. Although hard at work in finishing the last volume of Audubon's work, I will now and then have time to look at this matter; and here let me in anticipation state some of my objections. . . . . But I am overrun with calls of duty, and have written this under all kinds of interruptions. I shall be most sorry if my opposition to your theory would produce the slightest interruption to our good feeling, as I regard you, in your many works, as a benefactor to your country, and an honor to science. I feel confident that I can scatter some of your facts to the winds — yet in others you will be very apt to trip up my own heels; so let us work harmoniously together. At the English Universities they have wranglers, but no quarrellers."

This seems manly and friendly, and Morton, feeling it to be such, was very much gratified. He certainly never could have regarded it as a prelude to an attack upon himself; yet such it was. The next spring (1850) witnessed the publication of Dr. B.'s book on Unity, as well as his Monograph on Hybridity, in the Charleston Medical Journal, in both of which Morton is made the object of assault and attempted ridicule. The former work I have already referred to, (p. xlvi.) The author starts with what amounts, under the circumstances, to a broad and unequivocal confession of ignorance of his topic — a confession which, however praiseworthy on the score of frankness, may be regarded as wholly supererogatory; for no reader of ordinary intelligence can open the book without perceiving the fact for himself. His reading seems to have been singularly limited,* while the topic, involving, as it does, the characteristics of remote races, &c., demands a wide and careful consultation of authorities. For one who is confessedly neither an archæologist, an anatomist, nor a philologist, to attempt to teach Ethnology on the strength of having, many years ago, read on the subject a single work — and he scarcely recollects what — is a conception as bold as it is original. His production required no notice, of course, at the hand of Morton. On the special subject of Hybridity, however, he was entitled to an attentive hearing as a gentleman of established authority, particularly in the mammalian department of Zoology. Had he discussed it in the spirit foreshadowed by his letter, and which Morton anticipated, there would have been no controversy, but an amicable comparison of views, advancing the cause of science. But his tone was arrogant and offensive. Not only to the general reader in his book, but also to Morton in his letters,

* "In preparing these notes we have even resolved not to refer to Prichard—who, we believe, is justly regarded as one of our best authorities—*whose work we read with great interest some years ago,* (and which is allowed even by his opponents to have been written in a spirit of great fairness,) and many of whose arguments we at the time considered unanswerable." (p. 16.)

"After this work was nearly printed, we procured Prichard's Natural History of Man — *his other works we have not seen.* We were aware of the conclusions at which his mind had arrived, but not of the process by which his investigations had been pursued." (p. 304.)

Now, as the Natural History was not published until 1843, it could hardly be the book read "some years ago" (prior to 1849); especially as Dr. B. confesses ignorance "of the process, &c." [*supra.*] That must have been one of the earlier volumes of the *Physical Researches*, commenced in 1812, probably the very first, which leaves the subject short of the point to which Blumenbach subsequently brought it. But Dr. B. assures us again, that other work of Prichard than the Natural History he "has never seen." Then he never saw any, before writing his own book! His memory is certainly extremely vague. It is safe to conclude, however, that he undertook to write upon this difficult subject without the direct consultation of a single authority:—the result is what might be readily anticipated.

does he speak *de haut en bas*, as if, from the height of the pulpit, he was looking down upon men immeasurably removed from him by his sacred office. This faulty manner perhaps results from his profession, as does his verbose and declamatory style. But this consideration will not excuse the patronizing way in which he addresses one of higher scientific rank than himself. He reminds Morton of the countenance he has heretofore given him,—that he even subscribed for his book! The authorities relied upon by the latter he treats with supreme contempt, individually and collectively, characterizing them as pedantic, antiquated, and "musty."* All this is carried through in a bold, dashing, off-hand way, calculated to impress forcibly any reader ignorant of the matter under discussion. It argues the most confident self-complacency and conviction of superiority on the part of the writer, and doubtless his admiring readers shared the feeling. For a short season there was quite a jubilation over the assumed defeat of the physicists.

But there is an Italian proverb which says, *Non sempre chi cantando viene, cantando va!* and which Dr. B. was destined to illustrate. To his first paper Morton replied in a letter dated March 30th, 1850, the tone of which is calm, dignified, and friendly. He defends his authorities, accumulates new evidence, and strengthens and defines his position. This called forth Dr. B.'s most objectionable letter of June 12th, 1850, also published in the Charleston Journal, and in which he entirely passes the bounds of propriety. No longer satisfied with his poor attempts at wit, which consist almost exclusively in the use of the word "old" and its synonymes, he becomes denunciatory, and even abusive. He charges Morton with taking part in a deliberate conspiracy, having its ramifications in four cities, for the overthrow of a doctrine "nearly connected with the faith and hope of the Christian, for this world and for eternity." In another paragraph, (p. 507,) he says, that *infidelity* must inevitably spring up as the consequence of adopting Morton's views. Now, we all know that when gentlemen of Dr. B.'s cloth use that word, they mean war *usque ad necem.* Its object is simply to do mischief and give pain. It cannot injure

* Dr. Bachman's contempt for everything "old" is certainly very curious in one so likely, from calling and position, to be particularly conservative. Nor is this his only singularity. His pertinacious ascription of a remote date to every one whose name has a Latinized termination, reminds one of the story told of the backwoods lawyer, who persisted in numbering "old Cantharides" among the sages of antiquity. He is particularly hard upon "old Hellenius," never failing to give him a passing flout, and talking about raising his ghost. The writings of Dr. B. do not indicate a very sensitive person, yet even he must have felt a considerable degree of the sensation known as *cutis anserina*, when he received the information, conveyed in Morton's quietest manner, that "old Hellenius," with others of his so-called "musty" authorities, were his own contemporaries! The work of Chevreul, which he disposes of in the same supercilious way, bears the extreme date of 1846!

the person attacked, so far as the scientific world is concerned — for there the phrase can now only excite a smile — but it may impair his business or his public standing, or, still worse, it may enter his domestic circle, and wound him through his tenderest sympathies. Was such the intention in the present case? Charity bids us think otherwise; and yet the attack has a very malignant appearance. To Morton it occasioned great surprise and pain. He answered it calmly in a paper in the same Journal, entitled *Additional Observations*, &c. He is unwavering in the assertion of his opinion; and, inasmuch as its triumphant establishment would be his own best justification, he piles up still more and more evidence, often from the highest authorities in Natural History. The personalities of Dr. B. he meets and refutes briefly, but with firmness and dignity, declining entirely to allow himself to be provoked into a bandying of epithets. His conduct was in striking contrast with that of his reverend opponent; and, while it exalted him in the estimation of the learned everywhere, showed the latter to be a stranger to the courtesies that should characterize scientific discussion. More of a theological polemic than a naturalist, he uses the tone and style proverbially displayed by the former, and is offensive accordingly. He has his punishment in general condemnation and impaired scientific standing. In the mean time, Morton was stimulated to a determination to exhaust whatever material there was accessible in regard to Hybridity. Dr. Bachman he dropped entirely after the second letter; but he announced to his friends his intention of sending an article regularly for each successive number of the Charleston Journal, so long as new matter presented. Two only of these supplementary communications appeared, the last being dated January 31st, 1851.

But the solemn termination of all these labors was near at hand. Never had Morton been so busy as in that spring of 1851. His professional engagements had largely increased, and occupied most of his time. His craniological investigations were prosecuted with unabated zeal, and he had recently made important accessions to his collection. He was actively engaged in the study of Archæology, Egyptian, Assyrian, and American, as collateral to his favorite subject. His researches upon Hybridity cost him much labor, in his extended comparison of authorities, and his industrious search for facts bearing on the question. In addition to all this, he was occupied with the preparation of his contribution to the work of Mr. Schoolcraft, and of several minor papers. Most of these labors were left incomplete. The fragments published in this volume will show how his mind was engaged, and to what conclusions it tended at the close. For it was now, in the midst of toil and usefulness, that he was called away from us. Five days of illness — not considered alarming at first—had scarcely prepared his friends for the sad event, when it was announced, on the 15th of May, that Morton was no more! It was too true—he had left vacant among us a place that cannot soon be filled. Peacefully and calmly he had gone to his eternal rest, having accomplished so much in his short space of life, and yet leaving so much undone, that none but he could do as well!

So lived and so died our lamented friend. While we deplore his loss, however, we cannot but perceive that few men have been more blessed in life than he. His career was an eminently prosperous and successful one. Very few have ever been so uniformly successful in their enterprises. He established, with unusual rapidity, a wide-spread scientific fame, upon the white radiance of which he has, dying, left not a single blot. His life was also a fortunate and happy one in its more private relations. His first great grief came upon him, precisely a year before his own decease, in the loss of a beloved son, to whom he was tenderly attached. No other cloud than this obscured his clear horizon to the last. That he felt it deeply there can be no doubt; but he had, at his heart's core, the sentiment that can rob sorrow of its bitterness, and death of its sting. To that sentiment he has given utterance in these lines; and, with their quotation, I conclude this notice, the preparation of which has been to me a labor of love, and the solace, for a season, of a bed of suffering.

Jan. 1854. H. S. P.

CONSOLATION.

What art thou, world! with thy beguiling dreams,
Thy banquets and carousals, pomp and pride!
What is thy gayest moment, when it teems
With pleasures won, or prospects yet untried?

What are thy honors, titles and renown,
Thy brightest pageant, and thy noblest sway?
Alas! like flowers beneath the tempest's frown,
They bloom at morn,—at eve they fade away!

A few short years revolve, and then no more
Can Memory rouse them from their resting-place;
The joys we courted, and the hopes we bore,
Have pass'd like shadows from our fond embrace.

But is there nought, amid the fearful doom,
That can outlast the wreck of mortal things?
There is a spirit that does not consume,
But mounts o'er ruin with triumphant wings.

And thou, Religion! like a guardian star
Dost glitter in the firmament on high,
And lead'st us still, tho' we have wander'd far,
To hopes that cheer, and joys that never die!

And if an erring pilgrim on his way
Casts but a pure, a suppliant glance to Heaven,
"Fear not—benighted child"—he hears thee say—
"For they are doubly blest that are forgiven!"

SKETCH

OF THE

NATURAL PROVINCES OF THE ANIMAL WORLD AND THEIR RELATION TO THE DIFFERENT TYPES OF MAN.

BY LOUIS AGASSIZ.

Messrs. Nott and Gliddon.

Dear Sirs:—In compliance with your request that I should furnish you with certain scientific facts respecting the Natural History of Man, to which you are now devoting particularly your attention, I transmit to you some general remarks upon the natural relations of the human family and the organic world surrounding it; in the hope that it may call the attention of naturalists to *the close connection there is between the geographical distribution of animals and the natural boundaries of the different races of man*—a fact which must be explained by any theory of the origin of life which claims to cover the whole of this difficult problem. I do not pretend to present such a theory now, but would simply illustrate the facts as they are, to lay the foundation of a more extensive work to be published at some future time. Nor is it my intention to characterize here all the zoological provinces recognized by naturalists, but only those the animals of which are known with sufficient accuracy to throw light upon the subject under consideration. Of the marine animals, I shall therefore take no notice, except so far as they bear a special relation to the habits of uncivilized races or to the commercial enterprise of the world. The views illustrated in the following pages have been expressed for the first time by me in a paper, published in French, in the *Revue Suisse* for 1845.

Very truly, yours,

Ls. Agassiz.

Cambridge, Mass., Dec. 19th, 1853.

There is one feature in the physical history of mankind which has been entirely neglected by those who have studied this subject, viz., the natural relations between the different types of man and the animals and plants inhabiting the same regions. The sketch here presented is intended to supply this deficiency, as far as it is possible in a mere outline delineation, and to show that *the boundaries, within which the different natural combinations of animals are known to be circumscribed upon the surface of our earth, coincide with the natural range of distinct types of man.* Such natural combinations of animals circumscribed within definite boundaries are called *faunæ*, whatever be their home — land, sea, or river. Among the animals which compose the fauna of a country, we find types belonging exclusively there, and not occurring elsewhere; such are, for example, the ornithorhynchus of New Holland, the sloths of America, the hippopotamus of Africa, and the walruses of the arctics: others, which have only a small number of representatives beyond the fauna which they specially characterize, as, for instance, the marsupials of New Holland, of which America has a few species, such as the opossum; and again others which have a wider range, such as the bears, of which there are distinct species in Europe, Asia, or America, or the mice and bats, which are to be found all over the world, except in the arctics. That fauna will, therefore, be most easily characterized which possesses the largest number of distinct types, proper to itself, and of which the other animals have little analogy with those of neighboring regions, as, for example, the fauna of New Holland.

The inhabitants of fresh waters furnish also excellent characters for the circumscription of faunæ. The fishes, and other fluviatile animals from the larger hydrographic basins, differ no less from each other than the mammalia, the birds, the reptiles, and the insects of the countries which these rivers water. Nevertheless, some authors have attempted to separate the fresh water animals from those of the land and sea, and to establish distinct divisions for them, under the name of fluviatile faunæ. But the inhabitants of the rivers and lakes are too intimately connected with those of their shores to allow of a rigorous distinction of this kind. Rivers never establish a separation between terrestrial faunæ. For the same reason, the faunæ of the inland seas cannot be completely isolated from the terrestrial ones, and we shall see hereafter that the animals of southern Europe are not bound by the Mediterranean, but are found on the southern shore of that sea, as far as the Atlas. We shall, therefore, distinguish our zoological regions according to the combination of species which they enclose, rather than according to the element in which we find them.

If the grand divisions of the animal kingdom are primordial and independent of climate, this is not the case with regard to the ultimate local circumscription of species: these are, on the contrary, intimately connected with the conditions of temperature, soil, and vegetation. A remarkable instance of this distribution of animals with reference to climate may be observed in the arctic fauna, which contains a great number of species common to the three continents converging towards the North Pole, and which presents a striking uniformity, when compared with the diversity of the temperate and tropical faunæ of those same continents.

The arctic fauna extends to the utmost limits of the cold and barren regions of the North. But from the moment that forests appear, and a more propitious soil permits a larger development of animal life and of vegetation, we see the fauna and flora, not only diversified according to the continents on which they exist, but we observe also striking distinctions between different parts of the same continent; thus, in the old world, the animals vary, not only from the polar circle to the equator, but also in the opposite direction — those of the western coast of Europe are not the same as those of the basin of the Caspian Sea, or of the eastern coast of Asia, nor are those of the eastern coast of America the same as those of the western.

The first fauna, the limits of which we would determine with precision, is the arctic. It offers, as we have just seen, the same aspects in three parts of the world, which converge towards the North Pole. The uniform distribution of the animals by which it is inhabited forms its most striking character, and gives rise to a sameness of general features which is not found in any other region. Though the air-breathing species are not numerous here, the large number of individuals compensates for this deficiency, and among the marine animals we find an astonishing profusion and variety of forms.

In this respect the vegetable and animal kingdoms differ entirely from each other, and the measure by which we estimate the former is quite false as applied to the latter. Plants become stunted in their growth or disappear before the rigors of the climate, while, on the contrary, all classes of the animal kingdom have representatives, more or less numerons, in the arctic fauna.

Neither can they be said to diminish in size under these influences; for, if the arctic representatives of certain classes, particularly the insects, are smaller than the analogous types in the tropics, we must not forget, on the other hand, that the whales and larger cetacea have here their most genial home, and make amends, by their more powerful structure, for the inferiority of other classes. Also, if the animals of the North are less striking in external ornament — if their colors are less brilliant — yet we cannot say that they are more uniform, for though their tints are not so bright, they are none the less varied in their distribution and arrangement.

The limits of the arctic fauna are very easily traced. We must include therein all animals living beyond the line where forests cease, and inhabiting countries entirely barren. Those which feed upon flesh seek fishes, hares, or lemmings, a rodent of the size of our rat. Those which live on vegetable substances are not numerous. Some gramineous plants, mosses, and lichens, serve as pasture to the ruminants and rodents, while the seeds of a few flowering plants, and of the dwarf birches, afford nourishment to the little granivorous birds, such as linnets and buntings. The species belonging to the sea-shore feed upon marine animals, which live, themselves, upon each other, or upon marine plants.

The larger mammalia which inhabit this zone are—the white bear, the walrus, numerous species of seal, the reindeer, the musk ox, the narwal, the cachalot, and whales in abundance. Among the smaller species we may mention the white fox, the polar hare, and the lemming. The birds are not less characteristic. Some marine eagles, and wading birds in smaller number, are found; but the aquatic birds of the family of palmipedes are those which especially prevail. The coasts of the continents and of the numerous islands in the arctic seas are peopled by clouds of gannets, of cormorants, of penguins, of petrels, of ducks, of geese, of mergansers, and of gulls, some of which are as large as eagles, and, like them, live on prey. No reptile is known in this zone. Fishes are, however, very numerous, and the rivers especially swarm with a variety of species of the salmon family. A number of representatives of the inferior classes of worms, of crustacea, of mollusks, of echinoderms, and of medusæ, are also found here.

Within the limits of this fauna we meet a peculiar race of men, known in America under the name of Esquimaux, and under the names of Laplanders, Samojedes, and Tchuktshes in the north of Asia. This race, so well known since the voyage of Capt. Cook and the arctic expeditions of England and Russia, differs alike from the Indians of North America, from the whites of Europe, and the Mongols of Asia, to whom they are adjacent. The uniformity of their characters along the whole range of the arctic seas forms one of the most striking resemblances which these people exhibit to the fauna with which they are so closely connected.

The semi-annual alternation of day and night in the arctic regions has a great influence upon their modes of living. They are entirely dependent upon animal food for their sustenance, no farinaceous grains, no nutritious tubercles, no juicy fruits, growing under those inhospitable latitudes. Their domesticated animals are the reindeer in Asia, and a peculiar variety of dog, the Esquimaux dog, in North America, where even the reindeer is not domesticated.

Though the arctic fauna is essentially comprised in the arctic circle, its organic limit does not correspond rigorously to this line, but rather to the isotherme of 32° Fahr., the outline of which presents numerous undulations. This limit is still more natural when it is made to correspond with that of the disappearance of forests. It then circumscribes those immense plains of the North, which the Samoyedes call *tundras*, and the Anglo-Americans, *barren lands.*

The naturalists, who have overlooked this fauna, and connected it with those of the temperate zone, have introduced much confusion in the geographical distribution of animals, and have failed to recognize the remarkable coincidence existing between the extensive range of the arctic race of men, and the uniformity of the animal world around the Northern Pole.

The first column of the accompanying tableau represents the types which characterize best this fauna; viz., the white or polar bear, the walrus, the seal of Greenland, the reindeer, the right whale, and the eider duck. The vegetation is represented by the so-called reindeer-moss, a lichen which constitutes the chief food of the herbivorous animals of the arctics and the high Alps, during winter.

To the glacial zone, which incloses a single fauna, succeeds the temperate zone, included between the isothermes of 32°, and 74° Fahr., characterised by its pine forests, its amentacea, its maples, its walnuts, and its fruit trees, and from the midst of which arise like islands, lofty mountain chains or high table-lands, clothed with a vegetation which, in many respects, recalls that of the glacial regions. The geographical distribution of animals in this zone, forms several closely connected, but distinct combinations. It is the country of the terrestrial bear, of the wolf, the fox, the weasel, the marten, the otter, the lynx, the horse and the ass, the boar, and a great number of stags, deer, elk, goats, sheep, bulls, hares, squirrels, rats, &c.; to which are added southward, a few representatives of the tropical zone.

Wherever this zone is not modified by extensive and high table-lands and mountain chains, we may distinguish in it four *secondary* zones, approximating gradually to the character of the tropics, and presenting therefore a greater diversity in the types of its southern representation than we find among those of its northern boundaries. We have first, adjoining the arctics, a *sub-arctic* zone, with an almost uniform appearance in the old as well as the new world, in which pine forests prevail, the home of the moose; next, a *cold temperate zone*, in which amentaceous trees are combined with pines, the home of the fur animals; next, a *warm temperate zone*, in which the pines recede, whilst to the prevailing amentaceous trees a variety of evergreens are added, the chief seat of the culture of our fruit trees, and of the wheat; and a *sub-tropical zone*, in which a number of tropical forms are combined with those characteristic of the warm temperate zone. Yet there is throughout the whole of the temperate zone one feature prevailing; the repetition, under corresponding latitudes, but under different longitudes, of the same genera and families, represented in each botanical or zoological province by distinct so-called *analogous or representative species*, with a very few subordinate types, peculiar to each province; for it is not until we reach the tropical zone that we find distinct types prevailing in each fauna and flora. Again, owing to the inequalities of the surface, the secondary zones are more or less blended into one another, as for instance, in the table-lands of Central Asia, and Western North America, where the whole temperate zone preserves the features of a cold temperate region; or the colder zones may appear like islands rising in the midst of the warmer ones, as the Pyrenees, the Alps, &c., the summits of which partake of the peculiarities of the arctic and sub-arctic zones, whilst the valleys at their base are characterised by the flora and fauna of the cold or warm temperate zones. It may be proper to remark, in this connection, that the study of the laws regulating the geographical distribution of natural families of animals and plants upon the whole surface of our globe differs, entirely, from that of the associations and combinations of a variety of animals and plants within definite regions, forming peculiar faunæ and flora.

Considering the whole range of the temperate zone from east to west, we may divide it in accordance with the prevailing physical features into — 1st, an *Asiatic* realm, embracing Mantchuria, Japan, China, Mongolia, and passing through Turkestan into 2d, the *European* realm, which includes Iran as well as Asia Minor, Mesopotamia, northern Arabia and Barbary, as well as Europe, properly so called; the western parts of Asia, and the northern parts of Africa being intimately connected by their geological structure with the southern parts of Europe; * and, 3d, the *North American* realm, which extends as far south as the table-land of Mexico.

With these qualifications, we may proceed to consider the faunæ which characterize these three realms. But, before studying the organic characters of this zone, let us glance at its physical constitution. The most marked character of the temperate zone is found in the inequality of the four seasons, which give to the earth a peculiar aspect in different epochs of the year, and in the gradual, though more or less rapid passage of these seasons into each other. The vegetation particularly undergoes marked modifications; completely arrested, or merely suspended, for a longer or shorter time, according to the proximity of the arctic or the tropical zone, we find it by turns in a prolonged lethargy, or in a state of energetic and sustained development. But in this respect there is a decided contrast between the cold and warm portions of the temperate zone. Though they

* For further evidence that Iran, Asia Minor, Mesopotamia, Northern Arabia and Northern Africa, belong naturally to the European realm, see *Guyot's* Earth and Man.

are both characterized by the predominance of the same families of plants, and in particular by the presence of numerous species of the coniferous and amentaceous plants, yet the periodical sleep which deprives the middle latitudes of their verdure, is more complete in the colder region than in the warmer, which is already enriched by some southern forms of vegetation, and where a part of the trees remain green all the year. The succession of the seasons produces, moreover, such considerable changes in the climatic conditions in this zone, that all the animals belonging to it cannot sustain them equally well. Hence a large number of them migrate at different seasons from one extremity of the zone to the other, especially certain families of birds. It is known to all the world that the birds of Northern Europe and America leave their ungenial climate in the winter, seeking warmer regions as far as the Gulf of Mexico and the Mediterranean, the shores of which, even those of the African coasts, make a part of the temperate zone. Analogous migrations take place also in the north of Asia. Such migrations are not, however, limited to the temperate zone; a number of species from the arctic regions go for the winter into the temperate zone, and the limits of these migrations may aid us in tracing the natural limits of the faunæ, which thus link themselves to each other, as the human races are connected by civilization.

The temperate zone is not characterized, like the arctic, by one and the same fauna; it does not form, as the arctic does, one continuous zoological zone around the globe. Not only do the animals change from one hemisphere to another, but these differences exist even between various regions of the same hemisphere. The species belonging to the western countries of the old world are not identical with those of the eastern countries. It is true that they often resemble each other so closely, that until very recently they have been confounded. It has been reserved, however, for modern zoology and botany to detect these nice distinctions. For instance, the coniferæ of the old world, even within the sub-arctic zone, are not identical with those of America. Instead of the Norway and black pine, we have here the balsam and the white spruce; instead of the common fir, the *Pinus rigida;* instead of the European larch, the hacmatac, &c.; and farther south the differences are still more striking. In the temperate zone proper, the oaks, the beeches, the birches, the hornbeams, the hophornbeams, the chestnuts, the buttonwoods, the elms, the linden, the maples, and the walnuts, are represented in each continent by peculiar species differing more or less. Peculiar forms make, here and there, their appearance, such as the gum-trees, the tulip-trees, the magnolias. The evergreens are still more diversified,—we need only mention the camelias of Japan, and the kalmias of America as examples. Among the tropical forms extending into the warm temperate zone, we notice particularly the palmetto in the southern United States, and the dwarf chamærops of southern Europe. The animal kingdom presents the same features. In Europe we have, for instance, the brown bear; in North America, the black bear; in Asia, the bear of Tubet: the European stag, and the European deer, are represented in North America by the Canadian stag, or wapiti, and the American deer; and in eastern Asia, by the musk-deer. Instead of the mouflon, North America has the big-horn or mountain sheep, and Asia the argali. The North American buffalo is represented in Europe by the wild auerochs of Lithuania, and in Mongolia by the yak; the wild-cats, the martens and weasels, the wolves and foxes, the squirrels and mice (excepting the imported house-mouse), the birds, the reptiles, the fishes, the insects, the mollusks, &c., though more or less closely allied, are equally distinct specifically. The types peculiar to the old or the new world are few; among them may be mentioned the horse and ass and the dromedary of Asia, and the opossum of North America; but upon this subject more details may be found in every text-book of zoology and botany. We would only add that in the present state of our knowledge we recognise the following combinations of animals within the limits of the temperate zone, which may be considered as so many distinct zoological provinces or faunæ.

In the *Asiatic realm*,—1st, a north-eastern fauna, the *Japanese fauna;* 2d, a south-eastern fauna, the *Chinese fauna*, and a central fauna, the *Mongolian fauna*, followed westwards by the *Caspian fauna*, which partakes partly of the Asiatic and partly of the European zoological character; its most remarkable animal, antelope saiga, ranging west as far as southern Russia. The Japanese and the Chinese faunæ stand to each other in the same relation as southern Europe and north Africa, and it remains to be ascertained by farther investigations whether the Japanese fauna ought not to be subdivided into a more eastern insular fauna, the *Japanese fauna proper*, and a more western continental fauna, which might be called the *Mandshurian* or *Tongousian* fauna. But since it is not my object to describe separately all faunæ, but chiefly to call attention to the coincidence existing between the natural limitation of the races of man, and the geographical range of the zoological provinces, I shall limit myself here to some general remarks respecting the Mongolian fauna, in order to show that the Asiatic zoological realm differs essentially from the European and the American. In our Tableau, the second column represents the most remarkable animals of this fauna; the bear of Tubet (ursus thibetanus), the musk-deer (moschus moschiferus), the Tzeiran (antilope gutturosa), the Mongolian goat (capra sibirica), the argali (ovis argali), and the yak (bos grunniens). This is also the home of the Bactrian or double-hunched camel, and of the wild horse (equus caballus), the wild ass (equus onager), and another equine species, the Dtschigetai (equus hemionus). The wide distribution of the musk-deer in the Altai, and the Himmalayan and Chinese Alps, shows the whole Asiatic range of the temperate zone to be a most natural zoological realm, subdivided into distinct provinces by the greater localization of the largest number of its representatives.

If we now ask what are the nations of men inhabiting those regions, we find that they all belong to the so-called Mongolian race, the natural limits of which correspond exactly to the range of the Japanese, Chinese, Mongolian and Caspian faunæ taken together, and that peculiar types, distinct nations of this race, cover respectively the different faunæ of this realm. The Japanese inhabiting the Japanese zoological province; the Chinese, the Chinese province; the Mongols, the Mongolian province; and the Turks, the Caspian province; eliminating, of course, the modern establishment of Turks in Asia Minor and Europe.

The unity of Europe, (exclusive of its arctic regions,) in connection with south-western Asia and northern Africa, as a distinct zoological realm, is established by the range of its mammalia and by the limits of the migrations of its birds, as well as by the physical features of its whole extent. Thus we find its deer and stag, its bear, its hare, its squirrel, its wolf and wild-cat, its fox and jackal, its otter, its weasel and marten, its badger, its bear, its mole, its hedgehogs, and a number of bats, either extending over the whole realm in Europe, western Asia, and north Africa, or so linked together as to show that in their combination with the birds, reptiles, fishes, &c., of the same countries, they constitute a natural zoological association analogous to that of Asia, but essentially different in reference to species. Like the eastern realm, this European world may be sub-divided into a number of distinct faunæ, characterized each by a variety of peculiar animals. In western Asia we find, for instance, the common camel, instead of the Bactrian, whilst Mount Sinai, Mounts Taurus and Caucasus have goats and wild sheep which differ as much from those of Asia, as they differ from those of Greece, of Italy, of the Alps, of the Pyrenees, of the Atlas, and of Egypt. Wild horses are known to have inhabited Spain and Germany; and a wild bull extended over the whole range of central Europe, which no longer exists there. The Asiatic origin of our domesticated animals may, therefore, well be questioned, even if we were still to refer western Asia to the Asiatic realm; since the ass, and some of the breeds of our horse, only belong to the table-lands of Iran and Mongolia, whilst the other species, including the cat, may all be traced to species of the European realm. The domesticated cat is referred by Rüppell to felis maniculata of Egypt; by others, to felis catus ferus of central Europe; thus, in both cases, to an animal of the European realm. Whether the dog be a species by itself, or its varieties derived from several species which have completely amalgamated, or be it descended from the wolf, the fox, or the jackal, every theory must limit its natural range to the European world. The merino sheep is still represented in the wild state by the mouflon of Sardinia, and was formerly wild in all the mountains of Spain; whether the sheep of the patriarchs were derived from those of Mt. Taurus, or from Armenia, still they differed from those of western Europe; since, a thousand years before our era, the Phœnicians preferred the wool from the Iberian peninsula to that of their Syrian neighbours. The goats differ so much in different parts of the world, that it is still less possible to refer them to one common stock; and while Nepaul and Cashmere have their own breeds, we may well consider those of Egypt and Sinai as distinct, especially as they differ equally from those of Caucasus and of Europe. The common bull is derived from the wild species which has become extinct in Europe, and is not identical with any of the wild species of Asia, notwithstanding some assertions to the contrary. The hog descends from the common boar, now found wild over the whole temperate zone in the Old World. Both ducks and geese have their wild representatives in Europe; so also the pigeon. As for the common fowls, they are decidedly of east Asiatic origin; but the period of their importation is not well known, nor even the wild species from which they are derived. The wild turkey is well known as an inhabitant of the American continent.

Now, taking further into account the special distribution of *all* the animals, wild as well as domesticated, of the European temperate zone, we may sub-divide it into the following eight faunæ:—1st, *Scandinavian fauna;* 2d, *Russian fauna;* 3d, *The fauna of Central Europe;* 4th, *The fauna of Southern Europe;* 5th, *The fauna of Iran;* 6th, *The Syrian fauna;* 7th, *The Egyptian fauna;* and 8th, *The fauna of the Atlas.* The special works upon the zoology of Europe, the great works illustrative of the French expeditions in Egypt, Morocco, and Algiers, the travels of Rüppell and Russeger in Egypt and Syria, of M. Wagner in Algiers, of Demidoff in southern Russia, &c. &c., and the special treatises on the geographical distribution of mammalia by A. Wagner, and of animals in general by

Schmarda, may furnish more details upon the zoology of these countries.

Here, again, it cannot escape the attention of the careful observer, that the European zoological realm is circumscribed within exactly the same limits as the so-called white race of man, including, as it does, the inhabitants of south-western Asia, and of north Africa, with the lower parts of the valley of the Nile. We exclude, of course, modern migrations and historical changes of habitation from this assertion. Our statements are to be understood as referring only to the aboriginal or ante-historical distribution of man, or rather to the distribution as history finds it. And in this respect there is a singular fact, which historians seem not to have sufficiently appreciated, that the earliest migrations recorded, in any form, show us man meeting man, wherever he moves upon the inhabitable surface of the globe, small islands excepted.

It is, farther, very striking, that the different sub-divisions of this race, even to the limits of distinct nationalities, cover precisely the same ground as the special faunæ or zoological provinces of this most important part of the world, which in all ages has been the seat of the most advanced civilization. In the south-west of Asia we find (along the table-land of Iran) Persia and Asia Minor; in the plains southward, Mesopotamia and Syria; along the sea-shores, Palestine and Phœnicia; in the valley of the Nile, Egypt; and along the southern shores of Africa, Barbary. Thus we have Semitic nations covering the north African and south-west Asiatic faunæ, while the south European peninsulas, including Asia Minor, are inhabited by Græco-Roman nations, and the cold, temperate zone, by Celto-Germanic nations; the eastern range of Europe being peopled by Sclaves. This coincidence may justify the inference of an independent origin for these different tribes, as soon as it can be admitted that the races of men were primitively created in nations; the more so, since all of them claim to have been *autochthones* of the countries they inhabit. This claim is so universal that it well deserves more attention. It may be more deeply founded than historians, generally, seem inclined to grant.

The third column of our Tableau exhibits the animals characteristic of the temperate part of the European zoological realm, and shows their close resemblance to those of the corresponding Asiatic fauna; the species being representative species of the same genera, with the exception of the musk-deer, which has no analogues in Europe.

Though temperate America resembles closely, in its animal creation, the countries of Europe and Asia belonging to the same zone, we meet with physical and organic features in this continent which differ entirely from those of the Old World. The tropical realms, connected there with those of the temperate zone, though bound together by some analogies, differ essentially from one another. Tropical Africa has hardly any species in common with Europe, though we may remember that the lion once extended to Greece, and that the jackal is to this day found upon some islands in the Adriatic, and in Morea. Tropical Asia differs equally from its temperate regions, and Australia forms a world by itself. Not so in southern America. The range of mountains which extends, in almost unbroken continuity, from the Arctic to Cape Horn, establishes a similarity between North and South America, which may be traced also, to a great degree, in its plants and animals. Entire families which are peculiar to this continent have their representatives in North, as well as South America, the cactus and didelphis, for instance; some species, as the puma, or American lion, may even be traced from Canada to Patagonia. In connection with these facts, we find that tropical America, though it has its peculiar types, as characteristic as those of tropical Africa, Asia, and Australia, does not furnish analogues of the giants of Africa and Asia; its largest pachyderms being tapirs and pecaris, not elephants, rhinoceroses, and hippopotami; and its largest ruminants, the llamas and alpacas, and not camels and giraffes; whilst it reminds us, in many respects, of Australia, with which it has the type of marsupials in common, though ruminants and pachyderms, and even monkeys, are entirely wanting there. Thus, with due qualification, it may be said, that the whole continent of America, when compared with the corresponding twin-continents of Europe—Africa or Asia— Australia is characterized by a much greater uniformity of its natural productions, combined with a special localization of many of its subordinate types, which will justify the establishment of many special faunæ within its boundaries.

With these facts before us, we may expect that there should be no great diversity among the tribes of man inhabiting this continent; and, indeed, the most extensive investigation of their peculiarities has led Dr. Morton to consider them as constituting but a single race, from the confines of the Esquimaux down to the southernmost extremity of the continent. But, at the same time, it should be remembered that, in accordance with the zoological character of the whole realm, this race is divided into an infinite number of small tribes, presenting more or less difference one from another.

As to the special faunæ of the American continent, we may distinguish, within the temperate zone, a *Canadian fauna*, extending from Newfoundland across the great lakes to the base of the Rocky mountains, a fauna of the *North American table-land*, a fauna of the *North-west coast*, a fauna of the *middle United States*, a fauna of the *southern United States*, and a *Californian fauna*, the characteristic features of which I shall describe on another occasion.

When we consider, however, the isolation of the American continent from those of the Old World, nothing is more striking in the geographical distribution of animals, than the exact correspondence of all the animals of the northern temperate zone of America with those of Europe: all the characteristic forms of which, as may be seen by the fourth column of our Tableau, belong to the same genera, with the exception only of a few subordinate types, not represented among our figures — such as the opossum and the skunk.

In tropical America we may distinguish a *Central American fauna*, a *Brazilian fauna*, a *fauna of the Pampas*, a *fauna of the Cordilleras*, a *Peruvian fauna*, and a *Patagonian fauna;* but it is unnecessary for our purpose to mention here their characteristic features, which may be gathered from the works of Prince New Wied, of Spix and Martius, of Tschudi, of Pöppig, of Ramon de la Sagra, of Darwin, &c.

The slight differences existing between the faunæ of the temperate zone have required a fuller illustration than may be necessary to characterize the zoological realms of the tropical regions and the southern hemisphere generally. It is sufficient for our purpose to say here, that these realms are at once distinguished by the prevalence of peculiar types, circumscribed within the natural limits of the three continents, extending in complete isolation towards the southern pole. In this respect there is already a striking contrast between the northern and the southern hemisphere. But the more closely we compare them with one another, the greater appear their differences. We have already seen how South America differs from Africa, the East Indies, and Australia, by its closer connection with North America. Notwithstanding, however, the absence in South America of those sightly animals so prominent in Africa and tropical Asia, its general character is, like that of all the tropical continents, to nourish a variety of types which have no close relations to those of other continents. Its monkeys and edentata belong to genera which have no representatives in the Old World; among pachyderms it has pecaris, which are entirely wanting elsewhere; and though the tapirs occur also in the Sunda Islands, that type is wanting in Africa, where in compensation we find the hippopotamus, not found in either Asia or America. We have already seen that the marsupials of South America differ entirely from those of Australia. Its ostriches differ also generically from those of Africa, tropical Asia, New Holland, &c.

If we compare further the southern continents of the Old World with one another, we find a certain uniformity between the animals of Africa and tropical Asia. They have both elephants and rhinoceroses, though each has its peculiar species of these genera, which occur neither in America nor in Australia; whilst cercopitheci and antilopes prevail in Africa, and long-armed monkeys and stags in tropical Asia. Moreover, the black orangs are peculiar to Africa, and the red orangs to Asia. As to Australia, it has neither monkeys nor pachyderms, nor edentata, but only marsupials and monotremes. We need therefore not carry these comparisons further, to be satisfied that Africa, tropical Asia, and Australia constitute independent zoological realms.

The continent of Africa south of the Atlas has a very uniform zoological character. This realm may however be subdivided, according to its local peculiarities, iuto a number of distinct faunæ. In its more northern parts we distinguish the fauna of the Sahara, and those of Nubia and Abyssinia; the latter of which extends over the Red Sea into the tropical parts of Arabia. These faunæ have been particularly studied by Rüppell and Ehrenberg, in whose works more may be found respecting the zoology of these regions. They are inhabited by two distinct races of men, the Nubians and Abyssinians, receding greatly in their features from the woolly-haired Negroes with flat broad noses, which cover the more central parts of the continent. But even here we may distinguish the fauna of Senegal from that of Guinea and that of the African Table-land. In the first, we notice particularly the chimpanzee; in the second, the gorilla. There is no anthropoid monkey in the third. The fifth column in our Tableau gives figures of the most prominent animals of the genuine West African type. A fuller illustration of this subject might show, how peculiar tribes of Negroes cover the limits of the different faunæ of tropical Africa, and establish in this respect a parallelism between the nations of this continent and those of Europe. We are chiefly indebted to French naturalists for a better knowledge of the Natural History of this part of the world. In the sixth column of our Tableau we have represented the animals of the Cape-lands, in order to show how the African fauna is modified upon the southern extremity of this continent, which is inhabited by a distinct race of men, the Hottentots. The zoology of South Africa may be studied in the works of Lichtenstein and Andrew Smith.

The East Indian realm is now very well known zoologically, thanks to the efforts of English and Dutch naturalists, and may be subdivided into three faunæ, that of Dukhun, that of the Indo-Chinese peninsula, and that of the Sunda Islands, Borneo, and the Philippines. Its characteristic animals, represented in the seventh column of our

Tableau, may be readily contrasted with those of Africa. There is, however, one feature in this realm, which requires particular attention, and has a high importance with reference to the study of the races of men. We find here upon Borneo (an island not so extensive as Spain) one of the best known of those anthropoid monkeys, the orang-outan, and with him as well as upon the adjacent islands of Java and Sumatra, and along the coasts of the two East Indian peninsulæ, not less than ten other different species of Hylobates, the long-armed monkeys; a genus which, next to the orang and chimpanzee, ranks nearest to man. One of these species is circumscribed within the Island of Java, two along the coast of Coromandel, three upon that of Malacca, and four upon Borneo. Also, eleven of the highest organized beings which have performed their part in the plan of the Creation within tracts of land inferior in extent to the range of any of the historical nations of men! In accordance with this fact, we find three distinct races within the boundaries of the East Indian realm: the Telingan race in anterior India, the Malays in posterior India and upon the islands, upon which the Negrillos occur with them. Such combinations justify fully a comparison of the geographical range covered by distinct European nations with the narrow limits occupied upon earth by the orangs, the chimpanzees, and the gorillas; and though I still hesitate to assign to each an independent origin (perhaps rather from the difficulty of divesting myself of the opinions universally received, than from any intrinsic evidence), I must, in presence of these facts, insist at least upon the probability of such an independence of origin of all nations; or, at least, of the independent origin of a primitive stock for each, with which at some future period migrating or conquering tribes have more or less completely amalgamated, as in the case of mixed nationalities. The evidence adduced from the affinities of the languages of different nations in favor of a community of origin is of no value, when we know, that, among vociferous animals, every species has its peculiar intonations, and that the different species of the same family produce sound as closely allied, and forming as natural combinations, as the so-called Indo-Germanic languages compared with one another. Nobody, for instance, would suppose that because the notes of the different species of thrushes, inhabiting different parts of the world, bear the closest affinity to one another, these birds must all have a common origin; and yet, with reference to man, philologists still look upon the affinities of languages as affording direct evidence of such a community of origin, among the races, even though they have already discovered the most essential differences in the very structure of these languages.

Ever since New Holland was discovered, it has been known

as the land of zoological marvels. All its animals differ so completely from those of other parts of our globe, that it may be said to constitute a world in itself, as isolated in that respect from the other continents, as it truly is in its physical relations. As a zoological realm, it extends to New Guinea and some adjacent islands. New Holland, however, constitutes a distinct fauna, which at some future time may be still further subdivided, differing from that of the islands north of it. The characteristic animals of this insular continent are represented in the eighth column of our Tableau. They all belong to two families only, considering the class of mammalia alone, the marsupials, and the monotremes. Besides these are found bats, and mice, and a wild dog; but there are neither true edentata, nor ruminants, nor pachyderms, nor monkeys, in this realm, which is inhabited by two races of men, the Australian in New Holland, and the Papuans upon the Islands. The isolation of the zoological types of Australia, inhabiting as they do a continent partaking of nearly all the physical features of the other parts of the world, is one of the most striking evidences that the presence of animals upon earth is not determined by physical conditions, but established by the direct agency of a Creator.

Of Polynesia, its races and animals, it would be difficult to give an idea in such a condensed picture as this. I pass them, therefore, entirely unnoticed. The mountain faunæ have also been omitted in our Map from want of space.

Before closing these remarks I should add, that one of the greatest difficulties naturalists have met with, in the study of the human races, has been the want of a standard of comparison by which to estimate the value and importance of the diversities observed between the different nations of the world. But (since it is idle to make assertions upon the character of these differences without a distinct understanding respecting the meaning of the words constantly used in reference to the subject), it may be proper to ask here, What is a species, what a variety, and what is meant by the unity or the diversity of the races?

In order not to enter upon debatable ground in answering the first of these questions, let us begin by considering it with reference to the animal kingdom; and, without alluding to any controverted point, limit ourselves to animals well known among us. We would thus remember that, with universal consent, the horse and ass are considered as two distinct species of the same genus, to which belong several other distinct species known to naturalists under the names of zebra, quagga, dauw, &c. The buffalo and the bull are also distinct species of another genus, embracing several other foreign species. The black bear, the white bear, the grizzly bear, give another example of three different species of the same genus, &c. &c. We might select many other examples among our common quadrupeds, or among birds, reptiles, fishes, &c., but these will be sufficient for our purpose. In the genus horse we have two domesticated species, the common horse and the donkey; in the genus bull, one domesticated species and the wild buffalo; the three species of bear mentioned are only found in the wild state. The ground upon which these animals are considered as distinct species is simply the fact, that, since they have been known to man, they have always preserved the same characteristics. To make specific difference or identity depend upon genetic succession, is begging the principle and taking for granted what in reality is under discussion. It is true that animals of the same species are fertile among themselves, and that their fecundity is an easy test of this natural relation; but this character is not exclusive, since we know that the horse and the ass, the buffalo and our cattle, like many other animals, may be crossed; we are, therefore, not justified, in doubtful cases, in considering the fertility of two animals as decisive of their specific identity. Moreover, generation is not the only way in which certain animals may multiply, as there are entire classes in which the larger number of individuals do not originate from eggs. Any definition of species in which the question of generation is introduced is, therefore, objectionable. The assumption, that the fertility of cross-breeds is necessarily limited to one or two generations, does not alter the case; since, in many instances, it is not proved beyond dispute. It is, however, *beyond all question* that individuals of *distinct* species may, in certain cases, be productive with one another, as well as with their own kind. It is equally certain that their offspring is a half-breed; that is to say, a being partaking of the peculiarities of the two parents, and not identical with either. The only definition of species meeting all these difficulties is that of Dr. Morton, who characterizes them as *primordial organic forms*. Species are thus distinct forms of organic life, the origin of which is lost in the primitive establishment of the state of things now existing, and varieties are such modifications of the species as may return to the typical form, under temporary influences. Accepting this definition with the qualifications just mentioned respecting hybridity, I am prepared to show that the differences existing between the races of men are of the same kind as the differences observed between the different families, genera, and species of monkeys or other animals; and that these different species of animals differ in the same degree one from the other as the races of men—nay, the differences between distinct races are often greater than those distinguishing species of animals one from the other. The chimpanzee and gorilla do not differ more one from the other than the Mandingo and the Guinea Negro: they together do not differ more from the orang than the Malay or white man differs from the Negro. In proof of this assertion, I need only refer the reader to the description of the anthropoid monkeys published by Prof. Owen and by Dr. J. Wyman, and to such descriptions of the races of men as notice more important peculiarities than the mere differences in the color of the skin. It is, however, but fair to exonerate these authors from the responsibility of any deduction I would draw from a renewed examination of the same facts, differing from theirs; for I maintain distinctly that the differences observed among the races of men are of the same kind and even greater than those upon which the anthropoid monkeys are considered as distinct species.

Again, nobody can deny that the offspring of different races is always a half-breed, as between animals of different species, and not a child like either its mother or its father. These conclusions in no way conflict with the idea of the unity of mankind, which is as close as that of the members of any well-marked type of animals; and whosoever will consult history must remain satisfied, that the moral question of brotherhood among men is not any more affected by these views than the direct obligations between immediate blood relations. Unity is determinal by a typical structure, and by the similarity of natural abilities and propensities; and, unless we deny the typical relations of the cat tribe, for instance, we must admit that unity is not only compatible with diversity of origin, but that it is the universal law of nature.

This coincidence, between the circumscription of the races of man and the natural limits of different zoological provinces characterized by peculiar distinct species of animals, is one of the most important and unexpected features in the Natural History of Mankind, which the study of the geographical distribution of all the organized beings, now existing upon earth, has disclosed to us. It is a fact which cannot fail to throw light, at some future time, upon the very origin of the differences existing among men, since it shows that man's physical nature is modified by the same laws as that of animals, and that any general results obtained from the animal kingdom regarding the organic differences of its various types must also apply to man.

Now, there are only two alternatives before us at present:—

1st. Either mankind originated from a common stock, and all the different races with their peculiarities, in their present distribution, are to be ascribed to subsequent changes—

an assumption for which there is no evidence whatever, and which leads at once to the admission that the diversity among animals is not an original one, nor their distribution determined by a general plan, established in the beginning of the Creation; — or,

2d. We must acknowledge that the diversity among animals is a fact determined by the will of the Creator, and their geographical distribution part of the general plan which unites all organized beings into one great organic conception: whence it follows that what are called human races, down to their specialization as nations, are distinct primordial forms of the type of man.

The consequences of the first alternative, which is contrary to all the modern results of science, run inevitably into the Lamarkian development theory, so well known in this country through the work entitled "Vestiges of Creation;" though its premises are generally adopted by those who would shrink from the conclusions to which they necessarily lead.

Whatever be the meaning of the coincidence alluded to above, it must in future remain an important element in ethnographical studies; and no theory of the distribution of the races of man, and of their migrations, can be satisfactory hereafter, which does not account for that fact.

We may, however, draw already an important inference from this investigation, which cannot fail to have its influence upon the farther study of the human races: namely, that the laws which regulate the diversity of animals, and their distribution upon earth, apply equally to man, *within the same limits* and *in the same degree;* and that all our liberty and moral responsibility, however spontaneous, are yet instinctively directed by the All-wise and Omnipotent, to fulfil the great harmonies established in Nature.

L. A.

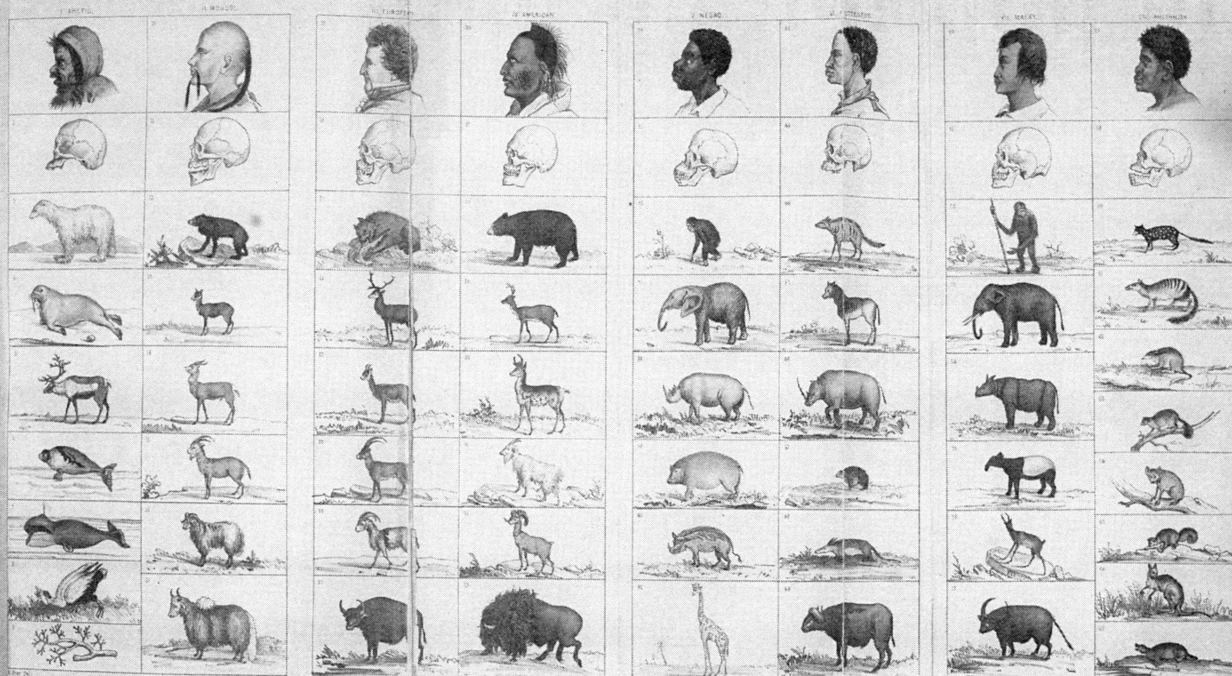

…ableau to accompany Prof. Agassiz's "Sketch." — Nott & Gliddon's Types of Mankind, 1854.

EXPLANATIONS

OF THE

TABLEAU ACCOMPANYING PROF. AGASSIZ'S SKETCH.

I.—ARCTIC REALM.

1. Head — *Eskimaux.* [FRANKLIN: *2d Exp. Pol. Sea*; 1828; i. pl. 13.]
2. Skull — *Eskimaux.* [MORTON: *Cr. Amer.*; p. 70. No. 1.]
3. White Bear (*Ursus maritimus*). [CUVIER: *Règne Anim.*; Atlas, Mamm., pl. 30, fig. 3.]
4. Walrus (*Trichecus Rosmarus*). [CUVIER: *op. cit.*; pl. 45, fig. 1.]
5. Reindeer (*Cervus Tarandus*). [CUVIER: *op. cit.*; pl. 87, fig. 2.]
6. Harp Seal (*Phoca grœnlandica*). [SHAW: *Zool.*; Mamm., i. pl. 71.]
7. RightWhale (*Balæna Mysticetus*). [CUVIER: *op. cit.*; pl. 100, fig. 1.]
8. Eider Duck (*Anas mollissima*). [AUDUBON: *Birds*; 1843; vi. pl. 405, fig. 1.]
9. Reindeer-moss (*Cenomyce rangiferina*). [LOUDON: *Enc. Plants*; p. 969, No. 15,636.]

II.—MONGOL REALM.

10. Head — *Chinese.* [HAM. SMITH: *Nat. Hist. Human Species*; 1848; pl. 10, "Mongol."]
11. Skull — *Chinese.* [CUVIER: *op. cit.*; pl. 8, fig. iii.]
12. Bear (*Ursus thibetanus*). [SCHREBER: *Säugthiere*: iii. pl. 141 DD].
13. Musk-deer (*Moschus moschiferus*). [CUVIER: *op. cit.*; pl. 86.]
14. Antilope (*Antilope gutturosa*). [SCHREBER: *op. cit.*; pl. 275.]
15. Goat (*Capra siberica*). [SCHREBER: *op. cit.*; pl. 281.]
16. Sheep (*Ovis Argali*). [CUVIER: *Iconographie*; i. pl. 44 bis, fig. 1.]
17. Yak (*Bos grunniens*). [VASEY: *Ox Tribe*; 1851; p. 45.]

III.—EUROPEAN REALM.

18. Head—CUVIER's portrait. [*Règne Anim.*; Atlas, Mamm.; "Medalion."]
19. Skull — *European.* [CUVIER: *op. cit.*; pl. 8, fig. 1.]
20. Bear (*Ursus Arctos*). [SCHREBER: *op. cit.*; pl. 139.]
21. Stag (*Cervus Elaphus*). [SCHREBER: *op. cit.*; pl. 247 A.]
22. Antilope (*Antilope Rupicapra*). [SCHREBER: *op. cit.*; pl. 279.]
23. Goat (*Capra Ibex*). [SCHREBER: *op. cit.*; pl. 281 C.]
24. Sheep (*Ovis Musimon*). SCHREBER: *op. cit.*; pl. 288 A.]
25. Auerochs (*Bos Urus*). [VASEY: *op. cit.*; p. 40.]

IV.—AMERICAN REALM.

26. Head — *Indian Chief.* [MAX. PR. DE WIED: *Travels*; pl. 3.]
27. Skull — *Mound in Tennessee.*— [MORTON: *Cr. Amer.*; pl. 55.]
28. Bear (*Ursus americanus*). [SCHREBER: *op. cit.*; pl. 141 B.]
29. Stag (*Cerv. virginianus*). [SCHREBER: *op. cit.*: pl. 246 B.]
30. Antilope (*Ant. furcifera*). [*U. S. Pat. Off. Rep.* 1852; pt. ii. pl. 1.]
31. Goat (*Capra americana*). [*U. S. Pat. Off.*; pl. 6.]
32. Sheep (*Ovis montana*). [*U. S. Pat. Off.*; pl. 5.]
33. Bison (*Bos americanus*). [*U. S. Pat. Off.*; pl. 7.]

V.—AFRICAN REALM.

34. Head — *Mozambique Negro.*— COURTET DE L'ISLE: *Tableau Ethnog. du Genre Humain*; 1849; pl. 5.]
35. Skull—*Creole Negro.* [LATHAM: *Varieties of Man*; p. 6.]
36. Chimpanzee (*Troglodytes niger*). [CUVIER: *Règne An.*; pl. ii. fig. 1.]
37. Elephant (*Elephas africanus*). CUVIER: *Règne anim.*; i. p.]
38. Rhinoceros (*R. bicornis*). [SMITH: *South Africa*; pl. 2.]
39. Hippopotamus (*H. amphibius*). [SMITH: *South Africa*; pl. 6.]
40. Wart-Hog (*Phacochœrus Æliani*). [SCHREBER: *op. cit.*; pl. 326 A.]
41. Giraffe (*Cameleopardalis Giraffa*). [CUVIER: *Iconographie*: i. pl. 43.]

VI.—HOTTENTOT FAUNA.

42. Head—*Bushman.* [HAM. SMITH: *Nat. Hist.*; pl. 13.]
43. Skull—*Bushman.* [HAM. SMITH: *op. cit.*; pl. 2.]
44. Hyena Genet (*Proteles Lalandii*). [*Mém. du Muséum*; xi. p. 354.]
45. Quagga (*Equus Quagga*) [SCHREBER: *op. cit.*; pl. 317.]
46. Rhinoceros (*R. Simus*). [SMITH: *South Africa*; pl. 19.]
47. Cape Hyrax (*Hyrax capensis*). [SCHREBER: *op. cit.*; pl. 240.]
48. Ant-eater (*Orycteropus capensis.*) [*Nouv. Dict. d'Hist. Naturelle*; xxiv. p. 182.]
49. Cape Ox (*Bos caffer*). [VASEY: *Ox Tribe*; p. 86.]

VII.—MALAYAN REALM.

50. Head — *Malay.* [WARD: *Nat. Hist. of Mankind*; 1849; p. 54.]
51. Skull — *Malay.* [DUMOUTIER: *Atlas Anthropol.*; pl. 37, fig. 5.)
52. Orang-Utan (*Pithecus Satyrus*). [TEMMINCK: *Monographies*; ii. pl. 41.]
53. Elephant (*Elephas indicus*).— [SCHREBER: *op. cit.*; pl. 317 CC.]
54. Rhinoceros (*R. sondaicus*). [HORSFIELD: *Zool. Researches*; 1824.]
55. Tapir (*Tapirus malayanus*).— [HORSFIELD: *op. cit.*]
56. Stag (*Cervus Muntjac*). HORSFIELD: *op. cit.*]
57. Ox (*Bos Arnee*). [VASEY: *Ox Tribe*; p. 111.]

VIII.—AUSTRALIAN REALM.

58. Head—*Alfouroux.* [CUVIER: *op. cit.*; pl. 8, fig. 1.]
59. Skull — *Alfouros.* [HAM. SMITH: *Nat. Hist.*; pl. 2.]
60. Spotted Opossum (*Dasyurus Vir.*). [SCHREBER: *op. cit.*; pl. 152 B.]
61. Ant-eater (*Myrmecobius fasciatus*). [*Trans. Zoological Soc.*; ii. p. 154.]
62. Rabbit (*Perameles Lagotis*).— [WATERHOUSE: *Marsupials*; i. pl. 13.]
63. Phalanger (*Phalangista vulpina*). [WATERHOUSE: *op. cit.*; i. pl. 8.]
64. Wombat (*Phascolarctos cinereus*). [SCHREBER: *op. cit.*; pl. 155 A.]
65. Squirrel (*Petaurus sciureus*).— [WATERHOUSE: *op. cit.*; i. p. 33.]
66. Kangaroo (*Macropus giganteus*). [WATERHOUSE: *op. cit.*; i. p. 62.]
67. Duck-bill (*Ornithorhynchus paradoxus*). [WATERHOUSE: *op. cit.*; i. p. 26.]

Note.— Adhering as closely as possible to the written instructions of Prof. AGASSIZ, the annexed Tableau was drawn and tinted, under my own eye, in the Library of the Academy of the Natural Sciences at Philadelphia. Every effort at correctness has been made; although, owing to unavoidable reduction to so small a scale, the *coloring* especially can be but suggestive.

To Prof. JOSEPH LEIDY, Dr. WM. S. ZANTZINGER, and Major JOHN LE CONTE, who most obligingly gave me the advantage of their aid and counsel in selecting the originals of these figures, must be ascribed the merit of carrying Prof. Agassiz's conception into detailed effect. (January, 1854.)

G. R. G., *Corr. Mem. Acad. Nat. Sciences.*

EXPLANATIONS

OF THE

MAP ACCOMPANYING PROF. AGASSIZ'S SKETCH.

I.—ARCTIC REALM—inhabited by HYPERBORÆANS; and containing:—
AAA—an *Hyperborean* fauna.

II.—ASIATIC REALM—inhabited by MONGOLS; and subdivided into:—
B—a *Mandchurian* fauna } in the temperate range of the zone.
C—a *Japanese* fauna }
D—a *Chinese* fauna, in the warmer part.
E—a *Central-Mongolian* fauna.
F—a *Caspian* (western) fauna.

III.—EUROPEAN REALM—inhabited by WHITE-MEN; and divided into:—
G—a *Scandinavian* fauna.
H—a *Russian* fauna.
I—a *Central-European* fauna.
J—a *South-European* fauna.
K—a *North-African* fauna.
L—an *Egyptian* fauna.
M—a *Syrian* and an *Iranian* fauna.

IV.—AMERICAN REALM—inhabited by AMERICAN INDIANS.
NORTH AMERICA—divided into:—
N—a *Canadian* fauna.
O—an *Alleghanian* fauna, or fauna of the Middle States.
P—a *Louisianian* fauna, or fauna of the Southern States
Q—a *Table-land* fauna, or fauna of the Rocky Mountains.
R—a *Northwest-Coast* fauna.
S—a *Californian* fauna.
CENTRAL AMERICA—subdivided into:—
T—a *Main-land* fauna.
U—an *Antilles* fauna.
SOUTH AMERICA—divided into:—
V—a *Brazilian* fauna.
—a *Pampas* fauna.
X—a *Cordilleras* fauna.
Y—a *Peruvian* fauna.
Z—a *Patagonian* fauna.

V.—AFRICAN REALM—inhabited by NUBIANS, ABYSSINIANS, FOOLAHS, NEGROES, HOTTENTOTS, BOSJESMANS; and divided into:—
aa—a *Saharan* fauna.
bb—a *Nubian* fauna.
cc—an *Abyssinian* fauna (extending to Arabia).
dd—a *Senegalian* fauna.
ee—a *Guinean* fauna.
ff—an *Afric-Table-land* fauna.
gg—a *Cape-of-Good-Hope* fauna.
hh—a *Madagascar* (diverging) fauna.

VI.—EAST-INDIAN (or MALAYAN) REALM—inhabited by TELINGANS, MALAYS, NEGRILLOS; and divided into:—
ii—a *Dukhun* fauna.
jj—an *Indo-Chinese* fauna.
kk—a *Sunda-Islandic* fauna (including Borneo and the Philippines).

VII.—AUSTRALIAN REALM—inhabited by PAPUANS, AUSTRALIANS; and divided into:—
ll—a *Papuan* fauna.
mm—a *New-Holland* fauna.

VIII.—POLYNESIAN REALM—inhabited by SOUTH-SEA ISLANDERS; and containing:—
nn, *nn*—*Polynesian* faunæ.

N. B. It has not been in my power to follow Prof. Agassiz's instructions in regard to the *coloring* of this map, the scale adopted being too small.—G. R. G.

MAP TO ACCOMPANY PROF. AGASSIZ'S "SKETCH."

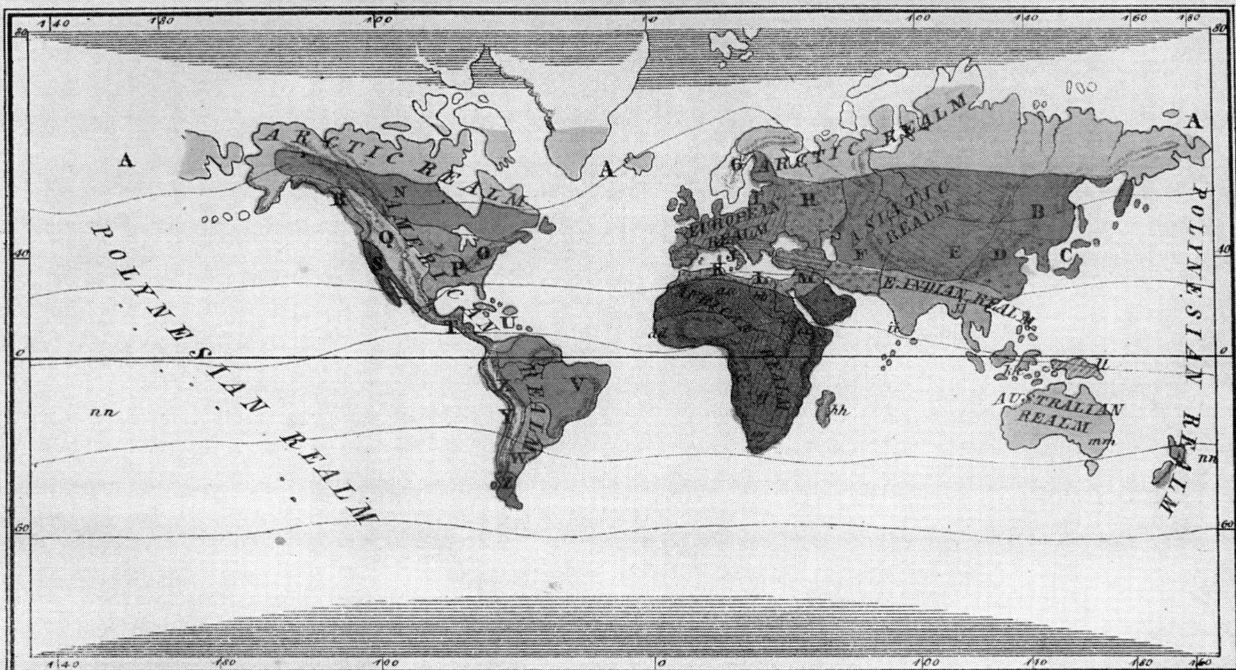

Nott & Gliddon's Types of Mankind, 1854.

TYPES OF MANKIND.

INTRODUCTION.

MR. LUKE BURKE, the bold and able Editor of the *London Ethnological Journal*, defines Ethnology to be "a science which investigates the mental and physical differences of Mankind, and the organic laws upon which they depend; and which seeks to deduce from these investigations, principles of human guidance, in all the important relations of social existence."[1] To the same author are we indebted not only for the most extensive and lucid definition of this term, but for the first truly philosophic view of a new and important science that we have met with in the English language.

The term "Ethnology" has generally been used as synonymous with "Ethnography," understood as the Natural History of Man; but by Burke it is made to take a far more comprehensive grasp—to include the whole mental and physical history of the various Types of Mankind, as well as their social relations and adaptations; and, under this comprehensive aspect, it therefore interests equally the philanthropist, the naturalist, and the statesman. Ethnology demands to know what was the primitive organic structure of each race?—what such race's moral and psychical character?—how far a race may have been, or may become, modified by the combined action of time and moral and physical causes?—and what position in the social scale Providence has assigned to each type of man?

"Ethnology divides itself into two principal departments, the *Scientific* and the *Historic*. Under the former is comprised every thing connected with the Natural History of Man and the fundamental laws of living organisms; under the latter, every fact in civil history which has any important bearing, directly or indirectly, upon the question of races — every fact calculated to throw light upon the number, the moral and physical peculiarities, the early seats, migrations, conquests or interblendings, of the primary divisions of the human family, or of the leading mixed races which have sprung from their intermarriages."[2]

Such is the scope of this science — born, we may say, within our own generation — and we propose to examine mankind under the above two-fold aspect, while we point out some of the more salient results towards which modern investigation is tending. The press everywhere teems with new books on the various partitions of the wide field of Ethnology; yet there does not exist, in any language, an attempt, based on the highest scientific lights of the day, at a systematic treatise on Ethnology in its extended sense. MORTON was the first to conceive the proper plan; but, unfortunately, lived not to carry it out; and although the present volume falls very far below the just requirements of science, we feel assured that it will at least aid materially in suggesting the right direction to future investigators.

The grand problem, more particularly interesting to all readers, is that which involves the *common origin* of races; for upon the latter deduction hang not only certain religious dogmas, but the more practical question of the equality and perfectibility of races — we say "more practical question," because, while Almighty Power, on the one hand, is not responsible to Man for the distinct origin of human races, these, on the other, are accountable to Him for the manner in which their delegated power is used towards each other.

Whether an original diversity of races be admitted or not, the *permanence* of existing physical types will not be questioned by any Archæologist or Naturalist of the present day. Nor, by such competent arbitrators, can the consequent permanence of moral and intellectual peculiarities of types be denied. The intellectual man is inseparable from the physical man; and the nature of the one cannot be altered without a corresponding change in the other.

The truth of these propositions had long been familiar to the master-mind of JOHN C. CALHOUN; who regarded them to be of such paramount importance as to demand the fullest consideration from those who, like our lamented statesman in his day, wield the destinies of nations and of races. An anecdote will illustrate the pains-taking laboriousness of Mr. Calhoun to let no occasion slip whence information was attainable. Our colleague, G. R. GLIDDON, happened to be in Washington City, early in May, 1844, on business of his father (United States' Consul for Egypt) at the State Department; at which time Mr. Calhoun, Secretary of State, was conducting diplomatic negotiations with France and England, connected with the annexation of Texas. Mr. Calhoun, suffering from indisposition, sent a message to Mr. Gliddon, requesting a visit at his lodgings. In a long interview which ensued, Mr. Calhoun stated, that England pertinaciously continued to interfere with our inherited Institution of Negro Slavery, and in a manner to render it imperative that he should indite very strong instructions on the subject to the late Mr. WM. R. KING, of Alabama, then our Ambassador to France. He read to Mr. Gliddon portions of the manuscript of his celebrated letter to Mr. King, which, issued on the 12th of the following August, ranks among our ablest national documents. Mr. Calhoun declared that he could not foresee what course the negotiation might take, but wished to be forearmed for any emergency. He was convinced that the true difficulties of the subject could not be fully comprehended without first considering the radical difference of humanity's races, which he intended to discuss, should he be driven to the necessity. Knowing that Mr. Gliddon had paid attention to the subject of African ethnology; and that, from his long residence in Egypt, he had enjoyed unusual advantages for its investigation, Mr. Calhoun had summoned him for the purpose of ascertaining what were the best sources of information in this country. Mr. Gliddon, after laying before the Secretary what he conceived to be the true state of the case, referred him for further information to several scientific gentlemen, and more particularly to DR. MORTON, of Philadelphia. A correspondence ensued between Mr. Calhoun and Dr. Morton on the subject, and the Doctor presented to him copies of the *Crania Americana* and *Ægyptiaca*, together with minor works, all of which Mr. Calhoun studied with no less pleasure than profit. He soon perceived that the conclusions which he had long before drawn from history, and from his personal observations in America, on the Anglo-Saxon, Celtic, Teutonic, French, Spanish, Negro, and Indian races, were entirely corroborated by the plain teachings of modern science. He beheld demonstrated in Morton's works the important fact, that the Egyptian, Negro, several White, and sundry Yellow races, had existed, in their present forms, for at least 4000 years; and that it behoved the statesman to lay aside all current speculations about the origin and perfectibility of races, and to deal, in political argument, with the simple facts as they stand.

What, on the vital question of African Slavery in our Southern States, was the utilitarian consequence of Calhoun's memorable dispatch to King? Strange, yet true, to say, although the English press anxiously complained that Mr. Calhoun had intruded *Ethnology* into diplomatic correspondence, a communication from the Foreign Office promptly assured our Government that Great Britain had no intention of intermeddling with the domestic institutions of other nations. Nor, from that day to this, has she violated her formal pledge in our regard. During a sojourn of Mr. Calhoun, on his retirement from office, with us at Mobile, we enjoyed personal opportunities of knowing the accuracy of the above facts, no less than of receiving ample corroborations illustrative of the *inconvenience* which true ethnological science might have created in philanthropical diplomacy, had it been frankly introduced by a CALHOUN.

No class of men, perhaps, understand better the practical importance of Ethnology than the statesmen of England; yet from motives of policy, they keep its agitation studiously out of sight. DR. PRICHARD, when speaking of a belief in the diversity of races, justly remarks—

"If these opinions are not every day expressed in this country [England], it is because the avowal of them is restrained by a degree of odium that would be excited by it."[3]

Although the press in that country has been, to a great extent, muzzled by government influence, we are happy to see that her periodicals are beginning to assume a bolder and more rational tone; and we may now hope that the stereotyped errors of Prichard, and we might add, those of Latham,[4] will soon pass at their true value. The immense evils of false philanthropy are becoming too glaring to be longer overlooked. While, on the one hand, every true philanthropist must admit that no race has a right to enslave or oppress the weaker, it must be conceded, on the other, that all changes in existing institutions should be guided, not by fanaticism and groundless hypotheses, but by experience, sound judgment, and real charity.

"No one that has not worked much in the element of History can be aware of the immense importance of clearly keeping in view the differences of race that are discernible among the nations that inhabit different parts of the world. In practical politics it is certainly possible to push such ethnographical considerations too far; as, for example, in our own cant about Celt and Saxon, when Ireland is under discussion; but in speculative history, in questions relating to the past career and the future destinies of nations, it is only by a firm and efficient handling of this conception of our species as broken up into so many groups or masses, physiologically different to a certain extent, that any progress can be made, or any available conclusions accurately arrived at.

"The NEGRO, or African, with his black skin, woolly hair, and compressed elongated skull; the MONGOLIAN of Eastern Asia and America, with his olive complexion, broad and all but beardless face, oblique eyes, and square skull; and the CAUCASIAN of Western Asia and Europe, with his fair skin, oval face, full brow, and rounded skull: such, as every school-boy knows, are the three great types or varieties into which naturalists have divided the inhabitants of our planet. Accepting this rough initial conception of a world peopled everywhere, more or less completely, with these three varieties of human beings or their combinations, the historian is able, in virtue of it, to announce one important fact at the very outset, to wit: that, up to the present moment, the destinies of the species appear to have been carried forward almost exclusively by its Caucasian variety."[5]

In the broad field and long duration of Negro life, not a single civilization, spontaneous or borrowed, has existed, to adorn its gloomy past. The ancient kingdom of Meroë has been often pointed out as an exception, but this is now proven to be the work of Pharaonic Egyptians, and not of Negro races. Of Mongolian races, we have the prolonged semi-civilizations of China, Japan, and (if they be classed un er the same head) the still feebler attempts of Peru and Mexico. What a contrast, if we compare with these,

"Caucasian progress, as exhibited in the splendid succession of distinct civilizations, from the ancient Egyptian to the recent Anglo-American, to which the Caucasian part of the species has given birth."

Nor when we examine their past history, their anatomical and physiological characters, and philological differences, are we justified in throwing all the Indo-European and Semitic races into one indivisible mass.

"Our species is not a huge collection of perfectly similar human beings, but an aggregation of a number of separate groups or masses, having such subordinate differences of organization that, necessarily, they must understand nature differently, and employ in life very different modes of procedure. Assemble together a Negro, a Mongol, a Shemite, an Armenian, a Scythian, a Pelasgian, a Celt, and a German, and you will have before you not mere illustrations of an arbitrary classification, but positively distinct human beings — men whose relations to the outer world are by no means the same."

"In all, indeed, there will be found the same fundamental instincts and powers, the same obligation to recognized truth, the same feeling for the beautiful, the same abstract sense of justice, the same necessity of reverence; in all, the same liability to do wrong, knowing it to be wrong. These things excepted, however, what contrast, what variety! The representative of one race is haughty and eager to strike, that of another is meek and patient of injury; one has the gift of slow and continued perseverance, another can labour only at intervals and violently; one is full of mirth and humour, another walks as if life were a pain; one is so faithful and clear in perception, that what he sees to-day he will report accurately a year hence; through the head of another there perpetually sings such a buzz of fiction that, even as he looks, realities grow dim, and rocks, trees, and hills, reel before his poetic gaze. Whether, with phrenologists, we call these differences craniological; or whether, in the spirit of a deeper physiology, we adjourn the question by refusing to connect them with aught less than the whole corporeal organism — bone, chest, limbs, skin, muscle, and nerve; they are, at all events, real and substantial; and Englishmen will never conceive the world as it is, will never be intellectually its masters, until, realizing this as a fact, they shall remember that it is perfectly respectable to be an Assyrian, and that an Italian is not necessarily a rogue because he wears a moustache."[6]

Looking back over the world's history, it will be seen that human progress has arisen mainly from the war of races. All the great impulses which have been given to it from time to time have been the results of conquests and colonizations. Certain races would be stationary and barbarous for ever, were it not for the introduction of new blood and novel influences; and some of the lowest types are hopelessly beyond the reach even of these salutary stimulants to melioration.

It has been naively remarked that —

"Climate has no influence in permanently altering the varieties or races of men; destroy them it may, and does, but it cannot convert them into any other race; nor can this be done by an act of parliament; which, to a thoroughgoing Englishman, with all his amusing nationalities, will appear as something amazing. It has been tried in Wales, Ireland, and Caledonia, and failed."[7]

Not enough is it for us to know who and what are the men who play a prominent part in these changes, nor what is the general character of the masses whom they influence. None can predict how long the power or existence of these men will last, nor foretell what will be the character of those who succeed them. If we wish to predict the future, we must ascertain those great fundamental laws of humanity to which all human passions and human thoughts must ultimately be subject. We must know universal, as well as individual man. These are questions upon which science alone has the right to pronounce.

"Where, we ask, are the historic evidences of universal human equality, or unity? The farther we trace back the records of the past, the more broadly marked do we find all human diversities. In no part of Europe, at the present day, can we discover the striking national contrasts which Tacitus describes, still less those represented in the more ancient pages of Herodotus."[8]

And nowhere on the face of the globe do we find a greater diversity, or more strongly-marked types, than on the monuments of Egypt, antedating the Christian era more than 3000 years.

Dr. James Cowles Prichard, for the last half century, has been the grand orthodox authority with the advocates of a common origin for the races of men. His ponderous work on the "Physical History of Mankind" is one of the noblest monuments of learning and labour to be found in any language. It has been the never-exhausted reservoir of knowledge from which most subsequent writers on Ethnology have drawn; but, nevertheless, as Mr. Burke has sagely remarked, Prichard has been the "victim of a false theory." He commenced, when adolescent, by writing a graduating thesis, at Edinburgh, in support of the *unity of races*, and the remainder of his long life was devoted to the maintenance of this first impression. We behold him, year after year, like a bound giant, struggling with increasing strength against the cords which cramp him, and we are involuntarily looking with anxiety to see him burst them asunder. But how few possess the moral power to break through a deep-rooted prejudice!

Prichard published no less than three editions of his "Physical History of Mankind," viz.: in 1813, 1826, and 1847. To one, however, who, like ourselves, has followed him line by line, throughout his whole literary life, the constant changes of his opinions, his "special pleading," and his cool suppression of adverse facts, leave little confidence in his judgment or his cause. He set out, in youth, by distorting history and science to suit the theological notions of the day; and, in his mature age, concludes the final chapter of his last volume by abandoning the authenticity of the Pentateuch, which for forty years had been the stumbling-block of his life.

Dr. Prichard's defence of the Book of Genesis, in the *Appendix* to the fifth volume of his "Researches," is certainly a very extraordinary performance. He denies its genealogies; denies its chronology; denies all its historical and scientific details; denies that it was written by Moses; admits that nobody knows who did write it; and yet, withal, actually endeavours "to show that the sacred and canonical authority of the Book of Genesis is not injured."

We confess that we cannot understand why one half of the historical portion of a book should be condemned as false and the other received as true, when both stand upon equal authority. Nor do we think that his dissection of other parts of the Old Testament leaves them in much better condition, as regards their account of human origins. Behold a sample:

"The time of Ezra, after the Captivity, was the era of historical compilation, soon after which the Hebrew language gave way to a more modern dialect. There are indications that the *whole* of the Sacred Books passed under several recensions during these successive ages, when they were, doubtless, copied, and recopied, and *illustrated by additional passages*, or *by glosses*, that might be requisite, in order to preserve their meaning to later times. Such passages and glosses occur frequently in the different Books of Moses, and in the older historical books, and we may thus, in a *probable way*, account for the presence of many explanatory notices and comments, of comparatively later date, which, unless thus accounted for, would add weight to the hypotheses (?) of some German writers, who *deny the high antiquity of the Pentateuch*."[9]

On the degree of orthodoxy claimed by the erudite Doctor in respect to chronology, the following extract will speak for itself:

"Beyond that event [arrival of Abraham in Palestine,] we can never know how many centuries, nor even how many thousands of years, may have elapsed since the first man of clay received the image of God, and the breath of life. Still, as the thread of genealogy has been traced, though probably with many great intervals, the whole duration of time from the beginning must apparently have been *within moderate bounds*, and by no means so wide and vast a space as the great periods of the Indian and *Egyptian fabulists*."

Instead of thus nervously shifting his scientific and theological grounds from year to year, how much more dignified, and becoming to both science and religion, would it have been, had Prichard simply followed facts, wherever they might lead in science; and had he frankly acknowledged that the Bible really gives no history of all the races of Men, and but a meagre account of one? He was indeed the victim of a false theory; and we could not but be struck by the applicability of the following pencil-note to his first volume (1813), written on the margin, just forty years ago, by the late distinguished Dr. Thomas Cooper, President of South Carolina College:

"This is a book by an industrious compiler, but an inconclusive reasoner; he wears the orthodox costume of his nation and his day. No man *can* be a good reasoner who is marked by clerical prejudices."

Alas! for his fame, Dr. Prichard continued to change his costume with the fashion; and some truths of the Universe, most essential to

Man, have thereby been kept in darkness, that is, out of the popular sight, by erroneous interpretations of God's works.

Albeit, in his last edition, Prichard evidently perceived, in the distance, a glimmer of light dawning from the time-worn monuments of "Old Egypt," destined eventually to dispel the obfuscations with which he had enshrouded the history of Man; and to destroy that darling unitary fabric on which all his energies had been expended. Had he lived but two years longer, until the mighty discoveries of LEPSIUS were unfolded to the world, he would have realized that the honorable occupation of his long life had been only to accumulate facts, which, properly interpreted, shatter everything he had built upon them. In the preface to vol. iii., he says:

"If it should be found that, within the period of time to which historical testimony extends, the distinguishing characters of human races have been constant and undeviating, it would become a matter of great difficulty to reconcile this conclusion [*i. e.* the unity of all mankind,] with the inferences already obtained from other considerations."

In other words, if hypotheses, and deductions drawn from analogies among the lower animals, should be refuted by well-ascertained facts, demonstrative of the absolute independence of the primitive types of mankind of all existing moral and physical causes, during several thousand years, Prichard himself concedes, that every argument heretofore adduced in support of a common origin for human families must be abandoned.

One of the main objects of this volume is to show, that the criterion-point, indicated by Prichard, is now actually arrived at; and that the diversity of races must be accepted by Science as a *fact*, independently of theology, and of all analogies or reasonings drawn from the animal kingdom.

It will be observed that, with the exception of Morton's, we seldom quote works on the Natural History of Man; and simply for the reason, that their arguments are all based, more or less, on fabled analogies, which are at last proved by the monuments of Egypt and Assyria to be worthless. The whole method of treating the subject is herein changed. To our point of view, most that has been written on human Natural History becomes obsolete; and therefore we have not burthened our pages with citations from authors, even the most erudite and respected, whose views we consider the present work to have, in the main, superseded.

Such is not our course, however, where others have anticipated any conclusion we may have attained; and we are happy to find that Jacquinot had previously recognized the principle which has overthrown Prichard's unitary scheme:

"If the great branches of the human family have remained distinct in the lapse of ages, with their characteristics fixed and unalterable, we are justified in regarding mankind as divisible into *distinct species*."[10]

Four years ago, in our "Biblical and Physical History of Man,"[11] we published the following remarks:—

"If the *Unity* of the Races or Species of Men be assumed, there are but three suppositions on which the *diversity* now seen in the white, black, and intermediate colors, can be accounted for, viz.:

"1st. A *miracle*, or direct act of the Almighty, in changing one type into another.

"2d. The gradual action of Physical causes, such as climate, food, mode of life, &c.

"3d. Congenital, or accidental varieties.

"There being no evidence whatever in favor of the first hypothesis, we pass it by. The second and third have been sustained with signal ability by Dr. Prichard, in his Physical History of Mankind."

Although, even then, thoroughly convinced ourselves that the second and third hypotheses were already refuted by facts, and that they would soon be generally abandoned by men of science, we confess that we had little hope of seeing this triumph achieved so speedily; still less did we expect, in this matter-of-fact age, to behold a *miracle*, which exists too, not in the Bible, but only in feverish imaginations, assumed as a scientific solution. Certain sectarians[12] of the evangelical school are now gravely attempting, from lack of argument, to revive the old hypothesis of a miraculous change of one race into many at the Tower of Babel! Such notions, however, do not deserve serious consideration, as neither religion nor science has anything to do with unsustainable hypotheses.

The views, moreover, that we expressed in 1849, touching Physical Causes, Congenital Varieties, &c., need no modification at the present day; but, on the contrary, will be found amply sustained by the progress of science, as set forth in the succeeding chapters. We make bold to add an extract from our opinions published at that time:—

"Is it not strange that all the remarkable changes of type spoken of by Prichard and others should have occurred in remote antehistoric times, and amongst ignorant erratic tribes? Why is it that no instance of these remarkable changes can be pointed out which admits of conclusive evidence? The civilized nations of Europe have been for many centuries sending colonies to Asia, Africa, and America; amongst Mongols, Malays, Africans, and Indians; and why has no example occurred in any of these colonies to substantiate the argument? The doubtful examples of Prichard are refuted by others, which he cites on the adverse side, of a positive nature. He gives examples of Jews, Persians, Hindoos, Arabs, &c., who have emigrated to foreign climates, and, at the end of one thousand or fifteen hundred years, have preserved their original types in the midst of widely different races. Does nature anywhere operate by such opposite and contradictory laws?

"A few generations in animals are sufficient to produce all the changes they usually undergo from climate, and yet the races of men retain their leading characteristics for ages, without approximating to aboriginal types.

"In fact, so unsatisfactory is the argument based on the influence of climate to Prichard himself, that he virtually abandons it in the following paragraph: 'It must be observed,' says he, 'that the changes alluded to do not so often take place by alteration in the physical character of a whole tribe simultaneously, as by the *springing up* of some new *congenital* peculiarity, which is afterwards propagated, and becomes a character more or less constant in the progeny of the individuals in whom it first appeared, and is *perhaps* gradually communicated by intermarriages to a whole stock or tribe. This, it is obvious, can only happen in a long course of time.'

"We beg leave to fix your attention on this vital point. It is a commonly received error that the influence of a hot climate is gradually exerted on successive generations, until one species of mankind is completely changed into another; a dark shade is impressed on the first, and transmitted to the second; another shade is added to the third, which is handed down to the fourth; and so on, through successive generations, until the fair German is transformed, by climate, into the black African!

"This idea is *proven to be false*, and is abandoned by the well-informed writers of all parties. A sunburnt cheek is never handed down to succeeding generations. The exposed parts of the body alone are tanned by the sun, and the children of the white-skinned Europeans in New Orleans, Mobile, and the West Indies, are *born* as fair as their ancestors, and would remain so, if carried back to a colder climate. The same may be said of other *acquired* characters, (except those from want and disease.) They die with the individual, and are no more capable of transmission than a flattened head, mutilated limb, or tattooed skin. We repeat, that this fact is settled, and challenge a denial.

"The only argument left, then, for the advocates of the *unity* of the human species to fall back upon, is that of '*congenital*' varieties or peculiarities, which are said to spring up, and be transmitted from parent to child, so as to form new races.

"Let us pause for a moment to illustrate this fanciful idea. The Negroes of Africa, for example, are admitted not to be offsets from some other race, which have been gradually blackened and changed in moral and physical type by the action of climate; but it is asserted that, 'once in the flight of ages past,' some genuine little Negro, or rather many such, were born of Caucasian, Mongol, or other light-skinned parents, and then have turned about and changed the type of the inhabitants of a whole continent. So in America: the countless aborigines found on this continent, which we have reason to believe (see Squier's work) were building mounds before the time of Abraham, are the offspring of a race changed by accidental or congenital varieties. Thus, too, old China, India, Australia, Oceanica, etc., all owe their types, physical and mental, to *congenital* or *accidental varieties*, and all are descended from Adam and Eve! Can human credulity go farther, or human ingenuity invent any argument more absurd? Yet the whole groundwork of a common origin for some nine or ten hundred millions of human beings, embracing numerous distinct types, which are lost in an antiquity far beyond all records or chronology, sacred or profane, is narrowed down to this 'baseless fabric.'

"In support of this argument, we are told of the Porcupine family of England, which inherited for some generations a peculiar condition of the skin, characterized by thickened warty excrescences. We are told also of the transmission from parent to child of club feet, cross eyes, six fingers, deafness, blindness, and many other familiar examples of congenital peculiarities. But these examples merely serve to disprove the argument they are intended to sustain. Did any one ever hear of a club-foot, cross-eyed, or six-fingered *race*, although such individuals are exceedingly common? Are they not, on the contrary, always swallowed up and lost? Is it not strange, if there be any truth in this argument, that no race has ever been formed from those congenital varieties which we *know* to occur frequently, and yet races should originate from congenital varieties which cannot be proved, and are not believed, by our best writers, ever to have existed? No one ever saw a Negro, Mongol, or Indian, born from any but his own species. Has any one heard of an Indian child born from white or black parents in America, during more than two centuries that these races have been living here? Is not this brief and simple statement of the case sufficient to satisfy any one, that the diversity of species now seen on the earth, cannot be accounted for on the assumption of congenital or accidental origin? If a doubt remains, would it not be expelled by the recollection of the fact that the Negro, Tartar, and white man, existed, with their present types, at least one thousand years before Abraham journeyed to Egypt as a supplicant to the mighty Pharaoh?

"The unity of the human species has also been stoutly maintained on psychological grounds. Numerous attempts have been made to establish the intellectual equality of the dark races with the white; and the history of the past has been ransacked for examples, but they are nowhere to be found. Can any one call the name of a full-blooded Negro who has ever written a page worthy of being remembered?"

The avowal of the above views drew down upon us, as might have been expected, criticisms more remarkable for virulence of hostility, than for the scientific education of the critics. Our present volume is an evidence that we have survived these transient cavils; and while we have much satisfaction in submitting herein a mass of *facts* that, to the generality of readers in this country, will be surprising, we would remind the theologist, in the language of the very orthodox Hugh Miller (*Footprints of the Creator*), that

"The clergy, as a class, suffer themselves to linger far in the rear of an intelligent and accomplished laity. Let them not shut their eyes to the danger which is obviously coming. The battle of the evidences of Christianity will have, as certainly to be fought on the field of physical science, as it was contested in the last age on that of the metaphysics."

The Physical history of Man has been likewise trammelled for ages by arbitrary systems of Chronology; more especially by that of the Hebrews, which is now considered, by all competent authorities, as altogether worthless beyond the time of Abraham, and of little value previously to that of Solomon; for it is in his reign that we reach their last positive date. The abandonment of this restricted system is a great point gained; because, instead of being obliged to crowd an immense antiquity, embracing endless details, into a few centuries, we are now free to classify and arrange facts as the requirements of history and science demand.

It is now generally conceded that there exist no data by which we can approximate the date of man's first appearance upon earth; and, for aught we yet know, it may be thousands or millions of years beyond our reach. The spurious systems, of Archbishop Usher on the Hebrew Text, and of Dr. Hales on the Septuagint, being entirely broken down, we turn, unshackled by prejudice, to the monumental records of Egypt as our best guide. Even these soon lose themselves, not in the primitive state of man, but in his middle or perhaps modern ages; for the Egyptian Empire first presents itself to view, about 4000 years before Christ, as that of a mighty nation, in full tide of civilization, and surrounded by other realms and races already emerging from the barbarous stage.

In order that a clear understanding with the reader may be established in the following pages, it becomes necessary to adopt some common standard of chronology for facility of reference.

An esteemed correspondent, Mr. Birch, of the British Museum, aptly observes to us in a private letter—"Although I can see what is *not* the fact in chronology, I have not come to the conclusion of what *is* the truth." Such is precisely our own condition of mind; nor do we suppose that a conscientious student of the subject, as developed under its own head at the close of this volume, can at the present hour obtain, for epochas anterior to Abraham, a solution that must not itself be vague for a century or more. Nevertheless, in Egyptian chronology, we follow the system of Lepsius by assuming the *age of* MENES at B. C. 3893; in Chinese, we accept Pauthier's date for the 1st *historical dynasty* at B. C. 2637; in Assyrian, the results of Layard's last Journey indicate B. C. 1250 as the probable extreme of that country's monumental chronicles; and finally, in Hebrew computation, we agree with Lepsius in deeming Abraham's era to approximate to B. C. 1500. Our *Supplement* offers to the critical reader every facility of verification, with comparative Tables, the repetition of which is here superfluous.

To Egyptology, beyond all question, belongs the honor of dissipating those chronological fables of past generations, continued belief in which, since the recent publication of Chev'r Lepsius's researches, implies simply the credulity of ignorance. One of his letters from the Pyramids of Memphis, in 1843, contained the following almost prophetic passage:[13]

"We are still busy with structures, sculptures, and inscriptions, which are to be classed, by means of the now more accurately-determined groups of kings, in an epoch of highly-flourishing civilization, as far back as the *fourth Millennium before Christ*. We cannot sufficiently impress upon ourselves and others these hitherto incredible dates. The more criticism is provoked by them, and forced to serious examination, the better for the cause. Conviction will soon follow angry criticism; and, finally, those results will be attained, which are so intimately connected with every branch of antiquarian research."

We subscribe without reservation to the above sentiment; and hope we shall not be disappointed in the amount of "angry criticism" which we think the truths embodied in this volume are calculated to provoke. Scientific truth, exemplified in the annals of Astronomy, Geology, Chronology, Geographical distribution of animals, &c., has literally fought its way inch by inch through false theology. The last grand battle between science and dogmatism, on the primitive origin of races, has now commenced. It requires no prophetic eye to foresee that science must again, and finally, triumph.

It may be proper to state, in conclusion, that the subject shall be treated purely as one of science, and that our colleague and ourself will follow facts wherever they may lead, without regard to imaginary consequences. Locally, the "Friend of Moses," no less than other "friends of the Bible" everywhere, have been compelled to make large concessions to science. We shall, in the present investigation, treat the Scriptures simply in their historical and scientific bearings.

On former occasions, and in the most respectful manner, we had attempted to conciliate sectarians, and to reconcile the plain teachings of science with theological prejudices; but to no useful purpose. In return, our opinions and motives have been misrepresented and vilified by self-constituted teachers of the Christian religion! We have, in consequence, now done with all this; and no longer have any apologies to offer, nor favors of lenient criticism to ask. The broad banner of science is herein nailed to the mast. Even in our own brief day, we have beheld one flimsy religious dogma after another consigned to oblivion, while science, on the other hand, has been gaining strength and majesty with time. "Nature," says Luke Burke, "has nothing to reveal, that is not noble, and beautiful, and good."

In our former language,

"Man can *invent* nothing in science or religion but falsehood; and all the truths which he *discovers* are but facts or laws which have emanated from the Creator. All science, therefore, may be regarded as a revelation from HIM; and although newly-discovered laws, or facts, in nature, may conflict with religious *errors*, which have been written and preached for centuries, they never can conflict with religious *truth*. There must be harmony between the works and the words of the Almighty, and wherever they *seem* to conflict, the discord has been produced by the ignorance or wickedness of man."

J. C. N.

MOBILE, *August*, 1853.

PART I.

CHAPTER I.

GEOGRAPHICAL DISTRIBUTION OF ANIMALS, AND THE RACES OF MEN.

HAVE all the living creatures of our globe been created at one common point in Asia, and thence been disseminated over its wide surface by degrees, and adapted to the varied conditions in which they have been found in historical times? or, on the other hand, have different genera and species been created at points far distant from each other, with organizations suited to the circumstances in which they were originally placed?

Two schools have long existed, diametrically opposed to each other, on this question. The *first* may be termed that of the Theological Naturalists, who still look to the Book of Genesis, or what they conceive to be the inspired word of God, as a text-book of Natural History, as they formerly reputed it to be a manual of Astronomy and Geology. The *second* embraces the Naturalists proper, whose conclusions are derived from facts, and from the laws of God as revealed in his works, which are immutable.

Not only the authority of Genesis in matters of science, but the Mosaic authenticity of this book, is now questioned by a very large proportion of the most authoritative theologians of the present day; and, inasmuch as its language is clearly opposed to many of the well-established facts of modern science, we shall unhesitatingly take the benefit of this liberal construction. The language of Scripture touching the point now before us is so unequivocal, and so often repeated, as to leave no doubt as to the author's meaning. It teaches clearly that the Deluge was *universal*, that every living creature on the face of the earth at the time was destroyed, and that *seeds* of all the organized beings of after times were saved in Noah's Ark. The following is but a small portion of its oft-repeated words on this head: —

"And the waters prevailed exceedingly upon the earth, and all the high hills that were under the whole heaven, were covered. * * * Fifteen cubits upward did the waters prevail and the mountains were covered. * * * And all flesh died that moved upon the earth, both of fowl, and of cattle, and of beast, and every creeping thing that creepeth upon the earth, and every man. All in whose nostrils was the breath of life; of all that was in the dry land. * * * And Noah only remained alive, and they that were with him in the Ark." [14]

Now we reiterate that speech cannot be more explicit than this; and if it be true, it must apply with equal force to *all* living creatures — animals as well as mankind. It is really trifling with language to say, that the Text does not distinctly convey the idea that all the creatures of our day have descended from the seed saved in the Ark; or that they were all created within a certain area around the point at which Adam and Eve are supposed first to have had their being.

Although the same general laws prevail throughout the entire Fauna and Flora of the globe, yet in the illustration of our subject, we restrict our remarks mainly to the class of *Mammifers*, because a wider range would lead beyond our prescribed limits.

It has been a popularly-received error, from time immemorial, that degrees of latitude, or in other words, temperature of countries, were to be regarded as a sure index of the color and of certain other physical characters in races of men. This opinion has been supported by many able writers of the present century, and even in the last few years by no less authority than that of the distinguished Dr. Prichard, in the "*Physical History of Mankind.*" A rapid change, however, is now going on in the public mind in this respect, and so conclusive is the recent evidence drawn from the monuments of Egypt and other sources, in support of the permanence of distinctly marked types of mankind, such as the Egyptians, Jews, Negroes, Mongols, American Indians, etc., that we presume no really well-informed naturalist will again be found advocating such philosophic heresies. Indeed, it is difficult to conceive how any one, with the facts before him, (recorded by Prichard himself,) in connection with an Ethnographical Map, should believe that climate could account for the endless diversity of races seen scattered over the earth from the earliest dawn of history.

It is true that most of the black races are found in Africa; but, on the other hand, many equally black are met with in the temperate climates of India, Australia, and Oceanica, though differing in every attribute except color. A black skin would seem to be the best suited to hot climates, and for this reason we may suppose that a special creation of black races took place in Africa. The strictly white races lie mostly in the Temperate Zone, where they flourish best; and they certainly deteriorate physically, if not intellectually, when removed to hot climates. Their type is not in reality changed or obliterated, but they undergo a degradation from their primitive state, analogous to the operation of disease. The dark-skinned Hyperboreans are found in the Frigid Zone; regions most congenial to their nature, and from which they cannot be enticed by more temperate climes. The Mongols of Asia, and the aborigines of America, with their peculiar types, are spread over almost all degrees of latitude.

So is it with the whole range of Mammifers, as well as birds, and other genera. The lightest and the darkest colors — the most gorgeous and most sombre plumage, are everywhere found beside each other; though brilliant feathers and colors are commoner in the tropics, where men are generally more or less dark.

Every spot on the earth's surface, from pole to pole — the mountains and valleys, the dry land and the water — has its organized beings, which find around a given centre all the conditions necessary for their preservation. These living beings are as innumerable as the conditions of the places they inhabit; and their different stations are as varied as their instincts and habits. To consider these stations under the simple point of view of the distribution of heat on their surface, is absolutely to see but one of the many secondary natural causes that influence organized beings.

Amidst the infinitude of beings spread over the globe, the Class of Mammifers stands first in organization, and at its head Zoologists have placed the *Bimanes* (Mankind). It is the least numerous, and its genera and species are almost entirely known.

This class is composed of about 200 genera, which may be divided into two parts. 1st. Those whose habitations are limited to a single Zone. 2d. Those, on the contrary, which are scattered through all the Zones. There would at first seem to be a striking contrast between these two divisions; on the one side, complete *immobility*, and on the other, great *mobility;* but this irregularity is only apparent, for when we examine attentively the different genera, we find them governed by the same laws. Those of the first division, whose habitat is limited, are in general confined to a *few species;* while those of the second, on the contrary, contain *many species*, but which are themselves confined to certain localities, in the same manner as the fewer genera of the first division. Thus we find the same law governing *species* in both instances. We will cite a single example out of many. The White Bear is confined to the Polar regions, while other ursine species inhabit the temperate climates of the mountain chains of Europe and America; and finally, the Malay Bear, and the Bear of Borneo, are restricted to torrid climates.

We may then consider the different species of Mammifers as ranged under an identical law of geographical distribution, and that each species on the globe has its limited space, beyond which it does not extend; and that every country on the globe, whatever may be its temperature, its analogies, or differences of climate, possesses its own Mammifers, different from those of other countries, belonging to its region alone. There are apparent exceptions to this law, but they are all susceptible of explanation.[15]

A few species are really common to the two continents, but only in the Arctic region. America and Asia are there united by icy plains, which may be easily traversed by certain animals; and, while the White Bear, the Wolf, the Red Fox, the Glutton, are common to both, the continents and climates may there be really considered as one. We shall show, as we proceed, that with a few exceptions in the Arctic region, the Faunæ and Floræ of the two continents are entirely distinct, and that even the Temperate Zones of North and South America do not present the same types, although they are separated by mere table-lands, presenting none of the extremes of climate encountered in the Tropic of Africa.

But this immobility, imposed by nature on its creatures, is illustrated in a still more striking manner if we turn to those Mammifers that inhabit the *ocean*, where there are no appreciable impediments, none of those infinitely varied conditions which are seen upon land, even in the same parallels of latitude. The temperature of the ocean varies all but insensibly with degrees of latitude; and among the immense crowd of animals that inhabit it, we find numerous families of Mammifers. Although endowed with great powers of locomotion, and notwithstanding the trifling obstacles opposed to them, they are, like animals of the land, limited to certain localities. The genera *Calocephalus*, *Stemmatopes* and *Morse*, are peculiar to the Northern Seas. In the Southern, on the contrary, we find the genera *Otarie*, *Stenorynchus*, *Platyrynchus*, &c. Other species inhabit only hot or temperate regions.

The various species of Whales and Dolphins, despite their prodigious powers of locomotion, are confined each to regions originally assigned them; and, while there is so little difference of temperature in the ocean, that a human being might, in the mild season, swim with delight from the North Temperate Zone to Cape Horn, along either coast of America, there is no degree of latitude in which we do not discover species peculiar to itself.

After a resumé of these and many kindred facts, M. Jacquinot uses this emphatic language:

"To recapitulate, it seems to us, after all we have said, that we may draw the following conclusions, viz., that all Mammifers on the globe have a habitation, limited and circumscribed, which they never overleap; their assemblage contributes to give to each country its particular stamp of creation. What a contrast between the Mammifers of the Old and New World, and the creations, so special and so singular, of New Holland and Madagascar!"

9

Facts, therefore, point to numerous centres of creation, wherein we find creatures fixed, with peculiar temperaments and organizations, which are in unison with surrounding circumstances, and where all their natural wants are supplied. But the strongest barrier to voluntary displacements would seem to be that of *instinct* — that force, unknown and incomprehensible, which binds them to the soil that has witnessed their birth.

While passing these sheets through the press, we have enjoyed the privilege of perusing *The Geographical Distribution of Animals and Plants*,[16] by our valued friend, CHARLES PICKERING, M. D., Naturalist to the United States' Exploring Expedition under Captain Wilkes. This is to be "regarded as an introduction to the volume on Geographical Distribution, prepared during the voyage of the Expedition," and published in Volume IX. of the same compendium.

In connection with our own work, the utterance of Dr. Pickering's views is most opportune; because, with thorough knowledge of Egypt, derived from personal travels, and acquaintance with hieroglyphical researches, he has traced the Natural History of that country from the remotest monumental times to the present day. The various pictorial representations of Faunæ and Floræ are thereby assigned to their respective chronological epochas; and, inasmuch as they are identified with living species, they substantiate our assertions regarding the unexceptional *permanence of types* during a period of more than 5000 years. Dr. Pickering's era for "the commencement of the Egyptian Chronological Reckoning" being B. C. 4493,[17] we find ourselves again in unison with him upon general principles of chronological extension.

The gradual introduction of foreign animals, plants, and exotic substances, into the Lower Valley of the Nile — the extinction of sundry species once indigenous to that soil, during the hundred and fifty human generations for which we possess contemporaneous registry — and the infinitude of proofs that such changes could not have been effected without the intervention of these long historical ages — are themes which Dr. Pickering has concisely and ingeniously elaborated: and although our space does not permit the citation of the numerous examples duly catalogued by him, it affords us pleasure to concur in the following results, viz.:

> "That the names of animals and plants used in Egypt are Scriptural [*i. e.* old Semitish] names. Further, in some instances, these current Egyptian names go behind the Greek language, supply the meaning of obsolete Greek words, and show international relationship, the more intimate the further we recede into antiquity." [18]

It will become apparent, in its place, that the philological views now held by Birch, De Rougé, and Lepsius, upon the primeval introduction of Semitic elements in Egypt, are confirmed by these independent researches of Pickering into the Natural History of Egyptian animals and plants, as we trust will be now demonstrated through the monumental evidences of human physiology.

Let us next turn to the races of Mankind in their geographical distribution, and see whether they form an exception to the laws which have been established for the other orders of Mammifers. Does not the same physical adaptation, the same instinct, which binds animals to their primitive localities, bind the races of Men also? Those races inhabiting the Temperate Zones, as, for example, the white races of Europe, have a certain degree of pliability, that enables them to bear climates to a great extent hotter or colder than their native one; but there is a limit beyond which they cannot go with impunity —they cannot live in the Arctic with the Esquimaux, nor in the Tropic of Africa with the Negro. The Negro, too, (like the Elephant, the Lion, the Camel, &c.,) possesses a certain pliability of constitution, which enables him to enter the Temperate Zone; but his Northern limit stops far short of that of natives of this Zone. The higher castes of what are termed Caucasian races, are influenced by several causes in a greater degree than other races. To them have been assigned, in all ages, the largest brains and the most powerful intellect; *theirs* is the mission of extending and perfecting civilization—they are by nature ambitious, daring, domineering, and reckless of danger—impelled by an irresistible instinct, they visit all climes, regardless of difficulties; but how many thousands are sacrificed annually to climates foreign to their nature!

It should also be borne in mind, that what we term Caucasian races are not of one origin: they are, on the contrary, an amalgamation of an infinite number of primitive stocks, of different instincts, temperaments, and mental and physical characters. Egyptians, Jews, Arabs, Teutons, Celts, Sclavonians, Pelasgians, Romans, Iberians, etc., etc., are all mingled in blood; and it is impossible now to go back and unravel this heterogeneous mixture, and say precisely what each type originally was. Such commingling of blood, through migrations, wars, captivities, and amalgamations, is doubtless one means by which Providence carries out great ends. This mixed stock of many primitive races is the only one which can really be considered cosmopolite. Their infinite diversity of characteristics contrasts strongly with the immutable instincts of other human types.

How stands the case with those races which have been less subjected to disturbing causes, and whose moral and intellectual structure is less complex? The Greenlander, in his icy region, amidst poverty, hardship, and want, clings with instinctive pertinacity to his birthplace, in spite of all apparent temptations—the Temperate Zone, with its luxuries, has no charm for him. The Africans of the Tropic, the Aborigines of America, the Mongols of Asia, the inhabitants of Polynesia, have remained for thousands of years where history first found them; and nothing but absolute want, or self-preservation, can drive them from the countries where the Creator placed them. These races have been least adulterated, and consequently preserve their original instincts and love of home. This truth is illustrated in a most remarkable degree by the Indians of America. We still behold the small remnants of scattered tribes fighting and dying to preserve the lands and graves of their ancestors.

We shall have more to say, in another chapter, on the amalgamation of races, but may here remark, that the infusion of even a minute proportion of the blood of one race into another, produces a most decided modification of moral and physical character. A small trace of white blood in the negro improves him in intelligence and morality; and an equally small trace of negro blood, as in the quadroon, will protect such individual against the deadly influence of climates which the pure white-man cannot endure. For example, if the population of New England, Germany, France, England, or other northern climates, come to Mobile, or to New Orleans, a large proportion dies of yellow fever: and of one hundred such individuals landed in the latter city at the commencement of an epidemic of yellow fever, probably half would fall victims to it. On the contrary, negroes, under all circumstances, enjoy an almost perfect exemption from this disease, even though brought in from our Northern States; and, what is still more remarkable, the mulattoes (under which term we include all mixed grades) are almost equally exempt. The writer (J. C. NOTT) has witnessed many hundred deaths from yellow fever, but never more than three or four cases of mulattoes, although hundreds are exposed to this epidemic in Mobile. The fact is certain, and shows how difficult is the problem of these amalgamations.

That negroes die out and would become extinct in New England, if cut off from immigration, is clearly shown by published statistics.

It may even be a question whether the strictly-white races of Europe are perfectly adapted to any one climate in America. We do not generally find in the United States a population constitutionally equal to that of Great Britain or Germany; and we recollect once hearing this remark strongly endorsed by HENRY CLAY, although dwelling in Kentucky, amid the best agricultural population in the country. KNOX[19] holds that the Anglo-Saxon race would become extinct in America, if cut off from immigration. Now, we are not prepared to endorse this assertion; but inasmuch as nature works not through a few generations, but through thousands of years, it is impossible to conjecture what time may effect. It would be a curious inquiry to investigate the physiological causes which have led to the destruction of ancient empires, and the disappearance of populations, like Egypt, Assyria, Greece, and Rome. Many ancient nations were colonies from distant climes, and may have wasted away under the operation of laws that have acted slowly but surely. The commingling of different bloods, too, under the law of hybridity, may also have played an important part. Mr. LAYARD tells us that a few wandering tribes only now stalk around the sites of the once-mighty Nineveh and Babylon, and that, but for the sculptures of SARGAN and SENNACHERIB, no one could now say what race constructed those stupendous cities. But let us return from this digression.

To this inherent love of primitive locality, and instinctive dislike to foreign lands, and repugnance towards other people, must we mainly attribute the fixedness of the unhistoric types of men. The greater portion of the globe is still under the influence of this law. In America, the aboriginal barbarous tribes cannot be forced to change their habits, or even persuaded to successful emigration: they are melting away from year to year; and of the millions which once inhabited that portion of the United States east of the Mississippi river, all have vanished, but a few scattered families; and their representatives, removed by our Government to the Western frontier, are reduced to less than one hundred thousand. It is as clear as the sun at noon-day, that in a few generations more the last of these Red men will be numbered with the dead. We constantly read glowing accounts, from interested missionaries, of the civilization of these tribes; but a civilized *full-blooded* Indian does not exist among them. We see every day, in the suburbs of Mobile, and wandering through our streets, the remnant of the Choctaw race, covered with nothing but blankets, and living in bark tents, scarcely a degree advanced above brutes of the field, quietly abiding their time. No human ingenuity can induce them to become educated, or to do an honest day's work: they are supported entirely by begging, besides a little traffic of the squaws in wood. To one who has lived among American Indians, it is in vain to talk of civilizing them. You might as well attempt to change the nature of the buffalo.

The whole continent of America, with its mountain-ranges and table-lands—its valleys and low plains—its woods and prairies—exhibiting every variety of climate which could influence the nature of man, is inhabited by one great family, that presents a prevailing type. Small and peculiarly shaped crania, a cinnamon complexion, small feet and hands, black straight hair, wild, savage natures, characterize the Indian everywhere. There are a few trivial exceptions, easily accounted for, particularly on the Pacific coast.

The eastern part of Asia presents a parallel case. From 65° north latitude to the Equator, it presents the greatest inequalities of surface and climate, and is peopled throughout by the yellow, lank-haired Mongols; the darkest families lying at the North, and the fairest at the South. Their crania, their instincts, their whole moral and physical characteristics, distinguish them from the American race, which otherwise they most resemble.

The other half of this northern continent, that is to say Europe and the rest of Asia, may be divided into a northern and a southern province. The first extends from the Polar region to 45° or 50° north latitude—from Scandinavia to the Caspian Sea; and contains a group of men with light hair, complexion fair and rosy, and blue eyes. The second or southern division, running north-west and south-east, stretches from the British Isles to Bengal and the extremity of Hindostan—from 50° to 8° or 10° north. This vast area is covered by people with complexions more or less dark, oval faces, black smooth hair, and black eyes.

Now, it is worthy of remark, that since the discovery of America, and during several centuries, the fair races have inhabited North America extensively, while the dark races, as the Spaniards, have occupied South and Central America, and Mexico; both have displaced the Aboriginal races, and yet neither has made approximation in type to the latter, nor does any person suppose they could in a hundred generations. And so with the Negroes, who have lived here through eight or ten generations. We have no more reason to suppose that an Anglo-Saxon will turn into an Indian, than imported cattle into buffaloes. We shall show, in another chapter, that the oldest Indian crania from the Mounds, some of which are probably several thousand years old, bear no resemblance to those of any race of the old continent.

When we come to Africa, we shall perceive various groups of peculiar types occupying their appropriate zoological provinces, which they have inhabited for at least 5000 years. But, having to develop some new views respecting Egypt in another place, we shall take up the races of the African continent *in extenso*.

Taking leave, for the present, of continents, let us glance for a moment at New Holland. This immense country, extending from latitude 10° to 40° south, attests a special creation—its population, its animals, birds, insects, plants, etc., are entirely unlike those found in any other part of the world. The men present altogether a very peculiar type: they are black, but without the features, woolly heads, or other physical characters of Negroes. Beyond, we have Van Diemen's Land, extending to 44° south latitude, which presents a temperate climate, not unlike that of France; and what is remarkable, its inhabitants, unlike those of New Holland, are black, with frizzled heads, and very similar to the African races.

Not far from New Holland, under the same parallels, and extending even farther south, we find New Zealand; where commences the beautiful Polynesian race, of light-brown color, smooth black hair, and almost oval face. This race extends from 50° south, descends to the equator, then remounts to the Sandwich Islands, 20° north—scattered over islands without number—encircling about half the globe—without presenting any material differences in their color or forms—in a word, in their zoological characters.

India affords a striking illustration of the fallacy of arguments drawn from climate. We there meet with people of all shades, from fair to black, who have been living together from time immemorial. We have the well-known testimony of Bishop Heber, and others, on this point; and Desmoulins adds, "The Rohillas, who are blonds, and situated south of the Ganges, are surrounded by the Nepauleans with black skins, the Mahrattas with yellow skins, and the Bengalees of a deep brown; and yet the Rohillas inhabit the plain, and the Nepauleans the mountains."[20] Here we have either different races inhabiting the same climate for several thousand years without change; or the same race assuming every shade of color. Of this dilemma, the advocates of unity may choose either horn.

We might thus recite innumerable facts to the same effect, but the labor would be superfluous.

The different shades of color in races have been regarded, by many naturalists, as one of their most distinctive characters, and still serve as the basis of numerous classifications; but M. Jacquinot thinks too much importance has been attached to colors, and that they cannot be relied upon. For example, all the intermediate shades from white to black are found in those races of oval face, large facial angle, smooth hair, etc., which Blumenbach has classed under the head *Caucasian*. Commence, for example, with the fair Fins and Sclavonians with blond hair, and pass successively through the Celts, Iberians, Italians, Greeks, Arabs, Egyptians, and Hindoos, till you reach the inhabitants of Malabar, and you find these last to be as black as Negroes.

Among the Mongols, likewise, we encounter various shades. Amid the Africans there exist all tints, from the pale-yellow Hottentots, Bushmen, and dusky Caffres, to the coal-black Negro of the Tropic and confines of Egypt. In short, the black color is beheld in Caucasians,

Negroes, Mongols, Australians, etc., while yellows or browns are visible throughout all the above types, as well as among Americans, Malays, and Polynesians.

In the present mixed state of the population of the earth, it is perhaps impossible to determine how far this opinion of Jacquinot may be correct. We possess certainly many examples to prove that color has been permanent for ages; while, on the contrary, it is impossible to show that the complexion of a pure primitive stock has been altered by climate. As before stated, we conceive that too much importance has been given to arbitrary classifications, and that the Caucasian division may include innumerable primitive stocks. This fact is illustrated further on, particularly in the history of the Jews, whose type has been permanent for at least 3000 years. We have no reason to believe that the Hebrew race sprang from, or ever originated, any other type of man.

We therefore not merely regard the great divisions of Caucasian, Mongol, Malay, Negro and Indian, as primitive stocks, but shall establish that History, Anatomy, Physiology, Psychology, Analogy, all prove that each of these stocks comprehends many original subdivisions.

Let us acknowledge our large indebtedness to Prof. Agassiz, who has given the most masterly view of the geographical distribution of animals written in our language, or perhaps in any other. Not a line can be retrenched from his already condensed articles without inflicting a wound, and we take much pleasure in referring the reader to them.[21] He shows, conclusively, that not only are there numerous centres of creation, or zoological provinces, for our pending geological epoch, but that these provinces correspond, in a surprising manner, to those of former epochas; thus proving that the Creator has been working after one grand and uniform plan through myriads of years, and through consecutive creations.

"It is satisfactorily ascertained at present, that there have been many distinct successive periods, during each of which large numbers of animals and plants have been introduced upon the surface of our globe, to live and multiply for a time, then to disappear and be replaced by other kinds. Of such distinct periods — such successive creations — we know now *at least about a dozen*, and there are ample indications that the inhabitants of our globe have been successively changed at more epochs than are yet fully ascertained."

In the earliest formations, but few and distant patches of land having emerged from the mighty deep, the created beings were comparatively few, simple, and more widely disseminated; but yet many distinct species, adapted to localities where they were brought into existence, are discovered. In the more recent fossil beds, we find a distribution of fossil remains which agrees most remarkably with the present geographical arrangement of animals and plants. The fossils of modern geological periods in New Holland are types identical with most of the animals now living there. Brazilian fossils belong to the same families as those alive there at the present day; though in both cases the fossil species are distinct from the surviving ones. If, therefore, the organized beings of ancient geological periods had arisen from one central point of distribution, to be dispersed, and finally to become confined to those countries where their remains now exist in a fossil condition; and if the animals now living had also spread from a common origin, over the same districts, and had these been circumscribed within equally distinct limits; we should be led to the unnatural supposition, argues AGASSIZ, that animals of two distinct creations, differing specifically throughout, had taken the same lines of migration, had assumed finally the same distribution, and had become permanent in the same regions without any other inducement for removal and final settlement, than the mere necessity of covering more extensive ground, after they had become too numerous to remain any longer together in one and the same district.

Now it would certainly be very irrational to attribute such instincts to animals, were such a line of march possible; but the very possibility vanishes, however, when we reflect upon the wide-spread physical impediments opposing such migrations, and that neither the animals nor plants of one province can flourish in an adverse one. No Arctic animals or plants can be propagated in the Tropics, nor *vice versa.* The whole of the Monkey tribe belong to a hot climate, are retained there by their temperaments and instincts, and cannot by any ingenuity of man be made to exist in Greenland. The same rule applies to the aboriginal men of the Tropical and the Arctic regions.

That the animals and plants now existing on the earth must be referred to many widely-distant centres of creation, is a fact which might, if necessary, be confirmed by an infinite number of circumstances; but these things are nowadays conceded by every well-informed naturalist; and if we have deemed it necessary to illustrate them at all, it is because this volume may fall into the hands of some possibly not versed in such matters.

Another question of much interest to our present investigation is —Have all the individuals of *each species* of animals, plants, &c., descended from a single pair? Were it not for the supposed scientific authority of *Genesis* to this effect, the idea of community of origin would hardly have occurred to any reflecting mind, because it involves insuperable difficulties; and science can perceive no reason why the Creator should have adopted any such plan. Is it reasonable to suppose that the Almighty would have created one seed of grass, one acorn, one pair of locusts, of bees, of wild pigeons, of herrings, of buffaloes, as the only starting-point of these almost ubiquitous species?

The instincts and habits of animals differ widely. Some are solitary, except at certain seasons; some go in pairs; others in herds or shoals. The idea of a *pair* of bees, locusts, herrings, buffaloes, is as contrary to the nature and habits of these creatures, as it is repugnant to the nature of oaks, pines, birches, &c., to grow singly, and to form forests in their isolation. In some species males—in others, females predominate; and in many it would be easy to show, that, if the present order of things were reversed, the species could not be preserved—locusts and bees, for example: the former appear in myriads, and by far the greater number of those produced are destroyed; and though they have existed for ages, a naturalist cannot see that they have increased, nor can he conceive how one pair could continue the species, considering the number of adverse chances. As regards bees, it is natural to have but one female for a whole hive, to whom many males are devoted, besides a large number of drones.

Again, Agassiz gives this striking illustration:—

> "There are animals which are impelled by nature to feed on other animals. Was the first pair of lions to abstain from food until the gazelles and other antelopes had multiplied sufficiently to preserve their races from the persecution of these ferocious beasts?"

So with other carnivorous animals, birds, fishes, and reptiles. We now behold all their various species scattered through land and water in harmonious proportions. Thus they may continue for ages to come.

Hybridity has been considered a test for species; but, when we come to this theme, it shall be proven that, in many instances, what have been called *varieties* are really distinct species: hence, that hybridity is no test. All varieties of dogs and wolves, for example, are prolific *inter se;* yet we shall prove that many of them are specifically distinct, that is, descended from different primitive stocks at distant points of the globe. Agassiz has beautifully illustrated the fact by the natural history of lions. These animals present very marked varieties, extending over immense regions of country. They occupy nearly the whole continent of Africa, a great part of Southern Asia, as, formerly, Asia Minor and Greece. Over this vast tract of country several varieties of lions are found, differing materially in their physical characters: these varieties also are placed remotely from each other, and each one is surrounded by entirely distinct Faunæ and Floræ: natural facts confirming the idea of totally distinct zoological provinces. It will readily be conceded by naturalists, that all the animals found in such a province, and nowhere else, must have been therein created; and although lions may possess in common that assemblage of characters which has been construed into evidence of community of *species*, yet it by no means necessitates community of *origin*. The same question here arises as in considering the varieties of mankind, with regard to the definition of the term *species*. We hold that a variety which is permanent, and which resists, without change, all known external causes, must be regarded as a primitive species — else no criteria exist by which science can be governed in Natural History.

Monkeys afford another admirable illustration, and are doubly interesting from the fact of their near approach to the human family. The following paragraph is one of peculiar interest: —

"As already mentioned, the monkeys are entirely tropical. But here again we notice a very intimate adaptation of their types to the particular continents; as the monkeys of tropical America constitute a family altogether distinct from the monkeys of the old world, there being not one species of any of the genera of Quadrumana, so numerous on this continent, found either in Asia or Africa. The monkeys of the Old World, again, constitute a natural family by themselves, extending equally over Africa and Asia; and there is even a close representative analogy between those of different parts of these two continents — the orangs of Africa, the Chimpanzee and Orilla, corresponding to the red orang of Sumatra and Borneo, and the smaller long-armed species of continental Asia. And what is not a little remarkable, is the fact that the black orang occurs upon that continent which is inhabited by the black human race, while the brown orang inhabits those parts of Asia over which the chocolate-colored Malays have been developed. There is again a peculiar family of Quadrumana confined to the Island of Madagascar, the Makis, which are entirely peculiar to that island and the eastern coast of Africa opposite to it, and to one spot on the western shore of Africa. But in New Holland and the adjacent islands there are no monkeys at all, though the climatic conditions seem not to exclude their existence any more than those of the large Asiatic Islands, upon which such high types of this order are found. And these facts, more than any other, would indicate that the special adaptation of animals to particular districts of the surface of the globe is neither accidental nor dependent upon physical conditions, but is implied in the primitive plan of creation itself. Whatever classes we may take into consideration, we shall find similar adaptations, and though perhaps the greater uniformity of some families renders the difference of types in various parts of the world less striking, they are none the less real. The carnivora of tropical Asia are not the same as those of tropical Africa, or those of tropical America. Their birds and reptiles present similar differences. The want of an ostrich in Asia, when we have one, the largest of the family, in Africa, and two distinct species in Southern America, and two cassowaries, one in New Holland and another in the Sunda Islands, shows this constant process of analogous or representative species, repeated over different parts of the world, to be the principle regulating the distribution of animals; and the fact that these analogous species are different, again, cannot be reconciled to the idea of common origin, as each type is peculiar to the country where it is now found. These differences are more striking in tropical regions than anywhere else. The rhinoceros of the Sunda Islands differs from those of Africa, and there are none in America. The elephant of Asia differs from that of Africa, and there are none in America. One tapir is found in the Sunda Islands; there are none in Africa, but we find one in South America. . . . Everywhere special adaptation, particular forms in each continent, an omission of some allied type here, when in the next group it occurs all over the zone."

The same authority has so well expressed his opinion on another point, that we cannot resist the temptation of making an additional extract.

"We are thus led to distinguish special provinces in the natural distribution of animals, and we may adopt the following division as the most natural First, the Arctic province, with prevailing uniformity. Second, the Temperate Zone, with at least three distinct zoological provinces — the European Temperate Zone, west of the Ural Mountains; the Asiatic Temperate Zone, east of the Ural Mountains; and the American Temperate Zone, which may be subdivided into two, the Eastern and Western, for the animals east and west of the Rocky Mountains differ sufficiently to constitute two distinct zoological provinces. Next, the Tropical Zone, containing the African Zoological province, which extends over the main part of the African continent, including all the country south of the Atlas and north of the Cape colonies; the Tropical Asiatic province, south of the great Himalayan chain, and including the Sunda Islands, whose Fauna has quite a continental character, and differs entirely from that of the Islands of the Pacific, as well as from that of New Holland; the American Tropical province, including Central America, the West Indies, and Tropical South America. New Holland constitutes in itself a special province, notwithstanding the great differences of its northern and southern climate, the animals of the whole continent preserving throughout their peculiar typical character. But it were a mistake to conceive that the Faunæ, or natural groups of animals, are to be limited according to the boundaries of the mainlands. On the contrary, we may trace their natural limits into the ocean, and refer to the Temperate European Fauna the eastern shores of the Atlantic, as we refer its western shores to the American Temperate Fauna. Again, the eastern shores of the Pacific belong to the Western American Fauna, as the western Pacific shores belong to the Asiatic Fauna. In the Atlantic Ocean there is no peculiar Oceanic Fauna to be distinguished; but in the Pacific we have such a Fauna, entirely marine in its main character, though interspread with innumerable islands, extending east of the Sunda Islands and New Holland to the western shores of Tropical America. The islands west of this continent seem, indeed, to have very slight relations, in their zoological character, with the western parts of the mainland. South of the Tropical Zone we have the South American Temperate Fauna and that of the Cape of Good Hope, as other distinct zoological provinces. Van Diemen's Land, however, does not constitute a zoological province in itself, but belongs to the province of New Holland by its zoological character. Finally, the Antarctic Circle encloses a special zoological province, including the Antarctic Fauna, which, in a great measure, corresponds to the Arctic Fauna in its uniformity, though it differs from it in having chiefly a maritime character, while the Arctic Fauna has an almost entirely continental aspect.

"The fact that the principal races of men, in their natural distribution, cover the same extent of ground as the same zoological provinces, would go far to show that the differences which we notice between them are also primitive."

These facts prove conclusively that the Creator has marked out both the Old and New Worlds into distinct zoological provinces, and that Faunæ and Floræ are independent of climate or other known physical causes; while it is equally clear that in this geographical distribution there is evidence of a Plan — of a design ruling the climatic conditions themselves.

It is very remarkable, too, that while the races of men, and the Fauna and Flora of the Arctic region, present great uniformity, they follow in the different continents the same general law of *increasing dissimilarity* as we recede from the Arctic and go South, irrespectively of climate. We have already shown that, as we pass down through America, Asia, and Africa, the farther we travel the *greater is the dissimilarity* of their Faunæ and Floræ, to their very terminations, even when compared together in the same latitudes or zones; and an examination will show, that differences of types in the human family become more strongly marked as we recede from the Polar regions, and reach their greatest extremes at those terminating points of continents where they are most widely separated by distance, although occupying nearly the same parallels of latitude, and nearly the same climates. For instance, the Fuegians of Cape Horn, the Hottentots and Bushmen of the Cape of Good Hope, and the inhabitants of Van Diemen's Land, are the tribes which, under similar parallels, differ most. Such differences of races are scarcely less marked in the Tropics of the earth; as testified by the Negro in Africa, the Indian in America, and the Papuan in Polynesia. In the Temperate zone, we have in the Old World the Mongolians and the Caucasians, no less than the Indians in America, living in similar climates, yet wholly dissimilar themselves.

History, traditions, monuments, osteological remains, every literary record and scientific induction, all show that races have occupied substantially the same zones or provinces from time immemorial. Since the discovery of the mariner's compass, mankind have been more disturbed in their primitive seats; and, with the increasing facilities of communication by land and sea, it is impossible to predict what changes coming ages may bring forth. The Caucasian races, which have always been the representatives of civilization, are those alone that have extended over and colonized all parts of the globe; and much of this is the work of the last three hundred years. The Creator has implanted in this group of races an instinct that, in spite of themselves, drives them through all difficulties, to carry out their great mission of civilizing the earth. It is not reason, or philanthropy, which urges them on; but it is destiny. When we see great divisions of the human family increasing in numbers, spreading in all directions, encroaching by degrees upon all other races wherever they can live and prosper, and gradually supplanting inferior types, is it not reasonable to conclude that they are fulfilling a law of nature?

We have always maintained *diversity* of origin for the whole range of organized beings. If it be granted, as it is on all hands, that there have been many centres of creation, instead of one, what reason is there to suppose that any one race of animals has sprung from a single pair, instead of being the natural production of many pairs? And, as was written by us many years ago, "if it be conceded that there were two primitive pairs of human beings, no reason can be assigned why there may not have been hundreds." [22]

Agassiz thus expresses himself: —

"Under such circumstances, we should ask if we are not entitled to conclude that these races must have originated where they occur, as well as the animals and plants inhabiting the same countries, and have originated there in the same numerical proportions and over the same area in which they now occur; for these conditions are the conditions necessary to their maintenance, and what among organized beings is essential to their temporal existence must be at least one of the conditions under which they were created.

"We maintain that, like all organized beings, mankind cannot have originated in single individuals, but must have been created in that numerical harmony which is characteristic of each species. Men must have originated in *nations*, as the bees have originated in swarms, and, as the different social plants, have covered the extensive tracts over which they have naturally spread."

We remarked, in the commencement of this chapter, that M. Agassiz had presented his views in such a condensed and irrefragable manner, that it would be impossible to attempt a *resumé*, or to do him justice without repeating the whole of his article; but although we have already borrowed freely, we cannot refrain from a concluding paragraph, our object being rather to give a synopsis, or "posting up" to date, of facts illustrative of our subject, than to claim any great originality: if we can bring the truth out, our goal is attained.

"The circumstance that wherever we find a human race naturally circumscribed, it is connected in its limitation with what we call, in natural history, a zoological and botanical province — that is to say, with the natural limitations of a particular association of animals and plants — shows most unequivocally the intimate relation existing between mankind and the animal kingdom in their adaptation to the physical world. The Arctic race of men, covering a treeless region near the Arctics in Europe, Asia, and America, is circumscribed, in the three continents, within limits very similar to those occupied by that particular combination of animals which are peculiar to the same tracts of land and sea.

"The region inhabited by the Mongolian race is also a natural zoological province, covered by a combination of animals naturally circumscribed within the same regions. The Malay race covers also a natural zoological province. New Holland again constitutes a very peculiar zoological province, in which we have another particular race of men. And it is further remarkable, in this connection, that the plants and animals now living on the continent of Africa south of Atlas, within the same range within which the Negroes are naturally circumscribed, have a character differing widely from that of the plants and animals of the northern shores of Africa and the valley of Egypt; while the Cape of Good Hope, within the limits inhabited by Hottentots, is characterized by a vegetation and a Fauna equally peculiar, and differing in its features from that over which the African race is spread.

"Such identical circumscriptions between the limits of two series of organized beings so widely differing in men and animals and plants, and so entirely unconnected in point of descent, would, to the mind of the naturalist, amount to a demonstration that they originated together within the districts which they now inhabit. We say that such an accumulation of evidence would amount to demonstration; for how could it, on the contrary, be supposed that man alone would assume new peculiarities and features so different from his primitive characteristics, whilst the animals and plants circumscribed within the same limits would continue to preserve their natural relations to the Fauna and Flora of other parts of the world? If the Creator of one set of these living beings had not also been the Creator of the other, and if we did not trace the same general laws throughout nature, there might be room left for the supposition that, while men inhabiting different parts of the world originated from a common centre, the plants and animals associated with them in the same countries originated on the spot. But such inconsistencies do not occur in the laws of nature.

"The coincidence of the geographical distribution of the human races with that of animals, the disconnection of the climatic conditions where we have similar races, and the connection of climatic conditions where we have different human races, shows further, that the adaptation of different races of men to different parts of the world must be intentional, as well as that of other beings; that men were primitively located in the various parts of the world they inhabit, and that they arose everwhere in those harmonious numeric proportions with other living beings which would at once secure their preservation and contribute to their welfare. To suppose that all men originated from Adam and Eve, is to assume that the order of creation has been changed in the course of historical times, and to give to the Mosaic record a meaning that it was never intended to have. On that ground, we would particularly insist upon the propriety of considering Genesis as chiefly relating to the history of the white race, with special reference to the history of the Jews."

Zoologically, the races or species of mankind obey the same organic laws which govern other animals: they have their geographical points of origin, and are adapted to certain external conditions that cannot be changed with impunity. The natives of one zone cannot always be transferred to another without deteriorating physically and mentally. Races, too, are governed by certain psychological influences, which differ among the species of mankind as instincts vary among the species of lower animals. These psychological characteristics form part of the great mysteries of human nature. They seem often to work in opposition to the physical necessities of races, and to drive individuals and nations beyond the confines of human reason. We see around us, daily, individuals obeying blindly their psychological instincts; and one nation reads of the causes which have led to the decline and fall of other empires without profiting by the lesson.

The laws of God operate not through a few thousand years, but throughout eternity, and we cannot always perceive the why or wherefore of what passes in our brief day. Nations and races, like individuals, have each an especial destiny: some are born to rule, and others to be ruled. And such has ever been the history of mankind. No two distinctly-marked races can dwell together on equal terms. Some races, moreover, appear destined to live and prosper for a time, until the destroying race comes, which is to exterminate and supplant them. Observe how the aborigines of America are fading away before the exotic races of Europe.

Those groups of races heretofore comprehended under the generic term Caucasian, have in all ages been the rulers; and it requires no prophet's eye to see that they are destined eventually to conquer and hold every foot of the globe where climate does not interpose an impenetrable barrier. No philanthropy, no legislation, no missionary labors, can change this law: it is written in man's nature by the hand of his Creator.

While the mind thus speculates on the physical history of races and the more or less speedy extermination of some of them, other problems start up in the distance, of which the solution is far beyond the reach of human foresight. We have already hinted at the mysterious disappearance of many great races and nations of antiquity.

When the inferior types of mankind shall have fulfilled their destinies and passed away, and the superior, becoming intermingled in blood, have wandered from their primitive zoological provinces, and overspread the world, what will be the ultimate result? May not that Law of nature, which so often forbids the commingling of species, complete its work of destruction, and at some future day leave the fossil remains alone of man to tell the tale of his past existence upon earth?

CHAPTER II.

GENERAL REMARKS ON TYPES OF MANKIND.

WE propose to treat of Mankind, both zoologically and historically; and, in order that we may be clearly understood, it is expedient that we should define certain terms which will enter into frequent use as we proceed.

TYPE.—The definition of H. Cassini, given in Jourdan's *Dictionnaire des Termes*, is adopted by us, as sufficiently precise:—

"*Typical* characters are those which belong only to the majority of natural bodies comprised in any group, or to those which occupy the centre of this group, and in some sort serve as the *type* of it, but presenting exceptions when it approaches its extremities, on account of the relations and natural affinities which do not admit well-defined limits between species."

In speaking of Mankind, we regard as *Types* those primitive or original forms which are independent of Climatic or other Physical influences. All men are more or less influenced by external causes, but these can never act with sufficient force to transform one type into another.

SPECIES.—The following definition, by Prichard, may be received as one of the most lucid and complete:—

"The meaning attached to the term *species*, in natural history, is very definite and intelligible. It includes *only* the following conditions: namely, *separate origin and distinctness of race, evinced by a constant transmission of some characteristic peculiarity of organization.* A race of animals or of plants marked by any peculiar character which it has constantly displayed, is termed a 'species'; and two races are considered specifically different, if they are distinguished from each other by some characteristic which the one cannot be supposed to have acquired, or the other to have lost, through any known operation of physical causes; for we are hence led to conclude, that tribes thus distinguished have not descended from the same original stock.

"This is the import of the word *species*, as it has long been understood by writers on different departments of natural history. They agree essentially as to the sense which they appropriate to this term, though they have expressed themselves differently, according as they have blended more or less of *hypothesis* with their conceptions of its meaning."

"VARIETIES," continues Prichard, "in natural history, are such diversities in individuals and their progeny as are *observed to take place* within the limits of species.

"PERMANENT VARIETIES are those which, having once taken place, continue to be propagated in the breed in perpetuity. The *fact* of their origination *must be known by observation or inference*, since, the proof of this fact being defective, it is more philosophical to consider characters which are perpetually inherited as *specific* or *original*. The term *permanent variety* would otherwise express the *meaning which properly belongs to species*. The properties of species are two: viz., original difference of characters, and the *perpetuity of their transmission*, of which only the latter can belong to permanent varieties.

"The instances are so many in which it is doubtful whether a particular tribe is to be considered as a distinct species, or only as a variety of some other tribe, that it has been found, by naturalists, convenient to have a designation applicable in either case."[23]

Dr. Morton defines *species* simply to be "*a primordial organic form*."[24] He classes species, "according to their disparity or affinity," in the following provisional manner: —

"REMOTE SPECIES, of the same genus, are those among which hybrids are never produced.

"ALLIED SPECIES produce, *inter se*, an infertile offspring.

"PROXIMATE SPECIES produce, with each other, a fertile offspring."

GROUP. — Under this term we include all those proximate races, or species, which resemble each other most closely in type, and whose geographical distribution belongs to certain zoological provinces; for example, the aboriginal *American*, the *Mongol*, the *Malay*, the *Negro*, the *Polynesian groups*, and so forth.

It will be seen, by comparison of our definitions, that we recognize no substantial difference between the terms *types* and *species*—permanence of characteristics belonging equally to both. The horse, the ass, the zebra, and the quagga, are distinct *species* and distinct *types:* and so with the Jew, the Teuton, the Sclavonian, the Mongol, the Australian, the coast Negro, the Hottentot, &c.; and no physical causes known to have existed during our geological epoch could have transformed one of these types or species into another. A *type*, then, being a pristine or primordial form, all idea of common origin for any two is excluded, otherwise every landmark of natural history would be broken down.

It has been sagaciously remarked by Bodichon: —

"That when a people writes its history, time, and often space, have placed them very far from their origin. It is then composed of diverse elements, and its national traditions are altered: there happens to it that which occurs to the man who has arrived at adult age — the remembrance of his early years has seized upon his imagination more than upon his mind, and incites him to cast over his cradle a coloring, brilliant, but deceptive. Thus some pretend they are descended from Abraham, others from Æneas, some from Japhet, some from stones thrown by Deucalion and Psyche: the greatest number from some god or demigod — Pluto, Hercules, Odin."[25]

It may then be truly said, that we possess no data by which science can at all approximate to the epoch of man's first appearance upon earth; for, as shown in our chronological essay, even the Jewish history, whose fabulous chronology is so perseveringly relied on by many, does not reach back to the early history of *nations*. It cannot now reasonably be doubted, that Egypt and China, at least, existed *as nations* 3000 years before Christ; and there is monumental evidence of the simultaneous existence of various Types of Mankind quite as far back. Inasmuch as these types are more or less fertile *inter se*, and as they have, for the last 5000 years, been subjected to successions of wars, migrations, captivities, intermixtures, &c., it would be a vain task at the present day to attempt the unravelling of this tangled thread, and to make anything like a just classification of types; or to determine how many were primitive, or which one of them has arisen from intermixture of types. This difficulty holds not alone with regard to mankind, but also with respect to dogs, horses, cattle, sheep, and other domestic animals, as we shall take occasion to show. All that ethnography can now hope to accomplish is, to select some of the more prominent types, or rather groups of proximate types, compare them with each other, and demonstrate that they are, and have always been, distinct.

A vulgar error has been sedulously impressed upon the public mind, of which it is very hard to divest it, viz., that all the races of the globe set out originally from a single point in Asia. Science now knows that no foundation in fact exists for such a conclusion. The embarrassment in treating of types or races is constantly increased by false classifications imposed upon us by prejudiced naturalists. It is argued, for example, that all the Mongols, all the African Negroes, all the American Indians, have been derived from one common Asiatic pair or unique source; whereas, on the other hand, there is no evidence that human beings were not sown broadcast over the whole face of the earth, like animals and plants: and we incline to the opinion of M. Agassiz, that men were created in *nations*, and not in a single pair.

Since the time of Linnæus, who first placed man at the head of the Animal kingdom and in the same series with monkeys, numerous classifications of human races have been proposed; and it may be well to give a rapid sketch of a few of them, in order to show the difficulties which encompass the subject, and how hopelessly vague every definitive attempt of this kind must be, in the present state of our knowledge.

Buffon divides the human race into *six* varieties—viz., Polar, Tartar, Austral-Asiatic, European, Negro, and American.

Kant divides man into *four* varieties—White, Black, Copper, and Olive.

HUNTER, into *seven* varieties; METZAN, into *two*—White and Black; VIREY, into *three;* BLUMENBACH, into *five*—viz., Caucasian, Mongol, Malay, Negro, and American; DESMOULINS, into *sixteen* species; BORY DE ST. VINCENT makes *fifteen* species, subdivided into races.

MORTON classifies man into *twenty-two* families; PICKERING, into *eleven* races; LUKE BURKE, into *sixty-three*, whereof twenty-eight are distinct varieties of the *intellectual*, and thirty-five of the *physical* races.

JACQUINOT[26] divides mankind into *three* species of a *genus homo*—viz., *Caucasian*, *Mongol*, and *Negro*.

The *Caucasian*, says Jacquinot, is the only species in which white races with rosy cheeks are found; but it embraces besides sundry brunette, brown, and black races—not regarding *color* as a satisfactory test of race. The principal races which he includes under the Caucasian head are, the Germanic, Celtic, Semitic, and Hindoo. The latter differ much in color, some being black, and others fair, comprising all intermediate shades, and are probably a mixture of different primitive stocks.

The *Mongol* species embraces the Mongol, Sinic, Malay, Polynesian, and American.

The *Negro* species comprehends the Ethiopian, Hottentot, Oceanic-Negro, and Australian. The *Ethiopian* race comprises those Negroes inhabiting the greater part of Africa, having black skins, woolly heads, &c.; Hottentots and Bushmen exhibiting light-brown complexions.

This classification of M. Jacquinot is supported by much ingenuity. In many respects it is superior to others; and inasmuch as some classification, however defective, seems to be indispensable, his may be received, as simple and the least objectionable. Like all his predecessors, however, who have written on anthropology, he seems not to be versed in the monumental literature of Egypt; and, therefore, he classes together races which (although somewhat similar in type), having presented distinct physical characteristics for several thousand years, cannot be regarded as of one and the same species, any more than his Caucasians and Negroes.

Though many other classifications might be added, the above suffice to testify how *arbitrary* all classifications inevitably must be; because no reason has yet been assigned why, if two original pairs of human beings be admitted, we should not accept an indefinite number; and, if we are to view mankind as governed by the same laws that regulate the rest of the animal kingdom, this conclusion is the most natural, no less than apparently most in accordance with the general plan of the Creator. We have shown that sundry groups of human beings, presenting general resemblances in physical characters, are found in certain zoological provinces where everything conveys the idea of distinct centres of creation; and hence, we may conclude that mankind only constitutes a link in Nature's great chain.

But many of our readers will doubtless be startled at being told that *Ethnology* was no new science even before the time of Moses. It is clear, and positive, that at that early day (fourteen or fifteen centuries B. C.), the Egyptians not only recognized, and faithfully represented on their monuments, many distinct races, but that they possessed their own ethnographic systems, and already had classified humanity, as known to them, accordingly. They divided mankind into *four* species: viz., the Red, Black, White, and Yellow; and, what is note-worthy, the same perplexing diversity existed in each of their quadripartite divisions which still pervades our modern classifications. Our divisions, such as the *Caucasian*, *Mongol*, *Negro*, &c., each include many sub-types; and if different painters of the present day were called upon to select a pictorial type to represent a man of these arbitrary divisions, they would doubtless select different human heads. Thus with the Egyptians: although the *Red*, or Egyptian, type was represented with considerable uniformity, the White, Yellow, and Black, are often depicted, in their hieroglyphed drawings, with different physiognomies; thus proving, that the same endless variety of races existed at that ancient day that we observe in the same localities at the present hour. So far from there being a stronger similarity among the most ancient races, the dissimilarity actually augments as we ascend the stream of time; and this is naturally explained by the obvious fact that existing remains of primitive types are becoming more and more amalgamated every day.

There are several similar tableaux on the monuments; but we shall select the celebrated scene from the tomb of SETI-MENEPHTHA I. [generally called "Belzoni's Tomb," at Thebes], of the XIXth dynasty, about the year 1500 B. C., wherein the god HORUS conducts *sixteen* personages, each *four* of whom represent a distinct type of the human race as known to the Egyptians; and it will be seen that Egyptian ethnographers, like the writers of the Old and New Testaments, have described and classified solely those races dwelling within the geographical limits known to them. We cannot now say exactly how far the *maximum* geographical boundaries of the ancient Egyptians extended; for their language, the names of places and names of races in Asia and Africa, have so changed with time that a margin must be left to conjecture; although much of our knowledge is positive, because the *minimum* extent of antique Egyptian geography is determined.

FIG. 1.

The ancient Egyptian division of mankind into four species—fifteenth century B. C.

A B C D

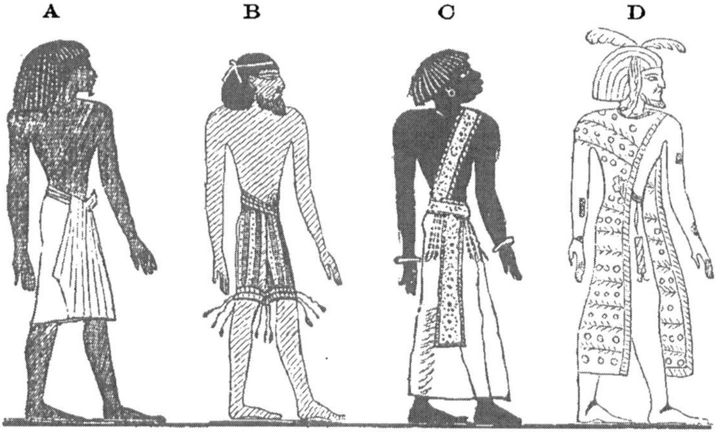

Red. Yellow. Black. White.

The above figures, which may be seen, in plates on a folio scale, in the great works of Belzoni, Champollion, Rosellini, Lepsius, and others, are copied, with corrections, from the smaller work of Champollion-Figeac.[27] They display the *Rot*, the *Namu*, the *Nahsu*, and the *Tamhu*, as the hieroglyphical inscription terms them; and although the effigies we present are small, they portray a specimen of each type with sufficient accuracy to show that *four* races were very *distinct* 3300 years ago. We have here, positively, a scientific *quadripartite* division of mankind into *Red*, *Yellow*, *Black*, and *White*, antedating Moses; whereas, in the Xth chapter of *Genesis*, the symbolical division of "SHEM, HAM, and JAPHET," is only *tripartite*—the Black being entirely omitted, as proved in PART II. of this volume.

The appellative "*Rot*" applies exclusively to one race, viz., the *Egyptian;* but the other designations may be somewhat generic, each covering certain groups of races, as do our terms Caucasian, Mongol, &c.; also including a considerable variety of types bearing general resemblance to one another in each group, through shades of color, features, and other peculiarities, to be discussed hereafter.[28]

EXPLANATION OF FIG. 1.

A—This figure, together with his three fac-simile associates, extant on the original painted relievo, is, then, typical of the *Egyptians;* who are called in the hieroglyphics "*Rot*," or Race; meaning the Human race, *par excellence.* Like all other Eastern nations of antiquity—like the Jews, Hindoos, Chinese, and others—the Egyptians regarded themselves alone as the chosen people of God, and contemptuously looked down upon other races, reputing such to be Gentiles or outside-barbarians. The above representation of the Egyptian type is interesting, inasmuch as it is the work of an *Egyptian* artist, and must therefore be regarded as the Egyptian ideal representation of their own type. Our conclusion is much strengthened by the fact, that the same head is often repeated on different monuments. This and the other portraits of the Egyptian type to which we allude, were figured during the XVIIIth dynasty of ROSELLINI; and possess, to Ethnologists, peculiar interest, from the fact of their vivid similitude to the *old* Egyptian type, (subsequently resuscitated by LEPSIUS), on the earlier monuments of the IVth, Vth, and VIth dynasties; at the same time that these particular effigies offer a marked dissimilarity to the Asiatico-Egyptian type, which becomes common on the later monuments of the XVIIth and subsequent dynasties; that is, from 1500 B. C. downwards.

B — This portrait is the representative of that Asiatic group of races, by ethnographers termed the *Semitic.* The hieroglyphic legend over his head reads "*Namu;*" which, together with "Aamu," was the generic term for *yellow*-skinned races, lying, in that day, between the Isthmus of Suez and Tauric Assyria, Arabia and Chaldæa inclusive.

C — *Negro* races are typified in this class, and they are designated, in the hieroglyphics, "*Nahsu.*" The portrait, in colour and outline, displays, like hundreds of other Egyptian drawings, how well marked was the Negro type several generations anterior to Moses. We possess no actual portraits of Negroes, pictorially extant, earlier than the seventeenth century before Christ; but there is abundant proof of the existence of Negro races in the XIIth dynasty, 2300 years prior to our era. Lepsius tells us that African *languages* antedate even the epoch of MENES, B. C., 3893; and we may hence conclude that they were then spoken by Negroes, whose organic idioms bear no affinity to Asiatic tongues.

D — The fourth division of the human family is designated, in the hieroglyphics, by the name "*Tamhu;*" which is likewise a generic term for those races of men by us now called *Japethic,* including all the *white*-skinned families of Asia Minor, the Caucasian mountains, and "Scythia" generally.

But we shall return to this Egyptian classification in another chapter. Our object, here, is simply to establish that the ancient Egyptians had attempted a systematic anthropology at least 3500 years ago, and that their ethnographers were puzzled with the same diversity of types then, that, after this lapse of time, we encounter in the same localities now. They of course classified solely the races of men within the circumference of their own knowledge, which comprehended necessarily but a small portion of the earth's surface. Of their contemporaries in China, Australia, Northern and Western Asia, Europe, and America, the Pharaonic Egyptians knew nothing; because all of the latter types of men became known even to Europe only since the Christian era, most of them since 1400 A. D.

We have asserted, that all classifications of the races of men heretofore proposed are entirely arbitrary; and that, unfortunately, no data yet exist by which these arrangements can be materially improved. It is proper that we should submit our reasons for this assertion. The field we here enter upon is so wide as to embrace the whole physical history of mankind; but, neither our limits nor plan permitting such a comprehensive range, we shall illustrate our views by an examination of one or two groups of races; premising the remark that, whatever may be true of one human division—call it Caucasian, Mongol, Negro, Indian, or other name—applies with equal force to all divisions. If we endeavor to treat of mankind zoologically, we can but follow M. Agassiz, and map them off into those great groups of proximate races appertaining to the zoological provinces into which the earth is naturally divided. We might thus make some approach towards a classification upon scientific principles; but all attempts beyond this must be wholly arbitrary.

"*Unity of races*" seems to be an idea introduced in comparatively modern times, and never to have been conceived by any primitive nation, such as Egypt or China. Neither does the idea appear to have occurred to the author of *Genesis*. Indeed, no importance could, in Mosaic days, attach to it, inasmuch as the early Hebrews have left no evidences of their belief in a future state, which is never declared in the Pentateuch.[29] This dogma of "unity," if not borrowed from the Babylonians during the captivity of the Israelites, or from vague rumors of *Budhistic* suavity in the sixth century B. C., may be an outgrowth of the charitable doctrine of the "Essenes;"[30] just as the present Socialist idea of the "*solidarité* of humanity" is a conception borrowed from St. Paul.

The authors have now candidly stated their joint views, and will proceed to substantiate the facts, upon which these deductions are based, in subsequent chapters; unbiassed, they trust, by preconceived hypotheses, as well as indifferent to other than scientific conclusions.

With such slight modifications as the progress of knowledge — especially in hieroglyphical, cuneiform, and Hebraical discovery — may have superinduced since the publication of his *Crania Ægyptiaca*, in 1844, they adopt the matured opinions of their lamented friend, Dr. Samuel George Morton, as, above all others, the most authoritative. In the course of this work, abundant extracts from Morton's writings render unmistakeable the anthropological results to which he had himself attained; but the authors refer the reader particularly to Chapter XI. of the present volume, containing "Morton's inedited manuscripts," for the philosophical and testamentary decisions of the Founder of the American School of Ethnology.

CHAPTER III.

SPECIFIC TYPES—CAUCASIAN.

WHAT is meant by the word "*Caucasian?*" Almost every Ethnologist would give a different reply. Commonly, it has been received, since its adoption by Blumenbach, as a sort of generic term which includes many varieties of races. By some writers, all these varieties are reputed to be the descendants of *one* species; and the manifest diversity of types is explained by them through the operation of physical causes. By others, the designations *Caucasian*, *Mongol*, *Negro*, &c., are employed simply for the convenience of grouping certain human varieties which more or less resemble each other, without paying due, if any regard, to specific characters. Under the head *Caucasian* are generally associated the Egyptians, the Berbers, the Arabs, the Jews, the Pelasgians, the Hindoos, the Iberians, the Teutons, the Celts, the Sclavonians: in short, all the so-called Semitic and Indo-Germanic races are thrown together into the same group, and hence become arbitrarily referred to a common origin.

Now, such a sweeping classification as this might have been maintained, with some degree of plausibility, a few years ago; when it was gravely asseverated that climate could transform one type into another: but inasmuch as this argument, apart from new rebutting data, revealed through the decyphering of the monuments of Egypt and of Assyria, is now abandoned by every well-educated naturalist, (and, we may add, enlightened theologian,) it is difficult to conceive how it can any longer be accepted with favor. We know of no archæologist of respectable authority, at the present day, who will aver that the races now found throughout the valley of the Nile, and scattered over a considerable portion of Asia, were not as distinctly and broadly contrasted at least 3500 years ago as at this moment. The Egyptians, Canaanites, Nubians, Tartars, Negroes, Arabs, and other types, are as faithfully delineated on the monuments of the XVIIth and XVIIIth Dynasties, as if the paintings had been executed by an artist of our present age.

Some of these races, owing to the recent researches of Lepsius, have even been carried backwards to the IVth Dynasty; which he places about 3400 years before Christ. It becomes obvious, consequently, that all the countries known to Egyptians in those remote ages presented types which were as essentially different then as they now exhibit. It is equally certain, that the Pharaonic Egyptians repudiated all idea of affinity to these coetaneous races; and it would seem to follow, as a corollary, that the other parts of the world were contemporaneously occupied by many aboriginal species. Ancient history nowhere acquaints us with habitable countries known to be uninhabited, and the earliest discoverers always found new types in distant lands. Hence, nothing short of a *miracle* could have evolved all the multifarious Caucasian forms out of one primitive stock; because the Canaanites, the Arabs, the Tartars and Egyptians, were absolutely as distinct from each other in primeval times as they are now; just as they all were then from co-existent Negroes. Such a miracle, indeed, has been invented and dogmatically defended; but it is a bare postulate, unsupported by the Hebrew Bible, and positively refuted by scientific facts. The Jewish chronology, (fabricated, as we shall render apparent, after the Christian era,) for the human family, since the Deluge, carries us back, according to Usher's computation, only to the year 2348 B. C.; or, at farthest, according to the Septuagint version (whose history we shall see is somewhat apocryphal), to 3246 B. C.; but the monuments of Egypt remove every shadow of doubt, by establishing that not merely races but *nations* existed prior to either of those imaginary dates. If then the teachings of science be true, there must have been many centres of creation, even for *Caucasian* races, instead of one centre for *all* the types of humanity.

The multiform races of Europe, with trifling exceptions, have been classed under the Caucasian head; and it has been assumed for ages, that each of these races must have been derived from Asia. It is strange, moreover, that naturalists should have spent their time in studying remote, barbarous and obscure tribes, while they have passed in silence over the historical races, lying close at hand: nevertheless, we think this branch of our subject may be readily elucidated by analyzing those types of mankind which surround us.

It is to M. Thierry and M. Edwards, the one honorably known as an historian and the other as a naturalist, that we are indebted for the first philosophical attempt to break in upon this settled routine. They have penetrated directly into the heart of Europe, and by a masterly examination of the history and physical characteristics of long-known races, have endeavored to trace them back to their several primitive sources.

Ancient Gaul is the chosen field of their investigations; and, although we admit that, from the very nature of the case, it is impossible at this late day to arrive at definite results, yet their facts are so fairly posited, and their deductions so interesting, as to command attention; no less than to induce the belief that their plan, if persevered in, may lend most efficient aid in classifying the races of men. They have at least shown, conclusively, that very opposite types have dwelt together in Europe for more than two thousand years; that time and identical physical causes have not yet obliterated or blended them; and that, while nations may become expunged, there is every reason to believe that primitive diversities are rarely, if ever, wholly effaced.

Inasmuch as the labors of these gentlemen stand unparalleled, and possess very important bearings upon certain opinions long held by ourselves, and which we are about to develop, no apology need be offered for the following extended *resumé* of their combined labors.

Cæsar begins his commentaries with—

"All Gaul is divided into three parts, of which one is inhabited by the *Belgians*, another by the *Aquitanians*, and the third by those who, in their own language, call themselves *Celts*, and who in our tongue are called Galls (*Galli*). These people differ among themselves by their language, their manners and their laws."[31]

To these three divisions, taken in mass, he applies the collective denomination of *Galli*, corresponding to the French term *Gaulois*.

Strabo confirms this account, and adds that the *Aquitanians* differ from the Celts, or *Galli*, and from the Belgians, not only in language and institutions, but also in conformation of body; and that they resemble much more the *Iberians;* while he regards the Celts and the Belgians as of the same national type, although speaking different dialects. There are, however, valid reasons for doubting the latter opinion.

From their physical character and language, Strabo considers the Aquitanians, as well as the Ligurians, who occupied a part of the coast of France, to be a branch of the Iberians,[32] the ancient people of Spain. These *Iberes*, or "people *beyond*," seem to have been transplanted, from time immemorial, on the soil of France, and are still beheld, distinct from all other men, in the modern *Basques*.

In consequence of their position on the coast of the Mediterranean, the *Ligurians* became known to ancient navigators before the other populations of Gaul. Greek historians and geographers speak of them in very early times. They figure among the barbarous allies of the Carthaginians, as far back as 480 B. C. Thierry adopts, enforcing by many proofs, the opinion that the Aquitanians and Ligurians were both of the *Iberian* stock, and also that they were alien to the Gallic family, properly speaking.[33]

These races disposed of, Thierry says that the Celts, or Galli, and the Belgians remain to be examined; and he views them as two branches of the same ethnic trunk:—

"Two fractions of the same family, isolated during many ages, developed separately, and become, by means of their long separation, distinct races. The *Galls*, or Celts, were the most ancient inhabitants of the country, and it is from them that it derives its name: and an idea of their antiquity may be obtained from the statement that 'the *Celts* subjugated Spain in the sixteenth century B. C. The Galls made a descent on Italy, under the name of *Ombræ*, about two centuries after; and the Roman antiquaries designate these ancestors of the Ombrians by the name of *Old Galls*.' . . . In short, we should consume much time, were we to cite all the authorities at command, to prove that the Galls were the most ancient population. On the contrary, the word *Belgians* is comparatively modern: it is found, for the first time, in CÆSAR; and they are recognized under the name of *Cimbrians*, in 113 B. C."

It seems tolerably well established, that the *Belgians* invaded Gaul on their first advent from the North, and that the Celts were driven before them. The Belgians settled in the north of Gaul and in Italy, where they were not only located by ancient historians, but where, according to Thierry and Edwards, they are still resident. The Celts, routed, and impelled to the South and East, took refuge in mountains, peninsulas, and islands—historical facts also elucidated by DE BROTONNE.[34]

M. Thierry has shown that the Armoricans and the Belgians are an identical people, and that the Welsh of Great Britain are also derived from the same stock. Prichard, it is true, does not concur in this opinion; but Thierry, so far as we can perceive, is thoroughly sustained in his views by French, German, and other continental writers. He places the entrance into Gaul of the conquering Belgians between the years 349 and 290 B. C. The Armoricans appertained to the same stock, but their establishment in Gaul was still more ancient.

The Celts, or *Galls* proper, according to M. Thierry as well as to ancient historians, were already inhabitants of Gaul about 1500 B. C., or previously to the time of Moses. They then existed as a nation, warring with other races around them; nor can a conjecture be formed as to the number of centuries, anterior to this date, during which they had occupied that territory.

The *Pre-Celtic* researches of WILSON,[35] among the *peat-bogs* of the British Isles, have carried the existence of man in England and Scotland back to ages immensely remote; at the same time that those of BOUCHER DE PERTHES, amid the alluvial stratifications of the river *Soame*,[36] indicate a still more ancient epoch for the cinerary urns, bones, and instruments, of a primordial people in France; who, if geological observations be correct, are yet posterior to the *silex*-evidences of human entity on the same spots before the "diluvial drift." These facts correspond with the exhumations of RETZIUS, in Scandinavia,[37] and the human vestiges discovered in European caves.[38]

But, leaving such points to another section (ably handled by our colleague, DR. USHER,) it remains now for us to ask, who were the *Belgians?* M. Thierry shows, from an elaborate historical investigation, that the *Cimbri*, who played so important a part in the history of early Europe, were of the same race as the Belgians; and that old writers, coeval with the time of ALEXANDER, or fourth century B. C., place this race on the Northern Ocean, in Jutland. Between the years 113 and 101 B. C., the Cimbri were set in motion, and eventually devastated Gaul, Spain, and Italy. It is a striking fact, that, in this invasion, when they reached Northern Gaul, where the Belgians were already seated, the latter immediately joined them, as allies, against the Celts; and it seems to be clearly proven that the Cimbri and the Belgians spoke dialects of the same language.

This Cimmerian race was diffusely scattered through the north of Europe, and even into Asia Minor, at an early period.

"Down to the seventh century before our era, the history of the Cimbri near the Euxine remains enveloped in the fabulous obscurity of Ionian traditions; it does not commence with any certainty before the year 631 B. C. This epoch was fruitful in disturbances in the west of Asia and east of Europe."

About this time, it is to be inferred from Herodotus, the Genesiacal GoMRi, *Gomerians*, or *Kymri*, abandoned the Tauric Chersonesus, and marched westward.[39]

We pretend not to afford a complete analysis of M. Thierry's able work. He has tracked out, with vast research, the settlements and subsequent history of the various Caucasian races of ancient Gaul; and to him we refer the reader for corroboration of the facts we are succinctly sketching. The *resumé* at the end of his Introduction explains his general conclusions. He considers the following points to be unanimously demonstrated by authorities:—

"Two great human families furnished to Gaul its ancient inhabitants: viz., the *Iberian* and the *Gallic* (*Gauloises*) families. The Aquitanians and Ligurians appertained to the *Iberian* family. The Gallic family occupied, out of Gaul, the British Isles. It was divided into two branches or races, presenting, under a common type, essential differences of language, manners, and institutions, and forming two individualities widely separated."

M. THIERRY, notwithstanding, asserts that the Cimbri and Celts were branches of the same family; but this we doubt. They were both fair, and strikingly contrasted with the dark-skinned, black-haired, and black-eyed *Iberians:* M. EDWARDS, however, proves that their physical characters were exceedingly different. No proof can be adduced of their common origin, beyond some affinity between their languages: arguments that we shall show to be no longer satisfactory evidence of aboriginal consanguinity.

"The first branch had preceded, in Gaul and the neighboring Archipelago, the dawn of history. The ancients considered them as autochthones. From Gaul they extended to Spain, Italy, and Illyria. Their generic name was *Gael*, or rather a word which the Romans rendered by *Gallus*, and the Greeks by *Galas* and *Galatēs*. The latter had improperly attributed to the whole stem the denomination of *Celt*, which properly belonged only to its southern tribes. The second branch, colonized in the west of Europe since historic times, was represented in Gaul by the Armoricans and Belgians, and by their descendants in the British Isles. *Armorican* was a local designation; *Belgian*, the name of a belligerent confederation; *Cimbri*, the name of a race. The relative position of the two Gallic branches was as follows: the Cimbrian branch occupied the north and west of Gaul—the east and south of Britain; the Celtic branch, on the contrary, the east and south of Gaul, and the west and north of the British Isles."

It becomes apparent, then, from the facts detailed, and which no historian will question, that the territory of ancient Gaul was occupied, some 1500 years B. C., by at least *two* distinctly-marked Caucasian races—the Celts and the Iberians: the one fair-skinned and light-haired; the other a dark race; and each speaking a language bearing no affinity to that of the other—precisely, for instance, as the Euskaldune of the present Basques is unintelligible to Gaelic tribes of Lower Brittany. But history justifies us in going beyond this dual division. Each *type* was doubtless a generic one, including many subordinate types. There are no data to warrant the conclusion that either of these stocks was an ethnic unit. It will be made to appear, when we come to the monuments of Egypt, that various Caucasian types existed in Egypt and Asia 2000 years before the most ancient Celtic history begins; and the same diversity of races, without question, prevailed simultaneously in Europe.

Let us inquire whether some positive information cannot be obtained with regard to the types of primitive European races. The work of Edwards, to which we have already alluded,[40] stands in many respects unrivalled. The high reputation of its author as a naturalist guarantees his scientific competency; and he has directed his attention into an unexplored channel. After perusing Thierry's *Histoire des Gaulois*, of which we have just spoken, M. Edwards made a tour of France, Belgium and Switzerland (*i. e.* ancient Gaul), and Italy, engaged in careful study of the present diversified races, in connection with their ancient settlements; and he asserts that now, at the end of 2000 years, the types of the Belgians (Cimbri), the Galls or Celts, the Iberians or Aquitanians, and the Ligurians, are still distinctly traceable among their living descendants, in the very localities where history at its earliest dawn descries these families.

Gaul has been the receptacle of other races than those named, but these were comparatively small in popular multitude; and although a great variety of types is now visible, yet M. Edwards contends that such exotic constituents of later times form but trivial exceptions, and that *three* major types stand out in bold relief.

Edwards upholds sundry physiological laws to account for this preservation of types; and a few shall be noticed incidentally, as we go on. He lays down a fundamental proposition, the importance of which will be at once recognized:—

"Where there is no natural repugnance to each other, and races meet and mix on equal terms, the *relative number* of the two races influences greatly the result: the type of the lesser number may disappear entirely. Take, for example, a thousand white families and one hundred black ones, and place them together on an island. The result would be, that the *black* type would after a while disappear, although there is reason to believe that traces of it would 'crop out' occasionally during a very long time. Where two fair-skinned races are brought into contact, the extermination of one would probably sooner be effected; nevertheless, even here, it is impossible to destroy the germ entirely. The Jews form a convincing illustration of the influence of the larger over the smaller number. This, from the time of Abraham to the present, has been a more or less adulterated race; yet its type has been predominant, is preserved, and is likely to be for ages to come. Such a law is well illustrated in the lower animals. Cross two domestic animals of different races; take the offspring, and cross it with one of the parent stocks; continue this process for a few generations, and the one becomes swallowed up in the other.

"Even where two races meet in *equal* numbers, which is an extreme supposition, in order to make a uniform type they would have to pair off uniformly, one race with another, and not each race to intermarry among themselves. This equilibrium could not be maintained; and without it, each race would preserve its own type.

"There is another tendency in nature, that interests us here particularly, and which has been curiously and ingeniously illustrated by M. Coladon, of Geneva. He bred a great many *white* and *gray* mice, on which he made experiments by crossing constantly a white with a gray one. The product invariably was a *white* or a *gray mouse*, with the characters of the pure race: 'point de métis, point de begarrure, rien d'intermédière, enfin le type parfait de l'une ou de l'autre variété. Ce cas est extrème, a la verité; mais le précédent ne l'est point moins; ainsi les deux procédés sont dans la nature: aucun ne règne exclusivement.'"[41]

The habit of reflecting on the relations in which primitive races are found, induces us to consider the following as the conditions which may make one or the other of these effects preponderate. Where races differ considerably, which animals do whenever they are of different species, (like, for example, the horse and the ass, the dog and the wolf or fox,) their product is constantly *hybrid.* If, on the other hand, they are very proximate, (*très voisines*, says M. Edwards,) they may not give birth to mixtures (*mélanges*), but reproduce pure or primitive types.

On examining facts closely, the greatest conformity is encountered precisely where we perceive, at first glance, the strongest contrast. In the crossing of *widely different* races, the hybrid presents a type diverse from that of the mother; notwithstanding certain conformities. So also when two *proximate* races reproduce the one and the other primitive type, the mother gives birth to a being which differs from herself. Behold here an uniformity of facts; but remark likewise, that in this last crossing, the mother produces a being more like herself than in the former case. She departs then less from the general tendency of nature, which is the propagation of the same types.

"In the higher order of animals, the two sexes concur in the formation of two individuals which represent them; thus the mother gives birth sometimes to one made in her own image—at others to one after the image of the father. Here she produces two very distinct types, notwithstanding their relations, and to such a point that the male and female of the same species often differ more between themselves, than one or the other differs from individuals of the same sex, in proximate species. This is so true, that the male and its female, among animals whose habits there has been no opportunity of examining, have frequently been classified as distinct species; insects and birds especially have furnished numerous examples.

"It is manifest that the observations of M. Coladon belong to this order of facts, considered in their general bearing; as the mother produces two types, of which one represents that of her own race, and the other the physical characters of the race of the father. Other examples of the same kind might be presented, but this is sufficiently striking.

"The most important consideration is, that the same phenomena are seen in the human races, and, further, in the same conditions indicated. Those human races which differ most produce constantly hybrids (*métis*). It is thus that a mulatto always results from the mixture of white and black races. The other fact, of the reproduction of two primitive types, when the parents are of two proximate (*voisines*) varieties, is less notorious, but is not, on that account, the less true. The fact is common among European nations. We have had frequent occasions to notice it. The phenomenon is not constant—but what of that? Crossing sometimes produces fusion, sometimes the separation of types; whence we arrive at this fundamental conclusion: that people appertaining to varieties of different, but proximate races, in vain unite, in the hypothetical manner we have described above; a portion of the new generations will preserve the primitive types."

These facts are no less true than curious; and every American, especially, has the means at hand for verifying them. When a white man and a negress marry, the product is a *mulatto* or intermediate type. When a white man and white woman marry, the one having *dark* hair, eyes and complexion, with one cast of features, and the other *light* hair and eyes, and fair complexion, with different features, some of the children will generally resemble one parent, some the other; while others may present a mixed type, being a reproduction of the likeness of an ancestor (generally forgotten) of either parent.

Every race, at the present time, is more or less mixed. A nation, that is, a numerous population, may be dispossessed of, and displaced from, a large extent of its territory; but this is extremely rare—savages alone furnishing almost all such examples. In America, witness the Indians driven before the whites, without leaving a trace behind them. There is a fixed incompatibility between civilized and savage man: they cannot dwell together. On the Old Continent, it is not now a question of savages; science has there to deal at most with *barbarians;* that is, people possessing the commencements of civilization. Otherwise, it would be neither the interest of conquerors to drive them all off, nor is it *their* inclination to abandon their native soil; of which history affords abundant proof. Mythology, fable, and Utopian philanthropy, have traced imaginary pictures; but history nowhere shows us a people who, first discovered in the savage state, afterwards invented a civilization, or learned the arts of their discoverers. The monuments of Egypt prove, that *Negro* races have not, during 4000 years at least, been able to make one solitary step, in

Negro-land, from their savage state; the modern experience of the United States and the West Indies confirms the teachings of monuments and of history; and our remarks on *Crania*, hereinafter, seem to render fugacious all probability of a brighter future for these organically-inferior types, however sad the thought may be.

There is abundant evidence to show that the principal physical characters of a people may be preserved throughout a long series of ages, in a great part of the population, despite of climate, mixture of races, invasion of foreigners, progress of civilization, or other known influences; and that a *type can long outlive its language, history, religion, customs, and recollections.* The accession of new people multiplies races, but it does not confound them: their numbers are increased by those which the intruders introduce, and also by those which they create by commingling; but all these incidents, nevertheless, still leave the old type in existence.

In tracing, at this late day, ancient types of men, we shall, of necessity, meet chiefly with those of great and powerful nations, that have been able to maintain themselves more or less inviolate, through a thousand difficulties, by their force or knowledge. Small and feeble fractions of humanity have generally been swallowed up and obliterated, like the Guanches of the Canary Isles. The world now advances in civilization more rapidly than in former times, and mainly for the substantial reason that the higher types of mankind have so increased in power that they can no longer be molested by the inferior; nor, arguing from the past and present, can we doubt that a time must come, when the very memory of the latter will survive solely on the page of history. The days of the aborigines of America are numbered; no victorious Tartar-hordes will ever set foot again on European soil; and the white races, or *Iapetidæ*, have commenced the career of Oriental conquest, and already "dwell in the tents of Shem."

Examinations of Roman history throw important light on this subject. The Empire was crushed by successive hordes of barbarians; but still their numbers, compared to the population of Italy, have been much overrated. The human waves of Visigoths, Vandals, Huns, Herules, Ostrogoths, Lombards, and Normans, rolled successively into Italy; and yet, it may be asked, what vestiges remain, in Italy itself, of these barbarian surges? The first three passed over it like tornados. The two next, within a short time, had to contend with the Goths, and were expelled from the country; and of the whole conglomerate mass but small fragments were left, too insignificant materially to influence the native Italic types. The Lombards, on the contrary, remained, and have implanted their name on a portion of Italy. The Normans were numerically but a handful. Gaul changed its government and name under the Franks; however, the army of Clovis was small; while William the Conqueror subjugated England with 60,000 men: but, as if to illustrate our axioms of the indelibility of type and the vigor of the *white* race, not a head in Christendom that, legitimately, wears a crown—not an individual breathes in whose veins flows blood acknowledged to be "royal," but traces his or her genealogy to this Norman colossus, WILLIAM THE CONQUEROR ![42]

Such are some of the great conquests of European antiquity that have considerably affected the condition of men and things, but which, notwithstanding, have not produced much alteration in the type of the conquered people. Some mixture of types is still seen — here and there the alien races "crop out," but the indigenous thousands have swallowed up the exotic hundreds.

Conquests are often merely political, resulting in territorial annexation or in tributary accessions, where little or no mingling of races takes place. Other examples there are, where the conquerors continue to pour into a country from time to time, and thereby greatly influence native types. It is thus that the Saxons, taking possession of England, have perpetuated their race: but it is ever the higher type that in the end predominates.

"The ignorant Turk, you say, subjected without difficulty the intellectual and lettered Greeks; the ferocious Tartar handcuffed the polished and learned Chinese; the violent Mongol bent under his scimetar the head of the studious Brahman; the Vandal, finally, ravaged Rome and Italy, then the centre of European civilization. Take care not to accuse the sciences of a humiliation entirely due to despotism, which alone degrades and debases human hearts. Certainly, no one exposes his life to defend a government he abhors and despises. * * * Perhaps a new vanquisher may be more generous; he cannot, at any rate, display himself more atrocious and more cruel than those monsters, in their infamies."[43]

Creative laws, as we have said, work by myriads of ages. Six centuries have not elapsed since *Turks*, *Tartars*, and *Mongols*, appeared in Europe. The *Vandal* had already disappeared. At every point of the European continent, the remnants of these Central-Asiatic swarms are melting away before the higher Caucasian types, wherever complete subserviency to the latter does not suspend the extermination of the former. Were it not that politics are eschewed in the present volume, events of the past five years might supply signal examples.

In characterizing *types*, M. Edwards justly regards form and size of the head, and the traits of the face, as most important: all other criteria are delusive and changeable; such as hair, complexion, stature, &c., though not to be neglected. Even these are less mutable, we think, than M. Edwards supposes. There are many examples of complexion and hair resisting climates for centuries, without the slightest alteration; and, in fact, we know of no authentic instance where a radical change of complexion or hair has been produced.[44]

We have mentioned that, in order to put the question to a practical test, M. Edwards made a journey through France, Italy, Belgium, and Switzerland. In passing through Florence, he took occasion to visit the Ducal gallery, to study the *ancient Roman type.* He selected, in preference, the busts of the early Roman emperors, because they were descendants of ancient families. They, too, are so alike, and withal so remarkable, that they cannot be mistaken. Augustus, Tiberius, Germanicus, Claudius, Nero, Titus, &c., exemplify this type in Florentine collections. The following is his description: —

"The vertical diameter of the head is short, and, consequently, the face broad. As the summit of the cranium is flattened, and the inferior margin of the jaw-bone almost horizontal, the contour of the head, viewed in front, approaches a *square.* The lateral parts, above the ears, are protuberant; the forehead low; the nose truly aquiline, that is to say, the curve commences near the top and ends before it reaches the point, so that the base is horizontal; the chin is round, and the stature short." [A sailor came to my office, a few months ago, to have a dislocated arm set. When stripped and standing before me, he presented this type so perfectly, and combined with such extraordinary development of bone and muscle, that there occurred to my mind at once the beau-ideal of a Roman soldier. Though the man had been an American sailor for twenty years, and spoke English without foreign accent, I could not help asking where he was born. He replied in a deep strong voice, "In *Rome,* sir!" — J. C. N.]

This is the characteristic type of a Roman; but we cannot expect now to meet with absolute uniformity in any race, however seemingly pure. Such a type M. Edwards found to predominate in Rome and certain parts of Italy at the present day. It is the original type of the country, which has swallowed up all intruders, has remained unchanged for 2000 years, and probably existed there from the epoch of creation.

The Etruscans present an extraordinary historical enigma. Science knows not whence they came, nor whence their institutions, arts, or language — whether, indeed, they were indigenous to the Italian soil, or strangers. We can trace their civilization far beyond that of Rome — more than 1000 years B. C. Citations from Etruscan archæologists, to this effect, are given further on. Some of their descendants now resemble Romans, but they present a mixed type. The well-known head of DANTE affords an illustration, peculiar, and strikingly typical; for it is long and narrow, with a high and developed forehead, nose long and curved, with sharp point and elevated wings. [Here is the portrait in question, to afford an idea of its style; which, however, requires to be studied upon designs of a larger scale.] M. Edwards was

FIG. 2.

DANTE.[45]

struck by the great frequency of this type in Tuscany (ancient Etruria), among the peasantry; in the statues and busts of the Medici family; and also amid the illustrious men of the Republic of Florence, in their effigies and bas-reliefs. This type is well marked since the time of Dante, as doubtless long before. It extends to Venice, and is visible over a large extent of country. In the Ducal palace, M. Edwards had occasion to observe that it is common among the Doges. The type became more predominant as he approached Milan; hence he traced it through a great part of France, and through the settlements of the ancient Cymbri or Belgæ, who, Thierry has shown, occupied Cis-Alpine and Trans-Alpine Gaul. The physical characteristics of the present population, therefore, correspond exactly with the historical colonies; showing that the ancient type of this wide-spread people, the *Cymbri*, has been preserved for more than 2000 years.

After visiting and analyzing thoroughly the population and history of Italy, M. Edwards next investigated Gaul, passing by the southern and western part, where Thierry places the Basques or ancient Ligurians. In the other parts of France, as we have seen, there existed, at a remote epoch, two great families, differing in language, habits and social state; and these two formed the bulk of the ancient population. Examination ascertains that two dominant types even yet prevail throughout the kingdom, too saliently marked and distinct from each other to be confounded. There have been many conquests and comminglings of races; but inasmuch as the greater number has swallowed up the lesser, no very obvious impression has been produced by these causes. Of the two families, the *Galls*, or Celts, and the Cymbri, or Belgæ, the former should be the most numerous, because they are the most ancient, and had covered the whole country before the entrance of the latter: in consequence, we find that the type with round heads and straight noses, that of the *Galls*, has prevailed over that of the Cymbri.

Oriental Gaul was occupied by the Galli proper of Cæsar, whom Thierry denominates "*Galls*." Northern Gaul, including the Belgica and Armorica of Cæsar, on the other hand, was occupied by the Cymbri. The population of Eastern Gaul — the *Gauls* proper — according to the historical facts, ought to be the least mixed, because the Belgæ never penetrated among them by force of arms, but took quiet possession of their outskirts, along the northern parts of the country.

"In traversing the part of France which corresponds to Oriental Gaul, from north to south, viz.: Burgundy, Lyons, Dauphiny, and Savoy, I have distinguished (says M. Edwards,) that type, so well marked, to which we have given the name of *Galls*."

He thus describes the type of the *Gall:*

"The head is so round as to approach the spherical form; the forehead is moderate, slightly protuberant, and receding towards the temples; eyes large and open; the nose, from the depression at its commencement to its termination, almost straight — that is to say, without any marked curve; its extremity is rounded, as well as the chin; the stature medium. It will be seen that the features are perfectly in harmony with the form of the head."

In the northern part of Gaul, the principal seat of the Belgæ, you again encounter the same striking coincidence.

"In a previous journey I traversed a great part of the coast of *Gallia Belgica* of Cæsar, from the mouth of the Somme to that of the Seine. It was here that I distinguished, for the first time, the assemblage of traits which constitutes the other type, and often to such an exaggerated degree that I was very forcibly struck; the long head, the broad, high forehead; the curved nose, with the point below and wings tucked up; the chin boldly developed; and the stature tall."

M. Edwards has pursued this type in its various settlements, with numerous and valuable scientific results. He concludes a division of his subject with the following strong language:

"Without the preceding discussions, and the facts we have just unravelled, how could we recognize the *Gaulois* in the north of Italy, among the *Sicules*, the *Ligures*, the *Etruscans*, the *Venetes*, the *Romans*, the *Goths*, the *Lombards?* But we possess the thread to guide us. First, whatever may have been the anterior state, it is certain, from your researches (M. Thierry's), and the unanimous accord of all historians, that the *Peuples Gaulois* have predominated in the north of Italy, between the Alps and Apennines. We find them established there in a permanent manner, according to the first lights of history. The most authentic testimony represents them with all the characters of a great nation, from this remote period down to a very advanced point of Roman history. Here is all I demand. I have no need to occupy myself with other people who have mingled with them since; to discuss their relative numbers—the nature of their language—the duration of their establishment. It is sufficient for me to know that the GAULOIS have existed in great numbers. I know the features of their compatriots in Trans-Alpine Gaul. I find them again in Cis-Alpine Gaul."

It has often struck us, that, even in the heterogeneous population of our United States, we could trace these European ancient races. The tall figure and aquiline nose of the Cymbrian are generally seen together; while the traits of the Gaul are more frequently accompanied by short stature.

The Celts and Cymbri have spread themselves extensively through Eastern Europe, beyond the limits of Gaul and Italy: but, for our objects their pursuit being irrelevant, we resume the explorations of M. Edwards; who, after his survey of Western, takes a glance at several other races of Eastern Europe, although he does not claim to have analyzed these with the same rigorous detail as those of Gaul.

The *Sclavonic* type, another of the thousand-and-one Caucasians whose types stretch beyond the reach of history, is thus described by our observant ethnologist; and it seems to be just as distinct and sharply marked over half of Europe, as that of the Jews everywhere:

"The contour of the head, viewed in front, approaches nearly to a square; the height surpasses a little the breadth; the summit is sensibly flattened; and the direction of the jaw is horizontal. The length of the nose is less than the distance from its base to the chin; it is almost straight from the depression at its root, that is to say, without decided curvation; but, if appreciable, it is slightly concave, so that the end has a tendency to turn up; the inferior part is rather large, and the extremity rounded. The eyes, rather deep-set, are perfectly on the same line; and when they have any particular character, they are smaller than the proportion of the head would seem to indicate. The eyebrows are thin, and very near the eyes, particularly at the internal angle; and from this point, are often directed obliquely outwards. The mouth, which is not salient, has thin lips, and is much nearer to the nose than to the top of the chin. Another singular characteristic may be added, and which is very general: viz., their small beard, except on the upper lip. Such is the common type among the Poles, Silesians, Moravians, Bohemians, Sclavonic Hungarians, and is very common among the Russians."

This type is also frequent through eastern Germany, and although it has become much mixed with the German, their separate historical settlements may yet be followed, and the two races traced out and identified, like those of the Celts and Cymbri in Gaul.

History, from its commencement, has mentioned immense Caucasian populations, ranging throughout northern and eastern Europe and western Asia, to the confines of Tartar and Mongol races. From their remoteness, and the absence of communication, little was known anciently about them; and even at the present day, they are looked upon as "outside barbarians," exciting trivial interest among general readers. This group, however, at all times, has comprised the most numerous of all the fair-skinned races upon earth: intellectually equal to any others. To give the reader an idea of the actual extent of Sclavonic races, we subjoin statistics, as quoted by Count Krasinski, from the Sclavonian Ethnography of Schafferick:—

	Russia.	Austria.	Prussia.	Turkey.	Cracow.	Saxony.	Total.
Moscovites, or Great Russians	35,314,000	......	......	......	......	......	35,314,000
Little Russians, Ruthenians	10,370,000	2,774.000	......	......	......	......	13,144,000
White Russians....	2,726,000	......	......	......	......	......	2,726,000
Bulgarians	80,000	7,000	......	3,500,000	......	......	3,587,000
Servians and Illyrians ...	100,000	2,594,000	......	2,600,000	......	......	5,294,000
Croats.................	......	801,000	......	......	......	......	801,000
Carinthians	......	1,151,000	......	......	......	......	1,151,000
Poles	4,912,000	2,341,000	1,982,000	......	130,000	......	9,365,000
Bohemians and Moravians	......	4,370,000	44,000	......	......	......	4,414,000
Slovacks in Hungary ...	......	2,753,000	......	......	......	......	2,753,000
Lusatians, or Wends ...	......	......	82,000	......	......	60,000	142,000
Total............	53,502,000	16,791,000	2,108,000	6,100,000	130,000	60,000	78,691,000

From the same *North British Review* we extract sufficient to illustrate our own views; but nothing adequate to evince the ability of the best article we have met with on these *Shlaves*.

"Much confusion has been produced by the constant use in books of words denoting the supposed state of flux and restlessness in which the early nations of Europe lived. The natural impression, after reading such books, is, that masses of people were continually coming out of Asia into Europe, and driving others before them. . . . But care must be taken to confine these stories of wholesale colonization to their proper place in the ante-historic age. For all intents and purposes, it is best to conceive that at the dawn of the historic period the leading European races were arranged on the map pretty much as they are now. Regarding the Slavonians, at least, this has been established; they are not, as has generally been supposed, a recent accession out of the depths of Asia, but are as much an aboriginal race of Eastern, as the Germans are of Central Europe. In short, had a Roman geographer of the days of the Empire advanced in a straight line from the Atlantic to the Pacific, he would have traversed the exact succession of races that is to be met in the same route now. First, he would have found the Celts occupying as far as the Rhine; thence, eastward to the Vistula and the Carpathians, he would have found Germans; beyond them, and stretching away into Central Asia, he would have found the so-called Scythians — a race which, if he had possessed our information, he would have divided into the two great branches of the Slavonians or European Scythians, and the Tatars, Turks, or Asiatic Scythians; and, finally, beyond these, he would have found Mongolian hordes overspreading Eastern Asia to the Pacific. These successive races or populations he would have found shading off into each other at their points of junction; he would have remarked also a general westward pressure of the whole mass, tending toward mutual rupture and invasion, the Mongolian pressing against the Tatars, the Tatars against the Sclavonians, the Slavonians against the Germans, and the Germans against the Celts.

"The Slavonians, we have said, are an aboriginal European branch of the great Scythian race."[46]

One of the most striking examples in history of preservation of type, after the Jews, is that of the Magyar race in Hungary. Completely encircled by Sclavonians, they have been living there for 1000 years, speaking a distinct language, and still presenting physical characters so peculiar as to leave no doubt of their foreign origin.

"Head nearly round, forehead little developed, low, and bending; the eyes placed obliquely, so that the external angle is elevated; the nose short and flat; mouth prominent, and lips thick; neck very strong, so that the back of the head appears flat, forming almost a straight line with the nape; beard weak and scattering; stature small."[47]

This picture, which is a faithful description of a modern Hungarian of the Magyar race, corresponds with the accounts given of this people by older writers, and of the ancient Huns.

History teaches that the Huns settled in Hungary in the fifth century after Christ, and to these succeeded a body of the Magyars, under Arpad, in the ninth. The type of the two races was identical. This type, so peculiarly exotic, is totally unlike any other in Europe. It belongs to the great Uralian-Tatar stem of Asia. The derivation is conceded by every naturalist, from Pallas to the present day: but it is a curious fact that, although differing in type, the Magyars speak a dialect of the language of the *Fins;* and the two races must have been associated in some way at a remote epoch, previously to the settlement of the Magyars in Hungary. DE GUIGNES had traced other connections, making also the grand error of confounding the *Huns* with the Chinese *Houng-nou:* but that identity of language is no irrefragable argument in favor of identity of race, will be a positive result of the researches in this volume.

Grecian annals afford an instructive lesson in the history of types of mankind. We trace her circumstantial history, with sufficient truthfulness, some centuries beyond the foundation of Rome, and her traditions back to about the epoch of Moses. This we can do with enough certainty to know, that Hellenic Europe was then populated, and marching toward that mighty destiny which has been the wonder and object of imitation of all subsequent ages. Who were the people that achieved so much more than all others of antiquity? And what was there in climate and other local circumstances that could produce such intelligence, coupled with the noblest physical type? Or, we may ask, did Greece owe her marvellous superiority to an indigenous race? The *Hellenes* and *Pelasgi* are the two races identified with her earliest traditions; but when we appeal to history for their origin, or seek for the part that each has played in the majestic drama of antiquity, there is little more than conjecture to guide us. Greece did not come fairly within the scope of M. Edwards's researches, yet he has ventured a few note-worthy observations, in connection with the point before us. He thinks the same principles that governed his examination of Gaul may be applied to Greece; and that the Hellenes and Pelasgi might be followed, ethnologically, like the Celts and Cymbri. Everybody speaks of the *Greek type*, regarded as the special characteristic of that country, referring it to a beau-ideal conformation. Nevertheless, all ancient monuments of art in Greece exhibit a wide diversity of types, and this at every period of their sculpture. M. Edwards draws a happy distinction between the *heroic* and the *historic* age of Greece: the first, if chiefly fabulous, has doubtless a semi-historical foundation; the latter is the true *historic* age—although no people of antiquity appears to have conceived the "historical idea" correctly; nor is it popularly understood, even at the present day, among ourselves.

"Most of the divinities and personages of the *heroic* times," says M. Edwards, "are formed on the same model that constitutes what we term the *beau-ideal*. The forms and proportions of the head and features are so regular that we may describe them with mathematical precision. A perfectly oval contour, forehead and nose straight, without depression between them, would suffice to distinguish this type. The harmony is such that the presence of these traits implies the others. But such is not the character of the personages of truly *historic* times. The *philosophers*, *orators*, *warriors*, and *poets*, almost all differ from it, and form a group apart. It cannot be confounded with the first—I will not attempt to describe it here. It is sufficient to point it out, for one to recognize at once how far it is separated. It greatly resembles, on the contrary, the type which is seen in other countries of Europe, while the former is scarcely met with there."

To facilitate the reader's appreciation of the differences betwixt the *heroic* and the *historic* types, the following heads are selected:

FIG. 3 — *Heroic* type; especially No. 4.[48]

1 2 3 4 5

FIG. 4 — *Historic* type.

LYCURGUS.[49]

FIG. 5.

ERATOSTHENES.[50]

FIG. 6.

ALEXANDER THE GREAT.[51]

FIG. 7.

PHILIP ARRIDÆUS.[52]

FIG. 8.

CLEOPATRA.[53]

The lineaments of Lycurgus and Eratosthenes, excepting the beard, are such as those one meets with daily in our streets; and the same applies to the other familiar personages whose portraits we present.

"Were we to judge solely by the monuments of Greece, on account of the contrast I have pointed out, we should be tempted to regard the type of the fabulous or heroic personages as ideal. But imagination more readily creates monsters than models of beauty; and this principle alone will suffice to convince us that it has existed in Greece, and the countries where its population has spread, if it does not still exist there."

The learned travellers, MM. DE STACKELBERG and DE BRONSTED, have journeyed through the Morea, and closely investigated the population. They assert that the *heroic* type is still extant in certain localities.[54] Here, then, there has been a notable preservation of a peculiar type—within a small geographical space—through time, wars, famines, plagues, immigrations, multifarious foreign conquests; although the Greeks of the *historic* type are, out of all proportion, the most abundant at the present day; which is precisely what, under the circumstances, an ethnographer would have expected.

"Nul peuple n'a conservé avec plus de fidélité la langue de ses aieux. Nul peuple n'a conservé plus d'usages, plus de coutumes, plus de souvenirs des temps antiques; au milieu d'eux les murs d'Argos, de Mycène et de Tyrinthe, qui dejà du temps d'Homère étaient d'une haute antiquité, sont encore debout: des Rapsodes parcourent encore le pays, et chantent avec le même accent et les mêmes paroles, les événements memorables: eux-mêmes sont l'image de ceux que ces souvenirs rappelent avec tant de force; et la ressemblance des traits est rehaussée par la similitude des événements. S'ils ne représentent pas sous le rapport de la civilisation leurs ancêtres des beaux siècles de la Grêce, ils représentent ceux qui les ont aménés."

Of the two types indicated, it is positive, M. Edwards thinks, that the first (*heroic*) is pure: but not certain that the second (*historic*) is. It may be, that the latter is the result of a mixture of the first with some other, the elements of which are now unknown to us; because it does not seem to be sufficiently uniform to be original. Albeit, if we set forth with M. Edwards to hunt for the required elements of modification through Greece, (giving to this name its most extensive sense)—

"We discover a people that has not been sufficiently studied. They speak a language peculiar to themselves. It is not known whence they come, nor when they established themselves there. The *Albanians* seem to be in some respects in Greece, what the Basques are on the two sides of the Pyrenees, the Brètons in France, the Gaels in England, and those who speak the Erse in Scotland and Ireland—a remnant of ancient inhabitants. Why not regard them as such, if it be true that we can find no trace of their foreign origin in their traditions, history, nor in the comparison of language? Why may they not be descendants of the *Pelasgi?*" [They call themselves "Skippetar;" but their Turkish name is *Arnaoot.*]

This ethnological question of *heroic* and *historic* types, mooted by Edwards, is worthy of careful study; but we must pass on.

M. Bodichon, a surgeon distinguished for fifteen years in the French army of Algeria, examines the races of Europe from another point of view; throwing considerable light on this abstruse subject, confirmatory of the very early, no less than permanent, diversity of types in the populations of Gaul and other European countries.

After establishing the insufficiency of Philology in tracing the origin of races, Bodichon makes the following forcible remarks in vindication of Physiology, as a more certain instrument of analysis:

"To throw light upon the question of *origins*, it is necessary to appeal to a science more precise, and founded on the nature of the object which we examine. This science is the *Physiology* of races, or, in other words, a knowledge of their moral and physical characters. Through Physiology has been established the existence of antediluvian beings, their genera, their species and their varieties; by it also we shall discover the origin of races of men, even the most mysterious. Through it we shall one day be able to classify populations as surely as we now class animals and plants: history, philology, annals, inscriptions, the monuments of arts and of religion, will be auxiliaries in these researches. Herein we consider its indications as motives of certitude, and its decisions as a criterion."[55]

The first inhabitants of southern and western Europe, according to his system, belonged to *two* very distinct races; but that region, from time to time, received many accretions from other tribes, mainly Oriental, such as Phœnicians, Pelasgians, Cretans, Rhodians, Hellenes, Carthaginians, Phocians, Saracens, Huns, &c.

His generic characters of the two primitive races may be gathered from the comparative columns we subjoin; and, although, at this late day, it is impossible to separate completely elements so interblended, we think there is much truth in his observations, and refer at the same time to a book that teems with solid material for reflection.

"BLOND RACE.	"BROWN RACE.
"Head generally large, of elongated, and often square, form; eyes blue, or bordering on blue; hair and beard blond, often red, but without Albinism.	"Head generally small, of round, but rarely square, form; eyes black or brown, or bordering on these colors; hair and beard black, sometimes red; but then there is Albinism, which is a pathological state.
"Stature tall, and skin fair. In love, natural chastity, with inclination to sentiment rather than sensuality.	"Short stature, and brown skin. In love, sensuality more developed than sentiment.
"Aptitude to unite in great assemblies, to make leagues, to choose a system of political unity, to live under the monarchical form.	"Aversion to all unitary systems, for great assemblies or leagues. Peculiar disposition to live in a social state by provinces.
"Fond of navigation, long voyages, adventurous expeditions.	"Tenacious of their locality; opposed to distant expeditions.
"Commenced by the pastoral or nomadic state, have been developed in plains, on the borders of great rivers, on the coasts of large bodies of water, and in countries which possess natural modes of communication.	"Have commenced by the agricultural state, and fixed habitations. Have been developed in mountains, islands, and countries, lacking natural channels of communication. Have at all times been addicted to the exploration of mines.

"In war, prefer cavalry to infantry, the attack to defence, open movements to ambuscades, pitched battles to small combats.

"Rush impetuously into danger.

"Unreserved, gay, fond of noise, orations, strong drinks, and good eating. Frank and naive.

"Minds naturally open to doubt, to examination, to discussion. Tolerant, and hold to the religious idea rather than to forms.

"Seek strangers, novelties, and ameliorations. Inconstant, violent, and impetuous, but easily forgive injuries.

"Are eminently sympathetic, initiatory, marching incessantly towards new ends.

"From its origin, has been under the influence of cold climates.

"Its faculties develop in the North.

"It produces, in preference, savans, reformers, creators of systems—philosophers: men whose genius is manifested by profound meditations, by elevated reason, by *sang froid*, by coldness and investigation. Thus, Bacon, Luther, Descartes, Liebnitz, Newton, Cuvier, Washington, and Franklin.

"Predominance of the aristocratic element, and political influence accorded to women.

"Its varities are, the *Celtic*, which is divided into the Gaelic, Belgic, and Cymbric; then the *Germanic*, divided into Germans, Franks, Vandals, Goths, Angles, Saxons, Scandinavians, and other blue-eyed nations, which have played so important a part in the formation of the modern nations of Europe.

"Of Asiatic origin, it penetrated Europe from the East and North; thus, the Volga and the Baltic.

"Considered in relation to the countries where we first see them, they are *Strangers*."

"In war, prefer infantry to cavalry, defence to attack, ambuscades to open movements, and guerillas to pitched battles.

"Await danger with firmness.

"Uncommunicative, sober. Perfidious and reserved.

"Credulous, intolerant, fanatical; attached to religious forms rather than the idea; and reject discussion, doubt, and inquiry.

"Hold strongly to ancient usages; feel a repugnance with regard to strangers.

"Unsympathetic; possess, to an extreme point, the genius of resistance; tend peculiarly to immobility and isolation.

"From its origin, has been under the influence of hot climates.

"Its faculties develop in the South.

"It produces, in preference, orators, warriors, artists, poets: men whose genius manifests itself by the exaltation of sentiments and ideas, by enthusiasm, a rapid conception. Thus, Hannibal, Cicero, Cæsar, Michelangelo, Tasso, Napoleon.

"Predominance of the democratic element, and little political influence granted to women.

"Its varieties are, the *Atlantes*, divided into Libyans and Berbers; next, the *Iberians*, divided into the Sicanians, Ligurians, Cantabrians, Asturians, Aquitanians, and other people of brown skins, who have played an important part in the formation of the ancient nations of Europe.

"Aborigines of Atlantis [?]; penetrated Europe from the South and West; thus, Spain and the Ocean.

"Considered in relation to the countries where we first see them, they are *Autocthones*."

M. Bodichon, with most writers, thinks that the *blond* race entered Europe originally from Asia, and many strong reasons support this position, in respect to those races found in Gaul and in countries north of it, during the recent times of the Greeks and Romans. Older races, notwithstanding—fated like our American aborigines—may have been exterminated by them, or have become amalgamated with them. He supposes these blond immigrants from Asia to have been of the same race as the *Hyksos*, who conquered and took possession of Egypt some 2000 years B. C.; but our modifications of this view, from the study of her monuments, will appear in their place.

"On arriving in Gaul, the Gaels found the banks of the Rhone, the Garonne and the Loire, in possession of a people who spoke a different language and had different usages. They, from time immemorial, had crossed the Pyrenees, and held the soil as first occupants. They were *Iberians*."

About the time alluded to, there seems to have been a great commotion among the white races of Asia; and the Gauls or Celts, and perhaps the Hyksos, (whose name means "royal shepherd,") may have been diverging streams of the same stock. Dr. Morton points out a head, often repeated on the monuments of Egypt, which he regards as of Celtic stock. These people, called "Tokkari" in hieroglyphics, are prisoners in a sea-fight of RAMSES III., of the XXth dynasty, about the thirteenth century B. C. They are, without question, the *Tochari* of STRABO. In his manuscript "Letter to Mr. Gliddon," Dr. MORTON reputes these people to

FIG. 9.[56]

"Have strong *Celtic* features; as seen in the sharp face, the large and irregularly-formed nose, wide mouth, and a certain harshness of expression, which is characteristic of the same people in all their varied localities. Those who are familiar with the Southern Highlanders (of Scotland) may recognize a speaking resemblance."[57]

But the interest in them is greatly enhanced by cuneiform discovery.

FIG. 10.

Here are the same "Tokkari," from Assyrian monuments of the age of SENNACHERIB, about B. C. 700.[58]

It is, to say the least, a very remarkable fact, that we find upon Egyptian monuments, beginning from the XVIIth dynasty, B. C. 1600, portraits in profusion, corresponding in all particulars with the blond races of Europe, whose written history opens as far west as Gaul and Germany: and now Assyrian sculptures present us with the same blond races in the VIIth and VIIIth century before our era.

When the two races first met in Europe, the *blond* from the south-east and the *dark* from the west, they encountered each other as natural enemies, and a severe struggle ensued. The Gaels finally forced their way into Spain, and established themselves there; became more or less amalgamated with the darker occupants, and were called the *Celt-Iberians*. These two types have ever since been commingling; but a complete fusion has not taken place, and the types of each are still clearly traceable. One pristine population of the British Isles was probably *Iberian;* and their type is still beheld in many of the dark-haired, dark-eyed and dark-skinned Irish, as well as occasionally in Great Britain itself.

The enormous antiquity of the Iberians in Europe is admitted on all hands; but their origin has been a subject of infinite disputes. Their type, both moral and physical, is so entirely distinct from that of the ancient fair-skinned immigrants from Asia, that it would be unphilosophical to claim for both a common source, in the present state of knowledge.

DUPONCEAU long ago wrote of the *Basque*, living representative of the *Iberian* tongue—

"This language, preserved in a corner of Europe, by a few thousand mountaineers, is the sole remaining fragment of, perhaps, a hundred dialects, constructed on the same plan, which probably existed, and were universally spoken at a remote period, in that quarter of the world. Like the bones of the mammoth, and the relics of unknown races which have perished, it remains a monument of the destruction produced by a succession of ages. It stands single and alone of its kind, surrounded by idioms whose modern construction bears no analogy to it."

We borrow the quotation from PRICHARD,[59] who has profoundly investigated the theme; and this idea of the antiquity of the *Basque* or "Iberic" tongue, termed "Euskaldune" by its speakers, is eloquently exemplified by LATHAM.

"Just as, in geology, the great primary strata underlie the more recent superimposed formations, so does an older and more primitive population represent the original occupants of Europe and Asia, previous to the extension of the newer, and (so to say) secondary—the Indo-Germans.

"And just as, in geology, the secondary and tertiary strata are not so continuous but that the primary formations may, at intervals, show themselves through them, so also do the fragments of the primary population still exist—discontinuous, indeed, but still capable of being recognized.

"With such a view, the earliest European population was once homogeneous, from Lapland to Grenada, from Tornea to Gibraltar. But it has been overlaid and displaced: the only remnants extant being the Finns and Laplanders, protected by their Arctic climate, the Basques by their Pyrenean fastnesses, and, perhaps, the next nation in order of notice. The Euskaldune is only one of the isolated languages of Europe. There is another—the Albanian."[60]

There was, truly then, an *Iberian* world before the *Celtic* world.[61]

"Persons," continues Bodichon, "who have inhabited Brittany, and then go to Algeria, are struck with the resemblance which they discover between the ancient Armoricans (*the Brétons*) and the Cabyles (*of Algeria*). In fact the moral and physical character is identical. The Bréton of pure blood has a bony head, light yellow complexion, of bistre tinge, eyes black or brown, stature short, and the black hair of the Cabyle. Like him, he instinctively hates strangers. In both the same perverseness and obstinacy, same endurance of fatigue, same love of independence, same inflexion of voice, same expression of feelings. Listen to a Cabyle speaking his native tongue, and you will think you hear a Bréton talking Celtic."

The Brétons to this day form a striking contrast with the people around them, who are—

"Celts, of tall stature, with blue eyes, white skins and blond hair—they are communicative, impetuous, versatile; they pass rapidly from courage to timidity, and from audacity to despair. This is the distinctive character of the Celtic race, now, as in the ancient Gauls.

"The Brétons are entirely different: they are taciturn; hold strongly to their ideas and usages; are persevering and melancholic; in a word, both in *morale* and *physique*, they present the type of a southern race—of the *Atlanteans* [Atalantidæ, *Berbers?*]."

The early history of the world is so enshrouded in darkness, that science leaves us to probabilities in all attempts to explain the manner of the wandering of nations from primitive seats.

"Formerly," says Bodichon, "northern Africa was joined to Europe by a tongue of land, afterwards divided by the Straits of Gibraltar. The *ensemble* of the Atlantic countries formed the [imaginary] island of *Atlantis*. Is it not probable that the *Atlanteans*, following the coast, penetrated Spain, Gaul, and reached Armorica? In contact with the Celts, may they not have adopted some of their usages? These African tribes, too, might have reached Europe by sea. The Atlanteans, among the ancients, passed for the favorite children of Neptune; they made known the worship of this god to other nations—to the Egyptians, for example. In other words, the Atlanteans were the first known navigators. Like all navigators, they must have planted colonies at a distance—the Brétons (*race Brétonne*) in our opinion sprang from one of them."[62]

Our historical proofs of the early diversity of Caucasian types in Europe might be greatly enlarged; but the fact will be admitted by every candid student of ancient history, who, to the propositions that we have already supported by cumulative testimony, will add those more recently established in Scotland, through the inestimable researches of Dr. DANIEL WILSON and his erudite fellow-laborers:

"The Celtæ, we have seen reason to believe, are by no means to be regarded as the primal heirs of the land, but are, on the contrary, comparatively recent intruders. Ages before their migration into Europe, an unknown Allophylian race had wandered to this remote island of the sea, and in its turn gave place to later Allophylian nomades, also destined to occupy it only for a time. Of these antehistorical nations, Archæology alone reveals any traces."[63]

For our immediate objects, however, the acknowledgment that Europe and Asia Minor were covered, at epochas antecedent to all record, by dark as well as by fair-skinned races, suffices. The farther back we journey chronologically, the more conflicting become the tribes, and the more salient their organic diversities; and no reflecting man can, at the present day, cast his eye upon the infinitude of types now extant over this vast area, and disbelieve that their originals were already located in Europe in ages parallel with the earliest pyramids of Egypt, nor that some of them were indigenous to the European soil. The reader will hardly controvert this conclusion, after he has followed us through the types of mankind depicted upon ancient monuments.

CHAPTER IV.

PHYSICAL HISTORY OF THE JEWS.

This historical people furnishes so striking an example of the permanence of a *Caucasian* type, throughout ages of time, and in spite of all the climates of the globe, that we assign it a chapter apart; and if indelibility of type be a test of *specific* character, the Jews must be regarded as a primitive stock.

If the opinion of M. Agassiz, which coincides with what we have long maintained, viz., that mankind were created in *nations*, be correct, it follows that, in reality, there is no such thing as a pure *Abrahamic race;* but that this so-called "race" is made up of the descendants of many proximate races, which had their origin around "Ur of the Chaldees."

We have already set forth that the various zoological provinces possess their groups of proximate species of animals, plants, and races of men; which differ entirely from those of other provinces. In like manner, around the waters of the Tigris and Euphrates, for an indefinite distance, and extending westward to the land of Canaan on the Mediterranean, were grouped certain races bearing a general resemblance to each other, although of distinct origins. This is not simply a conjecture; because we see these races painted and sculptured on the monuments of Assyria and Egypt. The striking resemblance of physical characters among the whole of them is unmistakeable, and wherever the portrait of another foreigner to their stock is introduced, the contrast is at once evident.

Let us, in the first place, take a glance at the history of the Jews, as given by their own chroniclers. In *Genesis*, chap. xi., we are told that Abraham, their great progenitor, is descended in a direct line from Shem, the son of Noah. Only ten generations intervene between Shem and Abraham; and the names, ages, and time of birth of each, being given by the Hebrew writers themselves, we are enabled to ascertain, with much precision, the length of time they estimated between the Jewish date of the flood and the birth of Abraham. According to the Hebrew text, which must be regarded as the most authentic, it was 292 years.

It is certainly reasonable to infer that Abraham inherited, through these few generations, the type of Shem and Noah (supposing the latter to be historical personages); for there are many examples where races have preserved their types for a much longer time; and the Jews themselves, as we shall show, have maintained their own type, from the epoch assigned to Abraham, down to the present day. The era of Abraham has been variously estimated, from 1500 even to 2200 years B. C.; which would give to his descendants at least one hundred generations, according to the common rules of vital statistics.

It should be kept in view that we are here treating the Book of Genesis according to the vulgar understanding of its language. In PART II., and in the SUPPLEMENT, it is shown that a far different construction has been adopted by the best scholars of the day; who regard the so-called *ancestors* of Abraham as geographical names of *nations*, and not as individuals.

The inadequacy of King James's Version to express literally the meaning of Hebrew writers, compels us to follow the Bible of CAHEN, Director of the Israelite School of Paris, and one of the ablest translators of the day. This work, printed under the patronage of LOUIS-PHILIPPE, commenced in 1831, and completed its twenty-two volumes in 1848: "*La Bible, Traduction Nouvelle, avec l'Hébreu en regard; accompagné des points-voyelles et des accens-toniques, avec des notes philologiques, géographiques et littéraires; et les variantes des Septante et du texte Samaritain.*" There is nothing like it in the English language; nor shall we discuss Old Testament questions with those who are unacquainted with CAHEN and the *Hebrew Text*. Neither must the reader infer, from our general conformity with the ordinary mode of expression, that we regard the documents of Genesis otherwise than from the scientific point of view.

The country of Abraham's birth was Upper Mesopotamia, between the waters of the Tigris and Euphrates, not very far from the site of Nineveh; and, after his marriage with Sarai, his history thus continues:—

"And Terah took Abram, his son, and Lot the son of Haran his son's son, and Sarai his daughter-in-law, his son Abram's wife; and they went forth together from Ur of the Chaldees [AUR-KaSDIM], to go into the land of Canaan; and they came unto Haran and dwelt there, and the days of Terah were 205 years, and Terah died in Haran.

"Now IeHOuaH said unto Abram, Get thee *out of thy country and from thy birth-place* and from thy father's house, unto a land which I will show thee. And I will make of thee a great nation, and I will bless thee, and I will aggrandize thy name, and thou shalt be a blessing." [64]

Accordingly, Abraham and Lot, with their families and their flocks, journeyed on, "and in the land of Canaan they arrived." "And IeHOuaH appeared unto Abram and said, Unto thy seed will I give this land."

They were soon driven to Egypt, by a grievous famine, to beg corn of the Pharaoh who then ruled over that country; but, after a short sojourn there, they returned to the Promised Land, and pitched their tents again on the very spot from which they had been taken. "And the Canaanite and the Perizzite then dwelled in the land."

Abram and Lot soon separated; and "Abram struck his tents, and came, and established himself in the grove of Mamre, which is near Khebron, and there he built an altar to IeHOuaH." In his eighty-sixth year of age, Abram's Egyptian concubine HAGAR (whose name means *desert, stone*) gave birth to ISHMAEL; who, launched into Arabian deserts, became the legendary parent of Bedouin tribes; while, to us, he is the earliest Biblical instance of the mixture of two types — *Semitic* and *Egyptian*.

Then the patriarch's name was changed: "Thou shalt no longer be called ABRaM (*father of high*-land); thy name shall be ABRaHaM (*father of a multitude*), because I have rendered thee parent of many nations."[65]

SARAH, at ninety years of age, gave birth to ISAAC, ITsK*h*aK, "laughter." Her own name, also, had previously been changed: "Thou shalt no longer call her SaRaI [ladyship], her name is now SaRaH [a woman of *great fecundity*]."[66] She died at the age of one hundred and twenty-seven years, and was buried in the family cave, which Abram had purchased in Canaan. Wishing then to dispose of his son Isaac in marriage, Abraham said to his *most aged slave*, "I will make thee swear by IeHOuaH, God of the skies and God of the earth, that thou shalt not take *for my son* of the *daughters* of the *Canaanite* [nether-landers] amongst whom I dwell, but thou shalt go into *my country*, and to *my birth-place*, to take a woman for my son Isaac."[67] And, accordingly, the *slave* went back into Mesopotamia, unto the city of Nahor, and brought Rebecca, the cousin of Isaac, whom the latter married.

The next link in the genealogy is Jacob; who, after defrauding his brother Esau of his birthright, retired, from prudential motives, into the land of his forefathers, and there married Leah and Rachel, the two daughters of Laban. Isaac lived to be one hundred and eighty, and Jacob one hundred and forty-seven years old; and they were both deposited in the family cave, or mausoleum. So tenacious were they of their customs, that Jacob, after being embalmed with great ceremony, was carried all the way back from Egypt, as was afterwards his son Joseph, to repose in the same family burial-place; which, our *Supplement* shows, is not a cave called "Machpelah," but "the cavern of the field *contracted for*, facing Mamre."

Here closes the history of those generations which preceded the departure of the Israelites for Egypt; and the evidence is clear, up to this epoch, as to the extreme particularity (ISHMAEL being outlawed) with which they preserved the purity of their blood, as well as the custom of "sleeping with their fathers."

Who the Canaanites were has been amply treated in Part II. It suffices here to note that *Knâ* means "low;" and that Canaanites, as *lowlanders*, were naturally repugnant, at first, to the ABRaM*idæ*, or "highlanders" of Chaldæan hills.

Let us follow this peculiar people through the next remarkable page of their history. The whole sept amounted to seventy persons in number, viz.: Jacob and his eleven sons, who, with their families, by the invitation of Joseph, the twelfth, migrated to Egypt; and were thereupon settled in the land of Goshen, apart from the Egyptians. Thus secluded, they must have preserved their national type tolerably unchanged down to the time of the Exodus, when they carried it back with them to the land of Canaan. Exceptional instances fortify the rule: else why should the genesiacal writer particularize the marriage of JOSEPH with ASNeiT*h* (the *devoted to* the goddess *Neith*), daughter of POTIPHAR (PET-HER-PHRE, the *belonging to* the gods *Horus* and *Ra*—"priest of On," *Heliopolis*), an Egyptian woman?[68] JUDAH had begotten illegitimate children by the Canaanite SHUAH;[69] MOSES, born, and educated in Egypt so thoroughly as to be called a "*Mizrite-man*,"[70] had wedded an Arabian ZIPPORAH, Tsi-P*h*RaH (literally, *daughter of the* god *Ra*), the daughter of JETHRO, a pagan "priest of Midian:"[71] and, besides the GouM AâRaB, *Arab-horde* (falsely rendered "mixed multitude"[72]), that journeyed with the Sinaic Israelites, and with whom there must have been illicit connexions, there was at least one son of an *Egyptian man*, by an *Israelitish woman*, in the camp.[73] Other examples of early Hebrew proclivity can be found; but these suffice to indicate exceptions to the law afterwards promulgated. Under the command of Joshua, the land of Canaan was conquered, and divided amongst the twelve tribes; and from that time down to the final destruction of the Temple by Titus (70 A. D.), a period of about 1500 years, this country was more or less occupied by them. They were, however, almost incessantly harassed by civil and foreign wars, captivities, and calamities of various kinds; and their blood became more or less adulterated with that of Syro-Arabian races around them; the type of whom, however, did not differ materially from their own.

We shall not impose on the patience of the reader, by recapitulating the long list of evidences which are found in history, both sacred and profane, to prove the comparative purity of the blood of the Israelites down to the time of their dispersion (70 A. D.). The avoidance of marriages with other races was enjoined by their religion, and this custom has been perpetuated, in an extraordinary degree, through all their wanderings, and under all their oppressions, down to the present day.

But, while all must agree that the Jews have, for ages, clung together with an adhesiveness and perseverance unknown, perhaps, to any other people, and that their lineaments, in consequence, have been preserved with extraordinary fidelity; it must, on the other hand, be admitted that the race has not entirely escaped adulteration; and it is for this reason that we not unfrequently see, amongst those professing the Jewish religion, faces which do not bear the stamp of the pure Abrahamic stock. We have only to turn to the records of the Old Testament, to find proofs, on almost every page, that the ancient Hebrews, like the modern, were but human beings, and subject to all the infirmities of our nature. Even those venerable heads of the Hebrew monarchy, whose names stand out as the land-marks of sacred history, were not untarnished by the moral darkness which covered the early inhabitants of the earth.

The history of the connubial life of the patriarchs, Abraham and Jacob, presents a picture quite revolting to the standard of our day. After the promulgation of the Mosaic laws, the Israelites were expressly forbidden to intermarry with aliens; and yet the injunction was often disregarded. Abraham, besides his *Arab* wife KETOURAH, and Joseph, as just shown, had both taken women from among the Egyptians; and Moses had espoused an Arab (Cushite?). David, the man after God's own heart, long after the promulgation of the *law*, not only had his concubines, but so far forgot himself as to commit adultery with Bathsheba, the wife of Uriah, the Hittite; and, after murdering the husband, married her, and she became the mother of the celebrated Solomon. Next, on the throne, came Solomon himself, whose career, opening with murder, closed in Paganism. He also married an Egyptian (a princess); enjoying, besides, seven hundred other wives and three hundred concubines: for "King Solomon loved many strange women, together with the daughter of Pharaoh — women of the *Moabites*, *Ammonites*, *Edomites*, *Sidonians*, *Hittites*, and of other nations:"[74] and so promiscuous was his philogamy, that some commentators have imputed scandal even to the "Queen of Sheba," the sombre belle of Southern Arabia. Even the noble-hearted Judah, the "*Lion's Whelp*," the last column of the twelve that stood erect in the sight of Jehovah, and whose especial mission it was to regenerate and raise up the fallen race in purity and power, even he, not only wedded an impure Canaanite, but was tempted to crime by his own daughter-in-law, disguised as a harlot, on the road-side; and, so far from repenting the sin, he had two children by her. Nor need we remind the reader of the unfortunate affair of Sarah with *Pharaoh*, and again with *Abimelech*.

We might thus go on, and multiply examples of similar import from Jewish annals; but to us it is much more pleasing to draw the veil of oblivion over the depravity of those primitive days, and to remember only the noble moral precepts bequeathed us by the kings and prophets of Judea. These, however, are historical facts, having important bearings on the subject before us, and must not, therefore, be passed over in silence. They show clearly that the ancient Israelites were restrained by no moral force which could keep their genealogies pure; but, in comparison with every other people, there is enough to justify us in believing that their pedigrees are to be relied on for a long series of generations. Those among Jews of the present day who preserve what is regarded as the national type, must necessarily be of *pure blood;* while those who do not, must be traced up to foreign alliances.

Fig. 11.

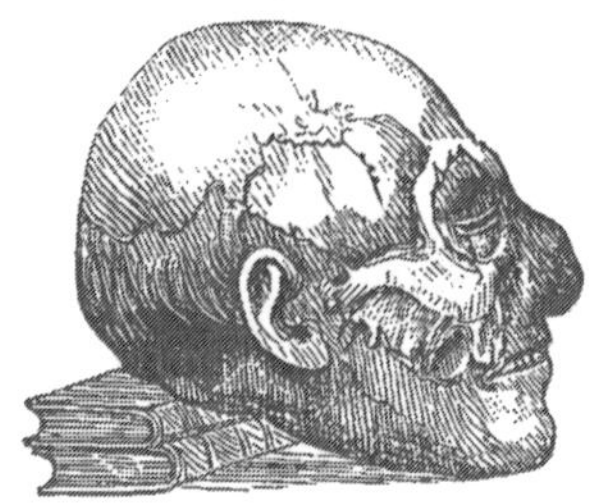

Fig. 12.

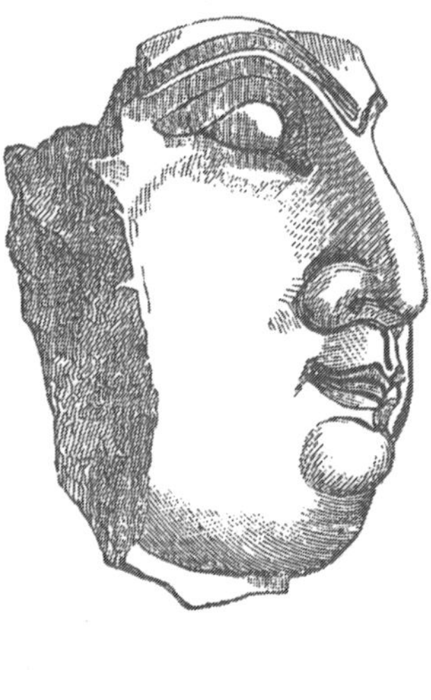

It will illustrate the indelibility of the Abrahamic type to present here a *mummied* Shemitish head, from Morton's collection.[75] Being bituminized, the skull cannot be much older than the time of Moses — say, fifteenth century B. C. Nor, inasmuch as general mummification ceased about 300 years after Christ, can it be less than 1500 years old. From its style and Theban extraction, it may be referred to Solomonic days[76] — yet, how perfectly the Hebrew type is preserved!

Fresh from exhumations in the father-land of Abraham, we add a higher variety of the same type — *Part of a Colossal Head from Kouyunjik.*[77] Its age is fixed between the reign of Sennacherib and the fall of Nineveh, about the seventh century B. C. And still, after 2500 years, so indelible is the type, every resident of Mobile will recognize, in this Chaldæan effigy, the fac-simile portrait of one of their city's most prominent citizens, who is honored alike by the affection of his co-religionists, and the confidence of the community which has just elevated him to a seat in the National Councils.

All written descriptions of early times, relative to the Jewish race, concur in establishing the permanence of their type. We are informed, by modern travellers, that the same features are common in Mesopotamia, their original seat, and also scattered through Persia, Afghanistan, &c.; the direction in which, we are taught by the annals of modern times, some descendants of the ten tribes were dispersed, long after the Assyrian captivity in the eighth century B. C. In short, the Jewish features meet one in almost every country under the sun; but it is worthy of special remark, that Hebrew lineaments are found in no region whither history cannot track them, and rarely where their possessors do not acknowledge Jewish origin. Nor will the fact be questioned, we presume, that well-marked Israelitish features are never beheld out of that race; although it has, as we shall show, been contended that Jews in certain climates have not only lost their own type, but have become transformed into other races!

The number of Jews now existing in the world, (of those that are regarded as descendants in a direct line from, and maintaining the same laws with, their forefathers, who, above 3000 years ago, retreated from Egypt under the guidance of the lawgiver, Moses,) is estimated by Weimer, Wolff, Milman,[78] and others, variously, from three to five millions. In all climates and countries, they are recognized as the same race. Weimer, whose statistics are lowest, gives the following:—

"AFRICA.—They are scattered along the whole coast, from Morocco to Egypt, besides being found in many other parts. Morocco and Fez, 300,000; Tunis, 130,000; Algiers, 30,000; Gabes or Habesh, 20,000; Tripoli, 12,000; &c. Total, 504,000.

"ASIA.—In Mesopotamia and Assyria. The ancient seats of the Babylonian Jews are still occupied by 5,270 families, exclusive of those of Bagdad and Bassora. Asiatic Turkey, 330,000; Arabia, 200,000; Hindostan, 100,000; China, 60,000; Turkistan, 40,000; Province of Iran, 35,000; &c. Total, 738,000.

"EUROPE.—Russia and Poland, 608,000; European Turkey, 321,000; Germany, 138,000; Prussia, 134,000; Netherlands, 80,000; France, 60,000; Italy, 36,000; Great Britain, 12,000; &c. Total in Europe, 1,918,053."

In AMERICA, Milman averages them at 6000 only; but this was certainly very far below the mark, even when his book was published, and they have since been increasing, with immense rapidity. We should think that an estimate of 100,000, for North and South America, would not be an exaggeration.

This sketch suffices to show how the Judaic race has become scattered throughout the regions of the earth; many families being domiciliated, ever since the Christian era, in climates the most opposite: and, yet, in obedience to an organic law of animal life, they have preserved, unchanged, the same features which the Almighty stamped on the first Hebrew pairs created. It may be well to denounce, as vulgar and unscriptural, the notion that the features of the Jews are attributable to a subsequent miracle, or that God has put a *mark* upon them, by which they may be always known, and for the mere purpose of distinguishing them from other races. If we are correct in carrying their type back to times preceding the Exodus, this superstition must fall to the ground. The Almighty, no doubt, individualized all human races, from the beginning.

It is admitted, by ethnographers of every party, that mankind are materially influenced by climate. The Jewish skin, for example, may become more fair at the north, and more dark at the tropics, than in the Land of Promise; but, even here, the limit of change stops far short of approximation to other types. The complexion may be bleached, or tanned, in *exposed parts* of the body, but the Jewish *features* stand unalterably through all climates, and are superior to such influences.

Nevertheless, it is stoutly contended, even at the present day, that Jews, in various parts of the world, have been *transmuted into other types.* Several examples (so supposed) have been heralded forth to sustain the doctrine of the Unity of the human species. We have examined, with care, all these vaunted examples, and feel no hesitation in asserting that *not one* of them possesses any evidence to sustain it, while the proof is conclusive on the opposite side.

The most prominent of these mendacious instances is that of the *black Jews* in Malabar; and this has been confidently cited by all advocates of the doctrine of Unity, down to the Edinburgh Review, 1849. Prichard, in his great work, has dodged this awkward point, in a manner that we are really at a loss to understand. In the second edition (1826) of his "Physical History of Mankind," he stated the facts with sufficient fairness; whereas, in the last, he suppresses them entirely, and passes over them without uttering one word in support of *his* previous assertions — merely saying that there is "no evidence" to show that the *black Jews* are *not Jews.* We shall here introduce testimony to prove our position, that the subjoined facts, though familiar to our author, are eluded by him with most ominous silence.

Under the protection and patronage of the British government, the Rev. CLAUDIUS BUCHANAN, D.D., late Vice Provost of the College of Fort William, in Bengal; well known for his learning, fidelity, and piety; visited and spent some time amongst the *white* and the *black Jews* of Malabar, near Cochin, in 1806–7–8; and the testimony given in his "Asiatic Researches" is so remarkable, and the subject so important, that we venture a long extract. The "Jerusalem, or white

Jews," he tells us, live in *Jews' town*, about a mile from Cochin, and the "*ancient, or black Jews*," with small exceptions, inhabit towns in the interior of the province.

"On my inquiry (continues Dr. Buchanan) into the antiquity of the white Jews, they first delivered me a narrative, in the Hebrew language, of their arrival in India, which has been handed down to them from their fathers; and then exhibited their ancient brass plate, containing their charter and freedom of residence, given by a king of Malabar. The following is the narrative of the events relating to their first arrival:—

"'After the second Temple was destroyed, (which may God speedily rebuild!) our fathers, dreading the conqueror's wrath, departed from Jerusalem—a numerous body of men, women, priests and Levites—and came into this land. There were among them men of repute for learning and wisdom; and God gave the people favor in the sight of the king who at that time reigned here, and he granted them a place to dwell in, called *Cranganor*. He allowed them a patriarchal jurisdiction in the district, with certain privileges of nobility; and the royal grant was engraved, according to the custom of those days, on a plate of brass. This was done in the year from the creation of the world 4250 (A. D. 490); and this plate of brass we still have in possession. Our forefathers continued at *Cranganor* for about one thousand years, and the number of heads who governed were seventy-two. Soon after our settlement, other Jews followed us from Judea; and among them came that man of great wisdom, Rabbi Samuel, a Levite, of Jerusalem, with his son, Rabbi Jehuda Levita. They brought with them the *silver trumpets* made use of at the time of the *Jubilee*, which were saved when the second Temple was destroyed; and we have heard, from our fathers, that there were engraven upon those trumpets the letters of the Ineffable Name. There joined us, also, from Spain and other places, from time to time, certain tribes of Jews, who had heard of our prosperity. But, at last, discord arising among ourselves, one of our chiefs called to his assistance an Indian king, who came upon us with a great army, destroyed our houses, palaces and strongholds, dispossessed us of Cranganor, killed part of us, and carried part into captivity. By these massacres we were reduced to a small number. Some of the exiles came and dwelt at Cochin, where we have remained ever since, suffering great changes, from time to time. There are amongst us some of the children of Israel (Beni-Israel), who came from the country of Ashkenaz, from Egypt, from Tsoha, and other places, besides those who formerly inhabited this country.'

"The native annals of Malabar confirm the foregoing account, in the principal circumstances, as do the Mahommedan histories of the later ages; for the Mahommedans have been settled here, in great numbers, since the eighth century.

"The desolation of Cranganor the Jews describe as being like the desolation of Jerulem in miniature. They were first received into the country with some favor and confidence, agreeably to the tenor of the general prophecy concerning the Jews—for no country was to reject them; and, after they had obtained some wealth, and attracted the notice of men, they are precipitated to the lowest abyss of human suffering and reproach. The recital of the sufferings of the Jews at Cranganor resembles much that of the Jews at Jerusalem, as given by Josephus. [Exactly! Notice also the "72" governors, and the "7" kings.—G. R. G.]

"I now requested they would show me their brass plate. Having been given by a native king, it is written, of course, in the *Malabaric* language and character, and is now so old that it cannot well be understood. The Jews preserve a Hebrew translation of it, which they presented to me; but the Hebrew itself is very difficult, and they do not agree among themselves as to the meaning of some words. I have employed, by their permission, an engraver, at Cochin, to execute a fac-simile of the original plate on copper. This ancient document begins in the following manner, according to the Hebrew translation:—

"'In the peace of God, the King, which hath made the earth according to his pleasure—To this God, I, AIRVI BRAHMIN, have lifted up my hand and have granted, by this deed, which many hundred thousand years shall run—I, dwelling in Cranganor, have granted, in the thirty-sixth year of my reign, in the strength of power I have given in inheritance, to JOSEPH RARBAN—'"

(Here follow several privileges, &c.)

"What proves the importance of the Jews, at the period when this grant was made, is, that it is signed by seven kings as witnesses. (The names are here given.)

"There is no date to the document, further than what may be collected from the reign of the prince, and the names of the royal witnesses. Dates are not usual in old Malabaric writings. One fact is evident, that the Jews must have existed a considerable time in the country before they could have obtained such a grant. The tradition, before-mentioned, assigns for the date of the transaction the year of the creation 4250, which is, in Jewish computation, A. D. 490. It is well known that the famous Malabaric king, CORAM PERUMAL, made grants to the Jews, Christians, and Mahommedans, during his reign; but that prince flourished in the eighth or ninth century."

Archæologically, the date assigned to this document is a manifest imposture, for any epoch anterior to 900 years after Christ. That change of religion from Brahminism to Judaism cannot metamorphose *Hindoo* renegades into *Jews*, is evident from what follows.

Speaking of the *black Jews*, Dr. Buchanan thus continues:—

"Their Hindoo complexion, and their very imperfect resemblance to the European Jews, indicate that they have been detached from the parent stock, in Judea, many ages before the Jews in the west, and that there have been intermarriages with families *not Israelitish*. I had heard that those tribes, which had passed the Indus, had assimilated so much to the customs and habits of the countries in which they live, that they sometimes may be seen by a traveller without being recognized as Jews. In the interior towns of Malabar, I was not always able to distinguish the Jew from the Hindoo. I hence perceived how easy it may be to mistake the tribes of Jewish descent among the Affghans and other nations, in the northern parts of Hindostan. The white Jews look upon the black Jews as an *inferior race*, and as not of *pure* caste, which plainly demonstrates that they do not spring from a common stock in India." [79]

The evidence of Dr. Buchanan can scarcely leave room for a doubt that the white Jews had been living at least a thousand years in Malabar, and were still *white Jews*, without even an approximation, in type, to the Hindoos; and that the *black Jews* were an "inferior race"—"not of *pure* caste"—or, in other words, adulterated by dark *Hindoos*—Jews in doctrine, but not in stock.

But we have another eye-witness, of no less note, to the same effect, namely, Joseph Wolff, a Christianized Jew, whose authority is quoted in places where modern Jews are spoken of. He assures us,[80] that the black Malabar Jews are *converted* Hindoos, and at most a mixture only of the two races. Similar opinions have been expressed by every competent authority we have seen or can find quoted; and even Prichard, in his laborious work, while he slurs over all these facts with the simple remark that there is "no evidence" in favor of Buchanan's opinion, ventures to give not a single authority to rebut him, and offers not a solitary reason for doubting his testimony. And, we say it with regret, that this is but one of Dr. Prichard's many unfair modes of sustaining the doctrine of the unity of mankind. We may add, also, that the opinions of Buchanan and Wolff are those of all Judæans of our day, as far as we have been able to ascertain them. Mr. ISAAC LEESER, the learned and estimable editor of the "*Occident*," at Philadelphia, in answer to our inquiries, thus writes: —

"You may freely assert that, in all essentials, the Jews are the same they are represented on the Egyptian monuments; and a comparison of 3500 years ought to be sufficient to prove that the intermediate links have not degenerated. . . . The black Jews of Malabar are not a Jewish race, according to the accounts which have appeared from time to time in the papers. They are most likely *converts* to Judaism, who, never having intermarried with the white Jews, have retained their original Hindoo complexion, and, I believe, language."

Although this letter of Mr. Leeser was written in haste, and not for publication, his well-known respectability and talent lend so much weight to any thing he would utter about his co-religionists, that we cannot forego the pleasure of giving another and longer extract from it. He says: —

"In respect, however, to the true Jewish complexion, it is *fair;* which is proved by the variety of the people I have seen, from Persia, Russia, Palestine, and Africa, not to mention those of Europe and America, the latter of whom are identical with the Europeans, like all other white inhabitants of this continent. All Jews that ever I have beheld are *identical in features;* though the color of their skin and eyes differs materially, inasmuch as the Southern are nearly all black-eyed, and somewhat sallow, while the Northern are blue-eyed, in a great measure, and of a fair and clear complexion. In this they assimilate to all Caucasians, when transported for a number of generations into various climates. [?] Though I am free to admit that the dark and hazel eye and tawny skin are oftener met with among the Germanic Jews than among the German natives proper. There are also red-haired and white-haired Jews, as well as other people, and perhaps of as great a proportion. I speak now of the Jews north — I am myself a native of Germany, and among my own family I know of none without blue eyes, brown hair (though mine is black), and very fair skin — still I recollect, when a boy, seeing many who had not these characteristics, and had, on the contrary, eyes, hair, and skin of a more southern complexion. In America, you will see all varieties of complexion, from the very fair Canadian down to the almost yellow of the West Indian — the latter, however, is solely the effect of exposure to a *deleterious* climate for several generations, which changes, I should judge, the texture of the hair and skin, and thus leaves its mark on the constitution — otherwise the Caucasian type is strongly developed; but this is the case more emphatically among those sprung from a German than a Portuguese stock. The latter was an original inhabitant of the Iberian Peninsula, and whether it was preserved pure, or became mixed with Moorish blood in the process of centuries, or whether the Germans contracted an intimacy with Teutonic nations, and thus acquired a part of their national characteristics, it is impossible to be told now. But one thing is certain, that, both in Spain and Germany, conversions to Judaism during the early ages, say from the eighth to the thirteenth century, were by no means rare, or else the governments would not have so energetically prohibited Jews from making proselytes of their servants and others. I know not, indeed, whether there is any greater physical discrepancy between northern and southern Jews than between English families who continue in England or emigrate to Alabama — I rather judge there is not."

Mr. Leeser professes not to have paid any special attention to the physical history of the Jews; but, nevertheless, his remarks corroborate very strongly two important points: 1st, That the Jews merely undergo those temporary changes from climate which are admitted by all ethnographers; and 2d, that they have occasionally mingled in blood with Gentile races; amalgamations that account for any visible diversity of type amongst them.

And that we have sought for information among the best informed of the Hebrew community in the United States, may be inferred from the subjoined letter of an authority universally known, and by all respected. His testimony confirms Mr. Leeser's, no less than that of every Hebrew we have been able to consult.

"The black Jews of Malabar are not descendants of Abraham, Isaac, and Jacob, but are of *Hindoo origin*. At Cochin, there are two distinct communities of Jews: one, white, was originally settled at Cranganor, but when the Portuguese became too powerful on that coast (A. D. 1500 to 1590) removed to Cochin. These Jews have been residents in India considerably above 1000 years, but still retain their Jewish cast of features, and, though of dark complexion, are not black. They never intermarry with the second community, also Jews, but black, of Hindoo origin, and, according to tradition, originally bondmen, but converted and manumitted some 300 years ago. Though of the same religion, the two races are, and keep distinct. In the interior of Africa, many Negroes are found who profess to be Jews, practise circumcision, and keep the Sabbath. These are held to be the descendants of slaves who were converted by their Jewish masters, and then manumitted. All the Jews in the interior of Africa who are of really Jewish descent, as, for instance, in Timbuctoo, the Desert of Sahara, &c., though of dark complexion, are not black, and retain the characteristic cast of features of their race—so they do likewise in China.

"J. C. Nott, M. D., Mobile." "Yours, &c. M. J. Raphall.

We think it is now shown satisfactorily that the "Black Jews" of India are *not* Jews by race, any more than the Negro converts to Judaism known to exist at Timbuctoo, or the many Moorish adherents to the Hebrew faith scattered throughout the States of Barbary. There are authors living who insist that the aborigines of our American continent are lineal descendants of the lost *ten tribes*, which have run so wild in our woods as to be no longer recognizable! Other examples of Jewish physical transformation have been alleged, but they are even less worthy of credit than the preceding. The Jews of Abyssinia, or *Falashas*, as they are called, may be noticed. They do not present the Jewish physiognomy, but are, doubtless, composed of mixed bloods, Arabian with African, and converts. Before us lies a pamphlet by Dr. Charles Beke, the very erudite Abyssinian traveller.[81] This essay was read on the 8th of February, 1848, before the Syro-Egyptian Society of London, and Dr. Beke's standing as an orientalist requires no comment. His information was obtained from the Falashas themselves; his opinion formed in presence of the speakers.

"There is, however, no reason for imagining that these Israelites of Abyssinia, who are known in that country by the name of *Falashas*, are, as a people, the lineal descendants of any of the tribes of Israel. Their peculiar language, which they still retain, differs entirely from the Syro-Arabian class to which the Ethiopic and Amharic, as well as the Hebrew and Arabic, belong, and is cognate with, and closely allied to, the existing dialects spoken by the

A'gaus of Lasta and the A'gaumider: a circumstance affording a strong argument in support of the opinion that all these people are descended from an aboriginal race, which has been forced to give way before the advances of a younger people from the opposite shores of the Red Sea — first in Tigrè, and subsequently in the countries adjacent to Bàb-el Mandeb.

"It is not till about the tenth century of the Christian era that we possess any history of the Israelites of Abyssinia, as a separate people; and even then the particulars respecting them, which are to be gathered from the annals of the country as given by Bruce, must, in the earlier portions at least, be received with great caution."

Bruce, in the second volume of his Travels, gives an interesting account of this people. He regards them really as Jews, but expresses sundry doubts, and thinks the question must be determined by future *philological researches.* Such researches have been made since his day, and the decision of Beke is recorded above. Even Prichard did not credit Bruce's narrative.

The history of the *ten tribes* affords also conclusive evidence of the influence of Jewish intermixtures with alien races. In the eighth century B. C., they were conquered, and carried captive, by Tiglathpilesar and Shalmanasar, into the north-western parts of the Assyrian empire; their places being supplied by foreign colonists from that country. These, with a few remaining Israelites, formed the Samaritans of after times; but the ten tribes have been scattered, and most of them lost by Assyrian amalgamations, or absorption into cognate Chaldæan tribes.

"The Affghans, as before remarked, bear strong marks of the Jewish type, and are doubtless descended from the ten tribes. . . . The Affghans have no resemblance to the Tartars who surround them, in person, habits, or language. Sir William Jones (and this opinion is now prevalent) is inclined to believe that their descent may be traced to the Israelites, and adds, that the best-informed Persian historians have adopted the same opinion. The Affghans have traditions among themselves which render it very probable that this is the just account of their origin. Many of their families are distinguished by names of Jewish tribes, though, since their conversion to *Islam,* they conceal their descent with the most scrupulous care; and the whole is confirmed by the circumstance that the *Pushto* has so near an affinity with the Chaldaic that it may justly be regarded as a dialect of that tongue. They are now confounded with the Arabs."[82]

This quotation is a fair specimen of the fabulous ethnography current among orthodox *littérateurs* of our day. There is no Biblical or historical basis for the first assumption: the second is a misapprehension, attributing to Judaism that which is due to Islamism in the last 1000 years; and the third is explained by linguistic importations, Persic and Arabian; because the *Pushto* is a Medo-Persian branch of Indo-European languages. Prichard himself treats Affghan derivation from the Israelites with a sneer[83] — but the reader is referred to our *Supplement* for further citations on the subject, from the works of thorough orientalists, who unite in testifying that the Semitic element in Affghanistan, out of the synagogues, is exclusively ***Arabian.***

Fig. 13.

The portrait of Dost-Mohammed[84] blends Semitic features with those of the true *Affghan;* and suffices to illustrate the similitudes perceived by tourists who, partial to a theory of the "ten tribes'" journey into Tartary, have been blinded to the palpable diversities of osteological structure, which even Arab blood has not obliterated.

We have thus gone over the physical history of the Jewish race; and, although the argument is very far from being exhausted, we think enough has been said to satisfy any unprejudiced mind that this species has preserved its peculiar type from the time of Abraham to the present day, or through more than one hundred generations; and has therefore transmitted directly to us the features of Noah's family, which preceded that of Abraham, according to the so-termed Mosaic account, by only ten generations.

If, then, the Jewish race has preserved the type of its forefathers for 3500 years, in all climates of the earth, and under all forms of government—through extremes of prosperity and adversity—if, too, we add to all this the recently developed facts (which cannot be negatived), that the Tartars, the Negroes, the Assyrians, the Hindoos, the Egyptians, and others, existed, 2000 years before the Christian era, *as distinct as now;* where, we may ask, is to be found the semblance of a scientific argument to sustain the assumption of a common Jewish origin for every species of mankind?

Accounts of the *Gipsies* offer such curious analogies with those of the Israelites, that it may not be out of place to add a word respecting them.

"Both have had an Exodus; both are exiles, and dispersed among the gentiles, by whom they are hated and despised, and whom they hate and despise, under the names of Busnees and Goyim; both, though speaking the language of the gentiles, possess a peculiar tongue, which the latter do not understand; and both possess a *peculiar cast of countenance,* by which they may be without difficulty *distinguished from all other nations;* but with these points the similarity terminates. The Israelites have a peculiar religion, to which they are fanatically attached; the Romas (Gipsies) have none. The Israelites have an authentic history; the Gipsies have no history — they do not even know the name of their original country."

This isolated race is involved in mystery, owing to absence of traditions; though, from their physical type, language, &c., it is conjectured that the Gipsies came from some part of India, but at what time, and why, cannot now be determined. It has been said that they fled from the exterminating sword of the great Tartar conqueror, Timùr Leng (Tamerlane), who ravaged India in 1408–'9 A. D.; but there will be found, in BORROW's work, very good reason for believing that they might have migrated, at a much earlier period, north, amongst the Sclavonians, before they entered Germany and other countries where we first trace them. However, we know with certainty that, in the beginning of the fifteenth century (about the time of Timur's conquest), they appeared in Germany, and were soon scattered over Europe, as far as Spain. They arrived in France on the 17th of August, 1427 A. D. Their number now, in all, has been estimated at about 700,000, and they are scattered over most countries of the habitable globe — Europe, Asia, Africa, South America, and some few in North America. "Their tents are pitched on the heaths of Brazil and the ridges of the Himalaya hills; and their language is heard in Moscow and Madrid, in London and Stamboul." "Their power of resisting cold is truly wonderful, as it is not uncommon to find them encamped in the midst of the snow, in slight canvass tents, where the temperature is 25° to 30° below the freezing point according to Reaumur;" while, on the other hand, they withstand the sultry climes of Africa and India.[85]

The Gipsies are the most prominent of numerous and diverse tribes diffused in little groups over the four continents, to whom Prichard's term "Allophylian races" would properly apply. A list might be made of them; their occurrence in islands, remote valleys and mountain-fastnesses, or even amid dense populations, being far more frequent than is generally supposed. In the absence of all record beyond that of modern days, (their existence known only by their discovery,) we refrain from the labor of enumeration, with the sole remark, that to us they all are mementos of the permanence of type, athwart vicissitudes certainly endured, but unrecorded by themselves: each being a relic of some primitive type of man, generally displaced from its geographical centre of creation, that, having served in days of yore the purposes of the Creator, is now abandoned (with so many others, now lost like the *Guanches*) to its fate, scarcely affording history sufficient for an epitaph.[86]

But it is time to illustrate the subject monumentally; and the words of an illustrious countryman will usher in the facts with which none are better conversant than himself. After alluding to changes wrought by climate on domestic animals and plants, DR. PICKERING maintains: —

"Not so however with the human family. Notwithstanding the mixtures of race during two centuries, no one has remarked a tendency to a development of a new race in the

United States. In Arabia, where the mixtures are more complicated, and have been going on from time immemorial, the result does not appear to have been different. On the Egyptian monuments, I was unable to detect any change in the races of the human family. Neither does written history afford evidence of the extinction of one physical race of men, or of the development of another previously unknown."[87]

Proceeding retrogressively, and closely as the theme can be elucidated, we present the only bas-relief which, throughout the entire range of hieroglyphical or cuneiform discovery hitherto published, in all probability represents *Jews*.

FIG. 14.

(2 *Kings* xviii. 14; *Isaiah* xxxvi. 2. About 700 B. C.)

"*Jewish Captives from Lachish*" (Fig. 14), disinterred from Sennacherib's palace at Kouyunjik, is the title given to the original by its discoverer,[88] who says —

"Here, therefore, was the actual picture of the taking of Lachish, the city, as we know from the Bible, besieged by Sennacherib, when he sent his generals to demand tribute of Hezekiah, and which he had captured before their return. . . . The captives were undoubtedly Jews — their physiognomy was strikingly indicated in the sculptures; but they had been stripped of their ornaments and their fine raiment, and were left barefooted and half-clothed."

Allowance made for reduction to so small a scale, the ethnological character of this bas-relief is not so strikingly effective in respect to true Hebrew physiognomy, as it is (when compared with other Chaldæan effigies) to show the pervading character of many Syrian and Mesopotamian races 2500 years ago.

FIG. 15.

These *Elamites* (Fig. 15) probably, if not Arabs, "*loading a camel*,"[89] belong to the same age, and supply one variety; while here

"*Captives employed by Assyrians*"[90] (Fig. 16), furnish another.

FIG. 16.

Divested of beard, other "*captives in a cart*"[91] (Fig. 17) portray characteristics verging toward an upland, or *Armenian*, expression; at the same time that these upon

FIG. 17.

an undated "Babylonian cylinder"[92] (Fig. 18), too minute in size for ethnographical precision, indicate more of wild Arab lineaments: an inference which the low-land site of Babylon, where Mr. Layard found it, may justify. If we contrast these last with (Fig. 19), an *Egyptian* artistic idea of a "Canaanite" (KANĀNA — *barbarian*),[93] the prevalence of this so-called Semitic type from the Euphrates, through Palestine, to the eastern confines of the Nile, becomes exemplified, back to the twelfth and fifteenth centuries B. C., as thoroughly as ocular observation can realize similar features in the same regions at the present day.

FIG. 18.

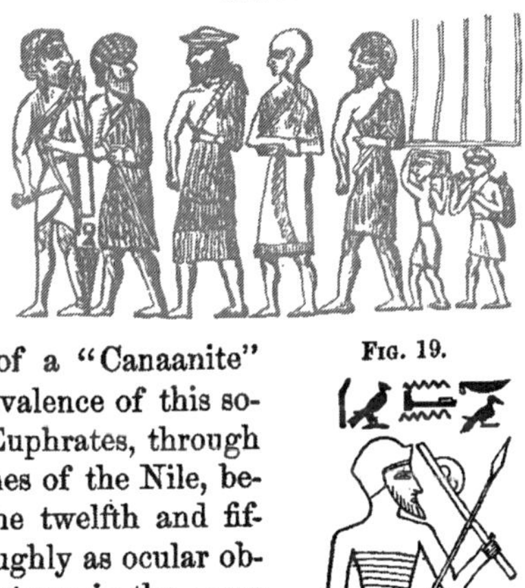

FIG. 19.

Each "canon of art,"[94] in Egypt and in Assyria, was dogmatically enforced (let it be remembered) upon principles entirely different: the former, or anterior, being primitive, and dependent rather upon its relations to *graphical* expression, more rigidly approximates to the ante-monumental age of "picture-writing." In the latter, we behold a developed, and consequently more florid, style of art; which, if nothing else existed to demonstrate the truth of this inherent law of artistic progression, would of itself classify monumental Assyria as, chronologically, a *succedaneum* of Egypt; and vindicate De Longpérier's conclusions of Assyrian modernness, no less than Rawlinson's acknowledgments of Egyptian antiquity.[95]

The combined action of art and of the prevalence, in and around Mesopotamia, of a preponderating type which approaches the beau-ideal of Semitic humanity, may be seen by comparing the *captives* of Assyrian triumphs with the common soldiery of Ninevite armies. Thus, this *Syrian* (Fig. 20), with his leathern scull-cap, whom a pass-

Fig. 20.

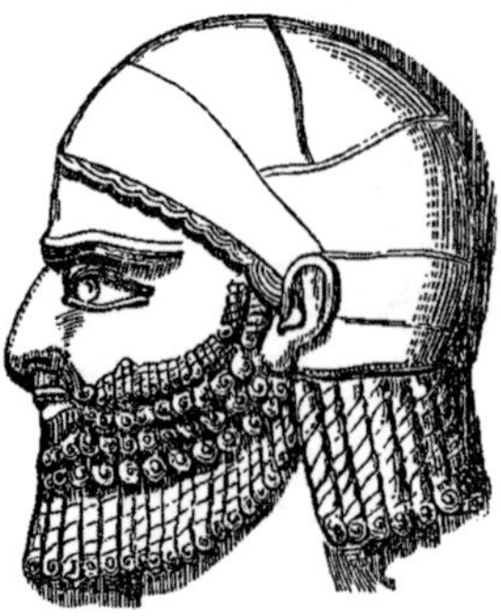

Syrian Captive.[96]

Fig. 21.

Assyrian Soldiers.[97]

age in Herodotus identifies with the people "Milyæ,"[98] or else of adjacent Cilicia, could not otherwise be distinguished from common Assyrian spearmen (Fig. 21) attacking a stronghold which, if not in Samaria, belongs to the same mountainous region. Both drawings are from Khorsabad, and the expeditions of Sargan, late in the eighth century B. C.

But it is in the likenesses of the patricians and of royalty wherein, partly owing to more pains-taking treatment by artists, and partly to a higher caste of race, that the pure Assyrian type becomes vigorously "*scolpito.*"

Sargan's minister, (Fig. 22) probably his *Vizeer*, displays the same noble blood as the King (Fig. 23) himself.[99]

Above all the portraits of Ninevite sovereigns discovered, that of Sargan is the most interesting; 1st, because it was the first royal likeness unearthed from Khorsabad by Botta;[100] 2ndly, because it was the first whose cuneatic legends were ascribed to the besieger of *Ashdod* by a most felicitous guess of Löwenstern;[101] and 3dly, because it was the first identified of those sublime sculptures that, rescued from perdition by French munificence, arrived in Europe,

FIG. 22.

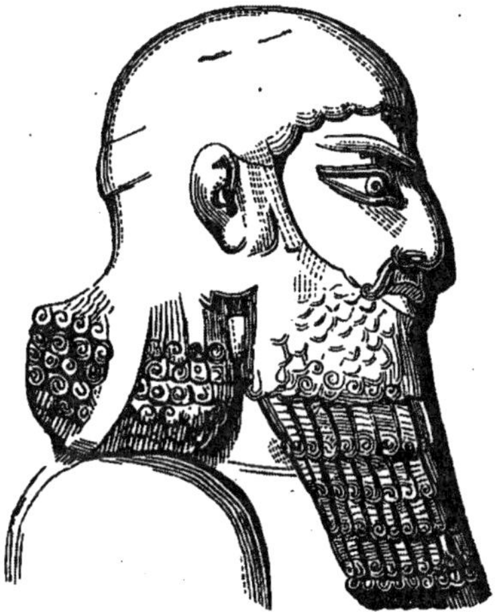

THE VIZEER.

FIG. 23.

THE KING.

and once again tower majestically in the Louvre Museum,[102] after some 2515 years of oblivion.

We present a rough tracing (Fig. 24) of BOTTA's earliest lithographs, wherein the head-dress is tinted red, like the original bas-relief.

FIG. 24.

SARGAN, (*Isaiah*, xx. 1).
B. C. 710 to 668.

It was established, twenty years ago, by ROSELLINI, that, in Egyptian art, the andro-sphinxes (human head on lion's body, symbolical of royalty,) always bear the *likenesses* of the kings or queens in whose reign they were chiselled. Thus, were the features of the Great Sphinx at the pyramids of Memphis adequately preserved, we should probably behold the lost portrait of AAHMES, founder of the XVIIth dynasty, in the seventeenth century B. C.; to whom, under the Greek form of *Amasis*, a tradition in PLINY's time still attributed this colossus.[103] The symbol "sphinx," by the Greeks reputed to be *female*, and by WILKINSON to be always *male* in Egypt, has the body of a lion when (*e. g.* in the splendid granite Sphinx of RAMSES at the Louvre,) it typifies the king; or of a lioness, (as in MAUT-HEM-WA's at Turin,) when the queen. Another rule of Egyptian art is, that the human faces of Divinities wear the portrait of the reigning monarch. Now, in Assyrian sculpture—an offshoot of Nilotic art—the same rules hold good. Those gigantic human-headed bulls, and those superb winged-gods, of scenes in which human-faced

FIG. 25.

SARGON.

deities are introduced, assume the *portraits* of the sovereigns in whose age they were carved: truths easily verified by comparison of the folio plates of FLANDIN or of LAYARD. In consequence, regretting the necessity for reduction of size, we submit, from one of the winged-bulls at Paris[104] the likeness (Fig. 25) of him whose cuneatic legend reads:—"SARGON, great king, puissant king, king of the kings of the land of *Assour*"—*Ashur*, or Assyria—of whom ISAIAH relates—"In the year that Tartan came unto Ashdod (when SARGON, the king of Assyria, sent him,) and fought against

FIG. 26.[105]

FIG. 27.

SENNACHERIB—B. C. 700.

Ashdod, and took it;" events of the seventh century before Christ.

To complete the series, we add a royal head, (Fig. 26) of the same times, but name unknown to us, surmounting a *winged-lion;* its only peculiarity being the ponderous nose.

Not less curiously valuable, whether in its historical, biblical, or ethnographic associations, is the portrait (Fig. 27,) of Sargan's son—"SENNACHERIB, on his throne before Lachish."[106]

We have already beheld (Fig. 14) his Jewish captives. Mr. LAYARD unfolds, through translation of this king's cuneiform inscriptions, points of the grandest scriptural interest[107]—"Hezekiah, king of Judah," says the Assyrian king, "who had not submitted to my authority, forty-six of his principal cities, and fortresses and villages depending upon them, of which I took no account, I captured, and carried away their spoil. I *shut up* (?) himself within Jerusalem, his capital city."

FIG. 28.

We commenced at the seventh, and now advance into the eighth century, B. C.

A "Bas-relief, (Fig. 28) representing PUL, or TIGLATH-Pileser," from Nimroud,[108] places us about the year B. C. 750.

Here the same high type is preserved in the features of the king, his bearded chariot-driver, and his depilated eunuch: while inscriptions that contain the name of "Menahem, king of Israel," tributary to Assyria,[109] evince the intimate relations already existing between that emigrant branch of the *Abrahamidæ* domiciliated in Judæa, and the indigenous stem still flourishing in Chaldæa, whence they had issued about 1000 years before. The same type is carried back to the tenth century B. C., by this copy (Fig. 29) of the statue of SARDANAPALUS I.[110]; whose era falls about 930 years before ours.

FIG. 29.

"On the breast is an inscription nearly in these words:—after the names and titles of the king, 'The conqueror from the upper passage of the Tigris to Lebanon and the Great Sea, who all countries, from the rising of the sun to the going down thereof, has reduced under his authority.' The statue was, therefore, probably raised after his return from the campaign in Syria"—where, the *Tyrians, Sidonians, Arvadites*, and others, acknowledged his suzerainty.

An epoch has now been reached that is more ancient than the registry of Hebrew annals,[111] by a century, perhaps; and hence they cease to throw light, for times anterior to SOLOMON, upon nationalities outside the topographical boundaries of Palestine. But, where Judæan chronicles are silent, when cuneiform records falter, the hieroglyphics of Egypt supply abundance of ethnological information, and enable us to demonstrate the perpetual indelibility of this (let us call it, for mere convenience sake,) *Chaldaic* type. Already, "half-breeds," between Nilotic and Euphratic populations, must have been numerous. Palestine was the neutral-ground of contact; and SOLOMON's wedding with the "daughter of Pharaoh" shows that Abrahamic royalty only followed a matrimonial practice familiar to the Israelites since that patriarch's first visit to Egypt; which duly received Mosaic sanction in the law—"Abhor not the MiTsRI (*Egyptian*):"[112] benignantly providing for its prolific consequences by adding the clause—"The *children* that are born of them, at the third generation, shall enter into the assembly of IeHOuaH."

Mr. Birch was the first to establish, five years ago,[113] the intimate connexions between Egypt and Assyria, in the tenth century B. C.; the very age of Solomon's marriage with an Egyptian princess, and of the punishment inflicted, about 971–'3, by SHESHONK upon Jerusalem, "in the fifth year of Rehoboam." The kings of Egypt during the XXIId or *Bubastite* dynasty, were proved, by this erudite palæographer, to bear not Egyptian, but *Assyrian* names: thus, SHESHONK, *Shishak*, was assimilated to the "Sesacea" of Babylon; OSORKON to *Serak, Saracus*; the son of Osorkon II. was shown to be a NIM-ROT, *Nimrod;* and the appellative TAKELLOTH, TKLT, of the hieroglyphics, to contain DiGLaT*h*, which is the same river *Tigris* that is embodied in the royal Assyrian name of TIGLATH-*Pileser*.

Here is a mute witness of those events and those times—GOT-THOTHI-*Aunk* (Fig. 30), "Chief of the Artificers," at Thebes,[114] who died, according to inscriptions on his cerements, in the "Year X" of the reign of King Osorkon III.; that is, he was alive in the year 900 B. C.! His complete *mummy* lies in the Anatomical Museum of the University of Louisiana, New Orleans; and we shall describe it in the proper place: our object at present being merely to indicate an atom of the ethnological abundance that Egypt and Assyria supply. And the reader will realize the harmony of these archæological researches, when he beholds the *portrait* of the king (Fig. 31) in

Fig. 30.

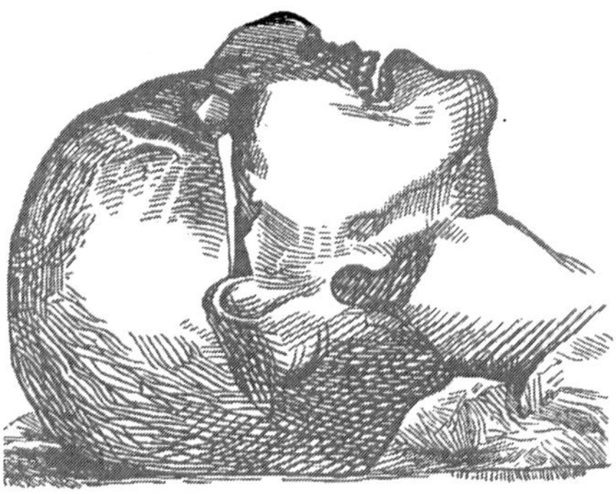

Fig. 31.

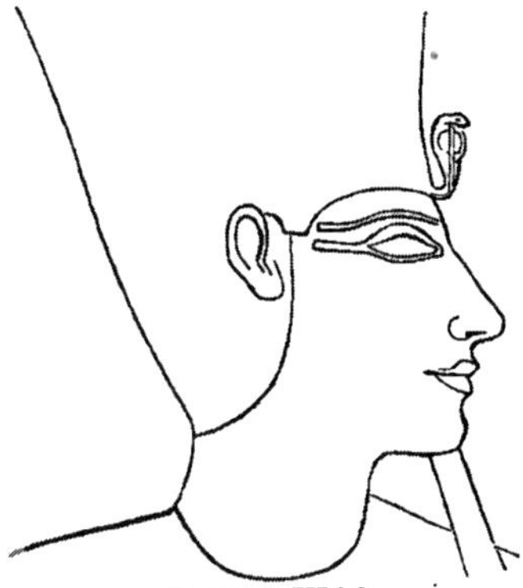

Osorkon III.[115]

whose reign this mummy was made. Leemans published a date of the IXth, and Bunsen one of this Pharaoh's XIth regnal year. The legend on the mummy has added another of his Xth.

Several coincidences have been ingeniously put together by Mr. Sharpe;[116] but, while we refer to Layard's *Second Expedition*,[117] for realizations of the almost-prophetic science of Birch, the latter's opportune discovery of the relationship of Ramses XIV., by marriage, to the daughter of the Semitic "King of *Bashan*,"[118] is merely noted here, because it will be elucidated under the chapter on Egypt. In the following Asiatic prisoners, recorded among the foreign conquests of Amunoph III., at Soleb,[119] there is no difficulty of recognizing—

Fig. 32.

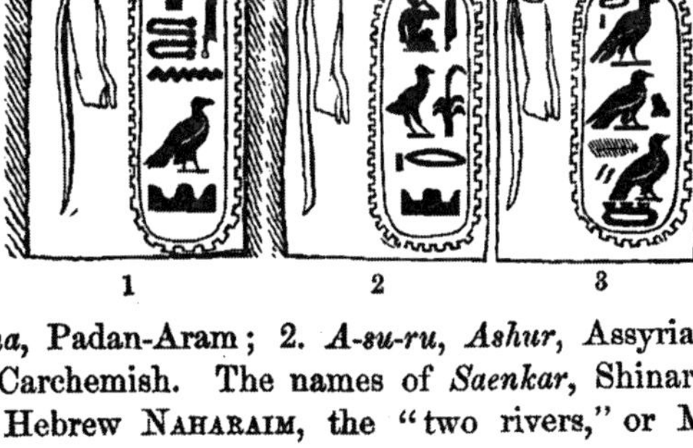

1 2 3

1. *Pa-ta-na*, Padan-Aram; 2. *A-su-ru*, *Ashur*, Assyria; 3. *Ka-ru-ka-mishi*, Carchemish. The names of *Saenkar*, Shinar, and *Naharaina*, in Hebrew Naharaim, the "two rivers," or Mesopotamia,

hieroglyphed in the same Pharaoh's reign, have long been familiar to Egyptologists; and thus Assyrian data and connexions with the Nile are positively carried back to the XVIIth dynasty, and the sixteenth century B. C.

But although, amid the ruins of Babylon itself, nothing has been yet disclosed of an earlier date than NEBUCHADNEZZAR, B. C. 604; and no genealogical list, not to say contemporaneous monument, older than B. C. 1250,[120] at Nineveh; hieroglyphics of an ancestor of AMUNOPH III., viz., THOTMES III., prove the existence of both *Babylon* and *Nineveh*, as tributaries to the Pharaohs, at least one generation earlier, or about 1600 years B. C.[121] This king, in an inscription more recently translated by Birch, is said to have "erected his tablet in *Naharaina* (Mesopotamia), for the extension of the frontiers of *Kami* (Egypt)."[122]

The sixteenth century B. C., according to Lepsius's system of chronology, touches the advent of Abraham and later sojourn of his grandson Jacob's children in the land of Goshen. Relations of war, commerce, and intermarriage, between the people of the Nile and those from the Tigris and Euphrates, in these times, were incessant. Semitic elements (as we shall see in the gallery of royal Egyptian portraits further on) flowed from Asia into Africa in unceasing streams. The *Queens* of Egypt, especially, betray the commingling of the *Chaldaic* type with that indigenous to the lower valley of the Nile; and, although we shall resume these evidences, the reader will recognize the blending of both types in the lineaments of Queen AAHMES-NEFERARI (Fig. 33), wife of Amunoph I., son of the founder of the XVIIth dynasty, about 1671 B. C. Hers is the most ancient of regal feminine likenesses identified;[123] and of it Morton wrote, "Perhaps the most *Hebrew* portrait on the monuments is that of Aahmes-Nofre-Ari."[124]

FIG. 33.

Having thus traced back the *Chaldaic* type into Egypt before the arrival of Abraham, first historical ancestor of the Jews, we have proved the perpetuity of its existence, through Egyptian and Assyrian records, during 3500 years of time, down to our day. But the Jewish type of man must have existed in Chaldæa for an indefinite time before Abraham. After all, he was merely *one* emigrant; and his ancestral stock, at 1500 B. C., must have amounted to an immense population. We hold, without hesitation, that 2000 years before

Abraham, there had already been intermarriages between the *Chaldaic* and the Egyptian species. No ethnographer but will perceive, with us, the Jewish cross upon Egyptians of the IVth Memphite dynasty, 3500 years B. C., say about 5400 years ago: and such amalgamations must then have been far more ancient. Examine the following—(Figs. 34, 35): we shall revert to them by-and-by.

FIG. 34.[125]

FIG. 35.

We shall yet be able to sketch out the durability of the cognate *Arabian* race 2000 years earlier than ISHMAEL, son of Abraham, when we deal with Egyptian primitive relations with Asia; and as, for thirty-five centuries (not to say fifty-five, when the *Chaldaic* blood first appears), Jews and Arabs have been monumentally coexistent and distinct in type, therefore the demonstration of the existence of the latter people 5500 years ago will naturally imply the simultaneous presence of the former in their Mesopotamian birth-place; although neither from Assyrian nor Hebrew records can we produce annals to that effect—simply because such chronicles, if any were kept, have not reached our modern day.

Before quitting, for the present, Semitish immigrations into Africa, we may allude to early Phœnician colonization of Barbary, as another prolific source of comminglings between *Chaldaic* and *Berber*, or Atalantic, types. These must have preceded, by centuries, the foundation of Carthage, estimated at B. C. 878; and, in those days (the *camel* not having been introduced into Africa before the first or second century B. C.), the Sahara desert being absolutely impassable, the Atalantidæ of the Barbary coast held no communication with Negro races of inland Africa. The subject is discussed in Part II. of this volume.

The illiterate advocates of a pseudo-negrophilism, more ruinous to the Africans of the United States than the condition of servitude in which they thrive, multiply, and are happy, have actually claimed St. Augustine, Eratosthenes, Juba, Hannibal, and other great men, as historical vouchers for the perfectibility of the *Negro* race, because born in Africa! It might hence be argued that "birth in a stable makes a man a horse." We submit the following portraits.

FIG. 36.

ERATOSTHENES[126] (Fig. 36), born at the Greek colony of Cyrene, on the coast of Barbary, about 276 B. C. What more perfect sample of the Greek *historical* type could be desired?

HANNIBAL[127] (Fig. 37), son of *Hamilcar Barcas*, born at Carthage, about B. C. 247. The highest "Caucasian" type is so strongly marked in his face, that, if his father was a Phœnico-Carthaginian, one would suspect that his mother, as among the Ottomans and Persians of the present day, was an imported *white* slave, or other female of the purest Japhetic race.

FIG. 37.

FIG. 38.

FIG. 39.

JUBA[128] (Fig. 38), son of *Hiempsal*, king of Numidia, ascended the throne about B. C. 50. If not *Berber* (and we have no means of comparison), the Arab type predominates in his countenance; and that this closely approximated to the true *Tyrian*, or Phœnician, is evident by comparing it with the features of an ancient citizen of Tyre (Fig. 39), figured at Thebes, in the reign of Ramses III., of the XXth dynasty, during the thirteenth century B. C.[129]

Abundant illustrations of the permanence of type, in other varieties of Semitish races, will be given in due course; but, on our road to Persia, let us indicate a *Syrian* form, in this mountaineer of Lebanon[130] (Fig. 40), from the conquests of the same Ramses; and contrast it with a genuine *Cushite Arab*, or *Himyarite*[131] (Fig. 41), who appears in the tomb of Seti-Meneptha I., about 1400 years B. C.

Fig. 40.

Fig. 41.

As we cross through Chaldæa, we again encounter (Fig. 42) the true Jewish type in the land of its origin. A full-length figure of this individual will be given in a succeeding Chapter; and it is the more curious, inasmuch as we behold in its design an Egyptian artist's conception of a *Chaldee* during the fifteenth century B. C.; that is, about 500 years before any cuneiform monuments yet found, and 600 years before any Jewish records, now known, were inscribed or written.

Fig. 42.

Persian monumental ethnography, (like the native, the Hebrew, and the Greek chronicles of that Iranian land,) can but commence with Cyrus;—that mighty name, which, until recent hieroglyphical and cuneatic discoveries threw open the portals of ages anterior, marked the grand terminus of historical knowledge concerning Oriental events and nations. We accompany the following series with Rawlinson's translation of the Persepolitan arrow-headed legends.

FIG. 43.

BAS-RELIEF OF CYRUS.[133]

"I am Cyrus, the King; the Achæmenian."[132]

Such is the simple epitaph of sterling greatness, on the ruined pilasters of Murghàb, or *Parsagadæ*, adjacent to the tomb of CYRUS: built about B. C. 528.

The abraded condition of the face (Fig. 43) enables us merely to distinguish that high-class type, which the grandson of a *Mede* (Astyages) and a *Lydian* (Mandane, sister of CRŒSUS), and the son of a *Persian*, would naturally present.

Singularly enough, the effigy wears an *Egyptian* (Kneph-Osiris) head-dress; which confirms LETRONNE'S argument of the very intimate relations between Persia and Egypt, before the conquest by Cambyses.[134]

FIG. 44.

BAS-RELIEF OF DARIUS.[136]

FIG. 45.

BAS-RELIEF OF XERXES.[138]

"I am Darius, (Fig. 44) the great King, the King of Kings, the King of Persia, the King of (the dependent) provinces, the son of Hystaspes, the grandson of Arsames, the Achæmenian."[135]

We see DARIUS in the attitude of uttering that noble address, which stands inscribed on the vast cuneiform *Tablet of Behistùn*, cut about 482 B. C.

"Xerxes, the great King, the King of Kings, the son of King Darius, the Achæmenian."[137]

We are uncertain whether the effigy (Fig. 45) be not that of his son, ARTAXERXES: but, ethnologically, the point is immaterial; for the Persic type of the line of Achæmenes is rigorously preserved in these sculptures of Persepolis.

"This is the face (Fig. 46) of the (Mazdæan) servant of Ormuzd, of the god SAPOR, king of the kings of the Iranians and of the non-Iranians, of the race of the gods; son of the (Mazdæan) servant of Ormuzd *Ardeshir*, king of the kings of Iran, of the race of the gods; grandson of the god *Babek*, king." [139]

FIG. 46.

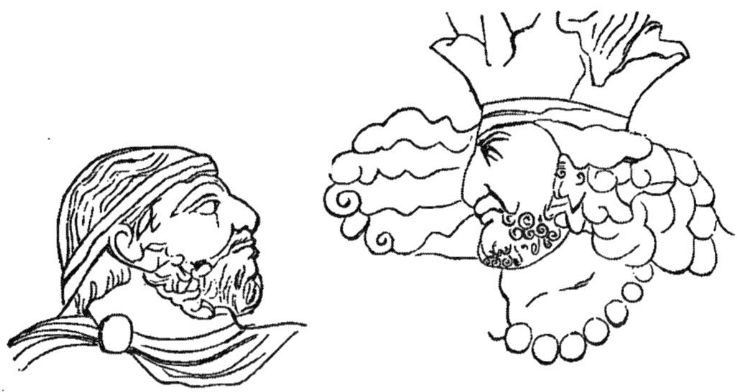

ROMAN. SAPOR.[140]

This *Greek* version of the trilinguar inscription carved upon SHAPOOR's horse at Nakshi-Redjeb, near Persepolis, is the more precious, because it served to GROTEFEND, 1802, the same purpose that the triglyphic *Rosetta Stone* answered to YOUNG, in 1816. The latter became the finger-post to CHAMPOLLION LE JEUNE's deciphering of all Egyptian hieroglyphics; just as the former to RAWLINSON's of all cuneiform writings.

Our heads, however, are taken from the bas-relief of the same king SHAPOOR, Sapor, at Nakshi-Roustam: where a *Roman* suppliant, no less a personage than the captive emperor VALERIAN, kneels in vain hope of exciting Persian humanity. The scene refers to events of about A. D. 260; when, under the Sassanian dynasty, art had wofully declined. The contrast, notwithstanding, between the Persian and the Roman, is here preserved; and still more effectively in another tableau[141] at Chapour.

Among the prisoners of DARIUS at Behistùn, the nations carved on his rock-hewn sepulchre at Persepolis, and the troops supporting the throne of XERXES, may be seen many varieties of the Median, Persian, and Chaldæan races; although, in the latter instances, the absence of names prevents identification: but this son of the desert, (Fig. 47) of the age of SAPOR,[142] affords a variant, with some Arabian lineaments, that we are inclined to refer to Beloochistàn, or the Indian side of the Persian Gulf.

Still nearer to the Indus do we assign the first of two effigies (Figs. 48, 49) painted in Egypt about 1800 years previously. The second

FIG. 47.

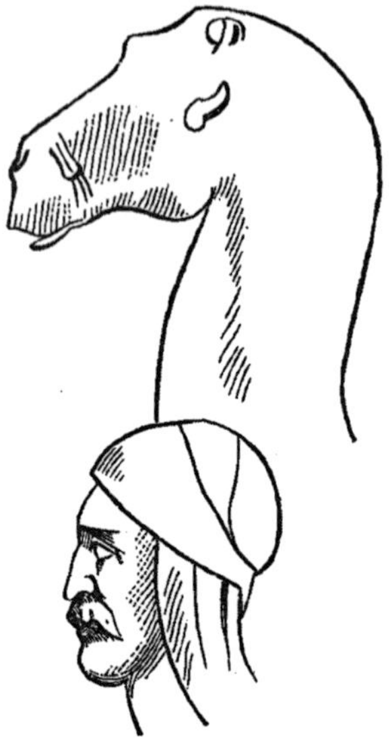

FIG. 48.

FIG. 49.

may even, perhaps, approach the Himalayan range. They are from the "Grand Procession" of THOTMES III., in the sixteenth century B. C., to be elucidated hereinafter.

He (Fig. 48) leads an elephant, which, like that on the *Obelisk of Nimroud*,[143] points towards Hindostanic intercourse; and his features, surmounted by the straw hat, are peculiarly Hindoo.

The other (Fig. 49) carries an elephant's tooth, at the same time that he leads a bear—by MORTON denominated an *Ursus Labiatus*—and a certain *Arian* cast of countenance favors the vague geographical attribution we adopt for him.

FIG. 50.

Finally, to establish the diversity of Asiatic types, in every age parallel with the Jewish, here is a *Tartar* (Fig. 50) from the conquests of RAMSES II.,[144] painted at Aboosimbel in the fourteenth century B. C. His face is unmistakeable; as are those of his associates, some of whom wear their hair long, in the same tableau.

The question of the "Chinese" (unknown to any nation west of the Euphrates prior to the Christian era,) has been settled in our *Supplement;* and it suffices here to note that, the custom of shaven heads, with scalp-lock, is essentially Tartar. The Chinese always wore their hair long until compelled to shave their heads by the present dynasty of Mantchou-Tartars;[145] and the Turkish branch of those hordes introduced this usage in the modern Levant.

Reader! we have followed the *Chaldaic* type from Mesopotamia to Memphis; and thence, via Carthage, through Palestine, Syria, Arabia, Assyria, and Persia, until it disappeared; when, looking towards the Caspian and the Indus, we descried the cradle-lands of Arian, Tartar, and Hindoo races. May we not now consider *permanence of type* among JEWS, for more than 3000 years, to be a matter proved? and with it, the simultaneous existence in the same countries of every variety of type and race visible there now, ever distinct during the same period?

The monuments of Egypt and Assyria, history and the Bible, have enabled us to ascend to the age of Abraham, first historical progenitor of the Israelitish line, and demonstrate the indelibility of the Jewish type from his era downwards. The sculptures of the IVth dynasty have also exhibited the admixture, or engraftment of the same Chaldaic type upon native families of Egypt at a date which is some 2000 years beyond Abraham's era upwards.

Other analogical proofs will appear in the sequel; but, in the interim, the Jews themselves are living testimonies that their type has survived every vicissitude; and that it has come down, century by century, from Mesopotamia to Mobile, for at least 5500 years, unaltered and, save through blood-alliance with Gentiles, unalterable.

CHAPTER V.

THE CAUCASIAN TYPES CARRIED THROUGH EGYPTIAN MONUMENTS.

In a preceding chapter, portions of the European group, generically styled the "Caucasian," were traced backwards through *historical* times. This sketch was followed by a *resumé* of the Physical History of the Jews, whose annals constitute the boundary of written history, by supplying the most ancient literary link that connects us with remoter monumental periods. We now propose to track this Caucasian type onwards, through the stone records of Egypt, up to the earliest of such documents extant.

The incipient history of the Israelites is indissolubly woven with that of Egypt; nor could we separate the two if we would. Although the earliest positive synchronism, or ascertained era of contact, between these people, is the year 971 B. C.; viz.: the conquest of Judæa under Rehoboam by Shishak or *Sheshonk*—nevertheless, there are other periods of intercourse much earlier in date, which may be reached approximately: and while, on the one hand, Egyptian monuments, so far as known synchronisms extend, bear testimony to the historical truth of Jewish records posterior to Solomon, these, on the other, furnish evidence in favor of the reliability of the hieroglyphics. The histories of Abraham, of Joseph, of Jacob and his descendants, and of Moses, all bear witness to the antiquity, grandeur, and high civilization attained by Egypt's *Old Empire* before the birth of the first Hebrew patriarch: but when we compare the genealogical and chronological systems of the two people, as well as their respective physical types, there is really nothing in common between them. Abraham, according to the Rabbinical account, is but the tenth in descent from Noah; his birth occurring 292 years after the Deluge: but, substituting the more critical computation of Lepsius, Abraham must have lived in the time of AMUNOPH III., *Memnon*, of the XVIIIth dynasty, about 1500 years B. C. Now, the epoch of MENES, the first Pharaoh of Egypt, is placed by the same *savant* at 3893 B. C., or some 2400 years before Abraham.

The epoch of Abraham has ordinarily, indeed, been computed by Biblical commentators, a few centuries farther back than the date assigned to him by Lepsius; but we are inclined to adopt the estimate of this superior authority, for the following simple reasons:—There are but five generations—viz.: ISAAC, JACOB, LEVI, KOHATH, AMRAM—between Abraham and Moses; and the era of the latter is now approximately fixed in the fourteenth century B. C. By adding to the latter age—assuming the Exodus, when Moses was 80 years old, at B. C. 1322[146]—the average duration of life for five generations, the time of Abraham falls about 1500 B. C. It may be objected that people in olden times were gifted with a longevity immeasurably greater than our modern generations; but this presumption is contradicted by a thoroughly-established fact, that the Egyptians, whose ages are recorded on the hieroglyphical tombstones for twenty centuries before Abraham's nativity, and whose mummied *crania*, of generations long anterior to this patriarch, abound, lived no longer than people do now. Another proof, likewise, that numerical errors have always existed in the Book of Genesis, is the fact, that the manuscript Texts differ irreconcilably in respect to the ages of the Patriarchs; while these extraordinary ages are rendered nugatory by the physiological laws governing human life. If farther proof be wanted, it may be gathered from the story of Abraham and Sarah. Though *contemporary with every one of her ancestors back to Noah himself*, (all of whom, according to Genesis,[147] lived from 205 to 600 years), yet

Sarah, when told, in her ninetieth year, that she should bear a child, laughed twice, having never heard of such an occurrence! But, even admitting such superhuman longevities for the Patriarchs, that does not mend the difficulty; for, after all, there are but *ten generations* between Abraham and Noah, to set off against no less than *seventeen dynasties* of Egypt, each of which included many kings, whose united ages exceed 2000 years.

The following is the popular view of the genealogy of Abraham: the scientific results of Hebraical inquiry into which are discussed in *Part III.* of our work.

1. *Shem.*	2. *Arphaxad.*	3. *Salah.*	4. *Eber.*
5. *Peleg.*	6. *Reu.*	7. *Serug.*	8. *Nahor.*
	9. *Terah.*	10. *Abraham.*	

Now, as we have stated, Abraham was not only contemporary with this ancestry, but, according to the Jewish system, 58 years old when Noah himself died; and yet, when he visits Egypt, he meets with no acquaintances nor kindred there; but, on the contrary, he finds a great empire, composed of millions of strange people; and beholds standing around him pyramids and temples, erected by this more ancient and distinct race — with records, hieroglyphical and hieratic, written in a language to him foreign, stretching back more than 2000 years before his birth. The reasons, then, are obvious, for passing over that part of Egyptian history subsequent to B. C. 1500, and for commencing our analysis of the monuments with those of the XVIIth dynasty, (of Lepsius—XVIIIth, of Rosellini,) which was contemporary with Abraham. Although Jewish chronicles, as they have reached us, beyond this Abrahamic point are all confusion, it will be seen that Egyptian monuments afford vast materials, bearing upon some Types of Mankind, in Asia and Africa, whose epoch antedates, by twenty centuries, that of the *Father* of the Abrahamidæ.

It is now known to every educated reader that the Egyptians from the very earliest times of which vestiges remain, viz., the IIId and IVth dynasties, were in the habit of decorating their temples, royal and private tombs, &c., with paintings and sculptures of an historical character; and that a voluminous, though interrupted, series of such hieroglyphed monuments and papyri is preserved to the present day. These sculptures and paintings not only yield us innumerable portraits of the Egyptians themselves, but also of an infinitude of foreign people, with whom they held intercourse through wars or commerce. They have portrayed their allies, their enemies, their captives, servants, and slaves; and we possess, therefore, thus faithfully delineated, most if not all the Asiatic and African races known to the Egyptians 3500 years ago — races which are recognized as identical with those that occupy the same countries at the present day.

We shall commence our illustrations by a series of royal portraits of the XVIIth and succeeding dynasties. They are faithfully copied, on a reduced scale, from the magnificent *Monumenti* of Rosellini. Although reasons will be produced hereinafter for regarding this line of Pharaohs as of mixed Asiatic origin (*i. e.* not of the pure Egyptian type proper), yet they will serve admirably as a basis whence to continue tracing, upwards, our *Caucasian types*. Not only are all these heads of high Asiatic or Caucasian outline, but several of their features strongly betray the Abrahamic cross.

When the celebrated VISCONTI printed, in Italy, his "*Greek and Roman Iconography*," containing the *portraits* of the most famous personages of classical antiquity, he lamented the absence of *Egyptian* portraits; little expecting that, a few years later, Rosellini [148] should publish a complete gallery of likenesses of Pharaohs and Ptolemies from the monuments of the Nile; still less could either of those great scholars foresee that, ere one generation elapsed, we should possess the portraits of Sennacherib and other Assyrian monarchs from the palaces of Nineveh!

Mankind have always, and in every country (China, from most ancient times, particularly), taken extreme interest in knowing the features of those who have been renowned in story. Pliny praises the 700 portraits collected by VARRO. Solomon, or the writer of *Wisdom*,[149] says, "Whom men could not honor in presence, because they dwelled afar off, they took the *counterfeit* of his visage, and made an express image of a king whom they honored;" and while to Grecian art we owe the perpetuation of the sublime busts of their worthies back to the fourth century B. C., we can no longer tolerate the illusion, now that we possess the likeness of Prince MERHET (to be exhibited in due course) who lived about 5300 years ago, that LYSISTRATUS, who flourished in the 114th Olympiad, was either the first portrait-sculptor or moulder. Such sparse remains of Hellenic art as appertain to the sixth century B. C. differ altogether from the perfection of later ages, and betray the stiffness of antiquity. They correspond in style to the old *Lycian* sculptures, which are known derivatives of Assyrian art; and it is sufficient to glance at the effigies of Ninevite kings and nobles, so splendidly illustrated in the *folio* plates of Botta and of Layard, to be convinced that the art of *portrait-taking* ascends, in Assyria at least, to the tenth century B. C.; while, in Egypt, its origin precedes the oldest pyramids — because, at the IVth dynasty, the *likenesses* of individuals are repeated times out of number in their tombs, as any one can verify by opening Lepsius's *Denkmäler*.

The general exactitude of Egyptian iconography being now a matter beyond dispute, we have only to remind the reader, while submitting the following selections, that, if he makes allowance for want of perspective in antique Egyptian art, wherein the *eye* is always presented in full, he will find the profiles admirably truthful. Moreover, he will be struck with the likenesses from father to son in each family group — which is another guarantee of artistic fidelity; at the same time that the infusion of new blood in each dynasty, and the consequent alteration of lineaments, are apparent to every eye.

PHARAONIC PORTRAITS.[150]

AMUNOPHITES AND THOTMESITES.—*New Empire*—XVIIth Theban dynasty — commencing at B. C. 1671 (Lepsius), with AAHMES, *Amasis;* whose portrait being unknown, we begin with his son's. Our ethnological conceptions are very briefly given under each head, leaving the reader to emend where we may not have seized the exact definitions.

FIG. 44.

AMUNOPH I.
(A *Grecian* countenance.)

His wife. ☞

FIG. 45.

AAHMES-NOFRE-ARI.
(Strong *Semitic* features.)

FIG. 46.

THOTMES I.
(Strikingly *Hellenic.*)

Son of the above. ☜

His wife. ☞

FIG. 47.

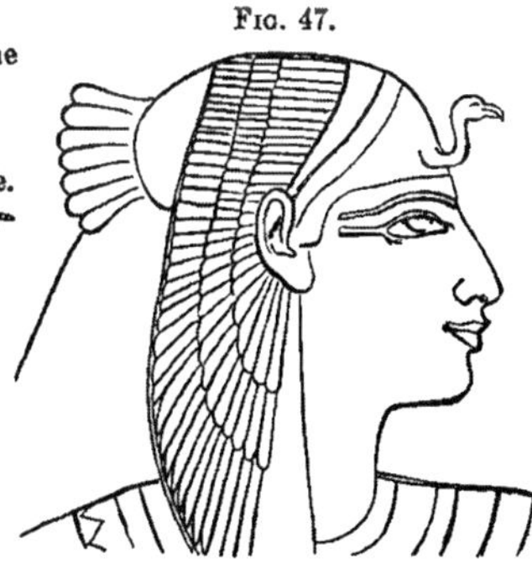

AAHMES.
(Absolutely *Jewish.*)

Fig. 48.

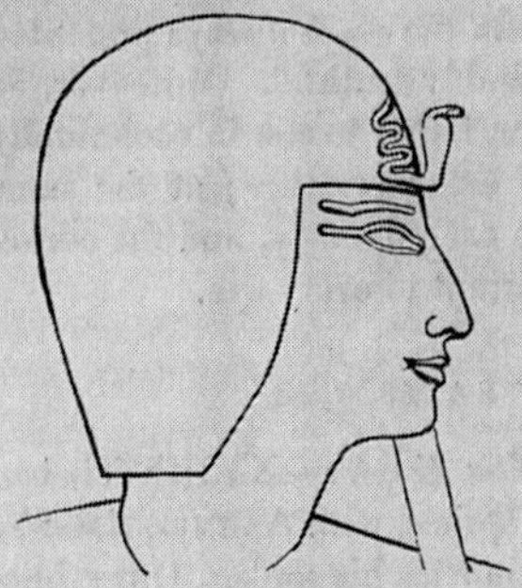

Thotmes II.
(Blends his father's with his mother's face.)

Son of Thotmes I. and Aahmes. ☜

His son. ☞

Fig. 49.

Thotmes III.
(Preserves the same character.)

Fig. 50.

Amunoph II.
(Unites *Egyptian* with *Hellenic*.)

Son of Thotmes III. ☜

His son. ☞

Fig. 51.

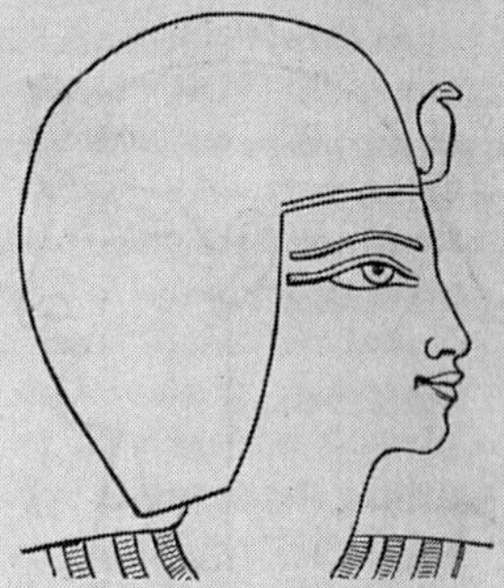

Thotmes IV.
(Returns to the *old Egyptian* form.)

Fig. 52.

Maut-Hemwa.
(*Nubian? Cushite*-Arab?)

Thotmes IV. marries a foreigner. ☜

Their son has foreign features. ☞

Fig. 53.

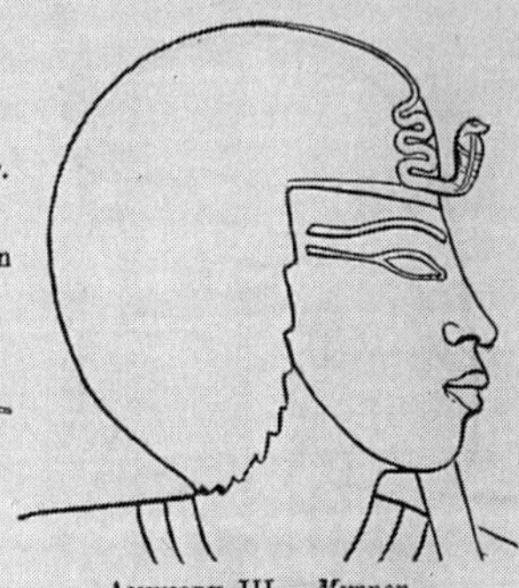

Amunoph III. *Memnon.*
(A *hybrid*, but not of Negro intermixture.)

Fig. 54.

Taia.
(*Egyptian.*)

Wife of Amunoph III. ☞

(Further comminglings with foreigners occur, and the *Disk-heresy* begins.)

Son of Amunoph III. ☞

Fig. 55.

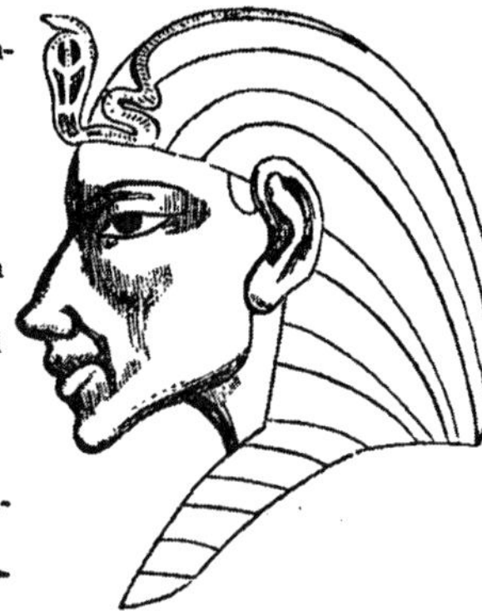

Amunoph IV. *Beχen-Aten.*[151]
(Anomalous features.)

At the close of the XVIIIth dynasty, and just before the inauguration of the XIXth, intervenes a period of anarchy, technically known to Egyptologists as the "Disk Heresy;" wherein the above extraordinary personage (Fig. 55) plays a not less extraordinary part. He turned the orthodox priests out of the sanctuaries—abolished the polytheistic orisons to Egypt's ancient gods—and introduced during his reign (followed for a short time by successors), the worship of the *sun's disk.* These events took place in Upper Egypt, during the fifteenth century B. C.; or some time before the birth of Moses, according to the emended Biblical chronology of Lepsius.

Fig. 56.
After anarchical times.

Horus.
(A lineal descendant from Thotmes III., whose *Semitic* ancestors he reproduces.)

And the XVIIIth *Dynasty ends in usurpations.*

XIXth Dynasty—*New Family*—Ramesides—about B. C. 1525.

Fig. 57.

Ramesu. *Ramses I.*
(Græco-Egyptian ?)

His son, a youth. ☛

Fig. 58.

Seti-Meneptha.[152]
(Mother unknown; but the *Semitic* caste reappears.)

Fig. 59.

Seti-MenEptha I.
(Not a good likeness ?)

Seti-Meneptha as king, but juvenile. ☚

Another portrait of the same at a mature age. ☛

Fig. 60.

Seti-Menептha I.
(More like his *youthful* style.)

Fig. 61.

Tsira.
(Entirely Jewish.)

The wife of Seti-Meneptha I. ☚

The son of Seti-Meneptha I. and Tsira. ☛

Fig. 62.

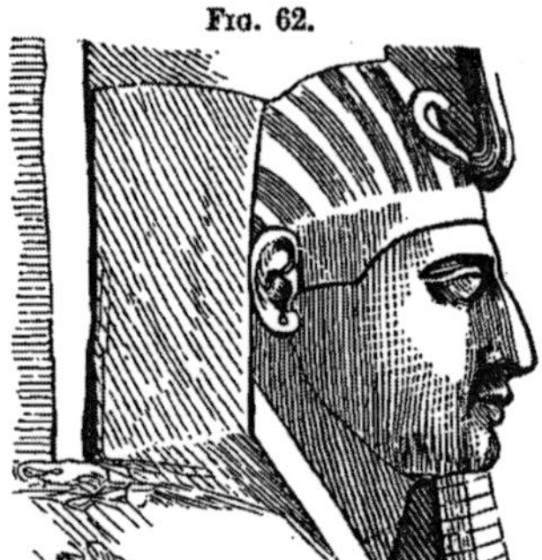

Ramses II., the *Great.*[153]
(His features are as superbly *European* as Napoleon's, whom he resembles.)

Fig. 63.

Nofre-Ari.
(Very high-caste lineaments.)

Wife of Ramses II. ☞

A daughter of Ramses II. by another wife. ☞

Fig. 64.

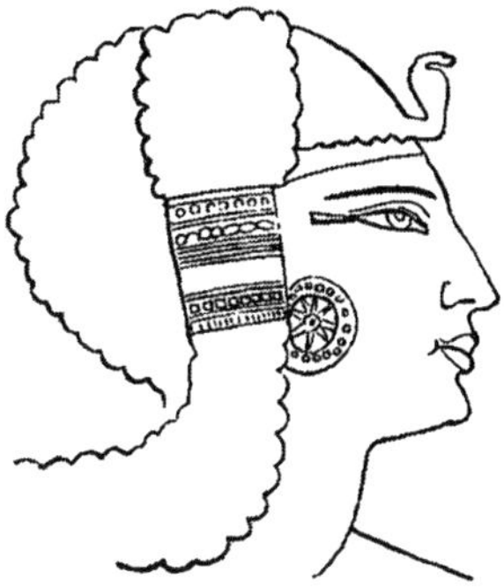

Bottante.
(Chiefly *Semitic.*)

Fig. 65.

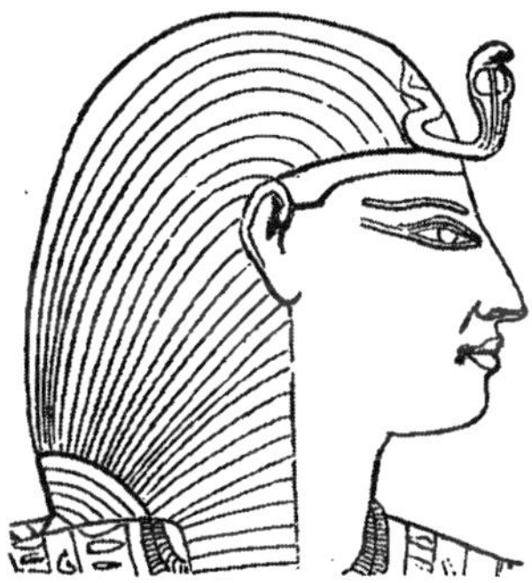

Menephtha II. *Menephthes.*
(Lepsius's Pharaoh of the *Exodus*.[154])
[*Egypto*-Semitic.]

13th son of Ramses II. ☞

After several Rameses, Uerri ascends the throne. ☞

Fig. 66.

Uerri. *Ramerri.*
(*Semitico*-Egyptian.)

And the XIXth dynasty ends about 1300 B. C.

We pass over the various portraits of the XXth and XXIst dynasties; because, where identified, the type is the same, except that it is in the *females* that we perceive the Asiatic caste of race most prominently; a fact of singular ethnographical import. We renew the illustrations at about 971–3 B. C., with the portrait of *Shishak*, conqueror of "Jerusalem," as recorded at Karnac; and "in the fifth year of Rehoboam," as chronicled by the Hebrew writers.

XXIId Dynasty—MANETHO'S "Bubastites;"

Proved by Mr. Birch to have *Assyrian* names; but the Pharaonic stock has now become so mixed, that it is difficult to determine whether the Hellenic, the Semitic, or the Egyptian preponderates.

FIG. 67.

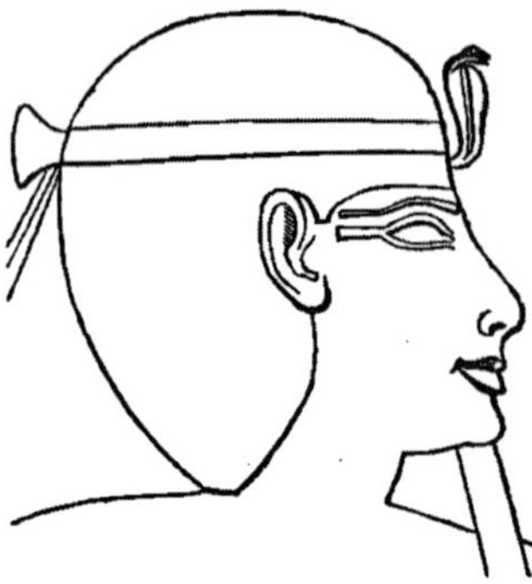

SHESHONK I.

FIG. 68.

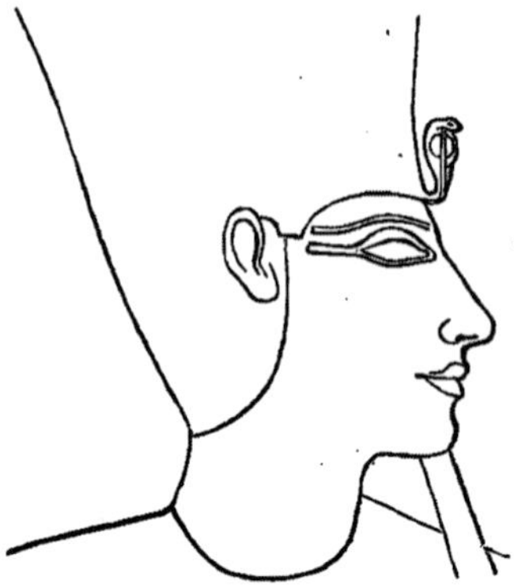

OSORKON III.

There are little or no remains of the XXIIId or XXIVth dynasties; but, in order to show that the so-called "Ethiopian" dynasty had no *Negro* blood in their veins, we subjoin their three portraits. Dr. Morton calls them "Austro-Egyptians;" and we opine that they may be derived from an Egyptian colony, crossed with *Old Beja* (Begawee), or perhaps with *Cushite*-Arabian blood.

XXVth Dynasty— B. C. 719 to 695.

FIG. 69.

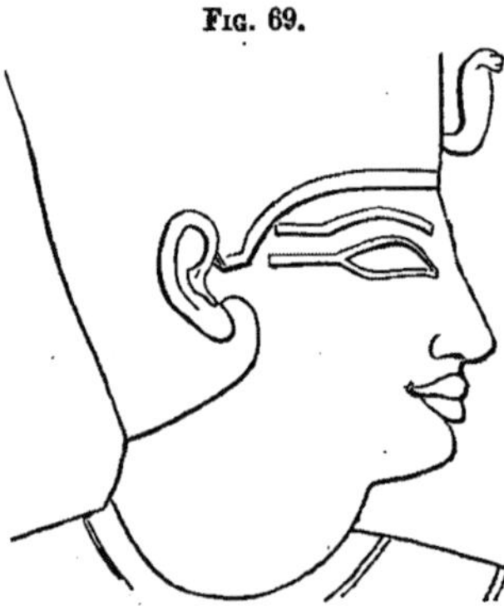

SHABAK-*Sabaco.*
(Meroite ?)

FIG. 70.

SHABATOK-*Sevechus.*
(Pharaoh *Sua.* 2 *Kings*, xvii. 4.)

FIG. 71.

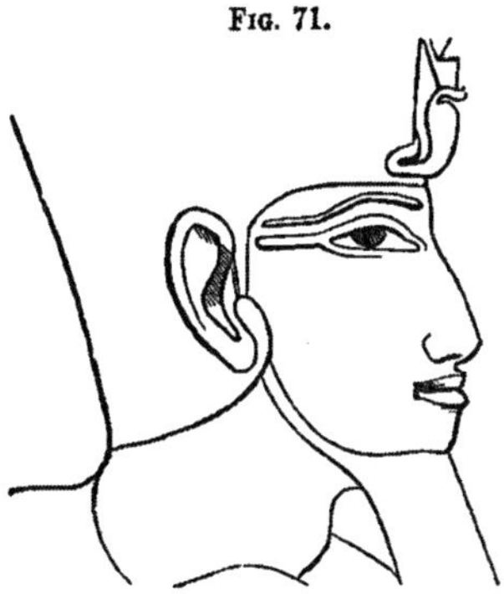

TAHRAKA-*Tirhaka.*
("Melek-KuSh." 2 *Kings*, xix. 9.)

It is unnecessary, for ethnological purposes, to continue the series of Egyptian portraits down to the Ptolemies, and ending with CLEOPATRA (already given, *Fig.* 8, page 104,) and her son by JULIUS CÆSAR, CÆSARION. The reader can behold the whole of them in Rosellini's magnificent folios. Having presented the royal likenesses, to serve as evidence of Egyptian artistic accuracy, we shall now investigate the *foreign nations* with whom the men, whose portraits we have just seen, were acquainted; together with such others as their ancestors had known during twenty centuries previously.

It will become apparent, in a succeeding chapter, that even as far back as the IVth dynasty, B. C. 3500, the population of Egypt already exhibited abundant instances of mixed types of African and Asiatic origins; at the same time that the language then spoken on the Lower Nile, and recorded in the earliest hieroglyphics, also presents evidence of these amalgamations. The series of Royal portraits just submitted not only demonstrates this commingling of races, but shows that Asiatic intruders had, at the foundation of the New Empire, to a great extent, supplanted, in the royal family at least, the indigenous Egyptians. Their foreign type is vividly impressed upon the iconographic monuments. So much do the Pharaonic portraits of the XVIIth, XVIIIth, and XIXth dynasties resemble those of the later Greek and Roman sovereigns, that the eye passes through the long series given by Rosellini without being arrested by any striking contrast between the former and the latter. Although the common people were also greatly mixed, the Egyptian type proper, nevertheless, among them, predominated over the Asiatic. Even admitting that the autocthonous Egyptian race was always, down to the Persian conquest, B. C. 525, the ruling one, yet the royal families of the Nile, as in other countries, become modified by marriages with alien races.

We know, through classical history, of numerous alliances between the Ethiopians and Egyptians. Solomon too, an Asiatic, married an Egyptian princess; and we have mentioned other instances of Jewish predilection for the women, no less than for the "flesh-pots, of Egypt."

Mr. Birch[155] has recently furnished some quite novel particulars concerning the matrimonial alliance of a Pharaoh of the XXth dynasty (probably Ramses XIV.) with an Asiatic princess of *Bukhitana;* to whom was given the title of "*Ra-neferu,* the king's chief wife." With regard to the exact locality in Asia of this country, although it might be *Ecbatana* in Media, Birch takes it to be the celebrated *Bashan* mentioned in Deuteronomy (iii. 1, &c.) This tablet, brought from the temple of Chons at Karnac, in 1844, by M. Prisse, is so intensely curious that we extract two of Birch's translations, adding interlineary explanations:—

"*Line* 5. 'Then the chief of Bukhitana [*Bashan?*] caused his tribute to be brought; he gave his eldest daughter [to the King of Egypt] . . . . in adoring his majesty, and in promising her to him: she being a very beautiful person, his majesty prized her above all things.'

"*Line* 6. 'Then was given her the title [?] of Ra-neferu, the king's chief wife, and when his majesty arrived in Egypt, she was made king's wife in all respects.'"

Here, then, is a positive example of the marriage of an Egyptian king with an *Asiatic* female, that entirely corroborates the intermixture of races we derived from the physical aspects of the royal portraits. Whether the hieroglyphic *Bashten*, or *Bakhtan*, be the Bashan of Palestine or Median Ecbatana, to ethnology the fact is the same; and probabilities favor, in either case, the lady's *Semitish* extraction. It is with regret that we cannot digress about the cure wrought upon this lady's sister, "Benteresh" [Hebraicè, *Daughter* of the *Resh*, chief, or king], who was "possessed by devils;" but her name, being Arabic no less than Hebrew, settles, philologically, her Semitic lineage.

It may be worthy of passing notice to the reader, that the conventional color by which the Egyptians always represented their own males was *red*, and their own females, *yellow;* and that, with few exceptions, other races were painted in such different colors as the artist deemed most conformable to their cuticular hues. Why were exceptions made? Was it because the Egyptians, in such instances, had formed marriage connections with some of these races, and ennobled them, therefore, with the *red* color? Our Figs. 41, 82, and 88, belonging to the fourteenth and fifteenth centuries B. C., are, in ROSELLINI, thus represented in *red;* showing, perhaps, that they were esteemed as equals,[156] or that they belonged to cognate Hamitic affiliations.

Let us now select for examination a few monumental heads of the various *foreign* races so faithfully portrayed. It will then be apparent that the same *diversity* has ever existed among the so-called *Caucasian* species, up to the very earliest monuments of above fifty centuries ago.

By way of general introduction to this vast subject, we present one group wherein *three* distinct *types* of mankind are grasped by a *fourth*.

FIG. 71. *bis*, [167]

Ramses II., in the fourteenth century B. C. (or during the early part of the lifetime of Moses), at the temple of Aboosimbel in Nubia, symbolizes his Asiatic and African conquests in a gorgeously-colored tableau. He, an *Egyptian*, brandishes a pole-axe over the the heads of *Negroes*, *Nubians* (Baràbera), and *Asiatics*, each painted in their true colors: viz., black, brick-dust, and yellow flesh-color; while, above his head, runs the hieroglyphic scroll, "The beneficent living god, guardian of glory, smites the *South;* puts to flight the *East;* rules by victory; and drags to his country all the earth, and all foreign lands." Ramses inclusive, here, to begin with, are *four* types of men — one mixed, two purely African, and one true Asiatic, co-existent at 1400 years B. C., or some 3350 years ago. Their geography extends from the confluence of the Blue and White Niles, beyond the northern limit of the tropical rains, in Negro-land; down the river to Egypt, and thence to the banks of the Euphrates. Precisely the same four types occupy the same countries at the present day.

We next proceed to examine the Asiatic class; but it should be remembered that we are about to trace retrogressively, into the very night of antiquity, various races—say, an indefinite point of time, more than 5000 years anterior to our age; and that languages, together with the names of people and of places, have so changed, that it is in these days impossible to identify, in several instances, either the nations or their habitats, except *en masse.* Often, the *type* alone, which has never altered, remains to guide us. It were irrational to be surprised at these difficulties. We must ever bear in mind the confusion of races and countries seen among the Hebrew, Greek, and Roman historians, and even in our geographies of much later ages. If *classical* topography be so often vague, that of the primeval hieroglyphics may well be still more so.

Most of our illustrations are taken from the great works of Rosellini and Lepsius; but we subjoin references to other hierological commentators.

Fig. 72.

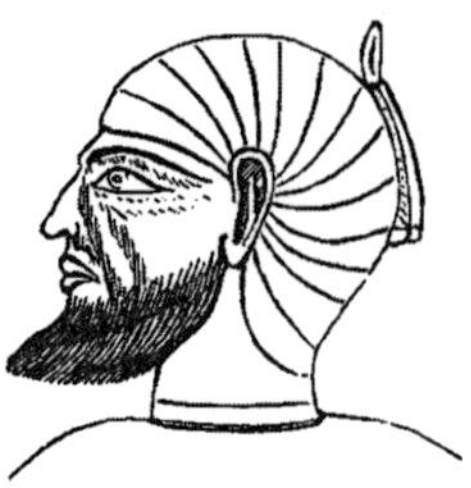

This head (Fig. 72), one of several similar, is taken from the Nubian temple of *Aboosimbel,* by Lepsius placed in the fourteenth century B. C. They appear on a tableau wherein Ramses II., during the fifth year of his reign, attacks a fortress in *Asia,* which, it is believed, belonged to a tribe of people called the *Romenen,* ReMeNeN, near the "land of Omar;"[158] probably mountaineers of the Tauric range, and, in any case, not remote from Mesopotamia.

The *Romenen* are a branch of the *Lodan-nou,* or "Ludìm," Lydians; by which general designation are known, on the monuments, divers *Asiatics* inhabiting Asia-Minor, Syria, Assyria, and adjacent countries; probably, Rosellini thinks, this side of the Euphrates: but we incline, with Morton, to consider that Fig. 72 "represents ancient *Scythians,* the easternmost Caucasian races; who, as history informs us, possessed fair complexions, blue eyes, and reddish hair." Contrasted with the other Asiatics, grouped in Fig. 71, it affords a very distinct type. The lower and most salient of the latter profiles presents, as Morton has duly noted, "a finely-marked Semitic head, in which the forehead, though receding, is remarkably voluminous and expressive."[159] An additional reason for supposing that Fig. 72 does not belong to Semitic races on the Euphrates, is the fact that it offers no resemblance to the true *Chaldæan,* or indigenous type, beheld on the royal monuments of Nineveh or Babylon; but may possibly be recognized among their prisoners of war or foreign nations.

FIG. 73.

Allowance made for difference between Egyptian and Assyrian art, coupled with the proviso that the Ninevite sculptors were by no means so precise in ethnic iconography as those of Egypt, we reproduce here a head (Fig. 73), from the sculptures of Khorsabâd, by way of comparison: noting the identity of the head-dress, which is a *leathern cap*. (*Vide infra*, page 128).

West of the Euphrates, more or less of the Jewish type prevailed. The heads, of which Fig. 72 is a specimen, represent a race which, some 1400 years B. C., was distinct from contemporaneous Mesopotamian families. People with yellowish skins, blue eyes, and reddish hair, are certainly not of Semitic extraction; and, judging from the physiognomy of this man and his associates, these were probably cognate Scythian tribes, inasmuch as they do not differ among themselves more than individuals of any Caucasian nation of our day. It is known that Scythic tribes settled in Syria, and even at *Scythopolis*, in Judæa; nor do we employ the term "Scythian" here in a sense more specific than as distinct from "Semitic" and from "Hamitic" populations.

OSBURN figures this head, classing it as one of the Canaanitish "Zuzim;" but we certainly should not regard blue eyes, red hair, eye-brows, and beard, as characteristic of Canaanites, nor of any other Hamitic families situate in this region of country, west of the Euphrates. The same author calls our Asiatic, FIG. 71 *bis*, a "Moabite of Rabbah," and describes him among the *Hittites;* but he likewise has classed our Fig. 93 as a Hittite; and we cannot imagine how heads so entirely different could be deemed identical by an ethnologist.

FIG. 74.[160]

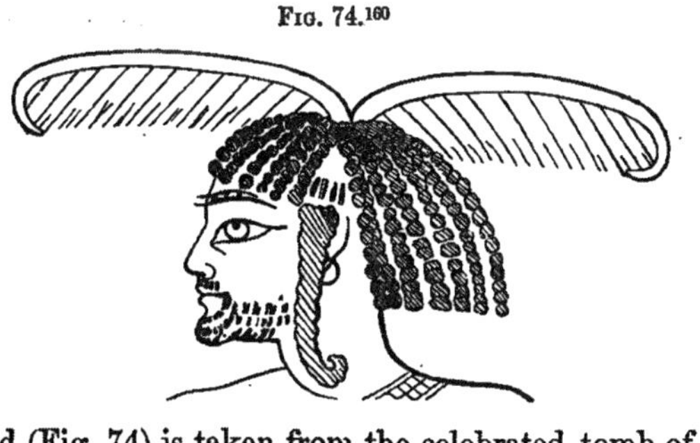

This head (Fig. 74) is taken from the celebrated tomb of SETI-ME-

FIG. 75.

NEPTHA I., of XIXth dynasty, about the fifteenth century B. C. We have already alluded, when speaking of classifications of races, to this scene, and illustrated it in Fig. 1. The god Horus is represented, conducting sixteen personages, in groups of four; each of which groups represents a distinct division of the human family; and these divisions include all the races known to the Egyptians. Our full length (Fig. 75) is a reduced copy of the same personage; but taken from the Prussian,[161] whereas the head (Fig. 74) is from the Tuscan work.

A similar scene occurs in the tomb of Ramses III. of the XXth dynasty, in which the same divisions are kept up; but the individuals selected differ in race from the preceding, though bearing a certain generic resemblance. As before stated, each Egyptian division, like our generic designations — Caucasian, Mongol, Negro, &c., contained many proximate types.

Although previously published in his colored folio plates by the indefatigable Belzoni, the ethnological importance of this tableau, in the sepulchre of SETI I., was not perceived until Champollion-le-Jeune visited Thebes in 1829; nor, indeed, to this day, has its quadripartite classification of mankind been adequately appreciated. Some writers have mistaken its import altogether; while none, that we know of, have deduced from it the natural consequence, that Egyptian ethnographers already knew of *four* types of mankind — *red*, *black*, *white*, and *yellow* — several centuries before the writer of Xth *Genesis;* who, omitting the *black* or Negro races altogether, was acquainted with no more than *three* — "Shem, Ham, and Japheth."

Champollion, with his consummate acuteness, at once pronounced this scene to represent

> "The inhabitants of the four quarters of the world, according to the ancient Egyptian system: viz., 1st, the inhabitants of Egypt; 2d, the Asiatics; 3d, the inhabitants of Africa, or the blacks; and 4th, the Europeans."

We merely object to the term "Europeans," instead of "*white* races;" because, in the fifteenth century B. C. there was no necessity for travelling out of Asia Minor in quest of *white* men; nor could the Egyptians, at that time, have possessed much knowledge of Europe.

To our eye, Fig. 74 marks a *type* of the *white* races in the fifteenth century B. C. The particular *nation* to which he belongs is the *Rebo* of hieroglyphics; probably the *Rhibii* of the classics.

Figure 76[162] is from another part of the tomb of SETI I., also dating about 1500 years B. C. This head, in Rosellini's colored plates, presents all the lineaments of a Himyarite Arab, except the *blue* eye; which, possibly, may be a mistake of the artist. "Himyàr" means *red*, and the Pisan copy is colored red. Upon reference, notwithstanding, to the great Prussian work,[163] wherein, it is to be assumed, the colors of the original paintings are reproduced with greater accuracy, this face is of a light *brown* complexion, with black eyes and beard. While, perhaps, it is not possible (considering the numerous transfers of copies between ancient originals in Egypt and their multiplied reproductions in modern plates,) always to avoid discrepancies, it will be remembered that the *crimson* or *scarlet* tints, adopted by the Egyptians for their own males, is purely conventional—that is, being impossible in real nature—so that, whether the skin be colored red or brown, the osteological structure of the features remains the same; and these are genuine *Arab*.

FIG. 76.

Morton remarks, in his MS. letter:—

"This is the very image of a Southern Arab, with his sharp features, dark skin, and certain national expression, admirably given in the drawing."

As such, his effigy furnishes another antique type of man.

This head (Fig. 77) (*vide supra* page 108, *fig.* 9,) has been already compared with the *Tochari* of Strabo and of the Ninevite sculptures. There is nothing to favor Osburn's theory, that this man and his maritime associates were *Philistines;* nor to oppose Morton's, that they exhibit *Celtic* features. We present it, without comment, as another evidence of the ancient diversity of "Caucasian types:" and with an indication of the incompatibility of this man's features with any tongue not a congener of that class bearing the name of "Indo-European." He cannot, therefore, be a *Philistine*.

FIG. 77.

From the prisoners of RAMSES III., of the XXth dynasty, thirteenth century B. C., we take Fig. 78: sculptured on the base of his pavilion at Medeenet-Haboo.[164] A fracture in the wall has obliterated the hieroglyphics, so that there is no name for him; but adjacent to him are prisoners of the *Tokkari* or *Tochari*. He may be a mountaineer

Fig. 78.

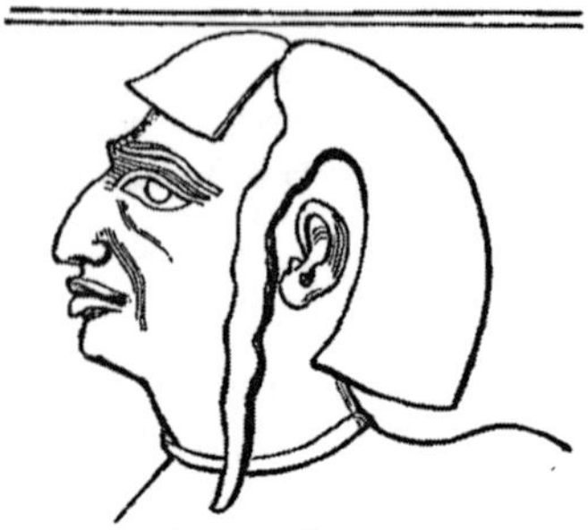

Ancient Asiatic.

Fig. 79.

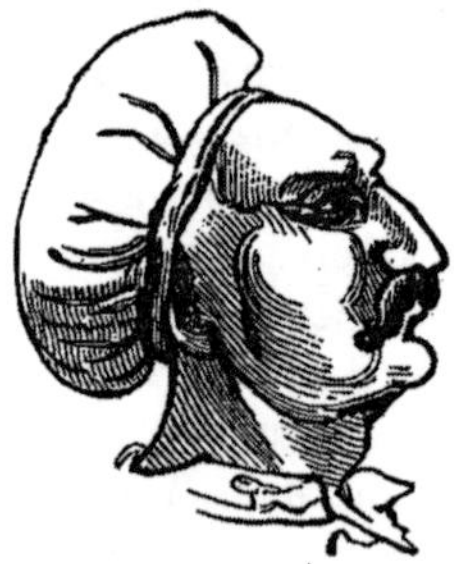

Modern Kurd.

of the Taurus chain; because he bears a strong resemblance to modern Kurdish families; seen by comparing this profile with the head of a *Kurd* (Fig. 79), from the work of Hamilton Smith. To our minds, here is a strong example of *permanence of type* through 3000 years; whilst the name "Kurdah," *Kurds*, is read in ancient cuneiform, by De Saulcy, upon Assyrian inscriptions.

Asiatic conquests of Ramses II. yield us Fig. 80; within the fourteenth century B. C., preserved at Bèyt-el-Wàlee.[165] Mr. Birch's detailed account of this important historical document is accompanied by colored drawings, in which the victories of that monarch over various Asiatic and African races are represented with amazing truthfulness and spirit. The head itself possesses a Semitic caste, blended, perhaps, with Arian elements.

Fig. 80.

Fig. 81.

Another captive (Fig. 81) from the Asiatic conquests of Ramses III.

at Medeenet-Haboo.[166] Wilkinson reads the name "Lemanon," identical with *Lebanon;* which is probable, inasmuch as Birch agrees; whilst Osburn, by reading *Hermonites,* fixes their locality at Mount Hermon, anti-Libanus, in the north-east of Palestine. This characteristic specimen is essentially Semitic, of the Syrian form.

FIG. 82.

Fig. 82 belongs to the "Grand Procession" of the age of THOTMES III., of the XVIIth dynasty, 1600 B. C.[167] No head in our whole catalogue has, perhaps, caused as much archæological debate; nor is our knowledge of his race and country as yet satisfactory.

Rosellini figures this head without comment. Champollion Figeac copies it, but his explanations lead to no tangible result. Hoskins has beautifully colored the whole file (sixteen persons in number) of these tributary people, regarding them as natives of *Meroë*, in Ethiopia; but subsequent researches, by Lepsius and others, render such estimate of Meroite antiquity radically wrong. We now know that, in the time of Thotmes III., the only civilized points in Nubia were those occupied by *Egyptian* garrisons. The Meroë of Greek annalists did not then exist.

Wilkinson accurately designs the whole scene, but without colors; thereby rendering it less clear, in an anthropological point of view; but his hieroglyphics are more exact, and he observes:—"The people, *Kufa* (which is their name), appear to have inhabited a part of *Asia*, lying considerably to the north of the latitude of Palestine; and their long hair, rich dresses, and sandals of the most varied form and color, render them remarkable among the nations represented in Egyptian sculpture." Birch calls them "the people of *Kaf* or *Kfou*, an Asiatic race;" placing them near Mesopotamia. Prisse denominates them, "le peuple de *Koufa* (race Asiatique, peinte en rouge)."

From the foregoing we may conclude — 1st, that these *Koufa* were *Asiatics;* 2d, that they resided near Mesopotamia; 3d, that, as they are painted *red* on the monuments, they presented certain affinities with the Egyptians, confirmed by the physiological characteristics of the latter race observed by Morton—"shortness of the lower jaw and chin;" and 4th, that, if they be *Cushites*, they are of the Hamitic stem. They are probably of the KUS*h*-ite families of Arabia, cognate to the Egyptians (perhaps allied by royal marriages), who in consequence honored them with the *red* color. Inasmuch as they bring a tribute of *golden* vessels, they may have had access to the Arabian *Ophir;* and as they carry *elephants' teeth*, they had communication with the Indies, or with Africa. Judging from their portraits, they certainly belonged not to any of the Abrahamic or Chaldæan tribes. They bear, furthermore, considerable resemblance to those primeval heads we shall exhibit in a succeeding chapter as illustrative of the type of the founders of the Egyptian empire; and slightly also to the later Egyptian type (*Rot*), as represented by Theban artists in their quadruple classification of races. These *Koufa* may possibly have been the descendants of an Egyptian colony, near the Persian Gulf: like that of Colchis, if we can trust Herodotus, in Asia Minor.

FIG. 83.

This figure is from the conquests of Seti-Meneptha I., fifteenth century B. C., at the temple of Karnac.[168] The people come under the generic class of *White* races; and their tribe is called *Tohen*, by Rosellini. The same head, in one of the tombs, appears as the type of White races in the quadrupartite division of which we have already spoken. Birch calls them *Tohen*, *Tahno*, or *Ten-hno* — "evidently belonging to the white blood, or Japhetic family of mankind." Morton, in his MS. letter, writes, "they present Pelasgic features; but the blue eye, reddish hair, and harsh expression, are not unlike the Scythian race." The Egyptians seem to have entertained towards them an excess of hatred, and to have slaughtered them with more fury than any other people. But we leave their exact race and country an open question, although their *Caucasian* features cannot be mistaken.

FIG. 84.

We have compared this (Fig. 84) and the next (Fig. 85) with the Jewish type (*vide supra*, p. 140). Rosellini gives no explanations. Supposed, by Champollion, to be *Lydians* — their name reading *Ludannu*, or *Rot-n-no*. This head belongs to the same Grand Procession of Thotmes III., so effectively colored in Hoskins; but we have copied Rosellini's outline, as more correct.[169] Hoskins again perceives "white slaves" of the king of his *Ethiopia!* Osburn terms them *Arvadites;* but Birch, refuting both opinions, puts these people down as *Cappadocians*, or Leuco-Syrians; which seems more rational, did not an *elephant's* tooth suggest some geographical obstacle. The man leads an animal—disputed, whether it is a *bear* or *lion*, the drawing being so very defective. He also carries an elephant's tusk. Morton figures this head as Indo-Semitic, or Indo-Persian; and all attending circumstances assign him a habitation between Persia and the Upper Indus.

FIG. 85.

Another from the same scene as the preceding figure.[170] He wears a light dress and straw hat, and leads an elephant: conditions indicative of a southern climate. Morton observes—"This is a yet more striking *Hindoo*, in whom the dark skin, black eye, delicate features, and fine facial angle, are all admirably marked. The presence of the elephant assists us in designating the national stock, while the straw hat sends us to the Ganges"—or, much nearer, to the Indus?

Peculiar interest attaches to both of the above effigies; the latter of which enables us to carry the existence of a *Hindoo* national type back to the sixteenth century B. C. Although no written Hindostanic monuments are extant of an age coetaneous with even the sixth century prior to our era, native traditions, zoological analogies, and admissions of the more sceptical Indologists, justify our considering the *Hindoos* to have inhabited their vast peninsula as early as the Egyptians did the shores of their Nile, or any other type of men its original centre of creation, whether in Asia, Africa, Europe, America, or Oceanica.

We now come to that Egyptian tableau the most frequently alluded to, and which has prompted much nonsensical, if pious, discussion.

FIG. 86.

The head (Fig. 86) is one of the "*Brickmakers*," from the tomb of an architect—"Prefect of the country, Intendant of the great habitations, ROKSHERE"—of the time of Thotmes III., XVIIth dynasty, sixteenth century B. C.[171] We copy from Rosellini, who thought them *Israelites;* but, according to the chronology of Lepsius, they antedate JACOB; though they may be a cognate race—perhaps some of his ancestry. Wilkinson honestly observes:—

"To meet with *Hebrews* in the sculptures cannot reasonably be expected, since the remains in that part of Egypt where they lived have not been preserved; but it is curious to discover *other foreign captives* occupied in the same manner, overlooked by similar 'task-masters,' and performing the very same labors as the Israelites described in the Bible."

The same author again insists —

"They are not, however, Jews, as some have erroneously supposed, and as I have elsewhere shown."

Notwithstanding the palpable anachronism and contradicting figurative circumstances, certain evangelical theologers have wasted much crocodilean grief over these unfortunate and oppressed, however apochryphal, Israelites; forgetting, in their exceeding-great-thankfulness over a wondrous "confirmation," to weep for the *Egyptian* brickmakers, who toil in the same scene.

The following items may assist the reader in forming an independent opinion: —

1st. The hieroglyphics do not mention the name or country of these brickmakers.

2d. The scene is not an *historical record;* but a pictorial illustration of brick-making, among other constructive arts that embellished the tomb of an architect, at *Thebes* — that is, 500 miles from "Goshen."

3d. The people wear no *beards* — their little chin-sprouts are but the usual unshaven state of Egyptian laborers, no less than of peasantry everywhere.

4th. They are a Semitic people — possibly, with their beards cut off in Egyptian slavery; but whether Canaanites, Hebrews, Arabs, Chaldæans, or others, cannot be determined.

5th. There is not the slightest *monumental evidence* that the *Jews* (in the manner described by the writers of Genesis and Exodus) were ever in Egypt at all! Their *type*, however, had existed there, 2000 years before Abraham's birth.

6th. These brickmakers are not more Jewish, in their lineaments, than Egyptian Fellàhs of Lower Egypt at the present day, where the Arab cross is strong. Indeed, they greatly resemble the living mixed race, who now make Nilotic bricks, every day, at Cairo, exactly as these brickmakers did 3500 years ago, and think nothing of it.

Finally — if these brickmakers are claimed to be *Israelites*, we can have no objection, because their effigies will corroborate the permanence of the Jewish type for 3500 years: if they be not, to us they answer just as well—being tacit witnesses of the durability of Semitic features in particular, no less than proofs of one more form of ancient Caucasian types in general.

The next head (Fig. 87), we now submit, is really out of place among our *Caucasian* group; but, from the man's associations, he may have a position here. We are induced to portray his singular type for another reason: viz., that, being represented in the same picture with foreign allies, as well as with native Egyptian soldiers, it serves to

FIG. 87.

illustrate the correctness of Egyptian outline drawing, and also the minute knowledge their artists had of various types of mankind at that early day. The people of whom this is a sample have been reputed by many to be ancient *Chinese*. There are much better reasons for believing them to be *Tartar* tribes; which form the geographical link between Mongols and Caucasians—aboriginal consanguinity with either excluded.

Morton took this head for *Mongolian;* and too hastily adopted ancient Egypto-Chinese connexions, on the faith of certain pseudo-antique Chinese "vases;" which, not manufactured prior to A. D. 1100, could not have been found in Theban tombs shut up 2000 years before.

Under the heading of "Alphabetical Origins," our *Supplement* establishes that the Chinese, before the Christian era, possessed no knowledge whatever of nations whose habitats lay north and west of Persia. The splendid tableau from which the above ethnographic record is taken, contains many heads of the same type—some of which are shaven, except the *scalp-lock* on the crown; while others, though adorned with the thin moustache, wear the hair long and untouched by scissors. Now, it can be seen, by reference to Pauthier, that the *Mantchou-Tartars*, in A. D. 1621–'27, forced the Chinese to shave their heads, and wear the pig-tail. Previously, the Chinamen had worn their hair long. This scalp-lock (called *Shoosheh*, by the Arabs), therefore, is a Tartar custom; and inasmuch as in the reign of Ramses II., fourteenth century B. C., China and Chinese were equally unknown to the Egyptians, Jews, or Assyrians, we must suppose that these fair, oblique-eyed, and scalp-locked enemies of Ramses, were *Tartars*, or a branch of the great easterly Scythian hordes.[172]

Osburn repeats this scene, calling the people *Sheti*, whilst striving to restrict their habitat to Canaan, in which he signally fails. Birch's more consistent geography carries them to the Caspian, where Tartars would naturally be found; to which critical induction we may add the recent opinions of Rawlinson, De Saulcy, Hincks, and Löwenstern, that the Tartar, or "Scythic," element in cuneatic inscriptions, especially of the Achæmeno-*Median* style, establishes the proximity of Turkish (call them Tartar or Scythic, for the terms are still vague) tribes to Persia at a much earlier period than ethnologists had heretofore suspected.

As such, this effigy (Fig. 87) exemplifies the remotest Asiatic people depicted on Pharaonic monuments, in days parallel with Moses, during the fourteenth century B. C.

Ramses II., at Beyt-el-Wâlee—fourteenth century B. C.—grasps the subjoined foreigner (Fig. 88) by the hair of his head. Considered, by Rosellini, to be typical of the "Tohen," a people of Syria: whereas Morton deemed him a "Himyar-ite-Arab."[173] We have naught to oppose; and may add, that his red (*Himyàr*) color affiliates him with the Arabian KUS*h*-ites.

FIG. 88.

FIG. 89.

As the type of *Yellow* races, (Fig. 89) stands in the tomb of Ramses III., XXth dynasty, about thirteen centuries B. C.[174] Nothing is certain respecting the history of the people he represents; but Osburn perhaps is right in calling him an ancient *Tyrian:* everything—features, *purple* dress, &c.—harmonizes with this view, adopted by us in a preceding chapter. (*Infra*, p. 136.)

FIG. 90.

An identical type, possibly from another Phœnician colony, is met with about 150 years earlier. From the Theban tomb at Qoornet Murraï, of the time of AMUNTUONCH (*Amenanchut* of Birch), we select (Fig. 90) one instance of the many, to illustrate physiological similitudes,[175] that time has not extinguished, along the present coasts of Palestine, in the fishermen of Sour and Sèyda (Tyre and Sidon), even to this day.

This great Asiatic chief (Fig. 91) is killed, in single combat, by Ramses II.; the colored original being drawn on a magnificent tableau, at Aboosimbel.[176] Rosellini makes him one of the Scythian "Tohen," beyond the Euphrates; and Morton deems him "Pelasgic." His features depart essentially from the Semitic cast; and the face offers the earliest instance wherein Egyptian art has figured the *eye closed.*

Fig. 91.

In this instance, as in many others, our copy is *reversed;* but such inadvertencies do not affect ethnographic precision.

Fig. 92.

We detach Fig. 92 from the bas-reliefs of Ramses III., XXth dynasty, at Medeenet Haboo; where he is called "Captive prince of the perverse race of the inimical country of *Sheto*, living in captivity."[177] Morton, very naturally, holds him to be a "variety of the Semitic stock;" and *Sheto*, if read *Kheto*, signifies a Hittite; using the Biblical term K*h*eT*t* in its widest acceptation.

Fig. 93.

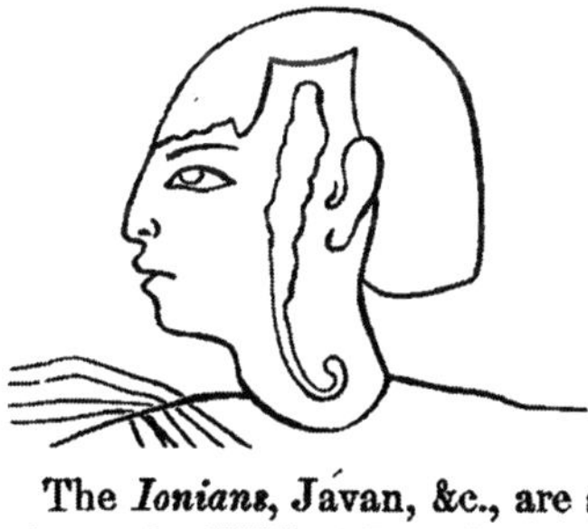

As the type of *White* races, Fig. 93 appears in one of the Theban tombs; and, name unknown, is conjectured, by Rosellini, to be "an ancient example of the Greeks of Asia Minor, and especially of *Ionians.* To strengthen this conjecture, I recall how among the monuments of Thotmes V. [IV.], and of Meneptha I., mention is made of this people."[178]

The *Ionians*, Jávan, &c., are sufficiently discussed in our Part II., where the IUN of Xth Genesis is analyzed; but "Yavan," and the "people of Yavan," as Grecian tribes of the seventh century B. C., occur repeatedly upon the monuments of Nineveh. Morton takes him to be "Pelasgic." In his MS. letter, he adds:—

"This head presents us with the true Hellenic line of nose and forehead; for, although the latter is more receding than we continually see in the Greek heads, it forms an uninterrupted line with the nose. The black hair is in unison with the other traits; but the red tint of the eye [perhaps an error of artist?] is not so readily accounted for. The facial angle, moreover, in this head, is little short of a right-angle."

FIG. 94.

For the sake of comparison, we first give Lepsius's copy of the enlarged head (Fig. 94) of the standard type of *Yellow* races, from the quadripartite division in Seti's tomb, described in a former place. Beneath it, (Fig. 95) is a reduction of one of the same four persons at full length. Opposite, we put Rosellini's copy (Fig. 96), for the express purpose of indicating an error in the *Tuscan* work which the Prussian has removed: referring to our note[179] for explanations.

FIG. 95.

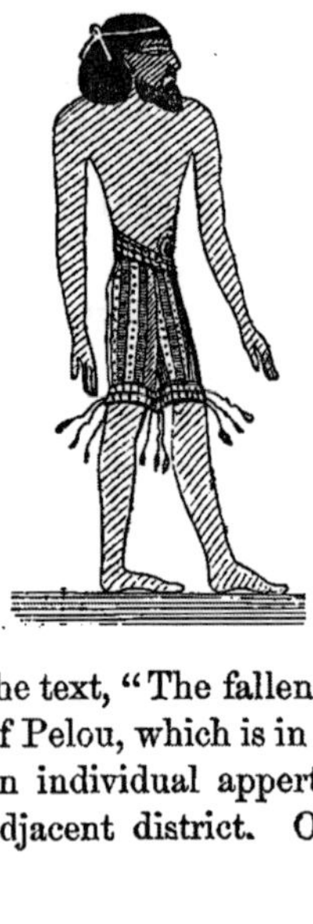

FIG. 96.

Numerous are the comrades of Fig. 97 in the conquests of Ramses II., at Bèyt-el-Wàlee, XIXth dynasty, fourteenth century B. C. Birch considers them tribes of *Canaan;* because, at Karnac, the same people are called, in the text, "The fallen of the *Shos-sou*, in their elevation on the fortress of Pelou, which is in the land of *Kanana*."[180] And the next (Fig. 98) is an individual appertaining to another set of prisoners, from some adjacent district. Osburn figures them as *Jebusites;* to which we

FIG. 97.

FIG. 98.

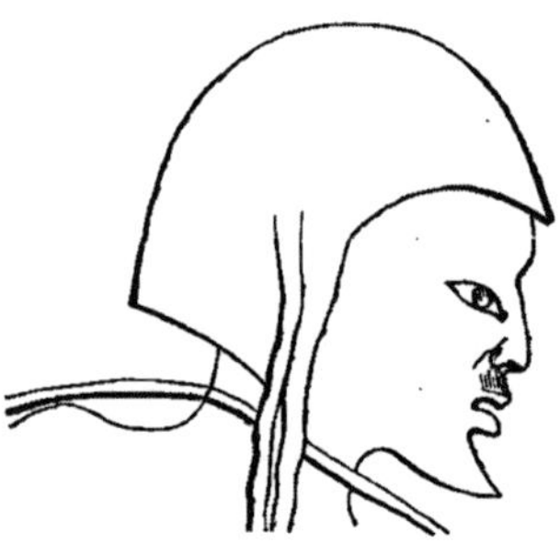

offer no objection; and thus we should behold one of the inhabitants of ante-Judaic Jerusalem, IeBUS or *Jebus*: before its capture by JOSHUA, and long prior to the expulsion of the *Jebusian* from Mount Zion by the prowess of DAVID.

FIG. 99.

FIG. 100.

Both the head and the full-length figure, here presented, illustrate four personages identical in all respects.[181]

They are the type of the *Yellow* races, in one of the tombs coeval with Mosaic times. Rosellini, who wrote before the Persian and the Ninevite arrow-heads were deciphered, suggested their resemblance to the sculptures of Assyria and Persepolis. They portray, certainly, strong Chaldæan affinities, cognate with the Hebrew race; and their elegant green dresses, embroidered with skilful taste, show a very polished people. Osburn figures them as *Hamathites*—citizens of *Hamah*, between Damascus and Aleppo, ever renowned for their beautiful manufactures, brocades, shawls; together with those richly-colored silk-and-cotton goods, now dear to Levantine merchants as "Allàgias;" nor does his view militate against ours. Champollion-Figeac gives this effigy, with the conjecture of his brother that they are *Medes*, corresponding to Persepolitan relievos. Chaldæa seems to be the centre-point of all these authorities; and we have classified, elsewhere, this head among Jewish tribes.

Belonging to the same sculptures of the thirteenth to fifteenth centuries B. C., and located geographically in the same Syrian provinces, we group together *six* more specimens of varieties of this all-pervading Semitic type. Representatives of ancient Sidonians, Aradians, and so forth, along the coast of Syria, and on the spurs of Lebanon, each one still lives in thousands of descendants, who now throng the Bazàars of Sèyda, Beyroot, Tripoli, Latachia, Antioch and Aleppo. Substitute the turban for the military casque and civic cap; and, in the same localities, still speaking dialects of the same

Semitish tongues, you will recognize in the "*Shawàm*," people of *Shàm*, or Syria (*Sh*eMites), — as the Arabs still designate the *Damascenes* technically, and the *Syrians* generally — the very men whose ancestral images were chiselled by Diospolitan artists not less than 3200 years agone.

Fig. 101.[182]

Fig. 102.[183]

Fig. 103.[184]

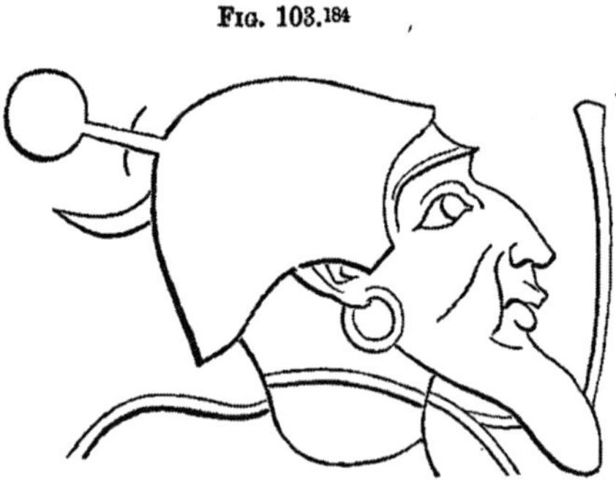

Fig. 104.[185]

Fig. 105.[186]

Fig. 106.[187]

Here let us pause. Thirty varieties, more or less, of the *Caucasian* type, solely among ancient foreigners to Egypt, have now been submitted to the reader. They have been taken, almost at random, from the *Monumenti* of Rosellini, with occasional reference to the *Denkmäler* of Lepsius: and their epochas range between the thirteenth and the seventeenth centuries B. C.; a period of about 400 years, including, moreover, whatever era is assignable to Moses. There is *diversity* enough among them to satisfy the most exacting, that men, in the same times and countries, were just as distinctly marked as they are now in the Levant, after some 3300 years; and hence, again, it follows that, in the same lands, time has produced no change, save through amalgamation; because, in the streets of Cairo, Jerusalem, Damascus, Beyroot, Aleppo, Antioch, Mosul, and Bagdad, every one of these varieties strikes your vision daily.

Mark, too, that the whole of these diversified Oriental families occupied a very limited geographical area; viz.: from the river Nile eastward to the Tauric range of mountains; at most, to the western borders of the Euxine and Caspian Seas, and across from the Mediterranean to the Persian Gulf—the Indus, perhaps, inclusive. This superficies constitutes but a petty segment of the earth. Neither have we yet looked beyond such narrow horizon, whether for Mongols, Malays, Polynesians, Australians, Americans, Esquimaux; nor for Finnish, Scandinavian, endless European, Uralian, and other races, with the above types necessarily coexistent, although to old Pharaonic ethnography utterly unknown! Observe likewise, that, Egypt deducted, Africa and her multifarious types are yet untouched.

How, we feel now emboldened to ask, have the defenders of the *Unity*-doctrine met the above facts? The answer is simple. By suppressing every one of them.

Dr. Prichard published the third edition of the IId volume of his *Researches into the Physical History of Mankind*, in 1837, at the vast metropolis of London, surrounded with facilities unparalleled. He devotes fifty-nine pages to the "Egyptians;"[188] yet, beyond a passing sneer at Champollion-le-Jeune,[189] whose stupendous labors were then endorsed by the highest continental scholars—De Sacy, Humboldt, Arago, Bunsen, &c.—he never quotes a single hierologist! Now-a-days, every archæologist knows that three-fourths of those very writers whom Prichard does cite on *Egypt* have been consigned to the "tomb of the Capulets." Now, in 1837, Rosellini's *Plates* and *Text*, comprehending almost every pictorial fact by us brought forward, had been published—in great part, for above four years, commencing in 1832–3. Common enough was the Tuscan work in London, to say naught of Paris, close at hand. How could Prichard ignore the existence also of these identical subjects in CHAMPOLLION's folio *Monuments d'Egypte?* But, worse than that, viewing the question merely as one of scientific knowledge and good faith, Prichard continued to publish, volume III. in 1841; volume IV. in 1844; and volume V. in 1847. The world seems exhausted to prove his unitary-hypothesis. He never reverts to *Egyptian* archæology, nor reveals one iota of all these splendid discoveries. Why? Because they flatly contradict him, and the antiquated school of which he was the steel-clad war-horse.

Who forced Prichard, at last, either to accept hieroglyphical discoveries in some of their bearings upon the Natural History of Man, or to become placed, so to say, without the pale of scientific anthropology?

Our countryman, Morton,—a student who, deprived of every facility in Egyptian matters until 1842, printed, in 1844, his "*Crania Ægyptiaca,* or Observations on Egyptian Ethnography, derived from Anatomy, History, and the Monuments;" and thereby founded the true principle of philosophical inquiry into human origins.

Prichard (in justice to his memory let us speak,) acknowledged Morton's work in the handsomest manner,[190] although not in the "Researches." But, how came it that Prichard should have allowed an American savan (cut off by the Atlantic from all his own unbounded facilities,) to anticipate him? In truth, only because Egyptian archæology had shattered Prichard's *unity*-doctrine from the weather-vane to its foundations.

Having disposed thus of their champion, weaker sustainers of "unity" who have pinned their creed on his obstinacy, adding their own blindness to his cecity, may be passed over, without distressing the reader by recapitulation of shallow arguments and unphilosophical crudities. Numbers of their books lie on our shelves undusted, because there is not a monumental *fact* to be culled from the whole of them. Nor shall we do more than allude to the opinions of the learned MURE,[191] or of the erudite, though mystical, HENRY,[192] who endeavored to confine all these Asiatic wars of the Pharaohs to the valley of the Nile; because, as neither scholar could read a *hieroglyphic,* they debated upon that which they did not understand; and, in consequence, uttered views that are now entirely superseded by later Egyptologists, to whose pages we make a point of referring those who may choose to criticise the bibliographical ground-work of "Types of Mankind."

But we have not finished with the monuments.

M. PRISSE's copy of the heterodox king, *Atenra-Bakhan* (*Beχ-en-Aten*), now proved to be AMUNOPH IV., need not here be repeated. Its reduced fac-simile may be consulted (*supra,* page 147); while every reference required is thrown into a note:[193] and, inasmuch as one of the writers (G. R. G.) was present at the temple of Karnac, 1839–40, when the original stone was found, and the design made, we can vouch for the accuracy of Prisse's copy of this unique bas-relief. We mention this, because it differs, though not materially, from the later reproductions of the same portrait in Lepsius's *Denkmäler*:[194] a divergence accounted for by the fact that the French original lay at Thebes, whereas the Prussians copied others at *Tel-el-Amarna*, 200 miles off: nor is it to be expected that ancient Egyptian portrait-sculptors could multiply likenesses of a man more uniformly similar among themselves, than can our own artists, or even *daguerréotypists*, at the present day. In proof of how artists differ, we here

FIG. 107.

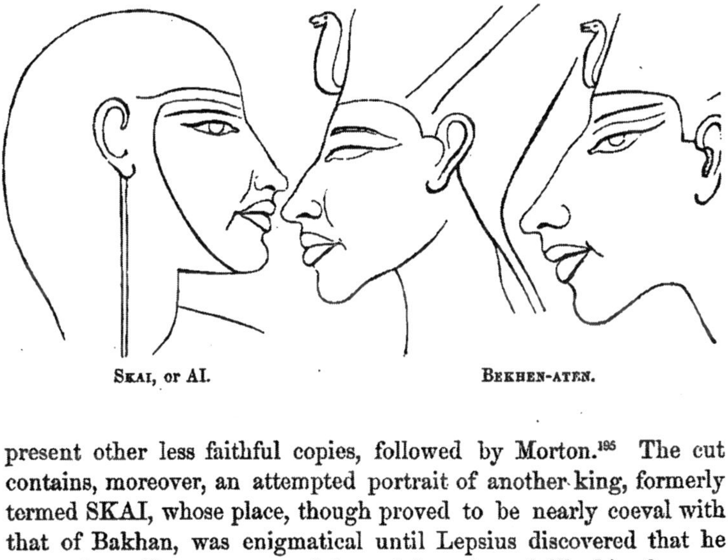

SKAI, or AI. BEKHEN-ATEN.

present other less faithful copies, followed by Morton.[195] The cut contains, moreover, an attempted portrait of another king, formerly termed SKAI, whose place, though proved to be nearly coeval with that of Bakhan, was enigmatical until Lepsius discovered that he was an immediate successor of the arch-heretic, and, like him, became effaced from the monuments when Amun's priests regained the upper hand.[196]

"This king, AI, was formerly a private individual, and took his sacerdotal title into his cartouche at a later period. He appears with his wife in the tombs of Amarna, not unfrequently as a noble and peculiarly-honored officer of king Amunoph IV.; that puritanical sun-worshipper, who changed his name into that of 'Bech-en-Aten'"—*i. e. Adorer of the sun's disk.*

In Rosellini's copy,[197] the features of this king AI are atrocious. Lepsius has since pronounced *Beχ-en-aten* to be Amunoph IV., son of Amunoph-*Memnon.* Ethnologically, his strange countenance attests very mixed blood; but nothing of the Negro in either parent. His face is Asiatic, typifying no especial race; but it is one of those accidental deviations from regularity that anatomists are familiar with, especially among mongrel breeds. We have seen in our Pharaonic gallery that Amunoph III. (Fig. 53) himself was not of pure Egyptian stock.

We now take a long and portentous stride in Egyptian history; viz.: from the XVIIth back to the XIIth dynasty, a period obscure for about four centuries. The country during this hiatus seems to have been greatly disturbed by wars, conquests, by *Hyksos*-migrations of population, and other agitating causes; and hence arises the lack of monuments to guide our investigations. In ethnographical materials, especially, there is almost an entire blank. But with the XIIth dynasty, one of the most effulgent periods of Egyptian history bursts upon us; and we can again, with ample documents, take up our Caucasian type, and pursue it upwards along the stream of time.

According to Lepsius, the XIIth dynasty closed about the year 2124 B. C. If we add to this the summation for the *eight* kings, given in the Turin Papyrus, of "213 years, 1 month, and 15 days,"[198] this dynasty commenced about the year 2337 B. C.; which is only some *eleven* years after Usher's date for the Deluge, when most good Christians imagine that but *eight* adults, four men and four women (with a few children), were in existence! The monuments of this dynasty afford abundant evidence not only of the existence of Egypto-Caucasian races, but of Asiatic nations, as well as of *Negroes* and other African groups, at the said diluvian era.

FIG. 108.

"*Thirty-seven Prisoners*" of Beni-Hassan.

FIG. 109.

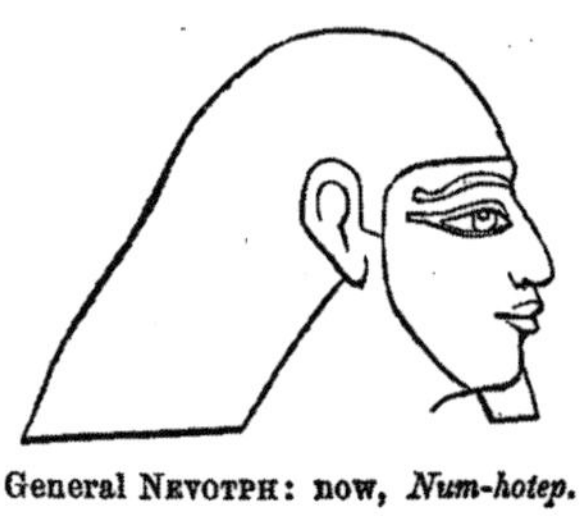

General NEVOTPH: now, *Num-hotep.*

Let us dispose first of Fig. 110. It is one of three recently published by Lepsius; characterized by *red* hair, and distinct from No.

108, whose hair is black. We refer to the *Denkmäler*[199] for their colored portraits, adding Lepsius's comments below.

Fig. 110.

Asiatic, from Beni-Hassan.

The head (Fig. 108)[200] on the preceding page, from the celebrated tombs of Beni-Hassan, so often alluded to by Egyptologists, represents one of a group of personages, generally known as the "*thirty-seven prisoners of Beni-Hassan.*" The scene has been repeatedly and variously explained, by Champollion, Rosellini, Wilkinson, Champollion-Figeac, Birch, and Osburn—leaving aside the trashy speculations of mere tourists; for, as usual, there have been printed many extravagant theories as to the country and condition of these "thirty-seven prisoners." They were, indeed, supposed, by orthodox credulity, to represent the visit of Abraham to Egypt, or else the arrival of Jacob and his family. More critical authorities have beheld in them Israelitish wanderers, Ionian Greeks, Hyksos, and what not. But, alas! all Jewish partialities received a death-blow when it was proved, through the discovery of the XIIth dynasty, that this tableau had been painted at Beni-Hassan several generations before Abraham's birth! The first rational account, in English, of this scene was put forth by Mr. Birch, in 1847. He says:—

"An officer of USR-T-SEN I., as recorded in his tomb at Benihassan, received in the sixth regnal year of that monarch, by royal command, a convoy of thirty-nine (37) *Mes-segem*, foreigners, headed by their *hyk*, or leader, AB-SHA. These were of the great Semitic family, called, by the Egyptians, "*Aamu.*"[201]

This lection he confirms in 1852—

"The *Mes-stem* foreigners, who approach the nomarch Neferhetp, come through the Arabian Desert on asses."[202]

Lepsius had described the impressions made upon him, at first sight of this unique series:—

"In these remarks, I am thinking especially of that very remarkable scene, on the grave of *Neheru-se*-NUMHETEP, which brings before our eyes, in such lively colors, the entrance of Jacob with his family, and would tempt us to identify it with that event, *if chronology would allow us*, (for Jacob came under the Hyksos [*i. e.*, centuries later]), and *if we were not compelled to believe that such family immigrations were by no means of rare occurrence.* These were, however, the forerunners of the Hyksos [and of the Israelites], and doubtless, in many ways, paved the way for them."[203]

From the excellent translation of Lepsius's *Briefe* by Mr. Kenneth B. H. Mackensie,[204] we extract the following particulars, referring at the same time to the Prussian *Denkmäler*[205] for exquisite plates of these splendid sepulchres:—

"It must then have been a proud period for Egypt—that is proved by these mighty tombs alone. It is interesting, likewise, to trace in the rich representations on the walls, which put before our eyes the high advance of the peaceful arts, as well as the refined luxury of the great of that period; also the foreboding of that great misfortune which brought Egypt, for several centuries, under the rule of its northern enemies. In the representations of the warlike games, which form a characteristically recurring feature, and take up whole sides in some tombs, which leads to a conclusion of their general use at that period afterwards disappearing, we often find among the red or dark-brown men, of the Egyptian and southern races, very light-colored people, who have, for the most part, a totally different costume, and generally red-colored hair on the head and beard, and blue eyes, sometimes appearing alone, sometimes in small divisions. They also appear in the trains of the nobles, and are evidently of northern, probably of Semitic, origin. We find victories over the Ethiopians and Negroes on the monuments of those times, and therefore need not be surprised at the recurrence of black slaves and servants. Of wars against the northern neighbors we learn nothing; but it seems that the immigration from the north-east was already beginning, and that many foreigners sought an asylum in fertile Egypt in return for service and other useful employments. . . . I have traced the whole representation, which is about eight feet long, and one-and-a-half high, and is very well preserved through, as it is only painted. The Royal Scribe, Nefruhotep, who conducts the company into the presence of the high officer to whom the grave belongs, is presenting him a leaf of papyrus. Upon this the sixth year of King Sesurtesen II. is mentioned, in which that family of thirty-seven persons came to Egypt. Their chief and lord was named Absha, they themselves Aama, a national designation, recurring with the light-complexioned race, often represented in the royal tombs of the XIXth dynasty, together with three other races, and forming the four principal divisions of mankind, with which the Egyptians were acquainted. Champollion took them for Greeks when he was in Benihassan, but he was not then aware of the extreme antiquity of the monuments before him. Wilkinson considers them prisoners, but this is confuted by their appearance with arms and lyres, with wives, children, donkeys, and luggage; I hold them to be an immigrating Hyksos-family, which begs for a reception into the favored land, and whose posterity perhaps opened the gates of Egypt to the conquering tribes of their Semitic relations."

The writer (G. R. G.), who had explored all these localities in 1839, with Mr. A. C. Harris, would mention, that immediately above Beni-Hassan (at the *Speos-Artemidos*, overlooked by Wilkinson from 1823 to '34), a defile through the precipitous hills leads from the Nile into the Eastern Desert, and thence trends through the Wâdee-el-Arabah to the Isthmus of Suez: as, indeed, may be perceived in RUSSEGGER's map,[206] before us. At the Egyptian mouth of this ravine are remains of walls, &c., that once blocked the passage; and, in ancient times, here doubtless was a military post, to prevent nomadic ingress into the cultivated lands without the *surveillance* of the police. Owing to the intricacies of the limestone ravines in this part of the Eastern Desert, any strangers, becoming entangled in these intersections, would, in the end, *débouche* at this pass, and be at once arrested by the guard. It is thus that, without speculative notions, we arrive at the conclusion that these "thirty-seven foreigners" (although the artist has drawn but fifteen—men, women, and children) were merely *Arabian* wanderers; who, motives unknown, entered Egypt during the twenty-third century B. C. Natural history, heretofore too frequently left aside by archæologists, not only confirms our view, but indicates the Peninsula of Mount Sinai, if not as their homestead, at least as the road by which they came. The reason we are about to give establishes two things: 1st, the minute accuracy of Egyptian draughtsmen in the XIIth dynasty, 4200 years ago; 2dly, the prompt acuity of Prof. Agassiz, in April, 1853.

At the house of their friend, Mr. A. Stein, of Mobile, the authors were looking over his copy of the noble Prussian *Denkmäler*, when Prof. Agassiz, the moment we reached this plate (*ubi supra*), pointed out the "*Capra Siniaca* — the goat with semicircular horns, laterally compressed," as the first animal; and the "*Antilope Saiga*, or gazelle of temperate Western Asia," as the second: animals offered in propitiatory tribute to General Num-hotep, by Absha, the *Hyk*, chief, of these *Mes-segem*, foreigners.

Our Fig. 109 presents the likeness of the excellent governor of the province; and the contrast, between their yellow Semitic countenances and his rubescent Egyptian face, spares us from fears that consanguinity will be claimed for them.

At least two types, then, of Caucasian families — the one Semitish, and the other Egyptian — were distinct from each other, and coexistent, 4200 years ago. If *two*, why not more? Why not each one of all the primitive types of humanity now distinguishable in Asia, Africa, Europe, America, or Oceanica? Science and logic can assign no negative reason: dogmatism, which excludes both, will doubtless continue to worry the hapless "general reader" with many.

We must span, for want of intervening ethnographic monuments, the gulf that separates the XIIth from the VIth dynasty, assuming the latter at about 2800 years B. C. Here again, however, our Caucasian type reappears not only perfectly marked, but identical with many of the heads we have already beheld among the royal portraits of the XVIIth and succeeding dynaties. Lepsius's precious *Denkmäler* yields us the following: —

Fig. 111.[207]

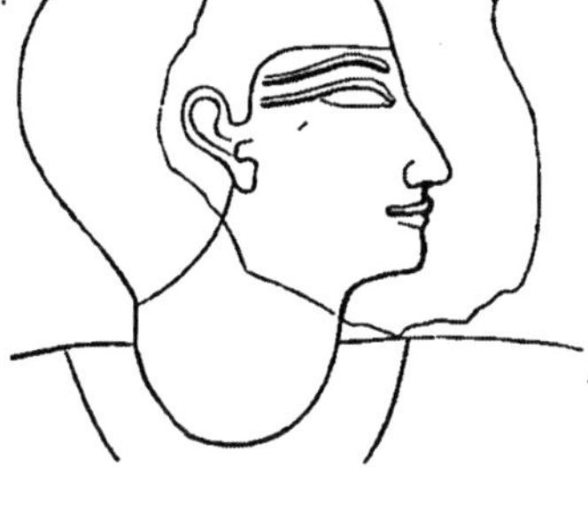

Fig. 112.[208]

The above heads are from patrician tombs of the VIth dynasty, which, according to Lepsius, commenced about the year 2900 B. C. Concerning the type of these, and numerous other effigies of this epoch, admirably figured by the same author, there can be no dispute; but, the plates being unaccompanied by text, we are unable to supply historical details of the personages represented in these early dynasties. Lepsius himself will ere long elucidate them.

The following two (Figs. 113 and 114) are selected as examples of the same type, in the anterior Vth dynasty, and are Egypto-Caucasians, no less clearly defined. In Fig. 113, the facial angle is actually *Hellenic.*

FIG. 113.[209]

FIG. 114.[210]

Lastly, here are some of the earliest portraits of the human species now extant — effigies 5300 years old.

FIG. 115.[211]

1

FIG. 116.[212]

2

FIG. 117.[213]
3

FIG. 118.[214]
4

The preceding four heads are all from painted sculptures in tombs of the IVth dynasty; which commenced at Memphis, according to Lepsius, about 3400 years B. C. The second and third of these heads assimilate closely to many of those already given of XVIIth and XVIIIth dynasties; demonstrating that mixed Caucasian types inhabited Egypt from the first to the last of her surviving monuments. We have stated our reasons, in another place, for regarding this special physiognomy to be commingled with foreign and Asiatic elements; and not representative, consequently, of the *aboriginal* Egyptian stem. The third of these heads is strongly Chaldaic in its outlines; and we think there is little reason to doubt that the ancestral Mesopotamian stock of Abraham had long been mingling its blood with the royal and aristocratic families of Egypt; because, in the IVth, Vth, and VIth dynasties, we find two distinct types sculptured on the monuments—the one African or *Negroid*, and the other Asiatic or *Semitic*. Of course, when speaking of Abraham's *ancestral stock*, the reader will understand that we make no reference to this patriarch's individuality. To us, his name serves merely to classify some proximate or identical *Chaldaic* family of man, originally connected with a common Euphratic centre of creation, of which the existence very likely preceded Abraham's birth by myriads of ages.

Our fourth portrait (Fig. 118) is the only one we can identify, and its associations are most interesting. Prince and Priest MERHET—probably a relative, if not son, of King SHOOPHO, *Cheops*, builder of the Great Pyramid,—is the man whose tomb, transferred from Memphis to Berlin, and now built into the Royal Museum, has escaped the vicissitudes of time for above fifty-two centuries. His bas-reliefed visage has endured almost intact; whilst, of the "chosen people," every Hebrew *portrait*, from Abraham to Paul, has been expunged from human iconography. In his lineaments, we behold the pure

Egyptian type, which we shall endeavor to render more obvious through lithographs that are genuine fac-similes of stamps made, on the monuments themselves, by the hand of Lepsius, at Berlin.

Meanwhile, it is worthy of notice, that, in the ratio of our descent from the sculptures of the IVth dynasty, through the *Old Empire*, our conventionally-termed "Chaldaic" type supplants the Nilotic to such an extent, that, under the *New* Empire, and among the aristocracy of the land, it almost entirely supersedes the African type of incipient times. The admixture, in these later ages, of such Asiatic blood, may be due to the so-called *Hyksos;* who commenced, even before the time of MENES, intruding upon, and settling in Egypt. Alliances and intermixtures of races, similar to those seen at the present day, have operated among nations in all ages, and everywhere that men and women have encountered each other on our planet.

Four instances may be consulted in Lepsius's *Denkmäler*, of Egyptian monarchs who have left at the copper-mines of Mt. Sinai, on *Stelæ*, inscribed with hieroglyphical legends, their bas-relief effigies; representing each king in the act of braining certain foreigners: whose pointed beards, aquiline noses, and other Semitish characteristics, combine with the Arabian locality to identify them as *Arabs*. We give entire (Fig. 119, A) a specimen of the earliest Tablets—"NUM-SHUFU

FIG. 119.[215]

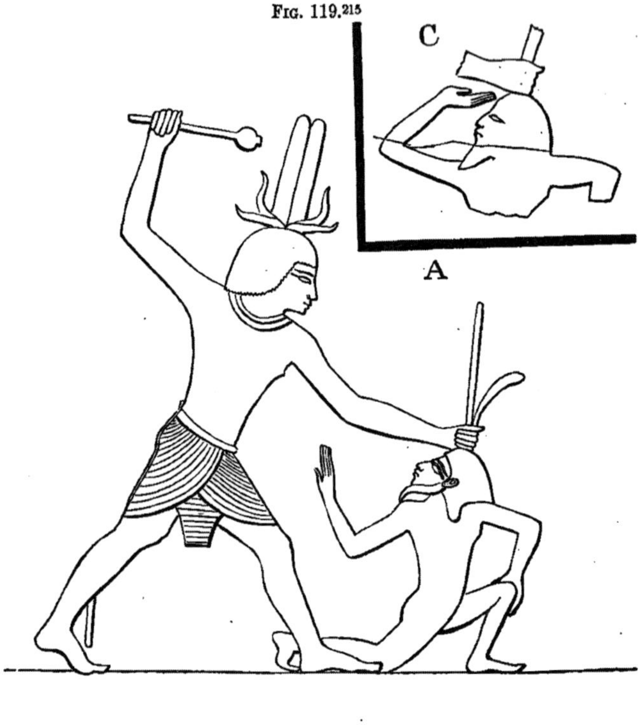

stunning an Arab-*barbarian;*" and the head of another smitten by "SENUFRU;" both kings of the IVth dynasty, during the thirty-fourth century B. C.

The other two examples (by us not copied) are identical in style, but a little posterior in age; one being of the reign of king SHORE, (or *Resho*) in the Vth, and the other of MERIRA-PEPI, in the VIth dynasty. A fifth example might be cited of the IVth, but it is of the same SENUFRU mentioned above.[216]

Here then are represented Egyptian Pharaohs striking Asiatics; and here, we are informed epistolarily by Chev. Lepsius, is the remotest monumental evidence of two distinct types of man; although, an analytical comparison of such antipodean languages as the ancient *Chinese* with the old Egyptian, of the Atlantic *Berber* with the Medic of DARIUS's inscriptions, of the Hindoo *Pali* with the Hebrew of HABBAKUK, and a dozen others we might name, would result in establishing for each of these distinct tongues such an enormous and independent antiquity, as to leave not a shadow of doubt that all primitive African and Asiatic races existed, from the Cape of Good Hope to China, as far back as the foundation of the Egyptian Empire, and long before. It is in the IVth Memphite dynasty, however, that we find the oldest sculptural representations of man now extant in the world.

In the above figures *two* primordial types, one Asiatic and the other Egyptian, stand conspicuous. If then, as before asserted, *two* races of man existed simultaneously during the IVth dynasty, in sufficient numbers to be at war with each other, their prototypes must have lived before the foundation of the Empire, or far earlier than 4000 years B. C. If two types of mankind were coetaneous, it follows that all other Asiatic and African races found in the subsequent XIIth dynasty must have been also in existence contemporaneously with those of the IVth, as well as with all the aboriginal races of America, Europe, Oceanica, Mongolia—in short, with every species of mankind throughout the entire globe.

CHAPTER VI.

AFRICAN TYPES.

Our preceding chapters have established that the so-called *Caucasian* types may be traced upwards from the present day, in an infinite variety of primitive forms, through every historical record, and yet farther back through the petroglyphs of Egypt (where we lose them, in the mediæval darkness of the earliest recorded people, some 3500 years before Christ), not as a few stray individuals, but as populous nations, possessing distinct physical features and separate national characteristics. We now turn to the African types, not simply because they present an opposite extreme from the Caucasian, but mainly because, from their early communication with Egypt, much detail, in respect to their physical characters, has been preserved in the catacombs and on the monuments.

In our general remarks on *species*, we have shown that no classification of races yet put forth has any foundation whatever in nature; and that, after several thousands of years of migrations of races and comminglings of types, all attempts at following them up to their original birth-places must, from the absence of historic annals of those primordial times, and in the present state of knowledge, be utterly hopeless. This remark applies with quite as much force to Negroes as to Caucasians: for Africa first exhibits herself, from one extreme to the other, covered with dark-skinned races of various shades, and possessing endless physical characters, which, being distinct, we must regard as primitive, until it can be shown that causes exist capable of transforming one type into another. The Negroes may be traced on the monuments of Egypt, with certainty, as nations, back to the XIIth dynasty, about 2300 years B. C.: and it cannot be assumed that they were not then as old as any other race of our geological epoch.

In order to develop our ideas more clearly, we propose to take a rapid glance at the population of Africa. We shall show, that not only is that vast continent inhabited by types quite as varied as those of Europe or Asia, but that there exists a regular *gradation*, from the Cape of Good Hope to the Isthmus of Suez, of which the Hottentot and Bushman form the lowest, and the Egyptian and Berber types the highest links;

that all these gradations of African man are indigenous to the soil; and that no historical times have existed when the same gradations were not.

When we compare the continent of Africa with the other great divisions of the world, it is apparent that it forms a striking contrast in every particular. Its whole physical geography, its climates, its populations, its faunæ, its floræ, &c., are all peculiar.) Upon examination of maps of Europe, Asia, and America, we see indeed, in each continent, great diversities of climate, soil, elevations of surface, and other phenomena; still no natural barriers exist so insurmountable as to prevent the migrations and comminglings of races, and consequent confusion of tongues and types: but in Africa the case is quite different. Here stand obstructions, fixed by nature, which man in early times had no means of overcoming. Not only from the time of Menes, the first of the Pharaohs, to that of Moses, but from the latter epoch to that of Christ, Africa, south of the Equator, was as much a *terra incognita* to the inhabitants of Europe, Asia, Egypt, and the Barbary States, as certain interior parts of that continent are to us at the present day. We know that, long after the Christian era, the nautical skill necessary for exploring expeditions, no less than for the transportation of emigrants to those distant latitudes, was wanting; and we have only to turn to any standard work (RITTER'S, for instance) on Ancient Geography, to be satisfied of these facts. It is equally certain that what is now termed "Central Africa" could not have been reached by caravan from the Mediterranean coast, before the introduction of *camels* from Asia, through Egypt, into Barbary. The epoch of this animal's introduction is now known to antedate the Christian era but a century or two. It is contended, by the advocates of a common origin for mankind, that this African continent was first populated by Asiatic emigrants into Egypt; that these immigrants passed on, step by step, gradually changing their physical organizations, under climatic influences, until the whole continent, from the Mediterranean to the Cape of Good Hope, was peopled by the various tribes we now behold scattered over that enormous space. But such an hypothesis can hardly be maintained, in the face of the fact asserted by Lepsius, and familiar to all Egyptologists, that *Negro* and other races already existed in Northern Africa, on the Upper Nile, 2300 years B. C. — existed, we repeat, in despite of natural barriers which could not have been passed by any means previously known; and, moreover, that all truly African races have, from the earliest epochas, spoken languages radically distinct from every Asiatic tongue. Linguistic researches have established that, prior to the introduction of Asiatic elements into the Lower Valley of the Nile, the speech of the ante-monumental Egyptians could have borne no affinity towards the latter. Lepsius, Birch, and De Rougé — our highest philological authorities in this question — coincide in the main principle, that the lexicology deduced from the earliest hieroglyphics exhibits two elements: viz., a primary, or *African;* and a secondary, or Asiatic, superimposed upon the former. It is also certain that, Syro-Arabian engraftments being deducted from the present *Nubian* and the *Berber* vernaculars spoken above and westward of Egypt, these languages are as purely African now as must have been the idiom uttered by the Egyptian ancestry of those who raised the pyramids of the IVth dynasty, 5300 years ago.

Such are the results of archæology, applied by that school of Egyptian philologists which alone is competent to decide upon the language of the hieroglyphics. They harmonize with the physiological conclusions we have reached through monumental iconography. But, requesting the critical reader to accompany us upon a map of the African continent, such as those contained in the *Physical Atlases* of Berghaus, or Johnston, we propose commencing at the Cape of Good Hope, and following the African races from Table Rock to the Mediterranean. Our limits do not permit a detailed analysis, nor is such necessary, as the few prominent facts we shall present are quite sufficient for the purpose in hand, and will at once be admitted by every reader who is at all competent to pursue this discussion.

What is now called *Cape Colony* lies between 30° and 35° of south latitude. It rises, as you recede from the coast, into high tablelands and mountains, and possesses a comparatively temperate and agreeable climate; nevertheless, it is here that we find the lowest and most beastly specimens of mankind: viz., the *Hottentot* and the *Bushman.* The latter, in particular, are but little removed, both in moral and physical characters, from the orang-outan. They are not black, but of a yellowish-brown (*tallow-colored*, as the French term them), with woolly heads, diminutive statures, small ill-shapen crania, very projecting mouths, prognathous faces, and badly formed bodies; in short, they are described by travellers as bearing a strong resemblance to the monkey tribe. They possess many anatomical peculiarities, known to physiologists if not recapitulated here. LICHTENSTEIN, one of our best authorities, in describing this race, says: —

"Their common objects of pursuit are serpents, lizards, ants, and grasshoppers. They will remain whole days without drinking; as a substitute, they chew succulent plants: they do not eat salt. They have no fixed habitation, but sleep in holes in the ground or under the branches of trees. They are short, lean, and, in appearance, weak in their limbs; yet are capable of bearing much fatigue. Their sight is acute, but their taste, smell, and feeling, are feeble. They do not form large societies, but wander about in families."

The *Hottentots* have been supposed by many to belong to the same race as the Bosjesman or Bushmen; and although we do not partake of this opinion, the point is too unimportant to our purpose to justify critical discussion here. In most particulars, the physical characters of Bushmen and Hottentots do not differ greatly — the Hottentots exhibit much of the orang character of the Bushmen, and their females often present two very remarkable peculiarities or deformities: viz., humps behind their buttocks, like those on the backs of dromedaries, and a disgusting development of the *labia pudendi.* (See an example in the *Hottentot Venus*, figured in our Chapter XIII.)

The complexion of the Hottentots is compared by travellers to that of a person "affected with jaundice" — "a yellowish-brown, or the hue of a faded leaf" — "a tawny buff, or fawn-color." Barrow relates that—

"The hair is of a very singular nature — it does not cover the whole surface of the scalp, but grows in small tufts, at certain distances from each other, and when clipped short has the appearance and feel of a hard shoe-brush, except that it is curled and twisted into small round lumps, about the size of a marrowfat pea. When suffered to grow, it hangs on the neck in hard-twisted tassels, like fringe."

The Hottentots are also very strongly distinguished from all other races by their singular language. Their utterance, according to Lichtenstein, is remarkable for numerous rapid, harsh, shrill sounds, emitted from the bottom of the chest, with strong aspirations, and modified in the mouth by a singular motion of the tongue. The name for it is commonly "gluckings." The peculiar construction of the vocal organs of this race greatly facilitates the formation and emission of these sounds, which to other species of men would be very difficult. [We had the pleasure, two years ago, at a meeting of the Ethnological Society in New York, to hear some specimens of this language from Prof. HALDEMANN, of Pennsylvania, who possesses an extraordinary talent for imitating sounds, and we can readily believe that the Hottentot vocalization has no affinity with any other in existence. — J. C. N.]

The next race we encounter, after leaving the Cape, is the Kafirs, or *Caffres.* They are not only found along the coast to the north-east in Caffraria, but extend far beyond, into the interior of Africa. They display certain affinities with the *Fulahs*, *Foolahs*, or *Fellatahs*, who are prolonged even into Northern Africa — whence an opinion that the two races are identical; but the fact, to say the least, is a matter of great doubt. The Caffres are traced northward, under various names; and their language and customs are very widely spread. Though they are now encountered in considerable numbers near the Cape, their original seat is doubtful. In geography, Central

Africa is yet a *terra incognita*, and we cannot, therefore, fix their birth-place with precision, however manifest may be the Caffrarian link in the chain of gradation we have assumed. Albeit, they resemble the true Negro much more than the Hottentot; whilst, both intellectually and physically, they are greatly superior not only to Hottentots, but to many Negro tribes on the Slave-Coast. They possess some knowledge of agriculture and the use of metals; they dress in skins, and live in towns. Descriptions of the Caffres, by different writers, vary considerably; and it is probable that several closely allied though diverse types have been included under this general appellation. No one has had better opportunities for studying this race, or can be more competent, than Lichtenstein, and we shall therefore adopt his description.

"The universal characteristics of all the tribes of this great nation consist in an external form and figure, varying exceedingly from the other nations of Africa: they are much taller, stronger, and their limbs better proportioned. Their color is *brown*; their hair black and woolly. Their countenances have a character peculiar to themselves, and which does not permit their being included in any of the races of mankind above enumerated. They have the high forehead and prominent nose of the Europeans, the thick lips of the Negroes, and the high cheek-bones of the Hottentots. Their beards are black, and much fuller than those of the Hottentots."

This race, it will thus be seen, is a very peculiar one, combining both moral and physical traits of the higher and the lower African races. Widely disseminated, they exhibit such singular affinities with opposing, such strange differences from proximate, Africans, that it is impossible to fix them to one locality: at the same time, being, like all savage races, without a history, we are unable to say, with any probability, to what latitude or to which coast they belong.

When, however, taking our departure from the Cape (the central regions of the continent being unknown), we continue our examination along the eastern and western coasts, as far as the transverse belt, just beyond the Equator, which separates the two great deserts, Northern and Southern, we find a succession of well-marked types, seemingly indigenous to their respective localities. Along the Easttern coast we encounter the various tribes inhabiting Inhambane, Sabia, Sofala, Botonga, Mozambique, Zanguebar, &c., each presenting physical characters more or less hideous; and, almost without exception, not merely in a barbarous, but superlatively savage state. All attempts towards humanizing them have failed. Hopes of eventual improvement in the condition of these brutish families are entertained by none but missionaries of sanguine temperament and little instruction. Even the *Slaver* rejects them.

If we now go back to Cape Colony, and thence pass upwards along the Western coast, we meet with another, equally diversified, series of Negro races, totally distinct from those of the eastern side, inhabiting Cimbebas, Benguela, Angola, Congo, Loango, Matembas, and Guinea; where we again reach the Equator. These are all savage tribes, but little removed, in physical nature and moral propensities, from the Hottentots. Anything like a detailed analysis of them would be but an unprofitable repetition of descriptions, to be found in all travellers' accounts, exhibiting pictures of the most degraded races of mankind. In a word, the whole of Africa, south of 10° N. lat., shows a succession of human beings with intellects as dark as their skins, and with a cephalic conformation that renders all expectance of their future melioration an Utopian dream, philanthropical, but somewhat senile.

North of the Equator, and dividing the two great Northern and Southern deserts, we fall in with a belt of country traversing the whole continent of Africa, terminating on the east with the highlands of Abyssinia — on the west with the uplands of Senegambia; and, between these two points, including part of the *Soodàn*, Negro-land proper, or Nigritia. About 10° N. lat. stretches an immense range of mountains, which are supposed to run entirely across the continent, and to form an insurmountable barrier between the Southern Deserts and the Northern Sahara. Throughout this region, we behold an infinitude of Negro races, differing considerably in their external characters. The annexed extracts from Prichard, bearing upon this subject, contain some important facts requiring comment.

"The whole of the countries now described are sometimes called Nigritia, or the Land of Negroes — they have likewise been termed *Ethiopia*. The former of these names is more frequently given to the Western, and the latter to the Eastern parts; but there is no exact limitation between the countries so termed. The names are taken from the races of men inhabiting different countries, and these are interspersed, and not separated by a particular line. Black and woolly-haired races, to which the term Negro is applied, are more predominant in Western Africa; but there are also woolly-haired tribes in the East: and races who resemble the Ethiopians, in their physical characters, are found likewise in the West. We cannot mark out geographical limits to these different classes of nations; but it will be useful to remember the difference in physical characters which separates them. The Negroes are distinguished by their well-known traits, of which the most strongly marked is their woolly hair; but it is difficult to point out any common property characteristic of the races termed Ethiopians, unless it is the negative one of wanting the above-mentioned peculiarity of the Negro: any other definition will apply only in general, and will be liable to exceptions. The Ethiopian races have generally something in their physical character which is *peculiarly African*, though not reaching the degree in which it is displayed by the black people of Soudan. Their hair, though not woolly, is commonly frizzled, or strongly curled or crisp. Their complexion is sometimes black, at others, of the color of bronze, or olive, or more frequently of a dark-copper or red-brown; such as the Egyptian paintings display in human figures, though generally of a deeper shade. In some instances, their hair, as well as their complexion, is somewhat brown or red. Their features are often full and rounded — not so acute and salient as those of the Arabs; their noses are not flattened or depressed, but scarcely so prominent as those of Europeans; their lips are generally thick or full, but seldom turned out like the thick lips of Negroes; their figure is slender and well shaped, and often resembling that form of which the Egyptian paintings and statues afford the most generally known exemplifications. These characters, though in some respects approaching towards those of the Negro, are perfectly distinct from the peculiarities of the mulatto or mixed breed. Most of these nations, both classes being equally included, are originally *African*. By this I do not mean to imply that their first parents were created on the soil of Africa, but merely that they cannot be traced, by historical proofs, from any other part of the world, and that they appear to have grown into clans or tribes of peculiar physical and social character, or that their national existence had its commencement in that continent." [217]

The above paragraph establishes that Prichard, in accordance here with our own views, cuts loose the population of the basin of the Nile from all the Negro races scattered between Mount Atlas and the Cape of Good Hope. In fact, one of Prichard's great objects, throughout his "Researches," is to show that there exists a regular *gradation of races*, from the highest to the lowest types, not only in Africa, but throughout the world. The learned Doctor spared no labor, for forty years, to prove that this gradation is the result of *physical causes*, acting, as he says, "during chiliads of years," upon one primitive Adamic stock. We, on the contrary, contend, that many primitive types of mankind were created in distant zoological provinces; and, that the numerous facts, ignored by Dr. Prichard, which have lately come to light from Egyptian monuments and other new sources, confirm this view. In fact, Prichard himself, in the fifth or final volume of his last edition, virtually abandons the position he had so long and so ably maintained.

The range of mountains which bounds Guinea on the north is supposed, by Ritter and other distinguished geographers, to be the commencement of a huge chain which trends across the continent about the tenth degree, connecting itself with the so-called "Mountains of the Moon," on the East; [218] and thus constituting an impassable wall, athwart the continent, between the North and the South. Certain it is that the whole of Africa south of this parallel was utterly unknown 600 years ago to any writers, sacred or profane—the coast, on either side, until reached by navigators, in quite modern times—the interior, or central portion of this mountain-land, continues to be less known than even the moon's.

One interesting fact, however, is clear: viz., that when, passing onwards from the South, we overleap this stupendous natural wall, [219] we are at once thrown among tribes of higher grade; although continuing still within the region of jet-black skins and woolly heads. The excessively prognathous type of the Hottentots, Congos, Guinea-Negroes, and so forth, is no longer, we now perceive, the prevailing type north of this mountain-range. We here meet with features approaching the Caucasian coupled with well-formed bodies and neatly-turned limbs; improved cranial developments, and altogether a much higher intellectual character. Here, likewise, the rudiments of civilization are met with for the first time in our progress from the South. Here and there, though surrounded by pastoral nomadism, many of the tribes are rude agriculturists; manufacturing coarse cloth, leather, &c.; knowing somewhat of the use of metals, and living in towns of from ten to thirty thousand inhabitants. It must be conceded, however, that most of this progress is attributable to *foreign immigration and exotic influences.* In the fertile low-countries, beyond the Sahara deserts, watered by rivers which descend northwards from water-sheds upon the central highlands, Africa has contained, for centuries, several Nigritian kingdoms, founded by Mohammedans; while many Arabs, and many more Atlantic Berbers, have settled among the native tribes. To these influences we should doubtless ascribe the maintenance of their Muslim religion and infant civilization: for it is indisputable that the rulers (petty kings and aristocracy) are not of pure Negro lineage.[220]

This superiority of races north of the mountain-range does not extend to all indigenous tribes; for Denham and Clapperton describe some of the tribes around Bornou and Lake Tchad as extremely ugly, savage, and brutal. It would seem that nature preserves such aboriginal specimens in every region of the globe: as if to demonstrate that *types* are independent of physical causes, and that species of men, like those of animals, are primitive.

We have also numerous accounts, from Bruce, Rüppel, Cailliaud, Linant, Beke, Werne, Combes et Tamisier, Rochet d'Héricourt, Russegger, Mohammed-el-Tounsy, Lepsius, and other explorers, of Sennâar, Dar-Four, Kordofân, Fazoql, of the wild Shillooks, &c., bordering on the White Nile and its tributaries, and of the western slopes of Abyssinia; and they concur in representing most of these superlatively barbarous tribes as characterized by Negro lineaments, more or less well marked. Of such unaltered types we see many authentic samples depicted on the Egyptian monuments of the XVIIth dynasty; and we find that some are referred to in the hieroglyphical inscriptions as early as the XIIth. Indeed, the first authentic evidences extant of Expeditions, made to penetrate towards the Nile's unknown sources, date with the XIIth dynasty, about 2300 B. C.; when Sesourtesen III. had extended his conquests up the river at least as high as *Samneh*, in Upper Nubia, where a harbor, or arsenal, and a *temple* (the former repaired by the Amenemhas, and the latter rebuilt by Thotmes III.), with other remains, prove that the Pharaohs of the XIIth dynasty had established frontier garrisons. But, as the *Tablet* of *Wâdee Halfa* contains the names of nations undoubtedly Nigritian, and inasmuch as there are abundant arguments to prove that the habitat of Negro races anciently, as at this day, never approximated to Egypt closer than, if as near as, the northern limit of the *Tropical Rains*, we can ascend without hesitation to the age of Sesourtesen I.; and confidently assert that, in the twenty-third century B. C., the knowledge possessed by the Pharaonic Egytians concerning the upper regions of the Nile extended to points as austral as that derived between A. D. 1820 and 1835, by civilized Europe, from the *Ghàzwas*, or slave-hunts, of Mohammed-Ali.[221] Time has transplanted some of these upper Nilotic families, over a few miles, from one district to another; but that such movements have entailed no physical mutations of race, we shall perceive hereinafter.

We have already stated, that Senegambia, on the west of *Central Africa*, like the eastern extremity at Abyssinia,[222] rises into mountains and elevated table-lands — physical characters which usually accompany higher grades of humanity than those of the burning plains below. It is here that we find sundry of the superior (so-called) Negro races of Africa: viz., the Mandingos, the Fulahs, and the Iolofs. The *Mandingos*, a very numerous and powerful nation, are remarkable among the African races for their industry and energy; and, of the genuine Negro tribes, have perhaps manifested the greatest aptitude for mental improvement. They are the most zealous and rigid Mohammedans on the continent. Agriculturists, cattle-breeders, cloth-manufacturers, living in towns, they possess schools, engage in extensive commerce, and use Arabic writing. Goldberry, Park, Laing, Durand, and other travellers, coincide in the statement that these Mandingos are less black, and have better features, than Negroes; indeed, Goldberry, who is good authority, says they resemble dark *Hindoos* more than Negroes.

The *Fulahs*[223] are a still more peculiar people, whose history is involved in much obscurity. They are supposed, by many authorities, to be a mixed race. Their type and language are totally distinct from all surrounding Africans. According to Park and others, they rank themselves among white people, and look down upon their neighbors as inferiors; at the same time, they are always the dominating families, wherever found. The contradictory descriptions of travellers lead us to suspect some diversity of physical characters among these Fulahs, or Fellatahs. They are not black, but of a *mahogany* color, with good features, and hair more or less straight, and often very fine. They are commercial, intelligent, and, for Africans, considerably advanced in the civilization they owe to Islamism and the Arabs.

The *Iolofs*, between the Senegal and Gambia, the most northerly

Negro nations on the West coast, are represented to be the comeliest of all Negro tribes.

"They are always well made [says Goldberry]; their features are regular, and like those of Europeans, except that their nose is rather round, and their lips thick. They are said to be remarkably handsome — their women beautiful. The complexion of the race is a fine transparent *deep black*; their hair crisp and woolly."

Here, again, is a combination of physical characters which contradicts the alleged influence of climate; because the Iolofs, and some other races north, are jet-black, while the Fulahs, and others, under and south of the Equator, are comparatively fair.

We shall show, in another place, that history affords no evidence that education, or any influence of civilization that may be brought to bear on races of inferior organization, can radically change their physical, nor, consequently, their moral, characters. That the brain, for example, which is the organ of intellect, cannot be expanded or altered in form, is now admitted by every anatomist; and Prichard, in recapitulating his results as to the races of Central Africa, makes the following important admission: —

"On reviewing the descriptions of all the races enumerated, we may observe a relation between their physical character and moral condition. *Tribes having what is called the Negro character in the most striking degree are the least civilized.* The Papels, Bisagos, Ibos, who are in the greatest degree remarkable for deformed countenances, projecting jaws, flat foreheads, and for other Negro peculiarities, *are the most savage and morally degraded* of the nations hitherto described. *The converse of this remark is applicable to all the most civilized races.* The Fúlahs, Mandingos, and some of the Dahomeh and Inta nations have, as far as form is concerned, nearly European countenances, and a corresponding configuration of the head. . . . In general, the tribes inhabiting elevated countries, in the interior, are very superior to those who dwell on low tracts on the the seacoast, and this superiority is manifest both in mental and bodily qualities." [224]

The truth of these observations is sustained by all past history, backed by every monument. Much as the success of the infant colony at Liberia is to be desired by every true philanthropist, it is with regret that, whilst wishing well to the Negroes, we cannot divest our minds of melancholy forebodings. Dr. Morton, quoted in another chapter, has proven, that the Negro races possess about nine cubic inches less of brain than the Teuton; and, unless there were really some facts in history, something beyond bare hypotheses, to teach us how these deficient inches could be artificially added, it would seem that the Negroes in Africa must remain substantially in that same benighted state wherein Nature has placed them, and in which they have stood, according to Egyptian monuments, for at least 5000 years.

Prichard's herculean work is so replete with interesting facts and valuable deductions, that we are tempted, almost at every page, to make extracts. The following *resumé* is certainly decisive in establishing the entire want of connexion between *Types* and *Climate.*

"The distinguishing peculiarities of the African races may be summed up into four heads; viz.: the characters of complexion, hair, features and figure. We have to remark—

"1. That some races, with woolly hair and complexions of a deep black color, have fine forms, regular and beautiful features, and are, in their figure and countenances, scarcely different from Europeans. Such are the Iolofs, near the Senegal, and the race of Guber, or of Hausa, in the interior of Sudan. Some tribes of the South African race, as the darkest of the Kafirs, are nearly of this description, as well as some families or tribes in the empire of Kongo, while others have more of the Negro character in their countenances and form.

"2. Other tribes have the form and features similar to those above described: their complexion is black or a deep olive, or a copper color approaching to black, while their hair, though often crisp and frizzled, is not the least woolly. Such are the Bishari and Danakil and Hazorta, and the darkest of the Abyssinians.

"3. Other instances have been mentioned in which the complexion is black and the features have the Negro type, while the nature of the hair deviates considerably, and is even said to be rather long and in flowing ringlets. Some of the tribes near the Zambezi are of this class.

"4. Among nations whose color deviates towards a lighter hue, we find some with woolly hair, with a figure and features approaching the European. Such are the Bechuana Kafirs, of a light brown complexion. The tawny Hottentots, though not approaching the European, differ from the Negro. Again, some of the tribes on the Gold Coast and the Slave Coast, and the Ibos, in the Bight of Benin, are of a lighter complexion than many other Negroes, while their features are strongly marked with the peculiarities of that race."

These observations, Prichard thinks, cannot be reconciled with the idea that the Negroes are of one distinct species; and that the opinion sustaining the existence, among them, of a number of separate species, each distinguished by some peculiarity which another wants, might be more reasonably maintained. The latter supposition he conjectures, however, to be refuted by the fact that *species* in no case pass so insensibly into each other. It will appear, notwithstanding, when we come to the questions of *hybridity* and of *specific* characters, that Prichard's doctrine, besides being in itself a *non sequitur*, is overthrown by positive facts.

Prichard himself tells us, "there are no authentic instances, either in Africa or elsewhere, of the transmutation of other varieties of mankind into Negroes."[225] We have, however, he continues, examples of very considerable deviation in the opposite direction. The descendants of the genuine Negroes are no longer such: they have lost in several instances many of the peculiarities of the stock from which they spring. To which fallacies we reply, that vague reports of misinformed travellers alone support such assertion. Our remarks on the *Permanence of Types* establish, that what physiological changes Prichard and his school refer to climatic influences, are indisputably to be ascribed to *amalgamation* of races.

Let us now travel through Nigritia, and ascend the table-lands of

Abyssinia; where another climate, another Fauna, another Flora, and another Type of Man, arise to view. Here, for the first time since our departure from the Cape of Good Hope, we stand among tribes of men who are actually capacitated to enjoy a higher stage of civilization; and, although we have not yet reached God's "noblest work," we have happily waded through the "slough of despond" in human gradations of Africa.

Reader! let us imagine ourselves standing upon the highest peak in Abyssinia; and that our vision could extend over the whole continent, embracing south, east, north and west: what *tableaux-vivants* would be presented to the eye, no less than to the mind! To the south of the Sahara we should descry at least 50,000,000 of Nigritians, steeped in irredeemable ignorance and savagism; inhabiting the very countries where history first finds them — vast territorial expanses, which the nations of the north, in ancient times, had no possible means of visiting or colonizing. Do we not behold, on every side, human characteristics so completely segregated from ours, that they can be explained in no other way than by supposing a direct act of creation? Upon the moral and intellectual traits of such abject types no impression has been made within 5000 years: none can be made, (so far as science knows,) until their organization becomes changed by—silliest of desperate suppositions—a "miracle." Turn we now towards the *north*. There we behold the tombs, the ruined temples, the gigantic pyramids of Pharaonic Egypt, which, braving the hand of time for 5000 years past, seem to defy its action for as many to come. These monuments, moreover, were not only built by a people differing from all others of Asia and Europe, in characters, language, civilization, and other attributes; but diverging still more widely from every other human type. Positive evidence, furthermore, exists, that Negroes, at least as far back as the XIIth dynasty, in the twenty-fourth century B. C., dwelt contemporaneously in Africa: which is parallel with (B. C. 2348) the era ascertained, to a fraction by Rabbinical arithmetic, for NOAH's Flood; when all creatures outside of the Ark, except some fishes, had found a watery grave! But we pursue our journey.

Abyssinia, according to TELLEZ, is called by its inhabitants *Alberegran* or the "lofty plain;" by which epithet they contrast it with the low countries surrounding it on almost every side. It is compared by the Abyssinians to the flower of the *Denguelet*, which displays a magnificent corolla surrounded by thorns — in allusion to the many barbarous tribes who inhabit the numerous circumjacent valleys and low lands.[226]

The highlands of Abyssinia, properly so called, stretch from the southern provinces of Shoa and Efat, which are not far distant from

Enarea under 9°, to Tscherkin and Waldubba under 15° N. lat.; where they make a sudden and often precipitous descent into the stunted forests occupied by the Shangalla Negroes. From east to west they extend over 9° of longitude. Rising at the steep border or terrace of Taranta from the depressed tract along the Arabian Gulf, they reach the mountains of Fazolco, Dyre and Touggoula; which overhang the flat, sandy districts of Sennâar and the valleys of Kordofan. (RITTER.)

The researches of Bruce, Salt, Ritter, and Beke, have shown that the high country of Habesh, Abyssinia, consists of three terraces or distinct table-lands, rising one above another; and of which the several grades or ascents present themselves in succession, to the traveller who advances from the shore of the Red Sea.[227]

The plain of *Baharnegash* is first met after traversing the low and arid steppe of Samhard, inhabited by the black *Danâkil* and *Dumboeta*, where the traveller ascends the heights of Taranta.

The next level is the kingdom of Tigré, which formerly contained the kingdom of Axum. Within this region lie the plains of Enderta and Giralta; containing Chelicut and Antalow, principal cities of Abyssinia. The kingdom of Tigré comprehends the provinces of Abyssinia westward of the Tacazze, of which the larger are Tigré and Shire towards the north, Woggerat and Enderta and the mountainous regions of Lasta and Samen towards the south.

High Abyssinia—*kingdom of Amhara*—is a name now given to the realm of which Gondar is the capital, and where the Amharic language is spoken, eastward of the Tacazze. Amhara proper is a mountain province of that name to the southeast, in the centre of which was Tegulat, the ancient capital of the empire; and, at one period, the centre of civilization of Abyssinia. This province is now in the possession of the Galla; a barbarous people who have overcome the southern parts of Habesh. The present kingdom of Amhara is the heart of Abyssinia, the abode of the Emperor or Negush. It contains the upper course of the Blue Nile. The climate is delightful—perpetual spring; and the mean elevation about 8000 feet. The upland region of Amhara, or rather the province of Dembea, breaks off towards the northeast, by a mountainous descent into the plains of Sennâar and lower Ethiopia. On the outskirts of the highlands, and at their feet, are the vast forests of Waldubba and Walkayat, abounding with troops of monkeys, elephants, buffaloes and wild boars. The human inhabitants of these tracts and the adjoining forests, and likewise of the valleys of the Tacazze and the Angrab, are Shangalla Negroes, who in several parts environ the hill-country of Abyssinia.[228]

Races inhabiting Abyssinia.—Several different races inhabit the old empire of the Negush or Abyssinian sovereign, who are commonly included under the name of *Habesh* or Abyssinians. They differ in language, but possess a general resemblance in their physical characters and customs. Whether they really are of unique origin is a question which science has no data for settling. Those who believe that the Hebrew and the Hottentot (as well as camels and cameleopards) are of one and the same stock, will unhesitatingly answer in the affirmative.

1. *The Tigrani, or Abyssins of Tigré.*—These are the inhabitants of the kingdom of Tigré, on the east of Tacazze—speaking the *lingua Tigrana.*

2. *The Amharas.*—They have for ages been the dominant people of Abyssinia, and speak the widely-spread *Amharic* language.

3. *The Agows.*—There are two tribes bearing this appellation, who speak distinct tongues, and inhabit different parts of the country.

4. *The Falashas.*—This race has much puzzled ethnographers, and their history is involved in obscurity. They possess strong affinities with the Fulahs on the western coast, and have not only been supposed by many to be of the same stock, but both have been regarded as identical with the Kafirs (Caffres) of Southern Africa. The Falashas are Jews in religion, though their language has no affinity with the Hebrew; and they use the Gheez version of the Old Testament.

5. *The Gafats* are another tribe, possessing a language of their own.

6. *The Gongas and Enareans* have also a language distinct from all the above.

There are other tribes which might be enumerated, speaking languages hitherto irreconcilable.[229] Whether these really present affinities, or whether some of them be not radically distinct, are questions yet undetermined.

Physical Characters.—Human races of the plateaux of Abyssinia are said to resemble each other, although it is admitted on all hands that they vary considerably in complexion and features.

Prichard, who has brought all his immense erudition to bear on these families, cuts them loose entirely from Negro races; and classes them under the head of *Ethiopians;* who, we shall see, have been very improperly confounded with *Negroes.* After treating on the general resemblance, in physical characters, of these nations, he concludes—

"By this national character of conformation, the Abyssinians are associated with that class of African nations which I have proposed to denominate by the term *Ethiopian*, as *distinguishing them from Negroes.* The distinction has indeed been already established by

Baron Larrey, Dr. Rüppell, M. de Chabrol, and others. Some of these writers include in the same department the Abyssins, the native Egyptians and the Barabra, separating them by a broad line from the Negroes, and almost as widely from the Arabs and Europeans. The Egyptians or Copts, who form one branch of this stock, have, according to Larrey, a 'yellow, dusky complexion, like that of the Abyssins. Their countenance is full without being puffed; their eyes are beautiful, clear, almond-shaped, and languishing; their cheek-bones are projecting; their noses nearly straight, rounded at the point; their nostrils dilated; mouth of moderate size; their lips thick; their teeth white, regular, but a little projecting; their beard and hair black and crisp.'[230] In all these characters, the Egyptians, according to Larrey, agree with the Abyssins, and are distinguished from the Negroes."

The Baron enters into a minute comparison of the Abyssinians, Copts, and Negroes; concluding that the two former are of the same race; and supporting this idea with Egyptian sculptures and paintings, and the crania of mummies.

M. de Chabrol, describing the Copts, says that they evince decidedly an African character of physiognomy; which, he thinks, establishes that they are *indigenous* inhabitants of Egypt, identifying them with the ancient inhabitants:—

"On peut admettre que leur race a su se conserver pure de toute mélange avec le Grecs, puisqu'ils n'ont entre eux aucun trait de ressemblance."[231]

[This must be taken with many grains of allowance; for the present Copts are hybrids of every race that has visited Egypt: at the same time that his "African physiognomy" evidently means no more than that the character of countenance termed *Ethiopian* is not that of the Negro.—G. R. G.]

Dr. Rüppell has also portrayed the Ethiopian style of countenance and bodily conformation as peculiarly distinct from the type both of the Arabian and the Negro. He describes its character as more especially belonging to the Baràbra, or Berberins, among whom he long resided; but he says that it is common to them, together with the Ababdeh and the Bishari, and in part with the Abyssinians. This type, according to Rüppell, bears a striking resemblance to the characteristics of the ancient Egyptians and Nubians, as displayed in the statues and sculptures in the temples and sepulchral excavations along the course of the Nile.

The complexion and hair of the Abyssinians vary very much: their complexion ranging from almost white to dark brown or black; and their hair, from straight to crisp, frizzled, and almost woolly. Hence the deduction, if these are facts, that they must be an exceedingly mixed race. Dr. Prichard, in defining the Abyssinians, has taken much pains, as we have said, to prove that they, together with families generally of the eastern basin of the Nile, down to Egypt inclusive, not only are not Negro, but were not originally Asiatic races; displaying somewhat of an intermediate type, which is nevertheless essentially *African* in character. To us, it is very gratifying to see this view so ably sustained; because, regarding it as an incontrovertible fact, we have made it the stand-point of our argument respecting the origin of the ancient Egyptians, whose effigies present this *African type* on the earliest monuments of the *Old* Empire more vividly than upon those of the *New*. This autochthonous type, as we shall prove, ascends so far back in time, is so peculiar, and withal so connected with a primordial tongue — presenting but small incipient affinity with Asiatic languages about 3500 years B. C. — as to preclude every idea of an Asiatic origin for its aboriginally-Nilotic speakers and hieroglyphical scribes.

Languages of Abyssinia. — In tracing the history of this country, we find the Gheez, or Ethiopic, the Amharic, and other Abyssinian languages. It is no longer questionable, that the Gheez or Ethiopic — idiom of the Ethiopic version of the Scriptures, and other modern books which constitute the literature of Abyssinia — is a *Semitic* dialect, akin to the Arabic and Hebrew.

"There is no reason to doubt [says Prichard], that the people for whose use these books were written, and whose vernacular tongue was the Gheez, were a Semitic race. How, and at what time, the highlands of Abyssinia came to be inhabited by a Semitic people, and what relations the modern Abyssinians bear to the family of nations, of which that people were a branch, are questions of too much importance, in African ethnography, to be passed without examination."

The Gheez is now extant merely as a dead language.

The Amharic, or modern Abyssinian, has been the vernacular of the country ever since the extinction of the Gheez, and is spoken over a great part of Abyssinia. It is not a *dialect* of the Gheez or Ethiopic, as some have supposed, but is now recognized to be, as Prichard affirms, "a language fundamentally distinct." It has incorporated into itself many words of Semitic origin; but accidents of recent date do not alter the case, as concerns the former existence of local Abyssynian idioms, non-Asiatic in structure. So with the Atlantic Berber language, which has likewise become much adulterated by foreign grafts: yet Venture, Newman, Castiglione, and Gräberg de Hemso, have fully proved that it is essentially, and in the primary or most original parts of its vocabulary, a speech entirely apart, and devoid of any relation whether to Semitic or to any other known language. The same remark applies with equal truth to the Amharic, which was probably an ancient *African* tongue, and one of the aboriginal idioms of the inhabitants of the south-eastern provinces of Abyssinia. Prichard winds up his investigation with the following emphatic avowal, so that we may consider the question settled: — "The languages of all these nations are essentially distinct from the Gheez and every other Semitic dialect." Our own general conclusion from the premises is, that, while the Abyssinians are absolutely distinct, on the one hand, from every Negro race, they are, on the other, equally distinct, in type and languages, from all Asiatic races; and they must therefore be regarded as autocthones of the country where they are now found.

On the south and south-east of Abyssinia there exist other races which might be enumerated; the Gallas, for example, with brown complexion, long crisp hair, and features not unlike the Abyssinians. Also, the Danakil, the Somauli, &c. — none of whom are Negroes: their types being intermediate — long hair, skins more or less dark, good features, &c.; all partaking far more of the *Ethiopian* than of the *Negro*. [No Abyssinian natives having fallen under the writer's personal eye, he cannot pronounce upon them with the same confidence that he speaks of Negroes; but his colleague, Mr. Gliddon, whose twenty-odd years' residence in Egypt, individual aptitude of observation, and extensive Oriental knowledge, render his opinions of some weight in these Nilotic questions, refers to the exquisite plates of Prisse d'Avennes[232] for what may be considered the most perfect expression of this Abyssinian type. We accept M. Prisse's life-like sketches the more readily, inasmuch as they harmonize with the best accounts we have read, and with our own ethnological deductions, through analogy, of the characteristics that Abyssinians must present.—J. C. N.]

On resuming our line of march, then, north towards Egypt, we turn our backs upon the *Soodan*, "*black* countries," ever the true land of Negroes; and descend from the Abyssinian highlands on the north-west and north, along the borders of Gondar and Dembea. Here, again, we meet divers scattered tribes, with black skins and woolly heads — varieties of the intrusive *Shangalla*, who now are found not only on the west, but on the northern borders of Habesh; while on the south-east we descry the *Dobos*. In Sennâr we again encounter Negro tribes — the Shilooks and the Tungi; inhabiting the islands of the Bahr-el-Abiad, above Wâdee Shallice. Fully described by Seetzen, Linant, Lord Prudhoe, Russegger, and others; they present Negro types more or less marked. This fact might seem to contradict our statement with regard to the primitive localities of Nigritian races. We look upon such *minutiæ*, however, as unimportant; because, contending simply for a *gradation* of African races, a few hundred miles, within the same upper Nilotic basin, do not affect the main principle. Dr. Rüppell, than whom there is certainly no better authority on this question, corroborates our assumption, by asserting that the present stations of those Negro races are not their ancient abodes. He assures us that —

"The Shilukh Negroes are a numerous and widely spread people, in the country of Bertal, bordering on Fertit, and to the southward of Kordofan, beyond the tenth degree of latitude, *whence they have dispersed themselves*, towards the East and North, along the course of the White Nile."

Prichard furthermore admits, that "the people of Sennàar are no longer Negroes," quoting M. Cailliaud to sustain himself; and adding the latter's description of the physical character of the races of Sennàar in general: —

"Les indigènes du Sennaar ont le teint d'un brun cuivré; leurs cheveux, quoique crépus, diffèrent de ceux des vrais Nègres: ils n'ont point, comme ceuxci, le nez, les lèvres, et les joues, saillantes — l'ensemble de leur physioguomie est agréable et regulier."

Cailliaud further remarks, that —

"Among the inhabitants of the kingdom of Sennaar, and the adjoining countries to the south, the results of mixture of race, in the intermarriage of Soudanians, Ethiopians, and Arabs, were frequently to be traced."

He holds, as does also Cherubini,[233] that *six* distinct castes are well known in that country, the names and descriptions of which they give.[234]

After a careful review of most leading authorities on the races of Africa, we have arrived at the conclusion that, upon ascending the table-lands of Abyssinia, at the south and west, we bid adieu to the true Negro-land (believing that every dispassionate inquirer must come to results identical). Which departure taken, we find, along the descending waters of the Nile, only some few scattered Negro types, who have wandered from their indigenous and more austral soil. Dr. Prichard, we have stated, fully recognizes the *gradation* of African races for which we have been contending, but he attributes it entirely to the operation of physical causes — assigning imaginary reasons, unsubstantiated by even the slenderest proof, and in negation of which we hope to adduce overwhelming testimony.

Nubians. — Next in order, we must glance at the races inhabiting Nubia and other countries between Abyssinia and Egypt, about whom much unnecessary confusion has existed, simply because few European travellers among them have been competent physiologists. One people who inhabit the valley of the Nile above Egypt, and from that country to Sennàar, give themselves the appellation of *Berberri* (in the singular). By the Arabs, they are termed *Nuba* and *Baràbera*. The same people in Egypt, whither they immigrate in large numbers, are by Europeans called *Berberins*. These races, through similarity of name, have been erroneously confounded with the *Berbers* of the Barbary States; but they differ in language, features, and every essential particular.[234] The Nubians constitute altogether a group of peculiar races, differing from Arabs, Negroes, or Egyptians — possessing a physiognomy and color of their own. They speak languages peculiar to themselves; in which, from the time of Moses, they were hieroglyphed as BaRaBeRa, no less than as NUBA. They are in the habit of coming down to Egypt, where their offices are wholly menial; and among other articles of traffic, some clans bring Negroes procured from the caravans of Sennàar, and are commonly known at Cairo under the name of *Gellabs*, "fetchers," or slave-dealers.

The discrepancy in the descriptions given of this Nubian race by travellers, demonstrates that there exists among them considerable variety of colors; and hence, at once, we feel persuaded of no little mixture of races. Denon describes them as of a "shining jet-black," but adds, "they have not the smallest resemblance to the Negroes of Western Africa." Other travellers speak of them as copper-colored, or black, with a tinge of red, &c. The fact is, the mothers are often pure negresses, and their children mulattoes of all shades. Their proper physical character is, we think, well described by M. COSTAZ:—

"La couleur des Barâbras tient en quelque sorte le milieu entre le noir d'ébène des habitans de Sennaar et le teint basané des Egyptiens du Sayd. Elle est exactement semblable à celle de l'acajou poli foncé. Les Barâbras se prévalent de cette nuance, pour se ranger parmi les blancs. . . Les traits des Barâbras se rapprochent effectivement plus de ceux des Européens que de ceux des Nègres: leur peau est d'un tissu extrêmement fin — sa couleur ne produit point un effect désagréable; la nuance rouge, qui y est mêlée, leur donne un air de santé et de vie. Ils différent des Nègres par leur cheveux, qui sont longs et legèrement crépus sans être laineux.

Dr. Rüppell's very scientific account of the races inhabiting the province of Dongola contains the following:—

"The inhabitants of Dar Dongola are divided into two principal classes: namely, the Barabra, or the descendants of the old Ethiopian natives of the country, and the races of Arabs who have emigrated from Hedjas. The ancestors of the Barabra, who, in the course of centuries, have been repeatedly conquered by hostile tribes, must have undergone some intermixture with people of foreign blood; yet an attentive inquiry will still enable us to distinguish among them the old national physiognomy, which their forefathers have marked upon colossal statues and the bas-reliefs of temples and sepulchres. A long oval countenance; a beautifully curved nose, somewhat rounded towards the top; proportionally thick lips, but not protruding excessively; a remarkably beautiful figure, generally of middle size, and a brown color, are the characteristics of the genuine Dongalawi. These same traits of physiognomy are generally found among the Ababdi, Bishari, a part of the inhabitants of the province of Schendi, and partly also among the Abyssinians."

Many of the Baràbra speak Arabic, and with an accent ever "*sui generis;*" but very few free Arabs consider it respectable to learn Berberree, which they affect to despise as *Rutàna*, a "jargon." Both races keep themselves separate; and marriage connexions between them, entailing disgrace upon the Arab, are, at the present day, of so rare occurrence, that Berberri *husbands* at Cairo are only adopted for one day, in cases of "triple divorce."[235] There are many citations of Arab historians to support the conclusion that some septs of these so-termed

Baràbra derived their origin from a country westward of the Nile, and not far from Kordofàn. A doubt thus arises not only, as above mentioned, with regard to Negroes, but whether some Nubians themselves did not come originally from the west of the White Nile. This opinion, confirmed to some extent by affinity of language and by modern traditions, is contradicted, apparently, by the monuments:— 1st, Egyptian monarchs of the XVIIIth dynasty conquer the *Nouba*, no less than the *Baràbera*, in their expeditions of the fourteenth and fifteenth centuries B. C. 2d, The portraits of these Ancient Nubians exhibit precisely the same traits, whilst occupying, 3500 years ago, the same topographical habitats, as their descendants at the present day; and the nostalgic tendencies of the modern *Berberri* are so notorious, that voluntary displacements on his part seem improbable.

In Part II. of this volume, under the head of KUS*h*, the reader will meet with ample investigations: although, beyond general accuracy, a minutely-exact geographical settlement of these Nubian groups is not essential to anthropology; because, whether in the Lower or Upper Nubias, or in Kordofàn, they lie now, where their progenitors ever did, along the Nile; that is, between the Egyptians at the north and the Negroes at the south. And, after all, their mightiest dislocations are confined within an area of 500 miles, up or down a single river. To us they are, consequently, merely *Nubian* aborigines.

The population of Kordofàn now consists of three races at least, who are physically distinct, each speaking different languages:— 1. Bedouin Arabs from the Hedjàz. 2. Colonists from Dongola. 3. Original natives of the country, who call themselves *Nouba*, whereas, in race, they are genuine Negroes. We dwell not, however, on exotic races; but upon the Nubians proper: whose type is independent of this chaos of national names, often erroneously given *to* them, as well as misappropriated by them. Dr. Prichard says:—

"The descent of the modern Nubians or Barabra, from the *Nouba* of the hill country of Kordofàn, seems to be as well established as very many facts which are regarded as certain by writers on ethnography."

But the *Baràbra* are not Negroes; their hair, though slightly frizzled and crisp, is long and not woolly: and Prichard's surmise of any great Nubian displacements since Pharaonic times, was doubted by Morton,[236] and is overthrown by facts we owe to Birch.[237] Burckhardt, Cailliaud, and other travellers who have visited this part of Africa, tell us that the *Noubas*, who are Negroes, do not here resemble in form, features, hair, complexion, &c., other Negroes of the west coast, but approximate more closely to the type of Baràbra or true Nubians. It is clear that there exists some strongly-marked difference between the *Nouba* of Kordofàn and the *Baràbra* of Nubia; which Dr. Prichard is at a loss whether to attribute to climate or to comminglings of races. Of the two opinions the latter is the only reasonable one; because the Nubians or modern Baràbra are the representatives of an original indigenous stock; whose normal position stands northward of pure Negro races.

The inhabitants of Dar-Four and Fezzàn exhibit some striking peculiarities, but we shall pass them by, as non-essential to our present objects, with the observation that, while the former approximate the Nubian, the latter verge towards the Atlantic Berber type.

The Eastern Nubians, or *Bisharine* or *Bejawy* Race.—To the eastward of Nubia, throughout the deserts and denuded hill-country east of Egypt, we encounter different tribes and nations, all supposed to belong to the same race, which is one of the most widely-spread in Ethiopia, stretching from the Eastern desert at Thebes, to the Somauli-country below Shoa. The *Bishari* are the most powerful of these clans. The *Hadharebe*, to the southward of the Bishari, and the Ababdeh, to the northward, belong, it is believed, to the same stock. Under the appellation *Hadharebe* are included numerous tribes, which it would be tedious and useless to enumerate.[238] *Suàkim*, or Suàkin, is their principal settlement; and of this place and its inhabitants Burckhardt supplies an ample account.

> "The Suakiny have, in general, handsome and expressive features, with thin and very short beards; their color is of the darkest brown, approaching black, but they have nothing of the Negro character of countenance."[239]

To the same excellent observer we are indebted for a fact that, seized upon to sustain the exploded idea of physical changes through climate, in reality affords the happiest illustration of the mode through which types of man become naturally effaced; viz.: by foreign amalgamations. The town of Suàkim; in Ptolemaic times *Berenice;* and containing (970 B. C.) the ancestors of the same *Sukkiim*[240] that now reside in its neighborhood; exhibited in Burckhardt's day a triple population, viz.: native *Hadharebe*, Arabs from the opposite coast, and the descendants of some Turkish soldiery left there by Sooltan Seleem. "The present race," says Burckhardt, "have the African features and manners, and are in no way to be distinguished from the Hadherebe."[241]

Turkish soldiery cohabit with the females of every land in which they are posted; and, while they rarely carry their own women with them, of all points of Ottoman conquests, *Suàkim*, on the African desert-coast of the Red Sea, would be the least likely to have been occupied by Turkish married couples. In consequence, Seleem's garrison there, after the subjugation of Egypt in A. D. 1517, adopted as wives and concubines the females of the *Hadharebe;* and in less than ten generations, down to the period of Burckhardt's travels, their descendants had been already absorbed into the aboriginal masses whence the mothers had been drawn.[242] Sustainers of "unity," who once snatched franticly at *Turks* metamorphosed, by climate, into Africans, are welcome henceforward to what capital they can evolve from Burckhardt's narrative.

The country of the Bishari reaches from the northern frontier of Abyssinia, along the course of the river Mareb, which flows through the northern forests of the Shangallah to the Belàd-el-Taka and Atbara, where dwell the Hadendoa and Hammadab, said to be the strongest tribe of the Bishari race. Tribes of the Bishari reach northward as far as Gebel-el-Ottaby in the latitude of Derr, where the Nile, after its great western bend, turns back towards the Red Sea; they occupy all the hilly country upon the Nile from Sennàar to Dar Berber and to the Red Sea. (PRICHARD.) Travellers do not give a flattering account of their social condition. Burckhardt states: "The inhospitable character of the Bisharein would alone prove them to be a true African race, were this not put beyond all doubt by their language." Rüppell declares that the physical character of the Bishari is very like that of the Baràbra. Burckhardt again observes, "The Bishari of Atbara, like their brethren, are a handsome and bold race of people. I thought the women remarkably handsome; they were of a dark brown complexion, with beautiful eyes and fine teeth; their persons slender and elegant." Hamilton, who saw a few of them during his short stay about Assouàn and Philæ, yields very much the same account, with the commentary, that many of them are beheld with "a cast of the Negro, others with very fine profile." Prichard makes the following just and significant remark on this description: "This sort of variety in physiognomy is observed by almost every traveller in the *eastern* parts of the continent, from Kaffirland to Nubia and Egypt." Now, on the *west*, the population has been cut off, by deserts and other natural impediments, from all foreign admixtures, in consequence of their isolated position; while, on the *east*, they have been subjected from time immemorial to adulteration from Semitic immigrants. Both the Bishari and Ababdeh have been somewhat adulterated with Arab blood; and, doubtless, far more so through Negresses, their slaves. They may, however, be considered a tolerably pure *African* race, inasmuch as the marks of adulteration are not by any means universal; at the same time they have preserved their native tongue, while the Arabic idioms have supplanted other languages around them.

The *Ababdeh* occupy the country to the northward of the Bishari; viz.: from the parallel of Derr to the frontiers of Egypt, and in the eastern desert as far northward as Qosseyr: they were scarcely known previously to the French Expedition to Egypt. M. du Bois Aymè, a member of Napoleon's Egyptian commission, affords the earliest description of the Ababdeh: —

"Les Abâbdeh sont un tribu nomade, qui habitent les montagnes situées a l'orient du Nil, au sud de la vallée de Qoçeyr. Ils diffèrent entièrement, par leur mœurs, leur language, leur costume, leur constitution physique, des tribus d'Arabes, qui, comme ceux ci, occupent les deserts qui environnent l'Egypte. Les Arabs sont blancs, se rasent la tête, sont vetus. Les Abâbdeh sont noirs, mais leur traits ont beaucoup de ressemblance avec ceux des Européens. Ils ont les cheveux *naturellement bouclês*, mais point laineux."

Belzoni, who knew them well, says their complexions are naturally of a dark chocolate; their hair quite black; their teeth fine and white, protuberant and very large.

It will be seen, from what precedes, that considerable is the discrepancy among descriptions by travellers of these Ababdeh and Bishareen, as well as of other races. This arises, doubtless, from two facts: 1, That they are a mixed population, descended from several primitive races; 2, That they have been described at different topographical points.

The following observations of M. Prisse—whose residence among these tribes in Upper Egypt counts years where others reckon months, or, more frequently, weeks, is a guarantee for the accuracy of his ethnological drawings — completely demonstrate the truth of our deductions: —

"The manners of the Bedjah described by Arab authors are even yet those of these populations, who, under the name of Ababdeh, of Bishari, or Bichareen, and others less known, inhabit the same countries at this day. . . . . . In 1836, out of 500 men (Ababdeh) of the tribe, assembled at Louqsor for the transportation of wheat to Cosséir, nearly 100 Arabs were found, who had married Ababdeh girls to avoid the conscription and the taxes. . . . . . The Ababdeh have a peculiar idiom, which seems to be that of the aborigines, or the ancient Ethiopians. . . . . . The *Bishari* commence at the north, where the Ababdeh finish, and extend to the south as far as the vicinity of Souakim. They occupy all that chain of mountains which runs along the eastern coast of Africa, and that seems to be the cradle of all these wandering septs, living in grottoes, and designated in consequence under the name of *Troglodytes*. They derive their origin from the Blemmyes, a nomad people of the environs of Axum, which the love of pillage drew towards Egypt [that is, in Roman times; when Coptic annals recount the ravages as low as Esneh of the *Bal-n-Moui*, "Eye-of-Lion," or *Blemmyes*. [243]] The manners of the Bishari differ little from those of the Ababdeh, with whom, nevertheless, they are ever at war. . . . . . Their language has drawn nothing from the Arabic, and seems to approach the Abyssinian and the Berber [*i. e. Berberee.*] This people, truly *indigenous to Africa*, is cruel, avaricious, and vindictive; these dispositions are restrained by no law, human or divine."[244]

We copy (Fig. 120) one of Prisse's engravings. It exhibits the perfect *Bishari*, but differs too slightly from the Ababdeh characteristics not to exemplify both tribes equally well.

Fig. 120.

Among Dr. Morton's papers we find the copy of a letter, addressed from the *Isle of Philæ*, Sept. 15, 1844, by Chev. Lepsius, to our erudite countryman, the late JOHN PICKERING, of Boston. Being inedited, and mentioned only by one writer[215] that we know of, we translate such passages as bear upon Nubian subjects, not merely for their intrinsic value, but in tribute to the memory of the profoundest native philologist that our country has hitherto produced.

"I have no need, certainly, to insist, as regards yourself, upon the high importance which linguistic researches always possess in ethnographical studies. I have not neglected, either, to study, to the extent that time permitted, the different tongues of the Soudàn, whenever I could find individuals who were in a state to communicate anything about their own language, through the medium of Arabic. The three principal tongues which I have studied in this manner, and of which I now possess the grammar and vocabulary, sufficiently complete to give an idea of their nature, are — the *Nobinga*, or Nouba, ordinarily known under the strange name of Berber, which is spoken in three different dialects in the valley of the Nile, from Assouàn to the southern frontier of the province of Dongola, as also in certain parts of Kordifal (this is the true pronunciation in lieu of *Kordofàn*): 2d, The *Kongàra*, or language of Dar-Four, a very extended speech of Negroes, of which until now even the name was unknown: 3d, The *Bégawìe*, or the language of the *Bicharîba*, who occupy the country west of the Nile from 23° to 15°, and principally the fertile province of Taka. The most interesting among these three tongues is, without doubt, the third. The grammar causes it to be recognized without difficulty as *appertaining to the great family of Caucasian languages*, as I think I was the first to demonstrate of the Egyptian tongue (in 1835, by comparison of the pronouns; in 1836 by that of the names of number); and as known concerning the Abyssinian tongue. This fact alone proves that the primitive origin of all these people, of this eastern part of Africa, must have been in Asia. [We do not perceive why such deduction necessarily follows. "Caucasian" is a term that physiology must abandon, as a misnomer productive of confusion; but the above was penned in haste, nine years ago, and the erudite writer may since have seen occasion, as we have ourselves, to modify first impressions]. . . . Finally, this tongue becomes to us of a far higher importance, through the circumstance that I think I shall be able to prove that the same people, who now speak this tongue, formerly inhabited the *Isle of Meroë*; built the temples and the pyramids, of which we still there find the ruins. . . . The people who ruled then, in this great kingdom, called themselves *Béga* (Bedja); a name which is now entirely lost as the name of a people, but which originated the name of the tongue *Bégawìe*, of which I have spoken above. . . . One facilely perceives at once, by many well-preserved paintings, that the people who built the pyramids [of Meroë] were a *red* people, or, rather, very reddish [*bien rougeâtre*], as might have been expected if they spoke veritably a Caucasian language. But nothing presents itself to the most scrupulous investigations that could lead us to suspect that a single one of the monuments [of Meroë] might ascend higher than the first century after J. C. The greater part belong, without doubt, even to much later times; and we must place the most flourishing epoch of Meroë nearly at the second or third of our era. And, not only upon the Isle of Meroë, but in all Ethiopia, from one end to the other, there is not the slightest trace, I will not say of a primitive civilization anterior to the Egyptian civilization, as has been dreamed, but not even whatsoever of an *Ethiopian* civilization, properly so called."[216]

These most scientific views of Chev. Lepsius were communicated to us long ago; and they have materially aided our endeavors to discriminate between the true and the false, the certain and the improbable, in *Ethiopic* problems; about which, we grieve to say, considerable mystification is still kept up between the Northern and the Southern States of our Federal Union, which a little reading might remove.

On the northern coast of Africa, between the Mediterranean and the Great Desert, including Morocco, Algiers, Tunis, Tripoli, and Bengazi, there is a continuous system of highlands, which have been included under the general term *Atlas*, anciently *Atalantis*, now the Barbary States. This immense tract, in very recent geological times, was once an *Island*, with the ocean flowing over the whole of the Sahara; thus cutting off all land-communication between Barbary, on the Mediterranean, and the remote plateaux of Nigritia. Throughout Barbary we encounter another peculiar group of races, subdivided into many tribes of various shades, now spread over a vast area, but which formerly had its principal, and probably aboriginal, abode, along the mountain-slopes of Atlas. The tribes have different appellatives in different districts: *e. g.*, the *Shillouhs*, now a separate people,[247] have been included under the general name of *Berbers* or *Berebbers:* but from the primitive Berbers the north of Africa seems to have derived the designation of *Barbary* or *Berberia*, "Land of the *Berbers*." To speak correctly, the real name of the Berbers proper is *Mazirgh;* with the article prefixed or suffixed, T-*amazirgh*, or *Amazirgh*-T: meaning, *free*, *dominant*, or "*noble* race." Their name, in Latin mouths, was softened into *Masyes*, *Masiges*, *Mazici*, &c.; and in Grecian, into Μαζυες, as far back as Herodotus (*lib.* iv. 191). These people have spoken a language unlike any other from time immemorial; and, although it has been a fruitful theme of discussion, yet no affinity can be established between its ancient words, stripped of Phœnician and Arabic, and any Asiatic tongue. We have every reason to feel persuaded that the Berbers existed in the remotest times, with all their essential moral and physical peculiarities. In a word, the reader of Part II. of this work will see, that there exists no ground for regarding them in any other light than as the autocthones of Mount Atlas and its prolongations. The Berber was, probably, as Mr. W. B. HODGSON (of Savannah — one of the highest authorities in Berber lore,) remarks, the language which "Tyria Bilingua" was obliged to learn in addition to a Carthaginian mother-tongue, the Punic or Phœnician speech. We know that this people, with their language stamped upon the native names of rivers, mountains, and localities, have existed apart for the last 2500 years; and inasmuch as Egypt, back to the time of Menes, barred their intercourse by land with races on the eastern side of the Suez isthmus, there is every reason to believe that the Berbers existed, at that remote date, in the same state in which they were discovered by Phœnician navigators, previously to the foundation of Carthage. At the time of Leo Africanus, the Berber was the language of all Atlas. It has remained so since, except where crowded out by Arabic. They are an indomitable nomadic people, who, since the introduction of *camels*, have penetrated, in considerable numbers, into the Desert, and even as far as Nigritia. These Berbers are the Numidians and Mauritanians of classical writers, by the Romans termed "*genus insuperabile bello;*" and French Algeria can testify to the indelible bellicosities of the living race.

We gather from SHAW, that —

"The tribes who speak this language have different names: those of the mountains belonging to Morocco are termed *Shilloukhs;* those who inhabit the plains of that empire, dwelling under tents, after the manner of Arabs, are named *Berber;* and those of the mountains belonging to Algiers and Tunis call themselves *Cabaylis*, or *Gebalis*" [a designation which is merely *Qabâil*, Arabic for a "tribe," when not *Gebâylee*, "mountaineer."]

A fourth and prominent branch must be added to this division: viz., the *Tuaryk*, who are now widely spread over the Sahara and its oases, and on both banks of the Niger.

Mr. HODGSON, long resident officially in the Barbary States, who has devoted much time, talent, and learning, to this subject, seems to have settled the question, that all these Berber races (except such few as have adopted the Arabic) speak dialects of the same language. In consequence, it has been assumed, by Prichard and others of the Unity-school, that they must all be of a common origin. But, while of this there is no evidence beyond a community of languages, the manifest diversity of physical characters would prove the contrary. Some of these clans are white; others black, with woolly hair; and there is no fact better established in ethnography, than that physical characters are far more persistent than unwritten tongues. The great mass of the Berber tribes have, in all likelihood, substantially preserved their physical as well as moral characters since their creation; although they have been to some extent subjected to adulterations of blood. The Phœnicians, Greeks, Romans, and Vandals, successively, founded colonies in the Barbary States: but they built and inhabited towns for commercial purposes — mixed little socially with the people — never resided in the interior, and have disappeared from the scene, leaving nearly imperceptible traces behind them. Arabs have since overrun the country, but their numbers have been small, compared with the natives; and, except during and since Saracenic culture in the towns, they have generally preserved their nomadic habits — keeping much aloof from the indigenous Barbaresques; and there is not merely no reason for thinking that Arabia has exercised great influence on the Berber type, but circumstances rather indicate Barbary's action over the Arab colonists. The ruling tuition of the Arabs, the genial vitality of *Islàm*, and the constant reading of the Koràn, have had the effect of spreading the *Arabic language* much faster and farther than Arabian blood. In some of the more civilized cities—Morocco, Fez, &c.—Arabic is the only tongue spoken among the patrician Berbers; thus affording another evidence of the utter fallacy of arguments in favor of the *identity of origin* or *consanguinity* of races based solely upon *community of language.*

The Mohammedan in Africa, like the Christian religion elsewhere, is spreading its own languages over races of all colors: just as did Shamanism, Budhism, or Judaism, in many parts of Asia, during ages past. Many Jews are scattered throughout Barbary, but especially in the empire of Morocco, where their number is estimated at 500,000. Some black blood too has infiltrated from the South.

No little difference exists in descriptions of the physical characters of Barbary Moors (corruption of the Latin *Mauri*), no less than concerning the native tribes of Atlas now diffused over the Sahara. Prichard says —

"Their figure and stature are nearly the same as those of the Southern Europeans; and their complexion, if darker, is only so in proportion to the higher temperature of the countries which they inhabit. It displays, as we shall see, great varieties."

The influence of climate is here again boldly assumed by Prichard, without one particle of evidence. What reason is there to suppose that climate influences Berbers, any more than it does Mongols, American Indians, or other races, who, each with their typical complexions, are spread over most latitudes? Moreover, the complexion of the Berbers does not, in very many cases at least, correspond with climate. The same action, we presume, operates in Barbaresque localities that seems to prevail in various parts of the earth; and which we have insisted upon in our general Remarks on Types. The Berber family, at present, appears to be made up of many tribes, presenting a sort of generic resemblance, but differing specifically, and possessing physical characteristics that are original, and not amenable to climatic influences any more than those which denote the Jew, the Iberian, or the Celt.

We submit a few examples of Atalantic physical characters, as described by various travellers. JACKSON informs us, that—

"The men of Temsena and Showiah are of a strong, robust make, and of a *copper-color*—the women beautiful.... The women of Fez are fair as the European, but hair and eyes always dark.... The women of Mequinas are very beautiful, and have the *red and white complexion of English women*."

ROZET gives the annexed description of the Moors:—

"Il existe cependant encore un certain nombre de familles, qui n'ont point contracté d'alliances avec des étrangers, et chez lesquelles on retrouve les caractères de la race primitive. Les hommes sont d'une taille au dessus de la moyenne; leur démarche est noble et grave; ils ont les cheveux noirs; la peau *un peu basanée*, mais plutôt blanche que brune; le visage plein, mais les traits en sont moins bien prononcés que ceux des Arabes et des Berbères. Ils ont généralement le nez arrondi, la bouche moyenne, les yeux tres ouverts, mais peu vifs; leurs muscles sont bien prononcés, et ils ont le corps plutôt gros que maigre."

SPIX and MARTIUS, the well-known German travellers, depict them as follows:—

"A high forehead, an oval countenance, large, speaking black eyes, shaded by arched and strong eyebrows; a thin, rather long, but not too pointed, nose; rather broad lips, meeting in an acute angle; thick, smooth, and black hair on the head and in the beard; *brownish-yellow complexion;* a strong neck, joined to a stature greater than the middle height, characterize the natives of Northern Africa, as they are frequently seen in the streets of Gibraltar."

M. ROZET recounts, that—

"The Berbers or Kabyles of the Algerine territory are of middle stature; their complexion is *brown*, and sometimes almost black (*noirâtre*); hair brown and smooth, rarely blond; they are lean, but extremely robust and nervous, very well-formed, and with the elegance of antique statues; their heads more round than the Arabs'."

Lieutenant WASHINGTON declares—

"The Moors are generally a fine-looking race of men, of middle stature, disposed to become corpulent; they have good teeth; *complexions of all shades*, owing, as some have supposed, to intermixture with Negroes, though the latter are not sufficiently numerous to account for the fact."

He describes the Shillouhs or Shilhas as having *light complexions*.

PRICHARD thus sums up his inquiries:—

'It seems, from these accounts, that the nations whose history we have traced in this chapter, *present all varieties* of complexion; and these variations appear, *in some instances at least*, to be *nearly in relation to the temperature*."

With all his inclination that way, however, it is evident that he himself cannot make his own climatic theory fit.

Our reasonings are based upon comparison of Barbaresque families diffused over a vast superficies—comprising tribes now more or less commingled, and in all social conditions, civic, agricultural, and nomadic. We may mention, although we exclude, as too local and modern to be important out of towns on the seaboard, the combined influences of European *captives*, at Salee, Tangiers, Algiers, Tunis, Tripoli, Bengazi, and other privateering principalities; which circumstances, in the maritime cities, have blended every type of man that could be kidnapped around the Black Sea, Mediterranean, and Eastern Atlantic, by Barbary pirates. [As an illustration — Mr. Gliddon tells us, that, in 1830, just after the French conquest of Algiers, the hold of a Syrian brig, in which he sailed from Alexandria to Sidon, was occupied by one wealthy Algerine family, fleeing from Gallic heresies to Arabian Islâm, anywhere. Exclusive of servants and slaves, there were at least fifty adults and minors, under the control of a patriarchal grand or great-grandfather. Of course, our informant saw none of the grown-up females unveiled; but, while the patriarch and some of the sons were of the purest white complexion, their various children presented every hue, and every physical diversity, from the highest Circassian to a Guinea-Negro. In this case, no Arabic interpreter being needed, it was found that each individual of the worthy corsair's family, unprejudiced in all things, save hatred towards Christendom in general and Frenchmen in particular, had merely chosen females irrespectively of color, race, or creed.—J. C. N.]

HODGSON states —

"The Tuarycks are a *white* people, of the Berber race. . . . The Mozabicks are a remarkably *white* people, and are mixed with Bedouin Arabs. . . . The Wadreagans and Wurgelans are of a *dark bronze*, with *woolly hair* . . . are certainly not pure Caucasian, like the Berber race in general. . . . There is every probability that the Kushites, Amalekites, and Kahtanites, or Beni-Yoktân Arabs, had, in obscure ages, sent forward tribes into Africa. But the first historic proof of emigration of the Aramean or Shemitic race into this region is that of the Canaanites of Tyre and of Palestine. This great commercial people settled Carthage, and pushed their traders to the Pillars of Hercules."[248]

Upon these various branches of a supposed common stock, there have been engrafted some shoots of foreign origin; for, amidst a uniformity of language, there exist extraordinary differences of color and of physical traits — at the same time, are we sure of this alleged uniformity of speech itself? Now, we repeat, history affords no well-attested example of a language outliving a clearly-defined physical type; and, in a preceding chapter, we fully instanced how the Jews, scattered for 2000 years over all climates of the earth, have adopted the language of every nation among whom they sojourn — thus affording *one* undeniable proof of our assertion, not to mention many others one might draw from less historical races.

Mr. Hodgson is a strenuous advocate of an extreme antiquity for the Berbers, or Libyans: —

"Their history is yet to be investigated and written. I yet maintain the opinion advanced some years ago, that these people were the *terræ geniti* — the aboriginal inhabitants of Egypt, prior to the historic or monumental era, and before the Mizraimites and their descendants, the Copts."[249]

In our Part II., these skilful inferences are singularly reconciled with the monuments and history, and from an altogether different point of view. When we remember how, in Hebrew personifications, MIZRAIM was the grandson of NOAH, and how Lepsius traces the Egyptian Empire back nearly 4000 years before Christ, a claim of such antiquity for the Berbers is certainly a high one, although, according to our belief, not extravagant; for we regard the Berbers as a primitive type, and therefore as old as any men of our geological period. Hodgson confirms his statement, by abundant proofs, that "the grammatical structure of the Berber dialects is everywhere the same;" and, in allusion to the affinities among these languages, avers: —

"Yet, with all this identity of a peculiar class of words and similarity of some inflections, adjunct particles, and formations — *the three most ancient and historical languages, Arabic, Berber, and Coptic, are essentially distinct.*"

With perfect propriety, our friend might have added the Chinese speech, which is equally peculiar, and can be traced monumentally farther back than either the Arabic or the Berber — if not, certainly, so far as that ante-monumental tongue which is prototype of the Coptic. It seems to us, that no one can read PAUTHIER's several works on Chinese history, language, and literature, without coinciding in this opinion; and every one can verify that the languages of America, according to GALLATIN, DUPONCEAU, and other qualified judges, are radically distinct from every tongue, ancient or modern, of the Old Continent.

Our ethnological sweep over the African Continent, from the Cape of Good Hope northwards to the Nubias on the right hand, and to Barbary on the left, incomplete as it is — wearisome, to many readers, as it may be — has brought us to the confines of *Egypt*. In that most ancient of historical lands we propose to halt, for a season; devoting the next chapter to its study. But, by way of succinct recapitulation of some results we think the present chapter has elicited, we would inquire of the candid reader, whether, at the present moment, the human races indigenous to Africa do not present themselves, on a map, so to say, *in layers?* Whether the most southern of its inhabitants, the Hottentots and Bushmen, are not the lowest types of humanity therein found? And lastly, whether, in the ratio of our progress towards the Mediterranean, passing successively through the Caffre, the Negro, and the Foolah populations, to the Abyssinian and Nubian races on the east, and to the Atalantic Berber races on the west, we have not beheld the Types of Mankind rising, almost continuously, higher and higher in the scale of physical and intellectual gradations?

Such are the phenomena. *Climate*, most certainly, does not explain them; nor will any student of Natural History sustain that each type of man in Africa is not essentially homogeneous with the fauna and the flora of the special province wherein his species now dwells.

Two questions arise:—1st, Within human record, has it not *always* been thus? and 2d, Do the *Egyptians*, northernmost inhabitants of Africa, obey the same geographical law of physical, and consequently of mental and moral, progression?

Our succeeding chapters may suggest, to the reflective mind, some data through which both interrogatories can be answered.

CHAPTER VII.

EGYPT AND EGYPTIANS.

Our survey of African races, so far, has been rapid and imperfect, but still we hope it is sufficiently full to develop our idea of *gradation* in the inhabitants of that great continent. A more copious analysis would have surpassed our limits, while becoming unnecessarily tedious to the reader. Prichard has devoted a goodly octavo of his "*Physical History*" to these races alone; whereas we can afford but a few pages.

We now approach Egypt, the last geographical link in African Ethnology. She has ever been regarded as the mother of arts and sciences; and, strange as it may seem, Science now appeals to her to settle questions in the Natural History of Man, mooted since the days of Herodotus, the father of our historians.

When we cast a retrospect through the long and dreary vista of years, which leads to the unknown epoch of Man's creation, in quest of a point of departure where we can obtain the first historical glimpse of a human being on our globe, the Archæologist is compelled to turn to the monuments of the Nile. The records of India cannot any longer be traced even to the time of Moses. Hebrew chronicles, beyond Abraham, present no stand-point on which we can rely; whilst their highest pretension to antiquity falls short by 2000 years of the foundation of the Egyptian Empire. The

Chinese, according to their own historians, do not carry their true historic period beyond 2637 years before Christ. Nineveh and Babylon, monumentally speaking, are still more modern. But, Egypt's proud pyramids, if we are to believe the Champollion-school, elevate us at least 1000 years above every other nationality. And, what is more remarkable, when Egypt first presents herself to our view, she stands forth not in childhood, but with the maturity of manhood's age, arrayed in the time-worn habiliments of civilization. Her tombs, her temples, her pyramids, her manners, customs, and arts, all betoken a full-grown nation. The sculptures of the IVth dynasty, the earliest extant, show that the arts at that day, some 3500 B. C., had already arrived at a perfection little inferior to that of the XVIIIth dynasty, which, until the last five years, was regarded as her Augustan age.

Egyptian monuments, considered ethnologically, are not only inestimable as presenting us *two* types of mankind at this early period, but they display other contemporary races equally marked — thus affording proof that humanity, in its infinite varieties, has existed much longer upon earth than we have been taught; and that physical causes have not, and cannot transform races from one type into another.

Among former objections against the antiquity of Egyptian monuments, it has been urged, that such numerous centuries could not have elapsed with so little change in people, arts, customs, language, and other conditions. This adverse charge, however, does not in itself hold good, because the fixedness of civilization, or veneration for the customs of ancestors, seems to be an inherent characteristic of Eastern nations. Through the extensive portion of Egyptian history which is now known with sufficient certainty, we may admit a comparative adhesion to fixed formulæ, and an indisposition to change: but no Egyptologist will deny that, during nearly 6000 years, for which monuments are extant, the developing mutations in Egyptian economy obeyed the same laws as in that of other races — with this signal advantage in the former's favor, that we possess an almost unbroken chain of coetaneous records for each progressive step. Oriental history anteceding Christian ages (when viewed through the eye-glasses of pedagogues who rank among CARLYLE'S "doleful creatures,") looms monstrously, like a chaotic blur, precisely where archæology, using mere naked eyes, has long espied most luminous stratifications: and human developments, requiring "chiliads of years," even yet are popularly restricted to the action of one *patriarchal* lifetime. For ourselves, referring to the works of the hierologists for explanation, we would readily join issue with objectors upon the following heads: —

IVth DYNASTY — B. C. 3400.	*Egyptian developments down to the* CHRISTIAN ERA.
1st. LANGUAGE — Only 15 articulations, ...	developed, in the Coptic, to 31 letters.
2d. WRITING — Hieroglyphics, ...	then Hieratic, next Demotic, and lastly *Coptic*.
3d. ARCHITECTURE — Pyramids, ...	then temples with *Doric*, and lastly with every kind of column.
4th. GEOGRAPHY — Egypt proper, ...	then, gradually, knowledge as extensive as that of the Evangelists.
5th. ZOOLOGY—No horses, camels, or common fowls,	then, every animal known to Aristotle.
6th. ARTS — No chariots, ...	then, all vehicles generally used by the ancients.
7th. SCIENCES — No bitumenized mummies, .	then, every form, with many kinds of foreign drugs, &c.

8th. ETHNOLOGY, *Native* — 1st. Egyptian type, then
2d. Egypto-Asiatic,
3d. Egypto-Negroid.
Foreign — IVth dynasty — *Arabs.*
XIIth dynasty — *Arabians, Libyans, Nubians, Negroes.*
XVIIIth dynasty — *Canaanites, Jews, Phœnicians, Assyrians, Tartars, Hindoos, Thracians, Ionians, Lydians, Libyans—Nubians, Abyssinians, Negroes.*
And, thence to *Oriental mankind*, as known to the Greeks in ALEXANDER's day.

We might extend this mnemonical list through many other departments of knowledge; but, until these positive instances of development be overthrown, let us hear no more fables about "*stationary* Egyptians."

It was, however, only through alien rule, introduced in later times by Persians, Greeks, Romans, Arabs, and Turks, that all old habits were uprooted. Look at India and China; which countries, according to popular superstitions, seem to have been stereotyped some three or four thousand years ago: yet, what enormous changes does not the historian behold in them! Nevertheless, every type is more or less tenacious of its habits; and we might cite how the Arabs, the Turks, and, still more, the Jews, now scattered throughout all nations of the earth, cling to the customs of their several ancestries: but, as we are merely suggesting a few topics for the reader's meditation, let us inquire, what was the *type* of that Ancient Egyptian race which linked Africa with Asia? This interrogatory has given rise to endless discussions, nor can it, even now, be regarded as absolutely answered. For many centuries prior to the present, as readers of ROLLIN and of VOLNEY may remember, the Egyptians were reputed to be *Negroes*, and Egyptian civilization was believed to have descended the Nile from *Ethiopia!* Champollion, Rosellini, and others, while unanimous in overthrowing the former, to a great extent consecrated the latter of these errors, which could hardly be considered as fully refuted until the appearance of Gliddon's *Chapters on Ancient Egypt*, in 1843, and of Morton's *Crania Ægyptiaca*, in 1844. The following extract presents the first-named author's deductions:—

"The importance of confining history to its legitimate place—to *Lower* Egypt—is evident:

"1st. Because it was in Lower Egypt that the Caucasian children of Ham must have first settled, on their arrival from Asia.

"2d. Because the advocates of the theory which would assert the *African* origin of the Egyptians say that they rely chiefly on history for their African, or Ethiopic, predilections.

"3d. Because the same theorists assume, that we must begin with *Africans*, at the top of the Nile, and come downward with civilization; instead of commencing with *Asiatics* and *White men*, at the bottom, and carrying it up.

"I have not as yet touched on ethnography, the effects of climate, and the antiquity of the different races of the human family; but I shall come to those subjects, after establishing a chronological standard, by defining the history of Egypt according to the hieroglyphics. At present, I intend merely to sketch the events connected with the Caucasian children of Ham, the Asiatic, on the first establishment of their Egyptian monarchy, and the foundation of their first and greatest metropolis in Lower Egypt.

"The African theories are based upon no critical examination of early history—are founded on no Scriptural authority for early migrations—are supported by no monumental evidence, or hieroglyphical data, and cannot be borne out or admitted by practical common sense. For civilization, that never came *northward* out of benighted Africa, (but from the Deluge to the present moment has been only partially carried into it—to sink into utter oblivion among the barbarous races whom Providence created to inhabit the Ethiopian and Nigritian territories of that vast continent,) *could* not spring from Negroes, or from Berbers, and *never did*.

"So far, then, as the record, Scriptural, historical, and monumental, will afford us an insight into the early progress of the human race in Egypt, the most ancient of all civilized countries, we may safely assert, that history, when analyzed by common sense—when scrutinized by the application of the experience bequeathed to us by our forefathers—when subjected to a strictly impartial examination into, and comparison of, the physical and mental capabilities of nations—when distilled in the alembic of chronology, and submitted to the touchstone of hieroglyphical tests, will not support that superannuated, but untenable, doctrine, that civilization originated in Ethiopia, and consequently among an African people, by whom it was brought down the Nile, to enlighten the less polished, therefore inferior, Caucasian children of Noah, the Asiatics; or, that we, who trace back to Egypt the origin of every art and science known in antiquity, have to thank the sable Negro, or the dusky Berber, for the first gleams of knowledge and invention.

We may therefore conclude with the observation that, if civilization, instead of going from *North* to *South*, came (contrary, as shown before, to the annals of the earliest historians and all monumental facts) down the "Sacred Nile," to illumine our darkness; and, if the Ethiopic origin of arts and sciences, with social, moral, and religious institutions, were in other respects *possible*, these African theoretic conclusions would form a most astounding exception to the ordinations of Providence and the organic laws of nature, otherwise so undeviating throughout all the generations of man's history.

"I have already stated that Sir J. Gardner Wilkinson's critical observations, during his long residence in Egypt, and his comparisons between the present Egyptians and the ancient race, as depicted in the monuments, had led him to assert the *Asiatic* origin of the early inhabitants of the Nilotic valley. The learned hierologist, Samuel Birch, Esq., of the British Museum, informed me, in London, that he had arrived at the same conclusion—while to his suggestion I am indebted for the first idea 'that the most ancient Egyptian monuments lie *North*.' The great naturalists, Blumenbach and Cuvier, declared, that all the mummies they had opportunities of examining presented the Caucasian type. M. Jomard, the eminent hydrographer and profound Orientalist, in a paper on Egyptian ethnology, sustains the *Arabian*, and consequently the *Asiatic* and *Caucasian*, origin of the early Egyptians; and his opinions are more valuable, as he draws his conclusions independently of hieroglyphical discoveries. On the other hand, Prof. Rosellini, throughout his '*Monumenti*,' accepts and continues the doctrine of the *descent* of civilization from Ethiopia, and the *African* origin of the Egyptians. Champollion-Figeac supports the same theory, which his illustrious brother set forth in the sketch of Egyptian history presented by him to Mohammed-Ali, in 1829 (published in his '*Letters from Egypt and Nubia*'), wherein he derives the Ancient Egyptians, according to the Grecian authorities, from Ethiopia, and considers them to belong to 'la race Barabra,' the *Berbers* or *Nubians*. Deeming the original *Baràbra* to have been an *African* race, engrafted at the present day with Caucasian as well as Negro blood, I reject *their* similitude to the monumental Egyptians *in toto*, and am fain to believe that Champollion-le-Jeune himself had either modified his previous hastily-formed opinion, or, at any rate, had not taken a decided stand on this important point, from the following extract of his eloquent address from the academic chair, delivered May 10, 1831:—C'est par l'analyse raisonnée de la langue des Pharaons, que l'ethnographie *décidera* si la vieille population égyptienne fut d'origine *Asiatique*, ou bien *si elle descendit*, avec le fleuve divinisé, des plateaux de l'Afrique centrale. On décidera en même temps si les Egyptiens n'appartenaient point à une race distincte; car, il faut le déclarer ici [in which I entirely agree with him], contre l'opinion commune, les *Coptes* de l'Egypte moderne, regardés comme les derniers rejetons des anciens Egyptiens, n'ont offert à mes yeux ni la couleur ni aucun des traits caractéristiques, dans les linéaments du visage ou dans les formes du corps, qui pût constater une aussi noble descendance.'"[250]

[These views received considerable extension in Mr. Gliddon's *Otia Ægyptiaca*;[251] and our colleague's enthusiastic concurrence in the work now put forth, in our joint names, sufficiently attests his adoption of our personal modifications, derived especially from Anatomy, compared with the more recent hieroglyphical discoveries.—J. C. N.]

Others, however, though not so decidedly out-spoken in tone, had rejected African delusions. Thus, Pettigrew,[252] following Blumenbach and Lawrence, had previously alluded to the probability of the ascent of civilization, introduced by an Asiatic people, along the Nile, from north to south. De Brotonne,[253] succeeded by Jardot,[254] ably sustained the Asiatic colonization of Egypt against the Nigritian hypothesis of Volney;[255] and, a hundred years ago, the academician De Fourmont[256] declared, "The Egyptians, for the three-fourths, issued either out of Arabia or Phœnicia; . . . Egypt being composed of Chaldæan, Phœnician, Arab people, &c., but especially of these last."

Morton, drawing from his vast resources in craniology, skilfully combined with history and such monuments as were deciphered in 1842, terminated his *Crania Ægyptiaca* with the subjoined conclusions — the utterance of which commenced a new era in anthropological researches:—

"The Valley of the Nile, both in Egypt and Nubia, was originally peopled by a branch of the Caucasian race.

"These primeval people, since called the Egyptians, were the Mizraimites of Scripture, the posterity of Ham, and directly affiliated with the Libyan family of nations.

"The Austral-Egyptian or Meroite communities were an Indo-Arabian stock, engrafted on the primitive Libyan inhabitants.

"Besides these exotic sources of population, the Egyptian race was at different periods modified by the influx of the Caucasian nations of Asia and Europe: Pelasgi, or Hellenes, Scythians, and Phœnicians.

"The Copts, in part at least, are a mixture of the Caucasian and the Negro, in extremely variable proportions.

"Negroes were numerous in Egypt, but their social position in ancient times was the same as it now is: that of servants and slaves.

"The present Fellahs are the lineal and least mixed descendants of the Ancient Egyptians; and the latter are collaterally represented by the Tuariks, Kabyles, Siwahs, and other remains of the Libyan family of nations.

"The modern Nubians, with a few exceptions, are not the descendants of the monumental Ethiopians, but a variously mixed race of Arabs and Negroes.

"The physical or organic characters which distinguish the several races of men are as old as the oldest records of our species."

Such were the best and most natural results of ethnography prior to Lepsius's unanticipated exhumations at Memphis, in 1842–'3; but the latter's discoveries did not become accessible to the authors' joint studies until 1850. We can now assert, with the plates of his splendid *Denkmäler* before us, that, notwithstanding the labors of our predecessors, they have left many doubts and difficulties still hanging around the primitive inhabitants of Egypt. Not only her written traditions, but her monumental history, as far back as it has been traced, prove that, from the *Menaic* foundation of the Empire, she had been engaged in constant strifes with foreign nations of types very different from that of her own aboriginal population, and that she has been often conquered and temporarily ruled by foreigners. Hence the consequence, *prima facie*, that the blood of her primitive inhabitants must have become greatly adulterated.

Morton's *Crania Egyptiaca* issued in 1844; at which day the discoveries of Lepsius were in progress, but not published; at the same time that the works of Rosellini, Champollion, Wilkinson, &c.—then the best sources of information respecting the monuments — did not extend, with the exception of some meagre materials of the XIIth dynasty (by all three scholars then supposed to be the XVIIth), beyond the XVIIIth, or about 1600 B. C. All these complicated data were, nevertheless, most admirably worked up by our revered friend; and he showed conclusively that, while there existed a pervading "Caucasian" Type, which he regarded as the *Egyptian* proper, the population already, at the XVIIIth dynasty, was a very mixed one, comprising many diverse Asiatic and African elements.

Did archæological science now solely rely, as before Champollion's day, upon the concurrent testimony of early Greek writers, we should be compelled to conclude that the Egyptians, previously to the Christian era, were literally *Negroes;* so widely do such Græco-Roman descriptions vary, and so strangely in their writings do Egyptian attributes diverge, from the *Caucasian* type. A passage in HERODOTUS has been often cited; and it possessed the more weight, inasmuch as he travelled in Egypt; and because his authority is generally reliable in such matters as fell beneath his personal observation. Of the people of *Colchis* he says, that they were a colony of Egyptians; supporting his assertion, unique among ancient authorities, by the argument that they were "black in complexion and woolly-haired."[257]

PINDAR also, copying the Halicarnassian, in his fourth Pythian Ode, speaks of the Colchians as *black*. In another passage, when retailing the fable of the Dodonian Oracle, Herodotus again alludes to the swarthy complexion of the Egyptians, as if it were exceedingly dark, or even black. ÆSCHYLUS, in the Supplices, mentions the crew of an Egyptian bark seen from the shore. The person who espies them concludes they must be Egyptians from their *black* complexion:

> "The sailors too I marked,
> Conspicuous in white robes their sable limbs."

Prichard has collected ample Greek and Latin testimony, of similar import, to show that the Egyptians were *dark*. His erudition renders any further ransacking of the Classics here supererogatory: but we may remark that the Greek terms might often apply with equal propriety to a jet-black Negro, or to a brown or dusky Nubian. The various names given to Egypt and her people, together with the mistakes of translators, are, however, analyzed in our Part II., where we treat upon "Mizraim;" and therefore a pause to discuss them now would be superfluous.

Prichard sums up in the following strong language:—

> "From comparing these accounts, some of which were written by persons who had travelled in Egypt, and whose testimony is not likely to have been biassed in any respect, we must conclude that the subjects of the Pharaohs *had something in their physical character approximating to that of the Negro.*"

In opposition to which classical opinions, BEKE, in a paper "*On the Complexion of the Ancient Egyptians,*"[258] had set forth:—

1st. The negative testimony of the Hebrew Scriptures—how JOSEPH'S brethren, when they first saw him in Egypt, supposed him to be an *Egyptian*:[259] how alliances with the Egyptians were permitted by the Israelitish lawgiver:[260] how an Egyptian woman was the mother of the heads of two of the tribes of Israel:[261] another the wife of Solomon, &c.:

2d. That "a description given by Lucian, in one of his Dialogues, ('Navigium, seu Vota,') of a young sailor on board an Egyptian vessel, who, besides being *black*, is represented as *having pouting lips and spindle-shanks"* — rather proves an exception to the usual tint of the Egyptian people:

3d. The incontrovertible evidence of the paintings, and mummy-cases.

We place these discussions of the learned in juxta-position; although new facts supersede the necessity for recurring to past disputations.

That the skins of Egyptians, in Grecian times, were much darker than those of Greeks and other white races around the Archipelago, there can be no question; nor that this complexion was accompanied sometimes with curly or frizzled hair, tumid lips, slender limbs, small heads, with receding foreheads and chins, which, by contrast, excited the wonder or derision of the fair-skinned Hellenes. But, while it must be conceded that Negroes, at no time within the reach even of monumental history, have inhabited any part of Egypt, save as captives; it may, on the other hand, be equally true, that the ancient Egyptians did present a type intermediate between other African and Asiatic races; and, should such be proved to have been the case, the autocthones of Egypt must cease to be designated by the misnomer of "Caucasian."

Whatever the complexion of the real Egyptians may have been, all authorities agree that the races south of Egypt were and are darker; and it is equally clear that the local habitats of Negroes in early times, having ever been the same as they are now, render it geographically impossible that Egyptians could be confounded with distinct types of men, never voluntarily resident within 1200 miles of the Mediterranean.

The Egyptians, on their oldest monuments, always painted their males in *red* and their females in *yellow;* thus adopting in their painted sculptures, (in order to demarcate themselves from foreign nations around them,) colors which, of course, were conventional. That there was considerable diversity of color among the denizens of Egypt need not be doubted, inasmuch as we now find parallel diversity of hues among Berbers, Abyssinians, Nubians, &c. The "Ethiopians" were always darker than the Egyptians proper, as their Greek name (αιθω, *burn*, and ωψ, *face*) of "sun-*burned faces*" implies. In the Ptolemaic papyrus published by Young,[262] and cited by Morton, one of the parties to a sale of land, PSAMMOUTHES, is described as being of a *dark*, while the four others are stated to possess *sallow*, complexions. Rosellini supposes the Egyptians to have been of a *brown* or *reddish-brown* color (*rosso-fosco*) like the present inhabitants of Nubia; but Morton thinks this remark applicable only to Austral Egyptians, and not to the inhabitants of Egypt proper, except when arising from intermixture of races.

In the *Crania Ægyptiaca*, Dr. Morton had laid much stress upon an observation of Ammianus Marcellinus, quoting but a line. Among his inedited MSS. for an improved edition of that work, we find the whole citation as he intended that it should appear:—

> "The following paragraph embraces all of this author's remarks, which only make us lament that he had not been more full and explicit: 'Homines autem Ægyptii *plerique subfusculi* sunt, et *atrati*, magisque mœstiores, gracilenti et aridi, ad singulos motus, excandescentes, controversi et reposcones acerrimi. Erubescit apud eos si quis non inficiando tributa, plurimas in corpore vibices ostendat.' (*Rerum gestarum, lib.* xxxii.)"

But, as the Doctor critically notices, it is difficult to associate the idea of a *black* skin with the fact related by the same writer, that the Egyptians "blush and grow red."

Investigation of this point, in 1844, impressed upon our judicious ethnographer's mind, results which he defines as follows:—

> "From the preceding facts, and many others which might be adduced, I think we may safely conclude that the complexion of the Egyptians did not differ from that of the other Caucasian races, in the same latitudes. That, while the higher classes, who were screened from the action of the sun, were fair, in a comparative sense, the middle and lower classes, like the modern Berbers, Arabs, and Moors, presented various shades of complexion, even to a dark and swarthy tint, which the Greeks regarded as black, in comparison with their own."

So much contradiction is patent in the opinions of the early Greek writers, with regard to the complexion and physical characters of the Egyptians, and the dubiousness has been increased to such an inextricable extent by the opposing scholasticisms of modern historians, yoked with the "first impressions" of unscientific tourists, that the only inference we can attain is, that the Egyptians of the New Empire—that is, from the XVIIth dynasty downwards—were a *mixed* population; presenting considerable varieties of color and conformation. Morton took the whole question out of the hands of the Greeks and their subsequent copyists, when he appealed directly to the iconography of the sculptures, and to the mummied remains of the old population found in the catacombs. Before pursuing, therefore, the monumental history of the Egyptian type into the earliest times, let us endeavor to see what were its physical characters subsequently to the *Restoration* in the seventeenth century B.C.; and afterwards we can better compare them with the pictorial and embalmed vestiges of earlier date.

Although it will be shown that Dr. Morton, since the publication of his *Crania Ægyptiaca*, had made important modifications in some of his opinions, there are others which have withstood triumphantly the test of time. When he published in 1844, his object was to describe and figure the people of Egypt as they appear on the monuments and exist in the sepulchres. Whatever the physical type of the anterior population may have been, previously to the date of his materials, had nothing to do with the task proposed. He was dealing exclusively with known facts, and we cannot but admire the sagacity with which, for the first time in Egyptian ethnology, Morton brought order out of a chaos — universally seen among authors prior to 1844. Considering that he had before him but a few monuments of the XIIth dynasty (in his day called the XVIIth *of Manetho*), and nothing of earlier date, his analysis of these, and of the XVIIIth and succeeding dynasties, must remain an imperishable attestation to his genius.

In order to institute comparisons between the population of these later dynasties with that upon the sculptures of the Old Empire, since discovered, extracts at length from the *Crania Ægyptiaca* will place before the reader the ideas of our great craniologist, together with abundant exemplifications of the type of man prevalent in Egypt during the New Empire.

"The monuments from Meroë to Memphis, present a pervading type of physiognomy, which is everywhere distinguished at a glance from the varied forms which not unfrequently attend it, and which possess so much nationality, both in outline and expression, as to give it the highest importance in Nilotic ethnography. We may repeat that it consists in an upward elongation of the head, with a receding forehead, delicate features, but rather sharp and prominent face, in which a long and straight or gently aquiline nose forms a principal feature. The eye is sometimes oblique, the chin short and retracted, the lips rather tumid, and the hair, whenever it is represented, long and flowing.

"This style of features pertains to every class, kings, priests and people, and can be readily traced through every period of monumental decoration, from the early Pharaohs down to the Greek and Roman dynasties. Among the most ancient, and at the same time most characteristic examples, are the heads of Amunoph the Second and his mother, as represented in a tomb at Thebes,[263] which dates, in Rosellini's chronology, 1727 years before our era. In these effigies all the features are strictly Egyptian, and how strikingly do they correspond with those of many of the embalmed heads from the Theban catacombs!

FIG. 121.

FIG. 122.

"A similar physiognomy preponderates among the royal Egyptian personages of every epoch, as will be manifest to any one who will turn over the pages of Champollion and Rosellini. The head of Horus [see our Fig. 56] is an admirable illustration, while in the portraits of Rameses IV., [III., of Lepsius] and Rameses IX., the same lines are apparent, though much less strongly marked. How admirably also are they seen in the subjoined juvenile head, (Fig. 123) which is that of a royal prince, copied from the very ancient paintings in the tomb of Pehrai, at Eletheias.[264] So also in the face of Rameses VII. (Fig. 124), who lived perhaps one thousand years later in time.

Fig. 123.

Fig. 124.

"I observe that the priests almost invariably present this physiognomy, and, in accordance with the usage of their caste, have the head closely shaven. When colored they are red, like the other Egyptians. The subjoined drawing (Fig. 125), which is somewhat harsh in outline, is from the portico of one of the pyramids of Meroë,[265] and is probably one of the oldest human effigies in Nubia. They abound in all the temples of that country, and especially at Semneh, Dakkeh, Soleb Gebel-Berkel, and Messoura.[266]

"From the numberless examples of similar conformation, I select another of a priest from the bas-relief at Thebes, which is remarkable for delicacy of outline and pleasing serenity of expression.[267] (Fig. 126).

"So invariably are these characters allotted to the sacerdotal caste, that we readily detect them in the two priests who, by some unexplained contingency, become kings in the XXth dynasty. Their names read Amensi-Hrai-Pehor and Phisham on the monuments; and the accompanying outline is a fac-simile of Rosellini's portrait of the latter personage, who lived about 1100 years before the Christian era.[268] In this head the Egyptian and Pelasgic characters appear to be blended, but the former preponderate. (Fig. 127).

"The last outline (Fig. 128) represents a modification of the same type, that of the *Harper* in Bruce's tomb at Thebes. The beautiful form of the head and the intellectual character of the face, may be compared with similar efforts of Grecian art. It dates with Rameses IV.[269]

Fig. 125.

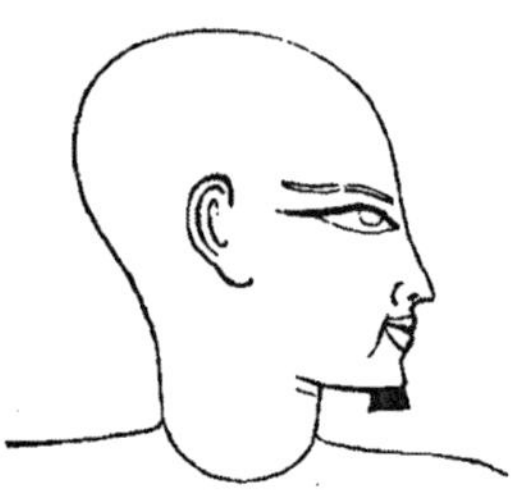

Fig. 126.

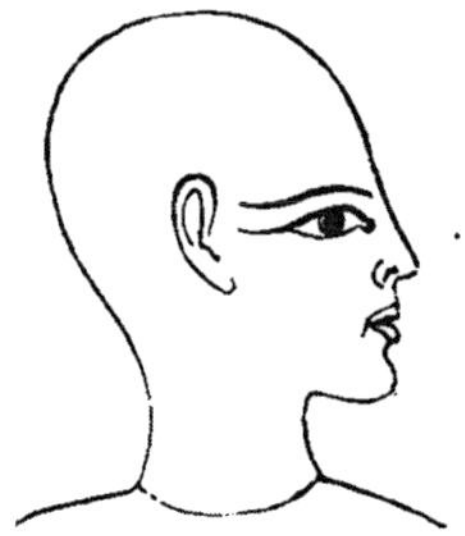

Fig. 127.

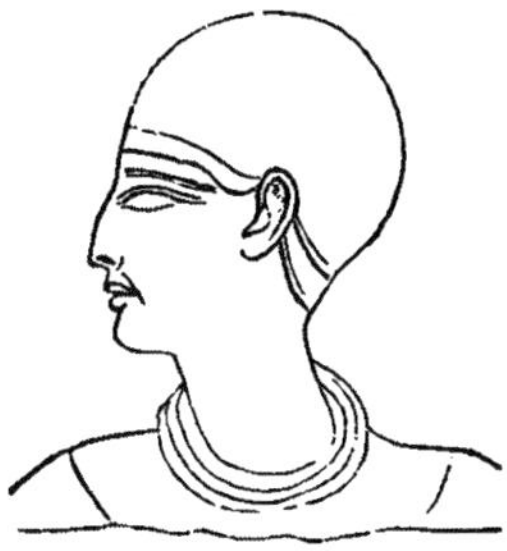

Fig. 128.

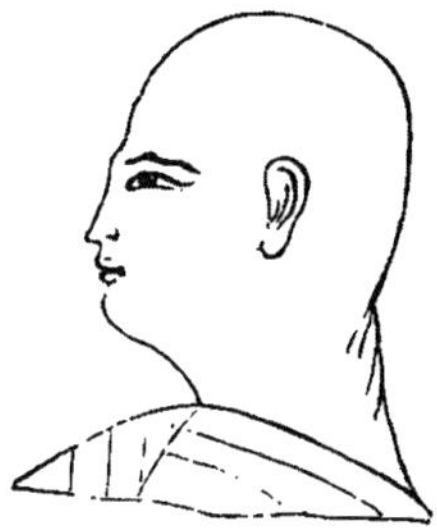

"As I believe this to be a most important ethnograpic indication, and one which points to the vast body of the Egyptian people, I subjoin four additional heads of priests (Figs. 129, 130, 131, 132,) from a tomb at Thebes of the XVIIIth dynasty. We are forcibly impressed with the delicate features and oblique eye of the left-hand personage, and with the ruder but characteristic outline of the other figures, in which the prominent face, though strongly drawn, is essentially Egyptian.[270]

Fig. 129.

Fig. 130.

Fig. 131.

Fig. 132.

"The annexed outlines (Fig. 133), which present more pleasing examples of the same ethnographic character, are copied from the tomb of Titi, at Thebes, and date with the remote era of Thotmes IV.[271] They represent five *fowlers* in the act of drawing their net over a flock of birds. The long, flowing hair is in keeping with the facial traits, which latter are also well characterized in the subjoined drawings (Figs. 134, 135, 136, 137), derived from monuments of different epochs and localities.

Fig. 133.

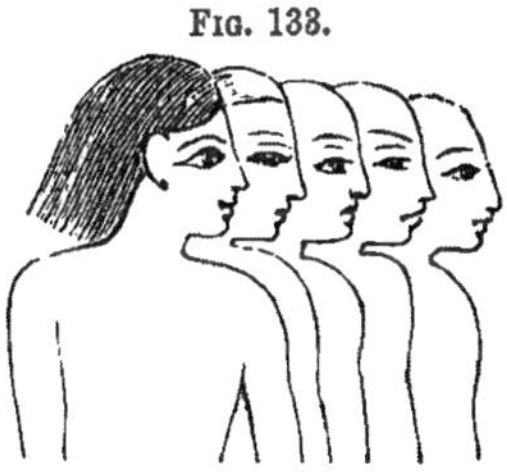

Fig. 134.

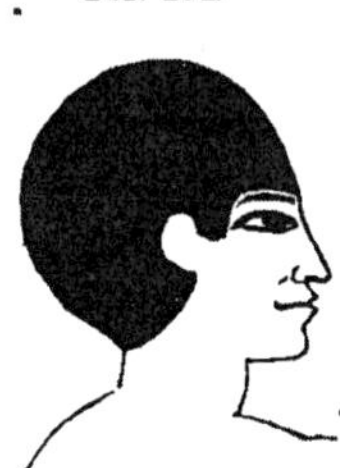

Fig. 135.

Fig. 136.

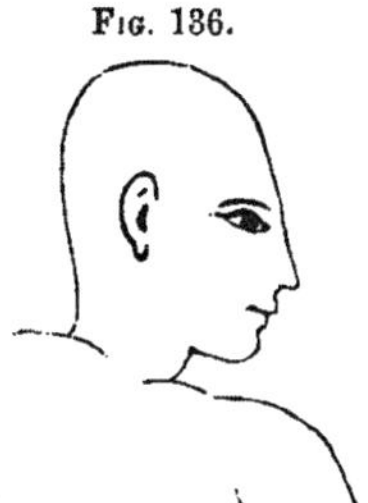

Fig. 137.

"Fig. 134 is the head of a *weaver*, from the paintings in the very ancient tomb of Roti and Menoph at Beni-Hassan, wherein the same cast of countenance is reiterated without number.[272]

"Fig. 135, a *wine-presser*, is also from Beni-Hassan, and dates with Osortasen, more than 2000 years before the Christian era.[273]

"Fig. 136 is a *cook*, who, in the tomb of Rameses IV, at Thebes, is represented with many others in the active duties of his vocation.[274]

"Fig. 137. I have selected this head as an exaggerated or caricatured illustration of the same type of physiognomy. It is one of the *goat-herds* painted in the tomb of Roti, at Beni-Hassan.[275]

"The most recent of these last four venerable monuments of art dates at least 1450 years before our era: the oldest belongs to unchronicled times; and the same physical characters are common on the Nubian and Egyptian monuments down to the Ptolemaic and Roman epochs.

"The peculiar head-dress of the Egyptians often greatly modifies, and in some degree conceals, their characteristic features; and may, at first sight, lead to the impression that the priests possessed a physiognomy of a distinct or peculiar kind. Such, however, was not the case, as a little observation will prove. Take, for example, the four following draw-

Fig. 138.

Fig. 139.

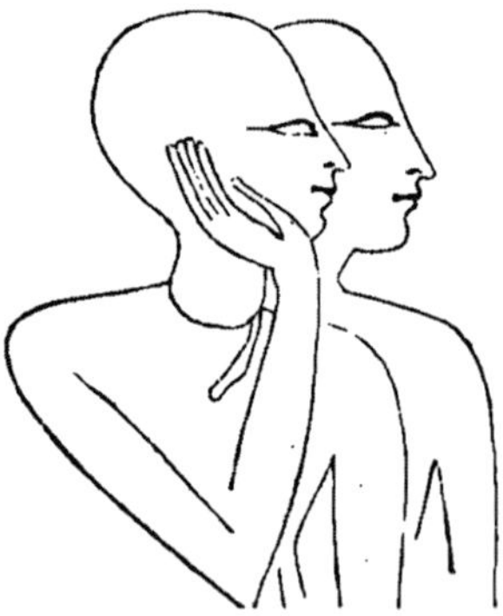

ings, from a Theban tomb, in which two mourners (Fig. 138) have head-dresses, and two priests (Fig. 139) are without them. Are not the national characteristics unequivocally manifest in them all?"[276]

Such, textually, are Morton's words, with the sole exception that, while preserving his references, we have substituted our own *numerals:* but, for the express object of removing, once for all, current impressions of Egyptian affinity with Negro races, we intercalate a relevant series of illustrations, and group into one page various heads from the *Crania Ægyptiaca* — five of which (Figs. 140—144) appertain to females of different classes, and two (Figs. 145 and 146) to males; indicating underneath each the vocations in which they are severally represented on the monuments. Apart from their facial angles and high-caste configuration, it is their long *hair* to which the attention of Negrophilism is more particularly invited.

Fig. 140.

A Mourner.

Fig. 141.

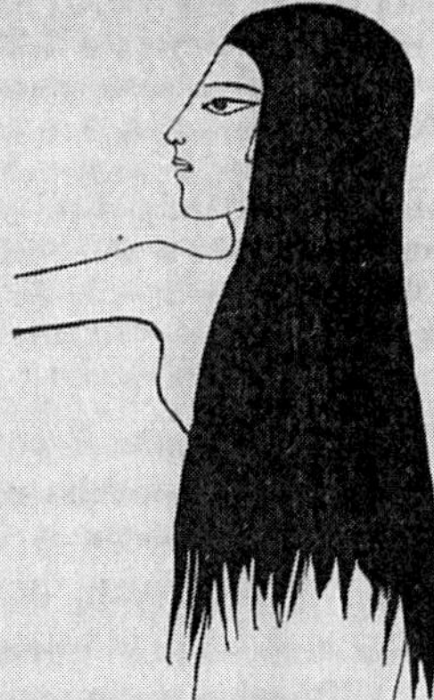

A Mourner.

Fig. 142.

A Lady *coiffée.*

Fig. 143.

A Mourner.

Fig. 144.

A Female Athlete.

Fig. 145.

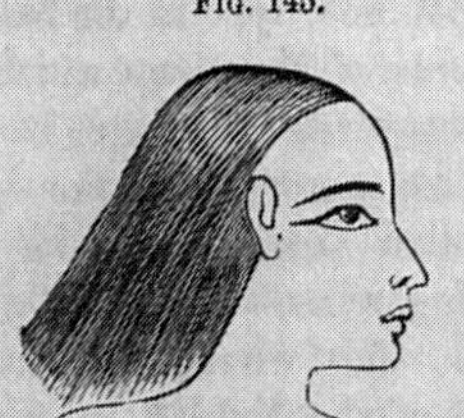

A Carpenter.

Fig. 146.

A Rustic-wrestler.

"It is thus that we trace this peculiar style of countenance, in its several modifications, through epochs and in localities the most remote from each other, and in every class of the Egyptian people. How different from the Pelasgic type, yet how obviously Caucasian! How varied in outline, yet how readily identified! And, if we compare these features with those of the Egyptian series of embalmed heads, are we not forcibly impressed with a striking analogy not only in osteological conformation, but also in the very expression of the face? . . . No one, I conceive, will question the analogy I have pointed out. This type is certainly *national*, and presents to our view the *genuine Egyptian physiognomy*, which, in the ethnographic scale, is intermediate between the Pelasgic and Semitic forms. We may add, that this conformation is the same which Prof. Blumenbach refers to the *Hindoo* variety, in his triple classification of the Egyptian people.[277] And this leads us briefly to inquire, who were the Egyptians?"

That this "*genuine Egyptian physiognomy*" was the preponderant type, seen throughout the whole monumental period known to Morton, cannot be questioned; but we do not think it is so universal in the royal families as in the other classes. There is such a want of portraits and other information of the dynasties between the XIIth and XVIIth, that we know little or nothing of the predominant type of those intermediate times. But it is highly probable, owing to Hyksos traditions, that the royal families of that period, called the "Middle Empire," were in great part Asiatics; and we are certain that, after the Restoration, marriages with foreigners were not uncommon. Alliances of this kind occurred in the XXth and preceding dynasties; and it is but reasonable to conclude that such had been the custom of the country in earlier times; inasmuch as the Bible has helped us to prove the same habits respecting *Jewish* amalgamations with denizens of the Nile.

In order that the reader may be enabled to judge for himself of the characteristics of the royal families, we have already exhibited some of their portraits, back to the XVIIth dynasty. It is evident to us, that these portraits do not fully correspond to Dr. Morton's *Egyptian Type*, but that, on the contrary, they are eminently Asiatic, and not African. However, it cannot be denied that the pervading type, throughout Egypt proper, was the one described by him; though we are not prepared to admit this as the then-common type in the Nubias, or so high up as Meroë. The monuments of Meroë, on which his opinions were based, have since been discovered to be mere bastard and modern copies of those of Egypt. This country, until the eighth century B. C., formed part of the Egyptian Empire; and its later edifices were built by consecutively ruling races—Egypto-Meroïte, then Nubian, and lastly Negro-Nubian. But we have abundant reason for opining that the populations of the Nubias, in ancient times, were what (Arab elements deducted) they are now: viz., types intermediate between Negroes and Egyptians; viewing the latter such as we behold them at the XVIIIth dynasty, or about 1500 B. C.

We read the *Crania Ægyptiaca*, with intense interest, so soon as it was published; and, down to the time when Lepsius's plates of the IVth, Vth, and VIth dynasties appeared, we had not ceased to regard Morton's *Egyptian type* as the true representative of that of the Old Empire; but the first hour's glance over those magnificent delineations of the primeval inhabitants produced an entire revolution in the authors' opinions, and enforced the conviction that the Egyptians of the earliest times did not correspond with our honored friend's description, but with a type which, although not *Negro*, nor akin to any Negroes, was strictly *African* — a type, in fact, that supplied the long-sought-for link between African and Asiatic races.

There are no portraits, yet discovered, older than the IVth dynasty, or the thirty-fifth century B. C.; and although what may be called a *Negroid* type preponderates at that period, yet the race, even there, is already a mixed one; and we distinguish many heads which are clearly Asiatic — possessing, as we have shown (*ante*, Figs. 34, 35), Semitish features. The history of Egypt from the XIIth to the XVIIth dynasty is so mutilated, that, for this interregnum, there is but little material for definite opinions. Lepsius, upon Manethonian tradition, states, that during this time the bulk of native Egyptians were driven up the Nile by Asiatic races, and retired into Nubia; and that when the Hyksos were expelled, their Pharaonic conquerors came down the river. It is not probable that every individual of the Hyksos race, however, could have been driven out; and when we compare the monumental portraits of the IVth, Vth, and VIth dynasties with those of the XVIIth and XVIIIth, we cannot doubt that an immense amount of Asiatic blood remained in the country, notwithstanding these expulsions. Lepsius considers that those Asiatic Shepherds impressed their type and language upon the native race, although the Egyptian people and their tongue still remained essentially African. It should be observed that, if Hyksos invasions be accepted as historical, so must the many centuries of the intruders' sojourn; and during MANETHO's five hundred and eleven years, or sixteen generations, these warriors must have found abundant leisure to stamp their paternity upon the offspring of Egyptian women, whose sentiments of chastity have never been other than somewhat lax.

But the *Negroid* type of the earlier dynasties seems never to have become extinguished, notwithstanding the immense influx of Asiatics into Egypt; which has been going on, literally for thousands of years, to the present hour. It may be received, in science, as a settled fact, that where two races are thrown together and blended, the type of the major number must prevail over that of the lesser; and, in time, the latter will become effaced. This law, too, acts with greater force where a foreign is attempted to be engrafted upon a native type aboriginally suited to the local climate. The Fellahs of Upper and Middle Egypt, at the present day, continue to be an unmistakeable race, and are regarded by most travelled authorities as the best living representatives of the ancient population of Egypt. [Mr. Gliddon, resident in Egypt for more than twenty years, may certainly be accepted as competent authority respecting the physical characteristics of the present inhabitants, whose idioms and customs in all their ramifications have been familiar to him from boyhood. He assures us, that the predominant type of the modern Fellah, *i. e.*, peasant (deducting Arab blood), is just as identical with the majority of portraits on the earliest monuments, as Morton concluded by comparing the crania of ancient mummies with Fellah-skulls from the present cemeteries. To render the latter point obvious, we subjoin, from the *Crania Ægyptiaca*, an authentic series of both. The practised eye of the anatomist will at once recognize the similitudes between the ancient and the modern heads, and detect in these last the osteological divergences produced by *Arab* infiltrations: —

Fig. 147.

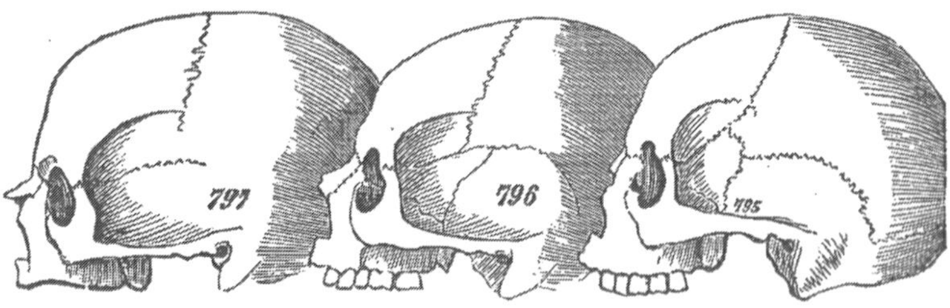

Ancient Crania, "from the front of Northern Brick Pyramid of Dashour."

Fig. 148.

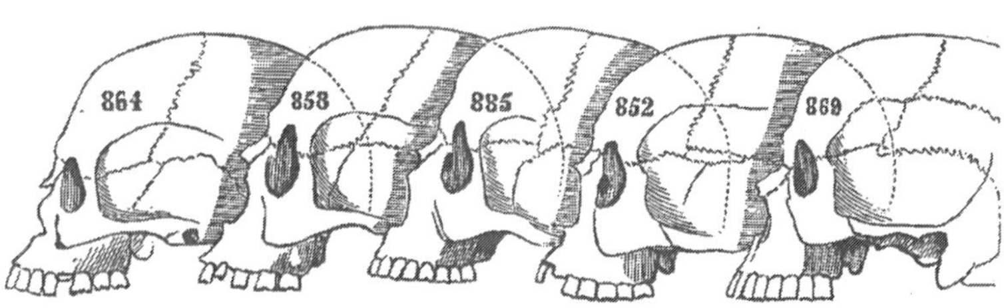

Ancient Crania, from Thebes; by Morton termed "Negroid Heads," whereas to us they yield rather the *Old* Egyptian type.

FIG. 149.

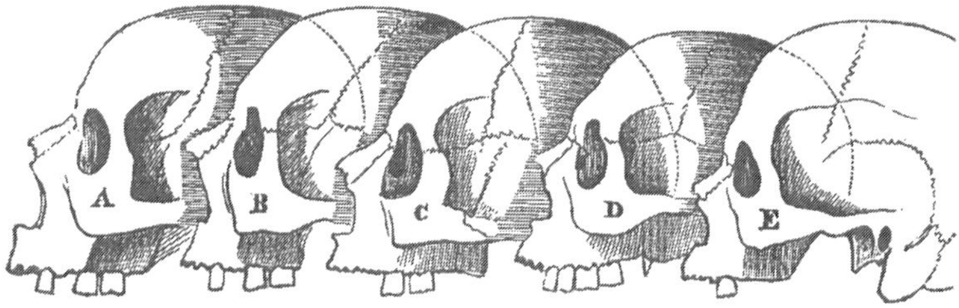

MODERN SKULLS — "the Fellahs," of Lower Egypt.

FIG. 150.

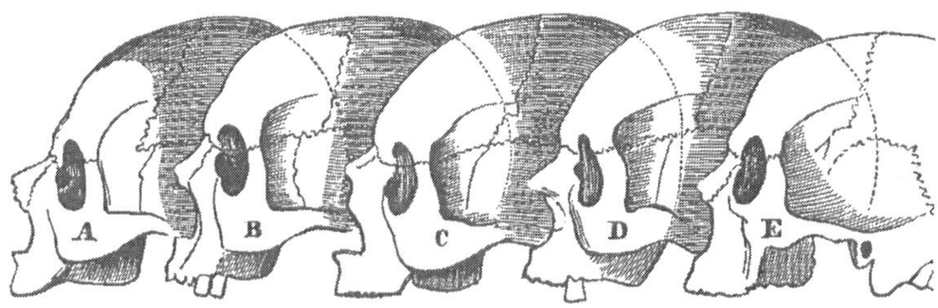

MODERN SKULLS — "the Arabs;" *Bédawees* of the Isthmus of Suez.

FIG. 151.

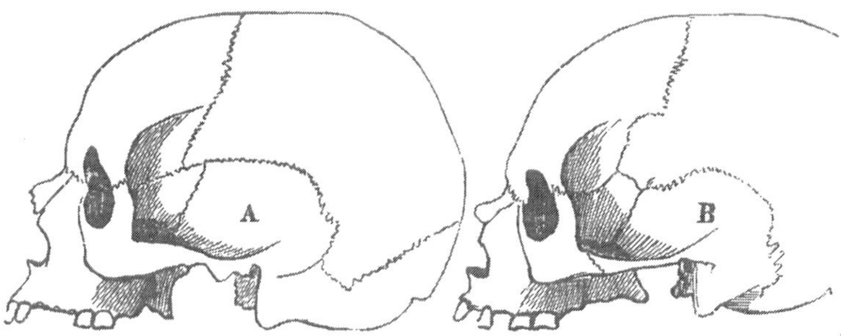

MODERN SKULLS — "the Copts;" from their Christian cemeteries.

With these positive data before him, the reader will be the better able to follow our general argument. — J. C. N.]

But we have not yet done with the *Egyptian Type* as understood by Morton; which, although without question popularly prevalent under the New Empire, was not, we think, the predominant type of the royal families. This last, to our eyes, as portrayed in Rosellini's *Iconography*, is clearly Asiatic: and not only Asiatic, but Semitic; and not merely Semitic, but strongly Abrahamic, or, to repeat our adopted term, *Chaldaic*. From the XIIth to the XVIIth dynasty (a period of some 511 years, according to Manetho, in Josephus), Egypt must have been subjected to extraordinary disturbing causes, which, however terrible to her denizens, to us, at the present day, are shrouded by darkness, and as if circumscribed within a moment of time. Ample evidence is now exhumed of the minuteness and fidelity with which the Egyptians, before and after the Hyksos-period, recorded events and delineated the physical characters of their own people, as well as of the foreigners with whom they held intercourse; but during this hiatus our monuments are comparatively few, and sculptured portraits, to guide the ethnographer, are wanting. The XVIIth dynasty (about 1761 B. C., according to Lepsius) opens to view with a completeness and splendor truly astounding; and from this point downward, for more than 1000 years, (we cannot too often insist upon with general readers,) there are ample materials for studying the natural history as well of Asiatic as of African humanity. In the magnificent plates of Rosellini, faithful representations of these painted sculptures are preserved; and in order that the reader might judge of the quantity of materials and the correctness of our deductions, we selected (*ante*, pp. 145—150) a copious series of the Royal Portraits of the XVIIth and XVIIIth dynasties. We have also illustrated how the same physical characteristics prevail, in profusion, down to the XXVth dynasty, when the so-called *Ethiopian* sovereigns come in for a brief season, to change a dynastic family, but not the national type.[278]

In the absence of parallel history (the "Middle Empire," or *Hyksos*-period, separating us from the XIIth dynasty), nothing remains beyond genealogical tablets and papyri to guide us, as to the ancestral origin of Pharaonic families of the New Empire, except their physical type, depicted or carved upon coeval monuments. There is a family-contour about them all, which at once indicates to the observer that they were of high "Caucasian" caste, with but little African of any grade, except what was derived from *Old* Egyptian lineage.

Having enlarged sufficiently upon the Egyptian race, as portrayed upon the sculptures of the New Empire, coetaneously with the times of Abraham, Moses, Solomon, and Josiah; (or, from about sixteen centuries before our era down to the apogee of Assyria's glory); none can now doubt that Pharaonic Egypt, at least among royalty, nobility, and gentry, exhibited in those generations a very mixed type, wherein Asiatic elements predominated over the Nilotic. Let us next take a retrogressive leap, over the *Hyksos*-period, from the XVIIth to the XIIth dynasty, and inquire, *What was the type of Egyptians under the Old Empire* — that is, backwards, from about the twentieth century before Christ? But before doing so, fairness renders it incumbent on the part of one of the authors [G. R. G.], whose province it is to superintend "Types of Mankind" as it passes through the press, to give place to some general observations of his absent colleague. The former, immediately in contact with their lamented friend, Dr. Morton, at Philadelphia, until within a few weeks of his demise in 1851, naturally became more conversant with the great ethnographer's matured views; whereas Dr. Nott's residence at Mobile restricted his studies within his own resources: so that what of merit and originality may attach to the following analysis of the *Old Egyptian* type, belongs to his individual ratiocinations.

[On the publication of Dr. Morton's *Crania Ægyptiaca*, we studied it carefully, and compared it, step by step, with the works of Champollion and Rosellini. No other conclusion than the one adopted by him, viz., that the physical traits which he had assumed as characteristic of the Egyptians were really and truly typical of the first settlers of Egypt, resulted from our researches; but, after several years, the *Denkmäler* of Lepsius, (the first *livraisons* of which reached us about two years ago,) essentially modified our former conclusions. Examination of these plates, and a more thorough investigation of the subject, have satisfied us, that the Egyptian *type* as known in 1844 to Morton, existed no longer in its pristine purity, but, after the XIIth dynasty, was absolutely an amalgam of foreign (chiefly Asiatic) stocks, engrafted on an antecedent and aboriginal *African type;* that the latter, although not Negro, was Nilotic; and that it constituted the true connecting *grade* between African and Asiatic races. When Mr. Gliddon and the writer again met, at Mobile, above eighteen months ago, after five years' separation, we mentioned this conclusion to him; and he placed in our hands various letters, received by him between the years 1846 and 1851, from Morton; through which it became evident that the Doctor himself had also so far changed his opinions as to feel assured that the primordial Egyptians were not an Asiatic, but an aboriginal population, indigenous to the Nile-land, although he says nothing of their primitive *Negroid* type: the ultimatum which our personal researches had then attained. We afterwards wrote to Chevalier Lepsius, informing him of the impression his *Old Egyptian* portraits had left on our mind, and were much gratified to learn, from his reply, that our new convictions accorded with his own. A very obliging letter also, from Mr. Birch, enables us to add his valid authority to arguments hereinafter presented, without, in either case, infringing upon the sanctity of private correspondence. — J. C. N.]

Although Dr. Morton had insisted strongly upon his conventional *Egyptian type*, nevertheless, a critical perusal of his work will show that, even in 1844, he felt by no means certain as to its Asiatic origin — glimmerings of the light that was ere long to break through "Egyptian darkness" already dawning upon the mind of our acute anthropologist. In the *Crania*, he says: —

"We have already alluded to the opinion of Prof. Ritter and others, that the old Bejas and modern Bishareens were derived from the Berber or Libyan stock of nations. I am ready to go farther, and adopt the sentiment of the learned Dr. Murray, that the Egyptians and monumental Ethiopians were of the same lineage, and probably descended from a Libyan tribe.

"This view of the case [he continues] at once reconciles the statement of Champollion, Rosellini, Heeren, and Rüppell, that they could detect the *Nubian* physiognomy everywhere on the monuments; but, at the same time, it supersedes the necessity of their inference that Nubia was the cradle of civilization, and that the arts, descending the river, were perfected in Egypt."

In further support of the common origin of the Egyptians, Berbers, and other tribes of Northern Africa, Morton refers to evidences furnished by Ritter, Heeren, Shaler, Hodgson, &c. — showing how "the Libyan or Berber speech was once the language of all Northern Africa," and infinitely more ancient than the *Coptic* — probably as old as the monumental language of Egypt's pyramidal period.

[For the sake of perspicuity, and to convey to the reader some idea of the chronological order of linguistic developments in Egypt, it may be well to mention, that the name *Coptic* (*i. e.* Christian *Jacobite*) represents the vernacular Egyptian from the seventh century after Christ back to about the Christian era; that *Demotic*, or Enchorial, refers to the colloquial idiom thence used backwards to the seventh century B. C.; that *Hieratic*, or Sacerdotal, means only the cursive character in which the "*lingua sancta*" of the old *hieroglyphics* was written, in every age, back to at least the VIth dynasty, or 2800 years B. C.; and finally, that the *hieroglyphics*, "sacred sculptured characters," represent that antique tongue which was the speech of Egypt when, long prior to the pyramids of the IVth dynasty (that is, centuries anterior to 3500 years B. C.) phonetic hieroglyphs succeeded an earlier *picture-writing*. With the reservation that where our Anglo-Saxon tongue counts centuries, the language of Egypt reckons up its thousands of years, if we were to call the English of Thackeray, Bulwer, and Irving, "Coptic" — that of the forty-seven translators of King James's Version, "Demotic" — that of Chaucer, "Hieratic," and that of the old Doom's-day Book, "Hieroglyphic," we should perceive, in modern English, some of the linguistic gradations and some phases in the writings of Egypt during 4000 monumental years, down to the introduction of Christianity into the Valley of the Nile.[279] Consequently, all philologers who, when comparing *Coptic* with Atalantic Berber dialects, imagined they were dealing with *ancient* Egyptian lexicography, have committed, *ipso facto*, a wondrous anachronism; and science must set their futile labors respectfully aside—LATHAM's inclusive. G. R. G.]

We must remark, in passing, that Dr. Morton's mind had not yet freed itself from the old, arbitrary, divisions of races, and that he here attempted to force into one common stock many African races which in themselves merely constitute a group of proximate, but quite distinct, types. But, it is interesting to observe the change gradually working in a brain so eminently reflective, as new archæological facts offered themselves to its well-disciplined scrutiny; nor can we adequately express our admiration at the simple-hearted honesty with which Morton sacrificed many hard-earned opinions, in the ratio that the field of Egyptian science widened before his contemplation. We derive extreme pleasure in offering some instances.

On the 26th of February, 1846, but two years after his *Crania Ægyptiaca* had appeared, in a letter to Gliddon at Paris, he thus utters thoughts which it seems had been half-formed for years previously, though proofs were yet wanting to mould them into definitive shape:—

> "I am more than ever confirmed in my old sentiment, that Northern Africa was peopled by an indigenous and aboriginal people, who were dispossessed by Asiatic tribes. These aborigines *could not* have been Negroes, because the latter were never adapted to the climate, and are nowhere now, nor ever have been, inhabitants of these latitudes. Were they Berabra?—or some better race, *more nearly allied to the Arabian race?*"

This gleam of light received expression long previously to the publication of any of the pictorial results of Lepsius's Expedition. To our view, Morton here struck the true key to the type of the Egyptian population of the New Empire. They were *then* already a mixed race, derived from Asiatic superpositions upon the aboriginal people of the lower Nile. From the dawn of monumental history, which antedates all chronicles, sacred or profane, we see the whole basin of the Nile, together with that part of Africa lying north of the Sahara, inhabited by races unlike Asiatics, and equally unlike Negroes: but forming in anthropology a connecting link, and, geographically, another *gradation*. To say nothing of Egyptians proper, such were and are the Nubians, the Abyssinians, the Gallas, the Barâbra, no less than the whole native population of the Barbary States; which last, in those ancient days, were absolutely cut off, through want of *camels*, from communication with Nigritia athwart the Saharan wastes.

About the time the preceding letter was penned, Dr. Morton was in correspondence with a very distinguished savan in Paris — our mutual friend, M. le Dr. BOUDIN, latterly Médecin en chef de l'armée des Alpes — who proposed to translate and republish the *Crania Ægyptiaca.* The work was to be rewritten; and we have before us its MS. emendations for a second edition. Writing to Gliddon, then in London, in May, 1846, Morton holds the following language: —

"In this work I maintain, without reservation, the following among other opinions—that the human race has not sprung from one pair, but from a plurality of centres; that these were created *ab initio* in those parts of the world best adapted to their physical nature; that the epoch of creation was that undefined period of time spoken of in the first chapter of Genesis, wherein it is related that God formed man, 'male and female created he *them;*' that the deluge was a mere local phenomenon; that it affected but a small part of the then-existing inhabitants of the earth; that these views are consistent with the facts of the case, as well as with analogical evidence."

In another letter to Gliddon, at New York, December 14, 1849, we read: —

"By the hands of the person to whom you confided them, I last night received Lepsius's "Chronologie," and the tin case of fac-simile drawings.[280] These, when studied in connection with the Egyptian heads [*skulls*], and especially with the small series sent me [from Memphis] by your brother William [seventeen in number, and very ancient,], compel me to recant so much of my published opinions as respects the *origin* of the Egyptians. They *never came from Asia,* but are the indigenous or aboriginal inhabitants of the valley of the Nile. I have taken this position in my letter to Mr. J. R. Bartlett (*New York Ethnological Soc. Journal,* I.): every day has verified it, and your drawings settle it forever in my mind. It has cost me a mental struggle to acknowledge this conviction, but I can withhold it no longer." [See confirmations in the MSS. of Dr. Morton; *infra,* Chap. XI.].

Again, to the same, January 30, 1850: —

"You allude to my altered views in Ethnology; but it all consists in regarding the Egyptian race as the indigenous people of the valley of the Nile. Not Asiatics in any sense of the word, but autocthones of the country, and the authors of their own civilization. This view, which you will recollect is that of Champollion, Heeren, and others [excepting only that they do not apply the word *indigenous* to the Egyptians], in nowise conflicts with their Caucasian position; for the *Caucasian group* had many primordial centres, of which the Egyptians represent one."

Here, then, we behold the matured and deliberately-expressed opinion of Dr. Morton, that the earliest monumental type of Egyptians was not Asiatic, but that of an *aboriginal African race.*

A few months ago the writer (J. C. N.) addressed the Chevalier Lepsius, stating the impressions relative to what we shall call a *Negroid* type, left on our mind by an examination of his plates of the IVth dynasty. We received from him a most obliging and comprehensive letter: an extract below indicates its nature.

We ought to premise that the Chevalier, like Baron von Humboldt,[281] is a sustainer of the *unity* of races, for linguistical and other reasons to be detailed by his own pen some day. We wish here simply to present the results of some of his "*linguistique*" researches — a department of science in which he is so justly renowned. His reply to our interrogatory begins — "Je laisse de coté le point de vue théologique qui n'a rien à faire avec la science." Our clerical adversaries need not lean, therefore, upon savans whose sole object is *scientific truth;* nor, for ourselves, can we refrain from admiring the philosophic tone with which such intelligences as Agassiz, Lepsius, and Morton, have pursued it.

"Vous parlez d'une gradation des peuples du continent d'Afrique depuis le Cap jusqu'à dans le nord. Il y'a un fait bien curieux, que les langues des Hottentots et des Bushmans sont essentiellement différentes des langues de tout le reste du continent jusqu'à l'équateur. Et ce qui est, peut-être, encore plus curieux, leur langue porte quelques traits charactéristiques, qui ne se retrouvent que dans les langues du nord-est de l'Afrique. . . . . . . Tout le continent Africain avait, selon mon idée, dans un certain temps, une population parente, et les langues par conséquent analogues aussi. Plus tard les peuples Asiatiques immigraient du nord-est. Le mélange des races produisait ce large bandeau de peuples et de langues dispersés et apparemment incohérens qui se trouvent maintenant entre la ligne et le 15me degré lat. nord. Ces langues ont perdu leur caractère Africain sans acquérir le caractère Asiatique; *mais le fond des langues et du sang est Africain*. . . . . .

"Je comprends ce que vous appelez un type negroïde dans les figures Egyptiennes, et je n'ai rien contre cette observation; mais cela n'empêche pas que leur caractère principal ne soit Asiatique. Pendant le temps des Hyksôs, la race ancienne se changeait considerablement."

We repeat that Prof. Lepsius declares, in the same letter, his confirmed belief in the unity of races; but the occurrences he speaks of must antedate the era by him defined for the foundation of the Egyptian Empire, 3893 years B. C., as Frenchmen express it, by "des millions et des milliards d'années."

Not less do we esteem, on these archaic subjects, the high authority of Mr. Birch, of the British Museum; who, in a private letter (to J. C. N.), dated October, 1852, writes: —

"You are, I agree, quite right as to the *intermediate relation* of Egypt to the Asiatic and Nigritian races. Benfey and others have already, I think, pointed out that the so-called Semitic languages are principally spoken in Africa, and the hieroglyphs are of Semitic connection—resembling the Semitic languages in the construction and *copia verborum;* at the same time they differ in many essential points, and have a fair claim to be considered a separate species of language. The astounding fact is, that Egyptian civilization was the oldest—and that the Assyrian and other nations have left no remains to compare with them in respect of time."

It cannot fail to be remarked, that certain of the portraits on the earliest pyramidal monuments already represent a very mixed people; and, consequently, it is clear that Egypt, for anterior centuries unnumbered, must have been, so to say, the battle-ground of Asiatic impinging against African races. Some of the heads we have selected as illustrative of the antiquity of a high "Caucasian" type, might readily pass unnoticed at the present day in the streets of London, Paris, or New York; while others, again, are so strictly African, that the typical difference cannot be mistaken. It is note-worthy, besides, that many of these Egypto-Caucasian heads are not only strongly Semitic, but even Abrahamic in type: thus affording support to legends running through the fragments of Manetho, and his mutilator, JOSEPHUS, as to connections between the Hyksos and the early population of Canaan. The same *Chaldaic* features beheld in some of the royal likenesses of the XVIIth, XVIIIth and XIXth dynasties, are seen upon the sculptures of the IVth, Vth and VIth.

Philological science generally admits that the roots of the modern Coptic language are, in the main, (alien engraftments deducted) the same as those of the "lingua sancta," or Old Egyptian tongue, spoken by the priesthood and educated classes, from Roman times, through all dynasties, back to the earliest Pharaohs, when the latter was the colloquial idiom of every native. As a medium of oral communication, the Coptic language ceased to be used in the twelfth century, and the last person who could speak it is said to have died in A. D. 1663:[282] but an old Egyptian (G. R. G.) avers that he met with good authority for its decease about ninety years ago, with a priest, in the Thebaid.

The ἱερὰ διάλεκτος,[283] *sacerdotal dialect*, or antique language, affords one of the strongest evidences of the high antiquity of the early population of Egypt, and also of their Nilotic or aboriginal emanation. Egypt has been, literally, for many thousands of years, the *football* of foreign conquerors; and her primordial language became infiltrated, from age to age, with Arabic, Persian, Greek, Libyan, Latin, and words of other tongues, known to us only at a later stage of development; but, when these exotic *injecta* are abstracted, there remains, nevertheless, a stone-recorded vernacular, possessing all the marks of originality, and in itself totally distinct from the utmost circumference of Asiatic languages. The proper names of very few Nilotic objects, natural or artificial, in primitive hieroglyphics, are really identical with the vocalization of Syro-Arabian languages; and their Egyptian structure is characteristically different; being monosyllabic, in lieu of the posterior *triliteral* shape in which Semitic tongues have come down to us. "If all these languages be kindred, BENFEY, who has compared them most elaborately, holds, they must have split off from a parent stock, not only at a period too remote for all historical or monumental evidence, but even for plausible conjecture."[284] Such, in brief, are the current opinions of Lepsius, Birch, of Bunsen, Hincks, De Saulcy, Lanci, and other eminent authorities of the day, as regards Egypt: supported, moreover, by the philological discoveries of Rawlinson, Hincks, and De Longpérier, in cuneiform Assyria; and by the studies of Gesenius, Ewald, Munk, and Fresnel, in Shemitish palæography. It is the deduction of Lepsius, that Egypt had possessed an African population, and a Nilotic language, before the foundation of the Old Empire; and that various disturbing causes superimposed, gradually, an Asiatic type and Semitic dialects upon the anterior people of the Lower Nile, without obliterating the aboriginal frame-work which, as well in type of man as in speech, was exclusively African.

Affinities, tending to establish a remote contemporaneousness, have been traced among various languages of Northern Africa: and Hodgson, quoted in the last chapter, long ago put forth the doctrine that the *Berber* speech, as now extant, had preceded the Coptic of Christianized Egypt. He insisted that many old names of places, divinities, &c., along the Nile, were Berber, and neither Coptic nor Semitic. Allowance made for some slight anachronisms, in terms rather than in facts, we think our learned countryman's arrow has not flown wide of the target.

The high antiquity formerly claimed for civilization in India, and many coincidences of doctrine and usages that, imagined by Indologists, have entirely vanished from Egypt since her hieroglyphics have become readable, had led Prichard, and other scholars less eminent, to connect the Ganges with the Nile: but, so far from any evidence of intercommunication, we have nothing to show that the nations on these two rivers, in the time of Solomon, much less of Moses or Abraham, were even acquainted with each others' existence. The ancient Egyptians never surmised a Hindostanic origin for their own nation; they believed themselves to be, in the strictest sense, *autocthones*, natives of the soil. Nor do East-Indians (since WILFORD's misconceptions became exposed) possess any tradition of having received an Egyptian or sent forth a Hindoo colony.[285] Moreover, the rumored resemblances between the languages of India and Egypt—Sanscrit and Coptic—compared in their modern phases, are few and slight, where not altogether factitious. The whole genius of both, and almost their entire stock of words, are entirely different. The hieroglyphic system of Egypt is clearly indigenous to the valley of the Nile, whilst not even a legendary tale remains to show that such mode of writing ever prevailed in India.

When we reflect that this hieroglyphic writing is found in high perfection on the earliest monuments extant, viz.: those of the IVth dynasty, 3400 years B. C., and, therefore, must have existed many centuries previously; that the figure of every animal, plant, or thing, delineated in these hieroglyphics, is *Nilotic* to the exclusion of every foreign idea; and that Egyptian economy in manners, customs, arts, &c., must have been radically diverse from those of all other races, at the time such writing received its incipient projection; — when, too, we remember the fact that, the physical characters of each type of man in India and Egypt were different, and that no physical causes but amalgamation have ever transformed one race into another, it is impossible to resist the conviction that these Gangeatic and Nilotic races have always been, that which, modern fusions deducted, they are now, *distinct*.

The Egyptians, for instance, had practised circumcision from time immemorial, long before Abraham adopted this mark after his visit to Egypt, in common with the later Ethiopic tribes; but this Nilotic rite was not practised in India, until introduced by Mohammedan conquests. So, again, with regard to "castes," heretofore almost insolently obtruded, in order to identify Egyptian with Hindostanic customs! It will be news to some coryphæi of the unity-doctrine, when they are taught, in our Part III., that the "caste-system" has never existed along the Nile, and that, on the Ganges, it is a very modern invention.

To the extreme climatic dryness of Egypt are we mainly indebted for the preservation of her monumental history. While the remains of Greece, Rome, and other nations, none of them 3000 years old, crumble at first touch, Egypt's granitic obelisks, at the end of 4000 years, have not yet lost their polish; and had all the early monuments of that country been spared by barbarian hands, we should not now, after fifty-three centuries, have to accuse *Time* as the cause of disputations over the history of the old Empire.

That MENES of *This* was the first mortal king of Egypt, is one of the points in which classical authorities, Herodotus, Manetho, Eratosthenes, and Diodorus, agree with the genealogical lists upon tablets and papyri; and we must regard him as the first historical founder of an empire, which, for untold ages previously, had been approaching its consolidation. His reign is placed by Lepsius at 3893 years B. C.; and although criticism grants that this date may be a few centuries below or above the true era, yet there is so much irrefragable evidence of the long duration of the empire prior to the fixed epoch of the XIIth dynasty, 2300 years B. C., that any error, if there be such, in his chronological computations, cannot be very great, while almost immaterial to our present purposes. The august name of MENES is gloriously associated with the building of Memphis, the oldest metropolis, with foreign conquests, with public monuments, with the progress of the arts and of internal improvements. To admit the possibility of such legislative actions, a numerous population and a long preparatory civilization must have preceded him: to say nothing of the contemporary nations with which this military Pharaoh held intercourse, that must have been at least as old as the Egyptians themselves. To one who knows anything of the topography of the Nile-land, it need not be told that the science of hydraulic engineering, in particular, must have existed in high perfection before the Lower Valley of the Nile could have been studded to any extent with towns on the alluvium: because this stream had to be controlled by dykes, canals, sluices, and similar works, long before the soil on its banks could be uniformly cultivated; and, what an antiquity do not these facts necessitate!

But, whatever uncertainty may hang over the first three dynasties (of which coetaneous records are now lost), when we come to the IVth—

"We may [in the language of the Rev. John Kenrick] congratulate ourselves that we have at length reached the period of undoubted cotemporaneous monuments in Egyptian history. The pyramids, and the sepulchres near them, still remain to assure us that we are not walking in a land of shadows, but among a powerful and populous nation, far advanced in the arts of life; and, as a people can only progressively attain such a station, the light of historic certainty is reflected back from this era upon the ages which precede it. . . The glimpse which we thus obtain of Egypt, in the fifth century after Menes, according to the lowest computation, reveals to us some general facts, which lead to important inferences. In all its great characteristics, Egypt was the same as we see it 1000 years later. A well-organized monarchy and religion elaborated throughout the country. The system of hieroglyphic writing the same, in all its leading peculiarities, as it continued to the end of the monarchy of the Pharaohs." [286]

Bas-reliefs beautifully cut, sepulchral architecture, and pyramidal engineering—reed-*pens*, *inks* (red and black), papyrus-*paper*, and chemically-prepared *colors!*—these are proud evidences of the Memphitic civilization of fifty-three centuries ago, that every man with eyes to see can now behold in noble folios, published by France, Tuscany, and Prussia; and concerning which any one, not an ignoramus through education, or a blockhead by nature, can acquire adequate knowledge by merely reading those English, French, German, or Italian works, printed within the last fifteen years, and abundantly cited at the end of this volume, which are at the present hour very accessible to all intelligent readers, everywhere but on the bookshelves of primary seminaries. This reservation made, we appeal, through these popular works, to the most ancient sculptures, in hopes of ascertaining—What was the *Type* of the primitive Egyptians?

Let our departure be taken, in this inquiry, from one of those four effigies extant in the sepulchral habitation of Seti I., before alluded to (*vide ante*, p. 85, Fig. 1), which establishes what Egyptian art considered, in the fifteenth century B. C., the *beau-ideal* of the Egyptians themselves. Beneath the head (Fig. 152) we place a reduction of one of the same full-length figures (Fig. 153), which, on the original, is colored in deep *red*. The reader has now before his eye the *standard effigy*, typical of the Egyptian race, such as the "hundred-gated" Thebes exhibited in her streets about 3400 years ago.

FIG. 152.[287]

FIG. 153.

FIG. 154.[288]

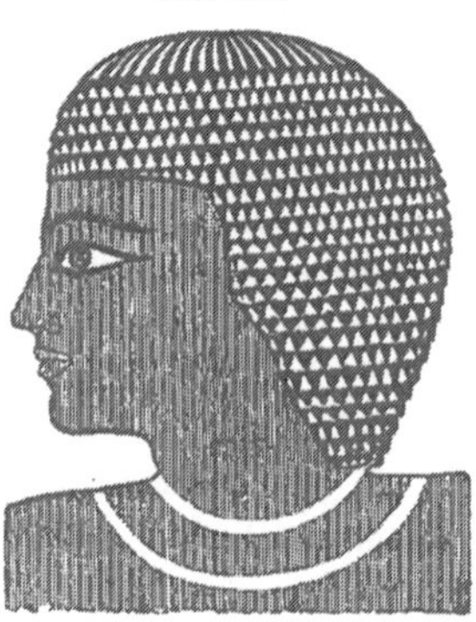

This head we regard as a most interesting one, in connection with the Egyptian type; because it givés the Egyptian idea of their own people, whom the accompanying hieroglyphics call the RoT, that is, "*race*," *par excellence*—viewed by the Egyptians as the only human species, to the exclusion of "outside barbarians" of every nation around the "land of purity and justice."

Now, although this effigy was designed, at Thebes, as typical of the Egyptian nation during the XVIIIth dynasty, to us it seems rather to be the long-settled *type* of that race, handed down from early times; for, assuredly, it does not correspond with the royal portraits of the New Empire, which, we have seen, were strongly Semitic in their lineaments, and therefore chiefly Asiatic in derivation.

This RoT, if placed alongside the iconographic monuments of the IVth, Vth, and VIth dynasties, is closely analogous to the predominant type of that day; which fact serves to strengthen our view that the Egyptians of the early dynasties were rather of an African or *Negroid* type—resembling the *Bishari*, in some respects, in others, the modern *Fellah*, or peasantry, of Upper Egypt. To show its analogy to the primitive stock, we reproduce a better copy of the colored head of Prince MERHET (Fig. 154), "Priest of Shufu" builder of the great pyramid, and probably his son (*supra*, p. 177, Fig. 118). More than 1700 years of time separate the two sculptures, and yet how indelible is the type!

Fig. 155 is taken from the temple of Aboosimbel—Wars in Asia of Ramses II., XVIIIth dynasty, during the fourteenth century B. C. This head is one of a group of full-length portraits of the same type, and they are *Egyptian* picked soldiers of the royal body-guard—pro-

Plate I

THE PROPRIETOR_ Most Ancient Tomb extant (IV.th Dynasty, B.C. 3500.) now in the Royal Museum, Berlin.

[NOTT & GLIDDON'S Types of Mankind 1853.]

FIG. 155.[289]

bably *Calisirians*: a word which means "young guard," and also persons wearing the *calasiris*, "fringed tunic."[290]

[The pictorial illustrations designed in 1842 for Gliddon's Lectures having required a critical study of every head then known upon the monuments, we will here introduce an extract from his *Ethnographic Notes*, written eleven years ago — when, without theory to sustain, he could have no idea that his private memoranda would become available to anatomists in the year 1853. — J. C. N.]

"These are *Egyptian* soldiers, of the royal body-guard — probably *Hermotybians*, or *Calasirians*; but, as the latter name seems derivable from the Coptic SHELOSHIRI, *young*, and since these soldiers are young men, it is likely that they represent *Calasirians* of the royal guard — like the young guard of Napoleon, or the *Yenèe-cheri* (corrupted by Europeans into *Janisaries*), 'new guard' of the Ottomans. The *Hermotybians* were the *veterans* — the old guard, in whose charge were the fortresses.

"Now, as these soldiers were quartered in, and chiefly drafted from, *Lower* Egypt, this soldier is a good specimen of the 'thews and sinews' of Egypt. See his athletic build, his muscular frame, and look of bull-dog determination — the very *beau-ideal* of a soldier! This man is precisely similar to the mass of the *Fellàhs* of Lower Egypt at this day, especially on the Damiata branch, and I could pick thousands in these provinces to match him; whereas, above *Middle* Egypt, as you approach Nubia, this type disappears, to be replaced by lank, tall, dark, spare men, until the Fellàh merges in the Nubian races, above Esnè. I therefore contend that this soldier is a perfect specimen of the picked men of Lower Egypt, B. C. 1560. He shows the superiority of the people of Lower Egypt in *that* day; while, as he is *identical* with the picked men of the Fellàhs of *Lower* Egypt at the *present* day, it follows that very great changes have not taken place, in 3500 years, between the *ancient* and *modern* Lower Egyptians; and supports my assertion that, apart from a certain amount of Arab-cross (easily explained, and easily detected), it is in *Lower Egypt*, among the *Fellàhs*, you will find the descendants of the ancient race — more than among the *Copts* (whose females are, and have been, the '*Gussarèeyeh* of Nations'); and infinitely more than among the half-witted, dissolute, corrupt, and mongrel *African* race of *Baràberas*."

Morton's comparison of ancient and modern skulls confirms this view; and it will remove some erroneous notions from the reader of Osburn,[291] to mention an indisputable proof of the Egyptian origin of those guards — that is, the fact that they are painted *red* in the tableau at Aboosimbel.

Now, a remark made by us when speaking of the last race (RoT), applies equally to this figure: viz., that although both are representations of Egyptians, drawn and colored by an *Egyptian* artist, during the XVIIIth dynasty, yet this soldier does not display the same type as the legitimate line of royal portraits, from AMENOPH I. downwards. There is nothing Asiatic about his physiognomy — on the contrary, it perpetuates the African or *Negroid* type of the first dynasties.

Fig. 156.

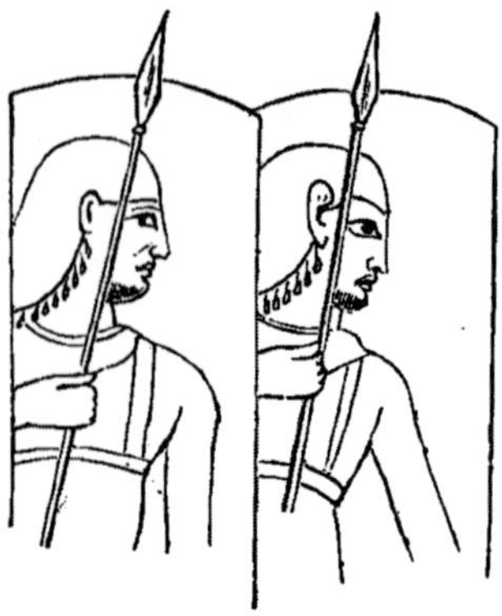

Nevertheless, already the military caste of Egypt was a mixed one; for here are two soldiers (Fig. 156), from another brigade, who, as Morton observed, present rather the Hellenic style of feature.[292]

So too, allowance made for very possible inattentions on the part of European copyists, where the subject was not *royal* iconography, do some of the following heads of lower classes of people (Figs. 157–161), also selected by Morton:—

Fig. 157.

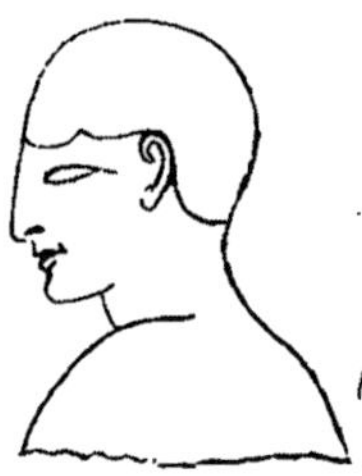

Artisan.

Fig. 158.

Leather-dresser.[294]

Fig. 159.

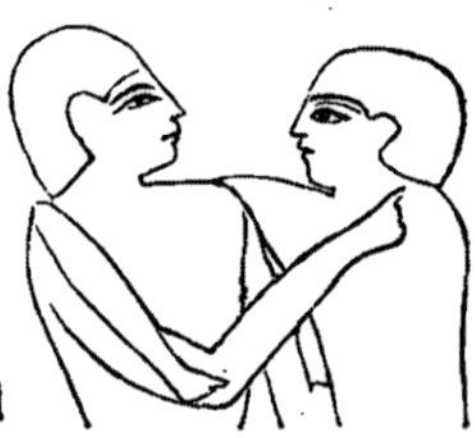

Wrestlers.

Fig. 160.

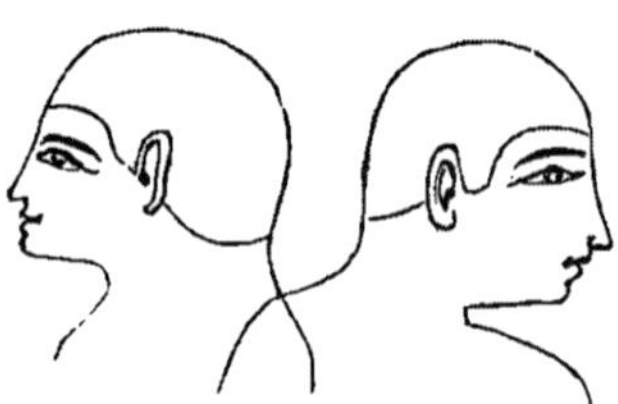

Peasants.[295]

Fig. 161.

Servants.[296]

The modern *Fellàhs*, constituting the mass of the common people of the country, have not even yet become sufficiently adulterated for their ancestral type to be extinguished, inasmuch as the same preponderating characteristics can be traced, backwards, from the living race, through five millennia of stone-chroniclings, to the earliest times.

Plate II.

MANEFRU, THE PROPRIETOR, 1st or 17th Dynasty, B.C. 3000, from his Tomb, now in the Royal Museum, Berlin

[NOTT & GLIDDON'S *Types of Mankind* 1854]

It is fair to conclude that these *Fellâhs* really preserve much of the aboriginal Egyptian type. Such type bears not the slightest resemblance (except in casual instances, themselves doubtful, when we first see it in the IVth dynasty, about 3400 B. C.) to any Asiatic race, and must therefore have been inherent in that indigenous race which was created to people the Valley of the Nile.

The authors esteem it a very high privilege that "Types of Mankind" should be the first work to remove all doubts upon the *type* of the earliest monumental Egyptians. Further discussion becomes superseded by the publication of the annexed lithographic Plates I., II., III., and IV. Being fac-similes of the most ancient human heads now extant in the world, and transfer-copies of impressions stamped, by the hand of Chevalier Lepsius himself, upon the original bas-reliefs preserved in the Royal Museum of Berlin, their intrinsic value in ethnography cannot be overrated; at the same time that, like an axe, these effigies cleave asunder *facts* and *suppositions* as to what primordial art at Memphis, above 5000 years ago, considered to be the "canonical proportions" ascribable to the facial and cephalic structure of the *heads* of the Egyptian people themselves.

Prefacing our exposition of the guarantees the lithographs possess for exactitude and authenticity with the remark, that these portraits belong to the tombs of princely, aristocratic, and sacerdotal personages, who lived during the IVth, Vth, and VIth Memphite dynasties, we proceed to state how such illustrations (alike precious from their enormous antiquity and for their unique excellence) have been obtained.

Attendants on Mr. Gliddon's Archæological Lectures in the United States have been informed, yearly, from 1842 to 1852,[297] of the discoveries of the Prussian Scientific Mission to Egypt: in every case, before the winter of 1849, far in advance of detailed publication, whether in America or in Europe. In that year, the first volume of Lepsius's quarto *Chronologie der Ægypter* was quickly followed by the first *livraisons* of the folio *Denkmäler aus Ægypten und Æthiopien* — the former judiciously constructing the chronological and historical framework within which the stupendous facts unfolded by the latter are enclosed. To facilitate popular appreciation of the magnitude of these Prussian labors and discoveries, Lepsius put forth, at Berlin, in 1852, his octavo *Briefe aus Ægypten, Æthiopien,* &c.; which, translated and ably annotated by Mr. Kenneth Mackenzie, being now equally accessible to every reader of our tongue, renders any account here of these Nilotic explorations superfluous, beyond mentioning that *four* of the most ancient tombs discovered at Memphis by Lepsius, independently of his vast collection of other materials, were taken to pieces on the spot, with the utmost care, and became rebuilt into the Royal Museum at Berlin.

Invited by Chevalier Lepsius to visit,[298] and inspect personally, antiquarian treasures endeared by a lifetime's Egyptian associations, Mr. Gliddon was at once so struck with the ethnographic importance of these sepulchral bas-reliefs, that he solicited *paper-impressions* of a few heads for the joint and future studies of Dr. Morton and himself; and, on the 10th of May, 1849, he had the gratification of assisting Chevalier Lepsius to make numerous *estampages;* while, to insure perfection and authenticity, the paper was stamped upon the sculptures by the Chevalier's own hands.

One singular fact, illustrative of the superior antiquity of these tombs of pyramidal magnates to any heretofore described by Egyptologists, may here be mentioned. Laid bare, through excavation, at a depth of many feet below the rocky surface, and emptied of the sand with which they had become refilled since their desecration by unknown hands (probably *Saracenic*) centuries ago, the *relievos* presented themselves in colors so vivid as to appear "fresh and perfect, as if painted only yesterday;" but, despite every precaution, on removing each slab into the open air, the painted stucco-superficies fell off—leaving, however, the uninjured *low-relief* (about the sixth of an inch) sculpture to endure long as time shall respect the Berlin Museum. Now, in the dry climate of Memphis, Egyptian colors known to range from 2500 to 4000 years old, where not exposed to the dew, or to the Etesian winds, still adhere on the wall of tombs in their pristine freshness and brilliancy. Well, therefore, is an antiquity of at least 5300 years for these now colorless *relievos* (imperiously demanded also by their hieroglyphical and other conditions) corroborated by their exceptional friability. With his wonted foresight, Lepsius had caused the colored sculptures to be copied by his draughtsmen, *in situ*, before removal; and in the *Denkmäler*,[299] their gorgeous paintings may still be admired.

On the writer's (G. R. G.'s) return to London, these *estampages*, after being outlined, were transferred upon tracing-paper by his wife's accurate pencil, in duplicate, for Dr. Morton and himself. The originals, as acknowledged by the Doctor in a foregoing letter (p. 232, *ante*), were duly passed on to his cabinet, where their inspection completed that revulsion of earlier views toward which his progressive studies had long been leading. The second copy, shaded and colored in imitation of the limestone originals, has often embel-

Plate III

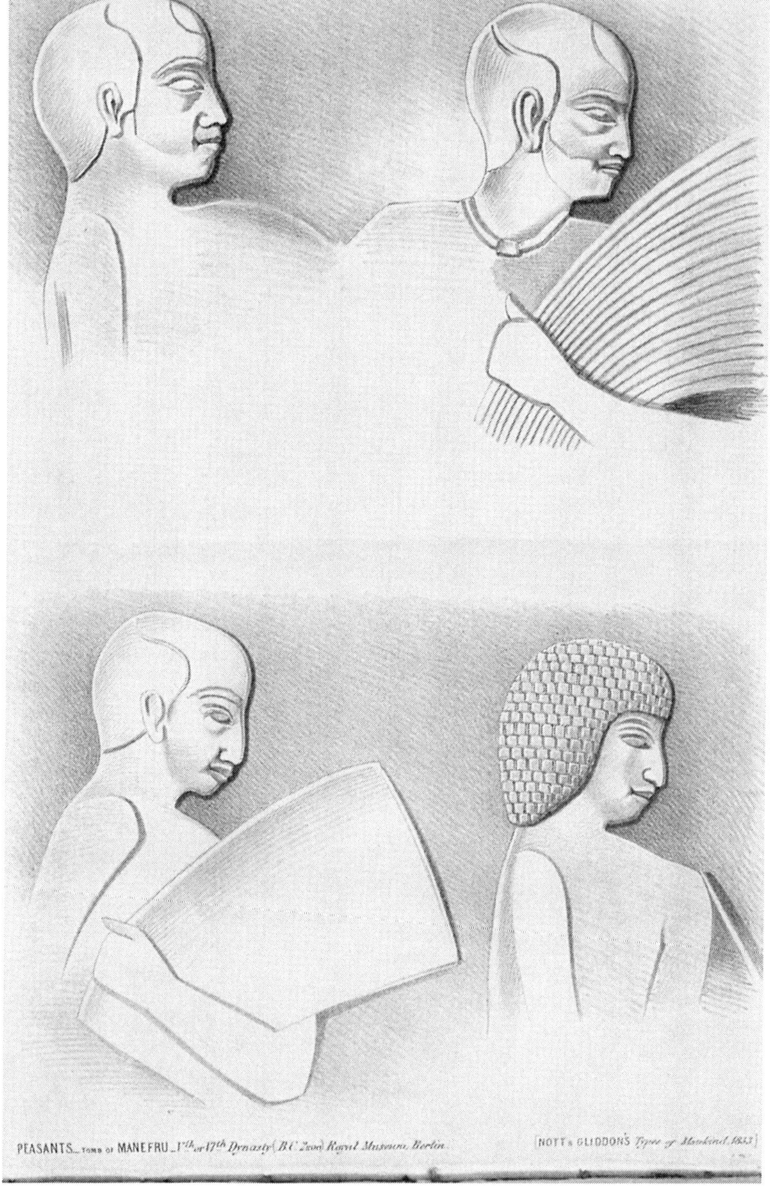

PEASANTS... TOMB OF MANEFRU _ 1th or 17th *Dynasty (B.C. 2000) Royal Museum, Berlin.*

[NOTT & GLIDDON'S *Types of Mankind, 1853*]

lished Mr. Gliddon's lecture-rooms when "Egyptian Ethnology" was the topic of his address.

When the authors projected the present work, at Mobile, in the spring of 1852, they acquainted Chevalier Lepsius, among other European colleagues, with their respective desiderata, archæological or ethnographical. Answering one of Gliddon's letters, the Chevalier complaisantly remarks: —

"BERLIN, 1 *Novembre*, 1852.

... "Pour les individus vous ne pouvez vous fier que sur les *empreintes* que vous avez; et si vous en desirez je vous en enverrai encore d'avantage. ... Les empreintes des bas-reliefs et les plâtres des anciennes statues sont, à ce qu'il me parait, les seuls matériaux utiles pour étudier l'ancien caractère des Égyptiens; et même pour ceux-là il faut admettre qu'on pourrait se tromper sur plusieur traits qui paraissent être surs, parceque le *canon* [that is, the *canon of proportion* accorded by Old Egyptian art to the human figure.— G. R. G.] reçu pouvait s'écarter en quelques points de la vérité, comme dans la position haute de l'oreille."

We have to record our joint obligations for the receipt, in August of the present year, of the second collection of stamps promised in the above letter; and it is from careful comparison of the duplicate originals with their tracings, that the models for our lithographic plates were designed. We feel confident, therefore, that our lithographs are *fac-similes*—submitting them to Chevalier Lepsius for comparison with the original bas-reliefs, while taking the liberty to urge upon his scientific attention, no less than upon that of possessors of such remains generally, the benefit they would confer upon ethnological studies, were they to publish similar fac-similes, where the lithographer, copying the *original* monument under their own critical eyes, would attain precision from which the Atlantic debars art in this country.

Abstraction made of the divergence from nature in the "high position of the ear," to which the above epistolary favor alludes, as a subject set at rest by Morton;[300] and repeating our previous notice of false delineation of the *eye* in Egyptian profiles: there remains no doubt that the *facial outlines*, and, where naked, the *cranial conformation*, in these most antique of all known sculptures, are rigorously faithful. Without hesitation, these heads may be accepted by ethnography as perfect representations of the *type* of Egyptians under the Old Empire.

Assuming such to be facts—and, beyond accidents of some trivial slip of a pencil, none can dispute them but the unlettered in these sciences — we may now claim as positive that the originals of our fac-simile heads date back, as a minimum, from 3000 to 3500 years before Christ, or to generations deceased above 5000 years ago; at which time Egypt had already existed for many centuries as a powerful empire, borne along on full tide of civilization: and, let us ask, what trace of an *Asiatic* type does the reader perceive in these hoary likenesses? How distinct, physiologically, are these heads from the royal portraits of the New Empire! Does not the low, elongated head; the imperfectly-developed forehead; the short, thick nose; the large, full lip; the short and receding chin; with their *tout-ensemble*, all point to *Africa* as the primeval birth-place of these people? When, too, we look around and along this ancient valley of the Nile at the present day, and compare the mingled types of races, still dwelling where their fathers did—the Fellàhs, the Bishariba, the Abyssinians, the Nubians, the Libyans, the Berbers (though they are by no means identical among each other), do we not behold a group of men apart from the rest of human creation? and all, singularly and collectively, inheriting something in their lineaments which clusters around the type of ancient Egypt? A powerful and civilized race may be conquered, may become adulterated in blood; yet the *type*, when so widely spread, as in and around Egypt, has never been obliterated, can never be washed out. History abundantly proves that human language may become greatly corrupted by exotic admixture—nay, even extinguished; but physiology demonstrates that a *type* will survive tongues, writings, religions, customs, manners, monuments, traditions, and history itself.

Dr. Morton's voluminous correspondence with scientific men throughout both hemispheres is replete with interest, exhibiting as it does so many charming instances of that philosophical *abandon*, or freedom from social rigidities, which characterizes true devotees to science in their interchanges of thought. There is one epistle among these, that almost electrified him[301] on its reception, bearing date "Alexandria, Dec. 17, 1843." It is invested with the signature of a voyager long "blanched under the harness" of scientific pursuits; who, as Naturalist to the United States' Exploring Expedition, had sailed round the world, and beheld *ten* types of mankind, before he wrote, after exploring the petroglyphs of the Nile:—

"I have seen in all eleven races of men; and, though I am hardly prepared to fix a positive limit to their number, I confess, after having visited so many different parts of the globe, that I am at a loss where to look for others."[302]

Qualified to judge, through especial training, varied attainments, and habits of keen observation that, in Natural History, are preeminent for accuracy, the first impressions of the gentleman from whose letter to his attached friend we make bold to extract a few sentences, (preserving their original form,) are strikingly to the point:

SERVANT WITH AN OX — TOMB OF MANEFRU,

V.th or VI.th Dynasty (B.C. 2800) Royal Museum, Berlin.

A PEASANT — TOMB OF SPETKHEMKA,

IV.th or V.th Dynasty (B.C. 3000) Royal Museum, Berlin.

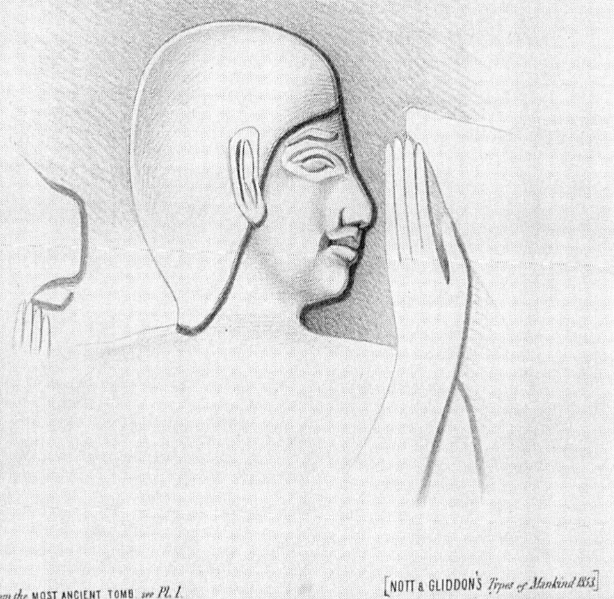

A SERVANT *from the* MOST ANCIENT TOMB *see Pl. I.*

"DEAR MORTON:

"This is the fourth day I have been in the land of the Pharaohs. . . . . . . Well, now for the Egyptian problem.

"Your October letter is now before me, and the left-hand drawing bears a most astonishing resemblance to my long-legged valet, Ali! (whom I intend to get daguerreotyped, if such a thing can be found at Cairo). The Robber Race has swept away everything at Alexandria; — nevertheless, by means of a *specimen* here and there, I had not been three hours in the country before I arrived at the conclusion, that the ancient Egyptians were neither Malays nor Hindoos, but ———————————————————

———————————————————————————————

——— Egyptians. . . . . .

Yours, truly,

"CHARLES PICKERING."

So inferred CHAMPOLLION-LE-JEUNE;[303] so pronounced MORTON, after a formal recantation of his published views; so, finally and deliberately, think the authors of this volume; viz.: that the primitive Egyptians were nothing more nor less than — EGYPTIANS.

Objectors must restrict themselves henceforward merely to cavils as to the antiquity of these Egyptian records. In Part III. their claims to reverence are superabundantly set forth. For ourselves we are content to rest the chronological case upon the authority of Baron ALEXANDER VON HUMBOLDT: —

"The valley of the Nile, which has occupied so distinguished a place in the history of Man, yet preserves authentic portraits of kings as far back as the commencement of the IVth dynasty of Manetho. This dynasty, which embraces the constructors of the great pyramids of Ghiza, Chefren or Schafra, Cheops, Choufou, and Menkara or Menkerés, commences more than 3400 years B. C., and twenty-four centuries before the invasion of Peloponnesus by the Heraclides."[304]

CHAPTER VIII.

NEGRO TYPES.

"When the prophet Jeremiah[305] exclaims, 'Can the *Ethiopian* change his skin, or the leopard his spots?' he certainly means us to infer that the one was as impossible as the other."—MORTON'S MSS.

"Niger in die (quodam) exuit vestes suas, incepitque capere nivem et fricare cum ea corpus suum. Dictum autem ei fuit: quare fricas corpus tuum nive? Et dixit (ille): *fortasse albescam.* Venitque vir (quidam) sapiens, (qui) dixit ei: O tu, ne affige te ipsum; fieri enim potest, ut corpus tuum nigram faciat nivem, ipsum autem non amittet nigredinem."—LOCMANI FABULA XXIII: *translated from the Arabic by Rosenmüller.*[306]

HAD every nation of antiquity emulated Egypt, and perpetuated the portraits of its own people with a chisel, it would now be evident to the reader that *each type of mankind*, in all zoological centres of man's creation, is by nature as indelibly permanent as the stone-pages upon which Egyptians, Chinese, Assyrians, Lycians, Greeks, Romans, Carthaginians, Meroïtes, Hindoos, Peruvians, Mexicans, (to say naught of other races,) have cut their several iconographies. How instantaneously would vanish pending disputes about the *Unity* or the *Diversity* of human origins!

Contenting ourselves at present with the now-acquired fact, that the Egyptians, according to monumental and craniological evidences, no less than to all history, written or traditionary, were really *autocthones* of the Lower Nile, we think the question as to their "type" has been satisfactorily answered. In reply, furthermore, to our previous interrogatory, whether this ancient family obeyed the same law of "gradation" established for other African aborigines; we may now observe, that the Egyptians, astride as it were upon the narrow isthmus which unites the once-separate continents of Africa and Asia, figure, when the Aurora of human tradition first breaks, as at one and the same time, the *highest* among African, and (physiologically, if not perhaps intellectually) as the *lowest* type in West-Asiatic *gradations*.

Were we to prosecute our imaginary journey northwards, the dark *Cushite*-Arabs would naturally constitute the next grade, and the ancient Canaanites probably the one immediately succeeding. The primitive group of Semitic nations would be found to have aboriginally occupied geographical levels commencing with Mount Lebanon and rising gradually in physical characters as we ascend the Tauric chain — passing, almost insensibly, into the Japethic or whitest races (also possessing their own *gradations*), until the highest types of prehistoric humanity would reveal their birth-places around the *Caucasus*.

But, dealing mainly with the Natural History of Man, elucidated through new archæological data, the scope of our work permits no geographical digressions beyond the Caucasian mountains. We have already insisted that the term "Caucasian" is a misnomer, productive of infinite embarrassments in anthropology; because a name in itself specifically restricted, since the times of Herodotus, to *one* locality and to *one* people, has become misapplied generically to types of mankind whose origins have no more to do with the mountains of *Caucasus* than with those of the moon. Would it not be ridiculous to take, for example, the name "Englander" (a compound of *Angl* and *land* — "man of the *land* of the *Angli*"), and to classify under such an appellative, Hebrews, Egyptians, Hindoos, &c.? That "Caucasian" is equally fallacious, will be made clear to the reader, in Part II., under the article on MaGUG; but we anticipate a portion of the philological argument by mentioning, that the Hellenized name CAUC-ASOS means simply the "*Mountain* of the *Asi*;" being the Indo-Germanic word *Khogh*, signifying "mountain," prefixed to the proper name of a nation and a race: viz., the *Aas*, *Asi*, *Jases*, *Osseth*, or *Osses*; who, dwelling even yet at the foot of that CAUC-ASOS where, from immemorial time, their ancestors lived before them, would be astonished to learn that European geographers had bestowed their national name upon the whole continent of *Asia*, and that modern ethnologists actually derive a dozen groups of distinct human animals from the *mountain* ("Khogh") of which such *Asi* are aborigines![307]

FIG. 162.

White races — JAPHETH.

Turning our backs upon the Caucasus, and retracing our steps toward Africa, let us incidentally notice the recognition by ante-Mosaic Egyptian, and by post-Mosaic Hebrew, ethnographers, of the general principle of *gradation* among such types of mankind as lay within the horizons of their respective geographical knowledge. The Egyptians, for instance, in their quadripartite division of races, already explained (*ante*, p. 85, Fig. 1), assigned the most northerly habitat to the "*white* race," of which we here reproduce the standard type (Fig. 162) — one of the four designed in the tomb of Seti I., about 1500 B. C.

Precisely does the writer of Xth *Genesis*, as set forth elaborately in Part II., follow the same system, in his tripartite division; inasmuch as he groups the "*Affiliations* of JAPHETH," that is, his "*white* races," between the Tauric chain of mountains and the Caucasian, along and within the northern coast of Asia Minor to the Black Sea.

FIG. 163.

Yellow races — SHEM.

So, again, Egyptian ethnography chose, for the standard-type of "*yellow* races," four effigies which entirely correspond, in every desideratum of locality, color, and physical conformation, with those families classified, in Xth *Genesis*, as the "*Affiliations* of SHEM;" and like the Hebrew geographer, the Theban artist must have known, that the *yellow*, or Semitic, groups of men occupied countries immediately south of the "*white* races," and stretching from the Taurus to the Isthmus of Suez, including the river-lands of the Tigris and Euphrates, together with the Arabian Peninsula.

The specimen illustrative of these groups of yellow-skinned races here presented in Fig. 163, is also, like the following (Figs. 164, 165), a reproduction from the four figures before shown on page 85.

Equally parallel is the Jewish classification, in respect to the "*Affiliations* of HAM" (Fig. 164), with those "*red* races" among which the Egyptians placed the RoT, or themselves. To the latter, K*h*aM was nothing but the hieroglyphical name of Egypt proper; K*h*eMe, or K*h*iMe, "the *dark* land" of the Nile; corrupted by the Greeks into "Chemmis" and "Chemia," and by us preserved in such words as "*chem*-istry" and "al-*chem*-y," both Egyptian sciences; while, in Hebrew geography, K*h*aM, signifying *dark*, or *swarthy*, merely meant all those non-Shemitish families which, under the especial cognomina of *Cushites*, *Canaanites*, *Mizraimites*, *Libyans*, *Berbers*, and so forth, formed that group of proximate types situate, aboriginally, east and west of the Nile, and along its banks north of the first cataract at Syene. Our wood-cut illustrates the *Egyptian* standard-type of these populations.

FIG. 164.

Swarthy (or red) races — HAM.

But here the analogy between the earlier Egyptian and the posterior Hebrew systems ceases. *Nigritian* races, never domiciled nearer to Palestine than 1500 miles to the south-westward, did not enter into the social economy of the Solomonic Jews, any more than into that of the Homeric Greeks; and, if not perhaps absolutely unknown, Negroes were then as foreign to, and remote from, either nation's geography, as the Samoïdans or the Tungousians are to our popular notions of the earth's inhabitants at the present day. In consequence, (as it is thoroughly demonstrated in Part II.), the writer of Xth Genesis omits *Negro* races altogether, from his tripartite classification of humanity under the symbolical appellatives of "Shem, Ham, and Japheth;" whereas the Egyptians of the XIXth dynasty, about 1500 years B. C., having become acquainted with the existence of *Negroes* some eight centuries previously (when Sesourtasen I., of the XIIth dynasty, about B. C. 2300, pushed his conquests into Upper Nubia), could not fail to include this *fourth* type of man in their ethnological system; because the river Nile was the most direct *viaduct* through which the Soodàn, Negro-land, could be reached, or Negro captives procured.

FIG. 165.

Black races.

With this preliminary basis, calling attention to the effigy (Fig. 165) by which they personified Negroes generally, we proceed to draw from the ancient stone-books of Egypt such testimonies concerning the *permanence of type* among Nigritian races as they may be found to contain.

FIG. 166.

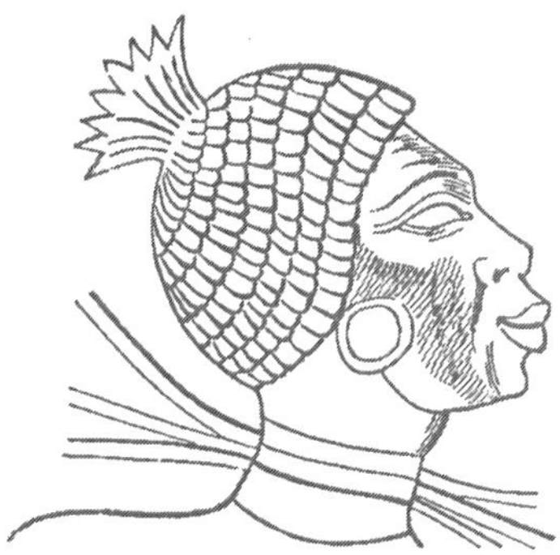

Our Negro (Fig. 166) is from the bas-reliefs of Ramses III. (XXth dynasty, thirteen centuries B. C.), at Medeenet-Haboo, where he is tied by the neck to an Asiatic prisoner. The head, in the original, is now uncolored; and it serves to show how perfectly Egyptian artists represented these races.[308] We quote from Gliddon's *Ethnographic Notes*, before referred to: "This head is remarkable, furthermore, as the *usual type* of two-thirds of the Negroes in Egypt at the present day." And any one living in our Slave-States will see in this face a type which is frequently met with here. We thus obtain proof that the Negro has remained unchanged in Africa, above Egypt, for 3000 years; coupled with the fact that the same type, during some eight or ten generations of sojourn in the United States, is still preserved, despite of transplantation.)

The following representation (Fig. 167) is traced upon a spirited reduction by Cherubini.[309] It is a double file of Negroes and *Baràbra* (Nubians), bound, and driven before his chariot by Ramses II., at Aboosimbel. This picture answers well as a complement to the two

FIG. 167.

preceding; for we here have the brown *Nubian*—a dark one, and a light-colored family—admirably contrasted with the jet-black Negro; thus proving that the same divisions of African races existed then as now, above the first cataract of the Nile at Syene.

FIG. 168.

One of the same series (Fig. 168), on a larger scale, taken from Rosellini.[310] It should be observed that he is shaded *browner* than the next head (Fig. 169); thereby showing the two commonest colors and physiognomical lineaments prevalent among Nubian *Baràbra* of the present day; who, whether owing to amalgamation, or from original *type*, approach closer to the Negro than do the adjacent tribes—*Ababdeh*, *Bisharíba*, &c.

The same group supplies a lighter (cinnamon) shaded sample of a Nubian *Berberri* (Fig. 169); whose name in the Arabic plural is *Baràbra*. The identical designation, BaRaBaRa, is applied to the same people in the sculptures of several Pharaohs of the XVIIth and XVIIIth dynasties, 1500 years B. C.[311]

Fig. 169.

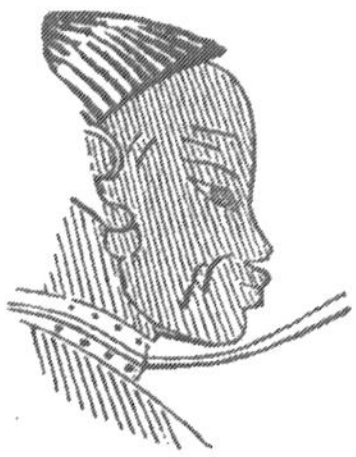

Fig. 170.

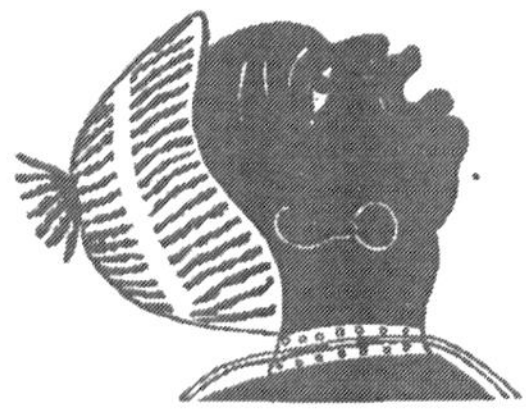

To render the contrast more striking, we place in juxta-position an enlarged head (Fig. 170) of the last Negro from the above prisoners. The face is ingeniously distorted by the Egyptian artist, who represents this captive bellowing with rage and pain.

One of Mr. Gliddon's personal verifications on the Nile is here worthy of note. He observed that the fusion between Nubian and modern Arab races is first clearly apparent, exactly where nature had placed the boundary-line between Egypt and Nubia: viz., at the first cataract. Here dwell the *Shellàlees*, or "cataract-men" — descended, it is said, from intermixture between the Saracenic garrisons at Assouàn and the women of Lower Nubia. Persian, Greek, and Roman troops had been consecutively stationed there, centuries before the Arabs; while European and American tourists at the present day coöperate vigorously to stem the blackening element as it flows in from the South. The *Shellàlees* count perhaps 500 adults and children; and they are mulattoes of various hues, compounded of Nubian, Arab, Egyptian, Turkish, and European blood; whilst, incidentally, Negresses enter as slaves among the less impoverished families—their cost there seldom exceeding fifty dollars. But, the predominating color, especially among the female *Shelallèeyeh*, is a light cinnamon; and in both sexes are seen some of the most beautiful forms of humanity; as may be judged from the "Nubian Girl," so tastefully portrayed by Prisse d'Avesnes.[312]

Fig. 171.[313]

This (Fig. 171) is the type of the NaHSU (*Negroes*), on a larger scale, among the four races in the tomb of SETI-MENEPTHA I.; before spoken of, and delineated at full length on pages 85 and 249, *supra.*

Beautifully drawn and strikingly contrasted, see two of the nine Asiatic and African heads (Fig. 172) smitten by king, SETI I., at

FIG. 172.[314]

Karmac. The Negro's features are true to the life, if we deduct the ancient defective drawing of the eye; as must be done in all copies of Egyptian art.

We next present (Fig. 173) one of the many proofs that Negro *slavery* existed in Egypt 1500 years B. C. An Egyptian scribe, colored

FIG. 173.[315]

red, registers the black slaves; of which males, females, and their children are represented; the latter even with the little tufts of wool erect upon their heads: while the leopard-skin around the first Negro's loins is grotesquely twisted so as to make the animal's tail belong to its human wearer.

In connection with this scene, which is taken from a monument at Thebes, Wilkinson remarks:—

"It is evident that both white and black slaves were employed as servants; they attended on the guests when invited to the house of their master; and from their being in the families of priests as well as of the military chiefs, we may infer that they were purchased with money, and that the right of possessing slaves was not confined to those who had taken them in war. The traffic in slaves was tolerated by the Egyptians; and it is reasonable to suppose, that many persons were engaged, as at present, in bringing them to Egypt for public sale, independent of those who were sent as part of the tribute, and who were probably, at first, the property of the monarch; nor did any difficulty occur to the Ishmaelites in the purchase of Joseph from his brethren, nor in his subsequent sale to Potiphar on arriving in Egypt."

In his comments on the antiquity of "eunuchs," Gliddon has extended these analogies of slavery among the Hebrews, and other ancient nations.[316]

We might thus go on, and add numberless portraits of Negro races. Hundreds of them are represented as slaves, as prisoners of war, as fugitives, or slain in large battle-scenes, &c.; all proving that, as far back as the XVIIth dynasty, B. C. 1600, they existed as distant nations, above Egypt.

Taken at random from the plates of Rosellini, the three subjoined portraits (Figs. 174, 175, 176) are submitted, to fortify our words.

Fig. 174.

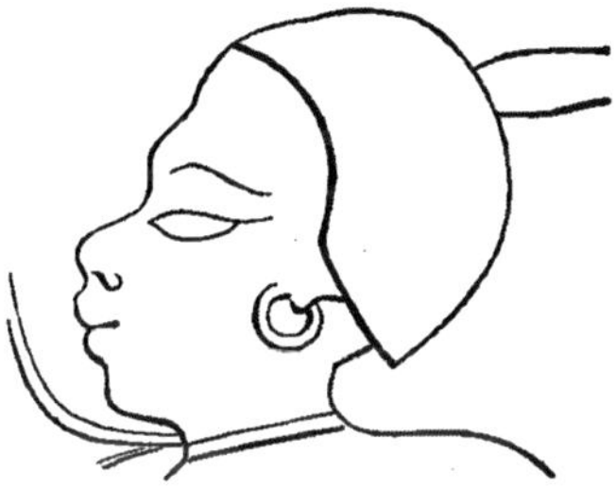

Fig. 175.

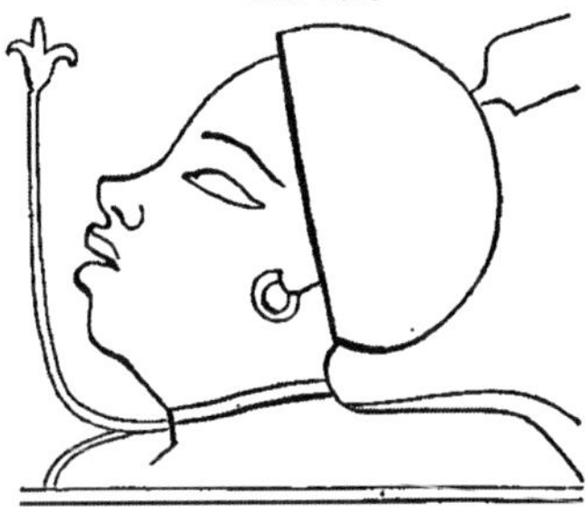

The *lotus*-bud at the end of their halters means the word "south," in hieroglyphical geography: while their varieties of physical conformation suffice to show that anciently, as at this day, the basin of the upper Nile included many distinct Negro races.

Fig. 176.

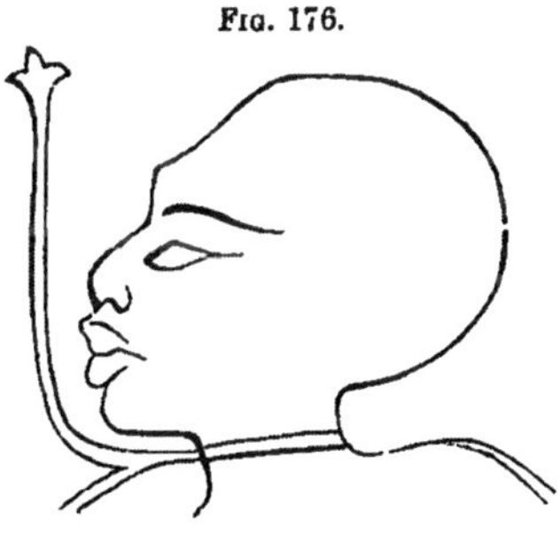

It has been for several years asserted[317] by the authors of the present volume, and it is now finally demonstrated in Part II., that *Negro* races are never alluded to in ancient Jewish literature; the Greek word "Ethiopia" being a false interpretation of the Hebrew KUS*h*, which always meant *Southern Arabia*, and nothing but the *Cushite*-Arabian race.

The Greeks, of course, were unacquainted with the existence of *Negroes* until about the seventh century B. C.; when PSAMETIK I. opened the ports of Lower Egypt to Grecian traffickers. Their "Ethiopians," sun-*burned-faces*, before that age, were merely any people darker than a Hellene—Arabs, Egyptians, and Libyans, from *Joppa* (Jaffa) westward to Carthage: nor, camels being unknown to the Carthaginians, as well as to the early Cyreneans, could *Negroes* have been brought across the Sahara deserts into the Barbary States, until about the first century before the Christian era. The only channel to the natural habitat of Negro races, (which never has lain geographically to the northward of the *limit of the Tropical rains*, or about 16° N. lat.,) until camels were introduced into Barbary, after the fall of Carthage, was along the Nile, and through Egypt exclusively. The Carthaginians never possessed Negro slaves, excepting what they may have bought in Egyptian bazaars; of which incidents we have no record. It is worthy of critical attention, that in the *Periplus of* HANNO, and other traditionary voyages outside the Pillars of Hercules, while we may infer that these Carthaginian navigators (inasmuch as they reached the country of the *Gorillæ*, now known to be the largest species of the chimpanzee,) must have beheld Negroes also; yet, after passing the *Lixitæ*, and other "men of various appearances," they merely report the whole coast to be inhabited by "Ethiopians."[318] Now, the Punic text of this voyage being lost, we cannot say what was the original *Carthaginian* word which the Greek translator has rendered by "Ethiopians;" so that, even if *Negroes* be a very probable meaning, these Atlantico-African voyages prove nothing beyond the fact that, in HANNO's time, B. C. five or six centuries, there was already great *diversity* of races along the north-western coast of Africa, and that all of them were *strange* to the Carthaginians.

It is now established, moreover, that the account given by HERODOTUS of the *Nasamonian* expedition to the country of the Garamantes, never referred to the river Niger, but to some western journey into Mauritania; as we have explained in Part II.

Apart, then, from a few specimens of the Negro type that, as curiosities, may have been occasionally carried from Egypt into Asia, there was but one other route through which Negroes, until the times of SOLOMON, could have been transported from Africa into Asiatic countries; viz.: by the Indian Ocean, Persian Gulf, and Red Sea. We have diligently hunted for archæological proofs of the existence of a *Negro* out of Egypt in such ancient times, and have found but two instances; dependent entirely upon the fidelity of the superb copies of TEXIER, and of FLANDIN.

In Texier's work[319] we think a *Negro*, (in hair, lips, and facial angle,) may be detected as the last figure, on the third line, among the foreign supporters of the throne of one of the Achæmenian kings at Persepolis. There is nothing improbable in the circumstance; for the vast Satrapies of Persia, in the fifth century B. C., extended into Africa. The more certain example we allude to is found in the sculptures of Khorsabad, or Nineveh;[320] and probably appertains to the reign of SARGAN, B. C. 710–668. It is a solitary figure of a beardless Negro with woolly hair, wounded, and in the act of imploring mercy from the Assyrians.

Turn we now to Roman authority.

Latin description of a NEGRESS, *written early in the second century after* C.

"Interdum clamat Cybalen; erat unica custos;
Afra genus, tota patriam testante figura;
Torta comam, labroque tumens, et fusca colorem;
Pectore lata, jacens mammis, compressior alvo,
Cruribus exilis, spatiosa prodiga planta;
Continuis rimis calcanea scissa rigebant."

"In the meanwhile he calls Cybale. She was his only [house-] keeper. African by race, her whole face attesting her father-land: with crisped hair, swelling lip, and blackish complexion; broad in chest, with pendant dugs, [and] very contracted paunch; her spindle-shanks [contrasted with her] enormous feet; and her cracked heels were stiffened by perpetual clefts."

Egyptian delineation of a NEGRESS, *cut and painted some* 1600 *years before the Latin description.*

FIG. 177.

To Mr. Gustavus A. Myers, (an eminent lawyer of Richmond, Va.,) are we indebted for indicating to us this unparalleled description of a *Negress;* no less than for the loan of the volume in which an unapplied passage of VIRGIL[321] is contained. Through it we perceive that, in the second century after C., the physical characteristics of a "field," or agricultural, "Nigger" were understood at Rome 1800 years ago, as thoroughly as by cotton-planters in the State of Alabama, still flourishing in A. D. 1853.

Time, as every one now can see, has effected no alteration, even by transfer to the New World, upon African types (save through amalgamation) for 3400 years downwards. Let us inquire of the Old continent what metamorphoses time may have caused, as regards such alleged transmutations, upwards.

About the sixteenth century B. C., Pharaoh HORUS of the XVIIIth dynasty records, at Hagar Silsilis, his return from victories over Nigritian families of the upper Nile.[322] The hieroglyphical legends above his prisoners convey the sense of—"KeS*h*, barbarian country, perverse race;" expressive of the Egyptian sentimentalities of that day towards Nubians, Negroes, and "foreigners" generally.

Among his captives is the Negress already portrayed (Fig. 177); to whose bas-reliefed effigy we have merely restored one of the colors now effaced by time. We present (Fig. 178) a head indicative of her male companions, traced upon Rosellini's size; our reduction of her full-length figure being taken from the Prussian *Denkmäler.*[323]

Fig. 178.

Here, then, is a Negress, sculptured and painted in Egypt about B. C. 1550, whose effigy corresponds with Virgil's description at Rome a little after A. D. 100; which female is identical with living Negresses, of whom American States, south of "Mason and Dixon's line," could produce many hundreds in the present year, 1853.

Have 3400 years, or any transplantations, altered the NEGRO race?

When treating of the "Caucasian" type, we were obliged to jump from the XVIIth back to the XIIth dynasty, owing to the lack of intervening monuments, since destroyed by foreign invaders. The same difficulty recurs with regard to Negro races. In fact, our materials here become still more defective; for, although in the XIIth dynasty abundant hieroglyphical inscriptions attest the existence of *Negro* nations, no portraits seem to be extant, of this epoch, upon whose coetaneous date of sculpture we can rely. That Negroes did, however, exist in the twenty-fourth century B. C., or contemporaneously with Usher's date of the Flood, we shall next proceed to show.

Aside from the Tablet of Wady Halfa, cut by Sesourtasen I., of the XIIth dynasty, (*supra*, p. 188,) we quoted from Lepsius (*supra*, p. 174), a paragraph illustrative of the diversity of types at this early period, of which the following is a portion rendered from his *Briefe:*

"Mention is often made on the monuments of this period of the victories gained by the kings over the Ethiopians and Negroes, wherefore we must not be surprised to see *black* slaves and servants."

Mr. Birch kindly sent us, last year, an invaluable paper, wherein the political relations of Egypt with Ethiopia are traced by his masterly hand, from the earliest times down to the XIXth dynasty. The "Historical Tablet of Ramses II.," from which the most recent facts are drawn, dates from the sixteenth year of a reign, that lasted upwards of sixty years.[324] The subjoined extract is especially important, not only because demonstrative of the existence of *Negroes* as far back as the XIIth dynasty, but also because it establishes the extended intercourse which Egypt held at that remote day (B. C. 2400–2100) with numerous Asiatic and African races.

"The principal inducements which led the Pharaohs to the south were the valuable products, especially the minerals, with which that region abounded. At the early period of the IVth and VIth Egyptian dynasties, no traces occur of Ethiopian relations, and the frontier was probably at that time Eileithyia (El Hegs). So far indeed from the Egyptian civilization having descended the cataracts of the Nile, there are no monuments to show that the Egyptians were then even acquainted with the black races, the Nahsi as they were called.[325] Some information is found at the time of the XIth dynasty. The base of a small statue inscribed with the name of the king *Ra nub Cheper*, apparently one of the monarchs of the XIth dynasty, whose prenomen was discovered by Mr. Harris on a stone built into the bridge at Coptos, intermingled with the Enuentefs, has at the sides of the throne on which it is seated Asiatic and Negro prisoners. Under the monarchs of the XIIth dynasty, the vast fortifications of Samneh show the growing importance of Æthiopia, while the conquest of the principal tribes is recorded by Sesertesen I. at the advanced point of the Wady Halfa. The most remarkable feature of this period are the hydraulic observations carefully recorded under the last monarchs of the line, and their successors the Sebakhetps of the XIIIth dynasty. A tablet in the British Museum, dated in the reign of Amenemha I. has an account of the mining services of an officer in Æthiopia at that period. 'I worked,' he says, 'the mines in my youth; I have regulated all the chiefs of the gold washings; I brought the metal penetrating to the land of Phut to the Nahsi.' It is probably for these gold mines that we find in the second year of Amenemha IV. an officer bearing the same name as the king, stating that he 'was invincible in his majesty's heart in smiting the Nahsi.' In the nineteenth year of the same reign were victories over the Nahsi. At the earliest age Æthiopia was densely colonized, and the gold of the region descended the Nile in the way of commerce; but there are no slight difficulties in knowing the exact relations of the two countries.

"The age of the XVIIIth dynasty is separated from the XIIth by an interval during which the remains of certain monarchs named Sebakhetp, found in the ruins of Nubia, show that they were at least Æthiopian rulers. The most important of the monuments of this age is the propylon of Mount Barkal, the ancient Napata, built by the so-called S-menken, who is represented in an allegorical picture vanquishing the Æthiopians and Asiatics. The XVIIIth dynasty opened with foreign wars. The tablet of Aahmes-Pensuben in the Louvre records that he had taken 'two hands,' that is, had killed two Negroes personally in Kish or Æthiopia. More information, and particularly bearing upon the Tablet of Rameses, is afforded by the inscription of Eilethyia, now publishing in an excellent memoir by M. de Rougé, in the line, 'Moreover,' says the officer, 'when his majesty attacked the Mena-en-shaa,' or Nomads, 'and when he stopped at *Penti-han-nefer* to cut up the Phut, and when he made a great rout of them, I led captives from thence two living men and one dead (hand). I was rewarded with gold for victory again; I received the captives for slaves.' During the reign of Amenophis I., the successor of Amosis, the Louvre tablet informs that he had taken one prisoner in Kash or Æthiopia. At El Hegs, the functionary states, 'I was in the fleet of the king — the sun, disposer of existence (Amenophis I.), justified; he anchored at Kush in order to enlarge the frontiers of Kami, he was smiting the Phut with his troops.' Mention is subsequently made of a victory, and the capture of prisoners. It is interesting to find here the same place, Penti-han-nefer, which occurs in a Ptolemaic inscription on the west wall of the pronaos of the Temple of Philæ, where Isis is represented as 'the mistress of Senem and the regent of Pent-han-nefer.' From this it is evident that these two places were close to each other, and that this locality was near the site more recently called Ailak or Philæ. The speos of this monarch at Ibrim, the chapels at Tennu, or the Gebel Selseleh, show that the permanent occupation of Nubia at the age of the XVIIIth dynasty extended beyond Philæ. Several small tesseræ of this reign represent the monarch actually vanquishing the Æthiopians.

"The immediate successors of Amenophis occupied themselves with the conquest of Æthiopia. There is a statue of Thothmes I. in the island of Argo, and a tablet dated on the 15 Tybi of his second year at Tombos. The old temple at Samneh was repaired and dedicated to Sesertesen III., supposed by some to be the Sesostris who is worshipped by Thothmes III. as the god Tat-un, or 'Young Tat.' It is at the temple of Samneh that the first indication occurs of that line of princes who ruled over Æthiopia, by an officer who had served under Amosis and Thothmes I., in which last reign he had been appointed Prince of Æthiopia. The reign of Thothmes III. shows that *Kush* figured on the regular rent-roll of Egypt. The remains of the mutilated account of the fortieth regnal year of the king is mentioned as '240 ounces' or 'measures of cut precious stones and 100 ingots of gold.' Subsequently 'two canes' of some valuable kind of wood, and at least '300 ingots of gold,' are mentioned as coming from the same people. It appears from the tomb of Rech-sha-ra, who was usher of the Egyptian court at the time, and who had duly introduced the tribute-bearers, that the quota paid from this country was bags of gold and gems, monkeys, panther-skins, logs of ebony, tusks of ivory, ostrich-eggs, ostrich-feathers, camelopards, dogs, oxen, slaves. The permanent occupation of the country is at the same time attested by the constructions which the monarch made, at Samneh, and the Wady Halfa. At Ibrim, Nehi, prince and governor of the South, a monarch, seal-bearer, and counsellor or eunuch, leads the usual tribute mentioned as 'of gold, ivory, and ebony' to the king. *Set*, or Typhon, called '*Nub*' or '*Nub-Nub*,' Nubia, instructs him in the art of drawing one of those long bows which these people, according to the legend, contemptuously presented to the envoys of Cambyses. The successor of this monarch seems to have held the same extended territory, since, in the fourth year of his reign, these limits are mentioned, and some blocks with the remains of a dedication to the local deities. One of the rock temples at Ibrim was excavated in the reign of Amenophis II. by the Prince Naser-set, who was 'monarch' (*repa ha*), 'chief counsellor' (*sabu shaa*), and 'governor of the lands of the south.' The wall-paintings represent the usual procession of tribute-bearers to the king, with gold, silver, and animals, some of whom, as the jackals, were enumerated. The same monarch continued the temple at Amada, and a colossal figure of him, dedicated to Chnumis and Athor, and sculptured in the form of Phtha or Vulcan, has been found at Begghe, and in the fourth year of his reign the limits of the empire are still placed as Mesopotamia on the north, and the Kalu or Gallæ on the south.

"In the reign of his successor Thothmes IV. a servant of the king, apparently his charioteer, states he had attended the king from Naharaina on the north, to Kalu, or the Gallæ, in the south.

"The constructions of this monarch at Amada and at Samneh, show that tribute came at the same time from the chiefs of the Naharaina on the north, and also from Æthiopia. This is shown by the tombs of the military chiefs lying near the hill which is situate between Medinat Haboo and the house of Jani, one of whom had exercised the office of royal scribe or secretary of state, from the reign of Thothmes III. to that of Amenophis III. The reign of his successor, the last mentioned monarch, is the most remarkable in the monumental history of Egypt for the Æthiopian conquests. The marriage scarabæi of the king place the limits of the empire as the Naharaina (Mesopotamia) on the north, and the *Karu* or *Kalu* (the Gallæ) on the south. Although these limits are found, yet it is evident from the number of prisoners recorded that the Egyptian rule was by no means a settled one. They are Kish, Pet or Phut, Pamaui, Patamakai Uaruki, Taru-at, Baru, . . . kaba, Aruka, Makaiusah, Matakarbu, Sahabu, Sahbaru, Ru-nemka, Abhetu, Turusu, Shaarushak, Akenes, Serunik Karuses, Shaui, Buka, Shau, Taru Taru, Turusu, Turubenka, Akenes, Ark, Ur, Mar.

Amongst these names will be seen in the list of the Pedestal of Paris that of the Akaiat or Aka-ta, a name much resembling that of the Ath-agau, which is still preserved in the Agow or Agows, a tribe near the sources of the Blue Nile. Amenophis appears by no means to have neglected the conquests of his predecessors, and his advance to Soleb, in the province of El Sokhot, and Elmahas, proves that the influence of Egypt was still more extended than in the previous reigns.

"In the reign of Amenophis, Æthiopia appears to have been governed by a viceroy, who was an Egyptian officer of state, generally a royal scribe or military chief, sent down for the purpose of administering the country; the one in this reign bore the name of Merimes, and appears to have ended his days at Thebes, as his sepulchre remains in the western hills. He was called the *sa suten en Kush*, or prince of Kush, which comprised the tract of country lying south of Elephantina. In all the Ethnic lists this Kash or Æthiopia is placed next to the head of the list, 'all lands of the south,' and its identity with the Biblical Kush is universally admitted. It is generally mentioned with the haughtiest contempt, as the vile Kush (*Kash kh'aas,*) or Æthiopia, and the princes were of red or Egyptian blood. They dutifully rendered their proscynemata to the kings of Egypt."[326]

[Substantial reasons may be found in our Part II. for questioning a somewhat unlimited extension of the Biblical KUS*h*, which certain opponents might draw from Mr. Birch's language. The hieroglyphical name for Negroes is *Nahsu*, or *Nahsi;* and, on the other hand, the Egyptian (not the *Hebrew*) word KiS*h*, KeS*h*, KaS*h*I,[327] was applied to the ancient *Baràbra* of Nubia, between the first and second cataracts, specifically; and sometimes to all *Nubian* families, generically. The vowels *a*, *e*, *i*, *o*, in antique Egyptian no less than in old Semitic writings, when not actually inserted, are entirely vague: nor is the hieroglyphical word ever spelt *k*U*sh*, like the Hebrew designation "Cush;" which is maltranslated by "Ethiopia," because it denotes Southern Arabia. — G. R. G.]

The authors regret that their space compels them to abstain from reproducing the archæological references with which Mr. Birch supports his erudite conclusions.

Ethnological science, then, possesses not only the authoritative testimonies of Lepsius and Birch, in proof of the existence of Negro races during the twenty-fourth century B. C.; but, the same fact being conceded by all living Egyptologists, we may hence infer that these Nigritian types were contemporary with the earliest Egyptians. Such inductive view is much strengthened by a comparison of languages; concerning the antiquity of which we shall speak in another chapter.

To one living in, or conversant with, the Slave-States of North America, it need not be told, that the Negroes, in ten generations, have not made the slightest physical approach either towards our aboriginal population, or to any other race. As a mnemonic, we here subjoin, sketched by a friend, the likenesses of two Negroes (Figs.

FIG. 179.

FIG. 180.

179, 180), who ply their avocations every day in the streets of Mobile; where anybody could in a single morning collect a hundred others quite as strongly marked. Fig. 179 (whose portrait was caught when, chuckling with delight, he was "shelling out corn" to a favorite hog) may be considered caricatured, although one need not travel far to procure, in daguerreotype, features fully as animal; but Fig. 180 is a fair average sample of ordinary field-Negroes in the United States.

Mr. Lyell, in common with tourists less eminent, but in this question not less misinformed, has somewhere stated, that the Negroes in America are undergoing a manifest improvement in their physical type. He has no doubt that they will, in time, show a development in skull and intellect quite equal to the whites. This unscientific assertion is disproved by the cranial measurements of Dr. Morton.

That Negroes imported into, or born in, the United States become more intelligent and better developed in their *physique* generally than their native compatriots of Africa, every one will admit; but such intelligence is easily explained by their ceaseless contact with the whites, from whom they derive much instruction; and such physical improvement may also be readily accounted for by the increased comforts with which they are supplied. In Africa, owing to their natural improvidence, the Negroes are, more frequently than not, a half-starved, and therefore half-developed race; but when they are regularly and adequately fed, they become healthier, better developed, and more humanized. Wild horses, cattle, asses, and other brutes, are greatly improved in like manner by domestication; but neither climate nor food can transmute an ass into a horse, or a buffalo into an ox.

One or two generations of domestic culture effect all the improvement of which Negro-organism is susceptible. We possess thousands of the second, and many more of Negro families of the eighth or tenth generation, in the United States; and (where unadulterated by white blood) they are identical in physical and in intellectual characters. No one in this country pretends to distinguish the native son of a Negro from his great-grandchild (except through occasional and ever-apparent admixture of white or Indian blood); while it requires the keen and experienced eye of such a comparative anatomist as Agassiz to detect structural peculiarities in our few African-born slaves. The "improvements" among Americanized Negroes noticed by Mr. Lyell, in his progress from South to North, are solely due to those ultra-ecclesiastical amalgamations which, in their illegitimate consequences, have deteriorated the white element in direct proportion that they are said to have *improved* the black.

But, leaving aside modern quibbles upon simple facts in nature, (so often distorted through philanthropical panderings to political ambition), we select, from Abrahamic antiquity, two other heads (Figs. 181, 182) which, although not Negroes, constitute an interesting link in the gradation of races; being placed, geographically and physically, between the two extremes.

Fig. 181.

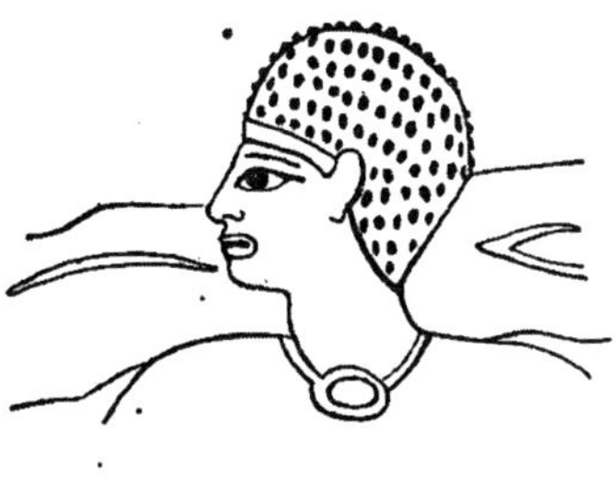

This specimen (Fig. 181) is from the "Grand Procession" of Thotmes III.—XVIIth dynasty, about the sixteenth century B. C. The original leads a leopard and carries ebony-wood: and his skin is *ash-colored* in Rosellini.[328] The same scene is given in Hoskins's *Ethiopia*, where this man's person is improperly painted *red*.[329] He is again figured without colors by Wilkinson,[330] no less than by Champollion-Figeac.[331] He is another sample of those "*gentes subfusci coloris*"—abounding around Ethiopia, above Egypt—neither Negro, Berberri, nor Abyssinian; but of a race affiliated probably to the latter; judging, that is, by characteristics alone, in the absence of hieroglyphical explanations now effaced by time.

Fig. 182.

Here we behold (Fig. 182), undoubtedly, a true *Abyssinian*, who should be represented, as he is at Thebes, *orange-color*.[332] We have the valid authority of Pickering[333] on this point; who concludes his chapter on Abyssinians as follows:—

"It seems, however, that the true Abyssinian (as first pointed out to me by Mr. Gliddon) has been separately and distinctly figured on the Egyptian monuments: in the two men leading the camelopard in the tribute procession of Thoutmosis III.; and this opinion was confirmed by an examination of the original painting at Thebes."

Pickering's *Races of Men* contains a beautiful *cinnamon*-colored portrait of an Abyssinian warrior, taken by Prisse; and, as before remarked, offers to the reader a good idea of the living type of this people.

It is worthy, too, of special note, that the above Fig. 182 is represented, in the Theban procession, leading a *giraffe;* which animal is not met with nearer to Egypt than Dongola; a fact that fixes his parallel of latitude along the Abyssinian regions of the Nile. Such heads seem to confirm the fidelity of Egyptian draughtsmen, together with the correctness of their ethnographical conceptions and varied materials. Our Abyssinian head exhibits the same form and color as the present race of that country, even after the lapse of 3300 years; and it stands as another proof of the *permanence of human types.*

Conceding the extreme probability of Birch's conjecture, that the Negro captives discovered by Mr. Harris belong to the XIth dynasty, (which thus would place the earliest known effigies of Negroes in the twenty-fourth or twenty-fifth century B. C.,) we cannot lay hold of the indication as a stand-point; because the sculpture may (through circumstances of recent masonry) be assigned to a later age. But, of one fact we are made certain by Birch's former studies:[334] viz., that the officers or superintendents appointed by the Pharaohs to regulate their Nubian provinces, were invariably *Egyptians*, painted *red*, and never Nigritians of any race whatever. The title "Prince of KeS*h*" was that of Egyptian viceroys, or lord-lieutenants, nominated by the Diospolitan government to rule over distant territories occupied by Nubians and Negroes of the austral Nile.

In the Theban tomb, opened previously to 1830 by Mr. Wilkinson, (about the epoch of which the theory of an Argive, "Danaus,"[335] led him into some odd hallucinations), and critically examined in 1839–'40 by Harris and Gliddon, there was an amazing collection of Negro scenes. A Negress, apparently a princess, arrives at Thebes, drawn in a plaustrum by a pair of humped oxen — the driver and groom being red-colored Egyptians, and, one might almost infer, eunuchs.[336] Following her, are multitudes of Negroes and Nubians, bringing tribute from the Upper country, as well as black slaves of both sexes and all ages, among which are some *red* children, whose *fathers* were Egyptians. The cause of her advent seems to have been to make offerings in this tomb of a "royal son of KeS*h* — Amunoph," who may have been her husband. The Pharaoh whose prenomen stands recorded in this sepulchral habitation is an Amenophis;[337] but, beyond the fact that his reign must fall towards the close of the XVIIIth

FIG. 183.

FIG. 184.[338]

dynasty, and about the times of the "disk-heresy," we were not aware that his place could be determined, until we opened the *Denkmäler;* where the major portion of these varied African subjects, unique for their singularity and preservation, are reproduced in brilliant colors. We have already chosen a Semitic head, deemed by us to present Phœnician affinities (*supra*, p. 164, Fig. 90), from sculptures of the same times. We here repeat it (Fig. 183), for the sake of contrasting its type with a Negro, and a Nubian apparently (Fig. 184), taken from the *ménagerie* of African curiosities above mentioned. We say *apparently*, because the slighter shade, given by Egyptian artists to figures grouped closely together, sometimes arises from the necessity of distinguishing the interlocked limbs, &c., of men of the same color. Instances may be found, of this attempt at perspective, in various colored scenes indicated in the notes,[339] so that the unblackened face in our Fig. 184 may be that of a Negro also.

For the sake of illustrating that, even in Ancient Egypt, *African slavery* was not altogether unmitigated by moments of congenial enjoyment; not always inseparable from the lash and the hand-cuff; we submit a copy of some Negroes "dancing in the streets of Thebes" (Fig. 185), by way of archæological evidence that, 3400 years ago, (or before the Exodus of Israel, B. C. 1322), "de same ole Nigger" of our Southern plantations could spend his Nilotic sabbaths in saltatory recreations, and

> "**Turn about, and wheel about, and** *jump Jim Crow!*"

Before closing our comments upon "Ethiopians," it is due to the memory of the author of *Crania Ægyptiaca* not to omit some notice of two

FIG. 185.[340]

problems that attracted his penetrating researches. The first concerns the ancient Meroïtes; the second, that mixed family in which, under the name of "Austral-Egyptians," Morton perceived some possibly-*Hindoo* affinities. Commencing with the former question, we recall to mind how the discoveries of the Prussian Scientific Mission (*supra*, p. 204), in and around the far-famed Isle of Meroë, have relieved archæologists from further discussions as to the illusory antiquity of a realm that, previously to the eighth century B. C., was merely a Pharaonic province and an Egyptian colony; and which, moreover, did not become important, as an independent kingdom, until Ptolemaic times. It was not, however, until after the publication of his *Ægyptiaca* (of which Chevalier Lepsius received a first copy, together with Gliddon's *Chapters*, under the pyramid of Gebel Birkel, in Ethiopia itself[341]), that Dr. Morton was informed, by the Chevalier directly, of results so demolishing to the learned theories of Heeren, Prichard, and other scholars. Unhappily for science, death arrested the hand of our illustrious friend before it could register the emendations consequent upon such immense changes in former historical opinions. Although one of the authors (G. R. G.) has, in the interim, enjoyed the advantage of beholding, at Berlin, the sculptures brought from Ethiopia, and of hearing Chevalier Lepsius's criticisms, *viva voce*, upon Meroïte subjects, we deem ourselves peculiarly unfortunate that the *Denkmäler*, so far as its *livraisons* have reached us, has not yet comprised copies of these newly-discovered bas-reliefs. We are unable, at present, therefore, to demonstrate to the reader, by the reproduction of portraits of Queen CANDACE and her *mulatto* court, the true causes why the civilization of Meroë declined, and finally became extinguished: viz., *owing to Negro amalgamations*, during the first centuries of our era. This fact may serve as a topic for some future *Appendix* to our volume.

FIG. 186.

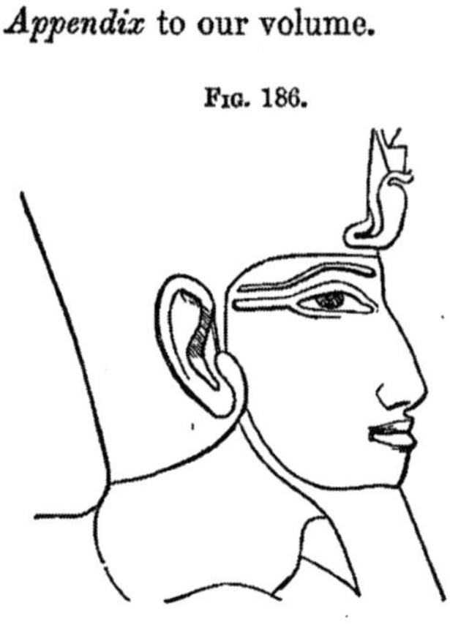

To obviate, however, any argument respecting Meroïte affinities with regard to Negro races in anterior times, we reproduce the portrait of Manetho's "Ethiopian" sovereign, Tirhaka (*supra*, p. 151, Fig. 71); the "Melek-KUS*h*, or *Cushite king* (2 Kings, xix. 9); contemporary with the Assyrian Sennacherib, whose likeness has also been submitted under our Fig. 27 (*supra*, p. 130.)

Nor did the high-caste lineaments of these "Ethiopian" princes, and the total absence of Nigritian elements in the physiognomies of all Meroïtes, as known in 1844, escape Morton's attention.[342] His comments on the accompanying effigies from Meroë suffice.

FIG. 187.[343]

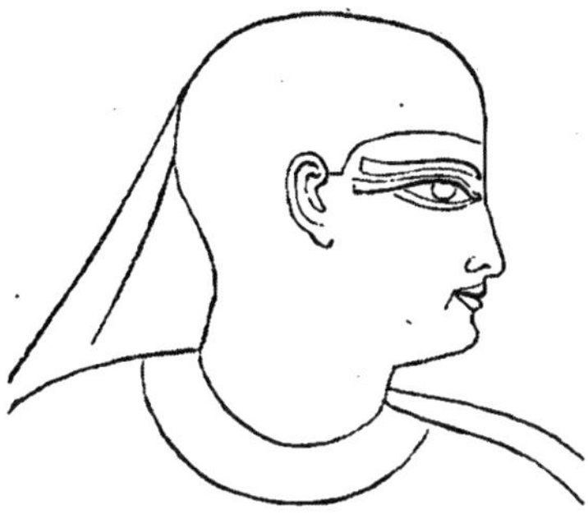

FIG. 188.[344]

"The one on the left hand [Fig 87] (that of an unknown king), has mixed lineaments, neither strictly Pelasgic nor Egyptian; while the right-hand personage [Fig. 188], who appears to be a priest doing homage, presents a countenance which corresponds, in essentials, to the Egyptian type, although the profile approaches closely to the Grecian. The annexed head [Fig. 189—is] also a king, bearing some resemblance to the one above figured."

FIG. 189.[345]

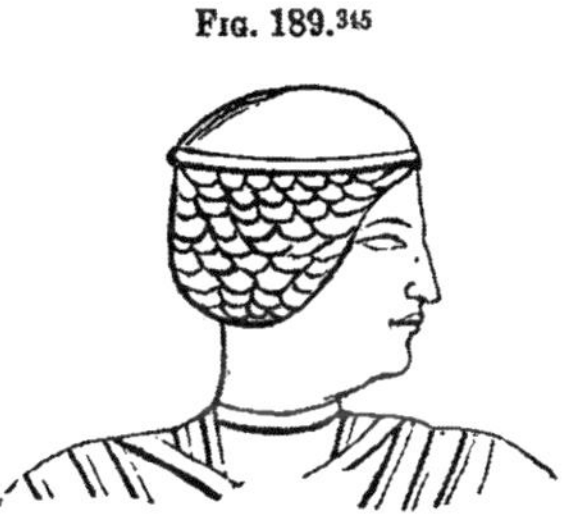

With regard to the "Hindoo" resemblances perceived by Morton in certain Egyptian crania of his vast collection, while we will neither affirm nor deny them, the authors cannot but think that their lamented colleague was herein biassed, rather by traditionary data (even yet supposed to be historical), than by anatomical evidences which, at any rate, do not strike our eyes as salient. Indeed, we know personally that, had Morton lived, Prichard's scholastic learning, but pertinacious ignorance of hieroglyphical Egypt, would have been dealt with as by ourselves, under full recognition of the one, and through respectful exposure of the other. Part III. of our volume renders it unnecessary to dwell, in this place, upon Sir W. Jones's Oriental erudition, or upon Col. Wilford's self-delusions, in respect to now-exploded connections between ancient India and primordial Egypt.

The Greek tradition (Latinicè) runs as follows: "*Æthiopes,* ab Indo fluvio profecti, supra Ægyptum sedem sibi eligerunt."[346] But, who are these *Ethiopians?* At most, Asiatic "sun-*burned* faces"—some people, darker in hue than Greeks, who emigrated from the Indus. The era, assigned for their migration to countries south of Egypt, is attributed to that of one among many Pharaohs, called by Grecian narrators "Amenophis;" and the legend reaches us through a Byzantine monk, *the Syncellus* (writing 2000 years after the events), at once the most diligent, and the least critical, compiler the seventh century of our era produced. To say the least, the historical surface we tread on trembles, as though it floated over a quagmire. These doubts suggested, we submit extracts from the *Crania Ægyptiaca*:—

"I observe, among the Egyptian crania, some which differ in nothing from the Hindoo type, either in respect to size or configuration. I have already, in my remarks upon the ear, mentioned a downward elongation of the upper jaw, which I have more frequently met with in Egyptian and Hindoo heads than in any other, although I have seen it occasionally in all the races. This feature is remarkable in two of the following five crania (A, B), and may be compared with a similar form from Abydos."[347]

Fig. 190.

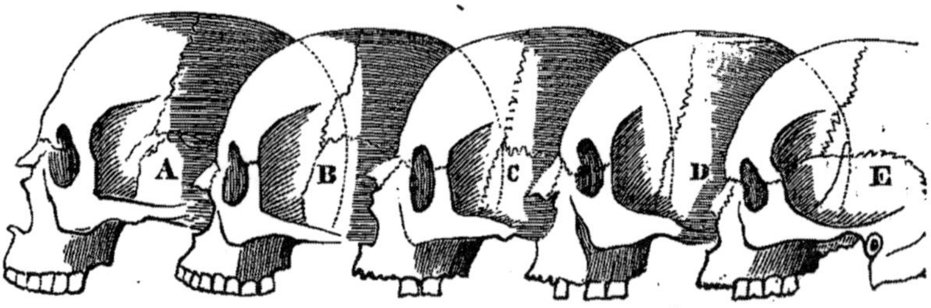

Fig. 191.

"It is in that mixed family of nations which I have called Austral-Egyptian that we should expect to meet with the strongest evidence of Hindoo lineage; and here, again, we can only institute adequate comparisons by reference to the works of Champollion and Rosellini. I observe the Hindoo style of features in several of the royal effigies; and in none more decidedly than in the head of Asharramon (Fig. 191), as sculptured in the temple of Debôd, in Nubia. The date of this king has not yet been ascertained; but, as he ruled over Meroë, and not in Egypt, (probably in Ptolemaic times [B. C. 200–300],) he may be regarded as an illustration of at least one modification of the Austral-Egyptian type.

Fig. 192.

"Another set of features, but little different, however, from the preceding, is seen among the middling class of Egyptians as pictured on the monuments, and these I also refer to the Hindoo type. Take, for example, the four annexed outlines (Fig. 192), copied from a sculptured fragment preserved in the museum of Turin. These effigies may be said to be essentially Egyptian; but do they not forcibly remind us of the Hindoo?"

So great is our respect for Morton's judgment; such manifold experiences have we acquired of his perceptive acuteness in craniological anatomy, that we should prefer the affirmatory decisions of others relative to this Hindoo-Meroïte problem, to any negation on our own parts.

The preceding brief digressions enable us to leave Meroë, and resume with a more positive, because osteological, proof of the perdurable continuance of the Negro type.

This semi-embalmed cranium of a *Negress* (Fig. 193), from Morton's cabinet, is preserved at the Academy of Natural Sciences in Philadelphia. Beyond the fact that mummification ceased towards the fifth century of our era; and that, being from an ancient tumulus at the sacred Isle of Beghe, the female owner of the annexed skull may have been a domestic slave of some "Ethiopian" worshipper at the shrine of Osiris, on the adjacent Isle of Philæ; all that can be said as to the antiquity of our specimen confines it to a period between the fourth century B. C. (when Pharaoh NECTANEBO founded the temple of Philæ), and the extinction of embalming, coupled with the substitution of Christianity (as understood by "Ethiopians,") for the religion of Osiris, about the fifth century after C.[349] Fifteen hundred years may, therefore, be assumed as the reasonable lapse of time since this aged Negress was consigned to the mound where hundreds of other Osirian pilgrims lie, coarsely swathed in bitumenized wrappers. The specimen is *unique* in the annals of Egyptian embalmment; inasmuch as no other purely-Negro vestiges have as yet turned up in tumuli or catacombs.

FIG. 193.[348]

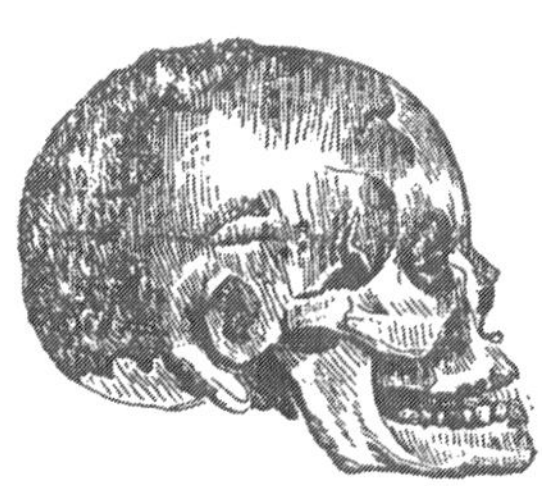

Trivial to many as the incident may seem, Science, nevertheless, can make "these dry bones speak" to the following points. First, they establish Nigritian indelibility of type, even to the woolly hair; because, our American cemeteries could yield up thousands of heads identical with this woman's. Secondly, they attest the comparative paucity of Negro individuals in Egypt during all ancient times; because, although the priests embalmed every native pauper, such Nigritian mummies have never, that we can learn, been discovered by ransackers of that country's sepulchres. And, thirdly, as this skull is a solitary exception, among millions of mummies disinterred, it demonstrates that the Egyptians possessed no craniological proximity to those Negro types with whom their existence was ever coeval. Indeed, this head was not found in Egypt proper, but immediately above the first cataract in Lower Nubia.

FIG. 194.

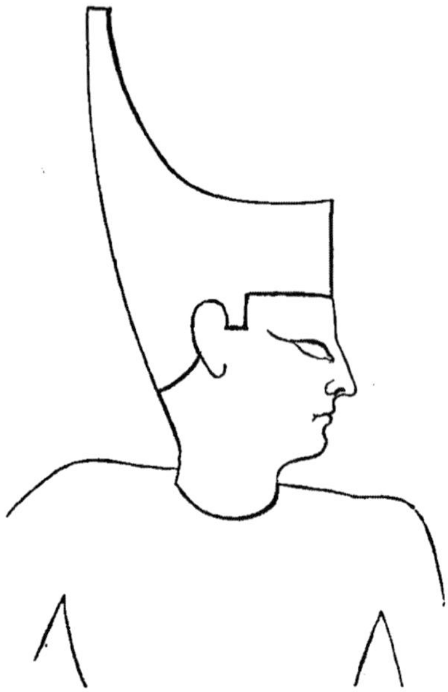

As Mr. Birch has mentioned, in the extract previously given, history reposes upon the ***Tablet of Wàdee Halfa*** for the conquest of Upper Nubia; and also for the earliest monumental rencontre with Negroes, by SESOURTESEN I., second king of the XIIth dynasty, near about 2348 years B. C.; which is the authorized date of the Deluge in King James's version. The tablet is small, and very much abraded; but, Morton having enlarged the royal portrait,[350] we repeat it here, for what it may be worth ethnologically. It proves, at least, that SESOURTESEN'S lineaments were anything but African.

The heads of austral captives, surmounting shields in which their national names are written, exist in this tablet, too mutilated for us to distinguish anything beyond the ***African*** contour of their features. Birch[351] reads their cognomina—

"1. *Kas*, or *Gas*.
2. *Shemki*, or *Temki*.
3. *Chasaa*.
4. *Shaat*.
5. *Khilukai;* or, perhaps the *Shilougis*, who now are called 'Shillouks'?"

It therefore becomes settled by the hieroglyphics, that the Egyptians had ascended the Nile, and had encountered *Negro*-races, at least as far back as the twenty-fourth century B. C.

We can now add a most extraordinary fact, since discovered by Viscount De Rougé, to the extracts we have culled from Birch's memoir. An inscription on the rocks near Samneh, in Nubia,[352] cut by Sesourtesen III. (of the same XIIth dynasty—about 2200 B. C.), in the "VIIIth year" of his reign, establishes that he had then extended the southern frontier of Egypt to that point, viz., the third cataract; whereas his predecessor, Sesourtesen I., had only guarded the passes at Wàdee Halfa, the second cataract, some 180 miles below. M. De Rougé,[353] with that felicitous acumen for which he is renowned, reads a passage in this inscription as follows:—

"Frontier of the South. Done in the year VIII., under King Sesourtesen [III.], ever living; in order that it may not be permitted to any *Negro* to pass by it in navigating" [down the river].

The repugnance of the Egyptians towards Nigritian races, exhibited in their epithet of "NaHSI—*barbarian* country, *perverse* race," becomes now a solid fact in primeval history; at the same time that the above inscription proves conclusively how, just about 4000 years ago, the geographical habitat of Negroes commenced exactly where it does at this day: viz., above the third cataract of the Nile.

We have shown, by their portraits, that the three "Ethiopian" kings (Sabaco, Sevechus, and Tarhaka) of the XXVth dynasty, B. C. 719–695), possess nothing Negroid in their visages. Meroë, as Lepsius has determined irrevocably, became an independent principality at a far later day; and, so soon as she was cut off from Egyptian blood and civilization, the influx of Negro concubines deteriorated her people, until, by the fifth century after Christ, she sank amid the billows of surrounding African barbarism, mentally and physically obliterated for ever.

To our lamented countryman, Morton, belongs the honor of first rendering these data true as axioms in the science of anthropology. Our part has been to demonstrate that the principles of his method were correct, as well as to support them with fresher evidences than he was spared to investigate. At the time of the publication of the *Crania Ægyptiaca*, the "Gallery of Antiquities in the British Museum"[354] had not reached him; consequently he was not then aware that the vast tableau from Beyt-el-Wâlee, out of which he had selected the following heads (Fig. 151) stands, moulded in facsimile and beautifully colored, on the walls of an Egyptian hall in that great Institution. The copy lies before us, elucidated by Mr. Birch's critical description. Here *Negroes* and *Nubians* are painted in all shades—blacks and browns; while the red (or color of honor) is given to the Egyptians alone.

With these emendations, which unfortunately the nature of our work does not permit us to portray in colors, Morton's own words and wood-cuts may appropriately close this chapter on the *Negro Type:*—

"For the purpose of illustration, we select a single picture from the temple (hemispeos) of Beyt-el-Wâlee, in Nubia, in which Rameses II. is represented in the act of making war upon the Negroes—who, overcome with defeat, are flying in consternation before him. From the multitude of fugitives in this scene (which has been vividly copied by Champollion[355] and Rosellini, and which I have compared in both), I annex a fac-simile group of nine heads, which, while they preserve the national features in a remarkable degree, present also considerable diversity of expression.

"The hair on some other figures of this group is dressed in short and separate tufts, or

FIG. 195.

inverted cones, precisely like those now worn by the Negroes of Madagascar, as figured in Botteller's *Voyage*.

"In the midst of the vanquished Africans, standing in his car and urging on the conflict, is Rameses himself; whose manly and beautiful countenance will not suffer by comparison with the finest Caucasian models. The annexed outline (for all the figures are represented in outline only), will enable the reader to form his own conclusions respecting this extraordinary group," which dates in the fourteenth century before the Christian era.[356]

FIG. 196.

The authors confidently trust, that the antiquity of Negro races, no less than the *permanence of Negro types*, during the (1853+2348) 4201 years that have just elapsed since Usher's Flood, are questions now satisfactorily set at rest in the minds of lettered and scientific readers. A parable, thrown back among our notes,[357] suffices to illustrate popular impressions in regard to the cuticular and osteological changes produced by *climate*, and in respect to the philological metamorphoses caused by *transplantation*, upon human races aboriginally distinct. It is not incumbent upon us to inquire, whether the delusions, generally current upon such very simple matters of fact, are to be ascribed to intellectual apathy among the taught, or to ignorance and mystifications among their teachers.

At the close of Chapter VI. (*supra*, p. 210), in reference to the permanency of Asiatic and African types in their respective geographical *gradations*, we asked, "Within human record, has it not *always* been thus?" Every national tradition, all primitive monuments, and the whole context of ancient and modern history, answer affirmatively for each of those parts of the *Old* continents hitherto examined. Deviations from the *historical* point of view requiring no notice, at the present day, by any man of science, it would be sheer waste of time to discuss them. We lose none, therefore, in passing over at once to that continent which no students of Natural History now miscall "the *New*."

CHAPTER IX.

AMERICAN AND OTHER TYPES.—ABORIGINAL RACES OF AMERICA.

THE Continent of America is often designated by the appellation of the *New World;* but the researches of modern geologists and archæologists have shown that the evidences in favour of a high antiquity, during *our* geological epoch, as well as for our Fauna and Flora, are, to say the least, quite as great on this as on the eastern hemisphere. Prof. Agassiz, whose authority will hardly be questioned in matters of this kind, tells us that geology finds the oldest landmarks here; and Sir Charles Lyell, from a mass of well-digested facts, and from the corroborating testimony of other good authorities, concludes that the Mississippi river has been running in its present bed for more than one hundred thousand years.[358] The channel cut by the Niagara river, below the Falls, for twelve miles through solid rock, in the estimation of the same distinguished author, as well as of others, gives no less satisfactory proof of the antiquity of the present relative position of continents and oceans.

Dr. Bennet Dowler, of New Orleans, in an interesting essay,[359] recently published, supplies some extraordinary facts in confirmation of the great age of the delta of the Mississippi, assumed by Lyell, Riddell, Carpenter, Forshey, and others. From an investigation of the successive growths of cypress forests around that city, the stumps of which are still found *at different depths, directly overlying each other;* from the great size and age of these trees, and from the remains of Indian bones and pottery found below the roots of some of these stumps, he arrives at the following conclusion:—

"From these data it appears that the human race existed in the delta more than 57,000 years ago; and that ten subterranean forests, and the one now growing, will show that an exuberant flora existed in Louisiana more than 100,000 years anterior to these evidences of man's existence."

The delta of the Alabama river bears ample testimony to the same effect. Along the Mobile river and bay we find certain shell-fish, whose relative positions are determined at present, as they always have been, by certain physical conditions, viz.: the *unio* and *paludina*, the gnathodon, and the oyster. The first are always found above tide-water, where the water is perfectly fresh; the second flourishes in brackish water alone; and the oyster never but in water that is almost salt. As the delta of the river has extended, they have each greatly changed their habitats. The most northern *habitat*, at the present day, for example, of the gnathodon, stands about Choctaw Point, one mile below Mobile; whereas we have abundant evidence that it formerly existed fifty miles above. The unio, paludina, and oyster have changed positions in like manner.

Immense beds of gnathodon shells are found, and in the greatest profusion, all along the coast of the Gulf of Mexico, where they have doubtless been deposited by Indians in former times. Great numbers of these beds exist on the Mobile bay, and along the river, for fifty miles *above* the city, where only a scattering remnant of the living species is still found. The Indians had no means for, and no object in, transporting such an immense number fifty miles up the river; and we must, therefore, conclude that the Mobile bay once extended to the locality of these upper "shell banks;" and that the Indians had collected them for food, near where these banks are now beheld. One strong evidence of this conclusion is gathered from the fact, that the different artificial beds of the unio, the gnathodon, and the oyster, are never here formed of a mixture of two or more shells; which would be the case if their locations had been near each other.

That these beds are of Indian origin is clear, from the fact that the shells have all been opened, and that we find in them the marks of fire, extending over considerable spaces—the shells converted into quick-lime, and mingled with charcoal, so that the successive accumulations of shells may be plainly traced.[360] Fish-bones and other remains of Indian feasts are common: *i. e.* fragments of Indian pottery; and of human bones, which can be identified by their crania.

Some of these beds are covered over by vegetable mould, from one to two feet thick, which must have been a very long time forming; and upon this are growing the largest forest trees, beneath whose roots these Indian remains are often discovered. It is more than probable, too, that these huge trees are the successors of former growths quite as large.

We cannot, by any conjecture, approximate, within many centuries, perhaps thousands of years, the time consumed in thus extending the delta of the Alabama river, and in producing the changes we have hinted at; nor dare we attempt to fix the time at which the Red men fed upon the gnathodons that compose the first beds to which we have alluded.

It is worthy also of special remark that the gnathodon, of which a few surviving specimens still endure along the Gulf coast of Florida, Alabama, and Mississippi, was once a living species in the Chesapeake bay; but has been so long extinct that it now exists there only in a fossil state. This would extend the living fauna very much farther back than the Chesapeake deposits: all our recent shells, or nearly all, being found in the pliocene, and many shells in still earlier formations. Such facts, with many others of similar import, which might be adduced, point to a chronology very far beyond any heretofore received: and who will doubt that, when the Mississippi, Alabama, and Niagara rivers first poured their waters into the ocean, a fauna and a flora already existed? and, if so, why did not man exist? They all belong to one geological period, and to one creation.

These authorities, in support of the extreme age of the geological era to which man belongs, though startling to the unscientific, are not simply the opinions of a few; but such conclusions are substantially adopted by the leading geologists everywhere. And, although antiquity so extreme for man's existence on earth may shock some preconceived opinions, it is none the less certain that the rapid accumulation of new facts is fast familiarizing the minds of the scientific world to this conviction. The monuments of Egypt have already carried us far beyond all chronologies heretofore adopted; and when these barriers are once overleaped, it is in vain for us to attempt to approximate, even, the epoch of man's creation. This conclusion is not based merely on the researches of such archæologists as Lepsius, Bunsen, Birch, De Longpérier, Humboldt, &c., but on those, also, of strictly-orthodox writers, Kenrick, Hincks, Osburn; and, we may add, of all theologians who have really mastered the monuments of Egypt. Nor do these monuments reveal to us only a *single* race, at this early epoch in full tide of civilization, but they exhibit faithful portraits of the same African and Asiatic races, in all their diversity, which hold intercourse with Egypt at the present day.

Now, the question naturally springs up, whether the aborigines of America were not contemporary with the earliest races, known to us, of the eastern continent? If, as is conceded, "Caucasian," Negro, Mongol, and other races, existed in the Old World, already distinct, what reason can be assigned to show that the aborigines of America did not also exist, with their present types, 5000 years ago? The naturalist must infer that the fauna and flora of the two continents were contemporary. All facts, and all analogy, war against the supposition that America should have been left by the Creator a dreary waste for thousands of years, while the other half of the world was teeming with organized beings. This view is also greatly strengthened by the acknowledged fact, that not a single animal, bird, reptile, fish, or plant, was common to the Old and New Worlds. No naturalist of our day doubts that the animal and vegetable kingdoms of America were created where they are found, and not in Asia.

The races of men alone, of America, have been made an exception to this general law; but this exception cannot be maintained by any course of scientific reasoning. America, it will be remembered, was not only unknown to the early Romans and Greeks, but to the Egyptians; and when discovered, less than four centuries ago, it was found to be inhabited, from the Arctic to Cape Horn, and from ocean to ocean, by a population displaying peculiar physical traits, unlike any races in the Old World; speaking languages bearing no resemblance in structure to other languages; and living, everywhere, among animals and plants specifically distinct from those of Europe, Asia, Africa, and Oceanica.

But, natural as this reasoning is, in favor of *American* origin for our Indians, we shall not leave the question on such debatable ground. There is abundant positive evidence of high antiquity for this population, which we proceed to develop.

In reflecting on the aboriginal races of America, we are at once met by the striking fact, that their physical characters are wholly independent of all climatic or known physical influences. Notwithstanding their immense geographical distribution, embracing every variety of climate, it is acknowledged by all travellers, that there is among this people a pervading *type*, around which all the tribes (north, south, east, and west) cluster, though varying within prescribed limits. With trifling exceptions, all our American Indians bear to each other some degree of family resemblance, quite as strong, for example, as that seen at the present day among full-blooded Jews; and yet they are distinct from every race of the Old World, in features, languages, customs, arts, religions, and propensities. In the language of Morton, who studied this people more thoroughly than any other writer:— "All possess, though in various degrees, the long, lank, black hair; the heavy brow; the dull, sleepy eye; the full, compressed lips; and the salient, but dilated nose." These characters, too, are beheld in the civilized and the most savage tribes, along the rivers and sea-coasts, in the valleys and on the mountains; in the prairies and in the forests; in the torrid and in the ice-bound regions; amongst those that live on fish, on flesh, or on vegetables.

The only race of the Old World with which any connection has been reasonably conjectured, is the Mongol; but, to say nothing of the marked difference in physical characters, their languages alone should decide against any such alliance.

"The American race differs essentially from all others, not excepting the Mongolian; nor do the feeble analogies of language, and the more obvious ones of civil and religious institutions and arts, denote anything beyond casual or colonial communication with the Asiatic nations; and even these analogies may, perhaps, be accounted for, as Humboldt has suggested, in the mere coincidence arising from similar wants and impulses in nations inhabiting similar latitudes."[361]

No philologist can be found to deny the fact that the Chinese are now speaking and writing a language substantially the same as the one they used 5000 years ago; and that, too, a language distinct from every tongue spoken by the Caucasian races. On the other hand, we have the American races, all speaking dialects indisputably peculiar to this continent, and possessing no marked affinity with any other. Now, if the Mongols have preserved a language entire, in Asia, for 5000 years, they should have likewise preserved it here, or to say the least, some trace of it. But, not only are the two linguistic groups radically distinct, but no *trace* of a Mongol tongue, dubious words excepted, can be found in the American idioms. If such imaginary Mongolians ever brought their Asiatic speech into this country, it is clear that their fictitious descendants, the Indians, have lost it; and the latter must have acquired, instead, that of some extinct race which preceded a Mongol colonization. It will be conceded that a colony, or a nation, could never lose its vocabulary so completely, unless through conquest and amalgamation; in which case they would adopt *another* language. But, even when a tongue ceases to be spoken, some trace of it will continue to survive in the names of individuals, of rivers, places, countries, &c. The names of Moses, Solomon, David, Lazarus, Isaac and Jacob, are still found among the Jews everywhere, although the Hebrew language has ceased to be spoken for more than 2000 years. And the appellatives Mississippi, Missouri, Orinoko, Ontario, Oneida, Alabama, and a thousand other Indian names, will live for ages after the last Red man is mingled with the dust. They have no likeness to any nomenclature in the Old World.

In treating of American races, our prescribed limits do not permit us to go into details respecting the infinitude of types which compose them. Our purpose at present is simply to bring forward such facts as may be sufficient to establish their origin and antiquity. The broad division of Dr. Morton, into two great families, which contrast in many points strongly with each other, is sufficiently minute, viz.: "The *Toltecan nations* and the *Barbarous tribes.*" This classification is somewhat arbitrary; but it is impossible, in our day, to establish any but very wide boundary-lines. Here, as in the Old World, wars, migrations, amalgamations, and endless causes, have, during several thousand years, disturbed and confused Nature's original work; and we must now deal with masses as we find them. In fact, our main object in alluding at all to the *diversity of types* among the aborigines of America, is to give another illustration of a position advanced elsewhere in this volume. We have shown that the major divisions of the earth, or its different zoological provinces, were populated by groups of races, bearing to each other certain family resemblances; notwithstanding that, in reality, these races originated in *nations*, and not in a single pair; thus forming proximate, but not identical species. The Mongols, the Caucasians, the Negroes, the Americans, each constitute a group of this kind. In our chapters on the *Caucasian* races, for example, we have shown how the Jews, Egyptians, Hindoos, Pelasgians, Romans, Teutons, Celts, Iberians, &c., which had all been classed under this common head, can be traced, as distinct forms, beyond all human chronology. The same law applies to the American races. Although every tribe has some characters that mark it as *American*, yet there are certain sharply-drawn distinctions, among some of these races, which cannot be explained by climatic influences. The Toltecan, and Barbarous tribes, taken separately, *en masse*, afford a good illustration, for they differ essentially in their moral and physical characteristics. The most prominent distinction between these two families results from comparison of their craniological developments. Dr. Morton, whose collection of human crania is the most complete in the world, bestowed unrivalled attention on

American races, and has given actual measurements of 338 Indian skulls, in which the two great divisions are almost equally represented.

1st. *The Toltecan Family* — comprising all the semi-civilized nations of Mexico, Peru, and Bogota, who, there is every reason to believe, were the builders of the great system of mounds found throughout North America. Of 213 skulls, Mexican and Peruvian, 201 belong to the latter — each having been obtained from the oldest burial-grounds and through the most reliable sources. On these heads, Morton makes the following striking comment: —

"When we consider the institutions of the old Peruvians, their comparatively advanced civilization, their tombs and temples, mountain-roads and monolithic gateways, together with their knowledge of certain ornamental arts, it is surprising to find that they possessed a brain *no larger than the Hottentot* or *New Hollander*, and far below the barbarous hordes of their own race." [We have shown, in our remarks on anatomical characters of races, that the Hottentot has a brain on the average 17 cubic inches less than the Teutonic race — the latter being 92, and the former 75 cubic inches.] "For, on measuring 155 crania, nearly all derived from the sepulchres just mentioned, they give but 75 cubic inches for the average bulk of brain, while the Teutonic, or highest developed white race, gives 92 cubic inches. Of the whole number, one only attains the capacity of 101 cubic inches — [the highest Teutonic in Dr. Morton's collection is 114 cubic inches] — and the minimum sinks to 58; the smallest in the whole series of 641 measured crania *of all nations*. It is important to remark, also, that the sexes are nearly equally represented: viz., 80 men and 75 women.

The mean of twenty-one Mexican skulls is seventy-nine, or five cubic inches above the Peruvian average; but the authenticity of this series is not so well made out as the other, and it may be too small for the establishment of a very correct mean.

2d. *The Barbarous Tribes.* — The semi-civilized communities of America seem at all times to have been hemmed in and pressed upon by the more restless and warlike barbarous tribes, as they are at the present day. We now see the unwarlike Mexican constantly pillaged by daring Camanches and relentless Apaches; who, since the introduction of horses, have become most fearful marauders, scarcely inferior to the Tartars or Bedouins of Asia.

On this series, collected both from modern tribes and ancient tumuli the most widely separated by time and space, Morton remarks: —

"Of 211 crania derived from the various sources enumerated in this section, 161 have been measured, with the following results: the largest cranium gives 104 cubic inches — the smallest, 70; and the mean of all is 84. There is a disparity, however, in the male and female heads, for the former are 96 in number, and the latter only 65.

"We have here the surprising fact, that the brain of the Indian, in his savage state, is far larger than that of the old demi-civilized Peruvian or ancient Mexican. How are we to explain this remarkable disparity between civilization and barbarism? The largest Peruvian brain measures 101 cubic inches; and the untamed Shawnee rises to 104; and the average difference between the Peruvian and the savage is nine cubic inches in favor of the latter. Something may be attributed to a primitive difference of stock; but more, perhaps, to the contrasted activity of the two races." [Here Dr. Morton might appear to endorse the

theory that cultivation of the mind, or of one set of faculties, can give expansion or increased size of brain. There is no proof of the truth of such a hypothesis. The Teutonic races, in their barbarous state, 2000 years ago, possessed brains as large as now; and so with other races. — J. C. N.]

Taken collectively, the American races yield an average mean, for the whole 338 crania, of only seventy-nine cubic inches, or thirteen below that of the Teutonic race.

The general law laid down by craniologists, that size of brain is a measure of intellect, would seem to meet with an exception here; but it is only apparent. A very satisfactory solution of the fact will be found in Mr. J. S. Phillips's *Appendix* to Morton's memoir on the *Physical Type of the American Indians;*[362] also, in Mr. George Combe's *Phrenological Remarks*, in the *Appendix* to Morton's *Crania Americana*. The appendix of Mr. Phillips, published after Morton's death, adds some new materials, which the Doctor had not time to work up before his demise. The additional crania make a little variation from the means or averages obtained by Morton, but too slight to influence the general conclusions. Mr. Phillips's closing observations are so well expressed that we are sure the reader will prefer them entire, to wit: —

"The average volume of the brain in the *Barbarous* tribes is shown to be from 83½ to 84 cubic inches, while that of the *Mexicans* is but 79, and in the Peruvians only 75; thus exhibiting the apparent anomaly of barbarous and uncivilized tribes possessing larger brains than races capable of considerable progress in civilization. This discrepancy deserves more investigation than time permits at present; but the following views of the subject may make it appear less anomalous: —

"The prevailing features in the character of the North American savage are, stoicism, a severe cruelty, excessive watchfulness, and that coarse brutality which results from the entire preponderance of the animal propensities. These so outweigh the intellectual portion of the character, that it is completely subordinate, making the Indian what we see him — a most unintellectual and uncivilizable man.

"The intellectual lobe of the brain of these people, if not borne down by such overpowering animal propensities and passions, would doubtless have been capable of much greater efforts than any we are acquainted with, and have enabled these barbarous tribes to make some progress in civilization. This appears to be the cerebral difference between the Mexicans and Peruvians on the one hand, and the Barbarous tribes of North America on the other. The intellectual lobe of the brain in the two former is at least as large as in the latter — the difference of volume being chiefly confined to the occipital and basal portions of the encephalon; so that the intellectual and moral qualities of the Mexicans and Peruvians (at least as large, if not larger than those of the other group) are left more free to act, being not so subordinate to the propensities and violent passions. This view of the subject is in accordance with the history of these two divisions: *barbarous* and *civilizable*. When the former were assailed by the European settlers, they fought desperately, but rather with the cunning and ferocity of the lower animals, than with the system and courage of men. They could not be subjugated, and were either exterminated, or continued to retire into the forests, when they could no longer maintain their ground. Had their intellect been in proportion to their other qualities, they would have been most formidable enemies. With the Mexicans and Peruvians the case has been the reverse. The original inhabitants of Mexico were entirely subjugated by the Aztecs, who appear to have been a small tribe in comparison with the Mexicans; and then they were all conquered and enslaved by a mere handful of Spaniards — although the Mexicans had the advantage over the barbarous tribes of concerted action, some discipline, and preparation, in which the latter were greatly deficient. The Mexicans, with small brains, were evidently inferior in resolution, in attack and defence, and the more manly traits of character, to the Barbarous races, who contested every inch of ground until they were entirely outnumbered. And at the present time, the Camanches and Apaches, though a part of the great Shoshonee division (one of the lowest of the races of North America), are continually plundering and destroying the Indians of Northern Mexico, who scarcely attempt resistance.

"Viewed in this light, the apparent contradiction of a race with a smaller brain being superior to tribes with larger brains, is so far explained, that the volume and distribution of their respective brains appear to be in accordance with such facts in their history as have come to our knowledge."

Again, Mr. Phillips remarks, of the Indians of the United States, that he has "grouped them, on a large scale, into families, according to language; and the result of measurement of the volume of brain is strikingly in accordance with the ascertained character of the different groups thus constituted. His arrangement is — 1st, Iroquois; 2d, Algonquin and Apalachian; 3d, Dacota; 4th, Shoshonees; 5th, Oregonians. Of the first division (the Iroquois), he observes: —

"The average internal capacity of the cranium in this group is about 8½ inches higher than the lowest types, and 4½ inches higher than the average — being 88¼ cubic inches. This result is strikingly in keeping with the fact that they were so completely the master-spirits of the land; that, at the time of the first settlement of this country by the white race, they were so rapidly subduing the other tribes and nations around them; and that, if their career of conquest had not been cut short by the Anglo-Saxon predominance, they bade fair to have conquered all within their reach."

He then states the measurements and characters of other families, in all of which the *morale* and *physique* most strikingly correspond.

These facts afford very instructive material for reflection. We here behold one race, with the larger, though less intellectual brain, subjugating the unwarlike and half-civilized races; and it seems clear, that the latter were destined to be either swallowed up or exterminated by the former. Who can doubt that similar occurrences had been going on over this continent for many centuries or even thousands of years? There are scattered over North America countless tumuli, which it is believed were built by races different from the savage tribes found around them on the advent of the whites, and an impenetrable oblivion rests upon these earth-works. There are many reasons for supposing that these mound-builders were either identical with, or closely allied to, the Toltecs; and, that they were driven south or exterminated by more savage and bellicose races, such as the Iroquois: for the traditions of the Mexicans point to the North as their original country.

At the present day, we see in America large settlements of Spaniards, French, Germans, &c., as well as Indians — all speaking their own languages; yet who doubts that in a century or two the Indians will be extinct, and the others swallowed up in the Anglo-Saxon tongue and type? Then, when the ethnographer shall undertake to analyze the population, what can he learn of the history of races that first overspread this continent, or what light upon the origins of lost or absorbed autocthones can he draw from the European dialects spoken by their destroyers? What will be the condition of this country two or three thousand years hence, we may ask, when we see Europe pouring its population into it from the East and Asia from the West? We can reason on the things of this world merely from what we see and know; and we must infer that a succession of events has been going on for ages, during ante-historic times, similar to those we encounter in the pages of written history. Human nature never changes, else it would cease to be human nature.

Now, how are we to explain these opposite intellectual and physical characters in the two great families of America, except by primitive cranial conformations, each aboriginally distinct? Certainly, no known facts exist leading to the conclusion that any particular mode of life can change the size or form of brain in man; while, on the contrary, we have abundant reason to be convinced that the size and form of brain play a conspicuous part in the advancement and destiny of races. The large heads, in many instances, having emerged from barbarism (Teutons, Celts, for example), within historical times, have reached the higher pinnacles of civilization, and everywhere outstripped and dominated over the small-headed races of mankind.

It is interesting here to note that the ancient Egyptians and Hindoos, who in very early times reached a considerable degree of civilization, had, like the Mexicans and Peruvians, much smaller heads than the savage tribes around them.[363] Each of these people give an internal mean-capacity of eighty cubic inches, which is but one inch above the average of American races. The Negro races, exclusive of Hottentots, yield an average of eighty-three inches.

If the Jews have lived during 1500 years in Malabar, the Magyars 1000 in Hungary, the Parsees as many ages in India, the Basques or Iberians in France and Spain for more than 3000, without material change — and, if the Anglo-Saxons and Spaniards have lived through ten generations in America without approximating the aboriginal type of the country, it is a reasonable inference that the intellectual and physical differences of the *Toltecan* and *Barbarous* tribes are not attributable to secondary causes, either moral or physical.

Mr. Squier makes the following philosophical remarks: —

"The casual resemblance of certain words in the languages of America and those of the Old World cannot be taken as evidence of a common origin. Such coincidences may be easily accounted for as the result of accident, or, at most, of local infusions, which were without any extended effect. The entire number of common words is said to be one hundred and eighty-seven; of these, one hundred and four coincide with words found in the languages of Asia and Australia, forty-three with those of Europe, and forty with those of Africa. It can hardly be supposed that these facts are sufficient to prove a connection between the four hundred dialects of America and the various languages of the other continent. It is not in accidental coincidences of sound or meaning, but in a comparison of the general structure and character of the American languages with those of other countries, that we can expect to find similitudes at all conclusive, or worthy of remark, in determining the question of a common origin. And it is precisely in these respects that we discover the strongest evidences of the essential peculiarities of the American languages: here they coincide with each other, and here exhibit the most striking contrasts with all the others of the globe. The diversities which have sprung up, and which have resulted in so many dialectical modifications, as shown in the numberless vocabularies, furnish a wide field for investigation. Mr. Gallatin draws a conclusion from the circumstance, which is quite as fatal to the popular hypothesis, respecting the origin of the Indians, as the more sweeping conclusion of Dr. Morton. It is the length of time which this prodigious subdivision of languages in America must have required, making every allowance for the greater changes to which unwritten languages are liable, and for the necessary breaking up of nations in a hunter-state into separate communities. For these changes, Mr. Gallatin claims, we must have the very longest time which we are permitted to assume; and, if it is considered necessary to derive the American races from the other continent, that the migration must have taken place at the earliest assignable period.

"The following conclusions were advanced by Mr. Duponceau, as early as 1819, in substantially the following language:—

"1. That the American languages, in general, are rich in words and grammatical forms; and, that in their complicated construction the greatest order, method, and regularity prevail.

"2. That these complicated forms, which he calls polysynthetic, appear to exist in all these languages, from Greenland to Cape Horn.

"3. That these forms differ essentially from those of the ancient and modern languages of the Old Hemisphere."[364]

The type of a race would never change, if kept from adulterations, as we have shown in the case of the Jews and other peoples. So with languages: we have no reason to believe that a race would ever lose its language, if kept aloof from foreign influences. It is a fact that, in the little island of Great Britain, the Welch and the Erse are still spoken, although for 2000 years pressed upon by the strongest influences tending to exterminate a tongue. So with the Basque in France, which can be traced back at least 3000 years, and is still spoken. Coptic was the speech of Egypt for at least 5000 years, and still leaves its trace in the languages around. The Chinese has existed equally as long, and is still undisturbed.

"An effort has been made by Mr. Blackie, Professor of Greek in the University of Edinburgh, to reform the pronunciation of Greek in that University. He is teaching his students to pronounce Greek as they do in Greece, insisting that it is not a dead, but a living language—as any one may see by looking at a Greek newspaper. Prof. Blackie gives an extract from a newspaper printed last year, at Athens, giving an account of Kossuth's visit to America, from which it is evident that the language of Homer lives in a state of purity to which, considering the extraordinary duration of its literary existence (2500 years at least), there is no parallel, perhaps, on the face of the globe. After noticing a few trifling modifications, which distinguish modern from ancient Greek, he states, as a fact, that in three columns of a Greek newspaper of the year 1852, there do not certainly occur three words that are not pure native Greek — so very slightly has it been corrupted from foreign sources."[365]

Although the nations of Europe and Western Asia have been in constant turmoil for thousands of years, and their languages torn to pieces, yet they have been moulded into the great heterogeneous Indo-European mass, everywhere showing affinities among its own fragments, but no resemblance to American languages. The subjoined extract from a paper of Prof. Agassiz admirably expresses new and most interesting views upon the natural origin of speech: —

"As for languages, their common structure, and even the analogy in the sounds of different languages, far from indicating a derivation of one from another, seem to us rather the necessary result of that similarity in the organs of speech which causes them naturally to produce the same sound. Who would now deny that it is as natural for men to speak as it is for a dog to bark, for an ass to bray, for a lion to roar, for a wolf to howl, when we see that no nations are so barbarous, so deprived of all human character, as to be unable to express in language their desires, their fears, their hopes? And if a unity of language, any analogy in sound and structure between the languages of the white races, indicate a closer connection between the different nations of that race, would not the difference which has been observed in the structure of the languages of the wild races — would not the power the American Indians have naturally to utter gutturals which the white can hardly imitate, afford additional evidence that these races did not originate from a common stock, but are only closely allied as men, endowed equally with the same intellectual powers, the same organs of speech, the same sympathies, only developed in slightly different ways in the different races, precisely as we observe the fact between closely allied species of the same genus among birds?

"There is no ornithologist who ever watched the natural habits of birds and their notes, who has not been surprised at the similarity of intonation of the notes of closely allied species, and the greater difference between the notes of birds belonging to different genera and families. The cry of the birds of prey, are alike unpleasant and rough in all; the song of all the thrushes is equally sweet and harmonious, and modulated upon similar rhythms, and combined in similar melodies; the chit of all titmice is loquacious and hard; the quack of the duck is alike nasal in all. But who ever thought that the robin learned his melody from the mocking-bird, or the mocking-bird from any other species of thrush? Who ever fancied that the field-crow learned his cawing from the raven or jackdaw? Certainly, no one at all acquainted with the natural history of birds. And why should it be different with men? Why should not the different races of men have originally spoken distinct languages, as they do at present, differing in the same proportions as their organs of speech are variously modified? And why should not these modifications in their turn be indicative of primitive differences among them? It were giving up all induction, all power of arguing from sound premises, if the force of such evidence were to be denied."[366]

To which may be added the familiar instance, that, although the Negro has been domiciliated in the United States for many generations among white people, he nevertheless, whether speaking English, French, or Spanish, preserves that peculiar, unmistakeably-*Negro*, intonation, which no culture can eradicate. So, again, who ever heard the voice of an Indian uttering English, and could not instantly detect the articulations of the Red man?

A review of the preceding facts shows conclusively, we think, that the Natural History of the American aborigines runs a close parallel with that of races in other countries. We have made but two divisions; but it is more than probable that each of these families, instead of springing from a single pair, have originated in many. But we have discussed this point elsewhere, and need not reopen it here.

Let us now glance at the history of those aboriginal races which made the only approach towards civilization. It is true that our materials are very defective in many particulars, yet enough remain to lead ethnologists to some important results.

No trace of an *alphabet* existed at the time of the conquest of the continent of America; but some tribes possessed an imperfect sort of picture-writing, from which a little archæological aid can be derived; though we are compelled to look chiefly to traditions, which are often vague, and to the light which emanates from the physical characters, antiquities, religions, arts, sciences, languages, or agriculture.

The decided structural connection which exists among the various Indian languages has been regarded as sufficient evidence, not only of the common origin of these languages, but of the races speaking them. The venerable Albert Gallatin, who devoted much time and talent to American ethnography, says: —

> "All those who have investigated the subject appear to have agreed in the opinion that, however differing in their vocabularies, there is an evident similarity in the structure of all the American languages, bespeaking a common origin."[367]

Now, we are not disposed to deny the close *affinity* of these languages, but we cannot agree that this affords any satisfactory proof of *unity* of their linguistic derivation. The conclusion, to our minds, is a *non sequitur*.

Let us assume, with Agassiz and Morton, that all mankind do not spring from one pair, nor even each race from distinct pairs; but that men were created in *nations*, in the different zoological provinces where history first finds them. The Caucasians, Mongols, Indians, Negroes, were, for example, created in large numbers, or in scattered tribes. What, let us ask, would necessarily be the result as regards types and languages? Various individuals of these tribes, having no language, would soon come in contact, either through proximity, or early wanderings. Unions would soon take place, and there would be a fusion of types, so as perhaps to change, more or less, each original; just as amalgamations have taken place among all historical nations, and are now going on in every country of the globe.

So with languages. As soon as individuals came in contact, they would necessarily commence the first steps towards forming a speech, as birds instinctively sing and dogs bark. The wants, and range of ideas of these tribes, would, for a long time, be very limited, and their vocabulary, thus formed, very meagre. The aboriginal races of America, though not identical, display a certain similarity in their physical and intellectual characters, as species of a genus in the animal kingdom possess certain physical characters and instincts in common; and it is probable that their primitive languages would, in consequence, more or less, resemble each other. This view is strengthened by the fact of general resemblance amongst American crania. But nothing in human anatomy can be more striking, than the wide difference in the conformation of the skulls of American and African races.

If two distinct races, created on incommunicable continents, had been left alone, originally, each to form its own languages independently of the other, is it not presumable, *à priori*, that there would accrue a much greater similarity among the tongues of the one race, on the same continent, than between these tongues and those spoken on the other continent by the other race? Especially, when the physical and moral characteristics of the former differ radically from those of the latter?

As, then, the crania of American races resemble each other, while differing entirely from those of African races, so do American and African languages differ from each other in structure and vocabulary; although both are in harmony with the various dialects spoken on their respective continents by races osteologically similar.

Whether the above proposition be true or false, all languages which, in their infant state, came together, would necessarily become fused into one heterogeneous mass. Let us illustrate this point a little farther. Suppose that, five thousand years ago, a country had existed large as Europe, covered by a virgin forest, and that the Creator had scattered over it tribes, bearing the type of the old Teutonic stock — each of whom commenced at once in forming a language — what would be the result in our day, after 5000 years of migrations, wars, amalgamations? Can any one doubt that these languages would be fused into one whole, quite as homogeneous as those of the aborigines of America? When we reflect that there is every reason to believe that this continent has been inhabited for more than 5000 years, such case becomes a much stronger one. Niebuhr, in one of his letters, expresses views very similar.[368]

"—— These great national races have never sprung from the growth of a single family into a nation, but always from the association of several families of human beings, raised above their fellow animals by the nature of their wants, and the gradual invention of a language; each of which families probably had originally formed a language peculiar to itself. This last idea belongs to Reinhold. By this I explain the immense variety of languages among the North American Indians, which it is absolutely impossible to refer to any common source, but which, in some cases, have resolved themselves into one language, as in Mexico and Peru, for instance; and also the number of synonyms in the earliest periods of languages. On this account, I maintain that we must make a very cautious use of differences of language as applied to the theory of races, and have more regard to physical conformation; which latter is exactly the same, for instance, in most of the Indian tribes of North America. I believe, farther, that the origin of the human race is not connected with any given place, but is to be sought everywhere over the face of the earth; and that it is an idea more worthy of the power and wisdom of the Creator, to assume that he gave to each zone and each climate its proper inhabitants, to whom that zone and climate would be most suitable, than to assume that the human species has degenerated in such innumerable instances."

Wiseman approaches the subject from a different point of view, offering another explanation for the dissimilarity of languages. He maintains that there are affinities among all languages, which can only be explained by original *unity*, but acknowledges, on the other side, certain radical differences, which are only to be explained by a miracle. He says, in Lecture second: —

"As the radical difference among the languages forbids their being considered dialects, or offshoots of one another, we are driven to the conclusion that, on the one hand, these languages must have been originally united in one, whence they drew their common elements, essential to them all; and, on the other, that the separation between them, which destroyed other and no less important elements of resemblance, could not have been caused by any gradual departure, or individual development — for these we have long since excluded — but by some violent, unusual, and active force, sufficient alone to reconcile these conflicting appearances, and to account at once for the resemblances and the differences."[369]

This view of the enigma would be much the most agreeable to many readers, inasmuch as, by the obtrusion of an unwarranted physical impossibility, it gets clear of that radical diversity of languages which philology has not yet been able to overcome. Such reasoning, however plausible at the time when it was written, will not stand the test of criticism in the year 1853. The facts revealed to us by the subsequent discoveries of Lepsius and others, require a much higher antiquity for nations and languages than the Cardinal had any idea of; and which is entirely irreconcilable with the Jewish date for the "confusion of tongues" at Babel, to which he plainly points. If that confusion of tongues in Genesis were even taken as literally true, it could neither have applied to all the nations of the earth, nor, particularly, to those inhabiting parts of the world unknown to Oriental geography in the time of Moses or Abraham; and this owing to exegetical reasons hereinafter set forth.

Clavigero, whose ability and opportunities confer upon his authority especial weight, gives the following chronology, derived from data obtained through Mexicans: —

	A. D.
The Toltecs arrived in Anahuac, or the country now called Mexico, migrating from the North	648
They abandoned the country	1051
The Chichemecs arrived	1170
The Acholchuans arrived about	1200
The Mexicans reached Tula	1296
They founded Mexico	1325

Here, then, we have the dates of successive migrations of these Toltecan races, from the seventh to the fourteenth century; and, although much doubt exists with regard to the accuracy of some of these dates, no one who investigates the subject will deny that they are sufficiently close for all practical purposes, and may be taken as the basis of chronological calculation. Clavigero, Gallatin, Humboldt, Prescott, Squier, Morton—in short, *all* authorities, are substantially agreed on this point. These Toltecan races, who it seems inhabited, though perhaps at different epochs, almost every portion of the present territory of the United States, must have been pressed upon by causes now unknown to us, and forced to migrate from their original abodes. They sought an asylum in the southern countries—Mexico, Central America, Peru; and here gave birth to the semi-civilization found at the time of the Spanish conquest. Gallatin, however, thinks it most probable that the Toltecan races and their civilization commenced in the tropic, and spread towards the north. Over an immense territory, bounded by the Atlantic and Pacific, the Gulf of Mexico and the Great Lakes, are scattered those countless mounds, on the origin of which the savage tribes surrounding them for the last three or four centuries have not even preserved a tradition.

"Not far from one hundred enclosures, of various sizes, and five hundred mounds, are found in Ross county, Ohio. The number of tumuli in the State may be safely estimated at ten thousand, and the number of enclosures at one thousand or fifteen hundred."[370]

From this single State, constituting but a small fraction of the surface over which they are scattered, may be formed some idea of the enormous number of these remains and of the ante-historical population which constructed them. These tumuli were of several distinct kinds, viz., sepulchral and sacrificial; dikes, fortifications, &c. Squier's investigations lead him to aver:—

"The features common to all are elementary, and identify them as appertaining to one grand system, owing its origin to a family of men moving in the same general direction, acting under common impulses, and influenced by similar causes."

These mounds, from their number and magnitude, present indisputable evidence of the existence of very large agricultural populations. How many centuries were these people increasing, migrating, and concentrating, around so many thousand widely-scattered nuclei?

How long was it before they possessed a density and command of labor requisite for such structures? How long, after building such national monuments, did they live around, before abandoning them? Were they not the same people who migrated into Mexico and Central America from the seventh to the thirteenth century A. C.? Surely, any reply to this view of the subject alone, in connection with the physical type of the race, must carry them back to times contemporary with the Pharaohs of Egypt.

Too valuable to be mutilated, a long extract from the standard work before quoted is here introduced.

"The antiquity of the ancient monuments of the Mississippi Valley has been made the subject of incidental remark in the foregoing chapters. It will not be out of place here to allude once more to some of the facts bearing upon this point. Of course, no attempt to fix their data accurately, from the circumstances of the case, can now be successful. The most that can be done is, to arrive at approximate results. The fact that none of the *ancient* monuments occur upon the latest formed terraces of the river-valleys of Ohio, is one of much importance in its bearing upon this question. If, as we are amply warranted in believing, these terraces mark the degrees of the subsidence of the streams, one of the four (which may be traced) has been formed since those streams have followed their present courses. There is no good reason for supposing that the mound-builders would have avoided building upon that terrace, while they erected their works promiscuously upon all the others. And if they had built upon it, some slight traces of their works would yet be visible, however much influence one may assign to disturbing causes—overflows, and shifting channels. Assuming, then, that the lowest terrace, on the Scioto river, for example, has been formed since the era of the mounds, we must next consider that the excavating power of the Western rivers diminishes yearly, in proportion as they approximate towards a general level. On the Lower Mississippi, where alone the ancient monuments are sometimes invaded by the water, the bed of the stream is rising, from the deposition of the materials brought down from the upper tributaries, where the excavating process is going on. This excavating power, it is calculated, is in an inverse ratio to the square of the depth — that is to say, diminishes as the square of the depth increases. Taken to be approximately correct, this rule establishes, that the formation of the latest terrace, by the operation of the same causes, must have occupied much more time than the formation of any of the preceding three. Upon these premises, the time since the streams have flowed in their present courses may be divided into four periods of different lengths — *of which the latest, supposed to have elapsed since the race of the mounds flourished, is much the longest.*

"The fact that the rivers in shifting their channels have in some instances encroached upon the superior terraces, so as in part to destroy works situated upon them, and afterwards receded to long distances of a fourth or half a mile or upwards, is one which should not be overlooked in this connection. In the case of the 'high bankworks,' the recession has been nearly three-fourths of a mile, and the intervening terrace or 'bottom' was, at the period of the early settlement, covered with a dense forest. This recession and subsequent forest growth must of necessity have taken place since the river encroached upon the ancient works here alluded to.

"Without doing more than to allude to the circumstance of the exceedingly decayed state of the skeletons found in the mounds, and to the amount of vegetable accumulations in the ancient excavations and around the ancient works, we pass to another fact, perhaps more important in its bearing upon the question of the antiquity of these works, than any of those presented above. It is, that they are covered with primitive forests, in no way distinguishable from those which surround them, in places where it is probable no clearings were ever made. Some of the trees of these forests have a positive antiquity of from six to eight hundred years. They are found surrounded with the mouldering remains of others, undoubtedly of equal original dimensions, but now fallen and almost incorporated with the soil. Allow a reasonable time for the encroachment of the forest, after all the works were abandoned by their builders, and for the period intervening between that event and the date of their construction, and we are compelled to assign them no inconsiderable antiquity. But, as already observed, the forests covering these works correspond in all respects with the surrounding forests; the same varieties of trees are found, in the same proportions, and they have a like primitive aspect. This fact was remarked by the late President HARRISON, and was put forward by him as one of the strongest evidences of the high antiquity of these works. In an address before the Historical Society of Ohio, he said:—

"'The process by which nature restores the forest to its original state, after being once cleared, is extremely slow. The rich lands of the West are indeed soon covered again, but the character of the growth is entirely different, and continues so for a long period. In several places upon the Ohio, and upon the farm which I occupy, clearings were made in the first settlement of the country, and subsequently abandoned and suffered to grow up. Some of these new forests are now, sure, of fifty years' growth; but they have made so little progress towards attaining the appearance of the immediately contiguous forest, as to induce any man of reflection to determine that at least ten times fifty years must elapse before their complete assimilation can be effected. We find, in the ancient works, all that variety of trees which give such unrivalled beauty to our forests, in natural proportions. The first growth, on the same kind of land, once cleared and then abandoned to nature, on the contrary, is nearly homogeneous, often stinted to one or two, at most three, kinds of timber. If the ground has been cultivated, the yellow locust will thickly spring up; if not cultivated, the black and white walnut will be the prevailing growth. . . . Of what immense age, then, must be the works so often referred to, covered, as they are, by at least the second growth after the primitive-forest state was regained?'

"It is not undertaken to assign a period for the assimilation here indicated to take place. *It must, however, be measured by centuries.*

"In respect to the extent of territory occupied at one time, or at successive periods, by the race of the mounds, so far as indicated by the occurrence of their monuments, little need be said, in addition to the observations presented in the first chapter. It cannot, however, have escaped notice, that the relics found in the mounds—composed of materials peculiar to places separated as widely as the ranges of the Alleghanies on the east, and the Sierras of Mexico on the west, the waters of the great lakes on the north, and those of the Gulf of Mexico on the south—denote the contemporaneous existence of communication between these extremes. For we find, side by side, in the same mounds, native copper from Lake Superior, mica from the Alleghanies, shells from the Gulf, and obsidian (perhaps porphyry) from Mexico. This fact seems to conflict seriously with the hypothesis of a migration, either northward or southward. Further and more extended investigations and observations may, nevertheless, serve satisfactorily to settle, not only this, but other equally interesting questions, connected with the extinct race, whose name is lost to tradition itself, and whose very existence is left to the sole and silent attestations of the rude, but oft imposing monuments, which throng the valleys of the West."

A dispassionate review of the evidences thus cursorily presented, in support of the contemporaneousness of American races with those first recorded on the monuments of the eastern world, when taken together, ought, we think, to satisfy any unprejudiced mind. Nor can anything be twisted out of the Jewish records to show that, at the time when many races were already formed in the old Levant, at least one distinct type of man did not exist on the Western Continent. But, to our minds, stronger than all other reasonings, not excepting the antithesis of languages, is that drawn from the antiquity of skulls.

The vertical occiput, the prominent vertex, the great interparietal diameter, the low defective forehead, the small internal capacity of the skull, the square or rounded form, the quadrangular orbits, the massive maxillæ, are peculiarities which stamp the American groups, more especially the Toltecan family, and distinguish them widely from any other races of the earth, ancient or modern.

As before remarked, these characters are seen to some extent in all Indians: although the savage tribes exhibit a greater development of the posterior portion of the brain than the Toltecs — thus supplying, in Natural History, the link of organism which assimilates the Barbarous septs of America to the savage races of the Old World.

An interesting fact was mentioned to us by an American officer, of high standing, who accompanied our army in its march through Mexico during the late war. Although his head, which we measured, is below the average size of the Anglo-Saxon race, he told us that it was with difficulty he could find, in a large hat-store at Matamoras, a single hat which would go on his head. Hats suited to Mexicans are too small for Anglo-Saxons: a fact corroborated by ample testimony. Throughout the winter season, in Mobile, at least one hundred Indians of the Choctaw tribe wander about the streets, endeavoring to dispose of their little packs of wood; and a glance at their heads will show that they correspond, in every particular, with the anatomical description just given. They present heads precisely analogous to those ancient crania taken from the mounds over the whole territory of the United States; while they most strikingly contrast with the Anglo-Saxons, French, Spaniards and Negroes, among whom they are moving.

It is impossible to say how long human bones may be preserved in a dry soil. There are some curious statements of Squier, and many more of Wilson,[371] respecting the barrows of the ancient Britons, where skeletons have been preserved at least 2000 years: —

"Considering that the earth around these skeletons is wonderfully compact and dry, and that the conditions for their preservation are exceedingly favorable, while they are in fact so much decayed, we may form some approximate estimate of their remote antiquity. In the barrows of the ancient Britons, entire, well-preserved skeletons are found, although possessing an undoubted antiquity of at least eighteen hundred years. Local causes may produce singular results in particular instances, but we speak now of these remains in the aggregate."[372]

From the ruins of Nineveh and Babylon we have bones of at least 2500 years old;[373] from the pyramids[374] and the catacombs of Egypt, both mummied and unmummied crania have been taken, of still higher antiquity, in perfect preservation; and numerous other proofs might be brought forward to the same effect: nevertheless, the skeletons deposited in our Indian mounds, from the Lakes to the Gulf, are crumbling into dust through age alone!

Speaking of the mound-builders, it is said:—

"The only skull incontestably belonging to an individual of that race, which has been recovered entire, or sufficiently well preserved to be of value for purposes of comparison, was taken from the hill-mound, numbered 8 in the map of a section of twelve miles of the Scioto Valley."

Squier's account continues:—

"The circumstances under which this skull was found are, altogether, so extraordinary as to merit a detailed account. It will be observed, from the map, that the mound above indicated is situated upon the summit of a high hill, overlooking the valley of the Scioto, about four miles below the city of Chilicothe. It is one of the most prominent and commanding positions in that section of country. Upon the summit of this hill rises a conical knoll, of so great regularity as almost to induce the belief that it is itself artificial. Upon the very apex of this knoll, and covered by the trees of the primitive forests, is the mound. It is about eight feet high, by forty or fifty feet base. The superstructure is a tough yellow clay, which, at the depth of three feet, is mixed with large, rough stones; as shown in the accompanying section, (Fig. 197).

"These stones rest upon a dry, calcareous deposit of buried earth and small stones, of a dark black colour, and much compacted. This deposit is about two feet in thickness, in the centre, and rests upon the original soil. In excavating the mound, a large plate of mica was discovered, placed upon the stones. . . . . Immediately underneath this plate of mica, and in the centre of the buried deposit, was found the skull figured in the plates (Figs. 198, 199). It was discovered resting upon its face. The lower jaw, as, indeed, the entire skeleton, excepting the clavicle, a few cervical vertebræ, and some of the bones of the feet, all of which were huddled around the skull, were wanting.

"From the entire singularity of this burial, it might be inferred that the deposit was a comparatively recent one; but the fact that the various layers of carbonaceous earth, stones, and clay were entirely undisturbed, and in no degree intermixed, settles the question beyond doubt, that the skull was placed where it was found, at the time of the construction of the mound. . . .

"This skull is wonderfully preserved; unaccountably so, unless the circumstances under which it was found may be regarded as most favorable to such a result. The imperviousness of the mound to water, from the nature of the material composing it, and its position on the summit of an eminence, subsiding in every direction from its base, are circumstances which, joined to the antiseptic qualities of the carbonaceous deposit enveloping the skull, may satisfactorily account for its excellent preservation."

A twofold interest attaches to the mound (Fig. 197), of which we offer a sectional tracing. On the one hand it indicates the pains

FIG. 197.

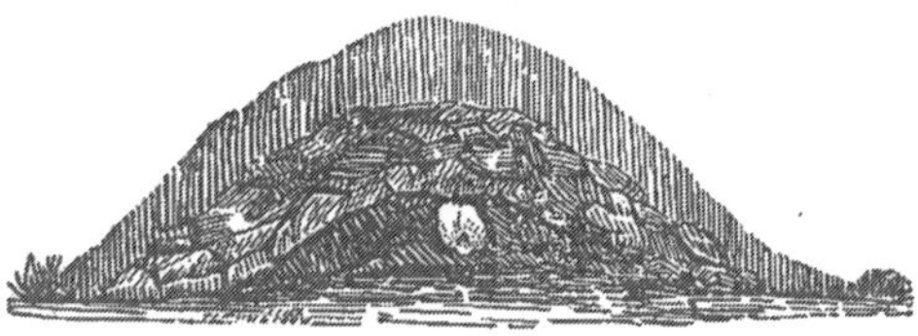

bestowed by ancient American man upon the dead; thus evincing considerable civilization: on the other, the central tumular position in which this unique cranium was discovered, establishes an ante-Columbian age for its builders, and segregates it entirely from the ruder sepulchres of our modern Indians.

We present a vertical and a profile engraving of this ancient skull, one exceedingly characteristic of our American races, although more

FIG. 198.

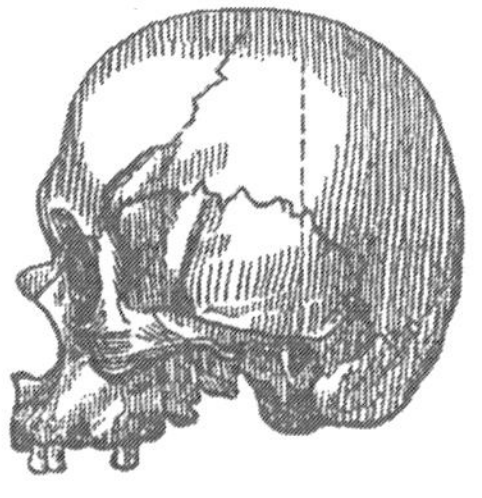

FIG. 199.

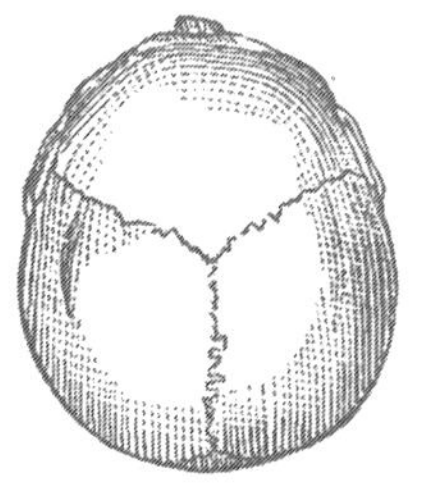

particularly of the *Toltecan;* having already stated that the *Barbarous* tribes possessed more development of the posterior part of the brain than the Toltecs. An examination of this skull will elicit the following characteristic peculiarities — forehead low, narrow, and receding; flattened occiput; a perpendicular line drawn through the external meatus of the ear, divides the brain into two unequal parts, of which the posterior is much the smaller; forming, in this respect, a striking contrast with other, and more particularly the Negro, races. Viewed from above, the anterior part of the brain is narrow, and the posterior and middle portion, over the organs of caution, secretiveness, destructiveness, &c., very broad, thus lending much support to phrenology: vertex prominent. [These peculiarities are confirmed by the numerous measurements of Dr. Morton, and by the observations of many other anatomists, as well as our own. Identical characters, too, pervade all the American races, ancient and modern, over the whole continent. We have compared many heads of living tribes, Cherokees, Choctaws, Mexicans, &c., as well as crania from mounds of all ages, and the same general organism characterizes each one. — J. C. N.]

FIG. 200.[375]

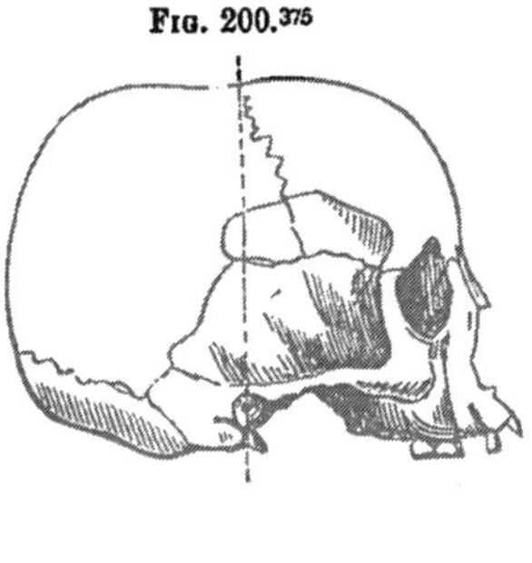

Any South-African race, compared with an American Indian, would exhibit a contrast almost as salient; but a *Bosjesman* (Fig. 200) from the Cape of Good Hope answers our purpose. Osteologically, they are as distinct from each other as the skull of a fossil hyena is from that of a prairie wolf; at the same time that each human cranium is emphatically typical of the race to which it appertains.

But, if comparison of an antique American cranium (Fig. 198) with the skull of a modern Bushman (Fig. 200), evolves instantaneously such palpable contrasts, still more extraordinary and startling are those which resile when we compare either or both with one of the primeval "*kumbe-kephalic*," or *boat-shaped* skulls (Figs. 201, 202),

Fig. 202.

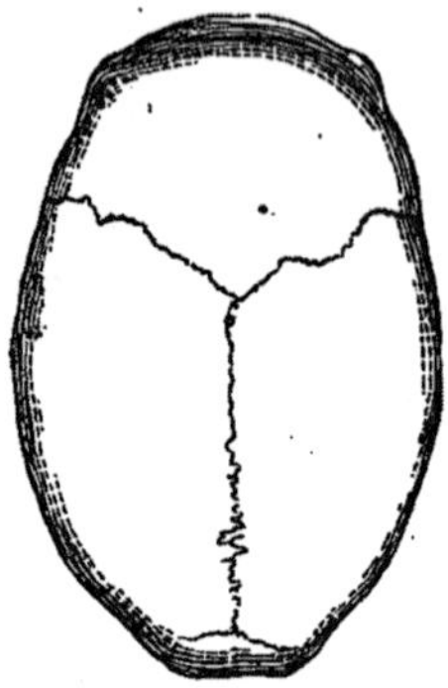

Fig. 201.

exhumed from the pre-Celtic cairns of Scotland.[376] Can anything human be more diverse than the osteological conformation of the most ancient type of man known in America from that of the primordial Briton? Be it duly noted, too, that while, on the American continent, the earliest cranium resulting from Squier's researches is every way identical (as we shall demonstrate hereinafter) with crania of the *Creeks*, and other Indian nations of our own generation, men of this *kumbe-kephalic* type occupied the British Isles long prior to the advent of those *brachy-kephalic* races, who were precursors of the old *Celts;* themselves, in Britain, antedating all history! Of this fact Wilson's *Archæology of Scotland* furnishes exuberant evidences; to be enlarged upon by us in dealing with "Comparative Anatomy."

Hamilton Smith and Morton have contended that no test is known by which fossil human are distinguishable from other fossil bones of extinct species.[377] The question, to say the least, is an open one; although none can aver that there are not human fossils as old as those of the mastodon and other extinct animals. The following extract from Morton's memoir is interesting, taken in connection with the American type:—

"It is necessary to advert to the discoveries of Dr. Lund, among the bone-caves of Minas Gerdas, in Brazil. This distinguished traveller has found the remains of man in these caverns associated with those of extinct genera and species of animals; and the attendant circumstances lead to the reasonable conclusion that they were contemporaneous inhabitants of the region in which they were found. Yet, even here, the form of the skull differs in nothing from the acknowledged type, unless it be in the still greater depression of the forehead and a peculiarity of form in the teeth. With respect to the latter, Dr. Lund describes the incisors as having an oval surface, of which the axis is antero-posterior, in place of the sharp and chisel-like edge of ordinary teeth of the same class. He assures us, that he found it equally in the young and the aged, and is confident it is not the result of attrition, as is manifestly the case in those Egyptian heads in which Professor Blumenbach noticed an analogous peculiarity. I am not prepared to question an opinion which I have not been able to test by personal observation; but it is obvious that, if such differences exist independently of art or accident, they are at least specific, and consequently of the highest interest in ethnology.

"The head of the celebrated *Guadaloupe skeleton* forms no exception to the type of the race. The skeleton itself, which is in a semi-fossil state, is preserved in the British Museum — but wants the cranium, which, however, is supposed to be recovered in the one found by M. L'Héminier, in Guadaloupe, and brought by him to Charleston, South Carolina. Dr. Moultrie, who has described this very interesting relic, makes the following observations: 'Compared with the cranium of a Peruvian presented to Professor Holbrook, by Dr. Morton, in the Museum of the State of South Carolina, the craniological similarity manifested between them is too striking to permit us to question their national identity, There is in both the same coronal elevation, occipital compression, and lateral protuberance, accompanied with frontal depression, which mark the American variety in general.'"

It seems clear, that the Indians of America are indigenous to the soil; but it does not follow, that in ancient times there might not have been some occasional or accidental immigrations from the Old World, though too small to affect materially the language or the type of the aborigines. There are several quite recent examples recorded, where boats with persons in them have been blown, from the Pacific islands and other distant parts, to the shores of America; and in this way may be explained certain facts, connected with language, which have been adduced as evidence of Asiatic origin for our Indians. But we protest, in the name of science, against the notion that any of these ancient possibilities have yet entered into the category of ascertained facts. On the contrary, all known anatomical, archæological, and monumental proofs oppose such hypothesis.

Possible, also, is it that the Northmen discovered this country several hundred years before Columbus, and held intercourse with it as far as Labrador; yet they have left no trace of tongue nor vestige of art.

Agriculture is acknowledged on all hands to have incited the first steps toward civilization, and, for some most curious facts on this head, the reader is referred to Mr. Gallatin's paper.[378] Was the agriculture found in America by the Whites, introduced at an early epoch from abroad, or was it of domestic origin? This question has excited much conjecture, and is an important one, as it necessarily involves the origin of American civilization. The following facts are certainly very significant: —

1. All those nutritious plants cultivated and used for food in the other hemisphere, such as millet, rice, wheat, rye, barley, and oats, as well as our domestic animals—horses, cattle, sheep, camels, goats, &c., were entirely unknown to the Americans.

2. Maize, the great and almost sole foundation of American civilization, is exclusively indigenous, and was not known to the other hemisphere until after the discovery of America.[379]

The kind of beans by the Spaniards called *frijoles*, still cultivated by the Indians in Mexico and Central America, is indigenous to our continent, and even now unused in the other.

If these facts be conceded, as they have heretofore been by all naturalists and archæologists, it will not be questioned that the agriculture of America was of domestic origin, as well as the semi-civilization of any Indian cultivators. These premises alone establish a primitive origin and high antiquity for the American races.

Inquiry into their astronomical knowledge, their arithmetic, division of time, names of days, &c., will show that their whole system was peculiar; and, if not absolutely original, must antedate all historical times of the Old World, since it has no parallel on record. The Chaldeans, the Chinese, the Egyptians, and other nations of the Eastern hemisphere, had divisions of time and astronomical knowledge more than 2000 years B. C.; nevertheless, among ancient or modern Indians, there remains no trace of these trans-Atlantic systems.

"Almost all the nations of the world appear, in their first attempts to compute time, to have resorted to lunar months, which they afterwards adjusted in various ways, in order to make them correspond with the solar year. In America, the Peruvians, the Chilians, and the Muyscas, proceeded in the same way; but not so with the Mexicans. And it is a remarkable fact, that the short period of seven days (our week), so universal in Europe and in Asia, was unknown to all the Indians, either of North or South America."[380] [Had this learned and unbiassed philologist lived to read Lepsius,[381] he would have excepted the Egyptians; who divided their months into *three decades*, and knew nothing of weeks of *seven days*. Neither did the Chinese, ancient or modern,[382] ever observe a "*seventh* day of rest." — G. R. G.]

"All the nations of Mexico, Yucatan, and probably of Central America, which were within the pale of civilization, had two distinct modes of computing time. The first and vulgar mode, was a period of twenty days; which has certainly no connection with any celestial phenomenon, and which was clearly derived from their system of numeration, or arithmetic, which was peculiar to them.

"The other computation of time was a period of thirteen days, which was designated as being the count of the moon, and which is said to have been derived from the number of days when, in each of its evolutions, the moon appears above the horizon during the greater part of the night. . . .

"We distinguish the days of our months by their numerical order — first, second, third, &c., day of the month; and the days of our week by specific names — Sunday, Monday,

&c. The Mexicans distinguished every one of their days of the period of twenty days, by a specific name—*Cipactli*, *Ehecatl*, &c.; and every day of the period of thirteen days, by a numerical order, from one to thirteen." [383]

These can be neither called weeks nor months — they were arbitrary divisions, used long before the Christian era, and no doubt long before the Americans had any idea of the true length of the solar year. This they arrived at with considerable accuracy, but, as we have reason to believe, not many centuries before the Spanish conquest. With regard to the origin of the astronomical knowledge of American races, there has been much discussion. Humboldt has pointed out some striking coincidences in the Mexican modes of computing time, names of their months, and similar accidents, with those of Thibet, China, and other Asiatic nations; which (were philology certainty, and old Jesuit interpretation safe,) would look very much as if they had been borrowed, and engrafted on American systems at a comparatively recent period. On the other hand, he has laid stress upon some of the peculiarities especially distinguishing the Mexican calendar, and which cannot be ascribed to foreign origin — such as the fact already mentioned, that the Mexicans never counted by months or weeks.

"What is remarkable too [says Humboldt], is, that the calendar of Peru affords indubitable proofs not only of astronomical observations and of a certain degree of astronomical knowledge, but also that their origin was independent of that of the Mexicans. If both the Mexican and Peruvian calendars were not the result of their own independent observations, we must suppose a double importation of astronomical knowledge — one to Peru, and another to Mexico — coming from different quarters, and by people possessed of different degrees of knowledge. There is not in Peru any trace of identity of the names of the days, or of a resort to the combination of two series. Their months were alternately of twenty-nine and thirty days, to which eleven days were added, to complete the year."

Now, if the Mexican calendar differed, "*toto cœlo*," from that of the Peruvian, it follows that their respective origins were distinct; and if neither, as Humboldt indicates, was constructed upon a foreign or Asiatic basis, how are any suppositions of antique intercourse between the two hemispheres justified by astronomy? Why, if the Peruvians did not borrow from the Mexicans, (their contemporaries on the same continent,) should they not have taught themselves, just as the Mexicans did their ownselves, systems as unlike each other as they are separated by nature, times, and spaces, from every one adopted by those types of mankind, whose physical structure is from these Americans utterly diverse?

Some of the astronomical observations of the Mexicans were also clearly local: the two transits of the sun, for instance, by the zenith of Mexico, besides others.

Assuredly the major portion, then, of the astronomical knowledge of the aboriginal Americans was of domestic origin; and any of the few points of contact with the calendars of the Old World, if not accidental, must have taken place at an exceedingly remote period of time. In fact, whatever may have come from the Old World was engrafted upon a system itself still older than the exotic shoots.

But, if it still be contended that astronomy was imported, why did not the immigrants bring an alphabet or Asiatic system of writing, the art of working iron, mills, wheel-barrows (all, with remembrance even of Oriental navigation, unknown in America)? Or at least the seeds of millet, rice, wheat, oats, barley, &c., of their respective botanical provinces or countries? Alas! sustainers of the *Unity*-doctrine will be puzzled to find one fact among American aborigines to support it.

In conclusion, we have but to sum up the facts briefly detailed, and these results will be clearly deducible, namely: —

1. That the continent of America was unknown not only to the ancient Egyptians and Chinese, but to the more modern Hebrews, Greeks, and Romans.

2. That at the time of its discovery, this continent was populated by millions of people, resembling each other, possessing peculiar moral and physical characteristics, and in utter contrast with any people of the Old World.

3. That these races were found surrounded everywhere by animals and plants specifically different from those of the Old World, and created, as it is conceded, in America.

4. That these races were found speaking several hundred languages, which, although often resembling each other in grammatical structure, differed in general entirely in their vocabularies, and were all radically distinct from the languages of the Old World.

5. That their monuments, as seen in their architecture, sculpture, earth-works, shell-banks, &c., from their extent, dissemination, and incalculable numbers, furnish evidence of very high antiquity.

6. That the state of decomposition in which the skeletons of the mounds are found, and, above all, the peculiar anatomical structure of the few remaining crania, prove these mound-builders to have been both ancient and indigenous to the soil; because American crania, antique as well as modern, are unlike those of any other race of ancient or recent times.

7. That the aborigines of America possessed no alphabet or truly-phonetic system of writing—that they possessed none of the domestic animals, nor many of the oldest arts of the Eastern hemisphere; whilst their agricultural plants were indigenous.

8. That their system of arithmetic was unique — that their astronomical knowledge, in the main, was indubitably of cis-Atlantic

origin; while their calendar was unlike that of any people, ancient or modern, of the other hemisphere.

Whatever exception may be taken to any of these propositions separately, it must be conceded that, when viewed together, they form a mass of cumulative testimony, carrying the aborigines of America back to the remotest period of man's existence upon earth.

The entire scope of argument on these subjects may be presented in the vigorous language of Lord KAIMES; expressing ideas entertained by himself and the authors in common, although more than seventy-nine years interlapse between their respective writings: —

"The frigidity of the North Americans, men and women, differing in that particular from all other savages, is to me evidence of a separate race. And I am the more confirmed in that opinion, when I find a celebrated writer, whose abilities no person calls in question, endeavoring in vain to ascribe that circumstance to moral and physical causes. *Si Pergama dextra defendi posset.*

"In concluding from the foregoing facts that there are different races of men, I reckon upon strenuous opposition; not only from men biassed against what is new or uncommon, but from numberless sedate writers, who hold every distinguishing mark, internal as well as external, to be the effect of soil and climate. Against the former, patience is my only shield; but I cannot hope for any converts to a new opinion, without removing the arguments urged by the latter.

"Among the endless number of writers who ascribe supreme efficacy to the climate, Vitruvius shall take the lead.[384] . . .

"Upon summing up the whole particulars mentioned above, would one hesitate a moment to adopt the following opinion, were there no counterbalancing evidence: viz., 'That God created many pairs of the human race, differing from each other both externally and internally; that he fitted these pairs for different climates, and placed each pair in its proper climate; that the peculiarities of the original pairs were preserved entire in their descendants — who, having no assistance but their natural talents, were left to gather knowledge from experience, and in particular were left (each tribe) to form a language for itself; that signs were sufficient for the original pairs, without any language but what nature suggests; and that a language was formed gradually, as a tribe increased in numbers and in different occupations, to make speech necessary?' But this opinion, however plausible, we are not permitted to adopt, being taught a different lesson by revelation: viz., That God created but a single pair of the human species. Though we cannot doubt of the authority of Moses, yet his account of the creation of man is not a little puzzling, as it seems to contradict every one of the facts mentioned above. According to that account, different races of men were not formed, nor were men framed originally for different climates. All men must have spoken the same language, viz., that of our first parents. And what of all seems the most contradictory to that account, is the savage state: Adam, as Moses informs us, was endued by his Maker with an eminent degree of knowledge; and he certainly must have been an excellent preceptor to his children and their progeny, among whom he lived many generations. Whence then the degeneracy of all men unto the savage state? To account for that dismal catastrophe, mankind must have suffered some terrible convulsion.

"That terrible convulsion is revealed to us in the history of the *Tower of Babel.*"[385] . . .

Babylon's Tower (it is known to cuneiform students of the present day) did not exist before the reign of NEBUCHADNEZAR; who built it during the seventh century B. C.[386] As the edifice does not concern Ethnology, we pass onward.

CHAPTER X.

Excerpta

FROM MORTON'S INEDITED MANUSCRIPTS.

[ALTHOUGH not in the mature shape in which Dr. Morton habitually submitted his reflections to the scientific world, and destitute, alas! of his own improvements, a contribution, so valuable to that study of Man which owes its present momentum to his genius, must not be overlooked in "Types of Mankind." With their joint acknowledgments to MRS. S. GEO. MORTON, for the unreserved use of whatever autographs their much-honored friend intended for eventual publication, the authors annex two fragmentary essays. Overcome by illness, the Doctor withdrew from his library on the 6th of May, 1851; leaving these, among other evidences of an enthusiasm for science which death alone could stifle. The authors take the more pleasure and pride in embodying such first rough-draughts, fresh as they flowed from his mind — not unstudied, but unadorned. Dr. Morton is here beheld in his office, writing down with characteristic simplicity, while disturbed by professional interruptions, the results of his incessant labor and meditation, couched in the language of truth.]

[MANUSCRIPT A.]

"*On the Size of the Brain in Various Races and Families of Man; with Ethnological Remarks. By* SAMUEL GEORGE MORTON, M.D.: *Philadelphia and Edinburgh.*"

The importance of the brain as the seat of the faculties of the mind, is preëminent in the animal economy. Hence the avidity with which its structure and functions have been studied in our time; for, although much remains to be explained, much has certainly been accomplished. We have reason to believe, not only that the brain is the centre of the whole series of mental manifestations, but that its several parts are so many organs; each one of which performs its peculiar and distinctive office. But the number, locality, and functions of these several organs are far from being determined: nor should this uncertainty surprise us, when we reflect on the slow and devious process by which mankind have arrived at some of the simplest physiological truths, and the difficulties that environ all inquiries into the nature of the organic functions.

In studying ethnology, and especially in comparing the crania of the several races, I was struck with the inadequacy of the methods in use for determining the size and weight of the brain. On these methods, which are four in number, I submit the following remarks:

1. The plan most frequently resorted to is that which measures the exterior of the head or skull within various corresponding points. We are thus enabled to compare the relative conformation in different individuals, and in this manner obtain some idea of the relative size of the brain itself. Such measurements possess a great value in craniology, and, we need hardly add, are the only ones that are available in the living man.

2. The plan of weighing the brain has been extensively practised in modern times, and with very instructive results. Haller found the encephalon to vary, in adult men, from a pound and a half to more than five pounds; and the Wenzels state the average of their experiments to range from about three pounds five ounces to three pounds ten ounces.*

The experiments of the late Dr. John Sims, of London, which, from their number and accuracy, deserve great attention, place the *average* weight of the recent brain between three pounds eight and three pounds ten ounces, or nearly the same weight as that obtained by the Wenzels. Of 253 brains weighed by Dr. Sims, 191 were adults from twenty years old to seventy, and upwards; and of the whole series, the lowest weighed two pounds, and the highest an ounce less than four pounds.†

Prof. Tiedemann, of Heidelberg, a learned and accomplished anatomist, has pursued the same mode of investigation. After giving the weight of fifty-two European brains, he adds that

"The weight of the brain in an adult European varies between three pounds two ounces and four pounds six ounces Troy. The brain of men who have distinguished themselves by their great talents are often very large. The brain of the celebrated Cuvier weighed four pounds, eleven ounces, four drachms, thirty grains, Troy; and that of the distinguished surgeon, Dupuytren, weighed four pounds ten ounces Troy. The brain of men endowed with but feeble intellectual powers, is, on the contrary, often very small, particularly in congenital idiotismus. The female brain is lighter than that of the male. It varies between two pounds eight ounces and three pounds eleven ounces. I never found a female brain that weighed four pounds. The female brain weighs, on an average, from four to eight ounces less than that of the male; and this difference is already perceptible in a new-born child." ‡

* Medico-Chirurg. Trans., xix. p. 351. † Idem, p. 259.

‡ Trans. of the Royal Soc. of London.

Sir W. Hamilton adds, that in the male about one brain in seven is found above four pounds Troy; in the female hardly one in an hundred.

These results are highly instructive, and furnish the average weight of the cerebral organs at the time of death; but whoever will examine the valuable tables of Dr. Sims, will observe that various circumstances may affect the weight of the brain, without, at the same time, modifying its size; viz.: extreme sanguineous congestion; fluids contained in the ventricles; interstitial effusion; extravasation of blood, and softening and condensation of structure. These morbid changes sometimes take place rapidly, while the absolute *bulk* of the brain remains unaltered. Again, the plan of weighing the encephalon must always be a very restricted one; and is not likely ever to be practised on an extensive scale, except in the Caucasian and Negro.

3. Another, but indirect, mode of ascertaining the weight of the brain, has been practised by Sir William Hamilton, who "examined about 300 human skulls, of determined sex, the capacity of which, by a method he devised, was taken in sand, and the original weight thus recovered." *

Respecting the process employed in these experiments I am not informed; and I agree with Dr. Sims, that the *weight* of the brain cannot be determined by ascertaining the capacity of the cranium, by any method, however accurate in itself.

More recently, Prof. Tiedemann has performed an elaborate series of experiments to determine the comparative weight of the brain in the different human races.

> "For this purpose," he observes, "I filled the skull through the foramen magnum with millet-seed, taking care to close the foramina and fissures, so as to prevent the escape of the seed, and at the same time striking the cranium with the palm of the hand, in order to pack its contents more closely. I then weighed the skull thus filled, and subtracted from it the weight of the empty one, and I thus determined the capacity of the cranium from the weight of the seed it was capable of containing." †

The results obtained by Prof. Tiedemann, like those of Sir William Hamilton, possess a great value in researches of this kind; yet, unfortunately, they are not *absolute* either as respects the size or weight of the brain; for it is evident that the second of these objects could only be obtained by employing a medium of the same density as the brain; and as to *capacity*, no method had, at that time (1837), been devised for obtaining it in cubic inches.

4. Seeing, therefore, that the several processes just described are not absolute, but only comparative in their results, without affording

* Essays and Heads of Lectures: by Dr. A. Monro, xxxix.

† Das Hein des Negers, &c. p. 21.

either the true weight or true bulk of the brain, I solicited my friend, Mr. John S. Phillips, to devise some more satisfactory method of obtaining the desired object; and this has been entirely successful in the following manner.

A tin cylinder was made, about two inches and three-fourths in diameter, and two feet two inches in height, standing on a foot, and banded with swelled hoops about two inches apart, and firmly soldered to prevent accidental flattening. A glass tube, hermetically sealed at one end, was cut off so as to hold exactly five cubic inches of water by weight, at 60° Fahrenheit. A float of light wood, well varnished, two and one-fourth inches in diameter, with a slender rod of the same material fixed in its centre, was next dropped into the tin cylinder. Then five cubic inches of water, measured in the glass tube, were poured into the cylinder, and the point at which the rod on the float stood above the top of the cylinder, was marked by the edge of a file laid across its top. And, in like manner, the successive gradations on the float-rod, indicating five cubic inches each, were obtained by pouring five cubic inches from the glass tube *gradatim*, and marking each rise on the float-rod. The gradations thus ascertained were transferred to a mahogany rod, fitted with a flat foot, and these were again subdivided by means of compasses to mark the cubic inches and parts.*

In order to measure the internal capacity of a cranium, the larger foramina must be first stopped with cotton, and the cavity then filled with leaden shot one-eighth of an inch in diameter, poured into the foramen magnum. This process should be effected to repletion; and for this purpose it is necessary to shake the skull repeatedly, and, at the same time to press down the shot with the finger, or with the end of the funnel, until the cavity can receive no more. The shot are next to be transferred to the tin cylinder, which should also be well shaken. The mahogany rod being then dropped into the tin cylinder, with its foot resting on the shot, the capacity of the cranium will be indicated by the number observed on the same plane with the top of the tube.

I thus obtain *the absolute capacity of the cranium, or bulk of the brain in cubic inches;* nor can I avoid expressing my satisfaction at the singular accuracy of this method; inasmuch as a skull of 100 cubic inches capacity, if measured any number of times with reasonable care, will not vary a single cubic inch.

On first using this apparatus, I employed, in place of shot, white-pepper seed, which possessed the advantage of a spheroidical form

---

* Crania Americana, 1839, p. 253.

and general uniformity in the size of the grains. But it was soon manifest that the utmost care could not prevent considerable variation in several successive measurements, sometimes amounting to three or four cubic inches. Under these circumstances, but not until all the internal capacity measurements of the *Crania Americana* had been made in this way, I saw the necessity of devising some other medium with which to fill the cranium; and after a full trial of the shot, have permanently adopted it, with the satisfactory results above stated.* These remarks will explain the difference between the measurements published in the *Crania Americana* and those obtained from the same skulls by the revised method.†

In an investigation of this nature, the question arises — At what age does the brain attain full development? On this point, there is great diversity of opinion. Professor Sömmering supposes this period to be as early as the third year. Sir William Hamilton expresses himself in the following terms: "In man, the encephalon reaches its full size about seven years of age. This," he adds, "was never before proved." The latter remark leads us to infer that this able and laborious investigator regarded his proposition as an incontestable fact. Professor Tiedemann assumes the *eighth* year as the period of the brain's maximum growth.

Dr. Sims, on the other hand, inferred from an extended series of experiments on the brain from a year old to upwards of seventy, that "the average weight goes on increasing from one year to twenty; between twenty and thirty there is a slight increase in the average; afterwards it increases, and arrives at the maximum between forty and fifty. After fifty, to old age, the brain gradually decreases in weight." These observations nearly correspond with those of Dr. Gall, but are liable to various objections.

Dr. John Reid has also investigated this question on a large scale and with great care. After weighing 253 brains of both sexes and of various ages, he arrives at the conclusion that the encephalon arrives at its maximum size sooner than the other organs of the body; that its relative size, when compared with the other organs, and to the entire body, is much greater in the child than in the adult; and that although the average weight of the male brain is absolutely heavier than that of the female, yet the average female brain, relative to the whole body, is somewhat heavier than the average male brain. Finally, he observes that his experiments do not afford any support to the proposition that the encephalon attains its maximum weight at or near the age of seven years. On this latter point, which is of

* Proceedings of the Academy of Nat. Sciences of Philad. for April, 1841.

† See my Catalogue of Skulls, 3d ed. 1849.

great importance in the present inquiry, I shall offer a few remarks. —The most obvious use of the sutures of the cranium is to subserve the process of growth, which they do by osseous depositions at their margins. Hence one of these sutures is equivalent to the interrupted structure that exists between the shaft and epiphysis of a long bone in the growing state. The shaft grows in length chiefly by accretions at its extremities; and the epiphysis, like the cranial suture, disappears when the perfect development is accomplished. Hence we may infer that the skull ceases to expand whenever the sutures become consolidated with the proximate bones. In other words, the growth of the brain, whether in viviparous or in oviparous animals, is consentaneous with that of the skull, and neither can be developed without the presence of free sutures.*

From these considerations, and from many comparisons, I cannot admit that the brain has attained its physical maturity at the age of seven or eight years; neither is there satisfactory evidence to prove that it continues to grow after adult age. It may possibly increase and decrease in size and weight after that period, without altering the internal capacity of the cranium, which last measurement will always indicate the maximum size the encephalon had attained at (the) period of its greatest development; for in those instances in which this organ has been observed in a contracted or shrunken state, in very old persons, the cranial cavity has remained to all appearance unaltered.†

We know that at, and often before, the age of sixteen years the sutures are already so firmly anchylosed as not to be separated without great difficulty, or even without fracture; whence we may reasonably infer that the encephalon has nearly, if not entirely, attained its

* I have in my possession the skull of a mulatto boy who died at the age of eighteen years. In this instance, the sagittal suture is entirely wanting; in consequence, the lateral expansion of the cranium has ceased in infancy, or at whatever period the suture became consolidated. Hence also the diameter between the parietal protuberances is less than 4.5 inches, instead of 5, which last is the Negro average. The squamous sutures, however, are fully open, whence the skull has continued to expand in the upward direction, until it has reached the average vertical diameter of the Negro, or 5.5 inches. The coronal suture is also wanting, excepting some traces at its lateral termini; and the result of this last deficiency is seen in the very inadequate —— of the forehead, which is low and narrow, but elongated below through the agency of the various cranio-facial sutures. The lamdoidal suture is perfect, thus permitting posterior elongation; and the growth in this direction, together with the full vertical diameter, has enabled the brain to attain the bulk of —— cubic inches, or about —— less than the Negro average. I believe that the absence or partial development of the sutures may be a cause of idiocy by checking the growth of the brain, and thereby impairing or destroying its functions. *See Proceedings of the Academy, for August*, 1841.

† Mr. George Combe, *System of Phrenology*, p. 83, is of the opinion that when the brain contracts, the inner table of the skull follows it, while the outer remains stationary.

growth; and I have therefore commenced my experiments with this period of life. I am aware that it cannot be as safely assumed for the nations who inhabit the frigid and temperate zones, as for some inter-tropical races — the Hindoos, Arab-Egyptians, and Negroes, for example; for these people are proverbially known to reach the adult age, both physically and morally, long before the inhabitants of more northern climates. But, if the average period of the full development of the brain could be ascertained in all the races, it would, perhaps, not greatly vary from the age of sixteen years.

It is evident that this age cannot be always positively determined in the dried skull; yet by a careful comparison of the teeth and sutures, in connection with the general development of the cranial structure, I have had little difficulty in keeping within the prescribed limit.

In classing these skulls into the two sexes, I have been in part governed by positive data; but in the greater number this question has been proximately determined by merely comparing the development and conformation of the cranial structure.

I have excluded from the *Table* the crania of idiots, dwarfs, and those of persons whose heads have been enlarged or otherwise modified by any obvious morbid condition. So, also, no note has been taken of individuals who blend dissimilar races, as the mulatto, for example — the offspring of the Caucasian and the Negro. Those instances, however, which present a mixture of two divisions of the same great race, are admitted into the *Table*. Such is the modern Fellah of the Valley of the Nile, in whom the intrusive Arab is engrafted on the Old Egyptian.

The measurements comprised in this *Memoir* have been derived, without exception, from skulls in my own collection, in order that their accuracy may at any time be tested by myself or by others. I have also great satisfaction in stating, that all these measurements have been made with my own hands. I at one time employed a person to assist me; but having detected some errors in his numbers, I have been at the pains to revise them all, and can now therefore vouch for the accuracy of these multitudinous data.

My collection at this time embraces [*] human crania, among which, however, the different races are very unequally represented. Nor has it been possible, for reasons already mentioned, to subject the entire series to the adopted measurement. Again, some of these are too much broken for this purpose; while many others are embalmed heads, which cannot be measured, on account of the presence of bitumen or of desiccated tissues. * * * * *

[* In May, 1851, about 837 skulls (*MS. addenda* to Catalogue of 1849). Since augmented by one or two dozen. — G. R. G.]

[MANUSCRIPT B.]

(*Origin of the Human Species.*)

Before proceeding to an analysis of these materials, I purpose to make a very few remarks on the origin of the Human Species as a zoological question, and one inseparably associated with classification in Ethnology.

After twenty years of observation and reflection, during which period I have always approached this subject with diffidence and caution; after investigating for myself the remarkable diversities of opinion to which it has given rise, and after weighing the difficulties that beset it on every side, I can find no satisfactory explanation of the diverse phenomena that characterize physical Man, excepting in the doctrine of an original plurality of races.

The commonly received opinion teaches, that all mankind have been derived from a primeval pair; and that the differences now observable among the several races, result from the operation of two principal causes:

1. The influence of climate, locality, civilization, and other physical and moral agents, acting through long periods of time. The manifest inadequacy of this hypothesis, led the late learned and lamented Dr. Prichard to offer the following ingenious explanation.

2. The diversities among mankind are mainly attributable to the rise of accidental varieties, which, from their isolated position and exclusive intermarriage, have rendered their peculiar traits permanent among themselves, or, in other words, indelible among succeeding generations of the same stock.

The preceding propositions, more or less modified and blended together, are by many ethnologists regarded as adequate to the explanation of all the phenomena of diversity observable in Man.

If, however, we were to be guided in this inquiry solely by the evidence derived from Nature, whether directly, in the study of man himself, or collaterally by comparison with the other divisions of the zoological series, our conclusions might be altogether different: we would be led to infer that our species had its origin not in one, but in many creations; that these were widely distributed into those localities upon the earth's surface as were best adapted to their peculiar wants and physical constitutions; and that, in the lapse of time, these races, diverging from their primitive centres, met and amalgamated, and have thus given rise to those intermediate links of organization which now connect the extremes together.*

* The doctrine of a plurality of original creations for the human family, is by no means

In accordance with this view, what are at present termed the *five races* would be more appropriately called *groups*. Each of these groups is again divisible into a smaller or greater number of primary races, each of which has itself expanded from a primordial nucleus or centre. To illustrate this proposition, we may suppose that there were several centres for the American groups of races, of which the highest in the scale are the Toltecan nations — the lowest, the Fuegians. Nor does this view conflict with the general principle, that all these nations and tribes have had, as I have elsewhere expressed it, a common origin; for by this term is only meant an indigenous relation to the country they inhabit, and that collective identity of physical traits, mental and moral endowments, language, &c., which characterise all the American races.*

The same remarks are applicable to all the other human races; but in the present infant state of ethnological science, the designation of these primitive centres would be a task of equal delicacy and difficulty.

It would not be admissible in this place, to inquire into the respective merits of these propositions; and we shall dismiss them for the present with a few brief remarks.

If all the varieties of mankind were derived from a single aboriginal type, we ought to find the approximation to this type more and more apparent as we retrace the labyrinth of time, and approach the primeval epochs of history. But what is the result? We examine the venerable monuments of Egypt, and we see the Caucasian and the Negro

---

new; for it was believed and expounded by a learned Rabbi of the Apostolic age, in a commentary (the *Targum*) on the Pentateuch. *Rev. J. Pye Smith, Relation between the Holy Scriptures and Geology*, p. 393.

I have invariably, when treating of this subject, avowed my belief in the *aboriginal diversity* of mankind, independently of the progressive action of any physical or accidental causes. The words of the Hebrew Targum are precisely to the point: "God created Man red, white, and black."

I now venture to give a fuller and somewhat modified *explanation of their origin*. See *Crania Americana*, p. 3; *Crania Ægyptiaca*, p. 37; *Distinctive Characteristics of the Aboriginal Race of America*, p. 36; and *Hybridity of Animals considered in reference to the question of the Unity of the Human Species*, in Amer. Journal of Science and Arts, 1847.

* Niebuhr expresses this idea admirably when he remarks, that it is "false reasoning" to say, "that nations of a common stock must have had a common origin, from which they were *genealogically* deduced." History of Rome, I., p. 37. In other words, people of a *common stock* may have had *several* or *many origins*. Such appears to be the fact not only with man, but with all the inferior animals. We are nowhere told the latter were created *in pairs*. "Male and female created He them" — and the same words are used in reference to the whole zoological series.

Prof. Bailey of West Point, one of the most successful microscopists of the present day, has shown, that the mud taken from some of the deep-sea soundings on the coast of the United States contains, in every cubic inch, hundreds of millions of living calcareous *Polythalmia*. Will any one pretend that these animals were created in pairs, or had their origin in Mesopotamia?

depicted, side by side, master and slave, twenty-two centuries before Christ; while *inscriptions* establish the same ethnological distinctions eight hundred years earlier in time. [387] Abundant confirmation of the same general principle is also found on the numberless vases from the tombs of Etruria; the antique sculptures of India; the pictorial delineations of the earliest Chinese annals; the time-honored ruins of Nineveh, and from the undated tablets of Peru, Yucatan, and Mexico. In all these localities, so far removed by space from each other, and by time from us, the distinctive characteristics of the human races are so accurately depicted as to enable us, for the most part, to distinguish them at a glance.

We earnestly maintain that the preceding views are not irreconcileable with the Sacred Text, nor inconsistent with Creative Wisdom as displayed in the other kingdoms of Nature. On the contrary, they are calculated to extend our knowledge and exalt our conceptions of Omnipotence. By the simultaneous creation of a plurality of original stocks, the population of the Earth became not an accidental result, but a matter of certainty. Many and distant regions which, in accordance with the doctrine of a single origin, would have remained for thousands of years unpeopled and unknown, received at once their allotted inhabitants; and these, instead of being left to struggle with the vicissitudes of chance, were from the beginning adapted to those varied circumstances of climate and locality which yet mark their respective positions upon the earth.*

I. THE CAUCASIAN GROUP.

THE TEUTONIC RACE.—I use this appellation in the comprehensive sense in which it has been employed by Professor Adelung; for the great divisions established by this distinguished scholar, though based exclusively on philological data, are fully sustained by comparisons in physical ethnology. Of the three great divisions, the Scandinavian lies chiefly to the north of the Baltic sea; the Suevic and Cimbric on the south.

1. The SUEVIC nations embrace the Prussians on one hand, the Tyrolese on the other; while between these lie the Austrians, Swiss, Bavarians, Alsatians, and the inhabitants of the Upper and Middle

* See Rev. J. Pye Smith: Relation between the Holy Scriptures and Geology, 3d. ed. pp. 398–400. Also, Hon. and Rev. William Herbert: *Amyrillidaceæ*, p. 338.

"Les livres Juifs n'entendent pas établir que leur premier homme ait été le père du genre humain, mais seulement celui de leur espèce privilégié. Il ne peut conséquemment y avoir aucune impieté à reconnaitre parmi nous plusieurs espèces qui, chaqune, auront eu leur Adam et leur berceau particulier." Bory de St. Vincent: *L'Homme*, I., p. 66.

Rhine. These nations once extended into the north-eastern section of Europe, whence they were driven by the Sclavonic tribes.

2. The CIMBRIC nations occupy western Germany, and among many subordinate families, embrace the Saxons, Frisians, Hollanders, &c.

3. The SCANDINAVIAN race is regarded by Adelung as a mixture of Suevic and Cimbric tribes. It includes the Danes, Swedes, Goths, and Icelanders; for although it is a disputed question, whether the Goths came from Scandinavia, or from the northern shores of the Baltic sea, the evidence preponderates in favor of the former opinion. The Vandals, however, appear to have been strictly a Suevic people.

Of these great divisions I possess but twenty-three skulls, of which twenty-one are used in the *Table*. Of this number, all but one have been obtained from hospitals and institutions for paupers, whence we may infer that they pertain to the least cultivated portion of their race. The proportion of males to females is twelve to nine.

The exception alluded to above is the skull of a Dutch gentleman of noble family, who was born in Utrecht, received a good education, was of convivial habits, and died at an early age, in the island of Java. I particularize this cranium, because it is by far the largest in my whole series; for it measures 114 cubic inches of internal capacity. Contrasted with this is a female Swedish head, kindly sent me, with several others, by Professor Retzius of Stockholm, which sinks to sixty-five cubic inches. Between these extremes the mean or average is ninety.

THE ANGLO-SAXONS. — The next division of the Teutonic race is the *Anglo-Saxon;* that remarkable people who have made their way with the sword, but marked their track with civilization. At an early period of the Christian era, *Angli* and *Saxones*, two powerful tribes, occupied the country between the Cimbrian peninsula, (now called Jutland,) and along the western shore of the Elbe to the termination of this river in the Baltic sea. These people commenced their piratical incursions to the coast of Britain in the fourth century, and were masters of the island as early as A. D. 449. They found it chiefly inhabited by the native Britons, who were CELTS; but these latter people had been for nearly 400 years under the dominion of the Romans, who had largely colonized the country; and so complete was this subjugation, that the Latin language was the colloquial speech of all Britain at the fall of the Roman empire, excepting among the Picts of the coast of Scotland.* From the period of the Anglo-Saxon invasion, the population became a blended mixture of the Celtic, Pe-

* Betham: Etruria Celtica, I. 4.

lasgic, and Teutonic races, among which the latter soon took the preponderance, and gave its language to the British Islands. The Norman conquest added another physical element of the Teutonic stock.

This fusion of three families into one, varying in degree in different sections of these islands, has given rise to a physiognomy varying in several respects from the Teutonic caste; while the cranium itself is less spheroidal, and more decidedly oval, than is characteristic of that people.

I have not hitherto exerted myself to obtain crania of the Anglo-Saxon race, except in the instance of individuals who have been signalized by their crimes; and this number is too small to be of much importance in a generalization like the present. Yet, since these skulls have been procured without any reference to their size, it is remarkable that five give an average of 96 cubic inches for the bulk of the brain; the smallest head measuring 91, and the largest 105 cubic inches. It is necessary, however, to observe, that these are all male crania; but, on the other hand, they pertained to the lowest class of society, and three of them died on the gallows for the crime of murder.

The Anglo-Americans conform, in all their characteristics, to the parent stock. They possess, in common with their English ancestors, a more elongated head than the unmixed Germans. The few crania in my possession have, without exception, been derived from the lowest and least cultivated portion of the community — malefactors, paupers, and lunatics. The largest brain has been ninety-seven cubic inches; the smallest, eighty-two; and the mean of ninety accords with that of the collective Teutonic race. The sexes of these seven skulls are, four male and three female.

Two or three circumstances connected with the ethnology of the Anglo-American race, seem to call for a passing notice on this occasion.

Mr. Haldemann has observed that when, in the last century, the color of the American Indian was supposed to be owing to climate, it was boldly insisted that the descendants of Europeans in this country had already made some progress in a change of color. Since that time an hundred years have elapsed; yet, I presume that no sensible person will maintain that they have brought with them any confirmation of the postulate in question.

Dr. Prichard has been informed that the heads of Europeans in the West Indies approach those of the aboriginal Indian in form, independently of intermixture. On this point I feel qualified to express an opinion. I passed three months in the West Indies, and visited eight of the islands, when slavery was everywhere in vogue (1834); and I can unhesitatingly declare that I saw nothing to confirm this assertion, which I regard as wholly idle and gratuitous. The only difference that occurred to me was, that the better class of English women had become paler, or whiter, and thinner, on account of the great and constant heat of the climate, and consequent neglect of exercise.

The observations of Dr. Pinkard, an intelligent English author,* correspond entirely with my own. He relates that he saw in the Island of Barbadoes (where I myself passed six weeks), an English family that had lived there through at least six generations; "and yet," he adds, "one would suppose them to have been born in Europe, so fine was the skin, so clear the complexion, and so well formed the features." Similar remarks have been made respecting the Mexican Spaniards, and the colonists of South America generally.

Although but —— skulls are included in the preceding Teutonic series, yet, when we take into consideration their variety and authenticity, and the fact that they have been collected without regard to size, I have no hesitation in assuming ninety cubic inches for the average of the brain in the Germanic family of nations; and I am further convinced that this standard is the highest among the races of men.

We should reasonably look for a preponderating brain in a race that is not more remarkable for its conquests and its colonies, than for the extent of its civilization; a race that has peopled North America, reduced all India to vassalage, and is fast spreading itself over Polynesia, Southern Africa and Australia; a race that is destined to plough the field of Palestine, and reap the harvests of the Nile.

THE SCLAVONIC RACE.—It is remarked by Dr. Prichard, that our acquaintance with the Germanic nations dates back three centuries before Christ; but the history of the Slavonic tribes begins nine centuries later. They are obviously the descendants of the ancient Sarmatians, and, among many smaller nations, at present embrace the Russians, Poles, Lithuanians, Bohemians, and Moravians.

I much regret that my cranial series possesses but a single example derived from this race,—the skull of a woman of Olmutz sent me by Prof. Retzius, and which measures only —— cubic inches. I record this deficiency in my collection, in the hope that some person interested in pursuits of this nature may be induced to provide me with materials for making the requisite comparisons. My impression is, that the Sclavonic brain will prove much less voluminous than that of the Teutonic race.

* Quoted by Rudolphi: Anthropologie, p. 153.

THE FINNISH RACE.—Among these people I consider the true type to be preserved in the Western Finns—the aboriginal inhabitants of Scandinavia, the predecessors of the Teutonic nations; for the Esthonians, the Tchudic tribes of Middle Russia and Permia, and, above all, the Ugrians of Siberia, have lived so long in contact with the Mongolian races, that they often present a very mixed physical character.* We should, therefore, be cautious in grouping these communities into a supposed cognate race, merely from analogies of language, which, however important as aids in ethnology, are often no better than blind guides.†

I am the more particular in making these remarks, because the Madjars of Hungary have been classed, not only with the Finns, but even with the Bashkirs and Votiaks of Siberia, upon no other grounds than those just mentioned.‡ But mark a single admitted fact: the Tchudish tribe of Metzegers speaks the *Turkish language*, and, for this reason, has been by some writers actually classed with the Tartar races, with whom they were supposed to be affiliated! And, since the stronger often gives its language to the weaker race, is it not most probable that the Bashkirs, Votiaks, and other tribes have derived their language, by adoption, from the contiguous Tchudic population?

Again, the present Madjars of Hungary entered that country in the middle of the ninth century, not to take possession of an uninhabited region, but to mingle with a numerous existing population; whence their characteristics, both of mind and body, must have undergone a remarkable change, and become highly improved.

History indicates the cause of these changes when it tells us, that when the Madjars arrived in Hungary they at once formed political alliances with the German princes, in order to check or expel "the common enemies of both nations, the Sclavonian races." It is to be inferred, as a matter of course, under these circumstances, that the intrusive Madjars formed social connexions, not only with the Sclavonians, whom they reduced to subjection, in the heart of Pannonia, but also with the surrounding German communities; and, in this

* For evidence of this kind in relation to the inhabitants of north-western Asia, even in very ancient times, see Herodotus, *Melpomene*, cap. cviii., and Dr. Wiseman's *Lectures*, pp. 103, 105. Pallas further informs us that the *Nogais*, who are decided Mongolians, are fast losing their natural traits *by intermarriage with the Russians.—Trav. in Russia*, p. 425.

† A single example, now before our eyes, will illustrate this proposition. "Two hundred years since, the Irish language prevailed over the whole province of Leinster. English was spoken only in the cities and great towns. At the present moment not one person in a thousand, even of the lowest rank of the natives of that district, understand Irish."—*Betham: Etruria Celtica*, i. 31. Here, then, are 2,000,000 of Celts, who, if judged solely by their spoken language, would be classed with the Anglo-Saxon race.

‡ Prichard: Researches, &c. iii. 326, 330.

manner, the blending of dissimilar stocks has produced the modified race so favorably known in the modern Madjar.

For the only skull I possess of this race I am indebted to Prof. Retzius, of Stockholm. It is that of a woman from the parish of Kerni, in Finland. It has all the characteristics of an unmixed European head, and measures eighty-six cubic inches of internal capacity.

THE PELASGIC RACE. — Every one knows that the Pelasgic tribes were the aboriginal inhabitants of Greece; that they, in the progress of time, and for unknown reasons, changed their name to Hellenes, and were thus the ancestors of the Greeks.

The Pelasgic occupation of Greece ascends into "the night of time." They may be regarded as the indigenous possessors, the *autocthones* of the soil. Indeed there is reason to believe that there was a civilization in Pelasgia long before that which history attributes to the Hellenic race, though generally attributed to the progenitors of that people; for a priest of Sais assured Solon (B. C. 400) that the Saitic writings accounted for an antecedent Grecian epoch of 8000 years; and that Greece had moreover possessed a great and beautiful city yet 1000 years earlier in time.*

Statements of this kind, which were once rejected on account of their seeming extravagance, now claim a respectful notice when viewed in connexion with the new lights of chronology. We are, indeed, compelled to acknowledge a great antiquity for a race that could produce the divine morality of Hesiod 900 years before Christ.

I do not use the term *Pelasgic* with ethnological precision, but in this designation place the Greeks and Romans, and their descendants in various parts of Europe — Greece and Italy, and, in more isolated examples, in Spain, France, and Britain. In the same category I place the Persians, Armenians, Circassians, Georgians, and many other kindred tribes, together with the Græco-Egyptians.

Of four adult *Circassian* crania brought me by Mr. Gliddon, two are male and two female. The former we may suppose, from appearances, to have been associated with a full share of manly beauty, and measure ninety and ninety-four cubic inches of internal capacity; the female heads measure seventy-nine and eighty; whence we obtain eighty-six cubic inches as the mean of all. One of these skulls, that of a woman who had passed the prime of life, is remarkable for the harmony of its proportions, and especially for the admirable conformation of the nasal bones.

I possess, through the kindness of Mr. Gliddon, two female *Parsee* skulls, which, though small, present a beautiful form. One measures eighty-nine cubic inches, the other only seventy-five.

* See the Timæus of Plato. Taylor's Trans. ii. p. 466. The accurate Niebuhr remarks that, "in very remote times the Peloponnesus was not Grecian."

It is a highly interesting fact, that whenever the ruling caste is represented in the statues and bas-reliefs of ancient Persia, the physiognomy always conforms to the Pelasgic type. A remarkable example is seen in the head of the first Darius (B. C. 500), sculptured on the Tablet of Behistun, and copied by Major Rawlinson. [*Supra*, Fig. 44]. Of the same character are the antique heads of Persepolis, Teheran and Chapoor. But we no sooner enter Assyria than the type is wholly changed for those in which the Semitic features are dominant, as seen at Nineveh, Khorsabad, and other places.

The arts have become the handmaid of ethnology; and it may be regarded as an axiom in this science, that the older the sculptures and paintings, the more perfect and distinctive are the cranial types they represent. Again, there is no evidence to prove that any one of the ancient races, simply as such, is older than another.

Of four adult *Armenian* skulls, three pertain to men; and the average size of the brain is but eighty-three cubic inches. I have felt some hesitancy in admitting these skulls in this place, for two reasons: 1st, because their characteristics incline almost as much to the Arab type as to the Pelasgic; and, 2dly, because the term Armenian is not always used in a strictly national sense in the East, but is applied to a class of merchants, whose ethnological affinities must be often very mixed and uncertain. But, inasmuch as these crania are inserted in my original *Table*, I will not now displace them.

Greek and Græco-Egyptian Heads.—Mr. Combe describes several ancient Greek skulls he had seen, as of large size, with a full development of the coronal and frontal regions. The head, in classic sculpture, is often small in comparison with the whole figure; whence the remark that a woman proportioned like the Venus de Medicis would necessarily be a fool. The same disparity has been noticed by Winkelmann in the Farnese Hercules; but in the Apollo Belvidere, [*infra*, Fig. 339] the perfect type of manly beauty, the head is faultless.

Whether this smallness of head was a reality among the Greeks, or only a conventional rule of art, has been a disputed question; but we may safely adopt the latter proposition. There can be no doubt, however, that the ancient Pelasgic was smaller than the modern Teutonic brain; and the proofs, which are derived, not from Greece itself, but from Egypt, are contained in the following section:

Of 129 embalmed heads in my collection, 22 present Pelasgic characters, and of these 18 are capable of measurement. Some of them present the most beautiful Caucasian proportions, while others merge by degrees into the Egyptian type; and I am free to admit that, in various instances, I have been at a loss in my attempts to classify these two great divisions of the Nilotic series. Hence it is that nine skulls, which in my original analysis were placed with the Pelasgic group, I have, on a further and more elaborate comparison, transferred to the Egyptian series.

The Greeks were numerous in Egypt even before the Persian invasion, B. C. 525, and their number greatly increased after the conquest by Alexander the Great, nearly 200 years later (B. C. 332). When the Romans, in turn, took possession of the country thirty years before our era, the Greeks had already enjoyed uninterrupted communication with it for five centuries. Their colonies were 300 years old; and it is, therefore, by no means surprising that the Egyptian-Greek population, which chiefly inhabited Lower Egypt, should be largely represented in the catacombs of Memphis. They are fewer in proportion in Theban sepulchres; and yet fewer as we ascend the Nile; and are hardly seen in the cemeteries of the rural districts. The peaceful occupation of the Delta by the Greeks, for a long period of time, must necessarily have caused an interminable mixture of the two races, and fully accounts for that blended type of cranial conformation so common in the catacombs.

It is further remarkable that these Græco-Egyptian heads, which I have separated from the other Nilotic crania by their conformation only, and consequently without any regard to size, present an average of eighty-seven cubic inches for the size of the brain; or, no less than seven cubic inches above that of the pure Egyptian race, and but three inches less than the average I have assumed for the Teutonic nations. Yet, no one of this series is of preponderating size; for the largest measures but ninety-seven cubic inches, while the smallest descends to seventy-four.*

Again, if we take the mean of the whole twenty-eight crania embraced in the present division, we find it to be eighty-six cubic inches.

THE CELTIC RACE.—The Celts who, with the cognate Gauls, at one

* Dr. J. C. Warren, of Boston, possesses two finely preserved *Roman* crania, from the ashes of Pompeii. It is many years since I saw them, but they appeared to be highly characteristic of this division of the Pelasgic race. The difference between the Roman and Greek heads is familiar to all observers, but it has not been satisfactorily explained. It may have arisen from alliances between the intrusive Pelasgic and some neighboring, but dissimilar tribe, in Italy. One of the first acts of the Romans was to seize the Sabine women, in order to people their infant colony. These Sabines, however, are said also to have been of Pelasgic origin; but that the rural population of Italy, at that period, embraced a large proportion of Celts, may be inferred from history and confirmed by the Etruscan vases; for wherever these relics, now so numerous, picture the sylvan deities, whether as fauns or satyrs, they are represented with marked Celtic features; while the higher and ruling caste, represented on the same vessels, has a perfect Grecian physiognomy. See Sir William Hamilton's *Etruscan Vases, passim.* The true Roman profile, however, is not unfrequent on the antique bas-reliefs of Persia. Flandin: *Voyage en Perse*, pl. 33, 48.

period, extended their tribes from Asia Minor to the British Islands, are now chiefly confined, as an unmixed people, to the west and southwest of Ireland, whence have been derived the six crania embraced in the *Table*. These range between ninety-seven as a maximum and seventy-eight as a minimum of the size of the brain; and the mean, which is eighty-sèven cubic inches, will probably prove to be above that of the entire race, and not exceed eighty-five.

France, Spain, and parts of Britain, partake largely of Celtic blood, but so variously blended with the Teutonic and Pelasgic branches of the Caucasian group as to form a singularly mixed population. If a series of crania could be obtained from the old Provincial divisions of France, they would constitute a study of extreme interest; for those of the northern section ought to conform in a marked degree to the German type, from their long intercourse (since A. D. 420) with the Franks, Burgundians, Visigoths, and other Teutonic tribes. Those in the south would present a greater infusion of the Roman physiognomy, with some Greek traits; while the intermediate communities would retain a marked preponderance of their primitive Celtic characteristics. For Cæsar restricts the true Continental Celts between the Garonne on the south and the Seine on the north: for although the genuine Gauls were a Celtic people, many German tribes bore the same collective name among the Romans, in the same way that all the nations of the far North were designated Scythians.

Europe was successively invaded by the Celtic, Teutonic, and Sclavonic races. The Celtic migration is of extreme antiquity, yet there can be no question that they displaced preëxisting tribes. Among the latter may be mentioned the Iberians of Spain, who are yet represented by a fragment of their race — the Basques or Euskaldunes of Biscay.

THE INDOSTANIC FAMILY. — No part of the world presents a greater diversity of human races than the country which bears the collective name of India. Exotic nations have repeatedly conquered that unfortunate region, and to a certain degree amalgamated with its primitive inhabitants. In other instances, the original Hindoos remain unmixed; and beside these, again, the mountainous districts still contain what may be called fragments of tribes which have taken refuge there, in remote times, in order to escape the sword or the yoke of strangers.

That peninsular India was originally peopled, at least in part, by races of very dark and even black complexion, is beyond a question. These people are stigmatised as Barbarians by their conquerors, the *Ayras* — a fair race, with Sanscrit speech, whose primal seats were in eastern Persia. They now occupy the country between the Himalaya mountains on the north, the Vindya on the south, and between the Indian ocean and the Bay of Bengal.* In this region, called *Ayra-Varta*, or India Proper, live those once-powerful tribes which it has taken the English more than half a century to subdue. The occupancy of India by these Persian tribes dates, according to M. Guigniaut, from the year 3101 before Christ, when also it is supposed the division of *castes* was instituted. [388]

Of thirty-two adult Indostanic skulls in my collection, eight only can be identified with tribes of the Ayra or conquering race; nor even in this small number is there unequivocal proof of the affinity in question. The largest head in the series, that of a Brahmin who was executed, in Calcutta, for murder, measures ninety-one cubic inches for the size of the brain — the smallest head, seventy-nine. Two others pertain to *Thuggs*, remarkable for an elongated form and lateral flatness. The mean of these Ayra heads is eighty-six cubic inches.

Contrasted with this people, and occupying the country adjacent to the Bay of Bengal, are the *Bengalees* — small of stature, feeble in constitution, and timid in disposition. They are obviously an aboriginal race, upon whom a foreign language has been imposed; and are far inferior, both mentally and physically, to the true Ayras. Weak and servile themselves, they are surrounded by warrior castes; and perhaps the most remarkable feature of their character is the absence of will, and implicit obedience to those who govern them.

Of these child-like people, my collection embraces twenty-four adult crania, of which the largest measures ninety cubic inches; the smallest, sixty-seven; and the mean of all is but seventy-eight.

All the Caucasian families of which we have spoken, belong to that vast chain of nations called *Indo-European*, in consequence of their having one common tongue, the Sanscrit, as the basis of their varied languages. This is also the *Japetic race*, and it extends from India proper in one direction to Iceland in the other.

THE SEMITIC FAMILY. — This group includes the Chaldeans, Assyrians, Syrians, and Lydians of antiquity, together with the Arabians and Hebrews.

The immense number of Jews in Egypt, even after the Exode (B. C. 1528), and especially during the Greek dominion of the Lagidæ,† would lead us to search for the embalmed bodies of this people in the catacombs; and hence it was no surprise to me to identify, with considerable certainty, seven Semitico-Egyptian heads, in all of which

* See President Salisbury's Discourse on Sanscrit and Arabic Literature: New Haven, 1843. The *Ayra race* derive their name from *Iran*, Persia.

† Josephus, B. XII. Chap. 2.

the Hebrew physiognomy is more or less apparent, and in some of them unquestionable. This identity is further confirmed by the fact, that the Jews in Egypt adopted the custom of embalming at a very early period of time (Genesis l. 26). And again, the two nations appear to have fraternized in a remarkable manner; for Adad married the sister of Pharaoh's wife, and one of Solomon's wives was the daughter of an Egyptian king, who is supposed to have been Osorkon. [389] To these facts we may add the marriage of Joseph, at a far earlier period of history, with a daughter of the priest of Heliopolis. For these reasons, I repeat, the Hebrew nation should be largely represented in the catacombs.

Five of my embalmed Semitic heads are susceptible of measurement, and give the low average of eighty-two cubic inches — the largest measuring eighty-eight; the smallest, sixty-nine.* In these crania, and also in others of existing Semitic tribes, I have looked in vain for the pit described by Mulder as situated on the outer wall of the orbit at the attachment of the temporal muscles; and consequently there is no trace of the corresponding elevation, also described by him, within the orbitar cavity.

I have had but little success in procuring the crania of the modern Semitic tribes; and for the three that I possess I am indebted to Mr. Gliddon. Of these, two are Baramka or Barmecide Arabs; the third, a Bedouin. The largest measures ninety-eight cubic inches; the smallest, eighty-four; and the mean is eighty-nine; but if we take the average of these eight Semitic heads, ancient and modern, it will be eighty-five inches.

I also received from Mr. Gliddon three additional skulls, from Cairo, which he was assured were those of Jews; [390] but their form has induced me to class them, perhaps erroneously, with the Fellahs of Egypt.†

The Nilotic Race. — In this designation I include the ancient Egyptians of the pure stock, and the modern Fellahs.

For the extensive series of Egyptian skulls in my possession, I am indebted to the kindness of Mr. Gliddon, Mr. A. C. Harris of Alexandria, in Egypt, Dr. Charles Pickering, and Mr. William A. Gliddon. Of these 129 embalmed heads, 83 present the Egyptian conformation; and of the latter number, 55 are capable of being measured.

I may here repeat a previous remark, that some of these crania present both Pelasgic and Egyptian lineaments, and thus form a transition between the two races; but I have classed them in one group or the other, according to the *preponderance* of national char-

* Crania Ægyptiaca, pp. 41 and 46, and the accompanying plates.

† Catalogue of skulls, Nos. 771, 772, 773.

acters. In the great majority of instances, however, the Egyptian conformation is detected at a glance.

The Egyptian skull is unlike that of any other with which I am acquainted. This opinion, which I long since announced,* has been fully confirmed by subsequent comparisons, and especially by the receipt of seventeen very ancient and most characteristic crania from tombs opened in 1842, at the base of the Great Pyramid, by Dr. Lepsius.†

It may be observed of these crania (for the rest of the series has been elaborately described in the *Crania Egyptiaca*), eleven at least are of the unmixed type, and present the long, oval form, with a slightly receding forehead, straight or gently aquiline nose, and a somewhat retracted chin. The whole cranial structure is thin, delicate, and symmetrical, and remarkable for its small size. The face is narrow, and projects more than in the European, whence the facial angle is two degrees less, or 78°. Neither in these skulls, nor in any others of the Egyptian series, can I detect those peculiarities of structure pointed out by the venerable Blumenbach, in his *Decades Craniorum;* and the external meatus of the ear, whatever may have been the form or size of the cartilaginous portion, is precisely where we find it in all the other races of men. The hair, whenever any of it remains, is long, curling, and of the finest texture.

On comparing these crania with many *fac-similes* of monumental effigies most kindly sent me by Prof. Lepsius and M. Prisse d'Avesnes, I am compelled, by a mass of irresistible evidence, to modify the opinion expressed in the *Crania Ægyptiaca*—viz.: that the Egyptians were an Asiatic people. Seven years of additional investigation, together with greatly increased materials, have convinced me that they were neither Asiatics nor Europeans, but aboriginal and indigenous inhabitants of the Valley of the Nile or some contiguous region:‡ peculiar in their physiognomy, isolated in their institutions, and forming one of the primordial centres of the human family.

Egypt was the parent of art, science, and civilization. Of these she gave much to Asia, and received some modifying influences in return; but nothing more. Her population, pure and peculiar in the early epochs of time, derived by degrees an element from Europe and Asia, and this was increased in the lapse of years, until the Delta became a Greek colony, with an interspersed multitude of Jews.

Effigies and portraits of Egyptian sovereigns and citizens are yet

---

* Crania Ægyptiaca, 1844.

† Proceedings of the Academy [of Nat. Sciences,] for October, 1844.

‡ This opinion, with some modifications, has been entertained by several learned Egyptologists—Champollion, Heeren, Lenormant, &c.

preserved in monuments that date back 5000 years,* and they conform, in all their characteristic lineaments, with the heads from the tombs of Gizeh and other Nilotic sepulchres.

Of the fifty-five Egyptian heads measured in the *Table*, it will be seen that the largest measures but ninety-six cubic inches of internal capacity, the smallest sixty-eight; and the mean of them all is but eighty. This result was announced in the *Crania Ægyptiaca*, and has been confirmed by the numerous additional measurements made since that work was published. Yet, on computing, by themselves, the fifteen crania from the ancient tombs of Gizeh, I find them to present an average of eighty-four cubic inches. The persons whose bodies had reposed in these splendid mausolea, were no doubt of the highest and most cultivated class of Egyptian citizens;† and this fact deserves to be considered in connexion with the present inquiry. To this we may add, that the most deficient part of the Egyptian skull is the coronal region, which is extremely low, while the posterior chamber is remarkably full and prominent.

The Fellahs.—The Arab-Egyptians of the present day constitute a population of more than 2,500,000; and that they are the lineal descendants of the ancient rural Egyptians, is proved by the form of the skull, the mental and moral character of the people, and their existing institutions, among which phallic worship is, even yet, conspicuous. Clot-Bey has drawn a graphic moral parallel between these two extremes of a single race, by showing that both were sober, avaricious, insolent, self-opinioned, satirical, and licentious. Contrasted with these defects in the old Egyptians, were the many household virtues, and that genius for the arts which has been a proverb in all ages.

When the Saracenic Arabs conquered Egypt in the seventh century of our era, an unlimited fusion of races was a direct and obvious con-

* Lepsius: *Chronologie der Ægypter*, p. 196. Dr. Lepsius dates the age of Menes, the first Egyptian king, 3893 before Christ, or 5743 years from the present time; and yet, in that remote time, Egypt was already possessed of her arts, institutions, and hieroglyphic language. The researches of the learned Chevalier Bunsen furnish conclusions nearly the same as those of Lepsius. Of the great antiquity of the Human Species there can be no question. In the words of Dr. Prichard, it may have been *chiliads of years*.

The ancient Egyptians appear to have had no doubts on this subject; for a priest of Sais, addressing Solon, spoke of "the multitude and variety of the destructions of the Human race which formerly have been, and again will be; the greatest of these, indeed, arising from fire and water; but the lesser from ten thousand other contingencies." — *Timæus of Plato: Taylor's Trans.* ii. 466.

† Dr. Lepsius did not desire to retain these crania, because they bore no collateral evidence of their epoch or national lineage. The bones were in great measure already denuded by time; and the appliances of mummification (which, in the primitive ages, consisted of little more than desiccating the body,) had long since disappeared. As heretofore observed, I judge these relics solely by their intrinsic characters.

sequence; but M. Clot-Bey has judiciously remarked, that the Arabs, nevertheless, present but a feeble element in the physical character of the great mass of people:—

"D'ou il résulte que l'Egyptien actuel tient beaucoup plus, par ses formes, par son caractère, et par ses mœurs, des anciens Egyptiens que des veritables Arabs; dont on ne trouve le type pur qu'en Arabie."*

The skull of the Fellah is strikingly like that of the ancient Egyptian. It is long, narrow, somewhat flattened on the sides, and very prominent in the occiput. The coronal region is low, the forehead moderately receding, the nasal bones long and nearly straight, the cheek-bones small, the maxillary region slightly prognathous, and the whole cranial structure thin and delicate. But, notwithstanding these resemblances between the Fellah and Egyptian skulls, the latter possess what may be called an *osteological expression*, peculiar to themselves, and not seen in the Fellah.

The Fellahs, however, do not appear to be the only descendants of the monumental Egyptians; for they exist also in Nubia, and westward, in isolated communities, in the heart of Africa. Of such origin I regard the Red Bakkari, so well described by Pallme. [391] So, also, the proper Libyans, the Tuaricks, Kabyles, and Siwahs, who, on the testimony of Dr. Oudney, and the more recent observations of Dr. Furnari, possess at least the physical traits of the Egyptian race:—

"Chez quelques unes des nombreuses [peuplades] qui habitent l'immense plaine du Sahara, chez les Touaricks, et chez quelques tribus limitrophes de l'Egypte, les yeux ecartés l'un de l'autre, sont long, coupés en amandes, à moitié fermés, et relevés aux angles extérieurs."

There are other reasons for supposing that the Libyan and Nilotic nations had a cognate source, though their social and political separation may date with the earliest epochs of time.

A few words respecting the *Copts*. Almost every investigation into the lineage of these people results in considering them a mixed progeny of ancient Egyptians, Berabera, Negroes, Arabs, and Europeans; and these characteristics are so variously blended, as to make the Copts one of the most motley and paradoxical communities in the world. The Negro traits are visible, in greater or less degree, in a large proportion of this people, and are distinctly seen in the three skulls in my possession. The two adult heads, which, on account of their hybrid character, are excluded from the *Table*, measure respectively eighty-five and seventy-seven cubic inches for the size of the brain, and consequently give the low average of eighty-one.

From the preceding observations it will appear that the Fellahs are the rural or agricultural Egyptians, blended with the intrusive Arabian stock; but the Copts, on the other hand, represent the descend-

* Aperçu Générale sur l'Egypte, i. p. 160.

ants of the old urban population, whose blood, in the lapse of ages, has become mixed with that of all the exotic races which have domiciliated themselves in the cities of Egypt. The mercenary licentiousness of the Copts is proverbial even at the present day.

I shall conclude these remarks on this part of the inquiry by observing, that no mean has been taken of the Caucasian races collectively, because of the very great preponderance of Hindoo, Egyptian, and Fellah skulls over those of the Germanic, Pelasgic and Celtic families. Nor could any just *collective* comparison be instituted between the Caucasian and Negro groups in such a *Table* as we have presented, unless the small-brained people of the latter division (Hottentots, Bushmen and Australians) were proportionate in number to the Hindoos, Egyptians, and Fellahs of the other group. Such a comparison, were it practicable, would probably reduce the Caucasian average to about eighty-seven cubic inches, and the Negro to seventy-eight at most, perhaps even to seventy-five; and thus confirmatively establish the difference of at least nine cubic inches between the mean of the two races.

II. THE MONGOLIAN GROUP.

The learned Klaproth, in his *Tableau de l'Asie*, has shown that before the year 1000 of our era, the Mongols were inconsiderable tribes in the northwest of Asia, and hence have erroneously had their name given to the most multitudinous of the five great divisions of the human family; but from an unwillingness to interfere with the generally adopted nomenclature of ethnology, I have used the word Mongolian in the comprehensive sense of Buffon and Blumenbach. It embraces nations of dissimilar features, among whom, however, there is a common link of resemblance that justifies the classification for generic purposes. Hence we group together the Chinese, the Kamtschatkans, and the Kalmucks.

I possess but eight Mongolian crania, and of these seven are Chinese—too small a number from which to deduce a satisfactory result. The largest of them measures ninety-one cubic inches, the smallest seventy; and they give an average of eighty-two. They are all derived from the lowest class of people; and it is not improbable that an average drawn, at least in part, from the higher castes, would approximate much more nearly to the Caucasian mean, perhaps to eighty-five cubic inches.

By the kindness of Prof. Retzius of Stockholm, I possess a single skull of a Laplander—a man of about forty years of age—whose brain measures no less than ninety-four cubic inches. The characteristics are obviously Mongolian, to which race the Lappes unquestionably belong. Dr. Prichard has produced philological evidence in proof of an opinion maintained by himself and some other learned men, that these people are *Finns*, who have acquired Mongolian features from a long residence in the extreme north of Europe. Yet, it must be remembered that, in former ages they lived much further south, in Sweden, and side by side with the proper Finns; whence has, no doubt, been derived any visible blending of the characters of the two races, and some affinities of language which are known and admitted by all.

This is a vital question in ethnology; and, although we have already made some remarks upon it, it may be allowable in this place to inquire how it happens that the people of Iceland, who are of the unmixed Teutonic race, have for 600 years inhabited their Polar region, as far north, indeed, as Lapland itself, without approximating in the smallest degree to the Mongolian type, or losing an iota of their primitive Caucasian features.*

A recent traveller,† equally remarkable for talent and enterprise, has briefly embodied the facts of this question in a manner sufficient to decide it in any unprejudiced mind. He declares that the Finns and Laplanders "have scarcely a single trait in common. The general physiognomy of the one is totally unlike that of the other; and no one who has ever seen the two could mistake a Finlander for a Laplander." The very diseases to which they are subject are different; and he quotes the learned Prof. Retzius of Stockholm for the fact, that the intestinal parasitic worms of the one race are different from those of the other. Finally, they differ almost as widely in their mental and moral attributes.

But, to show how little mere philology can be depended on in this and other instances, in deciding the affiliation of races, we may adduce the researches of the learned Counsellor Haartman. This eminent philologist has shown that the Carelians, who, from analogy of language, have hitherto been grouped with the proper Finnish race, belong to a totally different family, which invaded the region of the Lake Ladoga, and gave their name to the conquered country. This race, he adds, had a language of its own, which was lost in the course

---

* Desmoulins: *Hist. Nat. des Races Humaines*, p. 165. Were it not for the evidence of positive history, some future ethnologist might gravely insist that, because the Negroes of St. Domingo speak the French language, they are Frenchmen, to whom a tropical sun, altered aliments, and change of habits, have imparted the black skin, projecting face, and woolly hair of the African.

† A Winter in Lapland and Sweden: by Arthur de Capell Brooks, M. A., F. R. S. P.: London, 1827, p. 536–37.

of time, "and has been superseded by the Finnic, from the overpowering influence of the neighboring tribes."* Such evidence needs no commentary.

III. THE MALAY GROUP.

Besides the true Malays, the Malay race is composed of people of dissimilar stock; whence the opinion of M. Lesson, that those of the Indian Archipelago are a mixture of Indo-Caucasians and Mongols. That this amalgamation exists to a certain extent, there is no question; and in other instances they are variously blended with the indigenous or Oceanic Negro. Hence the origin of the Papuas of New Zealand, who are the littoral inhabitants of that continent.

Independently, however, of these mixed breeds, two great families are conspicuous—the Malays proper and the Polynesians—and to these pertain the twenty-three heads embraced in the *Table.*

The true Malays have a rounded cranium, with a remarkable vertical diameter and ponderous structure. The face is flat, the cheek-bones square and prominent, the ossa nasi long and more or less flattened, and the whole maxillary structure strong and salient. The twenty skulls in my possession have been collected with ethnological precision, and so much resemble each other, as to remind us of the remark of M. Crawford—that the true Malays are alike among themselves, but unlike among all other nations.

The largest of this series of skulls measures ninety-seven cubic inches, the smallest sixty-eight; and they give a mean of eighty-six: a large brain for a roving and uncultivated people, who possess, however, the elements of civilization and refinement.

Of the Polynesian Family I possess but three crania that can be measured, and they give a mean of eighty-three cubic inches. An extended series would probably show a larger average; but the brain of the Polynesian, if measured from skulls obtained to the eastward of New Zealand and the Marquesas islands, will prove smaller than that of the true Malay.

* *Trans. of the Royal Society of Stockholm, for* 1847. Egypt affords a remarkable example of the mutability of language; and Niebuhr (*Hist. of Rome,* i. p. 37) considers it proved that the Pelasgi, all the earliest inhabitants of the Peloponnesus, and many Arcadian and Attic nations, possessed originally a different language from the Greeks, and obtained the Hellenic tongue by adoption. He adds, that those Epirotes whom Thucydides calls Barbarians, "*changed their language, without conquest or colonization, into Greek.*" Diodorus and Cicero mention the same fact with respect to the Siculi, "although the Greek colonies in Sicily had only extended to a very few towns in the interior."—*Niebuhr, loco citat.*

IV. THE AMERICAN GROUP.

I have hitherto arranged the numberless indigenous tribes of North and South America into two great families: one of which, the *Toltecan*, embraces the demi-civilized communities of Mexico, Bogota, and Peru; while the other division includes all the Barbarous tribes. This classification is manifestly arbitrary, but every attempt at subdivision has proved yet more so. Much time and care will be requisite for this end, which must be based on the observations of D'Orbigny for South America, and those of Mr. Gallatin for the Northern [division of the] continent.

These subdivisions, after all, must be for the most part geographical; for the physical character of the American races, from Cape Horn to Canada, is essentially the same. There is no small variety of complexion and stature; but the general form of the skull, the contour and expression of the face, and the color and texture of the hair, together with the mental and moral characteristics, all point to a common standard, which isolates these people from the rest of mankind. The same remark is applicable to their social institutions and their archæological remains; for Humboldt has shown that the latter are marked by the same principles of art, from Mexico to Peru;* and Mr. Gallatin has decided, beyond controversy, that while their multitudinous tongues are connected by obvious links, they are at the same time radically different from the Asiatic or any other languages.

Mr. Gallatin finds this analogy among the American languages to extend to the Eskimaux — and he accordingly separates them from the Mongolian race, and regards them as a section of the great American family. This view may possibly be sustained by future inquiries; but the mere fact that the Eskimaux and the proximate Indian tribes speak dialects of one language, is of itself no proof that they belong to the same race. Thus, we may reasonably suppose that the Asiatic nomades, having arrived on this continent at various and distant periods, and in small parties, would naturally, if not unavoidably, adopt more or less of the language of the people among whom they settled, until their own dialect was finally merged in that of the Chippewyan and other Indians who bound them on the south.

When, on the other hand, famine, caprice, or a redundant population, has forced some of these people back again, across Behring's Strait, to Asia, they have carried with them the mixed dialect of the Eskimaux; whence it happens that the latter tribes and the Tchutch-

* Monuments, II. p. 5.

chi possess some linguistic elements in common: but here the analogy ceases abruptly, and is traced no farther.*

My collection embraces 410 skulls of 64 different nations and tribes of Indians, in which the two great divisions of this race are represented in nearly equal proportions, as the following details will show.

THE TOLTECAN FAMILY.—Of 213 skulls of Mexicans and Peruvians, 201 pertain to the latter people, whose remains have been selected with great care by the late Dr. Burrough, Dr. Ruschenberger, and Dr. Oakford. To the latter gentleman, I am under especial obligations for his kindness in personally visiting, on my behalf, the venerable sepulchres of Pisco, Pachacamac, and Arica. These cemeteries, at least the last two, are believed not to have been used since the Spanish conquest; and they certainly contain the remains of multitudes of Peruvians of very remote, as well as of more recent times.

Every one who has paid attention to the subject is aware, that the Peruvian skull is of a rounded form, with a flattened and nearly vertical occiput. It is also marked by an elevated vertex, great interparietal diameter, ponderous structure, salient nose, and a broad, prognathous maxillary region. This is the type of cranial conformation, to which all the tribes, from Cape Horn to Canada, more or less approximate. I admit that there are exceptions to this rule, some of which I long ago pointed out, in the *Crania Americana*, and others have recently been noticed among the Brazilian tribes by Prof. Retzius.

This rounded form of the head, so characteristic of the American nations, is in some instances unintentionally exaggerated by the simple use of the cradle-board, in common use among the Indians. * * * But on the other hand, whole tribes, from time immemorial, have been in the practice of moulding the head into artificial forms of singular variety and most distorted proportions. These were made the subject of the following experiment. * * *

[The] indomitable savages who yet inhabit the base of the Andes, on the eastern boundary of Peru, will no doubt prove to have a far larger brain than their feeble neighbors whose remains we have examined, from the graves of Pachacamac, Pisco, and Arica.

If we take the collective races of America, civilized and savage, we find, as in the *Table*, that the average size of the brain, as measured in the whole series of 338 skulls, is but 79 cubic inches.

In connexion with this subject, it may not be irrelevant to observe that the human cranial bones, discovered by Dr. Lund, in the cavern near the Lagoa do Sumidouro, in Brazil, and seemingly of a strictly fossil character, conform in all respects to the aboriginal American

* See my Inquiry into the Distinctive Characteristics of the Aboriginal Race of America, p. 27.

conformation;* thus forming a striking example of the permanence, we might say, immutability of the primordial type of organization, when this has not been modified by admixture with intrusive and dissimilar races.

I have no doubt that Man will yet be found in the fossil state as low down as the Eocene deposits, and that he walked the earth with the Megalonyx and Paleotherium. His not having been hitherto discovered in the older stratified rocks is no proof that he will not be hereafter found in them. Ten years ago, the Monkey-tribes were unknown and denied in the fossil state; but they have since been identified in the Himalaya mountains, Brazil, and England.†

[*End of Morton's MSS.*]

---

* Mémoire de la Soc. Roy. des Antiquaires du Nord, 1845–47, p. 73. See also Dr. Meigs's highly interesting communication on the Human Bones found at Santos, in Brazil, in Trans. of the Amer. Philos. Soc. for 1830; and Lt. Strain's Letter to me, in Proceedings of the Academy for 1844.

† Proofs of the vast antiquity of the earth, and of man's long sojourn upon it, multiply every day. The Hebrew chronology is a human computation from the Book of Genesis, and while it falls far short of the time requisite for the works of Man, is infinitely contracted when considered in reference to the creations of God. The Egyptian monuments, as we have seen, date far beyond the period allotted to the Deluge of Noah (which was evidently a partial phenomenon); and, on the other hand, the irresistible evidence of Geological Science realizes the sentiment of Plato — that Past time is an eternity.

"These views," observes Sir Charles Lyell, "have been adopted by all geologists, whether their minds have been formed by the literature of France, or of Italy, or Scandinavia, or England — all have arrived at the same conclusion respecting the great antiquity of the globe, and that too in opposition to their earlier prepossessions, and to the popular belief of their age."

All human calculations of time are futile in Geological and Ethnological inquiries. Epochs of vast duration are fully established by the nature of the organic remains of plants and animals that characterize the different formations; while the very intervals that separate these formations are evidences of other periods hardly less astonishing. In fact, Geological epochs present some analogy to Astronomical distances: the latter have been computed; the former are beyond calculation — and the mind is almost as incapable of realizing the one as the other. It cannot grapple with numbers which approximate to infinitude.

It is stated by Prof. Nichol, of Edinburgh, that "light travels at the rate of 192,000 miles in a second of time, and that it performs its journey from the Sun to the Earth, a distance of 95,000,000 of miles, in about eight minutes. And yet, by Rosse's great telescope, we are informed that there are stars and systems so distant, that the ray of light which impinges on the eye of the observer, and enables him to detect it, issued from that orb 60,000 years back." *Westminster Review*, 1846.

"In the beginning God created the Heavens and the Earth" — a sublime exordium, that points to an aboriginal creation, antedating the works of the *Seven Days*. Science has raised the veil of that ancient world, with all its numberless forms of primeval organization; but these are not noticed in the text, neither man, nor the inferior animals. When, however, we find the fossil remains of the latter so varied and so multitudinous, it is not inconsistent with true philosophy to anticipate the discovery of human remains among the ruins of that primal creation. In fact, I consider geology to have already decided this question in the affirmative.

[Unavailable, owing to its unfinished condition, the *Table* mentioned in the foregoing *Memoirs* is necessarily omitted. We cannot abstain, notwithstanding, from recalling the reader's attention — first, to the unqualified emphasis with which Dr. Morton's posthumous language insists upon an *aboriginal plurality of races;* and secondly, to the clear presentiments (engendered by his extensive researches in Comparative Anatomy) that our revered President of the Academy of Natural Sciences avows respecting the eventual discovery of *Man in a fossil state.*

Palæontological investigation had not fallen within the specialities of either author of this volume; and, in consequence, embarrassment was long felt by both, whether to mould what materials they possessed, concerning fossilized humanity, into a Chapter, or to relinquish a task in itself so indispensable to the nature of their work, no less than to the right understanding of Man's position in Creative history. The authors' hesitancy ceased when an accomplished friend, familiar with geological and other scientific literature, volunteered a digest of the most recent discoveries: nor will the general reader fail to be surprised, as well as edified, through the perusal of Dr. USHER's paper; which, with many acknowledgments on the part of J. C. N. and G. R. G., is embodied in the ensuing pages.]

CHAPTER XI.

GEOLOGY AND PALÆONTOLOGY, IN CONNECTION WITH HUMAN ORIGINS.

[CONTRIBUTED BY WILLIAM USHER, M. D., OF MOBILE.]

EVERY discovery in modern science tends to enlarge our ideas of the Universe, and to prove that the date of its creation is as far distant in the past, as the probable consummation of its destiny is remote in the future. Sir William Herschel has shown that there are stars in the heavens so distant, that the light by which they are visible to us has been myriads of years in its passage to the earth; and the wonderful powers of Lord Rosse's telescope have not, even yet, penetrated to the circumference of the starry sphere. It is the glory of astronomy to have demonstrated that the planetary bodies may retain their present movements undisturbed through a coming eternity; while chemistry illustrates the perpetual antagonism of the two great departments of organical nature on our globe, by which the vital properties of the atmosphere have been preserved for ages, as they may continue forever, unimpaired; and, finally, geology informs us that the earth has been, from the beginning, the theatre of constant and progressive changes, having for their object the fitting it for the support of the various races of beings which, in regular succession, have been its inhabitants.

The first great change in the condition of the earth was the condensation of its surface to a solid state, and the contraction of the newly-formed crust during the process of cooling; by which the Plutonic rocks of our system, the granite, porphyry and basalt, were formed in unstratified and crystallized masses. These underlie all the other rocks, and are sometimes forced up through them by the irresistible power of central heat. Their great eminences were separated by valleys filled with seas, (through the condensation of the circumambient vapors), along whose bottoms the stratified rocks were formed by the deposition of various mineral matters resulting from the disintegration of the primitive formations. The metamorphic rocks were thus formed; and, after becoming solidified by the heat of the cooling mass below them, were finally upheaved by the central force, and composed immense masses in different parts of the globe. Most of the considerable mountain ranges belong to this system. They rest upon a basement of granite, and have been thrown by the upheaving forces into positions inclining at all angles to the horizon. The upturned edges of these primary strata in many places show a thickness of fifteen or twenty miles — they were formed entirely from sediment produced by the disintegration of the hardest rocks, and by the gradual action of the elements; while their deposition, consolidation and elevation must have required periods of time which the mind shrinks from contemplating.

The Koran declares that the world was created in two days; and "Omar the Learned," for assigning a longer period, was obliged to fly from his country, to escape the disgrace of recanting his opinions. Happily, we live now under a more enlightened dispensation.

In these rocks we find no traces of organic remains to show that the earth was yet inhabited by living beings. But the creation of the earth consisted of a long succession of events, each occupying a distinct geological period, and leaving indelible records of its history in the solid crust of the globe. The creation of organized beings exhibits a similar succession — each race appearing as soon as the earth was prepared for its reception, continuing so long as the same state of things existed, and vanishing when the improvement of the earth had rendered it fit for the maintenance of a higher type of living creatures. All living creatures were exactly adapted through their organization to the peculiar localities they were placed in. They perished when the conditions necessary to their well-being were changed or ceased to exist.

In the next series of strata we find the earliest traces of those tribes of organized beings which occupied the primeval earth, and have left the monuments of their existence in the rocks which form their tombs. These primary fossiliferous strata are entirely of marine origin, having been formed at the bottom of the ocean; and they contain the remains of marine animals only. The types of these animals are easily recognized — they include representatives of all the great departments of the animal kingdom — but the species and even the genera are entirely lost. The animals, however, all belong to the lowest divisions of the different classes. Thus the radiata are represented by zoophytes, crinoidea and polyps — each the lowest in their respective classes. Mollusks, in like manner, exhibit only the lower types; articulata are mostly confined to trilobites; and fishes of the lowest forms are the sole representatives of the vertebrata: there are here no reptiles, no birds, and no mammals.

These primary strata are many thousand feet in thickness, and the organic remains imbedded in them, though belonging to a few species, show that animal life already existed in immense profusion, and extended over wide-spread regions of the globe. They flourished for countless generations, and their remains are found reposing in earth's earliest sepulchres.

In the next stage of the earth's history we have the Silurian system. Here the forms of life are more varied and abundant — species are multiplied; fishes now make their appearance in numbers and varieties corresponding with the improved conditions for their existence; and sea-plants are found among the fossils of this era. In the old red sandstone, the same orders are continued; new fishes are still more abundant, and all the silurian species have already disappeared. These fossils, again, are entirely distinct from the corresponding species of the carboniferous era which succeeds them. Not a single fish found in the old red sandstone has been detected, either in the silurian system on the one side or in the carboniferous on the other. Throughout all subsequent geological eras similar changes took place, and new species replaced the old at every new formation. In proportion as the earth approached its perfect state, the organic types became more complex; but the types originally created were never destroyed, they have been preserved through every succeeding modification and improvement, up to their highest manifestation in man. Regarding only the great, predominant groups of animals, M. Agassiz has classified the "Ages of Nature" as follows:—1. The primary or Palæozoic age, comprising the whole era preceding the new red sandstone, constituted the reign of fishes. 2. The secondary age, up to the chalk, constituted the reign of reptiles. 3. The tertiary age was the reign of mammals; and the modern age, embracing the most perfect of created beings, is the reign of man.*

A more minute classification would give us, since the first appearance of organized beings, not less than ten or twelve great groups of animals specifically independent of one another: so many entire races have passed away and been successively replaced by others; thus changing repeatedly the whole population of the globe.

The fossiliferous strata have been estimated to be eight miles in thickness. They were formed, like the metamorphic rocks, at the bottom of the sea, by sedimentary deposits, and afterwards upheaved in their consolidated form by central heat. Such a process, doubtless, must have been very slow: *e.g.* the hydrographic basin of the Tigris and Euphrates is 189,000 square miles; and the alluvial deposit along the course of those rivers, in the centre, is about 32,400 square miles in extent. The average rate of encroachment on the sea, at their mouths on the Persian Gulf, is about a mile in thirty years. During its season of flood, the Euphrates transports about one-eightieth of its bulk of solid matter; and the earthy portion carried by the Tigris past the city of Bagdad, was ascertained by Mr. Ainsworth to be one-hundredth of its bulk, or about 7150 pounds every hour.† But these rivers are insignificant compared with the Ganges, which hourly carries down 700,000 cubic feet of mud; or the Yellow river, in China, which transports 2,000,000 feet of sediment to the sea. Our own *Mesha-sebe*, "the Father of Waters," though purer than either of the rivers we have named, has already formed a delta 30,000 square miles in extent, and is yearly sweeping to the sea, from his many tributaries, the enormous amount of 3,702,758,400 cubic feet of solid matter. Yet, notwithstanding such immense deposits, it has been estimated that, if the sediment from all the rivers in the world were spread equally over the floor of the Ocean, it would require 1000 years to raise its bottom a single foot; or about 4,000,000 of years to form a mass equal to that of the fossiliferous rocks: and if, instead of merely the present extent of the sea, we include the whole surface of the globe in such estimate, the time required must be extended to 15,000,000 of years.‡ When we consider that these strata were formed at the

* Agassiz: Principles of Zoology, p. 189.

† Ainsworth: *Assyria, Babylonia and Chaldæa;* Euphrates Expedition, 1838, p. 111.

‡ Somerville: Physical Geography.

bottom of the sea, and thence upheaved by the operation of natural causes; and that in many cases this process has been more than once repeated; we may claim a very respectable antiquity for our planet, since such changes must have required a duration wholly incalculable.

We have seen that every great geological change was accompanied by the disappearance of existing species and the introduction of new: while the present geographical distribution of plants and animals coincides with the rise of those strata constituting the surface of the globe. All has been successive and progressive; plants and animals were produced in regular order, ascending from simple to complex; one law has prevailed from earth's foundations to its superficies; and thus our present species are *autocthonoi*, originating on the continents or islands where they were first found. Man himself is no exception to this law; for the inferior races are everywhere "glebæ adscripti."

Each of these orders of living beings occupied the earth for an appointed time, and gave way in turn to higher organizations. Fishes ruled over the primeval waters: as land gradually formed itself, they made way for the great amphibious reptiles. Just as fishes represent the first vertebrata of the sea, so reptiles are their earliest representatives on land. Reptiles presided over the formation of continents, and next came the birds. As huge reptiles of the sea were succeeded by the marine mammalia—the cetaceans—so, on the land, when mountain chains were thrown up and dry plains formed, leaving extensive marshy borders, monstrous wading birds, which have left but their footmarks behind them, succeeded the reptiles, and were followed in their turn by the amphibious mammals. Each epoch of the land, as of the sea, (whilst our "earth formed, reformed, and transformed itself,") was marked by the appearance of suitable inhabitants, necessary to the great plan of creation in preparing the globe for the reception of mankind.

The *tertiary* formation extends over most of Europe, and comprises those famous geological basins which are the sites of its principal cities, London, Paris, and Vienna; while, in America, it embraces nearly all the level region of the Middle and the Southern States. Its fossils comprise a mixture of marine, fresh-water, and land species, occurring in such succession as to show extensive alternations of sea and land; and giving reason to believe that large portions of the present surface of the land were covered with immense lakes, like Erie or Ontario. The animals of the tertiary period, while entirely different from those of the secondary, were similar to those now existing: marine animals no longer predominated in the creation — the higher orders of land animals had now appeared. The same advance is visible in all the great departments of animated nature. Of the radiates, the mollusks, and the articulata, the lower forms have entirely disappeared; and the tertiary species are frequently almost identical with those now living: among vertebrata, the enamelled fishes of the earlier epochs have been replaced by those with scales like the living species; and, in a word, the whole tertiary fauna resembles our present.

Another important change is noticed in the relative distribution of animals and plants. In the early history of the earth, the same animals were spread widely over the face of the globe; nearly the whole earth was covered with water, and a uniform temperature everywhere prevailed: none but marine animals existed, and there was nothing to prevent a great uniformity of type. In the tertiary era everything had altered — the earth's surface was varied with islands and continents, with mountains and valleys, with hills and plains; the sea, gathered into separate basins, was divided by impassable barriers. Here, accordingly, we find another great step towards the present condition of organized nature on the earth's surface: not only have higher orders of animals appeared, but they are confined within narrower limits. The fossils of the tertiary system, in different regions, are as distinct as the present faunæ and floræ of those countries. Each portion of the land, as it rose above the deep, became peopled with animals and plants best adapted to its occupancy; and the waters necessarily partaking of the physical change, the marine species which swarmed along the shores underwent a corresponding modification.

The earth was now inhabited by the great mammifers, whose constitution most nearly resembles that of mankind: where they existed, assuredly, man could have existed also. They approximate to humanity in their intelligence, their senses, their wants, their passions, their animal functions; and when they had "multiplied exceedingly," we may suppose that man would not be long in making his appearance. Here we meet for the first time with fossil monkeys; the type whose organization most closely assimilates to the human. It is only within a few years that fossil monkeys have been discovered, and their supposed absence was formerly cited as a proof of their recent origin. Monkeys, in still prevalent systems of creation, are supposed to have been coeval with, or at least but little anterior to, man; the absence of their organic remains being considered as satisfactory evidence that both men and monkeys were mere creations of yesterday! Fossil monkeys, nevertheless, have been found in England, France, India, and South America. In India, several different species have turned up in tertiary strata, on the Himalaya mountains. The French fossils, found in fresh-water strata of the tertiary era, belong to the gibbon or tailless ape, which stands next, in the scale of organization, to the orangs.

The American specimen, brought from Brazil by Dr. Lund, is referred to an extinct genus and species peculiar to that country. And the English fossils, belonging to the genus macacus and an extinct species, exhumed from the London clay, were associated with crocodiles, turtles, nautili, besides many curious tropical fruits.*

Only a few fossil quadrumanes have as yet been discovered; but a single one is sufficient to establish their existence. The number of animals preserved in rocky strata may bear but a small proportion to those which have been utterly destroyed. Thus, in the Connecticut sandstone, the tracks of more than forty species of birds and quadrupeds have been found distinctly marked. Some of these birds must have been at least twelve or fifteen feet high; and yet no other vestige of their existence has been discovered. They were the colossal residents of that valley for ages; they have all vanished; and had it not been for the plastic nature of the yielding sand whereon they waded along the river's banks, they would not have left even a footprint behind them. May there not be other creatures which have left no trace whatever of their existence? †

In each of the great geological epochas, life was quite as abundant as at the present day. All departments of the Animal Kingdom had their representatives, and some of them were even more numerous then than at present. Those immense tracts formed by zoophytes, and the incomprehensible masses of microscopic shells, would almost seem to favor the theory that the whole earth is formed of the débris of organized beings. Fossil fishes are far more plentiful than their living representatives; and more shells have been found in the single basin of Paris than now exist in the whole Mediterranean.‡ The remains of the giant reptiles show their exuberance; and now-extinct species of mammals must have at least equalled in numbers, as they far exceed in size, their living successors. Perhaps the most striking example is seen in the inexhaustible multitude of fossil elephants daily discovered in Siberia. Their tusks have been an object of traffic in ivory for centuries; and in some places they have existed in such prodigious quantities, that the ground is still tainted with the smell of animal matter. Their huge skeletons are found from the frontiers of Europe through all Northern Asia to its extreme eastern point, and from the foot of the Altai Mountains to the shores of the Frozen Ocean — a surface equal in extent to the whole of Europe. Some islands in the Arctic Sea are chiefly composed of their remains, mixed with the bones of various other animals of living genera, but of extinct species.§

* Lyell: Principles. † Hitchcock: Geology. ‡ Agassiz.

§ Lieut. Anjou's Polar Voyage.

In whatever way we may account for the series of geological changes thus cursorily enumerated, they must have required immense periods of time; and we have Mr. Babbage's authority for saying, that even those formations which are nearest to the surface have occupied vast periods, probably *millions* of years.* It is only with these latest formations, however, that we shall have any immediate concern.

The DILUVIUM, or *drift*, as now called, is almost universal in extent (except within the tropics); and is marked by deposits of clay and sand; and erratic blocks or boulders of all sizes, from common pebbles to masses thousands of tons in weight, occur at all levels up to the summits of lofty mountains, where no agency now in operation could have placed them. The drift abounds in fossil remains of animals; such as the elephant, mastodon, rhinoceros, hippopotamus, and other large mammalia: genera which, now living only in warm climates, must have then existed in England, France, Germany, and other northern countries. These animals were destroyed by the same inundations which left the deposits we call drift: yet the works and the remains of man have been found among them! These drift-formations are of immense antiquity, being in this country older than the basin of the Mississippi; and may be regarded as the last great transition in the earth's geological history.

All formations of the drift do not belong to one and the same period; nor were they produced by the same causes. According to the glacial theory of Prof. Agassiz, the climate of the northern hemisphere, which had been of tropical warmth, became colder at the close of the tertiary era. The polar glaciers advanced towards the south, leaving the marks of their passage in the ground and upon striated surfaces of rocks and mountains, whilst distributing on every side the blocks and masses they had entangled in their course: which last, with the finer detritus, were swept far and wide by torrents occasioned by the melting of these glaciers.

At other times, a sudden elevation of mountain-chains from beneath the surface of the sea, produced violent inundations of surrounding countries, and transported boulders and drift in every direction. The Alps furnish illustrations in point. They have been heaved up since the deposition of the tertiary strata; for those strata are found capping their summits or lying in their mountain-valleys; while the "drift" is seen scattered in all directions — on the range of the Jura, and over the plains of Lombardy. Blocks of granite, 10,000 cubic feet in size, have been found in the Jura mountains, 2000 feet above the Lake of Geneva. The rock in Horeb, from which

* Babbage: Bridgewater Treatise.

the leader in Israel miraculously drew water, is a mass of syenitic granite, six yards square, lying insulated upon a plain near Mount Sinai. There are displays of the drift in our own country, on a magnificent scale, but as our object does not require, nor our limits allow, more than a mere reference to this as an interesting stage in the earth's antiquity, we pass on.

Last comes the ALLUVIUM; that is, the formation along the margins of rivers and the deltas at their mouths, and the deposition of those superficial coverings of soil which have taken place since the earth assumed its present configuration of sea and land. Of the antiquity of the older formations, fossils have afforded unerring information; each set serving as medals to mark the epoch of their existence. The alluvium must be judged by comparison, and all we shall attempt is, to show that the earth, in its present condition, has been the habitation of man for many thousand years longer than people commonly suppose.

It appears, from recent observations,* that the hydrographic basin of the Nile (within the limits of rain), is about 1,550,000 square miles, and the whole habitable land of Egypt is formed of the alluvial deposits of the river. The Delta is of a fan-like form, narrow at its apex below Cairo, and spreading out as it extends towards the sea, until its outer border is about 120 miles in extent. The same immense deposits are still carried annually to the sea, yet the Delta has not perceptibly increased within the limits of history. Tanis, the Hebrew Zoan, at a very remote period of Egyptian annals, was built upon a plain at some distance from the sea; and its ruins may still be seen, within a few miles of the coast. The lapse of more than 3000 years, from the time of Ramses II., has not produced any great increase in the alluvial plain, nor extended it farther into the Mediterranean. Cities which stood, in his day, upon the coast, and were even then referred to the gods Osiris and Horus, may still be traced at the same localities; and Homer makes Menelaus anchor his fleet at Canopus, at the mouth of the Egyptus or Nile.† In short, we know that in the days of the earliest Pharaohs, the Delta, as it now exists, was covered with ancient cities, and filled with a dense population, whose civilization must have required a period going back far beyond any date that has yet been assigned to the Deluge of Noah or even to the Creation of the world.

The average depth of the Gulf of Mexico, between Cape Florida

---

* Beke, in Gliddon's Handbook to the Nile, 1849, p. 29; and, Map of the "Basin of the Nile."

† Wilkinson: Manners and Customs, i. p. 5–11; ii. 105–121: — Gliddon, *Chapters*, p. 42–3.

and the mouth of the Mississippi, is about 500 feet. Borings have been made near New Orleans to a depth of 600 feet, without reaching the bottom of the alluvial matter; so that the depth of the delta of the Mississippi may be safely taken at 500 feet. The entire alluvial plain is 30,000 square miles in extent, and the smallest complement of time required for its formation has been estimated at 100,000 years.* This calculation merely embraces the deposits made by the river since it ran in its present channel; but such an antiquity dwindles into utter insignificance when we consider the geological features of the country. The bluffs which bound the valley of the Mississippi rise in many places to a height of 250 feet, and consist of loam containing shells of various species still inhabiting the country. These shells are accompanied with the remains of the mastodon, elephant, and tapir, the megalonyx, and other megatheroid animals, together with the horse, ox, and other mammalia, mostly of extinct species. These bluffs must have belonged to an ancient plain of ages long anterior to that through which the Mississippi now flows, and which was inhabited by occupants of land and fresh-water shells agreeing with those now existing, and by quadrupeds now mostly extinct.†

The plain on which the city of New Orleans is built, rises only nine feet above the sea; and excavations are often made far below the level of the Gulf of Mexico. In these sections, several successive growths of cypress timber have been brought to light. In digging the foundations for the gas-works, the Irish spadesmen, finding they had to cut through timber instead of soil, gave up the work, and were replaced by a corps of Kentucky axe-men, who hewed their way downwards through four successive growths of timber — the lowest so old that it cut like cheese. Abrasions of the river-banks show similar growths of sunken timber; while stately live-oaks, flourishing on the bank directly above them, are living witnesses that the soil has not changed its level for ages. Messrs. Dickeson and Brown have traced no less than ten distinct cypress forests at different levels below the present surface, in parts of Louisiana where the range between high and low water is much greater than it is at New Orleans. These groups of trees (the live-oaks on the banks, and the successive cypress beds beneath,) are arranged vertically above each other, and are seen to great advantage in many places in the vicinity of New Orleans.

Dr. Bennet Dowler‡ has made an ingenious calculation of the last emergence of the site of that city, in which these cypress forests play

---

* Lyell's Principles of Geology, Cap. xv. † Lyell's Second Visit, Cap. xxxiv.

‡ Bennet Dowler: Tableaux of New Orleans, 1852.

an important part. He divides the history of this event into three eras:—1. The era of colossal grasses, trembling prairies, &c., as seen in the lagoons, lakes, and sea-coast. 2. The era of the cypress basins. 3. The era of the present live-oak platform. Existing types, from the Balize to the highlands, show that these belts were successively developed from the water in the order we have named: the grass preceding the cypress, and the cypress being succeeded by the live-oak. Supposing an elevation of five inches in a century, (which is about the rate recorded for the accumulation of detrital deposits in the valley of the Nile, during seventeen centuries, by the nilometer mentioned by Strabo,) we shall have 1500 years for the era of aquatic plants until the appearance of the first cypress forest; or, in other words, for the elevation of the grass zone to the condition of a cypress basin.

Cypress trees of ten feet in diameter are not uncommon in the swamps of Louisiana; and one of that size was found in the lowest bed of the excavation at the gas-works in New Orleans. Taking ten feet to represent the size of one generation of trees, we shall have a period of 5700 years as the age of the oldest trees now growing in the basin. Messrs. Dickeson and Brown, in examining the cypress timber of Louisiana and Mississippi, found that they measured from 95 to 120 rings of annual growth to an inch: and, according to the lower ratio, a tree of ten feet in diameter will yield 5700 rings of annual growth. Though many generations of such trees may have grown and perished in the present cypress region, Dr. Dowler, to avoid all ground of cavil, has assumed only two consecutive growths, including the one now standing: this gives us, as the age of two generations of cypress trees, 11,400 years.

The maximum age of the oldest tree growing on the live-oak platform is estimated at 1500 years, and only one generation is counted. These data yield the following table:—

"*Geological Chronology of the last emergence of the present site of New Orleans.*

	Years.
Era of aquatic plants	1,500
Era of cypress basin	11,400
Era of live-oak platform	1,500
Total period of elevation	14,400"

Each of these sunken forests must have had a period of rest and gradual depression, estimated as equal to 1500 years for the duration of the live-oak era, which, of course, occurred but once in the series. We shall then certainly be within bounds, if we assume the period of such elevation to have been equivalent to the one above arrived at; and, inasmuch as there were at least ten such changes, we reach the following result: —

	Years.
"Last emergence, as above	14,400
Ten elevations and depressions, each equal to the last emergence	144,000
Total age of the delta	158,400"*

In the excavation at the gas-works, above referred to, burnt wood was found at the depth of sixteen feet; and, at the same depth, the workmen discovered the skeleton of a man. The cranium lay beneath the roots of a cypress tree belonging to the FOURTH forest level below the surface, and was in good preservation. The other bones crumbled to pieces on being handled. The *type* of the cranium was, as might have been expected, that of the ABORIGINAL AMERICAN RACE.

If we take, then, the present era at	14,400 years,
And add three subterranean groups, each equal to the living (leaving out the fourth, in which the skeleton was found), ...	43,200
We have a total of	57,600 years.

From these data it appears that the human race existed in the delta of the Mississippi more than 57,000 years ago; and the ten subterranean forests, with the one now growing, establish that an exuberant flora existed in Louisiana more than 100,000 years earlier: so that, 150,000 years ago, the Mississippi laved the magnificent cypress forests with its turbid waters.†

In a note addressed to our colleagues, Nott and Gliddon, April 19, 1853, Dr. Dowler says: —

"Since I sent you the 'Tableaux,' several important discoveries have been made, illustrative and confirmatory of its fundamental principles in relation to the antiquity of the human race in this delta, as proved by works of art underlying, not only the live-oak platform, but also the second range of subterranean cypress stumps, exposed during a recent excavation in a cypress basin."

The cypress trees of Louisiana, and the antiquity claimed for them here, naturally remind us of the longevity of other trees in connexion with the antiquity of the present era. The baobab of Senegal, as is well known, grows to a stupendous size, and is supposed to exceed all other trees in longevity. The one measured by Adanson was thirty feet in diameter, and estimated to be 5250 years old. Having made an incision to a certain depth, he counted 300 rings of annual growth, and observed what thickness the tree had gained in that period; the average growth of younger trees of the same species was then ascer-

* Dowler: Tableaux of New Orleans. † Idem.

tained, and the calculation made according to the mean rate of increase. Baron Humboldt considered a cypress in the gardens of Chapultepec as yet older; it had already reached a great age in the reign of Montezuma, and is supposed to be now more than 6000 years old. If we could apply the criterion-scale of Dickeson and Brown, some of these trees might prove to be older still. These gentlemen counted 95 to 120 rings of annual growth in the cypresses of Louisiana, and say, moreover, that the ligneous rings in the cypress are remarkably distinct, and easily counted. Now the cypress measured by Humboldt was 40½ feet in diameter. A semi-diameter of 243 inches, multiplied by 95, the smaller number of rings to an inch, would give 24,036 years as the age of one generation of living trees. The harder woods are of very slow growth, and some of the huge mahoganies of Central America must be extremely old. The courbaril of the Antilles reaches a diameter of twenty feet, and is one of the hardest timber trees; and the ironwood, from the same data, may be ranked among the patriarchs of the forest.

Travellers have often been deterred from attempting to ascertain the age of remarkable trees by the apparent hopelessness of the task. To fell one of these giants of the woods was evidently impossible, nor was it an easy matter even to make such a section as would facilitate the calculation. This difficulty is now, happily, to a great extent removed, and scientific travellers can hereafter obtain measurements of the largest and hardest trees in the places of their growth. Mr. Bowman has devised an instrument something like a surgeon's trephine, which, by means of a circular saw, cuts out cylinders of wood from opposite sides of the tree, and thus furnishes the most satisfactory results.*

Having drawn the general reader's attention to a few geological † and botanical evidences of the incalculable lapse of time required for the existing condition of things upon our globe, let us endeavor to raise a corner of the veil which obscures human sight of epochas anterior to ours. Where our alluvial rivers flowed, where our present vegetation flourished, where our mammiferous animals abounded, science cannot assign, *à priori*, a reason why all our different species of mankind should not also have existed coetaneously. CUVIER (says Schmerling most truly,) does not contest the existence of man at the epoch in which gigantic species peopled the surface of the earth.‡ We content ourselves with lesser quadrupeds:

Fossil Dogs.—The dog has been the constant companion of man in

---

* J. Pye Smith.

† For the parallel antiquity of the Nile's deposits, *cf.* Gliddon, Otia Ægyptiaca, p. 61–69.

‡ Recherches sur les Ossemens Fossiles: Liege, 1833, i. p. 53.

all his migrations to distant regions of the earth, and has suffered from the same injustice which ignorance metes to his lord. The wise Ulysses has been ruthlessly referred to a consanguineous origin with the Papuan and the Hottentot; and the noble animal that died from joy on recognizing his master (when all Ithaca had forgotten the twenty years' wanderer), is left to choose a descent from the savage wolf or the abject jackal, and must perforce share its parentage with

> "Mongrel, puppy, whelp, and hound,
> And cur of low degree."

The monuments of Egypt have also shed new light upon the historical antiquity of both men and dogs, showing that the different races of each were as distinct 5000 years ago as they are to-day; and we now propose to inquire whether geology does not confer upon dogs a still more ancient origin.

Few questions in the history of fossil animals are more difficult to solve than that of dogs; for the differences between skeletons of the dog, the wolf, and the fox, are so trifling as to be almost undistinguishable. Indeed, some perceive no difference between them except in point of size. Consequently, when we meet with a fossil of the dog species, we are at a loss whither to refer it; and so strong are vulgar prejudices against the antiquity of everything immediately associated with man, that it is almost certain to be called a wolf, a fox, a jackal, or anything else, sooner than a common dog.

It does not appear that any canidæ have yet been found in the oolite, the earliest position of mammal remains; they are rare in the tertiary strata, and are chiefly met with in the caves of the pliocene, in the drift, and the alluvium.

Owen says that fossil bones and teeth extant in caves, and their association with other remains of extinct species of mammalia found in the same state, carry back the existence of the *canis lupus* in Great Britain to a period anterior to the deposition of the superficial drift. In the famous Kirkdale cave, Dr. Buckland discovered bones of a fossil canis associated with those of tigers, bears, elephants, the rhinoceros, hippopotamus, and other animals which Cuvier pronounced to belong to extinct species. Fossil bones of a species of canis, similarly associated with extinct animals, turned up in the cave of Paviland, in Glamorganshire; and the Oreston cavern furnished other examples. In all these cases it was difficult to designate the *species* of canis the fossils belonged to, and the Dog was never allowed the benefit of the doubt.

Cuvier, Daubenton and De Blainville inform us, that the shades of difference in canine skeletons are so slight, that distinctions are often more marked between two individual dogs, or two wolves, than between the various species. But, in spite of these difficulties, recognizable remains of the true dog, *canis familiaris*, have been frequently obtained. Dr. Lund discovered fossil dogs larger than those now living, in the cave of Lagoa Santa, in Brazil; associated, as we have elsewhere stated, with an immense variety of extinct species of animals, and in a position whose geological antiquity cannot be doubted. In this case the dog was partner with an extinct monkey; and a similar association has been found in a stratum of marl, surmounted by compact limestone, in the department of Gers, at the foot of the Pyrenees. Here the bones of a true dog were found, in company with the reliquiæ of not less than thirty mammiferous quadrupeds; including three species of rhinoceros, a large anaplotherium, three species of deer, a huge edentate, antelopes, and a species of monkey about three feet high. This fact is the more interesting, because fossil monkeys are almost as rare as fossil men in the fauna of the tertiary era; and, until recently, their existence was quite as strenuously denied. In the catalogue of the casts of Indian fossils, recently presented to the Boston Society of Natural History by the East India Company, we find two crania of canine animals from the Sivalik Hills, but have no information as to their species.

Dr. Schmerling has described several fossils of the true dog, which evidently belonged to two distinct varieties, notably differing from each other in size, as well as from the wolf and fox, whose bones, together with those of bears, hyenas, and other animals, reposed in the same locality. Cuvier, speaking of the bones of a fossil animal of the genus *canis*, found in the cave of Gaylenreuth, says that they resemble the dog more than the wolf, and that they are in the same condition with those of the hyenas and tigers associated with them: "they have the same color, the same consistence, the same envelop, and they evidently *date from the same epoch.*" Cuvier does not positively declare these remains to be those of the *dog:* he observes the caution which he exhibited, in 1824, when asked whether human bones had *yet* been discovered and *proved* to be coeval with those of extinct mammalia — "*Pas encore,*" was his simple reply.

In the quarries of Montmartre, Cuvier found the lower jaw of a species of canis, differing from that of any living species, and which we have the right to say belonged to an extinct species of dog. M. Marcel de Serres has described two species of dogs from Lunel Vieil. One he supposed to resemble the pointer, and the other was much smaller. The caves of Lunel Vieil are situated in a marine-tertiary limestone. In some dogs, the frontal elevation of the skull exceeds that of the wolf, and this characteristic is useful as a distinctive mark. The skull of a small variety of dog, with this mark well developed, was obtained from an English bone-cave, and submitted to Mr. Clift, who pronounced it to belong to a small bull-dog or large pug.

Our domestic dog has the last tubercular tooth *wider* than that of the wolf; which fact, together with slighter structure of the jaw, shows the dog to be less carnivorous. The teeth of the cave-dogs differ only in size from those of the common dog, being larger; and it appears almost certain that many of the fossil dogs were of a greater size than any of the varieties now common among us. This circumstance, together with their general similarity of structure, has doubtless led to their being almost universally designated as WOLVES. We read of wolves being constantly found in a completely fossilized state, associated with numerous extinct animals, and even with man himself; and considering the difficulty of distinguishing skeletons of the wolf from those of the dog, we have no doubt that many of these fossils belonged to man's natural companion — the dog.

Marcel de Serres observes, in reference to the large size of the fossil dogs which came under his observation, that they bear a stronger resemblance to the animal such as we may suppose him to have been before he came under the influence of man, than most of our domestic canes. Their stature is intermediate between the wolf and the pointer, their muzzle is more elongated, and all the parts of the skeleton are proportionally stronger. But there is no ground for assuming a specific unity among these fossil dogs, any more than among the domesticated races. A careful examination of the bones found in the caves has shown the existence of different sizes, and probably of different species; and inasmuch as we find, in the same caves, remains of animals which have suffered the greatest influence from man, *e. g.* the horse and ox, so we may reasonably infer that these dogs themselves have been contemporaneous with man; especially because no vestiges, either of domestic animals or dogs, have ever been found in countries uninhabited by mankind since the earliest human tradition. The gigantic size of fossil dogs appears less formidable to us than it probably did to M. de Serres, since Rawlinson has figured an enormous dog, from the sculptures of Nineveh, as large as the largest of the extinct animals, and Vaux assures us that a similar species is still living in Thibet. [*Infra*, Chap. XII.] Moreover, the skeleton of an immense dog was recently found in a cave at the Canaries, with remains of the extinct GUANCHES, and thence taken to Paris. Here, however the man may have met his death,

"His faithful dog still bears him company."

Very distinct traces exist, then, of at least four types of dogs, in fossilized state: the Canary dog, the pointer, the hound, and the bull-dog, together with a smaller animal, supposed by Schmerling to have been a turnspit. As we know some of these races to be hybrids, the list must be still further enlarged; for there can be no doubt that many other fossil canidæ appertained to different species of *dogs*. These species enjoy a very respectable antiquity; sufficient, we think, to destroy the claims of the wolf or the jackal to their common paternity: especially, when to our list of species is added the fossil dog discovered by Mr. W. Mantell, in the remote region of New Zealand, associated with the bones of the *Dinornis giganteus*. We have no doubt that MAN himself existed contemporaneously with these fossilized animals, and that both enjoyed an associated antiquity upon earth which has not yet been generally conceded, but cannot much longer be denied. As the hound, baying in our American woods, announces the presence of the hunter, so we may rest assured that a palæontological "fidus Achates" noiselessly implies the proximity of fossil *Man* himself.

Human Fossil Remains have now been found so frequently, and in circumstances so unequivocal, that the facts can hardly be denied; except by persons who resolutely refuse to believe anything that can militate against their own preconceived opinions. Cuvier remarked, long since, that notions in vogue (30 years ago) upon this subject would require considerable modification; and Morton left among his papers a record of his matured views still more emphatically expressed:—

> "There is no good reason for doubting the existence of man in the fossil state. We have already several well-authenticated examples; and we may hourly look for others, even from the upper stratified rocks. Why may we not yet discover them in the tertiary deposits, in the cretaceous beds, or even in the oolites? Contrary to all our preconceived opinions, the latter strata have already afforded the remains of several marsupial animals, which have surprised geologists almost as much as if they had discovered the bones of man himself." *

Human bones, mixed with those of lost mammifers, have been found in several places,—in England, by Dr. Buckland, in the famous cave of Wokey Hole, at Paviland, and Kirkby. The question, whether an equal antiquity should be assigned to such remains with that of extinct inferior species accompanying them — or, in other words, whether man lived at the same time with rhinoceroses, hippopotami, hyenas, and bears, whose entire species have disappeared from earth, bequeathing but their fossil remains to tell us that they once existed— was one of mighty import; and Dr. Buckland, Oxonian Professor, was loth to admit that these remains, human and animal, belonged to beings which had been swept from existence by the same catastrophe. Instances of human fossils had often been reported, but they

* Morton: Posthumous MSS.

were always treated with contemptuous neglect. A fossil skeleton, found in the schist-rock at Quebec, when excavating the fortifications, excited but a moment's incredulous attention; and the well-known Guadaloupe skeletons were pronounced recent, in a manner the most summary. Human bones are known to have been found in England, under circumstances which rendered their fossil condition probable; but, owing to prejudice or ignorance, they were cast aside as worthless, or buried with mistaken reverence. In some instances, they were used, with the limestone in which they were imbedded, to mend highways; and at all times were disposed of without examination, or apparent knowledge of their scientific importance. There is an instance, recorded by Col. Hamilton Smith, which, whether true or not, will serve to show a culpable indifference on this subject. A completely fossilized human body was discovered at Gibraltar, in 1748. The fact is related in a manuscript note, inserted in a copy of a dissertation on the Antiquity of the Earth, by the Rev. James Douglas, read at the Royal Society, in 1785. In substance, it relates that, while the writer himself was at Gibraltar, some miners, employed to blow up rocks for the purpose of raising batteries about fifty feet above the level of the sea, discovered the appearance of a human body; which they blew up, because the officer to whom they sent notice of the fact did not think it worth the trouble of examining! One human pelvis found near Natchez, by Dr. Dickeson, is an undoubted fossil; yet we are told that ferruginous oxides act upon an *os innominatum* differently than upon bones of extinct genera lying in the same stratum, lest natural incidents might give to man, in the valley of the Mississippi, an antiquity altogether incompatible with received ideas: and Sir Charles Lyell accordingly suggests a speedy solution of the difficulty, by saying that a fossilized *pelvis* may have fallen from an old Indian grave near the summit of the cliff. Attempts have been made to throw doubt upon every discovery of human fossils in the same manner; and the greatest ingenuity is exhibited in adapting adequate solutions to the ever-varying dilemmas. In the case of the fossils brought from Brazil, a human skull was taken out of a sandstone rock, now overgrown with lofty trees. Sir Charles Lyell again had recourse to his favorite Indian burying-ground; although this time it had to be sunk beneath the level of the sea, and become again upheaved to its present position. But, supposing all this to be true, what an antiquity must we assign to this Indian skull, when we remember the ancient trees above its grave, and reflect upon the fact that bones of numerous fossil quadrupeds, and, among others, of a horse (both found in the alluvial formation), must be of a more recent origin than the human remains!

Human fossil remains have been most commonly found in caves connected with the diluvium, usually known as ossuaries or bone-caverns. These caves occur, for the most part, in the calcareous strata, as the large caves generally do, and they have been, in all the instances we shall cite, naturally closed until their recent discovery. The floors are covered with what appears to be a bed of diluvial clay, over which a crust of stalagmite has formed since the clay bed was deposited; and it is under this double covering of lime and clay that the bony remains of animals are discovered. As the famous Kirkdale cavern may serve as a general type of caves of this description, we will here give a brief sketch of it: —

The Kirkdale cave is situated on the older portion of the oolite formation — in the coral-rag and Oxford clay — on the declivity of a valley. It extends, as an irregular narrow passage, 250 feet into the hill, expanding here and there into small chambers, but hardly enough anywhere to allow of a man's standing upright. The sides and floor were found covered with a deposite of stalagmite, beneath which there was a bed from two to three feet thick of sandy, micaceous loam, the lower part of which, in particular, contained an innumerable quantity of bones, with which the floor was completely strewn. The animals to which they belonged were the hyena, bear, tiger, lion, elephant, rhinoceros, hippopotamus, horse, ox, three species of deer, water-rat, and mouse — appertaining wholly to extinct species. The most plentiful were hyenas, of which several hundreds were found, and the animals must have been one-half larger than any living species. The bears belonged to the cavernous species, which, according to Cuvier, was of the size of a large horse. The elephants were Siberian mammoths; and of stags, the largest equalled the moose in size. From all the facts observed, Dr. Buckland concluded, that the Kirkdale cave had been for a long series of years a den inhabited by hyenas,* who had dragged into its recesses other animal bodies whose remains are there commingled with their own, at a period antecedent to that submersion which produced the diluvium; because the bones are covered by a bed of this formation. Finally raised from the waters, but with no direct communication with the open air, it remained undisturbed for a long series of ages, during which the clay flooring received a new calcareous covering from the droppings of the roof. Such is a general description of the bone-caves: but it does not apply to all of those which contained human fossils, as we shall presently see.

Apart from the geological formation they are found in, the only

* Buckland: Reliquiæ Diluvianæ.

method of judging of the age of bones is, by the proportions of animal and mineral matters which they retain. Where animal matter is present, the bone is hard without being brittle, and does not adhere to the tongue; when nothing but earthy matter remains, the bone is both brittle and adhesive. If we wish to be more particular in our examination, we treat the bone in question with dilute muriatic acid: the fossil bone, dissolving with effervescence, is reduced to a spongy flocculent mass: whereas the recent bone undergoes a quiet digestion, and after the removal of all the earthy matter, the gelatine still retains the form of the entire bone in a fibrous, flexible, elastic, and translucent state. If both solutions be treated with sulphuric acid, we obtain the same insoluble sulphate of lime from each.

Col. Hamilton Smith mentions several instances, occurring in England, where human bones were found kneaded up in the same osseous breccia, or calcareous paste, with those of extinct animals, wherein the most rigid chemical examination could detect no difference between them. In 1833, the Rev. Mr. M'Enery collected, from the caves of Torquay, human bones and flint knives amongst a great variety of extinct genera—all from under a crust of stalagmite, reposing upon which was the head of a wolf. Caves have been opened at Oreston, near Plymouth, in the Plymouth Hoe, and at Yealm Bridge, in all of which human bones were found, mixed with fossil animal remains. Mr. Bellamy subjected a piece of human bone, from the cave at Yealm Bridge, to treatment by muriatic acid, ascertaining that its animal matter had almost entirely disappeared; while the metatarsal bone of a hyena, from the same cave, *still* retained such an abundance of animal matter that, after separation of the earthy parts, this bone preserved its complete form, was quite translucent, and had all the appearance of a recent specimen. Pieces of human bone, from a sub-Appenine cavern in Tuscany, (probably not less than twenty-five or thirty centuries old, and which had all the appearance of being completely fossilized and even converted into chalk,) when subjected to the searching powers of such muriatic-acid test, revealed their recent origin. And human bones from the Brixham cavern, in England, were in like manner pronounced recent, though it was evident that they had been gnawed by hyenas or other beasts of prey. Not far from the cave whence these were taken, the thoroughly fossilized head of a deer was picked up. This test was also fairly tried in the case (to be presently cited) of sundry human fossils found in the Jura. MM. Ballard and de Serres compared them with some bones taken from a Gaulish sarcophagus, supposed to have been buried for 1400 years, but the fossil bones proved to be much the more ancient.

It may be granted, that Dr. Buckland was justified in concluding from the instances which came under his observation, that whenever human bones were discovered mixed with those of animals, they must have been introduced at a later period; but even Cardinal Wiseman admits that there are cases of an entirely different character.*

The cave of Durfort, in the Jura, has been examined and described by MM. Firmas and Marcel de Serres. It is situated in a calcareous mountain, about 300 feet above the level of the sea, and is entered by a perpendicular shaft, twenty feet deep. You enter the cavern by a narrow passage from this shaft, and there find human bones in a true fossil state, and completely incorporated in a calcareous matrix. A still more accurate examination, attended with the same results, was made, by M. de Serres, of certain bones found in tertiary limestone at Pondres, in the department of the Hérault. Here M. de Cristolles discovered human bones and pottery, mixed with the remains of the rhinoceros, bear, hyena, and many other animals. They were imbedded in mud and fragments of the limestone rock of the neighborhood; this accumulation, in some places, being thirteen feet thick. These human fossils were proved, on a careful examination, to have parted with their animal matter as completely as those bones of hyenas which accompanied them; and they furthermore came out triumphantly from a comparison with the osseous relics of the long-buried Gaul, as just related.

A fossil human skeleton is preserved in the Museum at Quebec, which was dug out of the solid schist-rock on which the citadel stands; and two more skeletons from Guadaloupe are deposited, one in the British Museum, and the other in the Royal Cabinet at Paris. The skeleton in the British Museum is headless; but its cranium is supposed to be recovered in the one found in Guadaloupe by M. L'Herminier, and carried by him to Charleston, South Carolina. Dr. Moultrie, who has described this very interesting relic, says that it possesses all the characteristics which mark the American race in general.† The rock in which these skeletons were found is described as being harder, under the chisel, than the finest statuary marble.

Dr. Schmerling has examined a large number of localities in France and Liege, particularly the "caverne d'Engihoul;" where bones of man occurred, together with those of animals of extinct species: the human fossils being found, in all respects, under the same circumstances of age and position as the animal remains.‡ Near these relics, works of art were sometimes disclosed; such as fragments of ancient urns, and vases of clay, teeth of dogs and foxes pierced with holes

* Lectures on the Connection between Science and Revealed Religion, by Nicholas Wiseman, D. D. London, 1849.

† Morton: Physical Type of American Indians. ‡ Recherches, I. pp. 59–66.

and doubtless worn as amulets. Tiedemann exhumed, in caverns of Belgium, human bones, mixed with those of bears, elephants, hyenas, horses, wild boars, and ruminants. These human relics were precisely like those they were associated with, in respect to the changes either had undergone in color, hardness, degree of decomposition, and other marks of fossilization. In the caves of France and Belgium, we often find, in the deepest and most inaccessible places, far remote from any communication with the surface, human bones buried in the clayey deposit, and cemented fast to the sides and walls. On every side, we may see crania imbedded in clay, and often accompanied by the teeth or bones of hyenas. In breccias containing the bones of rodents and the teeth of horses and rhinoceroses, we also meet with human fossils.

There are many other cases on record, of human remains being found associated with animal fossils, both in England and on the Continent. As well at Kitely as at Brixham, such associations have been noticed; and there can be little doubt that human fossils exist in caverns and formations beneath the present level of the sea: *e.g.* at Plymouth and other places, where remains of elephants have been washed up by the surf.

In the caverns of Bizé, in France, human bones and shreds of pottery turned up in the red clay, mixed with remains of extinct animals; and on the Rhine, they have been found in connection with skulls of gigantic bisons, uri, and other extinct species. The cave of Gailenreuth, in Franconia, is situated in a perpendicular rock, its mouth being upwards of 300 feet above the level of the river. Those of Zahnloch and Kühloch are similarly elevated; and the latter is supposed to have contained the vestiges of at least 2500 cavern-bears; while the cave of Copfingen, in the Suabian Alps, is not less than 2500 feet above the sea. These caves contained collections of human and of animal remains; while their elevation places them above the reach of any partial inundations. Ossuaries in the vale of Kostritz, Upper Saxony, are more interesting, because they have been more carefully studied. They are situated in the gypsum quarries; and the undulating country about them is too elevated to permit of their deposits having been influenced, in the least, by those inundations which are made to answer for such a multitude of sins. No partial inundation could possibly have disturbed them since the present geological arrangement; nor were there external openings or indications of any kind revealing the existence of an extensive cave within. The soil is the usual ossiferous loam, and the stalagmite rests upon it as in other caverns. Beneath these deposits, human and animal fossils have been discovered, at a depth of twenty feet. These deposits were first described by Baron von Schlotheim, who concludes his account with these remarks: —

"It is evident that the human bones could not have been buried here, nor have fallen into fissures during battles in ancient times. They are few, completely isolated, and detached. Nor could they have been thus mutilated and lodged by any other accidental cause in more modern times, inasmuch as they are always found with the other animal remains, under the same relations — not constituting connected skeletons, but gathered in various groups."

Besides those of man at different periods of life, from infancy to mature age, bones of the rhinoceros, of a great feline, of hyena, horse, ox, deer, hare, and rabbit, were found; to which owl, elephant, elk, and reindeer relics have since been added. Specimens of the human fossils are in possession of the Baron, of the Prince of Reuss, Dr. Schotte, and other gentlemen residing near the spot; and Mr. Fairholme, who visited Saxony expressly to satisfy himself of the facts by a careful examination of the locality, brought specimens to England, which he presented to the British Museum. It is worthy of being noted here, that the above bones were not all entombed in caverns or fissures, but that some human fossils were dug out of the clay, at a depth of eighteen feet, and eight feet below the remains of a rhinoceros.* Enough has thus been said upon fossil *Man* disinterred accidentally in that Old World which, in natural phenomena, is actually younger than the "New."

Crossing from Europe to our own continent, we behold, in the Academy of Sciences at Philadelphia, a fossilized human fragment, surpassingly curious, if of disputed antiquity: —

"Dr. Dickeson presented another relic of yet greater interest: viz., the fossil *Os innominatum* of the human subject, taken from the above-mentioned stratum of blue clay [near Natchez, Mississippi], and about two feet below the skeletons of the megalonyx and other genera of extinct quadrupeds; . . . that of a young man of sixteen years of age." † . . .

"Ten of these interesting relics [of the fossil *horse*], consisting of five superior and inferior molars, Dr. Dickeson relates, were obtained, together with remains of the *megalonyx, ursus*, the *os hominis innominatum fossile*, &c., in the vicinity of Natchez, Mississippi, from a stratum of tenacious blue clay, underlying a diluvial deposit." ‡

Aware of the critical objections to this fossil put forward by Lyell, we neither affirm nor deny its antiquity by mentioning that Morton, and other palæontologists, did not consider these demurrers conclusive: nor is much geological erudition requisite to comprehend that, under the atmospheric conditions in which a *horse* and a *bear* could inhale the breath of life, a human mammifer might equally well have respired it with them.

* Hamilton Smith: Natural History of the Human Species. Edinburgh, 1848; p. 93–107.

† Proceed. Acad. Nat. Sciences, Philad.; October, 1846, p. 107.

‡ Leidy: On the Fossil Horse of America, *op. cit.*, Sept. 1847, p. 265. *Vide*, also, Proceedings Acad. Nat. Sciences; Dec. 1847, p. 328.

How comes it that, with the exception of brief notices by Morton, the subjoined unequivocal instance of American fossil man has been generally overlooked for a quarter of a century? His fossil bones were discovered by Capt. J. D. Elliott, U. S. N., and are now in the Academy of Natural Sciences at Philadelphia: eight fossilized human relics, besides

"A specimen of the rock of which the mound is composed, and in which the skeletons are imbedded. It consists of fragments of shells united by a stalactic matter."

Dr. Meigs philosophically remarked, twenty-six years ago: —

The present specimens are particularly interesting, inasmuch as they belong to the American continent, and as adding another link to that chain of testimony concerning the early occupation of this soil, of which the remains are so few and unsatisfactory, but of which another link, a strong analogue exists in the Island of Guadaloupe, in good measure neglected or disregarded, on account of its loneliness or want of connection with similar facts." *

Here, then, is one "homo Diluvii *negator*," to be coupled with Dr. Dowler's sub-cypress Indian, who dwelt on the site of New Orleans 57,600 years ago.

The next most important and valuable contribution to this department of knowledge, in every point of view, has been made by the distinguished Danish naturalist, Dr. Lund, who has given an interesting account of the calcareous caves of Brazil, so peculiarly rich in animal remains. He discovered human fossils in *eight* different localities, all bearing marks of a geological antiquity. In some instances, the human bones were not accompanied by those of animals. In the province of Minas Geraes, human skeletons, in a fossil state, were found among the remains of forty-four species of extinct animals, among which was a fossil horse. This learned traveller discovered both the human and the animal reliques under circumstances which lead to the irresistible conclusion that all of them were once contemporaneous inhabitants of the region in which their several vestiges occur. With respect to the race of these fossil men, Dr. Lund found that the form of the cranium differed in no respect from the acknowledged American type; proper allowance being made for the artificial depression of the forehead. The peculiarity in the arrangement of the teeth has been noticed elsewhere.

In a cave on the borders of a lake called Lagoa Santa, Dr. Lund again collected multifarious human bones, in the same condition with those of numerous extinct species of animals. They belonged to at least thirty different individuals, of every age, from creeping infancy to tottering decrepitude, and of both sexes; and were evidently de-

* An Account of some Human Bones, found on the Coast of Brazil, near Santas; latitude 24° 30′′ S., longitude 46° W. By C. D. Meigs, M. D. Read 7th December, 1827: *Trans. Amer. Philos. Soc.;* Philad. 1830, iii. pp. 286–291.

posited where the bodies lay with the soft parts entire: immense blocks of stone with which Nature had partly covered them, bearing unanswerable testimony to the great revolutions which the cave had undergone since their introduction into it.

These bones were thoroughly incorporated with a very hard breccia, every one in the fossil state. A single specimen of an extinct family of apes, *callithrix primævus*, was found among them; but large numbers of rodents, carnivora, and tardigrades, were intermixed promiscuously with the human fossils. All their geological relations unite to show, that they were entombed in their present position at a time long previous to the formation of that lake on whose borders the cavern is situated; thereby leaving no doubt of the coexistence, in life, of the whole of the beings thus associated in death. These facts establish not only that South America was inhabited by an ancient people, long before the discovery of the New Continent, or that the population of this part of the world must have preceded all historical notice of their existence: they demonstrate that aboriginal man in America antedates the Mississippi alluvia, because his bones are *fossilized;* and that he can even boast of a geological antiquity, because numerous species of animals have been blotted from creation since American humanity's first appearance. The form of these crania, moreover, proves that the general *type* of races inhabiting America at that inconceivably-remote era was the same which prevailed at the period of the Columbian discovery: and this consideration may spare science the trouble of any further speculation on the modus through which the New World became peopled by immigration from the Old; for, after carrying backwards the existence of a people monumentally into the very night of time, when we find that they have also preserved the same TYPE back to a more remote, even to a *geological*, period, there can be no necessity for going abroad to seek their origin.

Thus much information, upon *fossil man* in America, was common property of the authors of this volume and the writer, until March, 1853: and such, in substance, were the consequent ethnological deductions in which they coincided. However convinced themselves, in regard to the real fossiliferous antiquity of the *os innominatum* unearthed by Dr. Dickeson from the bluffs near Natchez, they were aware of the conditions obnoxious to its special acceptance as evidence in court; and would, therefore, have cheerfully resigned, to their fellow-continentals of South America, the honor of exhibiting the oldest human remains upon the oldest continent, but for an unanticipated event, which enables North America to claim (in human palæontology at least) a republican equality.

Prof. Agassiz, during March and April, favored Mobile with a

Course of Lectures; the sixth of which (concisely, but admirably, reported in our "Daily Tribune" *) bore directly upon the themes discussed in *Types of Mankind*. The subjects of the present work were passed in daily review, while the Professor sojourned amongst us. We need not recapitulate the obvious advantages its readers in consequence derive. Its authors and the writer consider the following abstract to be, in all senses of the word, a *memorandum*: —

"Respecting the fossil remains of the human body I possess, from Florida, I can only state, that the identity with human bones is beyond all question; the parts preserved being the *jaws with perfect teeth*, and *portions of a foot*. They were discovered by my friend, Count F. de Pourtalès, in a bluff upon the shores of Lake Monroe, in Florida. The mass in which they were found is a conglomerate of rotten coral-reef limestone and shells, mostly ampullarias of the same species now found in the St. John river, which drains lake Monroe. The question of their age is more difficult to answer. To understand it fully, it must be remembered that the whole peninsula of Florida has been formed by the successive growth of coral reefs, added concentrically from north to south to those first formed, and the accumulation between them of decomposed corals and fragments of shells; the corals prevailing in some parts, as in the everglades; and in others, the shells, as about St. Augustine and Cape Sable. In all these deposits, we find remains of the animals now living along the coasts of Florida, sometimes buried in limestone as hard and compact as the rocks of the Jurassic formation. I have masses of this coral rock, containing parts of the skeleton of a large sea-turtle, which might be mistaken for turtle-limestone of Soleure, from the Upper Jura. Upon this marine-limestone formation and its inequalities, fresh-water lakes have been collected; inhabited by animals the species of which are now still in existence, as are also, along the shores, the marine animals, remains of which may be found in the coral formation. To this lacustrine formation belongs the conglomerate containing the human bones mentioned above; and it is more than I can do, to establish, with precision, the date of its deposition. This, however, is certain, that Upper Florida, as far south as the headwaters of the St. John, constituted already a prominent peninsula before Lake Okeechobee was formed; and that the whole of the southern extremity of Florida, with the everglades, has been added to that part of the continent since the basin has been in existence, in which the conglomerate with human bones has been accumulating. The question, then, to settle, (in order to determine the probable age of this anthropolithic conglomerate,) is, the rate of increase of the peninsula of Florida in its southward progress: remembering that the southernmost extremity of Florida extends for more than three degrees of latitude south of the fresh-water system of the northern part of the peninsula. If we assume that rate of growth to be one foot in a century, from a depth of seventy-five feet, and that every successive reef has added ten miles of extent to the peninsula, (which assumption is doubling the rate of increase furnished by the evidence we now have of the additions forming upon the reef and keys south of the mainland,) it would require 135,000 years to form the southern half of the peninsula.† Now, assuming further—which would be granting by far too much—that the surface of the northern half of the peninsula, already formed, continued for nine-tenths of that time a desert waste, upon which the fresh waters began to accumulate before the fossiliferous conglomerate could be formed, (though we have no right to assume that it stood so for any great length of time) there would still remain 10,000 years, during which, it should be admitted, that the mainland was inhabited by man and the land

* "The Lecture of Agassiz;" *Mobile Daily Tribune*, April 14, 1853.

† "Say 100,000 years, since which time at least the marine animals, now living along the coast of Florida, have been in existence; for their remains are found in the coral limestone of the everglades, as well as in that of the keys, and upon the reef now growing up outside of them."

and fresh-water animals, vestiges of which have been buried in the deposits formed by the fresh waters covering parts of its surface. So much for the probable age of our conglomerate. . . . L. AGASSIZ."

MAN, absolutely fossilized, exists therefore in North America.

We have shown that the alluvion of our river beds and deltas possesses an antiquity, which would permit of the existence of man upon the earth at a much more remote period than has been commonly assigned to him. We have given instances of his exhumation also in the fossil state. The human fossils of Brazil and Florida carry back the aboriginal population of this continent far beyond any necessity of hunting for American man's foreign origin through Asiatic immigration: and the body of one Indian beneath the cypress forests at New Orleans is certainly more ancient than the lost "tribes of Israel," to whom the American type has been rather fancifully attributed.

Man's vast antiquity can now be proved, moreover, by his works as well as by his fossil remains. Authentic relics of human art have been, at last, found in the diluvian drift. This drift, with its beds of rolled stones, the detritus of older rocks, its masses of sand and gravel, and the traces of its passage over mountain and plain in almost every region of the earth, is vulgarly regarded as furnishing irrefragable evidence of the Noachian deluge; as, indeed, every remarkable geological appearance was supposed to prove the universality of that visitation. The numerous bones of the elephant, the rhinoceros, and other extinct species of quadrupeds, occurring in this deposit, were commonly denominated "antediluvian remains," and assumed to be unquestionable vestiges of the "world before the flood!" Among *such* remains, in deposits clearly belonging to the diluvial epoch, traces of human industry are revealed, of an indisputable character. For these revelations from an earlier world we are chiefly indebted to the zeal and liberality of M. Boucher de Perthes, who has given us an extraordinary work on the primitive industry of man.* In 1835, M. Ravin † published a description of a "*Pirogue Gauloise*," found under the turf at Estrebœuf on the Somme; and in the same year M. Picard described an ornament made of the teeth of the wild boar, and some very ancient axe-sheaths, &c., disclosed in a similar situation near Picquigny. These researches, interrupted by the death of M. Picard, were subsequently resumed by M. Boucher de Perthes; who pursued them until 1849, when he published the result of his truly arduous labors.

M. de Perthes caused numerous excavations to be made in the Celtic

* Antiquités Celtiques et Antédiluviennes: Mémoire sur l'Industrie primitive, et les arts à leur origine: par M. Boucher de Perthes — Paris, 1849.

† Mémoires de la Société d'Emulation d'Abbeville — 1835.

burial-places, and in diluvian beds, over the departments of the Somme and Seine; besides examining all subterranean localities brought to light by the works of civil and military engineers, during a period of ten years. He did not succeed in finding fossil human remains in the diluvian deposits, but he has produced what he considers their equivalent: because, among relics of elephants and mastodons, and even below these fossils, at a depth where no archæologist had ever suspected traces of man, he discovered weapons, utensils, figures, signs, and symbols, which must have been the work of a surpassingly-ancient people.

Besides his researches in the diluvian beds, he opened many mounds and burial-places, Gaulish, Celtic, and of unknown origin, some of them evidently of extreme antiquity: and he describes successive beds of bones and ashes, separated from each other by strata of turf and tufa, with no less than five different stages of cinerary urns, belonging to distinct generations, of which the oldest were deposited *below* the woody or diluvian turf. The coarse structure of these vases, (made by hand and dried in the sun,) and the rude utensils of bone, or roughly-carved stone, by which they were surrounded, together with their position, announce their appertaining, if not to the earliest ages of the world, at least to a far more remote antiquity than has usually been assigned to such ceramic remains.

"In the various excavations made in the course of these inquiries, we become acquainted with successive periods of civilization, which correspond with the written history of the country. Thus, after passing through the first stratum of the soil, we come to relics of the middle ages; and then meet, in regular order, with traces of the Roman, the Gallic, the Celtic, and the diluvian epochs. It is always in the neighborhood of lakes and rivers that we find vestiges of the most numerous and ancient people. If their banks were not the earliest seats of human habitations, they were probably the most constant, and when once settled were seldom afterwards deserted. This was owing to water, the first necessary of life, and surest pledge of fertility; and to the abundance of fish and game, so indispensable to a hunting people. We may add, that all ancient people had a superstitious reverence for great waters, and made them the favorite resorts of their gods. On the banks of their rivers they deposited the ashes of chiefs and relatives, and there they desired to be buried themselves. The possession of these banks was, therefore, an object of general ambition, and became the continual subject of war and conquest. This explains the accumulation of relics which sometimes covers them, and which, on the banks of the Somme and the Seine, conducts us from the middle ages, through the Roman and the Gaulish soils, back to the Celtic period." *

We have nothing to do now with the comparatively-modern history of the Gauls; the excellent works of MM. de Caumont and Thierry may be consulted on that subject: our business is with the Celtic soil, the cradle of the people, the earth trodden by the primordial population of Gaul.

---

* Ibid. — Antiquités Celtiques.

"Here we naturally inquire, who were these mysterious Celts, these primitive inhabitants of Gaul? We are told that this part of Europe is of modern origin, or at least of recent population. Its annals scarcely reach to twenty centuries, and even its traditions do not exceed 2500 years. The various people who have occupied it, the Galls, the Celts, the Belgians, the Veneti, Ligurians, Iberians, Cymbrians, and Scythians, have left no vestige to which we can assign that date. The traces of those nomadic tribes who ravaged Gaul scarcely precede the Christian era by a few centuries. Was Gaul then a desert before this period? Was its sun less genial, or its soil less fertile? Were not its hills as pleasant, and its plains and valleys as ready for the harvest? Or, if men had not yet learned to plough and sow, were not its rivers filled with fish, and its forests with game? And, if the land abounded with everything calculated to attract and support a population, why should it not have been inhabited? The absence of great ruins would indicate that Gaul, at this period, and even much later, had not attained a high degree of civilization, nor been the seat of powerful kingdoms; but why should it not have had its towns and villages? or, rather, why should it not, like the steppes of Russia, the prairies and virgin forests of America, and the fertile plains of Africa, have been overrun from time immemorial by tribes of men, savages perhaps, but, nevertheless, united in families if not in nations?"

Those circles of upright stones, of which Stonehenge is the most familiar example, are admitted to be of great antiquity, but no one can tell how far back that antiquity may extend. They are found throughout Europe, from Norway to the Mediterranean; and they must have been erected by a numerous people, (being faithful exponents of a general sentiment,) since we find them in so many countries. They are commonly called Celtic or Druidical, but it would be hard to say on what authority; or, in what circumstances and for what purpose those mysterious Druids erected them. Having neither date nor inscription, they must be older than written language; for people who can write never leave their own names and exploits uncelebrated. The ancients were as ignorant on this subject as ourselves; and, at the period of the Roman invasion, the origin of those monuments was already shrouded in obscurity. Neither Roman historians nor Christian chroniclers have been able to throw any light upon their unknown founders. Even tradition is silent. Political or religious monuments, they were probably the first temples, the first altars, or the first trophies vowed to the gods, to victory, and to the memory of warriors; for among all people the ravages of war were deified before the benefits of peace: man has always venerated the slayer of man. The people who erected them are entirely forgotten; and they must have been separated from the living generations by an extreme antiquity, as well as by some great and overwhelming social revolution, probably involving the entire destruction of their nation. Being unable, then, to attribute these monuments either to the Rōmans or the Gauls, sciolists have ignorantly termed them Celtic or Druidic; not because they were raised originally by Druids, but because they had been used in the Druidical worship, though erected for other uses, or dedicated to other divinities. In like manner did the temples of Paganism afterwards serve for the solemnities of Christianity.

We have cited the example of these Celtic temples as a standard of comparison; for, if their antiquity is so extreme as to be entirely lost out of our sight, what date shall we assign to human works found at a considerable distance below their foundations? In the same soil upon which these druidical monuments stand, but many feet beneath their base, numbers of those stone wedges, commonly called Celtic axes, have been discovered; and these, with other similar instruments, only varying in the finish of their workmanship, according to the depth at which they are found, have been collected at different levels, even as low down as the diluvian drift.

The annexed cut represents a section of an alluvial formation at

FIG. 203.

ALLUVIAL DEPOSITES AT PORTELETTE, *showing the Arrangement of the Soil and the Sepultures.*

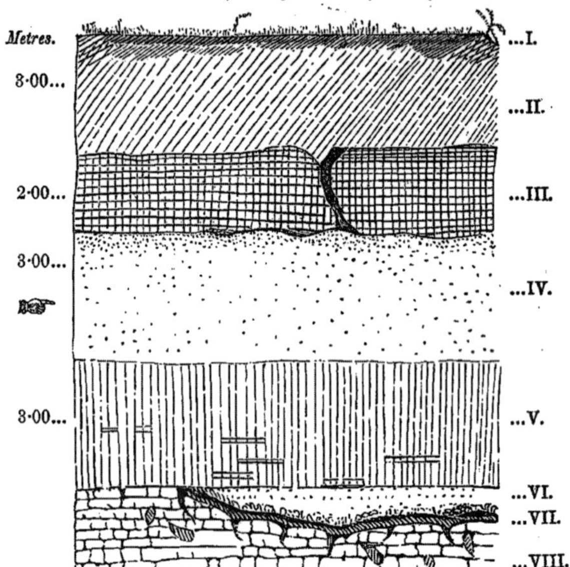

☞ Indicates the level of the actual waters of the Somme, whose depth is three metres.

I. Alluvial formation.
II. Vegetable soil — covering transported earth or rubble.
III. Calcareous tufa — porous, and containing compact masses.
IV. Muddy sand — blue, and very fine.
V. Turf — containing Celtic antiquities; indicated by ═.
VI. Muddy sand.
VII. Detrital diluvium — rolled silex, &c.
VIII. White chalk.

Portelette, on the Somme, where some beautiful specimens of Celtic axes were obtained. At a depth of nine feet, a large quantity of bones was found; and one foot lower, a piece of deer's horn, bearing marks of human workmanship. At twenty feet from the surface, and five feet below the bed of the river, three axes, highly finished, and perfectly preserved, turned up in a bed of turf. Some axe-cases of stag's horn were also discovered in the same bed. Near these objects was a coarse vase of black pottery, very much broken, and surrounded with a black mass of decomposed pottery — there were also large quantities of wrought bones, human and animal. The entire bones were those of the boar, urus, bull, dog, and horse; but none of man. In another locality, in the neighborhood of Portelette, the skull of a man was found. Here was evidently a Celtic sepulchre. The axes were entirely new, bearing no marks of use, and were doubtless votive offerings. This case is only cited to show that the same kind of utensils extend from the comparatively recent Celtic back to far remoter diluvian and antediluvian epochas. We annex sketches of the deer's-horn axe-cases (Figs. 204 and 205), because in the more

FIG. 204.

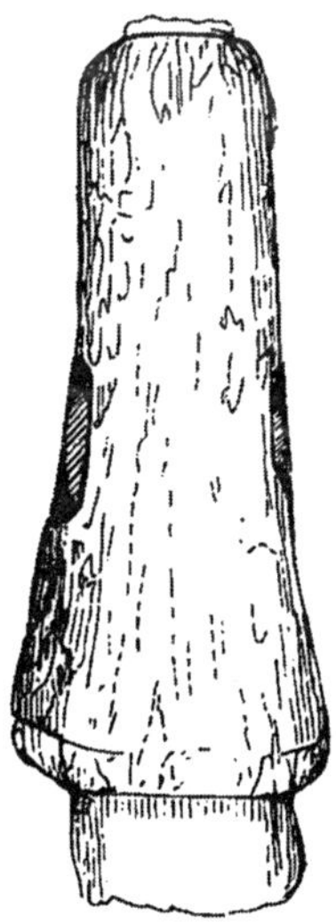

FIG. 205.

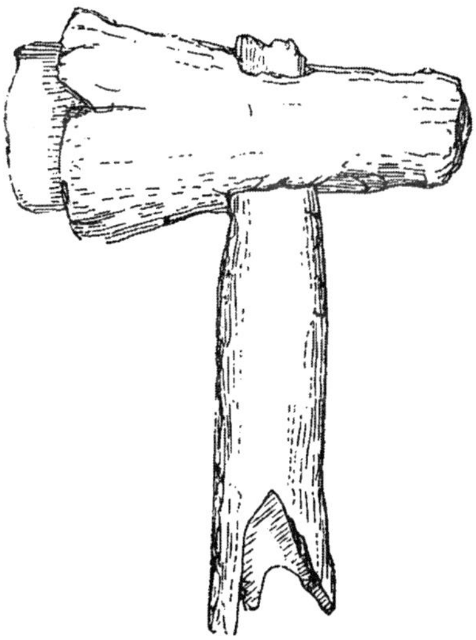

Celtic buck-horn "Axe-Cases."*

ancient excavations none were discovered. Fig. 204 is an axe-case made of the horn of a "stag of ten," and is six inches in length, two inches

* Boucher, Pl. I.

wide at one end, and a little more than one inch wide at the other. Around the opening intended to receive the stone, a line has been drawn by way of ornament. The axe is of grayish silex, polished along its whole length, and is three inches long, and one inch and a half wide. At the upper end of the case, broken remains of a large wild boar's tusk were firmly driven into the horn; while the axe itself was very loose, and seems always to have been so — the looseness being increased by its smooth polish. It was evidently intended to be thrown, or detached from the case, whenever a blow was struck with it. The handle of this axe was twenty inches long, made of oak, and in a tolerable state of preservation; but became reduced one-half in drying, by crumbling and splitting off in flakes. Carelessly worked, it had been hardened at both ends in the fire. This was the only wooden handle found — some being of bone, and many others entirely decomposed.

Fig. 205 was an axe-case and axe similar in most respects to Fig. 204, except its handle of horn.

A great variety of other instruments, made of deer's horn, occurred in this and other alluvial excavations; but as our main concern is with those of higher antiquity, we must pass them by without notice, and proceed to the diluvian vestiges.

In the gravel-pits of Menchecourt, on the Somme, M. de Perthes found a number of stone axes and other works, associated with the remains of extinct animals. The character of this formation is marked by erratic blocks and the organic remains which it contains: the erratic blocks being here represented by boulders of sandstone, and by massive flints, which have been visibly rolled and rounded, despite of their weight. Its organic remains are chiefly those of the elephant, the rhinoceros, hippopotamus, bear, hyena, stag, ox, urus, and other mammalia, of races either extinct or foreign to the present climate, belonging to the diluvian epoch. In the post-diluvian or alluvial formations already spoken of, only living or indigenous species are met with; and the human bones are mixed with scoriæ, worked metals, pieces of pottery, and other vestiges of the civilization of the period to which these buried men belonged. The alluvia, whatever be the materials which compose them, are easily recognized through the horizontal position of their beds. Such regular stratifications do not exist in the *Diluvial* formations. Here different sands, gravels, marls, broken and rolled flints, everywhere scattered in disturbed beds, and repeated at irregular distances, announce the movement of a great mass of water and the devastating action of a furious current. Indeed it is scarcely possible to be deceived in the diluvial character of these formations, or to confound them with a posterior deposit. Everything announces the diluvial origin of these beds at Menchecourt: the total absence of modern relics and of any remains of recent animals; the large lumps of silex; the scattered boulders; the pure sands (yellow, green, and black), sometimes in distinct layers, at other times mixed with the silex whose *couches*, descending to a great depth, rise again immediately to the surface of the soil. Such is the character of these formations; wherein we meet at every step the traces of an immense catastrophe, especially in valleys where the diluvian waters had precipitated the ruins accumulated in their course.*

M. Baillon, speaking of this locality, says:—

"We begin to find bones at the depth of ten or twelve feet, in the gravel of Menchecourt; but they are more plentiful at eighteen or twenty feet deep. Among them are bones which were bruised and broken before they were entombed, and others whose angles have been rounded by friction in water; but neither of these are found as deep as those which remain entire. These last are deposited at the bottom of the gravel bed; they are whole, being neither rounded nor broken, and were probably articulated at the time of their deposition. I found the whole hind leg of a rhinoceros, the bones of which were still in their proper relative position. They must have been connected by ligaments, and even covered with muscles, at the time of their destruction. The rest of the skeleton of the same animal lay at a small distance. I have remarked that whenever we meet with bones disposed in this manner—that is to say, articulated—we also find that the sand has formed a hard agglomeration against one side of them."

Subjoined is a list of the mammifers discovered by M. Baillon in the sands of Menchecourt: namely, elephant, rhinoceros, fossil horse (of medium size and more slender form than the living species), felis spelea, canis speleus, hyena, bear, stag, and bos bombifrons of Harlan. A scale from the neck of a great crocodile was also exhumed from gravel of Menchecourt, being only the third instance in which traces of that saurian had been found, thus associated, in Europe: once at Brentford in England, once in the diluvial beds of the Val d'Arno, and once at Menchecourt.†

We have said that, among these diluvian remains, (amid bones of elephants, rhinoceroses, and crocodiles, under many beds of sand and gravel, and at a depth of several feet below the modern soil,) vestiges of *human industry* had been met with; and we now give a section of the locality (Fig. 106) from which flint axes, agglutinated with a mass of bones and sand, were procured. These axes were taken from the ossiferous beds; one at four and a half metres, or nearly thirteen feet, and the other at nine metres, or about twenty-seven feet, below the surface. The character of the soil and of the superposed layers of compact sand, free from any appearance of modern detritus, forbids a supposition that they could ever have reached such a depth through accident since the formation of the bed itself, or by any infiltration from

* Boucher de Perthes; p. 217–246. † Cuvier: Ossemens Fossiles.

Section of the Gravel-Beds at Menchecourt.*

Fig. 206.

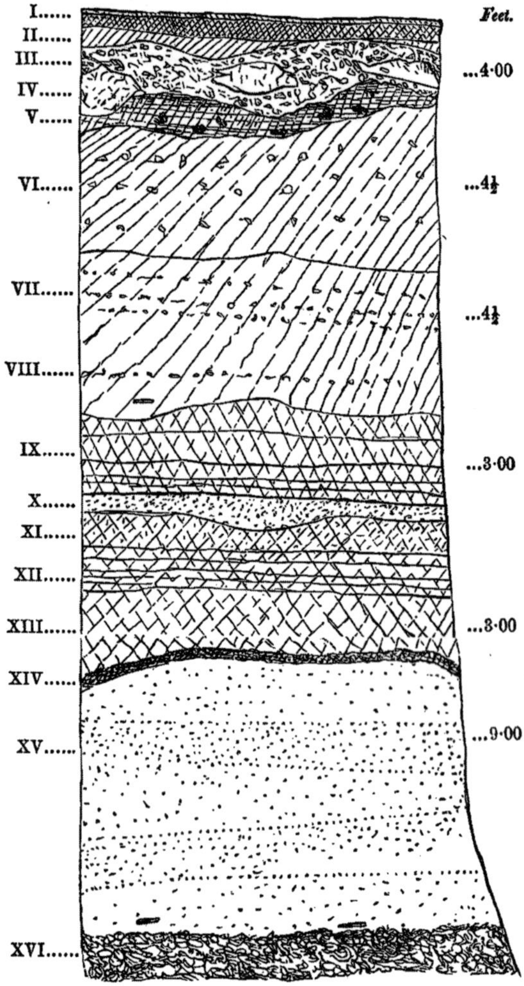

---

* *Modern*, or *Alluvial.*
- I. Superficial vegetable earth — humus.
- II. Lower vegetable — argillaceous.

Diluvian, or *Clysmian of Brongniart.*
- III. Brown clay.
- IV. Upper bed of silex — rolled and broken, with lumps of white marl and rolled chalk, in amygdaloid fragments.
- V. Compact ferruginous clay.

a superior level: because, in such cases, some trace must have been left of their occurrence. No doubt exists that those axes had lain in the same position ever since the fossilized bones were there, or that they were brought thither by the same causes.

Many other excavations were examined, as opportunities occurred; and stones bearing unmistakeable evidence of human workmanship were discovered so frequently in the *drift*, as to establish the fact beyond all room for question. The occurrence of similar axes in sepulchres of the Celtic era, might otherwise support the idea that they had found their way by subsidence from upper to lower levels; but the character of the formation, as before remarked, renders such contingencies highly improbable, if not impossible; and it seems much more likely that old diluvian remains were discovered by a more modern people, who adopted these ancient tools in later funebral ceremonies. But it is not necessary to assume either hypothesis: the same wants would suggest similar utensils. Forms, venerated as symbolical of any religious rite or sentiment, are very permanent, especially among a rude people: and, whether we suppose the more ancient race to have been entirely destroyed, and succeeded by another after a catastrophe, or the same type to have continued through that long period which must have elapsed between the diluvian and the Celtic epochas, the circumstance that the same instruments are found in both positions is not attended with any insuperable difficulties. Indeed, Indian axes, discovered by Mr. Squier in our Western mounds, are so precisely similar in form and material to those we have been describing, that one should not be much surprised at seeing them adduced, by some sapient advocate of the unity of human races, as decisive proofs of the Celtic origin of American Indians.

The annexed cuts (Figs. 207 and 208) represent different sections

Clysmien Limoneux of Brongniart.	*Limono-détritique.*	VI.	Marly clay, with broken flints, white externally.
		VII.	Marly sand, containing bones of mammifers.
	Clayey and sandy.	VIII.	Beds of rolled chalk, in pisiform fragments, mixed with siliceous gravel.
		IX.	White clay.
		X.	White sand.
		XI.	Gray sandy clay.
		XII.	Clay and sand, ochry, in veins.
		XIII.	Pure gray clay.
		XIV.	Ochry vein.
Clysmian detritic.	*Sandy.*	XV.	Alternate beds, slightly oblique, with shells and diluvian bones.
	Flinty.	XVI.	Lower bed of flints, rolled and broken.

— _ — These marks show the position of the flint-axes.

of a bank at Abbeville;* after excavations made by military engineers, while repairing the fortifications of the place. Here, in a bed of gravel some eight feet below the surface, fossil bones of an elephant were found; and, immediately below them, a flint knife; while at a still lower level, stone axes were discovered.

The existence of human works in Gallic diluvian drift, appears to be proven. Similar works have also been found in the alluvium of the same localities: and, inasmuch as the best geologists say that each of these formations may have occupied myriads of years, it will be interesting to trace connexions between the two periods. This we shall now attempt by an examination of some rude mementos of those ancient times entombed in mother earth. In later Celtic sepulchres, (besides stone axes, of regular shape and high polish,) numerous utensils wrought from deers' horns were discovered, of which we have given specimens when treating of axes.

---

* 1st. Section of Diluvian Beds at the Ramparts of Abbeville.

Fig. 207.

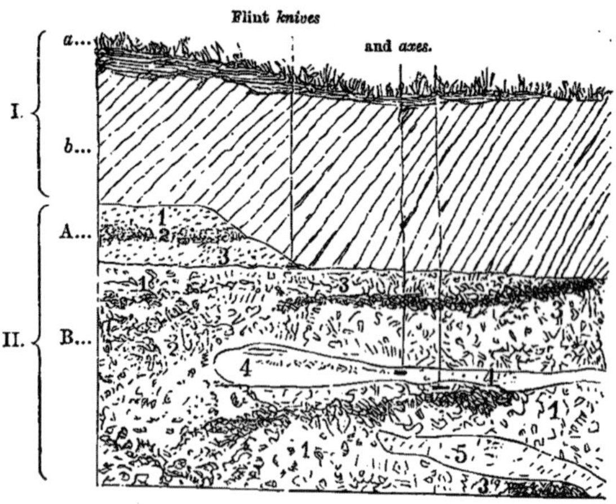

I. Recent.—Thickness 6 feet.
a. Vegetable mould.
b. Rubble.
II. Diluvian formation (clysmien Br.).
A. First bed—1½.
1. Yellow sand—argillo-ferruginous.
2. Silex, rolled and broken, mixed with gravel.
3. Green sand.
B. Second bed—détritique Br.—9·00.
1111. Masses of silex, rolled and broken, mixed with gravel and ferruginous sand. Below this mass the silex tends to form oblique beds.
2. The same silex, forming a large band in green sand.
3 3 3. The same silex, forming sinuous veins in black sand, colored by carbon from the decomposition of lignite.
4 4. Vein of white sand, containing a layer of silex and bands of clay.
5. Veins of green sand—16.
☰. Celtic instruments found in the diluvian mass.

Fig. 209.

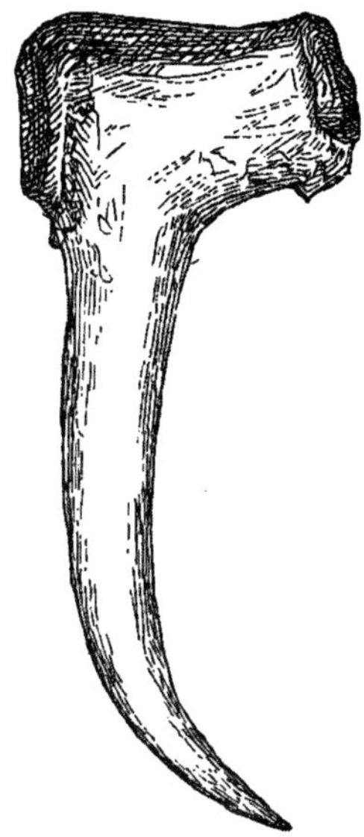

Celtic hammer, of buck-horn.*

An instance of the early use of deers' horn, (mentioned by Dr. Wilson in his Memoir on the pre-Celtic races of Scotland, read before the British Association for 1850,) may be here cited. Remains of a fossil whale have recently been exhumed in Blair Drummond Moss, seven miles above Stirling bridge, and twenty miles from the nearest point of the river Forth where by any possibility a whale could be naturally stranded. Nevertheless, a rude harpoon of deers' horn, found along with the cetaceous mammal, proves that this *fossilized whale* pertains to, and falls within, human historical periods; at the same time that it points to an era subsequent to man's first colonization of the British Isles.

Sketches of other instruments, made of the same material, equally illustrate the rude state of Celtic arts. Fig. 209, made of an antler and part of the horn attached to the head, was used as

---

2nd. Transverse Section — Abbeville ramparts.

Fig. 208.

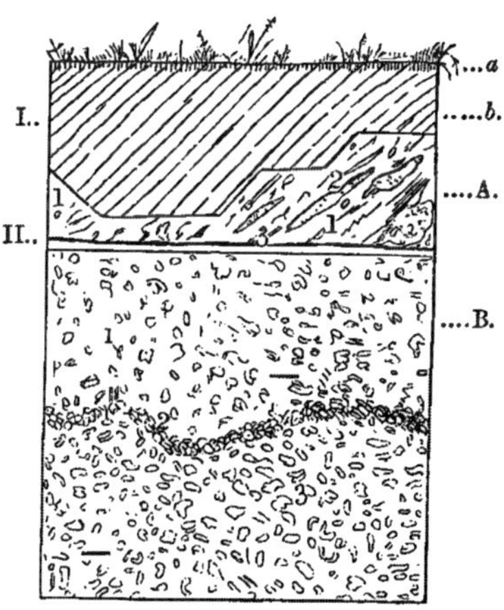

I. Recent.
  a. Vegetable earth.
  b. Transported earth.
II. Diluvian formation (clysmien Br.).
  A. First bed.
  1. Mixture of rolled silex and clay.
  2. Lumps and oblique veins of white sand, mixed with gravel and silex.
  3. Bed of ferruginous diluvian grit. Sand agglutinated by a cement of hydrated iron.
  B. Second bed. (Détritique Brong.)
  1. Masses of rolled silex, mixed with gravel.
  2. Sinuous band of silex (rolled) in black sand.
  3. Mass of silex and gravel, in brown ferruginous sand.
  ═. Celtic instruments contained in the mass of silex, covered with ferruginous sand; one set 3½ metres below the surface, the other at 5 metres 60 centimetres.

* Boucher, Plate III.

FIG. 210.

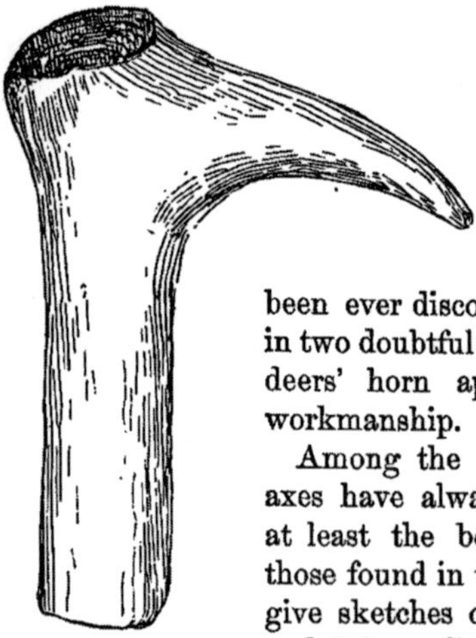

Celtic pickaxe, made of buck-horn.*

a hammer; and Fig. 210 is evidently intended for a pickaxe. Many other specimens, equally rude in design and execution, were found in these alluvial deposits; but, notwithstanding the most careful search, no traces of worked bones have been ever discovered in the diluvial beds; except in two doubtful instances, where fragments of *fossil* deers' horn appeared to show some traces of workmanship.

Among the weapons used by ancient people, axes have always been, if not the most common, at least the best known. We have spoken of those found in the Celtic sepulchres, and will now give sketches of a few of them. Figs. 211, 212 and 213 are Celtic axes. The first is composed of silex, the second of jade, and the third of porphyry: they are all of elegant form and perfect polish. This is the prevailing form; though the instruments vary in size from eight inches down to two inches and a half in length, with a proportionate width. An elegant little jasper axe (Fig. 214) is of the smaller size.

FIG. 211.

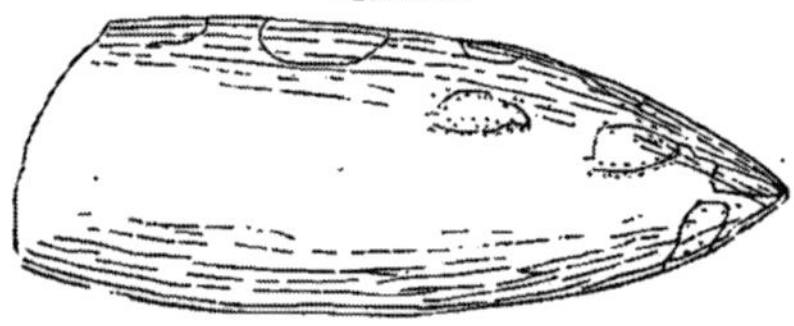

FIG. 212.

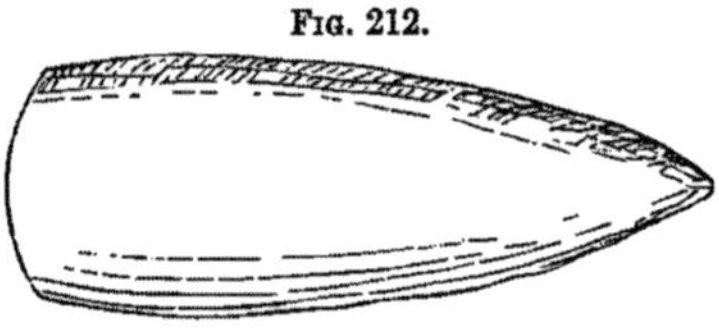

FIG. 213.

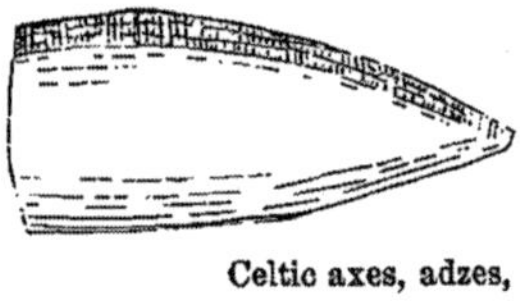

FIG. 214.

Celtic axes, adzes, &c.†

Serpentine is another common material, from its beautiful appearance and facility of workmanship: chalk and even bitumen are also frequently found moulded into the typical form. The subjoined (Figs. 215, 216, 217) appear to have been intended for amulets. Fig. 215 is of grit, two inches long, containing a rude representation of a human face, and pierced so as to be worn as an amulet. Fig. 216 is

* Boucher, Plate IV.

† Idem, Plate XIII.

FIG. 215.

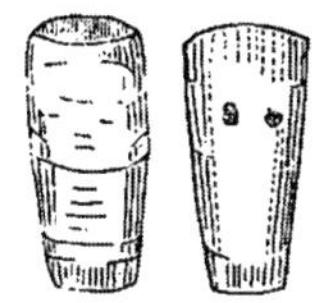

FIG. 216.

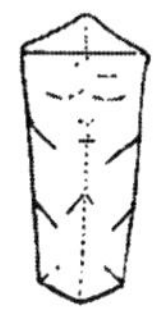

FIG. 217.

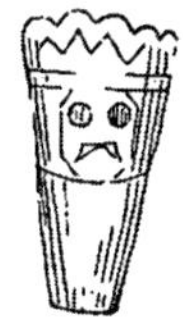

Celtic Amulets.*

of black basalt; and Fig. 217, which is more of the typical shape, is made of white marble, ornamented with small bas-reliefs, and pierced with holes for suspension as an amulet, or to facilitate fastening in a case. Several other specimens of different sizes, material, and finish, but all of the same general form, were found in the Celtic sepulchres, which it is unnecessary to our purpose to enumerate or describe.

Besides the axes, numbers of flints, wrought in the form of knives, were found in the Celtic depositories, and instruments of both kinds were also discovered in the diluvian deposites; the only difference between the Celtic and diluvian remains lying in the fineness of the workmanship, as the form and material were in both cases the same. Figs. 218, 219, and 220, represent axes from the diluvian deposites; and here it may be as well to remark, once for all, that the word *axe* is merely a conventional term, applied generally to all stones of a peculiar typical shape, and is not intended to convey the idea that those instruments were always used as weapons or as mechanical tools, as we shall take occasion to explain.

Figs. 221, 222, and 223, are sketches of Celtic knives; and Figs. 224, 225, and 226, are corresponding instruments of the diluvian epoch.

FIG. 218.

FIG. 219.

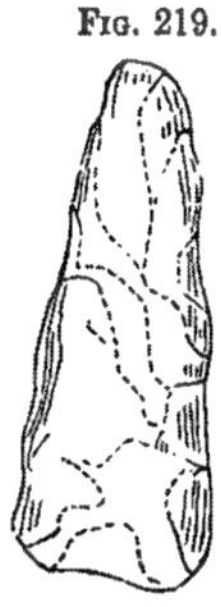

FIG. 220.

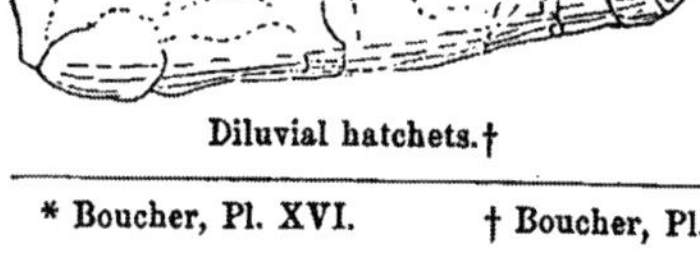

Diluvial hatchets.†

FIG. 221.

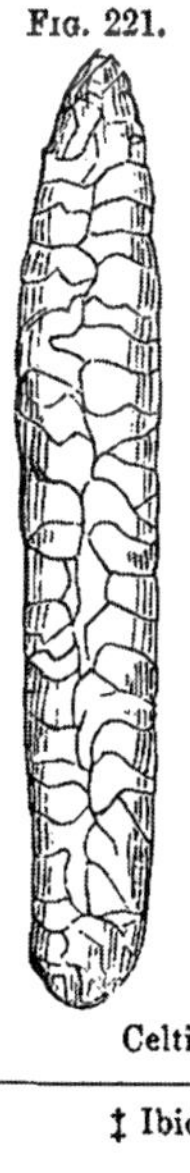

FIG. 222.

FIG. 223.

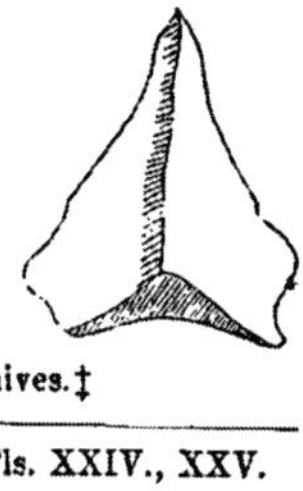

Celtic knives.‡

* Boucher, Pl. XVI.

† Boucher, Pl. XVII.

‡ Ibid., Pls. XXIV., XXV.

Fig. 224.

Fig. 225.

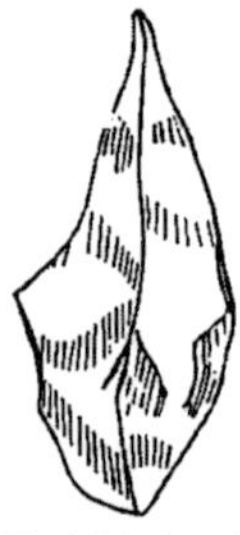

Fig. 226.

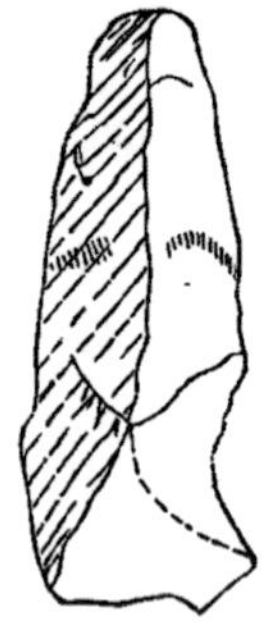

Diluvial knives.*

Besides the axes and knives, there were still other specimens of wrought silex and sandstone, which appear to have been used as symbols or signs connected with the rites of religion. Some of these were probably the original forms or models of the Celtic stones, so widely known; viz., *cromlechs, dolmens, lichavens,* &c. They certainly have the same shapes, and it is not easy to assign any other use or origin to them. Generally pyramidal or cubic in form, they are found, with little variation, from the oldest diluvian to the Celtic period,

Fig. 227.

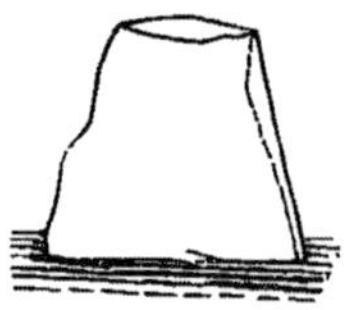

Fig. 228.

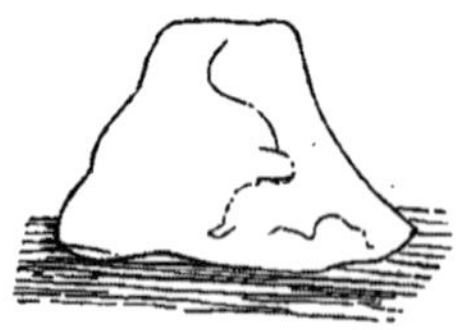

Fig. 229.

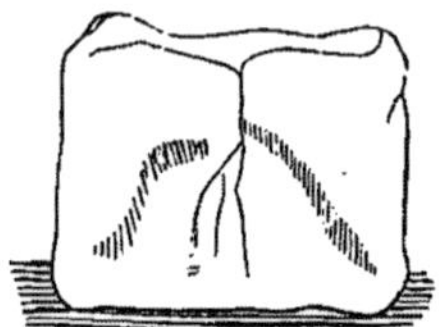

Fig. 230.

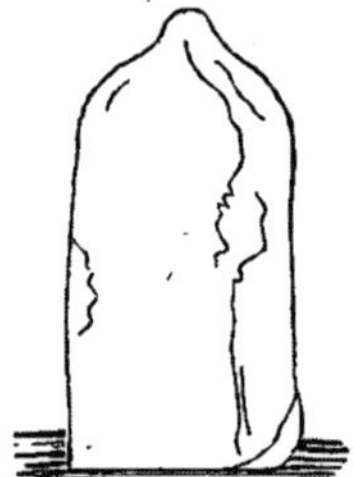

Druidical Monuments.†

and even down to near the Roman times. They are represented in Figs. 227, 228, 229, and 230.

* Boucher, Pl. XXVII. † Ibid., Pls. XXXIII. and XXXIV.

We should remember that many of the instruments we call *axes* were probably used only in sacrifices, and some, perhaps, merely as votive offerings or amulets; being too small, and made of materials too fragile, to have been of any use either as weapons or as tools. Moreover, they were fitted so slightly to their cases, that they must have become detached whenever a blow was struck, and would thus have been left in the wound, or, in case of sacrifice, would have dropped into the hole of the *dolmen* made to receive the blood of the victim. This superstition still exists among some savage tribes, who, in their human sacrifices, always leave the knife in the wound; and may perhaps be traced in the practice of Italian bravos, with whom it is a point of professional honor to leave the stiletto sticking in the body of the murdered man.

"The triangular axe was probably a form consecrated by custom among those rude tribes, like the crescent among the Turks. Being never employed as an instrument of death, except in sacrifices; when the sacrifice was consummated, on funereal occasions, it would be deposited near the urn containing the ashes of the chief they wished to honor, or under the altar of the god they would propitiate. At any rate, the permanence of so rude a state of art during so many ages, or perhaps so many hundreds of ages — from a period of unknown antiquity, separated from historic times by one of the great revolutions of the earth — and disappearing, not gradually, but suddenly; and either by death or conquest; to be succeeded by remains of the Roman era—indicates the existence of a people in a state of barbarism from which they would probably never have emerged. Inhabiting a country full of lakes and forests, they may have resembled the Indians of North America; or, to select a more ancient example, we may compare them to the nomadic tribes of Asia and Africa: the Tartars, Mongols, and Bedouins. The duration of their stationary state defies all speculation; since the most ancient traditions, especially of the pastoral Arabs, represent them precisely as we see them to-day, and there is no sensible difference between the tent of Jacob and that of a modern Shèykh." *

The supposition that these pre-Celtic populations of Europe may have resembled our North American Indians is exceedingly just, so long as similitudes are restricted merely to social habits, superinduced on both continents by the same natural causes; but that the aborigines of Europe were not, in any case, identical physiologically with the trans-Alleghanian mound-builders, has been already exemplified [*supra*, p. 291]. This leads us to the "*Pre-Celtic Annals of Scotland*" — one of those sterling works, replete with solid instruction, that reflects infinite honor on the "native heath," which Dr. Daniel Wilson has recently exchanged for a Canadian home. Whilst heartily welcoming such an accession of science to our continent, we lack space to do more than present the learned archæologist's results in the concisest form. Caledonia, in ages anterior to any *Celtic* traditions, appears to have been successively occupied by two types of man (heretofore unknown to historians), distinct from each other no

* M. Boucher de Perthes: Antiquités Celtiques.

less than from their Celtic destroyers; and this long prior to the Roman invasion of Britain. The most ancient of these extinct races, viz., the "*Kumbe-kephali*" (or, men with *boat*-shaped skulls), flourished during the earlier part of the "Primeval or *Stone* period;" and their successors, the "*Brachy-kephali*" (or, *short* heads) lived towards the latter part. Both became more or less displaced by intrusive Celts, during the subsequent "Archaic or *Bronze* period;" while these last gradually gave way before the precursors of Saxons, Angli, Scoti, Norwegians, &c., who usher in the "Teutonic or *Iron* period." Place the Roman invasion of Scotland in the year 80 A. D., and at what primordial era did Caledonia's aborigines begin?—With this exordium, let Caledonian archæology speak for itself:—

"Of the Allopylian colonists of Scandinavia, Professor Nillson assigns to the most ancient the short or brachy-kephalic form of cranium, with prominent parietal tubers, and broad and flattened occiput. To this aboriginal race, he conceives, succeeds another with a cranium of a more lengthened oval form, and prominent and narrow occiput. The third race, which Scandinavian antiquaries incline to regard as that of the bronze or first metallic period, is characterized by a cranium longer than the first and broader than the second, and marked by greater prominence at the sides. The last, Professor Nillson considers to have been of Celtic origin. To this succeeded the true Scandinavian race, and the first workers of the native iron ore.* . . .

FIG. 231.

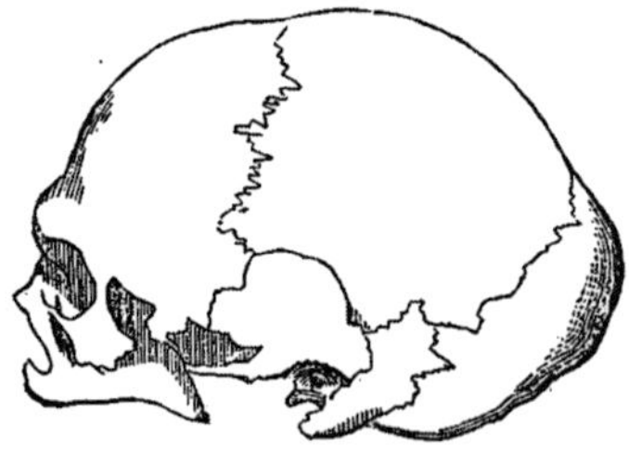

FIG. 232.

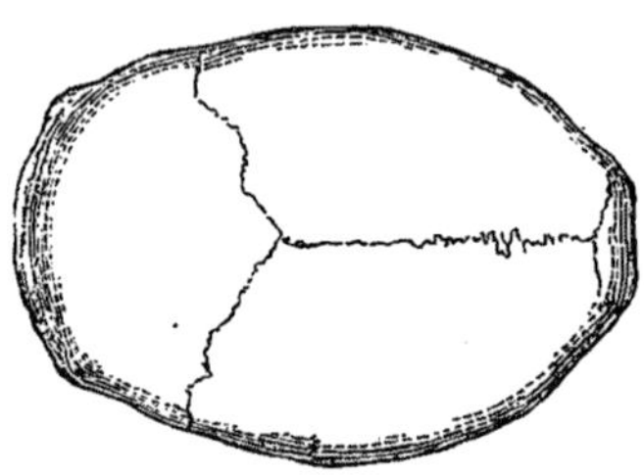

"No. 7. Nether Urquhart Cairn."

"Fortunately a few skulls from Scottish tumuli and cists are preserved in the Museums of the Scottish Antiquaries and of the Edinburgh Phrenological Society. A comparison of these with the specimens of crania drawn by Dr. Thurnam from examples found in an ancient tumular cemetery at Lamel Hill, near York, believed to be of the Anglo-Saxon period, abundantly proves an essential difference of races.† The latter, though belonging to the superior or dolicho-kephalic type, are small, very poorly developed, low and narrow in the forehead, and pyramidal in form. A striking feature of one type of crania from the Scottish barrows is a square compact form. . .

"No. 7 [Figs. 231 and 232] was obtained from a cist discovered under a large cairn at Nether Urquhart, Fifeshire, in 1835. An account of the opening of several cairns and tumuli in the same district is given by Lieutenant-Colonel Miller, in his 'Inquiry respecting the Site of the Battle of Mons Grampius.'‡ Some of them contained urns and burnt bones, ornaments of jet and shale, and the like early relics, while in others were found implements or weapons of iron. It is selected here as

* Primitive inhabitants of Scandinavia, by Professor Nillson of Lund.

† Natural History of Man, p. 193.

‡ Archæol. vol. iv. pp. 43, 44.

another example of the same class of crania. . . . The whole of these, more or less, nearly agree with the lengthened oval form described by Professor Nillson as the second race of the Scandinavian tumuli. They have mostly a singularly narrow and elongated occiput; and with their comparatively low and narrow forehead, might not inaptly be described by the familiar term *boat-shaped.* It is probable that further investigation will establish this as the type of a primitive, if not of the primeval nativé race. Though they approach in form to a superior type, falling under the first or Dolicho-kephalic class of Professor Retzius's arrangement, their capacity is generally small, and their development, for the most part, poor; so that there is nothing in their cranial characteristics inconsistent with such evidence as seems to assign to them the rude arts and extremely limited knowledge of the British Stone Period. . . .

FIG. 233.

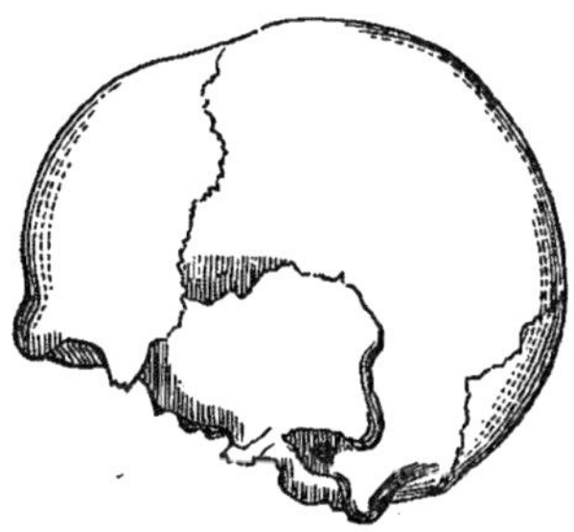

FIG. 234.

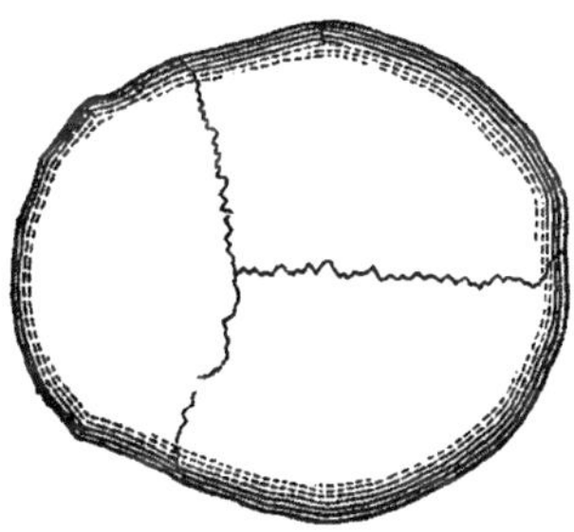

"No. 10. Old Steeple, Montrose."

"The skull, of which the measurements are given in No. 10 [Figs. 233 and 234], is the same here referred to, presented to the Phrenological Museum by the Rev. Mr. Liddell. It is a very striking example of the British Brachy-kephalic type; square and compact in form, broad and short, but well balanced, and with a good frontal development. It no doubt pertained to some primitive chief, or arch-priest, sage, it may be, in council, and brave in war. The site of his place of sepulture has obviously been chosen for the same reasons which led to its selection at a later period for the erection of the belfry and beacon-tower of the old burgh. It is the most elevated spot in the neighborhood, and here his cist had been laid, and the memorial mound piled over it, which doubtless remained untouched so long as his memory was cherished in the traditions of his people. . . .

"Few as these examples are, they will probably be found, on further investigation, to belong to a race entirely distinct from those previously described. They correspond very nearly to the Brachy-kephalic crania of the supposed primeval race of Scandinavia, described by Professor Nillson as short, with prominent parietal tubers, and broad and flattened occiput. In frontal development, however, they are decidedly superior to the previous class of crania, and such evidence as we possess seems to point to a very different succession of races to that which Scandinavian ethnologists now recognize in the primitive history of the north of Europe. . . .

"So far as appears from the table of measurements, the following laws would seem to be indicated:—In the primitive or elongated dolicho-kephalic type, for which the distinctive title of kumbe-kephalic is here suggested—the parietal diameter is remarkably small, being frequently exceeded by the vertical diameter; in the second or brachy-kephalic class, the parietal diameter is the greater of the two; in the Celtic crania they are nearly equal; and in the medieval or true dolicho-kephalic heads, the parietal diameter is again found decidedly in excess; while the preponderance or deficiency of the longitudinal in its relative proportion to the other diameters, furnishes the most characteristic features referred to in the classification of the kumbe-kephalic, brachy-kephalic, Celtic, and dolicho-kephalic types. Not the least interesting indications which these results afford, both to the ethnologist and the archæologist, are the evidences of native primitive races in Scotland prior to the intrusion of the Celtæ; and also the probability of these races having succeeded each other in a different order from the primitive colonists of Scandinavia. Of the former fact, viz., the existence of primitive races prior to the Celtæ, I think no doubt can be now entertained. Of the order of their succession, and their exact share in the changes and progressive development of the native arts which the archæologist detects, we still stand in need of further proof. . . .

"The peculiar characteristic of the primeval Scottish type appears rather to be a narrow prolongation of the occiput in the region of the cerebellum, suggesting the term already applied to them of *boat-shaped*, and for which the name of *Kumbekephalæ* may perhaps be conveniently employed to distinguish them from the higher type with which they are otherwise apt to be confounded. . . .

"The peculiarity in the teeth of certain classes of ancient crania above referred to is of very general application, and has been observed as common even among British sailors. The cause is obvious, resulting from the similarity of food in both cases. The old Briton of the Anglo-Roman period, and the Saxon both of England and the Scottish Lothians, had lived to a great extent on barley bread, oaten cakes, parched peas, or the like fare, producing the same results on his teeth as the hard sea-biscuit does on those of the British sailor. Such, however, is not generally the case, and in no instance, indeed, to the same extent in the skulls found in the earlier British tumuli. In the Scottish examples described above, the teeth are mostly very perfect, and their crowns not at all worn down. . . .

"The inferences to be drawn from such a comparison are of considerable value in the indications they afford of the domestic habits and social life of a race, the last survivor of which has mouldered underneath his green tumulus, perchance for centuries before the era of our earliest authentic chronicles. As a means of comparison this characteristic appearance of the teeth manifestly furnishes one means of discriminating between an early and a still earlier, if not primeval period, and though not in itself conclusive, it may be found of considerable value when taken in connexion with the other and still more obvious peculiarities of the crania of the earliest barrows. We perceive from it, at least, that a very decided change took place in the common food of the country, from the period when the native Briton of the primeval period pursued the chase with the flint lance and arrow, and the spear of deer's horn, to that comparatively recent period when the Saxon marauders began to effect settlements and build houses on the scenes where they had ravaged the villages of the older British natives. The first class, we may infer, attempted little cultivation of the soil. . . .

"Viewing Archæology as one of the most essential means for the elucidation of primitive history, it has been employed here chiefly in an attempt to trace out the annals of our country prior to that comparatively recent medieval period at which the boldest of our historians have heretofore ventured to begin. The researches of the ethnologist carry us back somewhat beyond that epoch, and confirm many of those conclusions, especially in relation to the close affinity between the native arts and Celtic races of Scotland and Ireland, at which we have arrived by means of archæological evidence. . . . But we have found from many independent sources of evidence, that the primeval history of Britain must be sought for in the annals of older races than the Celtæ, and in the remains of a people of whom we have as yet no reason to believe that any philological traces are discoverable, though they probably do exist mingled with later dialects, and especially in the topographical nomenclature, adopted and modified, but in all likelihood not entirely superseded by later colonists. With the earliest intelligible indices of that primeval colonization of the British Isles our archæological records begin, mingling their dim historic annals with the last giant traces of elder worlds; and, as an essentially independent element of historical research, they terminate at the point where the isolation of Scotland ceases by its being embraced into the unity of medieval Christendom." *

* Wilson: Archæol. and Prehist. Annals of Scotland; Edinb. 1851; pp. 163–187, 695–6.

Neither in Scotia nor in Scandinavia, then, any more than in Gallia, are lacking mute, but incontrovertible testimonies to the aboriginal diversity of mankind, as well as to human antiquity incalculably beyond all written chronicles. Ere long, "*Crania Britannica*, or Delineations of the Skulls of the Aboriginal Inhabitants of the British Islands, and of the Races immediately succeeding them," will vouch for existing evidences of the same unanswerable facts in England. The forthcoming work of Doctors Davis and Thurnam promises—

"Not merely to reproduce the most lively and forcible traits of the primeval Celtic hunter or warrior, and his Roman conqueror, succeeded by Saxon or Angle chieftains and settlers, and later still by the Vikings of Scandinavia; but also to indicate the peculiarities which marked the different tribes and races who have peopled the diversified regions of the British Islands."

We conclude this imperfect sketch with remarks, truthful as they are eloquent, of M. Boucher de Perthes, on the subject of these pre-Celtic resuscitations:—

"My discoveries may appear trifling to some, for they comprise little save crumbling bones and rudely sculptured stones. Here are neither medals nor inscriptions, neither bas-reliefs nor statues — no vases, elegant in form, and precious in material — nothing but bones and rudely polished flints. But to the observer who values the demonstration of a truth more than the possession of a jewel, it is not in the finish of a work, nor in its market-price, that its value consists. The specimen he considers most beautiful is that which affords the greatest help in proving a fact or realizing a prevision; and the flint which a collector would throw aside with contempt, or the bone which has not even the value of a bone, rendered precious by the labor it has cost him, is preferred to a Murrhine vase or to its weight in gold.

"The arts, even the most simple, those which seem born with nature, have, like nature herself, had their infancy and their vicissitudes; and industry, properly so called — that is, the indispensable arts — has always preceded the ornamental. It is the same with men as with animals; and the first nightingale, before he thought of singing or of sporting, sought a branch for his nest and a worm for food: he was a hunter before he became a musician.

"However great the number of ages which shroud the history of a people, there is one method of interrogating them, and ascertaining their standing and intelligence. It is by their works. If they have left no specimens of art, it is because they have merely appeared and vanished; or, even if they have continued stationary for any time, they must have remained weak and powerless. Experience proves that this total absence of monuments only exists among a transplanted people — among races who have been cast upon an abnormal soil and under an unfriendly sky, where they lingered out a miserable existence, always liable to momentary extinction. But among a people who had a country, and whom slavery and vice had not entirely brutalized, we may always find some trace, or at least some tradition of art, evanescent perhaps, but still sufficient to recal by a last reflection the physiognomy of the people, their social position, and the degree of civilization they had attained when that art was cultivated.

"Among these specimens of primitive industry, some belong to the present, and illustrate the material life; while others clearly refer to the future. Such are the arms and amulets which were intended to accompany their owners into the tomb, or even to follow them beyond the grave; for, in all ages, men have longed for an existence after death. In these tokens from the tomb — these relics of departed ages — coarse and imperfect as they appear to an artistic eye, there is nothing that we should despise or reject: last witnesses of the infancy of man and of his first footsteps upon earth, they present us with the only remains of nations who reared no columns nor monuments to record their existence. In these poor relics lie all their history, all their religion: and from these few rude hieroglyphics must we evoke their existence and the revelation of their customs. If we were engaged with Egyptians, Greeks, or Romans, people who have furnished us with chefs-d'œuvre which still serve as our models, it would be irksome to examine the ancient oak to find whether it had fallen before the tempest or the axe, or to argue whether the angle of a stone had been smoothed by the hand of man or the action of running water. But when the soil we explore has no other signs of intelligent life, and the very existence of a people is in question, every vestige becomes history. It is easy to conceive that of all the works of man in those ancient deposits, only such instruments of stone should remain. They alone were able to resist the action of time and decomposition, and above all of the waters which put the whole in motion. All these flints bear marks of mutual concussion and incessant friction, which silex alone could have resisted. The time when they were deposited where we now find them, was no doubt that of the formation of the bank itself: it must be separated from our epoch by an immense period, perhaps by many revolutions; and of all the monuments known upon earth, these are doubtless the *most ancient.*"

W. U.

CHAPTER XII.

HYBRIDITY OF ANIMALS, VIEWED IN CONNECTION WITH THE NATURAL HISTORY OF MANKIND.

[BY J. C. N.]

THE subjects embraced in this and the succeeding Chapter appertaining more to my individual studies than the rest, the reader will perceive that I generally speak in the first person; at the same time that every recognition is due to my colleague (G. R. G.) for material aid in the archæological department. Without further preface let me remark, that the importance of Hybridity begins to be acknowledged by all anthropologists; because, however imposing the array of reasonings, drawn from other sources, in favor of the *plurality* of origin, may seem, yet, so long as unlimited prolificness, *inter se*, of two races of animals, or of mankind, can be received by naturalists as evidence of specific affiliation, or, in other words, of common origin, every other argument must be abandoned as illusory.

We are told that, when two distinct species are brought together, they produce, like the ass and the mare, an unprolific progeny; or, at most, beget offspring which are prolific for a few generations and then run out. It is further alleged, that each of our own domestic animals (such as horses, dogs, cattle, sheep, goats, hogs, poultry, &c.)

is derived from a single Mesopotamian pair; and that the varieties of these, springing up spontaneously in diverse climates differ as widely as do the races of men. Hence an argument is deduced in favor of the common origin of mankind. The grand point at issue is here fairly presented: but reasons exist for dissenting from the above foregone conclusions.

In 1842 I published a short essay on *Hybridity*, the object of which was, to show that the White Man and the Negro were distinct "species;" illustrating my position by numerous facts from the Natural History of Man and that of the lower animals. The question, at that time, had not attracted the attention of Dr. Morton. Many of my facts and arguments were new, even to him; and drew from the great anatomist a private letter, leading to the commencement of a friendly correspondence, to me, at least, most agreeable and instructive, and which endured to the close of his useful career.

In the essay alluded to, and several which followed it at short intervals, I maintained these propositions: —

1. That *mulattoes* are the shortest-lived of any class of the human race.
2. That *mulattoes* are intermediate in intelligence between the blacks and the whites.
3. That they are less capable of undergoing fatigue and hardship than either the blacks or whites.
4. That the *mulatto-women* are peculiarly delicate, and subject to a variety of chronic diseases. That they are bad breeders, bad nurses, liable to abortions, and that their children generally die young.
5. That, when *mulattoes* intermarry, they are less prolific than when crossed on the parent stocks.
6. That, when a *Negro* man married a *white* woman, the offspring partook more largely of the Negro type than when the reverse connection had effect.
7. That *mulattoes*, like Negroes, although unacclimated, enjoy extraordinary exemption from yellow-fever when brought to Charleston, Savannah, Mobile, or New Orleans.

Almost fifty years of residence among the white and black races, spread in nearly equal proportions through South Carolina and Alabama, and twenty-five years' incessant professional intercourse with both, have satisfied me of the absolute truth of the preceding deductions. My observations, however, during the last few years, in Mobile and at New Orleans, where the population differs essentially from that of the Northern Atlantic States, have induced some modification of my former opinions; although still holding to their accuracy so far as they apply to the intermixture of the strictly *white* race (*i. e.* the Anglo-Saxon, or Teuton,) with the true *Negro*. I stated in an article printed in "De Bow's Commercial Review," that I had latterly seen reason to credit the existence of certain "*affinities* and *repulsions*" among various races of men, which caused their blood to mingle more or less perfectly; and that, in Mobile, New Orleans and Pensacola, I had witnessed many examples of great longevity among *mulattoes;* and sundry instances where their intermarriages (contrary to my antecedent experiences in South Carolina) were attended with manifest prolificacy. Seeking for the reason of this positive, and, at first thought, unaccountable difference between *mulattoes* of the Atlantic and those of the Gulf States, observation led me to a *rationale;* viz., that it arose from the diversity of *type* in the "Caucasian" races of the two sections. In the Atlantic States the population is Teutonic and Celtic: whereas, in our Gulf cities, there exists a preponderance of the blood of French, Italian, Spanish, Portuguese, and other *dark*-skinned races. The reason is simple to the historian. Our States along the Gulf of Mexico were chiefly colonized by emigrants from Southern Europe. Such European colonists belonged to types genealogically distinct from those white-skinned "Pilgrim Fathers" who landed north of Florida. Thus Spain, when her traditions begin, was populated principally by Iberians. France received a considerable infusion of the same blood, now almost pure in her Basque provinces. Italy's origins are questions in dispute; but the Italians are a dark-skinned race. Such races, blended in America with the imported Negro, generally give birth to a hardier, and, therefore, more prolific stock than white races, such as Anglo-Saxons, produce by intercourse with Negresses. Herein, it occurred to me, might be found a key to solve the enigma. To comprehend the present, we must understand the past; because, in ethnology, there is no truer saying than, "*Cœlum, non animam, mutant qui trans mare currunt.*" This sketch indicates my conceptions. I proceed to their development.

Bodichon, in his curious work on Algeria, maintains that this Iberian, or Basque population, although, of course, not Negro, is really an African, and probably a *Berber*, family, which migrated across the Straits of Gibraltar some 2000 years before the Christian era; and we might, therefore, regard them as what Dr. Morton calls a proximate race.

The Basques are a dark-skinned, black-eyed, black-haired people, such as are often encountered in Southern Europe; and M. Bodichon, himself a Frenchman, and attached as Surgeon to the French army during fifteen years in Algeria, holds, that not only is the physical resemblance between the Berbers and Basques most striking, but that they assimilate in moral traits quite as much; moreover, that their intonations of voice are so similar that one's ear cannot appreciate any difference. Singularly enough, too, the Basque tongue, while radically distinct from all European and Asiatic languages, is said to present certain affinities with the Berber dialects. The latter opinion, however, requires confirmation.

Subsequently to my incidental notices, Dr. Morton took up the entire question of hybridity, with his accustomed zeal; publishing his first two articles on it in *Silliman's Journal*, 1847; after which he continued a series of papers, in the *Charleston Medical Journal*, down to the time of his death in 1851. I attach little importance to my own labors on this subject, beyond that of attracting Dr. Morton to its investigation. None more than myself can honor him for the glorious triumph which his publications on this theme achieved for science. My object, then, being solely to place the question before the public as it actually stands, I shall use not only Dr. Morton's ideas, but his language, freely, throughout this chapter; merely extending to the *races of men* those principles of hybridity which Dr. Morton chiefly confined to known intermixture among the lower animals.

Hybridity, heretofore, has generally been treated as if it were a *unit;* whereas its facts are as susceptible of classification as any other series of physiological phenomena. For the terms *remote*, *allied*, and *proximate species*, there will be frequent call; and, in consequence, the reader is requested to look back (*supra*, p. 81) in this volume, to understand the meanings which, in common with Morton, I attach to them. Finding that the definitions customarily given of "species" apply as readily to mere varieties as to acknowledged species, the Doctor proposed the subjoined emendations: —

"As the result of much observation and reflection, I now submit a definition, which I hope will obviate at least some of the objections to which I have alluded: SPECIES — *a primordial organic form*. It will be justly remarked that a difficulty presents itself, at the outset, in determining what forms are primordial; but independently of various other sources of evidence, we may be greatly assisted in the inquiry by those monumental records, both of Egypt and Assyria, of which we are now happily possessed of the proximate dates. My view may be briefly explained by saying, that if certain existing organic types can be traced back into the 'night of time' as dissimilar as we now see them, is it not more reasonable to regard them as aboriginal, than to suppose them the mere accidental derivations of an isolated patriarchal stem, of which we know nothing? Hence, for example, I believe the dog-family not to have originated from one primitive form, but in many forms. Again, what I call a species may be regarded by some naturalists as a *primitive variety;* but, as the difference is only in name and no way influences the zoological question, it is unnecessary to notice it further." [392]

Morton himself has suggested the objection which really holds against his definition; and, for myself, I should prefer the following: SPECIES — *a type, or organic form, that is permanent; or which has remained unchanged under opposite climatic influences for ages.* The Arab, the Egyptian, and the Negro; the greyhound, the turnspit, and the common wild dog — all of which are represented on monuments of Egypt 4000 years old, precisely as they now exist in human and canine nature — may be cited as examples.

It is believed that the series of facts herein embodied will establish the natural existence of the following degrees of hybridity, viz.: —

1st. That in which hybrids never reproduce; in other words, where the mixed progeny begins and ends with the first cross.

2d. That in which the hybrids are incapable of reproducing *inter se*, but multiply by union with the parent stock.

3d. That in which animals of unquestionably distinct species produce a progeny which is prolific *inter se.*

4th. That which takes place between closely proximate species — among mankind, for example, and among those domestic animals most essential to human wants and happiness: here the prolificacy is unlimited.

There is, moreover, what may be called a *mixed form* of hybridity, that certainly has exerted very great influence in modifying some domestic animals; and which cannot be better expressed than in the language of Hamilton Smith: —

"The advances towards hybrid cases are always made by the domestic species to the wild; and when thus obtained, if kept by itself, and the cross-breed gradually becomes sterile, it does not prevent repeated intermixture of one or the other; and therefore the admission of a great proportion of alien blood, which may again be crossed upon by other hybrids of another source, whether it be a wolf, pariah, jackal, or dingo."[393]

Mankind, zoologically, must be governed by the same laws which regulate animals generally; and if the above propositions apply to other animals, no reason can be adduced in science why the races of men should be made an exception. The mere *prolificacy*, whether of human or of animal races, cannot therefore be received *per se* as proof of common origin in respect to either.

After the lapse of so many centuries, or, to repeat Prichard's language, chiliads of years, since the last Creation, it would be strange indeed did not many difficulties surround the question of hybridity: but one thing seems certain, viz., that as regards unity or plurality of origin, mankind, together with all our domestic animals, stand on precisely the same footing. The origin of our horses, dogs, cattle, sheep, goats, hogs, &c., no less than that of humanity, is wholly unknown; nor can science yet determine from how many primal creative centres, or from how many pairs, each may have originated. Our Chapter I., on the *Geographical Distribution of Animals*, has detailed (what is now conceded by naturalists whose authority is decisive), that, so far from a supposititious common centre of origin for *all* organized beings on our globe, there are in reality *many* specific centres or zoological provinces, in which the fauna and flora of each are exclusively peculiar.[394] The present volume establishes, through evidences varied as they are novel, that history finds the different races of mankind everywhere under circumstances which lead irresistibly to the conclusion, that humanity obeys the same laws which preside over the terrestrial distribution of other organized beings.

"A principal cause [well observes Jacquinot] of varieties among domestic animals is, the *blending* of dissimilar species among themselves; and it is this powerful agency which has contributed in the largest degree to obscure and entangle the question of the varieties of men and of domestic animals."

Passing over, as non-essential to the point immediately before us, the numerous examples illustrative of hybridity, in Dr. Morton's *first* and *second* degrees, we shall throw together a few of the more prominent instances of his *third* and *fourth*, in their direct bearings upon the plurality of the human species, in order to exemplify the question at issue.

EQUINE HYBRIDS.

The genus *equus* (horse) is divided by Cuvier into five species; viz.: the horse (*equus caballus*); the dzigguetai (*eq. hemonius*); the ass (*eq. asinus*); the zebra (*eq. zebra*); the couagga (*eq. quaccha*); the onagga, or dauw (*eq. montanus*).

So far as experiments prove, these all breed freely *inter se*; but the degrees of fertility among their various hybrid offspring, are matters yet to be determined.

Our common mules, or progeny of the ass and the mare, are the best known hybrids, and they are never prolific with each other; but there are a few instances recorded where mules have produced offspring when crossed on the parent stocks: such accidents being, as even Herodotus observed,[395] more common in hot climates than in cold.

The Hinny—

Offspring of the horse and she-ass—is rarely seen in the United States (but, we are told, is more frequent in Egypt, and in the Levant; where some hinnies are said to be even handsome): being a small, refractory, and (for draught) a comparatively useless animal, there is no practical object in our breeding them. I have seen one example in Mobile, very like a dwarfed, mean horse. The horse's likeness here greatly predominated: the head and ears were small, and precisely like its father's; the legs and feet were slender and small, like those of the mother; and the tail, as in the ass, was lank, with little hair. In the common mule, the head, on the contrary, resembles the ass. Judging by this example alone, it would seem as if the type of the sire predominated in hybrids. Such probable law, according to my observations, applies in some degree to the human hybrid. *Ex. gr.*, when the pure white man is crossed on the Negress, the head of their mulatto child ordinarily resembles more the father than the mother; but where a Negro man has been coupled with a white woman, in their offspring the color, the features, and the hair of the Negro father greatly preponderate. We cannot state, from observation, what may be the grade of intellect in the latter hybrid; but in a common *mulatto* the degree of intelligence is absolutely higher than in the full-blooded Negroes. About this deduction no dispute exists among medical practitioners in our Southern States, where means of verification are peculiarly abundant.

Not only do the female ass and the male onagga breed together, but a male offspring of this cross, with a mare, produces an animal more docile than either parent, and combining the best physical qualities, such as strength, speed, &c.; whence the ancients preferred the onagga to the ass for the production of mules.[396] This opinion, Mr. Gliddon says, is still prevalent in Egypt; and is acted upon more particularly in Arabia, Persia, &c., where the *gour*, or wild ass, still roams the desert. Cuvier had seen the cross between the ass and the zebra, as well as between the female zebra and the horse.

An important point should be borne in mind, viz.: that the ass is not the *proximate*, or nearest species, of the genus *equus*, compared with the horse; but that place Cuvier assigns to the *eq. hemonius*. Bell and Gray are even disposed to place the ass in a distinct genus. If, therefore, it were desired to experimentalize fairly, with the view of producing a *prolific* hybrid, the true horse should be coupled with the *eq. hemonius* in a proper climate, and under favorable conditions. This experiment, as far as we know, not having been properly tried, analogy warrants the suspension of a negative.

From the unlimited productiveness among the different races of horses, it has been boldly inferred that all horses have sprung from a solitary pair, possessing a common Mesopotamian origin, and therefore constituting a single species; but an assumption without proof, while valid reasons support the contrary, may be summarily dismissed. The elaborate and skilful researches of Hamilton Smith have thrown strong doubts over this superannuated idea of equine unity. He separates horses into five primitive stocks; which appear to constitute "distinct though oscillating species, or at least races, separated at so remote a period, that they claim to have been divided from the earliest times of our present zoology."[397] So true is this, that already two distinct species, if not more, of *fossil* horses exist in geological formations of this Continent, independently of the others familiar in European palæontology.[398]

About horses, Morton's later MSS. enable us to quote the following textually:—

"After an elaborate and most instructive inquiry into the natural history of the horse, Col. Hamilton Smith has arrived at the following conclusions, which we prefer to give in his own words: 'That there was a period when equidæ of distinct forms, or closely-approximating species, in races widely different, wandered in a wild state in separate regions, the residue of an anterior animal distribution, perhaps upon the great mountain line of Central Asia, where plateaux or table-lands, exceeding Armenian Ararat in elevation, are still occupied by wild horses; that of these some races still extant have been entirely subdued; such for example as the Tarpans, the Kirguise and Pamere woolly white race, and the wild horses of Poland and Prussia; that from their similarity, or antecedent unity, they were constituted so as to be fusible into a common, single, specific, but very variable stock, for the purposes of man, under whose fostering care a more perfect animal was bred from their mixture, than any of the preceding, singly taken. These inferences appear to be supported by the ductility of all the secondary characters of wild and domestic horses, which, if they are not admitted to constitute in some cases specific differences, where are we to find those that are sufficient to distinguish a wild from a domestic species? And with regard to different, though oscillating species, why should the conclusions be unsatisfactory in horses, when in goats, sheep, wolves, dogs, and other species, we are forced to accede to them?'"[399]

Some of these races still flourish in a wild state on the table-lands of Central Asia; at the same time that all have united to form, in domestication, very mixed and variable types.

A singular fact, which I have never seen noticed, is worthy of mention. The thorough-bred race-horse is rarely, if ever, beheld of a cream, or a dun color, or piebald. My attention, directed to this point for more than twenty years, as yet meets with no example; nor, through inquiry among turf-men, have I been able to hear of a single case where the pedigree was well authenticated. Horses of the above colors are exceedingly common in the United States; far more so, as I know from personal observation, than in England or France; and the only solution that occurs to me is, the supposition that the early Spanish emigrants may have brought over to America some breed of horses, distinct from the Arabian stock of England, or from any of the races of France and Belgium.

"When Cæsar invaded Britain he found there a race of indigenous ponies, with bushy manes and tails, and of a dun or sooty color, with the black streak on the spine which marks the wild races of northern Europe. This variety was known in a wild state for centuries after, and in every part of the island. This horse was subsequently amalgamated with the Roman and Saxon breeds, whence a great diversity of size and color in our own times.[400] These native British horses were the ancestors of the ponies now called Shetland, Scottish, Galloway, and by various other names."[401]

Naturalists remark that those animals, such as the ass, the camel, the dromedary, llama, &c., upon which the most sensible reasons are based for alleging a community of species, do not run into those endless and extreme varieties observable in dogs, horses, cattle, sheep, goats, or hogs.

Bovine Hybrids.

The ox tribe occupy, among naturalists, a position identical with that of the horse; many of our best authorities contending for plurality of species. The origin of our varied domestic races is wholly unknown, and the domestication of *cattle* antedates the earliest Egyptian monuments, together with the writer of *Genesis* [i. 24, 25, 26,] himself. The bison or American buffalo and our common cattle produce hybrid offspring which is unprolific *inter se;* but these hybrids reproduce without limit when coupled with the parent stocks; and this again furnishes another undeniable *degree* in the history of hybridity.

Caprine and Ovine Hybrids.

The weight of authority, as victoriously proven by Dr. Morton, decidedly favors plurality of species for our domestic goats and sheep. I shall not tax our readers with the details of the discussion, which they can find in the *Charleston Med. Journal*[402] (between his dispassionate science on the one hand, and the captious garrulity displayed by dogmatism on the other): but one of the most note-worthy examples of a prolific hybrid anywhere to be found in the range of natural history, must not be passed over; viz.: the offspring of *goats* and *sheep* when coupled together. The goat and the sheep being, not merely distinct species, but distinct *genera*, the example therefore becomes the more precious, whilst its authenticity is irrefragable: sustaining, furthermore, the authority of Buffon and Cuvier for the fertility of such hybrids, which are not only fertile with the parent stocks, but *inter se.*[403]

Another instance of hybridity, not less curious, and perfectly attested, is that of the *deer* and *ram*, quoted by Morton from Carl N. Hellenius, published in the Memoirs of the Royal Swedish Academy of Stockholm. After going through his experiments in detail, Hellenius concludes with the following summary: —

"I have thus, from this pair (female deer — *cervus capriolus*, and the male sheep — *ovis aries*), obtained *seven offsprings:* viz.,

"*Four* from the ram and deer — two of each sex.

"*Two* from the deer's first hybrid male offspring, viz., by crossing this latter animal with the Finland ewe; and by crossing this same male with the female offspring of the deer and ram.

"*One*, a ewe, by pairing the Finland ewe with one of her own progeny, from the first hybrid male derived from the deer and ram."

Hellenius furthermore gives a copious narrative of the form, fleece, and mixed habits of these animals, which were alive, healthy, and vigorous, when the account was published, and may be so still.

It is clear, from this unmistakeable testimony of Hellenius, that a mixed race of deer and sheep might be readily produced and perpetuated by bringing together *many pairs;* precisely as is done daily with the goats and sheep of Chili alluded to by the well-known naturalist and academician, M. Chevreul. Here we obtain a prolific hybrid again, from distinct *genera;* and, what is singular, the female progeny resembles the mother, and the male the father. Another fact to show the absurdity of querulous arguments drawn by the misinformed from "analogy."

The old and standard authority of Molina, in his Natural History of Chili, sustains the recent assertion of Chevreul,[404] in the *Journal des Savans*, as to the fact that the inhabitants of Chili, for a long time have been in the habit of crossing goats and sheep expressly with the view of improving their fleece in a hybrid progeny, whose prolificacy knows no limits.

CAMELLINE HYBRIDS.

Linnæus, Fischer, Ranzani, H. Smith, Lesson, Dumeril, Desmarest, Desmoulins, Quatrefages, Bory, Fleming, Cuvier, and all well-read naturalists of the present generation, regard the camel and dromedary as distinct species, and admit their prolificacy *inter se.* Buffon, in whose day Oriental matters were little known, denied that they are distinct species, simply on the ground that they are prolific. The Arabian camel and dromedary, no less than the *camelus bactrianus*, are figured on the monuments of Nineveh, at least 2500 years ago, precisely as we see them now. Our Fig. 15 (*supra*, p. 126) exhibits the single-humped species; and the rest are easily verified in the folio plates of Botta and Flandin, and Layard.

The following is extracted from one of many communications obligingly made to the authors by their honored friend Col. W. W. S. BLISS, U. S. A.; in whose person knowledge the most diversified and accomplishments of the highest order were combined with that military science and cool bravery which won universal admiration on the blood-stained field of *Buena Vista.* Alas! his eyes were closed by the writer's hands on the 5th of August, 1853.

"Eversmann, who is known as an investigator of Natural History in Bochara, remarks that *three different species of camel* are found there, all of which copulate together and bring forth prolific young.

"1. AIR is the *two-humped bactrian* (*camelus bactrianus*), with long wool.

"2. NAR is the *one-humped camel*, which Eversmann calls *camelus dromedarius*, but which is *camelus vulgarus*, the common Arabian camel; for the dromedary is only a particular breed, not a particular species.

"3. LUK is the name given to a camel with *one hump*, larger than the above, and having quite crisp, short, dark-brown wool.

"The copulation of camels, says the above-named naturalist and traveller (Eversmann), takes place in Bucharei in March and April, and between camels and bactrians, as well as the third race: its products are again prolific, self-propagating, foals. We might from this, as Buffon and Zimmermann have already done, infer the unity of genus and mere varieties of species; but apart from this, the number of humps at least seems to be no essential indication of species; for, says Eversmann, it cannot be determined beforehand whether the progeny of such crossing of races will have one or two humps: they are always bastards, and not of a pure species."[405]

SURINE HYBRIDS.

We dismiss this somewhat obscure theme by merely stating that, according to the best naturalists, sustained by Dr. Morton's critical essays, the weight of authority in favor of plurality of species predominates here also. So it does again, in respect to *Feline Hybrids.*

CANINE HYBRIDS.

No question, perhaps, in natural history has caused more controversy than that of the origin of *domestic dogs.* Our highest authorities have expressed most opposite opinions, and many are the important points yet at issue. Nevertheless, the last three years have accomplished much towards settling sundry pugnacious *dilettanti*, if not all scientific disputes. Some writers have derived all our dogs from the wolf: thus assigning to Noah's unaccountable predilections in behalf of a tame lupine *pair* ("species" unrecorded) the present existence of hyenas, jackals, foxes—laughing, or round-backed; big, or little; white, black, red, gray, or blue—as well as every kind and size of *dog*, from a Muscovite "muff-dog" to the colossal *St. Bernard;* now eaten by Chinamen and Sandwich Islanders; driven by Esquimaux; kicked by Muslim orthodoxy; whipped in English hunts; fondled by Parisian dames; abhorred by thieves and vagrants, if loved by shepherds, sportsmen, wagoners, and hostlers, besides all other honest men with their prattling children, universally since the Flood.

Others assert that dogs are animals absolutely not descended from the wolf, and also that they comprise many distinct species, created in many different zoological regions; whilst others, again, believe that all living dogs proceed from intermixtures of wolf, fox, jackal, and hyena—in short, from any *canidæ*, except from CANES.

As facts now stand, the opinion of Dr. Morton may probably be deemed the most correct. His convictions are, that the origin of domestic dogs is at least *threefold:* viz.—

1st. From several species of lupine and vulpine animals.

2d. From various species of wild dogs.

3d. From the blending of these together, with perhaps occasional admixture of jackal, under the influence of domestication.

A subject so replete with scientific interest in its general connections with other departments of natural history, and especially on account of its bearings on the physical history of man, renders it imperative that facts should here be presented somewhat in detail; and I shall again interweave without reserve the language of Dr. Morton.

Martin, in his *History of the Dog*, justly remarked that "the name *wolf* is a vague one, because there are various species of wolves in Europe, Asia, and America; and further, if each of these species has given rise to a breed of dogs in the different countries where they are found, then, as all domestic dogs promiscuously breed together, the advocate of the non-admixture of species is plunged into a dilemma." [406]

M. de Blainville, speaking of the experiments of Buffon on dogs and wolves, adopts the idea of distinct species for these animals; thereby leaving the inference that all dogs are not descendants from one primitive stock. The great naturalist tested the question as follows:

1st. He brought together a cur-dog and a she-wolf. The result of this union was a litter of four pups—two male, and two female. No difficulty occurred in procuring this cross.

2d. A male and a female of the first generation were coupled; whence four pups—of which two lived to maturity: a male and a female.

3d. The second generation being crossed, a third generation of seven pups was the consequence.

4th. A female of the third generation, crossed by her sire, gave birth to four pups, of which one male and one female lived.

Buffon sent two of such hybrids to M. Le Roi, Inspector of the Park at Versailles. Here they bred together, producing three pups. Two were given to the Prince de Condé — but of these no account remains. The third, retained by M. Le Roi, was killed in a boar-hunt. The father of these whelps was then mated with a she-wolf, who bore three pups. Here the report closes.[407]

"I have seen, in Moscow," says Pallas, "about twenty spurious animals from dogs and black wolves (*c. lycaon*). They are, for the most part, like wolves; except that they carry their tails higher, and have a kind of hoarse barking. They multiply among themselves; and some of the whelps are grayish, rusty, or even of the whitish hue of the Arctic wolves."[408] Crosses of this kind have been known from remote antiquity, and are called *wolf-dogs* (*c. pomeranus*). One of them is figured on an Etruscan medal of the second or third century before Christ. Ovid, describing the pack of Acteon, enumerates some thirty dogs, which appear to represent many different breeds; and he is careful to observe that one of them (*Napé*) sprang from a wolf; while another (*Lycisca*) is evidently the dog which Pliny refers to similar mixed bloods.

By a *feral* dog, is meant a domesticated dog which has run wild. Numberless are the instances of this kind, where dogs have become wild and multiplied; but in no instance, save through *lupine* admixture, have dogs ever been brought to resemble wolves. The dog of New Holland, called the *dingo*, is a reclaimed lupine, or wild dog. It is still found abundantly in the wild state in that country. Some naturalists consider the *dingo* to be a distinct species, or an aboriginal dog; others, a variety of the common dog. Australia, it should be remembered, possesses an exclusive *fauna* and *flora;* and the *canis dingo* would seem to be the aboriginal canine element pertaining to this special zoological province. The *dingo*, wild or tame, preserves its own physical characteristics when pure, but breeds freely with other dogs.

Systems of zoology mostly limit our North American wolves (exclusively of those of Mexico and California) to two species — *canis lupus* and *canis latrans*. But there is little reason to doubt that the *grey wolf* of Canada and other northern parts of this continent, is a different species from any of the Old World. Richardson adopts for it the name of *C. occidentalis*, and long ago hesitated about its relation to the *C. lupus*, because they differ both in conformation and character. Townsend describes the *giant wolf* as a distinct species, by the name of *C. gigas;* and Peale makes the same distinction.

While the dogs indigenous to North America, according to Morton, are derived from at least two species of wolves, which he considers, in common with Gray, Agassiz, Richardson and others, to be peculiar to our continent, the European race (although in some instances largely crossed by another wolf) is for the most part devoid of any such lupine mixture. The domestic dogs of Europe, when they assume the feral state, cannot be mistaken by naturalists for wolves. Besides, it will be proved further on, that the dog, the wolf, the jackal, and the hyena are figured as distinct animals on the monuments of Egypt, in company with many different races of dogs, as far back as 3500 years before Christ.

Dr. Morton held the Indian dogs of North America to be derived from at least two distinct species of wolves; that these two species have combined to form a third, or hybrid race, and that this last unites again with the European dog.

Sir John Richardson travelled over more than 20,000 miles of the northern regions of America; traversing 30° of latitude, and upwards of 50° of longitude; occupied for seven years in making observations. To him are we mainly indebted for the following facts: —

The Esquimaux Dog (*C. familiaris, Desm.*)

"The great resemblance which the domesticated dogs of aboriginal Americans bear to the wolves of the same country, was remarked by the earliest settlers from Europe, and has induced some naturalists of much observation to consider them to be merely half-tamed wolves. Without entering at all into the question of the origin of the domestic dog, I may state that the resemblance between the wolves of those Indian nations who still preserve their ancient mode of life, continues to be very remarkable; and it is nowhere more so than at the very northern extremity of the continent — the Esquimaux dogs being not only extremely like the grey wolf of the Arctic Circle in form and color, but also nearly equalling them in size."[409]

This famed Arctic voyager and naturalist adds, that he saw a family of these wolves, when playing together, occasionally carry their tails curved upwards; which seems to be the principal character which Linnæus supposed to distinguish the dog from the wolf.

Capt. Parry relates that his officers, seeing thirteen wolves in a single pack, mistook them for Esquimaux dogs; so complete was the resemblance. He observed, that when the wolf is tamed, the two animals will readily breed together.[410]

From these and other facts familiar to naturalists, it would appear that the Esquimaux dog is a reclaimed northern wolf (*canis occidentalis*).

"The common American wolf," Richardson observes, "sometimes shows a remarkable diversity of color. On the banks of the Mackenzie I saw five young wolves leaping and tumbling over each other with all the playfulness of the puppies of the domestic dog, and it is not improbable that they were all of one litter. One of them was pied, another entirely black, and the rest showed the colors of the common grey wolves."

So variable, however, are the external characters of the latter animal, both as to size and color, that naturalists have endeavored, at different times, to establish no less than five species in the northern part of America alone. Two of these, however (*C. ater* and *C. nubilus*), are generally regarded as mere varieties of the common grey wolf. Hence, it would naturally follow, that the domestication of these several varieties would develop a corresponding difference between our northern Indian and the more Arctic dogs of the Esquimaux; although both kinds may claim, in part, the same specific origin. Speaking of the wolves of our Sashatchewan and Copper-mine rivers, Richardson states: —

"The resemblance between the northern wolves and the domestic dog of the Indians is so great, that the size and strength of the wolf seems to be the only difference. I have more than once mistaken a band of wolves for the dogs of a party of Indians; and the howl of the animals of both species is prolonged, and so exactly in the same key, that even the practised ear of an Indian fails at times to discriminate between them.[411] At certain seasons they breed freely with the wolf, while, on other occasions, both male and female wolves devour the dogs as they would any other prey."

The Hare-Indian Dog (*C. familiaris lagopus*).

The author just quoted observes, that similitudes between this animal and the prairie-wolf (*C. latrans*) are "so great, that on comparing live specimens, I could detect no difference in form (except the smallness of the cranium), nor in the fineness of the fur, and the arrangement of its spots and color. In fact, it bears the same relation to the prairie-wolf, that the Esquimaux dog does to the great grey wolf (*C. occidentalis*)."[412]

Like the cognate wolf, these dogs vary considerably in color, size, and shape; [000] those on the Mackenzie river being so remarkably small, as to have been sometimes compared to the Arctic fox. In the Mandan country the dogs are larger; and are likewise assimilated by Say, the Prince de Wied, and other travellers, to the prairie-wolf.

"During my residence in the Michigan Territory, in the year 1831–32 (wrote Dr. J. C. Fisher to Dr. Morton), I on several occasions shot the Ojibeway or Indian dogs, by mistake, for the prairie-wolf, and supposed that I knew it well; but, after the frequent mistakes I made, I became very cautious about shooting them, lest I should kill more dogs. They were the common dogs of the Ojibeway, Pottawatomie and Ottawa tribes."

The North American or common Indian Dog (C. familiaris Canadensis).

"By the above title," says Richardson, "I wish to designate the kind of dogs which is most generally cultivated by the native tribes of Canada and the Hudson Bay countries. It is intermediate, in size and form, between the two preceding varieties; and by those who consider the domestic races of dogs to be derived from wild animals, this may be termed a cross between the prairie and gray wolves."

In the Appendix to Capt. Back's Narrative, Dr. Richardson subsequently observes, that "the offspring of the wolf and the Indian dog are prolific, and are prized by the voyagers as beasts of draught, being much stronger than the ordinary dog."[413] "This fact is corroborated," writes Morton, "by my friend Dr. John Evans, who has recently passed some time in the Mandan country, where the dogs, however, appear to be derived from the prairie wolf; and he assures me, that frequent and spontaneous intercourse between these dogs and the wolf of that country (which is now almost exclusively the *canis accidentalis*, or common gray wolf,) is a fact known to every one."

Again, the *canis Mexicanus*, or "Tichichi" of the Mexicans, by Humboldt said to be very much like this dog of the northern Indians, is also supposed to derive its parentage from a wolf.

The intermixture of these two species was indeed manifest to the acute perceptions of Richardson himself, who remarks, that it "seems to support the opinion of Buffon, lately advocated by Desmoulins, that the dog, the wolf, the jackal, and corsac, are, in fact, but modifications of the same species; or, that the races of domestic dogs ought to be referred, each in its proper country, to a corresponding *indigenous wild species*; and that the species thus domesticated have, in the course of their migrations in the train of man, produced by their various crosses with each other, with their offspring, and with their prototypes, a still further increase of different races, of which about fifty or sixty are at present cultivated."

Such doctrines accord with that adopted by Morton, who concludes his notice of wolf-dogs as follows:—"The natural, and to me very unavoidable, conclusion, is simply this, that two species of wolves (acknowledged to be distinct from each other by all zoologists) have each been trained into a domestic dog; that these dogs have reproduced not only with each other, but with the parent stocks, and even with the European dog, until a widely-extended hybrid race has arisen, in which it is often impossible to tell a wolf from a dog, or the dogs from each other."

We extract entire Morton's observations concerning

Aboriginal American Dogs, from vulpine and other sources.

"Besides the two indigenous wolf-dogs of the North, of which we have spoken (the Hare-Indian and Esquimaux races), and the third or mixed species (the common Indian dog), the continent of America possesses a number of other aboriginal forms, which terminate only in the inter-tropical regions of South America. One of these was observed by Columbus, on landing in the Antilles, A. D. 1492. 'These,' says Buffon, 'had the head and ears very long, and *resembled a fox in appearance*.' They are called *Aguara dogs* in Mexico, and *Alcos* in Peru.

"'There are many species,' adds Buffon, 'which the natives of Guiana have called *dogs of the woods* (*chiens des bois*), because they are not yet reduced, like our dogs, to a state of domestication; and they are thus rightly named, *because they breed together with domestic races*.'

"The wild Aguaras, I believe, are classed, by most naturalists, with the fox-tribe; but Hamilton Smith has embraced them in a generic group, called *dasicyon*, to which he and Martin refer four species. The latter zoologist sums up a series of critical inquiries with the following remarks: — 'It is almost incontestably proved, that the aboriginal Aguara tame dogs, and others of the American continent, which, on the discovery of its different regions, were in subjection to the savage or semi-civilized nations, were not only indigenous, but are the descendants of several wild Aguara dogs, existing cotemporary with themselves, in the woods or plains; and granting that a European race [as is the case since] had by some chance contributed to their production, the case is not altered, *but the theory of the blending of species confirmed.*' "[414]

Dr. Tchudi, one of the most distinguished zoologists of the present day, has paid especial attention to the character and history of two domesticated dogs of South America, which he regards as distinct species: —

1. *Canis Ingæ (Perro-dog, or Alco).*

The dog to which Tchudi gives this name is the same that the Peruvians possessed and worshipped before the arrival of the Spaniards, and is found in the tumuli of those people of the oldest epoch. It is so inferior, however, to the exotic breeds, that it is rapidly giving way to them, and an unmixed individual is now seldom seen; and they present "the undetermined form of the mixture of all the breeds that have been imported from Europe, and thus assume the shape of cur-dogs, or of a primitive species."[415]

We have already seen that the *Aguara*, or *fox-dogs*, of North America mingle freely with the indigenous dogs of this continent. The following facts are equally curious and valuable: -

2. *Canis Caribœus.*

Desmarest has given this name to the hairless dog, which, as Humboldt remarks, was found by Columbus in the Antilles, by Cortes in Mexico, and by Pizarro in Peru. Desmarest, if we mistake not, supposes this dog to be descended from the *c. cancrivorus*, a native species, which, according to Blainville, belongs to the section of true wolves. But Rengger, who had ample opportunities of deciding this question, regards it as an aboriginal wild dog, which the Indians have reduced to domestication; and he adds, in explanation, that it does not readily mix with the European species, and that the Indian tribes have, in their respective languages, a particular name for it, but none for any domestic animal of exotic derivation.[416]

This animal much resembles the Barbary dog (*canis Ægyptiacus*); but there is no ground but resemblance for supposing them to be of common origin.

Here then, once more, we may recognize two aboriginal dogs — one seemingly derived from the fox-tribe, or at least from fox-like wild dogs; the other, from an unknown source: yet both unite more or less readily with the exotic stocks, producing a hybrid race, partly peculiar in appearance, and partly resembling the mongrel races of Europe.

The Rev. Mr. Daniel states that Mr. Tattersall "had a terrier bitch which bred by a fox, and the produce again had whelps by dogs. The woodman of the manor of Mongewell, in Oxfordshire, had a bitch, his constant attendant, the offspring of a tame dog-fox by a shepherd's cur, and she again had puppies by a dog. These are such authentic proofs of the continuance of the breed, that the fox may be fairly added to the other supposed *original stocks* of these faithful domestics."[417]

Dr. Morton states that his friend Dr. Woodhouse, who had been much in Texas and on the frontier, had proven, by a comparison of skulls, skins, &c., that "the *Cayotte*, or jackal, of Texas and Mexico is a perfectly distinct species, to which Dr. W. gives the name of *canis pustor.*" They breed readily with European and Indian dogs — this fact is notorious.

The jackal coupled with the domestic dog, produces also a fertile offspring; yet they must be conceded to be a distinct species. Hunter records an example where the hybrid produced six pups; and one of these again brought five pups when lined by a terrier dog. There is no difficulty in producing or keeping up such a mixture; but there is no practical object in perpetuating it. To what extent the blood of the jackal was originally mingled with dogs, and how far it has influenced our present types, cannot now be determined, although we should imagine that the trace is lost.

"It seems rarely to happen that the mule offspring is truly intermediate in character between the two parents. Thus, Hunter mentions that, in his experiments, one of the hybrid pups resembled the wolf much more than the rest of the litter; and we are informed by Wiegamann, that of a litter lately obtained at the Royal Menagerie at Berlin, from a white pointer and a she-wolf, two of the cubs resembled the common wolf-dog; but the other was like a pointer, with hanging ears."[418]

Facts enough, and authorities enough have already been given, to prove, we think, to any unprejudiced mind, a plurality of origin for the numerous canine species, whose blood has become mingled in our domestic dogs. If this point be conceded by scientific men—to whom alone we appeal—an immense stride is at once made in the Natural History of Humanity; because, zoologically speaking, mankind and *canidæ* occupy precisely the same position. Grant that different species may produce offspring prolific *inter se*, and the dogma of the unity of human families can no longer be sustained, either by facts, or by analogies derivable from the rest of the animal kingdom. Science, we are persuaded, will grant this truth ere long.

MONUMENTAL HISTORY OF DOGS.

Whatever doubts may still linger in the reader's mind as to the diversity of *canine* species, we feel confident that they must give way before the new facts we are now about to present. Like the races of men, many races of dogs can be traced back, in their present forms, on the monuments of Egypt, from 4000 to 6000 years anterior to our day; and, inasmuch as there is no evidence that dogs did really all proceed from one stock, or that their different types, such as greyhounds, mastiffs, turnspits, &c., can be transformed into each other by physical causes; and, again, considering that all these canine types did preserve, side by side in Egypt, their respective forms for thousands of years, these animals must be regarded, by every naturalist, as specifically distinct.

Substantiating our doctrine with reduced fac-similes of these monumental dogs, we shall thereby enable the reader to form his own conclusions.

Hieroglyphic *for* "Dog"—(*Canis Lupaster ?*).

The dog was one of the figurative and symbolic forms used by the primordial Egyptians in their hieroglyphic writings; and may be traced on the inscriptions of the monuments from the earliest to the latest. Two forms were used, which seem to have been taken from very distinct races; and these, again, were totally unlike the beautiful *grey-hound* which is often seen upon contemporary monuments.[419]

Hieroglyphic writing had attained its full perfection at the IVth dynasty, and we possess abundant legends of the thirty-fifth century B. C.; but the *invention* of writing, as every hierologist declares, must inevitably antedate these monuments by many centuries; ascending certainly to the time of MENES, B. C. 3893; and, pictorially, to ages anterior. The pure hieroglyphics represent *things* in their appropriate shapes and colors; which things are all indigenous in Egypt, to the exclusion of any element foreign to the Nile. Among them is this hieroglyphic (Fig. 235) for "dog," which, like every other primitive sign, continued to mean "dog," down to the extinction of hieroglyphical writing, about the fifth century after C. Thus, one species of the *common dog*, at least, existed in Egypt 1500 years before Usher's *deluge;* to say nothing of the Archbishop's fabulous era for the world's creation.

FIG. 235.

This (Fig. 235) is called a *fox-dog* by Dr. Morton; not to be confounded, however, with the "fox-hound" of English kennels. It is found in the catacombs embalmed in great numbers through various parts of the country; and appears to have been "the parent stock of the modern red wild" (or *Pariah*) "dog common at Cairo and other towns in Lower Egypt." These dogs, Clot Bey observes, lead a nomadic life, and are invariably without individual masters. They are also found, semi-wild, on the confines of the desert. An interesting account of these Nilotic canidæ may be consulted in Martin's *History of the Dog* — and he properly regards them as a distinct species, that, we may add, has come down unaltered from immemorial time.

FIG. 236.

Persian Wild Dog.

A similar — we dare not say the same — species prevails throughout Barbary; and the Levant, from Greece and European Turkey, through Asia Minor, Syria, Palestine, Assyria, Persia, into Hindostan. They belong to civic communities, rather than to any particular person. If taken young into domestic keeping, when adult they instinctively abandon the house; and, if grateful for kindnesses, they will obey no master; but hang around the localities of their birth, neither enticeable into familiarity, nor expulsable from the precincts of their earliest associations. They are the *scavengers* of oriental cities; and Muslim charity, whilst shuddering at the unclean touch of a dog's *nose*, recognizes their utility, and protects them by municipal laws as well as by alimentary legacies. If love for their human acquaintances be not vociferous, their hatred to strangers is intensely so: and it is in the attitude of annoying intruders that the annexed *wild dog of Persia* (Fig. 236) is represented.

Dr. Pickering, in the letter from Egypt to Morton before cited [*supra*, p. 245], after viewing these semi-wild dogs with the critical eye of a naturalist, aptly remarks: — "By the way, *the dogs here I find all of one breed*,—the same, if my memory serve me, with a mummied skull presented by Mr. Gliddon [1840] to the National Institute at Washington:—with upright ears, and very much of a jackal, or small wolf, in appearance, — often, even in color. They bark, however, as I can well attest, like other dogs; — and if this be, as alleged by some, a matter of education, there seems to be here no danger of the loss of the art."

The Grey-hound

Is a very common animal throughout all Eastern nations, and presents great divergencies of external form. Several varieties, probably three, are seen on the monuments of

FIG. 237.

Grey-hound.

Egypt; and the specimen here delineated (Fig. 237) is from one of the tombs of the IVth dynasty, 3400 years B. C.[420] This dog is cotemporary with the hieroglyphic dog, and next to that is the oldest form of *grey-hound* we possess. There are now extant only the monuments of the IVth, Vth, and VIth dynasties in detail, and very few of other dynasties to the XIth inclusive; or we should, in all probability, have beheld portrayed many other varieties of dogs. Again, it is quite by accident that *dogs* are figured at all in the early pyramid days; because the Egyptian artist was not exhibiting a gallery of Natural History in these painted sepulchres, but merely introducing, with the likeness of the deceased proprietor, those things the latter had loved during his lifetime; among them the portrait of his favorite *grey-hound.* When arrived at the XIIth dynasty we find a very rich collection, because we happen to have stumbled upon the tomb of a great *dog-fancier.* It is worthy of remark, however, that although the Egyptians have accidentally represented almost the whole fauna of the Nile on the monuments, yet there were some common animals which never appear in sculptures now extant — as the wild ass, the wild boar, &c. Some dogs have likewise been left out, because there was no object in drawing them. Martin (*Hist. of the Dog*) informs us that a similar variety of grey-hound is very common still in Asia and Africa; and Mr. William A. Gliddon, who has spent years in the Indian Archipelago, informs me that a curl-tailed grey-hound of this form is quite common among the Dyaks of Borneo, and among the aboriginal inhabitants of the Malayan peninsula. They make good hunting dogs. Color—dark brown, with black spots.

The species of grey-hound given in the above sketch is often repeated on the monuments of the IVth, Vth, and VIth dynasties, with precisely the same characters—long, erect ears, curled tail, &c.; only the tail in some specimens is much shorter than in others, having evidently been cut.

FIG. 238.[421]

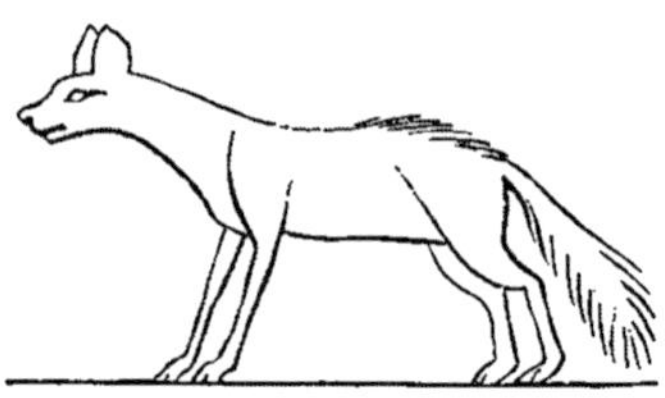

Wolf.

FIG. 239.[422]

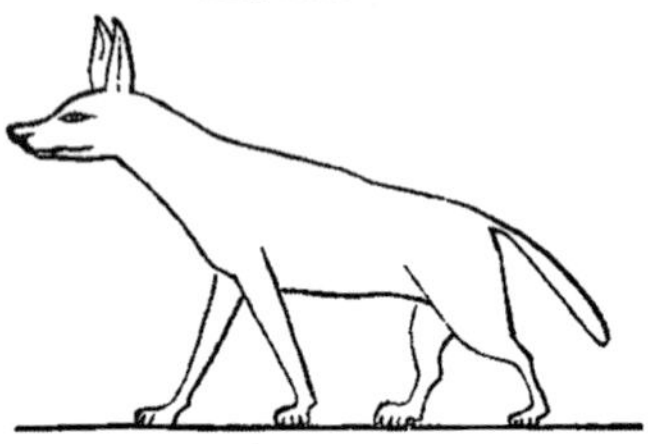

Hyena.

For the instruction of orthodox naturalists, who derive all *canidæ* from the Noachian pair of wolves, we submit the grandsire (Fig. 238) of the said lupine couple, who was alive in Egypt 3400 years B. C.; together with one of their hyena uncles (Fig. 239); and a jackal (Fig. 240) — their cousin in perhaps the forty-second degree.

FIG. 240.[423]

Jackal.

The scarcity of documents from the IVth to the end of the XIth dynasty, compels us to descend to the XIIth — 2400–2100 years B. C. Here we stand, not merely at a point which is several centuries before the birth of Abraham; but, at a day when, if the *deluge* occurred at B. C. 2348, the Egyptians, besides the wolves, hyenas, and jackals, in a wild state, possessed many kinds of dogs running about their houses, along with the *common dog* and *grey-hound*, preceding; whereas NOAH's seamanship, several hundred years afterwards, could only rescue *one pair* of wolves from drowning on the summit of Mount Ararat, thousands of feet above the line of perpetual glaciers.

The subjoined specimen (Fig. 241) of another species, is from the tomb of ROTI, who kept his kennel admirably stocked, during the XIIth dynasty. This dog is beautifully drawn and colored on the monument, and is one of the most superb canine relics of antiquity. Mr. Gliddon informs me that this is not only the common gazelle dog of Nubia at the present day, but that their ears are still cropped by the natives in the same way; as Prisse's drawing attests.[426]

FIG. 241.[424]

FIG. 242.[425]

We have not been able to find the portrait of an ancient rough hound, alluded to by Hamilton Smith; but here (Fig. 242) is the modern rough-haired grey-hound of Arabia, probably the same; and which will be interesting to the reader as a contrast to the other grey-hounds: it bears all the marks of a distinct species; but resembles the *Laconian* breed.

Another variety of grey-hound is said by Morton to be represented with rougher hair, and bushy tail, not unlike the modern Arabian grey-hound.

A grey-hound exactly like the English grey-hound, with semi-pendent ears, is seen on a statue of the Vatican at Rome.

Martin, whose work is full of instructive matter, says — "Now we have, in Modern Egypt and Arabia, and also in Persia, varieties of grey-hound closely resembling those on the ancient remains of art; and it would appear that two or three varieties exist — one smooth, another long-haired, and another smooth but with long-haired ears resembling those of a spaniel. In Persia, the grey-hound, to judge from specimens we have seen, is silk-haired, with a fringed tail. They were of a black color; but a fine breed, we are informed, is of a slate or ash color, as are some of the smooth-haired grey-hounds depicted in Egyptian paintings. In Arabia, a large, rough, powerful race exists; and about Akaba, according to Laborde, a breed of slender form, fleet, with a long tail, very hairy, in the form of a brush, with the ears erect and pointed — closely resembling, in fact, many of those figured by the ancient Egyptians. In Roumelia, a spaniel-eared race exists. Col. Sykes, who states that none of the domesticated dogs of Dukhun are common to Europe, observes that the first in strength and size is the Brinjaree dog, somewhat resembling the Persian grey-hound (in the possession of the Zoological Society), but more powerful. North of the Caspian, in Tartary and Russia, there exists a breed of large, rough grey-hounds. We may here allude to the great Albanian dog of former times, and at present extant, which perhaps belongs to the grey-hound family."[427]

The *grey-hound* can thus be distinctly traced back in several forms for 2000, and in one for more than 5000 years; and there is every reason to believe the Egyptian class embraced at least two, if not more, distinct species. Unlike all other dogs of the chase, they are almost destitute of smell, and pursue game by the eye alone. This deficiency of smell is connected with anatomical peculiarities, which must not be overlooked; because you cannot, by breeding, give a more powerful organ of scent to a grey-hound, without changing the animal into something else than a *grey-hound*.

The Hound.

Like the grey-hound, the *blood*, *stag*, and *fox* hounds, present many forms; and it is impossible, at the present day, to say whether they are varieties of one species, or whether they are derived from several primitive species. As far back as history can trace *hounds*, there seems to have been several very distinct animals of this kind. Our Egyptian monuments abound in hunting-scenes, in which hounds are represented in pursuit of wild animals of various kinds. These scenes are drawn oftentimes with great spirit; and the truthfulness of the delineations cannot be questioned, because they are perfectly true to nature at the present day, as will be seen by the subjoined drawings.

Fig. 243.[428]

This leash of hounds (Fig. 243) presents two varieties of the African *blood-hound;* one with erect, the other with drooping ears. They belonged to Roti's hunting-establishment, about the 22d century before Christ, at Beni-Hassan.

In Rosellini's colored copy of the same couple, here reduced in size, the off-dog is painted brick-dust; the near one is a light chestnut, with black patches.

Another of the same choice breed (Fig. 244), in full gaze.

Fig. 244.[429]

Fig. 245.[430]

Fig. 246.[431]

A fourth (Fig. 245), in the act of slaying a gazelle.

Here is a noble brace (Fig. 246), with the antelope they have captured, and their groom, returning to the kennel.

This (Fig. 247) is a variety of the same hound, pensively awaiting his dinner, about 4000 years ago.

Fig. 247.[432]

These hounds are a few specimens, selected from the several works of Lepsius, Rosellini, and Wilkinson. We could easily add a hundred more, not less characteristic. It is truly wonderful to compare these delineations, commencing as far back as the XIIth dynasty (twenty-third century B. C.), and extending down for 1000 years, with the common fox-hound and stag-hound of the present day — still more, with the African *blood-hound.*

In the *Grand Procession* of THOTMES III. (1550 B. C.), several of them are associated with the people and productions of the interior of Africa.[433] Again, in a later tomb at Gourneh, near Thebes, figured by Champollion. Dr. Morton says — "If we compare the oldest of these delineations, viz., those of Beni-Hassan, with the blood-hounds of Africa lately living in the Tower Menagerie in London, we cannot deny their identity, so complete is the resemblance of form and instinct."[434]

"On reading Mr. Birch's 'Observations on the Statistical Table of Karnac' (p. 56), I was much pleased to find this hound designated, beyond all question, in a letter of Candace, Queen of Ethiopia, to Alexander the Great, in which the former, among other presents to the Macedonian king, sends 'ninety dogs which hunt men' — *canes etiam in homines efferacissimos nonaginta.* And, that nothing may be necessary in explanation, the Queen further designates them as 'animals of our country.'"

The same *blood-hounds,* therefore, of which tribute was sent from the Upper Nile, in the sixteenth century B. C., had preserved their blood pure, down to B. C. 325, just as it is found at this day, in the same regions, after 3400 years.

Turnspit (*C. Vertagus.*)

Wilkinson, Blainville, Martin, and all, I believe, are agreed upon the identity of this dog. The portrait (Fig. 248), and others of the same well-marked character, are faithful representatives of the modern turnspit, which is still common in Asia and Europe.

FIG. 248.[435]

The figure above is from the tomb of ROTI, at Beni-Hassan, in the twenty-third century before Christ.

To the same ante-Abrahamic age (the XIIth dynasty) belongs this slut (Fig. 249), who stands under her master's chair, in his tomb at *El-Bersheh,* Middle Egypt. She is another species, but we hesitate in ascribing to it a name: although the *common-dog* of the Nile approaches nearest to the design.[437]

FIG. 249.[436]

Not only have we various other forms of dogs on the monuments of Egypt as far back as the XIIth dynasty, which, to our mind, cannot, from mere outline drawings, be satisfactorily identified with any of our European or American races; but, as we have shown, there also exist, in abundance, representations of wolves, jackals, hyenas, and foxes, each and all of which have been supposed to be progenitors of our domestic dogs — just as NOAH is said, by the same school of naturalists, to be the father of Jews, Australians, White-men, Mongols, Negroes, American aborigines, &c.

FIG. 250.[438]

Wolves.

As this animal has, by the majority of old-school naturalists, been believed to be the original parent of all dogs, we shall introduce here one specimen (Fig. 250) of a group of four *Egyptian* wolves, figured by Lepsius, from tombs of the IVth dynasty (about 3400 years B. C.). These Nilotic animals, which are different in species from European, are repeatedly seen, on sculptures of every epoch, sometimes chased by dogs, at other times caught in traps; in short, accompanied by so many corroborating circumstances as to leave no doubt that they were nothing but wild wolves. They are often depicted on the same monuments with dogs, ever perfectly contrasted.

Bull-dogs (*C. Molossus.*)

The term *molossus* has been rather vaguely applied by writers; but the type of the *bull-dog* is well understood. It is skilfully portrayed on a piece of antique Greek sculpture in the Vatican. M. de Blainville (in his *Ostéographie, Canis*, p. 74), states that the form and expression of the head are perfectly characteristic, even to the peculiar arrangement of the teeth. This species, too, is yet the common dog of Albania.

Mastiff (*C. Laniarius*).

We have nowhere yet met with this dog on the monuments of the Nile, although it must have been known to the Egyptians, through their constant intercourse with Assyria, in early times. The magnificent original of the sketch here given (Fig. 251) was taken from the *Birs Nimroud*, or Babylon, age of Nebuchadnezzar,[440] and would do honor to a prince of the present day. [His duplicate, we might almost say, is still alive; and belongs to my excellent friend Mrs. Jenkins, at Richmond, Va. — G. R. G.]

FIG. 251.[439]

Alexander, in his march to the Indus, received presents of dogs of gigantic stature, which were no doubt of the same family as the Thibetan mastiffs. To these dogs Aristotle applied the name of *leontomyx;* and they are figured on two ancient Greek medals — one of which, that of Segestus of Sicily, dates in the fourth or fifth century B. C.; the other, which is of Aquileia Severa, Dictator of Crete, is about two centuries later.[441]

Shepherd's Dog (*C. Domesticus*).

This dog, being (if a *Scotch* or *English* "shepherd-dog" be meant) altogether alien to the Nile at this day, is not figured on Egyptian monuments; but is doubtless very ancient in Europe. The earliest effigy, also mentioned by Aristotle, is preserved on an ancient Etruscan medal of unknown date, but probably as old as our Ninevite mastiff.

These remarks on the different species of dogs, faithfully delineated upon ancient monuments, might be very easily extended; but I have set forth enough to establish that the natural history of *dogs* and the natural history of *mankind* stand precisely in the same position. In whatever direction an inquirer may turn — wherever written history, monuments, analogies, or organic remains, exist to direct us—in every zoological province upon earth, I repeat, a specifically diverse fauna is encountered, in which distinct species, as well of mankind as of dogs, constitute a part.

The earliest monuments yet published by Lepsius are those of the IVth dynasty; and from these we here already have borrowed the "hieroglyphic" or *fox-dog*, the prick-eared *grey-hound*, the *blood-hound*, the *turnspit*, with other species; together with the wolf, the hyena, and the jackal. The Egyptian *fox* has not fallen under our eye at this early epoch, although it is seen on later monuments. Notwithstanding that the monuments of the earliest times do not exhibit every form of dogs that existed at the subsequent XIIth dynasty, their absence is no argument why these multifarious species did not exist from the very beginning; and while all the canine forms just mentioned must ascend even beyond the date of MENES, (which Lepsius places at the year 3893 B. C.,) science can perceive no reason to doubt that other unrecorded varieties of *canidæ* are quite as ancient as those of which fortuitous accident has preserved the pictorial register down to this day.

Concerning *fossil dogs*, the terrestrial vitality of which antedates Egyptian monuments by chiliads of years, Dr. Usher's enumeration (*supra*, Chap. XI.) of the numerous varieties discovered in geological formations, all over the world, precludes the necessity for saying more now, than that certain forms of true *canidæ* are primordial organic types; and, hence, utterly independent of alterations produced, in later times, by domestication.

Logical criticism will allow that, if specific differences among dogs were the result of climate, all the dogs of each separate country should be alike. Such, notoriously, is not the case; for the reader has just beheld several species of dogs, depicted (at various epochs, during 4000 years of coeval existence) on the monuments; which species are not only now seen in Egypt alive, but are permanent, always and everywhere, in other countries of climates the most opposite.

Indeed, "like begets like," to use dog-fancy terms; and a terrier is a *terrier*, and a dingo a *dingo*, all the world over, else language has no meaning; and wherever climatic action may be hostile to the permanency of either type, it does not transform the one into the other, nor into any species diverse from each: it kills them both outright, or their offspring within a generation or two. Thus, Newfoundlands perish within very limited periods after transplantation from American snows to African suns. Their short-lived whelps are as likely to become kittens as to be changed, by *climate*, into bull-pups. An interesting exception, nevertheless, should be observed:

viz., where dogs, becoming *wild*, return to a state of nature, they have, in the course of time, resumed very different types; say, shepherd's dog, Danish dog, grey-hound, terrier, and so on. "In other words, *they constantly tend to recur to that primitive type which is most dominant in their physical constitution; and it is remarkable, that in the Old World this restored type is never the* WOLF, *although it is sometimes a lupine dog, owing to the cause just mentioned.*'"

Where opposite types of dogs are bred together, and their hybrid progeny becomes again intermingled, all sorts of mongrel, degenerate, or deformed varieties arise; such as pugs, shocks, spaniels, &c.; which Cuvier calls "the most degenerate productions;" and they are found, by experience, "to possess a short and fleeting existence—the common lot of all types of modern origin." Such deformities arise in nature everywhere. There is one instance of dwarfish canine malformation, 4000 years old, in Lepsius's plate[442] of the XIIth dynasty; and embalmed monstrosities of other genera were found by Passalacqua.

Among North American Indian dogs, says Dr. Morton, "the original forms are very few, and closely allied; whence it happens that these grotesque varieties never appear. Neither have they any approximation to that marked family we call *hounds;* and this fact is the more remarkable, since the Indian dogs are employed in the same manner of hunting as the hounds of Europe, Asia, and Africa. Yet, this similarity of employment has caused no analogy of exterior form. No varieties like those so familiar in Europe, spring up *inter se* among them. They are as homogeneous as wolf-races, from whom they are descended; and Dr. Richardson quotes Theodat to show that the *common Indian dog* has not materially changed during two hundred and twenty years. Again, the same remark applies to the indigenous *aguara, alco,* and *techichi* dogs of Mexico and South America, which, before their admixture with European breeds, conformed to the types or species from which they sprung, without branching into the thirty *varieties* of Buffon, or the sixty of Brown."

In the words of Jacquinot, whose "Anthropologie"[443] is the ablest work on Man yet put forth in the French language, let me close these few, out of infinite, analogies in the animal kingdom, which space confines to the foregoing paragraphs on *dogs*. "Il est indubitable que les variétés du chien appartiennent à *plusieurs* types primitifs."

The facts above detailed establish, conclusively, that *Hybridity* is not a "unit;" or, in other words, they prove that different degrees of affinity exist in Nature, to be taken into account in all inquiries into the prolificacy of diverse "species." Equally certain is it, that climate and domestication affect animal species differently: some of them becoming variously modified in form and color—as horses, cattle, goats, sheep, fowls, pigeons, &c.; while others, to considerable extent, resist such physical influences—like the ass, the buffalo, the elk, the reindeer, pea-fowls, guinea-fowls, and so forth.

Now, it is equally singular and true, that these identical species, whence Natural History deduces very strong reasons for believing them to be derived from many primitive stocks, are those which undergo the greatest changes; whereas, on the contrary, other species, which equally good reasons induce us to regard as simple—that is, derived from one primitive stock—are precisely those in which the experience of ages chronicles the smallest alteration. This law (if it be such) seems to apply not merely to the lower animals, but also to mankind. In America, for example, where the autocthonous population has been isolated, very little variety is found among Indian tribes; whereas, in Europe, Asia, and Africa (more particularly in and around Egypt and India), we encounter infinite diversities among human beings, manifested in every form and by all colors.

The perplexing anomalies that beset this investigation may be illustrated by the following *resumé*, in which I have incorporated some very interesting facts, published by Dr. Alexander Harvey in the *London Monthly Journal of the Medical Sciences:*[444]

Instances are sufficiently common among the lower animals where the offspring exhibit, more or less distinctly, in addition to the characters of the male by which they were begotten, the peculiarities also of a male by which their mother had at some former period been impregnated: — or, as it has been otherwise expressed, where the peculiarities of a male animal, that had once held fruitful intercourse with a female, are more or less distinctly recognized in the offspring of subsequent connections of that female with other males. It is interesting to inquire whether this is a general law in animal physiology; and if it be, whether, and how far, it is modified in its operation in different animals, and under different circumstances: and it is of still more immediate interest to us to inquire whether, or not, the fact extends also to the human species. The facts bearing upon this subject may be most conveniently noticed—1st, in relation to the lower animals; 2d, in relation to the human species.

1. *In the Brute Creation.* — A young chestnut mare, seven-eighths Arabian, belonging to the Earl of Morton, was covered in 1815 by a quagga, which is a species of wild ass from Africa, and marked somewhat like a zebra. The mare was covered but once by the zebra; and, after a pregnancy of eleven months and four days, gave birth to a hybrid which had distinct marks of the quagga, in the shape of its head, black bars on the legs and shoulders, &c. In 1817, 1818, and 1821, the same mare, which had become the property of Sir Gore Ouseley, was covered by a very fine black Arabian horse, and produced successively three foals, all of which bore unequivocal marks of the quagga. A mare belonging to Sir Gore Ouseley was covered by a zebra, and gave birth to a striped hybrid. The year following the same mare was covered by a thorough-bred horse, and the next succeeding year by another horse. Both the *foals* thus produced were striped: *i. e.*, partook of the characters of the zebra. It is stated by Haller, and also by Becker, that when a mare has had a *mule* by an ass, and afterwards a *foal* by a horse, the foal exhibits traces of the ass. We can ourselves vouch for the truth of similar facts. A vast number of mules are bred in the United States, from the ass and the mare; and we have frequently seen colts from horses, out of mares, which had previously had mules; many of them were distinctly marked by the ass.

In these cases, the mares were covered in the first instance by animals of a different species from themselves. But cases are recorded of mares covered in every instance by horses, but by different horses on different occasions, where the offspring partook of the characters of the horse by which the impregnation was first effected. Thus, in several foals in the royal stud at Hampton Court, got by the horse *Acteon*, there were unequivocal marks of the horse *Colonel*—the dams of these foals had been bred from by Colonel the previous year. Again, a colt, the property of the Earl of Suffield, got by *Laurel*, so resembled another horse, *Camel*, "that it was whispered, nay even asserted at New Market, that he must have been got by Camel." It was ascertained, however, that the mother of the Laurel colt had been covered the previous year by Camel.

It has often been observed, also, that a well-bred bitch, if she have been impregnated by a mongrel dog, will not, although lined subsequently by a pure dog, bear thorough-bred puppies in the next two or three litters. The like occurrence has been noticed with the sow. A sow of a peculiar black-and-white breed was impregnated by a boar of the wild breed, of a deep chestnut color; the pigs produced were duly mixed, the color of the boar in some being very predominant. The sow being afterwards put to a boar of the same breed as her own, some of the produce were observed to be marked with the chestnut color that prevailed in the former litter: and, on a subsequent impregnation, the boar being still of the same breed as the sow, the litter was also observed to be slightly stained with the chestnut color. What adds to the value of the fact now stated is, that, in the course of many years' observation, the breed in question was never known afterwards to produce progeny having the smallest tinge of chestnut color. We may here remark that it is only in a state of domestication that animals produce offspring of various colors. When left entirely to the operation of natural causes, they never exhibit this sporting of colors; they are distinguished by various and often beautiful shades of color; but then each species is true to its own family type, even to a few hairs or small parts of a feather. It is needless to repeat examples of these facts — they are familiar to all rearers of animals; among cattle they are of every-day occurrence. There is another fact worthy of notice. It is well known to cattle-breeders, that the term of utero-gestation is much influenced by the sire — the calves of one bull will be carried longer in utero than those of another.

2. *In the Human Species.* — There are equally distinct breeds of the human family as of any of the lower animals; and it is affirmed that the human female, when twice married, bears occasionally to the second husband children resembling the first both in bodily structure and mental powers. Where all the parties are *of the same color*, this statement is not so easy of verification; but, where a woman has had children by two men of different colors, such as a black and a white man, it would be comparatively easy to observe whether the offspring of the latter connexion bore any resemblance to the former parent. Count Strzelecki, in his *Physical History of Van Diemen's Land*, asserts, that, when a native woman has had a child by a European male, "*she loses the power of conception, on a renewal of intercourse, with a male of her own race, retaining only that of procreating with the white men.*" "Hundreds of instances (says the Count) of this extraordinary fact are recorded in the writer's memoranda, *all occurring invariably under the same circumstances*, amongst the Hurons, Seminoles, Red Indians, Yakies (Sinaloa), Mendosa Indians, Auracos, South Sea Islanders, and natives of New Zealand, New South Wales, and Van Diemen's Land; and all tending to prove that the sterility of the female, which is relative only to one and not to another male, is not accidental, but follows laws as cogent, though as mysterious, as the rest of those connected with generation." In this sweeping assertion the Count may have been mistaken: a traveller could hardly have had opportunities for ascertaining a fact, which it must require years of careful observation to confirm. It is certain that no such thing exists between the whites and Negroes, the two races with which we are the most familiar; because examples are of frequent occurrence, where a Negress, after having had a child by a white man, has had a family by a husband of her own color.

Instances are cited, where a Negro woman bore mulatto children to a white man, and afterwards had by a black man other children, who bore a strong resemblance to the white father, both in features and complexion. It is supposed by some, that the influence, exerted on the generative system of a female of one race by sexual intercourse with the male of another, may be increased by repeated connexions; and Dr. Laing informs us of the case of an English gentleman in the West Indies, who had a large family by a Negro woman, and where the children exhibited successively, more and more, the European features and complexion. I have living with me a black woman, whose first child was by a white man:

she has had six children since, by a black husband, who are perfectly black, and unlike the first father; yet, it is a singular fact that these children, though strongly-marked Negroes, bear no family likeness to either father or mother—their physiognomy is as distinct as that of any two families of the same race. The children of a second husband may resemble the first sufficiently to attract attention, even where there is no striking contrast of color; thus Dr. Harvey cites a case where a lady was twice married, and had issue by both husbands. One of the children by the second marriage bears an unmistakeable resemblance to her mother's first husband; and what makes the likeness more discernible is, that there was a marked difference in features and general appearance between the two husbands.

The chain of facts herein by this time linked together, aside from many more of identical force that might easily be added, proves conclusively that prolificacy between two races of animals is no test of specific affiliation; and it therefore follows, as a corollary, that prolificacy among the different races of men carries with it no evidence of common origin. On the other hand, if it can be shown that the law of hybridity prevails between any two human races, the argument in favor of plurality of species would thereby be greatly strengthened.

I think that the genus *homo* includes many primitive species; and that these species are amenable to the same laws which govern species in many other genera. The species of men are all *proximate*, according to the definition already given; nevertheless, some are perfectly prolific; while others are imperfectly so—possessing a tendency to become extinct when their hybrids are bred together. At the beginning of this chapter I referred to my own observations, made some years ago, on the crossing of white and black races: and my investigations since that time, as well as those of many other anatomists, confirm the views before enunciated. So far as the races of men can be traced through osteography, history and monuments, the present volume establishes that they have always been distinct. No example is recorded, where one race has been transformed into another by external causes. *Permanence of type* must therefore be regarded as an infallible test of specific character. M. Jacquinot very dexterously remarks that, according to the theory of unity of races, a mulatto belongs to a "species" as much as any other human being, and that the white and black races would be but "varieties."

When two *proximate* species of mankind, two races bearing a general resemblance to each other in type, are bred together—*e.g.*, Teutons, Celts, Pelasgians, Iberians, or Jews—they produce offspring perfectly prolific: although, even here, their peculiarities cannot become so entirely fused into a homogeneous mass as to obliterate the original types of either. One or the other of these types will "crop-out," from time to time, more or less apparently in their progeny. When, on the other hand, species the most widely separated, such as the Anglo-Saxon with the Negro, are crossed, a different result has course. Their mulatto offspring, if still prolific, are but partially so; and acquire an inherent tendency to run out, and become eventually extinct when kept apart from the parent stocks. This opinion is now becoming general among observers in our slave States; and it is very strongly insisted upon by M. Jacquinot. This skilful naturalist (unread in cis-Atlantic literature) claims the discovery as original with himself; although erroneously, because it had long previously been advocated by Estwick and Long, the historians of Jamaica; by Dr. Caldwell;[445] by Professors Dickson and Holbrook, of Charleston, S. C.; and by numerous other leading medical men of our Southern States. There are some 4,000,000 of Negroes in the United States; about whom circumstances, personal and professional, have afforded me ample opportunities for observation. I have found it impossible, nevertheless, to collect such statistics as would be satisfactory to others on this point; and the difficulty arises solely from the want of chastity among mulatto women, which is so notorious as to be proverbial. Although often married to hybrid males of their own color, their children are begotten as frequently by white or other men, as by their husbands. For many years, in my daily professional visits, I have been in the habit of meeting with mulatto women, either free or slaves; and, never omitting an opportunity of inquiry with regard to their prolificacy, longevity of offspring, color of parents, age, &c., the conviction has become indelibly fixed in my mind that the positions laid down in the beginning of this chapter are true.

Hombron and Jacquinot have asserted on their own authority, as well as upon that of others, that this law of infertility holds also with the cross of the European on the Hottentot and Australian.

"Les quelques tribus qui se trouvaient aux environs de Port Jackson, vont chaque jour en décroissant, et c'est à peine si l'on cite quelques rares métis d'Australien et d'Européen. Cette absence de métis entre deux peuples vivant en contacte sur la même terre, prouve bien incontestablement la différence des espèces. On conçoit du reste que, si ces métis existaient, ils seraient bien faciles à reconnoître, et à différencier des espèces mères.

"A Hobart Town et sur toute la Tasmanie, il n'y a pas d'avantage de métis; tout ce qui reste des indigènes (quarante environ) à été transporté dans une petite île du détroit de Bass."[446]

The official reports published by the British Parliament confirm this statement as to Australia.

French and Spanish writers have maintained that, when the grade of *quinteroon* is arrived at, the Negro type is lost, and that such man becomes no longer distinguishable from the pure white. In some of the West India Islands this grade of slave by law becomes free. Now, it must be remembered that the Spaniards, and a certain proportion of the population of France, are themselves already as dark as any quinteroon, or even a quadroon; and thus it may readily happen that very few crosses would merge the dark into the lighter race: but, when the Anglo-Saxon and the Negro are brought together, no such result has been perceived, or hinted at, in the United States, where the latter amalgamation is going on upon an immense scale. Slaves of Southern States, seduced by delusive representations, are constantly making attempts to escape to free States; and would succeed without difficulty in most cases, were it not for their color: yet they have rarely, if ever, become so fair through white lineage as to escape detection. I am not sure that I ever saw at the South, one of such adult mixed-bloods so fair that I could not instantaneously trace the Negro type in complexion and feature. When we bear in mind the length of time during which the two races have been commingling in the United States, how are we to explain this fact? The only physiological reason that may be assigned is this: *the mulattoes, or mixed-breeds, die off before the dark stain can be washed out by amalgamation.* No other rational explanation can be offered.

Mr. Lyell speaks of some mulattoes he met with in North Carolina, whom, he says, he could not distinguish from whites; but, if any such examples exist, among the multiform crosses between Anglo-Saxons and Negroes, they must be extraordinarily few; because my half century's residence in our slave States should have brought me in contact with many instances. However, an Englishman, coming from an island where a Negro is a "rara avis," and running through the United States at Mr. Lyell's speed, could not become familiarized with these various grades, and therefore his eye might well be deceived. The great geologist certainly made many other decidedly erroneous observations in his American tour; quite innocently we all admit.

M. Gerdy claims (*Traité de Physiologie*) that primitive human species have all disappeared through amalgamations; giving a most erudite rehearsal of the wars and migrations which have influenced races, from the earliest times downwards: but it is a hard matter to wash out blood; and we oppose the fact, that the representatives of many original types still live: such as the Greeks (heroic type), the Basques, the Jews, the Australians, the Indians, and, above all, the Egyptians.

M. Jacquinot, whose ability and great opportunities for investigation add much weight to his authority, lays down the following conclusions: —

"1. A *species*, or race which represents it, is primitive, when all the individuals that compose it present the same physical characters, same color of skin, same type of face, same conformation, same kind of hair — notwithstanding the varieties of physiognomy of individuals, which vary to infinitude in all species.

"In a species, according to Cuvier, 'the children resemble the father and mother, as much as these resemble each other.'

"2. It is impossible, no matter how we produce crosses between species or races on the globe, to obtain a product which represents exactly one of the primitive types; that is to say, we shall never be able to construct, with all the pieces, a Negro, an American, a German, or a Celt.

"3. The species will separate from the primitive type, and will become the more altered by crosses with other species, in proportion as the individuals which compose it differ from each other, and as the types are more numerous.

"4. The greater the differences among individuals, the less the species which have produced them will be near (*voisines*) to each other, and *vice versâ*."[447]

The laws governing hybridity have as yet been but imperfectly studied. Some points of vital interest, connected with the crossing of races, have passed by without notice; for example, the relative influence of the male and the female on progeny. The physical characteristics of the common mule (offspring of the ass and mare) are well known. It partakes of the characters of both parents; but in the form of the head and ears, as well as in disposition, it inherits more of the ass than of the horse. The *bardeau*, or hinny (offspring of horse and she-ass) partakes, on the contrary, much more of the peculiarities of the horse — the head being small, closely resembling the horse; the ears short; the disposition rather that of the horse; and the voice is not a bray, but the neigh. The mule and hinny are almost as much unlike each other as the horse and ass. How far this rule may be applicable to other infertile hybrids, I am not prepared to say.

Where *proximate* species are bred together, the above rule, based upon *equidæ*, applies with less force; *e. g.*, the dog and wolf, or different species of dogs. I have seen pups from the cross of the cur-dog and wolf, which presented an *intermediate* type; but the following appears to show that a different breed of dog may produce a divergent result: —

"In the recent experiments of Wiegemann, in Berlin, of the offspring of a pointer and she-wolf, two resembled the father, with hanging ears, while the other was like a wolf-dog."[448]

When the grey-hound and fox-hound, the fox-hound and terrier, are coupled, their offspring partake rather of the half-and-half type.

We are unable to declare what shades of difference may arise from the manner of crossing canine males and females. A grey-hound possesses great speed, has a peculiar shape, and pursues his game by sight alone; being so destitute of smell as to be incapable of trailing it. The fox-hound, on the contrary, tracks game almost solely by scent, has little speed, but great endurance. Now, when fox-hound and grey-hound are bred together, their offspring is intermediate in form, in speed, in sense of smell, and in every attribute. Such law, I believe, holds with regard to all dogs, when thorough-bred.

Some years ago, I was intimate with a gentleman who owned a

fine pack of fox-hounds. Wishing to retain the sense of smell, and at the same time procure more speed, he commenced by crossing them with grey-hounds; and continued crossing until he obtained a stock of but one-eighth grey-hound, which dogs gave him all the qualities desired.

Now it would appear, from sundry facts already set forth under our "Caucasian" type, that even *proximate* species are not invariably governed by the same laws. Some species produce an intermediate type, like the dogs just cited; while others possess a tendency to reproduce each of the parent stocks. We may instance the white and gray mice, the deer and ram, no less than the fair and the dark-skinned races of men.

During a professional visit (which interrupted these lines) to the house of a friend, Mr. Garland Goode, my notice was attracted by some curious facts respecting the crossing of races. Among his slaves he owns three families, all crosses of white and black blood, as follows:—

1st. A woman, three-fourths white, married to a half-breed mulatto man. She had four children; the two first and the last of which were even more fair than the mother. The other presented a dark complexion — that of the father.

2d. A mulatto woman, half-breed, married to a full-blooded Negro man, not of the jettiest hue, although black. They had thirteen children; of which most were even blacker than the father, while two exhibited the light complexion of the mother.

3d. A mulatto man, married to a very black Negress. They had twelve children; and here again the majority of the children were coal-black, whereas two or three were as light in complexion as the father.

With respect to these examples, it is evident that, in the first case, white-blood predominated in the parents. In the two latter, the Negro blood was paramount. Thus, in three cases, the law of hybridity seems clearly to have been called into action. The children had a tendency to run into the type of the predominant blood: because, in the first example, white-blood preponderated in the children; in the two last, black-blood. Now, I do not consider this rule to be constant; but such examples are common. Mr. Lyell has again, in these matters, made statements upon exceptions to rules, and not, assuredly, upon the rules themselves.

Observations are wanting to settle many of the laws that govern the mixing of human species. In the United States, the mulattoes and other grades are produced by the connection of the white *male* with the *Negress;* the mulattoes with each other; and the white male with the *mulattress.* It is so rare, in this country, to see the offspring of a Negro man and a white woman, that I have never personally encountered an example; but such children are reported to partake more of the type of the Negro, than when the mode of crossing is reversed. I am, however, told that the progeny derived from a Negro father presents characteristics different from those where the male parent of mulattoes is white; and consequently I suspend decision.

Our ordinary mulattoes are nearly intermediate between the parent stocks; governed, apparently, very much by laws similar to those we have instanced in the grey-hound and fox-hound. They are, however, as before stated, less prolific than the parent stock; which condition is coupled with an inherent tendency to run out, so much so, that mulatto humanity seldom, if ever, reaches, through subsequent crossings with white men, that grade of dilution which washes out the Negro stain.

While speaking of dogs, we hinted, that the brain and nervous system, in animal nature, are so influenced by crossing, as to make instincts and senses partake of intermediate characters. The same law applies to human white and black races; for the mulatto, if certainly more intelligent than the Negro, is less so than the white man. His intelligence, as a general rule, augments in proportion to the amount of white-blood in his veins. This is invariably the case in the United States. In Hayti, *mulattoes* governed until exterminated by the blacks; and it is the mulatto element which now dominates, and always will govern in Liberia, until this experimental colony be annexed by Anglo-Saxons, or annihilated by native Negroes. Comparisons of crania alone substantiate this view, upon anatomical grounds; the past ratifies it, upon historical data: future Liberian destinies, if deduced from such premises, are not exhilarating. Again, in Africa itself, all Negro empires are ruled by the superior *Foolah* races.

It may be received, I think, as a fact, that in white races the intellect of children is derived much more from the mother than the father. Popular experience remarks, that great men seldom beget great sons; and it is equally true, that dull women do not often produce intelligent children. On the other hand, the mothers of great men almost invariably have been distinguished by vigorous natural intellects, whether cultivated or not. Now, it is singularly noteworthy, in connection with the above phenomena, that this doctrine seems to be reversed where black are crossed with white races. The intellect of a mulatto, child of a white male and a Negress, is certainly superior to that of the Negro; and I have pointed out, when speaking of the mule and bardeau, that the *form of the head is given by the sire.* Space now precludes my doing more than suggest inquiry into a new and interesting point, unfortunately not illumined by Morton's penetration.

Again and again, in previous publications, I have alluded to the fallibility of arguments drawn from analogy alone, while insisting that no true analogies can be said to exist. Every animal, from man to the worm, is governed by special physiological laws. Let me notice, *en passant*, the curious fact, that natural giants and dwarfs are next to fabulous in the animal kingdom, although frequent enough in the human family; subjoining an extract from one of my earlier articles on hybridity: —

"Catherine de Medicis amused herself and court by collecting, from various quarters, a number of male and female dwarfs, and forming marriages amongst them; but they were all unprolific. The same experiment was made by the Electress of Brandenburg, wife of Joachim Frederic, and with the same result. Geoffroy Saint Hilaire, in his researches, has been able to discover but one exception, the famous dwarf Borwilaski, and there are strong doubts about the faithfulness of his wife, who was a woman of full stature. Giants are likewise impotent, deficient in intellect, feeble in body, and short-lived. It is a remarkable fact, that giants and dwarfs proper are almost unknown in the animal kingdom, while they are common in all the races of men, and under all circumstances." [449]

Our chapter on *Geographical Distribution* alludes to one peculiar effect in the crossing of races, as illustrated by the blacks and whites in our Southern States: viz. —how the smallest admixture of Negro blood is equivalent to acclimation against yellow fever, being almost tantamount to complete exemption.

Much passes current, among breeders of domestic animals, about the improvements of breeds by crossing them; and similar ideas have been suggested by many writers, as applicable to the human family; but the notion itself is very unphilosophical, and could never have originated with any intelligent naturalist of thorough experience in such matters. It is *mind*, and mind alone, which constitutes the proudest prerogative of man; whose excellence should be measured by his intelligence and virtue. The Negro and other unintellectual types have been shown, in another chapter, to possess heads much smaller, by actual measurement in cubic inches, than the white races; and, although a metaphysician may dispute about the causes which may have debased their intellects or precluded their expansion, it can not be denied that these dark races are, in this particular, greatly inferior to the others of fairer complexion. Now, when the white and black races are crossed together, the offspring exhibits throughout a modified anatomical structure, associated with sundry characteristics of an intermediate type. Among other changes superinduced, the head of a mulatto is larger than that of the Negro; the forehead is more developed, the facial angle enlarged, and the intellect becomes manifestly improved. This fact is notorious in the United States; and it is historically exemplified by another: viz., that the mulattoes, although but a fraction of the population of Hayti, had ruled the island till expelled by the overwhelming jealousy and major numerical force of the blacks. In Liberia, President Roberts boasts of but one-fourth Negro blood; while all the colored chiefs of departments in that infant republic hold in their veins more or less of white-blood; which component had been copiously infiltrated, prior to emigration from America, into that population generally. If all the white-blood were suddenly abstracted, or the flow of whitening elements from the United States to be stopped, the whole fabric would doubtless soon fall into ruins; and leave as little trace behind as Herodotus's famous Negro colony of Colchis, or the more historical one of Meroë. From the best information procurable, we know that there has been a vast deal of exaggeration, among colonizationists at home, about this mulatto colony of Liberia abroad; nor, much as we should be gratified at the success of the experiment, can we perceive how any durable good can be expected from it, unless some process be discovered by which a Negro's head may be changed in form, and enlarged in size. History affords no evidence that cultivation, or any known causes but physical amalgamation, can alter a primitive conformation in the slightest degree. Lyell himself acknowledges: —

"The separation of the colored children in the Boston schools arose, not from an indulgence in anti-Negro feelings, but because they find they can in this way bring on both races faster. Up to the age of fourteen, the black children advance as fast as the whites; but after that age, unless there be an admixture of white-blood, it becomes in most instances extremely difficult to carry them forward. That the half-breeds should be intermediate between the two parent-stocks, and that the colored race should therefore gain in mental capacity in proportion as it approximates in physical organization to the whites, seems natural; and yet it is a wonderful fact, psychologically considered, that we should be able to trace the phenomena of hybridity even into the world of intellect and reason." [450]

To persons domiciled in our slave-States, it is really amusing to hear the many-toned hosannahs sung in Old England and in New England, over the success of the Republic of Liberia; while the world shakes with laughter at Frenchmen for attempting a *republic*, or any other stable form of government short of absolute despotism; as if Negroes were a superior race to the Franco-Gauls!

Robespierre gave, in palliation of his cruelties, that you could not reason with a Gallic opposition: the only way to silence it being through the guillotine. It would be a curious investigation to inquire, what was the type of those turbulent spirits? I have little doubt that each despot of the hour would be found to have been one of those dark-skinned, black-haired, black-eyed fellows, depicted so well [*supra*] by Bodichon; and if the imperial government were simply to chop off the head of every demagogue who was not a blond *white*-man, they might "get along" in France as tranquilly as in England, Germany, and the United States. *Dark*-skinned races, history attests, are only fit for military governments. It is the unique rule genial to their physical nature: they are unhappy without it, even now, at

Paris. None but the fair-skinned types of mankind have been able, hitherto, to realize, in peaceful practice, the old Germanic system described by Tacitus—"De minoribus rebus, principes consultant; de majoribus, omnes"—*omnes*, be it understood, signifying exclusively white men of their own type.

If these remarks be true in basis, it is evident, theoretically, that the superior races ought to be kept free from all adulterations, otherwise the world will retrograde, instead of advancing, in civilization. It may be a question, whether there is not already too much adulteration in Europe. Spain and Italy, where the darker races are in the majority, continue still behind in the march. France, although teeming with gigantic intellects, has been struggling in vain for sixty years to found a stable government—her population is tainted with bad elements; and wherever Portuguese or Spanish colonies attempt to compete with Anglo-Saxons, they are left astern, when not "annexed." It is the strictly-white races that are bearing onward the flambeau of civilization, as displayed in the Germanic families alone. Sir Walter Scott declares:—

"The government of Spain, a worn-out despotism, lodged in the hands of a family of the lowest degree of intellect, was one of the worst in Europe; and the state of the nobility in general (for there were noble exceptions) seemed scarcely less degraded. The incestuous practice of marrying within the near degrees of propinquity had long existed, with its usual consequences: the dwarfing of the body and the degeneracy of the understanding."[451] To which Mr. Percival Hunter adds, that "writers on lunacy attribute the insanity, or rather the innate idiocy, so frequent among certain Scotch families, to the old national practice of never marrying out of their clan."[452]

The civilization of ancient Rome, achieved by a very mixed race, although grand in its way, was, nevertheless, characterized throughout by cruelty, a certain degree of barbarism and want of refinement.

These crude elements of the laws of hybridity—laws by no means clearly defined in anthropological science—derive some illustration by contrasting the aristocracies of Europe. In England, where intermarriages between impoverished nobles of the Norman stock with wealthy commoners of the homogeneous Saxon, and where elevation of plebeians to the peerage, reinvigorate the breed, such patrician classes comprehend more manly beauty (Circassia, perhaps, excepted) than exists in the same number of individuals throughout the globe.

"What proportion," well asks the *Westminster Review*, "of the old Percy blood flows in the veins of those who claim the honor of the family's representation? The *fanatics* of 'blood,' *i. e.*, those who are not content to yield that reasonable amount of regard to it, which sense and sentiment both permit, should remember that when the main line has merged, again and again, into other families, the original blood must be but a small constituent of the remote descendant's personality.

"The great subverter of the aristocratic principle in the creation of peers, was Pitt. In fighting his battle against the Whigs, he availed himself immensely of the moneyed interest;

and rewarded the supporters of party with the honors of the crown. At every general election a batch was made: *eight* peerages were created in 1790; and in 1794, when a Whig defection to him took place, *ten* were created. Sir Egerton Brydges, a very accomplished man, both as a genealogist and a man of letters, published a special pamphlet on the point in 1798. He undoubtedly expressed the views of the aristocratic party when he said—

"'In every parliament I have seen the number augmented of busy, intriguing, pert, low members, who, without birth, education, honorable employments, or perhaps even fortune, dare to obtrude themselves, and push out the landed interest.'

. . . "What then is at present the portion of genuine aristocracy in the House of Lords? Calculations have been made by genealogists on this subject, of which we shall avail ourselves.

"The learned author of the *Origines Genealogicæ* analysed the printed peerage of 1828, and found that of 249 noblemen 35 'laid claim' to having traced their descent beyond the Conquest; 49 prior to 1100; 29 prior to 1200; 32 prior to 1300; 26 prior to 1400; 17 to 1500; and 26 to 1600. At the same time 30 had their origin but little before 1700. . . . Here then we have a result of one-half of the peerage being at all events *traceable* to a period antecedent to the Wars of the Roses. But of these a third only had emerged at all out of insignificance during the two previous centuries.

"Sir Harris Nicolas fixes as his standard of pretension in Family, the having been of consideration, baronial or knightly rank, that is, in the reign of Queen Elizabeth; and applying that test to the English Peerage in 1830, found that *one-third* of the body were entitled to it.

"There still remains in the male line, up and down England, a considerable number of landed families of very high antiquity; but the gradual decay and extinction of these is the constant theme of genealogists. Hear old Dugdale in the Preface to his Baronage in 1675.

"He first speaks of the Roll of Battle Abbey, and says of it:—'There are great errors or rather falsities in most of these copies. . . . Such hath been the subtilty of some monks of old.' But, speaking of his labors, generally, he has these more remarkable words:—

"'For of no less than 270 families, touching which this first volume doth take notice, there will hardly be found above *eight* which do to this day continue; and of those not any whose estates (compared with what their ancestors enjoyed) are not a little diminished. Nor of that number (I mean 270) above *twenty-four* who are by any younger male branch descended from them, for aught I can discover.'"[453]

Hence ethnology deduces, that the prolonged superiority of the English to any other aristocracies is mainly due to the continuous upheaval of the Saxon element: and, at such point of view, the social aspirations of Lord John Manners would seem to be as philosophical as his poetic effusions are unique:—

"Let arts and manners, laws and commerce, die;
But leave us still our old nobil*ity!*"

So, again, in Muscovy. German wives and Teutonic officers have metamorphosed the old Tartar nobility into higher-castes than IVAN and his court would have reputed to be ***Russian***. On the other hand, the recreant crew of *conti*, *baroni*, *marchesi*, in Spain, Portugal, Italy, Sicily, and parts of Southern Europe, include some of the most abject specimens of humanity anywhere to be found. The physical cause of this deterioration, from the historical greatness of their ancestral names, is said to be—"breeding in and in." Now, this may be true enough, as an apparent reason; but is there not a latent one? History shows that the families most degraded (in Portugal especially, where the lowest forms are encountered,) are compounded of Iberian, Celtic, Arab, Jewish, and other types — pure in themselves, but bad in the amalgam. Pride of birth, for centuries, has prevented them from marrying out of the circle of aristocracy. With rare exceptions, they are too mean in person to be accepted by the *white* nobility of Northern Europe. The consequence is, they intermarry with themselves; and, as in other mulatto compounds, the offspring of such mongrel comminglings deteriorate more and more in every generation. They cease to procreate, and there are some hopes that the corrupt breed is extinguishing itself. The Peninsular war, and the still more recent Don-Pedro-experiences, left on the mind of every foreign legionary concerned, the sentiment that, "if you take a Castilian, and strip him of all his good qualities, you will leave a respectable Portuguee." It is precisely the same with the *Perotes*, Greek aristocracy of Istamboul: on whom read Commodore Porter's "Letters from Constantinople, by an American." Such are unsolved enigmas in the rough-hewn conceptions we can yet form of human *hybridity*.

It seems to me certain, however, in human physical history, that the superior race must inevitably become deteriorated by any intermixture with the inferior; and I have suggested elsewhere, that, through the operation of the laws of hybridity alone, the human family might possibly become exterminated by a thorough amalgamation of all the various types of mankind now existing upon earth.

Sufficient having been said on the crossing of races, I shall close this chapter with a few remarks on the propagation of a race from a single pair, or what in common parlance is termed "*breeding in and in.*" It is a common belief, among many rearers of domestic animals, and one acted upon every day, that a race or stock deteriorates by this procedure, and that improvement of breed is gained by crossing. Whether such rule be constant or not, with regard to inferior animals, I am unprepared to aver — some authors having cited facts to the contrary. Science possesses no criteria by which it can determine beforehand the degree of prolificacy of any two species when brought together; and so differently are animals affected by physical agents, that actual experiment alone can ascertain the comparative operations of climate upon two given animals when moved from one zoological province to another — some becoming greatly changed, others but little, and man least of all. Recurring to our definitions of *remote*, *allied*, and *proximate* "species" [*supra*, p. 81], let us inquire what are the data as respects mankind.

Will any one deny that continued intermarriages among blood-relations are destructive to a race, both physically and intellectually?

The fact is proverbial. Do we not see it most fully illustrated in the royal families and nobility of Europe, where such matrimonial alliances have long been customary? The reputation of the House of Lords in England would long since have been extinct, had not the Crown incessantly manufactured nobles from out of the sturdy sons of the people. Cannot every one of us individually point to degenerate offspring which have arisen from family intermarriages for mere property-sake?

In early life, I witnessed a most striking example, in the upper part of South Carolina, where my father owned a country-seat. Almost the entire population of the neighborhood was made up of Irish Covenanters, who had moved to that country before the Revolutionary war. They had intermarried for many generations, until the same blood coursed through the veins of the whole of them; and there are many persons now living in South Carolina who will bear me out when I state, that the proportion of idiots and deformed was unprecedented in that district, of which the majority in its population was stupid and debased in the extreme. I could mention several other striking examples, beheld in higher life, but it would be painful to particularize.

And do not the instincts of our nature, the social laws of man, all over the civilized world, and the laws of God, from Genesis to Revelations, cry aloud against *incest?* Does not the father shrink with horror from the idea of marrying his own child, or from seeing the bed of his daughter polluted by her brother? Do not children themselves shudder at the thought? And can it be credited, that a God of infinite power, wisdom, and foresight, should have been driven to the necessity of propagating the human family from a *single pair*, and then have stultified his act by stamping incest as a crime?[454]

I do not believe that true religion ever intended to teach a common origin for the human race. "Cain knew his wife," whom he found in a foreign land, when he had no sister to marry; and although corruption and sin were not wanting among the patriarchs, yet nowhere in Scripture do we see, after Adam's sons and daughters, a brother marrying his sister.

It is shown, in our *Supplement*, that many of the genealogies of Genesis have been falsely translated, and otherwise misconstrued, in our English Bible; and that the names of Abraham's ancestors represent *countries* and *nations*, and not individuals. Moreover, nowhere in Genesis is the dogma of a future state hinted at: and its ancient authors could have had no object in teaching the modern idea of unity of races, when those writers themselves possessed no clear perceptions upon "salvation" hereafter.

In my remarks, five years ago, on "Universal Terms," reproduced and extended in this volume, I showed that the only text in the New Testament which refers directly to the unity of races, is that in *Acts*, where St. Paul says, that God "hath made of one blood all nations of men." I hold that no scientific importance should be attached to this isolated passage, inasmuch as the writer of *Acts* employed universal terms very loosely; at the same time that he knew nothing of the existence of races or nations beyond the circumference of the Roman Empire.

Dr. Morton, in one of his letters to me (Sept. 27, 1850), shortly before his demise, thus emphatically expressed himself:—

"For my own part, if I could believe that the human race had its origin in *incest*, I should think that I had at once got the clue to all ungodliness. Two lines of Catechism would explain more than all the theological discussions since the Christian era. I have put it into rhyme.

"*Q.* Whence came that curse we call primeval sin?
"*A.* From Adam's children breeding in and in."

The reader can now appreciate some of the contradictory phenomena that perplex the investigator of human *Hybridity*. I have purposely set them before him in juxtaposition. To me they appear irreconcileable; unless the theory of *plurality of origin* be adopted, together with the recognition that there exist *remote*, *allied*, and *proximate*, "species," as well of mankind as of lower animals.

Having speculatively alluded (*supra*, p. 80) to a possible *extermination of races* in an unknown futurity, I would here briefly justify such hypothesis by saying, that Nature marches steadily towards perfection; and that it attains this end through the consecutive destruction of living beings. Geology and palæontology prove a succession of creations and destructions previously to any effacements of Man; and it is contended by Hombron and other naturalists, that the inferior races of mankind were created before the superior types, who now appear destined to supplant their predecessors. Albeit, whatever may have been the order of creation, the unintellectual races seem doomed to eventual disappearance in all those climates where the higher groups of fair-skinned families can permanently exist.

The entire race of the Guanches, at the Canary Islands, was exterminated by the Portuguese during the thirteenth and fourteenth centuries; not a living vestige remaining to tell the tale. Some of the pre-Celtic inhabitants of Britain, Gaul, and Scandinavia, seem to have shared a similar fate: 16,000,000 of aborigines in North America have dwindled down to 2,000,000 since the "Mayflower" discharged on Plymouth Rock; and their congeners, the Caribs, have long been extinct in the West Indian islands. The mortal destiny of the whole American group is already perceived to be running out, like the sand in Time's hour-glass. Of 400,000 inhabitants of the Sandwich Islands, far less than 100,000 survive, and these are daily sinking beneath civilization, missionaries, and rum. In New Holland, New Guinea, many of the Pacific islands, and other parts of the world, the same work of destruction is going on; and the labors of proselytism are vain, save to hasten its accomplishment.

"Pourquoi cela?" asks Bodichon.[455] "*It is because their social state is a perpetual strife against humanity.* Thus, murder, depredations, incessant useless strifes of one against another, are their natural state. They practise human sacrifices and mutilations of men; they are imbued with hostility and antipathy towards all not of their race. They maintain polygamy, slavery, and submit women to labor incompatible with female organization.

"In the eyes of theology they are lost men; in the eyes of morality vicious men; in the eyes of humanitary economy they are non-producers. From their origin they have not recognized, and they still refuse to recognize, a supreme law imposed by the Almighty; viz.: the *obligation of labor.*

"On the other hand, all nations of the earth have made war upon the *Jews* for 4000 years: the Egyptians, the Assyrians, the Greeks, the Romans, &c.; — Christians and Mahommedans by turns; with innumerable cruelties, physical and moral: nevertheless, that race lives and prospers. Why? Because they have everywhere played their part in the progress of civilization.

"True philanthropy (insists Bodichon) should not tolerate the existence of a race whose nationality is opposed to progress, and who constantly struggle against the general rights and interests of humanity."

Omnipotence has provided for the renovation of manhood in countries where effeminacy has prostrated human energies. Earth has its tempests as well as the ocean. There are reserved, without doubt, in the destinies of nations, fearful epochs for the ravage of human races; and there are times marked on the divine calendar for the ruin of empires, and for the periodical renewal of the mundane features.

"In the midst of this crash of empires (says the philosophical VIREY), which rise and fall on every side, immutable Nature holds the balance, and presides, ever dispassionately, over such events; which are but the re-establishment of equilibrium in the systems of organized beings."

J. C. N.

CHAPTER XIII.

COMPARATIVE ANATOMY OF RACES.

[By J. C. N.]

"Craniorum inquam quibus ad gentilitias varietates distinguendas et definiendas nulla alia humani corporis pars aptior videtur, cum caput osseum (præterquam quod animæ domicilium et officina, imo vero interpres quasi et explanator ejus sit, utpote universæ physiognomiæ basin et firmamentum constituens) stabilitati suæ maximam conformationis et partium relativæ proportionis varietatem junctam habeat, unde *characteres nationum certissimas desumere licet.*" BLUMENBACH.

In examining the physical organization of races, the anatomist of the present day possesses many advantages over his predecessors: his materials for comparison are far more complete than theirs; and the admission now generally made by anthropologists, that the leading types of mankind now seen over the earth have existed, independently of all known physical causes, for some 5000 years at least, gives quite a new face to this part of the investigation.

It has been shown in preceding chapters that *permanence* of type must be considered the most satisfactory criterion of specific character, both in animals and plants. The races of mankind, when viewed zoologically, must have been governed by the same universal law; and the Jew, the Celt, the Iberian, the Mongol, the Negro, the Polynesian, the Australian, the American Indian, can be regarded in no other light than as distinct, or as amalgamations of very proximate, *species*. When, therefore, two of these species are placed beside each other for comparison, the anatomist is at once struck by their strong contrast; and his task is narrowed down to a description of those well-marked types which are known to be permanent. The form and capacity of the skull, the contour of the face, many parts of the skeleton, the peculiar development of muscles, the hair and skin, all present strong points of contrast.

It matters not to the naturalist how or when the type was stamped upon each race; its permanence makes it specific. If all the races sprang from a single pair, nothing short of a miracle could have produced such changes as contenders for "unity" demand; because (it is now generally conceded) no causes are in operation which can transmute one type of man into another. If, as for centuries it was supposed, the races became actually transformed when tongues were confounded at Babel, I presume this was effected by an instantaneous fiat of the Almighty; and when done it was "ipso facto" irrevocable. No terrestrial causes, consequently, could reverse HIS decree; nor, afterwards, metamorphose a white man into a Negro, or *vice versa*, any more than they could change a horse into an ass.

However important anatomical characteristics may be, I doubt whether the *physiognomy* of races is not equally so. There exist minor differences of features, various minute combinations of details, certain palpable expressions of face and aspect, which language cannot describe: and yet, how indelible is the image of a *type* once impressed on the mind's eye! When, for example, the word "Jew" is pronounced, a type is instantly brought up by memory, which could not be so described to another person as to present to his mind a faithful portrait. The image must be seen to be known and remembered; and so on with the faces of all men, past, present, or to come. Although the Jews are genealogically, perhaps, the purest race living, they are, notwithstanding (as we have shown), an extremely adulterated people; but yet there is a certain face among them that we recognize as typical of the race, and which we never meet among any other than Chaldaic nations.

If we now possessed correct portraits, even of those people who were contemporary with the founders of the Egyptian empire, how many of our interminable disputes would be avoided! Fortunately, the early monuments of Egypt, Assyria, Greece, Rome, &c., and even of America, afford much information of this iconographic kind, which decides the early diversity of types: but still, science is ill-supplied with these desiderata to afford a full understanding of the subject. Our first glimpse of human races, though dating far back in time, does not (we have every reason to believe with Bunsen,) reach beyond the "middle ages" of mankind's duration.

The very earliest monumental record, or written history, exhibits man, not in nomadic tribes, but in full-grown nations borne on the flood-tide of civilization. Even the writers of the Book of *Genesis* could not divest their imaginations of the idea of *some* civilization coeval with the creation of their first parents; because the man, A-DaM, gave names, in Paradise, "to all the *cattle*,"[456] BeHaiMaH; which implies either that, in the cosmogenical conception of those writers, some animals (oxen, horses, camels, and so forth,) had been already domesticated; or, writing thousands of years subsequently to animal domesticity, they heedlessly attributed, to ante-historic times past, conditions existing in their own days present. They could not conceive such a thing as a time when *cattle* were untamed; any more than archæology can admit that anybody could describe events prior to their occurrence.

[This is no delusion. Open Lepsius's *Denkmäler*, and upon the copies of monuments of the IVth Memphite dynasty, dating more than 2000 years before Moses, (to whom the Pentateuch is ascribed,) you will behold *cattle* of many genera—bulls, cows, calves, oxen, oryxes, donkeys (no *horses* or *camels*) — together with dogs, sheep, goats, gazelles; besides birds, such as *geese*, *cranes*, *ducks* (no common fowls), *ibises*, &c.; the whole of them in a state of entire subjection to man in Egypt; and none represented but those animals indigenous to the Nilotic zoological centre of creation.

Wherever we may turn, in ancient annals, the domestication of every *domesticable* animal has preceded the epoch of the chronicle through which the fact is made known to us; and, still more extraordinary, there are not a dozen quadrupeds and birds that man has tamed, or subdued from a wild to a prolifically-domestic condition, but were already in the latter state at the age when the document acquainting us with the existence, anywhere, of a given domestic animal, was registered. In these new questions of monumental zoology, Greece, Etruria, Rome, Judæa, Hindostan, and Europe, are too modern to require notice; because none of their earliest historians antedate, while some fall centuries below, Solomon's era, B. C. 1000. Verify, in any lexicons, upon all cases but *Jewish* fabled-antiquity, and no exception to this rule will be found sustainable against historical criticism. The monuments of *Assyria*, whose utmost antiquity may be fixed[457] about 1300 B. C., only prove that every tameable animal represented by Chaldæans (single and double humped camels, elephants, &c., inclusive) was already tamed at the epoch of the sculpture. Egyptian zoology has been cited. Chinese,[458] (in this respect the only detailed), proves that, in the times of the ancient writer, the domestication of six animals; viz.: the horse, ox, fowl, hog, dog, and sheep — was ascribed to Fou-hi's semi-historical era, about 3400 years before Christ.

When Columbus reached this country, A. D. 1492, he found no animals alien to our American continent, and none undomesticated that man could tame; and, when Pizarro overturned the Inca-kingdom, the *llama* had been, for countless ages, a tamed quadruped in Peru.

Geoffroi St. Hilaire is one of those authorities seldom controverted by naturalists. These, in substance, are his words: —

There are *forty species* of animals reduced, at this day, to a state of domestication. Of these, thirty-five are now cosmopolitan, as the horse, dog, ox, pig, sheep and goat. The other five have remained in the region of their origin, like the *llama* and the *alpaca* on the plateaux of Bolivia and Peru; or have been transplanted only to those countries which most approximate to their original habitats in climatic conditions; as the Tongousian reindeer at St. Petersburg. Out of the thirty-five domesticated species possessed by Europe, thirty-one originate in Central Asia, Europe, and North Africa. Only four species have been contributed by the two Americas, Central and Southern Africa, Australia and Polynesia; although these portions of the globe contain the major number of our zoological types. In consequence, the great bulk of tamed animals in Europe are of exotic origin. Hardly any are derived from countries colder than France: on the contrary, almost the whole were primitively inhabitants of warmer climates.[459]

We thus arrive at the great fact, that the domestication by man of all domestic animals antecedes every history extant; and, measured chronologically by Egypt's pyramids, most of these animals were already domesticated thirty-five centuries B. C., or over 5300 years ago. Indeed, the first step of primordial man towards civilization must have been the subjection of animals susceptible of domesticity; and, it seems probable, that the *dog* became the first instrument for the subjugation of other genera. And, while these preliminary advances of incipient man demand epochas so far remote as to be inappreciable by ciphers, on the other hand it is equally astounding, that modern civilization has scarcely reclaimed from the savage state even half-a-dozen more animals than were already domesticated at every point of our globe when history dawns.

Consequently, inasmuch as all these domestications, together with the perfecting of those arts and sciences that enabled king CHEOPS to build the Great Pyramid, occupied Egyptian humanity unnumbered ages before the IVth dynasty, or prior to B. C. 3400, we may well consider that the earliest monuments of Egypt represent but the "middle ages" of humanity, and not mankind's *commencements*. — G. R. G.]

There was, then, a time before all history. During that blank period, man taught himself to *write;* and until he had recorded his thoughts and events in some form of writing — hieroglyphics, to wit — his existence prior to that act, if otherwise certain, is altogether unattainable by us, save through induction. The historical vicissitudes of each human type are, therefore, unknown to us until the age of written record began in each geographical centre. Of these documentary annals some go back 5300 years, others extend but to a few hundreds. *Anatomy*, however, possesses its own laws independently of history; and to its applications the present chapter is devoted.

A minute and extended anatomical comparison of races, in their whole structure, would afford many curious results; but such detail does not comport with the plan of this work, and would be fatiguing to any but the professed anatomist. It is indispensable, however, that we should enter somewhat fully into a comparison of crania; and it may be safely assumed, as a general law, that where important peculiarities exist in crania, others equally tangible belong to the same organism.

While engaged on this chapter, I had the good fortune to welcome Prof. Agassiz in Mobile, where he lectured on the "Geographical Distribution of Animals," &c. The instruction derived from his lectures and private conversation on these themes, I here take occasion to acknowledge.

Prof. Agassiz's researches in embryology possess most important bearings on the natural history of mankind. He states, for instance, that, during the fœtal state, it is in most cases impossible to distinguish between the species of a genus; but that, after birth, animals, being governed by specific laws, advance each in diverging lines. The dog, wolf, fox, and jackal, for example — the different species of ducks, and even ducks and geese, in the fœtal state — cannot be distinguished from each other; but their distinctive characters begin to develop themselves soon after birth. So with the races of men. In the fœtal state there is no criterion whereby to distinguish even the Negro's from the Teuton's anatomical structure; but, after birth, they develop their respective characteristics in diverging lines, irrespectively of climatic influences. This I conceive to be a most important law; and it points strongly to *specific* difference. Why should Negroes, Spaniards, and Anglo-Saxons, at the end of ten generations (although in the fœtal state the same), still diverge at birth, and develop specific characters? Why should the Jews in Malabar, at the end of 1500 years, obey the same law? That they do, undeviatingly, has been already demonstrated in Chapter IV.; and while this sheet is passing through the press, a letter from my friend Dr. J. Barnard Davis (one of the learned authors of the forthcoming *Crania Britannica*), opportunely substantiates my former statement: —

"I find you have come to the same conclusions respecting them [the Jews] as myself. Seeing that the most striking circumstance adduced in the whole of Prichard's work was that of the change of the Jews to black in Cochin and Malabar; and finding Lawrence to state

Dr. Claud. Buchanan's evidence altogether on the other side, I was induced to inquire into the matter, and settle where the truth lay. I therefore wrote my friend Mr. Crawfurd, the author of the 'Indian Archipelago' and various other valuable works on the East, who cleared up the mystery at once. He said, he had often seen the Jews of Malabar serving in the ranks of our Sepoy regiments at Bombay, and that they are as black as the Hindoos of the same country, who are amongst the darkest people of India; that, although they have preserved the religion of Moses, they have intermixed with the natives of the country extensively, and it is probable, have little Semitic blood in their veins. He says, he knew Dr. Cl. Buchanan, who spent his Indian life in the *town of Calcutta*, except the single journey in which he saw the Indian Jews and Christians of St. Thomas." Little value can in consequence attach to this worthy churchman's ethnological authority.

Another of the preceding chapters (IX.) demonstrates how the aboriginal Americans present, everywhere over this continent, kindred types of specific character, which they have maintained for thousands of years, and which they would equally maintain in any other country.

Prof. Agassiz also asserts, that a peculiar conformation characterizes the brain of an adult Negro. Its development never goes beyond that developed in the Caucasian in boyhood; and, besides other singularities, it bears, in several particulars, a marked resemblance to the brain of the orang-outan. The Professor kindly offered to demonstrate those cerebral characters to me, but I was unable, during his stay at Mobile, to procure the brain of a Negro.

Although a Negro-brain was not to be obtained, I took an opportunity of submitting to M. Agassiz two native-African men for comparison; and he not only confirmed the distinctive marks commonly enumerated by anatomists, but added others of no less importance. The peculiarities of the Negro's head and feet are too notorious to require specification; although, it must be observed, these vary in different African tribes. When examined from behind, the Negro presents several peculiarities; of which one of the most striking is, the deep depression of the spine, owing to the greater curvature of the ribs. The buttocks are more flattened on the sides than in other races; and join the posterior part of the thigh almost at a right-angle, instead of a curve. The pelvis is narrower than in the white race; which fact every surgeon accustomed to applying trusses on Negroes will vouch for. Indeed, an agent of Mr. Sherman, a very extensive truss-manufacturer of New Orleans, informs me that the average circumference of adult Negroes round the pelvis is from 26 to 28 inches; whereas whites measure from 30 to 36. The scapulæ are shorter and broader. The muscles have shorter bellies and longer tendons, as is seen in the calf of the leg, the arms, &c. In the Negress, the mammæ are more conical, the areolæ much larger, and the abdomen projects as a hemisphere. Such are some of the more obvious divergences of the Negro from the white types: others are supplied by HERMANN BURMEISTER, Professor of Zoology in the University of Halle,[460] whose excellent researches in Brazil, during fourteen months (1850–'1), were made upon ample materials. Space limits me to the following extract: —

"If we take a profile view of the European face, and sketch its outlines, we shall find that it can be divided by horizontal lines into four equal parts: the first enclosing the crown of the head; the second, the forehead; the third, the nose and ears; and the fourth, the lips and chin. In the antique statues, the perfection of the beauty of which is justly admired, these four parts are exactly equal; in living individuals slight deviations occur, but in proportion as the formation of the face is more handsome and perfect, these sections approach a mathematical equality. The vertical length of the head to the cheeks is measured by three of these equal parts. The larger the face and smaller the head, the more unhandsome they become. It is especially in this deviation from the normal measurement that the human features become coarse and ugly.

"In a comparison of the Negro head with this ideal, we get the surprising result that the rule with the former is not the equality of the four parts, but a regular increase in length from above downwards. The measurement, made by the help of drawings, showed a very considerable difference in the four sections, and an increase of that difference with the age. This latter peculiarity is more significant than the mere inequality between the four parts of the head. All zoologists are aware of the great difference in the formation of the heads of the old and the young orang-outans. The characteristic of both is the large size of the whole face, particularly the jaw, in comparison with the skull; in the young orang-outan, the extent of the latter exceeds that of the jaw; in the old it is the reverse, in consequence of a series of large teeth having taken the place of the earlier small ones, which resemble the milk-teeth of man. In fact, in all men, the proportion between the skull and face changes with the maturity of life; but this change is not so considerable in the European as in the African. I have before me a very exact profile-drawing of a Negro boy, in which I find the total height, from the crown to the chin, four inches; the upper of the four sections, not quite nine lines; the second, one inch; the third, thirteen lines; the fourth, fourteen and one-quarter lines. The drawing is about three-quarters of the natural size; and, accordingly, these numbers should be proportionately increased. The strongly-marked head of an adult Caffre, a cast of which is in the Berlin Museum, shows a much greater difference in its proportions. I have an exact drawing of it, reduced to two-thirds of the natural size, and I find the various sections as follows: — the first is 11 lines; the second, 13; the third, 15; and the fourth, 18 lines. This would give, for a full-sized head of 7¾ inches, 15¾ lines for the crown; 19½ for the forehead: 22½ for the part including the nose; and 27 lines for that of the jaws and teeth. In a normal European head, the height of which is supposed to be 8¼, each part generally measures 2 inches, while the remaining ¼ may be variously distributed, in fractions, throughout lhe whoie.

"Any difference of measurement in the European seldom surpasses a few lines, at the most: it is impossible to find a case of natural formation where the difference between the parts of the head amounts, as in the Caffre, to one inch. I would not assert, that this enormous difference is a law in the Negro race. I grant, that the Caffre has the Negro type in its excessive degree, and cannot, therefore, be taken as a model of the whole African race: But, if the normal difference only amounts to half that indicated, it still remains so much larger than in the European, as to be a very significant mark of distinction between the races, and an important point in the settlement of the question of their comparative mental faculties.

"The peculiar expression of the Negro physiognomy depends upon this difference between the four sections. The narrow, flat crown; the low, slanting forehead; the projection of the upper edges of the orbit of the eye; the short, flat, and, at the lower part, broad nose; the prominent, but slightly turned-up lips, which are more thick than curved; the broad, retreating chin, and the peculiarly small eyes, in which so little of the white eyeball can be seen; the very small, thick ears, which stand off from the head; the short, crisp, woolly hair, and the black color of the skin — are the most marked peculiarities of the Negro head and face. On a close examination of the Negro races, similar differences will be found among them, as among Europeans. The western Africans, from Guinea to Congo, have very short, turned-up lips. They are ordinarily very ugly, and represent the purest Negro type. The southern races, which inhabit Loanda and Benguela, have a longer nose, with its bridge more elevated and its wings contracted; they have, however, the full lips, while their hair is somewhat thicker. Some of the individuals of these races have tolerably good, agreeable faces. A peculiar arch of the forehead, above its middle, is common among them.

"In the eastern part of Southern Africa, the natives have, instead of the concave bridge of the nose, one more or less convex, and very thick, flat lips, not at all turned-up. The Negroes of the East are commonly more light-colored than those of the West; their color tends rather to brown than to black, and the wings of their noses are thinner. The people of Mozambique are the chief representatives of this race — the Caffres also belong to it. The nose of the Caffre is shorter and broader than that of the others, but it has the convex bridge. The short, curly hair shows no essential deviation. The dark, brownish-black eyeball, which is hardly distinguishable from the pupil, remains constant. The white of the eye has in all Negroes a yellowish tinge. The lips are always brown, never red-colored: they hardly differ in color from the skin in the neighborhood; towards the interior edges, however, they become lighter, and assume the dark-red flesh-color of the inside of the mouth. The teeth are very strong, and are of a glistening whiteness. The tongue is of a large size, and remarkable in thickness. The ear, in conformity with the nose, is surprisingly small, and is very unlike the large, flat ear of the ape. In all Negroes, the external border of the ear is very much curved, especially behind, which is quite different in the ape. This curvature of the ear is a marked peculiarity of the human species. The ear-lobe is very small, although the whole ear is exceedingly fleshy.

"The small ear of the Negro cannot, however, be called handsome; its substance is too thick for its size. The whole ear gives the impression of an organ that is stunted in its growth, and its upper part stands off to a great distance from the head."

It may be objected against perfect exactitude in the above minutiæ, that races run insensibly into each other; but I contend, on the other hand, that *gradation* is the law, as illustrated in our Chapter VI.

Looking for a point of departure, in this brief anatomical comparison of types, one naturally turns to Egypt, where the most ancient and satisfactory materials are found: there lie not only the embalmed bodies of many races, deposited in catacombs several thousand years old, but all anatomical facts deducible from these are confirmed by those characteristic portraits of races, on the monuments, with which our volume abounds.

And here it is, that homage is more especially due to our great countryman, MORTON, whose *Crania Americana* and *Crania Ægyptiaca* created eras in anthropology. His acumen, in this department of science, is admitted by those who have studied his works; for, beyond all other anatomists, he enjoyed the advantage of possessing, in several departments, the most complete assortment of skulls in the world. His collections of American and Egyptian crania, especially, are copious, and of singular interest.

In 1844, Dr. Morton had received "137 human crania, of which 100 pertain to the ancient inhabitants of Egypt."[461] Seventeen additional of the latter reached his cabinet in the same year;[462] the more interesting as they were taken from tombs opened by Lepsius around the pyramids of the IVth dynasty; and, in some instances, may have been coeval with those early sepulchres. Through the enthusiastic coöperation of his many friends, about twenty-three more mummied heads[463] were added by 1851: so that his studies were matured over the crania of some 140 ancient, compared with 37 skulls of modern Egyptian races. Such facilities are as unexampled as the analytical labor bestowed upon them by the lamented Doctor was conscientiously severe. Possessors of his works, correspondence, and inedited manuscripts, my colleague and myself can now speak unhesitatingly upon Morton's testamentary views.

Morton very judiciously remarked, that the Egyptian catacombs do not always contain their original occupants; for these were often displaced, and the tombs resold for mercenary purposes; whence it happens that mummies of the Greek and Roman epochas have been found in those more ancient receptacles, which had received the bodies of Egyptian citizens of a far earlier date. This I conceive to constitute one of the greatest obstacles to investigation, for, save in four very probable instances, there is no positive evidence that he possessed a single mummy-head beyond the tenth century B. C.; although there are tombs that date more than 2000 years earlier, to which some of the Doctor's specimens doubtless belong, even if the proof be defective.

We have shown through the portraits on the monuments that the population of Egypt was already a very mixed one in the IVth dynasty; which Lepsius places at 3400 B. C. Dr. Morton confirms this conclusion by his anatomical comparisons. In the *Crania Ægyptiaca* he referred his series of Egyptian skulls to "two of the great races of men, the CAUCASIAN and the NEGRO:" subdividing the Caucasian class into three principal *types*, viz.: the *Pelasgic*, the *Semitic*, and the *Egyptian*.

Referring to his work for specification of the others, I confine my observations to the last.

"The *Egyptian* form (says Dr. Morton) differs from the Pelasgic in having a narrow and more receding forehead, while the face being more prominent, the facial angle is consequently less. The nose is straight or aquiline, the face angular, the features often sharp, and the hair uniformly long, soft, and curling. In this series of crania I include many of which the conformation is not appreciably different from that of the *Arab* and *Hindoo;* but I have not, as a rule, attempted to note these distinctions, although they are so marked as to have induced me, in the early stage of this investigation and for reasons which will appear in the sequel, to group them, together with the proper Egyptian form, under the provisional name of *Austral-Egyptian* crania. I now, however, propose to restrict the latter term to those Caucasian communities which inhabited the Nilotic valley *above* Egypt. Among the Caucasian crania are some which appear to blend the Egyptian and Pelasgic characters; these might be called the *Egypto-Pelasgic* heads; but without making use of this term, except in a very few instances by way of illustration, I have thought best to transfer these examples from the Pelasgic group to the Egyptian, inasmuch as they so far conform to the latter series as to be identified without difficulty."[464]

On reading over this classification several comments strike me as worthy of utterance. 1st. That, out of 100 crania presented in a tabular shape (*op. cit.* p. 19), only 49 are of the Egyptian form, while 29 are of the Pelasgic or foreign type; and of the crania from Memphis, ascertained to be the oldest necropolis, the Pelasgic prevail over the Egyptian in the proportion of 16 to 7. Those of Thebes are 30 Egyptian to 10 Pelasgic. This proves that the Egyptian population, if such classification be correct, was an exceedingly mixed one.

2d. The *Semitic* was, at all times, a type distinctly marked; and diverse both from the Pelasgic and the Egyptian, as our previous chapters illustrate.

3d. Hence, the conclusion is natural, that the earliest population of Egypt was a native African one, resembling closely Upper Egyptian Fellahs, and assimilating to the Nubian

(Berber) population: that this stock soon became intermingled with Arab and other Asiatic races of Semitic and Pelasgic type. Therefore, little confidence can be reposed upon any very minute classification of such a mixed people. Of craniological ability to distinguish a pure Pelasgic, Semitic, or African head, as a general rule, I do not doubt; but *blended* types must ever present difficulties. It is enough to know that we possess portraits of Pelasgic, Semitic and Egyptian types; and that the truthfulness of these portraits is attested by the crania of the catacombs.

With all his acuteness and experience in craniology, it is clear that Dr. Morton felt himself much embarrassed in making this classification. He has several times modified it in his different published papers; and it is seen above, that in his *Egyptian form* of crania, he "includes many of which the conformation is not appreciably different from that of the Arab and Hindoo."

To exemplify how much caution is necessary in classifications of this kind, it may be proper to refer to Morton's earlier opinion, that the *Austral-Egyptians* were greatly mixed with Hindoos, whose crania he thinks he can designate; adding, "That there was extensive and long-continued intercourse between the Hindoos and Egyptians is beyond a question," &c. Now, so great has been the advance of knowledge within the last five years, that, were Dr. Morton now alive, such doctrine would no longer be advocated by him; because it is generally conceded by Egyptologists—our best authorities—that facts are opposed to any such intercourse, until after the Persian invasion, B. C. 525.

Dr. Morton classified the crania procured (1838–'40) from each locality for his cabinet by my colleague Mr. Gliddon (then our Consul at Cairo), into the following series:—

First Series, from the Memphite Necropolis:			
	A. Pyramid of Five Steps	2	skulls.
	B. Saccara, generally	11	"
	C. Front of the Brick Pyramid of Dashour	3	"
	D. North-west of Pyramid of Five Steps	9	"
	E. Toora (quarries) on the Nile	1	"
Second Series, from	Grottoes of Maabdeh	4	"
Third " "	Abydos	4	"
Fourth " "	the Catacombs of Thebes	55	"
Fifth " "	Koum Ombos	3	"
Sixth " "	the Island of Beggeh, near Philæ	4	"
Seventh " "	Debôd, in Nubia	4	"

On the first series, Morton remarks:—"A mere glance at this group of skulls will satisfy any one accustomed to comparisons of this kind, that most of them possess the Caucasian traits in a most striking and unequivocal manner, whether we regard their form, size, or facial angle. It is, in fact, questionable whether a greater proportion of beautifully moulded heads would be found among an equal number of individuals taken at random from any existing European nation. The entire series consists of sixteen examples of the Pelasgic, and seven of the Egyptian form; a single Semitic head, one of the Negroid variety, and one of mixed conformation. Of the antiquity of these remains there can be no question," &c.

Reasons are then adduced for assigning a high antiquity to some of these heads, and, as relates to Mosaic contemporaneousness, they are certainly substantial; but still, science is very exacting; and I doubt that many more than the following can ascend to times anterior to the *Hyksos* period, say not earlier than B. C. 2000.

Excluding all *bitumenized* skulls, which, BIRCH has established[465] cannot be older than Egyptian conquests of Assyria, sixteenth century before Christ, the question stands open in favor of *four:* viz. —

C. — *Three* from the front of the Brick Pyramid of Dashour. Being in *woollen* wrappers, and desiccated rather than embalmed, they correspond with the human fragments found in the Third Pyramid, which, by BUNSEN,[466] are attributed to King *Menkera.* These may be of the Old Empire.

E. — *One* from Toora, on the Nile. There are grounds for supposing that the rectangular sarcophagi, at this locality, contained the bodies of quarry-men who cut stones for the pyramids.

Another criterion, in behalf of antiquity for these four crania, is the great diminution of animal matter; but, with regard to all the rest, probabilities militate against an *age* beyond the New Empire; and they range, consequently, from the sixteenth century before Christ downwards.

Besides the want of any positive data for the remainder, we have the fact stated by Morton, that the great majority of them *do not correspond with the Egyptian type in form, size, or facial angle;* as will be explained when I speak of the *Internal Capacity of Crania.*

FIG. 252.

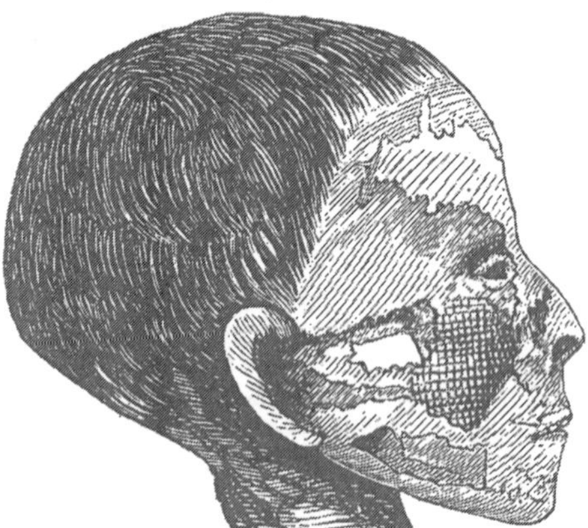

One head (Fig. 252), with Dr. Morton's commentary, will explain his idea of the *Egyptian type.*

"The subjoined wood-cut illustrates a remarkable head, which may serve as a *type* of the genuine Egyptian conformation. The long, oval cranium, the receding forehead, gently aquiline nose, and retracted chin, together with the marked distance between the nose and mouth, and the long, smooth hair, are all characteristic of the monumental Egyptian."

The *Crania Ægyptiaca*[467] here presents an "Ethnographic Table of 100 Ancient Egyptian Crania," arranged in the first place, according to their sepulchral localities; and, in the second, in reference to their national affinities — but, while preserving the subjoined comments, I prefer the substitution (overleaf) of a later and more extended synopsis.

"The preceding table speaks for itself. It shows that more than eight-tenths of the crania pertain to the unmixed Caucasian race; that the Pelasgic form is as one to one and two-thirds, and the Semitic form one to eight, compared with the Egyptian; that one-twentieth of the whole is composed of heads in which there exists a trace of Negro and other exotic lineage; that the Negroid conformation exists in eight instances, thus constituting about one-thirteenth part of the whole; and finally, that the series contains a single unmixed Negro." [*Vide, ante*, p. 267, Fig. 193 — the *Negress.*]

I have already mentioned, that, subsequently to the appearance of the *Crania Ægyptiaca*, a second lot of antique skulls arrived from Egypt. They had been collected by Mr. Wm. A. Gliddon, from some of the Memphite tombs opened by the Prussian Mission, in 1842–'3; and, although these heads may be a secondary or tertiary deposit in these sepulchres, which contained fragments of coffins and cerements as late as the Ptolemaic period, yet among them, as Morton has well observed [*supra*, pp. 318, 319], there are, very probably, some specimens of the olden time. Mr. W. A. G. took the precaution to mark, upon those skulls identifiable as to locality, the *cartouches* of the kings to whose reigns the tombs belonged; and the hoary names of Assa, Shore, and Akiu (*Heraku*),[468] carry us back to the IVth and VIth dynasties, or about 3000 years before Christ.

The reader may be gratified to peruse a condensation of Morton's digest (October, 1844) of their craniological attributes; and I have the more pleasure in reproducing his words, as they may be unknown or inaccessible to the majority of ethnologists.

"The following is an ethnographic analysis of this series of crania: —

Egyptian form	11
Egyptian form, with traces of Negro lineage	2
Negroid form	1
Pelasgic form	2
Semitic form	1
	17

"Remarks.—1. The *Egyptian* form is admirably characterized in eleven of these heads, and corresponds in every particular with the Nilotic physiognomy, as indicated by monumental and sepulchral evidences in my *Crania Ægyptiaca;* viz., the small, long, and narrow head, with a somewhat receding forehead, narrow and rather projecting face, and delicacy of the whole osteological structure. No hair remains, and the bony meatus of the car corresponds with that of all other Caucasian nations.

"Tw other heads present some mixture of Negro lineage with the Egyptian. . . .

"Of these thirteen crania, eleven are adult, of which the largest has an internal capacity of 93 cubic inches, and the smallest 76 — giving a mean of 86 cubic inches for the size of the brain. This measurement exceeds, by only three cubic inches, the average derived from the entire series of Egyptian heads in my *Crania Ægyptiaca.*

"The facial angle of the adult heads gives a mean of 82°; the largest rising as high as 86°, and the smallest being 78°. Two other heads are those of children, in whom the Egyptian conformation is perfect, and these give, respectively, the large facial angle of 89° and 91°. The mean adult angle is greater than that given by the large series measured in the *Crania Ægyptiaca.* . . .

"2. The *Negroid* head, as I have elsewhere explained, is a mixture of the Caucasian and Negro form, in which the latter *predominates*. . . . This head strongly resembles those of two modern Copts in my possession. It gives 81 cubic inches for the size of the brain, and a facial angle of 80°. . . .

"Of two *Pelasgic* heads, one is perfect, and well characterized in most of its proportions. It has an internal capacity of 93 cubic inches, and a facial angle of 80°. . . .

"The solitary *Semitic* head has rather the common Arab than the Hebrew cast of features. It measures internally 87 cubic inches, and has a facial angle of 79°.

"The ages of the individuals to whom these seventeen skulls pertained may be proximately stated as follows: 5, 7, 18, 20, 20, 25, 30, 40, 40, 40, 50, 50, 50, 50, 50, 50, 55."

"The result derived from this series of crania sustain, in a most gratifying manner, those obtained from the greater collection of 100 skulls sent me from Egypt, by my friend Mr. G. R. Gliddon, and which have afforded the materials of my *Crania Ægyptiaca*; and, without making further comparisons on the present occasion (for I design from time to time to resume the subject, as facts and materials may come to my hands), I shall merely subjoin my Ethnographic Table from the *Crania Ægyptiaca*, so extended as to embrace all the ancient Egyptian skulls now in my possession.

Ethnographic Table of one hundred and seventeen Ancient Egyptian Crania.

Sepulchral Localities.	No.	Egypt'n.	Pelasgic.	Semitic.	Mixed.	Negroid.	Negro.	Idiot.
Memphis	26	7	16	1	1	1	...	...
Ghizeh	17	11	2	1	2	1	...	...
Maabdeh	4	1	1	...	...	2	...	...
Abydos	4	2	1	1	...	...	...	...
Thebes	55	30	10	4	4	5	...	2
Ombos	3	3	...	...	...	...	...	...
Philæ	4	2	1	...	...	...	1	...
Debôd	4	4	...	...	...	...	...	...
	117	60	31	7	7	9	1	2

Internal Capacity of the Cranium.

The part of Dr. Morton's work bearing this superscription, I regard as one of his most valuable contributions to science, and it demands a close examination.

"As this measurement," says he, "gives the size of the brain, I have obtained it in all the crania above sixteen years of age, unless prevented by fractures or the presence of bitumen within the skulls; and this investigation has confirmed the proverbial fact of the *general smallness of the Egyptian head*, at least as observed in the catacombs *south of Memphis*. Thus, the Pelasgic crania, from the latter city, give an average internal capacity of 89 cubic inches; those from the same group from Thebes, give 86. This result is somewhat below the average of the existing Caucasian nations of the Pelasgic, Germanic, and Celtic families, in which I find the brain to be about 93 cubic inches in bulk. It is also interesting to observe that the Pelasgic brain is much larger than the Egyptian, which last gives an average of but 80 cubic inches; thus, as we shall hereafter see, approximating to that of the Indo-Arabian nations."[469]

"The largest head in the series measures ninety-seven cubic inches: this occurs three times, and always in the Pelasgic group. The smallest cranium gives but sixty-eight cubic inches; and this is three times repeated in the Egyptian heads from Thebes. This last is the smallest cranium I have met with in any nation, with three exceptions — a Hindoo, a Peruvian, and a Negro."

Morton then reduces his measurements of 100 ancient Egyptian crania into the subjoined tabular form:—

Ethnographic Division.	Locality.	Number of Crania.	Largest Brain.	Smallest Brain.	Mean.	
PELASGIC FORM....	Memphis	14	97	79	89	Mean, 88, C. I.
	Abydos	1	89	89	89	
	Thebes	5	92	82	86	
	Philæ	1	74	74	74	
SEMITIC FORM......	Memphis	1	88	88	88	Mean, 82,
	Abydos	1	69	69	69	
	Thebes	3	85	79	79	
EGYPTIAN FORM ...	Memphis	7	83	73	79	Mean, 80.
	Abydos	2	96	85	90	
	Thebes	25	95	68	80	
	Ombos	2	77	68	73	
	Debôd..........	3	82	70	75	
NEGROID FORM.....	Maabdeh	1	71	71	71	Mean, 79.
	Thebes	5	88	71	81	
NEGRO	Philæ	1	73	73	73	Mean, 73.

An examination of this table again brings to view the fact that the Pelasgic heads (which are foreign to Egypt, and possibly belonging to some of the so-called Hykshos,) predominate at Memphis; the point which invaders from Asia would first reach, and where they would be most likely to settle in ancient, no less than in present, times. The Pelasgic are here as 14 to 7, compared with the Egyptian form.

[Thus, Cairo, on the eastern bank, has but replaced Memphis on the western; at the same time that Tanis (*Zoan*), Bubastis (*Pibeseth*), and Heliopolis (*On*), owing to their proximity to the Isthmus of Suez, ever thronged with Asiatic foreigners. Here too, after the pyramidal period and the XIIth dynasty, was the land of Goshen — also, the *shepherd*-capital, Avaris; the frontier province whence issued, with Israel's host, that GouM-âRaB (exactly the same as *Goum-el-Arab*), "Arab-levy,"[470] mistranslated "mixed multitude;" and the scene of incessant Arabian relations, from Necho's canal down to Omar's, from the wars of Sesostris down to Mohammed-Ali's. In Coptic times this eastern province, now the *Sherqèeyeh*, was the *Tarabia* (the-Araby); in Saracenic, the *Khauf*;[471] and here, at this day, the modern Fellahs are almost pure *Arabs*.—G. R. G.]

At Thebes, higher up the river, the reverse is observed; the Egyptian form prevails over the Pelasgic in the proportion of 25 to 5. It is evident, also, that the size of the brain in the Pelasgic heads is much greater than that of the Egyptian type; and at Ombos, and Debôd in Nubia, the crania are still much smaller than those of the Egyptians. Such facts afford much plausibility to the idea, that the Pelasgic, as Dr. Morton terms them, or at least some large-headed superior race, had come into Egypt across the Isthmus of Suez, had taken possession of the country, and probably drove multitudes of the native Egyptians before their invading swarms. These Pelasgic heads, as before stated, resemble greatly the population of ancient Hellas, of the heroic age; and instead of migrating to Greece from Egypt in ancient times, similar tribes may have branched off from their original abode in Asia direct to the Peloponnesus. The latter view is strengthened by the fact that, in Greece, there are no traces of Nilotic customs, hieroglyphic writing, style of art, &c.; which would have been the case had that country been colonized by Egyptians.

These anatomical deductions, then, establish conclusively that, in proportion as we ascend the Nile through Middle Egypt, the Asiatic elements of the ancient crania diminish, to become replaced, after passing Thebes, by others in which African comminglings are conspicuous. Craniology, therefore, testifies to the accuracy of Lepsius's opinion, that the Hyksos invasion forced a large body of the Egyptians to emigrate to, and sojourn for a long period in, the Nubias.[472]

One grand difficulty, however, still remains with regard to the origin of the *Egyptian* type, as formerly understood, but since disavowed, by Morton. Thousands of paintings and sculptures on the monuments prove that ancient Egyptian faces often present a strong resemblance to the Grecian profile; but, according to the preceding table, there is a difference of eight cubic inches in the size of the crania of the two races! Were not the Egyptians, then, such as are represented on the monuments of the XVIIth and succeeding dynasties, a mixed Pelasgic and African race?

To the authors of this volume, in common with Morton's amended views, as before and finally set forth [*supra*, p. 245], the Egyptians had been once an aboriginally-Nilotic stock, pure and simple; upon which, in after times, Semitic, Pelasgic and Nubian elements became engrafted.

Our comments on monumental iconography [Chapters IV., V., VII., VIII.] have demonstrated that almost every type of mankind, of northwestern Asia, northern Africa, with some of southern Europe, is portrayed so faithfully, as to leave no doubt of the primitive existence of distinct races; some of which we are enabled to date back to the IVth dynasty, or 3400 years B. C. But it has been objected that the drawing of the Egyptians was imperfect or conventional, and therefore not to be relied upon. Such assertions, if again obtruded at the present day, would merely argue small acquaintance with the laws of Egyptian art;[473] because, however false may be the canonical position given to the *ear*, however defective the non-foreshortening of the *eye*, I defy BENVENUTO CELLINI himself to carve profiles more ethnologically-exact than those bas-relief effigies we possess, in myriads, from the IVth down to the XXIId dynasties. But, I proceed to give copies of various crania from the catacombs; which most triumphantly confirm all preceding asseverations concerning the accuracy of these Egyptian portrait-painters. The materials are drawn mainly from the collection of Morton, which I have examined carefully for myself. These heads, too, having been obtained in Egypt, direct from the tombs, by one of the authors of this volume, I can speak authoritatively, because all attendant circumstances are known to me.

"A large, elongate-oval head (Fig. 253), with a broad, high forehead, low coronal region, and strongly aquiline nose. The orbits nearly round; teeth perfect and vertical. Internal capacity 97 cubic inches; facial angle 77°. *Pelasgic form.*" [474]

FIG. 253.

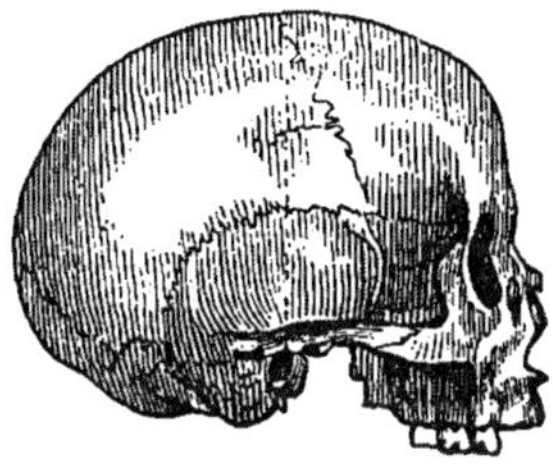

FIG. 254.

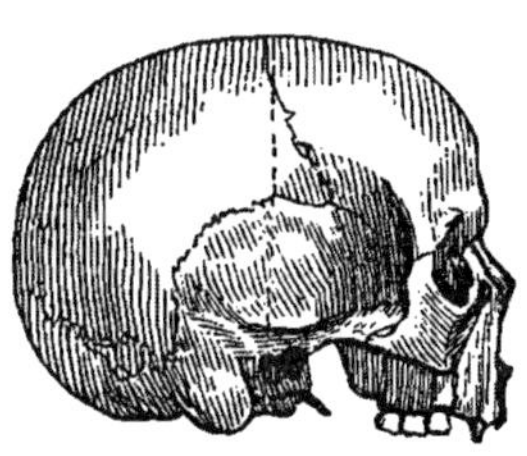

"A beautifully-formed head (Fig. 254), with a forehead, high, full, and nearly vertical, a good coronal region, and largely-developed occiput. The nasal bones are long and straight, and the whole facial structure delicately proportioned. Age between 30 and 35 years. Internal capacity 88 cubic inches; facial angle 81°. *Pelasgic form.*" [475]

FIG. 255.

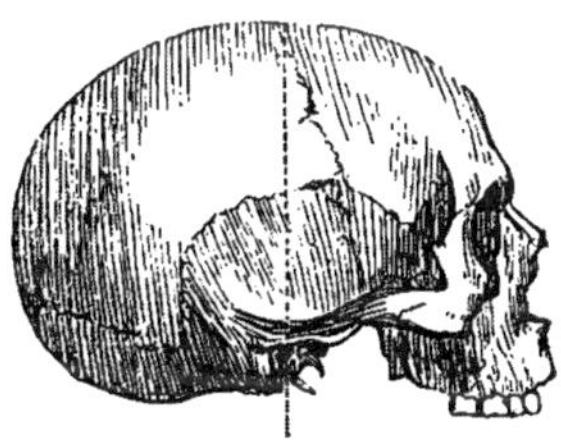

"Skull of a woman of twenty years (Fig. 255)? with a beautifully-developed forehead, and remarkably thin and delicate structure throughout. The frontal suture remains. Internal capacity 82 cubic inches; facial angle 80°. *Pelasgic form.*" [476]

"Head of a woman (Fig. 256) of thirty, of a faultless Caucasian mould. The hair, which is in profusion, is of a dark-brown tint, and delicately curled. *Pelasgic form,*" from Thebes.

The following series (Figs. 257, 258, 259, 260, 261), illustrates the *Egyptian* form.

FIG. 256.[477]

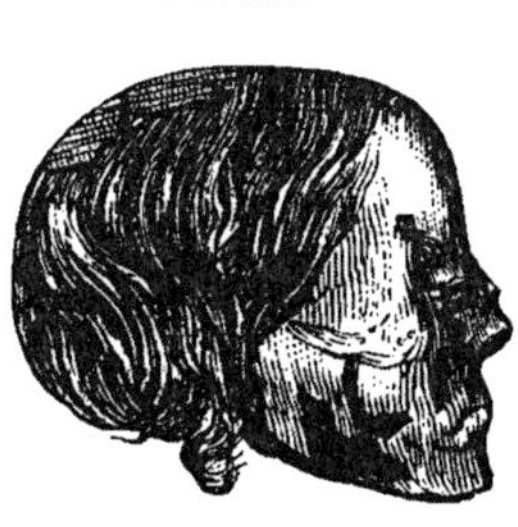

FIG. 257.[478]

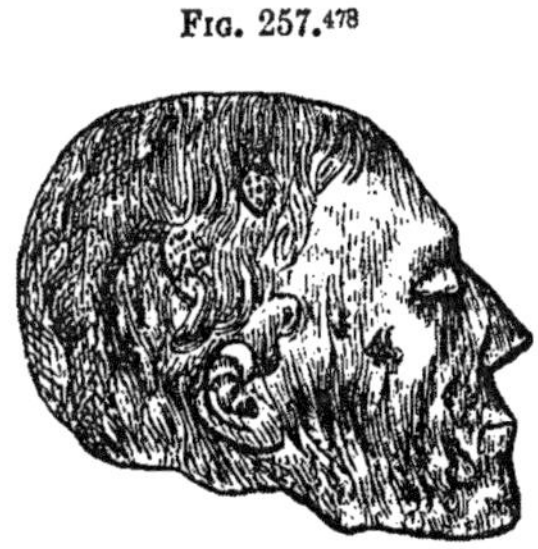

Fig. 258.[479]

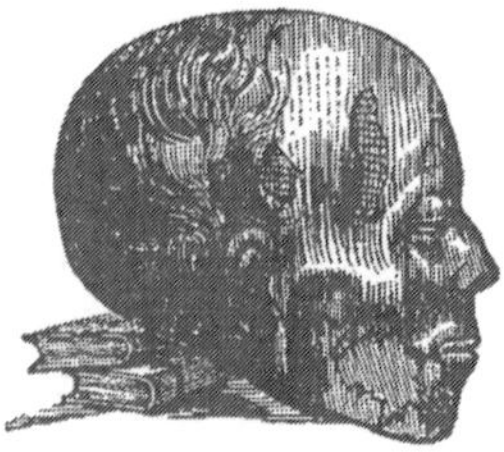

Fig. 259.[480]

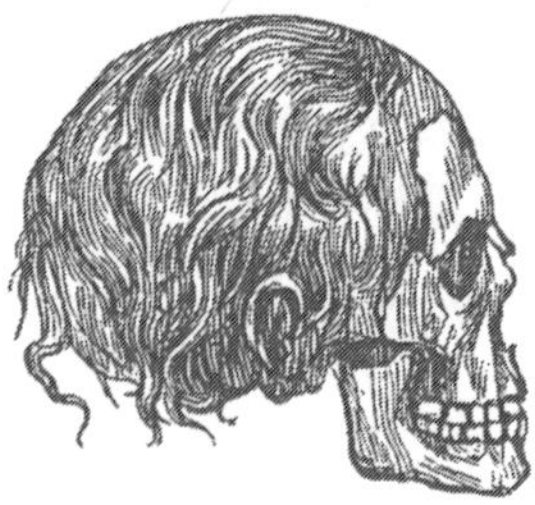

"An elongated head, with a broad, receding forehead, gently aquiline nose, and retracted chin, together with the marked distance between the nose and mouth, and the long, smooth hair, are all characteristics of the monumental Egyptian."

Of the *Semitic* form, foregoing chapters have supplied many portraits. One, out of numerous mummied crania, will suffice to illustrate its existence in the sepulchres of Egypt.

Fig. 260.[481]

Fig. 261.[482]

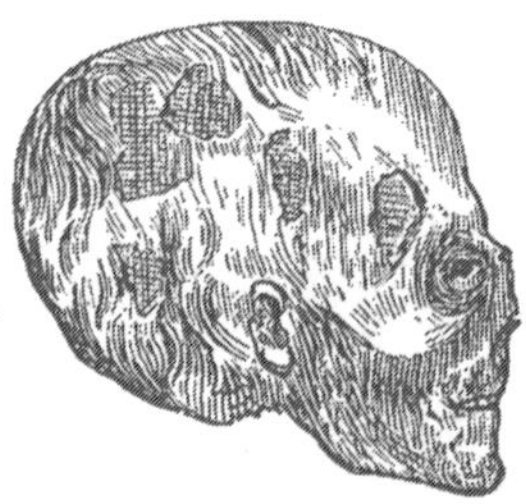

Fig. 262.

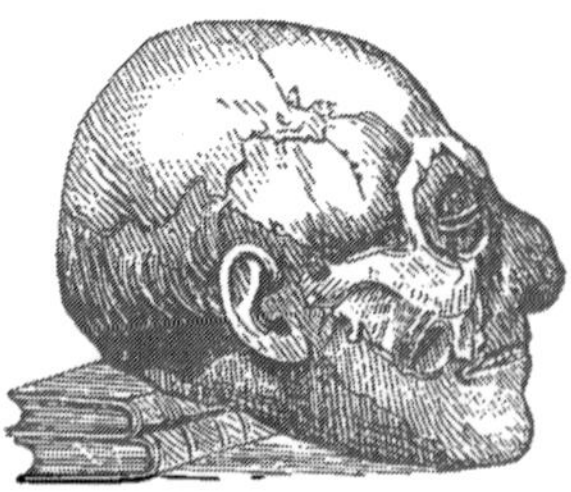

"This head" (Fig. 262), says Morton, "possesses great interest, on account of its decided *Hebrew* features, of which many examples are extant on the monuments" of Egypt; and we have already compared it with those of Assyria [*supra*, p. 116.]

"*The colossal head*" from Nineveh proclaimed the existence of a higher order of *Chaldaic* type upon Assyrian sculptures. The reader will be gratified to observe how faithfully ancient Chaldæa's tombs testify to the exactitude of her iconographic monuments; at the same time, he will perceive how art and nature conjointly establish the precision of modern anatomy's deductions.

The following sketch (Figs. 263 and 264) is a faithful reduction of an Assyrian skull, recently exhumed by Dr. Layard, from one of the ancient mounds, and now deposited in the British Museum. Its fac-simile drawing has just been most kindly sent me from England, by Mr. J. B. Davis, F. S. A., one of the authors of the *Crania Britannica* (a great work, which is shortly to be published). I have no history of the skull, beyond the facts above stated; but it is believed to be the representative of an ancient Assyrian. Speaking of the drawings, Mr. Davis says in his letter to me, "they are of the exact size of nature, and very faithful representations of the cranium."

It is much to be regretted that we have as yet no series of ancient skulls from Nineveh and Babylon, as they would throw great light upon the early connection between the races of Egypt and Assyria.

This skull is very interesting in several points of view. Its immense size confirms history by showing that none but a high "Caucasian" race could have achieved so much greatness. The measurements taken from the drawing are —

Longitudinal diameter,	$7\frac{3}{4}$	inches.
Transverse	" $5\frac{3}{8}$	"
Vertical	" $5\frac{1}{4}$	"

Fig. 263.

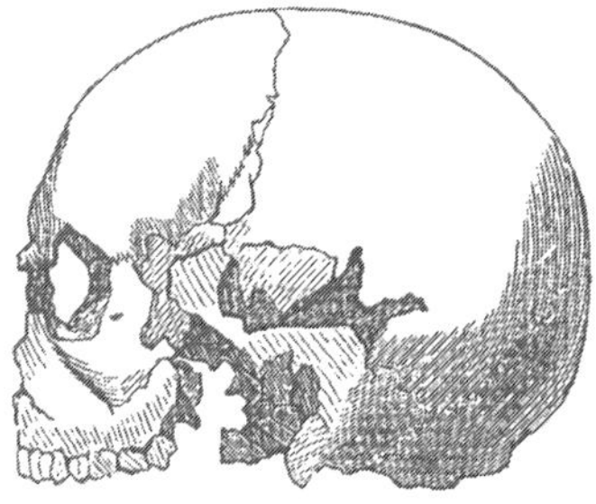

Ancient Assyrian.

It is probable that the parietal diameter is larger than the measurement here given; because, possessor of only front and profile views, I think these may not express fairly the posterior parts of the head. There are but two heads in Morton's whole Egyptian series of equal size, and these are "Pelasgic;" nor more than two equally large throughout his American series. Daniel Webster's head measured — longitudinal diameter, $7\frac{7}{8}$ inches; transverse, $5\frac{3}{4}$; vertical, $5\frac{1}{2}$: and comparison will show that the Assyrian head is but a fraction the smaller of the two.

Fig. 264.

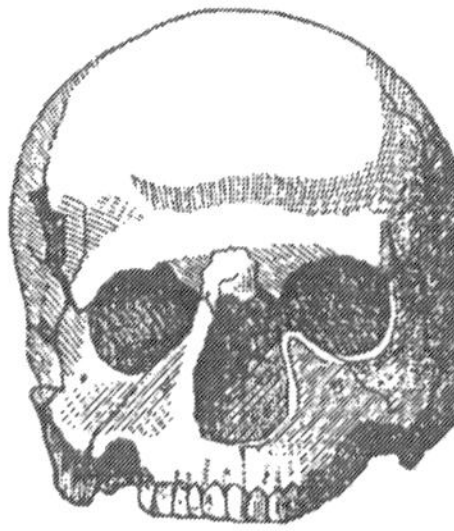

This Assyrian head, moreover, is remarkable for its close resemblance to several of Morton's Egyptian series, classed under the "Pelasgic form." It thus adds another powerful confirmation to the fact this volume establishes, viz., that the Egyptians, at all monumental times, were a mixed people, and in all historical ages were much amalgamated with Chaldaic races. Any one familiar with crania, who will compare this Assyrian head with the beautiful Egyptian series lithographed in the *Crania Ægyptiaca*, cannot fail to be struck with its resemblance to many of the latter, even more forcibly than anatomists will, through our small, if accurate, wood-cuts.

To vary these illustrations, while confirming the deductions already drawn, I borrow two admirably-preserved heads (Figs. 265 and 266)

Fig. 265.

Fig. 266.

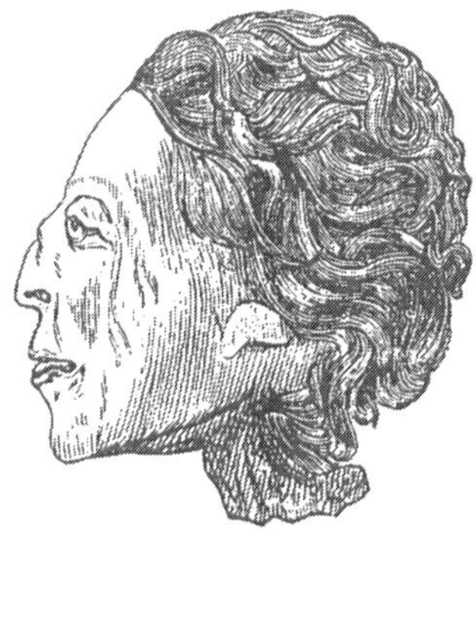

from Champollion-Figeac,[483] who has reduced them from the folio-plates of Napoleon's *Description de l'Egypte*. Fig. 266 yields the perfect Egyptian type.

From the mummy itself, now possessed by the University of Louisiana, at New Orleans, (and which I have personally scrutinized,) I present the most valuable specimen among all known to me; inasmuch as it is one of the extremely rare instances where the *date* of a deceased Egyptian can be positively determined by documentary evidence.

Fig. 267.

Portrait (Fig. 267) *of the Mummy of* Got-thothi-aunkh, "Chief of the Artificers," who died in the "Year X." of the reign of Osorkon III. A man between thirty and forty years of age, who was alive in the year B. C. 900; or, before a single stone yet discovered at ancient *Babylon* was inscribed with cuneatic characters. Here is the history of its transmission to this country:—

In 1845, Mr. Gliddon intimated, from Paris, to his friend Mr. A. C. Harris, the most influential resident in Egypt, his desire to procure a series of funereal antiquities to illustrate his Lectures in the United States. The letter fortunately overtook Mr. Harris during one of this gentleman's archæological visits at Thebes; where accident enabled him to obtain one admirable mummy, from the well-known Werda, in perfect condition. It was conveyed in his own yacht to Alexandria, with a dozen other human mummies collected at Thebes, Abydos, and Memphis, intended for Mr. Gliddon.

In 1846, after fruitless efforts to ship them, four were sequestrated at the Alexandrian Custom-house: Mohammed Ali, since 1835, having forbidden the exportation of Antiquities by any but agents of European powers.[484] An official application, made by the United States' Consul to the Viceroy failed; and, in 1849, these four mummies were found to have perished, through damp, in the Custom-house. Happily, Mr. Harris had preserved the most valuable specimen at his own residence.

In 1848, after Mohammed Ali's superannuation, permission to export Mr. Gliddon's collection was refused by Ibraheem Pasha. On his death, 1849, Mr. Harris's personal claims upon the courtesies of the Government obtained leave from Abbass Pasha; and the mummy, (with two others divested of their coffins), was forwarded to Liverpool, where the influential complaisance of Messrs. Baring Brothers obtained their transhipment to the United States, free of examination at the Quarantine and Custom-house. At New York, similar facilities were accorded to Mr. R. K. Haight; and, after five years of disappointments, Mr. Gliddon received these specimens in November, 1849.

Opened at Boston, June, 1850, in the presence of two thousand persons, by Prof. Agassiz, and a committee of sixteen of the leading physicians, these coffins yielded the embalmed corpse of the Theban Priest Got-thothi-aunkh, (*latinicè*, "Dixit Thoth, vivat!") who died in the tenth year of King Osorkon III., early in the ninth century B. C., or about 2750 years ago. The amusing equivoque of gender that occurred at its opening received satisfactory elucidation in the "Letter from Mr. Gliddon about the Papyrus found on the Boston Mummy," published in the *Boston Evening Transcript*, August 21st and 22d, 1850. A copy of this article is appended to the mummy, which, with all its documentary cerements, now lies open to inspection at the Anatomical Museum of the Louisiana University.

Fac-similes of all the hieroglyphical inscriptions on this mummy were forwarded by Mr. Gliddon to Mr. Birch; and the only material emendation of the former's readings, added by this erudite hierologist, is, that the legend on the papyrus designates the corpse as that of the "Chief of the *Artificers* of the abode of Ammon," *i. e.* Thebes.

Submitted, at Philadelphia, to the scientific scrutiny of the late Dr. Morton, this mummied body was not only pronounced to be "unequivocally identified with the reign of Osorkon III., by finding the *cartouche* or oval of that king stamped, in four different places, on a leather cross, placed diagonally on the thorax in front;" but the same authority also declares, "there are 130 embalmed Egyptian heads in the collection of the Academy, but none of them can be even approximately dated; whence the great interest that attaches itself to the present example."[485] And finally, on the 23d of January, 1852, the whole of these archæological facts have been confirmed, at New Orleans, by the personal investigation of Monsieur J. J. Ampère, whose opinions in Egyptology are decisive.[486] Mr. Gliddon pointed out to me, on this corpse, the only absolute confirmation, he says, of Scripture, with which long studies of Egyptian lore have made him personally acquainted. All male mummies comply with the ordinances of *Genesis* xli. 14; and with *Gen.* xvii. 11; *Exod.* iv. 25—but GOT-THOTHI's illustrates the accuracy of EZEKIEL's description of an "Egyptian"—xvi. 26; and xxiii. 19, 20.

FIG. 268. FIG. 269.

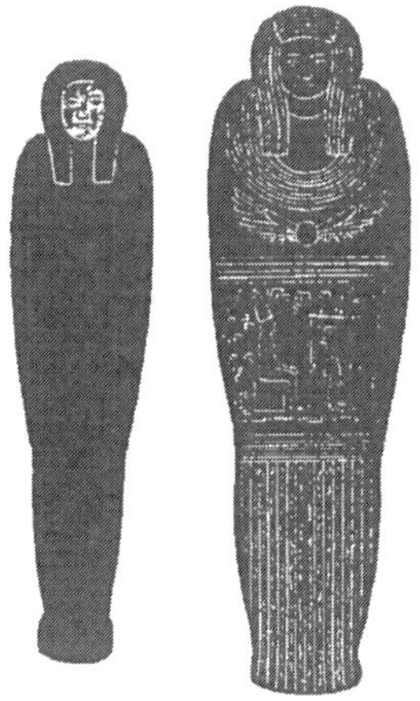

Inner Shell. Outer Case.

These Figs., 268 and 269, are copies of the mummy-cases. The face of the inner one is gilt; but *bitumen* had obliterated the legends.

That the influx of Asiatics into the Valley of the Nile commenced long before the foundation of the Empire under MENES—that is, prior to B. C. 4000—there can be no further question; and that amalgamations of foreign with the Nile's domestic races commenced at a pre-historic epoch, is now equally certain. Hence it is evident, that it must be often impossible to define some crania of these blended Egyptian races with precision, so great is the intermixture of primitive types. The facts however, drawn by Morton from the monuments and crania, prove, that the Egyptians-proper possessed small, elongated heads, with receding foreheads, and an average internal capacity of 80 cubic inches. Such view is fortified by the resemblance of this type to the modern native races of Egypt and surrounding countries; as the Fellahs, the Bedawees on both sides of the river and in the western oases, the Nubians, Berbers, &c. Their skulls have been already figured [*supra*, pp. 226, 227].

African-Negro Crania.

Our Chapter VIII. has already shown that Negroes are faithfully delineated on the monuments of the XVIIth dynasty, or B. C. 1600—1700; and that, although we produced no positive Nigritian *portraits* of earlier date, yet it is conceded that Negro tribes were abundant, along the Upper Nile, as far back as the XIIth dynasty; and *ergo*, they must have been also contemporary with the earliest settlers of Egypt.

FIG. 270.[487]

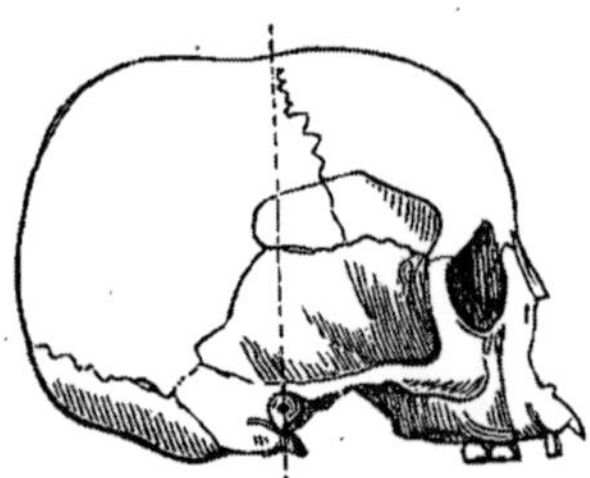

Bushman.

FIG. 271.[488]

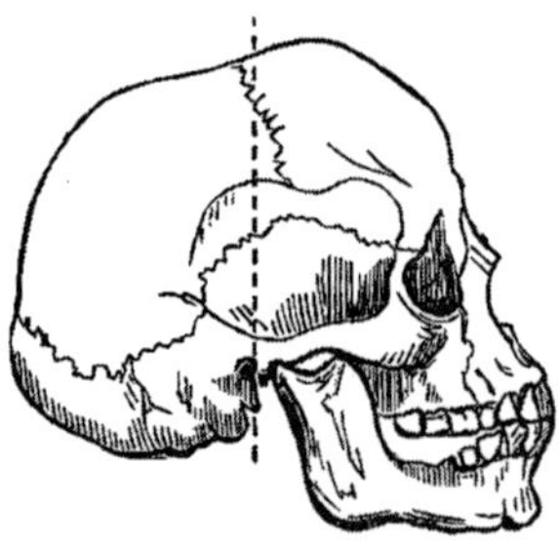

Mozambique.

Although Negro races present considerable variety in their cranial conformations, yet they all possess certain unmistakeable traits in common, marking them as Negroes, and distinguishing them from all other species of man. Prognathous jaws, narrow elongated forms, receding foreheads, large posterior development, small internal capacity, &c., characterize the whole group craniologically.

A few examples suffice to give the reader a good idea of their prominent characteristics, and will enable him to appreciate cranial distinctions between the varied Negro and other African types. (See Figs. 270–275.)

FIG. 272.[489]

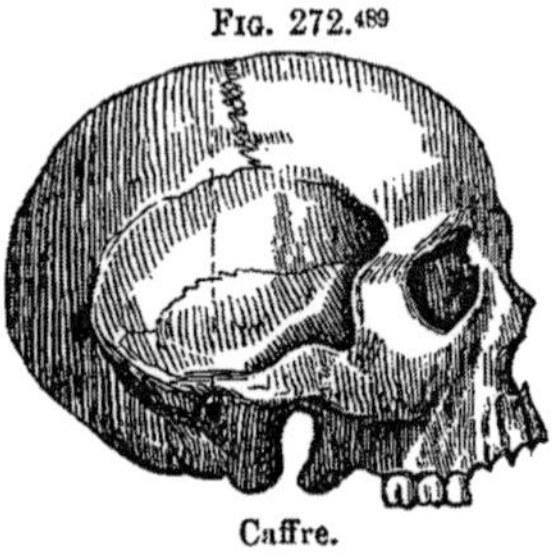

Caffre.

FIG. 273.[490]

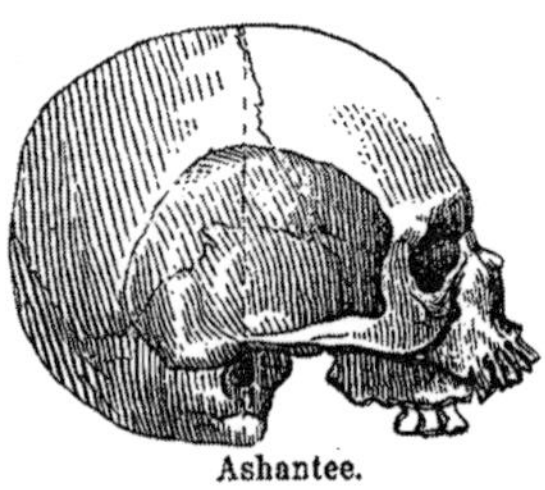

Ashantee.

It cannot fail to be noticed that the *Caffre* and the *Ashantee* exhibit far higher conformations than the rest; in accordance with recent historical events. They approach the *Foolah* "gradation."

FIG. 274.[491]

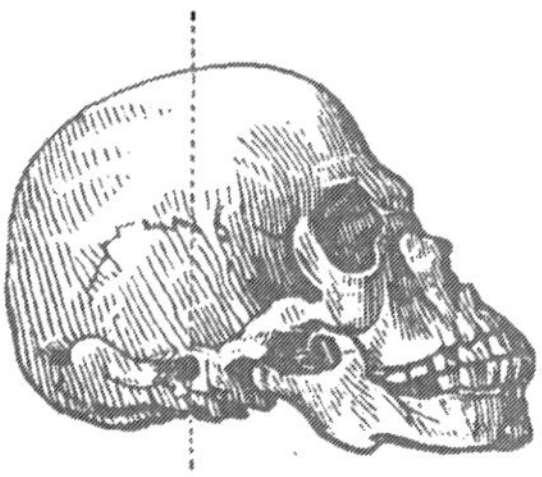

Creole Negro.

FIG. 275.[492]

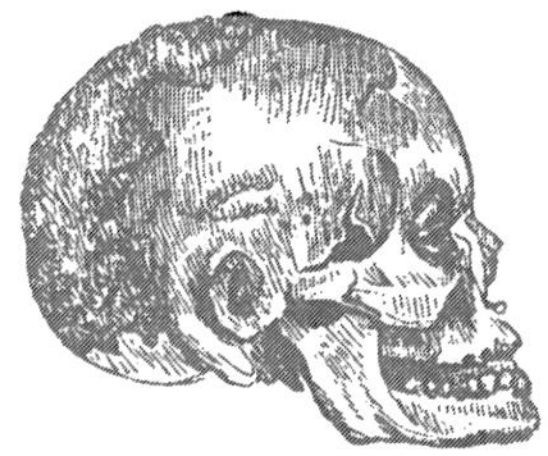

Mummied Negress.

Figure 276 is the portrait of a celebrated Hottentot female, which (seemingly, to Europeans) presents an extraordinary deformity. Some writers affirm that her bump, or hump, is an accidental freak of nature, or a peculiarity resulting from local causes. It is furthermore asserted, that such posterior development cannot be characteristic of any special race. But, while all these explanations are nullified by the fact that, around the Cape of Good Hope (and among Hottentot and Bushman races alone) similar retrotuberance is still quite common, it should not be forgotten that the proclivities of exotic Dutch Boors, combined with the action of local aborigines, have already modified the Hottentot and Bushman, and consequently divested both, to some extent, of their pristine uniformity. RITTER [*supra*, p. 380] shows that Arabian single, and Bactrian double-humped camels (although distinct "species"), when bred together, produce offspring sometimes with one, at others with two humps; and as the Hottentots are now a very mixed race, why should not the bump, once undeviatingly characteristic of the good old race, be frequently absent, or else diminished in volume, in the present generation?

FIG. 276.[493]

Hottentot Venus.

That the laws governing the phenomena of Nature, if as yet often inscrutable, are nevertheless perdurable, may be exemplified, monumentally, even through instances of idiocy or lunacy. Rosellini's plates, compared with Egyptian mummied skulls, and examined by the keen eyes of such comparative anatomists as Morton, furnish evidence that the natural deformities of humanity were appreciated, thousands of years ago, by Nilotic art; because the "sagacity of the Egyptian artist has admirably adapted this man's (Fig. 278) vocation to his intellectual developments, for he is employed in stirring the fire in a blacksmith's shop."[494]

FIG. 278.

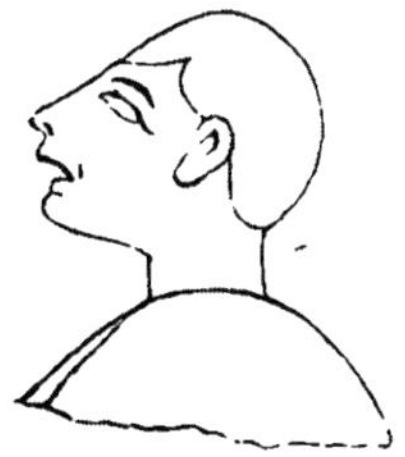

Sculptured Fool.

FIG. 277.

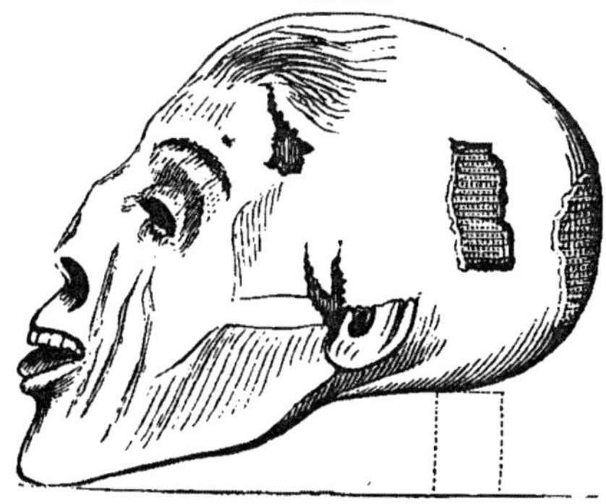

Mummied Idiot.

Oceanic Races.

Geographers divide our globe into Europe, Asia, Africa, America, and Oceanica. This last region has been subjected to many systematic divisions by different writers; but M. Jacquinot's are both simple and comprehensive: —

"1. Australia—embraces New Holland, and Tasmania or Van Diemen's Land.

"2. Polynesia—all the islands of the Pacific Ocean, from the west coast of America to the Philippines, and the Moluccas; comprising what have been termed Micronesia and Melanesia.

"3. Malaysia, or *East Indies*—Indian Archipelago; containing the Sunda, Philippine and Molucca Islands."

The three divisions together are termed Oceanica; and the races of men distributed over this vast area present an infinite diversity of types, which have also been variously classified. Prichard very justly remarks that these Oceanic types differ so much among each other, and from the inhabitants of the Old and New World, that it is now impossible to trace their origin.[495]

[Ethnographic knowledge of the whole of them does not antedate the sixteenth century. Thus, the existence of *Malay* tribes was unknown to Europe before their discovery by Lopez de Sequeira, in A. D. 1510, followed by Albuquerque about 1513. *Micronesians* were first seen by Ferdinand Magelhaens in 1520; *Polynesians* by Ruy Lopez de Villalobos in 1543, and by Alvaro de Mendana in 1595: while Abel Jansen Tasman, in 1642–3, sailed around Van Diemen's Land, seeing "no people, but some *smoaks*," and afterwards had some of his men killed by natives of New Zealand—which seems to be the first historic notice of *Australian* families. When we recollect that the *second* "voyage around the world" was not undertaken by Francis Drake before the year 1557,[496] it will be comprehended at once how very recent is the information which ethnology possesses of Malayan, Polynesian, and Australian types; whose separate existence, nevertheless, must be as ancient as that of the animals and plants of their respective provinces of creation.—G. R. G.]

As every classification of these races is wholly arbitrary, and inasmuch as any attempts at emendation would here be futile, I shall merely select for illustration a few of their more prominent types. We have shown, from the monuments of Egypt and other sources, that various distinct races of men stood, face to face, 5000 years ago, and that no physical causes have since transformed one type into another. We may, therefore, reasonably assume that these Oceanic races have ever been contemporary with others elsewhere, and were created where originally found by modern navigators. There is a more or less intimate connection, it is said, among most of the Polynesian tongues; but the Australian, whose type is altogether peculiar, Prichard declares, "is the only one whose language is known to be distinct."

Australians.

Australia comprises such immense superficies as to deserve the name of a continent; and, consequently, its inhabitants present considerable diversity of types. This is inferred from the contradictory accounts of travellers, who have described them at different geographical points. It should be remarked, that the natives of Australia, Van Diemen's Land, New Guinea, and some other of these islands, although differing in many particulars, are all so black in complexion as to have been termed Oceanic *Negroes*. They partake of the cranial conformation of African Negroes; displaying, like them, narrow, elongated heads, defective foreheads, small internal capacity, projecting jaws, &c.

Capt. WILKES, commander of the late U. S. Exploring Expedition, thus describes them:—

"The natives of Australia differ from any other race of men in features, complexion, habits, and language. Their color and features assimilate them to the African type: their long, black, silky hair has a resemblance to the Malays. The natives are of middle height, perhaps a little above it; they are slender in make, with long arms and legs. The cast of the face is between the African and the Malay; the forehead unusually narrow and high; the eyes small, black, and deep-set; the nose much depressed at the upper part, between the eyes, and widened at the base, which is done in infancy by the mother, the natural shape being of an aquiline form; the cheek-bones are high, the mouth large, and furnished with strong, well-set teeth; the chin frequently retreats; the neck is thin and short. The color usually approaches a deep umber, or reddish-black, varying much in shade; and individuals of pure blood are sometimes as light-colored as mulattoes. Their most striking distinction is their hair, which is like that of dark-haired Europeans, although more silky. It is fine, disposed to curl, and gives them a totally different aspect from the African, and also from the Malay and American Indian. Most of them have thick beards and whiskers, and they are more hairy than the whites."

JACQUINOT, of the French Exploring Expedition, gives a very similar description, except that "*leur couleur était d'un noir fuligineux assez intense.*" [497]

M. DE FREYCINET, who passed considerable time at different points of the country, describes these tribes in the same manner. He says: "The people everywhere assimilate. Their color varies from intense black to reddish black. Their hair is invariably black and smooth, though undulating, and never has the woolly appearance seen in other races." [498]

FIG. 279.[499]

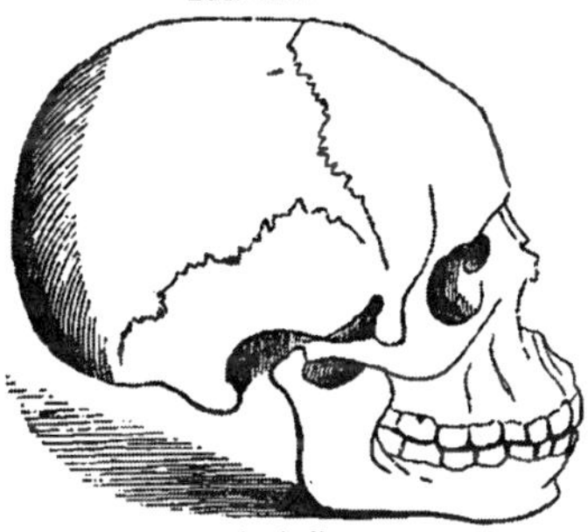

Australian.

FIG. 280.[500]

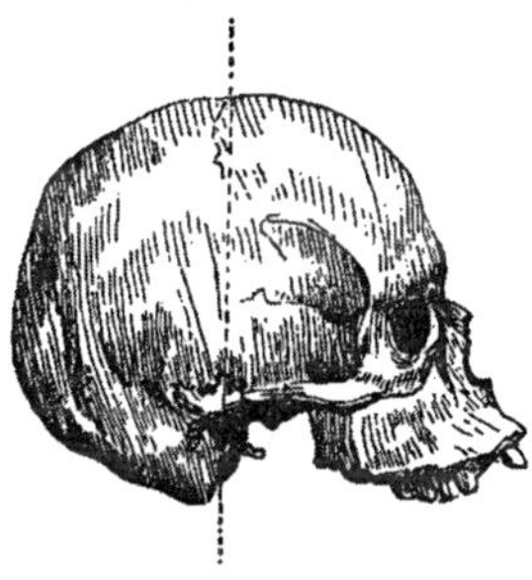

Australian.

"This man (Fig. 279), whose name was Durabub, was killed in a fray, after having himself killed two savages of a hostile tribe, A. D. 1841. His skull (adds Morton) is the nearest approach to the orang type that I have seen. Ætat. 40. J. C. 81."

Fig. 281 is from *la Baie Raffle*, coast of New Holland; taken from the Atlas of Dumoutier.

FIG. 281.[501]

Native of New Holland.

FIG. 282.[502]

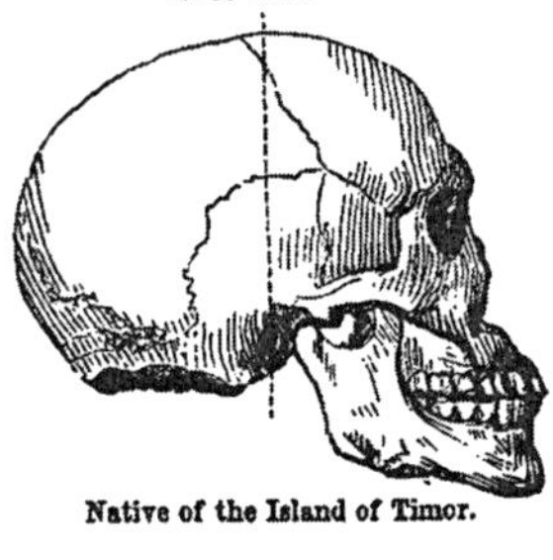

Native of the Island of Timor.

Fig. 282 — "Natif d'Amnoubang, Ile Timor."

To these heads from New Holland and the Island of Timor many others might be added, from the various works on the Physical History of Mankind. Our series, however, supplies fair specimens of these races, who represent the lowest grade in the human family. Their anatomical characteristics are certainly very remarkable. While, in countenance, they present an extreme of the prognathous type hardly above that of the orang-outan, they possess at the same time the smallest brains of the whole of mankind; being, according to Morton's measurements, seventeen cubic inches less than the brain of the Teutonic race. In my own collection I have a cast of the head figured above in Morton's catalogue; and, decidedly, it exhibits more of the animal than of man.

Tasmania, or Van Diemen's Land.

It is certainly an extraordinary fact, that this comparatively-small island, merely separated from Australia by a narrow channel, should be occupied by people of entirely different type. The tribes of New Holland, it has been just set forth, are more or less black, but possess fine, straight and silky hair; while their neighbors of Tasmania are thus described by Capt. Cook: —

"The color of the people of Van Diemen's Land is a dull black, and not quite so deep as that of the African Negroes. The hair is perfectly woolly. Their noses, though not flat, are broad and full. The lower part of the face projects a good deal."

The reader can select from the following 4 samples (Figs. 283 - 286) which he considers the worst expression of the most inferior grades of humanity.

Fig. 283.[503]

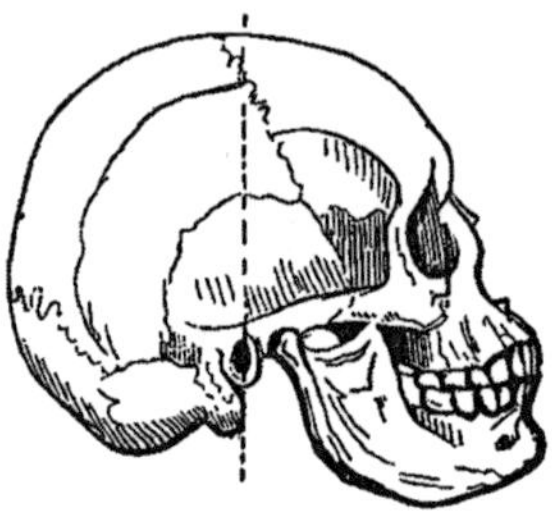

A. — Tasmanian.

Fig. 284.[504]

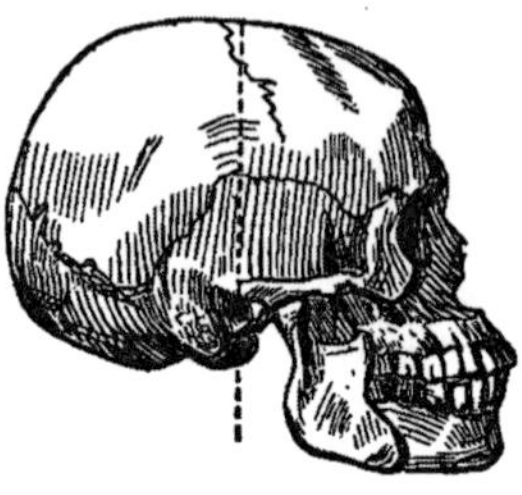

B. — Tasmanian.

Fig. 285.[505]

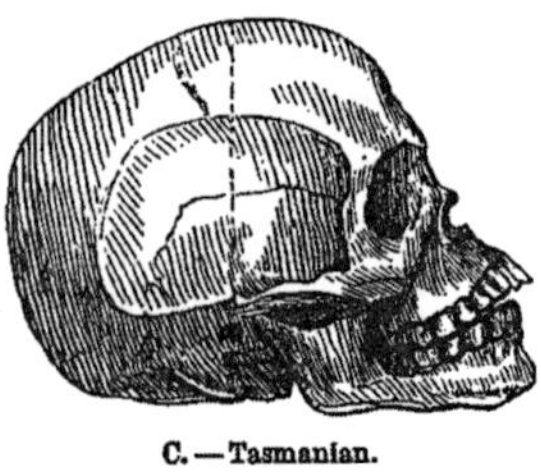

C. — Tasmanian.

Fig. 286.[506]

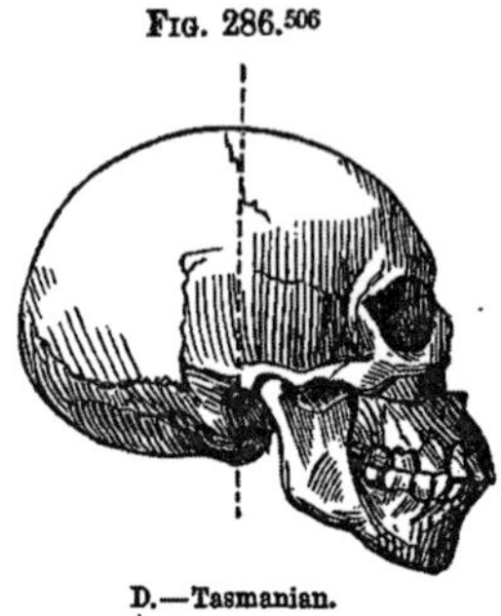

D. — Tasmanian.

Fig. A from Martin, and B from Dumoutier, compare well with the heads of Australians; and not less disagreeably.

Papuas, of New Guinea.

New Guinea is the largest of all these islands after New Holland. Numerous navigators, the old as well as the living, have described this people at various localities on the coast

The tribes appear everywhere to be substantially the same: skin more or less black, features Negro, hair woolly and formed into enormous tufts.

FIG. 287.[507]

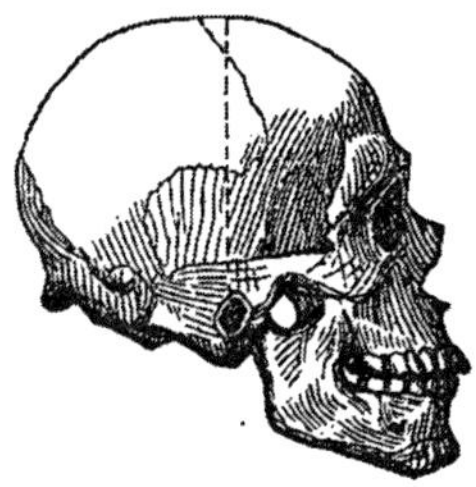

New Guinea-man.

This (Fig. 287) is a fair specimen of the inhabitants of New Guinea, which not only presents the Negro complexion, and features like the Australian, but also the woolly hair. We may consider this skull an average type of the Papuan race.

Harfours, or Alforians.

In Malaysia, under the names of Harfours, Alfours, Haraforas, &c., have been designated the inhabitants of the interior of the large islands, or mountain regions. But great diversity exists in the type of these families; and much confusion in descriptions. They seem generally to be a true Negro race, of the lowest order; and from their position in the interior, no less than from their degraded condition, they are, most probably, the true aborigines of many of these islands, who have been driven back by immigrants from other islands. One skull (Fig. 288) sufficiently represents them.

FIG. 288.[508]

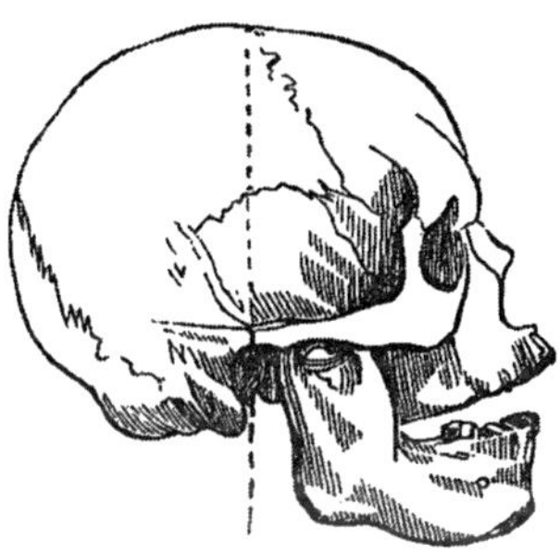

Alfour.

I shall not overload our pages with detailed descriptions of the various Oceanic Negro types inhabiting the smaller islands. Materials lack for satisfactory anatomical comparison. There is to be found in print very little to aid the craniologist, beyond the magnificent plates of Dumoutier, from which we have extensively borrowed; but his text has not yet been published; nor do drawings alone furnish the information required. All travellers and every anatomist agree, however, in placing these Oceanic Negroes at the bottom of the scale of races; and, at the same time, the Alforians are described as totally different from every group of Negroes on the African continent.

Therefore, the supposition of any community of origin between these Australasians and the true Nigritians — neither of them migratory races, and widely separated by oceans — would be too gratuitous to merit refutation. So also would be any hypotheses based upon climatic influences, when the zones of their respective habitats are as opposite in nature, as the races of Malaysia are distinct from those of Africa, and, at the same time, geographically remote.

Polynesian Race.

An elaborate account of this race may be found in Prichard's "Physical History of Mankind;" but I rely more particularly on the later work of M. Jacquinot; inasmuch as it is, in every respect, deserving of confidence and admiration: coming, besides, from a naturalist who has *seen* these tribes in their various localities:—

"The Polynesian race is well marked and distinct; it inhabits all Malaysia and the greater part of Polynesia, comprising the numerous islands separated by d'Urville under the name of Micronesia.

"The general characters of this race may be thus given:—Skin tawny, of a yellow color washed with bistre, more or less deep; very light in some, almost brown in others. Hair, black, bushy, smooth and sometimes frizzled. Eyes black, more split than open, not at all oblique. Nose long, straight, sometimes aquiline or straight; nostrils large and open, which makes it sometimes look flat, especially in women and children; in them, also, the lips, which in general are long and curved, are slightly prominent. Teeth fine; incisors large. Cheek-bones large, not salient; enlarging the face, which, nevertheless, is longer than wide."

Blumenbach describes the cranium thus: — "Summit of the head slightly contracted; forehead rather convex; cheek-bones not prominent; superior maxillary bone rather projecting; parietal protuberances very prominent."

Jacquinot declares that these characters are constant in all the individuals of the Polynesian race; and he says his description is confirmed by Forster,[509] Moerenhout,[510] Ellis,[511] Quoy et Gaimard, and others.

Most authors recognize three distinct races among the Polynesians: independent of those just described, they designate the inhabitants of the Carolines, or Micronesians, and the Malays; but M. Jacquinot regards this division as unfounded in nature. That there is considerable variety of types in these scattered islands is admitted; and the question reduces itself to, whether these islanders are really of one stock or of several. Anthropology perceives no reason for supposing that they are all descended from one pair; and I therefore regard them as a group of proximate races, like the numerous other groups already signalized on the earth's superficies. They have been separated, by some writers, on philological grounds; but I hold it to be a demonstrable, even if not demonstrated fact, that zoological characters are far more reliable than mere analogies of language; which (critically examined) are frequently less-real than fanciful.

After surveying the Polynesian race in detail, through all the islands, from the Philippines to New Zealand and the Sandwich, Jacquinot concludes:—

"Thus this race is found spread from 20° N. lat. to 50° S. lat.; that is to say, it occupies a space of about 3500 miles of latitude by 4500 of longitude. Certainly, within these extremes, the climate offers numerous variations. Some of these islands are flat, others mountainous; some are very fertile, others sterile; and, notwithstanding all these circumstances, the Polynesians remain the same everywhere. They are all in the same degree of civilization, of industry and intelligence; their color is not more dark under the equator than without the tropics—and everywhere we find some more brown than others.

"We repeat that, before such facts fall all theories respecting the influence of atmosphere and of climate.

"They prove also, in the clearest manner, that the Polynesians cannot be a hybrid race; because, if it were so, they could not preserve, in the numerous islands, a homogeneousness of character so perfect; there would necessarily be mixed breeds in different degrees, and showing every shade and grade. The Polynesian race then is *primitive*."

Fig. 289.

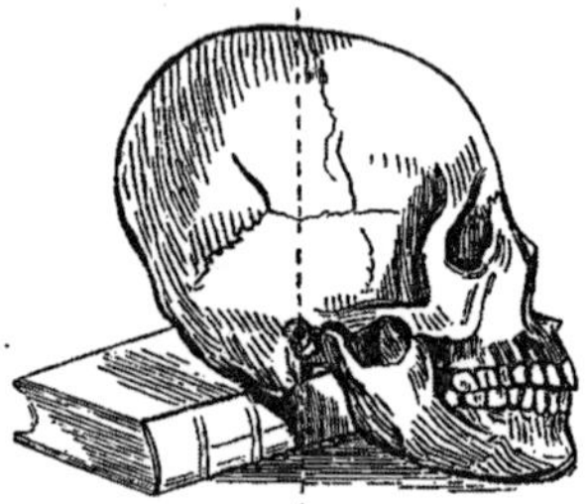

Sandwich Islander.

Fig. 290.

Vertical view.

The original of Fig. 289 died in the Marine hospital at Mobile, while under the charge of my friends Drs. Levert and Mastin; and the skull was presented to Agassiz and myself for examination, without being apprised of its history. Notwithstanding there was something in its form which appeared unnatural, yet it resembled more than any other race the Polynesian; and as such we did not hesitate to class it. It turned out afterwards that we were right; and that our embarrassment had been produced by an artificial flattening of the occiput; which process the

Islander, while at the hospital, had told Drs. Levert and Mastin was habitual in his family. The profile view displays less protuberance of brain behind, and the vertical view more compression of occiput, than belongs generally to his race; but still there remains enough of cranial characteristics to mark his Polynesian origin; even were not the man's history preserved, to attest the gross depravity of his animal propensities.

The first of these heads (Fig. 291) is an ancient *Guanche* from the Canary-Isles; and, though out of place here, is one of Dumoutier's series.—Besides being itself interesting, it contrasts still more powerfully with American aborigines.

The other five (Figs. 292–296) are Polynesians from different islands, presenting a strong family likeness to each other—receding foreheads; elongated heads; projecting jaws, ponderous behind, &c.

FIG. 291.[512]

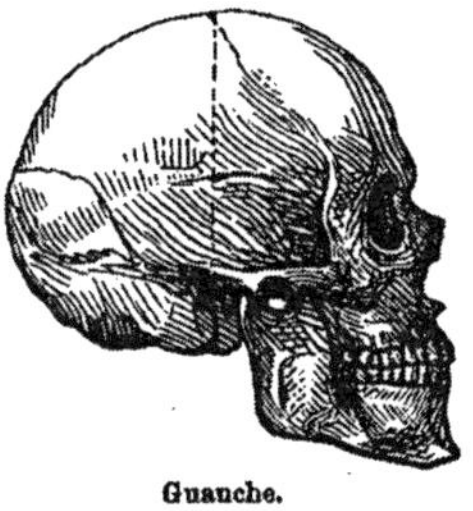

Guanche.

FIG. 292.[513]

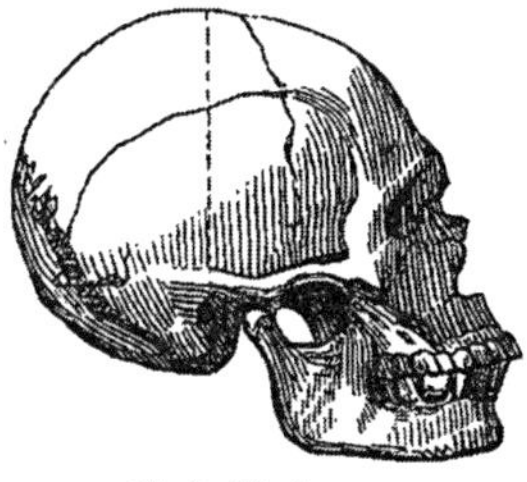

Nouka-Hivaian.

FIG. 293.[514]

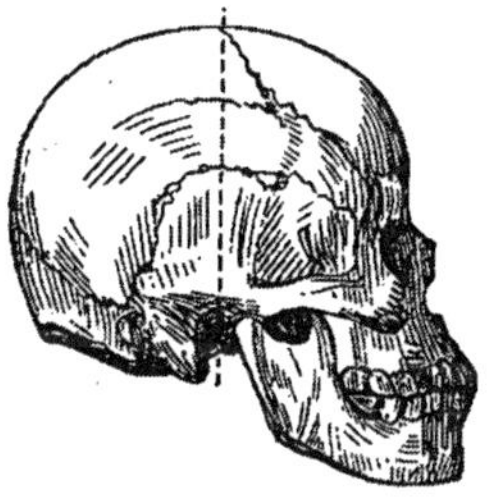

Taitian.

FIG. 294.[515]

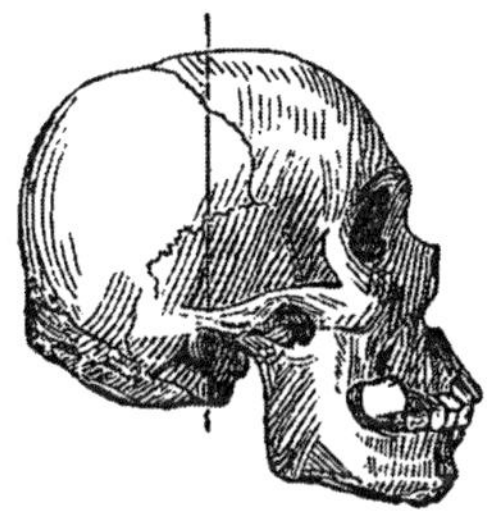

Tonga-Islander.

FIG. 295.[516]

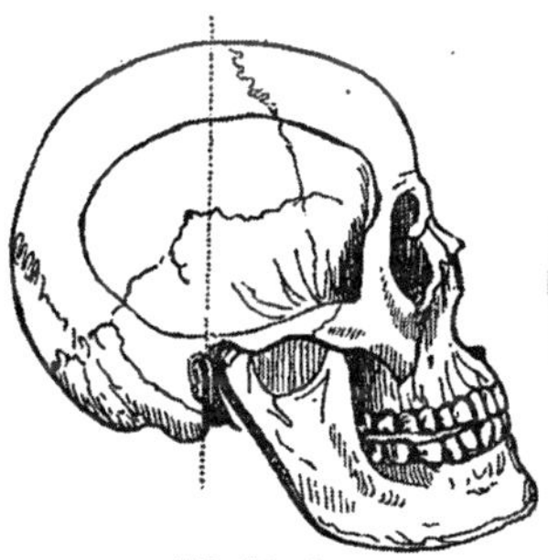

Fejee-Islander.

FIG. 296.[517]

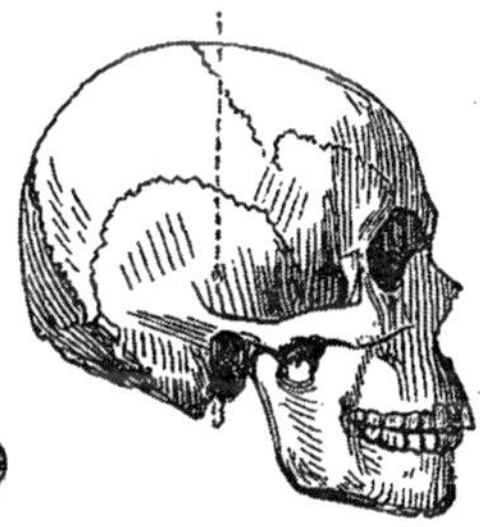

Sandwich-Islander.

I have pursued the Oceanic races, somewhat in detail, from the Indian seas across the whole extent of the Pacific Ocean to the shores of America; where another group of races, of entirely different type, remains yet to be described. My object in this tedious voyage has been, to place before the reader such material as might enable him to judge whether there is any proof, in this geographical direction, of migrations from the Old to the New World, that could account for its primitive manner of population. We have beheld, during our Oceanic travels, very opposite types in localities near to each other, as well as many distinct languages; and we have seen the same type as that of the Polynesians scattered throughout all climates, and yet speaking dialects of the same language.

It now remains to be shown that, (with perhaps some very partial exceptions along the Pacific coast,) the types of America are entirely distinct from those of Oceanica; and that American languages, civilizations, social institutions, &c., are utterly opposed to Oceanic influence, while differing, too, amongst each other. It is from the so-called Polynesian and Malay races that many writers have derived the population of America; yet in no two types of man do we find cranial characters more widely different. The heads which we have copied from the *Atlas* of M. le Docteur Dumoutier, (who accompanied M. Jacquinot in the Exploring Expedition of 1837–'8–'9–'40, of the Astrolabe and Zélée, sent out by the French government,) were all taken by the daguerreotype process, either from nature or from plaster-casts; and are therefore not only beautifully executed, but perfectly reliable. To the eye of the anatomist, these heads will be found to present a most striking contrast with those of the aboriginal Americans which we are about to produce. It is much to be regretted, however, that we have not complete measurements of these Oceanic heads, their various diameters, internal capacity, &c., after the plan adopted by Morton; but I presume such essentials will appear in full, when the text is published. It will be observed, furthermore, that the American heads differ more widely from all the Oceanic crania than they do even from those of the Chinese or true Mongol races, whence our American Indians are still supposed by fabulists to be derived. The Oceanic races, including even the Sandwich Islanders, when compared with our Indians, exhibit crania more elongated, more compressed laterally, less prominent at the vertex, and more prognathous, in type. American races, I shall render evident, are strongly distinguished by the very reverse of all these points, in addition to their own greatly-flattened occiput. Whilst running the eye, too, over Dumoutier's long series of Oceanic heads, I was struck by one remarkable difference: viz., the greater amount of brain behind the meatus of the ear than in the skulls of the aborigines of America; and the reader will notice *vertical lines*, rendering this fact obvious.

American Group.

The author of *Crania Americana* separated [*supra*, p. 276] the races of this continent into two grand divisions: viz., the Toltecan and the Barbarous tribes. That luminous paper — ***Inquiry into the Distinctive Characteristics of the Aboriginal Race of America***[518] — amply justified the traveller's adage, that "he who has seen one tribe of Indians, has seen all."

"The half-clad Fuegian, shrinking from his dreary winter, has the same characteristic lineaments, though in an exaggerated degree, as the Indians of the tropical plains; and these, again, resemble the tribes which inhabit the region west of the Rocky Mountains—those of the great Valley of the Mississippi, and those, again, which skirt the Eskimaux on the North. All possess alike the long, lank, black hair, the brown or cinnamon-colored skin, the heavy brow, the dull and sleepy eye, the full and compressed lips, and the salient, but dilated nose. . . . The same conformity of organization is not less obvious in the osteological structure of these people, as seen in the square or rounded head, the flattened or vertical occiput, the large quadrangular orbits, and the low, receding forehead. . . . Mere exceptions to a general rule do not alter the peculiar physiognomy of the Indian, which is as undeviatingly characteristic as that of the Negro; for whether we see him in the athletic Charib or the stunted Chayma, in the dark Californian or the fair Borroa, he is an Indian still, and *cannot be mistaken for a being of any other race.*"

And, above all anatomists, Morton had the best right to pronounce. We have seen [*supra*, p. 325] how his unrivalled "collection embraces 410 skulls of 64 different nations and tribes of Indians."

Time, moreover, from ante-historical — nay, even from *geological* epochas, down to the present hour, appears to have wrought little or no change on the physical structure of the American aborigines. Dr. Lund's communication to the Historical and Geographical Society of Brazil,[519] on the *human fossil* crania discovered by him in the Province of Minas Geraes, added to the published decisions of Dr. Meigs on the Santas fossilized bones, with those of Dr. Moultrie on the Guadaloupe fossilized head, settle that matter conclusively [*supra*, pp. 347, 350]: nor do the last-discovered fossilized *jaws with perfect teeth*, and *portions of a foot*, from Florida, now in the possession of Prof. Agassiz, negative this deduction; although such vestiges, still imbedded in conglomerate, may not be cited in the affirmative. Lund's language, as rendered by Lieut. Strain, U. S. N., is unequivocal: —

"The question then arises, who were these people? what their mode of life? of what race? and what their intellectual perfection? The answers to these questions are, happily, less difficult and doubtful. He examined various crania, more or less perfect, in order to determine the place they ought to occupy in the system of Anthropology. The narrowness of the forehead, the prominence of the zygomatic bones, the maxillary and orbital conformation, all assign to these crania a place among the characteristics of the American race. And it is known, says the Doctor, in continuation, that the race which approximates nearest to this is the Mongolian; and the most distinctive and salient character by which we distinguish between them, is by the greater depression of the forehead of the former. In this point of organization, these ancient crania show not only the peculiarity of the American race, but this peculiarity, in many instances, in an excessive degree; even to the entire disappearance of the forehead. We must allow, then, that the people who occupied this country in those remote times, were of the same race as those who inhabited it at the time of the conquest. We know that the human figures found sculptured on the ancient monuments of Mexico represent, for the greater part, a singular conformation of the head — being without forehead — the cranium retreating backward, immediately above the superciliary arch. This anomaly, which is generally attributed to an artificial disfiguration of the head, or the taste of the artist, now admits a more natural explanation; it being now proved by these authentic documents, that there really existed on this continent a race exhibiting this anomalous conformation. The skeletons, which were of both sexes, were of the ordinary height, although two of the men were above the common stature. These heads, according to the received opinions in Craniology, could not have occupied a high position in intellectual standing. This opinion is corroborated by finding an instrument of imperfect construction joined with the skeletons. This instrument is simply a smooth stone, of about ten inches iu circumference, evidently intended to bruise seeds or hard substances.

"In other caverns he has found other human bones, which show equally the characteristics of fossils, being deprived of all the gelatinous parts, and consequently very brittle and porous in the fracture."

Finally, the "Peruvian Antiquities" of Rivero and Tschudi[520] corroborate the above scientific view, viz., that the artificial disfigurement of the skull among the Inca-Peruvians and other South American families, owes its origin to the prior existence of an autocthonous race, in whose crania such (to us, seemingly) a deformity was natural: and thus the contradictory materials which induced Dr. Morton at first to deem this peculiarity to be congenital, and afterwards so exclusively artificial, become reconciled; while due regard is preserved to his truthful candor and craniological acumen.

FIG. 297.[521]

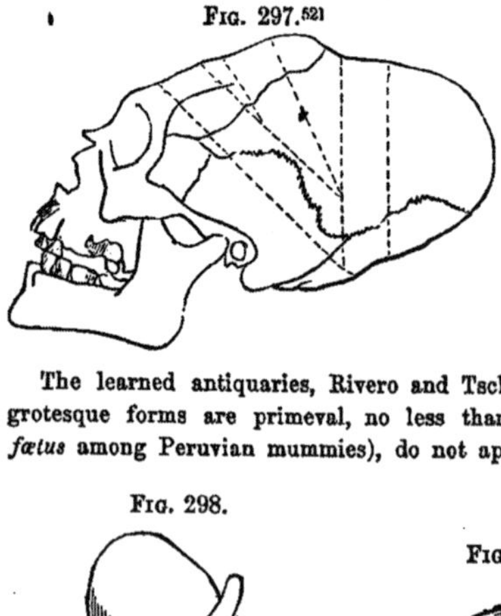

Of the *four* forms of the head among the Old Peruvians, which were produced by artificial means (as established by Morton, in *Ethnography and Archæology of the American Aborigines*, 1846), space restricts me to one example (Fig. 297), on which the "course of every bandage is in every instance distinctly marked by corresponding cavity of the bony structure;" and another form (Figs. 298, 299) is monumentally illustrated through DEL RIO's *Account of Palenque.*[522]

The learned antiquaries, Rivero and Tschudi, whose researches establish that these grotesque forms are primeval, no less than congenital (being exhibited even in the *fœtus* among Peruvian mummies), do not appear to have been aware that Dr. Morton had already classified the *four* varieties of such distortions, in a paper published five years previously to their work.[523]

FIG. 298.

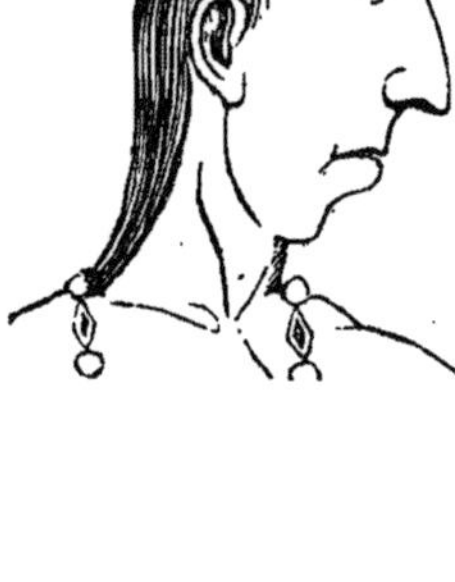

FIG. 299.

The compression of the head practised by various Indian tribes, although it causes distortion of the cranium in different directions, does not diminish the volume of the brain. This singular fact was announced many years ago by Prof. Tiedemann, and has since been abundantly confirmed by the multiplied observations of Morton. From the measurements of twenty-six Peruvian crania, all extremely distorted, some elongated, others conical, and others again flattened on the forehead and expanded laterally, he obtained a mean of 76 cubic inches, or one inch more than the Peruvian average. From twenty-one native skulls from Oregon, all more or less distorted by artificial means, he obtained a mean rather below the average of the barbarous tribes; but from the whole of his measurements of distorted crania, as derived from the Peruvian and Nootka-Columbian series collectively, he found the average volume of the brain to be 79 cubic inches, or precisely the mean of the whole American group of races. I may add that, as mechanical distortion of the skull does not lessen the volume of the brain, neither does it appear to affect the intellect.

These points established, I would remark, that the most striking anatomical characters of the American crânia are, small size, averaging but seventy-ninė cubic inches internal capacity; low, receding forehead; short antero-posterior diameter; great inter-parietal diameter; flattened occiput; prominent vertex; high cheek-bones; ponderous and somewhat prominent jaws. Such characteristics are more universal in the Toltecan than the Barbarous tribes. Among the Iroquois, for instance, the heads were often of a somewhat more elongated form; but the Cherokees and Choctaws, who of all modern Barbarous tribes display greater aptitude for civilization, present the genuine type in a remarkable degree. My birth and long residence in Southern States have permitted the study of many of these living tribes (a hundred Choctaws may be seen daily, even now, in the streets of Mobile), and they exhibit this conformation almost without exception. I have also scrutinized many Mexicans, besides Catawbas of South Carolina, and tribes on the Canada Lakes, and can bear witness that the living tribes everywhere confirm Morton's type.

One might, indeed, describe an Indian's skull by saying, it is the opposite in every respect from that of the Negro; as much as the brown complexion of the Red-man is instantly distinguishable from the Black's; or the long hair of the former differs in substance from the short wool of the latter.

The annexed sketches of three heads (Figs. 300–306) will, by comparison, illustrate this type better than language. Figs. 300 and 301, a Negro; Figs. 302 and 303, the head (in my possession) of a Cherokee Chief, who died while a prisoner, near Mobile, in 1837; and Figs. 305 and 306, the antique cranium from Squier's mound [*ubi supra*, p. 291.]

FIG. 300.[524]

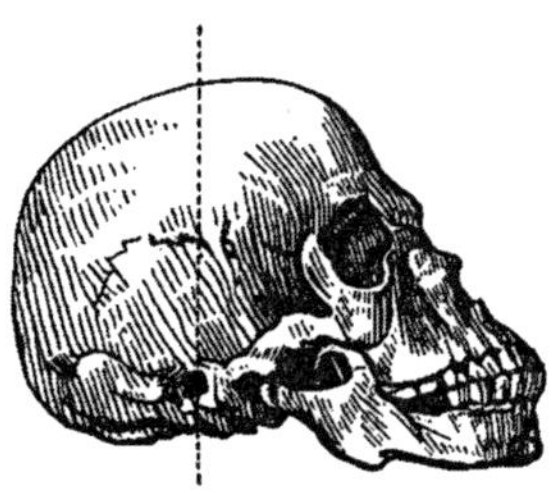

Negro — Profile View.

FIG. 301.

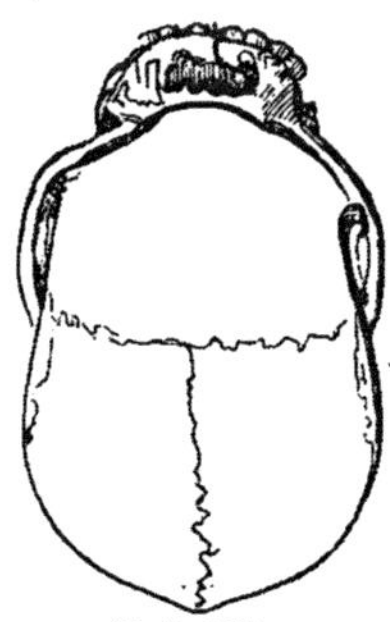

Vertical View.

I shall now proceed

FIG. 302.

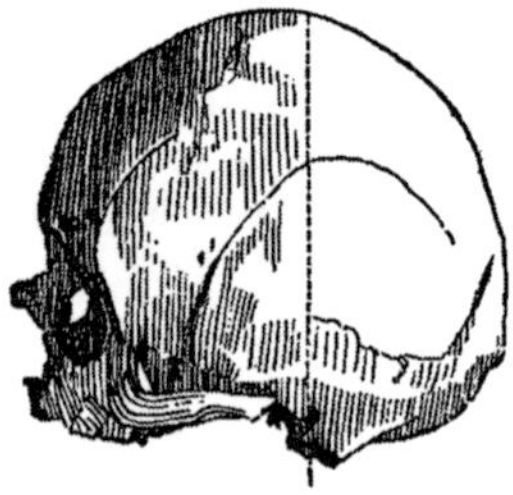

Creek Chief — Profile View.

FIG. 304.

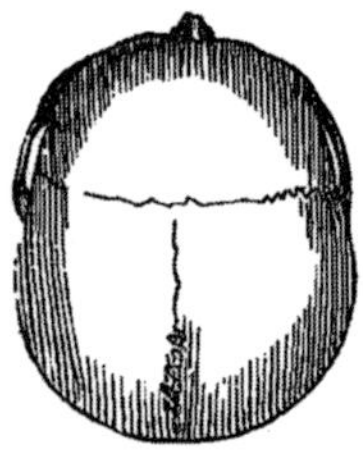

Vertical View.

FIG. 305.

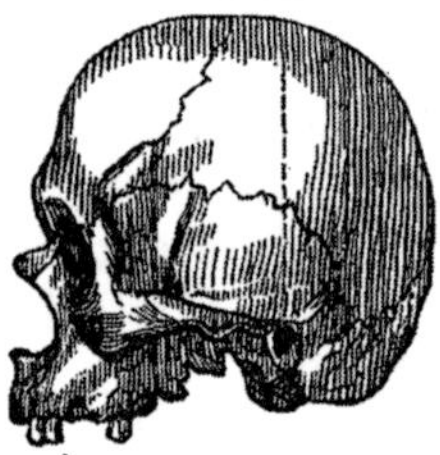

Mound-builder — Profile View.

FIG. 306.

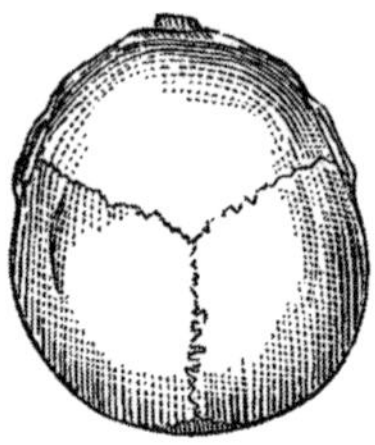

Vertical View.

to show, through faithful copies, that the type just attributed to the American races is found among tribes the most scattered — among the semi-civilized, and the barbarous — among living as well as among extinct races; and that no foreign race has intruded itself into their midst, even in the smallest appreciable degree: availing myself of some of the original wood-cuts of the *Crania Americana*, placed by Mrs. Morton's kindness at our disposal.

Peruvians, from Temple of the Sun.

This head (Fig. 307) from the Cemetery of Pachacamac, is characteristic of the American type, as will be seen at a glance: the parietal and longitudinal diameters being nearly equal; the vertex prominent.

FIG. 307.[525]

Peruvian—Profile View.

FIG. 308.

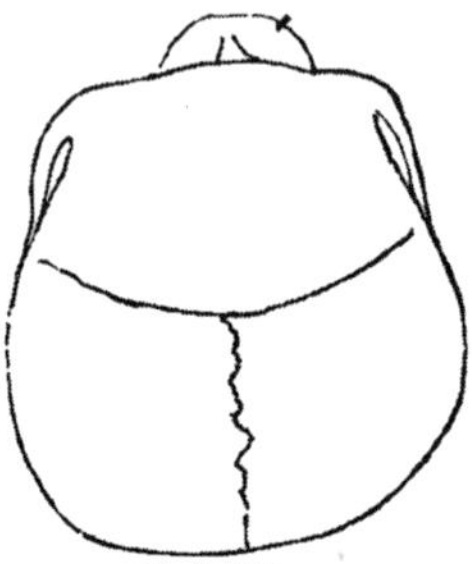

Vertical View.

FIG. 309.

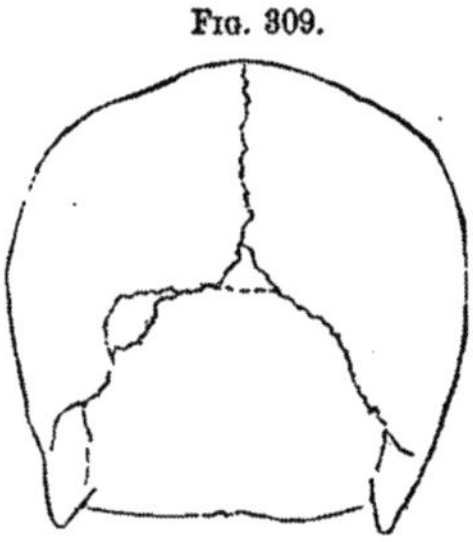

Back View.

Longitudinal diameter, 6 inches; parietal, 5·9; frontal, 4·4; vertical, 5. Internal capacity, 77 cubic inches.

FIG. 310.[526]

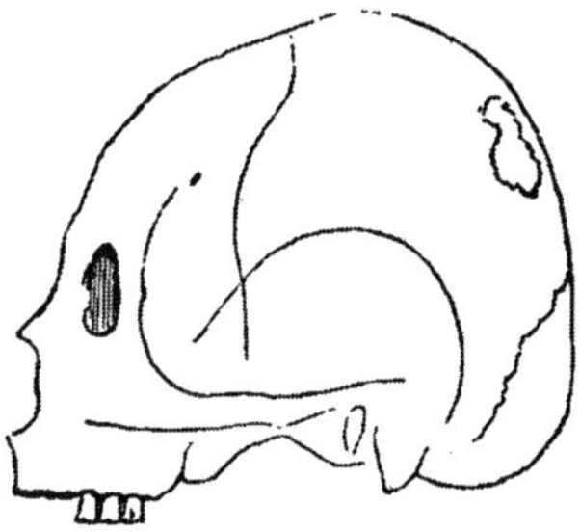

Peruvian.

Fig. 310, from the Inca Cemetery, is perfectly typical of the race.

Longitudinal diameter, 6·5 inches; parietal, 5·5; frontal, 4·6; vertical, 5·6. Internal capacity, 68·5 cubic inches.

Morton supplies the measurements of twenty-three adult skulls of the "pure Inca race," from the cemetery called Pachacamac, or the Temple of the Sun, near Lima; obtained and presented to him by Dr. Ruschenberger, U. S. N. As this sepulchre was reserved for the exclusive use of the higher class of Peruvians, it is reasonable to infer that the skulls thence disinterred belonged to persons of intelligence and distinction; although I am aware that Rivero and Tschudi express doubts that any of these can have belonged to royal Peruvian personages.[527]

The largest cranium of this series yields an internal capacity of 89·5 cubic inches, which is a fraction short of the Caucasian mean; while the smallest measures but 60. The mean of the whole is but 73 cubic inches.

The following examples of Mexican heads suffice to show the identity of the two races.

Mexicans.

FIG. 311.[528]

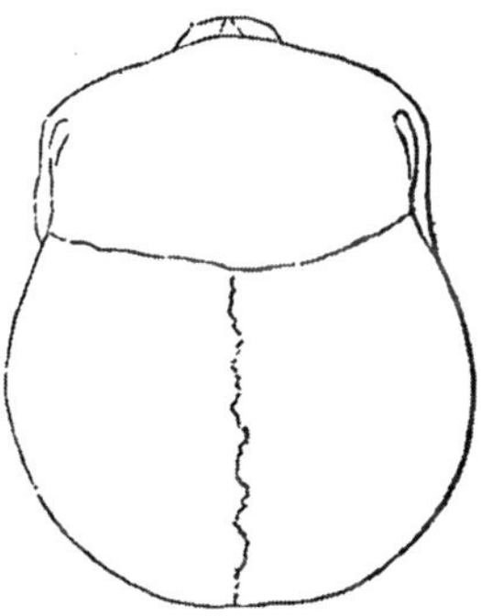

Mexican—Vertical View.

FIG. 312.

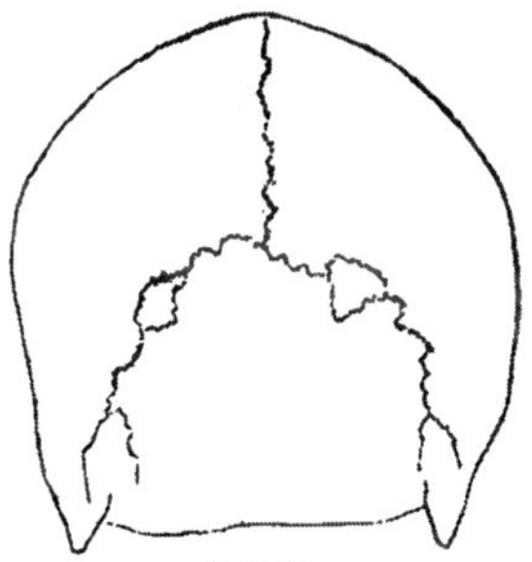

Back View.

This (Fig. 311) is a relic of the genuine Toltecan stock, having been exhumed from an ancient cemetery at Cerro de Quesilas, near the city of Mexico. It was accompanied by numerous antique vessels, weapons, &c., indicating a personage of distinction. This cranium was brought from the city of Mexico by the Hon. J. R. Poinsett, and by him presented to the Academy of Sciences of Philadelphia.

Longitudinal diameter, 7·1 inches; parietal, 5·7; frontal, 4·4; vertical, 5·2. Internal capacity, 83 cubic inches.

A remarkably-well characterized head (Fig. 313) from an ancient tomb near the city of Mexico, whence it was exhumed with a great variety of an-

FIG. 313.[529]

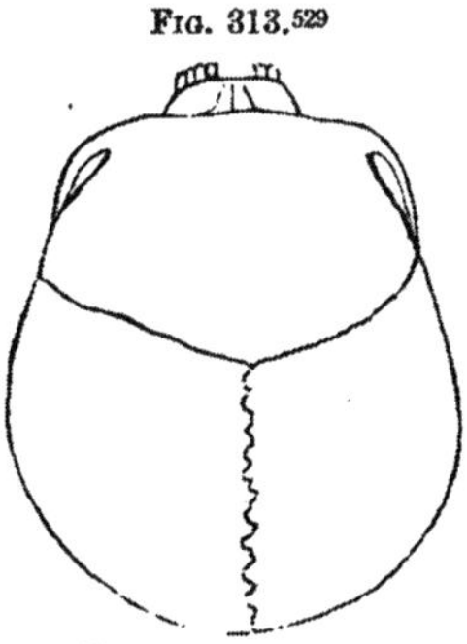

Mexican—Vertical View.

FIG. 314.

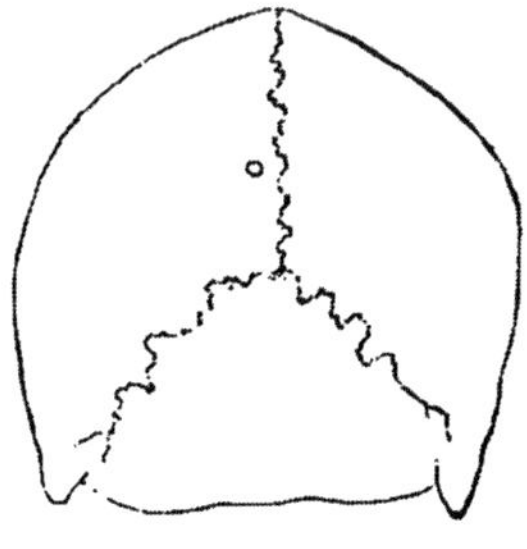

Back View.

tique vessels, masks, ornaments, &c. It is preserved in the collection of the American Philosophical Society. The forehead is low, but not very receding; the face projects, and the whole cranium is extremely unequal in its lateral portions. I had almost omitted the remark, that this irregularity of form is common in and peculiar to American crania.

Let us now track the American type into the Barbarous races. Among the Iroquois and some other tribes of both North and South America, heads of more elongated form are occasionally met with; but the type truly characteristic predominates largely among the *Creeks*—under which appellation were embraced most of the tribes of Alabama, Georgia and Florida. Having personally examined many of these nations, I can vouch for this fact. While Prof. Agassiz was in Mobile last spring, I took occasion to point out this cranial uniformity; and his critical eye detected no exception in at least 100 living Choctaw Indians whom we examined together in and around the city. *The modern Creek chief* [*supra*, Fig. 302] affords satisfactory evidence.

Seminole (*Creek Tribe*) *and Dacota* (*Sioux*).

FIG. 315.[530]

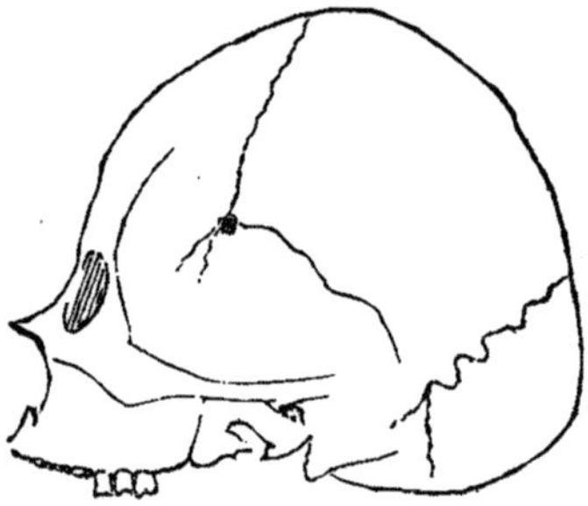

Seminole—Profile View.

FIG. 316.

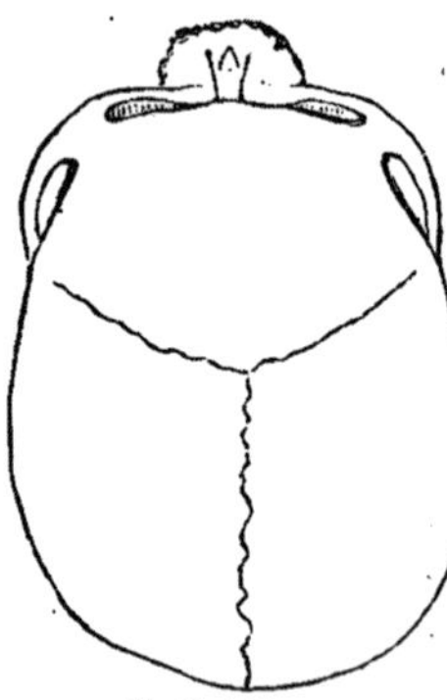

Vertical View.

FIG. 317.

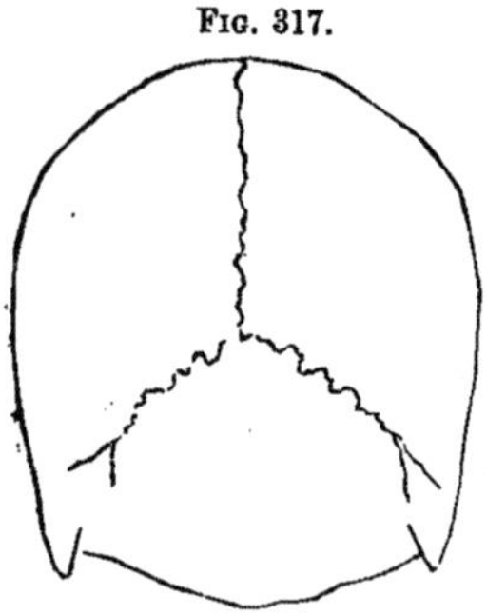

Seminole—Back View.

FIG. 318.[531]

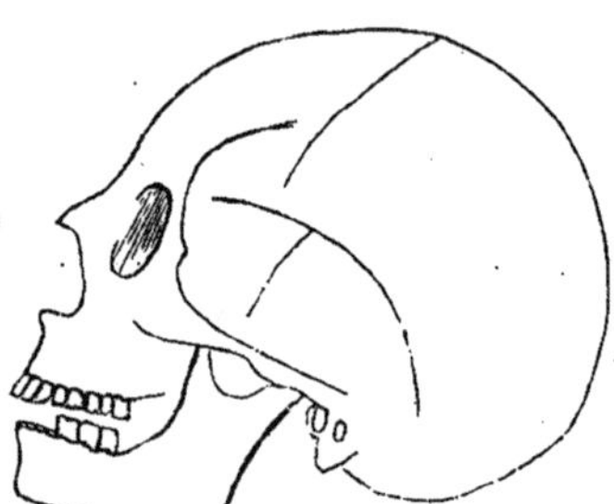

Dacota—Profile View.

Seminole warrior (Fig. 315) slain at the battle of St. Joseph's, 30 miles below St. Augustine, in June, 1836, by Capt. Justin Dimmick, U. S. Artillery. Longitudinal diameter, 7·3 in.; parietal, 5·9; frontal, 4·6; vertical, 5·8. Internal capacity, 93 cubic inches.

Fig. 318 is the head of a Sioux warrior; very characteristic of his tribe. Longitudinal diameter 6·7 inches; parietal, 5·7; frontal, 4·2; vertical, 5·4. Internal capacity, 85 cubic inches.

Reference to the *Crania Americana* will show that examples might be greatly multiplied, to prove that our Indian aborigines are everywhere comprehended under one group. I have already spoken of the ancient mounds and the mound-builders; have shown how numerous and widely-extended they are, and that they all belonged to the great Toltecan family. In addition to the cranium discovered by Squier [Fig. 198], I subjoin two more of these mound-skulls, selected from points separated by immense distance.

Skull from a Mound on the Upper Mississippi.

Skull (Fig. 319) taken from a mound seated on the high bluff which overlooks the Mississippi river, 150 miles above the mouth of the Missouri. There were six mounds, placed over each in a right line, commencing with a small one, only a few feet high, and terminating in another of eight or ten feet elevation and twenty in diameter. This skull was obtained from the fifth mound of the series. It is a large cranium, very full in the vertical diameter, and broad between the parietal bones.

FIG. 319.[532]

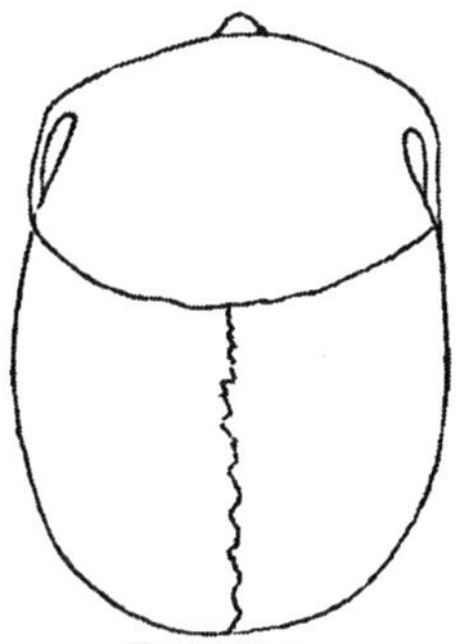

Vertical View.

FIG. 320.

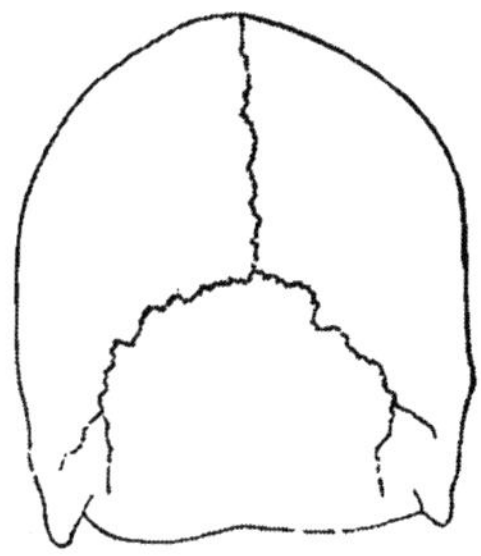

Back View.

Longitudinal diameter, 7·1 inches; parietal, 5·3; frontal, 4·8; vertical, 5·5. Internal capacity, 85·5 cubic inches.

Skull from a Mound in Tennessee.

This cranium (Fig. 321) was exhumed by the late distinguished Dr. Troost, of Nashville, Tennessee, from a mound in that State, at the junction of the French, Broad and Holston rivers. Many other mounds are found in this section of country. This skull is remarkable for its vertical and parietal diameters, flatness and elevation of the occiput. The facial angle is also unusually great.

FIG. 321.[533]

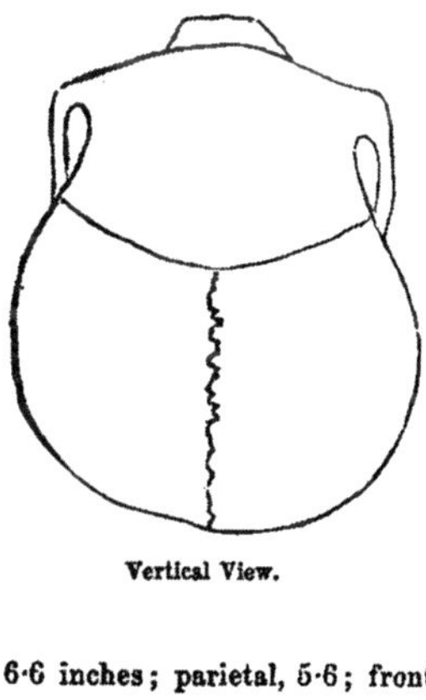

Vertical View.

FIG. 322.

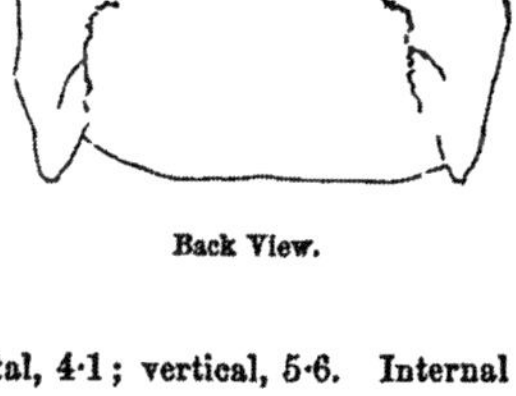

Back View.

Longitudinal diameter, 6·6 inches; parietal, 5·6; frontal, 4·1; vertical, 5·6. Internal capacity, 87·5 cubic inches.

To the reader have thus been submitted specimens of American skulls, from parts of the continent the most widely separated — some crania collected from the Toltecan, some from the Barbarous tribes of the present times, and others from ancient mounds and burial-places: and, although there are sundry minor varieties in the forms of crania — a few exceptions to the general rule, yet the type which I laid down as characteristic of this people, largely predominates over all others. It is everywhere peculiar, and bears no resemblance to any known nation of ancient or modern epochas throughout the world.

MEAN RESULTS, *selected from* MORTON'S TABLE.[534]

	Toltecan nations, including skulls from the mounds.	Barbarous nations, with skulls from the Valley of the Ohio.	American Race, embracing the Toltecans & Barbarous nations.	Flat-head tribes of Columbia River.	Ancient Peruvians.
Facial angle	75° 35′	76° 13′	75° 45′	69° 30′	67° 20′
Internal capacity in cu. in.	76·8	82·4	79·6	79·25	73·2

MONGOL-AMERICANS — ESKIMAUX.

The Polar family, which are identical on both continents, display one of the strongest possible contrasts with the aboriginal Americans; and no one can compare the crania of the two, and suppose that one continent was populated from the other through the Eskimaux channel. In fact, the Eskimaux are confined to a polar zone, as well in America as in Asia.

Dr. Morton obtained, from Mr. George Combe, four genuine Eskimaux skulls, of which figures are grouped below (Figs. 323–326). The eye at once remarks their narrow elongated form, the projecting upper jaw, the extremely flat nasal bones, the expanded zygomatic arches, the broad, expanded cheek-bones, and the full and prominent occipital region.

FIG. 323.

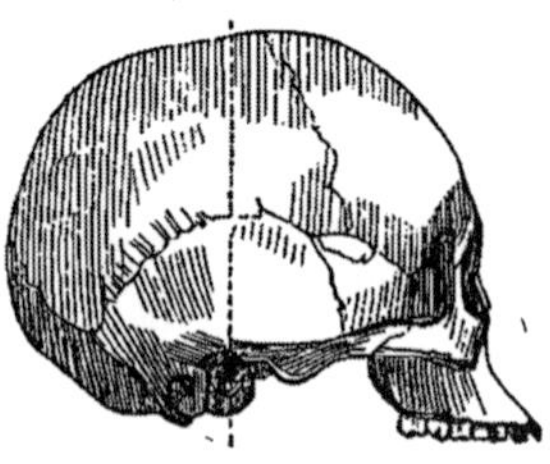

Eskimaux.

FIG. 324.

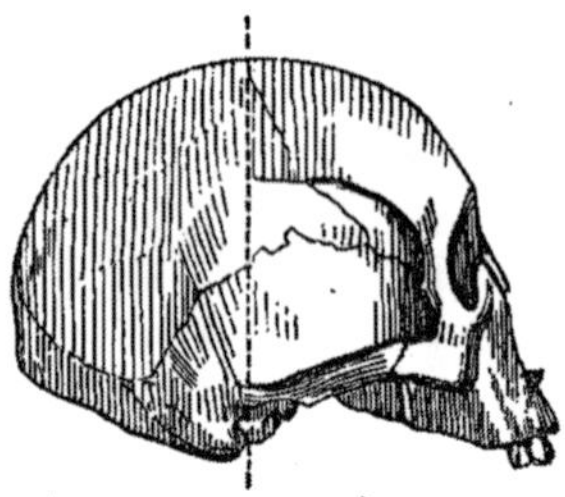

Eskimaux.

FIG. 325.

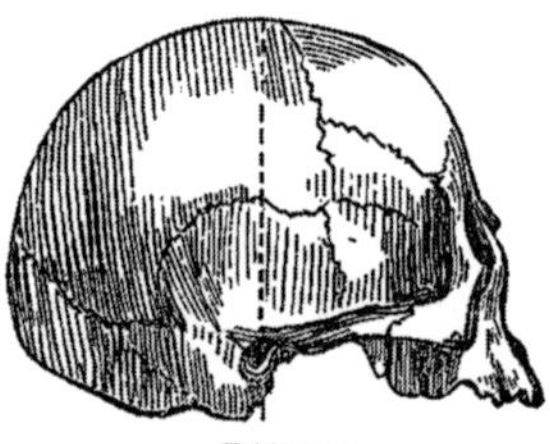

Eskimaux.

FIG. 326.

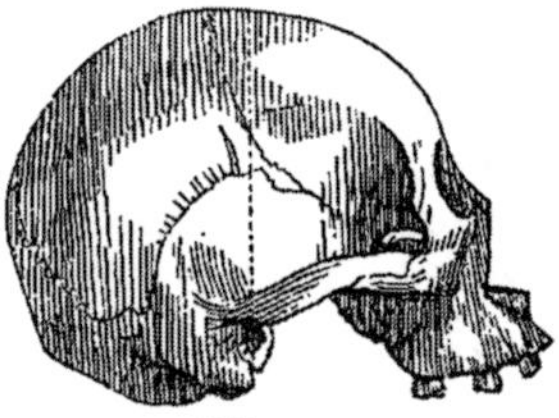

Eskimaux.

"The extreme elongation of the upper jaw contracts the facial angle to a mean of 73°, while the mean of 3 heads of the 4, gives an internal capacity of 87 cubic in., a near approach to the Caucasian average."[535] The diagrams here given will enable the reader to make his Eskimaux comparisons still more in detail. Fig. 323 is "from Davis's Strait, the largest head in the series, and the best frontal development. The nasal bones are so flat as to be scarcely perceptible." "On this skull (Fig. 324) is written the brief memorandum 'Found in the snow, by Capt. Parry.' In every particular, a well-characterized Eskimaux head." Fig. 325 was "found by Mr. John Turnbull, Surgeon, upon Disco Island, coast of Greenland, in the summer of 1825." And "this skull (Fig. 326) was obtained at Icy Cape, the northwest extremity of America, and is marked, 'from A. Collie, Esq., Surgeon of H. M.'s ship Blossom.'"

Nothing can be more obvious than the contrast between these Eskimaux heads and those of all other tribes of this continent. They are the only people in America who present the characters of an Asiatic race; and, being bounded closely on the south by genuine aborigines, they seem placed here as if to give a practical illustration of the irrefragable distinctness of races; together with an example, that modifications of human types are independent of any physical causes but direct amalgamation.

M. Jacquinot not only regards all the American races (exclusive of the Eskimaux) as one race, but as a branch of the same race as the Polynesians. He is very positive in this opinion, and rests it solely upon resemblance of type; at the same time acknowledging that, to the present day, no affinity between the languages of America and Polynesia has been discovered.[536] It is with reluctance that we differ from an authority we prize so highly; but, apart from the strange circumstance that M. Jacquinot was unacquainted with Morton's labors, we do so on materials furnished by M. Dumoutier, who was his *compagnon de voyage;* for which we refer to our remarks upon Polynesian crania. No anatomist, who has examined Dr. Morton's collection, or lived, as I have done, for half a century among Indian tribes, can subscribe to the opinion of M. Jacquinot; who does not appear to have bestowed adequate consideration upon American craniology, nor, indeed, upon our Indian questions generally.

Ethnography is yet unaware of its resources. The London "Times" of the 8th of October, 1853, publishes the despatches of Commander McClure, to the British Admiralty, through which the existence of *Arctic men* is announced, flourishing in a higher latitude than any other Eskimaux heretofore known:—"You will, I am certain, be very happy to learn that the Northwest Passage has been discovered by the Investigator, which event was decided on the 26th October, 1850, by a sledge-party over the ice, from the position the ship was frozen in. . . . We have been most highly favored, . . . in being able to extend our search in quest of Sir John Franklin over a very large extent of coast, which was not hitherto known, and found inhabited by a numerous tribe of Esquimaux, who had never ere our arrival seen the face of the white man, and were really the most simple, interesting people I ever met—living entirely by the chase, and having no weapons except those used for that object. The fiercer passions of our nature appeared unknown: they gave me a pleasing idea of man fresh from his Maker's hand, and uncontaminated by intercourse with our boasted civilization. All those who traded with the —— Company were found the greatest reprobates."

Annexed are given, by way of contrast, but without comment, two skulls (Figs. 327, 328) of the most prominent Asiatic types: viz., the *Tartar*, and the *Mongol*, which will show how greatly modern races differ; notwithstanding the

Fig. 327.[537]

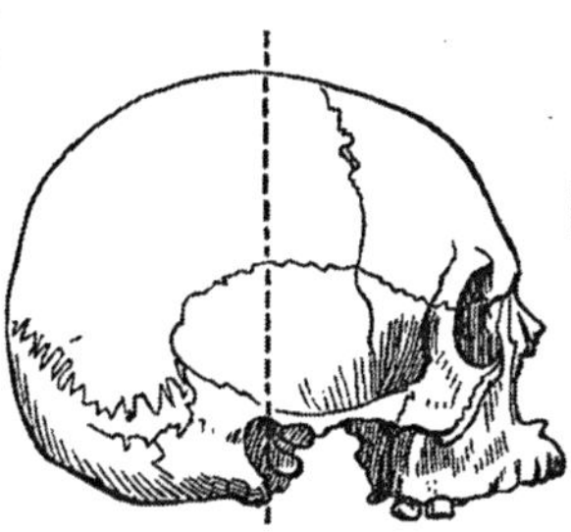

Chinese—Mongol.

Fig. 328.[538]

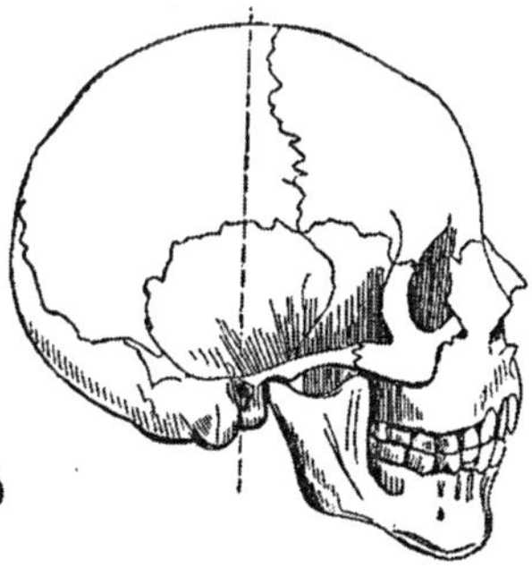

Tartar.

amalgamations which have been going on for several thousand years. These races all, unquestionably, antedate the foundation of the Egyptian Empire — proving how difficult it is to obliterate a type.

Thus far, in the Comparative Anatomy of Races, I have permitted myself to cull but a few of the more salient facts touching the races of Europe, America, Africa, and Oceanica, and already are my prescribed limits exhausted. Asia, with a population incomparably the most numerous of any division of the globe, and presenting an infinitude of widely different types, must be abandoned; although no terrestrial sphere affords a richer and more interesting field of research. However, I can scarcely regret the omission — regarding our side of the case to be sufficiently well made out.

All the types of mankind known to history or monumental researches vanish into pre-historical antiquity; and investigation shows that this remark applies with full force to the Mongolian group of Asia. Tartar races are distinctly portrayed on the monuments of the XIXth dynasty of Egypt; and a reference to our chapter on Chronology will prove that the Chinese Empire, with the same Mongolian types now seen, together with their peculiar language, institutions, arts, &c., were contemporary with the Old Egyptian Empire. Such facts confirm the only rational theory: viz., that races were created in each zoological province, and therefore all primitive types must be of equal antiquity.

Pauthier, whose work is the only veritable key to Chinese history and literature yet put forth in Europe, admirably remarks: — "Of all historical phenomena that strike the human understanding, and which it seeks to comprehend when wishing to embrace the whole of universal life, as well as the general development of humanity, the most curious and the most extraordinary is assuredly the indefinite existence of the Chinese Empire. Like the great river of Egypt, which veils to travellers one-half of its course, the grand empire of High Asia has only revealed itself to Europe after traversing an unknown region of more than forty ages of existence. It was during our Middle Ages — epoch of profound darkness in the West, and of immense movement in the East — that the noise of a colossal empire at the extremity of Asia reached European ears, simultaneously with the clangor of those Tartarian armies which (like an avalanche) then began to fall upon our panic-stricken Occident." [539]

Fig. 329.[540]

But the deficiency of *Mongolian skulls*, complained of by Morton, may, in part, be counterbalanced through *Chinese iconography*. The following selections are made merely with the view to illustrate *Mongolian* permanence of type.

A portrait (Fig. 329) of the *Miao-tseu*, "sons of the uncultivated fields" — the unsubdued and aboriginal savage tribes of China; whose existence recedes to the ante-historical times of Fo-HI (B. C. 3400), and descends to the present day, in various wild and mountainous regions of the empire, as well as among the hills near Canton. They have ever been reputed, by the Chinese, to be untameable, and, in this respect, resemble the aborigines of America. Paravey says he copied this figure from a Chinese work of 2400 plates, now in Holland.

Fig. 330.[541]

Portrait of KHOUNG-FOU-TSEU (Fig. 330), *Confucius*; born 551 years B. C.; whom the Chinese venerate as the "most saintly, the most sage, and the most virtuous, of human Institutors." His face, while Sinico-Mongol, possesses the massive lineaments of a great man.

Another form of Chinaman is beheld in the historian SSE-MA-THSIAN (Fig. 331), who, born B. C. 145, composed the grand history of the Empire, in 130 books.

Fig. 331.[542]

The work of Pauthier is illustrated by an infinitude of Chinese likenesses of all ages; and it is so very accessible in form and price, that we refer our readers to the original for proofs that, with the exception of the *pig-tail* introduced by the Tartars, the Chinese have not altered in the 4000 years for which we possess their records.

The subjoined (Figs. 332–335) are authentic Chinese portraits[543] of the ancient foreign people at the *four extremities*, or four cardinal points, of the Empire: —

Fig. 332 — "The men of *Tai-ping* (at the east) are humane, benevolent."

Fig. 333 — "The men of *Tan-joung* (at the south) are sage, prudent.

Fig. 334 — "The men of *Tai-moung* (at the west) are faithful, sincere"—*Indian* nations.

Fig. 332.

Fig. 333.

Fig. 334.

Fig. 335.

Fig. 335 — "The men of *Koung-thoung* (at the north) are warlike, valiant" — *Tartar* nations.

I have merely to remark, on these foreigners, that they represent varieties of the Mongol type, such as naturally belong to that centre of human creations; referring the reader to Pauthier's sketch of the "Relations of Foreign Nations with China,"[544] and to Jardot's "Tableau synoptique, chronologique, et par Race,"[545] for the best specification of ancient Mongol-Tartar subdivisions.

I conclude these few words on crania with some comments upon the following Table, taken from Morton's printed *Catalogue* (Philadelphia, 3d edition, 1849): —

TABLE, *showing the Size of the Brain in cubic inches, as obtained from the measurement of* 623 *Crania of various Races and Families of Man.*

RACES AND FAMILIES.	No. of Skulls.	Largest I. C.	Smallest I. C.	Mean.	Mean.
MODERN CAUCASIAN GROUP.					
Teutonic Family — Germans	18	114	70	90	
" " English	5	105	91	96	92
" " Anglo-Americans	7	97	82	90	
Pelasgic " Persians					
" " Armenians	10	94	75	84	
" " Circassians					
Celtic " Native Irish	6	97	78	87	
Indostanic " Bengalees, &c.	32	91	67	80	
Semitic " Arabs	3	98	84	89	
Nilotic " Fellahs	17	96	66	80	
ANCIENT CAUCASIAN GROUP.					
Pelasgic Family — Græco-Egyptians (catacombs).	18	97	74	88	
Nilotic " Egyptians (from catacombs).	55	96	68	80	
MONGOLIAN GROUP.					
Chinese Family	6	91	70	82	
MALAY GROUP.					
Malayan Family	20	97	68	86	85
Polynesian "	3	84	82	83	
AMERICAN GROUP.					
Toltecan Family — Peruvians	155	101	58	75	
" " Mexicans	22	92	67	79	
Barbarous Tribes — Iroquois					
" " Lenapé	161	104	70	84	79
" " Cherokee					
" " Shoshoné, &c.					
NEGRO GROUP.					
Native-African Family	62	99	65	83	83
American-born Negroes	12	89	73	82	
Hottentot Family	3	83	68	75	
Alforian Family — Australians	8	83	63	75	

Some classification of races, however arbitrary, seems to be almost indispensable, for the sake of conveying clear ideas to the general reader; yet the one here adopted by Dr. Morton, if accepted without proper allowance, is calculated to lead to grave error. Like Tiedemann, he has grouped together races which between themselves possess no affinity whatever — that present the most opposite cranial characters, and which are doubtless specifically different. In the "Caucasian" group, for example, are placed, among so-called *white* races, the Hindoos, the ancient and modern Egyptians, &c., who are *dark*. Our preceding chapters have shown that this group contains many diverse types, over which physical causes have exercised very little, if any influence.

Two important facts strike me, in glancing over this Table: — 1st, That the Ancient Pelasgic heads and the Modern White races give the same size of brain, viz., 88 cubic inches. 2d, The Ancient Egyptians, and also their representatives, the modern Fellahs, yield the same mean, viz., 80 cubic inches. The difference between the two groups being eight cubic inches.

Hence we obtain strong evidence, that time, or climate, does not influence the size of crania; thus adding another confirmation to our views respecting the *permanence* of primitive types. The Hindoos, likewise, it will be observed, present the same internal capacity as the Egyptians. Now, I repeat, that no historical or scientific reason can be alleged, why these races should be grouped together, under one common appellative; if, by such name, it is understood to convey the idea that these human types can have any sanguinous affiliation.

Again, in the *Negro* group — while it is absolutely shown that certain African races, whether born in Africa or in America, give an internal capacity, almost identical, of 83 cubic inches, one sees, on the contrary, the Hottentot and Australian yielding a mean of but 75 cubic inches, thereby showing a like difference of eight cubic inches. Indeed, in a Hottentot cranium, (now at the Academy of Natural Sciences in Philadelphia,) "pertaining to a woman of about twenty years of age, the facial angle gives 75 degrees; but the internal capacity, or size of brain, measures but 63 cubic inches, which, Dr. Morton remarked, was as small an adult brain (with one exception, and this also a native African) as he had ever met with;" so that, in reality, the average among Hottentots may be still lower.

In the American group, also, the same parallel holds good. The Toltecan family, our most civilized race, exhibit a mean of but 77 cubic inches, while the Barbarous tribes give 84; that is, a difference of seven cubic inches in favor of the savage.

The contrast becomes still more pronounced, when we compare the highest with the lowest races of mankind; viz.: the Teutonic with the Hottentot and Australian. The former family show a mean internal capacity of ninety-two, whilst the two latter have yielded but seventy-five cubic inches; or a difference of seventeen cubic inches between the skull of one type and those of two others! Now, it is herein demonstrated, through monumental, cranial, and other testimonies, that the various types of mankind have been ever permanent; have been independent of all physical influences for thousands of years; and, I would ask, what more conclusive evidence could the naturalist demand, to establish a specific difference between any species of a genus?

These facts, too, determine clearly the arbitrary nature of all classifications heretofore invented. What reason is there to suppose that the Hottentot has descended from the same stem as the African Mandingo, or Iolof, any more than from the Samoïdes of Northern Asia? or the Hindoo from the same stock as the Teuton? The Hindoo is almost as far removed in structure from the Teuton as is the Hottentot: and we might just as well class reindeer and gazelles together as the Teuton and Hindoo, the Negro and Hottentot. Can any naturalist derive a Peruvian from a Circassian? a Papuan from a Turk?

Dr. Morton's collection of crania, though extraordinarily copious in some races, is very defective in others; and, although his measurements doubtless approximate sufficiently to the truth to prove a wide difference in the form and size of crania, yet they are by far too few to afford perfectly accurate admeasurements. The first, or Teutonic group, for example, gives a mean of ninety-two cubic inches; and this average is based on the measurements of but thirty skulls; whereas 300 might not suffice to evolve a fair average of Germanic cranial developments.

In these anatomical statistics the science of anthropology is wofully deficient; nor can the vacuum be filled without the universal concurrence of physiologists. Morton's cabinet, the largest in the world, fails to supply adequate materials. In African, American, and Egyptian, types, it leaves little to be desired; but the great ethnographer himself frankly calls attention to its requirements: "For example, it contains no skulls of the Eskimaux, Fuegians, Californians or Brazilians. The distorted heads of the Oregon tribes are also but partially represented; while the long-headed people of the Lake of Titicaca, in Bolivia, are altogether wanting. Skulls also of the great divisions of the Caucasian and Mongolian races are too few for satisfactory comparison; and the Slavonic and Tchudic (Finnish) nations, together with the Mongol tribes of Northern Asia and China, are among the especial desiderata of this collection."[546]

Nevertheless, it is with some feelings of national and professional pride that I remind the reader how an American physician, unsupported by any government, and amidst incessant devotion to a most arduous practice, who "commenced the study of ethnology in 1830" without a single cranium, has bequeathed to posterity above 840 human skulls, and above 620 of the inferior animals, so thoroughly illumined by his personal labors, that, in the absence of fresher materials, science must pause before she hazards a doubt upon any result at which SAMUEL GEORGE MORTON had maturely arrived.

Deploring the absence of these cranial desiderata, the idea occurred to me that such deficiency might, in some degree, be supplied by hat-manufacturers of various nations; notwithstanding that the information derived from this source could give but one measurement; viz.: the *horizontal periphery*. Yet this one measurement alone, on an extended scale, would go far towards determining the general size of the brain. Accordingly, I applied to three hat-dealers in Mobile, and to a large manufacturer in Newark, New Jersey, for statements of the relative number of each size of hat sold to adult males. Their tables agree so perfectly, as to leave no doubt of the circumference of the heads of the white population of the United States. The three houses, together, dispose of about 15,000 hats annually.

The following table was obligingly sent me by Messrs. Vail and Yates of Newark; and they accompanied it with the remark, that their hats were sent principally to our Western States, where there is a large proportion of German population; also that the sizes of these hats were a little larger (about one-fourth of an inch) than those sold in the Southern States. This useful observation was confirmed by the three hat-dealers in Mobile. Our table gives—1st, the number, or size of the hat; 2d, the circumference of the head corresponding; 3d, the circumference of the hat; and, lastly, the relative proportion of each sold out of twelve hats.

Size—Inches.	Circum. of Head—Inches.	Circum. of Hat—Inches.	Rel. Proportion in 12.
6$\frac{7}{8}$	21$\frac{5}{8}$	22$\frac{5}{8}$	1
7	22	22$\frac{3}{4}$	2
7$\frac{1}{8}$	22$\frac{3}{8}$	23$\frac{1}{8}$	3
7$\frac{1}{4}$	22$\frac{3}{4}$	23$\frac{1}{2}$	3
7$\frac{3}{8}$	23$\frac{1}{8}$	23$\frac{7}{8}$	2
7$\frac{1}{2}$	23$\frac{1}{2}$	24$\frac{1}{4}$	1

All hats larger than these are called "extra sizes."

The average size, then, of the crania of white races in the United States, is about 22$\frac{1}{2}$ inches circumference, including the hair and scalp, for which about 1$\frac{1}{2}$ inches should be deducted; leaving a mean horizontal periphery, for adult males, of 21 inches. The measurements of the purest Teutonic races in Germany, and other nations of Europe, would give a larger mean; and I have reason to believe that the population of France, which is principally Celtic, would yield a smaller mean. I hope that others will avail themselves of better opportunities for comparison.

Dr. Morton's measurements of aboriginal American races present a mean of but about 19$\frac{1}{2}$ inches; and this mean is substantially confirmed by the fact stated to me by my friend, Capt. Scarritt, U. S. A. [*supra*, p. 289]. Although his head measures but 22 inches, it was with great difficulty that he found one hat amid several hundred to fit him; thus proving that the Anglo-American mean is equal to the *maximum* of the Mexican Indians; who are here, at Metamoras, more or less mixed, too, with Spanish blood.

Hamilton Smith states: — "We have personally witnessed the issue of military chacos (caps) to the Second West India regiment, at the time when all the rank and file were bought out of slave ships, and the sergeants alone being part white, men of color, Negroes from North America, or born creoles: and it was observed that scarcely any fitted the heads of the privates excepting the two smallest sizes; in many cases robust men of the standard height required padding an inch and a half in thickness, to fit their caps; while those of the non-commissioned officers were adjusted without any additional aid."[547]

My own experience abundantly proves the correctness of these facts in the United States, and my colleague, Mr. Gliddon, who resided two years in Greece, 1828–30, informs me that he saw hundreds of the Greek regulars, at reviews, drills, or on guard, who were compelled to wind a handkerchief around their heads to prevent their newly-adopted chacos, made for English soldiers, falling over their noses. The modern Greek head, like the Armenian, is somewhat sugar-loafed, owing to early compression by the turban.

The largest skull in Dr. Morton's collection gives an internal capacity of but 114 cubic inches; and we know that heads of this size, and even larger, are by no means uncommon in the Anglo-Saxon race. Dr. Wyman, in his post-mortem examination of the famed Daniel Webster, found the internal capacity of the cranium to be 122 cubic inches: and, in a private letter to me, he says, "The circumference was measured outside of the integuments, before the scalp was removed, and may, perhaps, as there was much emaciation, be a little less than in health." It was 23$\frac{3}{4}$ inches in circumference; and the Doctor states that it is well known there are several heads in Boston larger than Mr. Webster's.

Mr. Arnold, a very intelligent hat-dealer in Mobile, writes me in a note as follows: — "Frequently I have calls for the following sizes (measured from head)—24, 24$\frac{3}{4}$, and, about once a year, 25 inches."

I have myself, in the last few weeks, measured half-a-dozen heads as large and larger than Webster's; while a reference to Morton's tables will show that in his whole Egyptian group only one reaches 97 inches internal capacity; and, out of 338 aboriginal American skulls, but one attains to 101, and another to 104 cubic inches.

It has been asserted by Prof. Tiedemann of Heidleberg, that the brain of the Negro is as large as that of the White races; but Dr. Morton has refuted this opinion by a mass of facts which cannot be overthrown. He has, moreover, shown that Tiedemann's own tables contradict such deduction.

Tiedemann adopted the common error of grouping together, under the term *Caucasian*, all the White races (Egyptians, Hindoos, &c.); no less than all the African *dark* races under the unscientific term of *Negroes*. Now, I have shown, that the Egyptians and Hindoos possess about twelve cubic inches less brain than the Teutonic race; and the Hottentots about eight inches less than the Negro proper. I affirm that no reason can be assigned why the Hottentot and Negro should be classed together in their cranial measurements; nor the Teuton with the Hindoo. I can discover no data by which to assign a greater age to one type than to another; and, unless Professor Tiedemann can overcome this difficulty, he has no right to assume identity for all the races he is pleased to include in each of his groups. Mummies from catacombs of Egypt, and portraits from the monuments, exhibit the same disparity of size in the heads of races who lived 4000 years ago, as among any human species at the present day.

As Dr. Morton tabulated his skulls on a somewhat arbitrary basis, I abandon that arrangement, and present his facts as they stand in nature, allowing the reader to compare for himself.

Size of the Brain in Cubic Inches.

RACES.	I. C. Mean.	I. C. Mean.
Modern White Races;		
Teutonic Group	92	92
Pelasgic	84	88
Celtic	87	
Semitic	89	
Ancient Pelasgic	88	
Malays	85	83½
Chinese	82	
Negroes (African)	83	
Indostanees	80	
Fellahs (Modern Egyptians)	80	
Egyptians (Ancient)	80	
American Group;		
Toltecan Family	77	79
Barbarous Tribes	84	
Hottentots	75	75
Australians	75	

Absolute measurements array themselves into a sliding scale of ***seventeen*** cubic inches, between the lowest and the highest races. Here we behold cranial measurements as history and the monuments first find them; nor can such facts be controverted.

Let me again revert to the question of ***hybridity,*** in connection with endeavors to obtain accurate cranial statistics. The adulteration of primitive types, at the present day conspicuous among many races of mankind, renders precision, in regard to the commingled inhabitants of various countries, frequently impossible; especially wherever the *dark*-skinned races of Europe, and the lower grades of humanity elsewhere, have co-operated in mutual contaminations. Of the latter, our own continent supplies two deplorable regions, from which real philanthropy might take warning. Tschudi's "Travels in Peru" furnishes a list of the crosses resulting from the intermixture of Spanish with Indian and Negro races in that country. The settlement of Mexico by Spaniards took place at the same time, and the intermixture of races has been perhaps greater there than in Peruvian colonies. Mexican soldiers present the most unequal characters that can be met with anywhere in the world. If some are brave, others are quite the reverse — possessing the basest and most barbarous qualities. This, doubtless, is a result, in part, of the crossings of the races. Here is Tschudi's catalogue of such amalgamations in Peru: —

Parents.	*Children.*
" White father and Negro mother	Mulatto.
White father and Indian mother	Mestiza.
Indian father and Negro mother	Chino.
White father and Mulatto mother	Cuarteron.
White father and Mestiza mother	Creole — pale, brownish complexion.
White father and China mother	Chino-blanco.
White father and Cuarterena mother	Quintero.
White father and Quintera mother	White.
Negro father and Indian mother	Zambo.
Negro father and Mulatto mother	Zambo-Negro.
Negro father and Mestiza mother	Mulatto-oscuro.
Negro father and China mother	Zambo-Chino.
Negro father and Zamba mother	Zambo-Negro — perfectly black.
Negro father and Quintera mother	Mulatto — rather dark.
Indian father and Mulatto mother	Chino-oscuro.
Indian father and Mestiza mother	Mestizo-claro — frequently very beautiful.
Indian father and Chino mother	Chino-cola.
Indian father and Zamba mother	Zambo-claro.
Indian father and China-cholar mother	Indian — with frizzly hair.
Indian father and Quintera mother	Mestizo — rather brown.
Mulatto father and Zamba mother	Zamba — a miserable race.
Mulatto father and Mestiza mother	Chino — rather clear complexion.
Mulatto father and China mother	Chino — rather dark.

" To define their characteristics correctly," adds the learned German, " would be impossible; for their minds partake of the mixture of their blood. As a general rule, it may be fairly said, that they unite in themselves all the faults, without any of the virtues, of their progenitors; as men, they are generally inferior to the pure races; and as members of society, they are the worst class of citizens."

In Peru, be it also observed, these mongrel families are produced by the intermixture of two distinct types (*Indians* and *Negroes*) with a third (*Portuguese* and *Spaniards*), which I have shown to have been already corrupted by European comminglings, previously to their landing in South America. After all, in the United States, the bulk of mulatto grades is occasioned solely by the union of Negro with the Teutonic stock — *Indian* amalgamations being so unfrequent as to be rarely seen, save along the frontier.

This leads me to substantiate previous remarks on Liberia. " Gov. Roberts, of Liberia, a *fair mulatto*, and Russwarm, of Cape Palmas, are clever and estimable men; and we have in these two men unanswerable proofs of the capacity of the *colored* people for self-government.

" The climate of Western Africa cannot be considered as unwholesome to *colored* colonists. Every one must pass [*owing to the unacclimated exotic blood in his veins*] through the acclimating fever; but, now that more convenient dwellings are erected, so that the sick may be properly attended to, the mortality has considerably decreased. Once well through this sickness, the [*mulatto*] colonist finds the climate and the air suitable to his constitution; not so the WHITE man. The residence of a few years on this coast is certain death to *him*."

So far Commodore M. C. Perry, U. S. N., in his report on Liberia. Miss Frederika

Bremer adds, with that charming simplicity so peculiarly Swedish (Jenny Lind, Ole Bull, &c., have familarized Americans with its philanthropical self-sacrifices): — "It thus appears as if Liberia and Sierra Leone would become the nurseries from which the new civilization and more beautiful future of Africa would proceed. I cannot believe but that these [*mulatto*] plants from a foreign land must, before that time, undergo a metamorphosis — must become *more African*." [548]

The most inveterate anthropologist could not better foreshadow Liberian destinies!

And, as concerns the "beautiful" likely to arise in Africa when the half-civilized *mulatto* becomes re-absorbed into the indigenous Negro population, let me add, that, were *authority* necessary at this day to rebut the good-natured Abbé Grégoire's testimony in favor of mulatto-poesies, (and *such* posies!) ethnography might begin with Mr. Jefferson's. His *Notes on Virginia* contain this sentence: —

"Never yet could I find that a Black had uttered a thought above the level of plain narration; never saw even an elementary trait of painting or of sculpture."

I have looked in vain, during twenty years, for a solitary exception to these characteristic deficiencies among the Negro race. Every Negro is gifted with an ear for music; some are excellent musicians; all *imitate* well in most things; but, with every opportunity for culture, our Southern Negroes remain as incapable, in drawing, as the lowest quadrumana.

As before stated, the plan of this work does not permit a complete anatomical comparison of races; and I have merely selected such illustrations as I deem sufficient to demonstrate *plurality of origin* for the human family. A few others are subjoined, with a brief commentary. The "Caucasian," *Mongol*, and *Negro*, constitute three of the most prominent groups of mankind; and the vertical views of the following crania (Figs. 336–338) display, at a glance, how widely separated they are in conformation. How they differ in size and in facial angle has been already shown. So uniform are these cranial characters, that the genuine types can at once be distinguished by a practised eye.

If, as we have reiterated times and again, those types depicted on the early monuments of Egypt have remained permanent through all subsequent ages — and if no causes are now visibly at work which can transform one type of man into another — they must be received, in Natural History, as primitive and specific. When, therefore, they are placed beside each other (*e.g.* as in Figs. 336–338) such types speak for themselves; and the anatomist has no more need of protracted comparisons to seize their diversities, than the school-boy to distinguish turkeys from peacocks, or pecaries from Guinea-pigs.

Our remarks on African types have shown the *gradations* which, ever ascending in caste of race, may be traced from the Cape of Good Hope northward to Egypt. The same gradation might be followed through Asiatic and European races up to the Teutonic; and with equal accuracy, were it not for migrations and geographical displacements of these last, to which aborigines in Africa have been less subjected.

FIG. 336.[549]

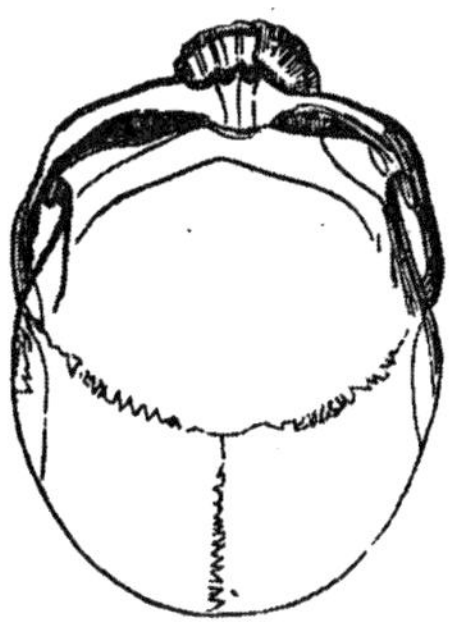

Caucasian.

FIG. 337.[550]

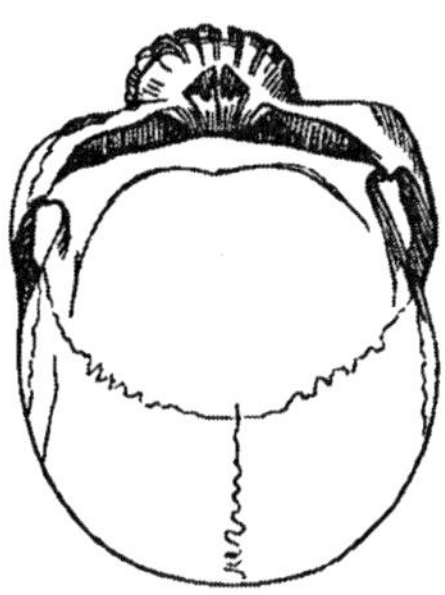

Mongol.

FIG. 338.[551]

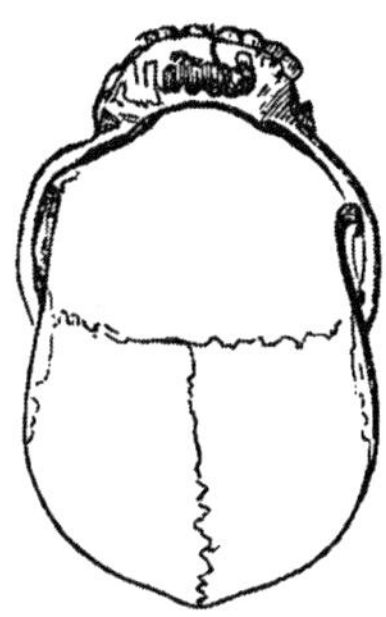

Negro.

Although I do not believe in the intellectual equality of races, and can find no ground in natural or in human history for such popular credence, I belong not to those who are disposed to degrade any type of humanity to the level of the brute-creation. Nevertheless, a man must be blind not to be struck by similitudes between some of the lower races of mankind, viewed as connecting links in the animal kingdom; nor can it be rationally affirmed, that the Orang-Outan and Chimpanzee are more widely separated from certain African and Oceanic Negroes than are the latter from the Teutonic or Pelasgic types. But the very accomplished anatomist of Harvard University, Dr. Jeffries Wyman, has placed this question in its true light:—

> "The organization of the anthropoid quadrumana justifies the naturalist in placing them at the head of the brute-creation, and placing them in a position in which they, of all the animal series, shall be nearest to man. Any anatomist, however, who will take the trouble to compare the skeletons of the Negro and Orang, cannot fail to be struck at sight with the wide gap which separates them. The difference between the cranium, the pelvis, and the conformation of the upper extremities, in the Negro and Caucasian, sinks into insignificance when compared with the vast difference which exists between the conformation of the same parts in the Negro and the Orang. Yet it cannot be denied, however wide the separation, that the Negro and Orang do afford the points where man and the brute, when the totality of their organization is considered, most nearly approach each other."[552]

The truth of these observations becomes popularly apparent through the following comparative series of likenesses. There are fourteen of them; and, by reference to the works whence they are chosen, the reader can verify the fidelity of the major portion. For the remainder, taken from living nature, the authors are responsible when vouching for their accuracy.

FIG. 339. — Apollo Belvidere.[553]

FIG. 340.[556]

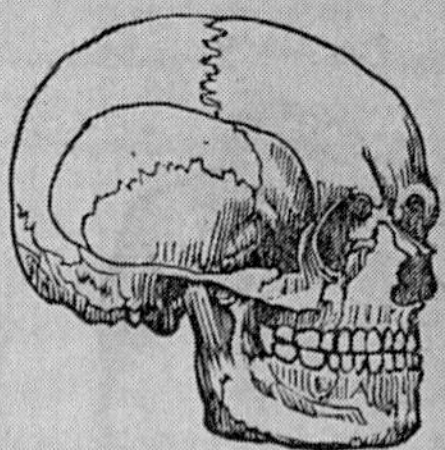

Greek.

FIG. 341. — Negro.[554]

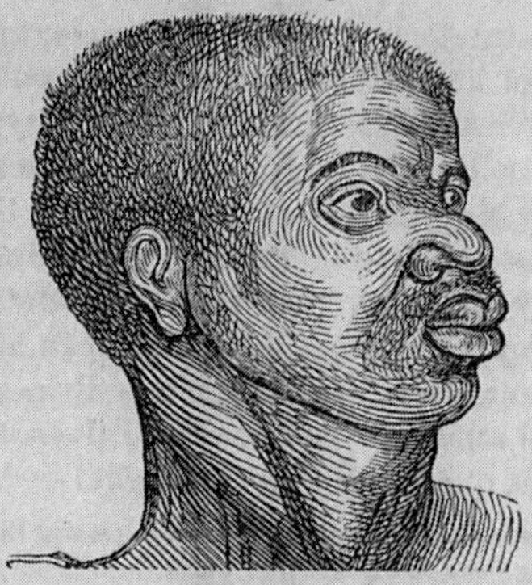

FIG. 342.[357]

Creole Negro.

FIG. 343. — Young Chimpanzee.[555]

FIG. 344.[558]

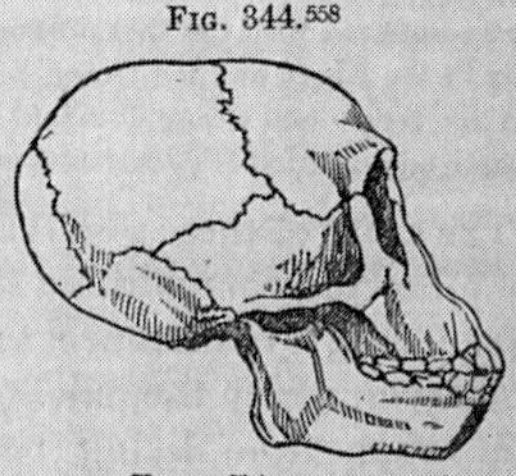

Young Chimpanzee.

Fig. 345.[559]

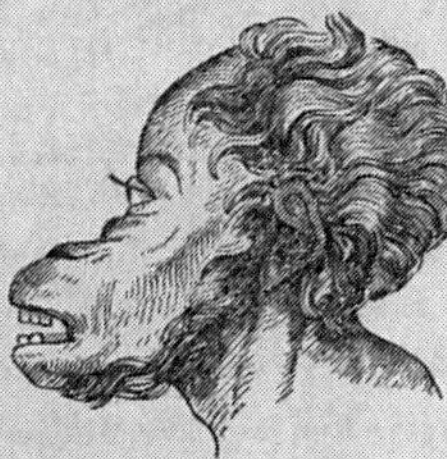

Orang-Outan.

Fig. 346.[561]

Hottentot Wagoner — Caffre War.

Fig. 347.[560]

Chimpanzee.

Fig. 348.[562]

Hottentot from Somerset.

Fig. 349.

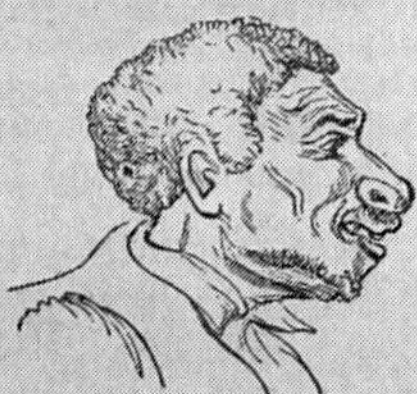

Mobile Negro, 1853.

Fig. 350.

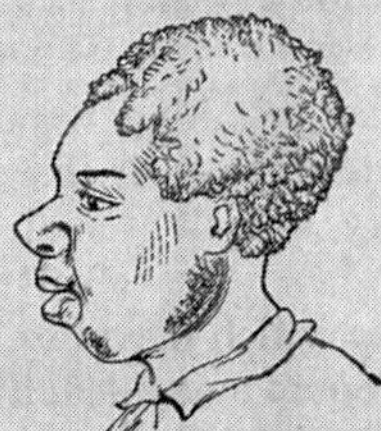

Mobile Negro, 1853.

Fig. 351.

Negro, 3200 years old [*supra*, pp. 250–251].

Fig. 352.

Nubian, 3200 years old.

It will doubtless be objected by some that extreme examples are here selected; and this is candidly admitted: yet, each animal type has a centre around which it fluctuates—and such a head as the Greek is never seen on a Negro, nor such a head as that of the Negro on a Greek. Absolute uniformity of type is not a law of Nature in any department: in the gradations of species, extremes meet, and are often confounded.

Morton's manuscripts supply an extract which shows, that "skeptical physicians" are not the only honest men who cannot descry unity of human origins in Nature's phenomena:—

"We fully concur with a learned and eloquent divine (the Hon. and Rev. William Herbert), that we possess no information concerning the origin of the different races of mankind, 'which are as different in appearance as the species of vegetables.' No one of these races has sprung up within the period of historical certainty; nor are we any better informed in respect to their 'innumerable languages, which cannot be reunited; and no person can show how or when any one of them arose, although we may trace the minglings of one with another in the later years of the world.'"[563]

Intellect.

I had intended to publish an entire chapter on the "Comparative Mental Characters of Races;" but our Part I. has already swelled beyond its prescribed limits; and, in consequence, although this field is a broad and fertile one, I must be content with a few brief remarks. It has been admirably observed by Dr. Robert Knox, that

"Human history cannot be a mere chapter of accidents. The fate of nations cannot be always regulated by chance; its literature, science, art, wealth, religion, language, laws and morals cannot surely be the result of mere accidental circumstances."[564]

It is the primitive organization of races, their mental *instincts*, which determine their characters and destinies, and not blind hazard. All history, as well as anatomy and physiology, prove this.

Reason has been called the "proud prerogative of man"—being the faculty which disunites him from the brute creation. Metaphysicians propose many definitions of *instinct* and of *reason;* and learned tomes have been written to show wherein the one differs from the other: and yet no true mental philosopher will contend that the line of demarcation can be drawn, nor can he point out where animal intellect ends and that of man begins. Even Prichard admits that animals do *reason*, and I might quote observations of the ablest naturalists to support him; but the following *résumé* suffices.

To judge the true nature of a "species" of animals, it must be viewed in its natural state; that is, unchanged either by domestication, or through foreign influences. To judge a "type" of the human family, it must also be studied separately; unadulterated in blood, and in the natural condition in which its instincts and energies have placed it. Our domestic animals, influenced by artificial causes, now differ exceedingly in *physique* and in *morale* from their primitive wild progenitors. The races of men are governed by similar laws. Intelligence, activity, ambition, progression, high anatomical development, characterize some races; stupidity, indolence, immobility, savagism, low anatomical development distinguish others. Lofty civilization, in all cases, has been achieved solely by the "Caucasian" group. Mongolian races, save in the Chinese family, in no instance have reached beyond the degree of semi-civilization; while the Black races of Africa and Oceanica, no less than the *Barbarous* tribes of America, have remained in utter darkness for thousands of years. Negro races, when *domesticated*, are susceptible of a limited degree of improvement; but when released from restraint, as in Hayti, they sooner or later relapse into barbarism.

Furthermore, certain savage types can neither be civilized nor domesticated. The *Barbarous* races of America (excluding the Toltecs), although nearly as low in intellect as the Negro races, are essentially untameable. Not merely have all attempts to civilize them failed, but also every endeavor to enslave them. Our Indian tribes submit to extermination, rather than wear the yoke under which our Negro slaves fatten and multiply.

It has been falsely asserted, that the *Choctaw* and *Cherokee* Indians have made great progress in civilization. I assert positively, after most ample investigation of the facts, that the pure-blooded Indians are everywhere unchanged in their habits. Many white persons, settling among the above tribes, have intermarried with them; and all such trumpeted progress exists among these whites and their mixed breeds alone. The pure-blooded savage still skulks untamed through the forest, or gallops athwart the prairie. Can any one call the name of a single pure Indian of the *Barbarous* tribes who — except in death, like a wild cat — has done anything worthy of remembrance?

SEQUOYAH, *alias* George Guess, the "Cherokee Cadmus," so renowned for the invention of an alphabet, was a half-breed, owing his inventive genius to his Scotch father. My information respecting these Cherokee tribes has been obtained from such men as Governor Butler, Major Hitchcock, Colonel Bliss, and other distinguished officers of our army — all perfectly conversant with these hybrid nations.

While, on the one hand, it must be admitted, that animals possess a limited degree of *reason*, it is equally true, on the other, that the races of men also have their *instincts*. They reason, but this "reason," as we term it, is often propelled by a blind internal force, which cannot be controlled. Groups of mankind, as we have abundantly seen, differ in their cranial developments; and their *instincts* drive them into lines diverging from each other — giving to each one its typical or national character.

The Egyptians, the Assyrians, the Jews, the Greeks, the Romans, the Celts, the Chinese, or the Hindoos, have not been solely guided by simple *reason*. Each type possessed, at the start, mental instinct, which, driving reason before it, determined each national character. The earliest civilization known to us is that of Egypt; and from this foundation, it is commonly said, all more modern civilizations are derived. Of this, science is by no means certain. From Egypt, the stream is supposed to have flowed steadily on, through Assyria, Palestine, Tyre, Persia, Greece, Rome, Gaul, Germany, Spain, Britain, until it crossed the Atlantic to our Federal Union. Certain it is, that Western Europe has rifted the bonds of barbarism only within recent historical times. European races, notwithstanding, possessed those cranial developments, and those moral instincts, which forced them to play their parts in the grand drama, as soon as the light penetrated to them, and that forms of government and stability became secured. The Celtic and the Germanic races required no gradual "expansion of brain," through successive educated generations. Created with the fullest "expansion," they only awaited opportunity to practise it. But, what has been the history of the dark races? When the stream originating in old Oriental civilization bounded across the Atlantic, instead of emulously drinking of its glorious waters, the aborigines of America have succumbed beneath its eddy, as though it exhaled an epidemic pestilence.

The Black-African races inhabiting the South of Egypt have been in constant intercourse with her, as we prove from the monuments, during 4000 years; and yet they have not made a solitary step towards civilization — neither will they, nor can they, until their physical organization becomes changed. With our verbal reservations about the term "Caucasian," [*supra*, p. 247,] the following paragraph, from the trenchant pen of THEODORE PARKER, speaks incontestable truths:—

"The Caucasian differs from all other races: he is humane, he is civilized, and progresses. He conquers with his head, as well as with his hand. It is intellect, after all, that conquers — not the strength of a man's arm. The Caucasian has been often master of the other races — never their slave. He has carried his religion to other races, but never taken theirs. In history, all religions are of Caucasian origin. All the great limited forms of monarchies are Caucasian. Republics are Caucasian. All the great sciences are of Caucasian origin; all inventions are Caucasian; literature and romance come of the same stock; all the great poets are of Caucasian origin; Moses, Luther, Jesus Christ, Zoroaster, Budha, Pythagoras, were Caucasian. No other race can bring up to memory such celebrated names as the Caucasian race. The Chinese philosopher, Confucius, is an exception to the rule. To the Caucasian race belong the Arabian, Persian, Hebrew, Egyptian; and all the European nations are descendants of the Caucasian race."

It is vehemently maintained, that mankind must be of common origin, because all men are endowed with more or less of reason, with some moral sense, and are impressed with the idea of responsibility to a Supreme Being; but the very statement of such proposition carries with it the conviction that it is simply an hypothesis, unsupported by facts. No line can be drawn between men and animals on the ground of "reason," and more than one of the savage races of men possess no perceptible moral or religious ideas.

If the Bible had been so construed as to teach that there were, from the beginning, *many* primitive races of men, instead of one, the psychological grades would doubtless have been regarded by everybody as presenting the plainest analogies when compared with the species of inferior animals. It would have been allowed at once, that beings so distinct in physical characters should naturally present diversity of mental and moral traits. All the species of *equidæ* exhibit certain habits and instincts in common, whilst differing in others. Amongst carnivora, the felines — such as lions, tigers, panthers, leopards, lynxes, cats — present a unity of moral and intellectual character, so to say, quite as striking as that displayed by the human family; and, scientifically speaking, there is just as much ground, at this point of view, for saying that all the felines are of one "species," as all the various types of mankind.

Nor can any valid argument be drawn from credence in a God, or in a future state. There exists among human races not the slightest unity of thought on these recondite points. Some believe in one God; the greater number in many: some in a future state, whilst others have no idea of a Deity, nor of the life hereafter. Many of the African, and all of the Oceanic Negroes, as missionaries loudly proclaim, possess only the crudest and most grovelling superstitions. Such tribes entertain merely a confused notion of "good spirits," whose benevolence relieves the savage from any fatiguing illustration of his gratitude; and an intense dread of "bad spirits," whom he spares no clumsy sacrifice to propitiate. Did space permit, I could produce historical testimonies by the dozen, to overthrow that postulate which claims for sundry inferior types of men any inherent recognition of *Divine Providence*—an idea too exalted for their cerebral organizations: and which is fondly attributed to them by untravelled or unlettered "Caucasians;" whose kind-hearted simplicity has not realized that diverse lower races of humanity actually exist uninvested by the Almighty with mental faculties adequate to the perception of religious sentiments, or abstract philosophies, that in themselves are exclusively "Caucasian."

Men and animals are naturally imbued with an instinctive fear of death; and it is perhaps more universal and more intense in the latter than the former. Man not only shudders instinctively at the idea of the grave, but his mind, developed by culture, carries him a step further. He shrinks from total annihilation, and longs and hopes for, and believes in, another existence. This conception of a future existence is modified by race and through education. Like the pre-Celtæ of ancient Europe, the Indian is still buried with his stone-headed arrows, his rude amulets, his dog, &c., equipped all ready for Elysian hunting-fields; at the same time that many a white man imagines a heaven where he shall have nothing to do but sing Dr. Watts' hymns around the Eternal throne.

It matters not from whatever point we may choose to view the argument, unity of races cannot be logically based upon psychological grounds. It is itself a pure hypothesis, which one day will cease to attract the criticism of science.

In a Review by GEO. COMBE of Morton's *Crania Americana*,[565] may be found a most interesting comparison of the brains of American aborigines with the European. Comparisons of any two well-marked types would yield results quite as striking. A few extracts are all we can afford from an article that, commanding the respect, will excite the interest of the reader.

"No adequately-instructed naturalist doubts that the brain is the organ of the mind. But there are two questions, on which great difference of opinion continues to prevail:—1. Whether the size of the brain (health, age and constitution being equal,) has any, and if so, what influence, on the power of mental manifestations? 2. Whether different faculties are, or are not, manifested by particular portions of the brain."

I believe that all scientific men concede that brains below a certain size are always indicative of idiocy, and that men of distinguished mental faculties have large heads.

"One of the most singular features in the history of this continent is, that the aboriginal races, with few exceptions, have perished, or constantly receded, before the Anglo-Saxon race; and have in no instance [not even Cherokee] either mingled with them as equals, or adopted their manners and civilization."

"Certain parts of the brain, in all classes of animals [says Cuvier[566]] are large or small, according to certain qualities of the animals."

"If then there be reason to believe that different parts of the brain manifest different mental faculties, and if the size of the part influence the power of manifestation, the necessity is very evident of taking into consideration the *relative proportions of different parts of the brain*, in a physiological inquiry into the connection between the crania of nations and their mental faculties. To illustrate this position, we present exact drawings of two casts from nature; one (Fig. 353) is the brain of an American Indian; and the other (Fig. 354) the brain of an European. Both casts bear evidence of compression or flattening out, to some extent, by the pressure of the plaster; but the European brain is the flatter of the two. We have a cast of the entire head of this American Indian, and it corresponds closely with the form of the brain here represented. It is obvious that the absolute size of the brain (although probably a few ounces less in the American) *might* be the *same in both;* and yet, if different portions manifest different mental powers, the characters of the individuals, and of the nations to which they belonged (assuming them to be types of the races), might be exceedingly different. In the American Indian, the anterior lobe, lying between

FIG. 353.

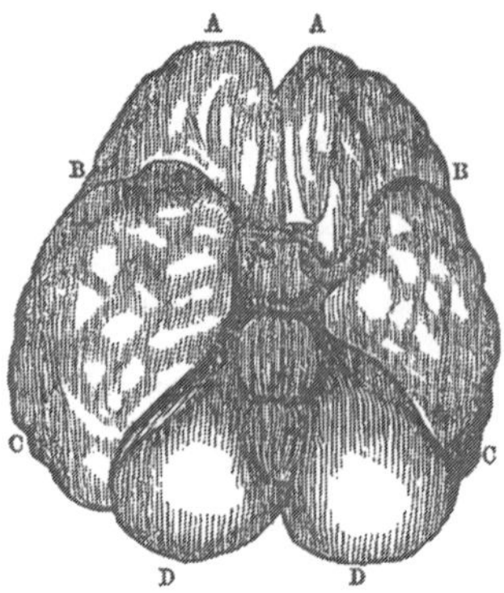

American Indian.

FIG. 354.

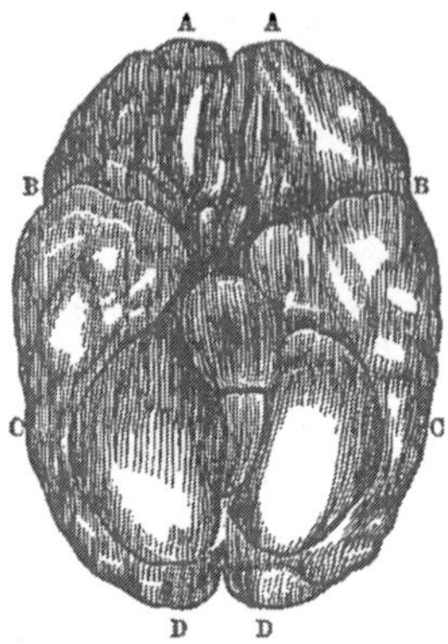

European.

A A and B B, is small, and in the European it is large, in proportion to the middle lobe, lying between B B and C C. In the American Indian, the posterior lobe, lying between C and D, is much smaller than in the European. In the American, the cerebral convolutions on the anterior lobe and upper surface of the brain, are smaller than in the European.

"If the anterior lobe manifest the intellectual faculties — the middle lobe, the propensities common to man with the lower animals—and the posterior lobe, the domestic and social affections — and if size influence the power of manifestation, the result will be, that in the native American, intellect will be feeble — in the European, strong; in the American, animal propensity will be very great — in the European, more moderate; while, in the American, the domestic and social affections will be feeble, and, in the European, powerful. We do not state these as established results; we use the cuts only to illustrate the fact that the native American and European brains *differ widely in the proportions of their different parts;* and the conclusion seems natural, that if different functions be attached to different parts, no investigation can deserve attention which does not embrace the size of the different regions, in so far as it can be ascertained."

Prof. Tiedemann admits that "there is, undoubtedly, a very close connection between the *absolute size* of the brain and the intellectual powers and functions of the mind;" asserting also that the Negro races possess brain as large as Europeans: but, while he overlooked entirely the comparative size of parts, Morton has refuted him on the equality in absolute size.

The above comparison of two human brains illustrates anatomical divergences between European and American races. Could a complete series of engravings, embracing specimens from each type of mankind, be submitted to the reader, his eye, seizing instantaneously the cerebral distinctions between Peruvians and Australians, Mongols and Hottentots, would compel him to admit that the physical difference of human races is as obvious in their internal brains as in their external features.

Let us here pause, and inquire what landmarks have been placed along the track of our journey. The reader who has travelled with us thus far will not, I think, deny that, from the facts now accessible, the following must be legitimate deductions: —

1. *That the surface of our globe is naturally divided into several zoological provinces, each of which is a distinct centre of creation, possessing a peculiar fauna and flora; and that every species of animal and plant was originally assigned to its appropriate province.*
2. *That the human family offers no exception to this general law, but fully conforms to it: Mankind being divided into several groups of Races, each of which constitutes a primitive element in the fauna of its peculiar province.*
3. *That history affords no evidence of the transformation of one Type into another, nor of the origination of a new and* PERMANENT *Type.*
4. *That certain Types have been* PERMANENT *through all recorded time, and despite the most opposite moral and physical influences.*
5. *That* PERMANENCE *of Type is accepted by science as the surest test of* SPECIFIC *character.*
6. *That certain Types have existed (the same as now) in and around the Valley of the Nile, from ages anterior to* 3500 *years* B.C., *and consequently long prior to any alphabetic chronicles, sacred or profane.*
7. *That the ancient Egyptians had already classified Mankind, as known to them, into* FOUR RACES, *previously to any date assignable to Moses.*
8. *That high antiquity for distinct Races is amply sustained by linguistic researches, by psychological history, and by anatomical characteristics.*
9. *That the primeval existence of Man, in widely separate portions of the globe, is proven by the discovery of his osseous and industrial remains in alluvial deposits and in diluvial drifts; and more especially of his fossil bones, imbedded in various rocky strata along with the vestiges of extinct species of animals.*
10. *That* PROLIFICACY *of distinct species,* inter se, *is now proved to be no test of* COMMON ORIGIN.
11. *That those Races of men most separated in physical organization — such as the* BLACKS *and the* WHITES *— do not amalgamate perfectly, but obey the Laws of Hybridity. Hence*
12. *It follows, as a corollary, that there exists a* GENUS HOMO, *embracing many primordial Types or "Species."*

Here terminates Part I. of this volume, and with it the joint responsibilities of its authors. It remains for my colleague, Mr. Gliddon, to show what light has been thrown by Oriental researches upon those parts of Scripture that bear upon the "Origin of Mankind."

J. C. N.

PART II.

CHAPTER XIV.

THE Xth CHAPTER OF GENESIS.

"Consilium igitur fuit tractatui de Paradiso pro appendice subnectere breué expositionem decimi capitis Geneseos de humani generis propagatione ex stirpe Noæ. Ex quâ non veteres modo sed et *nouitios interpretes horum ignoratione à sacri Scriptoris scopo sæpe aberasse pateret*. . . . Itaque hoc restat vnicum, vt ad sacram anchoram hoc est ad Scripturam confugiamus: Quæ non solum in genere docet *omnes homines ex vnô semine esse editos*, nempe ex Adamo in creatione, et post diluuium ex Noâ et tribus filiis, sed et recenset nepotes Noæ, et qui populi ex singulis ortum duxerint."

(PHALEG seu DE DISPERSIONE Gentium et Terrarum divisione facta in *ædificatione turris Babel* — auctore SAMVELE BOCHARTO; 1651.)[567]

Preliminary Remarks.

Two centuries intervene, as well as many thousand miles of land and water, between the completion of BOCHART's unsurpassable labors and the seemingly-audacious resumption of his inquiries in the present volume. The author of *Geographia Sacra* would smile, with more complacency perhaps than some of our readers, did he know that the edifice raised by his enormous erudition, in old scholastic Belgium, had been taken to pieces stone by stone; and, after a scrutinizing, but frugal, rejection of time-rotted superfluities, has been reverentially rebuilt, in the piny-woods of Alabama, on the rough, though beauteous, shore of Mobile Bay.

It is with some regret that, in order to compress their work into a portable *tome*, the authors lop away unsparingly the evidences of studies to which many months were conjointly and exclusively devoted: but, at present, they must content themselves with the briefest synopsis of *results*. Their references indicate the sources of all emendations proposed — by far the greater bulk of which (with the sole exception of MICHÆLIS's criticisms of seventy years ago)[568] arise from discoveries made by living Egyptologists, Hebraists, Cuneatic-students, and similar masters of Oriental lore. These references will establish, that, in the conscientious application of enlightened learning to the *Hebrew Text of Xth Genesis*, commentaries of the genuine English evangelical school have ever played an insignificant part. Where the latter sometimes happen to be right, their facts are taken — generally at second-hand, and mostly without acknowledgment—from Bochart; and wherever, more frequently, they are wrong, they have either ignored his text or the very-accessible criticism of Continental archæologists. Of trivial value in themselves, such popular commentaries possess less weight in science; and, having wasted their own time in hunting through dozens of them for a new fact or an original observation, the authors will spare the reader's by leaving them unmentioned.

> "*Priscorum mendax commenta est fabula vatum,*
> *Sincerumque nihil, nil sine labe fuit.*
> *Sordibus ex istis densa et caligine lucem*
> *Eruere, humanæ non fuit artis opus.*
> *Desperata aliis unus tentare* BOCHARTVS
> *Ausus, et ignotus primus inire vias.*"

"The ethnographic chart[569] contained in the tenth chapter of Genesis, presents," says Dr. Eadie, "a broad and interesting field of investigation. It carries us back to a dim and remote era — when colonization was rapid and extensive, and the princes of successive bands of emigrants gave their names to the countries which they seized, occupied, and divided among their followers. This ancient record has not the aspect of a legend which has arisen, no one can tell how, and received amplification and adornment in the course of ages. It is neither a confused nor an unintelligible statement. Its sobriety vouches for its accuracy. As its genealogy is free from extravagance, and as it presents facts without the music and fiction of poetry, it must not be confounded with Grecian and Oriental mythe, which is so shadowy, contradictory and baseless — a region of grotesque and cloudy phantoms, where Phylarchs are exalted into demigods, born of Nymph or Nereid, and claiming some Stream or River for their sire. The founders of nations appear, in such fables, as giants of superhuman form — or, wandering and reckless outcasts and adventurers, exhibiting in their nature a confused mixture of divine and human attributes; and the very names of Ouranos, Okeanos, Kronos, and Gaea, the occupants of this illusory cloud-land, prove their legendary character. In this chapter there is, on the other hand, nothing that lifts itself above vulgar humanity, nothing that might, nothing that did not happen in those distant and primitive epochs. The world must have been peopled by tribes that gave themselves and their respective regions those several names which they have borne for so many ages; and what certainly did thus occur, may have taken place in the method sketched in these Mosaic annals. No other account is more likely, or presents fewer difficulties; and, if we credit the inspiration of the writer of it, we shall not only receive it as authentic, but be grateful for the information which it contains. Modern ethnology does not contradict it. Many of the proper names occurring on this roll remain unchanged, as the appellations of races and kingdoms. Others are found in the plural or dual number, proving that they bear a personal and national reference (*Gen.* x. 13); and a third class have that peculiar termination which, in Hebrew, signifies a sept or tribe (x. 17)."[570]

The above scholar-like definition of what Dr. Hales styles "that most venerable and valuable Geographical Chart, *the tenth chapter of Genesis*,[571] indicates the absolute impossibility of obtaining satisfactory glimpses of a large portion of humanity's earliest migrations without discussing, at the very threshold of inquiry, that antique *document.* Apart from this fundamental classification of some human primordial wanderings, bootless indeed would be attempts to follow the cobweb threads of our own ancestral creepings, backward from America to Europe, and thence to their primitive European or Asiatic starting-points. Every aboriginal tradition we Anglo-Saxons cherish, is but a ray of morning light, flitting though it be, projected from the Aurora of our Eastern homes.

"The *Orient,* with her immense recollections that touch the cradle of the world, as this itself touches the cradle of the sun, with her seas of sand, beneath which nations lie forgotten, endures still. She preserves, yet living in her bosom, the first enigma and the first traditions of the human race. In history as in poetry, in religious manifestations as in philosophical speculations, the East is ever the antecedent of the West. We must therefore seek to know her, in order to become well acquainted with ourselves." [572]

But, before the historical character of this *Ethnic map* can be appreciated — before our unhesitating acceptance of it as a witness demonstrably credible — its antiquity, its nature, and its authorship, are indispensable points of preliminary inquiry.

The authors of the present work, impressed with the necessity of using the *Xth chapter of Genesis* as a "ground-text" for a large section of their anthropological researches, coincided in the opinion that an "Archæological Introduction to its study" ought to preface their adoption of its data. In consequence, it was decided, that the labor involved in such undertaking should be allotted to that one of the writers whose Oriental specialities naturally indicated him as performer of the task. Too complex in nature, no less than too bulky in size, to serve for a chapter in the text of "Types of Mankind," this *Archæological Introduction* now becomes a SUPPLEMENT to the work itself; thereby preserving its own unity, at the same time that to the reader it is equally accessible, being bound up in the same volume.

The perusal, then, of the SUPPLEMENT is recommended to the reader previously to his further continuation of this work; because the paragraphs upon Xth *Genesis,* hereto immediately following, are projected under the impression that such will be the natural course.

Which taken for granted, we place before us CAHEN'S *Genèse,*[573] for the Hebrew text of Xth *Genesis,* and proceed to its critical dissection. The method we shall adopt, if at first sight novel, will be found strictly archæological. It would be unphilosophic to set forth with any theory as to age, authorship, or true place, of this *document,* in the arrangement of the canonical books. These points can resile solely through exegetical analysis of the document itself; which — written in the *square-letter* Hebrew character (not invented prior to the third century after c.); divided into words (a system of writing not introduced in the earliest Hebrew MSS.—tenth century after c.); punctuated by the "Masora" (commencing in the sixth, and closing about the ninth century after c.); and subdivided into verses (not begun before the thirteenth century after c.)—now presents itself to our contemplation.

Section A.—ANALYSIS OF THE HEBREW NOMENCLATURE.

Omitting, for the present, any comment upon *verse* 1: "Behold the generations of the children of Noah, Shem, Ham, and Japheth; they had children after the deluge"—our point of departure is *verse* 2. "The children of Japheth," *eldest* of the three brethren; whose descendants, upon grounds to be justified hereinafter, we denominate

IAPETIDÆ, *or White Races.*

[Before proceeding, let me mention that, after our *Genealogical Table* was in type, Prof. Agassiz favored me with the loan of by far the most important work I have ever met with on Japethic questions: viz., *Voyage autour du Caucase, chez les Tcherkesses et les Abkhases, en Colchide, en Géorgie, en Armenie, et en Crimée,*[574] *par* FREDERIC DUBOIS DE MONTPEREUX. Extreme was my satisfaction to perceive that *our results* not only had been anticipated, but that they were so accurate as to demand no alterations of the Table. Following the profound researches of OMALIUS DE HALLOY,[575] and of Count JOHN POTOCKI,[576] the personal explorations of M. Dubois supersede everything printed on "Caucasian" subjects. I have made the freest use of his ethnological inquiries, as will be perceived under each Japethic name; but it is not in my power to convey to the reader adequate knowledge of the maps with which this magnificent folio *Atlas* is profusely adorned. On these, the successive displacements occasioned by the migrations, &c., of ancient "Caucasians" are so skilfully shown, that one's eye seizes instantaneously some 2500 years of history. To take GoMeR, or *Kimmerians*, as an example. Beginning in the

6th cent. B. C.—Pl.		VIII*a*.	gives	"Primitive Georgia before the invasion of the Scythians (Khazars)."
5th	"	IX.	"	"Scythia and Caucasus of Herodotus."
3d	"	X.	"	"Periplus of Scylax Caryandinian."
1st	"	XI*a*.	"	"Tauride, Caucasus, and Armenia of Strabo."
1st cent. A. C.	"	XII.	"	"Tauride, Caucasus, and Armenia of Pliny.'
2d	"	XIII.	"	"Arrian's Periplus of the Black Sea."
6th	"	XIV.	"	"Wars of the Romans and Persians."
10th	"	XV*a*.	"	"Massoudi's description of Caucasus," &c.

Now, on such maps, the transplantations of these *Kimmerians* can be followed, almost station by station: so minutely, that one might infer that GoMeR-*ians* became known to the Hebrew geographer after they had abandoned the northern Tauride to the Scythians, B. C. 633, and had settled about Paphlagonia, on the south-eastern side of the Black Sea. And so on with all the *Iapetidæ* of Xth Genesis. It need hardly be said that, in common with Bochart and ourselves, Dubois perceives *nations* and *countries*, and not individuals, in the Hebrew chart.—G. R. G.]

בני יפת—BNI-IP*h*T*t*—"Affiliations of JAPHET."—*Gen.* x. 2.

1. גמר—GMR—'GOMER.'

Essentially Indo-Germanic, this name, as well as all those of Japethites, is irresolvable into Semitish radicals; and its Hebrew lexicographic affinities, such as to '*complete, consume,*' &c., are rabbinical, spurious, and irrelevant.

(1 *Chron.* i. 5, 6) — "GOMER, and all his hordes—" (*Ezek.* xxxviii. 6). In Homer and in Diodorus, Κιμμεριοι; in Herodotus, Βοσπορος Κιμμέριος. In Josephus the *Galatæ* are called Γομαρεις; possibly also understood in the Scytho-Bactrian *Chomari, Comari,* of Ptolemy. These are, undoubtedly, the *Gomerians, Cimmerians, Crimeans,* who, under the various forms of *Cymr, Kymr, Kumero, Cimbri, Cambri,* and *Galatæ, Gael, Gauls, Kelts, Celts,* figure as a branch of *Celtic* migrations in later European history. If Celtic migrators be considered anterior to the age of Xth Genesis, we should not hesitate in adopting the Germanic *Sigambri, Sicambri*; or the *Gambrivii,* or the *Gamabriuni,* as memorials of 'Gomer.' Rawlinson evolves 'Tsimri' from the cuneatic legends of Khorsabad.

The name G*i*M*e*R*ian*, in endless forms, is scattered from Asia Minor to Scandinavia, for the following historical reason. About the year B. C. 633, the Scytho-Khazars expelled the Kimmerians from *Kimmericum.* One set of fugitives sought asylum in Western Europe; while the other skirted the eastern shores of the Black Sea; and, settling in and around Phrygia, became known to the writer of Xth Genesis. Bochart had happily remarked "Itaque omnibus expensis terra *Gomer* mihi videtur esse Phrygia, cujus portio est regio Κατακεκαυμένη." This word signifies the '*burnt*-district:' and Dubois thoroughly establishes that the volcanic nature of such Kimmerian localities explains all their mythic associations with the infernal waters, Styx, Phlegethon, Cocytus, Acheron, &c., which cluster around the naphtha-springs and mud-volcanoes of the present *Iénikalé.*

The Tauric Chersonesus, north of the Black Sea, would seem to have been the extremest geographical boundary assumed by the Hebrew writer; and by a simple transposition of letters, GMR (GRiMea) is still apparent in the name of this early Kimmerian halting-place, viz.: the *Crimea.*[577]

2. מגוג — MGUG — 'MAGOG.'

Indo-Germanic, or Scythic; and, therefore, not the Hebrew "he who *covers* and *dissolves.*" (*Gen.* x. 2; *Chron.* i. 5; *Ezek.* xxxviii. 2; xxxix. 6).

MAGOG is not associated with GOG until the times of Ezekiel, during the Captivity, from about 'the 30th year' of Nabopolassar, 595 B. C. down to 572 B. C. (*Ezek.* i. 1; xxxix. 17). In the post-Christian but uncertain age of the writer of the Apocalypse (between A. D. 95 and the Council of Laodicea, which rejected it as apocryphal, 360–369, A. D.,) 'GOG and MAGOG' appear together as *nations* (*Rev.* xx. 20); whereas, seven to eight centuries previously, GOG, "the Prince of *Rhos,* Meshech and Tubal," would seem to have been understood as the proper name of a *king.* King James's version (*Ezek.* xxxviii. 2, 3, &c.), by "Chief *prince* of Meshech and Toubal," effaces RAS (*i. e.* RHOS; the river *Araxes,* and the nation *Rhox*-Alani, or Alains), and perpetuates an error detected by Bochart 200 years ago.

Arab tradition, under the appellatives YADJOOJ and MADJOOJ, prolongs the union down to the seventh century after Christ; with the commentary, that they are two nations descended from Japheth; GOG being attributed to the Turks, and MAGOG to the *Geelân,* the Geli and Gelæ of Ptolemy and Strabo, and our *Alani.*

In ancient Greek and Latin, Γιγας, *Gygas,* read also *Gug*-as, signified *giant;* and oriental legend associated giants with Scythians in the north of Asia. MAGOG has been assimilated to the *Massagetæ* (perhaps *Massa*-Getæ, *Masian*-Getæ, of Mount *Masius*) who are to *Getæ* what MAGOG is to GOG; the prefixes of *ma* and *massa* being considered intensitives to indicate either the most honored branch of the nation, or the whole nation itself. Tacitus and Pliny mention the '*Chau*corum gentes,' and the *Chauci,* among powerful tribes in Germany at their day; and GOG may underlie these migrations.

EZEKIEL groups GOG with *Rhos, Toubal* and *Meshech;* and, inasmuch as Roxalani, Tibareni, and Moschii, no less than the transplanted Crimeans (GOMER), were geographically located in Asia Minor, between the Black Sea and the Caspian, the habitats of them all lay in that region. By Strabo, the country of *Gog-arene* (Gog-aïranian? *aïr* = man; '*man* of CAUC-asus'?) is placed near that of the *Moschi*. Josephus renders the name of MAGOG by *Scythians;* and Jerome, "Magog esse gentes Scythicas immanes et innumerabiles, quæ trans Caucasum montem et Mæotidem paludem, et prope Caspium mare ad Indiam usque tendantur."

But, ingenious as they are, such etymologies become henceforth superfluous through Dubois's excellent suggestions. The Hebrew word is *Ma*-GUG. The first syllable refers to the *Maïotes, Mœtes, Mates, Meotes:* tribes of the Sarmates, *royal*-Medes, Sauro-Madaï, (*i. e.*, Tauric Medians, transplanted from the Taurus to the east of the Caspian,) of the Sea of Azof. The second syllable, GUG, is simply the Indo-Germanic word *Khogh*, 'mountain' (as in the celebrated diamond, *Kôh-en-noor*, '*mountain* of light'); which has been preserved in the Hellenized name *Kauk*-asos, or *Cauc*-asus, from the time of Herodotus, B. C. 430; as also in the "inscription de Périsades, premier archonte du Bosphore, en 349 avant J.-C." Having thus fixed GUG to a 'mountain,' *Cauc*-asos, the root of ASOS is instantly recognized in the national name of the *Osses, Osseth, Yases, Aas, Asi;* whence the continent of 'Asia' derives its European designation. These *Osses*, or *As*, are traceable in the ancient *Jaxamates*, or Yas-Meotes, as perfectly as in the modern *Jazigees, Yasyghes* (or *Yas*-Djiks), 'Jaz-Djiks'; who now call themselves *Tcherkesses*, by us corrupted into 'Circassians.' They have been likewise termed *Ovsni, Acias, Akas*, and even *Kergis*, by the old travellers; and while the first syllable of their ante-historical name yet floats over the Sea of AS*of* (Azof), and lives in the Abkh-*Ases*-mountaineers, it has been borne to *Asaland* (land of the Asa) no less than to *Asgard* (city of the Asa), in old Scandinavia. In this manner ably sums up Dubois, "As far back as history mounts, she finds within the angle circumscribed between the Cauc-asus, the Palus Méotis, and the Tanais, an *Asia-proper*, inhabited by a people, 'AS,' of Indo-Germanic race:" and we discover, in the *Ma*-ïotes of the 'mountain' *Cauc*-asus, the long-lost and mystified *nation*, Ma-GUG, of Xth *Genesis*.

Thus, this collective name of MAGOG designated one of many barbarous Caucasian hordes, roaming of yore between the Euxine and the Caspian, including, probably, *Gothic* amid Scythic families; and GOG has left, even to this day, besides the living *Osses*, a trail still visible in the very etymon of his ancient homestead, the CAUC-*Asian* mountains.[578]

3. מדי — MDI — 'MADAI.'

Indo-Germanic, or Scythic. Not Hebrew, 'covering,' 'coat,' &c.

The LXX transcribe Μαδοι, in lieu of Μεδοι. The Persian word *madhya*, the 'middle,' its supposed derivation. Herodotus counted seven nations, and says their ancient name was *Arioi*, the 'braves'; that is, *Arii*, 'Arians.' It is probable, however, that the root *aïr*, which in Scythic tongues means 'man,' may have been assimilated to *Ari*, 'lion,' in the alien speech of Semitic nations. The name is spread over a vast area, from *Arhan*, 'Armenia,' through *Irân*, 'Persia,' to the conquering *Aryas, Ayras*, of Hindostan.

In primitive times, the *origines* of all nations were personified; and, according to Strabo, *Medus*, son of the mythological *Jason* and *Medea*, was the progenitor of the Medes. The name *Madah* occurs in the seventh century, written in Assyrian cuneiform, on sculptures from Khorsabad; and Rawlinson transcribes *Mâdiya* from the innumerable legends of Behistun and Persepolis, deciphered through his acumen.

Ragæ 'Media,' was called *Ruka* by the Egyptians of the XVIIIth dynasty; and perhaps *Matai* is Media itself.

The name *Mede* still survives in *Hamadan* (Ecbatana), just as that of *Arian* (Aria, Arii) in the HaRA of 1 *Chron.* v. 26.

They are the *Medes:* and further reference to Scriptural or to classical passages, in their case, is superfluous.[579]

4. יון — IUN — 'Javan.'

Indo-Germanic; and not from the Hebrew, 'mud,' or 'oppressor.'

In this instance, the *Masoretic points* (not added to the Text until after the fifth century of our era), and the modern Jewish reading of V for U, alone obscure a name whose literal meaning springs out at first glance.

"The barbarians called all Greeks by the name of *Ionians*," says the Scholiast on Aristophanes: and the Greeks revenged themselves by terming all other people *barbarians*.

The LXX correctly transcribe Ιωυαν; for Ιαονες is the older form in Homer; a name to be distinguished from the later Ιωνες, according to Pausanias. Herodotus recounts how the Athenians, previously called *Pelasgi*, received the name *Ionians*, from ION, son of *Xuthus;* the traditionary ancestor of the Ionian race.

In Daniel xi. 2, where King James's version renders *Grecia*, the original has IUN; but the age of this document not ascending earlier than B. C. 175–160, in the reign of Antiochus Epiphanes, we go back to the 27th March, B. C. 196, date of the coronation of Ptolemy Epiphanes at Memphis, recorded on the *Rosetta Stone;* where the word Ελληνικοις, in *Greek*, is rendered, on the corresponding *demotic* and *hieroglyphic* texts, by IUNiN: a name given by Egyptians to the Greeks at every age, back to the earliest records we possess in which *Ionians* are mentioned — documents anterior to Xth *Genesis* by some centuries, because ascending to the XVIIIth dynasty.

Upon the Assyrian monuments of Khorsabad, the same name, Jaounin, is read by cuneiform scholars, as early as the eighth century B. C.; and upon the Persian sculptures of the Achæmenidan dynasty, in the sixth century B. C., the *Greeks*, as YUNA, or *Ionia*, frequently appear.

Javanas, or *Yavanas*, is the Hindoo appellative of the Greeks, in the "Laws of Manou," who therein are classed among the *Soudras*, or 'degenerates'; and, although the fabulous antiquity of these Sanscrit records has sunk far below the pretensions of the so-called *Mosaic*, their compilation certainly ascends to the fourth century of our era, if not beyond. While, finally, among the Arabs, ancient and modern, *Yoonân* is the generic name for Greeks in general, and *Ionians* in particular.

By IUN, or *Ionian*, the writer of Xth *Genesis* seems to class the Greeks collectively, as far as they were known to him; and *Ionia*, on the western coast of Asia Minor, is the approximate limit of its geographical application.[580]

5. תֻבל — TtBL — 'Tubal.'

Indo-Germanic. Not the Hebrew, 'he who is *conducted*,' &c.

The LXX place before *Thubal* another son of Japheth, called *Elisa;* but Isaiah, by exiling "those who escape" to "*Tubal* and Javan, the *states* afar off," shows that, in the idea of the writer of the second (or spurious) part of the oracles ascribed to this prophet, *Thubal* ranked among distant northern nations of the gentile world. Connected, in Ezekiel, always with *Meshech*, by whom *Tubal* is immediately followed in Xth *Genesis*, these two nations of the "uncircumcised" must have lain close together in Hebrew geography.

Iberia, from the roots EBR, and υπερ, 'beyond,' or, so to say, 'the *yonderer*,' was the name of an Asiatic country east of Colchis, south of Caucasus, west of Albania, and north of Armenia; in short, corresponding to *Georgia* of the present day; classically denominated *Imeriti*. The substitution of B for M, at once changes the *Imeriti* into the *Iberiti:* to which prefixing the antique particle T, we obtain the *t-Ibarenes* of Herodotus and Strabo: a designation equivalent to *ultra*-Caucasians. The word *Iberian*, in the sense of 'yonderer,' was given to many remote nations by aliens to the formers' autocthonous traditions.

Identified as the Τιβαρηνοι of Strabo, who, by Herodotus, are located with the *Moschoi*, they seem to have been subject to *Gog*, CAUC-*Asus*, in the days of Ezekiel, and to have supplied slaves and brazen vessels to the bazaars of Tyre.

Through the common mutation of R for L, *Tubal* is fixed among the *Tibareni*, (about Pontus, on the south-east of the Black Sea, in the neighborhood of Colchis,) from ante-historical times down to the Christian era; and it is in vain, therefore, that Spanish orthodoxy, in efforts to affiliate its ancestry with some Genesiacal worthy, (confounding the Celto-*Iberes* with the *Iberians* of Asia,) should claim TUBAL as progenitor of *Spaniards*.

"The identity of Thobel, or Tubal, with the *Georgians*," holds Dubois, whilst substantiating Bochart, "is nowadays well recognized; because Flavius Josephus expressly says, that Tubal represented the Iberians of his time, the Iberians of Pliny, of Strabo, of Procopius, who are the Georgians of our day. The transition between *Tubal* and *Iberia* is the *Tibareni* of Herodotus. This name has never been, among the Georgians themselves, that of the nation; they give themselves the generic name of *Karthles:* but it has remained in their capital *Tbelissi*, our Tiflis." The root *υπερ*, *over*, 'ultra,' probably underlies *T-ibar-eni*, and its Hebraicized form of TɩuBaL; as well in the Hispanian *Iberes*, as in the Caucasian *Iberians*—both being a "people *beyond*." [581]

6. משך — MSK — 'MESHECH.'

Indo-Germanic. Not from the Hebrew, 'drawn with force,' &c.

Erroneously substituted for the Shemite *Mash* (in 1 *Chron.* 1. 17), and confounded with the Arabian *Meseq* (in *Psalm* cxx.), by the forty-seven translators of King James's version; mere analogy of sound has led some commentators to behold in MESHECH the parent of the *Muscovites*, incarnated founder of the city of *Moscow!* At the same time that the Arabic version transcribes *Khorassân!*

As above stated, "Tubal and Meshech" were deemed cognate nations by the writer of Xth *Genesis* and by Ezekiel; confirmed by Herodotus—Μοσχους μεν και Τιβαρηνους; and the concurrent testimony of Mela, Pliny, Stephanus, and Procopius, places the Μοσχοι, or Μεσχοι, on the *Moschian* range, adjacent to Iberia, (*Tubal*,) Armenia, and the Colchide, between the Black and Caspian seas; still called *Mesidji-dâgh*, or 'Meshech-mountains,' by the recent Turks. The *Misek* of Rawlinson's cuneatic inscriptions?

More ancient than classical, Hebraical, Assyrian, or other extant annals, is the name of MESHECH. Early as the age of Ramses II., in the fourteenth—fifteenth century B. C., or prior to the fugacious era of Moses, (even supposing the Xth chapter of *Genesis* to proceed from his individuality,) the *Maasu*, [Masii, Moschii,] whose cognomen is still preserved in "Mons *Masius*" of the Taurus chain, are chronicled on Egyptian papyri, inscribed in days contemporary with Ramses's reign.

'Meskhes' is the Georgian appellative for the people of Moskhike, or *Moschic*. They were a mixed population of primitive Phrygians (Thargamosians) and Medes, on the southern slope of Caucasus; who in classical geographies, as the *Mosunicoi*, *Mosynœci*, *Moschici*, are always neighbors of the Colchians, the Tibareni, the Khalybes, &c.; while Ezekiel, as above shown, groups together, in the land of *Gog* (*i. e.*, Caucasus), nations under the sway of the "Prince of Rhos, *Meshech*, and Tubal;" that is, the Araxians, the *Meskhes*, and the Iberians—inhabitants of that mountainous region.

MESHECH and *Moschi* are identified. [582]

7. תירס — TɩIRS — 'TIRAS.'

Indo-Germanic. Not hebraically, 'demolisher,' &c.

Occurring but twice, no light can be gathered upon this appellative from other Biblical sources than the context of *Gen.* x., and its repetition in 1 *Chron.* i. 5.

The Armenian historian, Moses Chorenensis, remarks—"Our antiquities agree in regarding *Tiras* not as the son of Japheth, but as his grandson."

Θραξ, 'Thracia,' is unanimously reputed to be the ethnological synonyme of *Thiras;*

and the river Τύρας, 'Tyras,' of Ptolemy, flowing into the Euxine, now called *Dniester*, to be its geographical, as *Thuras*, Mars, was its mythic, correspondent.

TIRoaS, and *Troas*, in western Mysia, so closely resembling each other, it is not impossible that the Troad is intended by the Hebrew writer; especially since the *Teucri* were perhaps of Thracian origin: but no reasonable objection can be raised to the usual attribution of *Tiras;* and Thrace, the *Thraces*, or *Thracians*, may be safely assumed as the "ultima Thule" of Hebrew knowledge, towards the north, in the time of the writer of Xth *Genesis;* whose dim horizon in that direction was doubtless similar to that of the Egyptians during the XVIIIth dynasty. *Sesostris* (in this narrative, Ramses II.) had pushed his conquests into Thrace, according to Herodotus and united classical tradition. *Thriksu*, 'Thracians,' are recorded in hieroglyphics at the ruined temple north of Esneh, among the conquests of Ptolemy Evergetes I.[583]

Gen. x. 3. — בני גמר — BeNI-GMR — 'Affiliations of the Crimea.'

8. אשכנז — ASKNZ — 'Ashkenaz.'

Indo-Germanic; and, although traced to a 'fire that distils,' so alien to Hebrew, that even Rabbinical philologers abandon it, as "obscure." In consequence, some perceive the parent of the *Germans!*

Oriental Jews call those of their co-religionists who are settled in Germany *Ashkenazìm*, which has been confounded with the ASKNZ of Xth *Genesis;* whereas the real source of this mistake lies in their intonation of the Indo-Germanic name, *Sassenach, Sascenak*, old form of our word *Saxon.*

ASKIN, ISQIN, in many dialectic varieties, is the national name of the *Basques;* and inasmuch as nobody seems to know whence they came to Biscayan neighborhoods, we pass on this suggestive similitude as cautiously as it was given to us.

Repeated in 1 *Chron.* i. 6, the "Kingdoms of Ararat, Minni, and *Ashchenaz*," seem to have been limitrophic in the time of Jeremiah — 629 to 588 B. C. — and hence the province termed *Asikinsene* by Strabo has been looked upon as its equivalent.

The Phrygians appear to have been anciently called *Ascanians;* and footprints of this migratory name are traceable throughout Bithynian vicinities, in *Sinus-Ascanius, Ascanius-lacus* and *amnis;* and likewise in Lesser Phrygia — *Ascania*, and *Ascaniæ-Insulæ.* Ascanius, son of Æneas, bore the original patronyme from Troas to Latium. Bordering on the Black Sea, these *Ascanian* similarities receive natural explanation through Pliny, "Pontus *Euxinus*, quondam AXENUS;" and Εὔξεινος, the *Euxine*, or Black Sea, preserves a mnemonic of *Ascanians* and *Ashkenaz.*

Rawlinson perceives analogies between *Askenaz* and the *Arzeskan* mentioned in cuneiform inscriptions of the Nimroud obelisk, the date of which is now assigned to about 860 B. C.

"Pontus," says Bochart, "olim *Ascenaz*, Græcè Ἄξενος, quasi inhospitalis dictus;" which wears very much the guise of an Hellenic play upon a foreign word. Potocki, followed by Dubois, "finds the *Askhanàz* (Rheginians of Flavius Josephus) in the Mysian-Askanians, who came from Great-Mysia, and established themselves in the Phrygia of Olympus: it was a Germanic colony." May not ASKN, as *Ascanian*, or as *Euxine* be an adjective to *aZ*, the *Asi?*

Suffice it for our purposes, to accept the southern coast of the *Euxine* as one of the pristine habitats of a people called Ashkenaz.[584]

9. ריפת — RIPTt — 'Riphath.'

Also Indo-Germanic; not 'medicine,' nor 'pardon.'

Owing to the slight distinction between the letters ר, *resh*, R, and ד, *daleth*, D, of the modern *square-letter* character in which the Hebrew text is written, some copyist has bequeathed to us a dilemma — whether the *Riphath* of *Gen.* x. 3, should be *Diphath*, or the *Diphath* of 1 *Chron.* i. 6, *Riphath!* Commentators agree, however, in preferring *Riphath;* and, while some, following the pseudo-Josephus, have identified the name with Great Britain, there are many claimants for *France!* The LXX read Ριφαθ, in Xth *Genesis.*

Josephus restricts the name to Paphlagonia; in which country Mela places the *Riphaces.*

Mons Niphates (snowy), in Armenia, through the substitution of N for R, has learned defenders. But the Ριπαια ορη, the *Riphæis montibus*, and the *Rhipæas* placed by Ptolemy where no *mountains* exist, near his imaginary sources of the Tanais, or Don, are the favorite localities chosen for *Riphath.*

To this view there are weighty objections. If the *Montes Rhipæi*, or *Hyperborei*, be the Ural chain, they were too remote even for the vision of geographers who wrote at least nine centuries later than the author of *Gen.* x. The mere accidental analogy of a proto-syllable — RIP-*ean* with RIP-*aTt* — when the second radically differs, (the only ground upon which the hypothesis rests,) cannot be allowed as negative proof against simpler reasons; especially when the geographical position of the Riphæan mountains, save as the tenebrous hyperborean limit of Greek geognosy, is utterly unknown.

The writer of Xth *Genesis* must have had some reason, more or less scientific, for the order in which he mapped out the nations he enumerates. In the present instance, among the "affiliations of the *Cimmerian*," or Crimea, he places *Riphath* between the *Euxine* (Ashkenaz) and *Armenia* (Togarma); confirmed by Latin writers who station the *Rhibii* east of the Euxine.

"*Riphath*," adds Dubois, from the authentic researches of Potocki, "is the veritable and most ancient name of the people Shlave. *Hénètes* and *Honoriates* are but translations of a Sclavonian word which signifies honored, distinguished." The Latins added a letter to *Enètes;* which, becoming *Venetes, Venedes, Vendes, Vinides*, and *Wends*, was the title of those *Wendo-Shlaves* from whom descended the ancient Prussians, together with the present Lithuanians, and whence *Venice* inherits her name.

Paphlagonia for the country, and *Riphaces* for its inhabitants, corroborated by the opinions of Josephus ond Mela, sufficiently define the position of RIPHATH.[585]

10. תגרמה — TtGRMH — 'TOGARMAH.'

Indo-Germanic, or Scythic; not, 'which is all bone'!

"They of the house of *Togarmah* traded," in the fairs of Tyre, "with horses, horsemen, and mules," in the time of *Ezekiel* xxvii. 14; and, based upon this text, Moses Chorenensis derives the Armenians, Georgians, &c., from THARGAMOS, grandson of Noah.

Its classical similitudes are visible in the *Trocmi, Trogmi*, about Pontus and Cappadocia; and, at the Council of Chalcedon, there was a bishop, τροχμαδων, of the *Trogmades.* Josephus makes *Aram, Minyas*, and *Khoul*, adjacent to *Togarmah.*

The name of Armenia now is *Arhan*, identical with IRAN, *Iriana*, original cradle of Persians.

The "History of Georgia," compiled in the reign of Vakhtang V., King of Karthli, in 1703–'21, is one of the rarest works. Dubois translates some curious extracts of its commencement: — "According to these traditions, the Armenians, the Georgians, the inhabitants of Rani (*Arran*), of Movakani (*Chaki, Chirvan*, and *Mougan*), of Hérèthi (*Cakheth*), the Lesgians, the Mingrelians, and the Caucasians, all descend from the same father, who was called THARGAMOS. This Thargamos was the son of *Tarchis*, son of *Avanan*, son of *Japhet*, son of *Noah*, and was a valiant man." Like Moses of Chorene, in the fifth century, Vakhtang wished to hitch his local traditions on to Biblical origins. The former historian metamorphosed the names *Zrouan, Didan*, and *Habe-*

dosth (which he found in an old Chaldæan volume), into "Shem, Ham, and Japheth;" and the race of Habedosth, *Merod*, *Sirath*, and *Thaklath*, became, in his pious hands, "Gomer, Thiras, and Thorgomus!" "It was thus that he reconciled the sacred with the profane, and that the *Haïk* of the ancient Chaldæan volume, son of *Thaklath*, was superimposed upon *Thorgomus*, as a descendant of Japheth." History abounds with similar fraudulent genealogies. Thus, skilfully observes Jardot, "Ràshid-ed-Deen, Vizir of the Emperor Gazan-Khàn, has left at the commencement of the fourteenth century, upon the origin of the *Mongols*, erroneous notions, which Arab, Turkish, and Persian historians have copied; and even Aboo 'l-Ghàzee, Governor of Kharizm, in 1654. Misguided by a false religious sentiment, Ràshid-ed-Deen attached the antique traditions of the nomad hordes of Asia to those of the Jews, as preserved in the Koràn: — *Japhet, son of Noah, transported himself to the East, and it is from him that descend the people of those countries, afterwards partitioned between two brothers, Tatar-Khàn and Mogoul-Khàn.* All this recital is fabulous, and does not correspond with any of the accounts furnished by the Chinese." Even in our day, the "Caucasian" missionary is stipended to instil into the ill-furnished crania of African Hottentots and Australian Papuas the fond hope that they are positively and lineally descended from *Ham!*

The *Turks* did not approach the Euphrates from their aboriginal hive on the confines of China until about 1000 A. D.; and consequently all ascriptions of the name *Togarmah* to them seem to be linguistically and historically fallacious. Whether in the appellative 'Turcoman' there be any demonstrable connexion, we will not aver or deny. But the Armenians, a primordial people upon their native mountains, call themselves "the house of *Thorgom;*" and there is no good reason to suppose that *Armenia* is not TOGARMAH.[586]

Gen. x. 4. — בני יון — BeNI-IUN — "Affiliations of IONIA."

11. אלישה — ALISH — 'ELISHAH.'

Indo-Germanic; not, 'God that gives help.'

Elisa, 'Elis,' on the coast of Peloponnesus, one of the earliest historical settlements of Greece, divides with *Hellas* the honor of being catalogued in Hebrew geography. The former, 'Ἦλις, or the *Elide*, would seem supported by EZEK. xxvii. 7 — "blue and purple from the isles of *Elishah;*" purple-bearing shells having been abundant, anciently, on the Laconian shore. The latter, Ἑλλας, whence Ἑλληνες became the national name for Greeks, does not appear to have possessed, in the times of Homer (whose disputed era cannot be much removed from that of the writer of Xth *Genesis*), the pan-Hellenic extension it had acquired about the fifth century B. C., when Herodotus and Thucydides flourished: having previously been restricted to a district and town of Thessaly. But, adds Grote, no sooner do we step beyond the "first Olympiad, 776 B. C., our earliest trustworthy mark of Grecian time," than the quicksands of mythical legend engulph the criteria by which the relationship of facts can alone be decided. Thus, to the Judaic compiler of Xth *Genesis*, IUN, *Ionia*, would seem to have been the parent of ELiSaH, *Elis*, or *Hellas*. On the contrary, Grecian tradition reverses the order; and *Ionia*, in Asia Minor, becomes an affiliation of Hellas, about 1050 years B C. There is no *Sh* in Greek alphabets, and consequently that articulation was foreign to the people. The author of Xth *Genesis* wrote A, L, I, S, H, in the unknown alphabet he used. ELISHAH, is not older than the Masora Rabbis. The LXX read 'Ελισά.

Either view, however, establishes a close affinity between *Ionians* and *Hellenes*, or *Eleans;* and Greeks in general, as well along the shores of the Morea as on the isles of the Archipelago, would adequately represent the geography of ALISH; but, in view of restricted knowledge (and no *Sh*), it seems more probable that *Æoles* and *Æolia*, in Asia Minor, were the nation and country intended by the writer of Xth *Genesis*.[587]

12. תרשיש — T*t*RSIS — 'TARSHISH.'

Indo-Germanic (?), or Semitic (?); not, 'contemplation.'

Perhaps, in endeavoring to attain the exact point of view of the author of Xth *Genesis*, this is the most enigmatical problem left to modern solution; although commentators of the present day slide over its difficulties, and range themselves under one of two schools: the first of which claims *Tartessus* on the Spanish, the second, *Tarsus* on the Cilician coast, to be the true locality.

The question is so far important, that in it is involved the occidental limit of the geographical knowledge of the Hebrews at the time when Xth *Genesis* was compiled; and, as customary, modern orthodoxy, which discovers the *Chinese* in the SINIM of *Is.* xlix. 12 — the *Negroes* in K*h*aM, *Ham*, of *Gen.* x. 1! and the "ten lost tribes of Israel" in the *American* aborigines, contends for the widest interpretation.

Scriptural texts require the word TARSHISH to be classed under three categories: —

A. — *Tarsus*, Ταρσος — now *Tarsous*, on the coast of Caramania — an ancient city on the river Cydnus: birth-place of Paul, and sepulchre of Julian. Between T*(*aRSIS of Xth *Genesis*, or other passages of the text, and T*a*RS*o*S, there is no difference, philologically, except a "mater lectionis," or vowel, which, in palæography, is vague. The *Masoretic points*, like the Greek tonic accents, are unauthoritative, beyond indicating the traditionary phonetism of post-Christian writers in either tongue: and the *Masora* commences only six centuries after Christ.

The amphibious adventure of Jonah, which, the Rev. Prof. Stuart says, "plainly savors of the miraculous," might possibly indicate the Spanish *Tartessus*, as the correspondent of *Tarshish* during the uncertain, but recent, age at which this prophetic book was composed — a treatise that must not be confounded with the scientific and more ancient document — Xth *Genesis*.

[The NaBI, 'JONAH,' rebelled against I*e*HO*ua*H's command, "go to Nineveh," and therefore encountered the fate from which Perseus delivered *Andromeda*, viz.: that of deglutition by "a great *fish*," or monstrous *cetus* — the *Whale*: which became a sempiternal emblem of icthyophagy, when, assuming the forms of *Cepheus* and *Cassiepea*, it ascended to the heavens, or, as *Glaucus*, descended to the sea. In 1850, a paragraph, started in the New York "Sunday Messenger" by Major NOAH, went the rounds of the religious and profane newspapers throughout the Union. It asserted that the portrait of the Prophet JONAH had been found on the walls of *Nineveh!* Here he is (Fig. 355).

FIG. 355.[588]

Ουαννες, *Oannes* (of Berosus) as IOANes; and *Jonah*, 'Jonas,' as IONAS; both being *i*-ON-*es* = 'the sun' — were identified long ago with *Dagon*, DAG-ON; *i. e.* the "sun in *pisces*," incarnated in this Assyrian fish-god. The same mythe lies in *Atergatis*, or *Derceto*, and especially in those Christian forgeries called the "Sibylline verses," beneath the acrostical Ιχθύς.

I should not hesitate, but for the above præternaturalities, in reading the *Tarsus* of Cilicia as the destination of the ship whereupon Jonah took his passage, and "*paid* the fare," on an obedient voyage from Joppa to Nineveh, (as a convenient route anciently, before *steam*-navigation, as now "cæteris paribus"), for compliance with the "tetragrammaton's" behests: but he spitefully "rose up to flee unto *Tarshish*, from the presence of ADONAI"; and, in consequence, while Jonah was righteously punished for his obduracy, it seems that his intention was to escape through a western, in lieu of proceeding in an easterly, direction; and therefore *Tartessus* of Hispania, or elsewhere so long as *Jonah* could realize a contrary, would appear to have been the country for which the vessel cleared, and wherein dwelt her consignees. — G. R. G.]

B.—*Tartessus*, Ταρτησσος, probably a Phœnician emporium, whether among the *Tartessii* in the vicinity of the present Cadiz, or at some other point within the Mediterranean, lay unquestionably in Spain. Hither Solomon and Hiram dispatched their commercial navies (1 *Kings* x. 22; 2 *Chron.* ix. 21); and thence, about the time of the Babylonish captivity (*Ezekiel* xxvii. 12; *Jeremiah* x. 9), *silver, tin, iron*, and *lead*, were imported, through Tyre, into the Levant. The presence of *silver, tin*, and *lead*, upon Egyptian mummies of every age back to the XVIIIth dynasty, establishes, beyond dispute, epochas far earlier than those of any Hebrew writers, Moses inclusive, for relations of trade between the Nile and whatever western regions, probably Spain, whence those articles were introduced: so, no doubts on relative antiquity need arise upon Iberian *Tartessus*. It corresponds perfectly to *Tarshish* in later parts of Hebrew annals. But there is a third element in the discussion, unknown to Anglo-Saxon divinity, which it is due to our contemporary Michel-Angelo Lanci, Professor of Sacred Philology at the Vatican, not to overlook.

C.—*Tarsis* does not proceed from *Tur-sus*; but from the old Semitic root *rasas*, preserved in Arabic, meaning 'to wet,' 'to lave.' With the primeval feminine article T prefixed to it, *Tarshish* means 'land laved by the sea,' that is, *the sea-shore*; and, in consequence, "vessels of *Tarshish*" often signifies *coasters*, irrespectively of any geographical attribution. For example—we should read, "thou breakest the *coasting-vessels*" (not ships of a place called *Tarshish*,) "with an east-wind." (*Ps.* xlviii. 7.) Again, "The kings of maritime states (*Tarshish*) and of inland regions (*Iîm*) shall present offerings." (*Ps.* lxxii. 10.) And finally, not to digress here on that most prolific theme, the mistranslations consecrated in King James's Version, compare "Sheba and Dedan, and the merchants of Tarshish, with all the *young lions* (!) thereof"—(*Ezek.* xxxviii. 13)—with Lanci's lucid *Italian* rendering: "The inhabitants of the strong places of *terra-firma*, Saba and Dedan, and the maritime merchandizers and their colonists will say to thee"—(*Gli abitatori de' forti luoghi di terra ferma, Saba e Dedan, e i mercatanti marittimi e i loro coloni diranno a te.*)

This derivation of *Tarshish*, from T-*rasas*, bears upon the geographical inquiry so far as concerns the marine position of a territory to which the name is applied.

The following passages are note-worthy in our discussion:—

1st.—(2 *Chron.* xx. 36.) Jehoshaphat "joined himself with him (Ahaziah) to make ships to go to *Tarshish*; and they made the ships at *Etsion-gaber*." Now, this arsenal lay near *Elath*, on the Elanitic arm of the Red Sea, not far from *Akaba*; and therefore, in those days, the Jews were not likely to have intended a circumnavigation of Africa to reach *Tartessus* in Spain! Nor is it probable that, after building galleys at enormous cost on the Red Sea, the Hebrews contemplated transportation backwards over the Isthmus to launch them again on the Mediterranean.

2d.—(1 *Kings* xxii. 48.) But we learn that "Jehoshaphat made ships of *Tarshish* to go to *Ophir* for gold: but they went not; for the ships were broken at Etsion-gaber." What other construction but "coasting voyages" will suit *Tarshish*, in the former passage? What other than "coasting vessels" could go by sea from Akaba to *Ophir* (on the Persian Gulf, as we shall see,) in the latter?

Here, then, without question, *Tarshish* refers to "coasters," or "maritime merchandizers," sailing down the Red Sea towards India, and not to Spain.

3d.—(2 *Chron.* ix. 21.) "For the king's (Solomon) ships went to *Tarshish* with the servants of Huram; every three years once came (back) the ships of *Tarshish*, bringing gold and silver, ShIN-HaBIM (*teeth*, of elephants?), KUPhIM (apes), and ThKIIM (peacocks?)." The parallel passage 1 *Kings* x. 22, enumerates the same articles, but has "fleet of *Tarshish*." So, "coasting vessels," and not a locality, seems intended by both writers. This is confirmed by Gesenius, who says that "a *ship of Tarshish*" meant "any large merchant vessel in general."

All the articles named, with one exception, might have been imported equally well from the African coast of the Gates of Hercules, opposite to the Spanish *Tartessus*, as from Southern Arabia, *Ophír*, &c.; because *elephants* abounded in Barbary, even in Roman times; while "*Apes*-hill," at Gibraltar, even now corresponds to the opposite Atlantic range, where *apes* are as common as African *baboons* in Arabia; whence the latter are brought now-a-days to Cairo.

But the exception excludes *Spain*, and all Northern Africa. The singular T*t*K, pointed *Thuk*, like its homonyme *Taoòk*, and *Taoòs*, in Arabic, Turkish, &c., is considered to mean 'peacock.' If so — and there is no actual impossibility that such a "rara avis" should have been brought *via* Arabia by the coasting trade — *India* is the country of *peacocks;* and therefore these birds were not procurable at *Tartessus*, in Spain, 1000 years B. C.

Peacocks are not impossible; but a new reading is submitted, equally destructive of Spanish *Tartessii* in these texts.

It is certain that *cocks* and *hens* (the common fowl), as well as *geese*, are never mentioned in the canonical writings of the Hebrews. Nor *fowls* in authentic works of Homer; nor by Herodotus. The Pharaonic *Egyptians* knew not the common fowl; using *geese*, *ducks*, and these birds' *eggs*, instead. But one instance of possibly a "*cock's* head," and that a stuffed specimen, occurs on Nilotic monuments. It is in the "Grand Procession" of tributes to Thotmes III., as Pickering first indicated. Etruscan vases, being of later manufacture, are no exception to the rule that the common fowl had not reached Europe, or Asia west and north of the Euphrates, or Africa, before the conquests of the Achemænians, B. C. 540, downwards. It is also positive, that the centres of creation for this bird are Indo-Chinese and Australasian; and that, like *peacocks*, they had to be imported into Arabia from India. Now, in Arabic, a *cock* is called 'Dèyk,' D*i*K. Stripped of the modern Masora, the Hebrew word is T*t*K, or D*i*K. May not the common fowl, in lieu of peacock, be alluded to in the above passages? It is as probable as *pheasant*, proposed by others; and about the same ages (B. C. 1110) *white pheasants*, probably from *Caffraria*, were received at the court of *Tching-wang*, in China; according to Pauthier.

Bochart, following Eusebius's Θαρσεῖς ἐξ ὧν Ἴβηρες — the Iberians of Spain — and the generality of English commentators, fix upon *Tartessus* as the equivalent for *Tarshish* of Xth *Genesis*. Continental orientalists of our day lean towards the Cilician *Tharsis*, *Tarsus;* upon the earlier authority of Josephus, and of Jonathan, the Chaldee paraphrast. And, without dogmatizing in the least upon either view, the order in which Ionic affiliations succeed each other — *Æolia*, *Tarshish*, *Kittim* the Cyprians, and *Rhodanim* the Rhodians — coupled with the geographical proximity of Rhodes and Cyprus to *Tarsous*, on the Caramanian coast, seems confirmatory of those opinions which select *Tarsus*, in Cilicia, as the locality indicated by the writer of Xth *Genesis* for TARSHISH. There is no difficulty with regard to the antiquity of Cilician *Tarsous;* because Mr. Birch read, long ago, "This is the vile slave from *Tarsus* of the sea," inscribed in hieroglyphics, during the thirteenth century B. C., over a captive of Ramses III.[589]

13. כתים — KT*t*IM — 'KITTIM'; plural of KiT*t*.

Language uncertain. Not, 'they that bruise,' or *gold;* nor, 'hidden," &c.

Three Mediterranean countries have been supposed by commentators to be figured by the various etymons of this word: *Italy*, *Macedonia*, and *Cyprus;* besides many "islands." The first, resting solely upon the fanciful analogies of Κετια, in Latium, and Κετος, a river near Cumæ, although supported by the erudition of Bochart, may now be dismissed without ceremony.

Kittim, as Μακετια, after Alexander's conquests had made Macedonia renowned, is the acceptation in which it appears in two latest books of the Hebrews — Daniel (xi. 30) and 1 Maccabees (i. 1); equally canonical in archæology.

The books belonging mainly to the period between Alexander (B. C. 330) and the Babylonish captivity — say, from Hilkiah's high-priesthood, about B. C. 630, downwards—give to *Kittim* a wider extension than can well be deduced from Xth Genesis; for Jeremiah (ii. 10) and Ezekiel (xxvii. 6) speak of the states or "isles of *Kittim:*" the latter with reference to works in *ivory* thence imported. Greece was celebrated for chryselephantine manufactures, certainly in the 30th Olympiad, 660 B. C., and perhaps before.

In the Hebrew text of the doubtful parts of Isaiah (lxvi. 19), *Tarshish* (Tarsus), *Phul* (probably Pam-*phylia*), *Lud* (Lydia), *Thubal* (Paphlagonia), *Javan* (Ionia), and *Kittim*, are grouped together; hence their proximity is inferable.

Josephus adopts the Oriental form of personification when he relates that "*Kethimus* possessed the island of *Kethima*, which now is called Cyprus; and from this, by the Hebrews, all islands and maritime places are termed Kethim."

Hence, modern researches unite upon the island of *Cyprus* as the centre-point of probabilities—*Citium*, χιτιον πολις, of Ptolemy, a city in Cyprus, now *Kiti;* and the Phœnician *Citiaci*, applied by Cicero; justifying the adoption. Confirmed, moreover, by Boeckh's Greek inscriptions, wherein 'איש כת, a 'man of KiT*t*,' is explained by Κιτιευς; a *Kitian*, or Cypriote.

But the true position of *Kitium*, as Cyprus, is now fixed by "coins of the anonymous kings of Cittium;" no less than by a cuneatic inscription of the time of the Assyrian king Sargon (recently found at Larnica, and conveyed to Berlin), which carries the name back to the eighth century B. C. Egyptian monuments, elucidated by Birch, enable us to behold it again in hieroglyphics of the thirteenth century B. C., where the "Chief of the *Khita*, as a living captive," surmounts one of the prisoners of Ramses III. Nor is this our earliest record; because the KeFa, portrayed in the "Grand Procession" of Thotmes III. [*supra*, p. 159, Fig. 82], are said to come "from the isles in the sea," *i. e. Cyprus;* and, again, "*Khefa* (Cyprus), *Khita* (Kettiæi)," stands registered in the sculptures of Amunoph III., at Soleb. So the people, and their island, are as old as the XVIIIth dynasty, or the sixteenth century B. C.

The inhabitants of *Cyprus* in particular, and of the adjacent coasts and islands in general, are undoubtedly the KiT*t*IM (*Cypriots*) of the later projector of Xth *Genesis*—a conclusion ratified by their propinquity to the nation immediately succeeding.[590]

14. דדנים—DDNIM—'DODANIM'; plural of *Dodan*.

Between Dodanim of Xth Genesis, and Rodanim of 1 Chron. i. 7, a literal discordance, produced by the error of some unknown transcriber, leaves the decision for posterity (as Cardinal Wiseman declares in respect to 1 *Tim.* iii. 16) to "rest on what judgment it can form amid so many conflicting statements!" Who, from the text alone, can tell whether we must read Rodanim in Xth Genesis, or Dodanim in 1 Chronicles? In consequence, conjecture has had full scope; and Bochart's ingenious assimilation of the river *Rhodanus*, Rhone, has been seized upon by a standard Anglican divine (Bishop Patrick, to wit), who beholds in *France* the country of the RODANIM! "Our old chroniclers," says Champollion-Figeac, "equally robust etymologists as able critics, do they not found the realm of *France* by *Francus*, one of the sons of Hector, saved expressly from the sack of Troy!" The Hungarians caused Attila to descend from Nimrod in a straight line; the *Danes*, from the *Danai* issuing from *Dodona*, crossed the *Danube*, to which they gave their name, and finally settled in the country they named *Danemark!*

Dodanim possesses advocates; and of course *Dodona*, in Epirus, site of Græcia's most ancient oracle, at once suggests that the *Dodonæi* must be the people intended. Nor, except its remoteness from the neighborhood of other proper names whose geography is tolerably positive, can a negation be absolutely demonstrated.

However, the Samaritan Pentateuch, reading *Rhodians* where the LXX have Ῥόδιοι, affords a preponderating vote in favor of the R. And, other conditions being equal, this fixes attention on the isle of *Rhodes;* by excluding the possibilities of D. Its early Grecian occupancy; its location between *Cyprus* and *Æolia;* and their common affiliation from *Ionia;* support the view that Ῥοδος, the roseate island of the *Rhodians*, was the habitat of the Genesiacal RODANIM.[591]

HAMIDÆ, or *Swarthy Races.*

בני חם — BNI-K*h*M — "Affiliations of HAM." — *Gen.* x. 6.

15. כוש — KUS — 'CUSH.'

By the LXX, and in the Vulgate, this word, whenever translated, is made to figure under the Greek form of Αιθιοπια, *Æthiopia.* Through Cruden's Concordance, it appears that *Cush* is transcribed in King James's Version as if in the primary Hebrew Text the name had occurred only *five* times: whereas, if we restore to its relative passages in the Text the original KUS, in every instance where in our version we find its supposed equivalents, '*Ethiopia*,' '*Ethiopian*,' '*Ethiopians*,' it will be perceived that *Cush* is repeated, (5+34=) *thirty-nine* times in the canonical Hebrew Scriptures.

It may occur to a simple believer in plenary inspiration to inquire, why, and upon what principle of logic or philology, the *translators* of our *authorized* version—"By Her Majesty's special command — appointed to be read in Churches" — took upon themselves the suppression of the Hebrew word KUS*h* thirty-four times, and its preservation only five? How happens it, that strict uniformity was not adopted; and that they did not either substitute *Ethiopia* all the way through, or preserve the original *Kush* in every instance; according to the consistent method of Cahen, in his much more accurate translation? To answer such queries is beyond human power, because the aforesaid translators did not know themselves: but some explanation may be found in the fact that, little versed in *Hebrew* literature, the fifty-four revisers, in 1603, followed the *versions*, and not the Text; as our Part III. thoroughly establishes.

Investigation must first be directed towards the Hebrew triliteral KUS. Its translation by the Greek word *Ethiopia* is a secondary inquiry. כוש, KUS, are its radicals; and must have been its components, at whatever time, and in whatever alphabet, anterior to the Hebrew *square-letter* (not invented until the third century after C.), the Xth chapter of Genesis was first written. The diacritical points, added by the Masoretes after the sixth century of our era, make its sound KUS*h*; whilst, as regards its original Hebrew phonetism, the terminal *Sh* is (Chaldaically) likely, and we adopt it in the form KUS*h*.

What did KUS*h* signify, in the mind of the compiler of Xth Genesis? There is not one *per mil* of our contemporary divinity-students who will not glibly reply — "*Ethipia*, to be sure — *Africa*, above Egypt"!

[Five years have passed since the authors of the present volume denounced such answer to be simply ridiculous (J. C. N.: *Biblical and Physical History of Man*, 1849, pp. 138–146;—G. R. G.: *Otia Ægyptiaca*, 1849, pp. 16, 133–4). Between replies so diametrically opposed there can be no reconciliation. One of the two must be absolutely false. Among the many, however, who have felt themselves called upon to contravene our assertions, not having hitherto met with one person really acquainted with the Hebrew *alphabet*, we may be excused by Hebraists from recognizing as "Biblical authorities" those teachers who (even the articulations of א, ב, ג, being to them unknown) are yet ignorant of the A, B, C, of Scriptural language, meanings, and history.

It was the authors' intention, when projecting "Types of Mankind," to publish an investigation of *Ethiopian* questions, sufficiently copious and radical as to leave few deductions ungrounded; and their MSS. were prepared accordingly: but, so much extra space has been occupied by Part I., that "copy," to the extent of some 200 of these pages, must be suppressed for the present. The reader will, in consequence, be lenient enough to accept dry *references*, in lieu of logical argument. If "truth" be the object of his search, we feel confident that our bibliographical indices will at any rate place such reader on the easiest route of verification. — G. R. G.]

Bochart's words show that we were not the first, by more than 1000 years, to claim

"Arabia" for KUSh, instead of "Ethiopia." "Chus alii Æthiopiam, alii Arabiam explicant. Priorem interpretationem præter Hebræos fere quotquot sint, etiam Græci sequuntur, et vulgatus interpres, et Philo, et Josephus, et Eusebius, et Hieronymus, et Eustathius in Hexæmeron, et author Chronici Alexandrini, et chorus patrum vniuersus. Arabs etiam nuper editus qui hic habet אלחבש Abasenorum seu Abissinorum terram, id est Æthiopiam. Posteriorem è veteribus, quod sciam, *solus* Jonathan, in cujus paraphrasi *Gen.* x. 6, pro Hebræo *Chus* est ערביא *Arabia*. . . . Ex iis quæ hactenus à nobis disputata sunt, credo constare luce clarius Chusæos in iis locis habitasse quæ supra indicauimus, nimirum supra Ægyptum ad Rubri maris sinum intimum, in parte *Arabiæ Petrææ et Felicis.*"

Circumscribed within a few pages, our part limits itself to the production of such atoms of new data as have been attained since Bochart's day: beginning with the four rivers of *Eden.*

"The name of the second river, Gihon; that which encompasseth all the land of KUSh" (*Gen.* ii. 13)—part of the *Jehovistic*, and consequently later document—may be dismissed from the discussion; because, relating to ante-diluvian epochas, its geography is unknown. If there ever was an universal *Deluge*, all land-marks were necessarily obliterated. If there was not, as some geologists now maintain, the *Bereshith* (from *Gen.* i. 1 to *Gen.* vi. 9, rabbinical division) ceases to contain history; and, when not accepted in the allegorical sense maintained by learned Christian fathers, must be abandoned, by science, to thaumaturgical ingenuity; while the KUSh of *Gen.* ii. remains to be sought for "near the isle *Utopia* of Thomas Morus. Utopia! expressive name!—invented by the satirical Rabelais (Pantagruel), and afterwards applied by the great Chancellor of England (Sir Thomas More) to the beautiful land (Oceana) of which he dreamed—this Greek noun seems made expressly to indicate the sole degree of latitude under which the poetic marvels of the grand Atalantic island (and of the *four rivers* in Eden) could have ever been produced. It has been believed," continues Martin, the ablest critic upon Plato, "that it [the river *Gihon*] might be recognized in the New World. No: it belongs to *another world*, which exists not within the domain of space, but in that of fancy."

In the geographical nomenclature of Xth Genesis, KUSh is the "son of *Kham*;" a name applied to *Egypt* and her colonial affiliations: of which some are African, and others, such as *Canaanites*, indisputably Asiatic. To which continent did the Hebrews refer the name KUSh?

In 1657, Walton, the upright and most proficient compiler of *Biblia Polyglotta*, inveighed against the notion that KUSh could be the African "Æthiopia;" citing the best scholars of his day to the same effect. So, again, Beroaldus, Bochart, and Patrick, following the Targum of Jonathan, the Chaldee paraphrast—third to eighth century after Christ—render KUSh by *Arabia*, on the subjoined, among other grounds:—

1st. Moses' wife is termed a KUShean (*Num.* xii. 13). Tsipora was a daughter of Jethro, the *Cohen* (priest) of Midian (*Exod.* ii. 16, 21; iii. 1); and Midianites being Arabians, here KUSh is Arabia. No other wife is given to Moses in the Pentateuch; nor can any supernaturalist so torture the plain words of its text as to prove, to a man of common sense, that Moses ever visited *Ethiopia* above Egypt. The Abbé Glaire, Doyen de la Sorbonne, whose two volumes—models of erudition and style that protestant divines would do well to imitate—lie before us, never resorts to such pitiful subterfuges.

2d. "I will make the land of *Mitzraim* a waste of wastes, from the tower of Syene even unto the frontier of KUSh." (*Ezek.* xxix. 10). Syene being *Assouân*, at the first cataract, on the border-line of (Ethiopia) Nubia and Egypt, the writer cannot mean "from Ethiopia to *Ethiopia*," but from Syene to KUSh, beyond the Isthmus of Suez, on the north-eastern frontier of Lower Egypt, and consequently here indicates *Arabia.*

Modern researches furnish more critical light. In the first place, Dr. Wells sustains, and, to a certain extent, demonstrates, that the word KUS*h* refers exclusively to the Asiatic "Ethiopia," and never to African localities; summing up his reasonings with, "the nation of Cush did first settle in *Arabia;* and the word is, generally, to be so understood in Scripture." In the second, believers in the *unity* of all mankind's descent from "Noah and his three *sons,*" must concede that *Nimrod,* and many other affiliations of KUS*h*, settled in Assyrian vicinities; even if offshoots did afterwards cross through *Arabia* into Africa, and there, owing to "effects of climate," originate *Nigritian* races; beginning with the comparatively high-caste *Berber,* and descending down to the lowest grade of *Bosjesman*—always along a sliding scale of deterioration, from the valley of the Nile to the Cape of Good Hope—where, unfortunately, 200 years of occupancy have not yet transmuted Dutch *Boers* into animals different from those left behind them in Holland and Flanders.

The text most triumphantly quoted to prove the African hypothesis is *Jerem.* xiii. 23.—"Can the *Ethiopian* change his skin, or the leopard his spots?" A glance at the Hebrew shows that here, as in other instances, the fifty-four revisers of King James's version blindly copied the LXX, or the Vulgate; because "Can the KUS*hean* change his skin" leaves the question vague until the real application of KUS*h* be determined. The same proclivity leads many divines to cite another text, from the so-called "Song of Solomon," in behalf of their negrophile theories.—"I (am) *black,* but comely. . . . Look not upon me, because I (am) *black,* because the sun hath looked upon me: my mother's children were angry with me; they made me keeper of the vineyards; (but) mine own vineyard have I not kept." (*Cant.* i. 5, 6.) The absence of notes of interrogation in Hebrew palæography, coupled with the philological inanity of modern translators of this ancient erotic ballad, perpetuates a delusion, removeable by Lanci's rendering:—"I (am) *browned,* but comely. . . . Look not [disparagingly] upon me that I (am) *browned* ["fosca" = tawny, dark], because the sun has *tanned* me: the sons of my mother [*i. e.* my step-brothers] becoming free to dispose of me [according to Oriental usage], posted me (as) custodian of vines; my own vine, have I not guarded [taken care of] it?" Besides, as it has been remarked on the above interrogatory of Jeremiah,—"If Cush means a Negro, then we have revelation to prove that climate will not change a Negro into a white man; if it means an Arab (dark) Caucasian, then it will not change a white man into a Negro!"—Indeed, the ultra-high-church orthodoxy of a living English divine, and profound, whilst fantastic, Orientalist, unhesitatingly endorses this critical view.—"Among the great land-marks of national descent, none, it may safely be affirmed, are *surer,* or *more permanent,* than those physical varieties of form, countenance, and color, which distinguish from each other the various *races of mankind.* . . . In Arabia, one of the earliest seats of post-diluvian colonization; a country rarely violated, and never occupied, by a foreign conqueror; and peopled, in all ages, by the same primitive tribes, . . . peculiarity of form and feature may be justly received, in any specific or authentic example, as evidence of identity of origin, little, if at all, short of demonstration. This principle we are enabled, by Scripture, to apply as an index to the *Arab* tribes descended from Cush, and especially to the posterity of his first-born, Seba."

If we had penned the above paragraph ourselves, we could not have embodied more forcibly Morton's decisive opinions on those "primordial organic forms," which are perpetuated to this day, as the Rev. Charles Forster, B. D., justly remarks, among "the various *races* of mankind."

After the citation of "Can the *Cushite* change his skin?" the geographer of Arabia proceeds:—"This *indelible* characteristic of race would seem to identify with the families of Cush the inhabitants of the southern coast" of Arabia. "Now, since the Cushites generally were distinguished by the *darkness* of their skin, and the Sebaim (*Isa.* xlv. 14), particularly, were noted for the procerity of their stature, if we find, in Arabia or its vicinity, a race uniting both distinctive marks, the probability certainly is not a low one, that, in that race, we recover a portion of the family of Seba." In testimony whereof, the reverend author quotes Burckhardt's description of the Dowaser tribe of Arabs — "*very tall men*, and *almost black*" — as well as passages from Chesney, Niebuhr and Wellsted, corroborating the *dark* complexion observed by these authoritative travellers among Bèdawees of the Persian Gulf; to whom we could add multitudes, were they needed.

Having indicated to the reader sufficient sources to substantiate the existence at this day, in Southern Arabia, of tribes *dark enough* to justify Jeremiah's simile (xiii. 23), we might proceed at once to the identification of KUS*h* in its geographical affiliations. Inasmuch, however, as one of the objects of the present work is to bring the archæological and ethnographical facts contained in Hebrew literature from out of a deplorable mysticism into the domain of science, there are other scriptural passages that claim priority of analysis.

1st. *Isaiah* (xi. 11) — "from Assyria, and from Egypt, and from Pathros, and from KUS*h*, and from Elam, and from Shinar, and from Hamath, and from the islands of the sea." Circumscribed within the geographical limits to be established for the Hebrew writers, *Southern Arabia* is here the equivalent of KUS*h*, because, otherwise, an immense peninsula, very familiar to them, would be omitted.

2d. *Isaiah* (xviii. 1, 2) — the prophet in Palestine here apostrophises *Egypt*. We have given Rosellini's rendering in Part III., and need merely now remark that "The rivers of KUS*h*" have no relation to the Nile, nor to "Ethiopia" above Egypt, but are the *torrens Ægypti*, the "streamlets of Mizraim"—the *Besor*, *Corys*, now "Wâdee el-Arish;" the winter-brook, or *Seyl*, which divides Palestine from Egypt at Rhinocorura. Indeed, this is, and has ever been, the boundary-line; the extremest West; beyond which, towards Africa, the word KUS*h* never passes, in the geography of the earlier Hebrews: and, from that occidental line, it stretches backwards to the Euphrates and its lower territories south-east of Syria. The term "earlier" Hebrews is used advisedly, to distinguish those parts of their literature that belong to times preceding the Captivity, from others composed during and after, when KUS*h* may have possessed a less restricted sense.

The most formidable objection to the Asiatic restriction of KUS*h* would seem to originate from 2 Chronicles (xiv. 9, 12; xvi. 8), where the rout of "Zerah *the* KUS*hean*," with a *million* of combatants, by Asa, is described — events attributed to the year 941 B. C. But this has been ably overthrown by Wells, sustained by the later work of Forster; who shows that *Gerar*, whither Zerah *the* KUS*hean* fled, "lay on the border of the Amalekites and Ishmaelites, between the kingdom of Judah and the wildernesses of Shur and Paran;" and, consequently, the scene lies in Arabia, and Zerah was some marauding potentate, probably *Shèykh* of a powerful Arab horde, whose foray was repelled into the "land of KUS*h*," Southern Arabia, whence he came. Saracus, moreover, (the classical transcription of Zerak-*us*,) was a proper name among *Kushean* dynasties descended from *Nimrod*, and also in Arabian traditions. To the Egyptologist, in consequence, the now-preposterous identification of Zerah *the* KUS*hean* with OSORKON (as *o*S*o*RK*on*, or SRK), second king of the XXIId dynasty of Bubastites, has long ceased to be of interest, because this text has no relation to Egyptian, any more to "Ethiopian," events.

The narrow circle of geography comprehended by all ancient nations situate around the Mediterranean as late as the *Persian period*, in the sixth century B. C., to which the Hebrews form no exception, forbids any such deduction as Jewish acquaintance with Nigritia. That analogy and comparison of the *literal* texts do not require KUS*h* to be sought out of South-western Asia in general, and Arabia in particular, in any Scriptural passages, could be shown text by text, did space allow. The "onus probandi" of the contrary may now be left to "le théologien" — for, as Letronne philosophically observed, "ici le rôle de l'hagiographe commence; celui de l'archéologue finit." "Le théologien," neatly declares Cahen, "en traduisant, ne perd jamais de vue son église, son temple, sa synagogue; borné par cet horizon, il allonge, raccourci, taille, entretaille, contretaille, les pensées de son auteur, jusqu'à ce qu'elles aient la dimension voulue pour entrer dans l'enceinte sacrée. Tel est *le faire du théologien; nous ne le blâmons pas; mais ce n'est pas le nôtre.*"

The reader, who may be pleased to verify the exactitude of the following *results*, will be enabled to do so through the references appended to this condensation of a complete chapter of our work, which lack of room compels us to curtail.

In hieroglyphics coeval with the XIIth dynasty at least, or 2200 years B. C., an African nation, situate immediately south of Egypt, always bore the following designation, in one of many dialectic forms — as "KS*h*I, *barbarian country*"; or spelt KAS*h*, KeS*h*, KiS*h*, or KS*h*; with or without the terminal I.

Fig. 356.[592]

K

S*h*

I

— *country, barbarian.*

The human portraits, wherever accompanying this name on the monuments, are invariably *Africans*, but more generally of the dark mahogany-colored Nubian than of the jet-black Negro type.

We contend that this proper name, which, indigenous to African *Nubia*, was ascribed by the ancient Egyptians to *Nubians* alone, has no relation (except through fanciful resemblances, produced in modern times, through corrupt vocalizations of Rabbis on the one hand, and of Copts on the other,) to the Hebrew word KUS, conventionally pronounced *Kush*, which, to the Jews, meant "Southern *Arabia*," and no country or nation out of Asia.

To render this clear, one must commence with a query — When, and how, was the Old Testament translated into *Coptic?* Quatremère, sustained by the old Coptologists, claims, "que la Bible avait été traduite sur le *texte hébreu* en langue Égyptienne." De Wette and the Hebrew exegetists aver, that "the origin of these versions (*Memphitic* and *Sahidic*) is probably to be referred to the end of the third and the beginning of the fourth century; for at that time Christianity seems first to have been extended to the Egyptian provinces [it had not even then reached the temple of *Osiris* at Philæ]. Both follow the Alexandrian version, but it is doubtful which of the two is the oldest."

The question is somewhat important, inasmuch as upon it hinges whether the Copts followed the LXX's Greek mistranslation of Αἰθιοπία, or the original Hebrew word KUS. There can be little doubt that such translators imitated the Alexandrian Version, and not the Text; and substituted *Ethaush* and *Koush* for "Æthiopia." Champollion gives P-KA-N-NGHOOSH, NEGOOSH, and ETHAUSH, from various Coptic topographical MSS., as synonymes for the Greek Αἰθιοπία, the Arabic *el-Habesh* (Abyssinia), and the vulgar Ethiopia; while Lenormant states — "the Coptic books employ the same expression (*Kousch*) that is frequently met with in its altered form, *Ethosch.*" Peyron and Parthey establish the same fact; but Lanci's deeper philology traces *Ethaosh* into two Semitic radicals, *heet* = 'form,' and *abes* = 'to-be-black."

Champollion's *Grammaire*, *Dictionnaire*, and *Notices Descriptives*, prove that the great master, whose discoveries were made through *Coptic*, always transcribes the ancient hieroglyphical KS*h* by the modern Coptic form of *Kousch*, or *Khoosh*. Hence, it has been universally taken for granted that Champollion's Coptic transcript of the old hieroglyphical African name of KiS*h* is identical with the Hebrew Asiatic KUS — that both are comprehended under the Greek maltranslation of "Ethiopia" by the LXX — and thus Arabs and Nubians, the Arabian Peninsula and the Upper Nile, Hamitic and Semitic distinct roots, have become jumbled up into "confusion worse confounded!"

Now, it so happens that the old hieroglyphical KS*h* is never written with a medial '*u*,' which is a radical "mater lectionis" in the Hebrew KUs — a strong point of dissimilarity to begin with. On the former word, Birch had critically remarked — "The term Kash is a fluctuating and uncertain territorial appellation: it is *supposed* to be the Kush of Scripture, the *Thosh* or *Ethosh* of the Copts, which, after all, is merely 'the frontier.'" We have already [*supra*, pp. 256–9] furnished abundant extracts from Mr. Birch's more recent definitions of KS*h*'s localities above Egypt.

But, in addition to the perplexing difficulties of archaic Egyptian and Hebrew names, and the anachronisms of modern philologers, there is a third element of medley, on which it behooves us to say a few words: viz., *Ethiopia*, and *Ethiopians*. Indeed, it is the prevalence of misconceptions upon the latter which lies at the bottom of mistakes concerning the former.

Already in A. D. 1657, the scholarship of Walton protested against "Ethiopian" delusions, with a citation from Waser—"Græci *Æthiopiam* deducunt ab *αἴθω cremo, uro*, et ὤψ, ὀπός, *facies, aspectus*, quia a solis vicinitate ita uruntur et torrentur, ut atro sint colore." Hence it is immediately perceived that *Ethiopian*, meaning simply a 'sun-*burned-face*," possessed at one time a generic application to the *color* of the human skin, and not an attribution to one specific geographical locality. During Homeric ages, by Αἰθίοψ, the fair-skinned Hellenes merely meant a foreigner *darker* than themselves; and, by Αἰθιόπια (the existence even of true *Negro* races being then utterly unknown to the Greeks) early Grecian geographers understood (not our modern "Ethiopia" above Egypt) the countries of all *swarthy* Asiatic and Barbaresque nations—Persians, Assyrians, Syrians, Arabs, Phœnicians, Canaanites, Jews, Egyptians, Carthaginians, and Libyans—especially those situate along the coast of the Mediterranean from the Orontes to Joppa.

This fact has been established beyond all controversy by the vast erudition of a Letronne, a Raoul-Rochette, and a Lenormant.[593] Its etymological truth can be verified in any Greek lexicon; while it is adopted, although not with sufficient archæological rigor, in the popular cyclopædias of Anthon and Kitto.

Want of space alone compels us to suppress many pages of extracts from the three first-named savans; through which it would become demonstrated that Αἰθίοπες, in all writers down to the fifth century B. C., meant nothing more than "visages brulés"; that is, "sun-*burnt-faces*." By way of example, take *Memnon*, who by Hesiod is termed Αἰθιόπων βασιλῆα, and by Homer, the most beautiful of men. Pausanias, Strabo, Diodorus, Æschylus, and Herodotus, affirm that he was an Asiatic demigod, probably from *Shusan*, or *Chuzistan*, on the confines of Persia. Now, Hesiod never meant that modern interpreters should understand that *Memnon* was "king of the *Ethiopians*"—of our Ethiopia above Egypt! The poet wrote that Memnon was "king of the *burnt-faces*;" that is, his followers were a *dark-skinned* people, such as the *Cushite*-Arabians are on Persian confines to this day. It is the same in Homer's "Eastern and Western *Æthiopians*"—again the same in Herodotus's *Ethiopians*, enrolled in the Persian army of Xerxes; some of whom were Asiatics, and others Africans—and, not to enumerate instances by the dozen, it is the same in Ælian's Indians (Hindoos), whom he terms *Æthiopians* also. In all these cases, the writers meant "sun-*burned-faces*" of the so-called "Caucasian" type; and it is but the inanity of modern *littérateurs* which ascribes any of the above *Æthiopians* to countries south of Egypt.

However, the time came, (after the Persian conquest, B. C. 525, and hardly before Ptolemaic days,) that Greek geographers, having discovered that there was a race "nigro nigrior" whose habitat lay south of Egypt, began to restrict *Æthiopia* and *Æthiopians* to the mahogany-colored *Nubians* and to the jet-black Negroes; and it is in this, the later specific, not in the older generic, sense, that scientific geographers understand a name which, without such reservation, is as vague as *Indians* (East and West Indies, and American aborigines!); as *Scythian* (from the Himalaya to the Baltic!); or, as that wretched term "Caucasian."

Now, it was during the prevalence of such geographical misconceptions—when *Africa* meant little more than Carthaginian and Cyrenaic territories along the face of Barbary; when *Asia* signified Asia Minor—in the interval between Eratosthenes the first scientific geographer, and Strabo the second—whilst Hindostan was termed *Ethiopia*, or *vice-versa*—pending the notions that the Nile and the Indus were one and the same stream; and that a circumambient ocean surrounded what little of a *flat* and stationary earth was known to Alexandrian science: — during such, and hundreds of similar cosmographical views since proved to be false, it was, we repeat, that the *Jews* of Alexandria, (having forgotten not only their parental Hebrew, but even the Chaldee dialect subsequently acquired through the Captivity,) caused the books of the Old Testament to be translated into *Greek;* in the form preserved to us under the mystic *No.* LXX, and by us consecrated as the *Septuagint:* translations fluctuating in date between B. C. 260, and B. C. 130.

Books of different origins, translated at different epochas, and by different persons, necessarily teem with imperfections; nor can uniformity be expected from literary labors under those circumstances, and in such uncritical times. Geographical criticism was certainly not a paramount object with any of these "uninspired" translators. They never foresaw archæological discussions that occur now, 2000 years after their day, in a language not formed for 1500 years later, by a distinct people, (whose infantine traditions attain not their Alexandrine lifetimes,) and on a Continent (6000 miles from Alexandria) whose existence was still undreamed of, even sixteen centuries after the original *Septuagint* MSS. were completed. In consequence, some of the Hellenizing Jews, or Judaizing Hellenes, when they met with the Hebrew word KUS*h*, simply transcribed it into Greek characters as Κοὺς, ΚΩC, or ΚΩΣ: others translated KUS*h* by Αιθιοπια — a word at that time equally applicable, etymologically in the sense of '*sun-burned faces*,' no less than geographically, to *India*, Persia, Arabia, and the *Nubias*, indifferently to its Asiatic or African association. And this explains why, after 2000 years, the imaginary sanctity of Hebrew and Greek *words*, accidentally preserved in recent MSS., or through Latin and other re-translations, and despite innumerable recensions, enables us yet to admire in King James's version the English transcript of *Cush* only five times, and its Alexandrian substitute, *Ethiopia*, some thirty-four [ubi supra]; at the same time that, in the far elder and original Hebrew Text (copies of which, only about 800 years old, have come down to us), Providence permits our counting the triliteral KUS*h* in about forty different places.

Under these circumstances (notoriously accessible to anybody who can read English), to quote the *Septuagint* authoritatively on doubtful relations of "Ethiopia," as if it had applied to Africa exclusively at the time when this Greek literary work was in progress, may be exceedingly praiseworthy on the part of professional hagiographers, but, archæologically, is "vox, et præterea nihil," leaving the radical issue untouched.

But there is yet one more rock of confusion to be indicated, upon which the adopters of Wilford's Puranic delusions, Faber's fantastic reconciliations, and Delafield's American extravaganzas, have always split. It occurs when, through disregard of philology and palæography, they prefix an S, or other sibilant, to the Hebrew KUS*h;* and, reading SKUCH, *Scuthi*, Σκυθαι, &c., make this patriarch the father of *Scythians*, *Sacæ*, Saxons, Scotchmen, and even of *American Indians!* One blushes to treat such absurdities seriously in A. D. 1853. Nevertheless, the disease is inveterate with many writers "à qui il ne manque rien que la critique;" and it behooves us to note our "caveat," because, as Bishop Taylor says, "it is impossible to make people understand their ignorance; for it requires *knowledge* to perceive it, and therefore he that can perceive it hath it not."

A dry recapitulation of the *results* of studies, that could not be presented in full under half this volume, together with references through which the reader may verify exactness, is all that the authors can now offer on the *hieroglyphical* KS*h*, the *Hebrew* KUS, and *Greek* Αιθιόπια.

1st. That the KeS*h* were African aborigines — probably similar to the *Barâbera* of the present day; but were not NAHSI, *Negroes*.

2d. That their habitat, from the XVIIth dynasty downwards, was closer to Egypt than that of any other Africans — probably Lower Nubia, because the KeS*h* are the first people encountered in Egyptian expeditions above Philæ.

3d. That their name, still preserved at Tutzis in *Kish*, was never KuS*h*, but KeS*h*, *Kish*, or *Kash*.

[Lower Nubia, nearest to Egypt, would seem to have been the residence of the *Kish*, or KeS*h*, anciently; just as we find a similar people, the *Barăbera* (who présent striking similarities), there now. A curious little fact comes in opportunely to support this position. The ruins of the ancient town of *Tutzis*, or Tusis, the military station "Dodecaschœni," are identified in the modern Gerf Hussèyn. A Coptic papyrus, found there in 1813, established that its former name was *Thosh;* and the similarity of this word with "Ethaush," the Coptic form of "Ethiopia," or *Koush* [ubi supra], was long ago pointed out by Wilkinson, who ascertained, moreover, that the present Nubian name of *Tutzis* is KISH.]

4th. That this appellative, *KeSh*, in hieroglyphics, refers to a special Nubian people, without the slightest relation, linguistically, geographically, or anthropologically, to *Tirhaka*, beyond the fact that, like his pharaonic predecessors, he conquered and ruled over them [*supra*, p. 264, Fig. 186.]

5th. That the African KeS*h* of the hieroglyphics are totally distinct from the Asiatic KUS*h* of the Hebrew writers, and are never implied by the latter in this term.

6th. That the confusion, still prevalent on this subject, proceeds from an insufficient examination of old Hebrew ethnic geography on the one hand, and of Egyptian records on the other, after starting with a fundamental error as to the Greek word "Æthiopia."

7th. That KUS*h* of Xth Genesis denotes *Arabia* in its widest sense, and Arabian tribes of *dark* complexion.

8th. That, except perhaps in two or three doubtful instances, in the later biblical books, where geographical precision is sacrificed to poetic license, the biblical word KUS*h* never crosses the Red Sea into Africa; and, even if it be sometimes coupled by a conjunction to *Phut*, and to *Lud*, it never embraces those races we term *Negro*—the context, in every case, being susceptible of more rational exegesis.

9th. That KUS*h* in Hebrew is radically distinct from the Nubian KeS*h* of hieroglyphics, as well as from the *Kish* of our present day.

10th. That KUS*h* is not Σκυθαι, *Skuth*, or *Scot!* does not include Scythic, Indo-Germanic, Tartar, Mongolian, or other races outlying the boundary of ancient Hebrew geography.

11th. That, excepting as regards its application to Asiatic tribes of *dark* complexion, KUS*h* cannot be rendered by Αιθιοπια, in the sense in which this Greek word was used during Ptolemaic times at Alexandria, and by ourselves, without leading to equivoque; but, if we restore to "Æthiopia" its old Homeric meaning of "sun-*burnt-faced*-people," there is no doubt that the KUS*h*, mentioned in parallel ages by Hebrew writers, were sometimes included among the *Eastern, i. e.* Asiatic, *Æthiopians* of Hesiod, Homer, and Herodotus.

12th. That, in archaic anthropology, *Æthiopian* is as vague an adjective (without specific warning, on the author's part, of the meaning he attaches to it) as *Scythian*, *Indian*, or *Caucasian*, and therefore had better be avoided by ethnographers.

13th. That the *Coptic* KHOUSH, and *Thaush*, or *Ethosh*, belong to post-Christian days, and represent "Ethiopia" in the corrupt sense in which the Hebrew name KUS*h* was already understood by the Hellenistic Jews called the LXX, and by Josephus. The former word, meaning *dark*, was naturally applied by Egyptian (Copts) *Jacobites* to African families and localities above the first cataract of the Nile; the latter, meaning "the *frontier*," and also (through dialectic mutations of K and T*h*), being a homonyme of KHOUS*h*, was a natural transcript of "Ethiopia;" a name which, from similarity of sound as much as from identity, in *Coptic* days, of association with Africa above Egypt, had been previously given to the *Nubias* by Alexandrian writers.

14th. Finally, that, unless *words* and *names* are restricted to the acceptation in which they were used by each writer in *his own age*, the natural history of humanity, greatly dependent as it is upon historical phenomena, can never rise to the level of a *positive* science; and that sublime sentence, "the proper study of mankind is *man*," mouthed by rote without perceptions of its lofty import, and still overlaid by theological clap-trap, will never reach practical realization.

To us, therefore, KUS*h* of Xth Genesis means *Asia* geographically, *Arabia* topographically, and the *dark Arabs* ethnologically. We pass on to classify KUS*hean* affiliations, in hopes that they will justify our *à priori* assumptions.[594]

KUS*h* as Arabian.

We have shown in the foregoing *résumé* that, amid geographical personifications of the Hebrews, KUS*h* was *Asiatic* generally, no less than *Assyrian* and *Arabian* espepecially. In consequence, it seems rational to seek for KUS*hean* origins among Arabic traditions, and Arab localities.

And here it is that the *Recherches Nouvelles* of Volney take precedence over all those made during the first quarter of the nineteenth century. Volney: "Un des hommes les plus pénétrants de ce siècle. . . . Si, parmi nous, Volney a profité des écrits de Richard Simon, ce n'est pas parceque Volney était imbu des principes de l'école matérialiste, mais à cause de l'instinct scientifique qu'il possédait profondément et qui, dans ses écrits, s'est souvent fait jour, en dépit même de ses préjugés philosophiques." Orthodoxy can find no fault with the words of Lenormant, whose views are eminently catholic, even in archæology. We gladly follow his example, when taking departure, in Arabian inquiries, from Volney. Nevertheless, since the peace of 1815, multitudes of scientific Europeans, profoundly versed in Arabic lore through arduous studies, or far more adventurous travels, have given to Arabian researches a propulsion similar to that received, since 1822, by Egyptian, and, since 1843, by Assyrian. *Primus inter pares* among the above, whether in the cabinet or on the road, ranks M. Fulgence Fresnel. Than his opinion French and German scholarship at this day recognizes none higher: because, in addition to a mind disciplined by thirty years of devotion to this speciality, no man, in Arabian investigations, has yet enjoyed M. Fresnel's facilities of actual observation. We select him, then, as our standard authority on KUS*h*, and *Cushites*: supporting it by the concurrence of distinguished Orientalists to whom his publications are familiar.

The arbitrary Ptolemaic repartition of the Peninsula into *Happy*, *Desert*, and *Petræan* Arabia, has long ago been abandoned by geographers. To the Arabs these foreign divisions were unknown. Into the varied districts designated by such alien names, old Arab tradition recognizes the introduction of three races, forming three distinct nationalities; whose several origins being lost in the night of time, Mohammedan writers have appropriated, through the Korân, Hebrew genealogies in the absence of history; so that it is now impossible to separate much of the exotic from the autocthonous. These three divers stocks of primitive *Arabian* nations, *i. e.*, âRaB, *Western* men — according to Ebn-Dihhiyah, followed by Fresnel and Jomard — were,

1st. The ARBA, or Aribah, *Arabs* par excellence — subdivided into nine tribes, claiming descent from Iram (*Aram* of *Gen.* x. 23), son of Shem: from whom the semi-Egyptian, semi-Hebrew, Ishmael is said to have learned Arabic!

2d. The MOUTA'ARIBA, *naturalized* and not pure Arabs; whose genealogies ascend to Qahtân (*Joktan* of *Gen.* x. 25), son of Heber, son of Salah, son of Arphaxad, son of Shem.

3d. The MOUSTAARIBA, still less pure Arabs; descendants of Ishmael, son of Abraham and Hagar.

These, in general, are reputed to be the *surviving* Arabs; in contradistinction to the lost tribes of Ad, Thamood, &c. &c., destroyed for their impieties, between the times of "the prophet Hood" (*Heber* of *Gen.* x. 24) and Abraham. "But the spirit of that entire table (*Gen.* x.), in which names of people, cities, and lands, are personified, leads us to conclude," says Gesenius, "that *Heber* was not an historical, but only a mythical personage, whose name was first formed from that of the people. This was, doubtless, the case with Ion, Dorus, and Æolus."

None of the above nations, however, attribute their descent to an *Hamitic* affiliation through KUS*h:* and Hyde sustains that the *Cushites* migrated from *Chusistàn*, or Susiana, to the shores of the Euphrates and Persian Gulf; whence it is probable their offshoots spread over Southern Arabia, and eventually crossed the Red Sea, in common with Arabs of the Semitic stock, into Abyssinia and other Upper Nilotic provinces.

With the *Ishmaelitish* tribes of Arabia, as they are not included in Xth Genesis, our inquiries have little to do. Their distribution has been worked up, as completely as the subject admits, by Forster; although the attentive comparisons of Fresnel result in but nine or ten nominal identifications of Arab tribes mentioned in the Bible, while above forty biblical tribes are wanting in the lists of the Arabs. The purely Semitish families of Xth Genesis are allotted their own places in our Essay. To determine KUS*hite* occupation of Arabia is our object, now that, except as "sun-*burned-faces*," they had no relation to African "Ethiopia," at the remote age of our historical horizon.

No one will dispute that, in the idea of the writer of XIth Genesis, the affiliations of SHEM, HAM, and JAPHETH, catalogued in the Xth, assembled, when "*the whole earth* was of *one* language," on the plain of *Shinar* (*Gen.* xi. 1, 2), whence they were dispersed by miraculous interposition. Among the number was KUS*h*, the father of NIMROD; and consequently *Asia*, on the banks of the Euphrates, was the primitive starting-place of himself and children, viewed as *men*. Conceding to orthodoxy their departure thence towards Africa, *Arabia* was inevitably their road and halting-place. The only differences between debaters are questions of time: our view being that the KUS*heans* remained there for indefinite ages, and that their African emigrations were partial, as well as chronologically recent; to be demonstrated, anon, by the Arabian concentration of their several descendants.

The many scriptural citations of our preceding remarks establish that KUS*hites* were still in Arabia at a far later period: a notable instance being ZERAH *the Cushite*, in the time of Asa; to place whom in Africa, because the *Lubìm* and *Cushìm* are united in 2 *Chron*. xvi. 8, when the *Cushìm* alone are recorded in the historical narrative (2 *Chron.* xiv. 8–14), merely to accumulate proofs that no confidence can be given to either account at all, is, to say the least, incautious. The KUS*heans* were yet in Arabia, at the time of Jeremiah's (xiii. 23) interrogatory, "Can the *Cushean* change his skin?" which contrast, we have shown, applies to the *dark* Arabian tribes, abounding in Arabia then as now. But, lest our application should be considered dubious, this fact must be contemplated from a more philosophic point of view.

It is acknowledged by the highest ethnological students of our generation, Prichard, De Brotonne, Jacquinot, Bodichon, Pauthier, and others, that wherever in Austral-Asiatic latitudes, Hindostan for example, tradition yet pierces through the gloom of time, the *dark*, or black, families of mankind (specimens of whom also survive there to our day) have invariably preceded colonizations by the *Whites*, or higher castes. It is also claimed by Kenrick, Bunsen, De Brotonne, and Lenormant, that the great *Hamitic* migration westwards through Arabia antedates the Semitic: in other words, that KUS*hites* were settled in Southern Arabia prior to the arrival of *Djourhomidæ*, *Joktanidæ*, or *Abrahamidæ* — Semitish tribes, like the Hebrews, of fairer complexion. The new doctrines advanced in this volume [*supra*, Chapter VI.] relative to the improving gradations of *type*, in humanity's scale, when we consider each family of mankind, one by one, from the Cape of Good Hope to the Caucasian mountains, show how a *dark* group of men ought to present itself in Arabia, as the immediate Asiatic successors of the swarthy Egyptians: *Egypt*-proper, according to ancient opinions, now corroborated by zoological facts, being far more Asiatic than African in its natural history and phenomena. What group answers all these conditions but the one to which, from immemorial time, the name of KUS*h* has been appropriately referred? Even as late as the fifth century after Christ, Syrian authors, cited by Assemani, designated *Himyarite* Arabs by the name of KUS*hites*.

And this brings us to the point where Fresnel's discoveries establish the entity of a *fourth* group of "Arabs," distinct from Semitish families, dating in Southern Arabia from ante-historical ages to the present hour.

Carsten Niebuhr, in 1763, first announced to Europe the positive existence in Southern Arabia of inscriptions which old Arab authors had characterized as *Musnad*, 'propped up,' and had considered anterior in age to Islâm, no less than to the present *Neskee* and its parent the *Cuphic* writing of Mohammed's day. De Sacy, 1805, with his usual acumen, investigated the subject; Seetzen, 1810; Gesenius, 1819; Kopp, 1822; and Hupfeld, 1825; chiefly from *Ethiopic* (Abyssinian) data, advanced its study; until Wellsted, 1834, and Crittenden, (officers attached to the East India Company's surveys,) discovered inscriptions of the highest interest, cut in the old Himyaritic alphabet, at *Hisn Ghoràb*, &c.

The learned critique of our friend Prof. W. W. Turner would greatly simplify an expository task, could we herein digress upon these Himyaritic inscriptions, the earliest date of which falls far below the Christian era. To his scathing refusal of "one particle of sympathy for Mr. Forster" viewed as translator (!) of the *Himyaritic*, we beg leave to add ours in respect to this gentleman's more recent "*Sinaic* Inscriptions—Voice of Israel from the Rocks of Sinai"; and to apply Turner's just strictures to both of the Rev. Mr. Forster's fabrications. "His wholly false and inconclusive method of deciphering the inscriptions, the bombastic strain in which he dilates on his achievements, and above all the disingenuous artifices by which he seeks to disguise the hollowness of his pretensions, render his performance [whether Himyaritic, or Sinaic, or, worse than either, his last pseudo-*hieroglyphical!*] deserving of all the ridicule and censure it has met with." It is sufficient now to mention, that Hunt's refutation also lies before us; together with the *Recherches sur les Inscriptions Himyariques de San'â, Khariba, Mareb*, &c., through which Fresnel's claim to the resuscitation of ancient Himyar is universally acknowledged.

M. Fresnel's IVth and Vth Letters to the *Journal Asiatique*, "Djiddah, Jan. and Feb. 1838," give a sprightly account of his rencontre with a "piratical grammarian" yclept *Moukhsin;* through whose and other fortuitous aids, he constructed the vocabulary of a still living tongue, spoken at *Zhafâr* and *Mirbât*, in Southern Arabia; which speech, now unintelligible to Semitic Arabs, is called *Ehkili* by native speakers, and *Mahri*, or *Ghràwi*, by surrounding tribes. This extraordinary language, whose existence was unsuspected until 1838 by modern philologers, possesses thirty-four to thirty-five *consonant* articulations, six pure *vowels*, and as many *nasal*—approximately, some forty-seven different sounds; among which three are utterly inexpressible in any European alphabet; and one is altogether too inhuman for any man but a true Zhafârite to enunciate! Of the twenty-eight articulations current during Mohammed's time in the Hedjàs, two have become superfluous in the vernacular Arabic (*Dàrig*) of Cairo; nevertheless the old Arabic alphabet of twenty-eight articulations is too poor, by nineteen phonetics, for tribes living at Mirbât and Zhafâr!

[They completely destroy, Fresnel states, "la symétrie du visage." Even Moukhsin thought the facial contortion ridiculous; though he told M. A. d'Abbadie that none of his tribe pronounced three of those letters on the *left* side of the mouth. "Pour rendre le son du ـث il faut chercher à prononcer un Z, en portant l'extremité de la langue sous les molaires supérieures du coté droit"—such is "*Himyaritic* euphony"! Having humbly endeavored, "in auld lang syne" at Cairo, to imitate my friend M. Fresnel's attempts to rival Moukhsin's mode of oral articulation, I was, and still am, at a loss to define the agonies of its intonation, otherwise than by reprinting how, "while (this letter) somewhat resembles the 'LL' of the Welsh, (it) *can* be articulated only on the *right side* of the mouth—being something between 'LLW,' a *whistle* and a SPIT!"—G. R. G.]

Gesenius had divided Semitish languages, classified as they are too vaguely, into three main branches:—

1st. The *Aramæan*, spoken in Syria, Mesopotamia, and Babylonia. This is again divided into East and West Aramæan; that is, the Chaldee and Syriac.

2d. The *Canaanitish*, or *Hebrew*, spoken in Palestine and Phœnicia. Of this the Punic is a descendant.

3d. The *Arabic*, of which the Æthiopic is a parallel branch. The Samaritan is a mixture of the Hebrew and Aramæan.

To the above, Fresnel's discoveries add a *fourth:* viz., the "Ehkèelee" of the inhabitants of Mirbât and Zhafâr; one which he considers among the richest and most ancient in the world—allied to the Ethiopic, but more archaic; preserved in Arabia by a peculiar family (long cut off from the rest of mankind by wild Bédawees of the Semitic stock, with whom, it is said, the Zhafârites never intermarry)—descended probably from the *Homeritæ;* in whose name classical annalists have preserved to us the original word *Himyar* (Arabicè, *Ahmar*), 'the *red*-men,' as the distinguishing title of the once-great *Himyarites* of Saba and Mariaba.

"He who enters Zhafâr *Himyarizes*," is an ancient Arab proverb, which shows that the Zhafârites were different, in some striking peculiarities, from Semitish tribes, and that visitors were constrained "to speak the language of the country;" as unintelligible even now to Ishmaelite and Joktanide Arabs as the *Basque* is to Frenchmen or Spaniards. Now, this tongue and the tribes that speak it, are considered by M. Fresnel to be the true relics of KUS*h;* owing as much to the abundance of words foreign to Arabic contained in its dialects, as to the singular characteristics of the speakers themselves; whose antiquity at *Zhafâr* reaches beyond all history. The daring of Dr. Arnaud, (who, at Fresnel's instigation, penetrated where no European ever reached previously to 1844, and copied multitudes of Himyaritic inscriptions on the ruined edifices of Sana, Khariba, and Mareb,) has confirmed, in all important respects, the existence of these human vestigies of KUS*hites* in their earliest Arabian homestead "even unto this day": and the men, their language and monuments, having now been found, our results on Xth Genesis may be finally tabulated as follows:—

1st. That by KUS*h* the Hebrew chorographer meant *dark* tribes of Southern Arabia, who probably inhabited that section of the peninsula prior to immigrations of strictly Semitish Arabs. They are the *Homeritæ* of Greek and Roman writers; *Himyarites* of Arab history; remnants of whom, speaking *Ehkîli*, still residing at Mirbât and Zhafâr, are living witnesses of the indelibility of primordial *types*.

2d. That other compilers of Scripture corroborate this view, and prove that in Hebrew geography the KUS*hîm*—bounded at the extreme west by the "rivers of *Cush*" on the Isthmus of Suez—spread across the peninsula to the banks of the Euphrates; perhaps eastwardly to *Chuzistân* and *Susiana*. Their settlements, as Forster has shown with commendable felicity, lay dotted around the Arabian coasts of the Red Sea and Persian Gulf; separated originally from the intrusive *Joktanides*, (as the writer of Gen. X. accurately remarks, v. 30), by a line drawn from "*Mesha*, as thou goest unto *Sephar*"—the former being the *Zames Mons* in Central Arabia of Ptolemy the geographer; the latter, Mount *Sephar*, at the extreme south-west of the peninsula, where in Ptolemy's time dwelt the *Sapharitæ;* and where at *Zhafâr*, Fresnel's researches (unquoted by Forster) prove their *Ehkîli* descendants to live still.

3d. That before future hagiographers place KUS*h* in *Africa*, as the Hebrew name for Nigritian races (of whom CUSH, scripturally and physically, is no more the father than Abraham himself), it might be well, perhaps, if they re-read their "Bibles" with a little attention; and not perversely close their eyes to the new lights that Oriental science is continually shedding upon an ancient code which, Lanci emphatically and truthfully observes, "is the more honored and revered as thought dives into it to illustrate and *comprehend* it."

As *Southern* Arabia, and as *dark* (*himyar*, 'red') Arabian tribes, KUS*h* takes his rightful position once more in Xth Genesis.[595]

16. מצרים — MTsRIM — 'Mizraim.'

Semitic; but certainly not the Hebrew 'tribulation,' &c.

As it stands, is the plural of MTsR. With the Masoretic points, added since the sixth century after Christ, it is a *dual*, Mitsraïm, meaning the *two* MTsRs. In the singular, MTsUR, it is the name (by modern natives referred also to the city of *Cairo*,) through which Egypt is designated in the form Muss'r, not merely by her present Arabicized people, but by all Oriental nations: and there being no dispute as to the application of MTsUR by Semitic races to the *land of Egypt*, from the present hour back to the remotest period for which we possess records, our genesiacal purposes would be served sufficiently on reading *Egypt* for MTsR*aïm*, were it not for foolish rabbinical notions, vulgarly current, that, misunderstanding the principle of Oriental personifications, still treat of "*Mizraim*" in Xth Genesis as if *he* had been really a *man*, "*son* of Ham," another individual! One might as reasonably maintain that all the *Russias*, or the "*two* Russias," mean a human being actually resident in Muscovy! Pandering to no such historical falsehoods, we briefly set the reader on the "royal road" to their refutation.

The earliest personification of *Matzur*, the singular of MTsRIM, is not in the Bible, but in Sanconiathon; a very ancient Phœnician writer, who flourished (none will dispute) some time *before* Philo Byblius, about the second century after c., translated into Greek such fragments of his works as reach our day through Athenæus, Porphyry, Eusebius, and other transcribers. Whether Sanconiathon be a mythe, as some maintain, or whether such a person really lived and wrote between St. Martin's adopted era, 1400 b. c., and Philo Byblius's age, is indifferent; so long as it remains historical, that, under the name "Sanconiathon," we possess some *exuviæ* of Phœnician traditions antedating Christian harmonizings, that cannot have been *written* alphabetically, according to the laws of palæography, earlier than the seventh to tenth century b. c., nor later historically than the second century after the Christian era. We have no hypothesis to sustain beyond establishing, through these fragments, that "Misor" was the ancestor of the Egyptian god Thoth, *Hermes-Trismegistus* (*Her-Mes* = 'begotten of Horus') of the Greeks; and consequently, that this Græco-Phœnician legend is our most valid authority for making a *man* out of the "two *Egypts*" — Upper and Lower — personified in Xth Genesis by commentators as Mitzraim.

The context of *Ps.* cv. 23, (and wherever else in canonical Hebrew records the singular form MTsUR occurs,) suffices to prove that, by MTsUR, each Jewish writer meant Egypt as a *country*. If the singular number, MTsUR, in Hebrew grammar and history, signifies merely a geographical locality, upon what principle can the dual or plural forms of the same word constitute a *man?*

Among the multitude of appellatives given to Egypt by other foreigners, the present name Muss'r reappears in the Phœnician Μυαρα — suspected to be an error of copyist for *Musra* — of Stephanus Byzantinus; in the Μεστραία of George the Syncellus; in the Messredj of the Persian "Boundehesch-Pahlevi"; and so on backwards to the Persepolitan cuneiform inscriptions of Darius, carved at Behistún early in the fifth century b. c., where it is orthographed M'udrâya. Two centuries earlier, the name MASR, or *Madr* (also Mesrahouan), is chiselled in Assyrian cuneatics on the thresholds of Khorsabad, among the conquests of Asarhaddon, between b. c. 709 and 667; and it may exist perhaps on older sculptures of the ninth century b. c., discovered by Rawlinson.

Albeit, 700 years b. c. are ample for our object; inasmuch as they prove that a singular form of the name *Muss'r* existed in Asia, in days parallel with, and probably anterior to, those passages in the Hebrew Text where MTsUR is its homonyme. Its dual or plural representative in Xth Genesis, MTsRIM, is either a later amplification, or meaning simply *the Muss'rites*, people of *Muss'r*, Egypt, excludes the supernatural idea that Mizraim was a *man*.

In this concrete sense of *Egyptians*, we find the correspondent of *Mizraim* in the

Μεστραιοι of Josephus, and of the Syncellus; but the latter uses it in his preface to a document, the *Old Chronicle*, which every scholar repudiates in some mode more or less decisive. Those who now pretend to accept the *Old Chronicle*, or the *Laterculus*, as genuine Egyptian, slur over Letronne's blighting criticisms. The hand of Judaizing Christian imposture stands out undisguisedly in the other portion of the Syncellus's chronography — where he commences his "Laterculus" with Μεστραιμ ο και Μηνης — *Mestraim* (for Mizraim) the same as MENES! That the first Pharaoh of Egypt, Menes, should be metamorphosed into MTsRIM, *the Egyptians*, of Xth Genesis, by a harmonizing monk of Byzantium some 800 years after Christ, and at least 4500 after the death of Menes, is not extraordinary, when one remembers the pious frauds of a school in which the Syncellus was neither the first nor the last ornament; but that writers in our day should reason from such and similar Greek-church literary juggleries, that *Mitsraim* of Xth Genesis was a *man*, instead of an Oriental personification of Egypt, merely proves such writers to possess, as Bunsen has it, "little learning, or less honesty." Our note [596] indicates volume and page wherein complete destruction of τὸ παλαιὸν χρονικόν, 'the Chronicle of the old times, or events,' may be found; and we are content to follow in the wake of Letronne, Biot, Matter, Barucchi, Böckh, Bunsen, Raoul-Rochette, Lepsius, Kenrick, Alfred Maury, &c. — all of whom, more or less earnestly, reject the *Old Chronicle*, uniting with Bunsen's condemnation of it and "similia, quæ hominis sunt Christiani, parum docti, at impudentissimi."

All Grecian antiquity, from Homer to Strabo, has designated Egypt by names in which no form of *Mitsraim* plays a part; nor can it be yet said that any true equivalent for the Semitic *Muss'r* has been discovered amid the numberless appellatives given to their own country by Egyptian hierogrammates. Leaving aside old fanciful analogies that might be retwisted out of Champollion's *Grammaire* and *Dictionnaire*, Dr. Hinck's ingenious TO-MuTeRI, 'Land of the *two* Egypts,' fell beneath the knife of Mr. Davyd W. Nash, who substituted TO-MuRE-KHAFTO, 'the beloved land of the *two* Egypts.' Syncellus's "Mestræans" was supposed by Lenormant to be a compound word — MES-*n*-RE, 'son of the sun': but, 1st, this has not been found as a proper name in hieroglyphics; and, 2dly, the word Μεστραια is but a modern Greek transcriber's corruption (not of an *Egyptian* name, but) of the *Hebrew* and foreign word *Mitsra-im.* Mr. Birch's "*Merter* (Mitzraim), is red under thy sandals," is the nearest approximation to *Muss'r* hitherto suggested; and saves discussion here of the various Hebraical solutions proposed by Rosellini, Portal, or Lanci; some of which would admirably explain why the *Hebrews* gave to Egypt the name of MTsRIM, but none of which prove that the Egyptian natives ever recognized such foreign designation — any nearer, philologically, than "Americus Vespucius" might, by some etymological gladiator, be wrenched out of our "Uncle Sam." We return, therefore, as in so many other instances, to Champollion's fiat of forty years ago: viz., that *Muss'r*, MTsUR, and MTsRIM, in all their forms, were probably alien to the denizens of the Nile, but were names given *to* Egypt and Egyptians by Semitic populations.

But one query remains. In the original idea of the writer of Xth Genesis, was MTsRIM a dual or a plural? The surviving punctuated Text (written or printed in the post-Christian *square-letter*) reads, dualistically, *Mitsraïm;* which would correspond perfectly to the Pharaonic division into "*two* Egypts," Upper and Lower — preserved still in the *Saeèd* and *Bahreèyeh* of the modern Fellaheen. We would submit, notwithstanding, that the *Masorete* diacritical marks float between A. C. 506, and the eleventh century (age of the earliest MSS. extant); and therefore such minute contingencies as a dual or a plural become, archæologically speaking, rather problematical. For ourselves, we think the plural form, *Mitsrìm*, most natural — 1st, because it is the Hebrew literal expression without the later and superfluous points; and, 2d, because the plural MiTsRìM, as the Israelitish name for *Egyptians*, amply satisfied all chorographic and ethnological exigencies whensoever Xth Genesis was projected.

"Misrajim," Bochart declared 200 years ago, "non est nomen *hominis.* Id non patitur forma dualis"; wherefore, denying that there ever was a *man* called "Mizraim," we read simply, for MiTsRIM — *the Egyptians*.[597]

17. פוט — P*h*UT — 'Phut.'

Hamitic; not the Hebrew 'fat,' 'despicable,' &c.!

That this is Barbary — *i. e.*, the African coast along the Mediterranean west of Egypt — no one doubts. Differences of opinion here resolve themselves into mere conjectures as to space.

The most salient feature of *Phut*, observable in Xth Genesis, is that this personification has no *children* — *i. e.*, colonies, or affiliations; which, coupled with the vague demarcations of *Phut* in other Scriptural passages (*Nahum* iii. 9), shows that to the Hebrews this name meant generally North-western Africa; embracing families of man too remote to be described. The word has since spread very extensively over Africa, if *Foute*, *Fouta*-Toro, *Fouta*-Bondou, *Fouta*-Djallon, &c., names of Fellatah States and tribes, be its derivatives; as *Fâs*, the kingdom of Fez, is, without question; nominally replacing the *Regio Phutensis* of Jerome's time; Ptolemy's city of *Foutis*; and Pliny's river *Phuth* flowing in Mauritania, the country which Josephus considers the equivalent of *Phut*. Indeed, there is no lack of old names, throughout the Moghreb, (part of which containing "*Putea* urbs, *Phut* flumen, *Phthia* portus, *Pythis* extrema," was anciently called *Futeya*), like *Phthamphu*, *Phthemphuti*, *Phautusii*, &c., to establish *Phut's* existence at all recorded ages, close to the *Loubîm*, *Lehabîm*, and similar Libyan designations in Xth Genesis.

Bunsen reads *Phut* as Mauritania; considering that the river *Phut* of Pliny is equivalent to the *Punt* of hieroglyphics; the N or M left out, as in *Moph* for Memphis, or *Shishak* for Sheshonk. Birch holds the hieroglyphical sign (which ascends in antiquity to the earliest monuments) to mean the "*nine bows*. This word has been read *Peti*, and supposed to be the Scriptural *Phut*, the Libyans or Moors; but it must be observed, that the hieroglyphical word *Peti* is always applied to a large unstrung bow, in ethnic names." Upon the cuneatic sculptures of Assyria, and among the conquests of Asarhaddon, De Saulcy has read — "Populum *Pout*, hos et gentes fœderatas."

As "P*h*eT-*kah*," or *bow-country*, or as "NiP*h*AT — countries," determined by *nine bows*, this name for the last quarter of a century has been identified with *Phut*, (or rather, comfounded with the NiP*haia*T — true representatives of the *Naphtukhîm* of Gen. x. 13,) in Egyptian sculptures of every epoch; and, without doubt, refers, in hieroglyphics, to Libyan families of *Amazirghs*, *Shillouhs*, &c., that under the present general denomination of *Berbers* stretch westwards from Lower Egypt to the Atlantic.

Deferring some critical minutiæ until we reach the *Naphtukhîm*, our opinion on *Phut* is, that in Xth Genesis it means those countries now called Barbary; while in other biblical texts it covers *Hamitic* affiliations along the Mediterranean face of Africa; to the exclusion of the more inland Negro races, by Hebrew chroniclers unmentioned.[598]

18. כנען — KNA*â*N — 'Canaan.'

Hamitic; not the Hebrew 'merchant,' 'tribulation,' &c.

Upon no terrestrial personification in Xth Genesis, except Cush and Nimrod, has more theory been piled upon hypothesis, than in respect to this luckless cognomen and the historical nations that bore it.

Assuming that the *Jehovistic* document of Genesis IXth was penned by the same individuality who compiled the chart of Genesis Xth, orthodox commentators, from the Rabbis and Fathers down to the uninspired annotators of our own generation, sorely vex themselves with Noah's inebriate malediction — "accursed be Kanaan. Let him be *â*BD-*â*BDIM, *slave of slaves*, to his brethren" — (Gen. ix. 25) — whereas, in the Text itself, Ham the father, not Kanaan the son, was the graceless offender. In Hesiod's

Greek version of the same Chaldæan mythe, hapless Οὐρανός, *Cœlus*, had infinitely more serious reasons for swearing at his unnatural son Κρόνος, *Saturnus;* while, as Cahen has duly noted on the Noachian curse, "this is the fourth malediction that one encounters in Genesis: the first being against a snake, the second against the earth, and the third against Cain."

Setting forth thence with a moral *non-sequitur*, commentators next attempt to justify a supposititious extermination of the guiltless grandson's innocent posterity, recorded by "writer 2d" — "but of the cities of these people (the *Canaanites*), which IeHOuaH thy God gives thee for heritage, thou shalt spare nothing alive that breathes" (*Deut.* xx. 16). Yet, despite this and similar omnipotent injunctions to obliterate poor KNAăN, we find "writer 3d" (*Josh.* xv. 63) attesting how "the children of Judah *could not drive* out" the Canaanites from Israel's holiest abode, Jerusalem, even "unto this day!" A fact explained by "writer 4th" (*Jud.* i. 19, 21), "because (the Canaanites) had chariots of iron"; at the same time that "writer 5th" (2 *Sam.* v. 7, 8, 9) bears witness that one band of Canaanites maintained the stronghold of Mt. Zion, *Jebus*, down to the reign of David. Even then, unscrupulously heroic as that monarch was, he was constrained, through political exigencies, chronicled by "writer 6th" (2 *Sam.* xxiv. 18, 24), to *buy* from a Canaanitish land-holder, "Aravna, the Jebusite," the identical "threshing floor" on the site of which Solomon, according to "writer 7th" (2 *Chron.* iii. 1, 3), erected a little paganish temple (smaller than its duplicate at *Hierapolis*) that, although only 90 feet long by 30 front, is estimated to have cost about 4000 *millions* of dollars — United States' currency.

Other sticklers for plenary inspiration who, in direct contravention of the plain words of Genesis IXth (favoring the notion that Ham, and not his son Canaan, was accursed), contend that, in consequence of such malediction, Ham became the progenitor of black (*Negro*) races, may be set aside as entirely ignorant of Scripture. Followers of the learned Dr. Cartwright's "*Canaan identified with the Ethiopian*" may be pleased to refer to the fac-simile portrait [*supra*, p. 127, Fig. 19] for confirmation of a doctrine which has the double misfortune of being physiologically and historically impossible, as well as wholly anti-biblical.

We appeal to the sober author of Xth Genesis for relief from such mental aberrations. His chorography (constructed some time after Joshua the son of Nun, or Nau, had expelled such Canaanitish tribes as survived massacre, or tolerated under the conqueror's yoke, along Israel's roads of march from Mount Sinai to Palestine) attests, *ex post facto*, that already in his time "the families of the KNAăNI (had been) *dispersed.*" (*Gen.* x. 18.) Large bodies of these people emigrated to Libya, where their names, traditions, and tongues, exist to this day. Procopius, in the sixth century A. C., mentions an inscription wherein *Phœnicians* recorded their flight into Africa, "from before the face of the brigand Joshua son of Naue:" and in the fourth century, St. Augustine, Bishop of Hippo, relates how, in his diocese, "Our rustics, being asked whence they were, responded, Punically, *Chanani.*" Now, it is a fact as certain as any in history, that the Punic-Carthaginians, their parents the Phœnicians, the Canaanites and the Hebrews, spoke one and the same tongue, but with slight idiomatic provincialisms of difference. "The term '*Hebrew* language' does not occur in the Old Testament," says Gesenius, "though it must have been common when part of it was written. Instead of this name, the language is usually termed the *language of Canaan* (*Isa.* xix. 18)." So far, indeed, from *Hebrew*, as philological science nowadays understands the term, deserving honors, owing to its supposititious antiquity, as the "lingua sancta" of Paradise (according to Usher, exactly B. C. 4002–3!), it is positive that Abraham, grandfather of Israel, when he emigrated from "Ur of the Chaldees," spoke, not in *Hebrew*, but, like his Mesopotamian tribe, in an *Aramæan* dialect. Israel's descendants, forgetting their mother-tongue, adopted afterwards, in Palestine, the speech of KNAăN; and, *calling* it "Hebrew," unwittingly sanctified the language of the "slave of slaves," instead of that of the true *Abrahamidæ!* During the Captivity, the

Jews again forgot *Kanaanitish* "Hebrew." Retempered by some seventy years' sojourn in the Euphratic regions of their primitive origin, they brought back with them a later idiom of that *Chaldæan* language which, modified by about 1500 years of time, was a lineal descendant of the pristine speech of Abraham, son of Terah, son of Nahor, son of Serag, son of Reu, son of Peleg; son (that is, *affiliation*) of *Eber* — not a *man*, but the geographical personification symbolized in Xth Genesis (21) by EBR, *ēber*; a name which, like its Greek form, *υπερ*, and its Latinized equivalent, *Iberian*, originally meant simply "the *yonder* land;" that is to say, Palestine; a country west of and *beyond* the river Euphrates! "*Hebrews*," as the foreign corruption of EBR, signifies nothing more than *men from* or *of the other side* — the *Yonderers*.

Every effort, therefore, made by orthodox Rabbis, Doctors, or Moolàhs, Jewish, Christian, or Muslim, to enhance the antiquity and holiness of the tongue they call *Hebrew*, only renders more venerable "the language of KNAăN": and thus, by exalting as theologians do, unintentionally, but positively, the "slave of slaves" above the chosen master, they enable the retributive justice of science to make inhumanity and superstition vindicate, in our nineteenth century, the memory of a much-injured people, who called themselves KNAăNI from ante-historical times down to a period far more modern than the Christian era.

The unceasing proclivity of the Israelites to adopt *Canaanitish* customs and worship, to intermarry with *Canaanitish* females, to dwell in peace with or among them — despite denunciations attributed to Moses and the Prophets — no less than the existence of Canaanites everywhere in Palestine after the Christian era: these facts (evident to every possessor of a "Concordance of the Old and New Testaments") merely prove the strong natural affinities of language and of physical organism common to both families. Nay, apart from supernaturalistic caprice, the only satisfactory mode of justifying such vehement declamations of hatred towards KNAăN, found in the writings of Hebrew reformers, is to acknowledge frankly, that human nature, rebelling against these homicidal proscriptions, often rendered them nugatory in practice.

Of the *eleven* affiliations of KNAăN, only five, the *Hethites*, *Yebousites*, *Emorites*, *Guirgasites*, and *Hivites*, were established within the petty territory of Palestine. Add to these the *Canaanites* (possibly descendants of another KNAăN) and the *Pherizites*, who were merely peasants; and we have the *seven* peoples which the Hebrews were enjoined to expel. (*Deut.* vii. 1; *Josh.* iii. 10.) The desire was stronger than the deed, for the Jews never entirely drove the *Canaanites* out, even of Jerusalem.

By classical historians, the KNAăNI were known under the general name of *Φοίνικες*, *Phœnicians;* and the LXX often substitute the latter name where the Hebrew Text reads *Kanaanites*. Herodotus and later authors assure us, that the Phœnicians came originally from the Persian Gulf; and the *Kanaani*, therefore, would not be indigenous to Palestine; but, nevertheless, they were "*already* in the land" (*Gen.* xii. 5) at the advent of the *Abrahamidæ*, and we regard them as autocthones.

Eusebius quotes Sanconiathon and his translator, Philo Byblius, for the fact that the Phœnicians called their country *Χνᾶ*, a contraction of KNAăN. On Phœnician coins the city of Laodicea is called *mother of Kanaan*. Older than numismatic record, more ancient than Hebrew annalists (Moses not excepted), more positively authentic than any source to which archæology can appeal, are the Egyptian monuments of Sethei-Meneptha I. and Ramses II.; whereupon KANANA-*land* is frequently mentioned among conquered Asiatic nations, from the seventeenth — sixteenth century B. C. downwards. And it may assuage pruriency in those who fancy the KNAăNI to have been *African* "Æthiopians," (though as "sun-*burned-faces*" they were certainly Asiatic,) to take another look at our portrait of a *Canaanite*, copied from sculptures anterior to the century in which the Mosaic Lawgiver is erroneously believed to have written the book called *Genesis*—a portrait, wherein the features establish that (apart from Canaan's priority of *speech* in the Hebraical "lingua sancta," as, eventually, "beatorum in cœlis") the inextinguishable laws of *type* prove the KNAǎNI, as history also testifies, to belong to the same zoological province of creation, though to a lower *gradation* of type, as the Abrahamidæ. Indeed, the root of KNǎ meaning 'low,' and that of ABRAM, 'high,' one may perceive the real cause of early antipathy between the *Canaanites* and the *Abrahamidæ* to lie in mutual repugnances between the indigenous "low-lander" and the intrusive "high-lander."

Palestine, in its widest geographical, no less than in its restricted rabbinical sense, is written history's cradle, and natural history's birth-place, for KNAǎN.[599]

בני כוש — BNI-KUS*h* — "Affiliations of KUSH."

19. סבא — SBA — 'SEBA.'

Perplexities are here occasioned by palæographical and phonetic differences between the letters S, S*h*, and S*s*.

Four separate nations or places, as Bochart reminds us, are mentioned in Genesis by names transcribed through *Seba* or *Sheba:* viz. —

A. — *Genesis* x. 7 — סבא — SBA, or *Seba*, affiliation of KUS*h*.
B. — " x. 7 — שבא — S*s*BA, or *Sheba*, affiliation of KUS*h* through RAAMAH.
C. — " x. 28 — שבא — S*s*BA, or *Sheba*, affiliation of S*h*eM through JOKTAN.
D. — " xxv. 3 — שבא — S*s*BA, or *Sheba*, affiliation of S*h*eM through ABRAHAM.

On these discrepancies Fresnel has wisely noted, that post-Mohammedan Arabs have likewise forged genealogies to match some of those in Xth Genesis; at the same time that different Hebrew annalists often contradict themselves, no less than current Arabian traditions. Various are attempts at reconciliation, to be consulted under our references to Volney, Lenormant, Munk, Jomard, and De Wette; but, upon the whole, Forster's appear to be the most successful, viewed geographically. To us, nevertheless, the only apparent difference between the *four* above-cited names is, that one (A.) begins with the letter *sameq*, S; and the other three (B., C., D.) with *sheen*, S*h*; that is, according to the Masorete points added to the modern *square-letter* manuscripts after the sixth century; because, those stripped away, *sheen* remains *Sseen*, or S*s*.

Abraham's grandchild, through Ketoura, the fourth S*h*BA (D.), is excluded from Xth Genesis, and, therefore, appertains not to our researches; except when noticing the confusion he produces in Arabian genealogies. Nor, for similar reasons, do we speculate on which of the four names might apply to the unknown region whence journeyed Solomon's "Queen of *Sheba*"; whom Josephus makes sovereign of Egypt and Ethiopia; and whom the *Abyssinians* have ever claimed as their own; her illegitimate son, by Solomon, being the legendary progenitor of all their kings. The gifts which this "illustrious inquirer after truth" made to King Solomon (1 *Kings* x. 10; 2 *Chron.* ix. 9) — estimated at $2,917,080, of U. S. coinage; besides any quantity of *spices* and *precious stones* — are enlarged upon by Forster, who considers this lady to have been "Queen of Yemen" in Southern Arabia. Indeed, "the offerings of the Queen of *Sheba*" are believed, by Mr. Wathen, to have enabled Rhamsinitus to build "the indestructible masses of the *pyramids*" of Egypt. Hoskins, of course, appoints this ubiquitous dame Queen of African Meroë: but Fresnel, commenting upon inscriptions brought by Dr. Arnaud from the *Hărăm-Bilkis*—a great elliptical temple, considered to be the "Sanctuary of the *Queen of Sheba*"—seems to have determined her Yemenite locality, as well as the name B-*Almakah;* by which, representing a form of Venus, she became subsequently deified by the Sabæans. Oriental tradition has consecrated, elsewhere, the voyages of princesses, about the same period that *Sheba's* queen and King Solomon interchanged affectionate courtesies. So struck, indeed, were the Jesuit missionaries with the resemblance between the journey made, about 1000 B. C., by "a princess named Si-wang-mou, *the Mother of the Western king* (who afterwards went to China, bearing presents to King Mou-wang") and Solomon's "queen of *Sheba*," that these pietists supposed the *Chinese* account to be *a mere travesty* of the Hebrew books of *Kings* or *Chronicles!* The era; many of the presents; the miraculous facilities of transportation over similar immense distances; and the manner in which the "Mother of the Western King and Mou-wang abandoned themselves, even at the end, to all the delights of joy and songs," curiously correspond. Still more singularly;—the Chinese book, in which these parallelisms are recorded, is called *Chi-i* (*i. e.* collection of what is neglected)—a name identical with the Hebrew *Dibré haiamim*, and the Greek *Paralipomena* (things left out): in which latter volume, under our English designation of "Chronicles," the queen of *Sheba's* visit was registered, like the Chinese story, by far later scribes, until copies became multiplied *ad infinitum*, through the blessing of moveable types.

Deeming, in common with the highest biblical exegetists of our age, Solomon's "queen of *Sheba*" to be less historical than Mou-wang's, we are fain to leave her out of the argument; no less than Josephus's opinion that African *Meroë* was intended by any "*Saba*" of Xth Genesis. Which doubts submitted, let us remember how Pliny assures us that the *Sabœans* stretched from sea to sea; that is, from the Persian to the Arabian Gulf: and, inasmuch as four distinct nations of Arabia are recorded under the appellative *Seba*, *Sheba*, *Sseba*, or *Saba*, it is uncertain whether any one of them can be specially identified at this day. Nevertheless, they are all circumscribed by the "Gezeeret-el-Arab," or *Isle of the Arabs;* and *Seba* (A.), the first of Genesis Xth, as a KUS*hite* affiliation, belongs to the *himyâr* (red), or *dark*-skinned race; — not improbably now represented by the tribes at *Mirbât* and *Zhafâr*, who still speak the old *Ehkhelee* tongue.

No objections militate against Forster's skilfully elaborated conclusion, "that the *Seba* or Sebaim of the Old Testament, and the Sabi or Asabi of (Ptolemy) the Alexandrine, denote one and the same people;" and that "the tract of country between Cape Mussendom and the mountains of Sciorm was originally the seat of Cushite colonies;" because, as Forster's *maps* and reasonings establish, Cape Mussendom was styled, by Ptolemy, "the promontory of the *Asabi*," near which now lies the town of *Câsean* (*Cushan* of Hebrew writers); and a littoral termed, by Pliny, "the shore of *Ham*," *Littus Hammœum*, now *Maham* [Ma-KhaM? *place* of HAM]; adjacent to which is a *Wâdee-Ham*, Valley of Ham; prove that, all around this centre, many local names, commemorative of KUS*hite* settlements, even yet exist.

Not to dogmatize, we conceive that *Omân*, province of Southern Arabia, suffices for the pristine habitat of our *Seba* (A.).[600]

20. חוילה — K*h*UILH — ʻHAVILAH.

Two *Havilahs*, both spelt exactly the same way, one KUS*hite* (v. 7), and the other *Joktanide* (v. 29), occurring in Xth Genesis, their separation is difficult: without harassing ourselves about the third — "Land of K*h*UILH," in *Gen.* ii. 11 — which, being ante-diluvian, concerns not human history.

Here again Forster is an excellent guide, because he does little more than copy Bochart. Assigning to the Joktanide *Havilah* the several districts bearing this name in Yemen, he naturally seeks for the KUS*hite* Havilah about the Persian Gulf, fixing upon the Bahrèyn islands as the pivot of inquiry; one of which still retains its original name, *Aval*. "In order to illustrate the ancient from the modern variations of the proper name Havilah, we must begin," he sensibly observes, "by removing the disguise thrown over it, in our English version of the Bible, by its being there spelled according to the Rabbinical pronunciation. The Hebrew word, written *Havilah* by adoption of the points, without points would read *Huile*, or *Hauile;*" and thereby its identity with the *Huaela* of Ptolemy; the *Huala* of Niebuhr; the *Aval*, *Aûal*, *Huale*,

Khau, Khalt, Khaul, Khaulàn, of modern Arabic, becomes transparent to general readers.

Thus, enlarging Bochart's ingenious comparisons, the Εὐιλάτ of the LXX; the *Chablasii* of Dionysius (Periegetes); the *Eblitæan* mountains of Ptolemy, still called *Aûal;* the *Chaulothei* of Erastosthenes, and the *Chaldæi* of Pliny; become resolved, by Forster, into the powerful tribe of the *Beni-Khâled:* whose encampments dot the Peninsula from Damascus to the Straits of Bab-el-mandeb; from Mekka, on the Arabian coast, round to the Persian Gulf and Mesopotamia; often on sites where some remembrance of their parental *Havilite* appellatives is traditionally preserved "unto this day."

"Se non è vero, almeno è ben trovato": and, in the present state of knowledge on Central Arabia — wonderfully small, our nineteenth century considered — if Carlyle's "hammer of Thor" might, perhaps, demolish Forster's picturesque edifice, we doubt that Thor himself could erect a substitute more solid.

Albeit, ethnology may well be content when Arabia, and especially the shores and islands of the Persian Gulf, preserve so many reminiscences of *three* "Havilahs;" among which, through closest application of the "doctrine of chances," some local habitation must still exist for the name and lineage of a KUS*hite* KHAUILAH.[601]

21. סבתה — SBT*t*H — 'SABTAH.'

What may have been the origin of the word *Saba,* which, simple or compound, has been preserved in Arabia by Hamitic and Semitic affiliations, from primordial times to the present, there appears to be no means now of ascertaining. Gesenius derives *Sabaism* from *Tsaba,* the heavenly 'host'; which, as concerns the root *Saba,* appears somewhat *ex post facto.* Arab migration carried this name into Abyssinia, if the *Sabæ* of Strabo be now represented by a town called *Essab;* so too Josephus imagines Meroë to have been called *Saba,* previously to its adoption of the name of Cambyses's sister; but Lepsius's Meroïte discoveries prove the whole story to be fabulous. Bochart, cautiously, traced *Sabatha, Sobota,* of Pliny, through *Sophtha,* an island in the Persian Gulf, to the *Massabathæ* on Median frontiers. Pliny, however, says "*Atramitæ* quorum caput *Sobotale* LX templa muris includens"; which fixes this city towards Hadramaut. Of the three Arabian sites where nominal remains of *Sabtah* are now traceable, Volney's adoption of Bochart's index seems most appropriate: that of Ptolemy's city, Σαφθα, *Saphtha, Sabbatha-metropolis,* on the coast of the Persian Gulf, in the province of Bahrèyn; where the *Saab* Arabs roam at present, as Forster's maps confirm.

"The Homeritæ," states the great hydrographer Jomard, "the Hadramitæ, the Chatramotitæ, the Sabæi, the Sapharitæ, the Omanitæ, the Maranitæ, the Miniæi, the Thamudeni, lived where nowadays even are the people of *Hemyar,* the people of *Hadramaut,* the people of *Saba* (or Mariaba), the people of *Dhafàr,* the people of *Oman,* those of *Mahrah,* those of *Mina,* of *Thamoud,* and many other peoples, of which the name, any more than the existence, does not appear to have suffered from time." And it will manifest the pains now bestowed by Orientalists to discover these Arabian localities, to add Fresnel's successes: — "The famous *emporium* of Kana is decidedly identified with Hisn-Ghorâb" — and "the town of *Kharibet,* discovered by M. Arnaud, is the last term of (Ælius Gallus's) Roman expedition (*Caripeta*)."

Though we cannot yet place our finger on the exact spot, there is no reason for seeking *Sabtah* elsewhere than among KUS*hite* affiliations colonized on the Persian Gulf. If not found already, the place and its tribes will soon be recovered by the zeal of Arabian explorers.[602]

22. רעמה — RA*á*MH — 'RAAMAH.'

Bochart's acuteness had settled upon Ρεγμα of the LXX; *Rhegama* of Ptolemy; *Regmapolis* and *Kolpos-Regma* in Steph. Byzantinus. This name is said by Strabo to signify 'straits'; which meaning singularly corresponds to the narrow entrance of the Persian Gulf, on the Arabian side of which Forster's maps fix *Raamah*, and its two colonies *Sheba* and *Dedan;* already grouped together by Ezekiel (xxvii. 20–22).

The inland province of *Mahrah* preserves the phonetic elements of *Raamah;* and there it is that, at *Mirbàt* and *Zhafâr*, Fresnel's discoveries of the *Ehkèelee* tongue, called also *Mahree*, establish the existence of a people, distinct from Semitish Arabs; survivors of the old Himyarite (*red*) stock: the *dark*-skinned Arabians of KUS*hite* lineage, represented by the swarthy *Dowàsir* tribes, as reported by Burckhardt and Wellsted.

These people were called *Rhaminitæ* and *Rhabanitæ* by Roman authors; and *Ramss*, an Arab port just inside the Persian Gulf, perfectly answers to the site of *Raamah* catalogued among KUS*hite* personifications in Xth Genesis.[603]

23. סבתכא — SBTtKA — 'SABTECHAH.'

"*Sabtaka* is thrown by Josephus into *Abyssinian Ethiopia;* by Bochart, into the Persic Carmania, under pretext of resembling *Samydake:* these two hypotheses seem to us vague and without proofs. Sabtaka has no known trace." So far Volney.

Yet Bochart's suggestion of B for M offers no palæographic difficulties; and if *Samedake* could be identified, SaBeTAKe might be *Sabteka*, situate in Kermàn, near the Persian Gulf.

"The *Sabatica Regio* of the ancients, a district apparently in the neighborhood of the Shat-al-Arab, is the only probable vestige I can discover," says Forster, "of the name or settlements of Sabtecha."

For our purposes, this excellent indication is sufficient. Personifying some locality or people of KUS*hite* origin, probably near the mouth of the Euphrates, the chorographic genealogist of Xth Genesis fixes *Sabteka* among Arabians of swarthy hue.[604]

24. שבא — SsBA — 'SHEBA.' "Affiliation of RAAMAH."

[Our SsBA second (B.), *ubi supra.*]

We have already stated the difficulties of distinguishing which of *four* Arabian SBAs — KUS*hite*, *Yoktanide*, and *Ketourite* or *Jokshanide* — are assignable now to the chart of Xth Genesis, more than twenty-seven centuries subsequently to its projection; but each one, by every process of reasoning upon facts, is circumscribed within *Arabian* denominations. If, on the one hand, time has rendered minute dissections nugatory, on the other it spares us the trouble of seeking elsewhere for historical lights.

Offshoots of RAAMAH, "*Sheba* and *Dedan*" stand contiguously, not only in Xth Genesis, but in Ezekiel (xxxviii. 13), and belong to the same neighborhoods; whilst Isaiah's KUS*h* and SeBA" (xliii. 3), united by a conjunction, serves to fix *Seba* among the dark-skinned Arabs, where the compiler of Xth Genesis had traced this name's genealogical affinities. But, at whatever age (probably *Esdraic; i. e.*, after return from captivity) the fragmentary documents now called "Genesis" were put together, "a sort of spirit of investigation and combination was also at work. We are indebted to this," continues De Wette, "for the genealogical and ethnographical accounts contained in the Pentateuch. They are designed in sober earnest, and are not without some historical foundation, but are rather the result of fancy and conjecture than of genuine historical investigation. To test the accuracy of the table of Genesis Xth, compare the following passages": —

Genesis X.	*Genesis* XXV.
7. "The sons of KUS*h*, Seba, and Havilah, and Sabtah, and Raamah, and Sabtecha. And the sons of RAAMAH; *Sheba* and *Dedan.*"	2. "*Abraham* [descendant of S*he*M] took a wife . . . Ketourah; and she bare him Zimran and *Jokshan*, Medan, and Midian, and Ishbak, and Shuah: and JOKSHAN begat *Sheba* and *Dedan.*"

Now, both texts concentrate "*Sheba* and *Dedan*" in Arabia. Nevertheless, the unostentatious care evidently bestowed upon his chorography by the practical compiler of Xth Genesis, favors his superior accuracy, and therefore we take his "*Sheba* and *Dedan*" to be the true colonial settlements of KUS*h*.

This is corroborated by Ezekiel (xxvii. 22) — "The merchants of *Sheba* and RAAMAH, they were thy merchants: they occupied in thy fairs with *chief of all spices*:" not merely referring to the rich productions of incense, myrrh, gums, and aromatics, raised in and exported from this part of Arabia then as now, but also to *spiceries* of India and its islands passing in transit through *Sabœan* hands: which, in Joseph's time (*Gen.* xxxvii. 25), were conveyed by inland caravan-portage to Gilead, whence *Ishmaelites* "with their camels bearing spicery and balm and myrrh," carried them to Egypt; and which "maritime merchandisers," under the name of *Tarshish*, had consigned to the Royal Firm of "Solomon, Hyram, & Co." by "coasters" up the Red Sea; and dispatched *via* Petra through this house's factors at Etsion-gaber: (cost of transhipments, freights, camel-hire, insurances, interests, brokerages, commissions, and *grattages*, no less than amount of shares or profits, to us unknown).

Forster skilfully compares the Plinean account of ÆLIUS GALLUS's expedition, "in the words of Gallus himself; the passage being, to all appearance, an extract from the report of that general to his master Augustus:"—"*Sabæos*, ditissimos sylvarum fertilitate odorifera, auri metallis, agrorum riguis, mellis ceroque proventu:" and moreover relates how, "On his arrival before Marsuabæ, the capital of the Rhamanitæ, Ælius Gallus, the Roman geographer informs us, learned from his prisoners that he was within two days' march of *the spice country*:" the very productions for which the Prophet of the Captivity had given celebrity to "*Sheba* and RAAMAH."

Hence, the geographer of Arabia succeeds in identifying the *Saba* of RAAMAH among the "*Sabæi*, with their capital Mar-Suaba or Sabe; whose locality is preserved and determined, in its modern topography, by the town of *Sabbia*, in the district of *Sabiê*;" mapped by him towards the southwestern extremity of the "Isle of the Arabs."

"A highly valuable confirmation of the identity of the modern province of Sabiê, and of its ancient inhabitants, the Rhamanite Sabæans, with the Cushite Raamah and Sheba, arises on our first reference to the 'Description de l'Arabie' [Carsten Niebuhr's]; where we find, in the Djebal, another *Sabbia*, a large town or village, seated in a district retaining, to this day, the patriarchal name of *Beni Khûsi*, or the sons of Cush. Another district, of the same name, *Beni Keis*, is noticed by our author in the Tehama. In the former district occurs a village named Beit el Khûsi [*house* of the KUS*hite*.] A third small district connects the name of Cush with that of his son Raamah; namely, that of Beni Khûsi, in the province or department of Rama. The city of Kusma, south of Rama, M. Niebuhr rightly conjectures to have derived its name and origin from Cush: a conjecture which receives strong light and confirmation from a remote quarter, in the corresponding denomination of Dooat el Kusma, a harbor of the ancient Havilah, near the head of the Persian Gulf; the acknowledged site of the earliest Cushite settlements"—i. e., of the true KUS*him* of all Israelitish chroniclers; affiliated from the personification KUS*h*, by which name the compiler of Xth Genesis figured those *swarthy* races that dwelt *ab initio* exactly where they do now, viz: in *Southern Arabia*.

More conclusive determinations, in primordial ethnology, than in this case of *Sheba* (B.), it would be hard to discover.[605]

25. דדן — DDN — 'DEDAN.'

Leaving aside nice discriminations between the duplex *Shebas* and *Dedans*, the one Hamitic and the other Semitic, we remark that, being a junior colony to *Sheba*, in Rhamanite affiliations, this *Dedan*, through analogy, might be fixed in Arabia, as we have seen in the preceding name, even without the precise words of Isaiah (xxi. 13):—"In the woodlands of *Arabia* shall ye lodge, O ye travelling companies of DDNIM," *Dedanians*: which obviates the necessity for seeking out of the Peninsula.

But the precise location of the geographical son of Raamah, and brother of the preceding Sheba, is fixed at the city and district of *Dadena*, just outside Cape Mussendom, on the Indian Ocean; and taking its natural station among KUSH*ite* tribes of Southern Arabia does not necessitate further research.[606]

With the exception of Nimrod (to be discussed as the next name), who, none will dissent, belonging to Assyrian history, can have no possible relation to *African* theories, here closes the genesiacal catalogue of KUS*hite* affiliations.

The educated reader who has followed us through Hebraical, Greek, Roman, Coptic and hieroglyphical sources, has now beheld every "Ethiopian" postulate on KUS*h* fall, one by one, beneath the knife of historical criticism. As one of the present authors indicated, ten years ago, and as both partially confirmed at a subsequent date by their several researches, the KUS*hites* of Xth Genesis could have been then, as they are now, once for all, glued permanently to *Arabia:* whence to detach them again will be a vain effort, should the reader be pleased to wield in their defence the weapons herein tendered him. That the present tiresome undertaking was needed, the reader can satisfy himself by opening any English *Commentary* on Scripture; and almost every English writer but Forster; who, following Bochart, has consistently vindicated the *Arabian* claims of *Kush*, to the exclusion of *African* fables: whilst henceforward the Ethnographer may calmly pursue his inquiries without necessarily exclaiming, when he stumbles upon the mistranslation "Æthiopia" in King James' version,

"Hic *niger* est; hunc tu, Romane, caveto."

[To my learned predecessors in KUS*hite* inquiries, who have uttered opinions without first employing archæological processes similar to those herein submitted respectfully to their consideration, I beg leave to quote Letronne:—"One regrets to see erudite and ingenious men, of zeal and perseverance most laudable, thus waste their time in pursuit of such vain chimæras, in allowing themselves to be led astray by assimilations the most whimsical and the most arbitrary. One might say, in truth, that, for them, Winckelmann and Visconti had never appeared on earth, so much do they deviate from the reserved and prudent method of these heroes of archæology; who, not pretending to know in antiquity but that which it is possible to explain through the aid of authentic monuments and of certain testimonies, knew how to stop, the moment they felt the ground fail beneath their tread. It is thereby that they arrived at so many positive results, and not at simple 'jeux d' esprit' or of erudition, that cannot sustain an instant's serious examination. Our new archæologists proceed quite otherwise: they take a monument perfectly obscure [like ÆTHIOPIA]; they *compare* it with a second, with a third, and again with others that are not less so; and, when they have placed side by side all these *obscurities*, they pleasantly figure to themselves that they have created *light*. Upon a first conjecture, they place a second, a third, and a fourth. Then, upon this conjecture, at the fourth generation, they erect an edifice, sometimes of appearance sufficiently goodly, because it is the work of architects who possess talent and imagination. This edifice may even endure, so long as nobody thinks of poking it with the tip of a finger; but the moment that criticism condescends to notice it, she has but to whiff thereon, and down it tumbles like a castle of cards."

To "nos adversaires," as the Abbé Glaire facetiously has it—viz: the biblical dunces in the United States, whose zeal in opposing the long-pondered, long-published views of Morton, Agassiz, Nott, Van Amringe, myself and others, has been more remarkable than literary courtesy, I now turn round for my own part, (after shattering their anti-Scriptural KUS*hite* illusions in regard to *Africa* and *Nigritian* families, for ever), and beg each individuality to accept the following citation; the more pertinent as it emanates from one of themselves: — "But, *I* confess that *I* have some considerable dread of the indiscreet friends of religion. *I* tremble," wrote the Rev. Sydney Smith, "at that respectable imbecility which shuffles away the plainest truths, and thinks the strongest of all causes wants the weakest of all aids. *I* shudder at the consequences of fixing the great proofs of religion upon any other basis, than that of the *widest investigation,* and the most *honest* statement of facts. [*Auree parole,* 'golden words,' as Lanci would say]. *I* allow such nervous and timid friends to religion to be the best and most pious of men; but a bad defender of religion is so much the more pernicious person in the whole community, that *I* most humbly hope such friends will evince their zeal for religion, by ceasing to defend it; and remember that not every man is qualified to be the advocate of a cause in which the mediocrity of his understanding may possibly compromise the dearest and must affecting interests of society." And if, in consequence, I discard their *Cushite* suppositions, I can only excuse myself in the words of Strauss: — "Les théologiens trouveront sans doute que l'absence de ces suppositions dans mon livre est peu chrétienne; moi (je) trouve que la présence de ces suppositions dans les leurs est peu scientifique." — G. R. G.]

27. נמרד — NMRD — 'Nimrod.'

Before us stands the sixth and last affiliation of KUS*h* — to whom the writer of Xth Genesis devotes more space than to any other personification secondary to the parental "Shem, Ham, and Japhet" — inasmuch as five of the modern and arbitrary divisions of the text, called *verses,* are especially set apart for Nimrod and his derivations. Hence we may infer that, in the mind of that writer, Nimrod's honor and glory were inherent elements. Now, the associations, the names of *cities* attributed to Nimrod, the language spoken in different dialects throughout the Mesopotamian vicinities of their several locations, and their geographical assemblagé in Babylonia and Assyria: — these considerations, we repeat, even were other histories silent, would lead archæology to suspect strong *Chaldæan* biases on the part of the compiler of Xth Genesis; and would increase the probabilities, to be enlarged upon ere we close this discussion, that Xth Genesis is either a transcript of an older Babylonian composition, or else was compiled by some Hebrew imbued, like Daniel for example, with "the learning and tongue of the *Chaldeans.*"

Such, *primâ facie,* would be the archæologist's deduction when, disengaging himself from prejudices, no less than from traditions of comparatively recent origin, he had sought to evolve facts from the letter of Xth Genesis itself: especially when to this text he adds the only other passage, (except, of course, the abridged parallel in 1 *Chron.* i. 10), in which Nimrod's name occurs throughout the canonical books, (viz: *Micah* v. 6); wherein "the land of Assyria . . . and the land of Nimrod" are Chaldaic synonymes for the same country.

But, when once the inquirer steps beyond these simple and natural limitations, what pyramids of falsehood and misconception intervene to prevent clear understanding of the words of Xth Genesis? and how baseless the fabrications upon which these pyramids rest!

A "mighty *hunter,*" whose imaginary deeds in *venerie* are still proverbial with modern "Nimrods," founds the grandest *cities.* The traditionary builder of a metropolis called *Babel* — BAB-EL, "gate of the *Sun*"; like the Ottoman "Sublime Porte" or the "Celestial Gates" of Chinese autocracy — "presto" becomes constructor of the "*Tower* of Babel;" when, so far as the letter of Genesis Xth and XIth be concerned, neither Nimrod, nor his innocent father KUS*h,* (save as two individuals out of "the whole earth," Gen. xi. 1), were more guilty in such impiety than KUS*h's* grandfather NOAH, who "lived after the flood three hundred and fifty years;" or than anybody else of the seventy-one or two persons — fathers, sons, grand-children, great grand-children, uncles, brothers, cousins, and what not — whose cognomina are enumerated in Xth Genesis.

Cramped within the factitious limits of biblical computation, English writers in particular, following neither Scripture nor true history, but the *Rabbis;* and unable to reconcile supposed Noachic orthodoxy with the sudden rise of so-called "idolatry," have seized, with rapturous eagerness, upon the earliest writer who is conjectured to have known anything more on the subject than we do ourselves; and these authorities behold in Josephus's Greco-Judaic hallucinations a clew to the enigma.

"It is vain we know that Nimrod became mighty, even to a proverb, if the nature and means of his elevation cannot be understood; or that Babylon was the beginning of his kingdom, unless we can find the means of learning for what purposes, and upon what principles, that city was established," reasons, somewhat illogically, the unknown author of *four* very scarce octavo volumes on this speciality,[607] in which we abortively hunted for a *fact:* so that, never having encountered any orthodox commentary on *Nimrod* in which principles of historical criticism were not more or less disregarded, we are reduced to the necessity of attempting to examine for ourselves: notwithstanding that the subjoined "views will doubtless excite astonishment in some, and displeasure in those who," avers Godfrey Higgins, the great Celtic antiquary, "while they deny *infallibility* to the Pope, write, speak, and act, as if they possessed that attribute."

To begin. Let us frankly disavow partialities, in the words which His Eminence, Cardinal Wiseman, aptly borrows from the great Adelung:—"Ich habe keine Lieblingsmeinung, keine Hypothese zum Grunde zu legen. Ich leite nicht alle Sprachen von Einer her. Noah's Arche ist mir eine verschlossene Burg, und Babylon's Schutt bleibt vor mir völlig in seiner Ruhe."

Through the common Oriental mutation of B for M, the word NMRD, of the Hebrew Text, becomes Νέβρωδ in the LXX, and Νεβρώδης in Josephus. Is it a modern or a primeval name? Cuneiform researches, so far as we yet know, have thrown no monumental light on the subject: but hieroglyphical do. Two Pharaonic princes of the XXIId dynasty—between B. C. 936 and 860—bore this appellative: one, son of OSORKON II., spells his name NIMROT; the other, son of TAKELOTH II., NMURT: and, Mr. Birch observes:—"As the Egyptians had no D, but employed the same homophone of the T to express this sound in foreign names, this name is unequivocally the Assyrian Nimroud, נמרד, the Νεβρώδης of the Septuagint, a word now known to signify *Lord* in the Assyrian, and unlikely to have been introduced into an Egyptian dynasty, except through intermarriage with an Assyrian house." Subsequent researches have not merely corroborated Mr. Birch's views on the intimate alliances between Egypt and Assyria, during the XXIId dynasty, but Rawlinson and Layard have established that cuneatic writings, and many other arts of Nineveh and Babylon, are long posterior to Egyptian hieroglyphics, and were the natural sequences of Egyptian tuition.

Monumental evidence, then, coetaneous in registration with the events recorded, carries the name NMRD, at a single bound, from its currency in parlance among the present natives of Assyria (as applied to places, such as *Nimroud, Birs Nimroud, Nimroud-dagh,* &c. &c.), back to the *tenth* century B. C., in hieroglyphics:—an age anterior, probably, to that of the Hebrew compiler, or translator, of Xth Genesis; but, while this fact corroborates his accuracy, it serves to sweep away sundry rabbinical and other cobwebs that hang between our generation and the primeval origin of the *word* itself.

What did NMRD, originally, *mean?* No reply can be accepted that does not, in a question involving such vast ramifications, first classify its components adverbially, under distinct heads:—

1st. *Philologically:*—We know not why the translation "Lord" results from arrow-headed investigations, and therefore relinquish discussion, on that ground, to such cuneatic philologues as Rawlinson, Hincks, De Saulcy, and others of the new school.

It may at once be acknowledged that Oriental traditions, of which the *Thalmudic*

Mishna and *Guemaras* of the present Israelites are but one rill out of many streams, concur in representing Nimrod as every thing haughty, tyrannical, and impious; but nothing can be produced to justify these gratuitous assumptions, earlier in date than Josephus; who merely hands us the rabbinical notions of his day (first century after Christ), when he calls Νεβρωδης the leader of those who strove to erect "Babel's tower;" and, as such, that he *rebelled* against Divine Providence. Now, before speculating, in opposition to the express words of Genesis Xth and XIth, what may have been NMRD's performances on that deplorable occasion, it ought to be first shown that the *fragment* termed "Genesis XIth, ver. 1–9," possesses real claims to be considered *historical*. This being as much out of our power as of any body else at the present day, Josephus's modern views upon NMRD's primordial *rebellion* serve merely to illustrate the proneness of the human mind to explain the impossible by inventing the marvellous. So we lay them aside, beyond the only historical fact resulting from Josephus, viz: that, in his age, NMRD was reputed to have been a *rebel*.

Such being the unique source whence flow all later theories upon KUS*h*'s heresies, and his *son's* enormities, we descend the main stream as we find it continued, "even unto this day," by the Rabbis:—"According to the Talmud (tr. *Chagiga*, ch. ii.), the name NMRD, *Nimrod*, is derived from MRD, *marad*, *to rebel*, because its writers suppose that he induced mankind to rebel against God. This, however, EBN EZRA does not seem willing to admit, but says—'Seek not a cause for every (Scriptural) name, where none is expressly mentioned;' on which his commentator (Ohel Joseph, *in loco*) remarks, 'if the name of Nimrod is derived from the cause stated in the Talmud, it ought to have been, not NMRD, *Nimrod*, but MMRD, *Mamred*.' But, according to Simones (*Onomast.* V. T. p. 472), the name *Nimrod* is composed of NIN, *offspring*, and MRD, *rebellion;* so that NIN-MRD means *filius rebellionis*. A portion of the name NIN survived in *Ninus*, under which appellation he is known to historians as the builder of Nineveh. . . . *He began to be a mighty one in the earth* (*Gen.* x. 8). 'Setting himself up against the Omnipotent, and seducing mankind from their allegiance to the Lord.' (Rashi.) The sacred historian intends here to point out to us the first beginning of those movements and convulsions in society, which led to the formation of states and dominions, especially to that of royalty [!]. And, inasmuch as these movements led to the overthrow of the previous state of things, the name of the man by whom these changes were first introduced, NMRD, *Nimrod*, from MRD, *Marad*, *to rebel*, is peculiarly expressive."[608]

There is—excuse the phrase!—a verdant lucidity about this series of *non-sequiturs* that justifies our tedious extract. In it we perceive the chain of *evidence*, as lawyers would say, through which Christian commentators obtain their first notions upon NMRD—"evidence" upon which each confounder erects his own favorite tower of BBL, *confusion*. "Nous en convenons," concedes the Abbé Glaire; "we agree that the fable of the Titans has some relation to the history of the tower of Babel; but may not one conclude from it that the Greek poets wished to *imitate* the legislator of the Jews, and surpass (enchérir sur) the veracity and simplicity of his recital?"

But, suppose somebody happened to entertain the idea that NMRD may not be derivable from the *Canaanitish* root MRD at all; what, if such case were proved, becomes of Nimrod's *rebellious* propensities?

To ascertain this possibility, a philologist must rise above the level of rabbinical hermeneutics.

We have seen that the word NMRD was a proper name among pharaonico-Assyrian individuals in the tenth century B. C.—an age anterior to most if not to all parts of Hebrew literature extant in our day. This bisyllabic quadriliteral (ceasing to remain any longer mere Hebrew) merges into the vast circumference of *Shemitish* tongues, of which Arabic is the most copious representative.

Now, foremost amid living Semitic lexicographers, stands Michel-Angelo Lanci, and his views are supported by students equally authoritative in their several specialities.

The substance of their researches is: — that the primeval speech whence all Semitish tongues have sprung was, aboriginally, *monosyllabic* in its articulations, and therefore at most *biliteral* in its alphabetical expression; whereas, at the present day, these languages, Hebrew and Arabic essentially, are *dissyllabic* and *triliteral*. "As vowel sounds," holds a supreme authority, Rawlinson, "are now admitted to be of secondary development, and of no real consequence in testing the element of speech, the roots of which are almost universally *biliteral;* the Babylonian and Assyrian [in which languages NMRD's name originated] being found in a more primitive state than any of the Semitic dialects of Asia open to our research [must be older]; inasmuch as the roots are free from the subsidiary element which, in Hebrew, Aramæan, and Arabic, has caused the *triliteral* to be regarded as the true base, and the biliteral as the defective one." Above one hundred examples are given by Lanci; proving how those words which rabbinical scholars suppose to be primordial Hebrew *radicals*, (*i. e.* of three letters), are but a secondary formation along the scale of linguistic chronology; because suffixes, prefixes, or medial elements, have become superposed, or interplaced, upon or within a pristine *monosyllable*. There was, then, a time before the period when the law of *triliterals* became formed; and while on the one hand the Hebrew tongue preserves abundant monosyllabic *reliquiæ* of that remoter age, on the other, the preponderance of *bisyllabic* roots in Jewish literature establishes that such literature arose *after* the law of *triliterals* had already become prevalent. This later age oscillates, it is true, between 700 B. C., and some centuries previously; but cannot, by incontrovertible ratiocination upon historical data, be carried back to *Mosaic* days — fourteenth century B. C. — a linguistic point in which all Oriental *philologers* of the new school coincide.

2*d. Archæologically.*—NMRD, therefore, older on Egyptian monuments than any Hebrew writings that have come down to us, was already, in the tenth century B. C., a matured importation from its native Assyria; where, doubtless, this proper name had existed long previously: being distinguished by the, probably-*Chaldæan*, projector of the chart of Xth Genesis, as the earliest traditionary founder of very ancient cities. To explain by a tri-literal verb, MRD, itself susceptible of reduction into an earlier *monosyllable*, the quadriliteral bi-syllabic proper name NMRD, although not absolutely impossible, presents many chances of involving its advocates in anachronisms; and most certainly would never have occurred to modern Orientalists, had it not been for the rabbinical legend current in Josephus's days, which, thousands of years after NMRD's age, and hundreds later than Xth Genesis, endeavored to reconcile Assyrian mythes with a Hierosolymite doctrine of genesaical origins. We have seen above, that the derivation of NMRD from MRD, *to rebel*, is considered speculative even by Talmudists themselves; and, with Gesenius's *Thesaurus*, the writer (G. R. G.) would undertake, upon legitimate principles of Semitic palæography,—such as the commonest mutations of D for N; B for M; L for R; T, *Th*, S, or *Sh*, for D, &c. — to draw a dozen, or more, happier, and quite as orthodox, significations for NMRD, Hebraically, than that ungrammatically twisted from MRD, which takes little or no account of the protogramme N.

Hear Lanci's more reasonable etymology. We give it regretfully, because without the ingenious arguments by which the Professor defends it in his *Paralipomeni*, and coupled with all the reservations due to philological intricacies of this archaic nature. The word NMRD is nonsense when wrung out from the verb MRD, *to rebel*. It is a compound of two distinct monosyllables, NM and RD. The former proceeds from the radical, preserved in Arabic, N*e*M, "to spread a good odor:" the latter from R*u*D, "to be responsible." N*i*MR*o*D means, Semitically (whether such was its pristine Assyrian acceptation or not), "*he-whose-royal-actions-correspond-to-the-good-odor* (*of his fame*)."

But, difficulties cease not here! In King James's version, as in all its MS. ancestors back to the LXX (where γίγας κυνηγός, a *hunting-giant*, is its wondrous paraphrase), the next verse (*Gen.* x. 9) states that NMRD was a "mighty *hunter!*" Upon this translation hang chiliads of commentaries. Leaving them in suspension, we again present Lanci's etymologies.

The Hebrew word TsID (translated *hunter*) is not in this case derivable from SAID, a *huntsman;* but comes from the Arabian verb WSD; instead of Arabicè SUD, Hebraicè TsUD, *to hunt.* Now, WaSaD means "to be *firm,*" to possess *consistency* and *stability;* which quality, applied to the vast domains assigned in Xth Genesis to Nimrod, makes the words GiBoR-TsID mean "*great-in-landed-tenements*"; and not "vigorous in the chase."

What of Assyrian mythology, on the question of Nimrod, may become exhumed eventually through cuneiform researches, it is useless yet to speculate upon. In the present state of science, Lanci's exegesis, grammatically as to Hebrew, philologically as to *Semitish* tongues, and far more sensibly in connection with the probable meaning of the writer of Xth Genesis, stands of itself, quite as well as, if not better than, the modern rabbinical notion of a "hunter." [Always ready for my own part to surrender any hypothesis the moment its irrationality is proven, I submit (for what I conceive to have been one of the intentions of the compiler of Xth Genesis) the following retranslation of his sentences, accompanied by notes to some extent justificatory.—G. R. G.]

The personage who wrote Xth Genesis is unknown. The language he adopted was *Canaanitish,* afterwards called "Hebrew." The age in which he flourished is obscure: the *alphabet* used by him still more so. His individual biases, beyond a supposable *Chaldaic* tendency, enter, as respects ourselves, into the vast family of human *conjectures.* The *media* through which this document, Xth Genesis, has been handed down, are, in a scientific point of view, suspicious. The vicissitudes (even when restricted to the Hebrew Text) through which the original manuscript has passed, in order to reach our eye in printed copies of King James's version, are not few: because, the oldest Hebrew manuscripts of Xth Genesis now extant do not antedate the tenth century A. C.; the Masorete diacritical marks, upon which orthodox commentaries mainly repose, were not invented before 506 A. C., nor perfected until some 800 years ago; and, finally, the *Ashouri, square-letter,* character of present Hebrew MSS. cannot possibly ascend to the second century of our era. It will therefore be conceded that, before the personal ideas of the first editor of Xth Genesis could have reached our individualities, *some* elements of uncertainty intervene; independently of errors of transcribers and of translators, from Hebrew into Alexandrian Greek; from both of these languages into Latin; from the three, in unknown quantities, into English: all conditions of doubt that cannot, nowadays, archæologically (and neither hagiographically nor evangelically) speaking, be altogether dodged. Upon such historical considerations, we opine, the algebraical chances of *mistakes,* in respect to Xth Genesis, are rather more numerous than those of exactitude in interpretation: albeit, Hebraically, the subjoined attempt at an English restoration can withstand criticism quite as well as, according to St. Paul, "Jannes and Jambres withstood Moses."

3d. *Biblically.*—Genesis X.

Verse 8. "And KUS*h* begat NMRD (NEM-RUD = *he-whose-royal-actions-correspond-to-the-good-odor of his fame*); he first began to be mighty upon earth:"

Ver. 9. "He was a *great-landed-proprietor* before (the face of) IeHOuaH; whence the saying—'like NMRD, *great-landed-proprietor* before (the face of) IeHOuaH:'"

Ver. 10. "And the beginning of his realm was BaBeL; and AReK, and AKaD, and KaLNeH, in the land of S*h*iNAâR."

Ver. 11. "From this land he himself (NMRD understood) went forth (*to*) AS*h*UR (*Assyria*), and built NINUeH and ReK*h*oBoT*t*-AâIR and KaLaK*h*."

Ver. 12. "And ReSeN between NINUeH and between KaLaK*h*; (he) *she* (Nineveh understood) the great city."

[The text, in verse 11, is ambiguous. It may be read, as in King James's version,

"Out of that land went forth Ashur;" but such rendering leaves out an essential member of the phrase, the word HHUA, '*he* himself,' before the verb "went forth," which can only refer to the antecedent Nimrod. On the other hand, as the literal text has "went forth Ashur," the preposition *to* must be interpolated; but not altogether arbitrarily, because learned Hebraists aver that this preposition is omitted in *Num.* xxxiv. 4, and in *Deut.* iii. 1, and yet its interpolation is obligatory to make sense.

Indifferent to either reading, I will merely mention that three new and distinct translations of Genesis, by eminent Hebraists (Glaire's, Cahen's, and De Sola's), read, "Nimrod went *to* Ashur (Assyria)" — that this last vindicates such explanation by unanswerable arguments, while most of them quote high scholarship in its favor; and, finally, that the Hebraical profundity of "N. M.," who defends this view in *Kitto's Cyclopædia*, is of more Germanic hue, and consequently deeper in Hebrew, if not perhaps in "geological" lore, than that of "J. P. S.," who opposes it. *Non nostrum tantas componere lites:* which future cuneiform discoveries alone can settle.—G. R. G.]

The probable ideas of the constructor of Xth Genesis on NMRD, may now be summed up: —

1st. That *Nimrod* was an affiliation of K*h*aM (Egypt?), swarthy, or *red*, race of mankind, through KUS*hite*, Arabian, lineage.

2d. That, unlike every other proper name, after "Shem, Ham, and Japheth," in Xth Genesis, each of which is a geographico-ethnological personification, NMRD is an *individual;* the only one in the whole chapter. Whether an actual hero, or a mythological personage, cannot be gathered from the text.

3d. That, whether "great in the chase" or not, neither Nimrod's *name* nor his deeds, nor any thing in Scripture, justifies our assumption that the writer of Xth Genesis did not entertain high respect for Nimrod's memory: on the contrary,

4th. This writer distinguishes NMRD from all his geographical compeers, as prominent "before IeHOuaH."

5th. That *Nimrod* was positively the earliest "great-landed-proprietor" known to the writer of Xth Genesis; who ascribes to NMRD the foundation of eight of the proudest cities along the Euphrates and Tigris—*Babel, Erech, Accad, Chalne, Nineveh, Rehoboth-Aïr, Kalah*, and *Resen.*

6th. And, finally, that the practical writer of Xth Genesis is innocent of the sin of causing those incomprehensible delusions about NMRD, which, commencing with Josephus's hypotheses, only 1800 years ago, pervade all biblical literature at the present day.

Two inferences might, however, be drawn from the said writer's peculiarities: — One, that the document, being *Jehovistic*, belongs to a later age than that immediately after Joshua; earlier than which, as shown further on, the mention of *Canaanitish* expulsions renders it archæologically impossible to place the writer: — the other is, that the writer not only was better informed upon *Babylonish* traditions than (to judge by his silence) upon those of other countries, but that he derived pleasure from the elevation of the former above the rest. Would not this imply *Chaldæan* authorship?

Now, whether Nimrod was originally a demigod, a hero, or a "hunting-giant;" whether, under such appellative, lie associations with Ninus, Belus, or Orion; or (were we to "travel out of the record," what we should first examine), whether he was not another form of the *Assyrian* Hercules, to be added to those so skilfully illustrated by Raoul-Rochette—these are speculations foreign to our subject, and we refrain from their present obtrusion.

The compiler of Xth Genesis, whose meaning we strive to comprehend, was satisfied to ascribe to NMRD the foundation of four *Babylonish* and four *Assyrian* cities; and, although the positions of some of these eight are not yet so positively fixed as might be desired, they group together in Mesopotamian vicinities; and thus the last affiliation of KUS*h* becomes placed in Asia—further removed from African "Ethiopia" than the whole, or any, of his geographical brethren.[609]

"Affiliations of the MTsRIM," or *Egyptians*.

27. לודים — LUDIM — 'LUDIM.'

We have already seen that *Mitsraïm*, read according to the Masorete punctuation, is a dual referable to the "Two Egypts," Upper and Lower; but, stript of the points which, after all, are but recent and arbitrary embellishments, that MTsRIm is a plural, meaning the *Miss'rites*, or the Egyptians.

The writer of Xth Genesis, therefore, in his system of ethnic geography, deemed these personified off-shoots from *Egypt* to be so many colonies or emigrations from that principal stock; and as such, we perceive that he suffixes to each name the plural termination IM; thereby testifying that he never foresaw modern assumptions in King James's version, that the LUDs, the AāNMs, the LHBs, &c., should have been *men;* one yclept Lud, another Anam, and so forth.

As grand-children of KheM (*Ham*), the hoary ithyphallic divinity of Egypt, these outstreams class themselves under the generic denomination of *Hamitic* families; and their habitats ought naturally to be sought for in regions contiguous to their ascribed focus of primitive radiations: without disregarding either, that the writer of Xth Genesis, by making them *cousins* of Palestinic *Kanaanites*, and of Arabian KUS*hites* (all issues from the same *Hamite* source), never supposed that they were, or could ever become, *Nigritian* races: upon which last "Type of Mankind" he, as well as every other writer in the Old Testament, observes the same judicious silence manifested throughout the Text towards *Tungouses*, *Esquimaux*, *Caribs*, *Patagonians*, *Papuans*, *Oceanians*, *Malays*, *Chinese*, and other human races; the discovery of whose terrestrial existence appertains to centuries posterior to the closure of the Hebrew canon, Xth Genesis inclusive, at some period not earlier than Alexander the Great, B. C. 332; nor posterior to B. C. 130, when the LXX translations were probably complete at Alexandria.

Hence, to judge by existing nomenclatures of tribes and places, LUD appears both on the Asiatic and Libyan flanks of lower Egypt. Thus, on the Syrian frontier, a few miles east of Yaffa, lay the site of *Loud*, Lydda, Diospolis; inhabited afterwards by Benjamites. So also Arabico-*Berber* traditions comprise the LaOUT*ah* among Sabian tribes of Yemen, reputed to have immigrated into Barbary. But, whether as exotics or *terrægeniti*, it is on the Libyan side of the Nile, prolonged on the southwestern littoral of the Mediterranean to the Atlantic — districts cut off through the absence of *camels* during primordial ages and by Saharan wastes, from contact with Nigritian families of remote austral latitudes — that the LUD*im* have left memorials of ancient occupancy.

Michælis long ago corrected Bochart, and suggested the probabilities that the *Luday*, situate near the river *Laud*, in Tingitana, were the *Ludim:* latterly confirmed by Gräberg de Hemso; who shows that the *Oluti*, *Oloti*, *Louat*, exist among Amazirgh tribes in those Mauritanian neighborhoods to this day; still admitting, too, the national prefix *ait*, "sons of," to their names (like Mac, Fitz, O', Ap, among ourselves), as they did of yore, when the Carthaginian Amon registered in his Periplus the *Ait-o-*LUD, "sons of Lud," or *Aitoloti;* resident in the same Barbaresque vicinities where the *Ludayas* of Spanish writers are now succeeded by the *Beni*-LOUD. There is no lack of vestiges of primeval LUDs to be met with in the very regions where analogy would lead us to look for them: and it is surprising that high authorities have altogether overlooked the facts.

[My former "Excursus (in *Otia Ægyptiaca*) on the origin of some of the *Berber* tribes of Nubia and Libya," suggested a ventilation of some disregarded ethnological data, preparatory to that of Xth Genesis, which, after five years' suspension, I am now endeavoring to accomplish. I then submitted authorities on two grand divisions of *Barbaresques* — a noun not derived from *Barbari*, barbarians, but from the aboriginal African name of BRBR — the *Shillouhs*, and the T-*Amazirgh* or Amazirgh-T; both readily traceable through the *Mazices*, *Macii*, &c., of Latin authors, back to the Μαζυες of Herodotus. — G. R. G.]

To render perspicuous the view we take of Barbaresque anthropology, it would be necessary to enlarge here upon generalities before scrutinizing each genesiacal name in detail; but space being wanting, we must curtail our MS. investigations.

Two human families, the *Shillouhs* and the *Mazirghs*, now called *Berbers*, have lain, either aboriginally or from antiquity beyond record, scattered from the Cyrenaica and oases west of Egypt, athwart the northwest face of Africa to the *Moghreb-el-Aksa*, or extremest west, of Marocchine territories on the Atlantic; and formerly even to the *Guanches*, now extinct in the Canary Isles. Estimated by Gräberg de Hemso at four millions of population in Morocco alone, these *Berber* families present differences as well as resemblances comparable to those visible between the *French* and the *Belgians*: they speak dialects of the old "lingua Atalantica," subdivided into *Berber* and *Shilha*; and intermarrying rarely between themselves, have also imbibed little or no alien blood through amalgamation with others.

Anciently they occupied exclusively that Atalantic zone of oases, littoral or inland, which lies between the Sahara deserts and the Mediterranean; now called *Barbary*; "Land of BERBERS," *Berberia*: and the remoteness of their residence along that tract so far surpasses historical negation, that geology alone may decide whether the *Berbers* can have witnessed those epochas when the now-arid Sahara was an inland sea. In any case, we may suppose that, in proportion as its salt-lacustrine barriers to communication with Nigritian plateaux became desiccated, the *Berber* tribes, driven from the coast by Punic, Kanaanitish, Greek, Egyptian, and other early invaders, spread themselves southwards; and, whilst their former invaders have been replaced by successive Roman, Vandal, Saracenic, Ottoman, and French establishments, that they themselves gradually crossed the Sahara; and now, under the name of *Tuaricks*, some offshoots of this main Atalantic stock, modified by the facilities such passage has afforded them of possessing *Negresses* in their hareems, roam along both banks of the Niger and around Lake Tchad.

But the southerly expansion of *Berber* families, except in partial and conjectural instances, is bounded chronologically by one great fact, overlooked though it be by most writers; which is, that, until the *camel* was introduced into Barbary from Arabia, the Saharan wilderness presented obstacles to nomadism almost insurmountable. Now, the *camel* was not imported into Barbary until Ptolemaic times. Mentioned in hieroglyphics only as a foreigner, and never used by the Pharaonic Egyptians, the earliest historical appearance of *camels* in Africa dates in the first century B. C. The vulgar notion of camel-diffusion over Barbary before the Ptolemies, is nowadays archæologically erroneous.[610]

It therefore follows that, whenever Xth Genesis was compiled, the Barbaresque affiliations of the MTsR*i*m could not have penetrated to the latitude of *Negro* races, south of the Sahara, by any other route than up the Nile — *Negroes* never having existed, in a state of nature, north of the limit of *tropical rains*. This long journey was not undertaken by the powerful MTsR*i*m themselves much before the XIIth dynasty, about B. C. 2300: so that the LUD*i*m, for example, like all their uncivilized brethren, driven away from the Nile by the Egyptians; restricted from southerly progress by the Sahara and the absence of *camels*, from northerly by the Mediterranean and the absence of ships (*Berber* habits being the reverse of nautical, and Tyrian privateersmen hovering on those coasts); were, down to Ptolemy Soter, B. C. 320 (as the utmost antiquity), confined in their nomadisms within Barbary between Egypt and the Atlantic littoral of Morocco. The lowest historical age possible for the compilation of Xth Genesis attains to the *Esdraic school*—the earliest (if the document be *Chaldaic*) may antedate Ezra by some centuries: but, logically, the more remote the antiquity claimed for this ethnic geographical chart, the less possible, physically, becomes intercourse between *Berber* tribes (athwart the Sahara and without *camels*) and the true Negro races of Central Africa.

Content with offering this dilemma, we pass onwards, and remark, that the *Berbers* were generically termed *Mauri* by the Romans, and *Moors* by "moyen age" writers; whilst, if we adopt Egypt as the geographical pivot of eccentric radiations, we shall find, that these Mauritanian *Berbers* on the west are to the *Egyptians* what we have shown the Arabian *Kushites* to be on the east, viz., "gentes subfusci coloris"; ÆTHIOPIANS, in its Homeric sense of sun-*burned-faces*. All of them were possibly distinguished by the *red* color on Nilotic monuments; and the term *Hamitic* would be, genesiacally, ethnologically, and geographically, the best designation for these races; were it not for modern *Negro* theories, which ignorance and charlatanism have foisted upon that mystified name we now spell "Ham." "One almost blushes," Agassiz has sarcastically observed, "to state, that the Fathers of the Church, in Northern Africa, have even more recently been quoted as evidence of the high intellectual and moral developments of which the *Negro* race is supposed to be capable, and that the monuments of Egypt have been referred to with the same view. But, we ask, have men who do not know that Egypt and Northern Africa have never been inhabited by Negro tribes, but always by nations of the Caucasian race, any right to express an opinion on this question?"

[Five years ago, Luke Burke's *Ethnological Journal*, and the writer's *Otia Ægyptiaca*, pointed out several analogies between some names of twenty-five *Berber* tribes mentioned by Ebn Khaledoon, and various other ethnic cognomina preserved by the writer of Xth Genesis. The former are certainly reliable, inasmuch as Ebn Khaledoon was a *Berber* himself and the historian of his nation: who contests their common descent from such legendary sources as Abraham, Goliath, Amelek, Afrikis, Himyar, and other fabulous origins; claiming, however, that the *Berbers* "descend from KESLOUJIM (Casluhim), son of MITZRAIM, son of HAM." So, also, through Mohammedan harmonizing, we meet, in the "*Rozit ul Suffa*," with a similar example of pious genealogical frauds—"God bestowed on Ham nine sons: *Hind*, *Sind*, *Zenj*, *Nowbo*, *Kanaan*, *Kush*, *Kopt*, *Berber*, and *Habesh!*"

It will be seen, further on, that the CASLUHIM undoubtedly dwelt in Barbary when Xth Genesis was written, as their descendants do "unto this day;" but it need scarcely be insisted upon, with the reader of these pages, that Ebn Khaledoon, an Arabicized Berber, no less than a most learned and conscientious Muslim, naturally felt anxious to connect his own pedigree with that of the genesiacal Patriarchs, to him rendered orthodox and respectable through the *Korân:* and the fact that, overlooking the Hebrew plural terminations, he deemed KESLOUDJIM (the *Shillouhs!*) to be a man, son of MITSRAIM (the *Egyptians!*), another individual, indicates his literary sources; while it serves to illustrate what we have maintained elsewhere, viz.: that the *Berbers* (their own indigenous traditions being unrecorded) appropriated instead the language and religious ideas of their civilizers, the Arabs; who certainly, when the *Korân* was composed, had never taken *Berber* origins into consideration.

Nevertheless, this sentimental bias of Ebn Khaledoon does not touch the archæological fact gained from his pages that, in his time, the LAOUTE are recorded, as one of twenty-five *Berber* tribes then inhabiting Barbary.

"Six hundred lineages of *Berbers*"—the enumeration of Marmol and of Leo Africanus—resolved themselves, about the fifteenth century of our era, into *five* main stems; who, already imbued with longings after Islamite respectabilities, *said* that their progenitors were Sabæans of Yemen: at the same time Leo adds the noteworthy remark, "*subfusci coloris sunt.*" The same quintuple division reappears in the "quinquegentani *Barbari*" of Roman writers of the fourth century; which is important, because it establishes an identical quinary repartition of *Berbers* prior to Mohammedan impressions; and, although it does not contradict, this fact renders it less likely that pagans or semi-Christians should have leaned towards an Arabian origin, before religious motives for such honorary attribution existed in *Berber* minds. To trace whence *Barbari*, or *Berbers*, from about 1400 years ago, through the "Misulani *Sabarbares*, Massylii" of Pliny; the *Sabouboures* of Ptolemy; and possibly, in some instances, the BARBAROI of Strabo, Diodorus, and Herodotus: to resolve the *Zilia, Zilca, Zelis, Salinsi, Zilzactæ, Massyli, Xilohes*, into the Μασσαιλιβυες = AMAZIG-*Libyans*, or the *Massæsylli* into AMAZIG-*Shillouhs;* and then to deduce the *Amazirghs* of the present day from the Μαζυες of Herodotus, B. C. 430: — these are tasks which, following chiefly Castiglione, have been already executed.

History, philology, and analogy unite, therefore, in establishing that the T-*Amazirghs*, or real *Berbers*, distinct in that day from Asiatics or Negroes, existed, about the fifth century B. C., in their own land of *Berberia*, now called Barbary. With the exception of their having embraced Islàm; exchanged the bow, for which they were celebrated long before that age, for the musket; added the *camel* to the horse; and appropriated *Arabic* words to make up for deficiencies in their native vocabulary; the *Berbers* of Mt. Atlas are precisely the same people now that they were twenty-five centuries ago; dwelling in the same spots, speaking the same tongues, and called by the same names, as we shall see presently.

We are now prepared to accept an opinion pronounced by a man of science eminently qualified to judge; which, coupled with Forster's attestation [*supra*, p. 483] of the indelibility of *color* as a criterion of type, when we recall how all *Berbers* "subfusci coloris sunt," ought to possess sufficient weight.

There is but one veritably indigenous race in Barbary, says Bodichon; viz., the GÆTULIAN?—"Ainsi, Atlantes, Atarantes, Lotophages, Occidentaux, Troglodytes, Maurusiens, Maures, Pharusiens, Garamantes, Augéliens, Psylles, Libyens, même Canariens, et toute cette multitude de peuples à qui les anciens donnent l'Afrique septentrionale pour patrie, se confondent en une seule et même race, la GÉTULIENNE." The Arabs, foreigners in Barbary, call the present descendants of this race "*Berbers* and *Kabyles*." Indeed, as tillers of the soil, *i. e.*, as human animals brought into direct contact with the *earth* of Barbary (rank with exhalations so mortiferous, even now, to Europeans), no type of humanity could have outlived, not to say flourished amid, the climatic and geological conditions of Atalantic Africa, but a few furlongs from the sea-beach, except the *Gætulian*. For proofs, read Dr. Boudin's *Lettres sur l'Algérie*.

Cut off from escape on the west by the ocean; on the north by the Mediterranean; on the south by the Sahara (once a sea also), and, until the Christian era, by the absence of *camels;* and on the east by the MTsRIM; these "quinquegentani *Berberi*" have survived the extinction of the *elephant*, together with the depressions of temperature consequent upon the destruction of their primeval forests: and, repugnant through natural constitution to any alien institutions but those of the *Koràn* (construed after their own liberal fashion), they remain now, what they were at their unknown era of creation, *Gætulians*, and nothing else.

Inquire of history.

Phœnicia planted her standards at the Carthaginian ports she occupied: Greece built her strongholds on the littoral of the Cyrenaica: Rome, prostrating all, sent her eagles further into Africa than any Europeans: Persia inscribed her westernmost tablet at Tripoli: Byzantium, after Belisarius's triumph, has been obliterated, even in name: Vandals, massacred in detail, or extinguished by climate more murderous to white races than Numidian arrows, have vanished, physiologically, like other heterogeneous foreigners on the sea-board: Ottoman and Frank invaders still surround their temporary havens with bastions strongest towards the mainland; and French prowess over the *Berber* race is confined to the latter's preparations for the next *razzia*. The *Saracens* alone, themselves "gentes subfusci coloris;" apostles of a genial polygamous religion;

speaking dialects of a tongue long familiar to *Berberic* ears through anterior Punic intercourse: — the *Arabs*, I repeat, cognate with the *Berbers* in nomadic restlessness and social habits, have ridden over the *Gætulians*, through them, and around them: but whilst from the first hour, A. D. 644, that the lances of Islâm penetrated into *Berberia*, the wise policy of its Arabian votaries associated the native *Berbers* in spoils and benefits mutually agreeable; the *Arab* himself, after twelve centuries of Barbaresque sojourn, has become far more *Berberized* as a MOGHRABEE than the *Berbers* have been *Arabicized*. And (asks the reader) what is the "ultima ratio" of all these successive influences upon mankind's Atlantic *type?*

Merely this: — that wherever the *Gætulian* has not (he has in Morocco) revindicated his national supremacy, he rather tolerates Arab encampments in the domains of his birth-right, than hospitably welcomes Arabian presence by practical fusion. "Mohammed" is their moral bond of Barbaresque unity — their common battle-cry. Implacable detestation of *Turks* and *Frenchmen* is the only chord of sympathy between Âbd-el-Kàder (*slave* of the *Puissant*), the heroic and betrayed *Shemite*, and that mulatto-cross between Arabico-Berbers and Negresses, exhibited in a beastly individuality called "the Emperor of *Morocco*." Hatred to aliens — to anybody but one of themselves, a *Berber* — is still the banner of *Gætulian* instincts.

If, then, Gætulian populations cannot have originated through imaginary importations of *Negroes* from the interior of Africa, nor from imaginary colonizations of *white* races from Europe, whence came they?

History being impartially silent, our alternative lies between *Arabian* immigrations as one possibility, and the autocthonous creation of *Berbers* for Barbary as the other. My own inquiries lend no support to the scientific probabilities of the former contingency. The latter it is not my province to discuss. — G. R. G.]

Viewing, therefore, *Gætulian* families as "une race apart," we proceed to ascertain their relation to the chart of Xth Genesis.

Their present name is *Berbers* in Mauritania, and *Shillouhs* towards the Cyrenaica.

In Ebn Khaledoon's "History of the *Berbers*," we have already noticed that one tribe of this race was called LAOUTE, or LAOUTEH. Cutting off the Arabic plural termination, there remains LAOUT; which, reduced to its simplest expression, vowels being vague, is LUT, or LUD; an appellative, as we have shown, traceable in Barbaresque nomenclatures at all times, back to where history is lost.

In Xth Genesis, the eldest-born of the affiliations of the MTsRim (or Egyptians), and who, therefore, in the idea of the writer, issued first and went furthest from the supposed parental hive, are the LUDIM. Removing the Hebrew plural suffix IM, there remains LUD. All commentators unite in deeming *Barbary* the geographical sphere of these emigrations.

To have shown that the Laouteh, LUDs, of Ebn Khaledoon, can be no others than the Ludim, LUDs, of Xth Genesis, is likewise to prove that *Gætulian* families are included in that ancient system of geography, and that the LUDIM probably occupied *Mauritania*. A conclusion which our inquiries into the habitats of their fraternal affiliations will fortify. In the meanwhile, we rejoice to learn from Gräberg de Hemso that the *Ludaya* tribe still furnishes the Sultan's body-guard in Morocco, and that their river Tagassa is yet called *Laud* and *Thaluda;* at the same time, that it is satisfactory to find such scholarship as Quatremère's sustaining how, "Dans les Loudés de Moïse, je reconnais la grande nation des *Lewata*, la plus puissante des tribus de race Berbère;" and thus ratifying our views upon the LUD*im* of Xth Genesis.[611]

28. ענמים — AâNMIM — 'ANAMIM.'

Of course, this is a tribe which (plural termination IM cut off) was called AâNM.

Viewed as *Aânams* the analogies falter, unless we adopt Bochart's speculative idea, that the Semitic word for *sheep*, GNM, be the root of this name. The *Num*-idians,

Nomades, have also furnished comparisons; which we dispute not, because it is in Barbary that commentators locate the people called ANM*ìm*.

Referring the reader to the "causes of verbal obscurity" in Oriental names, ably set forth by Forster and De Saulcy, there are few literal permutations more frequent than those of M and N: and hence it has been long remarked, that ANM is but an anagrammatic form of AMN. Under such view, the AMN-*ìm* become at once *Amonians;* and, from the ancient worshippers of the Egyptian deity AMN-*Kneph*, or NUM, at the "Oasis of Ammon" (now *Seewah*); through the *Nasamonitis*, *Nasamones;* to the *Amonians*, or the *Garamantes*, whether on the river Cinyphus near Tripoli, or on the *Gir;* the transition is more rapid than the results may appear precise.

Castiglione gives solid reasons why the *Macæ-Ammonii*, or *Macæ-Amnii*, should refer to Amazirgh-Ammonians; which term he supposes became in Greek mouths *Mes-ammones*, and thence *Nas-ammones*. Hence, the ANM*ìm* would naturally take their places among *Berber* tribes next to the LUDs, their kinsfolk.

The *Nasamones* of Herodotus and of later writers, read by Birch *Nahsu*-Amonians (*Negro*-Amonians?), were a very roving predatory race; who carried their name all over Barbary: but, without insisting upon any one family in whose name AMN is a component, it is for objectors, after perusing what follows, to show that the Barbaresque Anamim of Xth Genesis, cannot be represented by some offshoot of the *Gætulian* stem yet stretching between the Sahara and the Mediterranean.

For ourselves, while descrying the *Anamìm* in the *Berber* tribe of "*Enine*," catalogued by Ebn Khaledoon, we suggest that AâNM may underlie both the words "Nasamones" and "Numidians;" and this for a reason that no Orientalist acquainted with hieroglyphical permutations will disregard. Bunsen, following Ewald, proposed to read the name GUB, *Chub* [which nation Ezekiel (xxx. 5) associates with "KUS*h*, and *Phut* (Barbary) and *Lud*ìm (the *Ludayas*, as shown above, No. 27) and all the mingled people,"] as if such name had been written GNUB; and thence to apply it to *Nubia* — a country, we have proved, altogether unmentioned by Hebrew writers. Volney had perceived GUB in the Barbaresque *Cobbii* of Ptolemy, and we adopt his view as by far more natural, according to the context of Ezekiel. Nevertheless, Bunsen's very just remark of the frequent suppression of the N before G or K, in the transfer of Hamitic into Semitic proper names (*ex. gr.*, SHESHONK, *Shishak*), allows us to behold the âNuM of AâNM-IM in the GNUM-*idians* of classical history. If, however, with Bochart, we transcribe the Greek Νασαμονες into Hebrew letters, נשי אמ-ן; NàSI AM-N, or otherwise NàSI-ANuM-*ìm*; we observe that *Nàs* means "people" in Semitish tongues, and thereby such compound name becomes, in English, "*People* of NUM*idia*;" or else, "*People* of (the oasis of) AMoN:" in either case, the *Anamìm* of Xth Genesis.

But Bochart declared that these tribes were "Solinus's *Amantes*, and Pliny's *Hammanientes*, peoples beyond the Greater Syrtis;" and, reminding us that גר, GaR, means "to inhabit," he discloses at once the famed "*Garamantes* near to the fountains of the river Cyniphus." Now, let us add that this river is still called the *Gir*, or *Gar*, by living descendants of these very *Amantes*, who once were the Berber AâMaN-IM alluded to by the ancient Hebrew geographer.[612]

29. להבים — LHBIM — 'LEHABIM.'

The first orthodox English work we chanced to open, in quest of etymological meanings, has, "LEHABIM, *flames; or, which are inflamed;* or, *the points of a sword!*" and just below, "LIBYA, in Hebrew Lubim, *the heart of the sea;* or, *a nation that has a heart!*"

Let us seek elsewhere. Detaching the plural IM, through which the writer of Xth Genesis indicates that he means a *tribe*, the singular number of whom is LHB, we realize instantaneously how ignorant of Hebrew were the forty-seven translators of King James's version. This may be at once seen by their writing "Mizraim begat Ludim, and Anamim," &c., instead of "*the Luds and the Anams*" and so forth. Had they even suspected that IM was already a plural termination, they would not have *doubled* it by printing "Cherubims" for *Cherubs*, or "Seraphims" for *Seraphs!* What should we think of the French scholarship of a person who wrote *tableauxes?*

That these people were *Libyans* no commentator now doubts, although Bochart dissents; and that in LHB, the soft aspirate *he*, H, may be equivalent to such vowels as *a*, *e*, *i*, *o*, *u*, no palæographer will contest: nor that the LUB*im* of 2 *Chron.* (xii. 3; xvi. 8), of Nahum (iii. 9), and of Daniel (xx. 43), are the same as the LHB*im;* especially in Nahum's text, where a conjunction couples them to P*h*UT; already shown to have been a generic appellative for the whole of Barbary.

Λιβύη of the Homeric Greeks possessed a wider territorial extension than the *Libya* of the Romans; the former signifying Barbary in general; the latter the coast from Egypt to the Greater Syrtis: hence we may infer that the more precise information of Roman geographers rested upon better acquaintance with the localities where the LHBs were domiciled. T-LIBI is the homonyme in Coptic MSS; but perhaps in a sense restricted to tribes on the immediate west of the Nile's alluvium; which also suggests the easternmost limit of Libyan encampments.

Among the *Berber* tribes enumerated by Ebn Khaledoon occur the LeWaTaH; which word in Oriental palæography is the same as LeHaB-*atah;* and its analogies with LeHaB-*im* are salient. Arab tradition invests the present *Beni*-LeWA, of Amazirgh stock, with sufficient correspondences to resolve all these appellatives into the Λευάθαι, Λεβαυθαι, of Procopius, about the sixth century B. C.; not forgetting the *Languantan* of Corippus.

Any one investigating such subjects, without preconceptions, will recognise in the LHB*s* of Xth Genesis a nomadic population of *Gætulian* race, and of Barbaresque habitats.[613]

30. נפתחים — NP*h*T*t*K*h*IM — 'Naphtuhim.'

Before commencing analyses that arise through new resuscitations of Egyptology, it is desirable to remind the reader of a principle that governs our philological inquiries into 10th Genesis. Extremely simple, it is still, even where known, more or less disregarded by rabbinical writers.

The genesiacal writer's classification of nations is tripartite, under the titular headings "Shem, Ham, and Japheth;" and his lists, therefore, embrace *Semitic*, *Hamitic*, and *Japethic* families; corresponding [*supra*, pp. 85, 86] to the *yellow*, the *red*, and the *white* colors given by Egyptian ethnographers to such varieties of man as were known to them about the sixteenth century B. C.: but the Hebrew map excludes the *Negro;* which race, the fourth in the quadripartite ethnography of Thebes, is, on the monuments, painted *black*.

Arabian languages are necessarily represented in the proper names of nations belonging to the *Semitic* stock; the Egyptian "sacred tongue" is the most ancient and reliable nucleus for those of the *Hamitic;* while those of the *Japethic*, almost a distinct world, must belong either to the *Indo-Germanic* or to the *Scythic* class of human idioms.

To suppose that the "speech of *Kanaan*" (misnamed *Hebrew*) can answer the purpose of an "open Sessame" to the significations of all proper names in Xth Genesis, which the writer himself has carefully segregated from each other into *three* groups of tongues, spoken by *three* groups of humanity (in his day as in ours, from each other entirely distinct), is one of those aberrations that no educated person of our generation would be likely to boast of; if he reflected that, in considering *Hebrew* as a fitting key to any thing more than to one, the *Semitic*, of these three linguistic portals, he would be as great a dolt as if he sustained that *English* might be contained in a Chinese radical or in a Mandingo root.

No philologist at the present day, when he beholds in Xth Genesis the proper name NP*h*T*t*K*h*IM, would seek for its explanation in a Hebrew vocabulary; because a proper name belonging to the *Hamitic* group of languages ought first to be examined within the sphere of its own positive domiciliations; and it is only when these are wanting, or when comparative philology is the investigator's object, that speculative analogies of such an antique cognomen may be hunted for in the modern Arabic *Qamôos*, or other Shemitish lexicon.

NP*h*T*t*K*h*IM is a plural, of which the singular expression is NP*h*T*t*K*h*.

In Coptic days, according to authentic MSS., the western skirts of Lower Egypt, on the south of Lake Mareotis, *Marea, Mariout*, were called NIFAIAT; whence, deducting the plural prefix, NI, we obtain FAIAT as the Coptic vocalization of the hieroglyphical root F-T; or P*h*eT, meaning a *bow;* as we explained under the head P*h*UT. The occupants of these localities, along the desert ridges from *Marea* to *Ptiminhor* (now *Damanhoor*) spoke a *Berber* dialect, and not pure Egyptian; in this, resembling the inhabitants of the nearest oasis, that of Ammon, or Seewah, who, already in the time of Herodotus, 430 B. C., were a mixed "colony of Egyptians and *Ethiopians*," *i. e.*, *sun-burned*-faces; "subfusci coloris," like all *Berber* derivations. We have settled that the preceding affiliations of the MTsR*îm* occupied parts of Barbary, and belonged to branches of the great *Gætulian* trunk. We shall see that others of the Hamitic brethren did so likewise. What, then, more natural than to find, on the western flank of MT*s*R (Egypt) herself, the NIPHAIAT nomads of that race, speaking their national tongue, the *Berber?*

As usual, Champollion was the first to carry back the NIPHAIAT of Coptic Christian literature to the ancient Pharaonic monuments; confirmed by Rosellini, Peyron, &c., and since universally accepted by Egyptologists as designations of *Libya* and *Libyans*. But, without doubting in the least the Barbaresque application of the word, whether in its Coptic or in its hieroglyphical form, the original name P*h*-T-*kah* sometimes occurs in the singular number, "Bow-country," or plural "Nine-bow-country." Now, the same distinction holds in Xth Genesis, where P*h*UT refers to Barbary as a whole; and NP*h*T*t*K*h*IM, in which the same radical P*h*T is preserved, to *tribes* of the same Hamitic stock. May we not assign "Bow-country" to PHUT, and "Nine-bow-country" to the others? With this reservation, Hengstenberg is right in seizing upon *Niphaiat* as the probable representative of "Naphtuchim." It is easy to prove this identity. The Masorete punctuation, through which *Naphtoukhîm* is its present phonetism, commands no reverence; being merely the rabbinical intonation, in the sixth and later centuries after Christ, of a *foreign* proper name antedating them, and the writer of Xth Genesis himself, by unnumbered ages. All that science can now accept are the six letters — NP*h*T*t*K*h*IM.

The hieroglyphical root is P*h*-T; the later Copts added the medial vowels, and it became P*h*aiaT: to make it an Egyptian plural, the NI, or N, was prefixed, and NI-P*h*aiaT, thus formed, is simply *the*-P*h*aiaT-s — the proper name, as above shown, of a *Berber* tribe on the western frontier of Lower Egypt. But, Champollion's *Grammaire* tells us how, "in the graphical system, as in the Egyptian spoken tongue, the plural number (of nouns) was expressed by the *désinences* or terminations" — OU, or U: so that, Egyptologically, the name must have been orthographed NI-P*h*aiaTU. Such was the word that presented itself to the researches of the compiler of Xth Genesis, when he classified the MTsR*ite* "affiliations of K*h*aM, after their families, after their *tongues*, in their countries, in their nations" (*Gen.* x. 20). We have only to take the *square-letters* which the later Jews substituted for his own (unknown) calligraphy, and, inserting the omitted vowels, write them below the older Egyptian form — thus,

Ni-P*h*aiaTU,
Ni-P*h*aiaT*t*-uK*h*-IM,

to perceive that this diligent writer (not being conversant, unhappily, with Nilotic syntaxis) has suffixed the Hebrew plural, IM, to a proper name, NIPHAIATU, that was already in its indigenous *plural* form when it reached the chorographic bureau of Jerusalem or Babylon. Hence the following conclusions: —

1st. That *Egyptian* tongues and writings are older than Hebraical transformations of the name *Niphaiatu*.

2d. That the people *Niphaiatu* existed before Xth Genesis was written.

3d. That the Hebrew chorographer must have been unacquainted with the first elements of *Hamitic* tongues; else he could not have appended his own *Semitic* plural, IM, to a foreign name that was already pluralized by its national prefix NI, and suffix.U — a blunder to be paralleled in English by the vulgar *Cockneyism* of "post-'ses" for *posts*.

4th. That, as a consequence, the principle laid down at the beginning of this section, of examining *Hamitic*, *Shemitish*, and *Indo-Germanic* names by their respective languages, is both rational and useful.

But, the less "inspiration" that is required for the construction of an ethnic chart, the more admirable becomes the human skill and knowledge which, its antiquity considered, compiled such an excellent synopsis of the *nations* existing within the geographical horizon of its day.

The long-chased families of the NiP*h*aiaT*t*U-*kh*-(IM) have been *earthed*, at last, where Bochart indicated his "Naphtuhæi": viz., around Mareotic provinces on the confines of the MTsRIM, or Egyptians. They spoke *Berber* dialects, like the rest of their Barbaresque brethren; and may be safely assumed as ranking among the easternmost representatives of the great *Gætulian* race.

Nor are their vestiges wanting either in Arabic or in classical geographies. The twelfth tribe catalogued by Ebn Khaledoon is that of the NeP*h*USeH. T and S being palæographically identical, here is the Arabicized form of the same word, precisely; with its plural termination *e*H, in lieu of IM. The same name reappears in the sixth century of our era, and therefore before Arab invasions, in the *Nefusa*, or *Navusi*, of the Latin poet Corippus. And, to back assertions with authority, one of the greatest living Orientalists of France, Quatremère, while commenting on this passage of Xth Genesis, records: "Les *Naftouhis* répondent, je crois, à une des tribus Berbères, celle des *Nafzah*, ou celle des *Nafousah*."[614]

31. פתרסים — PT*t*RSIM — 'PATHRUSIM.'

Again stands before us an *Hamitic* word, and again we apply to it our rules of dissection; after lopping away the excrescent Hebrew IM, and thereby restoring this name to its native simplicity — PT*t*RS.

Orthodox lexicography reveals to an inquirer how the PATHROS mentioned by Ezekiel (xxix. 14; xxx. 14) means a 'mouthful of dew,' or 'persuasion,' or 'dilatation of ruin'!

The wonted acuteness of Bochart, two centuries ago, perceived that *Pathros*, a district in the Thebaid, would answer very well to the exigenda of PT*t*RS; and the Coptic researches of Champollion and Peyron established that the western side of the Nile, at Thebes, bore the names of *Patoures* (Phaturites), *Tathyrites*, *Pathurés*, and *Phatrous:* probably orthographed better by Parthey in *Papithourès*, because the name of *Thebes*, "P-API," as the "T*h*o-ReeS," south-land, is preserved in it. But with all deference, and without absolutely denying that the compiler of Xth Genesis may have meant *Pathros* in the Thebaid as the site of his PT*t*RS*im*, we cannot assent to such inference, for the following reason: —

"Dato il caso, e non concesso," that Moses, in the fourteenth century B. C., was the compiler of this chart — and orthodoxy itself claims no date more ancient — the MTsR*im* in that age, the XIXth dynasty, had been spread over the Nile's alluvium, for above 2000 years, "from *Migdol* to the Tower of Syene," and far more australly soon after the XIIth dynasty. Consequently, they had left to any people but themselves nothing but the *deserts* on either flank of the alluvials to roam along. *Pathros* was merely a suburban district in the "nome" of Thebes, then at the acme of her glory;

so that to construe the general meaning of Xth Genesis into such a paraphrase as, "out of the MTsRIm went forth a colony and founded *Pathros*, whence about the seventieth fraction of all humanity known to the Jews was called PT*t*RSIm," would be like saying (if for Thebes we read London, and French for Hebrew) that "out of the *Englishmen* went forth a colony and built *Waterloo bridge*, whence arose the grand nation called '*Vaterloos*.'" Besides, Wilkinson has critically noted, that *Pathyris*, or *Tathyris*, was so called after the goddess Athyr; and meant "*the* belonging to ATHYR," as the protectress of the western side of Thebes.

The obstacles to such interpretation increase just in the ratio that the compilation of Genesis Xth is brought down to a more historical epoch. It is evident from the context of the whole paragraph on the "affiliations of the MTsRIm," no less than from the ultra-Egyptian areas on which each one of these affiliations is naturally fixed, that such information as the Hebrew writer possessed on the PT*t*RSIm had led him to understand this tribe as extraneous to Egypt; and he did not locate their habitats in Egypt itself, because this country was already appropriated by the MTsRIm. Quatremère, and before him Golius, had perceived the physical impediments to the location of the PT*t*RSIm in upper Egypt: — "Les *Phatrousis* ont été, assez ordinairement, pris pour les habitants de la Thébaïde; mais cette conjecture ne me paraît pas admissible. En effet, Misraïm ayant été le père de l'Égypte inférieure se trouvaient naturellement rangé parmi ces descendants, sans qu'il fût necessaire d'indiquer d'une manière spéciale les habitants de telle ou telle partie de cette contrée. Si je ne me trompe, les *Phatrousis* du récit de Moïse nous representent les *Pharusiens*, qui occupaient une partie de ce qu'on nomme aujourd'hui l'Empire de Maroc."

This identification tallies with our views exactly. In classical geographies the *Pharusii* lie about Mauritania, east of the *Autololes;* and these last are identified with the *Berber* tribes of the AIT-o-LOT, "sons of Lud;" whom we have already proved to have been the genesiacal LUDIm. A Persian origin has been ascribed to the *Pharuses* since the time of Sallust; but probably upon no better authority than accidental resemblance of the word *Phars*, coupled with traditions of Achæmenidan invasions of the Cyrenaica; and its claims have been well contested by Lacroix. To behold the PT*t*SRIm of Xth Genesis in the *Pharusians* of Barbary is obnoxious to no difficulties, beyond the inconvenient presence of the letter T*t*, "tav" in the Hebrew transcription of the name; and this letter may be the old Hamitic *feminine article;* which clings to *Berber* words as tenaciously as "*atl*" does to proper names in Mexican languages. However, it has been shown above that these people must have resided beyond Egyptian territorial limits; and as one of many *brethren* in genesiacal personifications, the major part of whom are unquestionably *Barbaresques*, the PT*t*RSIm must lie to the west of Egypt also; and every reasonable requirement seems fulfilled in the *Pharusii*.

[Albeit, let me revert to a former etymology in "Otia Ægyptiaca;" which, while it does not conflict with a *Pharusian* derivation, exemplifies how a compound *Hamitic* name has become Hebraicized: for, in Berber nomenclature, *Pha*A*Rusians*, *Ma-Rusians*, *Ma* U*Ri*, and their endless Gætulian homonymes, all inflexions preceding the RA, or AUR, are but demonstrative aggregations to that omnific monosyllable; whose birthplace, according to D'Avezac, might lie among the "Divine AUR*itæ*," and whose tomb is not yet constructed in *MA*R*occo!*

The reduction I formerly proposed of PT*t*RSIm was this: — Pi is the universal Hamitic masculine article *the;* T*t* may be T*ho* or To, Coptic and hieroglyphic for *world;* RS, the Coptic RiS and hieroglyphic RiS, meaning the *south;* which connectedly read PiT*to*RiS, *the-world-south*, or "the southern world."

This is a designation appropriate enough to austral populations; and if the PiT*to*RIS-I*m* of Xth Genesis be lineal "affiliations of the MTsRIm," their *name* must be resolvable into Egyptian roots. In any case, the Hebrew writer added his plural IM to a word already formed in Northern Africa centuries before his day. — G. R. G.]

Whilst submitting the above dubious solution as preferable to any dependent upon a spurious *Masora*, we nevertheless consider the *Pharusii* of ancient Barbary to be the true PTtRSîm of Xth Genesis: confirming such opinion by two prophetic passages; 1st—"They of *Phares* (not Persians, but *Pharusii*) and of *Lud* and of *Phut* were in thine army," says *Ezekiel* (xxvii. 10) to the Tyrian masters of Barbary: 2dly, *Isaiah* (xi. 11) proves that he regarded *Pathros* to be a land entirely distinct from Egypt, when he wrote—"from Assyria, and from Egypt, and from PhTtuRiS, and from Cush," &c.[615]

32. כסלחים—KSLKhIM—'Casluhim.'

The ground here becomes less firm than that whereon we travelled in quest of the preceding tribes; not merely owing to the briars planted in our way by commentators, but also from the ambiguity of the text of Xth Genesis itself.

Let us commence by inquiring into the latter. King James's version, verse 14, has: "And Casluhim, (out of whom came Philistim,) and Caphtorim"; the plain English of which is, that a man called *Philistim* issued from another called *Casluhim*. The commas and parentheses being the conjectural punctuation and interpolation of King James's *translators*, we restore the text to its primitive simplicity, as closely as our alien language permits, thus: "And (the) KSLKhIM from whom issued (the) PhLSTt-IM and (the) KPhTtRIM." Of this the plain English is, that two families, the *Philistîm* and the *Kaphtorîm*, issued from the family of the *Kaslukhîm*.

In psychological speculations, it may not be of the slightest consequence whether either of these families did, or both of them did not. Our English Bible, as Taylor, the erudite translator of *Calmet*, declares, after freely acknowledging its manifold misconstructions, "suffices for all purposes of *piety*." But in matters of archæological, and essentially of anthropographical science, the English Bible is less safe than any standard translation of *Homer*, *Herodotus*, *Cicero*, or *Cæsar*; as our "Introduction to Xth Genesis" abundantly shows.

The question whether the *Casluhîm* were the progenitors of one or both families has amply occupied theological pens, rabbinical as well as Christian; but we may mention that Rosenmüller, Cahen, and Glaire, confirm our reading.

Let us endeavor to ascertain the affinities of the *father*-stock—the KSLKhIM. Excepting the Abbé Mignot, followers of the few errors rather than of the many truths of Bochart, had discovered, until latterly, nothing more apposite than that semi-historical Egyptian colony of *Colchians*, planted by one of the Sesostridæ in a section of Mingrelia whence Jason brought the golden fleece. Without doubting the mythico-astronomical basis of the latter event, we summarily dismiss the *Colchians*, as a colony of Egypt, for the very reason given by Herodotus in proof of their extraction: viz., that the former people were "*black* in complexion, and *woolly*-haired," which everybody knows the MTsRIM, or Egyptians, were not.

Now, the "Caucasian" *Egyptians* being impossible procreators for *Negro* Colchians, the former's "children," according to Xth Genesis, cannot have been "woolly-haired *blacks*" either; and, inasmuch as the KSLKhIM were "sons of the MTsRîm," they cannot have been the *Negroes* of Colchis. So we are compelled to look elsewhere.

Five of the affiliations of the Mitsrites—the *Ludîm*, *Aănamîm*, *Lehabîm*, *Nephtukhîm*, and *Pathrusîm*—having already found comfortable homes among Gætulian races in Barbary, it would seem unnatural if the sixth had not left some mementoes of coeval residence in the same regions, between the Sahara and the Mediterranean. Indeed, our *Berber* historiographer, Ebn Khaledoon, has told us [*supra*] that his nation "descends from *Kesloudjîm*," which name is but the Arabicized vocalization of KSLK*h*-*îm*. He, therefore, reputed the latter to be a Barbaresque family; and, in consequence, we proceed to test their appellative by an *Hamitic* touchstone.

Its protogramme K is a difficulty, but one of two explanations will remove it. The first is philological: viz., that all Orientalists know how such articulations as K*h*S, KS*h*, KS, glide into one another accordingly as they are enunciated by different tribes. Thus, in the very name before us, that which the native Berbers and Arabs pronounce *Shillouh*, an exotic Spaniard, Marmol, writes *Xilohes*. The writer of Xth Genesis, transcribing a *foreign* name in the unknown Hebrew alphabet he used, from six to *blank* centuries before the present *square-letter* character (in which we now have his text) was invented,—this Hebrew writer, we now repeat, when he placed a *sameq*, S, immediately after the *kaf*, K, probably meant the two letters to represent a *Berber* intonation of KS. In such case, interpolating vowels, we divide the word into KS*h*iLouK*h*-îm, and writing beneath it .... S*h*iLouH—-*s*, we instantly recognize the SHILLOUHS, one of the grand duplex divisions of *Gœtulian* families; the other being the *Berbers* [*ubi supra*]. In the Egyptian "sacred tongue" and character, such hieroglyphical signs as the "sieve," or the "garden," equally represent KS and SH; and if, according to orthodox interpretation, an individual yclept *Casluhîm* was really *son* of a man called MTsRaIM, the father's vernacular and writing must have regulated the child's baptismal nomen.

The second explanation is archæological; and although less likely, nay superfluous after the preceding remarks, it is submitted as another proof that the speech of the old MTsRIM, not having been the "lingua sancta" of *Shemite* families, serves to effect that which modern *Hebrew* never can aspire to: viz., a rational solution of the *Hamitic* word KSLK*h*.

"Every name determined by the sign KAH . . . is the proper name of a *province* or *country* more or less extended." This is Champollion's law of hieroglyphical writing; and so familiar to anybody who has read an Egyptological work, that one feels ashamed to pile up authorities.

If an ancient hierogrammateus had written the name of a people called *Shillouh*, he would have spelt it S*h*LUK*h*-KAH; that is, SHILLOUH-*country;* the determinative for *country* being inseparable from a geographical term. It is, then, possible that, on exportation to Jerusalem or Babylon where Xth Genesis was edited, the determinative *kah* may have become transposed from the end to the beginning of the word S*h*LK*h*, in order to suit the *Chaldaic* cuneiform system of writing; in which "determinatives" always *precede* the proper name; just as, in English, we usually say *country* of the SHILLOUHS in lieu of SHILLOUH-*country*. We have only now to suppose that a *Chaldæan* original, written in cuneiform, was transcribed by a Hebrew amanuensis into the *old* alphabet of the Jews; and the copies of this transcription recast, about two or three hundred years A. C., into the modern *square-letter* character—all things possible, and the latter event certain—to perceive that the initial K may be the relic of the sign "kah," now incorporated into a name that (supplying the vowels) we might read K*a*h-S*h*iLuKh, *land* of the SHILLOUHS. To which name, inasmuch as the Hebrew writer knew that it referred to a people and not to a man, he added the plural determinative IM, and thus has handed down to us a true signification of *Kasluhîm*, in "country of the SHILLOUHS." Still, we prefer the former explanation, because it is the simplest; and with these new lights continue the inquiry.

The learned Swede, so long Consul-General for his own and the Sardinian government at Tangiers, follows Ebn Khaledoon with his personal corroborative experience, when he deems the *Casluhîm* of Xth Genesis to be no others than the *Shillouhs;* already domiciled in Barbary previously to the intrusion of the first Phœnician colonists: indeed, he favors the opinion that they are autocthones. The conclusions, drawn by this eminent scholar from actual Marocchine observation, derive support from another quarter; nor will Orientalists question the vast profundity of Quatremère.

In his judicious critique of Hitzig he observes:—"Quant aux *Kaslouhis*, j'y reconnais les *Schelouh* qui, de nos jours encore, composent une grande division de la nombreuse nation dont les membres sont désignés, d'une manière abusive, par le nom de *Berbères;*

66

on conçoit que ces hommes, qui, dans tous les temps, se montrèrent avides de pillage, avaient, de bonne heure, parcouru l'Afrique pour y excercer leurs brigandages. Que, se trouvant attiré par l'appât des richesses de l'Égypte, ils aient tenté une incursion dans cette contrée, et réussi à s'en rendre maîtres, la chose n'a rien d'improbable. C'est ainsi qu'à des époques plus récentes nous voyons les *Mazices*, qui appartenaient à la même race, infester par leurs brigandages l'Égypte et les contrées voisines."

The *Shillouhs* (sufficiently for the purposes of this essay) have now been started in Morocco and followed to the confines of Egypt. In these wildernesses some of their advanced posts still reside. At the famed oasis of Jupiter Ammon, or *Seewàh*, the same phenomenon is witnessed at the present day for which this oasis was remarkable in the time of Herodotus, viz: the intermixture of Egyptian and *Berber* tribes. And just as its habitants then spoke Coptic and "Ethiopian" dialects, so now their speech is Arabic and *Shilha; i. e.*, the tongue of the *Shillouhs;* into which latter idioms Arabic continues to become the more and more absorbed, in proportion as from oasis to oasis one journeys westwards; until, little beyond words impressed with religious attributes remains of Arabic in the aboriginal tongue of the *Shillouh* votary of Islâm.

The KS*hi*LuK*h*-*ìm* of Xth Genesis resolve themselves, once for all, into the SHILLOUHS; one of the two main branches of the great *Gætulian* or Libyan family, race, or perhaps "species," of mankind. They inhabited Barbary when the ethnic chart of *Hamitic* stocks was compiled. They do so still, in the nineteenth century A. C.[616]

33. פלשתים — P*h*LST*t*IM — 'PHILISTIM.'

None will dispute that, according to the Text and the versions, these people proceed from out of the KS*hi*Lou-K*h*-*ìm*. Ergo, the *Philistìm* were of *Berber* stock, and must have migrated from a Gætulian birthplace into Palestine; a land which, to this day, consecrates in its name the remembrance of one of its earliest occupants, the *Philistines*.

Contrary to the general current of opinion, here we encounter, if the ethnic genealogies of Xth Genesis are historical (as we conceive them to be), a migration from Northern Africa to Asia; that is, from West to East. If we are to be told by "teologastri," that a man yclept *Casluhim*, on his way from Mount Ararat to Mount Atlas, was delivered in Palestine of another called *Philistim*, St. Augustine will reply for us "credo, quia *impossibile*." Can it be shown when the "Philistines" were not in Palestine?

The P*h*LST*t*-IM were in Palestine before the second Pylon of the temple of *Medeenet-Haboo* was erected at Thebes; else Ramses III. could not have recorded, in the thirteenth century B. C., "the POLISITE," among his Asiatic vanquished; by all hierologists recognized as the *Philistines*. They must have been also settled in Palestine before the advent of the *Abrahamidæ*, whose presence the Philistines never quietly tolerated; and these *Philistines* were sufficiently powerful, at the time of the Exode, for Israel's escaping helots to prefer a wearisome desert march by the Sinaic route, lest, peradventure the latter should "see war;" if their valor had tested the right of way through "the land of the P*h*LST*t*-*ìm*, although that was near." And, in their uncompromising abhorrence of later Hebrew domination (which they successfully resisted until Nabuchadnezzar crushed alike the intruder and themselves) the *Philistines* never belied their *Berber* antipathies to an alien yoke. Ἀλλόφυλοι, *Emigrants*, themselves, they seem never to have comprehended the legality of the charter through which other strangers in the same land claimed its exclusive possession: nor did Jewish holders of this supernatural title-deed ever collect physical force adequate to an eviction.

Leaving aside, as Pundit fabrications, those *Sanscrit* apocryphas through which Wilford traced Palestine to *Pali-stàn*, "country of the *Pali*" (Hales's endorsement notwithstanding); and by no means prepossessed in favor of any *Sanscrit* etymology for descendants of Hamitic *Shillouhs* in Palestine or elsewhere, after Quatremère's exposure of their impossibility — leaving aside all these Indomanias, we turn to the Abbé Mignot for some reasonable derivation of PLST*t*.

PLS, or *Felesh*, in Hebrew means *mud;* and the same bisyllable resiles from the Greek πηλος, and the Latin *Palus*. *Pelusium*, frontier city of Lower Egypt, towards Palestine (surrounded by marshes at the Pelusiac mouth), derived its foreign name from its *muddy* situation; being called SIN, *mud*, in Ezekiel (xxx. 15, 16), and *Teeneh*, mud, by the present Arabs. These coincidences, coupled with the fact that the PLST*t* dwelt between Pelusium and Palestine, led the ingenious Abbé to see, in the *miry* neighborhoods of their abode, the origin of the name *Philistine*. On the other hand, Munk draws the name from FLS, to *emigrate;* being the sense in which the LXX understood PLST*t*-*îm*, when they rendered it by αλλοφυλοι. Munk supports this hypothesis by the Ethiopic name of Jewish Abyssinians, the Falashas, or *emigrants*, *if* their name be Semitic.

These appear to be the most rational etymologies of many producible upon the old system, before hieroglyphics were translated; or rather, in Munk's instance, before rumors of Egyptian translations had reached an erudite Conservator of the Royal Library at Paris, even in 1845. Such attempts at solution must be abortive, because, revolving within a vicious and narrow circle of ideas, they all lean upon Hebraical explanations of that which the Hebraicized "language of Kanaan" cannot explain; and for the following reason: —

Upon Egyptian monuments, at a date long anterior to the compilation of Xth Genesis (never supposed by us to be *Mosaic*), the PLST*t*-*îm* are recorded. Their name is orthographed "POLIS*i*TE — *men* and *women*." Allowing vowels to be as vague in hieroglyphics as every one knows they are in *Hebrew*, here, notwithstanding, is a word of three or *four* syllables, represented by at least *four* radical letters, P, L, S, T; as well in the old Egyptian as in the very modern *square-letter* calligraphy. To this primitive name the Jews added IM, in order to make their plural, PLST*t*-*îm;* the *Philist-ines:* which word by the Masora is read *Phelesheth* in the singular; the final letter "tau" being inherent: that is, the T was already inseparable from the name thus chronicled at Thebes some three to more centuries before the consolidation of the Hebrew language itself; taking Solomon's era as the earliest and the Captivity as the latest points for pure Hebrew literature. This historical fact thrust before them, rabbinical scholars must pause, and settle with comparative philology the vital question of *biliterals* and monosyllables, ere they can make Egyptologists concede that the triliteral FLS, or PLS, is the root, not of a Semitic, but of an *Hamitic* nomen of this Barbaresque affiliation of the KSiLouK*h*-*îm;* because, in the *Hamitic* "language of KNAâN" (falsely called *Hebrew*); in cognate *Berber* tongues; and in old Egyptian; the prefix P, P*h*, F, no less than its Berber gradation into *OU*, *wa*, *w*, &c., is almost invariably the masculine article *the*, put before the noun it determines. We hold, therefore, that the hieroglyphical POLIS*i*TE is "*the*-OLIS*i*TE," or something similar; and while we pretend not to know either the meaning or the vowelled phonetism of this noun, the presence of the article P hatchets away such fabulous etymons as PLS. *mud*, or FLS. *stranger*. It remains for *Berber* scholars to discover nominal origins of the P-OLIS*i*TE among families of the *Gœtulian* race: our part contents itself with suggesting two indications supplied by Quatremère: —

1st. Ashdod, *Azotus*, was one of the five great cities of Philistia. In the time of Nehemiah (xiii. 23, 24), after return from Captivity, "the *Jews* had married wives of Ashdod," and "their children spake half in *the speech of Ashdod*, and could not speak in the Jews' language."

It is true that the Jews, (who, considering the sanctity of their lineage, have amazingly surpassed all nations in rapidity of linguistic mutation,) in the days of Nehemiah spoke *Chaldee;* but, it would appear from the context that *Hebrew*, i. e. the "speech of Kanaan," was the tongue which their "Pasha" (PK*h*H) sought to reinstil into them by means vehement, not to say singular. "I contended with them, and cursed them, and smote certain of them, and plucked out their hair!" says *Nehemiah* (xiii. 25).

Now, Ashdod's inhabitants were PLST*i*-*îm* Even as late as Nehemiah, B. C. 520—40, they had preserved their own tongue in Palestine. What more natural, what otherwise possible, than that an "affiliation of the KS*h*iLouK*h*s" should have spoken in some dialect of *Berber?*

2d. — The KS*h*iLouK*h*s, in Xth Genesis, are offshoots of the MTsR*ites*. Hear Quatremère:—"Quant à ce qui concerne l'influence de la langue Égyptienne sur celles des Philistins, nous en trouvons un vestige remarquable. Il existait, sur le rivage de la mer Méditerranée, un lieu situé à peu de distance de la ville de Gaza, dont il formait le port. Ce lieu était nommé *Maïuma*. Comme il avait acquis une grande importance, il fut, sous le règne des empereurs de Constantinople, séparé de l'évêché de Gaza, et devint un siége épiscopal distinct. Ce nom, dont M. Hitzig a cherché l'étymologie dans la langue Sanscrite, appartient indubitablement à la langue de l'Égypte. En retranchant la terminaison grecque, il se composa du mot [Coptic and hieroglyphic] MA *lieu* et de IOM *mer*. Cette denomination, qui désigne *un lieu maritime*, convient parfaitement à un port de mer:" and establishes the *Hamitic* vernacular of the people who named it. Who can these people have been but the *Philistines* who built Gaza?

Another consideration. We have seen that Gætulian races, descendants of K*h*aM, *dark*, are "gentes subfusci coloris;" and also that to half the population of the oasis of Ammon, who were not Egyptians, Herodotus gives the usual Greek name of "*sun-burned-faces*." Emigrants from such stock into Palestine were therefore physiologically *swarthy;* and such were the PTST*i*-*îm* who founded Joppa, settling along the coast from the Suez Isthmus to Mt. Carmel. Now, as Raoul Rochette has skilfully established, early Greek writers placed the cœlo-piscine adventure of "Perseus and Andromeda" at Joppa; "among the ÆTHI-OP*ians*," inhabitants of that city of *Philistia*. Had the PLST*i*-*îm* not been, like all *Berbers*, of the swarthy race, *Joppa* would not have been included in *Æthiopia*, "land of *burnt-faces*."

Sufficient has been said on the PLST*i*-*îm* to show that the traditions collected in Xth Genesis accurately ascribe these peoples' origins to Barbary. To reject this deduction is to deny the validity of Xth Genesis, backed as it is by every historical desideratum; without reserving a shadow upon which contrary hypotheses have been erected through imaginary *Sanscrit* analogies that possess, anthropologically speaking, about as much relation to a man of *Philistia*, as to "the man in the moon."

"If, (says Quatremère) as I have attempted to establish, the Philistines were originally of the west of Africa, it is probable that their idiom, primitively, belonged to that speech, improperly termed *Berber*, which is spoken even to-day in northern Africa, from Egypt to the shores of the Atlantic ocean. One may believe that, during their domination (?) in Egypt, the Philistines forgot their own language to adopt that of this country, or made of the two idioms a barbarous mixture. When they were established in Palestine, seeing themselves surrounded by nations that spoke the Semitic dialects, and with whom they had daily relations, either as friends, or as enemies, they must have still more achieved modifications or corruptions of their *lingua propria*."

Through the "Annals of Thotmes III," a most scientific paper which reaches us while correcting these pages, the antiquity of the *Philistines* can now be carried back to the sixteenth century B. C. Describing the hieroglyphical records of that Pharaoh, Birch reveals how there took place "another campaign against the fortress of Aranatu, that of Kanana, and the land of Tunép; Kadesh was once more attacked, and the campaign extended to Naharaina or Mesopotamia. The Tanai, a *Philistine* tribe who were conquered by Ramses III, the PALUSATA or *Philistines*, and the Gakhil or Galilæans, also contributed to the rent-roll, and the 'silver jug the work of the Kevau' refers to the celebrated metallic works of the Cyprians." Here the reader will recognize various geographical and ethnic names already mentioned in our present disquisition. Mr. Birch's surpassingly-great essay will show him many more.

And this is all we have to say on "P-OLIS*i*TE-*men* and *women;*" — except that orthodox Hebrew dictionaries propose, by way of explanation, "PHILISTINES, *those that dwell in villages!*" 617

34. כפתרים — KP*h*T*t*RIM — 'CAPHTORIM.'

The first born of a dilemma (previously stated) displays itself in the absolutely equivocal verse of the ethnic chart itself. Our construction is, that the *Caphtorîm* proceeded (like the Philistines) from out of the KS*h*iLouK*h*s: but if a Lanci were to object that every Mitsrite name, but that of the parenthetical *Philistîm*, is preceded by the demonstrative AT*t*, and were to insist that "W-AT*t*-KP*h*T*t*RIM" means "*and-all*-KP*h*T*t*R*ites*," we should yield at once that, in the Text, the latter are *sons*, not grandsons, of the MT*s*R*îm*. In mere hagiography a distinction so minute is of no importance; but in ethnography it makes all the difference whether the KP*h*T*t*R*îm* issued primarily from the Egyptians, or whether they are a secondary formation from among the KS*h*iLouK*h*s of Barbary; Gætulians who, like their brethren the *Philistines*, abandoned their birthplace, and went —— whither? Nobody knows!

Bochart pointed out a road to *Cappadocia*, along which English orthodoxy follows him as sheep do their leading-rams — chiefly because, having fixed the Negro *Casluhîm* in Colchis on the Euxine, Protestant divines consider that *his* brother, or *his* son, "*Caphtorim*," naturally took lodgings next door. Our restoration of the KS*h*iLouK*h*s to Barbary shatters that hypothesis, unless Cappadocia, like Colchis, can show to some Halicarnasian a population also "*black* in complexion, and *woolly*-haired." Strabo tells us that the Leuco-Syrians, *white*-skinned-Syrians, resided there. Michaelis thought of *Cyprus*, which Volney rejects; Calmet, first *Crete*, and afterwards *Cyprus*, which second thought is favored in Kitto's cyclopædia by "E. M." *Crete*, however, is adopted by the Germanic scholarship of "J. B. R."; and, based upon similar sources, by that of Munk. One regrets to disturb this happy uniformity; but, let a query or two be propounded — after recalling that, our preceding analyses having vindicated *Barbary* as the region, and *Gætulian* as the race, of *seven* "affiliations of the MTsR*îm*," the *eighth*, our KP*h*T*t*Rs, whether as offshoots of *Shillouhs* or of *Egyptians*, must have been likewise "gentes subfusci coloris"; speaking a dialect of *Hamitic* tongues; whose birthplace was also Northern Africa.

1st. How, in the remote age of these ante-historical migrations, could *Berber* races have got to Crete? By navigation? Not impossible, certainly; but, it is one thing to suppose a MR. *Caphtorim* tacking his frail bark, not along shore, but straight out 400 miles (against Etesian gales) to windward, to the Island of Candia; and another to explain the embarkation of a whole tribe of KP*h*T*t*Rs, for aught we know, as numerous as the *Pharusii* or the *Philistines*. Such a voyage, at such unnautical epochas, is rather more difficult to be conceived, in archæology, than some mistake of a copyist in writing that name which, as KPT*t*R (save in the Text, versions, and rabbinical commentors thereon), has never yet been localized.

2d. What vestiges are there in Crete, or in her traditions, of any such Barbaresque visitation? And why, after they had landed at Candia, did the KP*h*T*t*Rs abandon that splendid island *en masse*, and so thoroughly, that not a suspicion of their sojourn is to be found in Cretan, in classical, or in *Hamitic* traditions?

When these two questions have received a reasonable answer, we shall put our

3d, and last interrogatory — How comes it that, after all these improbabilities, the second voyage, from *Crete* to Palestine, is unrecorded?

It is true that three texts are quoted to identify the *Philistines* with Crete: — *Ezek.* xxv. 16, "I will stretch out my hand upon the *Philistines*, and I will cut off the K*h*RT*t*-*îm*." *Zeph.* ii. 5, "Woe unto the inhabitants of the seacoast, the nation of the K*h*RT*t*-*îm!* the word of IeHOuaH against you; O Kanaan, the land of the *Philistines*." 1 *Sam.* xxx. 14, 16, "We made an invasion south of the K*h*RT*t*-*îm*, . . . the land of the *Philistines*."

Now, if the resemblance of K*h*RT*t*I to *Crete* be the only reason for making those *Shillouh* affiliations, called P-OLISiTE in hieroglyphics, navigate from Barbary to Candia, and thence to Palestine — if this be all, why the same palæographical analogy might bring the K*h*RT*t*-*îm* from KhȧRT*t*-*oum*, the modern city on the juncture of the

Blue and White Niles! Unluckily for Crete, these texts merely show that K*h*RT*t*-*i*m was another name — a nickname perhaps — for a sept of *Philistines* in Palestine. David's life-guards were composed of K*h*RT*t*I and P*h*LT*t*I (2 *Sam.* viii. 18; 1 *Chron.* xviii. 17). They, with the GT*t*I (2 *Sam.* xv. 18), made up a corps of "600 men." Now, the latter being citizens of Gath, the union of all three tribes into a cohort renders their homogeneity, as native Palestinians, more than probable. But, none of these passages touch the *Kaphtorim;* whose name is distinct from that of the *Kherethim.*

But, it is said, three other texts confirm the *Cretan* theory: — *Deut.* ii. 23, "The *Âvim* that dwelled in villages as far as (Gaza?) *Âza,* the KP*h*T*t*Rs who issued from KP*h*T*t*R destroyed them and established themselves in their place." *Jerem.* xlvii. 4, "IeHOuaH will spoil the *Philistines,* the remnant of the *country* of KP*h*T*t*R." *Amos* ix, 7, "The *Philistines* from KP*h*T*t*R."

One must employ double-magnifying spectacles to see anything more here than that *Kaphtor* was some place whence *Philistines* came (far, or near, unrevealed); but, in what does all this concern the "Island of Candia"? Herodotus and Tacitus are quoted. The former merely says, that *Creta* was occupied by barbarous tribes until the time of Minos. This citation does not help *Caphtorim* out of the mire. The latter has "*Judæos, Cretâ insulâ profugos, novissima Libyæ insedisse memorant.*" He speaks of *Jews,* driven out of Candia, taking refuge in *Libya.* What has that incident to do with "*Philistines* from KP*h*T*t*R" in Palestine? Those who fancy that Hitzig or Movers, spite of their immense learning, and dexterity in placing one Indo-Germanic hypothesis alongside of another, have mended matters, will be edified by the perusal of Quatremère's critique of both. From it we translate: "It seems to me probable that the *Kreti* inhabited to the south of the country of the Philistines, upon the shores of the Mediterranean Sea, on the side which looks towards the frontiers of Egypt. And a passage of Herodotus (iii. 5) comes perfectly in support of my opinion. According to the Greek historian, 'from Phœnicia to the environs of Kadytis [Jerusalem], the country is inhabited by Syrians, called *Palestinians.* From Kadytis to the town of Ienusos, the market-places appertain to the Arabs; thence after, to the Lake Serbonis, dwell the Syrians.' This curious passage demonstrates that to the south of the country of the Philistines there was a coast sufficiently considerable occupied by *Arabs.* Now, inasmuch as the passages of the Bible show us these *Kreti* established in the same districts, I think they constituted an *Arab* tribe that the love of gain had fixed upon the shore of the Mediterranean, that they (the *Kreti*) had nothing in common either with the Philistines or with the Cretans."

Orthodox lexicography encourages a searcher with "CAPHTOR — a *sphere,* a *buckle,* a *hand,* a *palm, doves,* or *those that seek and inquire.*" We do, "et hinc illæ lachrymæ." The roots Kah-P-T*t*oR might signify "*the-Bull-land*"; but neither these, nor any others hitherto offered, having furnished a clew to the genesiacal KaP*h*T*t*oR-IM, we humbly place the name upon our "Table" coupled with the word "*unknown.*"

Volney, whose acuteness of perception is beyond all praise, simply says, "les *Kaphtorim* peuvent être les habitans de Gaza." Wherever may have been their abode in Palestine during later times, Xth Genesis makes them so many affiliations of K*h*aM, the *dark* (red) race, through the *Egyptians;* and consequently points to *Barbary* for their origin. Our "Affiliations of the MTsR*i*m" now arrange themselves as follows:

		Stock and Tongue.	Habitat.	Origin.
1.	*The* LUD,s	Berber	Mauritania	Barbary.
2.	" ÂMaN,s	"	Oases, &c.	"
3.	" LHaB,s	"	Libya	"
4.	" NiP*h*aiaT*t*,s	"	Mareoticum	"
5.	" P*h*T*t*RiS,s	"	Pharusia	"
6.	" KS*h*LouK*h*,s	"	All N.-W. Africa	"
7.	" P*h*iLiST*t*,s	"	Palestine	"?
8.	" KaP*h*T*t*oR,s	"?	"	"Unknown."

[All these families of mankind thus re-enter into the grand *Gætulian* group of North-western Africa: of which sundry races, through prehistorical migrations, had partially occupied Palestine in ages anterior to the arrival of the *Abrahamidæ*. The surpassing accuracy of the ancient compiler of Xth Genesis has now been triumphantly vindicated from a new quarter; and that which not a man of the ghostly schools, whence issued his reverence doctor smythe, has ever possessed the knowledge to expound rationally, herein becomes comprehensible through "Gliddon, skeptical views of, — *Index*, p. 401." — G. R. G.] [618]

"And KNAȧN begat" (*Gen.* x. 15.)

35. צידן — TsIDN — 'SIDON.'

One especial object of our Section A has been achieved in the preceding pages. It was, to rescue the maligned "affiliations of KUS*h*," and the mystified "affiliations of the MTsR*lm*," from the sloughs of despond into which ecclesiastical hands had plunged them. After fixing the former in Southern Arabia among the dark-red *Himyarites*, and the latter in Barbary among the "gentes subfusci coloris" of *Gætulian* origin, we can now look down complacently upon the Egyptian alluvium of the Nile — whether viewed as the true "Land of K*h*eM" (the god), divine procreator of the Egyptian race; or as the "Land of K*h*àM," the *swarthy* people — as the centre-point, whither converge the traditions and the anthropological similitudes of Arabian Asia and of Barbaresque Africa. Our remaining objects will be satisfied by a catalogue of the other cognomina in Xth Genesis, according to the latest views of archæological science; beginning with TsIDoN.

The *city* of Sidon is the simple meaning of our text; not an individual so christened: the vicissitudes of whose *Sidonian* inhabitants, "skilled in many arts," often lauded poetically by Homer, are celebrated prosaically in classic and biblical dictionaries. Its local name was *Sàyda* when the writer (G. R. G.) sojourned there in 1829 and 1830. Orthodox philology replies to our query, as to the signification of the word — "SIDON — *hunting, fishing, venison;*" of which heterodoxy can accept but the second term in this instance; because the Semitic roots of *sàyd*, "to chase," here refer, as Trogus Pompeius tells us, to the icthyologic facilities of the locality; "nam *piscem* Phœnices SIDON vocant." In ethnic classification *Sidon* derives prominence from having once been (*Gen.* x. 19) the easternmost limit of Kanaanitish occupancy; and "after many years," continues Trogus, "the Philistines of Askalon drove out the Sidonians, who sought refuge on the rocky islet upon which they founded *Tyre*."

From Justin, the epitomizer of Trogus's lost volumes, we descend to Bochart, and admire the subdued irony with which he disposes of commentators upon the word TsIDN: — "Quod vir qui in his literis paucos habuit æquales *admirationem* explicat vocem צידן *Sidon*, non sine admiratione legi." The most recent, and incomparably the best qualified archéologue who has journeyed "round the Dead Sea and in the Bible Lands," is De Saulcy. He remarks on "Saydah — This is undoubtedly the Σιδὼν πόλις καὶ λιμὴν (κλειστὸς) of Scylax, the Sidon of Pliny, the Σιδὼν of Strabo, who places it at 400 stadia from Berytus, the *Sidona* of Antonine's Itinerary, the *Sydone* of Peutinger's Table, and, lastly, the *Civitas Sidona* of the Pilgrim from Bordeaux. It would be quite useless to argue this identity, which proves itself."

Conformably to Xth Genesis, KNAȧN, parent of *Sidon*, was an affiliation of HAM; but, "according to M. Movers, the Kanaanians, called by the Greeks *Phœnicians*, were a people that appertained to the *Semitic* race; of which some tribes," says he, "at a time which preceded the commencement of our history, marched little by little, some coming from the north, by way of Syria; others, from the south, by way of Arabia; and, according to all appearances, achieved, after several centuries, their establishment, in a permanent manner, in Palestine. Called Kanaanians, from the word *Kanaan*, KNAȧN, which means *a low land*, by opposition to the term *Aram*, ARM, which expressed *a high land*, they composed, according to the recital of Moses, a single people, but divided into many nations," &c.

To this theory Quatremère judiciously objects, — that the opinion which attributes a *Semitic* origin to the Kanaanites (aside from its opposition to Xth Genesis, which he considers of *Mosaic* editorship) reposes uniquely upon the resemblance of the tongue spoken by the Kanaanites with the languages in vogue among other peoples to whom general consent now applies the name of *Shemitish*. He holds this basis to be unsafe; because all of the affiliations of Shem did not speak one language; notably the *Elamites*, of Persia; whose tongue differed entirely from that of Aramæans or Arabs: at the same time, surrounded as the KNAåNI ever were by Semitic influences, their language would necessarily imbibe such exotic idioms. Again, it is by Quatremère considered doubtful, either that KNAåN means *a low land*, or ARM a *high* one. Indeed, one might add that the final N in *Kanaan* may be a later addition to an original root, KNå; said to be the pristine name of the *Phoinikes*, Phœnicians; which is probably preserved through another form, viz.: *Beni-å*NK, "sons of ANAK;" who were not "Giants," as some commentators imagine. Such diversities of scientific opinion are here presented to exhibit some *problemata;* not to solve them.

To us the chart of Xth Genesis has proved a very trustworthy guide so far. It assigns an *Hamitic* origin to KNAåN; and consequently to the foundation of the city of *Sidon*. No facts known to us interfere with this natural view. During the eighth—ninth centuries B. C. the name of Sidon was already sculptured, according to Rawlinson and Layard, upon the monuments of Assyria; but the very conjectural identity, claimed by Osburn, of the S*h*AIRETANA, hieroglyphed on the Egyptian records of Ramses II., with the *Sidonians*, is now overthrown by Hinck's translation of a cuneatic register of Sardanapalus, wherein the "Sharutinian" city becomes situate "between Antioch and Aleppo." We have, moreover [*supra*, p. 239, Fig. 289], identified with Egyptian native soldiery of the royal guard the individual whom Mr. Osburn suspected to be a *Sidonian*. None dispute, however, that *Sidon* must have been a "city" whensoever Xth Genesis was written, so we proceed to the next name.[619]

36. חת — K*h*T*t* — 'HETH.'

The *Hittites* are well known. Of them the patriarchal Abraham (*Gen.* xxiii. 9, 17, 19) purchased not a *double* cavern, called *Machpelah;* but "the field *contracted for*." Thus, under the magic wand of such scholarship as that of the Vatican Professor of Sacred Philology, multitudes of mistranslated Hebrew words are replaced by their historical meanings. — "I boschi," says Lanci, "diventano *veneri*, le doppie spelonche spiegansi per *contratti*, i torrenti si cangiano in beneficii, le isole in *popoli e stati*, i topi in *virili vergelle*, le rondini in *puledri*, le voragini in *montagne*."

In hieroglyphics, the K*h*eT, variously euphonized, occur so often, back to the age of Thotmes III., or the sixteenth century B. C., that one need but refer to Mr. Birch's critical papers for authority. The "land of *Kheta*' among Egyptians seems to have meant that part of Palestine where we find the *Hittites* of Scripture; but the name K*h*eT also designated this very wide-spread people; who reappear, through Layard's researches, on the cuneatic inscriptions of Assyria, as the *Khatti* or *Khetta* of Syria. To us, and to the writer of Xth Genesis, K*h*eT*t* is not a man, but a *people* so called.[620]

37. יבוסי — IBUSI — 'JEBUSITE.'

In the book of *Judges* (xix. 10), a flagitious act is recounted, which chronologers assign to about the year 1406 B. C. The date seems too remote, but the earlier it is placed by commentators, the more certain will be the archæological deductions now about to be drawn.

A Levite "rose up and departed, and came over against *Jebus*, which is Jerusalem;" that is to say, the place had been known previously by the name of IBUS; but, in the time of the writer of *Judges*, was called Jerusalem, as a second name for one and the same locality; whence the Benjamites, who gave it this latter appellative, had failed to drive the *Jebusites* out, "even unto this day." (*Jud.* i. 21.) So *Joshua* (xviii. 28), *i. e.* the book so-called, has "and IBUS which is Jerusalem;" and without requiring further information, the following text corroborates what precedes: — (1 *Chron.* xi. 4), "And David and all Israel went to Jerusalem, which is IBUS, where the IBUSîm (were then) the inhabitants of the land."

Hence it is certain, that IBUS was a very ancient city, on the site of which the exotic Israelites founded a more recent one they named *Jerusalem* — literally, YeRuS, *heritage*, and S*h*aLaïM, *peace* (in the dual) — written YeRuS*h*aLaïM, and signifying, according to Lanci, "She who inherits two-fold peace."

IBUSI, in Xth Genesis, means therefore "a *man* of, or belonging to, IBUS," a *city;* and not the imaginary *son* of a man of that name. Around this topographical centre clustered the IBUSîm before the irruption of Israel's hosts into Kanaan. There the *Jebusites* manfully vindicated their nationality until David stormed their citadel, Mt. Zion; and here some of them remained long after their city was changed into *Jerusalem*, until the invader and the invaded were swallowed up by the Babylonians.

Now, whether a *tribe* called IBUSîm built a city and named it after a mythical ancestor, divine or human; or whether the anterior name of a city was adopted by a tribe, is what neither ourselves nor any one else can aver. Xth Genesis speaks of an Ibusian*;* just as it speaks of an inhabitant of any more celebrated but perhaps not more ancient city than IBUS, already in existence when Joshua entered Palestine.

Mr. Osburn's reading of "Jebusite," among the "thirty-seven prisoners of Beni-Hassan," has not survived criticism [*supra*, p. 173]; but M. De Saulcy recognizes *Gabusa*, or *Jebus*, upon the old cuneiform tablets at Lake Van. We note a "man appertaining to the *city* of *Jebus*" in the IBUSI of Xth Genesis, and pass onwards.[621]

38. אמרי — AMRI — 'AMORITE.'

Around half the circumference of the Lake Asphaltum, and from the Jordan northward to Mt. Hermon, once dwelt a people "of stature high as cedars, and strong as oaks" (*Amos* ii. 9), called the AMORîM: — cousins to the *Emîm*, *Rephaîm*, *Zuzîm*, *Zamzumîm*, *NiphiLîm*, and *Anakîm;* falsely rendered "giants" in the versions; all, according to the Vulgate translators, "monstra quædam de genere giganteo" (*Numb.* xiii. 33): some of whom were so tremendously tall, that Caleb's spies reported how "we were in our own eyes as *grasshoppers*, and such were we in *their* eyes." Nevertheless, astonishing as such human proportions seem, those of a thorough-bred Amorite surpassed them all; according to the orthodox stream of Hebraical traditions supplied by Cahen.

"When Og (the *Amoritish* king of Bashan) saw the Israelite camp, which had six parasangs (twenty-four miles) of extent, he said: I single-handed will undertake the combat with this people, that they do not to me as to Sihon. For this object he detached a mountain six parasangs (twenty-four miles) in breadth, and placed it on his head to heave it upon the Israelites. God caused an insect to come, which, piercing the mountain through the middle, caused *Og's* head to sink therein. He, wishing to disengage himself, could not manage it, because one of his teeth projected in front very considerably. Moses then seized an axe ten cubits (fifteen feet) in length, and jumping into the air to the height of ten cubits (fifteen feet), struck the giant on the ankle-bone of his foot. On falling, the corpse of Og touched the Israelite camp." To similar rabbinical stories Horace replied, "Credat Judæus Apella!" After all, in the Text, another and later writer, during whose day Og's iron bedstead was still exhibited at Rabbath, found, by actual measurement, that this "remnant of giants" had slept within an area of only thirteen and a half feet by six (*Deut.* iii. 11).

Among *Berber* tribes, the name OMARE, *Aâmare*, reappears in Ebn Khaledoon's list; but whether indigenously, or exotically through some ante-historical Kanaanitish or modern Arab affiliation (sons of Omar, or Aâmer?), others may better determine.

It is long since that Rosellini pointed out among the early Asiatic conquests of the XVIIIth dynasty, the "Land of OMAR:" but Birch first suspected this country to be that of the Palestinic *Amorite;* a conclusion enforced by Hincks, and developed by Osburn. There is a question still pending between hierologists and cuneiform decypherers in regard to the "citadel of ATesh" in the land of *Amaru*, which leaves it yet uncertain whether the river *Amoor*, "Jaxartes," or the nation *Amorite* in Palestine, is intended. Nor have the Palestinic travels of De Saulcy ascertained any ruins of a *city* called AMR, whence the AMoRI of Xth Genesis might be derived: although nothing can be more precious to the ethnologist than the "Figure of a *Moabite*" discovered by him on the "hybrid monument, in which the Egyptian and the Assyrian styles are intermingled," at Redjom-el-Aabed. Ignorance of Judaic topography here compels us merely to read an AMoR-*ian;* a man of, or belonging to, the city, country, or tribe, of AMR.[622]

39. גרגשי — GRGSI — 'GIRGASITE.'

This, together with the two preceding and all the following affiliations of KNAâN, has the termination I (*iod*); which in Semitic tongues commonly indicates *the-belonging-to* a place; for instance, *Muss'r* means Cairo; *Muss'r-i*, a Cairine. In Xth Genesis, this adjunct to a geographical proper name has precisely the same grammatical acceptation; and if science cannot always find the *place* alluded to, the fault lies at the door of travellers less qualified than a De Saulcy. GRGS-I signifies nothing more than a man *belonging-to* a locality once called GRGS; although its Palestinic situation still lacks a discoverer. Other books of the Hebrews are silent on this name; which was all that remained of a *Girgasite* even in the time of Josephus, 1800 years ago; unless "the country of the *Gergesenes*," mentioned by *Matthew* (viii. 28), contained other persons than those "possessed with devils."[623]

40. חוי — K*h*UI — 'HIVITE.'

A man "of, or belonging to," a place called K*h*U; now pronounced, through the modern *Chaldee* substitution of V for U, "K*h*aV." The K*h*UI*tes* rank among the *unexpelled* Kanaanites; because *Joshua* (xi. 19) suffered some of them to deceive him into a peace; and *Solomon* (1 *Kings* ix. 20, 21) exacted "bond-service" from others.

We must never forget, in viewing this name and its fellow-nomina, that time, distance, foreign and obsolete languages now reputed to be "sacred," combined with the singular mixture of scepticism and marvellousness instilled into our minds by juvenile education, lend an enchantment to these Kanaanitish people that would vanish, did we now possess the honor of their acquaintance. They all were petty tribes of a few thousands, at most of fewer myriads of population; comprised within an area so very insignificant, that St. Jerome, who travelled over Palestine (which had previously included the whole of these *nations*, and other people besides), wisely deprecates statistics: — "Pudet dicere latitudinem terræ repromissionis, ne ethnicis occasionem blasphemandi dedisse videamur." That criticism which, precursor of Niebuhr, the author of "Scienza Nuova," applied so successfully to early Roman, might equally well be adapted to early Jewish history—"What we may say about the *poetic geography* of the Greeks suits the *ancient geography* of the Latins. Latium possessed, without doubt, at the commencement, but a petty extent; inasmuch as, while employing two hundred and fifty *years* to conquer twenty different *peoples*, Rome during that time did not stretch out the frontier of her empire further than twenty miles round about." Among "the *cities* of the K*h*U-*im*" (2 *Sam.* xxiv. 7) we cannot yet place a finger upon that particular one whence hailed the "citizen" individualized in Xth Genesis.[624]

41. ערקי — A*á*RKI — 'ARKITE.'

A man of *Arka*, or *Acra;* a city the ruins of which are still seen at *Tel-Arka*, mound of Arka, between Tripoli and Antaradus; but *Akra* must have been already a city when Asar-adan-pal and Temenebar I. recorded its capture in the eighth—ninth century B. C.; else Rawlinson could not have discovered its cuneatic name.

[In former inquiries into the probable origin of some *Berber* names, that certainly present some Kanaanitish coincidences, I indicated the ERKYE of Ebn Khaledoon as homonymous. That some *Kanaanites* sought refuge in Barbary is undoubtedly historical; that some *Berbers* did once occupy Kanaan has been already shown. There is a strange blending of Gætulian and Arabian elements in Palestine anterior to the advent of the *Abrahamidæ*, underlying every record, which the supposition of a creative centre, distinct from that of *Euphratic* tradition, might possibly explain.—G. R. G.][625]

42. סיני — SINI — 'SINITE.'

A man "of, or belonging to the town of SIN," not far from *Acra*, on the slopes of Mount Lebanon. This name reappears among Ebn Khaledoon's *Berber* tribes as the ZIN-ata.[626]

43. ארודי — ARUDI — 'ARVADITE.'

A man of *Rowàyda* (as modern Syrians now designate the little island of *Aradus*), which town, with its continental neighbor *Antaradus*, was a famed Phœnician emporium. Every lexicon explains the familiar locality; but Osburn has the merit of indicating the people and their name hieroglyphed amid the conquests of Sethei I., and Ramses II.; fourteenth—sixteenth centuries B. C.; and Rawlinson that of reading the cuneiform inscriptions in which, during the eighth—ninth centuries B. C., the existence of *Aradus* is chronicled.[627]

44. צמרי — T*s*MRI — 'ZEMARITE.'

A man of the Phœnician town of *Simyra*, not far from Antaradus, on the western spur of Mount Lebanon; afterwards occupied by the Benjamites, who probably expelled its inhabitants—the T*s*MR-*ìm*. A similar name occurs among Ebn Khaledoon's *Berbers;* but, beyond this phonetic and therefore uncertain analogy, we here must emulate the laconic chorography, not merely of Xth Genesis, but of map-makers in general, having nothing to add to the investigations of Bochart.[628]

45. חמתי — K*h*MT*t*I — 'HAMATHITE.'

This is a man "belonging to a *city*" situate on the Orontes at the eastern frontier of Palestine, now called *el-Hámah* by Syrians. Although later Greeks termed it *Epiphaneia* during their dominion, the natives have always preserved its antique nomen. The LXX properly wrote Ε*μάθ*: as did Assyrians, six centuries before them, in cuneatic inscriptions deciphered by Rawlinson; while, at least four hundred years previously, Ramses III. had hieroglyphed the *Hamathites* among his Asiatic vanquished.

We would passingly notice that which, philologically speaking, is incontrovertible in regard to the Hebrew transcription of this name. The letter I, *iod*, has been shown above to be the demonstrative adjunct "of, or belonging to" a locality. T*t*, *tau*, in all ancient *Hamitic* idioms is the feminine article, *the;* prefixed or suffixed even now to abundant Berber nomina—*ex. gr.*, T-Amazirgh or Amazirgh-T. These cut away, the pristine monosyllable of K*h*aMaT*i*I is K*h*M; identical with K*he*M the name of *Egypt;* and also with K*h*aM the son of Noah, personified symbol of all *Hamitic* families. We have traced the *Philistines* to a Barbaresque source, although history dawns upon them in Palestine. The writer of Xth Genesis, whose authority has been found so unexceptionably safe hitherto, makes a K*h*aM-*ite* citizen on the frontier of Palestine descend from KNAâN; the figurative son of KUS*h* who was the figurative son of K*h*aM. The *Hamitic* article T is suffixed to the primitive *biliteral* name of a city, whose existence is carried back on Egyptian monuments to Mosaic epochas. There is no historical limit definable for the foundation of the *city;* none, most assuredly, for the antiquity of its *name.* But, archæology may draw, from other data, inferences that appear satisfactory: before considering which, justice to the memory of human greatness suggests a citation: —

"The man who has anticipated by a century the movements of mind towards modern sciences; who has raised up questions which, down to him, were considered to be resolved or to be insoluble; who has carried the investigations of a criticism the most intrepid into documents by all antiquity respected; who never bent himself before established prejudice; who has accomplished the double enterprise of destroying and of reconstructing universal history; who has treated upon all the sciences without being acquainted precisely with any one, and who bequeathed to each of them some fecund teaching; the man who has almost divined all the discoveries of the nineteenth century; who, appertaining to an age [1722] and to a country [Naples] wherein thought was never free, seemed to ignore that the saying of every thing to every body, was to expose himself to be comprehended by nobody; the man whose genius recalls the mighty intellects of Plato and of Aristotle, deserves to be followed step by step in the development of his glorious intelligence and in the vicissitudes of his long and unhappy life." That man was Vico. In "establishing the Principles" of historical criticism, he laid down, for the 107th rule: "the commencements of nations preceded the commencements of *cities.*" A hagiographer smiles at its infantine simplicity — let us raise a laugh at his.

We have seen that, *Sidon, Ibus, Arka, Sin, Aradus, Simyra,* and *Hamath,* were *cities.* We know that the terminal letter I, *iod,* to six of these seven names, produces, in Semitic idioms, exactly the same effect that our addition of an English "*ian*" changes them into a Sidon-*ian*, an Ibus-*ian*, an Ark-*ian*, a Sin-*ian*, an Arad-*ian*, a Simyr-*ian*, and a Hamath-*ian*. Ergo, these people derive their appellatives from *cities;* built, of course, before men could hail from them. What now — let us turn round and ask the smiling querist, as his face augments its longitude while diminishing its risible latitude,—what now becomes of your fables about those MEN called *Sidon, Ibus, Arka, Sin, Aradus, Simyra,* or *Hamath,* whom your schools have dared to find in Xth Genesis, as *sons*, forsooth [!], of another fabulous human being your philologers spell "Canaan"?

But, there is yet another deduction which the reader will draw at once from these premises, viz.: — that, inasmuch as a man could not be a *Hamathian* before the city of Hamath was built, the fact that the writer of Xth Genesis speaks of a K*h*aMaT*i*I, or *Hamathian*, proves that the document called "Xth Genesis" was written *after*, probably long after, this city had existed; and, therefore, that *he* (the writer aforesaid) never dreamed that modern logopœists would metamorphose his *cities* into so many human beings.

The age of the foundation of all these cities receding beyond historical chronology, we have said enough on the *Hamathian* and his compeers: but, while taking leave of the *cities* included in the terrestrial area called KNAâN, we likewise bid farewell to every commentator who perpetuates rabbinical superstitions about "Canaan" and his gigantic progeny. "These," says the chorographer of Xth Genesis, on closing his *Hamitic* list, — "These are the affiliations of K*h*aM [*i. e*, the *swarthy*], after their families, after their *tongues*, in their countries, and in their nations." (*Gen.* x. 20.)

Nothing can be plainer, nor more scientifically concise. In our journey from Babylon through Southern Arabia, and round by the shores of the Erythræan (red), Edomite or *Red* Sea, the dark *Himyarites* (red) have accompanied us, over the Suez Isthmus, into Egypt — the true "land of *Kh*à M" (dark); its ancient name preserved in *Chemmia* — abode of the *red* people, "par excellence." Thence, towards the west along Barbary we see the prolongations of the same *Hamitic* (dark) families, "gentes subfusci coloris," stretching between the Sahara desert and the Mediterranean, as far as Mauritania: whilst, towards the east, through Palestine, we behold the wrecks of an aboriginal population, linked by traditions and primitive speech to *Egypt* and to Barbary, "tinged with the *red* of Gætulian blood," and *Hamitic* under every aspect.[629]

We next take up the "Affiliations of SHEM."

"And unto S*h*eM (there was) issue." (*Gen.* x. 21—Hebrew Text.)

46. עילם — A*â*ILM — 'ELAM.'

Preceding generations have bent their intelligencies towards the elucidation of *Shemitish* subjects with more zeal, and therefore with more success, than towards that of Japethic or of Hamitic problems.

Owing partly to the fortuitous preservation of this family's chronicles in greater completeness than those of any people except the *Chinese;* still more, to the absence, until this century, of those immortal discoveries epitomized in two names, "CHAMPOLLION and RAWLINSON"; and, beyond any other stimulant of research, to doctrinal biases in favor of a select line that, under the name of Hebrews and Arabs, traces its pedigree backwards to a *biliteral* SM — owing, we repeat, to these historical accidents, we happen to know a little more about some of SM's posterity, their annals, habitats, and associations, than we do concerning other less respectable, because unrecorded, "Types of Mankind."

According to Ainsworth, geologist to the Euphrates Expedition, *Elymais,* country of the *Elymæi* (the capital city of which was also called *Elymais* when classical history first dawns upon its geography), was a Persian province, situate to the south of Media, between the river Tigris and the Persian Appenines, sloping downwards into Susiana and to the Persian Gulf. Tradition, through Polybius and Strabo, ascribes to its *Elymæan* inhabitants a northern origin; and Josephus calls them "the founders of the Persians": with whom they are often confounded in later Hebrew annals; for Persia and Persepolis are both called *Elam* (1 *Maccab.* vi. 12; 2 *id.* ix. 2). They were, however, in the days of Abraham, already occupiers of a *kingdom* called *Elam* (*Gen.* xiv. 1, 9); so that when, more than a thousand years later, the compiler of Xth Genesis registered A*â*ILM on his ethnic chart, he naturally meant the *country* which had been so called from times immemorial before him.

This country (generally, if improperly, included in the sections of territory comprehended by the term *Susiana*), is full of ancient cuneiform remains; both of the Persian and of the older Assyrian period: but, in 1846, one class of the cuneatic inscriptions there discovered, owing to "the number of new characters which they exhibit — characters for which no conjectural equivalent can be found either in the Babylonian or the Assyrian alphabet" — was denominated *Elymæan* by Rawlinson, being monuments distinct from their neighbors.

Under these circumstances, until Rawlinson or his emulous competitors shall breathe upon these "dry bones" of *Elymais,* "and say unto them, O ye dry bones, hear!" it is best not to hazard opinions on the unknown, which the next mail from Europe may perhaps render clear as day. We therefore merely indicate a discrepancy at present evident between modern philological and historical results and the *Semitish* genealogy of A*â*ILM-*ais,* in Xth Genesis. According to the latter, the A*â*ILM-*ites* should have spoken a dialect of the *Aramæan* class of languages: but, according to the former, as interpreted by Lenormant, Quatremère, Movers, and others, the affinities of

AâILM, cognate if not identical with the Persians, are *Arian*. It seems to us, however, that Löwenstern's solution is satisfactory. He shows how the primitive Elamites were of Semitic extraction, but that, in after times, Scythic conquerors superimposed in Elam their extraneous blood, tongues, and traditions; as the reader can verify in this author's learned papers. In the meanwhile, De Saulcy has read upon cuneatic inscriptions of the age of Asar-haddon, eighth century B. C., that this monarch was "rex populi Assur," and "rex populi *Elam*": and this is confirmed by Layard's Second Expedition, for "Sennacherib speaks of the army which defended the workmen being attacked by the king of *Elam* and the king of Babylon."

Our confidence in the compiler of Xth Genesis stands unshaken. If, as we have proved, his tabulation of the distant *Hamites* is so correct, how much better must a *Chaldæan* chorographer have been acquainted with the legendary origins of a Semitish AâILM-*ais*? [630]

47. אשור — ASUR — 'ASSHUR.'

While admitting the equivocal nature of the text of *Genesis* x. 11, we have given reasons [*supra*, p. 509] for reading — "From this land (*Shinar*) he himself (NiMRoD) went forth (to) ASUR (Assyria) and builded Nineveh," &c. Such lesson indicates that we have now before us a *geographical* name.

"It would be strange," critically remarks De Sola, "if ASHUR, a son of Shem (*Gen.* x. 22) were mentioned among the descendants of *Cham*, of whom Nimrod was one. It would be equally strange if the deeds of ASHUR were spoken of (in verse 11) before his birth and descent had been mentioned." The writer of Xth Genesis, a plain sensible man, compiling the Assyrian department of his chart not impossibly in ASUR itself, was not likely to have committed such a needless anachronism. Let us examine another text.

King James's version, *Genesis* ii. 14—"And the name of the third river *is* Hiddekel: that *is* it which goeth toward the east of Assyria." This text has opportunely received recent ventilation at Paris, in discussions between De Longpérier, an Orientalist as profound in biblical as in all archaic lore, and a learned dogmatist, M. Hoeffer. The ante-diluvian river, miswritten *Hiddekel* in our version, is, in the Text, H-DKL, *the*-DiKLe — a name that, through various historical transmutations, such as DiGLe, DidJLeh, TiGLe, and TiGRE (*Tigrâm*, in Persepolitan inscriptions), is inherited by us in its euphonized Latin form — the TIGRIS.

The Text therefore reads literally — *the* TIGRIS, "ipse vadens KDMT*t* (*ante*) ASUR;" Parisian debate turned upon the meaning of KDMT*t*; by English interpreters rendered "East;" — a translation which, if true, (as dogmatism had maintained,) would place the city of *Nineveh*, built in the land of ASUR (*Gen.* x. 11), on the west bank of that river; supposing always that the river lay to the *east* of it (Assyria). And thus "Holy Scripture" was triumphantly quoted to prove that, inasmuch as Nineveh was situate *west* of the Tigris, the vast exhumations of Botta, Layard, Place, and Rawlinson, on the *eastern* bank, which people fondly supposed to have been executed in ante-diluvian *Assyria*, not having been made on the site of Nineveh at all, the whole of these discoveries, in regard to *Nineveh*, fell to the ground!

But, Mrs. Rich and St. Jerome naively tell us — "It is one thing to write *history*, and another to write prophecy under the immediate effect of inspiration." If "a prophet is not without honor, but in his own country, and among his own kin, and in his own house" (*Mark* vi. 4); that is, among those mortals who happen to know him best; — the unfortunate scholar alluded to can hope for little elsewhere; since De Longpérier established:—

1st. That Herodotus has nowhere connected the Tigris with Assyria.

2d. That neither the Septuagint, nor the Vulgate, any more than the Hebrew Text, justifies such a reading as "East" in Genesis ii. 14.

3d. That KDMT*t* here meaning simply "en avant vers," the true signification of this passage must be, in English, "the Tigris, flowing *in front towards* (say *opposite*) Assyria."

Our digression introduces another difficulty. Between the land of ASUR in IId Genesis, and ASUR in Genesis Xth, rolls the Flood; which, contrary to the sophistries of the Rev. Dr. J. Pye Smith, we wholly agree with the "Friend of Moses," and the writer of Genesis VIIth, in considering to have been *universal*. If geology, in the XIXth century after Christ, discovers phenomena which prove Diluvian momentaneous universality to be impossible, so much the worse for *geologists*. But to attribute to Hebrew authors living long subsequently to the XIXth century B. C., the intrepid conceptions of modern geology, is to commit a most gross historical anachronism; besides inventing a doctrine utterly irreconcilable with the plain *square-letters* of the Hebrew Text. We would therefore merely inquire of the orthodox geologist whether he considers the land of ASUR, along which ran the river *Tigris* before the universal Flood, to have been specified (by Moses) proleptically or retroleptically? His reply would enlighten us upon one of two propositions. If this Hebrew "scholar and statesman," as the *Friend of Moses* terms him, had before his eyes, as some maintain, certain documents written by ante-diluvian patriarchs, then ASUR, in such manuscripts, must have been the geographical appellative of a *country* existing before the Flood; which country, after the waters had passed away, emerged as ASUR, along with its river *Tigris*, on the same terrestrial area, in order to be catalogued by the writer of Xth Genesis among other countries existing in his later day. Or, if Moses was enlightened upon events anterior to his lifetime through "Divine inspiration," then we possess the authority of the Most High (through Moses) for sustaining that, ASUR, having been the geographical name of a *country* years before the Deluge, and centuries before "ASHUR, son of SHEM," was born, the writer of Xth Genesis was right in mapping the "land of ASUR" as a *country*, according to its ante-fluviatile acceptation in Genesis ii. 14 — a country, too, wherein the masterly geological researches of Ainsworth could discover no traces of any Noachian Flood. That which remains certain is, that ASUR was already a *country*, according to the letter of Scripture itself, whensoever, or by whomsoever, or wheresoever, Xth Genesis was written; and, for our researches, "for us, that is enough." — "That you should wish to *call* MOSES author of the *Pentateuch*, or ESDRAS the restorer of this same work, I do not object," philosophically wrote St. Jerome.

The name of ASUR, in unpunctuated Hebrew, becomes AS*h*UR through rabbinical marks; and passing through different dialects and ages, as AT*t*UR, ATUR, ATUR*ia*, A*th*URA, ASSUR*ia*, &c., it is now written *Assyria* by ourselves. But, while modern Chaldee Jews have preserved in *Athour* the correspondent of *Ashour* as intonated by their forefathers, cuneiform scholars have discovered, in the land of AS*h*UR itself, the indigenous name, petroglyphed *Assour*, upon innumerable records disinterred from the mounds of Khorsabad and Nimroud.

Kings of the "country of ASUR" are now well-known personages to readers of Botta, Layard, Rawlinson, De Longpérier, De Saulcy, Hincks, Birch, Grotefend, Löwenstern, Oppert, Norris, Vaux, Eadie, or Bonomi; and having been found upon sculptures coeval with the epoch of Jehu, king of Israel, ASUR was already the name of Assyria early in the ninth century B. C.: an age, we think, nearly parallel with the compilation of Xth Genesis. These now-familiar topics need no pause; but some of those things which are less so demand notice in tracing ASUR to its primeval source. Rawlinson finds in *Assarac*, (Assarak, Asserah,) "god of *Assyria*" — the deified proto-patriarch of that land — called in the inscriptions "father of the gods," "king of the gods," "great ruler of the gods;" whose mythological characteristics are those of *Kronos* or *Saturn*. "I should suppose him, as head of the Pantheon, to be represented by that particular device of a *winged figure in a circle*, which was subsequently adopted by the Persians to denote ORMUZD, the chief deity of their religious system." And we may now leave hagiography to rejoice over possible connections between the divine *Assarac* and *Ashur* the son of SHEM, among those of other genealogies of Xth Genesis; which document Rawlinson does not consider anything more than "an historical representation of the great and lengthened migrations of the primitive Asiatic race of man." More recently we learn from Layard how — "*Asshur*, the king of the circle of the great gods," heads the list of the thirteen great gods of Assyria, at Nimroud. At Babylon, however, the god *Marduk* is termed "the great lord," "lord of lords," "elder of the gods," &c.; and *Ashur* no longer appears, being the god of upland Assyria, and not of the Babylonian plains.

The cuneiform documents upon which ASʰUR figures as a native mythological personage approach in antiquity the era of Moses. The hieroglyphical records in which *A-su-ru* occurs as the Egyptian name of *Assyria*, surpass, by two hundred years, the age of the Hebrew lawgiver, because Birch discovers it upon inscriptions of the time of Amunoph III [*supra*, p. 133, fig. 32]. Space now prevents the demonstration that, among its various symbolical meanings, A-SUR signifies also "*the-Bull*-land;" but the writer (G. R. G.) will publish the reasons elsewhere. In the interim, to the author of Xth Genesis, ASʰUR meant the *country* by us called *Assyria* — nothing more nor less.[632]

48. ארפכשד — ARPʰKSD — 'Arphaxad.'

"Arphaxad (ARPʰaKSaD; Sept. Ἀρφαξάδ), the son of Shem, and father of Salah; born one year after the Deluge, and died B. C. 1904, aged 438 years (*Gen.* xi. 12, &c)."

Requiescat in pace!

Such is the terse obituary notice,—unaccompanied by the customary poetical regrets, or general invitation to attend the funeral,—a divinity student encounters when, seeking for instruction about the Savior's genealogy, he opens Kitto's cyclopædia or Taylor's *Calmet* (the best English biblical dictionaries) at the name Arphaxad: and this is *all*. A noble cenotaph! We close those devout, not to say laborious, compendia, and turn to Volney's *Recherches Nouvelles*.

"A fifth people *of Sem is Araf-Kashd*, represented in the canton *Arra-Pachitis* of Ptolemy, which is a mountainous country, at the south of the Lake of Van, whence stream forth the Tigris and the Lycus or great *Zab*. This name signifies *boundary of the Chaldæan*, and seems to indicate that the Chaldæans, before Ninus, had extended themselves even thither. This Araph-Kashd, according to Josephus, was father of the Chaldæans; according to the Hebrew, he produced Shelah, whose trace, as *city*, and *country*, is found in the *Salacha* of Ptolemy. Shelah produced Eber, father of all the peoples *on the other side* of the Euphrates; but if we find him on *this side*, relatively to Judæa, we have the right to say that this antique tradition comes from Chaldæa." Our analyses of Xth Genesis entirely corroborate Volney's deductions of its Chaldaic derivation; and justify Lenormant's orthodox eulogies of him as "un des hommes les plus pénétrants de ce siècle." From the latter we take the following note— "Josephus had made, before Michælis, of *Arphaxad*, the father of the *Casdim* or Chaldæans. M. Bohlen explains *Arrapachitis* by the Sanscrit: *Aryapakschatà*, the country bordering upon *Aria*. This etymology is not unworthy of attention."

There is little to be added to Volney's definition; and that little confirms him. ARPʰ-KaSD — after dividing into two words that which in the Hebrew ancient Text (Synagogue rolls) runs letter after letter, "continuâ serie," along the whole line — yields us, as Michaelis first suggested, ARFA, the Arabic for *boundary*, and KASD, *Chaldæan*. The etymology is in unison with Aramæan origines; and Arphaxad was the *brother* of Aram: while Bochart's identification of it with the province of *Arrapachitis* of Ptolemy's geography also stands; but perhaps not with "nam quod Josephus et alii volunt Chaldæos olim ab eô dictos *Arphaxadæos* merum somnium est."

It is strange how Oriental tradition clings to the vicinities of Ararat as the mountainous birthplace of Chaldaic races. There we find the *Heden* (Eden) of Genesis IId, and "the house of Eden" extant in the time of the prophet Amos (i. 5); while another writer tells us how "Haran Canne, and *Heden*, have made traffic with what came from Seba, and Assyria learned thy traffic" (*Ezek.* xxvii. 23).

There, too, was the *Haïasdan* of the Armenians; and there the *Hadénéche* which Zoroaster ennobled by the title of the "pure Iran" because his birthplace was at Ourmi, on the border of Lake Ourmiah. "There," continues Dubois, "is the antique native-land of *Arpacsad* and of the Hebrews: and their patriarch Abraham, like Zoroaster, was born at Our, on the shores of Lake Ourmiah, in Chaldæa. There touches also Iràn, Arhan, the land of Persian mythes." In which connection let us likewise add, that the river *Akhourêan*, whose sources lie on the same chain, still bears the name of ARPA-TCHAI. But we suggest a melioration.

ARPHAKASD, as a *country* in Xth Genesis, is the parental source, through the province of *Salacha*, of EBER, *the yonderer;* and from the latter, according to the other document (*Gen.* xi. 18–26), sprang ABRAHAM, progenitor of the *Abrahamidæ;* born probably at *Our Kasdìm*, "*Ur* of the Chaldees," whence they issued "to go to the land of Kanâan." It is true that Mr. Loftus considers the enormous ruins of *Werka* to be the real "Ur of the Chaldees," now traditionally called "the birthplace of Abraham;" nor would the establishment of this fact result in any further alteration of our view than by proving (what is very likely) that ARP*h*a-KaSD was a different place from AUR-KaSDIM. The name "Chaldæan" is also ancient enough, having been found in cuneiform on the monuments of Nineveh.

Be all this as it may, there still remains *one* "*Ur* of the Chaldees," AUR-KSDIM in the text, which is unquestionably, as shown by Ritter and by Ainsworth, the present city and district of *Urhoi*, now *Orfa*, or URP*h*A (called, in Greco-Roman times, *Chaldæopolis*, *Antiochia*, *Callirhoe*, and *Edessa*), in *Diàrbekìr*. Allowing very common mutations of vowels, we behold in *Urfa*, or ARP*ha*, ARP*ha*-KaSD, "*Orfa* of the *Chaldæan*," the absolute solution of ARPHAXAD, no less than the earliest geographical source of the *Abrahamidæ*.

Thus, at every step, the chorographic exactitude of Xth Genesis is vindicated; and ARP*h*aKaSD, no more a fabulous human being, regains its legitimate heritage among the *countries* of the earth. To the "late *Mr.*" ARPHAXAD, "aged 438 years," we repeat our valedictory, "requiescat in pace!" [633]

49. לוד — LUD — 'LUD.'

The high road from Nineveh, in the land of ASUR, Assyria, conducts a traveller towards Asia Minor, through ARFA-KASD, *Chaldæan-Orfa*, into *Lydia;* — a name which, in its Greek spelling of Λυδια, faithfully transcribes the Hebrew LUD-*ia*.

This country derives its name, according to traditions collected by a native of Asia Minor, Herodotus of Halicarnassus, from Lydus, son of Atys; whose crown passed into the keeping of Hercules. This legend indicates the ante-historical ground we tread upon; and probably the intrusion of Hellenic *Hieraclidæ* upon an aboriginal Lydian population, affiliated with the Shemites. The recent explorations of Fellows and the Lycian monuments now rescued from perdition, establish, in the most convincing manner, the transitions of art in all its symbolism, through Asia Minor, from Assyria to Greece; and the mythe of the *Assyrian Hercules* serves as a faithful thread through the mazes of this labyrinth: which mythe, Grote observes, exhibits but the "tendency to universal personification"—being merely "Μυθος, *Saga* — an universal manifestation of the human mind."

But, from the premises, one deduction is solid, viz.: that Herodotus, than whom in Lydian questions there is no higher authority, makes Hercules succeed Lydus — the personified land of *Lydia*. Now, inasmuch as the mythe of *Hercules* antedates all chronology, it follows that Herodotus, who says that *Lydus* preceded the *Hieraclidæ*, looked upon the autocthonous name and traditions of *Lydia* as still more remote from his own day; B. C. 484–430. To us, therefore, the Halicarnassian's testimony, upon the ante-historical affairs of his native Asia Minor, would *ipso facto* outweigh any notices of

Lydia issuing from the "School of Esdras" in Palestine (foreign to Lydian blood, language, and traditions), should the latter contradict him: which, happily, they do not.

The compiler of Xth Genesis, educated, as we now begin to feel assured, amid the "learning of the Chaldees," attributes no affiliations to the geographical locality he designates LUD; any more than, in his classification of the senior *Hamidæ* (*ver.* 6), he ascribes descendants to P*h*UT; which, we have seen, is *Barbary*. This engenders the supposition that he knew little beyond the *names* of either; and that just as to him, composing his ethnic chart in some University of Chaldæa, P*h*UT appeared to be the most western geographical range of *Hamitic* migrations, so LUD probably seemed to lie among the most northerly of *Semitic*. As such, then, he duly registered them in his inestimable chorography.

Some centuries prior to the age of this venerable digest, the *Lydians* are mentioned in Egyptian hieroglyphics. In the Asiatic conquests of Sethei-Meneptha, and of Ramses II., to say nothing of later Pharaohs, associated with *Ionians*, *Riphæans*, and other well-known families of Asia Minor, we find the oft-recurring "Land of *Ludenu*," or "land of the upper *Luden*," and "of the lower *Luden*." This establishes the existence of *Lydia* and of *Lydians* at the XVIIIth dynasty, fourteenth—sixteenth centuries B. C.; in days anterior to and coeval with Moses; *i. e.*, much earlier than the compilation of Xth Genesis. But (to avoid Mosaic conflictions with Egyptian records) it is best perhaps to ascend a few generations beyond modern disputes upon the era of the Hebrew "scholar and statesman;" when by pointing out LUD and *Lydians* in chronicles appertaining to the anterior XVIIth dynasty, we show that Amunoph II., Thotmes III., and Amunoph III., successors of that "new king over Egypt which knew not Joseph" (*Ex.* i. 8), could not readily have heard of Moses's Lydian geography before the great lawgiver was born. Posterior in epoch to the former, and anterior to the latter dignitary, these Pharaohs of the XVIIth dynasty knew nothing about either Joseph or Moses.

Nor is history wanting to support the early spread of Egyptian arms into Asia Minor; for besides a confused aggregation of events of different ages to be met with in every classical lexicon under the head of "Sesostris," we have the authentic account of Tacitus that the Priests of Thebes read to the Emperor Germanicus, from hieroglyphical inscriptions, how "Ramses overcame Libya, Ethiopia, the Medes and the Persians, Bactriana, and Scythia, and held sway over the lands which the Syrians, Armenians, and neighboring Cappadocians, inhabit from Bithynia up to the Lycian Sea."

We cannot quote authority for the discovery of the name LUD in cuneiform writings; unless *Ludenu* be the same as the "Rutennu" of the "Grand Procession of Thotmes III." [*supra*, p. 159], which Birch fixes, in hieroglyphical geography, "north of the Great Sea," and compares with the Assyrian king Sargina's prisoners at Khorsabad.

However, LUD, being identical with *Lydia*, enters, like the rest, as a geographical appellative into the catalogue of Xth Genesis; and the cyclopædic notion that, from a *man* called LUD, "the Lydians in Asia Minor derived their name," ranks among the childish postulates belonging to an age of which science now hopefully discerns "the beginning of the end." [634]

50. ארם — ARM — 'ARAM.'

Orthodox lexicography informs us that ARAM means "*highness, magnificence; otherwise, one that deceives,* or *their curse.*" In this instance the erudition of "N. M." compensates for the meagre article by "J. P. S." in Kitto's cyclopædia.

It has been shown already that Quatremère doubts Mover's derivation of ARM; which the latter considers to mean *a high land*, in juxtaposition to KNA*ă*N, *a low land.* Still, the objection assigned by the former is inconclusive, because RM does actually signify *high;* and with the primeval masculine article *aleph*, A, prefixed, A-RM is *the-high.* Certain it is, also, that the geographical brother of Arpha-Kasd, "*Orfa* of the

Chaldæan," and of *Lydia*, must be sought for along the same Tauric uplands of Asia Minor; where ARM lay among the "mountains of the east" (*Numb.* xxiii, 7). In Punic, also, the same word means *high;* for M. Judas reads on Numidian coins, *Juba* ROUM *melkat* = "Juba, *highness* of the realm."

Diodorus's Αριμα ὄρη or *Arimi Montes*, suggest themselves at once; although authorities disagree upon their location, in Phrygia, Lydia, Mysia, Cilicia, or Syria: but Strabo and Josephus inform us that the Greeks called *Syrians* those people who called themselves *Aramæans:* and when Homer and Hesiod wrote, the Αριμοι extended to Phrygia, which they termed *Arimaïa.* Syria, therefore, in its widest acceptation, seems best to correspond to ARM, because the latter merges into *Mesopotamia;* and in Pliny and Pomponius Mela the name of Syria is applied to provinces even beyond the Euphrates and Tigris.

As the grand centre of *Shemitish* families, Syria still preserves the name of *Sh*eM in its Oriental appellative; being known to *Syrians* and the populations around them by no other title than BûR-Es-*Sh*àM, *land of Shem.* Arab geography explains this coincidence by reasons worthy of attention. SHAM means the *left hand*, and YEMEEN (*Yemen* in Arabia), the *right;* as, face directed to the East, an Arabian worshipped the rising sun; or looked back to ARM as the traditionary birthplace of his ancestry before, by emigration to Arabia, they had acquired the right to call themselves âRB, *western*-men. Damascus, *Es-Shâm el-kebeer*, "the great Sham," may perhaps be the focus of these ancient radiations: for its identity with ARAM is marked in the passage —"The ARaM*ians* of *Damascus* came to succor Hadadezer king of Sobah, &c. (2 *Sam.* viii. 5. 6) — the versions generally substituting *Syrians* for *Aramæans.*

So extensive was the range of ARM in ancient geography that, to distinguish its divisions, a qualifying name was generally appended to it: thus, *Sedeh*-ARM, the "field of Aram," *Padan*-ARM, the "plain of Aram," and ARM-*Naharaïm*, "Aram of the two rivers," refer to parts of Mesopotamia: ARM-*Damashk* was a Damascene territory; ARM-*Sobah*, probably Cilicia; ARM-*Maakah*, east of the Jordan; and ARM-*beth-Rekhub*, on which authorities vary. ARMI, an *Aramæan*, is a Syrian in one scriptural text (2 *Kings* v. 20). It is a Mesopotamian in another (*Gen.* xxv. 20).

Aramæan was the speech of the patriarchal Abrahamidæ, when abandoning ARP*ha*-KaSD, or its equivalent AUR-KaSD*îm* (Chaldæan *Orfa*, or *Ur* of the Chaldees), they arrived in the land of Kanaan; where, forgetting their ancestral idiom, they adopted and misnamed *Hebrew* "the language of Kanaan," or *Phœnician.*

Thus, from Arabia Deserta to the confines of Lydia, from Syria, over Mesopotamia, to Armenia, do we meet with infinite *reliquiæ* of *Aram:* without being able, after four or five thousand years of migrations, to mark on the quicksands of *Aramæan* geography any more specific locality for ARM, than SYRIA in its most extended sense.

Hieroglyphical researches do not aid us to a more definite ascription of ARM. In the Vatican Museum, the statue of a priest bears the inscription — "His majesty, King Darius, ever living, ordered me to go to Egypt, while his majesty was in ARMA": supposed to be *Assyria.* Nor, in Persepolitan cuneiform records or in those of Assyria, has any more positive identification of ARM been discovered and published than what may exist in *Arm'ina*, *Arama*, &c., considered to be Armenia — a country in whose name ARM is also preserved.

The writer of Xth Genesis may or may not have had more precise views upon ARM; which he set down with its parallels, *Assyria*, *Orfa*, and *Lydia*, on his invaluable chart, and then proceeded to tabulate those tribes of the Semitic stock that looked back upon the *land* of ARM as their birthplace.[635]

"And the affiliations of ARM."

51. עוץ — âUT*s* — 'Uz.'

In *Gen.* x. 23, the *four* names after ARM are called BeNI-ARM; *i. e.*, "sons of

Aram"; but, in 1 *Chron.* i. 17, the same four are catalogued as BeNI-S*h*eM; that is, "sons of *Shem.*"

Hence one of two conclusions is submitted to hagiography. Either the writer of Chronicles follows a different genealogical list from that of Xth Genesis — in which case we are at a loss to which document to ascribe "plenary inspiration"—or (as we maintain with every Orientalist) the word BeNI (sons) does not mean, whether in the former or in the latter text, the *bona fide* offspring of a *man* called Aram, or of a *man* called Shem; but simply a general *affiliation;* such as in English we comprehend by Wilkin-*son;* or by *Fitz*-Gerald, *Mc*-Donald, *O'*-Brien, *Ap*-Shenkyn, &c.

ǎUT*s*, first of the four, cannot well have been Shem's *son* and *grandson* at one and the same time; unless it be claimed that Shem wedded his own daughter: an escape not provided for in either text; and if it were, what becomes of Aram's paternity? Again, an imaginary human being called S*h*eM could not physically have been progenitor of a *country* called Aram. Common sense, however, based upon the spirit of familiar Oriental personifications, finds no contradiction between the authors of Xth Genesis and of 1 Chronicles; to whom ǎUT*s* and his three figurative brethren, as BeNI, "affiliations," were colonies or emigrants from an especial *land* termed ARaM; itself classified generically among countries occupied by *Shemitish* families.

This example, we presume, suffices to show the absurdity of seeing *human* individuals where the writer of Xth Genesis catalogued naught but *countries*, *cities*, and *tribes*, after the symbolical names "Shem, Ham, and Japheth." — But, our difficulties end not here.

Genesis X.	*Genesis* XXII.
V. 23—And *sons* of ARaM, ǎUT*s*, and K*h*UL, and GT*t*R, and MaS*h*.	*V.* 20 — Milcah has also given *sons* to Nahor thy brother. " 21 — ǎUT*s* his first born, and BUZ his brother, and KMUAL, *Father* of ARaM. " 22 — And KaSD—(i. e. *Chaldæa*) &c.
A *third* ǎUT*s* occurs among the descendants of Esau (*Gen.* xxxvi. 28).	

With three distinct personifications (above exhibited), each called ǎUT*s*, it is next to impossible for a commentator to avoid equivoques; and the country, or tribe, of one ǎUT*s* may be erroneously assigned to either of the two others; even without supposing mistakes in the two later genealogical lists; which discrepancies, however, do not otherwise concern us. Xth Genesis, in every instance, has stood the test of critical geography heretofore; and errors in this case are ours, not its venerable compiler's.

Nevertheless, in the second list (*Gen.* xxii.), ǎUT*s* becomes the uncle of ARAM; whereas in Xth Genesis he is the latter's son: while KaSD, *Chesed*, (singular of KaSDIM, *Chaldæans*,) unmentioned by the former author, figures, in the latter's list, among the descendants of Nahor, Abraham's brother.

It is to the *land*, called ǎUT*s* in Xth Genesis, that Job's residence is generally assigned, owing to its proximity to Chaldæa; wherefore the latter passage indicates a *country*, rather than a tribe — but in no case a *man*.

These triple chances of error, above noticed, compel archæology to be extremely wary in deciding to which of numerous Arabian resemblances of name we are to attribute the ǎUT*s* of Xth Genesis—or really "*land* of ǎUT*s*." Bochart ingeniously guessed the *Æsitæ, Ausitis, Ausite*, of Ptolemy, in the Syrian desert towards the Euphrates; where the Idumæan Arabs *Beni-Tamîn* have dwelt; to whom Jeremiah exclaims — "Rejoice thee, daughter of Edom, who livest in the land of ǎUTs." Lenormant follows Michælis in selecting Damascus.

In Arab tradition, *Owz* was the parent of the lost Addite tribes; and, assuming this wild legend to be historical, by dint of mistranslations Forster has raised a fabric of delusion exceeded only in extravagance by the same enthusiastic divine's *Sinaic inscrip-*

tions! It is in the ill-advised *Appendix* to his excellent Geography, entitled "Hadramûtic Inscriptions," that this erudite Orientalist lost his balance when supposing that, in these very modern *Himyarite* petroglyphs, he found himself "conversing, as it were, with the immediate descendants of Shem and Noah, not through the doubtful medium of ancient history, or the dim light of Oriental tradition, but in their own records of their own annals, 'graven with an iron pen, and lead, in the rock for ever!'" He translates the second line of Wellsted's short inscription as follows: "*Aws* assailed the Beni-Ac, and hunted [them] down, and covered their faces with blackness."

Happy, indeed, though not perhaps to the pious extent of the Rev. Mr. Forster, should we be to recognize âUT*s* in these inscriptions; but some trifling obstacles intervene. Suppose, for instance, that the Hadramautic inscription (No. 4), read into *Arabic*, should say nothing of the kind? *Ex. gr.*, that which Forster translates "*Aws* assailed the Beni-Ac," &c., should be, according to Hunt, "the effeminate youths are adorned and perfume their garments and strut proudly"! And suppose, that the language in which these inscriptions of Hisn Ghoràb are written, being the old Ehkèelee or Cushite tongue, does not admit of their being *transcribed* directly into Arabic idioms at all! Fresnel, the Himyarite discoverer "par excellence," gives the same inscription (No. 4), in Arabic *letters*, but has ventured no *translation*. These suppositions Forster, so far as we can learn, has never taken notice of; but goes on translating anything and everything into an Arabic "sui generis," with the same serene composure that Father Kircher, two centuries ago, read off at sight (!) those identical *Sinaic inscriptions* on which Forster has latterly exercised his orthodoxy without mentioning the labors of his Herculean prototype.

âUT*s*, under these circumstances, remains on our hands. Probabilities favor the *Æsitæ*, *Ausitis*, of Ptolemy the geographer; and Job's "*land* of âUT*s*," on the Arabian frontier of Chaldæa, seems to answer best to the *Aramæan* analogies of Xth Genesis. âUT*s*, we infer, was a *tribe*.[636]

52. חול — K*h*UL — 'HUL.'

We enliven the reader with orthodox lexicography as we proceed — "HUL, *pain, infirmity, bringing forth children, sand,* or *expectation!*"

Most authorities abandon K*h*UL in despair: but Grotius indicated that a Cœlo-Syrian city called *Chollæ* by Ptolemy might represent K*h*UL; and Bochart noticed the frequency of this word in the Armenian localities of *Cholua, Choluata, Cholimma,* and *Cholobetene;* which last might be an Hellenic corruption of K*h*UL-*Beth*, "house of K*h*UL." Recent researches favor the adoption of the "land of *Huleh*," in which is the Lake *Huleh*, at the north of Palestine.[637]

53. גתר — GT*t*R — 'GETHER.'

Koranic tradition execrates the memory of "*Thamoud*, son of GATHER, son of the *Aram*," among ante-historical tribes distinguished for their idolatry: but nothing can exceed the vagueness of these legends.

Gadara, the metropolis of the Peræa, east of the Jordan, and one of the cities of Decapolis, has been assumed to represent GT*t*R. Here the well-known miracle of the "swine" is said to have been performed. There are many other places whose names, with the slightest modifications, answer equally well: among them, *Katara*, a town and district placed by Ptolemy on the Persian Gulf, sufficiently important to have become the bishopric of *Gadara*.

Gaddir, in Kanaanitish dialects (according to Pliny and Solinus, also in the "Punica lingua") meaning a hedge, limit, boundary, or "a place walled-round," renders the confusion still more perplexing; for in countries traversed by Phœnician caravans, and occupied by their factors, any form of GT*t*R is as likely to have signified *frontier* or *station*, as to be derived from the *tribe* called GT*t*R in Xth Genesis.[638]

54. מש — MS — 'Mash.'

Besides the discrepancy, above removed, between Xth Genesis and the parallel in 1 *Chronicles* (i. 17), in regard to the affiliations of these four names from Shem, or from Aram; here is another, that cannot be explained save through an error of some copyist. Who can really tell whether we should transpose MSK*h* into Xth Genesis, or MS into 1 Chronicles? [*Supra*, p. 473.] Two reasons, however, seem to justify the accuracy of the former text: one that a MSK is already mentioned among the "sons of Japheth" (*ver.* 2); and therefore the repetition of a similar name amid the *Shemites* is improbable: the other that the chart of Xth Genesis is the "editio princeps," of older and more standard authority than the books called *Chronicles.*

The *Macæ,* on the peninsula of the Persian Gulf whereon now stands the derivative city of *Muscat* — the *Masæi* Arabs in Mesopotamia; the *Masani* near the Euphrates; and the *Massonitæ* of Yemen; might entice inquiries: but, we think their habitats somewhat distant from the localities where *Aramæan* tribes appear to group; especially as MSA, *Massa,* descended from Ishmael (*Gen.* xxv. 14), may well assert its right to the latter lineage.

We cannot amend the old view of Bochart and of Grotius, that this Aramæan tribe survives about Mt. *Masius;* along Xenophon's river *Masca;* in the *Masieni* of Stephanus, and perhaps the *Moscheni* of Pliny; all of which point to Upper Mesopotamia as the camping-ground of MaS*h*.[639]

"And ARP*ha*-KaSD engendered SLK*h*, and SLK*h* engendered âEBR" (*Gen.* x. 24).

55. שלח — SLK*h* — 'Salah.'

Orfa in Diàrbekìr has been already demonstrated to be the fountain-source *Arpha-Kasd,* "Chaldæan Urfa," and no other than the true AUR-KaSDIM, "Ur of the Chaldees;" whence flow the earliest traditions of the Abrahamidæ.

âEBR, the *yonderer,* third in descent, seems to show either that a displacement had taken place before the *name* itself could well have been assumed; or that the appellative "yonderer" is an *ex post facto* attribution—the consequence of a migration that had previously taken effect.

Between these two names, *Orfa* as a fixed geographical point, and *Êber* "he who has gone *beyond,*" stands SLK*h;* transcribed *Salah* in king James's version: perhaps in this instance with more propriety than according to the vulgar Masoretic *Shelah;* which is suggested as the marginal reading.

Sela of Ammianus Marcellinus, or *Sele* of Ptolemy, a city in Susiana, has received the concurrence of many commentators. Others consider SLK*h* unknown. If Volney's suggestion of the *city* and *territory* called *Salacha* by Ptolemy be not the most probable halting-place of the EBERi when they had left Chaldæan *Orfa,* the ignorance of every body consoles us for ours.[640]

56. עבר — ÊBR, or rather êiBR — 'Heber.'

[The impossibility of transcribing the letter *Gnain* of the Hebrews, *âin* of the Arabs, into any European alphabet, has been noticed by me long ago. As a general principle, I follow the rules of Lane in these substitutions; but unless a European *hears* the sound of *âin* orientally articulated, his imagination can realize its phonetism as little as his adult voice can enunciate it. — G. R. G.]

Etymologically, ÊBR signifies "one of the other side," or "the *yonder-land;*" whilst ÊBRI, a "*yonderer,*" or "a man from the other side," has precisely the same radical as the *Greek* Υπερ, Latinized into *Iber* (*Iberes,* Iberian); equivalent to *trans, ultra,* &c.

"HEBER (עבר, *one of the other side;* Sept. Ἔβερ and Ἑβερ), son of Salah, who became the father of Peleg at the age of 34 years, and died at the age of 464 (*Gen.* x. 24; xi. 14; 1 *Chron.* i. 25). His name occurs in the genealogy of Christ (*Luke* iii. 35). There is nothing to constitute HEBER *an historical personage;* but there is a degree of interest connected with him from the *notion*, which the Jews themselves entertain, that the name of Hebrews applied to them, was derived from this *alleged* ancestor of Abraham. No *historical* ground appears why this name should be derived from him rather than from any other personage that occurs in the catalogue of Shem's descendants; but there are so much stronger objections to every other *hypothesis*, that this perhaps is still the most probable of any which have yet been started."

If the authors of this volume had written the above scientific *exposé*, it would have been seized upon as another instance of "skeptical views" (save the mark!); but the initials "J. N." appended to the above article in Kitto are those of a profound Germano-Hebraist, the Rev. Dr. JOHN NICHOLSON of Oxford.

Archæologically, the name ÊBR marks a displacement, or dislocation, that must have occurred before such name could have been given or assumed.

Of such dislocation the earliest notice is the march of the *Abrahamidæ* from *Orfa-Chaldee* to Harran (probably *Carræ*), in Mesopotamia, and thence to Kanaan: where the Kanaanites gave to ABRAHAM, probably, the designation of ÊBR, as "he who comes from *yonder-land*,"—*transfluvianus*, or "from the other side" of the Euphrates—whence HEBREW, ÊBRI, became the cognomen of this family. Indeed, it is remarked that the title ÊBRIM, *yonderers*, Hebrews, was given to the Abrahamidæ by foreign nations. They called themselves *Israelites* after Jacob's wrestling match at *Phenuel;* and did not adopt that of "Hebrews" until many centuries later.

We are dealing, therefore, in Xth Genesis — a document compiled at least five, if not ten, hundred years subsequently to the arrival of the earliest Abrahamidæ in Kanaan — with a *people* upon whom the name ÊBR had been imposed, "nolens volens" on their own part. Had the chorographer of Xth Genesis been a man of Abrahamic pedigree, he would probably have designated his own nation by its most honored title, "Israelite;" but, far from that, a *Chaldæan* composing his ethnic map in Chaldæa, naturally gives to ÊBR its radical sense of "yonderer;" either because the Palestinic Abrahamidæ were so termed by surrounding populations, or because they were then, to him, as ÊBeR-îm, "people who had gone *beyond*" the Euphrates. That there is no "prefiguration" (*i. e.*, "cart before the horse") in Xth Genesis, has been proven by the names *Sidonian, Hamathian*, &c.; folks who could not well have been citizens of those cities, *Sidon, Hamath*, &c., until after the houses had been built: and inasmuch as these citizens are catalogued in the same document with ÊBR, the antiquity of the latter's registration is brought down to historical times; long ages after that emigration from Chaldæan *Orfa* into Palestine through which the foreign application of "yonderers," given to Abraham's descendants, had originated.

"Fama crescit eundo;" and Oriental mythos — after Judaism, a little before the Christian era, had penetrated into Arabia; and still more forcibly after Islamism, in the seventh century, had imbued pagan Arabians with extraneous traditions — assimilated ÊBER, now metamorphosed into a *man* and a *patriarch*, to the Arab prophet HOOD: who, in native Arabian tradition, plays a part somewhat like that which MOSES does in Jewish; being their earliest metahistorical Reformer. Who this HOOD probably is, the profound investigations of Fresnel clearly indicate:—

DʜU-NUAS, or *Zhu-Nawâz*, is the subject. "CAIRE, 12 *Mars*, 1845.

"The Greeks knew that Bacchus was Arabian, and have sought for the etymology of the name Διόνυσος, *Dionysus*, after their own fashion: they made of it 'the god of Nysa,' Nysa being a city of Arabia, or, as says Herodotus, of Ethiopia, where Bacchus was raised by the Nymphs. . . . . About forty miles to the east of *Zhafâr*, the most ancient of all their (Arabian) metropoles, and the site of the oldest Arabian civilization, is a mountain that Edrisi calls *Loûs*, and that the inhabitants of Mahrah call *Noûs*. . . . . This mountain of *Noûs*, near which is found, not the *Kabr Hoûd*, or tomb of Heber (ÊBR), but the *Kabr Sâleh* (that is to say, the tomb of the FATHER or HOUD, according to Arab notions) is the point where I place the birth of Bacchus; in other words, the point of departure for those civilizing conquests of which the Arabs have preserved the remembrance. These conquests are not the act of a single man, or if one might so express oneself, 'of a single Bacchus.' *Dhou-Ons* or *Dhou-Noûs* (in the oblique case, *Dhi-Ons* or *Dhi-Noûs*), *Dhou 'l Karneyn* (the man with the two horns), *Afrikis* (the god-father of Africa), *Lokman*, &c., &c., are to me so many personifications of Bacchus; and if you must absolutely have a religious idea pre-existent to Arab kings, a Bacchus outside of Yemenite dynasties, I should venture to tell you to seek for Bacchus in the tomb *Salch* (SLK*h*) [*Gen.* x. 24] under the *Djabal-Noûs*. Bacchus then will be the father of the patriarch Héber (ÊBR), of the *Abrahamidæ* and of the *Joktanidæ*.

"Will you mount up still higher? Διόνυσος is (Hebraicè) DU-ANOS*h*, *Dhou-Enosh* (the god of the vulgar), or lastly, Enos himself, ENOS, grandson of Adam.

"Agréez, monsieur, &c.,

"F. FRESNEL."

"À M. MOHL, *Journal Asiatique, Paris.*"

Our researches do not require our accompanying M. Mohl into antediluvian regions. We are satisfied when shown that EBR in Xth Genesis is the natural appellation of a *tribe;* better known to modern science as source of the *Abrahamidæ.*[641]

"And unto ÊBR were born two sons."

57. פֶּלֶג — PLG — 'PELEG.'

"And the name of one (was) PLG," explains the author of Xth Genesis, "because in his day the earth was *divided;*" literally, "PLG*ed*," *split*. In modern Arabic even, the identical word FLG means a "split," and "to split;" which again induces a smile at mystifications concerning a "sacred tongue," every third word of which exists in the Arabic *dàrig*, vernacular; every second in the *Nahwee*, or Koranic idiom; every one, in some form or other, by easily recognizable changes of consonant or vowel, in the *Qamoos* — the "Ocean" lexicon of Arabian literature. Any well-educated *Arab*, we fear not to maintain, who could first peruse in some European tongue a few philosophical works on *Hebrew* literature and comparative philology, would master the 5642 words counted (by Leusden) in this exaggerated Kananitish language, after devoting one day to its alphabet, in about a week. This doctrine no Shemitish Orientalist (no Lanci, no De Saulcy, no Quatremère, no Fresnel, no Rawlinson), will deny. "We have remarked in it," comments De Saulcy upon the *Toison d'Or*, a new Phœnician work by the Abbé Bourgade, "a passage the justness of which we ought to applaud; because, in order to write it, one must not have been scared by the scientific anathemas of certain too-exclusive savants. Here is this passage — 'It is therefore rational to make use of Hebrew, and of the other Aramæan idioms to explain the Punic: one may also use Arabic, another ramification of the Semitic family; sometimes even it is indispensable to have recourse to this language, *almost all Hebrew words being found within Arabic*, either without modification, or with very slight modifications, sometimes in the form, at others in the sense, but not *vice-versâ;* the language of the Korân being incontestably richer than that of the Bible.'"

On the historical monstrosities erected upon this verse of Scripture, it is not for us to dwell. *Pelagos*, the *Pelasgi*, and *Pelargos;* the "Sea," the "fossil people" as Niebuhr beautifully calls them, or the "Stork," do not concern an alien Semitic bisyllable, whose simplest essence is Anglicè a "split." We are loath to reject the Bochartian assimilation of *Phalga*, a town on the Euphrates, near *Charræ;* which town, some say, is *Haran*, built by Abraham's brother, after his own death at *Chaldæan-Orfa:* just in the same way that Moses posthumously describes his own ever-unknown burial-place, his wake of thirty days, &c. (*Deut.* xxxiv. 5–12): but we venture to submit the following doubts: —

1st. If by PLG, or P*h*LG, the editor of Xth Genesis meant what, in every instance but the mythological NMRD, is herein proved to have been a *country*, a *people*, or a *city*, then the parenthetical passage, "because in his day the earth was *split*," may be a gloss by some later hand,—rationally suggested through paronomasia of the triliteral PLG "split," combined with impressions formed upon other documents by such interpolator — the whole having been subsequently recast by the Esdraic school from which we inherit (every possible chance of intervening error and perversion inclusive) this *verse* of Xth Genesis.

2nd. If it were shown that a gloss must be as unlikely as it is dangerous to the claims of plenary inspiration; then, before we can perceive a necessity for supposing that the chorographer of Xth Genesis here alludes to the "Dispersion of mankind," we would inquire whether the words "(was) *split* the earth" do not refer to some local and terrestrial catastrophe—an earthquake, for instance—that, occurring simultaneously, may have become traditionally coupled with a PLG*ian* migration. A similar catastrophe, introduced into Manetho's text in a similar manner, occurred under Bochus, 1st King of the second Egyptian dynasty, when "a huge chasm" was made at Bubastis.

3rd, and lastly—If none of the above possibilities be satisfactory, then, falling back upon the indubitable orthodoxy of the Parisian Professor of Egyptian Archæology, we should perceive in the words "because in his day the earth (was) *split*," merely a partition of territory between the PLG*ian* and the *Joktanide* affiliations of ÊBR the "yonderer."—"Of the two sons of this Patriarch, the first, *Phaleg* (holds Lenormant), indicating that part of the nation that continued to wander in Upper Mesopotamia; *Iectan*, the second, shows us on the contrary the other portion of the same people which first set itself on a march towards the south." The verb "divide" occurs three times in the English version of Xth Genesis (5, 25, 32). It need scarcely be mentioned that, in the Hebrew, the play upon the word PLG "to split" presents itself only in verse 25. The other two passages use a distinct verb, NP*h*RDU, "they *dispersed*."

"Hypotheses non fingo" — and as everything beyond the name of PLG, "split," is an hypothesis, we leave hagiography to "split hairs" on the question: merely insisting here that PLG has no relation whatever to a "Dispersion of mankind."[612]

58. יקטן — IKTN — 'Joktan.'

The compiler of Xth Genesis closed the ancestral line of the *Abrahamidæ*, abruptly, with PeLeG, a "split." Yet to the pedigree of IKTN he devotes particular attention; for, besides cataloguing thirteen of the latter's descendants, he adds, "all these are sons of IKTN": and then fixes their dwelling-places.

Why this difference? Were his partialities Arabian? Did he know all about Arab migrations, and nothing of those of the *Abrahamidæ?* Had the writer been a "Hebrew of the Hebrews," he would scarcely have blocked the "royal line of David" at PLG, "a split"; and thereby left to another hand, in another document (*Gen.* xi. 18–26), at a later age, the task of linking Abraham's genealogy to his own ethnic map of nations and places. Here again, a *foreigner* to Judaism and Jews, our conjectural *Chaldæan* chorographer, "laisse percer le bout d'oreille." Such alien would not have greatly concerned himself with the *Abrahamidæ*, a petty tribe that had wandered off to Kanaan; and the writer of Xth Genesis did not: such alien would have taken much interest in the proceedings of the ever restless *Joktanidæ*, always harrying the Mesopotamian frontier; and the writer of Xth Genesis did.

IoKTaN, *Joktan*, *Yoktan*, or correctly *Qahtân*, the *Beni-Kahtân*—most ancient and renowned of all Semitish intruders upon the domains of Cushite-*Himyâr* — need no panegyrist. They have ground their lance-heads upon every pebble "from *Havilah* to *Shur*, that is before Egypt, as thou goest towards Assyria." Their woollen tents are pitched from "*Sephar*, a mount of the east," at the south-western extremity of Arabia, even unto the declivities of Persian Uplands. Their *Nedjdee* horses still chase the wild ass, "gour," over the wildest tracts of Arabia's *hâgar*, "stone," desert; their *dromedaries* are precious at Cairo, Mecca, Aleppo, Bagdâd, and Ispahân. From them issued Mohammed; whose *Korân* is the monotheistic code of religious and moral law to above one hundred millions of mankind in Europe, Asia, Africa, and India's islands: their tongue, "the pure *Korèysh*," for twelve centuries has been the envied attainment of poets, historians, and philosophers, of their own exalted race, and of its Arabian contemporaries during consecutive generations.

By "*Beni-Qahtân*," sons of IKTN, we have hitherto implied the *Joktanides* in general; but the great tribe in Arabia now calling itself *Beni-Kahtân* claims the direct lineage of this son of ÊBR. They are traced in the *Katanitæ*, *Kithebanitæ*, and *Kottabani*, of Ptolemy; the *Katabeni* of Dionysius; back to the *Cattabanes*, *Kattabanum*, of Eratosthenes in the third century B. C.: while their existence in Arabia is attested by the compiler of Xth Genesis many generations anterior to the age of the Cyrenian geographer.

With the admirable tabulation of the "Settlements of Joktan," and the maps that Forster has appended to his geography, the reader can verify for himself the accuracy of the following schedule of IoKTaN's affiliations.[643]

"And IoKTaN engendered"

59. אלמודד — ALMUDD — 'ALMODAD.'

The *Allumaeotæ*, *Almodæei*, Ἀ'λλουμαιῶται, of Ptolemy, a people of central Arabia Felix, represent ALMUDaD by general consent.[644]

60. שלף — SLP — 'SHELEPH.'

Ptolemy's *Salapeni*, *Salupeni*, the Greek transposition of "*Beni*-SeLePh," sons of SHELEPH, are equally certain: now represented by the tribe of *Metèyr?*[645]

61. חצרמות — KhTsRMUTt — 'HAZARMAVETH.'

Who, unacquainted with corrupt Chaldee vocalizations, foisted in the sixth century after Christ upon the old Hebrew Text (under the name *Masoretic points*), would see that the writer of Xth Genesis here wrote *Khàdramaut?* the very name which the Arabs still give to their province of *Hadramàut*, or *Khàzramôt*.

This name, "in the Septuagint version, is written *Sarmoth*, the first syllable being dropped; by St. Jerome (a well-versed Orientalist), in the Vulgate, written *Asarmoth;* the article being incorporated with the name, or the aspirate omitted, conformably with the dialect of the Nabathæans; by Pliny, *Atramitæ*, and *Chatramotitæ;* and by Ptolemy, *Adramitæ*, *Chathramitæ*, and *Chatramotitæ* or *Cathramonitæ*": no less than by Strabo. "So Hadramaut," comments Forster upon Bochart, "is modulated into Hazarmoveth, merely by the use of the diacritic points, . . . an artifice," says this learned and reverend Orientalist, "allowedly, of recent and rabbinical invention."

The tribe and territory of HADRAMAUT being fully identified in Xth Genesis; the only salient point of interest connected with its later history, is the mission — we follow Mr. Plate — of a "priest of Nagrane, the capital of Christian Hadhramaût," to *China*, in the seventh century of our era; whose successful voyage is attested by the bilinguar stone, in Chinese and Syriac (dated A. D. 782), discovered at *Si-Gan-Fú* in 1625; which inscription is reputed to be genuine.[646]

62. ירח — IRKh — 'JERAH.'

This tribe of Arabia, under the Arabic title of *Yàreb-ben-Qahtàn*, "*Yàreb* son of JOKTAN;" or of *Aboo-l'-Yemèen*, "father of Yemen;" was pointed out by Golius, upon Arab authority, as "Pater populorum Arabiæ Felicis; primus Arabicæ linguæ auctor." Forster, continuing his emendations of Bochart, states that IRKh "in the LXX, is written Ἰαρὰχ (*Jarach*); by St. Jerome, *Iare;* by the modern Arabs, *Jerhä* or *Serhä* (pronounced Jerc*hä*, Serc*hä*); and also, as shall presently be shown, *Sherah* or *Sheradje*,

Serene or *Zohran:*" — a name thrice registered by Ptolemy, "in his Insula *Jerachæorum*, on the Arabian Gulf, S. of Djedda, and in his Vicus *Jerachæorum*, on the Lar or Zar river, in the vicinity of the Persian Gulf; a town and an island bearing in common this proper name, although separated from each other by a space of 15°, or more than one thousand geographical miles!"

It was Bochart's acuity, as our author honestly remarks, that restored Ptolemy's νῆσος Ἱεράχων, previously rendered *insula accipitrum*, or "the Isle of Hawks," to its patriarchal origin; *insula Jerachæorum, i. e.*, "the island of the Beni Jerah." But this father of European commentators on Xth Genesis did more. He showed that the *Alilæi* of Agatharcides were identical, not merely with the tribe *Beni-Hilal* of the Nubian geographer; but also with Ptolemy's "insula Ierakiorum;" for the reason that *Hilal* means "moon" in Arabic, just as *Ierakh* does in Hebrew.

Most successfully does Forster exhibit the settlements of IeRaK*h* within "a vast triangle, formed by the mouth of the Zar river, on the Persian Gulf; the town of Djar (the *Zaaram reg.* of Ptolemy) on the coast of the Hedjàz, twenty English miles south of Yembo; and the district of Beni Jerah (part of the ancient Katabania), or the southwestern angle of the peninsula, terminating at the Straits of Bab-el-Mandeb;" and the probability that the great tribe, known as the *Minæi* in classical geography, belonged to IeRaK*h-ian* affiliations, is also by him perspicuously elucidated. [647]

63. הדורם — HDURM — 'Hadoram.'

By Fresnel this name is considered to be the same as *Djourhoum;* of whom Arabian tradition reckons an elder branch, the old *Jorhamites*, among extinct, and a younger, the Koranic *Jorhamites*, among existing families. *Jorham* is the "Arabum *Hejazensium* pater" of Pococke; and Bochart associated the name with the *Drimati* of Pliny, and with Cape *Corodamon;* which last, by the facile transposition of D for R, is Cape *Hadoramus*, or of HDURM. Volney accepts *Adrama* for their natural representative; confirmed by Forster in *Hadrama*. and thus, carried onwards through the classical *Chatramis*, *Dacharæmoizæ* of Ptolemy, to the *Dora* and *Dharræ* of Pliny; they are perpetuated in the modern town and tribe of *Dahra:* at the same time that *Ras-el-*Had now preserves one abbreviation of the name, and *Bunder-*Doram another — on the very promontory "Hadoramum" at the mouth of the Persian Gulf. [648]

64. אוזל — AUZL — 'Uzal.'

The native Jews of *Sanaa*, capital of Yemen, have abundantly borne witness that AUZaL was its ancient Arabian appellative, as, to this day, it is among themselves. The "*Javan* from AUZaL" of Ezekiel (xxvii. 19,) must be, therefore, as Volney and Forster unite in indicating, not Grecian *Ionia*, but a town in Yemen, now called *Deifân*. *Ocelis* of Ptolemy, *Ocila* of Pliny, recognizable in the modern *Cella;* together with *Ausara*, a town of the *Gebanitæ* or Yemenites; are relics of AUZaL long patent through the scholarship of Bochart. [649]

65. דקלה — DKLH — 'Diklah.'

In the *Dulkhelitæ* of Himyar, and the tribe *Dhu-'l-Kalaah* of Yemen, Orientalists perceive this affiliation of *Joktan;* that, perhaps, has carried along with it some remembrance of an ante-historical sojourn on the *Dikle*, or *Tigris:* if, as Bochart suggested, its name have no affinity to *nukhl*, a "palm tree." [650]

66. עובל — *á*UBL — 'Obal.'

Among nine names of existing Arab tribes identified by Fresnel with biblical appellatives (after the rejection of more than forty of the latter as irrecognizable) *Abil* is one. But, it seems more than probable that a branch of these *Joktanidæ* crossed the narrow straits of Bàb-el-Mandeb into Abyssinia, "Arabia Trogloditica;" and gave their patronymic âUBaL, to the *Aualites* Sinus, *Abalites* emporium, *Avalitæ*, and perhaps *Adoulitæ* (D for B), on the African coast of the Red Sea and Indian Ocean, recorded in classical geography. Volney sees them in Edreesee's *Hobal;* or in El-Hamza's *Obil*, that, with nine other tribes, succumbed, about 230 years A. C., in wars with ARDOUAN, Radowàn, king of Persia, better known as the Sassanian ARDISHEER-*Babegàn*.[651]

67. אבימאל — ABIMAL — 'ABIMAEL.'

ABI-MAL, in Arabic, is "*Father* of MAL;" the meaning of which is also "possession of *property*;" in allusion, perhaps, to the wealth accruing to this tribe from their occupancy of the myrrh, incense, balsam, and spice districts of Yemen.

They are the *Mali* of Theophrastus, the *Malichæ* of Ptolemy; surviving in the town *Malai*, or *el-Kheyf;* not far from the tomb of Mohammed at *Medeéneh*.[652]

68. שבא — SBA — 'SHEBA.'

The perplexities accruing to ethnic geography from the presence of *four* SBAs in the book of Genesis, three of them in the Xth chapter, have been set forth in our analysis of the *Hamitic Saba* of Himyar [*ubi supra*, p. 498]: nor is it possible to escape from confounding this *Joktanide's* properties with some of those that appertain to the former's inheritance.

Nothing daunted, Forster says, "the Joktanite Sheba gave its origin, and his own name, to the primeval and renowned kingdom of the Sabæans of Yemen." Perhaps he did. Possibly the *Cushite* SaBA may have done so before him. "Quien sabe?" Nevertheless, "the concurrent testimonies of Eratosthenes, Dionysius Periegetes, Priscian, Festus Avienus, and others of the ancients," collected by Bochart, place the *Sabæans* between the Minæi and the Katabeni, at *Sàba* and *Màreb:* whilst the notice by *Aboo'l-Feda* that "Mareb was inhabited by the *Beni-Kahtan*," or *Joktanidæ*, really favors our author's somewhat peremptory identification of this SBA.[653]

69. אופר — AUPR — 'OPHIR.'

A volume would not suffice to display the aberrations of intelligence printed on this name! Some are exposed in Kitto and in Anthon.

Munk very properly cuts short discussion by reminding those who see *Ophir* at Madagascar, Malacca, or Peru, that the writer of Xth Genesis places AUPR in the midst of the Arabian *Joktanidæ:* which doctrine Volney had previously sustained, and supported by vigorous researches that identified it with the ruined site of *Ophor* on the Persian Gulf.

Bochart and Michælis held the same judicious views; and Forster has left nothing more to be desired; by proving, once for all, that *Ofor*, a town and district of Oman, is the true AUP*h*iR of the Old Testament — that Pliny's "littus Hammæum ubi auri metalli" is the true *Gold Coast* of Solomon's expeditions — and that the whole of them are comprehended within the domains of the *Joktanidæ*.[654]

70. חוילה — K*h*UILH — 'HAVILAH.'

Our prefatory remarks on ASUR, and its ante-diluvian existence, apply with equal force to that "land of *Havilah* where (there is) gold," which, an universal Flood notwithstanding, now reappears exactly where it stood, antefluvially, on the *gold-coast* of Arabia.

We are not free, either, from chances of error in attributing to the present K*h*UILH (the *Joktanide* affiliation of Shem) some possessions that may have belonged to his namesake, K*h*UILH the *Cushite*.

However, the Nubian geographer indicated to Bochart (father of genesiacal geographers) the country of *Chaulan* in Arabia Felix; and Forster, with propriety selects the province of *Khaul*, south-east of Sanaa (*Uzal*); site of Pliny's tribe of *Cagulatæ;* now inhabited by the *Beni*-KHOLÂN. Its topography, moreover, in the immediate proximity of Omanite *gold* regions, satisfies the mineralogical exigenda of the prædiluvian "land of HAVILAH" demanded by the letter of *Gen.* ii. 11, 12; and insisted upon, as a preliminary step towards precision, by Volney.[655]

71. יוֹבָב — IUBB — 'JOBAB.'

The *Iobaretai* of Ptolemy, through the ready change of the Greek *b* into the Latin *r*, by a mistake of copyists, revealed themselves to Bochart as the *Jobabitæ* of Xth Genesis. But, "the flexible genius of the Arabic idiom" suffices to explain such difference of pronunciation; and Forster triumphantly points out "the Iobaritæ of Ptolemy, in *Beni*-JUBBAR, the actual name of a tribe or district, in the country of the Beni-Kahtan, south-east of Beishe, or Baisath Joktan, in the direction of Mâreb; and the original, or Scriptural form of this name, in *Beni*-JOBUB or JOBAB, the existing denomination of a tribe and district situated in the ancient Katabania, half-way between Sanaa and Zebid" — *Katabania* being the Greek inversion of *Beni-Qahtân*, the old JOKTANIDÆ. "All these are sons of JOKTAN;" wrote the venerable compiler of this precious ethnic chart, Xth Genesis, above 2500 years ago.[656]

We have shown that every name (but NIMROD's, which is mythological) in the Xth chapter of Genesis, excepting those of NOAH and "Shem, Ham, and Japheth," is a personification of *countries*, *nations*, *tribes*, or *cities*: — that there is not a single "*man*" among the seventy-nine cognomina hitherto examined. [N. B. The number 79 is obtained by adding the 8 *cities*, founded by Nimrod, to the 71 names above enumerated.]

Abundant instances are patent, even in king James's version, where Israel, or Jacob, is put for *all the Jewish community;* and so ASUR, for example, means *Assyria* in such passages as "ASUR shall come as a torrent; ASUR shall arise like a conflagration; JEHOVAH will raise up ASUR against *Moab*, against *Ammon*, against *Judah*, against *Israel*." Now, none will suppose that *Asur*, *Moab*, *Ammon*, or *Israel*, are individuals, human beings. It is evident that these are collective names, employed according to the genius of Oriental minds and tongues. And upon whose authority, let us ask, must we modern foreigners offend the spirit of old Oriental writers (apart from common sense itself), in order to find *men* in the seventy-nine ethnico-geographical appellatives of Xth Genesis?

That, in some instances, the name of an ante-historical founder of a nation has been perpetuated by the nation itself, no one denies. Classical history teems with such; *e. g.* HELLAS for the *Hellenes;* DORUS for the Dorians; LYDUS for the Lydians; but they are, in general, about as historical as AFRIKIS of the Arabs; whom the Saracens made the "Father of *Africa*," after they had learned the Latin name of this continent! In most cases, however, the nation or tribe invented a founder; to whom they gave the name of the *country* they happened to occupy: nor does archæology concede to the Hebrews any exemption from this universal law, merely for the sake of conformity to time-honored caprice.

But, if seventy-eight of the seventy-nine names in Xth Genesis are those of *countries*, *nations*, *tribes*, or *cities;* such is not the case with four others, catalogued as the parental NuK*h*, NOAH, and his three sons S*h*eM, K*h*aM, and IaP*h*eT*t*.

Our observations on these names limit themselves to guessing, as nearly as we can, what *may* have been meant by the writer of Xth Genesis.

1st. NuK*h* — (Noah), or NUK*h*, in Hebrew lexicons, among its various meanings, signifies *Repose* and also *Cessation*. We place the word "OBSCURITY" beneath it on our Genealogical Tableau. To the chorographer of Xth Genesis this name NK*h* symbolized, probably, a point of time so remote from his own day that he *ceased* to inquire further; and *reposed* from his labors in blissful ignorance, after having comprehended the vanity of human efforts to pierce that primordial gloom. If he did not, we do: and with the less regret, because an expounder (who says he knows all about it) can be met with at every street-corner.

2d. From the *unknown*, then, in the supposed idea of a Chaldæan writer, proceeded three grand divisions of mankind; already distributed, at the age of the compilation of Xth Genesis, each one "after his *tongue*, in their lands, after their nations." It became necessary, for his chorographic and ethnic objects, to classify them. He saw they were apparently divided into *three* cuticular colors; just as the Egyptians before him had perceived the same thing, when they classified *three*, of the four human varieties known to them, by the colors red, yellow, and white.

3d. He gave to them, or adopted through preceding traditions, the three names "S*h*eM K*h*aM and IaP*he*T*t*"; and called the nations within his horizon of knowledge by these terms, as much for convenience sake, as on account of their several and probable linguistic, physiological, geographical, and traditionary relationship to each other. The meaning which he attached to each of these proper names is utterly unknown; but modern lexicography speculates upon their acceptation as follows: —

A. K*h*aM is the ancient name of Egypt; centre point of the populations which the writer of Xth Genesis classified as BeNI-K*h*aM, "sons of Ham;" and which we call *Hamitic.* In Hebrew, K*h*M means *hot:* but, in Arabic, while HàM has the same acceptation, K*h*àM signifies *dark, swarthy:* perfectly applicable to the peoples that this name embraces in Xth Genesis. The Egyptians designated themselves as the *red* race; wherefore, for Hamitic types, we adopt the red color.

B. S*h*eM, in Hebrew, means *name* "par excellence." It is also supposed to possess the sense of *left* hand, in contrast to *Yemen*, the *right;* but this seems to be an "ex post facto" Arabian commentary. The Egyptians always gave shades of yellow to *Shemitish* races, in accordance with their cuticular color; and we adopt it for our classification.

C. IaP*he*T*t*. Such rabbinical explanations as "the man of the opening of the tent" belong to the domain of fable.

IAPETUS, son of Cœlus and Terra, was the Titanic progenitor of Greeks in their ante-historical MUTHOI; the "audax genus *Iapeti*" is a symbolical periphrasis for *white* races; and an ancient Greek proverb, του Ιαπετου πρεσβυτερος, "elder than Iapetus," indicates that the sense in which Grecians used it corresponds to our saying "older than Adam." It is not impossible that the writer of Xth Genesis, in his anxiety to discover an ancestor for *white* families, asked some Greek traveller, who replied "Ιαπετος." To ourselves, as anciently to the Egyptians, these families are white.

We conclude in the language of D'Avezac — "Far from admitting that *Genesis* wished to make all the ramifications of the great human family descend from the unique NOAH, we would voluntarily sustain the thesis, that the genesiacal writer only wished to designate the three great branches of *white* races, individualized for us in the three types Greek, Egyptian, and Syriac; whose respective traditions have preserved athwart ages, as an indelible testimony of the veracity of Moses [or, only of that of the unknown *writer* of Xth Genesis], the names of Japheth, of Ham, and of Shem: but, without entering digressionally into a question so vast, let us hasten to say that, to our eyes, the Biblical texts are very disinterested upon any doubts arising from that [doubt] as to the unity or multiplicity of species in the human genus."

Section B.—OBSERVATIONS ON THE ANNEXED GENEALOGICAL TABLEAU OF THE "SONS OF NOAH."

So far as the authors' reading enables them to judge, here, for the first time since Xth Genesis was composed, are tabulated, in a true *genealogical* form, all the ethnic and geographical names contained in that ancient document.

After the foregoing analysis of each name under *Section A.*, the reader requires no prolix remarks to perceive the utility of our Tableau; which, at a glance, exhibits *Father* NuK*h* (Noah), and his three *Sons*—his *Grandsons, Great-grandsons, Great-great-grandsons, Great-great-great-grandsons,* and *Great-great-great-great-grandsons*, according to their natural order. In this manner (the geography of the Hebrew Text being, once for all, defined,) it is to be hoped that science will be relieved from further discussion of main *principles*, whatever may be the light which future Oriental researches cannot fail to shed upon details.

Each *Name* is first displayed in the "square-letter" of the Hebrew Text, without the Masoretic points. Below it, in "Roman" capitals, is placed the conjectural vocalization of our modern, and colloquial, *English* imitation of ancient foreign words. Beneath is put, in "Italics," the spelling of each name as printed in king James's version. This is followed, in "Gothic" letters, with the *geographical* attribution of the several cognomina, conformably to the results attained through our *Section A.* And finally, under every one, in common "Roman" type, is represented the probable *country, nation, tribe, city, citizen,* and *personage* historical or mythic, to which the authors' studies ascribe each name.

"*Humanum est errare.*"

[The best parallel I have met with in ancient history of the conversion of symbolical and national names into *personages*, that might be assimilated to the Hebrew map in Genesis Xth, occurs in Tacitus.[657] Speaking of the Germans, he gives one of their antique myths (which, during his time, was current among them) in explanation of their figurative origins and tripartite distribution into races. "Celebrant carminibus antiquis, quod unum apud illos memoriæ et annalium genus est, TUISCONEM deum, terrâ editum, et filium MANNUM originem gentis conditoresque. MANNO tres filios assignant e quorum nominibus proximi oceano *Ingævones*, medii *Herminones*, cæteris *Istævones* vocantur."

TUISCO is the god *Mars.* MANNUS the Latinized form of our word "Man," in German *Mann:* "*ones*," is the euphonizing suffix to the primitive words *Ingæv, Hermin, Istæv.*

The learned Zeuss[658] has shown that *Ingæv* is the same as *Yngvi*, "noble;" ancient title of the royal race of Sweden. *Istæv*, also meaning "illustrious," is traced in *Astingi*, royal race of the Visigoths and Vandals: and *Hermin*, in old Gothic *airmun*, meant "the mighty ones."

1. *Hermin*-ones, (in Pliny, *Herminones*,) comprehended four tribes: the Suevi, Hermudiri, Chatti, and Cherusci. These clans occupied inland Germany.

2. *Ingæv*-ones. These embraced the Cimbri, the Teutones, and the "Chaucorum gentes;" inhabiting west and north-west Germany.

3. *Istæv*-ones — as the *Vindili* of Pliny, included the Burgundiones, Varini, Carini, and Guttones. Their place was north-eastern Germany.

For our purpose of simple illustration, it is not essential to detail the geographical territories assigned to these names; which, mutilated and corrupted by Roman orthography, preserve as little relation to an ancient *German* pronunciation as the Indo-Germanic names of GoMeR, MaGUG, &c., do in our authorized version after passing through Hebrew transcriptions, Septuagint corruptions, and the fabulous vocalizations of Jewish Rabbis of the Masora. What we are driving after becomes evident at once, so soon as we tabulate the *genealogy* of these tribes as we have done that of those in Xth Genesis.

Tuisco
MARS.
|
Mannus
MAN
|

Ingæv.	*Hermin.*	*Istæv.*
"Noble."	"Puissant."	"Illustrious."
North-west Germany.	*Central Germany.*	*North-east Germany.*
Cimbri,	Suevi,	Burgundians,
Teutones,	Hermundiri,	Carini,
Chauci.	Chatti,	Varini,
	Cherusci.	Gothones.

It would be easy to carry this method of illustration, which classifies the mythical, the geographical, and the patronymic personifications of nations in their true historical order, through the traditions of different races all over the world. We content ourselves by indicating to fellow-students the utility of a simple process that has solved many a "vexata quæstio" encountered in our personal researches: especially when studying the Persian genealogies of Firdoosi's *Shah-Nameh;* as we hope to show elsewhere. — G. R. G.]

Section C. — Observations on the accompanying "Map of the World."

1st. The parts in *black* indicate what the writer of Xth Genesis knew not: those *shaded* represent where his knowledge decreases; it being unfair, no less than impossible, to define his information by a sharp line. Other explanations are given on the Map itself.

2d. The great *alteration*, which our results superinduce, is the prolongation of his geographical knowledge (hitherto unsuspected) along the whole of Barbary, between the Mediterranean Sea and the Sahara desert. Former African delusions are curtailed at the First Cataract, *Syene;* southern extremity of the *Egyptians*, MiTsRIM, proper. The compiler of Xth Genesis knew nothing of "Ethiopia" above; nor is any austral land beyond *Egypt* mentioned by a single writer in the Old Testament; because *Chub* (*Ezek.* xxx. 5), GUB, conjectured by Bunsen, after Ewald, to be ɢNUB, *Nubia*, is an unnecessary effort when we can identify it with the Barbaresque *Cobii* of Ptolemy the geographer [*supra*, p. 515].

GENEALOGICAL TABLEAU OF XIII GENESIS: prepared for NOTT & GLIDDON's *Types of Mankind*, 1853, by G. R. G.

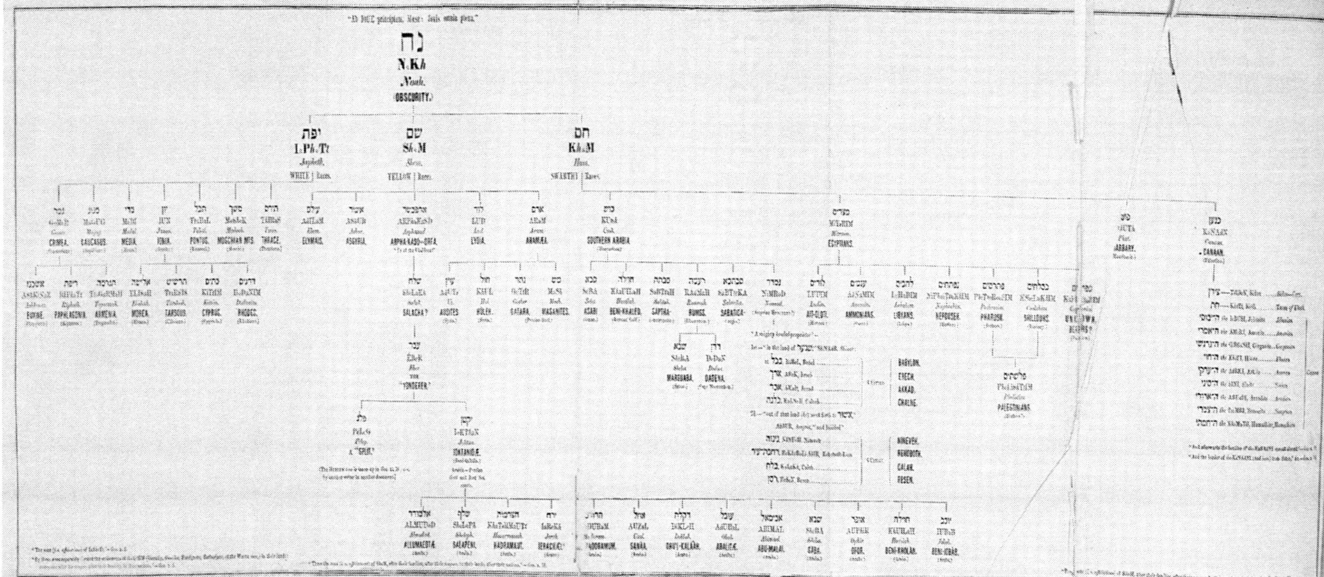

MAP OF THE WORLD.

on Mercator's projection, exhibiting the COUNTRIES more or less known to the ancient Writer of 10th GENESIS.

NOTT & GLIDDON'S Types of Mankind, 1853.

3d. The coast of Abyssinia is dotted *red* and *yellow*, because some KUS*hites*, besides the *Joktanide*, *â*UBaL, may have crossed the Red Sea. The latter lent his name to the *Avalites Sinus*, &c., on the African continent.

Section D.—THE XTH CHAPTER OF GENESIS MODERNIZED, IN ITS NOMENCLATURE, TO DISPLAY, POPULARLY AND IN MODERN ENGLISH, THE MEANING OF ITS ANCIENT WRITER.

Verse
1 Now these (are) the T*t*oLDTt-BNI-NuK*h*, (generations of the sons of CESSATION); S*h*eM yellow races, K*h*aM swarthy races, and IaPeT*t* white
2 races: unto them (were) sons after the deluge.* (The) affiliations of IaPeT*t*
white races; — Crimeâ = GoMeR, and Caucasus = MaGUG, and Media
= MeDI, and Ionia = IUN, and Pontus = T*t*uBaL, and Moschia =
3 MeS*h*eK, and Thrace = T*t*IRaS. And (the) affiliations of Crimea =
GoMeR; — Euxine = ASKiNaZ, and Paphlagonia = RIP*h*aT*t*, and Armenia
4 = T*t*oGaRMaH. And (the) affiliations of Ionia = IUN; — Morea = ALISaH,
and Tarsous = TaRSIS, Cypriots = KiT*t*IM, and Rhodians = RoDaNIM.
5 By these were dispersed the settlements of Ha-GOIM the (white barbarian)
hordes in their lands; every one after his tongue, after their families, in their
6 nations. And (the) affiliations of K*h*aM swarthy races; Dark Arabia† =
KUS*h*, and Egyptians = MiT*s*RIM, and Barbary = P*h*UT*h*, and Canaan =
7 KN*â*AN. And (the) affiliations of Dark Arabia = KUS*h*; — Asabia = SeBA,
and Beni-Khâled = K*h*aUILaH, and Saphtha-metropolis = SaBT*t*aH, and
Rumss = R*â*AMaH, and Sabatica-regio = SaBT*t*aKA: and (the) affiliations
8 of Rumss = R*â*AMaH; Marsuaba = S*h*eBA, and Dadena = DeDaN. And
Dark Arabia = KUS*h* engendered (the Assyrian Hercules?) = NeM-RuD,
9 he first began to be mighty upon earth. He was a great landed-proprietor
before (the face of) IeHOuaH; whence the saying, *like* NeM-RuD, (a) *great*
10 *landed-proprietor* before (the face of) IeHOuaH.‡ And (the) commencement of his
realm, Babylon = BaBeL, and Erech = AReK, and Accad = AKaD, and
11 Chalne = KaLNeH in the land of Mesopotamia = S*h*iN*â*AR. Out of that
land he (Nimrod) went forth [*to*] Assyria = AS*h*UR, and builded Nineveh =
12 NINUeH, and Rehoboth-*Lion* = ReK*h*oBoT*t*-*â*IR, and Calah = KaLaK*h*, —
and Resen = ReSeN between Nineveh = NINUeH and between Calah = KaLaK*h*
13 (he) *she* (Nineveh?) the great city). And (the) Egyptians = MiT*s*RIM engendered
the Ait-Oloti = LUDIM, and the Ammonians = ÂNaMIM, and the Libyans
14 = LeHaBIM, and the Nefousehs = NiP*h*aiT*t*uK*h*IM, — and the Pharusii =
P*h*aT*t*uRiSIM, and the Shillouhs = KS*h*iLouK*h*IM out of whom issued

* No *translation* is intended by the terms yellow, swarthy, and white races. We use them merely to evolve the ethnological *tripartite* classification of the writer.

† Dark Arabia serves for the dark CUSHITE (red-*Himydr*) Arabs.

‡ The mention of IeHOuaH makes this copy of the Ethnic Chart *Jehovistic*, and consequently recent, by every rule of exegesis. (PARKER'S *De Wette*, II., pp. 77-145.)

15 Philistines = P*h*eLiST*t*IM, and the Caphtors = KaP*h*T*t*oRIM. And Canaan
= KN*â*AN engendered Sidon = T*s*IDoN his first born, and Kheth = K*h*eT*t*,
16 and the Jebusian = IBUSI, and the Amorian = AMoRI, and the Girgasian
17 = GiRGaSI, And the Khuian = K*h*UI, and the Aocrian = *â*RKI, and the
18 Sinian SINI, — and the Aradian = ARUaDI, and the Simyrian = T*s*iMRI,
19 and the Hamathian = K*h*aMaT*t*I: (Afterwards the families of the Kanaanian
= KN*â*ANI (were) spread *abroad.*) And the boundary of the Kanaanian =
KN*â*ANI (had been) from Sidon = T*s*IDoN, towards *Gerar*, even to *Aâza*,
(round) by *Sodom*, and *Aâmora*, and *Admah*, and *Tseboim*, as far as *Lashâ*.
20 These (the) affiliations of K*h*aM swarthy races, after their families, after
21 their tongues, in their countries, in their nations. And to S*h*eM yellow races
also (there was) issue: he (is) the father of all (the) affiliations of (the)
22 Yonderer = ÊBeR, brother of IaP*h*eT*t* the elder. Affiliations of S*h*eM yellow
races. Elymais = *â*ILaM, and Assyria = AS*h*UR, and Chaldæan Orfa =
23 ARP*h*a-KaSD, and Lydia = LUD, and Aramæa = ARaM; — and (the) affilia-
tions of Aramæa = ARaM; Ausitis = *â*UT*s*, and Hûleh = K*h*UL, and
24 Gatara = GeT*t*uR, and Masonites = MaS. And Chaldæan Orfa = ARP*h*a-
KaSD engendered Salacha? = S*h*eLaK*h*; and Salacha = S*h*eLaK*h* engendered
25 (the) Yonderer = ÊBeR. And unto (the) Yonderer = ÊBeR were born two
affiliations; the name of one (was) (a) Split = PeLeG (because in his days the
earth was split), and (the) name of his brother (was) Joktàn = IoKTaN.
26 And Joktàn = IoKTaN engendered (the) Allumaæotæ = ALMUDàD, and (the)
Salapeni = S*h*eLeP*h*, and Hadramàut = K*h*aT*s*aRaMUT*t*, and (the) Jera-
27 chæi = IeRaK*h*, — and (Cape) Hadoramum = HaDURaM, and San*â*a =
28 AUZAL, and (the) Dhu'-l-Kalàah = DiKLeH, And (the) Abalitæ = *â*UBaL,
29 and Malai (el-Khyèf) = ABIMAL, and Sàba (Màreb) = SaBA, — and Ofor
AUP*h*iR, and (the) Beni-Kholàn = K*h*UILeH, and (the) Beni-Jobàb = IUBaB.
30 All these (are) affiliations of [*Qahtàn*] Joktàn = IoKTaN; — and their dwelling
(was) from Zames Mons = MeS*h*A, towards Mount Zaffàr = SeP*h*aRaH,
31 mountain of the East (or *mountain opposite?*).* These (are) (the) affiliations
of S*h*eM yellow races, after their families, after their tongues, in their lands,
32 after their nations. Such (are the) families of (the) *sons* of CESSATION = NuK*h*,
after their generations, in their nations; and from these were dispersed Ha-GOIM
= the hordes (the peoples) on the earth after the deluge.

(*Here ends the document.*)

The authors cannot but hope, after the evidences herein accumulated, that the impartial reader now agrees with them and with Rosellini, that "la serie dei nomi de' discendenti di Noè è una vera ricenzione geografica delle varie parti della terra;" so far as the world's surface was known to the writer of Xth Genesis.

Viewed by itself, as a document from all others distinct, incorporated by the Esdraic school into the canonical Hebrew writings, Xth Genesis is simply an *ethnic chorograph;* wherein three "Types of Mankind," generically classified as the red, yellow, and white, are mapped out — "after their families, after their tongues, in their countries, in their

* The word here is the same KDM upon which the analysis of De Longpérier was referred to under ASUR [*ubi supra*, p. 534].

nations." In every instance where monumental or written history has enabled us to check the writer's system, his accuracy has been vindicated. In not a few cases exactitudes, so minute as to be relatively marvellous, have been exhibited.

Our genealogical *table* displays the order in which this compiler supposed the different colonies, or affiliations, issued from each of the three parental stems. Our *retranslation* of Xth Genesis, by substituting, as far as possible, modern names for the same nations and countries, has enabled us to comprehend his literal meaning more clearly than when reading Hebraical appellatives now mostly obsolete, no less than veiled by an ancient and foreign mode of spelling them. And lastly, our transfer and redistribution of these seventy-nine cognomina, in a *map*, fix, within a few degrees of latitude and longitude, the boundary of this writer's geographical circumference; and thus indicate the horizon, so to say, of all the knowledge his "gazetteer" contains.

Learned and orthodox works have frequently defined this geography before; and with limitations of area quite as restricted as ours, as regards the sum total of terrestrial superficies. Because, if we have cut off, as not alluded to in Xth Genesis, the whole of *Nubia* above Egypt, and all Africa lying south of the northern limit of the Sahara deserts, our *map*, on the other hand, prolongs the writer's knowledge through Barbary, from Egypt to the Pillars of Hercules. Thus, upon the whole, our restoration is more extensive than that of Volney.

No savant whose opinion is worthy of respectful attention, but excludes all knowledge, on the part of the writer of Xth Genesis, of any portion of *Europe*, except the coasts of the Peloponnesus and of Thracia. All reasonable commentators, by cutting off "Scythia" at a line, drawn from the north-eastern apex of the Black Sea to the Caspian, deny that Xth Genesis includes *Russian Asia;* while none extend the geography of that document beyond a line drawn from the Caspian Sea to the mouth of the Indus, as an extreme; a frontier, to our view, quite unjustifiable, and by far too distant from a *Chaldæan* centre-point.

In consequence, we all agree that Hindostan and its mixed populations; China with her immense Mongol and Tartar hordes; and the Islands of the Indian Ocean; are entirely excluded from Xth Genesis. The lands of Malayana, Oceanica, Australasia, and the Pacific, having been discovered within the last three centuries, were of course unknown to the school of Esdras twenty-three hundred years ago. So was also the "New World;"—the vast American continent and its Islands, prior to the voyages of Columbus, and his successors. The most rigid orthodoxy, therefore, concedes that, upon *Finnish, Samoïde, Tongousian, Tartar, Mongol, Malay, Polynesian, Esquimaux, American*, and many other races, the writer of Xth Genesis is absolutely silent; that, every one of these peoples lay very far beyond the utmost area demonstrable through his chorography.

Nothing "heretical," then, accrues from our simple demonstration of the truth of that which the educated of all Christendom now-a-days insist upon.

But, the orthodox will even allow a little more. Beginning at the Cape of Good Hope, they will admit, that the compiler of Xth Genesis does not embrace that region, nor its inhabitants, the *Bosjesmans, Hottentots, Kaffres*, and *Foolahs*, in this ethnic geography. They will voluntarily renounce also, in the name of this genesiacal writer, acquaintance with any part of Africa more austral than a line drawn athwart its continent from *Senegal* on the western to Cape Gardafui on the eastern or *Abyssinian* coast. Thus much, we opine, no one "nisi imperitus" can hesitate to grant.

Upon reflection, in view of the impassabilities of the immense Sahara desert (first, geologically, when it was an inland *sea;* and secondly, zoologically, until the *camel* was introduced and propagated in Barbary, after the first century, B. C.), all scholars, we presume, will coincide with our limitation; and, by way of compensation for the additional knowledge which our analyses have secured for the author of Xth Genesis, along *Berberia*, Barbary, they will not insist upon his acquaintance with anything south of the northern edge of the *Sahara:*—the *oases* of Séewah, El-Khârgheh, &c., remaining, between orthodox readings and ours, "sub judice."

So far, to judge by published commentaries, there are no insurmountable obstacles to harmony between the most catholic interpreter of Xth Genesis and ourselves. "Nos adversaires" will now fairly confess that the battle-ground, upon which their and our opinions have to be fought, lies on a miserable strip of the *Nile's* deposits; along the countries we term, in common, the *Nubias.*

Yet, even here, reasonable persons—those who have of their own accord, and for the sake of truth, already abandoned the *Tchoudes, Finns, Samoïdes, Tongousians, Tartars, Mongols, Malays, Polynesians, Esquimaux, American-aborigines, Hottentots, Bosjesmans, Kaffres, Foolahs, Senegalians, Abyssinians,* the Sahara desert, &c., &c., as not included in Xth Genesis—such reasonable persons, we think, cannot make out, legally, a "casus belli" between our results and their individual preconceptions, upon matters so pitiful in geography as the *Nubias.*

They have read our analysis of KUS*h*. They have seen every affiliation of KUS*h* settled in *Arabia.* Now, if every affiliation of KUS*h* in Xth Genesis be *Arabian,* why must we seek for these KUS*h-ites* elsewhere? Indeed, if we both agree in classification, neither party has any other genesiacal *names* to dispute about.

KUS*h* and its affiliations being irrevocably determined in *Arabia,* and proved to have been generally of the Himyar-*red* stock, it would be as absurd to look for them in Nubia as on the Caucasian mountains. We know that until the XIIth and perhaps the XIth dynasty, the boundary of the MTsRim, *Egyptians,* was the 1st Cataract of Syene: and inasmuch as the *Nubias* were then little known to Egyptians, they were undoubtedly far less known to Asiatics.

Consequently, there was a time when *Nubia* herself was a "terra incognita." We have only to continue this Asiatic ignorance of Africa for a few centuries, and every one will allow that there is no improbability involved in the assertion that the *Nubias* were unrevealed to the compiler of Xth Genesis at Jerusalem, or at Babylon. His *map* proves that they were so; and, thus far, discussion is at an end.

With the *Nubias* vanishes the last possibility that *Negro* races were known to the writer of Xth Genesis. He never mentions them; nor indeed does any other writer in the canonical Scriptures, from *Genesis* to *Malachi.*

Negroes are, therefore, excluded from mention in the Old Testament; together with *Finns, Uralians, Mongols, Tartars, Malays, Polynesians, Esquimaux, American*-Indians, &c., &c. The *map* of Xth Genesis, under the heads "Shem, Ham, and Japheth," merely covers those families of mankind classified by the Egyptians, in the days of SETHEI-MENEPTHA, 15th–16th centuries B. C., into the yellow, the red, and the white human types.

Such is our conclusion. Science and reason confirm it. Xth Genesis proves it. Nevertheless, few persons beyond the circle of education exempt from ecclesiastical prejudice, will, for some time to come, accept this result! *Why?*

[Our *manuscripts* comprise critical answers to this query viewed in all its bearings upon the *Ante-Diluvian* Patriarchs, and upon the two pedigrees of ST. JOSEPH recorded in *Matthew* and *Luke.* Inasmuch, however, as their production here would necessitate a second volume to this work, we postpone their publication; remembering St. Paul's sage admonishments to Timothy and to Titus—"not to give heed to fables and endless genealogies"—"but avoid foolish questions and genealogies." (1 *Tim.* i. 4; *Titus* iii. 9: Sharpe's *New Testament,* "translated from Griesbach's Text;" London, 1844, pp. 380, 392–3).—G. R. G.]

CHAPTER XV.

BIBLICAL ETHNOGRAPHY.

Section E.—TERMS, UNIVERSAL AND SPECIFIC.

THERE is nothing in the language of the Bible which illustrates more strongly the danger of a too rigid enforcement of literal construction than the very loose manner in which *universal terms* are employed. Those who have studied the phraseology of Scripture need not be told that these terms are used to signify only a *very large amount* in number or quantity. *All*, *every one*, *the whole*, and such like expressions, are often used to denote a *great many*, or a *large portion*, &c. Examples may be found on almost every page of the Old Testament, but we will first select a few from the many scattered through the New. And we beg the reader to bear in mind the fact already established, viz., that neither the writers of the Old or New Testament knew anything of the geography of the earth much beyond the limits of the Roman empire, nor had they any idea of the spheroidal shape of the globe. Be it noted also that, in order to avoid the mistakes of the English AUTHORIZED VERSION, our quotations are borrowed from Sharpe's *New Testament* as closest to the original Greek.

In the account given by Matthew (iv. 8, 9) of the temptation of Christ, we have these words:

"Again the Devil taketh him on to a very high mountain, and showeth him *all the kingdoms of the world*, and their glory; and saith unto him; 'All these will I give thee, if thou wilt fall down and worship me.'"

Before accepting such words as "all the kingdoms of the world" in a *literal* sense, it may be well to peruse the commentary of Strauss, in his *Life of Jesus*:—

"But that which is the veritable stumbling-block, is the personal apparition of the Devil with his temptations. If even there could be a personal Devil, 't is said, he cannot appear visibly; and, if even he could, he would not have behaved himself as our Gospels recount it. . . . The three temptations are operated in three different places, and even far apart. It is asked, how Jesus passed with the Devil from one to the other? . . . The expressions, *the Devil takes him*, . . . *places him*, in Matthew—the expressions, *fetching*, *he conducted*, *he placed*, in Luke, indicate incontestably a displacement operated by the Devil himself; furthermore, Luke (iv. 5) saying that the Devil showed Jesus 'all the kingdoms of the world *in a moment of time*;' this trait indicates something magical. . . . Where is the mountain from the summit of which one can discover all the kingdoms of the earth? Some interpreters reply that by the *world*, COSMOS, one must understand Palestine only, and by *the kingdoms*,

BASILEIAIS, the isolated provinces and the tetrarchies of that country: a reply which is not less ridiculous than the explanation of those who say that the Devil showed to Jesus the world on a geographical map."[659]

In reference to these diabolical powers we may also be permitted to rejoice with our readers over the following fact, recently announced by the Rev. John Oxlee (Rector of Molesworth, Hunts, England) in his "Letters to the Lord Archbishop of Canterbury:"—

"In the *Chronicon Syriacum* of Bar Hebræus, we have it duly recorded, that, in the year of the Hegira 455, or of our Lord 1063, certain Curdean hunters, in the desert, brought a report into Bagdad; how that, as they were hunting in the desert, they saw black tents, with the voice of lamentation, weeping, and yelling; that, on their approaching them, they heard a voice saying: '*To-day died* BEELZEBUB, the Prince of the Devils; and every place where there is not lamentation for three days, we will erase from its very foundation.' . . . Hence it is apparent, even on the indubitable testimony of the devils themselves, that Beelzebub, the Prince of the Devils, died a natural death, nearly eight hundred years ago; and was lamented and bewailed, with all due honors, by the municipal authorities of Bagdad, Mosul, and other cities in the land of Senaar. There, then, let his mortal remains peaceably rest, never more to be disturbed, in the future, by human curiosity."[660]

We have a repetition of the previous passage in Luke, which should probably be taken in a figurative or allegorical sense; for although the evangelists had little idea of the extent or the shape of the earth, yet it cannot be maintained that Jesus or the devil were so ignorant as to suppose that a view of the world could be greatly extended by ascending a mountain. If we could take this language in a literal sense, it would at once settle the question as to the amount of geographical and ethnological knowledge of the evangelists. Here are some more instances of "universal terms" used loosely in a vague or general sense:—

(*Mat.* xii. 42)—"The queen of the South . . . . came from *the ends of the earth* to hear the wisdom of Solomon."

(*Luke* ii. 1)—"And it came to pass in those days that a decree went forth from Cæsar Augustus that *all the world should be registered.*"

(*John* xxi. 25)—"And there are also many other things which Jesus did, which if they should be written one by one, I do not think that *the world itself* would contain the written books.

(*Acts* ii. 5)—"And there were dwelling in Jerusalem Jews, devout men, *from every nation under heaven.*"

(*Acts* xiii. 47—quoting *Isaiah* xlix. 6)—"I have set thee to be a light of the Gentiles, that thou shouldest be for salvation *to the ends of the earth.*"

(*Rom.* x. 18—quoting *Ps.* xix, 4)—"Yes, verily, their sound went into *all the earth,* and their words *unto the ends of the world.*"

These examples will be quite sufficient to show the manner in which "*universal terms*" were used, and the necessity for measuring their extent by a proper standard. We now present a remarkable text, and the only one in the New Testament which alludes directly to the dogma of *unity* of races.

(*Acts* xvii. 26)—"And [God] hath made of one blood *all nations* of men to dwell on *all the face of the earth*, and hath determined the appointed seasons, and the bounds of their habitation." It will be noted that this saying of Paul is not autographed in his *Epistles*; but, as Hennell critically annotates, "rests mainly on the testimony of the author of *Acts*, who himself intimates that he is the same as the author of the third Gospel."[661]

Now, can any reason be assigned why a wider signification should be given to "universal terms" here than in the previous examples? Have we not seen, too, in the quotation just preceding this, the loose manner in which the same writer (St. Paul) uses such terms? Should not this paragraph, also, deserve the less credit, inasmuch as it has no parallel? It should be remembered that when St. Paul stood upon Mars's Hill and preached to the men of Athens, his knowledge of nations and of races did not extend beyond that of his hearers; and the expression, "*hath made of one blood all nations of men,*" was certainly meant to apply only to those nations about which he was informed; that is, merely the *Roman Empire.*

Leaving the New Testament we take up the Old, and such passages as these meet our eye:—

(1 *Kings*, xviii. 10)—As "IeHOuaH thy God liveth [most sacred form of Jewish oath], there is no nation or kingdom, whither my Lord hath not sent to seek thee; and when they said, '*He is* not there,' he took an oath [a certificate] of the kingdom, that they found thee not." If this text were to be taken literally, Obadiah's most solemn affidavit is here given that Ahab's emissaries had visited *China*, *Norway*, *Peru*, *Congo*,—in short, circumnavigated the whole globe, besides traversing it in every direction, during the tenth century B. C., in quest of Elijah!

(1 *Kings*, x. 24)—"And all the earth sought the face of Solomon, to hear his wisdom." Is this to be accepted *verbatim et literatim?* Must no allowance for poetic license be made, when David says,—"And the channels of the sea appeared, the *foundations of the world were discovered*" (2 *Sam.* xxii. 16).

Receding to previous chapters (that is, not written during earlier ages, but merely bound up in books placed anteriorly to *Kings* and *Samuel* in the present order of arrangement), we come to—"AND NOW KuL-HAReTs (the WHOLE earth) was of one LIP and of DeBeRIM AKhaDIM."—The last two words, plurals in Hebrew, cannot be literally rendered into English, as *ones words;* but the sense is "one language."

The whole context refers to an idea purely *Chaldæan*, and to a preternatural event exclusively *Babylonish;* viz., the city and the tower of BaBeL, which IeHOuaH "descended to see" after they were *built*. The two things, *tower* and *city*, are inseparable; and we perceive that the people "ceased to build the *city*," after they were "dispersed thence over the face of the WHOLE EARTH."

(*Gen.* xi. 1)—"On that account it was called BaBeL, because IeHOuaH there BeLeL (confounded) the LIP (speech) of the WHOLE EARTH." The root BLL means *to mingle*, to *talk-gibberish;* and, conformably to the favorite genius of Semitic d scription, the writer avails himself of a play upon words—*i. e.*, really "perpetrates a *pun*"—because the monosyllabic etymon of BaBeL, itself meaning "confusion," is the same as that of BeLeL.—We might say in English, "BABEL-*babble*," and thus realize part of the alliteration of BaBeL-BeLeL, while losing half its *double entendre;* because, BaBeL does not mean in English what it does in Semitish idioms, viz., "gibberish" as well as *confusion*. Another mode of conveying an idea of this play upon words would be, to translate BaBeL-BeLeL by "higgledy-piggledy." Poor, dreary, and mis-timed though such jocularity may seem to us, and inconsonant with the sanctity of the volume in which it is now found, nevertheless, no Orientalist will dispute the assertion, that similar *rebuses*, or *riddles*, are the delight of Eastern narrators;[662] while, by the Talmudic Rabbis, this pun was supposed to cover awful mysteries. Few persons are aware that, as the Text says nothing about the *destruction* of either city or tower, theologians derive their notions in this respect, not from the Bible, but from the spurious and modern tales of Hestiæus, of Polyhistor, of Eupolemus, and of the "Sibylline Oracles." The classical texts may be found in Cory's *Ancient Fragments*.

The reader, who has comprehended the principles of criticism, established further on in the *Archæological Introduction to Xth Genesis*, can now seize the historical value of this document (*Gen.* xi. 1–9) in a moment.

1st. It has no connection with what precedes or succeeds it; but breaks in, parenthetically, between what is now printed as the 32d *verse* of Chap. X. and the 10th of Chap. XI.: its apparent relation to either originating solely through modern, arbitrary, and therefore unauthorized, divisions into *chapters* and *verses*.

2d. Age and authorship unknown, its antiquity cannot ascend beyond the seventh—eighth century B. C., because its divine ascriptions are *Jehovistic;* nor could it well have been embodied into the book called "Genesis," earlier than about B. C. 420, by the Esdraic School; because, the mention of "the land of *Shinar*"—of "*brick* they had for stone (or rather L-ABNi, *for building*) and *bitumen* they had for mortar"[663] of the "*city;*—therefore the name of it was BaBeL (Babylon)"—carries us at once to plains between the *Shinar hills* and the Euphrates-river; to the *bricks* or Chaldæan mounds; to the bituminous springs of *Hit* (*His* of Herodotus, and hieroglyphic IS);[664] and to the Babylon of Nebuchadnezzar; than whom, although the name of a place called BBL is as old as Thotmes III. of the XVIIIth Theban dynasty, 1500—1600 B. C., nothing *cuneiform* yet found at Babylon is anterior.[665]

3d. What connections BàB-eL[666] "*Gate* of the SUN" (like the Chinese "celestial gates;" or their Mongol derivative, the Ottoman "Sublime Porte"), may have with this name's origin: whether BELUS the king; BAAL the god; or "*Bel* and the dragon;" are to be taken into consideration:—these curious inquiries, if familiar to our studies, are foreign to our present purposes and objects. But, "in sober sadness," let us ask—Can such words as KuL-Ha-AReTs (the *whole* earth) be accepted, by ethnological science in the nineteenth century, when contained in such an unhistorical document? At any rate, "Types of Mankind" must respectfully leave them aside.

"Isis! dea infelix, Nili remanebis ad amnem
Sola, carens et voce!"

The ignorant of all races and ages, especially inland-populations such as the Jews were, when a foreign tongue strikes their auricular nerves, do not suppose that the speaker is uttering sense, but believe that he is merely exercising his vocal muscles instinctively, in the same manner that *geese* "talk." The writer of *Matthew* is not free from this illusion; because, where our authorized mistranslation has "Use not vain repetitions, as the heathen *do;*" the original *Greek* reads—"And when ye pray, *babble* not as the heathen do" (*Mat.* vi. 7:—Sharpe, *N. T.*, p. 10). In the idea of the Hebrews, vouched for, according to De Sola, even by such mighty commentators as Rashi and Mendelssohn,[667] the "One language" at Babel was merely the "lingua sancta;" that is to say, all mankind there talked *Hebrew* at first; but (after the dispersion thence, when their speech was "confounded"), only SHEM's *sons* miraculously preserved the Hebrew tongue immaculate; "the rest of mankind" BABEL-*babbled* in gibberish!

The above hints are furnished to others. We feel as charitably disposed as Josephus did when writing.—"Now, as to myself, I have so described these matters as I have found them and read them; but if any one is inclined to another opinion about them, let him enjoy his different sentiments without any blame from me."[668]

Section F.—STRUCTURE OF GENESIS I., II., AND III.

Far more important, at an ethnological point of view, are the first *three* chapters of the book called "Genesis;" and to them we can here devote but a paragraph or two.

Our *Archæological Introduction*, in Part III., has pointed out their Esdraic age, and the *Persic* origin of some of the mythes they contain. All modern divisions into chapters and verses, of course, are to be abstracted; being mere European addenda. *Jewish* divisions of the book of Genesis are entirely different. They are *twelve* in number; of which the first SeDR—*Chapter* I. to *Chapter* VI., *verse* 9—is called the "Bereshith," *beginning*.[671]

To understand this "structural analysis of the book of Genesis," according to exegetical principles now universally recognized by Hebraists, we refer the reader to a masterly critique by Luke Burke,[672] and to the solid evidences supplied by De Wette.[673] The more salient characteristics distinguishing the two documents are, the words ELoHIM, in king James's version replaced by "God;" and IeHOuaH, for which our appellative "Lord" is substituted; neither of these two Hebrew divine names being *translated;* as the writer will demonstrate in some future treatise. The relative order of these documents becomes intelligible to the reader by being placed in juxtaposition. Our purpose now being merely the exhibition of some *structural* peculiarities not generally known, it is unnecessary to retranslate the whole three chapters, and impossible to justify herein our verbal interpretations. With Cahen's *Bible*, the reader can easily fill up gaps for himself in the former case: adequate explanations in the latter would require the publication of a volume of results which, obtained through ten years' incessant travel and study, G. R. G.'s *manuscripts* embrace. To the anthropologist, however, it will be satisfactory to behold the true place of the word A-DaM in these texts—אדם, says Cahen, "l'espèce humaine, singulier collectif." And, as concerns other questions, we must be content for the present to submit an observation written by the great Hellenist, R. Payne Knight, to his colleagues Sir Joseph Bankes and Sir W. Hamilton:—

"It must be observed that, when the ancients speak of *Creation* and destruction, they mean only formation and dissolution; it being universally allowed, through all systems of religion or sects of philosophy, *that nothing could come from nothing, and that no power whatever could annihilate that which really existed.* The bold and magnificent idea of a creation from nothing was reserved for the more vigorous faith, and more enlightened minds of the moderns; who need seek no authority to confirm their belief; for, as that which is self-evident admits of no proof, so that which is in itself impossible admits of no refutation."[674]

Pagan Saxon names of the *week-days*.	Ancient Oriental Planetary System.	Musical Note.	
Sun's daeg.	SOL.	E *mi.*	(*Chorus* 1st.)
Moon's daeg.	LUNA.	A *la.*	(*Chorus* 2d.)
Tiwe's daeg.	MARS.	D *re.*	(*Chorus* 3d.)
Woden's daeg.	MERCURY.	G *sol.*	(*Chorus* 4th.)
Thor's daeg.	JUPITER.	C *ut.*	(*Chorus* 5th.)
Friga's daeg.	VENUS.	F *fa.*	(*Chorus* 6th.)
Satur's daeg.	SATURN.	B *si.*	(*Benediction*)

"SABBATH," *Saturday*; commencing at sunset on Friday, and ending at sunset on Saturday.

DOCUMENT No. I. — GENESIS I.; II. 3.

"Elohim."

Harmonical Ode of Creative cosmogony — antique and scientific.

"In the beginning, ELoHIM created the (universality of) skies, and the (universality of) earth. And the earth was TtoHU — and — BoHU (literally — masculine and feminine principles dislocated, or confounded; paraphrastically — "*without form and a confused mass*"), and darkness was upon the face of the abyss, and the (breath) spirit of ELoHIM hovered (like a descending bird) over the face of the waters—

[*V.* 3, 4.]

"And it was ĕReB (*western* twilight) and it was BeKR (early dawn) — *Day* ONE!

[*V.* 6, 7.]

"And it was ĕReB (*western* twilight) and it was BeKR (early dawn) — *Day* SECOND!

[*V.* 9—12.]

"And it was ĕReB (*western* twilight) and it was BeKR (early dawn) — *Day* THIRD!

[*V.* 14—18.]

"And it was ĕReB (*western* twilight) and it was BeKR (early dawn) — *Day* FOURTH!

[*V.* 20—22.]

"And it was ĕReB (*western* twilight) and it was BeKR (early dawn) — *Day* FIFTH!

"And ELoHIM said, 'Let us make (the universality of) the A-DaM (THE-RED-man) after our image, like our likeness, and let him rule over the fish of the seas and over the bird of the skies and over the cattle and over all the [whole] earth and over all the crawler crawling upon the earth.' And ELoHIM created (the universality of) the A-DaM (THE-RED-man) after his image, after the image of ELoHIM created (he) them. And ELoHIM blessed them and ELoHIM said to them 'Be fruitful and multiply, and fill the (universality of) earth and subject it, and rule over fish of the seas and over bird of the skies and over all the living that crawls upon the earth.'

[*V.* 29—30.]

"And it was ĕReB (*western* twilight) and it was BeKR (early dawn) — *Day* the SIXTH!

[*Ch.* ii. *v.* 1, 2.]

"And ELoHIM blessed the (universality of) *day*-the-SEVENTH and sanctified it, because he ShaBaTt (rested, and *seventhed*) from all his work which ELoHIM created to act" — (*i. e.*, by its own organism henceforward).

FINIS.

DOCUMENT No. II. — GENESIS II. 4; III. 24.

"Jehovah."

Popular Creation of the World —later, and Persic.

"Such (the) generations (literally, *bringing-forths*) of the skies and the earth according to their creation, on (the) day IeHOuaH-ELOHIM made earth and skies.

[*V.* 5, 6.]

"And IeHOuaH-ELOHIM formed the (universality of) A-DaM (THE-RED-man) of dust from the A-DaMaH (THE-RED-earth) and breathed in (his) nostrils breath of life, and the A-DaM (THE-RED-man) became (a) living creature. And IeHOuaH-ELOHIM planted (a) garden in ĕDeN (or, *in*-DELIGHT) to (the) East, and there placed the (universality of) A-DaM (THE-RED-man) whom he had formed.

[*V.* 9—14.]

"And IeHOuaH-ELOHIM took the (universality of) A-DaM and placed him in (the) garden of ĕDeN (or, DELIGHT) to cultivate it and to guard it.

[*V.* 16—20.]

"And IeHOuaH-ELOHIM made the A-DaM (THE-RED-man) to fall (into a) great drowsiness, and he slept; and he took one of his ribs and filled-in flesh in place thereof. And IeHOuaH-ELOHIM constructed the rib which he had taken from the A-DaM (THE-RED-man) into AiShiH (woman — or ISE, ISIS) and brought her to the A-DaM (THE-RED-man).

[*V.* 20. *Ch.* iii. *v.* 19.]

"And the A-DaM (THE-RED-man) called (the) name of AiShaTtU (his wife, or ISeT, ISIS) KhiUaH (*life*), because she was (the) mother of all KhaIa (*living*).

[*V.* 21—23.]

"So he drove-out the (universality of) A-DaM (THE-RED-man); and he placed at (the) East to (the) garden of ĕDeN (*delight*) the (universality of) KeRuBIM (FIERY-DISKS), of which he made the CENTRAL-FLAME revolve to guard the road to (the) tree of the KhaIaIM (*lives*).

FINIS.

Our present object limiting itself to the *Creation of Man*, as set forth in the above two documents — each, the reader now perceives, distinct altogether the one from the other — we withhold (contrary to our habit) authorities for our arrangement of the "document *Elohim*." The Hebraist will concede that we have adhered with rigid fidelity to the Text; and that suffices until we resume biblical mysteries on a future occasion, when *authority* enough shall be forthcoming. Yet, to the curious investigator, we feel tempted to offer the "Air" of the *Music of the Spheres:*

If he be a musician, he can play it on a piano; if he is a geometrician, he will find its corresponding notes on the sides of an *equilateral triangle* added to the angles of a *square;* if he loves metaphysics, Plato will explain the import of *unity*, *matter*, *logos*, *perfection*, *imperfect*, *justice*, *repose;* while Pythagoras will class for him *monad*, *duad*, *triad*, *quaternary*, *quinary*, *senary*, and *septenary*. We hope to strike the OCTAVE note some day ourselves; but, in the meanwhile, should the reader be profound in astronomical history, and if he can determine the exact time when the ancients possessed *neither more nor less* than "five planets, besides the Sun and Moon," there are two archæological problems his acumen will have solved — 1st, the arithmetico-harmonical antiquity of the *number* 7; and 2d, the precise era beyond which it will thenceforward be impossible to carry back the composition of that ancient *Ode* we term "*Genesis* i—ii. 3."

Being of an epoch much more recent; arranged upon a geographical basis purely *Chaldæan;* and containing allusions to a *garden* of DELIGHT (like the famed "hanging-gardens" of Babylon, and the *paradisiacal* parks of Persia); the "Jehovistic document" throws little or no light upon ancient ethnography. A-DaM, as we shall see, never was intended by the Jehovistic writer, to be the *proper-name* "Adam," as the versions pretend. The woman AiS*h*aH (when the masoretic *points* or other arbitrary and modern diacritical marks are removed) becomes ASH, or (vowels being vague) ISE: identified with the Coptic ISE, as well as with the hieroglyphical appellative of that primordial ISI, whom the Greeks (through the addition of their euphonizing *Sigma*) made into the goddess ISIS: "for," says CLEMENS *Alexandrinus*, "in that which belongs to the *occult* the enigmas of the Egyptians are similar to those of the Hebrews." [675] One of the titles of this myrionymed goddess was "the universal *mother*;" and naturally so, "because she was the *mother* of all living" (*Gen.* iii. 20).

"I am," says ISIS, "*Nature;* parent of all things, the sovereign of the elements, the primary progeny of Time, the most exalted of the deities, the first of the heavenly gods and goddesses, the queen of the shades, the uniform countenance; who dispose with my rod the numerous lights of heaven, the salubrious breezes of the sea, and the mournful silence of the dead; whose single deity the whole world venerates in *many forms*, with various rites and many *names*. The Egyptians, skilled in ancient lore, worship me with proper ceremonies, and call me by my true name, Queen ISIS."

In consequence, the "document JEHOVAH" does not especially concern our present subject; and it is incomparable with the grander conception of the more ancient and unknown writer of Genesis Ist. With extreme felicity of diction and conciseness of plan, the latter has defined the most philosophical views of antiquity upon *cosmogony;* in fact so well, that it has required the palæontological discoveries of the XIXth century — at least 2500 years after his death — to overthrow his *septenary* arrangement of "Creation;" which, after all, would still be correct enough in general principles, were it not for one individual oversight, and one unlucky blunder; not exposed, however, until long after his era, by post-Copernican astronomy. The oversight is where he wrote (*Gen.* i. 6—8): "Let there be RaQIĕ;" i. e., a *firmament;* which proves that his notions of "sky" (solid like the concavity of a copper basin with *stars* set as brilliants in the metal),[677] were the same as those of adjacent people of his time: indeed, of all men before the publication of NEWTON'S *Principia* and of LAPLACE'S

Mécanique Céleste. The blunder is where he conceives that AUR, "light," and IOM, "day" (*Gen.* i. 14—18), could have been physically possible *three whole days* before the "two great luminaries," *Sun* and *Moon*, were created. These venial errors deducted, his majestic song beautifully illustrates the simple process of ratiocination through which—often without the slightest historical proof of intercourse—different "Types of Mankind," at distinct epochas, and in countries widely apart, had arrived, naturally, at cosmogonic conclusions similar to the doctrines of that Hebraical school of which his harmonic and melodious *numbers* remain a magnificent memento.

That process seems to have been the following. The ancients knew, as we do, that man *is* upon the earth; and they were persuaded, as we are, that his appearance was preceded by unfathomable depths of time. Unable (as we are still) to measure periods antecedent to man by any *chronological* standard, the ancients rationally reached the tabulation of some events anterior to man, through *induction*—a method not original with Lord Bacon, because known to St. Paul; "for his unseen things from the creation of the world, his eternal power and godhead, are clearly seen, *being understood by the things that are made*" (*Rom.* i. 20). Man, they felt, could not have lived upon earth without *animal* food; ergo, "cattle" preceded him; together with birds, reptiles, fishes, &c. Nothing living, they knew, could have existed without light and heat; ergo, the *solar system* antedated animal life, no less than the *vegetation* indispensable for animal support. But terrestrial plants cannot grow without *earth;* ergo, dry land had to be separated from pre-existent "waters." Their geological speculations inclining rather to the *Neptunian* than to the *Plutonian* theory—for Werner ever preceded Hutton—the ancients found it difficult to "divide the waters from the waters" without interposing a metallic substance that "divided the waters which were *under* the firmament from the waters that were *above* the firmament;" so they inferred, logically, that a *firmament* must have been actually created for this object. [*E. g.*, "The *windows* of the skies" (*Gen.* vii. 11); "the waters *above* the skies" (*Ps.* cxlviii. 4).] Before the "waters" (and here is the peculiar error of the genesiacal bard), some of the ancients claimed the pre-existence of *light* (a view adopted by the writer of Genesis Ist); whilst others asserted that "chaos" prevailed. Both schools united, however, in the conviction that DARKNESS — *Erebus* [678] — anteceded all other *created things.* What, said these ancients, can have existed before the "darkness?" ENS ENTIUM, the CREATOR, was the humbled reply. ELoHIM is the Hebrew vocal expression of that climax; to define whose attributes, save through the phenomena of creation, is an attempt we leave to others more presumptuous than ourselves.

"GOD," nobly exclaims De Bretonne, "has no need to strike our ears materially to make himself heard, our eyes to make himself seen. The first act of triumph of the spirit over matter is the discredit of emblems that have disguised the infinite God; and the first step towards truth is to recognize him *without image*, after having, for so long a period, modelled him after our own." [679]

What definition of the Godhead more sublime than that in the Hindoo *Vedas?*—

"He who surpasses speech, and through the power of whom speech is expressed, "know, O thou! that He is BRAHMA, and not these perishable things that man adores.

"He who cannot be comprehended by intelligence, and he alone, say the sages, "through the power of whom the nature of intelligence can be understood, know, "O thou! that He is BRAHMA, and not these perishable things that man adores.

"He who cannot be seen by the organ of vision, and through the power of whom the "organ of seeing sees, know, O thou! that He is BRAHMA, and not these perishable "things that man adores.

"He who cannot be heard by the organ of audition, and through the power of "whom the organ of hearing hears, know, O thou! that He is BRAHMA, and not "these perishable things that man adores.

"He who cannot be perceived by the organ of scent, and through the power of "whom the organ of smelling smells, know, O thou! that He is BRAHMA, and not "these perishable things that man adores." [680]

Phœnician, Chaldæan, and many other nations' cosmogonies present both striking resemblances and divergences. Some of them are compared with *Genesis*, very ably, by Palfrey;[681] from whom we borrow these words of the *Alexandrian* cosmogony of DIODORUS SICULUS — "This is not unlike what Euripides says, who was a disciple of Anaxagoras. For this is his language in the Melanippe:

'There was one aspect to sky and earth;
Then the secret powers doing their office
Produced all things unto the regions of light,
Beasts, birds, trees, the sea-flock,
Finally, men themselves.'"

But that which ancient philosophers attained through the laws of inductive reasoning, if to themselves clear and satisfactory, could not be conveyed in a form so indefinite to the intelligence of the illiterate, nor to children. Such undeveloped minds require *dogmatical* tuition. The teachers, so to say, had inductively ascended along an imaginary ladder, from *man* as its basis; until, having established some facts in nature antecedent to his terrestrial advent, they reached its top, when they recognized that there must be a FIRST CAUSE anterior to the "beginning:" but, so soon as these scientific results were to be conveyed to pupils, the dogmatical method became necessary: wherefore the preceptors reversed the order; and, commencing at the top of the supposititious ladder, they taught — "In the beginning ELoHIM *created*." Each rung, as they came down, marked, like degrees on a scale, the order in which previous induction had established the relative places of events; and thus every intellectual nation possessed *a* "Genesis." That of the Hebrew Elohistic writer possesses the superior merit of being a scientific hymn,[682] arranged in true accordance with the *septenary* scale of numerical harmonies.

Viewed as a literary work of ancient humanity's loftiest conception of Creative Power, it is sublime beyond all cosmogonies known in the world's history. Viewed as a narrative inspired by the Most High, its conceits would be pitiful and its revelations false; because telescopic astronomy has ruined its celestial structure, physics have negatived its cosmic organism, and geology has stultified the fabulous terrestrial mechanism upon which its assumptions are based. How, then, are its crude and juvenile hypotheses about *Human Creation* to be received?

Before answering this interrogatory, it may be instructive to peruse some Fathers of the Church:

1st. ORIGEN. — "To what man of sense, I beg of you, could one make believe, that the first, the second, and the third *day* of creation, in which notwithstanding an evening and a morning are named, could have existed without *sun*, without *moon*, and without *stars?* —that, during the first day, there was not even a *sky!* Who shall be found so idiotic as to admit that God delivered himself up like a man to agriculture, by planting trees in the garden of Eden situate towards the East; that one of those trees was that of life, and that another could give the science of good and evil? No one, I think, can hesitate to regard these things as *figures*, beneath which mysteries are hidden."[683]

The same patristic scholar adds elsewhere—"Were it necessary to attach ourselves to the letter, and to understand that which is written in the Law after the manner of the Jews or the populace, I should blush (*erubesco dicere*) to say aloud that it is God who has given us such laws: I should find even more grandeur and reason in human legislations; for example, in those of the Athenians, of Romans, or of Lacedæmonians."[684]

2d. CLEMENS *Alexandrinus* — "For your *Genesis* in particular was never the work of Moses."[685] — "Horum ergo scripta (Orphei et Hesiodi) in duas partes intelligentiæ dividuntur; id est, secundum litteram sunt ignobilis vulgi turba confluxit, ea vero quæ secundum allegoriam constant omnis philosophorum et eruditorum loquacitas admirata est."[686] St. Clement applies exactly the same principles to *Genesis* (xxvi.), where he exclaims — "O divine jesting! It is the same that Heraclitus attributes to Jupiter.

Abimelech is Jesus Christ, our king, who, from the heavens above, considers our sports, our actions of grace, our transports of joy."[687]

3d. St. AUGUSTINE — "There is no way of preserving the true sense of the first *three* chapters of Genesis, without attributing to God things unworthy of him, and for which one *must have recourse* to allegory."[688]

4th. St. JEROME — who, in his commentary upon Jeremiah, enforces the allegorical method — "Sive MOSEN dicere volueris auctorem Pentateuchi, sive Esdram ejusdem instauratorem operis, non recuso."[689]

Let the most philosophic of many truly-learned Rabbis close the list:—

MAIMONIDES — "There are some persons to whom it is repugnant to perceive a motive in a given law of the (divine) laws; they love better to find no rational sense in the commandments and prohibitions. That which leads them to this, is a certain feebleness they feel in their souls, but upon which they are *unable to reason*, and of which they know not how to give any account. This is what they think. If the laws should profit us in this (temporal) existence, and that they had been given to us for such or such a motive, it might very well be that they are the product of the reflection and of the intelligence of a *man of genius*: if, on the contrary, a thing possesses no comprehensible sense and that it produces no advantage whatever, it emanates, without doubt, from the Deity, because human thought could not lead to such a thing. One would say that, according to these weak minds, man is greater than his Creator; because *man* (according to them) speaks and acts while aiming at a certain object; whereas God, far from acting similarly, would order us, on the contrary, to do that which to ourselves is not of the least utility, and would forbid us from actions that cannot cause us the slightest damage." (Arabicè, '*Dellâlat el Khâyereen*; Hebraicè, *More Neboukhîm*; "Guide to the Strayers," ch. xxxi.: MUNK's Translation, Paris, 1833.)

They all — i. e., the Fathers of the first centuries — attributed a *double* sense to the words of Scripture, the one obvious and literal, the other hidden and mystical, which lay concealed as it were under the outward letter. The former they treated with the utmost neglect;[690] following St. Paul's authority — "For the *letter* killeth, but the spirit giveth life." — (2 *Corinth.* iii. 6.)

Section G. — COSMAS-INDICOPLEUSTES.

But, in the proportion that Hellenic learning faded in Alexandrian schools, so patristic talent and scholarship also deteriorated. That "Genesis" which, by the earlier Fathers, had been ascribed to EZRA rather than to MOSES, and the language of which, to more refined Grecian intellects, appeared too contemptible for Divinity unless construed in an *allegorical* sense, at length began to be accepted *verbatim et litteratim* by Christian writers: the strenuousness of orthodoxy, in any creed, increasing always in the ratio that mental culture declines. At last, arose a Monk who, unjustly forgotten by the Church though he be now, did more to petrify theological stolidity in Europe, for 800 years, with respect to the first three chapters of *Genesis*, than any human being but himself — COSMAS-*Indicopleustes*.

"He is," says the learned Mr. Sharpe, "of the dogmatical school which forbids all inquiry as heretical. He fights the battle which has been so often fought before and since, and is even still fought so resolutely, the battle of religious ignorance against scientific knowledge. He sets the words of the Bible against the results of science; he denies that the world is a sphere, and quotes the Old Testament against the pagan philosophers, to show that it is a plane, covered by the firmament as a roof, above which he places the kingdom of heaven. . . . The arguments employed by Cosmas were unfortunately but too often used by the Christian world in general, who were even willing to see learning itself fall with the overthrow of paganism. All knowledge was divided into sacred and profane, and whatever was not drawn from the Scriptures was slighted and neglected; and this perhaps was one of the chief causes of the darkness which overspread the world during the middle ages." [691]

To comprehend the force of these observations it may be well to preface our description of the *Topographia Christiana* by a few excerpts from Matter.[692]

The only Christian Father whose writings evince the humblest acquaintance with Egyptian studies, CLEMENS *Alexandrinus*, expressly says, that the "Egyptians taught the Greeks the movement of the planets round the sun;" and, since 1848, Egyptology can proudly add the extraordinary discoveries of Lepsius in hieroglyphical Astronomy, which are likely to be carried to results little expected, through Biot.[693]

About B. C. 603, Thales had observed an eclipse of the sun. He taught the *spheroidity* if not the sphericity of the earth; he knew the obliquity of the ecliptic; knew that the moon was illumined by the sun; and explained solar eclipses by the intervention of the lunar disc between the earth and the sun. In the succeeding century, Pythagoras sustained the *sphericity* of the earth, and its movement, with the planets, round the sun; and his disciples Leucippus and Democritus added some acquaintance with the rotary motion of the earth upon its axis. Eudoxus advocated similar doctrines. Now, Thales, Pythagoras, and Eudoxus, had studied under genuine hierogrammatists in Egypt.

The grand Stagyrite (who had not drunk of Nilotic waters) maintained the contrary; viz., that the sun revolved around the earth. In vain did Aristarchus strive to bring science back to truer principles. His voice was unheard for sixteen centuries. Hipparchus determined the precession of the equinoxes, &c., during the 2d century B. C.; but, his more important works being lost, "tulit alter honores;" because Ptolemy, a far better geographer than astronomer, has not revealed what of his great predecessor's views militated against his own celestial dogmas. In the early part of the 2d century, after C., Ptolemy had wofully retrograded from ancient Greco-Egyptian science; for he held to the absolute immobility of the earth, and made the sun revolve around our globe. Denouncing the contrary system as too ridiculous to merit attention, he gives his own reason for opposing it, viz., "that one always sees the *same* half of the sky"! "The earth," says Claudius Ptolemy, "is not only central, but also stationary. If it had an individual motion (upon its axis) such movement would be proportioned to its mass. It would, therefore, leave behind it the animals and other bodies, which would be carried into the air,—it would fly away from them, and escape from the sky! No object not fixed to the earth, no bird, could advance to the eastward with the same rapidity as the globe"! Unsuspected before Newton, the laws of gravitation and attraction could not ease Ptolemy's perplexities.

We have seen that the older and wiser Fathers of the Church (who must have been more or less read in the higher Grecian classics), unable to reconcile the *letter* of "Genesis" with what they well knew to be positive philosophy, had recourse, like Philo, to *allegorical* explanations: which means, simply, that they disbelieved genesiacal stories as revealed in the *Septuagint*, and therefore nullified them by inventing mystic hypotheses. They sustained, however, in their writings, no especial theory upon astronomy or geography: but, that with which Clemens, and Origen, and Anatolius, and Synesius, and Theophilus, and even Cyril, had refrained from meddling, was grasped, with Promethean audacity, by an itinerant trader of the sixth century after C.; whose temerarious zeal, when he had adopted monastic vows, was exceeded merely by his delicious stupidity; as we now proceed to prove. Cosmas, setting a Greek copy of "Genesis" before him, composed, upon that poor version's literal language, his *Topographia Christiana*.[694] Of *Hebrew* he had not an idea.

FIG. 357.

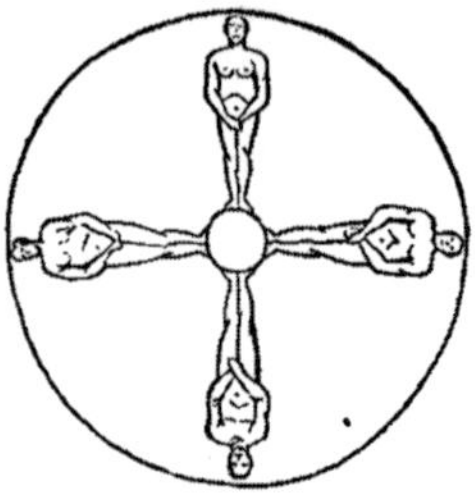

He, Cosmas aforesaid, commences with a practical demonstration of the absurdity of "Antipodes," — by drawing a figure like this :—

He then acutely observes :—"Cum figura hominis recta sit, qui fit ut quatuor illi eodem tempore stantes recti non sint; sed quocumque vertas eos, quatuor illi simul nunquam videantur; quomodo ergo fieri potest ut vanas illas mendacesque hypotheses admittamus? Quomodo ergo fieri potest ut eodem tempore pluvia in quatuor illos decidat? Quod ergo nec natura nec *mens nostra* admittere potest, id cur frustra supponitis?"—"Thus," continues Montfaucon, "Cosmas here and throughout Topographia Christiana, *ut et multi alii ex SS. PP. qui nec gravitatis centrum, nec astronomicas observationes, callebant.*"[695]

St. Augustine it was who had "*seen* folks with an *eye* in the pit of their stomachs;" so his testimony is unsafe; but Lactantius had beheld fewer marvels, and we quote him :— "Ineptum credere esse homines quorum vestigia sint superiora quam capita, aut ibi quæ apud nos jacent inversa pendere, fruges et arbores deorsum versus crescere. . . . Hujus erroris originem *philosophis* fuisse quod existimarint rotundum esse mundum."

For the sake of contrast with later patristric orthodoxy, let justice be meted out to some old rabbinical capacities. The most ancient authors of the *Guemara* were acquainted with the spherical form of the earth; for they say, in the Jerusalem Talmud, that Alexander the Great, going over the earth to conquer it, ascertained that it was *round;* and it is on that account that statuary represents him with a globe in his hand.[696] Albeit, there are Judaical authorities of higher antiquity in the *Zohar* — a book which probably antedates, but in any case approximates to, the Christian era[697] — whose knowledge of the more ancient systems of cosmogony led them to write as follows: — "In the book of Chamnouna *the Old* one learns, through extended explanations, that the earth turns upon itself in the form of a circle; that some (people) are above, and others below; that the aspect of all creatures changes according to the appearance of each place, while preserving nevertheless the same position: that such a country of the earth there is that is lighted, whilst such others are in darkness; the former have day when to others it is night; and there are some countries where it is constantly day, or, at least, where night lasts but a few instants."[698]

But such profanity was unintelligible to Cosmas. No ray of light, from scientific sources, could penetrate into a blockhead.

To him, the habitable earth is a plane surface, having the form of a parallelogram, of which the sides are double in length to the top and bottom. Inside this oblong square are *four* basins, the Mediterranean, the Caspian, the Red Sea, and the Persian Gulf. Outside the parallelogram the circumambient ocean surrounds the inner oblong-square, and separates it from the outer continents (primitively inhabited by Adam's family), from *paradise*, and from the "garden of Eden," which are situate upon a mountain at the East. Here dwelt our first parents, until the *ark* of Noah, during the deluge, ferried them over to the inner continent where we ourselves reside unto this day. Cosmas ignored whatever he could not find *in the Bible;* and, wiser than our modern theologers, this modest pattern for prurient orthodoxy never discovered *China*, Northern *Europe*, Central *Africa*, *America*, *Polynesia*, or *Australia*, in the canonical Scriptures. Let his *map*, and his own perspicuous language, explain true Mosaic cosmology. He begins with the exact Greek letter of *Genesis* i. 1: but his editor kindly furnishes the *Vulgate*:—"Scriptum est IN PRINCIPIO FECIT DEUS CŒLUM ET TERRAM. Primum itaque *cœlum* fornicatum."[699]

[N. B. My own tracing (made at the British Museum, in 1848, for personal remembrance) being too rough, we are indebted to the accomplished Mrs. Luke Burke for the *fac-simile* transcript, of which the above is a copy; reduced slightly more than one half. Typographical exigenda compel us also to transfer Cosmas's explanations from the *map*

Cosmas's *Map*. — Fig. 358. — "I. TABULA."

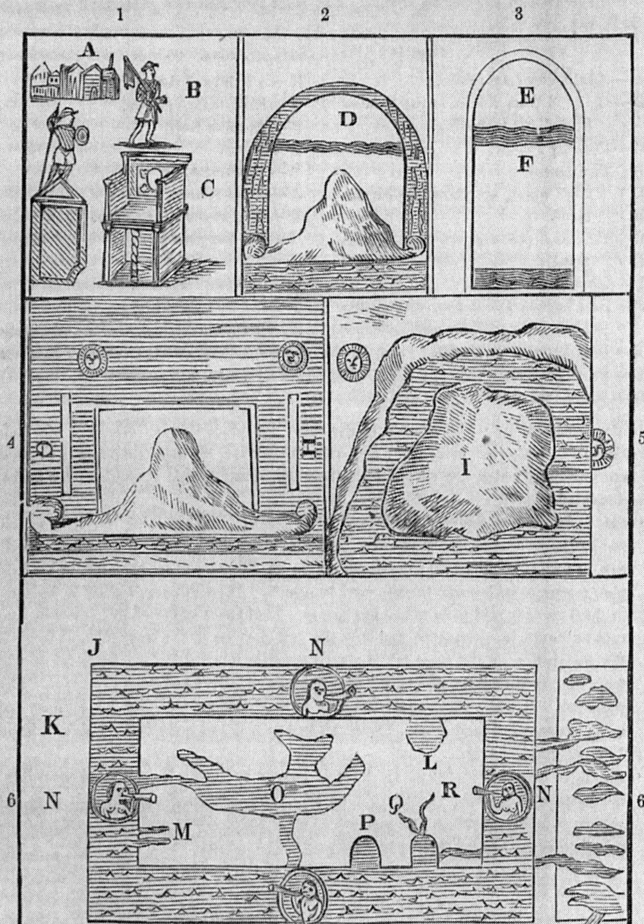

itself into our text; but the letters A, B, C, &c., indicate the place of each. As the work of Cosmas is exceedingly rare, we hope theological students will appreciate the pains taken to furnish them with so clear an illustration of what they still call "Mosaic" cosmogony. —G. R. G.]

COSMAS'S GREEK EXPLANATIONS.

A — Adulis city (*Abyssinia*).
B — the road from Adulis to the East — Ethiopians travelling.
C — Ptolemy's chair.
D — Firmament.
E, F — Waters which are above the Firmament.
G, H — Columns (to support the Firmament).
I — inhabited earth.
J — land beyond the Ocean, where men dwelt before the Deluge.
K — land beyond the Ocean.
L — Caspian Sea.
M — River Phison.
N — 4 Points of the compass.
O — Mediterranean Sea.
P — Arabian Gulf.
Q — Tigris.
R — Euphrates.
S — River Gihon.
T — land beyond the Ocean.
U — the Sun Occident.
V — the Sun Orient.
X — the Sun Occident.
Y — the Sun Orient.
Z — is Cosmas's picture of the Almighty looking down, and seeing that "it was good."

In the IVth book of "Topographia Christiana," the pious Cosmas describes his hydrographic and ecclesiastical principles; but, rich as they are, his argumentation is too prolix for our purposes, which are served by translating Montfaucon's synopsis of his author's elucidation of *Plate* I.

"*Fig.* 1. In the first figure, the city 'ADOULI or *Adulis* [in Abyssinia] (for it is so called in both ways by Cosmas) is shown. *Axumis*, which is two miles distant from the Red Sea, is situated to the East; for which reason an *Ethiopian* is represented, in his Ethiopian costume, taking the Axumis road to Adulis. Then Ptolemy's chair is delineated in the form it is said to have had by Cosmas. That [part of the chair] however, sculptured all over in characters, had only the last portion of the inscription added. But the inscription on the stone tablet placed opposite was finished—a fragment of which from the lower part together with its characters or letters had been destroyed. Above the stone tablet king Ptolemy EVERGETES himself is represented in his military attire as he appears in the picture. These things you will find more fully explained in page 140 and the following.

"*Fig.* 2. In the second figure the shape of heaven and earth is delineated according to the opinion of Cosmas and the old Fathers, who thought the earth, as it were, a *flat surface*, extending beneath and inclosed by *walls* on all sides; and that these walls were raised to an immense height, and finally arranged themselves into the form of a vault; while the *firmament* pervaded the higher part of the vault so that it (beatorum sedes) might be the seat of the Blest. [The same idea ('firmament,' Hebraicè SK*h*KIM K*h*ZKIM — literally, *solid skies*) occurs in *Job* xxxvii. 18. Thus Cahen renders — 'As-tu étendu avec lui les *cieux*, *solides* comme un miroir métallique?' And Noyes —

> —— 'Canst thou like him spread out the *sky*
> Which is *firm* like a molten mirror?' 700

But, under the firmament, they thought the sun, moon, and stars, were put in motion; and that a *conical* mountain of wondrous height rose up in the northern parts of the earth; and while the sun, performing his *circuit round the earth*, stood behind this mountain, there was night to those inhabiting the earth; but, on the other hand, it was *day* when the sun shone upon us on the reverse [i. e., on *our* side] of the mountain: and, in a similar way Cosmas reasons with respect to the moon and stars; see page 186 and the following.

"*Fig.* 3. Exhibits a prospective view of the universe; that is to say, of the heavens and the earth in the part where they are more closely drawn together; for Cosmas thought the earth was *square* and *oblong*, and the same is assumed with respect to the heavens. See page 186 and following.

"*Fig.* 4. Represents a conical mountain, and the earth, together with the sun and moon, *under* the firmament. But on the sides [*Job* ix. 6—âMUDIH—'*Pillars* (of the earth)'; *Job* xxvi. 11—'*pillars* of the skies'] are represented the *pillars* of heaven, with an inscription [in *Greek!*] upon the plan here presented—οἱ ςύλοι τοῦ οὐρανου—*the columns of the sky;* which columns, according to the opinion of Cosmas, I think to be those walls which arise on the sides from the earth up to the heavens (*Psalms* cxlviii. 4—'Ye WATERS that be *above* the *skies*').

"*Fig.* 5. The outline of the earth and its ἐκνογραφίαν are traced out. You may observe that Cosmas conjectured that the immensely-high conical mountain presented an obstacle where our earth could not, at the northern part, be so well inclosed by a right line; because its foundations on that side are *round*, as if they proceeded from a great promontory in the ocean.

"*Fig.* 6. Displays the rugged plain of the earth, such as Cosmas explains in many places; for he thought, as we have said before, that the earth was oblong, and its length twice as long as its breadth, and that an *ocean* surrounded the entire earth, as is here represented. But, beyond the ocean, there was yet *another* land adhering closely, on all sides, to the walls of heaven. Upon the eastern side of this *transmarine* land he judges that MAN WAS CREATED; and that there the *paradise of gladness* was located, such as here, on the eastern edge, is described: where it received our first parents, driven out of paradise to that extreme point of land on the sea-shore. Hence, upon the coming of the *deluge*, Noah with his sons was borne by the ark to this earth we now inhabit. The four *rivers*, he supposes, to be gushing up the spouts in paradise; with subterranean channels through the ocean, to our earth, and in certain places that they gush out anew. He considers that the Hyrcanian Sea [Caspian] is joined to the ocean; which we have elsewhere shown was the opinion of certain ancients.

"*Fig* 7. He briefly dispatches the whole machinery of the world, which, as the ancients thought, was composed of the *sky* and the *earth*. Its form he represents, with the conical mountain above alluded to. But Cosmas-Ægypticus deemed that the earth which we inhabit was always inclining from the north to the south. Albeit Cosmas contradicts himself. How can such a mass as that of heaven and earth stand, supported by nothing, since it is always pressed downward? He answers—the earth, inasmuch as it is ponderous matter by nature, seeks the bottom; but the igneous parts tend upward; therefore, when sky and earth are thus joined and cannot be torn asunder, the one pressing from above and the other from below, neither yielding to the other, the whole machine remains immovable and *suspended*. ['This is a grand argument,' says Mr. Burke, commenting in a private letter, 'and beats the Newtonian theory out and out! Only fancy; two forces shut up in a box, one pulling up, and the other pulling down, and the BOX, *in consequence*, remaining 'immota et suspensa!' This is, beyond exception, the brightest mechanical idea I have ever come across'].

"*Fig.* 8. He represents the conical mountain on that side which is turned adversely to the earth; where, when the sun arrives, night is produced to the earth's inhabitants. In the same place the *revolutions of the sun* are indicated by lines [upon the conical mountain]; whereby the various *seasons* of the year are caused. When, therefore, the sun arrives at the lower line, the nights then are longer, and it makes *winter*, τροπη, or revolution: the sun performing the major portion of his course *behind* the mountain. When, however, the sun comes to the middle line of the mountain, then the *equinox* is produced; the sun in performing his course having reached the equinoctial line. When, finally, the sun touches the uppermost line, then the *summer* revolution takes place, and he attains to the *tropic*. This is in conformity with the opinion of Cosmas, who describes the revolutions of the sun in these words—μεγάλη νὺξ, *great night;* μέση νὺξ, *middle night;* μικρὰ νὺξ *little night;* as you behold in the picture."

Through the above parody upon nature, Cosmas explained all celestial phenomena — the course of the moon, its phases and eclipses, as well as the sun's rotation round the earth's flat plain. The *Topographia Christiana* became the text-book of ecclesiastical orthodoxy, for above 800 years, down to Galileo; and Cosmas's caricature on the one hand, coupled with ignorance of the Hebrew text of Joshua (x. 12–14) on the other, induced the murder of Giordano Bruno.

Nevertheless, according to the literal language of the first IX chapters of "Genesis," Cosmas was not far from the truth. Were the ancient writers of those chapters to arise from the grave, and were they respectfully requested to indicate which commentary best represented their meaning — that of the *Topographia Christiana;* or those recent attempts "to make Moses sound in the faith of the geological section of the British Association for the Advancement of Science"[701] — they would unanimously claim the former as their own.

Happy middle-ages; when Europe made up in credulity what it lacked in intelligence! "They had neither looked into heaven, nor earth; neither into the sea, nor the land, as has been done since. They had philosophy without scale, astronomy without demonstration. They made war without powder, shot, cannon, or mortars; nay, the mob made bonfires without squibs or crackers. They went to sea without compass, and sailed lacking chronometers. They viewed the stars without telescopes, and measured altitudes without barometers. Learning had no printing-press, writing no paper, paper no ink; magnetism no telegraph, iron no rails, steam no boilers. The lover was forced to send his mistress a deal-board for a love-letter, and a billet-doux might be of the size of a trencher. They were clothed without manufactures, and the richest robes were the skins of formidable monsters. They carried on trade without books, and correspondence without postage: their merchants kept no ledgers; their shopkeepers no cash-books. They had surgery without anatomy, physicians without materia-medica; who gave emetics without ipecacuanha, and cured agues without quinine. They dispensed with lucifer-matches, coffee, sugar, tea, and tobacco"[702] — and, never having heard of the first three chapters of "Genesis," they believed in *Topographia Christiana!*

The *book* is scarcely known, now-a-days, to theologers; but its commentary (orally transmitted from father to son) survives all around us. We have conceived it our duty not to let the one continue without the other; and therefore have rescued from further oblivion the Mosaic chart of Cosmas.

Section H. — ANTIQUITY OF THE NAME "ADaM."

After what has been already set forth, there seems scarcely reason to answer an interrogatory, above propounded, relative to "human creation" as narrated in *Genesis.* Archæological criticism might finally rest upon *one* Hebrew word; viz. ADaM.

The philological law of *triliterals,* in Semitic tongues, has been touched upon during previous examinations of Xth Genesis. "Non omnia possumus" — and the authors must reiterate that, in order to keep within *one* volume, they have been forced to expurgate redundancies, often, they fear, at the sacrifice of perspicuity. In lieu of *extracts* from the pages of Lanci, Meyer, Gesenius, Neumann, Ewald, Wilhelm von Humboldt, Prichard, Bunsen,—in addition to those previously drawn from Rawlinson, De Saulcy, &c. — all corroborating our correctness, we must substitute *references* to their authoritative works.

The reader will observe, notwithstanding, that the bisyllable ADM cannot be a primitive but must be a *secondary* formation, according to the progressive scale of linguistic development. To reach the primary root, or monosyllable, within this triliteral word contained, an *affix,* a *suffix,* or a *medial*-letter, must be first removed. Among Hebraists of the highest modern school, on the European continent, the fact that "Adam" is a *dissyllabic* name alone suffices to prove that its possessor appeared on earth thousands of years subsequently to the primordial ages of humanity; because *in principio* man articulated but *monosyllables.* Or else (what is the same thing in result, no less than more positive) the Israelite who (in some form of *coin*-letter) wrote the word ADM, of *Genesis,* lived at a philological epoch when the pristine *monosyllables* had already (organically through development) merged into words of *two* syllables; and therefore, that writer committed an egregious anachronism when he retro-leptically ascribed a *triliteral* proper-name, or rather noun, to his first human progenitor.

The word ADM, or with an additional vowel, ADaM, is consequently to be divided into two separate words, A and DaM; or A-DaM. Now, A, *aleph,* is the primeval, Semitic, masculine article *A* = "the":[703] an article that, in Scripture, is prefixed to above forty masculine substantives; although, until recently, the fact was unperceived by Hebrew grammarians, or Jewish lexicographers.

In the next place, the word ADaM does not proceed, as the Rabbis suppose, from ADaMaH (*Gen.* ii. 7)—a *bisyllable* from a *trisyllable!*—but the latter is an extension of the former root, DaM (Arabicè, *Dem*), meaning *blood;* the color of which, being *red,* originated the secondary signification of DaM, as "red;" and "to be *red.*"

Consequently, A, the letter "*aleph,*" being the masculine article *the;* and the noun DaM meaning *blood,* or "red," we have only to unite these two words into A-DaM, to read *the-blood,* or THE-RED, in "Genesis;" which duplex substantive, applied to man, naturally signifies "*the-red*-man;" and, when applied to the *ground,* ADaMaH ("out of the dust" of which this *the-red*-man, ADaM, was moulded), it means *the-red-earth: i. e.,* that rubescent soil out of which the Jehovistic writer of Genesis IId imagined Hebrew man to have been fashioned by Creative artisanship. The BeNi-ADaM also, in Psalms (xlix. 2. Comp. *Ps.* lxii. 9: and contrast with BeNoT*t*-HaADaM, *Gen.* vi. 2), are reputed to be *patricians* of the pure Abrahamic stock; whereas the plebeians (including all those who are, like Anglo-Saxons, mere GOIM, *Gentiles*) belong altogether to a different and lower level . . . in the eye of IeHOuaH.

We adopt entirely the Italian rendering of the great interpreter of Sacred Philology at the Vatican; and think, with Lanci, that *il-rossicante,* "the-Blusher," is the happiest translation of the old Semitic particle and noun A-DaM.

How does this interpretation bear upon ethnography?

Reader! simply thus. As no "Type of Mankind" but the *white race* can be said (physiologically) to *blush;* it follows, that, according to the conception of the writers of Genesis (who were *Jews* and of the "white race"), not only did the first human pair converse between themselves, no less than with God and with the serpent, in pure *Hebrew,* but they were essentially A-DaM*ites* (*red*-man and woman) "blushers:" — and therefore, these Hebrew writers, never supposed that A-DaM and ISE (vulgaricè, Adam and Eve) could have been of any stock than of the *white* type—in short, Hebrews, *Abrahamidæ,* like themselves — these writers aforesaid.

Thus, through a few cuts of an archæological scalpel, vanishes the last illusion that any but *white* "Types of Mankind" are to be found in the first *three chapters* of the book called "Genesis."

The "Chinese" having been carefully removed further on from connection with the Mesopotamian SINIM of Isaiah (xlix. 12), nothing remains but to refer the reader to the *map* [*supra, p.* 552] we have given of Xth *Genesis* for the whole of Ethnography comprehended by the writers of the Old Testament: Strabo, who followed Eratosthenes about B. C. 15, furnishing every possible information upon what of geography was attainable, in the first century after C., by the writers of the New.

The present authors have asserted these results before.

"That part of the *map* colored deep-red includes all the world known to the inspired writers of the Old Testament; and this, with the part colored pale-red, includes all known to St. Paul and the Evangelists. — As we have no evidence that their inspiration extended to matters of science, and we know that they were ignorant of Astronomy, Geology, Natural History, Geography, &c. — what evidence is there that they knew anything of the INHABITANTS of countries unknown to them, viz.: Americans, Chinese, Hindoos, Australians, Polynesians, and other contemporary races?" — (J. C. N.: *Bibl. and Phys. Hist. of Man*; New York, 1849; "Map" and pp. 54-67.)

"These unhistorical *origines* of nations are now adverted to, as a prelude to the discussion of the Xth chapter of Genesis (see *Ethnological Journal*, No. VI., note, page 254), whereby it will be demonstrated that, under the *personifications* of "Shem, Ham, and Japheth," their fifteen *sons*, and seventy-one *grand-children*, the Hebrew geographers, whose ken of the earth's superficies was even more limited than that of Eratosthenes, about B. C. 240, have never alluded to, nor intended, Mongolian, Malayan, Polynesian, American, or Nigritian races." — (G. R. G.: *Otia Ægyptiaca*; London, 1849: p. 124, "note.")

Five years have since elapsed. Most of the conclusions advanced by the authors have been challenged. Whether those conclusions were based, or not, upon thorough investigation of each department of the subject, the reader of the present volume is now best qualified to decide.

PART III.

Supplement.

BY GEO. R. GLIDDON.

ESSAY I.

ARCHÆOLOGICAL INTRODUCTION TO THE Xth CHAPTER OF GENESIS.

"Scriptura primum intelligi debet grammaticè antequam possit explicari theologicè."
(Luther.)

"The Xth Chapter of Genesis—*Archæological Introduction to its Study*"—is the heading given, in our "Prospectus," to Part III. of this work.

To the generality of readers, educated under convictions that every process calculated to probe the historical evidences of the Hebrew Scriptures has heretofore been rigorously applied to them, an *Introduction* termed "archæological" may seem, to say the least, superfluous at the present day—while to not a few persons, the proposed method of examination may, at first sight, even wear the aspect of presumptuousness. Nevertheless, having announced the intention, it behooves us to justify it.

In common with other Protestants, since our earliest childhood, we have been assured that the Bible is the *word of God*—and that the inspiration of the writers of both Old and New Testaments rests upon testimony the most irrefragable. We have also been admonished in the language of the Apostle (1) to "*search* the Scriptures;" coupled with the corroborative exhortation, (2) "seek, and ye will find; knock, and it will be opened unto you."

Thus, on the one hand, asseverations the most positive fortify the inquirer who conscientiously examines whether the divine revelation of the Bible and the inspiration of its penmen are "built upon a rock;" at the same time that, on the other, the Gospels themselves invite him to search, seek, and scrutinize.

Supported by such authority, no legitimate objection can be sustained, by Protestants, against the employment of what we conceive to be the only method through which the historical validity of a given proposition can be thoroughly tested; nor will logical orthodoxy contest Vater's axiom—"*Faith in Christ can set no limits to critical inquiries; otherwise he would hinder the knowledge of Truth.*"

(1) *The good Tidings according to* John v. 39.

(2) *The good Tidings according to* Matthew, vii. 7; copied in *The good Tidings according to* Luke, xi. 9. We follow Sharpe: *The New Testament, translated from Griesbach's Text;* wherein "will" is substituted for the "shall" of king James's version.

Homo, according to Bacon, *naturæ minister et interpres, tantum facit et intelligit quantum de naturæ ordine re vel mente observaverit; nec amplius scit, aut potest.* A finite being, circumscribed within the intellectual horizon of the mundane age in which each individual lives, man can reason merely upon phenomena. *Quicquid enim*, wrote the immortal Newton, *ex phenomenis non deducitur hypothesis vocanda est; et hypotheses vel metaphysicæ, vel physicæ, vel qualitatum occultarum seu mechanicæ, in philosophia locum non habent.*

What is *Philosophy?* Etymologically, the "love of wisdom," and paraphrastically, the "love of knowledge;" multiform are the significations through which this sublime Greek word has travelled. From the ablest English historian (3) of its phases, we extract such paragraphs as will convey to the reader our individual perceptions of its import at this day.

"We shall find some obscurities cleared up, if we can master an accurate and comprehensive definition of Philosophy. The definition I have finally settled upon is this:—

"*Philosophy is the explanation of the Phenomena of the Universe.* By the term explanation, the subject is restricted to the domain of the intellect, and is thereby demarcated from religion, though not from theology.

"Philosophy is inherent in man's nature. It is not a caprice, it is not a plaything, it is a necessity; for our life is a mystery, surrounded by mysteries: we are encompassed by wonder. The myriad aspects of Nature *without*, the strange fluctuations of feeling *within*, all demand from us an explanation. Standing upon this ball of earth, so infinite to *us*, so trivial in the infinitude of the universe, we look forth into nature with reverent awe, with irrepressible curiosity. We must have explanations. And thus it is that Philosophy, in some rude shape, is a visible effort in every condition of man—in the rudest phase of half-developed capacity, as in the highest conditions of culture: it is found among the sugar-canes of the West Indies, and in the tangled pathless forest of America. Take man where you will—hunting the buffalo on the prairies, or immovable in meditation on the hot banks of the Ganges, priest or peasant, soldier or student, man never escapes from the pressure of the burden of that mystery which forces him to seek, and readily to accept, some explanation of it. The savage, startled by the muttering of distant thunder, asks, 'What is that?' and is restless till he knows, or fancies he knows. If told it is the voice of a restless demon, that is enough; the explanation is given. If he then be told that, to propitiate the demon, the sacrifice of some human being is necessary, his slave, his enemy, his friend, perhaps even his child, falls a victim to the credulous terror. The *childhood of man* enables us to retrace [archæologically] the infancy of nations. No one can live with children without being struck by their restless questioning, and unquenchable desire to have everything explained; no less than by the facility with which every authoritative assertion is accepted as an explanation. The History of Philosophy is the study of man's successive attempts to explain the phenomena around and within him.

"The first explanations were naturally enough drawn from analogies, afforded by consciousness. Men saw around them activity, change, force; they felt within them a mysterious power, which made them active, changing, potent: they explained what they saw, by what they felt. Hence the fetichism of barbarians, the mythologies of more advanced races. Oreads and nymphs, demons and beneficent powers, moved among the ceaseless activities of Nature. Man knows that in his anger he storms, shouts, destroys. What, then, is thunder but the anger of some invisible being? Moreover, man knows that a *present* will assuage his anger against an enemy, and it is but natural that he should believe the offended thunderer will also be appeased by some offering. As soon as another conception of the nature of thunder has been elaborated by observation and the study of its phenomena, the supposed Deity vanishes, and, with it, all the false conceptions it originated, till, at last, Science takes a rod, and draws the terrible lightning from the heavens, rendering it so harmless that it will not tear away a spider's web!

"But long centuries of patient observation and impatient guessing, controlled by logic, were necessary, before such changes could take place. The development of Philosophy, like the development of organic life, has been through the slow additions of thousands upon thousands of years; for humanity is a growth, as our globe is, and the laws of its growth are still to be discovered. . . . One of the great fundamental laws has been discovered by Auguste Comte — viz: *the law of mental Evolution* . . . which he has not only discovered,

(3) G. H. Lewes: *Biographical History of Philosophy;* London, 1846. The substance of our remarks may be found in vol. iv. pp. 245–262, under the heading of Auguste Comte, "the Bacon of the nineteenth century," and author of *Cours de Philosophie Positive.* The original source of this abstract may be found in Comte, vol. i. edit. Paris, 1830, "Exposition," pp. 3–5, 63, &c.; but we take Mr. Lewes's later definitions from *The Leader;* London, 1852; April 17, 24, and May 1. A profound thinker has recently done full honor to Mr. Lewes's work. (Vide McCulloh: *Credibility of the Scriptures;* Baltimore, 1852, vol. ii. pp. 454–458.)

but applied historically. . . . This law may be thus stated: "Every branch of knowledge passes successively through three stages: 1st, the *supernatural*, or fictitious; 2d, the *metaphysical*, or abstract; 3d, the *positive*, or scientific. The first is the necessary point of departure taken by human intelligence; the second is merely a stage of transition from the supernatural to the positive; and the third is the fixed and definite condition in which knowledge is alone capable of progressive development.

"In the attempt made by man to explain the varied phenomena of the universe, history reveals to us," therefore, "three distinct and characteristic stages, the *theological*, the *metaphysical*, and the *positive*. In the first, man explains phenomena by some fanciful conception suggested in the analogies of his own consciousness; in the second, he explains phenomena by some *à priori* conception of inherent or superadded entities, suggested in the constancy observable in phenomena, which constancy leads him to suspect that they are not produced by any *intervention* on the part of an external being, but are owing to the nature of the things themselves; in the third, he explains phenomena by adhering solely to these constancies of succession and co-existence ascertained inductively, and recognized as the *laws* of Nature.

Consequently, "in the *theological* stage, Nature is regarded as the theatre whereon the arbitrary wills and momentary caprices of Superior Powers play their varying and variable parts. . . . In the *metaphysical* stage the notion of capricious divinities is replaced by that of *abstract entities*, whose modes of action are, however, invariable. . . . In the *positive* stage, the invariableness of phenomena under similar conditions is recognized as the sum total of human investigation; and, beyond the laws which regulate phenomena, it is considered idle to penetrate."

"Although every branch of knowledge must pass through these three stages, in obedience to the law of evolution, nevertheless the process is not strictly chronological. Some sciences are more rapid in their evolutions than others; some individuals pass through these evolutions more quickly than others; so also of nations. The present intellectual anarchy results from that difference; some sciences being in the *positive*, some in the *supernatural* [or *theological*], some in the *metaphysical* stage: and this is further to be subdivided into individual differences; for in a science which, on the whole, may be fairly admitted as being positive, there will be found some cultivators still in the metaphysical stage. Astronomy is now in so positive a condition, that we need nothing but the laws of dynamics and gravitation to explain all celestial phenomena; and this explanation we know to be correct, as far as anything can be known, because we can predict the return of a comet with the nicest accuracy, or can enable the mariner to discover his latitude, and find his way amidst the 'waste of waters.' This is a *positive* science. But so far is meteorology from such a condition, that prayers for dry or rainy weather are still offered up in churches; whereas if once the *laws* of these phenomena were traced, there would be no more prayers for rain than for the sun to rise at midnight."

We have only to reverse the order, and apply its triple classification to individuals, and in the natural arrangement of the strata, tracing backwards from the *positive* to the *metaphysical*, from the latter down to the *supernatural*, we shall perceive that this last, at once the oldest stage and unhappily the most common, represents the least mature, the least educated, the most antiquated, state of human intelligence. In consequence, the mere *supernaturalist* believes anything and everything, however impossible.

"The *Metaphysician* believes he can penetrate into the *causes* and *essences* of the phenomena around him; while the *Positivist*, recognizing his own incompetency, limits his efforts to the ascertainment of those laws which regulate the succession of these phenomena."

In the quintuple classification of those sciences into which *Positive Philosophy* has hitherto been successfully introduced, M. Comte (1832–40) admits only Astronomy, Physics, Chemistry, Physiology, and Sociology. It strikes us that, at the present day, this division is more exclusive than the progression of knowledge any longer warrants. *Archæology*, for instance, we claim to have arrived at its *positive* grade; and although its laws are by no means popularly appreciated, to have become as certain in its results as any other human science. A brief exposition of its attributes may prepare the reader for a just recognition of its utility.

Αρχαιος, *antiquus*, "ancient," and Λογος, a "discourse," are Hellenic words—meaning, when *united*, in general acceptation, "discourse or treatise on the opinions, customs, and manners of the ancients." This is the definition of *Archæology* proposed by the sage Millin, (4),

(4) *Introduction à l'étude de l'Archéologie*; Paris, 1796; pp. 2, 20, 22.

adopted by Lenormant, (5) and recognized by all true scholars from Niebuhr to Letronne; especially among those intellectual giants who since Champollion's era have solved the chief enigmas of hieroglyphical and cuneatic records. *Archæography*, as distinct from archæology, according to Fabricius, (6) is a term which should be limited to the study of ancient monuments especially, whereas archæology embraces every process of investigation into all historical subjects. Dionysius Halicarnassensis, in the first century before C., and Josephus in the first century after, treated upon *Archæology*, but entirely neglected Archæography, or the study of monuments; whence their several incoherencies: the former, however, had some clear perceptions of the truth when he named Archæology "the science of primitive origins."

Albeit, the word has deviated somewhat from its pristine sense; for among the Greeks an *archæologist* signified a man who brought together the most ancient recollections of a given country; whereas, at the present day, the name is applied exclusively to him who, possessing intimate acquaintance with the *monuments* of a given ancient people, strives through the study of their characteristics to evolve facts, and thence to deduce logical conclusions upon the ideas, tastes, propensities, habits, and history of departed nations; many of the greatest and most essential of whom having left but fragmentary pages of their *stone-books*, out of which we their successors must reconstruct for ourselves such portions of their chronicles as are lost; no less than confirm, modify, or refute such others as have reached us through original, transcribed, or translated annals.

Archæology, so to say, has now become the "backbone" of ancient history; its relation to human traditions being similar to that of Osteology to Comparative Anatomy; or to what fossil remains are in geological science. An *Antiquary* is rather a collector of ancient relics of art, than one who understands them; but an *Archæologist* is of necessity an Antiquary who brings every science to bear upon the vestiges of ancient man, and thus invests them with true historical value. In short, an Archæologist is the *monumental* historian — the more or less critical dealer in and discoverer of historical facts, according as by mental discipline, diversified attainments, and the study of *things*, he acquires thorough knowledge of each particle preserved to his research among the *débris* of antique humanity.

Were the simplest rules of this science popularly taught, we should not have to prolong the lamentations of Millin at errors prevalent for want of a little archæological knowledge. He narrates how Baronius took a statue of Isis for the Virgin Mary — how the apotheosis of the Emperor Germanicus was mistaken for St. John the Baptist's translation to heaven — and how a cameo called "the agate of Tiberius," which represents the triumphs of this prince and the apotheosis of Augustus, came to be long regarded as the triumphal march of Joseph! Neptune and Minerva giving the horse and olive to man would not have been metamorphosed into Adam and Eve eating the forbidden apple; nor would a trumpery pottery toy have been considered by His Eminence Cardinal Wiseman (7) as a Roman memento of Noah's Ark after the universal flood, although among its animals were "thirty-five human figures!" Without archæology, says Millin, one is liable with the historian Rollin to speak of the *Laocoon* as a lost monument — to dress up Greek heroes in Roman garments — to adorn Hercules with a *perruque à la Louis XIV!* Æsop, at the court of Crœsus, would hardly have addressed himself to a colonel in French uniform; nor Strabo, in "Démocrite Amoureux," have pointed his quizzing-glass at steeples, and amused his leisure by making almanacs; neither would Horace call Servius Tullius "Sire;" nor Racine have invoked a goddess as "Madame" in his classic plays. (8)

More than half a century has elapsed since Millin wrote. Hundreds of archæologists have made their works accessible to the literary public. Yet so slow is the diffusion of

---

(5) *Archéologie*, par M. Ch. Lenormant, de l'Institut: *Revue Archéol.*; Paris, 1844; 1re partie, pp. 1–17.

(6) *Bibliotheca Antiquaria;* p. 181.

(7) *Connection between Science and Revealed Religion;* 1849; vol. ii. pp. 139–143.

(8) See many recent instances of antiquarian shams exposed by Letronne — "L'amulette de Jules César, le cachet de Sépullius Macer, le médaillon de Zénobie, le coffret d'Antinoüs, le sabre de Vespasien, et d'autres antiquités *modernes*" — *Mémoires et Documents; Rev. Archéol.;* Paris, 1849; pp. 192–223.

critical knowledge, that in our own land and hour, there are still some not uncultivated minds who imagine the *Aborigines* of this American continent to have descended from the "Lost Tribes of Israel"(9)—who see the *Runic* scribblings of Norsemen upon the Indian-scratched Rock of Dighton (10)—who, regardless of Squier's exposure,(11) yet suppose the local pebble manufactured for that *museum* since 1838, to attest *Phœnician* intercourse with the mound-builders of Grave Creek Flat (12)—and who, disdaining to refer to the long-published determination of its pseudo-antiquity, (13) still believe that the *gold seal-ring* of RA-NEFER-HET, a functionary attached to a building called, about the sixth century B. C., *after* King SHOOPHU, should have once adorned the finger of CHEOPS, builder of the Great Pyramid in the thirty-fourth century B. C. (14); thereby becoming 5300 instead of only some 2500 years old!

The instances around us of the misconceptions, which the slightest acquaintance with the rudiments of archæology would consign forever to oblivion, are inexhaustible. Would that some of them were less pernicious to moral rectitude! They offend our vision under the prostituted names of "*Portraits* of CHRIST" (15) — they excite one's derision in the ludicrous anachronisms of modern art current as "*Pictorial Bibles*" (16) — they bear witness to theological ignorance when *Chinese* are asserted to be referred to in the SINIM of Isaiah (17)—and they amount to idiocy when ecclesiastics continue disputing whether MOSES wrote a *resh*, R, or a *daleth*, D, in a given word of the Hebrew Pentateuch, notwithstanding that every archæologist knows that the *square-letter* characters of the present Hebrew Text (18) were not invented by the Rabbis before the second century *after* Christ; or 1600 years posterior to the vague age when IeHOuaH buried the Lawgiver "in a valley in the land of Moab opposite to Beth-peor; but no man has known his sepulchre *unto this day*."(19) But—"point de fanatisme même contre le fanatisme: la philosophie a eu le sien dans le siècle dernier; il semble que la gloire du nôtre devrait être de n'en connaître aucun." (20)

The above illustrations suffice to indicate some of the utilitarian objects of the science termed "Archæology;" which furnishes the only logical methods of attaining historical certainties. Its indispensableness to correct appreciations of biblical no less than of all other history, nevertheless, remains to be proved by its application. We shall endeavor to be precise in our experiments; but, must not forget that "precision is one thing, certainty another. An absurd or false proposition may be made very precise; and, on the other hand, although the sciences vary in degree of precision, they all present results equally certain." We propose to test the principles of archæological criteria by applying them to biblical studies, and to test the authenticity of *one chapter* of the Hebrew records through the former's application: and inasmuch as Truth must necessarily harmonize with itself, if archæology be a true science the Scriptures will prove it to be so incontestably; and if the Bible be absolute truth, archæology will demonstrate the fact. We need not perplex ourselves with apprehensions. It would imply but small faith in the *Bible* were we to suppose that arch-

(9) DELAFIELD: *American Antiquities.*

(10) *Transactions of the Royal Society of Antiquaries of Copenhagen*, 1840–'43. *Antiquitates Americanæ*, 1837; sect. xv.

(11) London *Ethnological Journal*: "Monumental Evidence of the Discovery of America by the Northmen critically examined" — Dec. 1848; pp. 313–324.

(12) SCHOOLCRAFT: New York *Ethnological Society's* Trans. 1845; vol. i. pp. 386–397.

(13) See "A Card": New York *Courier and Enquirer*, 12 Feb. 1853.

(14) ABBOTT: *Catalogue of a Collection of Egyptian Antiquities*, now exhibiting at the Stuyvesant Institute; New York, 1853; plate No. 1051, p. 64.

(15) Founded exclusively upon no more historical bases than the spurious "Letter of LENTULUS" — or derived from "Veronica's Sudarium"; ALBERT DURER, 1510,—vide COLE: *Passion of our Lord;* London, 1844.

(16) HARPERS', for instance; New York, 1842–'45.

(17) Rev. Dr. SMYTHE: *Unity of the Human Races;* 1840 — "And while even China (*Is.* li. [*sic*] 12, Sinim, a remote country in the S. E. extremity of the earth, as the context intimates) and the islands of the sea are specified" — p. 43. and note.

(18) GLIDDON: *Otia Ægyptiaca;* p. 112; and *infra*, further on.

(19) *Deuteronomy* xxxiv. 6 — CAHEN's translation.

(20) AMPÈRE; *Recherches, &c.*; Rev. des Deux Mondes; Sept. 1846, p. 738.

æological scrutiny could affect the divine origin insisted upon for the book itself by those who make it the unique standard of all scientific as well as of all moral knowledge.

Instead, however, of the ordinary mode in which biblical history is presented to us in books bearing the authoritative title of professed "Christian Evidences," the requirements of archæology demand that we should reverse the order of examination. In lieu, for instance, of asserting *à priori* that the *Creation of the world* took place exactly "on October 20th, B. C. 4005, the year of the *creation*" (21)—or sustaining, *ex cathedra*, with universal orthodoxy, that MOSES *wrote the Pentateuch*—it is incumbent upon us, while we deny nothing, to take as little for granted. If such be the era revealed by the Text, our process will lead us to that date, with at least the same precision through which Lightfoot (by what method is unknown), ascertained that *Anno Mundi* I, "VIth day of creation . . . his (Adam's) wife the weaker vessell: she not yet knowing that there were any devils at all . . . sinned, and drew her husband into the same transgression with her; this was about *high noone*, the time of *eating*. And in this lost condition into which Adam and Eve had now brought themselves, did they lie comfortlesse till towards the cool of the day, or *three o'clock afternoon*." (22) If the *Pentateuch* was originally penned in the Mosaic autograph, the proof will resile to our view, through archæological deductions, with the force of an Euclidean demonstration.

The analytical instruments of archæology are purely *Baconian;* viz: proceeding from the known to the unknown; through a patient retrogressive march from to-day to yesterday, from yesterday to the day before; and so on, step by step, backwards along the stream of time. Each fact, when verified, thus falls naturally into its proper place in the world's history; each event, as ascertained, will be found tabulated in its respective stratum. It is only when our footsteps falter, owing to surrounding darkness or to treacherous soil, that we may begin to suspect historical inaccuracies; but, at present, we have no right to anticipate any such doubts, considering the averments of œucumenic Protestantism, of the orthodox sects, that the *Bible is the revealed word of God.*

Our inquiries are directed to a single point. We desire to ascertain the origin, epoch, writer, characteristics, and historical value of but one document: viz.—*The* Xth *Chapter of Genesis;* familiar to every reader. It is presented, however, to our inspection as one of *fifty* chapters of a book called "Genesis"—this book being the first of *thirty-nine* (23) books that constitute the compendium entitled the "Old Testament;" and the latter is bound up in the same volume with another collection to which the name of "New Testament" is given: the whole forming together that literary work to which the designation of "*The* BIBLE" is reverentially applied in the English tongue—a name derived from *byblos*, the Greek name for *papyrus*, being the most ancient material out of which its derivative *paper* was made. *Byblos*, the Egyptian plant, gave to the Greeks their name for paper, and paper their name for "the book" in *το βιβλειον*. On adopting Christianity, the Greeks designated their earliest translation of the Hebrew Scriptures, TO BIBLEION, as *the book*—"par excellence;" which words we moderns have adopted into our national tongue in the form of "Bible."

With every desire on our part to obtain solution of our queries by the most direct road and in the shortest method, we do not perceive the possibility of detaching a solitary *chapter* of the Bible from the volume itself, until by archæological dissection we are enabled to demonstrate that such separation is feasible. In consequence, it behooves us to examine, with as much brevity as is consistent with perspicuity, the entire *Bible;* and, if we hold "all the books of the Bible (24) to be equally true," the Xth *chapter* of the first book will be found unquestionably to be true likewise.

Soliciting that the reader should divest his mind, as far as in him lies, of preconceived biases; we invite him to accompany us patiently through an investigation, in which the

(21) REV. DR. NOLAN: *The Egyptian Chronology Analyzed;* London, 1848, p. 392.

(22) *Harmony, Chronicle, and Order of the Old Testament*, &c.; London, 1647, p. 5.

(23) Mystic origin of the XXXIX "Articles" of the Anglican Church.

(24) POOLE: London *Literary Gazette*, 1849, p. 432—unaccountably suppressed in *Horæ Ægyptiacæ*, 1851.

subject banishes all ornament, but that cannot fail to elicit some portions of the truth.

The incipient steps of our analysis do not call for much expenditure of erudition. In popular Encyclopædias most of the preliminary information may be verified by the curious reader; for Calmet, Kitto, and Horne, contain catalogues of the various editions of the *Bible*, done into English, that have been put forth, during the last four centuries, from A. D. 1526 down to the present year.

At the sight of such catalogues of different *translations* said to proceed from one and the same original, few can refrain from asking, in all humbleness, why, if any one of them were absolutely correct, should there have been a necessity for the others? In the course of studies carried over many years, we have been at pains to compare sundry of the most prominent English translations (among them ancient as well as modern editions), not only with themselves, but often with the Latin, Greek, or Hebrew originals, of which each purports to supply a faithful rendering. They all differ! some more than others; but in each one may be found passages the sense of which varies essentially from that published by the others. Hence arose in our minds the following among other doubts.

Some of these *Translators* can have known little or nothing of *Hebrew* — or they must have translated from different originals — or, they did not consult the *Hebrew* Text at all, but rendered from the Latin or the Greek versions — or (what recurs with far more frequency), each *translator*, wherever the original was ambiguous, rendered a given passage in accordance with his own individual biases, or with the object of fortifying the peculiar tenets of his Church, Kirk, Conventicle, Chapel, or Meeting-house. Now, these discordant *Bibles* being thrust upon us, each *one* as the only and true "Word of God," it is humanly inconceivable that GOD should have uttered that Word in so many different ways, and thereby have rendered nugatory the comprehension of one passage, by permitting a translation, in significance totally distinct, of the self-same passage in other modern editions. For instance, that the reader may at once seize our meaning: there are few texts more frequently quoted, especially under circumstances where consolation is administered; there are none perhaps that have originated such Demosthenian efforts at pulpit-oratory, or have produced in some minds more of those extatic emotions "that the world cannot give," than the verse wherein Job ejaculates — "For I know *that* my Redeemer liveth." (xix. 25). The "*Multitude* of those who are called Christians," as Origen termed them in A. D. 253 (25); the "Simpletons, not to say the imprudent and the idiotic," of Tertullian, A. D. 245; (26) the "Ignorant" of St. Athanasius, A. D. 373 (27); and the "Simple believers" of the milder St. Jerome, A. D. 385 (28); have always imagined, in accordance with the lower scholarship of orthodoxy, that Job here foreshadows the Messianic advent of Christ. (29)

The context does not appear, philologically or grammatically, to justify such conclusion; inasmuch as the preceding verses (1 to 22) exhibit Job — forsaken by his kindred, forgotten by his bosom friends, alien in the eyes of his guests and of his own servants — overwhelmed with anguish at the acrid loquacity of Bildad the *Shuhite*, protesting vehemently against these accusations, and wishing that his last burning words should be preserved to posterity in one of *three* ways. To support our view, and to furnish at the same time evidences of different *translations*, we lay before the reader three renderings of verses 23 to 26. He can, by opening other translators, readily verify the adage that "doctors differ," although the *Hebrew* Text is identically the same throughout.

(25) *Commentary upon John:* and *Contra Cels.*, lib. viii..

(26) *Ad Praxeam*, sec. iii.

(27) *De Incarn. Verb. — contra Paul. Samosatæ.*

(28) *Comm. in Es.* xxxii.

(29) NOTES: *Op. cit.*, p. 147 — "That there is no allusion to Christ in the term [*redeemer*], nor to the resurrection to a life of happiness, in the passage, has been the opinion of the most judicious and learned critics for the last three hundred years; such as Calvin, Mercier, Grotius, Le Clerc, Patrick, Warburton, Durell, Heath, Kennicott, Doederlein, Dathe, Eichhorn, Jahn, De Wette, and many others."

I. King James's *Version.* The *italicized* words are the Translators'.

23 "Oh that my words were now written! oh that they were printed [*sic!*] in a book!
24 That they were graven with an iron pen and lead in the rock for ever!
25 For I know *that* my redeemer liveth, and *that* he shall stand at the latter *day* upon the earth.
26 And *though* after my skin *worms* destroy this *body*, yet in my flesh shall I see God."

The marginal reading, authority unknown, substitutes—"Or, *After I shall awake, though this* body *be destroyed, yet out of my flesh shall I see God.*" In the authorized version, by the interpolation of "worms," Job is made a believer in the resurrection of the body: in the margin, he believes that he shall behold God "out of the flesh;" that is, in the spirit! What did he believe?

II. Noyes, *New Translation of the Book of Job;* Boston, 1838; p. 37.

23 "O that my words were now written!
O that they were inscribed in a register!
24 That with an iron pen, and with lead,
They were engraven upon the rock for ever!
25 Yet I know my Vindicator liveth,
And will stand up at length on the earth;
26 And though with my skin this body be wasted away,
Yet in my flesh shall I see God."

Noyes (*Notes*, pp. 144–6) says—"Or we may render, *Yet without flesh I shall see God*"—and enumerates cogent "objections to the supposition that Job here expresses his confident expectation of a resurrection."

III. Cahen, "Job;" *La Bible*, Traduction Nouvelle, avec l'Hébreu en regard; Paris, 1851; pp. 86–7. We render the French literally into English.

23 "Would to God that my words were written! Would to God that they were traced in a book
24 With a burin of iron and with lead! that they were engraved for ever in the rock!
25 But I, I know that my 'redemptor' is living, and will remain the last upon the earth:
26 And after that my skin shall have been destroyed, this delivered from the flesh, I shall see God."

In the foot-note, Cahen explains that the Hebrew word גאלי, GALI, which he renders "mon rédempteur," proceeds from the verb GAL, "to deliver;" meaning likewise "revendiquer;" which corresponds to the *Vindicator* of Noyes. The idea of Job's hope of a *resurrection*, itself a mythological anachronism, is popularly derived from the LXX and the Greek Fathers, with ideas developed in the Latin Church after St. Jerome.

Thus the reader has now before him three specimens, amid the wilderness of *Translations*, wherein are involved theological dogmas of "resurrection of the body," "redemption of the soul," and the antiquity of "Messianic prefigurations"—questions of no slight religious importance; and yet, withal, unless he be profound in *Hebrew*, his opinion upon the merits of either rendering is alike worthless to himself and to others; nor can he conscientiously distinguish which is veritably the "word of God" among these triple contradictions. The ridiculous anachronism perpetrated in king James's *version* (*v.* 23) that makes Job wish that his words were "printed" (probably 2500 years before the art was invented!) (30) has long ago been pointed out; and is alone sufficient to destroy the alleged inspiration of that "authorized" verse. For ourselves we mourn that want of space compels the suppression of some archæological remarks on the "book of Job" (*ây*IUB—meaning "L'uomo iracondo che rientra con rossore in se stesso"). We derive them from studies at Paris, under our honored preceptor Michel-angelo Lanci, to whom we here renew the warmest tribute of respect and admiration.

To Anglo-Saxon Protestantism the biblical profundities of the "Professor of Sacred and Interpreter of Oriental Tongues at the Vatican" (31) since the year 1820, are entirely un-

(30) Nott: *Biblical and Physical History of Man;* 1849; pp. 136, 137.
(31) Gaetano Deminicis: *Biografia del Cavaliere D. Michel-angelo Lanci;* Fermo, 1840; p. 10.

known. Written in the purest Italian exclusively for the lettered—restricted to one edition of 125 copies for each work, at a cost of 125 *francs* ($25) per copy—and, for manifold reasons, artistically fashioned upon a plan not easily comprehended without an *oral key*—Lanci's enormous labors upon Semitic palæography, to the "profanum vulgus" of theology, must long remain sealed books. In 1848–9, no copy of the *Paralipomeni*, (32) nor of the *Seconda Opera Cufica*, (33) both published during 1845–7, at Paris (the latter at the expense of Nicholas, Czar of Muscovy), existed within the Library of the British Museum: notwithstanding that Lanci's volumes were for sale at two leading booksellers' in London; and that their absence at the Museum-Library had been formally notified to its unnational "Powers that be." (34) The *Vie Simboliche della Bibbia* (known to us in its author's manuscript) will not be published for a period incalculable, because dependent upon human longevity. Our mutual friend, Mr. R. K. Haight of New York, is, in the United States, the sole possessor of Lanci's works that we know of. (35)

History records that it was in consequence of the discrepancies, notorious among such *translations* into English as existed at the beginning of the seventeenth century, that, in the reign of king James, a new version of the Scriptures was published: which duly received the royal, ecclesiastical, parliamentary, and national sanction, and is now consecrated amongst us Anglo-Saxons as the unique and immaculate "Word of God"—the standard of faith among Protestant communities of our race throughout the world. It is, and ought to be, in the hands of every one; so that no obstacles to the verification of such quotations, as we shall have occasion to make, exist at the present day among readers of English. As the document we are in quest of, Xth Genesis, is contained within this volume, we are compelled by the rules of archæology first to examine the book itself; in order to obtain some preliminary insight into its history, its literary merits as a *Translation*, and the repute in which the latter point is held by those most qualified to judge.

To avoid mistakes arising from confusion of editions, we quote the title-page of the copy before us.—"THE HOLY BIBLE, containing the *Old* and *New Testaments*: translated out of the original Tongues; and with the former Translations diligently compared and revised, by His Majesty's Special Command. Appointed to be read in Churches. London:

---

(32) *Paralipomeni all' Illustrazione della Sagra Scrittura*; Paris, qto. 2 vols.; 1845.

(33) *Seconda Opera Cufica — Trattato delle simboliche rappresentanze Arabiche e della varia generazione de' Musulmani caratteri sopra differenti materie operati*; Parigi, 1846–'47; qto. 2 vols.

(34) Gliddon: *Otia Ægyptiaca*; London, 1849; p. 17, note; see also p. 110.

(35) Through the Chevalier's epistolary kindness, I am enabled to correct a former mistake, into which other authority had led me; and I gladly seize occasion to quote from one of numerous Italian autographs in my possession:—

"Roma, 18 *Ottobre*, 1851.

"*Car^mo Amico!*

"You say, in *Otia Ægyptiaca* (p. 31), that 'pyramid' is derived from *pi* and *haram*; the former being a Coptic article, the latter an Arabic word, combined even nowadays among the Arabs in [their name, EL-HaRaM, for] *pyramid*. This is not according to grammatical exactness; because *haram* is not altogether radical. The demonstrative [letter H] *he* is prefixed to it, which serves in lieu of the Coptic *pi*. *Ram* [Arabicè], RM, is the root (*altitude*). *Haram*, HRM, says, therefore, *the-altitude*; and it is a synonyme of the Coptic *pi-ram*, in which the *he*, H, that you have yoked to it, plays no part. The word *ram*, besides being a Semitic, is also a Coptic word, with the sense of *height*... But very huge seems to me the error of Ewald, in Bunsen, who presumes to explain a text of *Job* (iii. 14) by changing a *b* into *m*, and making a *HaraMòt* of his own out of the biblical *HaraBòt*.... I transcribe for you the complete article of mine, which on some occasion may be of aid to you:

"*Article taken from the 'Vie Simboliche del Vecchio e Nuovo Testamento' regarding a passage in Job*.... [We have not two pages to spare, and therefore are compelled to omit the acute philological reasonings of our valued preceptor.—G. R. G.] The said two verses, most entangled in the versions of others, through my inquiries now read—'Now should I have quiet with the kings and mighty-ones of the earth who already repose in their subterranean habitations; or with the princes who had gold and (who) caused their sepulchres to be filled with silver.' [Comp. Cahen, xv. p. 12.] ... I will not leave this argument without first giving you an illustration of that arduous verse 6 of Psalm ix.; in which, it appears to me, interpreters have strayed away from truth. Here recurs that *charabôt* which I explained. Now, if philologers are wise enough to accept my discovery, they will see that this sentence of the Psalm, in the place above-named, speaks with vibratory locution—'They closed to the enemy the subterranean abode in perpetuity: thou destroyedst the cities, and with these the memorial of those perished.'" [Compare *King James's Version!*] ...

"Aff^mo vostro, Michel-Angelo Lanci."

Printed by George E. Eyre and Andrew Spottiswoode, Printers to the Queen's Most Excellent Majesty, and sold at their Warehouse, 189, Fleet Street, 1844. [Nonpareil Reference, 12mo.]" The Dedication "To the most high and mighty Prince, James," states that His "Highness had once out of deep judgment apprehended how convenient it was, that out of the Original Sacred Tongues, together with comparing of the labours, both in our own, and other foreign Languages, of many worthy men who went before us, there should be one *more exact Translation* of the Holy Scriptures into the *English Tongue*."

It thus becomes patent that our copy is not printed in one of "the Original Sacred Tongues," but merely professes to be a "more exact *Translation*" into English than, at the date of its publication, 242 years ago, had previously appeared. Even conceding that the Holy Scriptures in the "Original Sacred Tongues" may have been revealed word for word by the Almighty, and granting that their *editio princeps* was a manuscript in the autographs of divinely-inspired Scribes, no reasonable person will deny the possibility that this English *translation* may embrace some errors—none among the educated will be so unreasonable as to insist upon the *infallibility* of its English translators, however erudite, however conscientious; nor perchance will claim *inspiration* for these worthies. Childishly credulous as we are by nature, and uncritical though the generality of us remain through education, no sane Anglo-Saxons, since the middle ages, allow "divine *inspiration*" to men of *their own race*. We accord the possibility of "inspiration" solely to members of a single family that lived a long time ago, and a great way off; whose descendants (although nowadays ranking among the best citizens of our cis-Atlantic Republic) are still abused by our kinsfolk across the water; and who, although contributors to our own and the latter's welfare and glory, are yet debarred, as unworthy, from a voice in the British Parliament: and all this, forsooth, in the same breath of acknowledgment that we derive our most sacred Code of Religion, Morals, and Laws, from their *inspired* ancestors! and whilst, based upon our modern notions of their ancient creed, we nasally vociferate that they and ourselves are "of one *blood* as brothers"!

Our copy, such as it is, may be accepted without hesitation as a lineal descendant of the primary *authorized* version in the English language, wrested from the Lords Spiritual and Temporal through the intelligence of our ancestors, quickened by the Reformation; who bled for the same rights that we their posterity can now assert, in the free United States of America and in Great Britain (without even the merit of boldness), viz. the right to examine the Scriptures, and everything else, for ourselves, and to express our opinions thereon in the broad light of heaven.

Archæologically speaking, in order to insure minute exactness, it would be imperative to collate, year by year, and edition by edition, the whole succession of copies of our "authorized version"; and, by retracing from the exemplar on our table backwards to that first printed in black-letter during the reign of king James, to ascertain whether any and what changes, beyond variations in typography, may have been introduced. But such dreadful labor is, to the writer, impossible for want of the series; ungenial to his tastes as well as unnecessary for his objects. He contents himself with the assertion that there are many differences between such copies of divers editions that have fallen in his way, although considered by others of little or no moment; being chiefly *marginal*, as in the superadded and spurious chronology; or *capitular*, as in the apocryphal headings to chapters, &c.; neither of which can have any more to do with the original "word of God," than the printer's name, the binding, or the paper.

As *positivists* in Philosophy while archæologists in method, we clear the table of these comparatively-trivial disputations; and bounding retrogressively over the interval that divides our generation from that of His Majesty King James, the reader is requested to take with us the historical era of the promulgation of the "authorized version" as a common point of departure; viz.: A. D. 1611.

The most ancient printed copy of king James's *version*, that has been accessible to us, lies in the British Museum. It contains a memorandum by the Rev. Dr. Horne to the effect that the *title-pages* are of the primary edition of the year 1611, but that the rest appertains to that of 1613. The whole folio is printed in black-letter. Its frontispieces are literary gems; and so faithfully portraying the symbolism of Europe's "moyen age" in their astrologico-theological emblems, that every antiquary must deplore that castigating zeal which has effaced such quaint expressions of ancestral piety, to substitute for them, in some of our current copies, typographical whims that cannot pretend even to the venerable halo of bygone days. The title-page to the Old Testament is embellished by vignettes, among which figure the *Lion*, *Man*, *Bull*, and *Eagle*; (36) ancient signs for the solstices and equinoxes. Moses is truthfully represented, as in Michel-angelo's statue, with his characteristic horns; according to the *Vulgate* of Exod. (xxxiv. 29, 30, 35), "*cornuta* esset facies sua," which preserves one sense of the Hebrew KRN, *horn*. The zodiaco-heraldic arms of the "12 Tribes" of Israel are also preserved; (37) together with a variety of other symbols, archæologically precious. That of the New Testament is still more curious, inasmuch as it exhibits the esoteric transmission (perceived even as late as at that time by learned reformers in England) of certain antique symbolisms of Hebrew Scriptures into those of the Orientalized Greeks or Hellenized Jews. The "4" solstitial and equinoctial signs of the "4 *seasons*" remain, but are now attached to the figures of the "4" Evangelists; while the zodiaco-heraldic arms of the "12 *Sons of Jacob*" (*Gen.* xlix. 1, 28), whence the "12 *Tribes of Israel*," lie parallel with and officiate as "pendants" to the "12 Apostles," each with his symbolical relation to the "12 months" of the year, &c.—the whole, indeed, saving its uncouth artistic execution, so vividly solar and astral in conception, as to betray that primeval Ægypto-*Chaldaic* source whence students of hieroglyphical and cuneiform monuments,—exhumed and translated more than two centuries subsequently to the publication of our English "editio princeps"—now know that the types of this imagery are derived. The reader, who seeks throughout our modern editions in vain for the once-consecrated embellishments of ages past, may now perceive that we are not altogether ill-advised when hinting that great liberties have been taken with the authorized English Bible between A. D. 1611, era of its first promulgation, and those copies ostensibly represented in the current year (1853) to be its lineal and unmutilated offspring. Theologically, however, these variants through omission or commission are not of the same importance as they seem to be archæologically, nor need we dwell upon them now.

The accuracy of this English version, and its fidelity to the original *Hebrew* and *Greek* MSS., must rest upon the opinion we can form of its Translators; legalized by the royal seal and confirmed by an act of Parliament. With the value of the two last authorities, regal or parliamentary, in questions of purely-philological criticism and of strictly-literary knowledge, we American Republicans may be excused in declaring that we have nothing to do. Until it is proved to our comprehension that the acquaintance of those worthy M. P.'s with the "original sacred tongues" was profound, and that they devoted one or more Sessions to the verification of the minute exactness of the volume they endorsed, their fiat upon the literary merit of the book itself carries with it no more weight in science than, to bring the case home, could the Presidential signature to an act of Congress authorizing the printing in *Arabic*, at national expense, of the Mohammedan *Korân*, in the year 1853, be accepted as a criterion or even voucher of such huge folio's historical or philological correctness.

To us the only admissible evidence of the exactitude of king James's version, as a faithful exponent of the "word of God" (originally written, and closed some 1500 years before that monarch's reign, in *Hebrew* and in *Greek*), must be twofold—*historical*, and *exegetical:* the former, by establishing the learning, oriental knowledge, critical skill, and integrity of the men; the latter, by demonstrating that rigid examination will fail to detect errors in the performance itself. Of this duplex evidence we now go in quest; remarking at the outset,

---

(36) Conf. SALVERTE: *Sciences Occultes;* i. pp. 46, 47. Comp. *Ezekiel* i. 10, with *Apocalypse* iv. 7. RICHELLINI: *Franc-maçonnerie;* Paris, 1842; i. p. 324, pl. 4, fig. 1.

(37) Conf. KIRCHER: *Œdipus Ægyptiacus;* Rome, 1653; vol. ii. part 1. p. 21. DRUMMOND: *Œdipus Judaicus;* London, 1811; plate 15—"Dissertation on XLIXth Chapter of Genesis":—and LANCI: *Paralipomeni, passim.*

that, inasmuch as (precise date unknown) the gift of "divine inspiration" is said by Protestants to have ceased about 1750 years ago with the last *Apostle*, nobody claims for these English Translators any supernatural assistance during the progress of their pious labors; and, therefore, in matters appertaining to the merely-human department of linguistic scholarship (whilst we doubt not their excellence as men, their attainments, nor their good faith), we must concede the chance that their production, owing to man's proneness to err, may be found to fall short, in a literary point of view, of the standard by which a similar performance would be judged were a *new Translation* of the Old Testament "authorized," after the same fashion, at the middle of this XIXth century.

I. The Historical Testimony.

In the year 1603, owing to the enormous defects recognized in all popular *translations* then current, the revision that had been ordered in the days of Elizabeth was carried into effect by James. *Fifty-four* of the most learned graduates of the Universities of Oxford and Cambridge were appointed to the task, *seven* of whom died before the work was completed: (38) among the last, Lively, (39) the best if not the only *Hebraist* on the translation, whose labors were of short duration; and, "much weight of the work lying upon his skill in the Oriental tongues," his loss was irreparable; because the surviving *forty-seven* translators rejected the assistance of the only remaining Hebraist in England, viz., "Hugh Broughton, fellow of Christ College, Cambridge, who had certainly attained a great knowledge in the *Hebrew* and Greek tongues." Indeed, says the very learned Bellamy, (40) from whom we derive the fact, "it was well known that there was not a critical Hebrew scholar among them; the Hebrew language, so indispensably necessary for the accomplishment of this important work, having been most shamefully neglected in our Universities; and, as at this day [1818], candidates for orders were admitted without a knowledge of this primary, this most essential branch of biblical learning. It was, as it is at present, totally neglected in our schools, and a few lessons taken from a Jew in term-time, whose business is to *Judaize*[!], and not to Christianize, serve to give the character of the Hebrew scholar," in England.

In consequence, then, of the inability of the *forty-seven* translators to read one (and the *oldest*, the *aboriginal* "divine word") of those "sacred tongues" of which their servile dedication makes parade, "it appears they confined themselves to the Septuagint (Greek) and the Vulgate (Latin); so that this was only working in the harness of the first translators: no translation (excepting perhaps Luther's, 1530—1545), from the original Hebrew only, having been made for 1400 years," says Bellamy.

"If we turn," continues elsewhere this outspeaking writer (whose erudition *nemo nisi imperitus* will contest), "to the translations made in the early ages of the Christian Church, we approach no nearer the truth; for as the common translations in the European languages were made from the modern Septuagint and the Vulgate, where errors are found in these early versions they must necessarily be found in all the translations made from them."

Whether the *Vulgate* and the *Septuagint* versions are faultless will be considered anon. Our present affair is with king James's *translation*, and certainly appearances are not flattering.

We learn from Fuller, (41) how at once, on its first apparition, objections were raised against its accuracy in England; but as these emanated chiefly from Romanist scholarship, in those days of reformation at a discount, their validity is slurred over by Protestant ecclesiastics. Gradually, as Hebraical scholarship struggled into existence — that such

---

(38) Fuller: *Church History;* 1655; pp. 44–46.

(39) *Ibid*, p. 47 — and Horne: *Introd. to the Crit. Stud. of H. Scrip.;* 1838; ii. pp. 70, 80; note 5.

(40) *The Holy Bible, newly translated from the Original Hebrew; with notes critical and explanatory;* London, 1818, 4to — published by the subscriptions of Royalty, Nobility, and Clergy; but never completed, and now out of print. Our quotations are from the "general preface."

(41) *Church History;* pp. 58, 59 — also Horne: *Introd.;* ii. pp. 76-78.

giants as Walton,(42) 1657, had redeemed the Oriental wisdom of Oxford — the voice of the great Dr. Kennicott (43) was uplifted a century later, 1753–9, protesting vehemently against the perpetuation of fallacies which the *forty-seven* translators' ignorance of Hebrew had spread over the land through king James's *version*. He commences — "The reader will be pleased to observe, that, as the study of the Hebrew language has only been *reviving* during the last hundred years," (44) &c. — that is, only since the time of Walton, his predecessor: — which passage implies that fifty years previously to the latter's epoch, 1657, (*i. e.*, at the time of the forty-seven translators, 1603–11), the study of Hebrew was all but defunct, or rather it had scarcely yet begun to exist; that is, in *England*.

This point was considered so familiar to every general reader, that no hesitation was felt when stating it, 1849, with reference to the same question, (45) in the following words: "Now the Hebrew language in 1611 had been a dead language for more than two thousand years, and though these men (the forty-seven translators aforesaid) were renowned for their piety and learning, yet very few, if any of them, were competent to so important a task. In fact, the Hebrew language may be said only to have been recovered within the last century by modern Orientalists: and from the ignorance of these very translators of the original language, the Old Testament was taken mostly from the Greek and Latin versions, viz: the *Septuagint* and *Vulgate*. Being, then, a translation of bad translations, which had passed through numerous copyings, how could it come down to us without errors?"

Nevertheless, want of ordinary information on Scriptural literature prompted a reviewer, (with intrepidity characteristic of that undeveloped stage of the reasoning faculties which, in accordance with Comte's positive philosophy, has been already classed as "the theological,") to indite these remarks: — "Dr. Nott, again, speaks disrespectfully of the English version of the Scriptures. He makes the astounding assertion that 'the Hebrew language may be said only to have been recovered within the last century, by modern Orientalists.' Most surprising is it that any one should believe that the Jews should have wholly lost a knowledge of their ancient and sacred tongue; and that a knowledge of it should only have been recovered by modern Orientalists, displays an amazing want of reading and scholar-like accuracy, and a credulity exceedingly rare, *except in an unbeliever*." (46)

"Mutato nomine, de te fabula narratur!" Under the head of KNâAN [*supra*, p. 496], the "Association" may find a series of facts on the permutations, which the so-called "Lingua Sancta" of the Israelites has undergone, still more "astounding," where we took occasion to repeat and enlarge upon the positions of Dr. Nott's "Reply." In the meanwhile, the "ipse dixit" above quoted of Kennicott, that a century and a half posterior to the *forty-seven* translators of king James's version, the study of Hebrew was only "reviving," may, by some, be considered as authoritative as that put forth, in 1850, in proof of the united scholarship of an "Association."

"This only is certain, that, in Nehemiah's time, the people still spoke Hebrew; that, in the time of Antiochus Epiphanes and the Maccabees, the Hebrew was still written, though the Aramæan was the prevalent language; and, on the contrary, about this time, and shortly after Alexander the Great, even the learned Jews found it hard to understand difficult passages of the old writings, *because the language had ceased to be a living speech*. The reign of the Seleucidæ, and the new influence of an Aramæan people, seem gradually to have destroyed the last traces of it;" (47) and this about two thousand years ago!

---

(42) *Biblia Sacra Polyglotta* — complutentia Textus Originalis — Hebraicos cum Pentat. Samarit., Chaldaicos, Græcos, Versionumque Antiquarum — Samarit., Græc. Sept., Chaldaicæ, Seriacæ, Lat. Vulg., Arabicæ, Æthiopicæ, Persicæ.

(43) Author of *Vetus Testamentum Hebraicum*; cum variis Lectionibus; Oxon. 1780; and of *Dissertatio Generalis in Vetus Test. Heb.*; 1780.

(44) I. *Dissertation — State of the printed Hebrew Text of the O. Test. considered*; Oxford, 1753; p. 307.

(45) NOTT: *Op. cit.*; p. 134.

(46) The Rev. Dr HOWE, in *The Southern Presbyterian Review*, "conducted by an Association of Ministers;" Columbia, S. C.; vol. iii. No. 3.; Jan. 1850 — refuted by Dr. NOTT: "Chronology, Ancient and Scriptural," in *Southern Quarterly Review*; Nov. 1850.

(47) GESENIUS, apud *Parker's De Wette*: i., *Appendix*, p. 457 — compare also p. 221.

Such is the position of *Hebrew* in the world's philological history as a *spoken* tongue: yet, "a knowledge of that language which is contained in the scanty relics of the Old Testament has been preserved, though but imperfectly, by means of *tradition.* Some time after the destruction of Jerusalem in the Palestine and Babylonian schools, and after the eleventh century in those of Spain, this tradition was aided by the study of the Arabic language and its grammar. Jerome learned the Hebrew from Jewish scholars. Their pupils were the restorers of Hebrew learning among the Christians of the sixteenth century;" (48) that is, on the *continent;* for, with the exception of Lively, who died, and Hugh Broughton, whose aid was refused, history does not record any man deserving the name of a *Hebraist* in England, even during 1603–11. Finally, "the name *lingua sancta* was first given to the ancient Hebrew in the Chaldee version [made long after the Christian era, when *Hebrew* had orally expired,] of the Old Testament, because it was the language of the sacred books, in distinction from the Chaldee, the popular language, which was called *lingua profana.*" (49)

These citations here seem indispensable, lest dogmatism, peeping from out of its theological chrysålis, should feel itself again called upon to "astound" a reader by charging us with errors of its own commission: otherwise an apology would be due for this excursus. We return to Dr. Kennicott.

After setting forth the causes of mistaken renderings in king James's version, he declares — "A *New Translation*, therefore, prudently undertaken and religiously executed, is a blessing, which we make no doubt but the Legislature [!] within a few years will grant us." (50) Six years later, finding his humble prayer unheeded, he comes out clamorously against "our authorized version": claiming that some of the earlier English translations were more faithful and literal, (51) and backing his appeal with the subjoined among other examples:

Luke xxiii. 32. Christ made a *malefactor!* "And there were also two other malefactors led with him to be put to death;" instead of "two *others*, malefactors." The *Greek* reads simply, "And two others, evil-doers." (52)

Judges xv. 4. Three hundred *foxes* tied tail to tail, instead of wheaten *sheaves* placed end to end! "And Samson went and caught three hundred foxes, and took firebrands, and turned tail to tail, and put a firebrand in the midst between two tails." The *Hebrew* is, "And Samson went and gathered three hundred sheaves of wheat, and taking torches and turning (the sheaves) end to end, set a torch in the midst between two ends." (53)

1 *Kings* xvii. 6. Elijah not fed by *ravens*, but by *Arabs!* "And the ravens brought him bread and flesh," &c. In the *Hebrew*, "And the ÔRBIM (*â*RaB-*î*m) brought him bread and flesh." Kennicott thinks *Orbîm*, inhabitants of Oreb, or Orbo—"villæ in finibus Arabum," says St. Jerome: but, *Arabs* seem to us more natural and correct. In no contingency "crows"! (54)

It is superfluous now to continue our excerpta from Kennicott, or narrate how it comes to pass that, owing to nice appreciations of the Text that none of them could construe, the *forty-seven* (in Psalms cix.) have made pious king David (disputed author of that

---

(48) De Wette: *Parker's transl.;* Boston, 1843; i. p. 128 — cited by Nott, in the "Reply." Comp. also, Palfrey: *Academical Lectures on the Jewish Scriptures;* Boston, 1838; i. pp. 8–20 — "It is out of the question for any man to suppose, that he can be acquainted with Hebrew as familiarly and thoroughly, as he may be with Latin and Greek."

(49) Conant's *Gesenius:* Hebrew Grammar; New York, 1846; p. 23.

(50) *Op. cit.;* p. 567. Cf., also, Munk: *Palestine;* Paris, 1845; pp. 433–436.

(51) II. *Dissertation;* Oxford, 1759; pp. 579, 580, *seq.*

(52) Sharpe: *N. Test.;* p. 165.

(53) John Dove: *Vindication of the Hebrew Scriptures*; London, 1771 — in his furious assault upon the "Authorized Version," and lamentations at English ignorance of Hebrew, also derides the "foxes"; p. 71, *seq.* Glaire: *Livres Saints Vengés;* Paris, 1845; ii. pp. 57, 58, contests the "fagots" — but vide Cahen: vi. pp. 68, 69, note 4.

(54) Glaire: *Op. cit.;* ii. p. 85, reads "Arabes"; but Cahen, viii. p. 77, "corbeaux" — acutely adding, "Universa historia fabularum plena est."

rhapsody) (55) utter such fearful imprecations against his foes; when, in the "original sacred tongue," he actually complains that his enemies are heaping these outrageous maledictions upon himself!

Well might the Reverend Doctor quote Michælis — "I am amazed when I hear some men vindicate our common readings with as much zeal as if the editors had been inspired by the Holy Ghost!" Still better does he terminate his earnest work with supplications for a *new* Hebrew Text, and for a *new* English "authorized" *translation.*

Reader, these things were published at Oxford and disseminated over Great Britain about ninety-four years ago — not in expensive folios veiled through the dead languages, but in two English *octavos* — not by a "skeptic" whose indignation at any kind of imposture impels him to spurn it, but by that Church of England Divine, collator of six hundred and ninety-two ancient Hebrew biblical manuscripts, (56) whose folios, together with the *Biblia Polyglotta* of his illustrious precursor, Walton, are the only *English* labors on the Scriptures that receive homage from continental erudition, as performances on a par with the colossal researches of Germans, Frenchmen, and Italians, even unto this day!

Kennicott passed away. Other scholars followed in his footsteps. From a few of the latter we extract what they have left in print respecting king James's version, with a prefatory citation from Bellamy, to whom we owe the collection.(57)

"It is allowed by the learned in this day and every Christian nation, that the authorized translations of the sacred Scriptures, in many places, are not consistent with the original Hebrew. A few extracts are here given, from some of our most learned and distinguished writers, who were decidedly of opinion, that a New Translation of the Scriptures was absolutely necessary; not only on account of the great improvement in our language, but because the *Translators* have erred respecting things most essential. The following are some of the eminent men who have left their testimony concerning the necessity of a new translation:—

'Were a version of the Bible executed in a manner suitable to the magnitude of the undertaking, such a measure would have a direct tendency to establish the faith of thousands. . . . Let the Hebrew and Christian prophets appear in their proper garb: let us make them *holy garments* for glory and for beauty; . . . *the attempts of individuals should be promoted by the natural patrons of sacred learning.*' — (Bishop NEWCOMBE.)

'Innumerable instances might be given of faulty translations of the divine original. . . . An accurate translation, proved and supported by sacred criticism, would quash and silence most of the objections of pert and profane cavillers.' — (BLACKWELL'S *Sac. Class. Pref.*, 1731.)

'Our English version is undoubtedly capable of very great improvements.' — (WATERLAND'S *Script. Vindicated*, Part 3, p. 64.)

'Nothing would more effectually conduce to this end, than the exhibiting the Holy Scriptures themselves in a more advantageous and just light, by an accurate revisal of our vulgar translation.' — (Dr. LOWTH'S *Visitat. Sermon*, at Durham, 1753.)

'The common version has many considerable faults, and very much needs another review.' — (*Biblioth. Lit.*, 1723, p. 72.)

'The Old Testament has suffered much more than the New, in our Translation.' — (DODDRIDGE'S *Pref. to Family Expositor.*)

'Many of the inconsistencies, improprieties, and obscurities, are occasioned by the translators' misunderstanding the true import of the Hebrew words and phrases, showing the benefit and expediency of a more correct and intelligent translation of the Bible.' — (PILKINGTON'S *Remarks*, 1759, p. 77.)

'The version now in use in many places does not exhibit the sense of the Text; and mistakes it, besides, in an infinite number of instances.' — (DURELL'S *Crit. on Job*, 1772, *Pref.*)

'That necessary work, a New Translation of the Holy Scriptures.' — (LOWTH'S *Prelim. Dissert. to Isaiah*, p. 69.)

(55) Cf. DE WETTE: ii. pp. 520–529 — and CAHEN: xiii. p. 247, "Sommaire," and p. 249, note 20.

(56) *Diss. Gen. in Vet. T. Heb.*; 1790: Tables, pp. 110–112.

(57) *Op. cit.*: "General Preface"; 1818.

'Whoever examines our version in present use, will find that it is ambiguous and incorrect, even in matters of the highest importance.' — (Prof. SYMOND'S *Observations on the Expediency of revising the present Version*, 1789.)

'At this time, a New Translation is much wanted, and universally called for.'—(GREEN'S *Preface to Poetical Parts of the New Test.*)

'Great improvements might now be made, because the Hebrew and Greek languages have been much better cultivated, and far better understood, since the year 1600.' — (Dr. KENNICOTT'S *Remarks*, &c., 1787, p. 6.)

'The common version has mistaken the true sense of the Hebrew in not a few places. Is it nothing to deprive the people of that edification which they might have received, had a fair and just exposition been substituted for a false one? Do we not know the advantages commonly taken by the enemies of Revelation, of triumphing in objections plausibly raised against the Divine Word, upon the basis of an unsound text or wrong translation?' —(BLANEY'S *Prelim. Disc. to Jeremiah*, 1789.)

'They [the *forty-seven*] are not acquainted with the Hebrew, without which no man should pretend to be a critic upon the writings of the Old Testament. It has some peculiar properties and idioms which no other language has, with which every critic should be acquainted. . . . The Hebrew is fixed in nature, and cannot change. . . . He should be acquainted with the genius of the Hebrew tongue, and with its manner of expressing spiritual things, under their appointed images in nature.' — (ROMAINE'S *Works*, vol. v. p. xvi.)

'It is necessary that translations should be made from one time to another, accommodated to the present use of speaking or writing. This deference is paid to the heathen classics, and why should the Scriptures meet with less regard?' — (PURVER.)

'The common English translation, though the best I have seen, is capable of being brought, in several places, nearer to the original.' — (WESLEY.)

For other arguments, continues our author, see Bishop Newcombe's "Chief reasons in support of a corrected English translation of the Scriptures for national use:" adding on his own account: —

"Notwithstanding all that has been done, the translators have left it [our version] defective in *mood, tense, person, gender, infinitive, imperative, participles, conjunctions*, &c.; and in many instances, almost in every page, we find verses consisting in a great part of *italics;* in some, a third part; in others, nearly half; as may be seen in the Bibles where the words *for which there is not any authority in the original* are always so marked."

Descending into works of less exclusive circulation, what do we encounter?

"It is not to be denied that a translation of Holy Scripture, if undertaken in the present day, would have many advantages superior to those which attended king James's translation. The state of knowledge is much improved. . . . Our language has undergone some changes in the course of two centuries, by which it has varied from being precisely the same as when our translators wrote. Many words which were then polite and elegant, are now vulgar, to say the least. . . . Nor can we refrain from complaining also of the negligent manner in which the press has been conducted in all our public editions: what should be printed in poetry is set as prose; what should be marked as a quotation, or a speech, reads like a common narrative. . . . And this perplexity is occasionally increased by improper divisions of chapters and verses, which but too often separate immediate connection. . . . Undoubtedly, the present version is sufficient to all purposes of *piety*."—(TAYLOR'S *Calmet's Dictionary of the Holy Bible* — voce "Bible.")

"It is needless to pronounce a formal encomium on our authorized version. The time, learning, and labor expended on it were well bestowed. It far surpasses every other *English* version of the entire Bible in the characteristic qualities of simplicity, energy, purity of style, as also in *uniform fidelity* [!] to the original. A revision of it, however, is wanted, or rather a *new translation* from the Hebrew and Greek, based *upon it* [!]"—("S. D.," in KITTO, ii. p. 919.)

"No less than 30,000 various readings (58) of the Old and New Testament have been

---

(58) Say rather, with the Rev. Prof. MOSES STUART — "Investigation has dissipated this pleasant dream. In the Hebrew MSS., that have been examined, some 80,000 *various readings* actually occur, as to the Hebrew consonants. How many as to the vowel-points and accents, no man knows. And the like to this is true of the New Testament"—(*Crit. Hist. and Defence of the O. Test. Canon;* Andover, 1835; p. 192.) "Nemo est, qui in uno aliquo codice, sive MSto sive impresso, textum incorruptum exhiberi arbitratur. Riderent docti; si quis codicem aliquem cum istis Apostolorum autographis, in omnibus, consentire dixerit"—(KENNICOTT: *Dissert. Gen.;* par. 13, p. 6.)

discovered; . . . and putting alterations made knowingly, for the purpose of corrupting the text, out of the question, we must admit, that from the circumstances connected with transcribing, some *errata* may have found their way into it; and that the sacred Scriptures have in this case suffered the same fate as other productions of antiquity. . . . In the last 220 years, critical learning has so much improved, and so many *new manuscripts* have come to light, as to call for a revision of the present authorized version." — (SEARS, *Hist. of the Bible*, 1844, pp. 651, 665.)

"The *second* thing which I would strongly recommend, is constantly to study and peruse the Original Scriptures; the Old Testament in the Hebrew, and the New Testament in the Greek. . . . There is no such thing as any *written* Word of God independent on the word of man. The Lord Jehovah may have uttered the whole Law from Mount Sinai; and, yet, Moses may not have accurately recorded it. . . . In like manner, the Gospel may have been fully preached by Christ; and, yet, the Evangelists may not have fully recorded it. . . . One painful conviction is, that the plain import of the Word of God has been most *fantastically*, *ignorantly*, and *wilfully* perverted, as well in the translation as in the interpolations. . . . Many gross *perversions*, not to say mistranslations, of the Sacred Text have been occasioned by dogmatical prejudices and sectarian zeal."—(REV. JOHN OXLEE, *Letters to the Archbishop of Canterbury*, London, Hatchard, 1845; pp. 117, 137–8.)

Fuerunt autem, relates Kennicott, *qui de hac re aliter senserunt:* among the non-extinct is the Rev. Dr. Horne, who makes the fiercest battle in defence of "our authorized version;" quoting many writers on the opposite side to ours, whose combined "association," like the one prelauded, fails in authority for want of *Hebraical* knowledge in its parts; but, when the best is done for it, he naively remarks on our translation — "It is readily admitted that it is not immaculate; and that a revision, or *correction*, of it is an object of desire to the friends of religion" — and then the reverend gentleman breaks forth in rhapsodical glorifications and thanksgivings, *that it is not worse!* (59)

Nor are the erudite among Christians alone the denouncers of king James's version. Anglicized Israelites hold it in estimation equally low, to judge by the following Editorial:

"*What we should like to see at the World's Fair.*—It would give us a great deal of pleasure to see at the World's Fair a correct English version of the Bible, resting upon the solid fundament of the results of modern criticism; reaching the elevation of modern science, and being accomplished by men of a thorough scholastic education, and free from every foreign influence, who take the letter for what it is without paying any regard to authorities, and without coming to the task with a certain quantity of prejudices. Such a work would reconcile science and religion; it would reclaim many an erring wanderer to the straight path of truth; it would evaporate many a prejudice and a superstition; it would greatly modify many sectarian views, and would closely unite the men of opposite nations. It appears, however, that the men for this task are not yet among the mortals; for the theologians come to the Bible with an established system, which must lead them away from the true import of letters, where they find again their own system whenever it can be done conveniently; and where their sentiments frequently overbalance their critical judgment." —(*The Asmonean*, New York, July 22, 1853.)

Thus we might go on, citing work after work wherein, if king James's version is not denounced for its *perversions* of the "original sacred tongues," its erroneous readings are more or less apologetically but thoroughly confirmed by many instances in which the erudition and fairness of the authors compel them to *substitute* their own translations for those of our "authorized" copy. Notable examples may be seen in the recent work of our much-honored fellow-citizen, Dr. McCulloh. (60).

Albeit, as said before, if our version were decently accurate, why should so many laborious men run the risks of incurring some theological obloquy, coupled with pecuniary loss, in efforts to *correct* the false renderings of that superannuated edition by publishing emendatory *retranslations* in *English?* Among the many we have consulted may be cited:

"The HOLY BIBLE, according to the established Versions, with the exception of the substitution of the *original Hebrew names*, in place of the words LORD or GOD, and of a few corrections thereby rendered necessary. (London, 1830; Westley and Davis.)"

This book, however, seems to have closed at 2 *Kings*. The uninitiated may be informed

---

(59) *Op. cit.*; ii. pp. 77–83.

(60) *Credibility of the Scriptures*; Baltimore, 1852. See particularly vol. ii. Appendix, "On the Human Soul," pp. 465–489.

that the word "Lord" of our version renders merely the *Dominus* of the Vulgate, and the Κυριὸς of the Septuagint, and does not directly *translate* the original Hebrew word IeHOuaH; the latter being suppressed, by "His Majesty's special command," in the "authorized" copies, only 6846 *times!* The number of times it occurs in the *Hebrew Text* are 6855: (61) on which hereafter. Another is: —

"The HOLY BIBLE, containing the *authorized* version of the Old and New Testaments, with *twenty thousand* [*!*] emendations. (London, 1841; Longman, Brown & Co.)"

Its *title* attracted our notice, as savoring of a *Tauric* genus known as Hibernian; aptly illustrated in that "same old knife which belonged to 'my grandfather,' after having received thirteen new handles and seventeen new blades." The *preface* justified our first impressions, when we read — "This is our AUTHORIZED ENGLISH VERSION, which is characterized by unequalled fidelity, perspicuity, simplicity, dignity, and power. . . . No one has *yet detected a single error* [in it!!!] in reference to those great and vital truths in which all Christians agree." After which, where the utility of 20,000 *emendations?* Suffice it, that, maugre this huge amount, not perceiving any of the catalogue of "emendations" hereinafter submitted to the reader, we refrained from its purchase, after a morning's examination.

A third, which we have long possessed through the kindness of its publishers, merits attention, and is ushered by a most excellent preface: —

"The HOLY BIBLE, being the English version of the Old and New Testaments, made by order of King James I., carefully *revised and amended*, by several Biblical Scholars. (Sixth edition, Philadelphia: J. B. Lippincott & Co., 1847.)"

After a brief sketch of preceding translations into English, from 1290 to 1611, the *preface* states — "From these facts, and from comparing the translation of king James with those which preceded it, nothing is more obvious, than that the common version is but a revision of those executed by Tindal, Coverdale, and others, and that, however excellent it may be, the paramount praise, under God, is due to WILLIAM TINDAL and MILES COVERDALE." In the above sentiments we heartily concur; having enjoyed opportunities, in the course of our studies, of comparing some points in both of the latters' self-sacrificing editions with the so-called "revision" of the *forty-seven.* Αυτοδιδακτοι, however, like Abderitan DEMOCRITUS, in some branches of Oriental philology; and possessing, furthermore, an apparatus tolerably complete of *continental* criticism in biblical matters; we prefer direct references to the *Hebrew Text*, now rendered accessible in a very handy form, and illumined by Cahen's most useful parallel French translation. (62)

From the nature of these premises it will be seen that, save under the scientific point of view and for the general cause of human enlightenment, the writer, as an individual, is not urgent in exacting another "authorized" version of Texts to which he has acquired (what any man who really is serious in such matters can acquire as he has) access for himself. At the present day that in Protestant countries, such as Great Britain and the United States, it has become a common practice to *worship* king James's translation, and "study divinity;" that our English version, with all the unnecessary deviations from its Hebrew prototype, is reverenced by the masses as a "fetiche," or viewed with a relic of that semi-idolatrous awe refused by Protestants to crucifixes, pictures, or images, our observations may perhaps seem indecorous to those who choose to cramp their intellects and continue to ignore the splendid results of continental exegesis. We should regret the fact, the more so because offence is unintentional; but, "the epoch of constraint has passed away [in these United States] for ever: a freeman will be free in all things; material and political emancipation suffice no longer for him. He knows that there is a sublimer liberty, that of thought and belief. It is with sorrow that he beholds those sweet illusions fleeting away

(61) WALTON: *Bibl. Polyg.*; Prolog. C. 8, § 8, p. 275. HORNE: *Op. cit.*; i. p. 38. But, above all, LANCI: *Paralipomena*; 1845; *passim.*

(62) LA BIBLE: *Traduction Nouvelle*; 22 octavo volumes; Paris, 1831–'51.

that whilom had been the charm of his childhood; but reason exacts it, and he sacrifices his illusions upon the altar of *truth*." (63)

Of that wherein the aspirations of a Newcombe, a Lowth, and a Kennicott (to say nothing about others of the best of England's biblical critics), have been baulked, it would be at this day egregious folly to entertain further hopes, viz: that the British Lords, Spiritual and Temporal, will, in our generation at least, permit such a radically-correct *re-translation* of the Hebrew Scriptures as would supersede the vulgar version "appointed to be read in churches." The Universities, especially the *Oxonian*,—part of whose support depends, like some institutions on this side of the water,—upon a "Book Concern," would oppose such violation of vested privileges. By the evangelical dissenting sects, sundry of whose various hierarchies derive subsistence from those very linguistic quibbles that a *new* standard version would obliterate, such a proposition would be repelled with devout horror. *Exeter Hall* shudders, even at the thought: "Bible Societies" whine that the reign of Anti-Christ is come indeed. As positivists we lament not that our brief span of life will have been measured, long before a *new* English version may be "authorized;" because, through the slow but unerring laws of human advancement in knowledge, by the time that *theologists* shall have accomplished their metaphysical transition and have awakened to the stern realities of the case, the development of science will have rendered any *new translation* altogether supererogatory among the educated who are creating *new religions* for themselves.

In the utterance of these long-pondered thoughts, though written years ago, we have been somewhat anticipated by our learned friend McCulloh; (64) with a quotation from whose admirable chapter on the "Value of Translations" we conclude this *historical* division of the two-fold evidence.

"No emendation however of our common translation would affect the revelations made in the Scripture, upon any subject which Jehovah has directly addressed to the understanding or consciences of mankind, whether as regards their faith or practice. That a new translation would considerably affect our theological creeds, or our ecclesiastical institutions, there is no doubt; but this again is a most desirable object if such things are not accordant to the undoubted word of God. No Christian in his senses can wish to remain under any error respecting the import of Jehovah's revelations; and hence nothing can be more absurd than to oppose a correction of our common translation, on the ground that it would overturn some of the inventions that theologians have heretofore constructed upon the comparatively defective Hebrew or Greek Texts upon which that translation has been made.

"The popular objections of unlearned persons to the amendment of our present translation, however, are often, unfortunately for Christianity, sustained by learned men and accomplished scholars, whose interests or whose prejudices are too deeply involved in the present condition of things to be willing to admit of any innovation. Their creeds, institutions, and ecclesiastical establishments, for the most part, were constructed contemporaneously by divines or statesmen of similar theological or ecclesiastical views with those who made our authorized version. To change the terms or texts of Scripture that have been heretofore used as the basis for ecclesiastical institutions, or theological assumptions concerning divine truths, are shocks too violent, either for the pride or self-interests of men, to acquiesce in willingly. . . . . Dr. Vicesimus Knox, (65) of the Church of England, says, 'For my own part, if I may venture to give an opinion *contrary to that of the profound collators of Hebrew Manuscripts*, I cannot help thinking a new translation of the Bible an attempt *extremely dangerous and quite unnecessary*. Instead of serving the cause of religion, which *is the ostensible motive* for the wish, *I am convinced that nothing would tend more immediately to shake the basis of the* ESTABLISHMENT' (*i. e.*, of the Church of England). 'Time,' says the reverend gentleman, 'gives a venerable *air* to all things. Sacred things acquire *peculiar* sanctity by long duration.'"

And finally, the unlettered dogmatist who, possessing no knowledge of the real merits of the topics before us, would thrust into court "his" *opinion*, may as well be told by the reader, that:—

"At the rational point of view, a sentiment such as is termed Christian conscience, a

(63) MUNK: *Examen*, in CAHEN'S *Exodus*; p. iv.

(64) *Op. cit.*; i. pp. 281, 283.

(65) *Annual Obituary*; vi. p. 352; — *Op. cit.*; p. 283, note.

sentiment that reposes upon suppositions, has no voice in scientific discussions; and, every time that it would meddle with them, it ought to be called to order through the simple dictum: *Taceat mulier in ecclesia.*" (66)

II. — The exegetical Evidence.

"Eh! datevi pace, o teologoni di vecchia scuola, che la verità vuol risplendere anche a traverso di quel denso velo che la ignoranza di alcuni di voi si presume di opporle. Intanto per apprendimento vostro fatevi or meco a leggere qualche altro versetto in cui . . . sarà pure una di quell' esse novità che a' preoccupati leggitori fanno strabuzzare occhi e naso aggrinzare." (67)

The foregoing section has prepared the reader for the "experimentum crucis" to which we now propose submitting various passages of king James's version, by way of testing the vaunted accuracy of its *forty-seven* translators. Three of these instances have been already indicated; (68) one of which, wherein Job longed that his speech should be "*printed* in a *book*," was noticed above.

For convenience sake, having now a few more of these literary curiosities to present, we will tabulate them under alphabetical signs, and prefix to this initial gem the letter

A. — *Job* xix. 23.

One almost blushes to make this imbecility more palpable to general intelligence by recalling to mind that *block*-printing was unknown to Europe prior to A. D. 1423, and printing in *types* before 1457 — although the former invention existed, according to Stanislas Julien, (69) in *China* at A. D. 593, and the latter about 1041. Yet, by this "translation," the patriarch must have foreshadowed the art six to ten centuries previously to the advent of Christ! Like every writer comprised in the Old Testament Canon, Job knew as much of *China* as they all did of America; that is, to be frank, just nothing at all. How *forty-seven* able-bodied men could have overlooked this blunder while "correcting proof," surpasses comprehension; unless we ourselves perpetrate another anachronism, as well as a pitiful conundrum, and suppose that "Job-printing" may have suggested some inappreciable affinity between the Anglo-corrupted name of that venerable Arab and the glorious art. What more simple than to have *printed* what the "original sacred tongues" read, "*inscribed* in a *register?*"

B. — *Job* xxxi. 35. [N. B. The first citations always present the textualities of king James's version.]

> "Oh that one would hear me! behold, my desire *is, that* the Almighty would answer me, and *that* mine adversary had written a book."

Can human intelligence understand what possible connection Job's supplication, that God should reply to him, can have with his individual craving that his own unnamed enemy should have indited a *book?* If this text be "divinely inspired" in king James's version, then "the Lord have mercy upon his creature" *archæology!* Because, were these words authentic, logic could prove: —

1. That, at least 2500 years ago, polemical works in the form of "books" were not unknown even in Arabia.
2. That, inasmuch as Job could have no benevolent motive in such wish, vexed as he felt at the aggravations heaped upon his distressing afflictions by his proverbial *comforters*, and knowing, as he must necessarily have done, the power which a Reviewer has over an *author*, he longed, with vindictive refinement, as the most terrible retribution to be inflicted upon an adversary, that his particular enemy should actually write a *book*, in order that Job might *review* him; probably, as Horace Smith conjectured, "in the *Jerusalem Quarterly*."

---

(66) Paul: 1 *Corinthians* xiv. 34; — Strauss: *Vie de Jesus*; Littré's transl., Paris, 1840; ii. p. 378.
(67) Lanci: *Op. cit.;* i. p. 150.
(68) Nott; *Op. cit.;* pp. 136, 137.
(69) Communication to *L'Académie;* June 7 — London *Athenæum;* 19 June, 1847.

Cahen renders —

> "Alas! that I have not one who hears! Behold my *writing* — let the Almighty answer me — and the book edited by my adverse party." (70)

This version (for reasons to be elaborated elsewhere) is unsatisfactory, like all we have seen, but Lanci's; because among other oversights it does not afford due weight to the word TaU; vaguely rendered "sign" or "mark" in *Ezekiel* ix. 4. TaU is the name of the last letter in the post-christian *square-letter* alphabet of the Jews; which 142 years B. C., on the earlier Maccabee coinage was cruciform; sometimes like the *Latin*, at others like the *Greek* cross. (71) At the time when Ezekiel wrote in Chaldea, during the sixth century B. C., this *cruciform* letter was the one he must have used, no less than the shape of that "mark" which should be stamped upon the foreheads of the righteous. Its etymological and figurative meaning was "benediction" or "absolution;" just what its descendant, the "baptismal sign" (drawn with water on the foreheads of infants) signifies at this day. Ezekiel's TaU had no direct relation, beyond a distant resemblance in shape and perhaps an occult one in hierophantic mysteries, to the "Crux Ansata," or the sign for "Ankh," *eternal life*, of the more ancient Egyptian hieroglyphics; but its original is now-a-days producible from the *cuneiform* monuments of Assyria; though our demonstration of the fact must be reserved to other opportunities.

It is one thing to prove that the *forty-seven* were wrong in their appreciation of the "word of God:" quite another to emulate the presumptuous part of theologians and dictate dogmatically the English sense of ancient texts in themselves obscure. Our task limits itself to the former office in this essay; but, not to shrink from the utterance of what little we know, the following *free rendering* indicates a probable solution of this tortured passage, and combines Lanci's with other views:— says Job, "Who will give me one that will listen to me? [i. e., as my judge]. Behold! (here is) my TaU [i. e., he holds up masonically the *cruciform* emblem, as his "absolution"]. The Omnipotent will answer for me [i. e., guarantee me, be my surety, become responsible for me —" that I seek not to evade," *understood*]. And now let my opponent write down his charge [i. e., let my accuser, my calumniator, put his accusations into writing—" that everybody may see them," *understood*].

And, while on the subject of TaU, we may continue our expurgations with other examples.

C. — *Psalms* lxxviii. 41.

> "Yea, they turned back and tempted God, and limited the Holy One of Israel."

Bad as the Jews were, in this case they did precisely the contrary! "The Psalmist," says Lanci, (72) "celebrates in this canticle the marvels which the Lord had done in behalf of rebellious Israel; nevertheless, as the latter finished by conversion, God pardons him and spreads over the culprit the most ample bounties. Conversion, therefore, is the import of this verse, and then it is said—" they (became) converted, they supplicated the Puissant, and implored TaU [i. e., "absolution," or "benediction"] of the Holy of Israel."

D. — 1 *Samuel* xxi. 10—15.

> "And David arose; and fled that day for fear of Saul, and went to Achish the King of Gath. — And the servants of Achish said unto him, *Is* not this David the king of the land? did they not sing one to another of him in dances, saying, Saul hath slain his thousands, and David his ten thousands? — And David laid up these words in his heart, and was sore afraid of Achish the King of Gath. — And he changed his behavior before them, and feigned himself mad in their hands, and scrabbled on the doors of the gate, and let his spittle fall down upon his beard. — Then said Achish unto his servants, Lo, ye see the man is mad: wherefore *then* have ye brought him to me? — Have I need of madmen, that ye have brought this *fellow* to play the madman in my presence? shall this *fellow* come into my house?"

Reminding the reader that David, besides being the warrior-king, was Israel's *bard*, we let Lanci speak for himself:—" The LXX (Greek) made a periphrasis at the first verse, and

(70) *Op. cit.;* vol. xv. p. 143.
(71) Letronne: *Examen Archéologique;* 1846; plate i., and pp. 11-18.
(72) *Sagra Scrittura Illustrata;* Roma, 1827; ch. ix. Cahen, xiii. p. 175, note.

added to the (Hebrew) Text by twice mentioning the gates of the city, first to make David play upon his harp, and afterwards to cause him to fall against the said gates. There is perhaps no passage in Scripture that has been more completely denaturalized through the obscurity of a single word. It is evident that David had altogether a part more dignified, more reasonable, to adopt than to counterfeit a lunatic; and moreover that Achish did not display great esteem for his court by saying that madmen were not wanting in it. But the famous TaU, misunderstood, has thrown all interpreters into error. So we will give to it its veritable sense of *to bless;* to this we add that SHôAR [in Hebrew, as in vulgar Arabic now] does not signify 'door' in this passage, but *poetry*, as its Arabic root teaches: DALETH has the value of 'door' in the same sense that Chaldees and Arabs call 'doors' [*bâb, bibân*] or 'houses' [*bêyt, beyoôt*] the *strophes;* that is, those *commencements of chapters* and of *strophes* that we [Italians] call 'stanze' [and that in English is adopted for poetry in our word *stanzas;* a word that in Italian, like the above nouns in Oriental speech, has the double meaning of 'stanza' and 'chamber']. If it be insisted that David was raving, it will be, then, with *poetic* furor — the prophetic transport that animated him: but the Arabic root SHAGIâ, which signifies *to exhibit valor, bravery, courage*, accords much better with the context. These few rays of light ought to be sufficient to dissipate the thick tenebrosities which Translators have piled upon this divine narrative. We may thenceforward give to these verses a reasonable translation and worthy of the majesty of Scripture:— 'David arose, and fleeing on that day from the presence of Saul, came to Achish the king of Gath.—Then the servants of Achish said to him, 'And is not this David king of the earth? is it not in his honor that it was sung in chorus [not, at ancient *Fandangos!*]: Saul has killed a thousand, and David ten thousand!' — David weighing these words in his heart, feared greatly in presence of Achish king of Gath.—It was for this that in his presence, he [David] celebrated their power in a varied *hymn* and in inspired *verses;* and, at each *commencement of a strophe* he made TaU [i. e., he made 'benedictions'— he *blessed them*]; and already the *sweat* was dripping upon the chin's honor [i. e., upon his *beard*, in Oriental phraseology] when Achish interrupted him, and said to his servant: 'hearken to this man who affects inspiration [literally, '*comes* the inspired']; are *poets* [*bards, improvisatori*] wanting to me, that you must bring this one to celebrate my power? and shall (such as) he come into my house?' Nevertheless, David escaped, and took the road that conducted to the cavern of Adulla." (73)

Who seem most "cracked," David, or the bibliolaters of king James's version?

E. — *Leviticus* xi. 20.

"All fowls that creep, going upon *all* four, *shall be* an abomination to you."

To us, likewise! "Raræ aves," invaluable however to museums of Natural History. Not merely, were this prohibition authentic, did *four-legged-fowls* exist in the days of Moses, but the inhibition to eat them would now be worthless to a *Caraïte* Jew, because the breed is extinct. Cahen renders — "Every winged-insect [or literally, *flying-creeping* thing] that walks upon four [*claws, feet*, understood] is an abomination unto you."

Dwelling not upon *verse* 21, although marvelling how "legs" could be placed anatomically elsewhere than "above their feet," we refreshen ourselves with

F. — 2 *Kings*, vi. 25.

"And there was a great famine in Samaria: and, behold, they besieged it, until an ass's head was *sold* for fourscore *pieces* of silver, and the fourth part of a cab of dove's dung for five *pieces* of silver."

"Sternhold and Hopkins had great qualms
When they translated David's psalms";

but the sufferings of these poor men were infinitesimally small compared to those the *forty-seven* would have experienced had they partaken of that delicate repast, for about two-thirds of a pint of which the starving Samaritans paid such monstrous prices! *Pigeon's dung*, or "doves'-dung," owing to the quantity of ammonia it contains, is still used throughout

(73) *Op. cit.;* Ch. ix. § 3. CAHEN: vii. p. 86, preserves the old mistakes.

the East, in the absence of modern chemistry, to give temper to Damascene sword-blades, &c. It sharpens weapons, not appetites! Can one conceive a human stomach, however depraved by want, alimented upon "guano?" Bochart, (74) two centuries ago, showed that "pois chiches," in Italian *ceci*, in English "chick pea," — the commonest Oriental vetch, or pea, — is the rational interpretation of the word; and thus the only enigma preserved is, how *forty-seven* Englishmen could have committed a mistake so extraordinary. The obsolete word "cab" aptly illustrates how imperative it has become, through unavoidable changes of language within 250 years, to issue a re-translation in our current vernacular, lest the illiterate should think that "*cab*-riolets," 26 centuries ago, plied in the streets of Samaria! Superstition is gradually elevating the vulgar Cockney speech of the age of King James into our "lingua sancta;" and the translation authorized in his reign will some day become unintelligible and useless in the "Far West," except to those who possess glossaries wherewith to read it. Theologers would act wisely to consider these things, while we pass on to

G. —*Leviticus* xxi. 18 and 17.

> "He that hath a flat nose" — [is forbidden] — "approach to offer the bread of his God."

A *flat nose*, in the Abrahamic type of mankind, among their "Cohenîm" or priesthood, was, in the days of the Hebrew Lawgiver, as it is now among Israel's far-scattered descendants, too great a deviation of physical lineaments from the indelible standard of the race (portrayed as we exhibit them in our present work from the monuments of that epoch, and as we daily see them in our streets) not to excite suspicion that such cases testified to admixtures of foreign (75) and consequently of "impure blood"; and therefore to debar a priest with a "flat nose" from the Tabernacle was rational at their point of view. *Negro* families [as already demonstrated, *supra*] are unmentioned throughout the Hebrew Text; and negrophilism may accordingly rejoice that the rendering selected by the *forty-seven* cannot now be applied to the former "de jure," where it is notoriously (in the *Free* States of this Federation, especially) "de facto."

Happily — no thanks to our translators — "Snubs" of universal humanity may legally officiate at sanctuaries; the word K*h*RM (76) meaning only a "*mutilated* nose:" and the inhibition referring to noses injured by deformity, accident, disease, or law, (77) our apprehensions were futile, like their translation.

An ethnological item has been touched upon involuntarily, and now we may as well give ventilation to another much-abused text.

H. — *Song of Solomon*, i. 5, 6.

> "I *am* black, but comely, . . . Look not upon me because I *am* black, because the sun hath looked upon me: my mother's children were angry with me; they made me keeper of the vineyards; *but* mine own vineyard have I not kept."

The apocryphal "prologue" at the head of this chapter tells us that here the *Church* "confesseth her deformity"! It were well if, before printing this acknowledgment (which it is not for us to dispute), the "Establishment" had corrected the deformity of their *translation:* which has led our anglicized Nigritians to claim this supposititious bride of Solomon as a Venus of their own species! With equal reason, some commentators, even of modern

---

(74) SALVERTE; *Sciences Occultes*; i. p. 44. CAHEN (whose *notes* are infinitely more valuable than his textual translations), viii. p. 127, *note*, adds — "Selon plusieurs commentateurs, il s'agit ici d'une nourriture misérable, de quelque herbe à vil prix," &c.

(75) On returning from the Captivity, "the children of Habaiah, the children of Koz, the children of Barzillai, which took *one* [SIC, in our version!] of the daughters of Barzillai the Gileadite to wife, and was [! *idem*] called after their name," were, "as polluted, put from the priesthood" — (NEHEMIAH vii. 63, 64.)

(76) CAHEN: vol. iii. pp. 99, 100.

(77) "I cut off both his *nose* and ears," proclaims DARIUS, of Phraortes, and of Sitratachmes, at Behistun. (RAWLINSON: *Persian Cuneif. Inscrip.*; 1846; part i. p. 34.) Philanthropy need not shudder at atrocities of the fifth century B. C., for in Turkey such punishment is as common now as it was 3300 years ago, if MOSES wrote this passage.

times, (78) infer that she was "an Egyptian princess;" while others identify the lady with "Pharaoh's daughter;" for "King Solomon loved many strange women. . . . Moabites, Ammonites, Edomites, Zidonians, *and* Hittites," and what not! (79) It need hardly be mentioned that, the dynasty out of which the sage king selected additions to his *hareem* being yet unfound in hieroglyphics, the monuments of Egypt throw no light upon this otherwise very probable amalgamation. (80)

The "*Canticle of Canticles of which of Solomon,* that is to say, *one of the Canticles of Solomon,*" as Lanci literally interprets its epigraph, (81) has suffered much at the hands of the *forty-seven.* They, and others, lost sight of the simple fact (to be exemplified in its place), that, in the ancient Hebrew Text, divisions into *chapters, verses, words,* or by *punctuations,* are absolutely unknown; while, paralleled to this day in Arabic calligraphy, no *notes* of admiration, interrogation, &c., mark inflections of the sense. The context alone can indicate a query; so that a "crooked little thing which asks a question," added to fidelity of construction and acquaintance with Levant usages of the present hour, rescues our pretty Shulamite *brunette* from all Ethiopian hallucinations [*supra*, p. 483].

"I am *brown* (Italicè "fosca," dark, *tanned*) but pretty," says the girl coquettishly; then [deprecatingly to her swain], "Do not mind that I am *browned*, because the sun has tanned me; [which she explains by adding] the male-children of my mother [*i. e.* my *step-brothers;* who, in the East, control their maiden sisters after the father's death] having become free to dispose of me, placed me watcher of vines: ["don't you see?" *understood*] my own vine, have I not watched it?" (82)

One improvement heralds another: it is so in machinery: it is equally true in biblical hermeneutics, the moment a man's mind soars above the supernatural grade of ratiocination. From the simple proposition that they who expound the Scriptures should understand them, we hold that no one is competent to impugn these deductions who is unacquainted, not merely with the original Hebrew and Greek languages, but with the noble achievements of Continental exegesis. Hear a living Church of England dignitary: —

> "Those who advocate the free use of philology in the interpretation of the Scriptures, find their fiercest and most uncompromising opponents in the ranks of those who are slaves to the Puritanical *Bibliolatry,* so common in this country. According to this school, every word in the canonical books of the Old and New Testament (in king James's version) proceeds from a divine and miraculous inspiration. . . . By those who believe in the plenary and verbal inspiration of the (English) Scriptures, science in general and philological science in particular, are viewed with distrust, if not with abhorrence; and the more so, if this *bibliolatry* is combined with a certain amount of *ecclesiolatry.*" (83)

It is a pity, certainly; for if some expounders possessed the intelligence they would deplore their want of education: but we continue.

I. — *Habakkuk* ii. 11.

> "For the stone shall cry out of the wall, and the beam out of the timber shall answer it."

That a stone should cry out from a wall is an idea consonant with Oriental hyperbole; but that a *beam* should answer out of timber seems to be an unpoetical and far-fetched conception, as it presupposes the proximity of a "timber-yard" to the wall aforesaid. It furthermore is not in unison with the context; wherein the prophet, who "surpasses all which Hebrew poesy can offer in this department," (84) declaims against Chaldæan flagitiousness. The propriety of his metaphor resiles to view through Lanci's rendering and notes of interrogation.

---

(78) *The Friend of Moses;* New York, 1852; p. 468, note.

(79) 1 *Kings* iii. 1; xi. 1.

(80) Rosellini: on Osorchor of Manetho's XXIst dynasty.

(81) *La Sagra Scrittura;* ch. v. § 4. Cahen: xiv. 3, 4, has not seized the poet's meaning.

(82) Lanci: *Paralipomeni;* ii. p. 45.

(83) Phileleutherus Anglicanus: *A Vindication of Protestant Principles;* London, 1847; pp. 43, 44; — Gliddon: *Otia Ægyptiaca;* 1849; p. 93.

(84) De Wette: ii. p. 466.

"Peradventure, shall the *statue of stone* [an *Assyrian* bas-relief?] from the wall cry out? The *cricket* [scarabæus, or beetle] from out of the wood will it respond?" (85)

There is a verse of another prophet that Lanci restores, in which our *forty-seven* have metamorphosed *famines* into "young men," and *sorrows* into "maids"!

J. — ZECHARIAH ix. 17.

"Corn shall make the young men cheerful, and new wine the maids."

The "Sons of Temperance" may not be pleased with the moral, but the Daughters will not fail to appreciate an emendation that relieves their antique sisters from the charge of unfeminine indulgences.

The old *Vulgate* had translated — "For, what is the goodness of God, what is his glory, if not the corn of the elect, and the wine which fecundates the virgins?" Vatablus and Pagnini make "confusion worse confounded" by reading — "The corn which makes the young men sing, and the new wine of the girls." But, based upon *radicals* preserved in Arabic, our teacher proposes: —

"What is more sweet and more agreeable than corn in scarcities, and wine that fortifies in afflictions?" (86)

"Per saltum," inasmuch as in the chaos of our memoranda of *false-translations* orderly classification is inconvenient, while to our objects quite unnecessary, we open —

K. — *Genesis* xxiii. 9, 17, 19.

"The cave of Machpela" —

purchased by Abraham for Sarah's inhumation — to remark, that the word *Machpela* which, according to our authorized verity, seems a "proper name," is grammatically, in Semitic tongues, "a thing *contracted-for*;" so that, it is as vain for tourists in Palestine to search for *Machpela*, as for biblical chorographers to define its latitude and longitude. (87)

L. — 1 *Samuel* xix. 13.

"And Michal took an image, and laid *it* in the bed, and put a pillow of goat's *hair* for his bolster, and covered *it* with a cloth."

Manifold were the sins of David, but idolatry was certainly not one of the number; although scandalous suspicions have been rife in regard to this *image*. Commentators have likewise expounded how the *image* being laid in the bed, and covered up with the bed-clothes, the messengers supposed that the invalid whom they were sent to slay (*v.* 11) was asleep therein: but we are told: —

M. — 1 *Samuel* xix. 16.

"And when the messengers were come in, behold, *there was* an image in the bed, with a pillow of goat's *hair* for his bolster:" —

whence it is evident that the *forty-seven* deemed the "image" to be of the masculine gender. Their notions of an Oriental *bed* too must have been peculiar, in England, two hundred and fifty years ago, when a "pillow" was made to serve for a "bolster;" and such a hirsute contrivance! However, having commenced rolling down hill, they reach the bottom through a series of cascades that would excite Homeric smiles were not "God's word" the sufferer: as may be seen by the subjoined restitution; after comprehending that Michal, the astute daughter of king Saul, was a princess in whose "trousseau" were doubtless many of the crown regalia: —

"Michal took her casket full of jewels, and placed it upon the bed; whence were reflected magnificent splendors; and she hid them with a curtain [? *coverlid*]." . . . "The messengers having arrived, O surprise! the jewels [being] upon the bed, from their summits was thrown out a magnificence of splendors." (88)

(85) *Op. cit.*; i. p. 283; — CAHEN, xii. p, 115, also reads differently from our version; but see his *note* 11.

(86) *Sag. Scrit.*; ch. ii. § 1; — CAHEN, xii. p. 156, follows the Rabbis.

(87) *Paralip.*; i. p. 144.

(88) *Sag. Scrit.*; ch. vii. 4. The *note*, 13, of CAHEN, vii. p. 76, shows how the text puzzled him. LANCI, *op. cit.*, proves that in no place are TeRaPhIM "idols."

Humiliated at this sight, the assassins remembered that Michal was a royal daughter whose husband, escaped from their clutches, was just the man to reward them with a hempen neckcloth on his accession to the throne; so, apologizing for their intrusion, the emissaries withdrew.

Goats appear to have been favorites with our translators. Not content with transmuting jewels into "goat's *hair*" and filling the royal "bolster" with this rare, elastic, and odoriferous article, they must needs metamorphose one of the sublimest Hebrew names of Deity into a "*scape-goat*"!

N. — *Leviticus* xvi. 8, 10, 26.

> "And Aaron shall cast lots upon the two goats; one lot for the Lord, and the other for the scapegoat.... But the goat, on which the lot fell to be the scapegoat, shall be presented alive before the Lord, to make an atonement with him, *and* to let him go for a scapegoat into the wilderness.... And he that let go the goat for the scapegoat, shall wash his clothes," &c.

ÂZAZL — *âzazel* — is the Hebrew word. "This terrible and venerable name of God (says Lanci) through the pens of biblical glossers has been a *devil*, a *mountain*, a *wilderness*, and a *he-goat!*" (89)

It will give an idea of the lucidity of Rabbinical criticism, to quote the following: —

"Aben Esra, according to his habitual manner when he is in trouble, enunciates in the style of an oracle: 'If thou art capable of comprehending the mystery of *Azâzêl*, thou wilt learn also the mystery of his name; for it has similar associates in Scripture; I will tell thee by allusion one portion of the mystery; when thou shalt have thirty-three years, thou wilt comprehend us.' He finishes abruptly without saying anything more allegorically or otherwise." (90)

The ante-Christian Hebrew text was undivided into *words*. Our preceptor re-divides ÂZAZeL into two distinct nouns; ÂZAZ and EL. The latter, every sciolist knows, means the *strong*, the *puissant* par excellence, the *Omnipotent*. ÂZAZ, identical with the Arabic *âzâz*, has its radical monosyllable in âZ, "to conquer" and "to be victorious;" wherefore, ÂZAZ-*E*L signifies the "God of *victory*" — here used in the sense of the "*Author* of *death*," in juxta-position to I*e*HO*ua*H, the "*Author* of *life*:" to the latter of which *Authors* the Jews were enjoined to offer a *dead* goat; while, by contrast, to the former they were to offer a *live* one. Thus, death to the *Life-giver* — life to the *Death-dealer*. The symbolical antithesis is grand and beautiful.

For the sake of perspicuity we submit a *free* translation to the reader: — "And Aaron shall place lots upon the two he-goats; one lot to I*e*HO*ua*H, and one lot to ÂZAZ-*E*L.... And the he-goat upon which the lot has fallen to ÂZAZ-*E*L shall be placed *alive* before I*e*HO*ua*H, to become exempted by him, to be sent forth to ÂZAZ-*E*L in the desert.... And he who shall have led forth the he-goat to ÂZAZ-*E*L shall cleanse his clothes," &c. In verse 9, the other he-goat offered to I*e*HO*ua*H was to be *killed*.

Having thus entirely misapprehended the sense of the above passages, it was quite natural that our gifted translators, one *Divine Name* having vanished through their skill, should have been blinded to many others. Here is one of them: —

O. — *Job* xxi. 15.

> "What *is* the Almighty, that we should serve him? and what profit should we have, if we pray unto him?"

We have illustrated, under the preceding letter N, the splendor of antithesis which Hebrew literature conceived in the selection of *Divine Names*; and herein leniency may be accorded to the English interpreters, because neither they nor early or later scholiasts, could have anticipated a discovery due to the profoundest Semitic savant of our genera-

(89) *Sagra Scrittura*; ch. iii. § 1; — *Paralipomeni*; ii. p. 354.

(90) CAHEN: iii. p. 68. It may be well to warn cavillers that this subject has been studied. We do not agree in HENGSTENBERG'S idea (*Egypt and the Books of Moses*; pp. 169–184), that *âzazel* is "Satan." For parallelisms on the sacrifice of he-goats to the God-Preserver and the God-Destroyer, conf. RIGHELLINI (*Examen*; ii. p. 246); MOVERS (*Die Phœnizier*; i. p. 367); and MAURY (*Génies Psychopompes*; Aug. 1845; pp. 295, 296 — and *Personnage de la Mort*; Aug. 1847; pp. 325, 326) in the *Revue Archéologique*.

tion, the affable Professor (for thirty-nine years) of Sacred Philology at the Roman Vatican.(91)

The original of the substantive rendered "profit" is NUāIL — a noun which, occurring but once amid the 5642 (92) words preserved, in the Hebrew and Chaldee Bibles, to our day (fragments, so to say, of the ancient tongue) — is unique; and consequently its signification is recoverable solely through its extant radical in Arabian dialects. Its true root is *wāal*, "to be eminent"; and its sense, "the most *sublime*." The prototype of "Almighty" is textually S*h*aDaI; literally, "the most *valorous*." Let the reader now compare king James's version with the subjoined: —

"Who is the *most* VALOROUS (S*h*aDaI), that to him we must be servants? who the *most* SUBLIME (NUāIL), that we should go [out of our way] to meet him?"

Variety is pleasing, so we skip over to

P. — *Micah*, v. 2.

"But thou Beth-lehem Ephrata, *though* thou be little among the thousands of Judah, *yet* out of thee shall he come forth unto me *that is* to be ruler in Israel."

The emendation suggested relates principally to the word rendered "thousands," of which the singular, in the unpunctuated Hebrew, is ALUP*h*.

ALeP*h*, א, first letter of the Hebrew alphabet, in its Phœnician original is the tachygraph of a *Bull's head;* and its name is derived from that of the animal, because the *bull* is "leader" of the herd.(93) Hence ALeP*h* became a title as the "leader," general, dux, or *chief;* of which examples are numerous in the discrepant so-called "Dukes" of Edom, &c.; corruption of the Latin "dux, duces": which, with more propriety in English, should be rendered *chiefs*. Copying the Latin and Greek versions, without archæological knowledge of the Hebrew tongue, our translators have read *Elf-îm* "thousands," when *Chiefs* is its real meaning; thus: —

"And thou Bethlehem of Euphrata, [even] if thou art little among the CHIEFS of Juda, I will cause to issue from thee the dominator of Israel." (94)

Without regard to the fantastical and spurious headings to this Chapter in our version, we may add, that the reading of CHIEFS is as old as the second century B. C, when the LXX Greek version was made by the Hellenistic Jews of Alexandria; because about 68–69 A. D. the author of the "*Good Tidings according to Matthew,*" in citing the above passage from Micah, read "Princes"; (95) and he does not appear to have been acquainted (96) with the Hebrew Text. Paulus and De Rossi even contend that the speech of Christ, Χριστος, was Greek. (97) But, we wander from our theme.

Q. — *Isaiah* xviii. 1, 2.

"Woe to the land shadowing with wings, which *is* beyond the rivers of Ethiopia; — That sendeth ambassadors by the sea, even in vessels of bulrushes upon the waters, *saying*, Go, ye swift messengers, to a nation scattered and peeled, to a people terrible from their beginning hitherto; a nation meted out and trodden down, whose land the rivers have spoiled."

We cite this passage not with a view of destroying the interpretation of the *forty-seven*, in this instance excusable enough, but by way of elucidating how meritorious it would be to reconstruct their time-worn edifice, guided by the lights which Oriental, and particularly *Egyptian*, researches of our living generation cast upon subjects until this century utterly dark.

All interpreters here have been at fault. The LXX render 'Ουαί γῆς πλοίων πτέρυγες — i. e. *Væ terræ navium alis.* The Vulgate — *Væ terræ cymbalo alarum.* Cahen substitutes — "Ah!

(91) LANCI: *Op. cit.;* p. 354, &c.

(92) LEUSDEN, apud GESENIUS, in *Parker's De Wette;* i. p. 459; — MUNK: *Palestine;* p. 436.

(93) GESENIUS: *Script. Ling. Phœniciæ;* 1838; p. 19.

(94) *Sagra Scrit.;* ch. i. § 2; — "Trop petit pour être parmi les *chefs* de Iehouda," CAHEN: xii. pp. 96, 97 — see *note* 1.

(95) *Matt.* ii. 6; SHARPE'S *New Test.;* p. 3.

(96) HENNELL: *Origin of Christianity;* 1845; pp. 123, 124: and *Christian Theism;* pp. 82, 83.

(97) GESENIUS; *Heb. Sprache und Schrift;* 1815; p. 46.

pays sous l'ombrage des voiles'; (98) and the late Major Mordecai Noah actually read — "Hail! Land of the (American) *Eagle*"!

Rosellini (99) was the first to indicate that here the prophet apostrophizes *Egypt* under the metaphor of her national symbol —  — the "winged globe"; as Birch defines it, "emblem of KHEPER, the *Creator Sun*". (100) We subjoin the learned Pisan's emendation, with a few additions: —

FIG. 359.

"Ho! Land of the *Winged Globe* [Egypt]! which art beyond the rivers of KUSh [i. e. the "torrens Ægypti," on the Isthmus of Suez; *supra*, p. 484]: that sendest into the sea, as messengers, the canals of thy waters; and that navigatest with boats of *papyrus* on the face of the waves. Go, ye light messengers, to the *elongated* people [i. e. stretched out along the narrow alluvials of the Nile,] and *shaved* nation [the Egyptians were essentially a *shaven* population — vide *Genesis* xli. 14,]; to a people terrible from the time that was, and also previously; to the *geometrical* people [Geometry originated in Egypt], who treading [with their feet cultivate their fields]; whose lands the rivers will devastate [referring to some unfulfilled prophecy]."

R. — *Ecclesiastes* xi. 1—2.

> "Cast thy bread upon the waters, for thou shalt find it after many days.... Give a portion to seven, and also to eight; for thou knowest not what evil shall be upon the earth."

Unless there was some cabalistic *key* to the latter portion of these sentences, through which the Translators understood what *they* wrote, the super-refined meaning they attached to the numerals 7 and 8 surpasses our feeble comprehension: even Solomon, reputed author and great magician, could not unravel their knot. Let us substitute: —

"Cast thy bread where fruits are borne, because time will restore it with usury.... Give the measure (*porzione*) even to saturity and abundance, because thou knowest not what evil may come upon the earth." Here, comments Lanci, (101) the sage exhorts man to do good, and to charitable acts towards the poor who, satiated with abundant food, will cause to rain upon him, through the fervor of their prayers, ample benedictions during bad seasons. But, what can be expected from men who translate "*Tor, Sus*, and *Agùr*" — *ve* TtUR *ve* SUS *ve* âGUR,

S. — *Jeremiah* viii. 7, — by

> "the turtle and the crane and the swallow,"

— when the prophet meant "the *bull* and the *horse* and the *colt*"? (102)

T. — *Zechariah* v. 1, 2, 3.

> "Then I turned, and lifted up mine eyes, and looked, and behold a flying roll.... And he said to me, What seest thou? And I answered, I see a flying roll; the length whereof *is* twenty cubits, and the breadth thereof ten cubits.... Then said he unto me, This *is* the curse that goeth forth over the face of the whole earth; for every one that stealeth shall be cut off, *as* on this side according to it; and every one that sweareth shall be cut off *as* on that side according to it."

If the prophet had been so unfortunate as to receive the words of this angelic vision in *English*, he would have required a second revelation to understand its Translators' impenetrable meaning.

A "flying roll"! Think of a parchment synagogue *roll* (MeGiLaH, *Meghillà*), of such proportions, actually *flying* through the air! Consider the amount of inspiration it must

(98) IX. pp. 66, 67.

(99) *Monumenti Civili*; ii. pp. 394–403.

(100) GLIDDON: *Otia Ægypt.*; pp. 95, 96: — "It is *the Morning Sun*: it is often called *the beam of light which rises*, or '*comes out*,' *of the horizon*" — BIRCH: *Egyptian Inscription at the Bibliothéque Nationale*; R. Soc. Lit.; 1852; iv. p. 3.

(101) *Sag. Scrit.*; ch. iv. § 64. CAHEN: xvi. p. 129, *notes* 1, 2.

(102) *Paralip.*; ii. p. 391. The "seasons" should be "rutting-times — although CAHEN, x. pp. 30, 31, prefers the old reading.

have required to comprehend *which* side was mortiferous to thieves, which to swearers; for in Aristotelian logic, "if the one is the other, the other must be the one:" and remember that in the phrase "according to it" lies lost, forgotten, and entombed, *one-half* of the *ineffable Tetragrammaton* IHOH (JEHOVAH)! that most terrible, the most occult monosyllable of the palindromic name vocalized as ADONAI, the "Lord"! Here is the sense, *verbatim et litteratim:* —

"And turning myself, I raised my eyes, and saw: and behold a *whirling disk* [of fire—having a mystic relation to the Egyptian 'winged-globe,' emblem of KHEPER, the *Creator-Sun*]. (103) Then the angel said to me: 'What seest thou?' I answered, 'I see a *whirling disk* of twenty cubits in length and of ten in height' [its *wings* enlarging the lateral diameter]. And he said to me: 'This is the malediction [of God] which spreads itself upon the surface of the whole earth; verily, every thief by this [the *whirling disk*] *as (if) by* OH [deuterosyllable of IH-OH] shall be destroyed; and every perjurer by this [the *whirling disk*] *as (if) by* OH shall be destroyed.'" (104)

"The which, philologers will recognize as common sense and justness, if as much was not perceived by those wretched theologists (*teologastri*) who, in philological knowledge not surpassing the Hebrew alphabet, go hunting about through lexicons in order thence to spit forth a doctoral decision in people's faces"; says Lanci. (105)

But, as the time for the exposition of these recondite biblical arcana has not yet arrived, our meaning is best conveyed to the *Illuminati* (106) by amending

U. — *Psalms* xxxvii. 7,

> "Rest in the Lord, and wait patiently for him; fret not thyself because of him who prospereth in his way, because of the man who bringeth wicked devices to pass" —

as follows: — "Keep silence in (the secret of) IHOH, and take delight in it: dispute not with him who seeks to penetrate into the acquiring of it, nor with any vain man who attempts it." (107)

V. — *Psalms* cx. 1—7.

> "The Lord said unto my Lord, Sit thou at my right hand, until I make thine enemies thy footstool.— The Lord shall send the rod of thy strength out of Zion; rule thou in the midst of thine enemies. — Thy people *shall be* willing in the day of thy power, in the beauties of holiness from the womb of the morning; thou hast the dew of thy youth. — The Lord hath sworn, and will not repent, Thou *art* a priest for ever after the order of Melchisedek.—The Lord at thy right hand shall strike through kings in the day of his wrath.— He shall judge among the heathen, he shall fill *the places* with the dead bodies; he shall wound the heads over many countries.— He shall drink of the brook in the way: therefore shall he lift up the head."

This superb ode has by some been suspected to have been derived from hymns of pagan origin, sung during the season that Ezekiel (viii. 14) saw the "woman weeping for TtaM-UZ," about the winter solstice, or 21st December, where the Church almanacs place the anniversary of the *unbelieving* St. Thomas. They refer to the fact that St. Jerome's Vulgate renders TtaM-UZ by *Adonis*, favorite god of the Phœnicians in Palestine and Syria, to justify their reading of "Says JEHOVAH to ADONIS" (108)! Others, again, take MELCHISEDEK to be the *Melek-Sadyc*, the "just king," whose name SYDYC, with the title of "just" is preserved, by Sanconiathon, as the father of the *Cabiri*, &c. (109) St. Paul, however, cites this Psalm frequently in his *Epistle to the Hebrews*; and whoever put the headings to the former in our authorized version has asserted that its language can apply to no other than the Messiah. With all deference, the subjoined paraphrase of Lanci's close Italian

---

(103) See preceding page, under Q.

(104) LANCI: *Sag. Scrit.*; ch. iii. § 7; — *Paralipomeni*; i. p. 97, *seq.*; ii. p. 354; and *Lettre à M. Prisse*; 1847; p. 33. These views are later than CAHEN'S, xii. p. 144.

(105) *Paralip.*; i. p. 3.

(106) MACKAY: *Free-Mason's Lexicon*; 2d edit.; Charleston, S. C.; 1852; voce *Jehovah*, and *Name*: — also, ROCKWELL: *Discourse* before the G. L. of Georgia; Oct. 30, 1851; p. 27.

(107) *Paralip.*; i. p. 149; — CAHEN: xiii. p. 84, *note* 7.

(108) Compare PARKHURST: *Hebrew Lexicon*; voce "Adonai"; with ANTHON: *Class. Dict.*; 1841; pp. 26, 27; — also R. P. KNIGHT, to be cited hereafter.

(109) CORY: *Anc. Frag.*; pp. 8, 9, 13, 16; "Sanconiatho."

translation of the "Dixit Dominus," while it removes the senilities of the *forty-seven*, shows that the composer of that ode dedicated it to some contemporary *priest* called MELCHISEDEK, living at the time of its composition.

"Said IeHOuaH to my Lord: 'Sit thou on my right until I make of thy foemen a stool for thy feet'.—IeHOuaH from Zion will send the wand of thy glory: go, rule in the midst of thy foes.—Thy people will behold spontaneously, when thou shalt understand thy powerful qualifications for the splendor of the priesthood; from the womb, the germ of thy birth was mysterious.—IeHOuaH swore, nor does he retract his oaths: '*Thou, O Melchisedek, shalt be, upon my word, Priest* (a Cohen) *forever!*'—My Lord at thy right hand slew kings in the day of his furor—At the ruling amid the Gentiles, the confines having been passed by force, the chief of vastest land swooned—He will pour himself out more than a torrent through (its) course; wherefore will he raise his head." (110)

As every departure from the literal Italian entails another remove from the original Hebrew, grace is here purposely sacrificed to fidelity; but, from the general tenor of the context, owing to the distinctions observed by the writer between the use of the terms "Jehovah" and "my Lord," one might infer, that this poetical effusion commemorates some conquest over foreigners, with which the composer and his sacerdotal friend MELCHISEDEK were familiar; scenes in which the latter personage (named after the long-anterior "King of Salem") (111) had been an actor. We must console ourselves (under the expected charge that all this is mere conjecture) by reflecting how, if Lanci's shaft may have missed the bull's eye, the arrows of forty-seven able-bodied men flew wide of the target; and that another nail has been driven into the latters' version, which we shall have the satisfaction of "clinching" under the succeeding letters.

According to Cruden's laborious work, (112) the words "grove" and "groves" are "authorized" to re-appear in the English Bible about thirty-six times. Theologians of the lower grade naturally suppose that, in the "original sacred tongue," one single noun, repeated throughout the Text, as its substitute is in our version, must be the latter's representative. Vain illusion!

W. — *Genesis* xxi. 33.

"And *Abraham* planted a grove in Beer-sheba, and called there on the name of the Lord, the everlasting God."

He did nothing of the kind! He, ABRAHAM, "set up (אשל, ASeL) a *tablet* (or *stele*) in Beersheba, and (קרא, KaRA, *read;* also, *wrote*) *engraved* it with the name of IeHOuaH to perpetual duration." (113) Here, take note, the original for "grove" is ASeL.

X. — 2 *Kings* xxiii. 6.

"And he brought out the grove from the house of the Lord, without Jerusalem, unto the brook Kidron, and burned it at the brook Kidron, and stamped *it* small to powder," &c.

A word occurs frequently in the Text, written in two ways, *ă*ST*t*URT*t*, and *ă*S*h*T*t*RUT*t;* which is punctuated, by the Massora, *Astôret*, and *Ashtarôt*. At other times, according to the peculiar provincialism (*patois*) of each biblical writer, the same word appears in the form of ASeRA, or plural AS*h*eR-IM. These are all proper names of one person; and that person is no other than the *goddess* ASTARTE of the Palestinians; HATHOR of the Egyptians; *ă*TYR of the Himyaritic Arabs; the VENUS of Græco-Roman mythology, and of our vernacular. Now, here the word for "grove" is AS*h*eRaH: and our Translators' deed in rendering ASeL by "grove" in one place, and AS*h*eRaH by "grove" in another,

(110) *Paralip.;* ii. p. 110. How extensively obscure is the sense of this Psalm may be seen from CAHEN'S *notes*, xiii. pp. 251–256, 355, 356.

(111) *Genesis* xiv. 18. "Salem," commentators tell us, was the name of *Jerusalem*—YeRuS*h*aLaïM, from *Yerus*, "heritage," and *Shalaïm*, "peace," in the dual; literally, "She who inherits twofold peace" (*Paralip.; in loc.*). They also tell us that MOSES wrote *Genesis*, about the 14th—15th century B.C. Perhaps their archæological ingenuity will explain how it came to pass that the old town of *Jebus* was called "Salem" before it was taken by the Jews of JOSHUA (*Josh.* xviii. 28; *Judges* i. 21; xix. 10, 11; &c.), long after MOSES's death? Until they do, that MOSES wrote XIVth *Genesis* is simply impossible; as likewise the contemporaneousness of ABRAHAM with a "King of Salem." Such anachronisms betray the modern age of this chapter; and render the *older* MELCHISEDEK very like the Phœnicians' "SADYC the *Just*," whose place in history is mythological.

(112) *Concordance* — from 10th Lond. edit.; Philadelphia, 1841; p. 254.

(113) *Paralip.;* i. p. 97, *seq.*

is cecity, if not worse. We pass over, therefore, the extraordinary circumstance how JOSIAH could find a "grove" in a *house*, unless that grove was very small, or the house very large, which SOLOMON's *temple*, only ninety feet by thirty, was assuredly not—and how he could carry about and break up with facility an entire "grove" seems inexplicable. Not so when we read — "And he dragged the (wooden *statue* of) VENUS (AS*h*eRaH) (114) out of the house of IeHOuaH:" — a proceeding which begins to reveal to us, what some "teologastri" have ventured recently to doubt, (115) viz., the infamous *atrocities* of ancient Jewish templar worship; that we propose to lay bare in another place. "Ex abundantiâ," we give a correct but *modest* restoration of *verse* 7 of the same chapter, which intelligent readers can compare with the blundering performance of the *forty-seven*: — "And he (JOSIAH) broke down the little chapels of the *shameless* priests that were in the house of IeHOuaH, where the women spread perfumes before the *niches* of VENUS" — for, says *verse* 5 — the Jews "had burned incense to BAAL, to SHEMS, to the *Moon*, and to the *Signs of the Zodiac*, and to all the *Asterisms* of Heaven!"

It was the *discovery* (about 620 B. C.), to say the least, of the "Book of the Law" of MOSES, (116) lost and forgotten for some 700 years, which instigated the reforming JOSIAH to these vigorous measures: but pious iconoclasts had been shocked at similar abominations before; as the following text clearly exhibits; while it also relieves poor JOASH, the worthy father of the valiant GIDEON, from the accusation of idolatry that *forty-seven* men stimulate "simple believers" to hurl at his innocent head.

Y. — *Judges* vi. 25, 26.

> "And it came to pass the same night, that the Lord said unto him, Take thy father's young bullock, even the second bullock of seven years old, and throw down the altar of Baal that thy father hath, and cut down the grove that *is* by it:—And build an altar unto the Lord thy God upon the top of the rock, in the ordered place, and take the second bullock and offer a burnt sacrifice with the wood of the grove which thou shalt cut down."

Decency forbids that we should explain the sculptural obscenities that GIDEON's eyes beheld. Orientalists, whose studies may have led them into antique *pornography*, will comprehend us and the exactitude of the venerable Lanci's translation, (117) of which we submit a close but softened paraphrase: —

"And it was in that night that IeHOuaH said to him [Gideon]: 'Take the young bullock of thy father, and another bullock of seven years, and thou shalt fell, with the *altar* [supporter] of BAAL [the obscene God] that [bullock] which is thy father's; afterwards thou shalt break down the VENUS [ASHERA, the foul goddess] which was above it. Then thou shalt build up, in regular proportion [i. e., according to Mosaic rules], an altar to IeHOuaH, thy ELOH, on the summit of that [yonder] rock; and, taking the second bullock, thou shalt burn it in holocaust with the wood of the VENUS by thee broken up.'"

We may now inquire of the reader, in all good faith, whether, in every instance laid hitherto before his acumen, our emendations have not made plain sense of that which was utter nonsense; and whether the *Bible*, properly translated, is not a much loftier book, far grander, as regards mere literary excellence, than the version, "authorized" exactly 250 years ago, has ever made it appear?

If such be his candid opinion, he will feel a high gratification at the revisal, through the application of pure grammar and philology, of that imaginary text, on the authority of which the *Copernican* system was traduced by ecclesiastical ignorance; while the telescopic discoveries of the immortal Galileo, A. D. 1615, condemned, as "absurd, false in philosophy, and formally heretical, being contrary to the express word of God," nearly brought him to those fagots whereupon, only fifteen years before, Giordano Bruno's living

(114) CAHEN preserves "Aschera" in his translation (viii. p. 190, &c.); accurately remarking that, if the Rabbis bestowed more attention on "*Antiquités bibliques*" — "there would not be then less respect for the sacred writings, but they would no longer be regarded as the Pillars of Hercules of all civilization" (p. 205).

(115) *Inter alios*, the Rev. Dr. SMYTHE of Charleston, S. C.: *Unity*; p. 112, note.

(116) 2 *Kings* xxii. 8; and 2 *Chron*. xxxiv. 14.

(117) *Paralip.*; ii. 28–31. CAHEN: vi. p. 31, "Aschera."

body was calcined "ut quam clementissime et citra sanguinis effusionem, puniretur." (118) Had Lanci never turned his vast Semitic acquirements to any other Scriptural text but Joshua Xth, 12, 13, astronomical posterity should weave for him a wreath of laurels. But, to appreciate his labors, one must bestow a final smile of pity upon the *forty-seven.*

Z. — *Joshua* x. 12, 13, 14.

> "Then spake Joshua to the Lord in the day when the Lord delivered up the Amorites before the children of Israel, and he said in the sight of Israel, Sun, stand thou still upon Gibeon, and thou, Moon, in the valley of Ajalon.... And the sun stood still, and the moon stayed, until the people had avenged themselves upon their enemies. *Is* not this written in the book of Jasher? So the sun stood still in the midst of heaven, and hasted not to go down about a whole day.... And there was no day like that before it or after it, that the Lord hearkened to the voice of a man: for the Lord fought for Israel."

So far "authorized version!" and, in lieu of examining whether the ancient Text has been truthfully rendered, those among whom knowledge has not yet advanced beyond the theological grade are lavishly vituperative of scholars who, knowing the English translation of this passage to be an absurdity, despise the commentaries upon it as a sham.

To place the reader at our point of view, let us first ask the question—what is this "book of Jasher?" One of the twenty *lost* books of the Hebrews cited in the Old Testament, is the facile reply. "*The book of Jasher*, that is, *the Righteous.* (*Josh.* x. 13; 2 *Sam.* i. 18.) This book must have been of no very ancient date, for it contained the Lamentations of David on the death of Saul and Jonathan. A spurious work with this title has come down to us, containing the history recorded in the first seven books of the Old Testament." (119) According to Cahen (vii, pp. 121–124; 2 *Samuel* i. 17–27), the verse runs —

> "17. David composed this lament upon Saul and upon Jonathan his son. — 18. And ordered to be taught to the children of Judah [the elegiac Lament called] *the Bow;* behold, it is written in the book of Jasher."

Then *follows* the lament itself, from *verse* 19 to 27: in which David, in poetic strain, says (*v.* 22, 23) —

> "The *bow* of Jonathan never retreated;
> The sword of Saul never returned empty:
> (Oh) Saul and Jonathan!"

Consequently, David, about B. C. 1056, had composed this beautiful ode; and a later writer says, "behold, it is written in the *Book of Jasher;*" that is, David's ode is. Ergo, this *Book of Jasher* was a collection of poems compiled *after* B. C. 1056. Now, the writer of "Joshua Xth" quotes, from this same *Book of Jasher*, the passage which in king James's version runs — "So the sun stood still in the midst of heaven and hasted not to go down about a whole day;" continuing his citation down to "the Lord fought for Israel." Hence it is positive that "Joshua-*ben*-NUN," could not have been the author of the "Book of Joshua;" because, having departed this life about B. C. 1426, he could have known nothing of a subsequent collection of poems that contained the lamentations of David upon events that happened some 370 years after Joshua himself was dead and buried. Moses is the only man who is privileged by orthodoxy to describe his own demise: (120) a second instance cannot be tolerated. Now, this author of "the Book of Joshua" is utterly unknown, and its date is very *modern*, perhaps as low as the sixth century B. C.; (121) as are likewise the "Books of *Samuel.*"

The next point, to which attention is invited, regards the sentence—"*Is* not this written in the Book of Jasher?" *What* was written in the said book? Commentators, ignorant of Oriental usages, concur in the notion that those passages which *precede* the book cited, were contained in the said book. Such opinion is fallacious, because, as Orientalists know, it is the universal custom of Semitic writers to quote the authorities they introduce *before*

(118) HUMBOLDT: *Cosmos;* transl. *Otté;* New York, 1851; iii. p. 17.
(119) DE WETTE: i. p. 411.
(120) *Deuteron.* xxxiv. 5–12. N.B. The *dates* are from the margin of our English Bible.
(121) DE WETTE: ii. pp. 186–191; and p. 228, for *Samuel.*

the extracts or citations they make from the latter's works; so that, what *follows* the words "Book of Jasher" must be the quotation from that book.

The literary criticism of age, manner, and authorship, being briefly defined, we glance next at the topography; observing, that any proposed verifications of the latitude and longitude of *Gibeon* and *Ajalon* by tourists in modern Palestine are mere "traveller's tales:" for *Gabâ*-ON, "occultation of the sun," and *Aial*-ON, (122) "dawning of the sun," refer respectively, the former to the *West*, the latter to the *East*, as points of the compass. Now, suppose two towns, one on either side of a valley, opposite to each other; the one, *Gabâ*-ON, on the western summit; the other, *Aial*-ON, on the eastern; while a battle was raging between Israelites and Ammonites in the valley between and beneath. Suppose, again, by anticipation of the text (and you have as much right to suppositions, in this case, as the *forty-seven* collectively), that the twenty-four hours during which this fight went on occurred at an *equinox;* and that it so happened, by a singular juncture of the solar and lunar motions, that, at six o'clock P. M. precisely, the sun *set* in the West at the same apparent moment that a full moon *rose* in the East; you would have light for twenty-four hours in the valley; or twelve hours of sunlight through the day, and twelve hours of moonlight through the night. Such combinations are so natural, although rare, that if any tourist were to furnish an astronomer with the exact latitude and longitude of such a *valley* in Palestine, the latter could calculate the precise *day* when such celestial combinations occurred, and thus fix the *era* alluded to in the "Book of Joshua." Finally, in the Hebrew, these two lines are rhythmical, besides containing a play upon the words GBăUN and AILUN, by poetic license:—

> "To the eyes of Israel, O Sun! in the *hills* [B-GBăUN] even hide thyself:
> But thou, O Moon! be most resplendent in the [B-ăMKAILUN] *valley*."

We conclude with the lesson of that sage from whom both text and commentary are derived. (123)

"In precisely that day that IeHOuaH [the document is *Jehovistic*] delivered up the Amorean in face of the children of Israel, Joshua spake to IeHOuaH and said: TO THE EYES OF ISRAEL, O SUN! IN THE HILLS EVEN HIDE THYSELF: BUT THOU, O MOON! BE MOST RESPLENDENT IN THE VALLEY. And the sun set, and the moon endured until the multitude glutted (their) vengeance upon their enemies:—And is it not written in the book [entitled] *the Just?* [here follows the quotation] 'The sun which, running *along the meridional partition of the heavens* [*i. e.* along the equinoctial line], goes down [sets], was not as precise [true, exact], as by day, intent upon new-birth?' For certainly there was not before, nor after, a day equal to that in which, IeHOuaH having listened to the voice of man, IeHOuaH (himself) fought for Israel."

It may be prudent to observe that a passage in *Isaiah*, and another in *Ecclesiastes*, properly translated, lend no support to the supernaturalist commentary. That of *Habakkuk* (iii. 11) has no relation to the event; as, with "one longing, lingering look" at king James's *translation*, we prove by the subjoined rendering:—"Sun and moon set at their season: by the light of thy arrows they shall march, by the splendor of the lightning of thy lance." (Referring probably to a *night* attack.)

Thus vanishes "JOSHUA'S miracle!" The late Rev. Moses Stuart, than whom as a Hebraist, and upright champion of theology, none superior have yet appeared in these United States, supplies this definition of a "miracle"—"I have it before me, in a letter from one of the first philologists and antiquarians that Germany has produced. It is this: 'The laws of nature are merely developments of the Godhead. God cannot contradict, or be inconsistent with himself. But inasmuch as a miracle is a contradiction of the laws of nature, or at least an inconsistency with them, *therefore a miracle is impossible.*'" (124)

Reader! We have submitted *seriatim* to your judgment a positive example of the errors of our truly-vulgar version for every letter of the English alphabet. We have kept no

---

(122) Like *Beth*-ON—"House of the Sun"; or ON, the *Sun*, Hebrew name for *Heliopolis*.

(123) LANCI: *Paralipomeni;* ii. pp. 381–390. It is of no use to consult CAHEN on these passages, except for the *text* (points deducted); vi. pp. 38, 39.

(124) *Crit Hist. and Defence*, &c.; Andover; 1845; p. 19.

account of digressional instances of other blunders, made by the *forty-seven* translators 250 years ago; although these are numerous, they are thrown in to make weight. The whole are taken, almost promiscuously, from our biblical portfolio, referred to years gone by.(125) You may now begin to think that we may be serious, when we affirm that our theological armory contains *hundreds* more, to prove that king James's translators were not "inspired;" and that, whatever may be the fact as regards the "original tongues," the English version cannot be accepted by science as a *criterion* in matters concerning anthropology.

The ladder of time has been ascended to the year 1600, when our "authorized version" was not; but when many English translations, some in MSS., others in print, required but an act of Parliament to make them orthodox. With the former, chiefly *Saxon* versions, from Alfred the Great down to John Wycliff, our inquiries do not meddle; none of them having been seen by us: nor, indeed, do we take intense interest in the latter, save to remember how William Tyndal, "homo doctus, pius, et bonus," for *printing* the earliest English translation of the New Testament, in 1526, and of parts of the Old, was rewarded by strangulation and cineration in the year 1536. Copies of his work, together with that of Myles Coverdale, 1535, have been before us for examination; and it is a singular fact that, in the majority of cases, where king James's translators departed from the version of Tyndal, or more particularly from that of Coverdale, they commenced floundering in the mire; and that where they have appropriated the readings of either, it has been done without acknowledgment. Fuller, the Church historian of those times, says of Tyndal that "his skille in Hebrew was not considerable: yea, generally, learning in languages was then in y[e] infancie thereof"—and we have shown (*ubi supra*) that *Hebrew* scholarship was all but unknown in England until the generation of Walton; that is, half a century later than the emission of king James's standard version.

The period of English history embraced within the sixteenth century is distinguished on the one hand by the successive intellectual upheavals of the educated classes, each surge towering higher and higher; and on the other by the mind-compressing enactments of the "Lords Spiritual and Temporal" in the repeated erection of barriers that gradually sunk lower and lower. Tyndal's body was burnt; that of Grafton, (126) guilty of printing "Matthew's Bible," was incarcerated; the Inquisition at Paris merely confiscated 2500 copies of the edition afterwards known as "Cranmer's;" in 1546, an act of Parliament only forbade the possession and reading of either "Tyndal's" or "Coverdale's." The reaction now began to feel its weakness, the progressives their strength: and so long as the sacerdotal caste could keep before the popular mind a parliamentary idea that Tyndal's version was "crafty, false, and untrue," its sages, satisfied that resistance had begun to endanger the "Establishment," as it is still called, were preparing to give way. Unhappy Tyndal, as the first Englishman to trample upon theological impediments through *publication*, has ever remained the "bête noire" of High Church orthodoxy; nor, owing to the obfuscations of history by ecclesiastical writers, has his memory yet received from posterity the justice that it merits.

About 1542, an act permitting certain persons to possess the "Word of God," as we term it now, "*not being of Tyndal's translation*," was graciously issued. It provides—

"That no manner of person or persons after the first day of October, the next ensuing, should take upon him or them to read openly to others in any church or open assembly, within any of the king's dominions, the Bible or any part of the Scripture in English, unless he was so appointed thereunto by the king, or any ordinarie, on pain of suffering a month's imprisonment. Provided, that the Chancellor of England, captaines of the warres, the king's justices, the recorders of any city, borough, or town, the speaker of parliament, &c., which heretofore had been accustomed to declare or teach any good, virtuous, or godly exhortations in anie assemblies, may use any part of the Bible or holie Scriptures as they have been wont; and that every nobleman and gentleman, being a householder, may read,

(125) Nott: *Bibl. and Phys. Hist.;* 1849; p. 135.

(126) See Hunt, *History of Journalism*, 1850, for the legal barbarities then perpetrated upon Printers generally—*mutilations, hangings, drawings and quarterings, gibbets,* and *fagots!*

or cause to be read by any of his familie servants in his house, orchards, or garden, and to his own familie, anie text of the Bible or New Testament, and also every merchant-man, being a householder, and any other persons other than *women*, prentises, &c., might read to themselves privately the Bible. But no woman [except *noble-women* and *gentle-women*, who might read to themselves alone, and not to others, any texts of the Bible], nor artificers, prentises, journeymen, serving-men of the degrees of yomen or under, husband-men, or laborers, were to read the Bible or New Testament in Englishe to himself, or any other, privately or openly, upon paine of one month's imprisonment."

Three hundred years have effaced even the remembrance of such legislative prohibitions. The "general reader" of our day never dreams that "my Bible" was once forbidden to his plebeian use. He claps his hands at Missionary Meetings when it is triumphantly announced that myriads of *translations* of the Scriptures are yearly diffused among the Muslims, the Pagans, and other "heathen," printed in more languages than are spoken, in more alphabets than there are readers. Has it never struck him to inquire, when the clamor of gratulation has subsided, whether these myrionymed versions are correct? If they are, what is commonly the case, mere servile paraphrases of king James's *English* translation, as we have proven the latter's woeful corruptions (*ubi supra*), must not the mistranslations of that text be perpetuated and increased by transfer into another tongue? and if so, is not that one of the providential reasons why the spiritual effect of these versions among the "heathen" falls below that material one produced by drops of rain on the Atlantic? Or, if the Missionary translators of the Scriptures into *Feejee*, *Kamtchadale*, or *Patagonian*, possess (what is so rare, as to be a pleasant proverb) sufficient Hebraical erudition to translate into the above, or any other tongue, direct from the *Text*, do not these excellent men "ipso facto" confirm all we have asserted in regard to our "authorized" version, by leaving its interpretations aside?

There are (although few Anglo-saxons know it) human dialects, orally extant, wherein there is no name for "God," no appellative for "Heaven," because such ideas never entered the brain of those low "Types of Mankind" for which a *Missionary* version has been manufactured. The highly-cultivated Chinese remained impenetrable to the disputes, sustained by the learned Jesuits and the evangelical Dominicans with the quintessence of "odium theologicum," on the following heads: —

"1st., if, by the words *Thian*, and *Chang-ti*, the Chinese understand but the material sky, or if they understand the Lord of Heaven? — 2d., if the ceremonies made by the Chinese in honor of their ancestors or of their national philosopher *Khoung-tseu*, are religious observances or civil and political practices?" (127)

Unable to settle the first problem by reference to Chinese lexicons, those Catholic Missionaries submitted it to the decision of the Emperor Khang-hi; and the solution of the second dilemma was referred to the Pope!

Regarding this "Foreign Missionary" discussion from the same point of view, as here in the United States we should look upon a dispute between Chinese Bonzes as to what *we* mean by "Providence," or in what light *we* celebrate the "Anniversary of Washington"; and feeling the same sort of astonishment that would fill ourselves were we told, that by one Chinaman the first doubt had been submitted to His Excellency the President, and that the settlement of the latter had been left by the other Chinaman to His Holiness the *Dalai-Lama* of Thibet: — the wise and jocular Emperor wrote in autograph beneath the Pope's *Constitution*; —

"This species of decree concerns none but vile Europeans: how can it decide anything upon the grand doctrine of the *Chinese*, of whom these people in Europe do not understand even the language?"

And then enforced his jest by banishing both Jesuits and Dominicans, about 1721, to Macao Protestant successors in the Celestial Empire are still perplexed with the same linguistic obstacle; for about 1844, it was proposed to invent a *new* name for Deity, (that is, neither

(127) PAUTHIER: *Chine*; pp. 446—448.

Chinese nor English,) and compromise the matter by writing YAH; (128) while the papers have since held out hopes that the scruples of converted neophytes in China are about to be overcome by adopting "*Shin.*"

On the African coast the *Sooahelee* dialect, so restricted in its barbarous jargon that all its vocables implying civilization are borrowed from the *Arabic*, (129) a Missionary, who *translates* the "First three Chapters of Genesis" into the native tongue, can find no more euphonious rendering of our word "God" than MOOIGNIAZIMOONGO. (130) And, in America, no idea of "Original Sin" can be conveyed to an *Ottomi*-Indian, without the agglutination of monosyllables into TLACATZINTILIZTLATLACOLLI; nor will the last *Delaware's* heart experience "Repentance" until his mind has perceived the meaning of SCHIWELENDAMOWITCHEWAGAN. (131) But, we apologize for the digression.

During the second half of the sixteenth century, the frail hedge planted around the popular accessibility of the Scriptures vanished beneath the spades of the accumulating delvers for knowledge. At the Convocation of Hampton Court, in 1603, those measures were adopted that have placed the *Bible* before the people. Far, far, be it from us to undervalue the "Great Fact"—still farther to contest its vast educational utility. Would that *all* the "Sacred Books" of the East were equally accessible and equally read! The canonical literature of the Hebrews would be elevated infinitely beyond its present scientific estimation by such free comparisons; but not so its *English* "authorized" translation, and that is the only point for which these paragraphs contend.

In the years 1603–11, then, our Forty-seven Translators had before their eyes *many* English translations of the Old Testament. They possessed, furthermore, the *Latin* Vulgates, first printed in 1462, and revised in the *Sextine* edition of 1590, and the *Clementine* in 1592: together with numerous editions of the *Greek* Septuagint, both printed and manuscript. Their critical apparatus was copious enough wherewith to study the Original *Hebrew* Text, which lay before them in a variety of editions, more or less accurate, printed between the years 1488 and 1661; besides Jewish *Manuscripts*. If to their unquestioned knowledge of Latin and Greek, had been added a little Hebrew of the genuine school, which might very easily have been imported from the Continent, their version would have been better; but the confession of ignorance to themselves was as irksome, as to their race and country anti-national. They completed their labors without the contemporary aids within call; and "His Majesty's Special Command" has consecrated them for two hundred and forty-two years. "Undoubtedly, the present version is sufficient to all purposes of *piety*"; (132) our part is to show that it has long ceased to be adequate to the requirements of science.

It seems, therefore, considering the facilities they enjoyed, and still more the many they disdained, that errors so tremendous as those which modern criticism exposes should have been backed by orthodoxy with praises less extravagant; because, their *Hebraical* qualifications for the task being *nil*, the multiplicity of foreign versions, without that discriminating criterion, could but augment the multiplicities of their mistakes. (133)

The earlier English versions, if here and there superior to readings adopted by the Forty-Seven, were radically defective, owing to the same natural causes that precluded the possibility of making a direct translation from the Hebrew in 1611; viz.; small acquaintance with the vocabulary and grammar of the language itself. Fuller, for instance, infers that poor Tyndal rendered the Old Testament from the Latin, "as his friends allowed that he had no skille in Hebrew"; and the same authority explains that the reason why king James

(128) Dr. Bowring: in London *Literary Gazette.*

(129) Gliddon: *Otia;* p. 126.

(130) Rev. Dr. Krapf: *Jour. Amer. Oriental Soc.;* iii.; Boston 1847; pp. 261–274.

(131) Gallatin: *Trans. Amer. Ethnological Soc.;* New York, 1845; i. pp. 28–35.

(132) Taylor: in both the English and American editions of *Calmet's Dictionary*; voce "Bible."

(133) After this was written, a friend asked us to read "*The Translators Revived; a Biographical Memoir of the Authors of the English Version*"; by A. W. McClure; 12mo; New York, 1853. It merits nothing here beyond this mention, but a *review* in any newspaper is much at its author's service.

appointed Fifty-Four Translators was because "many and great faults" were already notorious amid the earlier translations.

The *Samaritan* text was unavailable to them for two reasons; one, that no copy had reached Europe until 1623, or twelve years later than the publication of king James's version; (134) the other, that those whose Hebraical accomplishments were so slender could have elicited nothing from any cognate Oriental idiom. It is superfluous, therefore, to speculate upon what philological feats our Forty-Seven might have performed through Samaritan contexts.

As the oldest of all "printed" books, A. D. 1462, the Latin *Vulgate* must have riveted the attention of men whose reverence for the invention induced them to carry the antiquity of moveable types back to the age of Job (xix. 23; *ubi supra*). With the numerous Latin versions, (135) made prior to St. Jerome, from the Greek, our translators did not trouble themselves; nor need we, because this first of Hebraists among the Fathers declares— "For the most part, among the Latins, there are as many different Bibles as copies of the Bible; for every man has added or subtracted, according to his own caprice, as he saw fit."

To remedy this evil, Jerome completed a retranslation of the Old Testament, directly from the Hebrew, between the years 385 and 405. (136) His contemporaries loudly protested against such profanity, lest it should sacrilegiously disturb that bibliolatry with which Christian communities then regarded the *Septuagint*; but, about 605, Pope Gregory invested it with respectability, by adopting its lections along with the old *Italic* version. The consequence was that the monastic scribes, having equal authority for either, began to correct the first by the second indiscriminately; and succeeded in fusing them both so inextricably into one, that the emendations of Alcuin in the ninth, of Lanfranc in the eleventh, and of Nicolaus in the twelfth centuries, failed to establish any uniformity among *manuscripts* which, in the words of Roger Bacon, "every reader alters to suit his own whim." Such was the state of the *Latin* version current until the sixteenth century, when Stephens undertook to castigate its errors in his printed editions: Clarius, in the meantime, submitting a schedule of 80,000 mistakes for the edification of the Council of Trent. However, on the unlettered side, fanciful substitutions; on that of scholarship, ruthless expurgations; impelled Sixtus V. to volunteer the office of "proof-reader:" and, in 1589, a copy of the Vulgate issued from the Vatican, wherein "eaque res quo magis incorrupte perficeretur, *nostra* nos *ipsi manu* correximus:" *i. e.*, the Vicar of God corrected the press himself. Alas! Such condescension only made the innumerable faults of that edition "notorious as ludicrous. Bellarmine luckily hit upon a plan to correct the errors, and save the infallibility of the Pontiff." New recensions were executed, "quod vix incredibile videbatur," in *nineteen days*; and the year 1592, during the apostolic vicarage of Clement VIII., brought out a standard Papal copy, wherein the odium of all errors patent in the former Pope's edition was charged upon the "printer's devil."

This Romanist *finality* abounds with misinterpretations if collated with the Hebrew Text; and when placed before the Forty-Seven, some ten years after its appearance, could only have served to lead them more astray; even if the fear of Papistry did not prevent adoption of such of its readings as attracted rather their fancy than their septi-quadrigentesimal criticisms. Consequently, the *Divine Afflatus* did not penetrate into king James's version through the *Vulgate;* which fact renders nugatory, as regards the Latin language, any inference derivable from their Preface in favor of the peculiar sanctity of this among the "Original Sacred Tongues" whence "one more exact translation" was by them made. Perhaps some streams of the apostolic imponderable reached our translators by transmission through the *Greek?*

At least three, and probably more, *printed* editions of the Greek *Septuagint* (137) were procurable by our Translators in the year 1603; independently of such *manuscripts* as they may have consulted; from the number of which last must be deducted the Codex-*Alexan-*

(134) KENNICOTT; *Dissert. Gen.;* p. 475.

(135) DE WETTE: i. pp. 183–191.

(136) *Ibid.;* i. p. 257, *seq.*

(137) DE WETTE: i. pp. 81–82.

drinus, (138) now in the British Museum; because it did not arrive in England until the year 1628. (139) The *printed* editions issued during the sixteenth century were naturally copies resulting from the collation of such *manuscripts* as to their respective editors were more or less accessible; and if the originals were defective the transcriptions must be still more so. We can utter no opinions on the critical value of the printed editions, before ascertaining what scholarship may have decided upon the archæological merits of the *manuscripts* themselves; nor is it in our power to enumerate what copies of the latter may or may not have been consulted by our translators; chiefly because our own note-books do not afford the *dates* at which many celebrated Greek MSS. were known throughout Europe. (140) We presume they used copies of the Codex-*Vaticanus* (printed in 1587, by Cardinal Caraffa), of which the antiquity is estimated by Kennicott at A. D. 387, while others suppose "a few years later;" (141) among them Montfaucon and Blanchini, who refer it to the fifth century. None of other Greek Codices extant can possibly antedate, in any case, the fourth century; for even the oldest, the Codex-*Cottonianus*, once conjectured to have been Origen's property, is now proved to have been calligraphed towards the end of the fourth or the commencement of the fifth century. Its fragments lie in the British Museum. (142) This falls within the lifetime of St. Jerome, A. D. 331–422; (143) who laments that, in his day, "the common (Greek) edition is different in different places, all the world over;" and reiterates, "It is corrupted everywhere to meet the views of the place and time, or the caprice of the transcribers." (144)

> "Thus it seems that, in the time of Jerome, *three* different editions of the LXX were in use under the sanction of the several churches, and with their authority, viz.: Origen's Hexapla in Palestine, the text of Hesychius in Egypt, and that of Lucian in Constantinople and its vicinity. No wonder the existing *manuscripts* have come down to us with so many corruptions." (145)

Such asseverations, when once recognized to be true in fact, suffice to damage the accredited uniformity of the *Greek* versions; but a little further inquiry will evince that it was impossible, through the very nature of human things, that any Hellenic translation from the Hebrew could be "inspired."

If, then, only four centuries after the Christian era, the Greek translation (finished about the year 130 B. C., at Alexandria) no longer existed in its "editio princeps," but its later recensions alone had flowed down to St. Jerome's time in three turgid streams, each one essentially *corrupt*, it follows that all MSS. now extant, no less than all *printed* editions made from such MSS., must be still more blemished, owing to later mistakes, than even the best exemplar known to St. Jerome. It is in this vitiated state that the *Septuagint* reached our translators in the year 1603: —

> "No one of these recensions is found pure; for they have flowed together, and become mixed also with the other Greek versions. . . . The criticism of the Seventy has hitherto advanced no farther — and perhaps it never can — than to a collection of the various readings. The editions hitherto published do not afford the true and exact text of the manuscripts." (146)

But, not merely does the *Greek* version falter in its historical traditions. Its deviations from the *Hebrew* original render objections to its plenary authenticity unanswerable.

"As a whole, this version is chargeable with want of literalness, and also with an arbi-

---

(138) WOIDE thinks its age to lie towards the end of the fourth; but if KENNICOTT selects A. D. 395, he reports other opinions as low as the ninth century (Ist *Dissert.*, pp. 306, 307).

(139) TAYLOR'S *Calmet;* voce "Bible."

(140) PORTER (*Principles of Textual Criticism*, Dublin, 1848) might supply deficiencies; but memory is treacherous, and we have not now his most excellent work: *vide Otia*, pp. 111–113.

(141) KENNICOTT: IId *Dissertation;* p. 407.

(142) HORNE: *Introd.;* i. pp. 105–107.

(143) ANTHON: *Class. Dict.;* voce "Hieronymus"; p. 625.

(144) DE WETTE: i. p. 181.

(145) *Ibid.;* p. 180.

(146) DE WETTE; i. pp. 181–183.

trary method, whereby something foreign to the text is brought in. In general, it betrays the want of an accurate acquaintance with the Hebrew language, though it furnishes many good explanations. (147)

"The character of this version is different, according to the different books. It is easy to distinguish five or six different translators. . . . Indeed, the real value of the Septuagint, as a version, stands in no sort of relation to its reputation. All the translators engaged in it appear to have been wanting in a proper knowledge of the two languages, and in a due attention to grammar, etymology and orthography. Hence they often confound proper names, and appellations, kindred verbs, similar words and letters, &c., and this in cases where we are not at liberty to conjecture various readings. The whole version is rather free than literal," &c. . . . The *Text* of the Septuagint has suffered greatly. Through the multitude of copies, which the very general usage rendered necessary, and by means of ignorant critics, the text of this version, in the third century, had fallen into the most lamentable state." (148)

"Although we cannot say from whom it (the LXX) emanated, it is certain that it is the work of one or several Jews of Egypt, of Greek education (if always our version called *the Seventy* be exactly the same as the one that was made at that epoch); because one may discover in it traces of that philosophy which afterwards developed itself among the Alexandrian Jews, and of which PHILO is for us the principal representative. It does not appertain to us to characterize here the translation under its philological aspect; we must content ourselves with establishing that, in many places, it differs sensibly from our Hebrew text, and that very often its variants agree better with the text of the Samaritans. Nevertheless, the latter does not sufficiently conform to the version of the Seventy, that one could imagine a common source for both compilations." (149)

It results from Talmudic exegesis that its authors, beyond vague impressions of errors contained in the Greek version, not only did not know, save through hearsay, the *Septuagint* themselves (although they suppose its Translators to have been seventy-two), but that it was impossible for the Palestinic Jewish Rabbis to read it, owing to their ignorance of the Greek tongue.(150) Not a word in the *Mishna* and the two *Guemeras* refers to Aristobulus, or Philo, or to the Apochryphal books; neither to the *Essenes*, nor to the *Therapeutæ*. The Jews of Palestine were separate people from those of Alexandria; and it was a concern exclusively interesting to the latter to defend the many false renderings of the Septuagint, of which remarkable examples are exhibited in the learned treatise of Franck, whence we condense some facts into a foot-note.(151) But hear Sharpe:—

"It will be enough to quote two passages from this (LXX) translation, to show how the Alexandrian Jews, by a refinement of criticism, often found more meaning in their Scriptures than ever entered the minds of the writers. Thus when the Psalmist, speaking of the power of Jehovah, says with a truly Eastern figure (*Psalms* civ. 4, *Text*), '*He maketh the winds his messengers, and the lightning his servants*,' (152) these translators change the

---

(147) *Ibid.*; p. 147.

(148) TAYLOR'S *Calmet*; voce "Versions."

(149) MUNK: *Palestine*; p. 487. Cf. also, AMPÈRE: *Recherches en Égypte*, &c., 2de part.; Rev. des D. Mondes, 1846.

(150) FRANCK: *La Kabbale:* Paris, 1843; pp. 273, 329.

(151) "Already the Thalmud had a vague knowledge (*Thalm. Babyl. Tract. Meguillah*; fol. 9, ch. i.) of the numerous infidelities of this antique translation [viz., of the LXX]. . . . Thus, when the sacred Text says positively (*Exod.* xxiv. 9, 10) that Moses, his brother, and the seventy elders, saw the God of Israel upon a throne of sapphire; according to the (Greek) translation, it is not God who was seen, but *the place which he inhabits.* When another prophet, Isaiah, sees the Lord seated on his throne and filling the temple with the folds of his robe (*Isaiah*, vi. 1), this too-material image is replaced by the *glory of God*. . . . When it concerns Adam and Eve, (the Greek interpreter) would carefully avoid saying, with the Text, that God created them male and female (*Gen.* i. 27); but this double character, these two halves of humanity, are united in *one and the same being*—"Ἄρσεν καὶ θῆλυ ἐποίησεν αὐτὸν. . . . . 'Who has created all things?' asks the Hebrew prophet (*Isaiah* lx. 26); 'Who has rendered them *invisible?*' says the Alexandrian interpreter" (FRANCK: *La Kabbale*; Paris, 1843; pp. 329–331). Our author furnishes several other examples of downright perversions committed by those Alexandrines called "the LXX": of which our space denies insertion. After our own conclusions were formed, it was most gratifying to find them all confirmed by RUBENSOHN ("Origin and Structure of the Septuagint"—*Christian Examiner*; Boston, March, 1853; pp. 165–187), who truthfully observes—"Such a version—if it should be thus designated—is not only conformable to the spirit of those times, but there are many indications that the Greek version was originally intended only as an auxiliary book for the use of the Alexandrian Jews."

(152) So also CAHEN, xiii. p. 229, and *note* 4—"des flammes brûlantes, ses ministres." St. PAUL too, although said to have been "a Hebrew of the Hebrews," follows the *Septuagint* in quoting this passage (*Epist. to the Hebrews*; i. 7) even to *Jews!* (SHARPE'S *New Test.*; p. 395)—a passage non-existent in the *Hebrew* Text.

sentence into a philosophical description of the spiritual nature of angelic beings, and say (in the Greek), '*He maketh his angels into spirits, and his servants into a flame of fire.*' Again, when the Hebrew text, in opposition to the polytheism with which the Jews were surrounded, says (Text, *Deut.* vi. 4), '*The Lord is our God, the Lord alone*' [literally, 'Hear, O Israel! IeHOuaH, our God, IeHOuaH (is) *one!*']; the translators turn it to contradict the Egyptian doctrine of a plurality of persons in the unity of the Godhead, (153) by which the priests said that their numerous divinities only made one God; and in the Alexandrian Greek this text says, '*The Lord our God is one Lord.*'" (154)

Should the reader now turn to the above passages in our "authorized" version, he will perceive that the *forty-seven* have rendered into English the exact words of the *Greek;* and thus he will behold a little of the damning evidence produceable that these worthies could not construe a simple line of the Hebrew Text; but have palmed off upon us, as genuine "inspiration," language that, being Alexandrian forgeries, cannot be Divine; confessions of creed that, not being in the original Hebrew, cannot be "inspired."

Here, as concerns king James's translation in its relations to the *Greek* versions, we might bring our inquiries to a close: the seal of condemnation has been so legibly stamped upon it. But, inasmuch as some data respecting the origin of these Grecian documents may be useful to our researches into the Hebrew Text, it is desirable to reach that epoch when the *Septuagint* had not yet been manufactured.

Ascending from St. Jerome in the IVth century to the great Origen in the IId, we find him complaining of the corruptions manifest in the Greek MSS. of his day — "But now there is obviously a great diversity of the copies, which has arisen either from the negligence of some transcribers, or the boldness of others—or from others still, who added or took away, as they saw fit, in making their corrections." (155)

"From the time of the birth of Christ to that of Origen," continues Eichhorn, "the Text of the Alexandrian version was lamentably disfigured by arbitrary alterations, interpolations, omissions, and mistakes. Justin Martyr had a very corrupt Text, at least in the minor Prophets." (156) He was decapitated in A. D. 164, having been converted about the year 132; thus sealing his convictions with his blood.

The works of Origen's predecessors in the first century, Flavius Josephus, born A. D. 37, and of Philo Judæus, who flourished about A. D. 40, exhibit through their citations, (both being Hellenized Jews writing in Greek rather for Grecian and Roman readers than for their own countrymen,) that some alterations had already been made in the copies of the Septuagint respectively used by them: at the same time that the writers of the New Testament, by quoting the *Greek* version, in lieu of the Hebrew, have invested the former with a traditionary sanctity, fabulous when claimed for extracts from the Old Testament not cited directly from the Hebrew Text. (157). Its discussion would lead us astray from the inquiry as to when and by whom the Original *Greek* translations were made; and the fact is noted merely to establish the existence of the latter, in what state of literal preservation no man can tell, at the Christian era.

"All we can determine with certainty is, — that the whole, or the greater part of the Old Testament, was extant in the Greek language in the time of Jesus the son of Sirach. [Sirach presupposes that 'the Law and the Prophets, and the rest of the books,' were already extant in his time; that is, in the 38th year, which is probably the 38th year of Evergetes II., about 130 B. C.]" (158)

This year before Christ 130 is recognized, nowadays, by all biblical scholars, to be the *minimum* epoch at which Greek versions of certain books of the Old Testament canon were already in circulation at Alexandria. Tradition, itself, claims no date for the existence of

---

(153) Compare BURNAP: *Expository Lectures;* Boston, 1845; p. 9; — and CHENEVIÈRE: *Système Théologique de la Trinité;* Geneva, 1831; *passim.*

(154) SHARPE: *Hist. of Egypt;* 1846; p. 196.

(155) DE WETTE: i. p. 165.

(156) DE WETTE: i. p. 166.

(157) STRAUSS: *Vie de Jesus;* and HENNELL: *Origin,* &c.; enlarge upon these themes.

(158) DE WETTE: p. 146; — also, STUART; *Crit. Hist. and Defence;* pp. 241, 423.

same circumstances earlier, as the *maximum*, than the reign of Ptolemy Philadelphus; and about 260 years B. C. suffice for a chronological stand-point that reconciles scientific probabilities. The medium suits well with the dispersion of some Hebrew exemplars after the saccage of the temple by Antiochus, B. C. 164; and is parallel with the literary restorations of the *Maccabees*.

To read (as we ourselves formerly did with confidence) the works of some leading English Divines in quest of information about the *Septuagint*, and the chronology erected upon its numerations, one would actually suppose, from the positive manner in which statements are put forward, that they had studied the subject! Hales, (159) for instance, assures us that *Seventy*, or Seventy-two, elders of the Jewish congregation, after the reception by the king of a copy of *Law* from Jerusalem *written in letters of gold*, sat down at Alexandria, and did the Hebrew into Greek in 72 days, "d'una sola tirata"; with many episodes equally romantic. Half a century has elapsed since any Continental critic of biblical literature who ventured to give further currency to such wretched stories would have been jeered into silence and overwhelmed with literary obloquy. The reader is referred to De Wette for facts and authorities, (160) and to Bunsen (161) for endorsement of the following sketch; after remarking that wherever the number "70," or its cabalistic equivalent "72," occurs in Jewish connections, it carries with it more cogent evidences of historical untruth than even the *forties*, or "Erbaïnàt," so common in Hebraical literature. (162)

The origin of the *Greek* version, stripped of verbiage and exaggerated traditions, was the natural consequence of the great influx of Jews — a people ever partial to the fleshpots of Egypt — into Alexandria, immediately upon the foundation of that city by Alexander the Great, about B. C. 332. Enjoying privileges under the early Ptolemies, the number of Jewish colonists constantly augmented: at the same time that incipient intercourse with their Greek fellow-citizens superinduced first the disuse and next the oblivion of that *Syro-Chaldee* idiom the Israelites had brought back with them, from Babylonish bondage, in lieu of the Old Hebrew orally forgotten; and led their Alexandrine descendants to adopt the *Greek* tongue, together with much of Grecian usages and Philosophy. They became *Hellenizing*-Jews (163) at Alexandria, without ceasing to be Hebrews in lineage or religion; just as their present descendants are *Germanizing*, *Italianizing*, or *Americanizing* Israelites, according to the country of their birthplace or adoption.

The conquests of the Macedonian are to us the most salient causes of the transmutations that took place throughout the Levant owing to the wide-spread of Grecian influences; but Pythagoras, Plato, and Herodotus, are earlier prominent expressions of Greek infiltration into Babylonia and Egypt during the fifth and sixth centuries B. C., which was far more exten-

(159) *Analysis of Chronology.*

(160) *Op. cit.*; i. pp. 136–144.

(161) *Egypt's Place in Universal Hist.*; 1848; i. pp. 184, 185.

(162) LEPSIUS: *Chronologie der Ægypter*; 1849; i. p. 365. We find the subjoined to the purpose among "Talmudical statements: — In *Megilla*, ix. *a*, we read the following account: 'Ptolemy the king called seventy-two old and wise men to Alexandria, and confined each in a separate room, without telling them the reason of their being called. He afterwards visited each of them, and directed them to write down in Greek the words of Moses. God inspired them with a sameness of ideas, so that their translations literally agreed.' In *Sophrim*, § 1, we read another passage: 'Five sages were called to Alexandria by the king Ptolemy, to translate the law into the Greek language; this day was as oppressive to Israel as the one when the golden calf was made, for they were unable to do justice to the subject. Then the king assembled seventy-two sages, and set them in seventy-two cells,' &c. .... In *Taanith* occurs the following passage, which also DE ROSSI quotes (*Imrai Binah*, § 7): 'There are certain days on which we fast on account of the law: such a day is the eighth day of Thebeth, because on that day the law was translated into the Greek under the second Ptolemy, king of Egypt, and darkness covered the earth for three days.'" — ("*Greek Versions of the Bible* — the passages extracted from LANDAU'S *Vorwort zum Aruch*" — *The Asmonean*; New York, 5 Aug. 1853.) Little historical criticism is required to perceive that the writers of these Talmudic legends, several centuries after Josephus, had merely given another shape to the same baseless tradition of the false Aristeas: and we may class JUSTIN MARTYR'S evidence (*Admonitione ad Græcos*) that "he *saw* the 72 cells into which the translators were locked up"; and EPIPHANIUS'S (*De mensuris et ponderibus*) that these cells were 36, each for two translators; — with St. AUGUSTINE'S, where he says "*Vidimus* — we have seen" men with an eye in the pit of their stomachs.

(163) According to Philo, the Jews exceeded a million at Alexandria alone (RAPAPORT'S *Erech Milin*; quoted in *The Asmonean*; New York, July 20, 1853).

sive commercially than until recently accredited; while Greek *condottieri* had been employed in Egypt from the seventh century by Psametticus: nor was Xenophon the first General, nor Ctesias the first Doctor, who volunteered their services to the Achæmenidæ of Persia. Into Jerusalem itself, Greek ideas had penetrated very soon after the erection of the Second Temple in the fifth century. These result from the history, and are stamped upon the *proper names* of the Jews of Palestine, particularly after Alexander's era. Nor were such Hellenic infiltrations without a certain influence upon the canonical literature of Judaism; for the "political satire" (164) entitled the "*Book* of DANIEL" betrays, through its *Greek* words, as much as by its exegetical adaptations, an author of the age of Antiochus Epiphanes, not earlier than the plunder of Jerusalem by that king about 164 years B. C. Continental scholarship long ago placed this fact beyond dispute; (165) and the Hebraical erudition of the late Rev. Moses Stuart (166) induced him to fortify it with his customary skilfulness.

So much nonsense still passes currently, in regard to the various dialects spoken by the Jews after their return from the Captivity, that we must here digress for a moment. Independently of books read and others cited, we have sought for information on these subjects from some of the most cultivated Hebrew citizens of the United States, and have invariably met with the kindest readiness to enlighten us. We possess not (merely because we omitted to ask for it) the sanction, of the many very learned Israelites consulted, to publish their honored names; but not on that account are the hints with which all have favored us the less appreciated by ourselves nor the less useful to readers. No interdict being laid by one of the writer's valued friends, Mr. J. C. Levy of Savannah, upon the many indices to knowledge for which his goodness has rendered us his debtor, we condense the substance of two recent communications; coupled with regrets that certain inexorable limits of typographical space should compress what ought to be in "Brevier" into "Nonpareil." (167)

(164) New York *Daily Tribune;* Feb. 10, 1853. The attribution to "Discoveries" at Babylon is fabulous. For that of the *Decalogue*, conf. GLIDDON, *Otia*, 1849; p. 19: — extended in New York *Sun*, "Historical Sketches of Egypt," Nos. 6, 7; Jan. 19 and 25, 1850.

(165) MUNK: *Palestine;* p. 420; — DE WETTE: ii. pp. 483–512; — CAHEN: *Notes on Daniel.*

(166) *Hints on the Interpretation of Prophecy;* Andover, 1842; pp. 71–108.

(167) EXTRACT 1.—"The information I promised barely is, that the Babylonian Captivity lasted from 538—486 B. C., when Zerubabel, with 50,000 men, went to Palestine with the permission of Cyrus. A second colony followed in the year 458, led by Ezra, under the reign of Artaxerxes Longimanus. He was, again, followed by Nehemiah, 444. During the Captivity, by good treatment, they adopted Babylonian customs and manners, and amalgamated with their conquerors (*Ezra* v.; *Nehemiah* xiii. 1–3), and forgot their native Hebrew. Besides this, the Samaritans speaking an Aramaic (Chaldaic) dialect, as well as the Syrians who ruled for a long time in Palestine, exercised great influence over the Jews; so that the Hebrew soon disappeared as the vernacular (*Nehemiah* xiii. 24) to yield to the Chaldaic, and the mother-tongue probably was the language of their real mothers. This may be best proved by the fact, that all civil acts, official documents, and legal formulas, were written in that language, and that the Talmud itself is written, to a great extent, in this tongue. Furthermore, numerous proverbs originating at this time, and popular books of that age, are all in the same language. The chief prayers of the Jewish Service, composed by Ezra, are in the Chaldaic language. Already at the consecration of the Temple on the 1st of the 9th month and in the 24 days of its duration, it was found necessary to accompany the reading of the Law with translations and *explanations* (*Nehemiah* viii. 8, 12); the latter being the beginnings and foundation of the Talmud, or traditional oral law, which was first prohibited to be written down, in order to preserve life and motion for the letter of holy writ. That this prohibition was afterwards transgressed much to the injury of the development of Judaism, and caused all schisms among the Jews, is well known. Had these explanations, which are mostly contradictory of each other, not been collected and made a code of, all strife might have been avoided.

"*Written Chaldaic translations* were in existence in the time of the Maccabees — the first known is that of ONKELOS, disciple of R. Gamaliel (53 after X), and fellow-student of the Apostle Paul. This translation is paraphrastical, especially in the prophetic and poetical parts of the Bible. More explanatory is that of JONATHAN-BEN-NGOOZIEL. A third translation is the *Targum Jerushalme* (Jerusalem translation), fragmentary, and exhibiting a commentary in accordance with the reigning ideas of the age. Macedonian and Egyptian rule in Palestine produced among the Jews Grecian manners, customs, and *ideas*, also language; so that translations of the Bible were soon necessary. The oldest mentioned is that of AKILAS, often referred to in ancient writings, to explain Chaldaic parts of the Bible; there you have the Greek translation of the LXX. Philo, Josephus, and other Jewish authors wrote in Greek, proving their ignorance of Hebrew by the blunders in translation and explanation of the Text. Greek technical terms are even to be found abundantly in the Talmud."

EXTRACT 2. — "I am not satisfied with the meagre reference given you regarding the ignorance of the Jews

Returning to the LXX.—Some precursory events had prepared Jewish Alexandrian immigrants for the adoption "nolens volens" of the Greek tongue and alphabet, consequent upon the oblivion of the Aramæan dialect which their progenitors had re-imported into Palestine. The children were growing up in ignorance of a "Law" their Alexandrian parents could no longer read in *Hebrew*. To have paraphrased that "Law" into *Syro-Chaldee*, like their brethren in Palestine and Babylonia, would at Alexandria have been useless; because the parents had forgotten Syro-Chaldee, and the children already talked *Greek*, by the reign of Ptolemy Philadelphus, B. C. 284–45. What more in unison with the instinctive characteristics of that "Type of Mankind" which, beyond all others (from the days of Abraham), changes its *language* with most facility, while it repels admixture of alien blood and tenaciously adheres to its own religion, than that one of its branches, the Alexandrian Hebrews, should cause the sacred writings of their forefathers to be translated into Greek? This was precisely that which they did, although the exact year of the commencement of such translations can no longer be fixed; but the style and idioms of the several books, to which, after collection into one canon, the name of *Septuagint* was subsequently given, indicate different times and divers hands. (168)

While confined to Judaism in Alexandria, this Greek translation was reputed orthodox by the Hellenizing Rabbis as much as the Hebrew Scriptures themselves; and more authoritative, because they could read no other. It was read in the Synagogues of that city, and wherever Jewish congregations were planted under similar Grecian circumstances; but a Greek version was of no use, and therefore of little value, to the Jews of Palestine, Syria, and Persia; who understood not the Greek tongue, but spoke *Chaldaic* "patois." The Greeks themselves, regarding all languages but their own as barbarous, Hebrew inclusive, never troubled their heads about the *Septuagint* until after apostolic missions had propagated the *New Testament*, composed in Greek by Hellenized Jews also; when the recurrence of quotations from the Old Testament, in the evangelical books, instigated its readers to reference to that Code; and as these Christianized readers were ignorant of Oriental idioms, of course the *Septuagint* version was the only one accessible to them: while, to give it an air of antiquity and of royal respectability of origin, both Græcized Jews and Judaizing Christians coincided in attributing its authorship to "70" translators, appointed (like our *forty-seven* English translators by king James) under the hand and seal of Philadelphus; whose encouragement of literature was testified by munificent donations (cost to himself, nothing) to the Alexandrian Library. A pseudo-Aristeas "reported" a fable so flattering to Alexandrine pride, to Jewish respectabilities, and to Christian orthodoxy; while the real tradition seems to have reached us in an account that the authors of the *Septuagint* were but "*five*:" (169) and so, veneration for the *Septuagint* increased from day to day in the ratio that time rolled onward, and that the remembrance of its natural origin faded from the "memory of the oldest inhabitant" of Alexandria; nor would the harmless legend have been disturbed, had not proselyting furor on the part of new converts to Christianity led them to provoke rabbinical susceptibility by appeals to the *Greek* version of the Old Testament in support of novel doctrines promulgated in the *New:* the two texts

---

everywhere of Hebrew after the Captivity.... I offer you what your opponents cannot object to—that is, the XIIIth Chapter of NEHEMIAH (the chronology of the book you know better then I do). Jewish or Christian chronology make it about 450 before X. This chapter will show you, that the Dragoman [Arabicè *Turgemán*, "Interpreter"] was necessary in reading the Book of the Law. Gibbon (vi. vol. chap. 50, p. 262) quotes, in a note, Walton (*Prolegomena ad Bibl. polyglot.*, pp. 34, 93, 97; also, Simon, *Hist. Critique du V. et du N. Testament*), to illustrate that the Bible was translated into Arabic at a much earlier period than the time he is treating of (about 550 after X); and he proves the fact 'from the perpetual practice of the Synagogue of expounding the Hebrew Lesson by a paraphrase of the vulgar tongue of the country.'... I think these very respectable authorities, if you need them." Mr. Levy's views are amply supported by GESENIUS (*Geschichte der Heb. Sprache*, &c.; p. 198).

(168) DE WETTE: i. p. 145;—TAYLOR's *Calmet;* voce "Versions."

(169) *Ibid.*; p. 150—*note* from the *Talmud*, Tract Sopherim, ch. i.—"The work of the *five* elders, who wrote the Law in Greek, in the time of King Ptolemy": unless they meant the *Pentateuch*, attributing one book to each elder? Conferre, also, the high Jewish authority of RAPAPORT, in "*Erech Milin*"—New York *Asmonean*; July 29, 1853.

having been made singularly harmonious; owing to scrupulous care on the part of the apostles to cite each passage according to its *Greek* coloring in the Septuagint; for a long time held in common to be canonical as well by Jews as by Greeks.

Bewildered for a time by these dexterous sophisms, and mystified through literary ambuscades which it required a Grecian intellect to comprehend, the worthy old Rabbis (taken in reverse) had no resource but to proscribe the *Septuagint*, and ostracize its readers. "The law in Greek! Darkness! *Three days fast!*" (170) Because, says the *Talmud*, "on that day, in the time of King Ptolemy, the Law was written in Greek, and darkness came upon the earth for three days." (171) Little by little, however, their perceptive faculties expanded to the true posture of affairs; and by proving incontinently that many things, which looked one way in the *Greek*, looked quite another in the Hebrew, the Rabbis soon defeated their assailants; routing them so repeatedly, that gradually the latter thought it safer to let such doughty controversialists alone: a method of repulsion continued with never-failing success by Israel's wide-spread posterity even now; who, when summoned by anxious "Missionaries for the Conversion of the Jews" to adopt a Trinitarian faith which Semitic monotheism (172) despises, have merely to show such well-meaning persons that king James's version does really copy the *Septuagint* rather than the Hebrew, to see these itinerant simplicities pocket their English Bibles and slink off. Some day, perhaps, when the rules of archæology through popular diffusion have augmented, all over Anglo-Saxondom, that mental element termed "common sense," sundry excellent persons, in the language of Letronne, "sentiront, je pense, l'inutilité, la vanité de leurs efforts." (173)

The above conclusions on the *Septuagint*, long known to scholars, if not previously expressed in print with the same "brutale franchise" habitual to writers who believe they speak the truth (so far as ratiocination can deduce logical results from known premises,—*humanum est errare*), have enfeebled its value—except for purposes of archæological restorations of the Hebrew text—to such degree that, in this discussion, the ablest theologians have advanced into the *positivist's* stage of philosophy. No scientific exegetist of the present generation—save for purposes aforesaid—perils his Continental reputation on the letter of any Greek version, unless *chronological* computations be the objects of his research. Another Essay (III.) of this book gives parallel tables wherein the *Septuagint* system is compared with others; but, to evince the numerical discrepancies between Text and versions, it suffices here to note, that, from the creation of Adam to the "Deluge," computations (based upon the Hebrew original, as now extant) generally yield 1656; upon the Samaritan Pentateuch, 1307; and upon the *Septuagint*, 2242 years.

The indefatigable labors of a profound Hellenist and Egyptological scholar, enable us to sweep away any *chronological* superstitions, yet in fashionable vogue, built upon the Septuagint:—

"The chief disagreement between the [Hebrew] original and the [Greek] translation is in the chronology, which the translators very improperly undertook to correct, in order to make it better agree with Egyptian history and the more advanced state of Alexandrian science. They only made the Exodus of Moses 40 years more modern; but they shortened

---

(170) Bunsen: *Op. cit.*; p. 185.

(171) De Wette: *Note*, p. 150; — Hennell: *Origin of Christianity*; pp. 454, 455, note.

(172) "Bear witness! God is *one*. He is the God eternal. He never has begotten, and was never begot" (*Kur'ân*; *Sura* cxii).

(173) *Recueil des Inscriptions*; Paris, 1843; Introd., i. p. xliii. We clip the following from the London *Inquirer*, 1853: "*The Cost of Converting a Jew.*—After some twenty years of labor — after the erection of a church on Mount Zion, at an enormous cost — after the expenditure of hundreds of thousands of pounds, the 'London Society for promoting Christianity among the Jews' (a mission presided over by a bishop and endowed by the joint efforts of the kingdoms of Prussia and England) produces as its fruits, according to its own statistics, a congregation of just *thirty seven* Jewish converts. During the whole of last year, the result of its labors was the conversion of *one* Jew. The cost of this one convert was the annual outlay at Jerusalem alone, besides the bishop's stipend, of £1228 expended on the mission, £445 on the church, £1173 on the hospital, and £400 (we beg pardon, £399 19*s*. 11*d*.; see *Report*, p. 111) on the house of industry. The Jerusalem Mission, then, if we add to its cost the £1200 per annum paid to Bishop Gobat, arising from the endowment, has actually, in the past year, baptized converts at the moderate rate of only £4443 7*s*. 2*d*. per head."

the residence of the Jews in Egypt by 275 years, allowing to it only the more probable space of 155 years. But having thus made the great Jewish epoch, the migration of Abraham out of Chaldæa, 315 years more modern, they thought it equally necessary to make such a large addition to the age of the world as the history of science and civilization, and the state of Egypt at the time of Abraham, seemed to call for. Accordingly, they added to the genealogies of the patriarchs neither more nor less than a whole Egyptian cycle [*Sothic-period*] (174) of 1460 years; or 580 between Adam and Noah, and 880 between Noah and Abraham, though in so doing they carelessly made Methuselah *outlive the Flood.* (175)

This plain matter-of-fact solution of the reasons why the *Septuagint* chronology differs from that of the Hebrew — between Adam and the *Deluge* — upon popular computations only 586 years! — relieves us from the bootless trouble of attaching any importance to opinions current at Alexandria among those successors of the *Founder* of chronology; who, with the original copies of MANETHO (176) before them, paid homage to his accuracy in their endeavors to assimilate their own foreign estimates of time to his.

Archæological rules also permit two deductions to be drawn from these premises:—

1st. That the differences of numerical results among early Christian and Judaical computators of the *Septuagint* proceed less from wilful perversions of numbers (as heretofore attributed to Josephus and others), than from radical discrepancies then existing between the *manuscript* consulted by one computator, and those exemplars whose numeration was followed by his compeers. This becomes obvious by comparing the eras severally reached by modern computations upon manuscript and printed copies now extant.

	Creation B. C.	Deluge B. C.
HALES's *Septuagint* computation—edition to us unknown—	5586	3246
Alexandrinus MS.	5508	——
Vaticanus MS.	5270	——
JOSEPHUS, on some lost MS.—probably	5555	3146

2d. That already in the time of Josephus, during the first century after Christ, the manuscript he followed must have differed in numeration from the parental *exemplars* of those transcriptions that, under the modern names of various codices, *Cottonianus, Alexandrinus, Vaticanus, Bezæ,* &c. (none earlier than A. D. 500), have reached our day; and *ergo* there must have been many corruptions and variants among *Septuagint* MSS., about and prior to the Christian era.

Hence we conclude, that it is as vain a task for computators, now-a-days, to recover more than a vague approximation of chronological notions (deducible from the *Septuagint*) current at Alexandria before the Christian era, as, after the foregoing analysis of the natural origin, history, and manifold corruptions of Greek codices, it would be to insist upon Divine authenticity for king James's version; on the plea that, in the majority of cases, its forty-seven translators rendered from the *Greek* of editions, or manuscripts, so rotten in basis as those of the *Septuagint.*

We proceed to the *Hebrew Text;* with the remark that, although we now know that it could have had little to do with the formation of our "authorized version," we shall examine it under the hypothesis (customarily put forward) that it had a great deal.

In the year 1603, at the time when king James authorized a new English translation, there were numerous printed editions of the *Hebrew Text* familiar to biblical scholars. That of Soncino, 1488, the first printed; of Brescia, 1494, used by Luther for his translation; Bomberg's, 1518–45; Stephens's, 1544–46; Munster's, 1546; are the most prominent of the number. Whether the translators consulted any, or what, Hebrew *manuscripts,* does not appear from works within our present reach. We have shown how trivial was their acquaintance with the language of the editions, and may be persuaded that they did not

(174) CHAMPOLLION-FIGEAC: *Egypte Ancienne;* 1840; pp. 236–240; — GLIDDON: *Chapters on Early Egyptian History;* 1843; pp. 50, 51, 52, 61; — LEPSIUS: *Chronologie;* 1849; i. pp. 165–180.

(175) SHARPE: *Op. cit.;* p. 196.

(176) BUNSEN: *Op. cit.;* pp. 50–96.

greatly distress themselves about the latter; for, a century and a half elapsed before Kennicott proclaimed how — "the Hebrew Bible was *printed* from the *latest*, and consequently the *worst* manuscripts;" (177) thus corroborating his previous acknowledgment — "that the Sacred Books have not descended to us, for so many ages, *without some mistakes and errors of transcribers.*" (178) He enlarges upon the certainty of corruptions in the *printed* Hebrew Text, powerfully refuting those who claim textual unity; and then passes on to establish the absurdity of attributing perfection, either, to the *manuscripts.* (179)

Of all men down to his epoch, 1780, Kennicott had the best right to speak decisively; his conclusions being drawn from the collation of no less than 692 *manuscripts* of the Hebrew text; whereof about 250 were collated by himself personally, and the remainder by Mr. Bruns, under his direction. Of the most ancient relics, but *two* were assigned by him to the tenth century after Christ; to the eleventh or twelfth centuries, only *three;* while all the rest ranged between the years 1200 and 1500 A. D. (180) The bulk of his work, its costliness and comparative rarity, combine with its Latin idiom to render it inaccessible to ordinary readers, save at second-hand. But few of the facts established by this great and upright scholar are popularly known; or they have been misrepresented, more or less, by some of the ecclesiastical mediums (181) through which they have reached the public eye. Cardinal Wiseman, (182) for example, would lead his readers to infer, that the innumerable variants and corruptions of the Hebrew Text, verified by Kennicott, were of small importance; and even the Rev. Moses Stuart (183) slurs lightly over those depreciatory results which it will be archæology's duty presently to enumerate, in saying: —

"Indeed, one may travel through the immense desert (so I can hardly help naming it) of Kennicott and De Rossi, and (if I may venture to speak in homely phrase) not find game enough to be worth the hunting." So again, "Have they (the Jews) added to, or diminished from, their Scriptures during all this period of 1800 years? Not the least. . . . *Their* Bible has remained inviolate."

Now, to continue the sagacious Professor's simile, the quantity of game to be found in a given wilderness frequently depends upon the keenness of the huntsman; its quality upon his individual tastes; some sportsmen being partial to *tomtits,* whilst others sigh that nothing fiercer than *grizzly-bears* encounters their ferine combativeness. And, with respect to the "inviolate" state of the Text, Kennicott shall speak for himself, after we have opened a volume of De Rossi.

G. Bernardo de Rossi, of Parma, was that august Italian critic who resumed investigation into the actual condition of the Hebrew Text at the point where his English predecessor had left off; recasting also (wherever the same MSS. could be reached by him) the work of the illustrious Oxonian. Written in Italian, and intended solely for the lettered, his books are not very familiar to the general reader. A quotation or two, therefore, may place matters in their proper light:

"Here it suffices to observe, that the totality of *manuscripts collated* is 1418, of editions 374; that to the English 577, and 16 Samaritan, I have added 825; of which my cabinet alone furnished 691, and 333 editions; besides the ancient versions, the commentaries, the works of criticism and other sources that are also themselves in the greatest number." (184)

In another work he states: — "Of the manuscript codices most ancient of the sacred Text" . . . the *oldest,* that of Vienna, dates in A. D. 1019; the next is Reuchlin's, of Carlsruhe; its age being A. D. 1038. There is nothing in manuscript of the Hebrew Old Testa-

(177) *State of the printed Hebrew Text;* 2d Dissert.; Oxford, 1709; p. 470.

(178) *Ibid.;* 1st Dissert.; 1753; Introd.

(179) *Ibid.;* pp. 234, 263.

(180) *Dissertatio Generalis in Vetus Testamentum Hebraicum;* Oxford, 1780; in folio; pp. 110–113.

(181) "By 'ecclesiastical persons' are understood such as are indeed subjects, yet their office and works is [*sic!*] in matters of Religion; they act *between* GOD *and man,* as messengers, and mediators between them. They deliver GOD'S *mind* to men; and offer men's prayers and *gifts* to GOD"; says the Rev. GEORGE LAWSON, *Protestant* Rector of More (*Politica Sacra et Civilis;* London, 1660; p. 230).

(182) *Connection between Science and Revealed Religion;* 1844; ii. pp. 168, 169.

(183) *Crit. Hist. and Defence of the O. T. Canon;* Andover, 1845; pp. 193, 239.

(184) *Compendio di Critica Sacra;* Parma, 1811; ii. p. 37.

ment now extant of an earlier date than the eleventh century after Christ. (185) And, "of the most ancient manuscripts of the Greek Text of the *New* Testament," . . . the *oldest* are the Alexandrian and Vatican, which may ascend to the fourth, but cannot be much later than the fifth century after Christ.

Considering such circumstances, our credulity is not strained by accepting what De Rossi asserts, as rather more authoritative than the fiats of some "teologini" we might name; for he, at least, had advanced by studious discipline to the *positive* stage of philosophy. These are his Italian views rendered into English:—under the head of "Premure degli Ebrei per loro Testo:"—

"It is known [?] with what carefulness Esdras, the most excellent critic they have had, had reformed [the Text] and corrected it, and restored it to its primary splendor. Of the many revisions undertaken after him none are more celebrated than that of the *Massoretes*, who came after the sixth century [ANNIS D.]; who, in order that the Text should not in after time become altered, and that it might be preserved in its integrity, numbered all the verses, the words, the letters of each book, together with their form and place. But their fatigues being well analyzed, one perceives that they had more in aim to fix the state of their Text, than to correct it; that, of infinite interesting and grave variants they do not speak: and that, ordinarily, they do not occupy themselves but with minutiæ of orthography of little or no weight: and all the most zealous adorers and defenders of the Massora, Christians and Jews, while rendering justice to the worthiest intentions and to the enormous fatigues of its first authors, ingenuously accord and confess that it [the Massoretic Text], such as it exists, is *deficient, imperfect, interpolated, full of errors;* . . . a most unsafe guide." (186)

Why, "the single Bible of *Soncino* [earliest printed Text] furnishes more than *twelve thousand* (variants)!" Which said, our authority continues through above eleven 8vo pages to deplore and make manifest "the *horrible state of the Text*," resulting from his own comparisons of 1418 Hebrew manuscripts, and 374 printed editions. Such being the truth, published a quarter-century before the Rev. Dr. Hales's "Analysis of Chronology," (187) the reader can qualify the following attestation of an ecclesiastic by what epithet he pleases:—

"It is not more certain that there are a *sun* and *moon* in the heavens, than it is, that not a single error of the press, or of a *Jewish* transcriber, has crept into the present copies of the *Masorete* Hebrew Text, to give the least interruption to its chronological series of years."

And yet, so devoid of consistency is this theologer, that he designates the *Hebrew* chronology as "spurious," and actually follows that of the *Septuagint!*

From the loud denunciations of one of the most learned Church-of-England Protestant divines, and the sterner sorrow of an Italian Catholic cenobite, turn we to the wild despair of the Hebrew Rabbis:—"Peruit consilium! Computruit sapientia nostra! Oblivioni traditæ sunt leges nostræ! Multæ etiam *corruptelæ*, et *errores*, ceciderunt in Legem nostram sanctam!" (188)

But Kennicott substantiates that the disorderly condition of the Hebrew Text, and its multitudinous vitiations, resile from the works, or are lamented in the language, of all claimants to biblical knowledge for 1700 years previously to the Rabbis and himslf; equivalent to 1730 prior to De Rossi. Here is a skeleton of his list, omitting citations:—"Justin Martyr, died A. D. 165—Tertullian, 220—Clemens Romanus, 102—Origen, 254—Eusebius Cæsarienensis, 340—Eusebius Emisenus, flourished 350—Ephraim Syrus, died 378—Hieronymus, 420." We pause to illustrate.

1st. King James's version.—PAUL, *Galatians*, iii. 13:—"for it is written, Cursed *is* every one that hangeth on a tree." [The English of the Greek passage in *Griesbach's text* is, apud Sharpe, "(for it is written; *cursed is every one that is hanged on a tree;*)"].

(185) *Introduzione alla Sacra Scrittura;* Parma, 1817; pp. 34, 47.

(186) *Compendio;* ch. iv. p. 7; and pp. 9-22. DE ROSSI furthermore proves these positions in his "Specimen Variarum Lectionum Sacri Textus"; Rome, 1782.

(187) *Analysis;* 2d edit.; 1830; i. p. 277.

(188) *Hebrew edition* of 1751; the preface, cited in *Dissert. Generalis;* p. 27.

2d. This is a quotation by the Apostle from *Deuteronomy* xxi. 23; which, in king James's version stands—"(for he that is hanged *is* accursed of God;)" [The French of Cahen reads—"car un pendu est une malédiction de Dieu" (v. pp. 93, 94); which conforms better to the context, and resembles current superstitious aversion to *gibbets*.]

Apart from illiteral citation, the New Testament, in this passage, leaves out the word ELoHIM, 'God.' Theologists who combat for "plenary inspiration" can doubtless answer the following interrogatories. If those words be Paul's (always provided for), did he quote from memory? then his recollection was faulty. If he copied the LXX, then, in his day, the Greek already differed from the Hebrew; and who can tell which of the two transcripts preserved the original reading?

The catalogue continues with—"Epiphanius, 403—Augustine, 430"—but we abridge twenty-two folio pages of extracts from later Christian writers, who protest to the same effect, into a line; epitomizing the series by one name—Ludovicus Capellus, founder of sacred criticism in 1650.

All the subjoined commentators vouch for inaccuracies in the Text: viz.—"Raymond de Pennaforti, 1250—Nic. Lyranus, 1320—Rudolphus Armachanus, 1359—Tostatus, 1450—Jacob Perez de Valentia, 1450—Marsilius Ficinus, 1450—Baptista Mantuanus, 1516—Zuinglius, 1528—Martin Luther, 1546—Bibliander, 1564," &c. The same corruptions are certified through the decrees of the *Council of Trent*, 1546; through the *Vulgate of Sixtus V.*, 1590; and through king James's version, 1604–1611: on which the Oxonian critic remarks (p. 50, § 108):—"To the AUTHORS of the *English version* that which is due: many examples prove that they did not always mind what they found in the Hebrew, but what they thought ought to be read therein: tantamount to that, in their opinion, the Hebrew Text was corrupt. This the reader evolves from twenty places:—*Gen.* xxv. 8: xxxv. 29: *Ex.* xx. 10: *Deut.* v. 14; xxvii. 26; xxxii. 43: *Jos.* xxii. 34: *Jud.* vii. 18—vid. com. 20—1 *Sam.* ii. 23: 2 *Sam.* iii. 7; v. 8; xxi. 19; xxiii. 8: 2 *Kings* xxv. 3: 1 *Chron.* vii. 6; ix. 41; xxiv. 23: *Ps.* xxxiv. 17; lxx. 1: *Isa.* xxviii. 12: *Ezech.* xxvi. 23."

After citing "Jos. Scaliger; the Buxtorfs, father and son, defenders of the purity of the text; Capellus; Glassius; Joseph Mede; Usher, Morinus, Beveridge, Walton, Hammond, Bochart, Hottinger, Huet, Pococke, Jablonski, Clericus, Opitius, Vetringa, Michaelis, Wolfius, Carpzovius, Joseph Hallet, Francis Hare"—Kennicott concludes (§ 132):—

> "Id autem a me maximè propositum fuit, ut ostenderem—produci posse testimonia multa et insignia, per intervallum fere 2000 annorum, ad probandas *mutationes* in Hebraicum Textum *invectas:* quanquam in contrariam sententiam, annis abhinc triginta, docti fere omnes abierint." (189)

One would have thought (to return to Prof. Stuart's metaphor), that this "immense desert" contained "game enough," in all conscience! but, in some men, the love of chase is insatiable. "Defence," as he justly observes, "would seem to be needed. The contest has become one *pro aris et focis*"—"truly become one, as I have said, *pro aris et focis*." (190)

> "It has become plain," frankly declares this lamented Hebraist, "that the battle which has been going on over most European ground these forty or fifty years past, has at last come even to us [alluding to the exegetical works of his learned and reverend New England colleagues, Noyes, Palfrey, Norton, Parker, &c.], and we can no longer decline the contest. Unbelief in the Voltaire and the Thomas Paine style we have coped with, and in a measure gained the victory. But now it comes in the shape of philosophy, literature, criticism, philology, knowledge of antiquity, and the like.[!] Hume's arguments against miracles have been *exhumed*, clothed with a new and splendid costume, and commended to the world by many among the most learned men in Europe. Before them, all revelation falls alike, both Old Testament and New." (191)

And, considering who these "most learned men" veritably are, it is not for us to question the uprightness of his outspoken recognition, that—

(189) *Dissertatio Generalis;* 1780; pp. 7, 8, 33–43, 55, *seq.*
(190) *Op. cit.;* pp. 3, 422.
(191) *Op. cit.;* p. 420.

"The unbelief that consistently sets aside the whole, shows a *more manly and energetic attitude of mind;* and, in my opinion, it is much more likely to be convinced at last of error, than he is who thinks that he is already a believer and is safe, while he virtually rejects from the Gospel all which makes a Gospel, in distinction from the teachings of Socrates, of Plato, of Plutarch, of Cicero, and of Seneca." (192)

We have quoted the highest contemporary authority of the Calvinist school; and impartiality requires that a member of the "Chiesa Cattolica Apostolica Romana" should make up for the mild notice taken of Kennicott's and De Rossi's researches by His Eminence the Cardinal.

If the man of science mourns, with as much fervor as the most devout, over the irrecoverable loss of Hebrew *manuscripts* of the Bible—of those precious documents that would have linked the *Bodleian codex* (about 800 years old, said to be the most ancient) (193) with the transcripts of Ezra's copy; and filled up the frightful chasm that now divides, in Hebrew palæography, the tenth century after Christ from the fifth century before his advent — to whose acts is he indebted, and by whom are his sorrows caused? Lacour shall answer:—

"At the commencement of the thirteenth century, it was expressly forbidden to the laity to possess the books of the Old and New Testament. The Church permitted only the Psalter, the Breviary, or the Hours of the Sainted Mary: and these books were required not to be translated into the vulgar tongue. Decrees of Bishops interdicted the use of grammar." (194) Other sources confirm this assertion.

Gregory the Great, A. D. 590, censured Didier, Archbishop of Vienna, for suffering grammar to be taught in his diocese; "boasting that he (himself) scorned to conform his latinity to grammatical rules, lest thereby he should resemble the *heathen.*" (195) In the ninth century, Alfred the Great laments that there was not a priest in England who really understood Latin, and, for ages after, English Bishops were termed "marksmen," because they could not sign their names otherwise than by a *cross!*

"In 1490, the Inquisition caused the Hebrew Bibles to be burned, that is to say, the work in default of the author; in the absence of Moses, his *Pentateuch.*" At Salamanca, the fiendish Dominican, Torquemada, reduced some 6000 Hebrew volumes to ashes; and besides such as were ravished from libraries in Spain and Italy, about 12,000 Talmudic rolls perished, *circa* A. D. 1559, in Inquisitorial flames at Cremona. (196) These unnameable deeds were induced by orthodox doubts that, the Hebrew Text, as represented in the *square-letter* copies, was ever quoted by the Apostles; (196) but, in those ages of darkness, little respect could have been paid to MSS. even of the *New* Testament; for such ancient copies as had been preserved, down to A. D. 1749, at Alcala in Spain, were sold to one Toryo, a pyrotechnist, as materials for sky-rockets. (197) Quintillian (*Inst. Orat.* i. 1), in the first century after Christ, complains that writing was neglected; but it was not until after the barbarian irruptions of the eighth century that "la crasse ignorance" prevailed in Western Europe. It is uncertain if even Charlemagne could write. The tenth to twelfth centuries exhibit Bishops, Abbots, Clerks, &c., incredibly ignorant: as even in earlier times, before the seventh century, at the Episcopal Conference of Carthage, the "brigandage" of Ephesus, and the Council of Chalcedon—at which last there were *forty* most incapable Bishops (LABBE, *Concil,* iv). Few Romish monks could read, in the eleventh; the laity began about the end of the thirteenth; but in the fourteenth, the number was small. (198)

From these fearful destructions (the Inquisitorial agents having acted in obedience to orders sent from Rome), Lacour draws a singular argument in behalf of his own free restorations of the Hebrew Text, maintaining:—

---

(192) *Op. cit.;* p. 320.

(193) KENNICOTT: 2d *Dissert.;* p. 317 — "*Laud,* A, No. 162," in catalogue Bodleian Library.

(194) ÆLOÏM: Bordeaux, 1828; i. p. 28.

(195) MANDEVILLE, apud TAYLOR; p. 34; — also, RIGHELLINI: *Examen;* iii. p. 537; — and VICO: *Scienza Nuova,* trad. MICHELET; ii. p. 67; for other examples.

(196) LACOUR: p. 29; — and KENNICOTT: *Dissert. Gen.;* p. 16

(197) MARSH's *Michaelis;* ii. p. 44.*

(198) Condensed from an excellent article on Alphabets, in vol. ix. pp. 727-739, of the great "Encyclopédie Catholique"; Paris, 1846: conducted by the Abbé GLAIRE and M. WALSH.

"That the Hebrew Text of the Bible, tried and condemned by the Holy Tribunal, burned as an act of faith at Seville, and in the Square of St. Stephen at Salamanca, proscribed during the sixteenth century, prohibited in the pulpits of Catholic preachers, declared dangerous, infected with Judaism, and causing those Christians who read it to Judaize likewise, finds itself—owing to this solemn condemnation from which it cannot be purged save through the adoption of a *new translation*—finds itself, I repeat, does this Text, to have lost the character and authority that, in the spirit of Christianity, the Fathers [only Origen and Jerome] attributed to it. One may, therefore, after all, study this Text in a new point of view, purely philosophical and philologic; and seek in it a new interpretation, without being scared at the sense which such interpretation may produce. The anathema with which it has been stricken has abandoned it to criticism and to the investigations of the world; *tradidit disputatione:* its testimony is no longer anything but mere human testimony, liable to error like all things that proceed from man." (199)

Conceding his premises, and allowing for his peculiarly catholic point of view, the deduction is logical; but they who deny Papal infallibility may continue to reverence the Hebrew Text just as if excommunication had never been pronounced upon it; notwithstanding the avowal of those manifold corruptions which, owing to these Inquisitorial holocausts of ancient *manuscripts*, it seems now humanly impossible to expunge. To persecutions and to the expulsion of the Jews from Spain, after 1491, the extinction of the most precious Hebrew exemplars may be, in part, attributed; for Muslim intolerance had never knowingly laid the hand of sacrilege upon documents which Christian charity has for ever destroyed. (200) MOHAMMED had built up his *Kur'ân* upon the monotheistic foundations of MOSES; (201) and his faithful disciples have been always too consistent, whatever barbarities they may have inflicted upon the Jews, to injure that chosen people's sacred *books*, and thereby stultify themselves. With reference to textual corruptions, says Kennicott (202 :—

"Hæc denique sunt verba eruditissimi Professoris J. A. Starck—'cum negari prorsus nequeat (si quidem luminibus uti, et antiquos libros ab omnibus præjudicatis opinionibus liberi inter se conferre velimus) *multa et ingentia σφαλματα inisse sacris libris;* qualia sunt, gravissimi in chronologicis errores; in historicis manifestæ contradictiones; numerorum exaggerationes; literarum, nominarum, sententiarum, omissiones, additiones, transpositiones: quæstio jure orietur—Unde tot tamque graves immutationes originem suam habeant? Et si gravissimis argumentis, quibus solis permota ita sentio, fides habenda est; prorsus omni caret dubio, Judæorum imprimis fallaciam et malevolam mentem accusandam esse, post librariorum inertiam et negligentiam.'"

To avoid mistakes we have given the Latin text, and now offer its straightforward signification in English:—

"Since it cannot altogether be denied (if indeed we free ourselves from all prejudiced opinions, and wish to compare ancient books with each other and to avail ourselves of the instructions of the learned,) that *many and enormous σφαλματα* [*lapsi*, mistakes] *exist in the sacred books;* such as, most grave errors in chronological (matters); manifest contradictions in historical; exaggerations in numbers; omissions, additions, transpositions of letters, of names, of sentences:—the question will naturally arise, Whence have such and so many serious mutations their origin? And if faith is to be placed in most weighty arguments, by which alone I am influenced, every doubt is altogether wanting, (that) first one must accuse the fallacious and malevolent mind of the Jews, (and) afterwards the inertness and negligence of librarians."

Such are the published *facts*. Yet one marvels at the ways of theology; on seeing the Rev. Prof. Stuart skip nimbly over that "immense desert" with his "gun, man, and dog," (*Arma virumque cano*,) and the *dégagé* air of a juvenile Nimrod, without finding "*game* enough to be worth the hunting;" and then asserting with equal frivolity, that the Jewish "Bible has remained *inviolate*"! How can the unlettered distinguish truth from error, when their Teachers mystify the plainest results that scholarship the most exalted, honesty the most unbending, and science the most profound, have striven to make public to all men for the last hundred years?

---

(199) LACOUR: *Op. cit.;* i. p. 33.

(200) SISMONDI, not now before me, gives many other examples of literary destructions in Italy, Portugal, and Spain.

(201) Compare LANE: *Selections;* pp. 183-225, 270, 271.

(202) *Op. cit.;* p. 33; note to § 76.

Nevertheless, a time has come in which opinions, that ignorance had laid down as fundamental *principles*, begin to compromise those institutional structures beneath which they were placed. Enlightened manhood in a free Republic is fast approaching the hour when such opinions will be openly recognized as nothing more than *opinions of ignorance*. To attempt to impede reform, when it is necessary, is to jeopard the whole system. To refuse to repair foundations whose vetustity perils an edifice, is to desire that the downfall of such edifice shall prove that its foundations are rotten. "Creeds," says Sharpe, speaking of the decrees of the œcumenic Councils, "composed in the dark have now to be defended in the light, and those who profess them have the painful task of employing learning to justify ignorance." (203)

A point has been now attained in this exposition, when a brief recapitulation of the halts made during our journey will enable us to dismiss king James's version from further consideration. We opine that the foregoing pages have established, upon archæological principles and adequately for the demands of positive philosophy, —

1st — by *authority* of the highest Biblical critics;

2d — by *exegetical* exposure of some of its false-translations;

3d — by *historical* testimony, that all versions in English, (being mere popular accommodations of defective editions printed in the "Original Sacred tongues,") have only perpetuated or increased whatever errors their antecedent editions contain;

4th — that because the *Latin Vulgate*, printed or manuscript, abounds in mistakes;

5th — that because the *Greek Septuagint*, if ever a faithful representative of the Hebrew original, is so no longer, in any printed editions or manuscript copies now known; and that tradition, well authenticated, proves its vitiated state as far back as the first century of the Christian era;

6th — that because the only men, Protestant, Catholic, or Rabbinical, whose decisions (owing to their respectively minute collation of every printed edition or manuscript exemplar of the *Hebrew Text*) can be weighty in the premises, have pronounced the whole of them to be radically, enormously, and irretrievably *corrupt*; —

in view of all of the above facts, we have a right to conclude that, our English "authorized *Translation*," made 250 years ago under circumstances naturally adverse upon documents so faulty, can claim, in science, no higher respect than we should accord to a poor translation of mutilated copies of Homer; and finally, that those individuals who are most clamorous in its praises only bear witness that they possess the least acquaintance with its origin and history, however familiar they may be with its contents.

But, universal orthodoxy, regardless of the collective researches of three centuries, insists upon our credence that Moses *wrote the Pentateuch*; and still stigmatizes those who respectfully solicit some evidences of this alleged authorship (a little more conclusive than ecclesiastical tradition) with terms intended to be opprobrious; of which, perhaps, the most courteous form in vogue nowadays is "skeptic." (204) If by this harmless vocable nothing more is implied than that a "skeptic" has, by laborious study, attained to the positive stage of philosophy, while "orthodoxy" vegetates in a sub-metaphysical stratum, it should be cheerfully endured; if not with Christian fortitude, at least with gentlemanly equanimity.

The real question, however, posited in logical shape, is this: —

The Hebrew Moses wrote the Hebrew Pentateuch. Did the Hebrew Moses write the Hebrew Pentateuch? If the Hebrew Moses wrote the Hebrew Pentateuch, where is the Hebrew Pentateuch the Hebrew Moses wrote?

For ourselves, we do not perceive what essential difference it would make, in positive philosophy, supposing even that *he did*: but, inasmuch as we have embarked in an inquiry

(203) *History of Egypt*; p. 490.

(204) The Rev. Dr. Smythe of Charleston, S. C.: *Unity of the Human Races*; Index, p. 401.

for the purpose of ascertaining the importance which progressive Ethnology must assign to *one document;* and this document happens to be the Xth *Chapter* of a Book called "Genesis," (which some vehemently protest is *Mosaic,* while others as flatly contradict them,) it behooves us to test certain points of these disputed allegations by archæological criteria; and, authority against authority, the citation of a few may help us in making ready for the voyage.

"And yet no one, I believe, has the pretension to understand perfectly the sense of *Genesis;* no one denies that the text of this book contains many parables, or Oriental allegories, of which the most skilful and the wisest of the Fathers of the Church have sought in vain for the meaning. — But, thanks to the massoretic points and to the susceptibilities of orthodoxy, things have come at the present day to such a pass, that if Moses himself arose from the tomb to cause all uncertainty to cease; if he interpreted his own book literally; if he expounded it as he had conceived it and reflected upon it; Jerusalem, Rome, Constantinople, and Geneva, [Great Britain, Germany, France, and the United States,] would convoke their Doctors of Divinity from all corners of the world, to prove to him — that he knows nothing about the genius of the Hebrew tongue — that his translation is contrary to the grammar and dictionary of Mr. *This* or Mr. *That* — that he does not possess even common sense — that he is an impious (fellow) whose book they had done perfectly right [*Rome's orders,* XIII–XVIth centuries] to burn; and that it is wonderful how he had not been served so himself in the other world." (205)

Having now fulfilled my published pledges to the reader, so far as relates to the exhibition of a few atoms of the vicissitudes through which the *Xth Chapter of Genesis* has travelled to reach our day, I am obliged to bring this "Archæological Introduction" to an abrupt close at this point. The reasons are these: —

When my colleague Dr. Nott, at Mobile (in April, 1852), agreed with me to erect a literary cenotaph "*To the* MEMORY *of* MORTON," it was mutually arranged that, in our division of labor, he would undertake the anatomical and physical department, embracing those subjects that belong to the *Natural Sciences;* while the execution of the archæological and biblical portions was to devolve upon myself.

No two men have ever worked together in the same harness with more perfect harmony of object. In the midst of professional engagements, whose onerous character none but the most laborious of the medical faculty can adequately appreciate, Dr. Nott, at the sacrifice of every instant of repose, succeeded in accomplishing, not merely all that appertains to his part of our enterprise as set forth in Part I., but also the revision of my studies as exhibited in Part II.: each of us, notwithstanding, being wholly responsible for whatever naturally falls within the specialities severally assumed, but neither of us being fairly amenable for mistakes in other than our own departments as above classified.

On the other hand — independently of three months, December 1852 to March 1853, spent by myself in travelling; and aside from all supervisions of the press since the 25th of August — I devoted nearly twelve months of day and night to the performance of my "specialité" of our joint undertaking; some of the fruits of which have been already submitted to the reader's criticism.

Resolved, in my own mind, to pursue inquiries into biblical questions, once for all, *usque ad necem,* my manuscripts have, I think, completely answered the Aristotelian proposition above stated as concerns the *Pentateuch.* Nevertheless, I postpone their publication: —

1st. Because they do not directly concern *Ethnology,* and the main subjects of this work.

2d. Because the printers assure me that my "copy" could not be condensed, satisfactorily, within 300 more of these pages: thereby rendering it impossible to keep "Types of Mankind" within one volume.

Ample, however, and far more gratifying than a dry archæological disquisition can be to the general reader, are the compensations which displace my own performances: and it is with unfeigned pleasure that, in order to make room for the papers of our collaborators, I

---

(205) LACOUR: ÆLOÏM; i. p. 180.

mutilate my own essays in substituting theirs. Perhaps it is for the best; because the nature of this work may elicit some hostile comments; and he is the prudent soldier who "keeps his powder dry." In consequence, I suppress about 300 of these pages, after submitting an outline of the *Periods* of misfortune which the canonical Hebrew Text has, to a great measure, survived, down to CAHEN's *Bible*, A. D. 1831–1849.

Walton, Kennicott, and De Wette (to say nothing of other sources), the reader perceives are tolerably familiar to us. To extract from their works is merely mechanical; but the fear of tedium warns us to be eclectic. In these matters it is our private opinion that, if Titans were again to pile Ossa upon Pelion, after rolling upon "Ossa the leafy Olympus,"(206) they would fail to startle, far less convince, those who lie below the *metaphysical* stratum of intellectual development; for, "as Jannes and Jambres withstood Moses, so do these men withstand the truth."(207) It will be more interesting to the enlightened reader to view a brief historical schedule of the *changes* which eighteen centuries have entailed upon the Hebrew Text—condensed principally from Kennicott's results in his *Dissertatio Generalis*:—

1st PERIOD, B. C.—"In most ancient times, the Hebrew Text was corrupt;" and the codex (say, "fragmentary books") used by the Greek interpreters of the Old Testament, at Alexandria, was undoubtedly Hebrew, but a copy not sufficiently emended. Even Buxtorf is obliged to admit—"Judæos a tempore Esdræ negligentiores fuisse circa textum Hebræum, et non curiosos circa lectionem veram."

The numerals were expressed by *letters*: the five *final* letters (*kaf*, *mim*, *nun*, *pay*, and *tsàde*) had not then been invented: the words were still *undivided*.

2d PERIOD, A. D. down to 500.—The texts were more corrupt in the time of Philo and Josephus. Neither in their day, nor in that of Origen, third century, were the *Commandments* (*Exod.* xx. 3–17) divided into ten, in the manner they are now. In Philo the division is *quinary*, after the fashion of Pythagoreans. About the latter epoch commences the Talmudic *Mishna*; and, in the fifth century, the *Gemara*; each of which books proves the increase of textual errors. So do the writings of the Fathers during all this age—notably St. Jerome; while the apostolic books demonstrate that the *Greek* differed, more or less, from the Hebrew original.

3d PERIOD, A. D. 500 to 1000.—Aside from the later and less reliable Fathers, two Hebraical works establish, that no expurgations of error had been made in the Text: viz., the *Robboth*, after A. D. 700, and the *Pirke Eliezar*, after 800. About the sixth century, the Rabbis of Tiberias commenced the "Masora": a labor that would not have been undertaken but for the reasons above given, and the wretched condition of the Text in their time; as proved by the multitudes of *Keri velo Kethib* (the read, but not the written) or *Kethib velo Keri* (the written, but not the read). (208)

4th PERIOD, A. D. 1000 to 1450.—The Jewish schools of Babylonia seek refuge in Spain about 1040; between which era and 1240 flourished the four great Rabbis. Their works prove not merely different readings, but absolute mistakes in copies of the Text: things then existing in manuscripts of the Old Testament now exist no longer, and *vice versa*; while the "Masora," itself, already in confusion inextricable, only rendered matters worse. It is of this age alone that we possess those Hebrew manuscripts by us called *ancient*—not one 900 years old!

5th PERIOD, A. D. 1450 to 1750.—Printing invented; the art was first applied to *Psalms* in the year 1477; and to the whole Hebrew Text in 1488; that entire edition, save one-third of a copy, being immediately burnt by Neapolitan Jews. But here, upon editions now following each other with rapid succession, the Rabbis begin their restorations and their lamentations. Continental scholars now set to work upon *Hebrew* in earnest, without professorships: whilst, in England, king James's version is a splendid

(206) VIRGIL: *Georg.*; i. 281.

(207) 2 *Tim.* iii. 8—apud SHARPE.

(208) DE WETTE: i. pp. 345, 353–358.

record of Professors without Hebraism, during the years 1603–'11. Fifty years later, Walton redeems the shame of Oxford; and yet, one hundred years later still, Kennicott himself chronicles — "the reader will be *pleased* to observe, that as the study of the Hebrew language has only been *reviving* during the last one hundred years:" (209) to end which sentence logically, we ourselves consider that there could be no "revival" where, in 1600, there was scarcely a *beginning;* and, ergo, that the Doctor's attestation must refer to incipient efforts, in his century commencing, to resuscitate the *Hebrew tongue* after twenty centuries of burial.

6th and present PERIOD, A. D. 1750 to 1853.

Taking Eichhorn as the grand point of departure, we find, after the lapse of a century, how, through the operations of that "*rational* method" of which he and Richard Simon were, among Christians, the first qualified exponents, the Hebraical scholarship of our own generation (proud of its hundred champions) has truly kept pace, on the European continent, with the universal progress of knowledge.

Nevertheless, on every side, we still see and hear the crocodile whimper how "nobody undertakes a *new* translation (into English) of Holy Scripture" commensurate with the imperious demands of all the sciences at present advancing — news of the onward steps made by each being actually transmitted through magnetic telegraphs (210) — and yet, withal, few men in America so blind as not to perceive that, even in evangelized England, such pecuniary superfluities as those said to have been realized through a "WORLD'S *Exhibition,*" are expended (God alone knows how or why) upon anything, or everything, rather than in behalf of a conscientious *revisal* of our ENGLISH BIBLE.

G. R. G.

ESSAY II.

PALÆOGRAPHIC EXCURSUS ON THE ART OF WRITING.

THE same imperious necessity that has constrained us to suppress the continuation of Part III., Essay I. (*supra*, p. 626), renders it obligatory to curtail our History of the "*Art of Writing*, from the earliest antiquity to the present day." This subject, perhaps the most vital in any researches into the antiquity of the Hebrew *Pentateuch*, has never yet publicly received adequate attention from modern scholarship. With ourselves it has been a favorite pursuit ever since 1844; (211) nor, did space permit the insertion of what we had prepared in manuscript for the present volume, should we not have taken some pride in the presentation of a series of facts and arguments that would entirely justify every point set forth in the accompanying *Tableau* [*infra*, pp. 630, 631].

(209) 1st *Dissert.;* 1753; p. 307.

(210) Rev. JOHN BACHMAN, D. D.'s *Doctrine of the Unity of the Human Race;* Charleston, S. C., 1850; p. 288 — "And even telegraphing to America, through the convenient wires of Mr. Gliddon, the yet unpublished discoveries of Lepsius." These discoveries have since been published, and much JOHN BACHMAN knows about them! MORTON'S refutations, in the Charleston *Medical Journal*, 1850–'51, render it quite unnecessary for me to waste more ink upon the extinguished author of the above "Doctrine." — G. R. G.

(211) Vide GLIDDON, in LUKE BURKE'S *Ethnological Journal*, No. ix.; London, Feb. 1849; pp. 400–416: — republished in *Otia Ægyptiaca;* London, Madden, 1849; pp. 99–115: — and, without *text*, but with some improvement of the "Table," in *Hand-book to the Panorama of the Nile;* London, Madden, 1849; pp. 41–45; under the heading of "Philology." Of this pamphlet, rather more than 3000 copies have been distributed in the United States, from Maine to Louisiana, and, accompanied by my oral Lectures, have somewhat familiarized American auditors with themes but little known in Europe beyond collegiate precincts.

As it is, we can merely recommend the reader, after viewing the three distinct geographical origins and independent developments of the art of writing, to study well the place which palæography now assigns to the modern *square-letter* (AS*h*URI) Hebrew alphabet of "22 letters;" while we discuss a few general principles, to be amply corroborated in detail on some future occasion.

Digressional Remarks on the ensuing Table.

I.—The *principle* followed (probably for the first time in palæographical disquisition) and exhibited through the annexed table, is a consequence of the work which it accompanies. As "Types of Mankind" tabulates the various species of the "genus homo" according to their several relations to the *Flora* and the *Fauna* of their respective centres of creation, the harmonious unison of all sciences,(112) when directed to the elucidation of a given fact, cannot be better exemplified than by cleaving into *three* well-ascertained masses the grand enigma of graphical *origines*.

We hold, without mental reservations, that history does not justify, archæology permit, or ethnology warrant, *any*, the slightest, intercourse, between Egypt and China prior to the days of Cyrus (as an extreme point); nor between either of these two primordial nations, and the Aborigines of that continent which, pronounced by Agassiz to be the *oldest* land, was unknown (from us trans-atlantically) to inhabitants of the Oriental hemisphere before Columbus. Some of the physical reasons are set forth in the present volume: and it is pleasing to find that *palæography* entirely corroborates results deduced from other investigations. To chivalrous opponents, "blanched under the harness" of scientific pursuits, we respectfully throw down our gauntlet upon three propositions: —

A — Prior to B. C. 500, Egypt had no intercourse with America or China.
B — " " America had no intercourse with China or Egypt.
C — " " China had no intercourse with Egypt or America.

Until some student, qualified through knowledge of the archæological actualities inherent in this triad of problemata (knowledge to be evinced by the weight in science of his demurrer), overthrows the *principle* upon which our table is erected, we shall not fear for its stability: nay, we offer to his use the weapons of our armory, by indicating the shortest path to verification of bibliothical accuracy.

II.—The researches of Gesenius (213) and of Champollion-Figeac (214) have been our points of departure in the construction of the *Table*. We have remodelled them by the lights which, in the former case fifteen, in the latter twelve, years of discovery demand; fusing the results of both authorities into one; and then separating the whole into *three* grand stems; 1st, HAMITIC, with its *Semitish* branches—2d, MONGOLIAN, with its offshoots—3d, AMERICAN, whose slender twigs were cut short, for ever, by Pizarro and by Cortez.

1st. The HAMITIC ORIGIN — start with Champollion le Jeune,(215) continue with Lepsius,(216) and close with Bunsen,(217) Birch,(218) Burgsch,(219) and De Saulcy.(220)

The *Semitic* streams have been followed in the subjoined order.

Aside from personal verification of the "old travellers" — Pietro della Valle, Chardin, Corneille le Brun, Kaempfer, Niebuhr, &c.; and of the later, Rich, Ouseley, Ker Porter, Kinnier, Morier, and Malcolm; the perusal of De Sacy, Tychsen, Münter, Grotefend, Saint

(212) Humboldt: *Cosmos;* Introduction to *French* edition; 1846; i. pp. 36–48.

(213) *Scrip. Ling. Phœn. Mon.;* 1837; pp. 62, 63, and Table of *Alphabets*, p. 64.

(214) *Paléographie Universelle;* 1841; i. p. 46 — "Tableau général pour servir à l'histoire de l'Écriture."

(215) *Grammaire Égyptienne;* 1836; — *Dictionnaire Égyptienne;* 1841.

(216) *Lettre à Rosellini* — Annali dell' Instituto di Corrispond. Archeol.; Roma, 1837; vol. ix.

(217) *Ægyptens Stelle in der Weltgeschichte;* 1845; vol. i. part 2d.

(218) In Bunsen's *Egypt's Place;* 1848; i. pp. 448–600; — and in Gliddon: *Otia Ægyptiaca;* 1849; pp. 113–115.

(219) Burgsch: *Scriptura Ægyptiorum dematica* ex papyris et inscriptionibus explanata; Berlin, 1848; — and *Numerorum apud veteres Ægyptios demoticorum doctrina;* Berlin, 1849.

(220) De Saulcy: *Lettre à M. Guigniaut;* Paris, 1843; — and *Analyse grammaticale du Texte Démotique du Décret de Rosette;* i., première partie, 1845.

THEORY OF THE ORDER OF DEVELOPMENT IN HUMAN WRITINGS.

"Primi per figuras animalium *Ægyptii* sensus mentis effingebant (ea antiquissima monumenta memoriæ humanæ impressa saxis cernuntur) et litterarum semel *inventores* perhibent; inde Phœnices, quia mari præpollebant, intulisse Græciæ, gloriamque adeptos, tanquam repererint, quæ acceperant."—*Tacitus*, Annal., lib. xi. c. 14.

PRIMORDIAL, or *ante-chronological* PERIODS—when incipient Humanity, requiring no records, had invented no form of *writing* (like the *Papuan*, *Eskimaux*, *Hottentot*, or *Patagonian* types at this day, A. D. 1853) .... B. C. 00,000

1st AGE; the PICTORIAL—current in the *ante-monumental* days of Egypt and China (as seen upon ancient *Peruvian* and *Mexican* monuments; and as practised now (1853) by *American Indians*, *Polynesians*, *African* and *Asiatic* barbarous tribes, &c.) 0,000

HAMITIC ORIGIN.

	B. C.
2d AGE; the Egyptian HIEROGLYPHICAL—earliest *monuments* extant, the pyramids and tombs of the IVth Memphite dynasty (say, with Lepsius)	3500
Secondary form—*Hieratic*—VIth dynasty	2800

SEMITIC STREAMS.

3d AGE; the Asiatic SEMI-ALPHABETIC—earliest *monuments* extant—*Cuneiform* Inscriptions: Assyro-Babylonian, partly ideographic, but chiefly phonetic	1000
4th AGE; the ALPHABETICAL—earliest Egyptian *monuments* extant (*i. e.* those indicating a close of transitions) are of the Tertiary form—*Demotic* papyri	600
Persepolitan *cuneiform*	530
Boustrophedon inscriptions; Grecian	650
Himyaritic	?
Phœnician	?

MONGOLIAN ORIGIN.

	B. C.
2d AGE; the Chinese IDEOGRAPHICAL—earliest *monuments* extant, the Inscription of Yu, with later remains in the *Kou-wen* character,	2278

CHINESE STREAMS.

	A. D.
3d AGE; *Japanese*—	
First form	200
Second form	840

Infiltrations of the *Semitic* element by Jewish exiles, Christian Syriac missions, and Muslim extensions—with some slight *Arian* influences thro' the *Sanscrit*—produce changes upon Mongolian conditions and originate the

4th AGE; Alphabet *Mongol*	1260
Mandchou	1600

Siamese forms, &c., &c.; some inclining toward Chinese, others rather toward *Sanscrit* affinities.

AMERICAN ORIGIN.

	B. C.
2d AGE; *Peruvian monuments*	?
Mexican monuments	?

[Ante-Columbian—principles unknown.]

The post-Columbian influences break all links, palæographically, with the past. What atoms of extraneous civilizations reach the *American* type of humanity, begin with the sixteenth century after Christ, and are simply European. Even the *Cherokee* alphabet is the invention of GEORGE GUESS, *Sequoyah*—a half-breed Scotchman.

"*Phœnices* primi, famæ, *si* creditur, ausi
Mansuram rudibus vocem signare figuris."
Lucan, Pharsal. iii. 220, 221.

"Quidam Cecropem Athenlensem, vel Linum Thebanum, et temporibus Trojanis Palamedem, Argivum, memorant, *sexdecim* litterarum formas —— reperisse." . . . "Quippe fama est, Cadmum, classe *Phœnicum* vectum, rudibus adhuc Græcorum populis artis ejus auctorem fuisse." — *Tacitus*, Annal. lib. xi. c. 14. [Vide also *Herodotus*, v. 57–8; *Diodorus*, iii. 66; *Pliny*, vii. 56; *Josephus*, Contr. Apion. i. 2.

SEMITIC STREAMS. — *Continued.*

ASSYRO-PHŒNICIAN, B.C. 700.

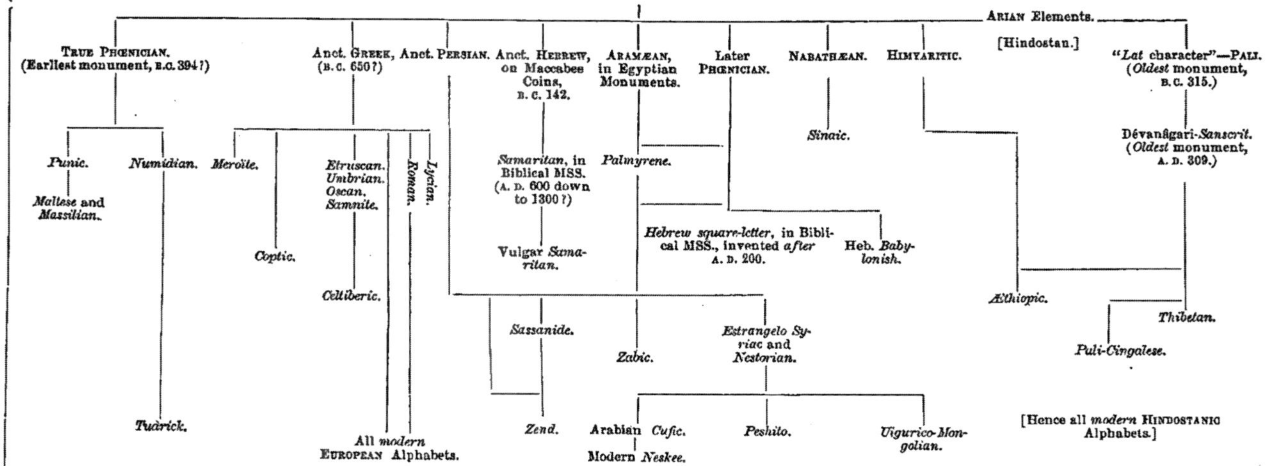

Martin, Rask, Burnouf, Lassen, and Westergaard; the possession of the major portion of the folio plates and texts of Botta, Flandin and Coste, Layard, Texier, &c.; a d the inspection of what of Assyrian sculptures were in London and Paris during 1849: (221) — our views upon *Assyro-Babylonian* writings take their departure and are derived from the series at foot, appended in the order of our studies.(222)

Egyptian hieroglyphical discoveries had long ago revealed the fact that, as early at least as Thotmes III, of the XVIIIth dynasty, about the sixteenth century B. C., the Pharaohs had overrun "Naharina," or Mesopotamia, with their armies. Accepted, like all new truths, with hesitation, since Rosellini's promulgation of the data in 1832; or at first entirely denied by cuneatic discoverers, who claimed a *primeval* epoch for the sculptures of Nineveh and Babylon; nothing at this day is more positively fixed in historical science than these *Egyptian* conquests over "Nineveh" and "Babel," at least three centuries before Derceto (the earliest monarch recorded in *cuneiform* inscriptions) lived; assuming Layard's last view to be correct, (223) that he flourished about B. C. 1250. At foot we present the order in which an inquirer may investigate the discoveries that have finally set these questions at rest; (224) while the following extracts from Rawlinson will render further doubts irrelevant: —

> "That the employment of the Cuneiform character originated in Assyria, while the *system of writing* to which it was adapted was *borrowed from Egypt*, will hardly admit of question: . . . the whole structure of the Assyrian graphic system evidently betrays an *Egyptian* origin. . . . The whole system, indeed, of homophones is *essentially Egyptian.*" (225)

It is upon such data that, without adducing other reasons derived from personal studies, we have made the earliest *Semitic* stream of our Table flow outwards from Egypt into ancient Mesopotamia — assigning the period of its Eastward flux, according to well-known conditions in *Egyptian* history, as bounded by the XIIth and XVIIIth dynasties: that is, between the twenty-second and sixteenth century B. C.; — which age, placed parallel with Archbishop Usher's scheme of biblical chronology, implies from a little before Abraham down to the birth of Moses. No Egyptologist will contest this view: the opinions of those who deny, without acquaintance with the works submitted, are "vox et præterea nihil."

---

(221) Three Archæological Lectures, on "Babylon, Nineveh, and Persepolis," delivered before the *Lyceum of the 2d Municipality* at New Orleans; 6th, 9th, 13th April, 1852; by G. R. G.

(222) BOTTA: *Lettres à M. Mohl;* Paris, 1845; — DE LONGPÉRIER and DE SAULCY, in *Rev. Archéol.;* 1844–1852; — LÖWENSTERN; *Essai de Déchiffrement de l'Écriture Assyrienne;* Paris, 1845; — BOTTA: *Sur l'Écriture Cunéiforme;* 1849; — RAWLINSON: *Tablet of Behistun;* 1846; — and *Commentary on Cuneiform Inscriptions;* 1850; — HINCKS: *On the Three kinds of Persepolitan Writing;* Trans. R. Irish Acad., 1847; — NORRIS: *Memoir on the Scythic Version of the Behistun Inscription;* and RAWLINSON'S communications; in Jour. R. Asiat. Soc., 1853; xv. part 1. Many other works upon this speciality, no less than upon the writings of every historical nation of antiquity, are cited in the manuscripts we suppress for lack of space. But, by anticipation of their future appearance, it would be injustice to an author "qui a puisé à des bonnes sources," not to recommend earnestly to the sincere inquirer after truth, a perusal of the first and only work in the English language which has grasped this vast subject in a manner commensurate with the progress of science. It arrived at the *Philadelphia Library*, and was kindly pointed out to us by our accomplished friend Mr. Lloyd P. Smith, after our own "Table" was already *stereotyped.* We have read it with admiration; and although upon *three* points, the hieroglyphical, the cuneiform, and especially the *Hebrew*, we might suggest a few critical — that is to say, more rigidly *chronological* — substitutions; yet, upon the whole performance we are happy to offer the warm commendations of a fellow-student. The reader will find it, in the meanwhile, an excellent adjunct to our "Table"; and the following extracts, with an interlineary commentary, suffice to indicate that Mr. Humphrey's views and our own differ upon but a single point: — "The world has now possessed a purely *alphabetic* system of writing for 3000 years or more [say rather, about 300 years *less*], and iconographic systems for more than 3000 years longer [say, considerably *more*]. . . . . There can be little doubt that the art of writing grew up independently in many countries having no communication with each other [entirely agreed]": (vide HENRY NOEL HUMPHREYS: *The Origin and Progress of the Art of Writing;* London, 1853; pp. 1, 3

(223) *Babylon; 2d Ex.;* 1853; p. 623.

(224) LETRONNE: *La Civilisation Égyptienne;* pp. 1–55; Extrait de la Revue des Deux Mondes; Feb., April, 1845; — BIRCH; *Statistical Tablet of Karnac; — Obelisk of Thotmes* III.; and on *Two Cartouches found at Nimroud;* Trans. R. Soc. Lit., 1846–'48; — GLIDDON: *Otia;* p. 103; — LAYARD: *Nineveh;* 1848; ii. pp. 153–235; — SHARPE, in *Bonomi's Nineveh;* pp. ——; — LAYARD: *Babylon;* 1853; pp. 153–159, 186–196, 280–282, 630; — and, particularly, BIRCH: *Annals of Thotmes* III.; London *Archæologia*, xxxv., 1853; p. 160, &c.

(225) *Commentary;* 1850; pp. 4–6.

Scholars, guided by the books cited for justificatory details, will find little to alter in the general features of these several *alphabetical* streams as their respective *monumental* rocks first pierce through the mists of traditionary history: except in one direction; viz.: where we have made a *Semitic* rivulet (probably through Chaldæan channels) commingle with "ARIAN elements" in Hindostan. "Indology" will protest against profaning the sanctified soil of *Indra* and *Brahma* with the mere "tail-race" of a *Semitic* pond, originally filled by the Nile! Shades of Wilford, Faber, Hales, and spirit of Edgar Quinet! In Germany, appeal will at once be made to Von Bohlen! In Wales, to Arthur James Johnes, Esq.! (226) Does not every body know, it will be said, that primordial civilization (unceremoniously kicked out of Ethiopic *Meroë* by Lepsius,) first dawned upon the Ganges? that Memphis, (if not also Palenque, and Copan,) received her holiest Penates at the hands of *Siva*, *Vishnu*, *Bhairava*, *Crishna*, or any other Indian Deity a pundit may invent? (227)

With all deference, after the first horrors excited by our outrage shall have calmed down into philosophical contempt, we beg to offer a quotation: —

"The people of Hindostan and the ancient nations of Europe came in contact at a single point. The expedition of Alexander the Great begins, and in some sort ends, their connexion. Even of this event, so recent and remarkable, the *Hindus* have no record; they have not even a *tradition* that can with certainty be traced to it." (228)

Our author, who stands out in bold relief among the *Sanscrit* scholars of England, wonders at the credulity of those who reject Chaldæan and Egyptian antiquity to worship Hindostanic; administering stern rebukes to writers who trust in the "absurdity of *Hindu* statements," — a people utterly "destitute of historical records."

The same historian, in Notes on the *Mudra Rákshana*, says: —

"It may not here be out of place to offer a few observations on the identification of Chandragupta and Sandracottus. *It is the only point on which we can rest with anything like confidence in the history of the Hindus*, and is therefore of vital importance in all our attempts to reduce the reigns of their kings to a rational and consistent chronology."

Turnour, (229) sums up his review of Hindoo literature with saying, —

"That there does not *now exist an authentic*, connected, and chronologically-correct Hindoo history; and that the absence of that history proceeds, not from original deficiency of historical data, but *from the systematic perversion* of those data adopted to work out the monstrous scheme upon which Hindoo faith is based."

The preceding extracts, we hope, may serve to break the fall of huge Indianist edifices from the highest peak of the Himalaya to a level but little expected by general readers. That we are not altogether freshmen in these Hindoo demolitions may be inferred from a passage, printed five years ago, which we now take the liberty of repeating, with its Italian preface: —

"Cadono le città, cadono i regni,
E l'uom d'esser mortal par che si sdegni!" (230)

"That the peninsula of Hindostan, thronged with varied populations, possessed great Empires and a high state of culture, in ages parallel with the earliest monuments of Egypt and China, upon whose civilizations India exerted, and from which she experienced influences, in the flux and reflux of Humanity's progressive development, no one, *nisi imperitus*,

---

(226) *Philological Proofs of the Original Unity and Recent Origin of the Human Race*; London, 1846; pp. 131–133. For "Celto-mania," this work out-Herods BETHAM'S! We can only observe with CHAMPOLLION (*L'Égypte sous les Pharaons*, 1814), of a *philologist* who derived the Greek name of Egypt from the *Gaelic* dialects of Lower Brittany — "Certainly, even admitting that the Greeks spoke *Bas-brêton*, there is some distance from AIGUPTOS to *Écou-ò-vet*."

(227) PRICHARD: *Egyptian Mythology*; 1819; p. 35, *seq.*; — HEEREN: *Hist. Res.*, *Indian Nations.*

(228) WILSON: *History of British India*; 1840; "Chronology and History of the Hindus;" i., book 2, ch. 1, pp. 163–169.

(229) Author of the "Buddhist Pali Historical Annals of Ceylon," called *Mahawanso*, "Royal Chronicles"; compiled from earlier sources in A. D. 302: if not *later*.

(230) METASTASIO: paraphrase of *S. Sulpicius's Letter to Cicero*; epist. v. lib. 4. The second line has been latterly rhymed — "E nel cader un c*****n par che si sdegni." The English is — "Cities fall, kingdoms fall; and (yet) man seems to scorn that he is mortal!"

will deny: but the hallucinations about early Brahmanical science in Astronomy, when their Zodiacs are *Greek*, their Eclipses calculated *backwards*, and their fabulous chronology is built upon *Chaldean* magianism, leave the historical antiquity of India prostrate beneath the axe of the *short*-chronologist. 'Un astronomo può, se vuole, far le tavole dell'ecclissi che avranno luogo di qui a cento-mila anni, se il mondo esisterà; e può ugualmente determinare lo stato, nel quale sarebbesi trovato il cielo centomil'anni fa, se il mondo esisteva:' (Testa, 'Dissertazione sopra due Zodiaci,' &c.; Roma, 1803, p. 23.) The Hindoos, in concocting their primeval chronology, merely added a *naught* to Babylonish cyclic reckonings;—4,320,000 years, instead of 432,000! (De Brotonne, 'Filiations des Peuples,' 1837; vol. i., pages 234 to 251, and 414.) See ample confirmations of the above view in the critical work of Wilson ('Ariana Antiqua,' 1841; pages 17, 21, 24, 419; 44, 45; and particularly page 439, wherein it is shown, that numismatic studies cease to throw light on Indian antiquities about the middle of the third century B. C.").

"When, therefore, the contenders for the ante-diluvian remoteness of the *forty-eight*-lettered *Sanscrit* Alphabet can produce any *stone*, or other record older than the 'column of *Allahabad* in honor of TCHANDRA-GOUPTA, *Sandracottus*,' cotemporary with SELEUCUS NICATOR, B. C. 315, it will be time enough for Hierologists, Sinologists, Hellenists and Hebraists, to take into account the pseudo-antiquity of *Sanscrit Alphabetical* literature." (231)

Our profession of faith in these matters, identical with the doctrines we hold at this day, shocked some literary prejudices. Nevertheless, it was based upon tolerably extensive perusal of works on Hindoo antiquities; and it is supported by the cuts and thrusts of a swordsman, whose trenchant blade, notched on the battle-fields of Hindostan, still preserves its keenness amid the bloodless strifes of archæological polemics — Lieut. Col. Sykes. (232)

From his matchless overthrow of European superstitions, in regard to Indian antiquity, we have already extracted two paragraphs containing the decisions of Wilson and Turnour. We now condense his own applications of cold steel to some of the vitalities of Hindostanic pretension.

There exists but *one* Sanscrit composition that can be called "history;" viz. the *Raja Taringini*, compiled A. D. 1148. It contains anachronisms of 796, and of 1048 years! Prior to the fifth century after C., "inscriptions in *pure Sanscrit* are entirely wanting" — the *earliest* Sanscrit inscription ascends to the fourth century, but it is impure in language and not orthographic. Between the tenth and seventeenth centuries of our era, Sanscrit inscriptions "roll in thousands!" The very Sanscrit *language*, in the polished form in which its literature reaches us, can no more be found *monumentally* in India, before the fifth century after C., than the English of Byron could appear in the days of Gower or Chaucer. In consequence, those Germanic writers who, in their assimilations (which are positive enough) of Greek, Latin, German, or other Indo-European idiom, forget that *Sanscrit* has undergone even greater transmutations than our Saxon vernacular has since the reign of Alfred, often commit philological oversights of sublime magnitude!

"Why are there not," asks Sykes, "the same tangible and irrefragable proofs extant of the Sanscrit as of the *Pali* language: the more particularly so as Brahmanism and Sanscrit have hitherto been believed to emanate from the fabled ages?"

Commencing his deep researches with the more recent Sanscrit inscriptions, and tracing them backwards as far as they recede, Prinsep (233) resolved the modern forty-eight *Deva-Nagari* characters absolutely into the primitive letters of the *old* inscriptions written in the "Lat" character and *Pali* language — the rencontre of graphical forms that approximated to the ancient *Pali* type increasing exactly in the ratio of the antiquity of each Sanscrit inscription. Of these last, the most *ancient* known dates A. D. 809; being just 624 years posterior to the *oldest Pali* inscription discovered throughout the Hindostanic peninsula!

Now, this oldest *Pali* inscription is found on the "column of *Allahabad*," whereupon it

---

(231) *Otia Æg.*; p. 110, and note.

(232) "Notes on the Religious, Moral, and Political State of Ancient India before the Mohammedan Invasion" —*Jour. R. Asiatic Soc.*; London, 1841; vol. vi. pp. 248–484.

(233) *Journal Asiatic Soc. of Bengal*; 1834–'41. Conf. *Jour. R. Asiatic Soc.*, 1853; xv. part i. p. xxv; for "Nassik Inscriptions," the date of the *cave* being only A. D. 338! Also, concerning *Arian* superpositions upon a dark autocthonous population of Hindostan, Gen. BRIGGS's Lecture "On the *Aboriginal* Race of India;" reported in London *Literary Gazette*, July 17, 1852.

was chiselled in the reign of Tchandra-Gupta, who is the *Sandracottus* of Greek history, coetaneous with Seleucus Nicator in the year B. C. 315. All India affords nothing, written *alphabetically*, more ancient; and this age is 220 years later than the alphabetic cuneiform of Persepolis; or above 300 years after the Greeks had already adopted the *Aleph* (alpha), *Beth* (beta), *Gimel*, (gamma), *Daleth* (delta), of the anterior *Phœnician* alphabet! The identification of "Sandracottus" is moreover proved by the next early inscriptions known in the *Pali* tongue; viz.: two edicts of PISADASI-*Asoka*, a king of India in the year B. C. 247; who refers to his contemporary ANTIOCHUS *the Great;* just 62 years after the *oldest* inscription, whose epoch stands parallel with SELEUCUS. Thus, palæographically, the antiquity of India has fallen, never to rise again: and, inasmuch as the Brahmans certainly stole their *Zodiac* from the post-Macedonian Greeks; and probably some Levitical ceremonials of MANOU from Jewish exiles; there is no reason whatever, yet published, against our theory, that *alphabetic* writing also reached Hindostan, through *Arian* channels, from those Semitic streams the source of which is now irrevocably traced back to HAMITIC *origines* in Egypt.

"All those ancient systems of Persic writing with which we are acquainted, although applied to Arian dialects, are obviously formed on a *Semitic* model. I may notice, in chronological succession, the writing on the Cilician Darics; the Arianian alphabet (of which the earliest certain specimen is the transcript of the Edicts of Asoka), with its derivatives, the numismatic Bactrian, and the character of the Buddhist topes; the Zend; the Parthian; exhibiting in the inscriptions of Persia at least three varieties; and the Pehlevi, lapidary, numismatic and cursive. These several branches of Palæography are all more or less connected. (234)

Thus much to justify our table. But, "Titius or Sempronius" exclaims, have we not the *Sanscrit Vedas*, the Epics *Mahabharata* and *Ramayana*, the "Laws of MANOU," and the *Puranas?* Did not Sir William Jones fix the age of the Vedas in the fifteenth century B. C.; that of the "Institutes of Menu" in the twelfth? (235) Were not similar opinions held by Colebrooke and Schlegel; and are they not supported by great Indianists of our own time? Conceded, gentlemen. Knowing nothing of Sanscrit ourselves, we are as little able to speak decisively as those *littérateurs* who will be most startled at our audacities. Linguistically, there are not twenty-five men in the world whose judgment, matured by comparative archæology, is really authoritative in this discussion. In the meanwhile, *palæographical* facts speak intelligibly to all educated minds. We might add that Professor Wilson thinks the *Vedas* may, in part, ascend almost to the sixth century B. C.: but Sykes's sabre is not wanting in our defence; so let us continue.

In the first place, it is historical, that the Brahmans, in their efforts to destroy Buddhism, dealt, by the *ancient* texts of Hindoo treatises on religion or traditions, precisely as the Inquisition did with Hebrew Scriptures that existed before the tenth century of our era— *i. e.*, destroyed them. In the second, two Chinese travellers in India—Fa-hian, in the fourth century, and Hiuan-thsang, in the seventh after Christ—have (unfortunately for Brahmanical respectability) chronicled how, in this interval of three hundred years, the disciples of Brahma had expanded, from an incipient bud, into that detestable flower in which *Sanscrit* literature portrays them—ever noxious as *Upas* blossoms. (236) Their accounts are confirmed by the Chinese encyclopædist, Ma-touan-lin; (237) who registers that, bout 502 A. D., the *Brahmans* were but a small sept among the Buddhists—"first among the tribes of *barbarians*." It may also be mentioned that, in the time of BUDDHA, sixth century B. C., the Hindoo population was classed already into those four grand divisions which attest, as

(234) RAWLINSON: *Behistun;* part i. pp. 43–44.

(235) We have recently re-read most of Sir W. JONES's Papers with increased reverence: for his immense erudition qualifies all dogmatic opinions attributed to him with "*ifs*" of his own. Before us lie PAUTHIER's *Livres Sacrés de l'Orient;* 1843: also MUNK: *Réflexions sur le Culte des Anciens Hébreux;* 1833; wherein the fifth book of MANOU is compared with *Leviticus;*—and other Sanscrit commentators "quos recensere supervacaneum esset." We have read BURNOUF: *Boudhisme,* and *Yaçna;* and nothing therein opposes, while much justifies, our view.

(236) REMUSAT; *Mélanges Asiatiques.*

(237) PAUTHIER: *Chine;* p. 381.

Pauthier well remarks, (238) "the diversity of races conquering and vanquished at a very early epoch;" viz: *Brahmans*, priests; *Kchatriyas*, soldiers; *Vaisyas*, tradesmen; and *Soudras*, serviles: (239) but the Chinese Fa-hian shows how, even in the fourth century after C., these divisions were merely *civil*, and not yet religious ordinances. In short, it is now certain that the "*caste*-system,"(240) which (it is likewise thoroughly established) was never known in Egypt, had not been invented in Hindostan until Brahmanical superstitions obtained predominance long after the Christian era. So again with respect to most of those prohibitions of animal sustenance, and other "unclean things," which some have supposed that Moses learned from primeval gymnosophists. Forbidden, for practical hygienic motives, among Pharaonic priests, Pythagoræan philosophers, and among Israelitish no less than Mohammedan Arabians, *pork* was equally proscribed by MANOU: (241) "The regenerate man who knowingly may have eaten mushroom, domestic *hog*, garlic, wild-cock, onion, or leek, shall be degraded." Now, as Sykes inquires, if the laws of MANOU had been in existence prior to the Christian era, how came it that BUDDHA died of dysentery from eating *pork*, and that *hog's* flesh should have been the aliment of early Brahmanical ascetics?

When enthusiastic Indologists shall have explained away the above palæographical and historical objections, they will be at leisure to defend the alleged antiquity of the *Sanscrit* books themselves. Here is a little thing calculated, as Lanci writes, to "scaponire i grattacapi." (242)

The "Puranas" claim for RAMA a date something like 867,102 years before their compilation. Bentley fixed the poem *Ramayana*, by its intrinsic evidences, at A. D. 291: and Wilson, together with the best Sanscrit critics, determines the age of the earliest "Puranas" between the eighth and ninth century after Christ. Such being the facts, Sykes educes as follows.

Sir W. Jones (Preface to the *Institutes of Menu*), assumed "that the *Vedas* must therefore have been written three hundred years before the Institutes of Menu, and these Institutes three hundred years before the Puranas." Then, Sykes's deadly sword gives point— as Wilson has proved, from internal evidence, that the "*Puranas* were written or compiled between the eighth and fourteenth centuries of the Christian era, it follows, according to Sir W. Jones's hypothesis, that the *Institutes of Menu* date from the fifth century (*Annis* D), and the *Vedas* from the second century." *Monumental* calligraphy supports this view; while the *Vishnu* Purana (dated by Wilson at A. D. 954) brings the polished Sanscrit language down as late as the tenth century. Analogy also, in adjacent countries, points to the same solution as to how Lamaism and Romanism present such striking identities. It is said by Father Georgi that "Writing, laws and religion were introduced into Thibet about the year 65 after Christ."(243) Thus, we learn that *Thibetan* pretensions, which have more affinity with those of Hindostan than of China, lend no support to Hindoo antiquity.

The geographical *names* in Hindoo literature wofully invalidate the antiquity of some books: because, if the mention of "Yavanas" (*Ionians*, IUNīm in Hebrew and in Assyrian cuneiform, *Yoonàn* in Arabic, and YUNIN in old Egyptian), does not positively prove a writer posterior to ALEXANDER, B. C. 330; that of "Tchinas" (inasmuch as the Celestial Empire was not called *Thsin*, China, before the year 250 B. C.), at once knocks down a book to times *after* that era.(244) So again, as Indo-Scythians did not penetrate into India before B. C. 125, allusion to the *Sakas* must proceed from an author who lived subsequently. Now, the *Ramayana* and the *Mahabharata* both speak of "Yavanas, Tchinas, and Sakas;" and ergo, the latter cannot well be older (aside from other reasons) than the

(238) *Lois de Manou;* Introd.: p. 22.

(239) *Id.;* book i., sloka 31.

(240) GLIDDON: *Otia:* p. 90.

(241) Book v. 19: — The reason why neither Judaism nor Islàmism ever made progress in *China* is owing to its inhabitants' fondness for little *pigs*. The same tastes render either religion utterly impossible at *Cincinnati*.

(242) "*Remove the obstinacy of head-scratchers.*"

(243) *Alphabetum Tibetanum;* apud DE BROTONNE: *Filiations;* i. p. 445.

(244) The fleets of HOANG-TI first visited the ports of Bengal about the year 280 B. C. (*Chine*, p. 2).

second century after Christ, nor the former earlier than the fifth; in no case can either antedate B. C. 250. But, wildly shriek our Brahmanists — the grottos of *Ellora*, *Elephanta*, *Adjunta*, &c.? Alas, gentlemen — Sykes says, not one antedates the ninth century after Christ! Even Prichard, following Prinsep, does not consider these caves earlier than "a century or two prior to the Christian era, when Buddhism flourished in the height of its glory from Kashmir to Ceylon." (245)

We delude ourselves, probably, with the belief that our opponents in biblical studies will concede that, in our hands, the knife of criticism is double-edged; and that we apply it equally to the notions of Hindoo as well as of Judæan commentators. In the last century it was the fashion to exalt *Sanscrit* literature at the expense of Jewish; greatly to the discomfort of orthodoxy. The latter may now console itself with the assurance, that its Hindostanic apprehensions were puerile — for, beneath the most ruthless scalpel, a "Book of the *Law* of MOSES" stands erect with vitality, in the sixth century B. C.; that is, 200 years before the oldest *Pali* document of India was inscribed by CHANDRAGUPTA.

With the judicious reflections of another *Sanscrit* authority we take leave of Hindostan; merely mentioning that our own analysis of Xth Genesis has entirely confirmed the doctrine broached by the learned Col. Vans Kennedy. (246)

"Although I do not derive all the nations of the earth from *Shem*, *Ham*, and *Japhet*, I still think that Babylonia [we read, ARIANA] was the original seat of the Sanscrit language and of Sanscrit literature. . . . But this error [i. e. the contrary hypothesis] necessarily proceeds from the assumption, that the first *eleven* chapters of Genesis give an authentic account of the creation and of the earlier ages of the world; which renders it necessary to insult common sense, and to disregard the plainest principles of evidence and reasoning, in order to prove that all the races of mankind and all systems of polytheism were derived from one and the same origin."

Those who have leaned upon Faber's broken reed would do well to peruse our author's *Appendix* — "Remarks on the Papers of Lieut. Col. Wilford contained in the Asiatic Researches." To others it may be satisfactory to know, that the earliest Greek mention of *India* (Sind) occurs in Æschylus, B. C. 525–456: while, about the same times (if Ezra compiled the "Book of Genesis," as patristic authority sustained), tradition — which, in our version (*Gen.* iv. 16), sends Cain into "the land of *Nod*, on the east of Eden" — probably consecrated some legendary rumor that the forlorn outcast had escaped to the *Hindus* — "*hi*NUD, towards the *East* of Eden," itself located in Mesopotamia; which Indian people are still called HINooD, by the Arabs. (247) *India* became known to Jews and Greeks after the former had been captive in Babylonia, and after the Persian invasions had given new ideas upon Asiatic geography to the latter.

FIG. 360.

Intending to publish other justifications of the correctness of our *Tableau* [*supra*, pp. 630, 631] on some future occasion, we suspend further discussion of the "*Semitic* streams," and merely submit specimens of that character upon which we have bestowed the name of "Assyro-Phœnician." If, as Dr. Layard states, some of these relics were positively found in the "chamber of records" opened by him at Kouyunjik, (248) and if, as he declares, they are really of the time of Sennacherib, B. C. 703 to 690, the reader beholds the very earliest known samples of *purely-alphabetic* writing hitherto discovered. They will become the more precious to his eyes, inasmuch as (in the contingency that Dr. Layard is certain that Fig. 360 belongs to Sennacherib's reign) here is the closest approximation to that (unknown) character in which the *oldest Hebrew books* of the Bible were originally written: which fact we shall demonstrate elsewhere. For

FIG. 361.

(245) *Researches*; 1844; iv. pp. 120, 121.

(246) *Researches into the Nature and Affinity of Ancient and Hindu Mythology*; 1831; pp. 368, 369; also pp. 406–422.

(247) MUNK: *Palestine*; p. 429.

(248) *Babylon*; 2d Exped., 1843; pp. 346, 591, 601, 606.

FIG. 362.

fear of misapprehensions, let us also note that the above *ancient* characters are entirely distinct in age from those on the *modern* and rabbinical "Bowls" (249) from Babylonia which Mr. Ellis's remarks might lead others than archæologists to invest with the halo of antiquity. They cannot attain even to the *third century after* C.; and, indeed, may descend to days after the Mohammedan conquests. Until we can resume the subject, the reader will find a place assigned to them in our Table under the heading of "Hebrew *Babylonish.*"

2d. MONGOLIAN ORIGIN.—We give this designation to a system of writings distinct organically, chronologically, linguistically, geographically, palæographically, ethnologically — in short, *aboriginally*—from any affinity with *Semitic* streams, or with the latter's common HAMITIC source. To comprehend us, the reader need but open the works of Pauthier; (250) without perplexing himself with other definitions, until he finds the former inconsistent with science, history, reason, and probability.

It is, however, from his *Sinico-Ægyptiaca* that the principles and examples of our author's critical results must be gathered; and, having advocated them on a former occasion, (251) we return to them with pleasure increased by subsequent verifications of their accuracy.

PAUTHIER'S THREE AGES OF WRITINGS.

"1st AGE.—The *figured* representation of objects and ideas; otherwise the *pictorial* age.

"Of this age we possess nothing that can be safely referred to primeval antiquity. All barbarous nations, like the tribes of North America, still strive to perpetuate their simple traditions by *pictures*.

"To this age, with a probable infusion of the *symbolical* element (although, as yet, whether of their lost languages, undeciphered writings, or chronology, it may be said that we literally *know* nothing), may perhaps be referred the *pictures* and so-called *hieroglyphs* of the ante-Columbian monuments of Mexico, Central America, and Peru.

"2d AGE.—The *altered* and *conventional* representation of objects; otherwise the *transition*-period; when the pictorial signs pass into the *symbolical*, and thence gradually into the syllabico-*phonetic*.

"To this age belong the *ideographic writings* of the Chinese secondary period, classified as follows: (252) 1st.—HIGH ANTIQUITY; B. C. 2637 to 3369—according to the *Chinese* annalists, the KOU-WEN, or *antique writing*. 2d.—MEDIUM ANTIQUITY; B. C. 820—the TA-TCHOUAN, or *altered image of objects*. 3d.—LOW ANTIQUITY; B. C. 227—the SIAO-TCHOUAN, or *image still more altered of objects*. 4th.—MODERN TIMES; B. C. 200 to A. D. 1123, and still in use—*four* kinds of current writing and typography.

"The above are formed upon principles presenting some few analogies, but in the main remarkable differences, when compared with the Egyptian *phonetic* system. (253) Under the same age may be classed the *hieroglyphical* and *hieratic* system of Egypt, the latter being a tachygraphy or *short-hand* of the former.

"Albeit that we have but very vague data in this respect, it is exceedingly probable that all writings began by being *figurative* and *syllabic* before they became purely *alphabetical*. Many alphabets, such as the *Sanscrit* alphabet, the *Ethiopic* alphabet, the *Persepolitan* (without speaking of the *Japanese* and *Coræan* alphabets), are still almost completely *syllabic*, and bear evident traces of a *figurative* origin. (254)

"3d AGE.—The purely-*phonetic* expression of the articulations of the human voice: otherwise the strictly *alphabetical* age; to which belong all writings which represent no more than the vocal elements of human articulations, reduced to their simplest expression; i. e., A, B, C, D, &c.

---

(249) *Op. cit.*; pp. 509–526; figs. 1, 3, 5, 6.

(250) 1st. *Sinico-Ægyptiaca*—Essai sur l'Origine et la Formation *Similaire* des Écritures Figuratives *Chinoise* et Égyptienne; Paris, 1842. 2d. *Systèmes d'Écritures Orientales et Occidentales*; 1838. 3d. *Chine Ancienne*, d'après les documents *Chinois*; 1837. 4th. *Civilisation Chinoise*—containing the Chinese Books, CHOU-KING, Y-KING, TA-HIO, TCHOUNG-YOUNG, LUN-YU, and MENG-TSEU; 1843.

(251) *Otia*; pp. 100–102.

(252) PAUTHIER: *Sinico-Ægyp.*; p. 24.

(253) *Op. cit.*: pp. 98 to 110.

(254) *Op. cit.*: p. 34; and on each alphabet, consult his "Orig. des Alphabets," *passim*.

"To this belong the *Enchorial, Demotic*, or *Epistolographic* characters of Egypt, detached from occasional figurative and symbolical signs."

Nothing to the student of Pauthier's work can be more clear than that the primeval type of Mongol man, whose centre of creation lies along the banks of the *Hoang-ho*, and that other (organically distinct) Hamitic type whose centre is the *Nile*, after each one in its own region had passed through all preliminary phases of its individual development, reached, at an age on either side equally beyond *traditions*, the power of recording things by *pictures;* just as the American Indian around us, spurning every inducement to profit by our graphical art, still traces on the bark of trees, on rocks, on buffalo-robes, those rude designs whereby he hopes to annihilate space and time in the transmission of his thoughts.

If it be granted that an Egyptian, or a Chinese, could singly arrive at the discovery of this the humblest stage of letters for himself, why refuse the same capacities to the other? One nation of the two, at least, must have discovered this pictorial art for itself, most certainly: how then attribute tuition of another world of man to either, when the graphical systems of both are radically different?

Nearly a century ago, after applying vigorous strictures to the theories of Needham and De Guignes (we might add Kircher, De Pauw, Paravey, Wiseman, indeed orthodoxy generally), who claimed that either China taught Egypt, or Egypt China, Bishop Warburton thus emphatically placed the question in its only philosophical light:—

"To conclude, the learned world abounds with discoveries of this kind. They have all one common original; the old inveterate error; that a similitude of customs and manners, amongst the various tribes of mankind the most remote from one another, must needs arise from some communication. Whereas *human nature*, without any help, will, in the same circumstances, always exhibit the same appearances." (255)

How, it may be asked, do we know that the *pictorial* was the first, or rather the anterior, age of writing in Egypt, or in China? Aside from all arguments of analogy that *pictures* are the rudimental writings of semi-barbarism at this day—already a vast step higher than the savage *Bosjesman, Papuan*, or *Patagonian*, has ever attained—it is proved, in Egyptian hieroglyphics of the most ancient and pure style,(256) by their being, as far as perfection of sculpture and vivid coloring can make each thing, the exact representatives of natural and artificial objects, every one indigenous in nature to the *valley of the Nile:* and utterly foreign elsewhere. In China, the pictorial epoch is reached by tracing backwards each mutation of characters, age by age, to the primitive KOU-WEN; which is a tachygraph, or abridgement, of natural or artificial productions, all autocthonous to the region of the *Hoang-ho.*

Of course, copies however rude of the same things must present certain identities, whether delineated in China, Egypt, or America; but just as a parent instinctively detects which of his children has scrawled a given form; or that a man betrays to others his individuality by his handwriting; so archæological practice enables an observer to point out the distinctive peculiarities of a given people's designs. The latter, moreover, tell whence they came by the very subjects figured. Thus, if, in a series of characters called "*Egyptian* of the IVth Memphite dynasty," a *camel*, a *horse*, a *cock*, were designed, the presence of either of these animals would prove the document to be a forgery; because camels, horses, and cocks, were unknown in the valley of the *Nile* for a thousand and more years later. In China, *cocks* and *horses* (257) were indigenous, like the silkworm, from the commencement of creation in this geological period; but, in her primitive pictures, there are no Egyptian *ibises*, nor *papyrus*-plants. No *rattlesnakes, magnolias*, or *bisons*, can be discovered in

---

(255) *The Divine Legation of Moses demonstrated;* 1766; 5th ed.; iii. p. 99.

(256) LEPSIUS: *Denkmäler;* for illustrations.

(257) There seems to be some doubt about the *horse* in China proper at an early period, because, about B. C. 900, this animal was imported from *Tartary* (*Chine*, p. 100). Nevertheless, FO-HI is said to have taught his people to raise the six domestic animals — *horse, ox, fowl, pig, dog*, and *sheep:* and under the three mythical "Hoangs," his antecedents, there was a period of time called the *horse* (PAUTHIER: *Temps Antérieurs au Chou-king;* LIT. SAC.; pp. 20, 33). We cite the *pictorial* horse merely by way of popular illustration.

the pictures of China, or of Egypt, because these things are indigenous to the American continent — until COLUMBUS, segregated from the entire Old World: neither will the Grecian *acanthus*, the African *lion*, or the Asiatic *elephant*, appear in the sculptures of Yucatan or Guatemala; simply because, to American man, these objects were unknown. Each centre of creation furnished to the human being created for it the models of his incipient designs. It was materially impossible for him, without *intercourse* with other centres, to be acquainted with things alien to the horizon of his nativity. An *ornithoryncus*, or a *kangaroo*, if found in a picture, would establish—1st, that such picture could not be Egyptian, Chinese, or American; and 2d, that it was made within the last two centuries — that is, since the discovery of Australia by European navigators. Payne Knight laid down the rules:—

"The similitude of these allegorical and symbolical fictions with each other, in every part of the world, is no proof of their having been derived, any more than the primitive notions which they signify, from any one particular people; for as the organs of sense and principles of intellect are the same in all mankind, they would all naturally form similar ideas from similar objects; and employ similar signs to express them, so long as natural and not conventional signs were used. . . . The only certain proof of plagiary or borrowing is where the animal or vegetable productions of one climate are employed as symbols by the inhabitants of another. . . . As commercial communication, however, became more free and intimate, particular symbols might have been adopted from one people by another without any common origin or even connexion of general principles." (258)

These few remarks suffice as suggestives, to the thoughtful and educated, of the radical distinctions which the first glance perceives when comparing the ancient sculptures of three aboriginal worlds of art, Egyptian, Chinese, or American. But, just as a physician's writings presuppose that his readers have passed beyond the elementary schoolroom, so it is not in "Types of Mankind" that any one need expect to find an archæological "Primer."

We return to the *ante-monumental* pictures of the Nile and the Hoang-ho — the former, long anterior to B. C. 3500; the latter, to B. C. 2300; being the *minimum* distance from our generation at which the graphical system of each river's denizens first dawns upon our view.

Impelled by the same human wants, though absolutely without inter-communication, the Mongol Chinese for his part, and the Hamitic Egyptian for his, attained, at periods unknown, the power of representing their several thoughts *pictorially*. Where they copied the same universal things — the *sun*, a *star*, a *goat*, a *pigeon*, a *snake*, a *tree* (though here even, in Flora and Fauna, already the two countries exhibit distinct "species"),— those copies necessarily resemble each other; although, in each, art betrays the individualities of a separate human type. Where the Chinaman, however, portrays a man, that man is a *Mongol:* where the Egyptian draws a human being, that being is an *Egyptian*.

No stronger exemplification of human inability to conceive that which is beyond the circumference of local experiences, can be met with, than in Squier's exhumations from the primeval mounds of the West.(259) Not merely is the *skull*, divested by time of its animal matter, osteologically identical with those of American Aborigines of this day; not only does every fragmentary relic which accompanies it limit that antique man's boundaries of knowledge to a space longitudinally between Lake Superior and the Gulf of Mexico, and laterally within the Alleghanian and the Rocky Mountains; — but, every *pipe-bowl*, or engraved article, that bears a human likeness, portrays an American *Indian*, and no other type: because man can imitate only what he knows. And finally, to bring the case home to our biblical researches, does not every line of the first *nine* chapters of Genesis prove that Hebrew writers never conceived, in speculation upon creative origines, anything alien to *themselves* and to their own restricted sphere of geography? At their point of view, the first *pair* of human beings conversed, at once, in pure *Hebrew:* — nay, the Talmudic books

(258) R. PAYNE KNIGHT: *Inquiry into the Symbolical Language of Ancient Art and Mythology;* Valpy's 8vo ed., 1818; par. 230, 231.

(259) *Ancient Monuments of the Mississippi Valley;* 1848: compare *wood-cuts*, pp. 194, 244–251.

show, that this divine tongue is to be the future language; the speech in which the "ultima ratio" will be meted out to all humanity in heaven!

"Concludam . . . verbis Rabbi Jehosuæ in *Talmud.* qui cuidam curiosè percontanti de statu resurgentium ad vitam æternam respondat, *Quando reviviscemus, cognoscemus qualis futurus sit eorum status.* Sic de futura lingua Beatorum in cœlis, quando reviviscemus, cognoscemus illam." (260)

Independently of one another, then, Mongolian man on the Hoang-ho, and Egyptian man on the Nile, each arrived for himself at *picture*-writing: yet, after casting a retrospective look at the relative epochas of both achievements, we behold that the difference between their chronological eras is almost as immense as when we, who in this day actually "*print* by lightning," see an Indian spend hours of lifetime in the effort to adorn a deer-skin with the uncouth record of his scalping exploits. At the time when Prince Mer-het (261) caused his sepulchre to be carved and painted with those exquisite hieroglyphs, that, through 16 *phonetic*, many *figurative*, and a few *symbolical* signs, relate his immediate descent from King Shoopho (262) builder of the mightiest mausoleum ever raised by human hand,—under the shadows of which great pyramid this (probably) son reposed: at that time, which, it is far more likely, ascends rather beyond than falls within the thirty-fifth century B. C., or 5400 years backward from our day—what was the state of civilization in China? Now, the most exacting of native *Chinese* archæologists will confess that their first Emperor Fo-hi (whose *name* emblematizes to the Chinese mind above 1000 years of meta-history, as that of Moses did to the Hebrew intellect in the age of *Hilkiah* the high-priest), (263) that this Fo-hi—*inventor* of writing, (264) through the legendary "8 *koua*"—scarcely floats upon the foam of tradition's loftiest surge: because, no Chinese scholar claims for Fo-hi's semi-mythical reign a date earlier than B. C. 3468; while conceding that perhaps it may have begun 600 years later.

And, if we compare *monuments*, then the *oldest* (265) written record of China claims no higher date than the "Inscription of Yu," estimated at B. C. 2278—being above 1000 years posterior to the Egyptian tomb of Mer-het, now in the Royal Museum of Berlin. All earlier Chinese documents being lost, the times anterior to Yu are, *palæographically*, blanks; but skepticism (scientific, not, the most obdurate, theological,) has no more reason to reject what of rational story pierces through the gloom of generations preceding, as concerns China, than we have to consider fabulous the British periods of the *Heptarchy*, although we cannot now individualize many events, and possess no Saxon "Saga" coeval with their occurrence.

A moment's pause will illustrate in what respect *Egypt's* monuments tower as loftily above Chinese antiquity, as *St. Peter's* at Rome above New York "Trinity Church." Our remarks are not directed to personages who, stifled beneath ante-metaphysical strata, read little and know less; but to readers who have perused, or will examine, the writings of at least Bunsen, Lepsius, Birch, and De Rougé; without disparagement of these scholars' ardent colleagues, too numerous for specification.

Whilst the pyramids and tombs of the IVth Memphite dynasty in Egypt stand, about B. C. 3500, at the uppermost terminus of that lengthy monumental chain—the coils of which, within a range of twenty miles, may still be unwound from Mohammed-Ali's mosque at Cairo, link by link, century by century, and stone by stone, back through all the vicissitudes of Nilotic annals, for 5400 years, till we touch the sepulchre of Prince Merhet—these pyramids, these tombs, themselves reveal infinite data upon ages to their construction long anterior; but, how long? Utterly unknown.

For instance, we here present the hieroglyphic for *scribe*, *writing*, or *to write*. It is compounded of the *reed*, calamus, or pen; the *ink*-bottle; and the scribe's *palette*, with two little cavities for his black and red inks. It may be seen

(260) WALTON: *Prolegomena*; ii. par. 25, p. 19.

(261) LEPSIUS: *Denkmäler*; and *supra*, p. 238; fig. 154.

(262) *Ibid.*; *Briefe aus Ægypten, Æthiopien*, &c.; Berlin, 1852; pp. 37, 38—"Superintendent of all constructions of the king."

(263) About B. C. 625—2 *Kings* xxii. 8; 2 *Chron.* xxxiv. 14.

(264) PAUTHIER; *Chine*; pp. 24–26.

(265) *Ibid.*; p. 53.

on all monuments of the IVth Dynasty:(266) and its presence proves that *writing* must have been common enough in Egypt during ages antecedent. So again, here is  —a roll of *papyrus*-paper, a volume, tied with strings—meaning a "Book." Its presence upon the monuments, not merely of the XIIth, but of the VIth, and even of the same old IVth dynasty, establishes that the invention of *paper*, and the usage of written *volumes*, antedate the earliest hieroglyphics now extant.

It would require an especial treatise to convey to readers any adequate idea of the copiousness of ancient Egyptian documents written on *papyrus*-paper existing and deciphered at the present day. There are some of the IVth (B. C. 3400) and succeeding dynasties down to the XIIth B. C. 2200) in legible preservation; but the great "age of the Papyri" belongs to the XVIIth and following dynasties;(267) that is, from the 17th century B. C. downwards. Independently of the thousands of copies of the "Book of the Dead," there are *poems, account-books, contracts, decrees, chronological lists, histories, romances, scientific essays*, —in short, it is really more difficult now to define what there is not, than to catalogue the enormous collections of *Papyri*, some written ages before Moses's birth, existing in European cabinets. At foot we indicate where the curious inquirer may satisfy himself upon the accuracy of this statement. (268) And if he wishes to behold the *transitions* of Egyptian writing from the hieroglyphic into the hieratic, he need only open Lepsius's *Denkmäler*.(269) We have no space to enlarge upon these facts here, which the writer's *Lecture-rooms* have exhibited in most of the chief cities of the Union.

All which premised, as facts at this day open to everybody's verification, the reader comprehends that, if *picture*-writing, as well on the Nile as on the Hoang-ho, was the first stage towards *phonetic* orthography; nevertheless, according to *monumental* evidences, the Egyptians had already been inscribing their thoughts in perfect *hieroglyphics*, "sacred sculptured characters," a thousand years before the Chinese had perfected a system of *ideographics*, to us represented by their primitive character KOU-WEN.

It is from Champollion's *Grammaire Egyptienne* (270) that the reader must draw clear definitions of Nilotic classifications into the *phonetic, figurative*, and *symbolical*, elements of calligraphy: and Mr. Birch's definition of Egypt's pristine 16 monosyllabic articulations— *a, b, f, g, h, i, k, m, n, p, r* × *l, s, t, sh, kh, u*,—is the most accessible to the English reader. (271) For *Chinese* analogies and discrepancies, as said before, there is no satisfactory work but the *Sinico-Ægyptiaca*.

Through their study the reader will glean how—starting both from the same springs, although chronologically and geographically distinct, viz., PICTURE-WRITING—the Egyptian rivulet, gushing forth naturally in one direction, formed the HIEROGLYPHICS; whence, in due time, through *Semitish* channels, streamed those mighty rivers that, from Chaldea, have watered Europe, Hindostan, Northern Asia, Africa, America, and Australia, with the refreshing rills of *Phœnicia's* alphabet: and how the Chinese fountain, its waters taking an opposite direction, created the IDEOGRAPHICS; which, cramped within gutters artificially if ingeniously conceived, have enabled the Chinamen to attain a system, it is true, essentially phonetic, and which, originating in a Mongolian brain, suffices for all the necessities of Mongol articulations: notwithstanding that A B C are as alien to its complex construction as our English language is remote from the agglutinations of an Indian, or the "gluckings" of a Hottentot. The Chinese never have had an *alphabet*. It is impossible, without organic changes which human history does not sanction, that the Sinico-Mongol ever can possess that, to us the simplest, method of chronicling our thoughts.

---

(266) LEPSIUS: *Chronologie*; i. p. 33;—*Todtenbuch*; 1842; Pref. p. 17;—BUNSEN: *Eg's Pl.*; i. p. 8.

(267) HINCKS: *Trans. R. Irish Acad.*; 1846.

(268) *Select Papyri*; published by the British Museum;—LEPSIUS: *Chronologie*; i. pp. 39, 40;—PRISSE, DE ROUGÉ, and CHAMPOLLION-FIGEAC'S papers, in the *Revue Archéologique*;—and BIRCH'S in *Trans. R. Soc. Lit.*, and in the *Archæologia*; &c.

(269) *Abth.*; ii. bl. 98, 99.

(270) A synoptical sketch is in GLIDDON: *Chapters*; 1843.

(271) GLIDDON: *Otia*; pp. 113-115; but better in LEPSIUS: *Vorläufige Nachricht*; 1849; p. 35.

In consequence of which reflections, fortified by the physical deductions elsewhere embodied in "Types of Mankind," we have assigned to MONGOL-*origins* a distinct column in our theoretical Tableau of human palæographic history.

For the objects of anthropology, the above explanatory remarks would be sufficient, were not notions current among those readers, who look to theology for biblical criteria, to metaphysics for archæological—1st., that the "Chinese" are recorded in Scripture; and ergo, that *Mongolian* races were familiar to Jewish writers; 2d., that "Chinese vases" have been found in tombs of the XVIIIth dynasty at Thebes; and ergo, that Egypt and China were in positive communication about the time of Moses. (272) So we digress.

Once upon a time an adage prevailed in literary controversies—*Cave hominem unius libri.* Through what impairing causes is to us unknown, but certain it is, that in proportion as one ascends in English theological literature to the Kennicotts, Warburtons, Lowths, Cudworths, Stillingfleets, Waltons, and other intellectual giants of that deceased school, so one's respect for divines and one's reverence for Scripture augment. They had *one* book to study professionally, and that book they knew well; because they actually read it.

It would appear that there are cycles of deterioration, as evident in theology as in the weather, to judge by what took place in China about A. D. 1368; and inasmuch as our inquiries first concern the Chinese, it is but fair that they should open proceedings.

The Emperor Houng-Wou, appalled at the degradation of scholarship consequent upon the tragic events that preceded him, one day convoked the "Tribunals of Literature" (equivalent to the French Ministère d'Instruction Publique), (273) and made to them a common sense speech, the pith of which is here in extract:

> "The ancients," said he, "the ancients used to write but few books, but they made them good. . . . Our modern *litterati* write a great deal, and upon subjects that cannot be of the slightest real utility. . . . The ancients wrote with perspicacity, and their writings were suited to the comprehension of everybody.
> . . . In former times their works were read with pleasure, and one reads them at this day [A. D. 1368, in China!] with the same.
> . . . You [addressing himself to the Censors of the Press], you, who stand at the head of literature, make all your efforts to restore good *sense:* you will never succeed but by imitating the ancients. (274)

In the days between Walton and Kennicott, a theological student who might have ventured to opine that the Chinese are mentioned in the Bible, would have been sent incontinently to read the Hebrew text of Isaiah. (275) When this task was executed (and, formerly, divinity students could read a little Hebrew), the young man would have found a place on the lowest form, by command of the Professor of History, for ignorance of the rudiments of his class. Shame would soon have impelled an ingenuous youth, of those days gone by, to cram his head with simple facts of which some of his elders in theology now seem unaware. (276)

Chinese history—in this question the most valid—proves that, until the year 102 after Christ, the Chinese never knew of the existence of any countries situate north and west of Persia. Between the years 89–106 A. D., in the reign of Ho-Ti, a vast Chinese army, under General Kan-Ying, detached by the Commander-in-Chief, Pan-tchao, halted on the shores of the Caspian Sea; (277) receiving the submission of the Tad-jiks (Persians) and

---

(272) Vide GLIDDON'S IVth *Lecture*—reported in "Daily Dispatch," March 18; and in "Richmond Examiner," March 21; Richmond, Va., 1851. Also, more extensively, in "The Union," Washington, D. C., April 25, 1851. The abusive writers alluded to in that discourse, as

"Mere youths in science, and to fame unknown,"

were the reverend authors of "Unity of the Human Races," 1850; of an article in the *Princeton Review*, 1851; and of a third article, the one prelauded [*supra*, p. 587], as emanating from an Ass. of Min. at Col., S. C.

(273) ED. BIOT: *Essai sur l'Instruction publique en Chine;* 1846.

(274) PAUTHIER: *Chine d'après les Documents Chinois;* pp. 393, 394.

(275) ISAIAH; xlix. 12.

(276) Rev. THOMAS SMYTHE, D.D.: *Unity of the Human Races;* 1850; p. 43;—Rev. Dr. HOWE: *Southern Presbyterian Review;* Columbia, S. C., No. 3, Jan. 1851; &c.

(277) REMUSAT: *Mém. sur l'Extension de l'Empire Chin. du coté de l'Occident;*—PAUTHIER, *Chine;* pp. 258-260.

of the *Asi* [*supra*, MaGUG, p. 471]. A powerful interest, however, incited these last to withhold correct information on western countries from the Chinese officer; viz.: that, hitherto, they had held the monopoly of the raw *silk* trade, by caravan, between China and the West; which silk, dyed and woven into then-priceless raiments by the Parthians, found its way occasionally to the grandees of Europe; and, on the other hand, one of the practical motives which carried Roman eagles to the Tigris, was a hope to discover the unknown source whence the crude material of these exquisite fabrics had reached Persia. It was during this, the most distant military expedition ever undertaken before Genghis-Khàn, that the Chinese heard, for the first time, of the existence, far west from the *Asi*, of the Roman Empire. Deterred from advance for its conquest by the discouraging report of the Parthians that his commissariat ought to be supplied for three years, the Chinese General renounced the enterprise, and returned to headquarters at Khotàn.

From the opposite direction, the arms of Rome had not been turned towards Persia until, about B. C. 53, Pro-Consul Crassus perished by Parthian arrows on the western frontier of Persia; some 155 years before the Chinese had penetrated to its south-eastern provinces. Within four years after the retrograde march of the Chinese armies, Parthia was invaded by Trajan, A. D. 106; and it was about that generation, a few years more or less, that the Romans first heard, through the Persians, of the remote country whence the silk came. (278) In A. D. 166, Antoninus sent the first Roman embassy to China; the hospitable reception of which is chronicled, by contemporary Chinese annalists, in the reign of their Emperor Houan-Ti.

No nations, then, situated to the north-west of Persia, so far as history or monuments relate, had ever heard of China; nor had the Chinese known anything about such nations until after the Christian era. Surmises to the contrary require, nowadays, to be justified by something more substantial than the *ipse dixit* of moderns, however erudite, whose opinions were formed before geographical criticism had fixed the boundaries of antique intercommunicational possibilities.

With this historical basis, let us take up the only word in the entire canon of Scripture, upon which living theologists have erected a fable, that the Chinese are mentioned in the Old Testament. Even king James's version suffices for this discussion: — "Behold these [the Jewish Babylonian exiles] shall come from far; and, lo, these from the north and from the west; and these from the land of *Sinim*." (279) "Our modern *litterati*," says the Emperor Houng-Wou, "write a great deal;" and sustain that *Sinim* means the Chinese; because, after stripping away the Hebrew plural IM, there remains the word SIN; and the native name of China is THSIN.

Now, the whole context of the prophet refers to the return of the Jews from bondage in Babylonia. It must, therefore, be in Mesopotamian vicinities that the SIN*s*—"inhabitants of SIN;" or, otherwise, "cities, districts, localities of" SIN—should be sought for, before traversing Central Asia, in such impassable ages, to recall from China unknown Jewish fugitives who might have escaped thither from Babylonia.

The root SIN of Isaiah is not SINI; (280) and, furthermore, that SIN*ian* was a Canaanite. Nor is it either of the "wildernesses of SIN" familiar to the Mosaic Israelites; because the first, (281) spelt with the letter *sameq*, lay close to Egypt: and the second (282) was T*s*IN, near the Dead Sea. Far less could it have meant the Egyptian city of *Pelusium;* called Sin, (283) or dialectically T*h*IN, anciently, as *Teen* now by the Arabs. Why travel to China, when Mesopotamia itself offers to every eye, in an excellent map, (284) at the

(278) On "Sérica," and the fact that little or nothing was known about it by writers antecedent to Claudius Ptolemy, in the second century after Christ; compare the excellent *critique* of ANTHON, *Class. Dict.*, voce "Seres."

(279) ISAIAH: xlix. 12.

(280) *Genesis;* x. 17; *supra*, p. 531.

(281) *Exodus;* xvi. 1; xvii. 1.

(282) *Numbers;* xiii. 21; — *Deuteronomy;* xxxii. 51; &c.

(283) EZEKIEL: xxx. 15, 16.

(284) FRASER: *Mesopotamia;* 1841; — XENOPHON: *Anab.;* lib. ii. 4.

mouth of the river Lycus, the vestiges of a city termed *Kainai* by Greeks, *Cænæ* by Romans, and *Senn* by Arabians? Or, if it be absolutely necessary to obtain SINIM (more SINs than one), add to the preceding *Senn* the site of *Sina*, (285) about fifty miles northeastward of Mosul; together with the "large mounds" called *Sen*, on the banks of the Euphrates, opposite Dair.

One, or two, or all of these localities, amply suffice for the extremest points whence the Jews were to be summoned from captivity; and, singly or collectively, they are comprehended in the LXX translation; where *Sinîm* is paraphrased by εκ γης Περσων — "from a land of the Persians."

Aside from the obvious adaptation of these places, near the Euphrates or the Tigris, to the natural sway of Nebuchadnezzar who captured the Jews, no less than of Cyrus and Artaxerxes who released them; it is physically impossible, as well as unhistorical, that ancient Jews should have been expatriated to China: a country none of their descendants ever reached until centuries after the Christian era. (286) It is equally out of the question that the Septuagint translators could have known anything of China — a land beyond the horizon of Alexandrian knowledge previously to the time of Trajan, about a century after c.; or some 230 years after the various Hellenistic-Jews, called the LXX [*ubi supra*], had completed their labors. Indeed, they pretend to nothing of the kind; for they well knew that the SINIM were in the "land of the Persians;" while Orientalists of the present day always understand, with the Chaldee paraphrast, "from the southern country" of Assyria, in that passage. (287)

We forbear from reagitating here the question elsewhere treated, whether there were really "twelve tribes" of Israel before the times of Sennacherib; nor what became of the ten said to have remained — where? Some moderns (288) claim that these Israelites marched round by Behring's Straits into America; and, after building the cities of ancient Mexico and Peru, have run wild in our woods—in short, unaccountably become our Indians. Others have sought for them in Affghanistan; (289) although the portraits of Dost-Mohammed, Shah-Soojah, and their fierce cavaliers, are as little Jewish in lineaments as are their speech, and still more their bellicose habits: for the Bible shows that the Jews of Palestine, except under supernatural circumstances, were beaten and enslaved by any adjacent tribe that happened to covet their persons or property. If ever supposititious offshoots of the "ten tribes" wandered as far as Cabul, Bokhara, Balkh, or Samarcand, they were Jews at their migration, and Jews they would have remained in type and in religion, if certainly not in language. Wolff found his compatriots everywhere. Indeed, we know, personally and positively, that had the reverend renegade not been a true Hebrew, he could never have traversed Central Asia in 1832–'5. But he narrates that the fathers of those who kindly welcomed him, on the score of his inextinguishable Judaism, had established themselves in Affghan provinces very long after the fall of Jerusalem. We also know that Arabs (to the Abrahamidæ closely allied) settled in Persia, Khorassan, Balkh, &c., ever since the Muslim invasion, one thousand years ago, having rarely intermarried with Tartars, remain physiologically distinct to this day. Yet while they have preserved the name, religion, and appearance of Arabs, they have lost their Arabian language. (290) So it is with the Hebrew nation in every clime—indelibility of physical type, coupled with a most pliant faculty for change of tongue. If, then, exactly "ten tribes" of Israel were swept away into Chaldea, they did but return to their aboriginal centre of creation; and (mixing voluntarily with no type of mankind but their own) they have naturally disappeared amid the

---

(285) LAYARD: *Second Expedition, Babylon;* 1853; *Map of Journeys;* and p. 297

(286) About 60,000 Jews are reputed to be there now; others reached Malabar about A.D. 490; — See NOTT: *Phys. Hist. of the Jewish Race;* 1850; pp. 12, 13; and *supra*, pp. 117-123.

(287) CAHEN: *Bible;* ix. p. 176, note 12.

(288) DELAFIELD: *American Antiquities.*

(289) DUBEUX: *Afghanistan;* pp. 65, 66.

(290) MALCOLM: *History of Persia;* 1815; p. 277; — MORIER: *Second Journey through Persia;* 1818; i. pp. 47, 48; — PICKERING: *Races;* 1848; p. 240.

waves of a homogeneous population. These opinions, long avowed by the authors, are confirmed by the views and new facts of Layard.(291)

But we finish with orthodoxy's "Chinese":—

From a previously small feod of the Celestial Gates, called *Thsin*, given by Hiao-Wang, about B. C. 909, to one of his jockeys, issued a line of princes whose constant acquisitiveness had enabled them, by the year B. C. 249, to incorporate a fifth part of the Chinese realm, and to extend over it their patronymic title of *Thsin*. Out of this stock sprung Thsin-Chi-Hoang-Ti, at once the Augustus and the Napoleon of China—founder of the fourth or *Thsin* dynasty, whose name signifies "the first absolute sovereign of the dynasty of *Thsin*." About B. C. 221, all the principalities of China were consolidated under his supreme sway; and, as a consequence, the name *Thsin* became, in common parlance, synonymous with the whole empire. Proud of his mighty exploits, although detesting the individual, the Chinese, from and after his day, adopting the word *Thsin* as typical of China itself, originated the Hindoo appellative "Tchina," whence we inherit our corrupt designation "China." Under these circumstances we tender to future sustainers of Chinese in Scripture a many-horned dilemma:—

Either the Prophet Isaiah (whose meaning is so naturally explained above) by the word SINIM does not refer to the Chinese, or inasmuch as the Chinese empire was not called *Thsin* previously to B. C. 221—which is about 450 years after Isaiah wrote—the verse 12 of chapter xlix of the book called "Isaiah" cannot possibly have been penned by Isaiah, but is the addition of some nameless interpolator: who must have lived, too, later than the first century after Christ, when the existence of China first became known, under its recent name *Thsin*, to nations dwelling west of the Euphrates. The writers called the "Seventy" knew nothing of this absurd Chinese attribution, as their "Land of the Persians" attests.

Were it not for them who thus had paraphrased SINIM between B. C. 260 and 130, the interpolation of a mere verse, after the year A. D. 100, in a prophetic book wherein whole chapters had been previously interpolated, would excite small surprise among biblical exegetists. "If, for example," writes the great Hebraist of the "Bibliothèque Impériale," (292) "in a prophetic book, bearing the name of Isaiah, they speak to you of the return from Babylonish exile; if they go so far as even to name Cyrus, who is posterior to Isaiah by about two centuries, be assured that it is not Isaiah who speaks." And if that explanation does not satisfy theological exigencies, then let some people bear in mind that the word SINIM occurs in the forty-ninth chapter of Isaiah; and that, according to the highest biblical critics of Germany, whose mouth-piece is the eminent Professor of Theology at Basle,(293) "the whole of the second part of the collection of oracles under Isaiah's name (xl.—lxvi.) is spurious." But they say Chinese vases have been found in tombs of the Mosaic age in Egypt; and, *ergo*, that China was known some 3300 years ago to the ancient Egyptians. The archæological interest of this alleged fact has been revived in the present year by two new phases:—

First. The presence at New York, among a variety of Egyptian antiquities, less authentic, of—

"No. 626.—A Chinese vase, with 17 others of different forms. All found in tombs. Some from Thebes; others from Sakharah and Ghizeh.

"These vases are curious, inasmuch as they prove the early communication between Egypt and China. *Vide* Rosoleni [*sic* for Rosellini]; Sir Gardner Wilkinson's Manners and Customs; Sir John Davis's Sketches of China, p. 72, and Revue Archœologique, by Mr. E. Prisse.

"No. 627.—A Chinese padlock, found in the tombs at Sakharah." (294)

This last *bijou* is a confirmation of ancient intercourse between Pharaonic Egypt and

(291) *Op. cit.*; pp. 373, 383–386.

(292) MUNK: *Palestine*; p. 420.

(293) DE WETTE: Parker's transl. ii. p. 336; and also HENNELL: *Origin of Christianity*; 1845; pp. 354, 355.

(294) "*Catalogue of a Collection of Egyptian Antiquities*, the property of Henry Abbott, M. D., now exhibiting at the Stuyvesant Institute, No. 659, Broadway, New York"; 1853; p. 44.

China, of which orthodox navigation may well be proud, especially now that two additional vases have been discovered since Joseph Bonomi, in his sly way, indicated the extreme rarity of such antiques at Cairo, 1843.

"No. 254.—Padlock, Chinese, said to be found at Sakhara.

"No. 255.—Thirteen Chinese bottles, of the usual form, and with the inscription in the Chinese characters; and three bottles of different shape, found in Egyptian tombs, both in Upper Egypt and Sakhara. The larger portion of this collection was found in Sakhara. Bottles exactly similar may be purchased in the perfume bazaar of Cairo; and in 1842 the Jannissary of the Prussian Mission purchased ten of them." (295)

Second. The deterration of two similar Chinese vases by Layard, one from the mound of Arban, and another from its vicinity. These are the more precious as they show the orthodox and primeval overland route of Egypto-Chinese intercourse by way of Assyria, in ages preceding the discovery of the monsoons, about A. D. 45, by the Greek pilot Hippalus.(296)

"In a trench on the south side of the ruin, was found a small green and white bottle, inscribed with Chinese characters. A similar relic was brought to me from a barrow in the neighbourhood. Such bottles have been discovered in Egyptian tombs, and considerable doubt [not the remotest] exists as to their antiquity, and as to the date and manner of their importation into Egypt. (*Note.* —Wilkinson, in his 'Ancient Egyptians,' vol. iii. p. 107, gives a drawing of a bottle precisely similar to that described in the text, and mentions one which, according to Rosellini, had been discovered in a previously unopened tomb, believed to be of the eighteenth dynasty. But there appears to be considerable doubt on the subject.) The best opinion now is, that they are comparatively modern, and that they were brought by the Arabs, in the eighth or ninth century, from the kingdoms of the far East, with which they had at that period extensive commercial intercourse. Bottles precisely similar are still offered for sale at Cairo, and are used to hold the kohl or powder for staining the eyes of the ladies." (297)

Since the conquest of Algeria, Parisian naturalists have been constantly employed by the French Government to collect every specimen of natural history that region affords. One of these enthusiastic savans, lamenting that his predecessors had exhausted the resources of the country, was supplied by the Zouaves with sundry live examples of a wild rat, the species of which was entirely unknown at the Jardins des Plantes. The soldiers called it *rat à trompe.* On arrival of these novelties at the Museum, (298) it was perceived that each rat was adorned by a flexible and hairy proboscis. In time these appendages happening to drop off, some assistant ascertained that the malicious Zouaves had inserted an amputated tail of one species of rat into the nasal cartilage of another! It behooves archæologists, therefore, to view any such marvels as Sinico-Nilotic "padlocks" with more than caution; for, as De Longpérier, the Conservator of the Louvre Museum, writes to De Saulcy, Director of the Musée d'Artillerie, "above all things, now-a-days, *gardons nous des rats à trompe.*"

Chinese vases, of the genus mentioned, having been familiar things to the writer ever since his boyhood's visit to Cairo in 1823, no less than during his official residence there from 1831 to 1841, it was against his wishes (while aiding his revered friend Morton with a few hieroglyphical indices in 1842–3) that the following passage ever saw the light without some qualifying reservation: "That the Chinese had commercial intercourse with the Egyptians in very early times, is beyond question; for vessels of Chinese porcelain, with inscriptions in that language, have been repeatedly found in the Theban catacombs. (Wilkinson's *Ancient Egyptians*, vol. iii. p. 108.)" (299) But Dr. Morton relied upon the accuracy of Wilkinson, and the latter upon that of Rosellini, (300) as to the matters of fact; at the

(295) BONOMI: *Catalogue* of ditto: Cairo, 1846; pp. 25, 26, 35. [Printed in London. We saw its proof-sheets there.]

(296) PLINY: lib. vi. p. 26.

(297) *Babylon:* p. 279.

(298) Vide *Histoire Naturelle de MM. les Professeurs aux Jardins des Plantes:* 12mo, Paris, 1847.

(299) *Crania Ægyptiaca:* 1844; p. 63.

(300) Compare CHAMPOLLION-FIGEAC: *Égypte Ancienne:* 1840; voce "Nechao," p. 369; and *Notice sur deux Grammaires de la Langue Copte:* June, 1842; pp. 7–10. The perusal of these two *critiques* might benefit the author of *Horæ Ægyptiacæ.*

same time that, in the United States, there was no sinologist to whom we could refer the inscriptions themselves. Nor, indeed, was it until the writer studied at Paris, (301) in the winter of 1845–6, that appeal had ever been made from the learned opinion of Davis. (302)

In the letter cited at foot, the Chinese scholar defends his view against the "Quarterly," (February, 1835); which maintained that these vases could not have been found in ancient Egyptian tombs — that the supposition of their being so found depended upon hearsay; neither Lord Prudhoe, Mr. Wilkinson, nor Mrs. Bowen (quondam Mrs. Col. Light), having seen those specimens they had purchased at Coptos and Thebes, extracted from any ancient tomb. To repel which attack, Davis exhibits a letter from Rosellini to the effect, that he saw one withdrawn from an ancient tomb during the Tuscan excavations at Thebes, in 1828–9. And thus, the only archæological process of determining the vastly important fact of Pharaonic intercourse with China, so far as depended upon these vases, stood over until, at the writer's suggestion, and in his presence, *four* specimens were submitted by his valued colleague, Prisse, at the latter's apartments, to their mutual friend, the high sinologue, Pauthier. It is also desirable to note, that the question of the authenticity of these vases arose amongst us at Paris, in consequence of their forming a prominent feature in the "Notice" which M. Prisse was at that time preparing of the identical "Collection of M. H. Abbott;" (303) — a collection that, rejected by Europe, has "fata profugus" since been transferred, with the augmentation of a Chinese padlock, in 1852, from Egypt to New York. "Iisdem in armis fui;" although M. Prisse's own doubts first prompted him to consult the opinion of so old an Egyptian fellow-sojourner as the writer.

M. Prisse had already projected the substance of the following in manuscript:

"It is pretended that these little flasks have been found in Egyptian tombs; but as the fact is contestable, I think it useful to discuss it. Whenever an error is met with in your path, says Bacon, fail not to eradicate it, as a traveller cuts down a bramble in passing. I ought to strain myself the more to destroy this error that I have aided in its propagation, by coöperating in the 'Collection of Dr. Abbott,' and by giving to N. L'Hôte two of those little flasks for the Royal Museum of the Louvre, where they figure under the title of 'Vases Chinois trouvés dans les tombeaux de l'Egypte par MM. Champollion et L'Hôte.' Champollion had bought one of these little vases at Thebes (*Monuments de l'Egypte et de la Nubie*, Pl. 424, No. 28.) N. L'Hôte received from me the two others; and none of them, to my knowledge, had been found in an Egyptian tomb. Rosellini, the only one who pretends to have found a similar one himself (*Monumenti Civili*, vol. iii. p. 397), in a tomb of which he makes the epoch ascend to the XVIIIth dynasty, is not an author very worthy of credit. Sir G. Wilkinson (*Man. and Cust.*, iii. p. 108) believes that these little flasks which held perfumes, had been brought into Egypt by the commerce of India, with which country the ancient Egyptians appear to have been in relation from a very remote epoch: but he does not discuss the authenticity of these vases. Upon the testimony of these two authors, and upon that of the Arabs, I had believed for a long time that these flasks issued from the excavations, and I bought many that I gave away. Soon after, a traveller having assured me that he had seen similar vases at some ports of the Red Sea, (304) I began to conceive doubts. Pressed by questions, the Arabs avowed to me that the greater number of these vases came from Qous, from Qeft and from Qosseyr, successive entrepôts of Indian commerce. This avowal seemed to me peremptory."

It was here that M. Pauthier's call with the writer led opportunely to the sequel.

"Nevertheless, the stability of the arts in China might have caused repetitions of the forms of these vases from early centuries; and the nature of the characters employed in the inscription could alone remove all objection. I consulted at Paris two learned sinologists, MM. Stanislas Julien and Pauthier, who assured me that the characters *thsao*, painted upon these vases, dated solely from the second century of our era. M. Pauthier has been pleased to indite a note upon this subject, which I hasten to publish in order to terminate the discussion."

From Pauthier's "Note upon the Chinese vases found in Egypt," we have condensed the

(301) Prisse: *Recherches sur les legendes de SCKAI:* Revue Archéol., 1845; pp. 457–475, note.

(302) *Lettre à M. Bunsen sur les Vases Chinois trouvés dans d'Anciens Tombeaux:* translated from the English in *Annali dell' Instituto di Corr. Archeol. di Roma*, 1836; p. 322, *seq.*, and plate G.

(303) *Notice sur le Musée du Kaire, et sur les Collections Égyptiennes de MM. Abbott, Clot Bey, et Harris:* Revue Archéol., 15 Mars, 1846; tirage à part, pp. 3–28, and wood-cuts, pp. 18, 19.

(304) Compare Pickering: *Races of Men and their Geographical Distribution:* 1848; p. 400.

subjoined. In his work, "The Chinese," under the article "Porcelain," Gov. J. F. Davis, of Hong-kong, refers to the exceptions taken by the Quarterly Review, citing Wilkinson and Rosellini for the fact of the discovery of such vases in Egyptian catacombs.

"M. Letronne, when giving account, in the Journal des Savans, (Nov. 1844, p. 665,) of the work of Mr. Wilkinson, thus expresses himself: 'The author believes in the Chinese origin of certain porcelain vases, found in the tombs at Thebes, of which one is of the XVIIIth dynasty. He gives the figures of four of these vases, with Chinese inscriptions, which Mr. Davis flatters himself with having read. We know that other sinologues doubt this origin. The fact deserves to be cleared up by a contradictory discussion. . . . There is nothing in it impossible, but it seems *little verisimilar*. . . . Yet, if these inscriptions are really *Chinese*, the fact must be accepted. All lies in that.'"

It is merely justice to Morton's memory here to remark that his "Crania Ægyptiaca" had appeared in the spring of 1844, at Philadelphia. Nor is his discrimination amenable, on questions alien to his special studies, to the charge of hastily adopting, in good faith, that which Parisian science had not begun to ventilate for six months later.

After stating that no sinologist doubted that these vases "are really and purely *Chinese*," M. Pauthier holds that all the question does "not lie in that;" and then eliminates the facts as follows:—

1. The inscriptions upon these vases are in the cursive Chinese character called *thsao*.
2. This cursive character was not invented in China until the second century after Christ. Hence "it is materially impossible that vases, bearing inscriptions in that writing, could have been manufactured and transported to Egypt in the time of the XVIIIth dynasty; that is to say, about 1800 years before the said epoch!"

   Gov. Davis, "well versed in the study of the vulgar Chinese (language), seems, like some other sinologues, to have completely neglected the study of Chinese archæology." Nevertheless, on the vase published by him (No. 4 of Wilkinson, and of M. Prisse), one reads easily:—
3. "*Ming youê soung tchoung tchao:* 'the brilliant moon is resplendent through the pines.'"
4. This is a line from a "strophe composed by Wang-gan-chi, who lived under the Soung dynasty, in 1068 of our era; and corrected in the last syllable by Sou-toung-po, who flourished fifty years later."
5. The highest antiquity of the cursive character on these vases being 200 years after Christ, and the verse written upon them being from an author who lived early in the twelfth century of the same era — it follows that the vases in question have been transported into Egypt since the year 1100 A. D. M. Pauthier gives reasons, from Chinese history, why some of them may have been brought back from China by Arabian embassies in the fifteenth century after Christ; to which age probably belong the two specimens recently exhumed from the Khabour mounds by Dr. Layard.

But, as the writer, and Mr. Bonomi, and M. Prisse, and others, have known for these twenty years, such vases abound in Egypt; especially after the annual return of the *Hadj*, or Mecca pilgrims, to Qossèyr and Cairo. The Mosaic Theban tombs are supplied through the former; the ante-Abrahamic catacombs of Memphite Saccàra through the latter mercantile channels; while the drug bazaars of Cairo and of Qenneh have always a stock on hand — price fluctuating, according to the demands of antiquaries, between two and a half and three and a half cents apiece, retail. Arab curiosity-mongers are thus enabled to furnish imbecilities travelling along the Nile with Sinico-Ægyptian vases even of ante-diluvian antiquity, on application. In the meanwhile, archæologists are aware of the sort of proofs of "early communication between Egypt and China" the New York collection embraces.

To close the digression. The reader will duly take note that the New York catalogue, above cited, refers to the "Revue Archœologique, by Mr. E. Prisse." The proprietor of the invaluable "Revue *Archéologique*" is M. Leleux; but while the author of the "catalogue" aforesaid mentions both the work and the savant whose inquiries, seven years ago, demonstrated a "Chinese vase with 17 others" to be, as antiquities, spurious; readers of that document need not wonder at the appropriate association, in the same unique cabinet, of *similia similibus.*

All obstacles to the appreciation of what we mean by "Mongolian Origin," in the theory of human graphical development, being now removed, but a few paragraphs are necessary to elucidate that section of the General Table devoted to

3d. AMERICAN ORIGIN.—To another department of "Types of Mankind" belongs the argumentative exhibition of those data, whereby the aboriginal groups of American humanity are disconnected from other centres of creation [*supra*, Chap. IX]. The purposes of our tableau are served by reference to Morton for the *craniological*, to Gallatin for the *philological*, and to Squier for the *archæological* bases of discussion.

It is unnecessary to reiterate the emphatic disclaimers of Dr. Morton, concerning any recognition by himself of such notions as an exotic origin for *American Indians*. Dr. Patterson's Memoir [*supra*, pp. xlvi–xlix] and our various *Chapters* [VII. p. 232; IX. p. 275; X. pp. 305–307, 324–326] have removed from Morton's cherished memory any further attributions to him of these philosophical heresies. (305)

The total segregation of American aborigines from other types of man throughout the rest of our globe, deduced in the present volume from the former's osteological peculiarities, animal propensities, geographical constitution, and what of history has been made *for* Indian nations by post-Columbian foreigners, results equally from the matured philology of Gallatin.

"I beg leave once more to repeat that, unless we suppose that which we have no right to do, a second miraculous interposition of Providence in America, the prodigious number of American languages, totally dissimilar in their vocabularies, demonstrates not only that the first peopling of America took place at the earliest date which we are permitted to assume, but also that the great mass of existing Indian nations are the descendants of the first [imaginary] emigrants; since we must otherwise suppose that America was peopled by one hundred different tribes, speaking languages totally dissimilar in their nature."(306)

Dr. Young it was who first made languages the subject of mathematical calculation:—

"It appears, therefore, that nothing could be inferred with respect to the relation of two languages, from the coincidence of the sense of any given word in both of them; and that the odds would be three to one against the agreement of two words; but if three words appear to be identical, it would then be more than ten to one that they must be derived in both cases from some parent language, or introduced in some other manner; six words would give more than seventeen hundred chances to one, and eight near one hundred thousand; so that, in these cases, the evidence would be little short of absolute certainty." (307)

Comparative philology now recognizes the grammatical structure of tongues as the sole criterion, which point we have explained in its proper place; but those whose minds have been led astray by the plausible application of arithmetical formulæ to the chances of intercourse between ante-Columbian American nations and the aborigines of Europe, Asia, Africa or Australasia—based upon vocabularies said to be coincident in about one hundred and eighty words—would do well to ponder upon the fiat of the greatest archæologist of our generation, Letronne:—

"Profound mathematicians have essayed, principally since Condorcet, to apply the calculus of probabilities to questions of moral order, and above all to the divers degrees of certitude in historical facts. They have flattered themselves upon ability to calculate how much might be bet against one, that a given event had or had not happened. Unfortunately, they have not seen that such a probability can yield but a result chimerical and illusory! In no case could it replace that conviction, intimate, absolute, admitting neither more nor less, which the examination of the diversified circumstances accompanying a real event produces. To those who may yet preserve any confidence in this abusive employment of mathematical analysis, I would venture the counsel that they should undertake to find out, through calculation, what new chance of probability is added by the fortuitous discovery of all these contemporaneous testimonies [such as Squier has disinterred from the primeval mounds of the West] which seem to emerge from the earth expressly to con-

(305) The substance of our remarks appeared, under the heading of "The Progress of Knowledge *versus* the Increase of Crime," in the New Orleans *Picayune*, June 12 and 19, 1853; signed G. R. G.

(306) *American Civilization:* Trans. Amer. Amer. Ethnol. Soc.; 1845; i. p. 179.

(307) *Experiments on the Pendulum:* Philos. Trans.; London, 1819; p. 7.

firm history. They will feel, I think, the uselessness, the vanity of their efforts; because that which results naturally from this unexpected accord, is not one of those definite probabilities estimable in numbers and in ciphers; it is a complete certitude which, with irresistible force, takes possession of every mind that is honest and exempt from prejudice." (308)

Not a solitary point of identity which cannot, at a glance, be explained by the rule — that similar causes operating upon similar principles produce everywhere the same effects— exists between the sculptured and architectural monuments of the Old World and those of the New, as known in 1853 to archæologists: not a tongue, habit, custom, mythe or idea found among the aborigines of America by Columbus, can be traced back to any anterior communication with other inhabitants of our planet. The real differences, moreover, in the geological constituents, the fauna, the flora, and the entire range of physical nature whence American man drew his artistic models, preponderate infinitely over those partial resemblances which, when not caused by the circumscribed necessities of all human things, are simply accidental—if accidents can occur in the organic laws of creative power.

Take up the works of Squier. (309) What relic of art, what natural object, what human or non-human thing, unearthed from those forest-clad mounds, is not solely and exclusively American? Run your finger along the map from the sub-polar limit of the Esquimaux down to the Terra del Fuego, and where, in published designs, of respectable authenticity, can you point out a fact, in native human economy, anterior to the fifteenth century after Christ, that compels your reason to travel off the American continent for its origin? We cannot find, at this day, pretensions to any but one. There is nothing, earnestly insists Mr. Squier, (310) even in the most curious of all mythological coincidences yet discovered between the Old and New Hemispheres, viz: the "serpent worship," that necessarily drives an archæologist away from this continent for explanation: the very figurative expression of this American mythe is, "ab ovo," a rattlesnake! Mr. Squier's subsequent pursuits in Europe (311) have opened, he tells us personally, hopeful prospects of filling up some gaps between tribes of Indians still extant and the Azteq and Tolteq scribes of ancient Mexico. He is now in Central America exploring untrodden ground; and may he succeed in his indefatigable restorations.

The possibility of Malayan, Polynesian, Japanese, or other shipwreck on the American Pacific coasts, having been established by such accident within our generation, is not disputed; but there are three common-place reasons that militate against the probability that contingencies of this sporadic nature had any the slightest influence in stocking this continent with its groups of Indian aborigines: 1st. No memento of any similar event exists in the speech, semi-civilization, art, or mythe, of the American world to induce such hypothesis; which originates simply in evangelical cravings — European fathers "of that thought." Nor, were it proven, could such petty accident establish intercourse; because these ancient castaways never returned home again; and (still stranger to relate) there are no "Indians" in the countries whence originally they sailed. 2d. In the ratio that antiquity is claimed for such a supposititious chance, so, owing to proportionate diminution of human navigatory ability, the physical possibilities of its occurrence become "fine by degrees, and beautifully less." 3d. As Morton long ago declared, "If the Egyptians, Hindoos, or Gauls have ever, by accident or design, planted colonies in America, these must have been, sooner or later, dispersed and lost in the waves of a vast indigenous population;" so that, Indians existing before the arrival of such metaphorical colonists, the old difficulty remains.

Of Irish or Welsh "Indians" it will be time enough to speak, when their "coprolites" —we dare not say their historical vestiges — are found, not merely on this continent, but west of the European "Ultima Thule" of established Celto-maniac migrations.

---

(308) *Recueil des Inscriptions Grecques et Latines de l'Égypte*: 1842; i., Introd., p. 63.

(309) *Observations on the Aboriginal Monuments of the Mississippi Valley*: New York, 1847; — *Ancient Monuments of the Mississippi Valley*: 1848; and, besides fragmentary papers, *Nicaragua*: 1852.

(310) *American Archæology*: "The Serpent Symbol;" 1851; pp. 170, 171.

(311) Sketched in the New York *Tribune*: 24 Nov. 1852.

Far be it from us to disparage the Icelandic researches of the "Royal Society of Northern Antiquaries at Copenhagen;" nor their "Scriptores Septentrionales Rerum Ante-Columbiarum." (312) Most laudable are their national resuscitations of "Sagas" recounting the voyages of Eric-rufus, or of Thorfinn Karlsefne; particularly those affording *American* proofs of that genealogy of Thorvaldsen, the great sculptor, back to the eleventh century after Christ. In our humble opinion, however, Thor, with his hammer, is much older; but, unable to seize the exact threads of connection between the "Fornmanna Sögur" of Iceland and the autocthones of the American continent, we are fain to leave their unravelling to the incredulous author of the "Monumental Evidences of the Discovery of America by the Northmen critically examined." (313)

We have said that to the evidences of non-intercourse between Ancient America and the other hemisphere there was but one exception. Here it is: —

In the printed "Inquiries respecting the History, present Condition and future Prospects of the Indian Tribes of the United States," circulated gratuitously by the Department of the Interior, (314) contributions are solicited from "persons willing to communicate the results of their reading or reflection." Applauding most heartily any Government action in the rescue of some mementoes of national tribes whose span of life is but short, we deem it the part of good citizenship to coöperate. Our respectful mite is tendered gratis.

"*Appendix* (Inquiries, p. 560): — 305. Is the Inscription found on opening the Grave Creek Mound, in Western Virginia, in 1839, alphabetic or hieroglyphic?"

Neither the one nor the other.

Originally a forgery — its disappearance from the "Museum" at Grave Creek is accounted for in the discovery of an imposture; its sempiternal reappearance, in an unique series of works, is due to individual idiosyncracy.

An old acquaintance of ours is this inscription; which was first started, about A. D. 1838, by some "Grave Creek Flat." (315) Flat at its origin, the Ohio pebble has become flatter through scholastic abrasions; and so terribly worn away, that the United States Department, at no trivial expense, is doomed to advertise perpetually for its recovery through official inquiries.

Already, before our sojourn at Paris, 1845–'6, the vast palæographic erudition of this inscription's composer had been exemplified by the reduction of its twenty-two rudimental apices, into four Greek, four Etruscan, five Runic, six Gallic, seven Erse, ten Phœnician, fourteen British, and sixteen Celtiberic letters; being no less than sixty-six chances drawn from twenty-two, that an Ohio pebble had made, in primeval times, an outward voyage to Europe and the Levant; and, after receiving the engraved contributions of eight antique nations, had recrossed the Atlantic to its pristine geological habitat.

Unhappily, we were too late. Our venerable friend, M. Jomard (having accepted a copy of this inscription, for the "Bibliothèque Royale," in scientific good faith), had already printed the learned and skilful analogies deducible between the scratches on this pebble and the Numidian alphabet. Other scholars, native and foreign, were misled; and there really seemed no prospect that the bewilderments produced by this contemptible petroglyph of a "Grave Creek Flat" should not become universal, when Squier's sudden mallet flattened it out forever, in 1848. (316) The pebble vanished from the Grave Creek Mound; and while, at this day, there is but one man who yet slumbers in a fool's paradise concerning it, we may echo its annihilator's felicitous dictum — "sic transit gloria moundi."

We have seen how the fabled communications between the ancient denizens of the Nile and those of the Hoang-ho have reposed upon Sinico-Ægyptian "vases" — to which has recently been added a "padlock"; and we now know the archæological worthiness of the *only*

(312) *Antiquitates Americanæ:* opera et studio Caroli C. Rafn; folio, Copenhagen, 1837.

(313) Squier: in Luke Burke's London *Ethnological Journal;* Dec. 1848; especially p. 319.

(314) *Office of Indian Affairs:* 4to, Washington, 1851.

(315) *Trans. Amer. Ethnol. Soc.:* 1845; i. pp. 369–420.

(316) London *Ethnological Journal: loc. cit.*

proof yet standing to sustain idiocratical theories of ante-Columbian intercourse between the American continent and any other centres of human creation on our terraqueous planet. Until something very different in calibre be discovered by future explorers, the section of our General Table devoted to AMERICAN ORIGINS will survive, as the plain result of palæographic science in Anno Domini 1853.

G. R. G.

ESSAY III.

MANKIND'S CHRONOLOGY—INTRODUCTORY.

Our brief inquiries into a subject which possesses such manifold ramifications may be conveniently heralded by an extract or two from the works of some learned contemporaries: —

"We must therefore acquiesce in the conclusion, that the *Hebrew* copies represent the original and authentic text of the book of Genesis. . . . On historical grounds, very formidable objections present themselves to the *Hebrew* Chronology. . . . The difficulties are still greater when the Mosaic chronology is applied as a measure to profane history. . . . It is not, however, in these difficulties alone that we find reason for doubting whether the genealogies of the book of Genesis, taken either according to the Hebrew or the Septuagint, furnish us with a real chronology and history. . . . No evidence, therefore, remains, by which we can fix the interval which elapsed between the origin of the human race and the commencement of the special history of each nation. . . . The consequence of the method which has been commonly adopted, of making the Jewish chronology the bed of Procrustes, to which every other must conform in length, has been, that credence has been refused to histories, such as that of Egypt, resting upon unquestionable documents; and we have voluntarily deprived ourselves of at least a thousand years, which had been redeemed for us from the darkness of ante-historical times." (317)

"From this discrepancy we may infer, securely as it seems to me, that the Biblical writers had no revelation on the subject of chronology, but computed the succession of times from such data as were accessible to them. The duration of time, unless in so far as the knowledge of it was requisite for understanding the Divine Dispensation, was not a matter on which supernatural light was afforded; nor was this more likely than that the facts connected with physical science should have been revealed. . . . The result of this part of our inquiry is, in the first place, that a much longer space of time must have elapsed than that allowed by modern chronologers between the age of Abraham and the Exode; (318) and, secondly, that generations have certainly been omitted in the early genealogies. . . . By some it will be objected to the conclusions at which I have arrived, that there exists, according to my hypothesis, *no chronology*, properly so termed, of the earliest ages, and that no means are to be found for ascertaining the real age of the world. This I am prepared to admit, and I observe that the ancient Hebrews seem to have been of the same opinion, since the Scriptural writers have always avoided the attempt to compute the period in question. They go back, as we have seen in the instance of St. Paul's computation, to the age of Abraham, at the same time using expressions plainly denoting that they make no pretension to accurate knowledge, and could only approximate to the true dates of events; but they have in no instance, as far as I remember, attempted to carry the computation of time further back, nor has any one writer alluded to the age of the world. . . . Beyond that event (the arrival of Abraham in Palestine) *we can never know how many centuries nor even how many chiliads of years* may have elapsed since the first man of clay received the image of God and the breath of life." (319)

(317) Rev. John Kenrick: *Primæval History*; London, 1846; pp. 56, 57, 58, 61, 62.

(318) The contrary is now held by the highest Egyptologists: viz.— there being but Isaac, Jacob, Levi, Kohath, and Amram —*five* generations, or about 165 years — between Abraham and Moses, this interval must be curtailed. Vide Lepsius: *Chronologie der Ægypter*; and *infra*.

(319) Prichard: *Researches into the Physical History of Mankind*; 1847; v., "Note on the Biblical Chronology," pp 557, 560, 569, 570.

"The Roman researches of Niebuhr had proved to me the uncertainty of the chronological system of the Greeks, beyond the Olympiads; and that even Eusebius's chronicle, as preserved in the Armenian translation, furnishes merely isolated, although important, data for the Assyrian and Babylonian chronology beyond the era of Nabonassar. Again, as regards the Jewish computation of time, the study of Scripture had long convinced me, that there is in the Old Testament *no connected chronology, prior to Solomon.* All that now passes for a system of ancient chronology beyond that fixed point, *is the melancholy legacy of the 17th and 18th centuries;* a compound of intentional deceit and utter misconception of the principles of historical research." (320)

With Germanic virility of diction, Bunsen further insists—

"This fact must be explained. To deny it, after investigation once incited and begun, would imply, on the part of such investigator, small knowledge and still smaller honesty." (321)

"But (il s'en faut) much is wanting, we are convinced of it, that religious truth should be thus tied to questions of literature or of chronology. Christian faith no more reposes upon the *chronology* of Genesis, than upon its *physics* and its *astronomy;* and besides, to restrain ourselves to the subject that occupies us, the career of examination has been largely opened to us by men who certainly were far from holding Christian orthodoxy cheap." (322)

Nor does our learned authority confine himself to mere assertion; because, within a year after the publication of the above passage, he illustrates the slight estimation in which he holds *Genesiacal* chronology in the following emphatic manner:—

"It must be known that I wish to make public a monument of which the interpretation, if this be admitted, will push back the bounds of historical certitude beyond everything that can have been imagined up to this day. . . . Because, one must not dissimulate, Manetho places king MENCHERES in the IVth dynasty; and the most moderate calculation, if one follows the ciphers of Manetho, makes the author of the third pyramid remount beyond the *fortieth* century before our era. A monument of six thousand years! And what a monument! . . . We obtain the sum of 63 years, which, joined to the 4073 years, result of the preceding calculations, would give, to the end of the reign of Mycerinus, *the date of* 4136 *before* J. C." (323)

That is, our author means, the third Pyramid was built in Egypt just 153 years before the world's *Creation*, and exactly 1809 years before the *Flood;* according to the "Petavian" chronology of that Catholic Church in which M. Lenormant is a most devout communicant.

We have thought it expedient to preface our chronological inquiries with the above four citations. Each of them will protect us, like an *Ægis* raised on the stalwart arm of Jove or of Pallas. We have selected, out of the multitude before us, the highest representatives of distinct schools; who, nevertheless, perfectly agree in rejecting Scriptural chronology:—

1st. The Rev. Dr. John Kenrick—author of many standard classical works, and of "Egypt under the Pharaohs," 1850,—one of the most brilliant Protestant scholars of England.

2d. James Cowles Prichard, M. D., F. R. S.—the noblest champion of the "Unity of the human species."

3d. Chev. Christian C. J. Bunsen—the successor of Niebuhr as Prussian Ambassador at the court of Rome, and of Wilhelm von Humboldt at that of St. James; the pupil of Schelling, and the friend of Lepsius. (324)

4th. Prof. Charles Lenormant—the companion and disciple of Champollion-le-Jeune; alike famed for Hellenic erudition, and for severe Catholicity; who now fills the chair of Egyptology, vacated by Letronne's demise, at the Collège de France. (325)

It will moreover be remarked that our quotations set up no claim, as yet, for the respect-

---

(320) BUNSEN: *Egypt's Place in Universal History;* London, 1848; i., Preface, pp. 1. 2.

(321) *Ibid.: Ægyptens Stelle in der Weltgeschichte;* Hamburg, 1845, i., Einleitung, pp. 6, 7—unaccountably omitted in *Egypt's Place* by the accomplished English translator.

(322) LENORMANT: *Cours d'Hist. Ancienne;* Paris, 1838; p. 122.

(323) LENORMANT: *Éclaircissements sur le Cercueil du Roi Memphite Mycerinus;* Paris, 1839; pp. 3, 6, 24.

(324) Read Dr. ARNOLD'S eulogies of this illustrious gentleman.

(325) GLIDDON: *Otia Ægyptiaca;* 1849; pp.) 91, 92.

ability of the chronological systems of other nations at the expense of Judaism. On the contrary, they bear with undivided force upon *Hebrew* computations, viewed for themselves alone.

Not less truthfully does the language of a profound thinker — expression of a fifth, and far more liberal philosophy, — set forth the effeteness of Jewish chronology. Luke Burke's writings are unmistakeable: his "Critical Analysis of the Hebrew Chronology" (326) is one of the most masterly productions our literature can boast. Curtailment is injustice to its author: to the reader garbled extracts would be unsatisfactory; and the sincere investigator knows where to peruse the whole. We content our present requirements with one specimen: —

"Such, then, is the character and importance of 'the most brilliant and important of Primate Usher's improvements in chronology!' [as Dr. Hales terms the fabulous notion that Abraham was *not* the eldest son of Terah!] It consists, first, of an argument that turns out to be groundless, in every one of its elements; and, which, if well founded, would prove the Old Testament to be one of the most absurdly written books in existence; and secondly, of an assumption which, apart from this argument, is wholly gratuitous and improbable; and which also, if admitted, would bear equally hard against the character of the very writings for the support of which it was invented. And it is by such arguments as these that grave and learned divines seek to ascertain the realities of ancient history, and endeavor to place chronology upon a rational and sure foundation! And it is to such as these that men of science are required to bow, at the risk of being deemed sceptical, dangerous, profane, &c., &c. For it must not be supposed that the present is an isolated or exceptional instance of theological argument. On the contrary, it is a rule. Volumes upon volumes have been written in precisely the same spirit — volumes numerous enough, and ponderous enough, to fill vast libraries. Until a comparatively late era, all historical criticism, on which Scriptural evidences could in any manner be brought to bear, was carried on in this spirit. Nothing else was thought of; nothing approaching to genuine independence would have been tolerated. And thus the human world rolled round, century after century; the brave trampled upon by slaves; the wise compelled to be silent in the presence of fools; the learned alternately serfs and tyrants, deluded and deluding, cheating themselves, and cheating others with sophistries which, upon any other subject, would disgrace even the mimic contests of schoolboys! For ourselves, we should feel a humiliation to contend with such sophistries seriously, and in detail, were we not firmly convinced that to do so is not merely the most legitimate, but also the only mode by which truth can be rendered permanently triumphant. Wit and sarcasm may obtain a temporary success, they may awaken minds otherwise prepared for freedom, but they are often unjust, usually unbenevolent, and consequently, in the majority of cases, they merely awaken antagonism, and cause men to cling with increased fondness to their opinions. Nothing but minute, searching, inexorable argument will ever obtain a speedy, or a permanent triumph over deep-seated prejudices." (327)

"But, fortunately," winds up another and a sixth formidable adversary to Hebrew computation — no less an archéologue than the great Parisian architect, Lesueur — "fortunately, questions of ciphers have nothing in common with religion. What imports it to us, to us Christians, who date so to say from yesterday, that man should have been thrown upon our globe at an epoch more or less remote; that the world should have been created in six days, or that its birth should have consumed myriads of centuries? Can God, through it, become less grand, his work less admirable? We are, since the last eighteen hundred years, dupes of the besotted vanity of the Jews. It is time that this mystification should cease." (328)

Italian scholarship speaks for itself:—(329)

"The Bible is, certainly, as the most to be venerated, so the most authoritative fount of history; but, in so many varieties of chronological systems, which are all palmed off by their authors as based upon indications of time taken from the Bible; in the very notable difference of these indications between the Hebrew and the Samaritan text, and the Greek version, and between the books of the Old and of the New Testament; finally, in the indecision, in which *the* CHURCH has always left such controversy, that, I do not see any certain standard, by which the duration of the Egyptian nation has to be levelled, unless this

(326) London *Ethnological Journal;* June, July, November, December, 1848.

(327) *Op. cit.;* pp. 274, 276.

(328) *Chronologie des Rois d'Égypte* — ouvrage couronné par l'Académie: Paris, 1848; pp. 304, 305.

(329) BARUCCHI, Director of the Museum of Turin; *Discorsi Critici sopra la Cronologia Egizia;* Torino, 1844; pp. 29, 43, 44, 147.

become determined through an accurate examination of all its historic fountains. . . . Leaving therefore aside anysoever system of biblical chronology; because, of the quantity hitherto brought into the field by the erudite none are certain, nor exempt from difficulties the most grave; and, because *the* CHURCH, to whose supreme magistracy belongs the decision of controversies appertaining to dogma and to morals, has never intermeddled in pronouncing sentence upon any one of the systems aforesaid, of which but one can be true, while all peradventure may be erroneous. . . . I shall finish by repeating in this place that which already I declared elsewhere, viz.: it is not my intention to combat any systems regarding biblical chronology; but inasmuch as, of these, not one is propounded as true under *the* CHURCH's infallible authority; I have placed all these (systems) aside in the present examining, in order to treat Egyptian chronology through the sole data of history and of Egyptian monuments."

Finally, we quote Lepsius:—(330)

"The Jewish chronology differs in a most remarkable manner from every other; and even in times as modern as those of the Persian kings the difference amounts to no less than 160 years, from known dates. Its several sources present but little difference among themselves. They count according to *years of the world;* a calculation which, as also IDELER (*Hand. d. Chron.* I. pp. 569, 578, 580), considers most probable, was invented, *together with the whole present chronology of the Jews*, by the Rabbi HILLEL HANASSI, in the year 344 after Christ: and thenceforward gradually adopted. They fix the creation of the world 3671 B. C.; and all agree, even Josephus, in the usual calculation of the Hebrew text. They fix the deluge at 1656, the birth of Abraham at 1948, Isaac's 2048, Jacob's 2108, Joseph's 2199, Jacob's arrival in Egypt 2238, Joseph's death 2309, years after Adam." . . . "The question is now, how must we explain this obvious dislocation of facts as compared with the true dates. IDELER has demonstrated that the introduction of the *era of the world*, and consequently of the whole system of chronology, must be ascribed to the author of the *Moleds*, (or 'New Moons,') and in general of the whole later Jewish calendar, the Rabbi HILLEL who flourished in the first half of the IVth century."

Reserving further extracts until we take up the *Hebrew* chronology, it here suffices to notice that MOSES, who lived about the fourteenth century B. C., is not amenable for numerical additions made, to books that go by his venerable name, about 1800 years after his death, by a modern *Rabbi.*

The unanimity of science in the rejection of any system of biblical computation might be exemplified by many hundred citations: either, of savans who, establishing grander systems more in accordance with the present state of knowledge, pass over the rabbinical ciphers in contemptuous silence; or, of divines who, like the Rev. Dr. Hitchcock (President of Amherst College, and Professor of Natural Theology and Geology) strive, vainly we opine, to reconcile the crude cosmology of the infantine Hebrew mind with the terrestrial discoveries of matured intellects like Cuvier, De la Beche, Murchison, Owen, Lyell, or Agassiz. Nevertheless, Calvinism in the pages of Hitchcock begins to affect a more amiable disguise than was worn by the magnanimous slayer of SERVETUS, or by the iconoclastic John Knox; to judge by the following admissions:—

"If these positions be correct, it follows that, as we ought not to expect the doctrines of religion in treatises on science, so it is unreasonable to look for the principles of philosophy in the Bible. . . . But a still larger number of [clerical] authors, although men of talents, and familiar, it may be, with the Bible and theology, have no accurate knowledge of geology. The results have been, first, that, by resorting to denunciation and charges of infidelity, to answer arguments from geology, which they did not understand, they have excited unreasonable prejudices and alarm among *common Christians* respecting that science and its cultivators; secondly, they have awakened disgust, and even contempt, among scientific men, especially those of sceptical tendencies [!], who have inferred that a cause which resorts to such defences must be very weak. They have felt very much as a good Greek scholar would, who should read a severe critique upon the style of Isocrates, or Demosthenes, and, before he had finished the review, should discover internal evidence that the writer had never learned the Greek alphabet." (331)

How true the latter part of this paragraph is, the reader has convinced himself by the perusal of our Essay I. [*supra*]; where the Hebraical knowledge of Calvinistic divines in Ame-

---

(330) *Chronologie der Ægypter:* "Kritik der Quellen," i. pp. 259, 360, 361, 362.

(331) *The Religion of Geology;* Boston, 1852; p. 3, and Preface, p. 7.

rica has been compared with that of coetaneous Lutherans and Catholics in Europe. Contentions between scramblers for the loaves and fishes may, however, be left to the diverted contemplation of the gatherers of St. Peter's pence. None of them have real bearing upon the science of mundane *chronology*, to which our present investigations are confined.

Until very recent times, it was customary, among chronologers, to follow the Judaic and post-Christian system in assigning eras to events; viz.: by assuming that a given occurrence had taken place in such a year (*Anno Mundi*) of the Creation of the world. This arrangement would have been absolutely exact, if the precise moment of Creation, according to the "book of Genesis," had been previously settled, or even conventionally agreed upon: but, unhappily, no two men ever patiently reckoned up its numerals and exhibited the same sum total; as will be made apparent anon, in its place. Besides, this arrangement was found by experience to be theologically unsafe; because, on the one hand, the Christian Fathers, by assuming the *Septuagint* computation, demonstrated that Jesus, appearing exactly in Josephus's 5555th year of the world, could be no other than the Χριστος, "the *anointed;*" (332) whilst, on the other hand, the Jewish Doctors, proving through computation of the *Hebrew* Text that the birth of Jesus had occurred in the year of the world 3751, demonstrated that he could not possibly be their MeS*h*aiaH. (333)

"There was an old tradition," says the profound Kennicott, (334) "alike common among Judæans and Christians, sprung from the mystic interpretation of Creation in six days, that the duration of the world should be 6000 years: that the Messianic advent should be in the *sixth* millennium; because he would come in the *latter days.* The ancient Jews, therefore, their chronology having been previously contracted, made use of an argument sufficiently specious, through which they did not recognize Jesus: for the *Messiah was to come in the sixth millennium;* but *Jesus was born* (according to the computation of time by them received) in the latter part of the *fourth millennium*, about the year of the world 3760 (*Seder Olam*, edit. Meyer; pp. 95 and 111). The very celebrated [Muslim-Arab] Abul-Pharagius, who lived in the XIIIth century, in his history of Dynasties, thus proffers a sentence worthy of remembrance; by Pococke so rendered into Latin:—'A defective computation is ascribed by Doctors of the Jews—For, as it is pronounced, in the Law and the Prophets, about the Messiah, he was to be sent at the ultimate times: nor otherwise is the commentary of the more antique Rabbis, who reject Christ; as if the ages of men, by which the epoch of the world is made out, could change. They subtracted from the life of Adam, at the birth of Seth, one hundred years, and added them to the rest of the latter's life; and they did the same to the lives of the rest of the children of Adam, down to Abraham. And thus it was done, as their computation indicates, in order that Christ should be manifested in the *fifth* [fourth, K.] millennary through accident in the middle of the years of the world; which in all, according to them, will be 7000: and they said, *We are now in the middle of this time, and yet the time designated for the advent of the Messiah has not arrived.*' The computation of the LXX also indicates, that Christ should be manifested in the sixth millennary, and that this would be his time. . . . The old *Italic* version, which, according to St. Augustine, was 'verborum tenacior cum perspicuitate sententiæ,' is the foundation of the *chronologia major* of the Latin Church, to this day (1780); for, 'in the Roman Martyrology, which is publicly chanted in church, on the 8th Jan., the Nativity of the Lord is thus announced to the people from the ecclesiastical table: *Year from the creation* 5099 (5199 in Martyrol. Rom. Antwerp. 1678, p. 388): and *from the deluge year* 2957 (Hod., p. 447)."

A quotation from a Christian work next to canonical will establish the belief of those early communities who lived nearest to the apostles:—the 5500 years, be it noted, had been, by Nicodemus, "found in the first of the seventy books, where Michael the archangel" had mentioned them to "Adam, the first man."

"13 By these five cubits and a half for the building of the Ark of the Old Testament, we perceived and knew that in five thousand years and half (one thousand) years, Jesus Christ was to come in the ark or tabernacle of the body;

14 And so our Scriptures testify that he is the Son of God, and the Lord and King of Israel.

15 And because after his suffering, our chief priests were surprised at the signs which were wrought by his means, we opened that book to search all the generations down to the generation of Joseph and Mary the mother of Jesus, supposing him to be the seed of David;

---

(332) Hennell: *Christian Theism;* 1845; pp. 82, 83.

(333) *Seder Olam Rabba*, composed about A. D. 130; apud Hales.

(334) *Dissertatio Generalis;* § 75, pp. 32, 33, 76.

"16 And we found the account of the creation, and at what time he made the heaven and the earth, and the first man Adam, and that from thence to the flood, were two thousand, two hundred, and twelve years.

17 And from the flood to Abraham, nine hundred and twelve. And from Abraham to Moses, four hundred and thirty. And from Moses to David the king, five hundred and ten.

18 And from David to the Babylonish captivity, five hundred years. And from the Babylonish captivity to the incarnation of Christ, four hundred years.

19 The sum of all which amounts to five thousand and a half (a thousand.)

20 And so it appears, that Jesus, whom we crucified, is Jesus Christ the Son of God, the true and Almighty God. Amen." (335)

The conclusive logic of this passage derives support from another ancient Christian document, wherein is given the reason why the end of the world was expected some time ago:—

"Consider, my children, what that signifies, he [God] finished [creating] them in six days. The meaning of it is this; that in six thousand years the Lord God will bring all things to an end." (336)

Such being the whole story, the reader has now to make choice of whichever of the following dates may suit his views upon the

Epochas of Creation.

Biblical Texts and Versions.	B. C.		B. C.
Septuagint computation	5586	Chinese Jews	4079
Septuagint Alexandrinus	5508	Some Talmudists	3761
Septuagint Vatican	5270	Vulgar Jewish computation	3760
Samaritan computation	4427	Seder Olam Rabba, great Chronicle of the World, A. D. 130	3751
Samaritan Text	4305	Rabbi Lipman	3616
Hebrew Text	4161	*Christian Divines.*	
English Bible	4004	Clemens Alexandrinus, A. D. 194	5624
Jewish Computations.		Hales, Rev. Dr.	5411
Josephus { Playfair	5555	Origen, ——, A. D. 230	4830
Josephus { Jackson	5481	Kennedy, Bedford, Ferguson	4007
Josephus { Hales	5402	Usher, Lloyd, Calmet	4004
Josephus { Universal History	4698	Helvetius, Marsham	4000
Talmudists	5344	Melancthon	3964
Seder Olam Sutha	4339	Luther	3961
Jewish computation	4220	Scaliger	3950
" "	4184		

These are mere excerpts of 120 different opinions, on the date of *Creation*, tabulated by Hales. (337) This list can easily be swelled to above 300 distinct and contradictory hypotheses. Between the highest epoch, B. C. 6984 (the Alphonsine tables), and the lowest, B. C. 3616 (Rabbi Lipman), there is the trifling difference of 3268 years!

It is but fair to set off Catholic against Protestant authorities, so we cull a few more instances from the learned pages of De Brotonne (338).—"Among authors who deny the eternity of the world, not one, from its creation to the advent of Jesus Christ, counts more than 7000 years, nor less than 3700." He also supplies a schedule of 70 more disputants, ranging between B. C. 6984 and 3740, from Riccioli; (339) but the subjoined are some of his own, *extra*.

	B. C.		B. C.
Suidas	6000	*Hebrew Text*	3834
Nicephorus, Constantinopolitanus	5500	St. Isidore	5336
Eusebius Cæsariensis	5200	Montanus	3849
St. Jerome, and Beda	3952	Vossius	5590
Hilarion	5475	Petavius (Romanist authority)	3983
St. Julian, and the LXX	5205		

(335) *Gospel of Nicodemus;* chap. xxii.—Apochryphal New Testament, pp. 51, 52.

(336) *General Epistle of Barnabas;* xiii. 4: *op. cit.*; p. 101.

(337) *Analysis:* i. p. 212.

(338) *Filiations et Migrations des Peuples:* Paris, 1827; 428–436.

(339) *Chronologia reformatâ:* pp. 290–292, 293.

Riccioli shows that computations upon different exemplars of the LXX oscillate, also, between a maximum of 5904 years B. C., and a minimum of 5054, for the *Creation* alone! Nevertheless, "Cœlum ipsum petimus stultitiâ." Not satisfied with human inability to define, through biblical or anysoever methods of reckoning, the age when Creative Power first whirled our incandescent planet from the sun's fire-mist, some intelligences, at the supernatural stage of mental development, have actually fixed the *month*, *day*, and *hour!*

"And now hee that desireth to know the yeere of the world, which is now passing over us this yeere 1644, will find it to bee 5572 yeeres just now finished since the Creation; and the year 5573 of the world's age, now newly begunne this *September at the Æquinox.*" (340) *Anno Mundi* I; "VIth *day* of Creation, . . . his (Adam's) wife the weaker vessell: she not yet knowing that there were any Devils at all . . . sinned, and drew her husband into the same transgression with her; this was about *high noone*, the time of eating. And in this lost condition into which Adam and Eve had now brought themselves, did they lie comfortlesse till towards the cool of the day, or *three o'clock* afternoone. . . . (God) expelleth them out of Eden, and so fell Adam *on the day* that he was created." (341)

"We do not speak of the theory set forth in a work entitled *Nouveau Système des Temps*, by Gibert father and son. This system, which is not so new as its title seems to announce, gives to the world only 3600 years of duration down to the 1st July, 1834; and makes Adam's birth 1797 years before J. C., on the 1st *July*." (342)

"It is, besides, generally allowed by Chronologists, that the beginning of the patriarchal year was computed from the autumnal equinox, which fell on *October* 20th, B. C. 4005, the *year* of the creation." (343)

But the Promethean intrepidity of orthodoxy is not content with mathematical demonstrations of the year, the month, the day, nor the hour of Creation. It ascends, in some extatic cases, far beyond! Thus, Philomneste heads an especial chapter with

"*Antégénésie*—What God was about *before* the creation of the world." (344)

Albeit, none of these profanations of science contain one solitary element, in regard to Creation, that is strictly *chronological*. "Passons au Deluge" (345)—let us descend to the Flood; and see what resting-place a "dove" could find amid these wastes of waters and of time. For the

EPOCHAS OF THE DELUGE,

out of sixteen opinions published by Hales—maximum, B. C. 3246; minimum, 2104; difference 1142 years—the following are singularly in accordance:—

	B. C.		B. C.
Septuagint version	3246	Vulgar Jewish computation	2104
Samaritan Text	2998	Hales	3155
English Bible	2348	Usher	2348
Hebrew Text	2288	Calmet	2344
Josephus	3146		

So are also the intervals of time assigned, by the subjoined computators, to mundane existence, between the Creation and the Flood. We borrow them from De Brotonne.

CREATION TO DELUGE.

	YEARS.		YEARS.
Josephus	2256	Later Rabbis, St. Jerome, Beda, Montanus, Scaliger, Origanus, Emmius, Petavius, Gordonus, Salianus, Torniellus, Hervartus, Philippi, Tirinus, Riccioli	1656
Suidas, Nicephorus, Eusebius, St. Julian, St. Isidore	2242	St. Augustine—"From Adam to the Deluge, according to our sacred books (*i. e.*, the LXX), there have elapsed 2242 years, as per our exemplars; and 1656, according to the Hebrews."	
Clemens Alexandrinus	2148		
Hilarion	2257		
Vossius, Riccioli	2256		
Cornelius a Lapide	1657		

(340) Rev. Dr. LIGHTFOOT: *Harmony of the Foure Evangelistes;* London, 1644; 1st part, Proleg., last page.
(341) *Ibid.: Harmony, Chronicle, and Order of the Old Testament;* London, 1647; p. 5.
(342) DE BROTONNE; *op. cit.;* ii. p. 160.
(343) Rev. Dr. F. NOLAN: *The Egyptian Chronology Analysed:* London, 1848; p. 392.
(344) *Livre des Singularités:* Dyme, 1841.
(345) DANDIN, in *Les Plaideurs:* iii. 54.

But these discrepancies are increased by the computations made, since 1623 A. D., upon MSS. of the *Samaritan* Pentateuch, which generally yield an interval between the Creation and the Deluge of years 1307.

The basis of all these calculations lies in the hyperbolical lives of the *ten antediluvian Patriarchs.* It will be seen, through the skilful synopsis of a learned divine, how admirably the numerals of the Hebrew and Samaritan texts correspond, not merely with each other, but with those of the Septuagint version, and of Josephus: —

"The following tabular schemes exhibit the variations; the numbers expressing the parent's age at the son's birth, except in the cases of Noah and Shem.(346)

Ante-Diluvian Patriarchs.	Hebr.	Samr.	LXX.	Josep.	Post-Diluvian Patriarchs.	Hebr.	Samr.	LXX.	Josep.
1. *Adam*	130	130	230	230	11. *Shem* (aged 100 at				
2. *Seth*	105	105	205	205	the Flood)	2	2	2	12
3. *Enos*	90	90	190	190	12. *Arphaxad*	35	135	135	135
4. *Cainan*	70	70	170	170	[Cainan spurious...	...	...	130	...]
5. *Mahalaleel*	65	65	165	165	13. *Salah*	30	130	130	130
6. *Jared*	162	62	162	162	14. *Heber*	34	134	134	134
7. *Enoch*	65	65	165	(1)65*	15. *Peleg*	30	130	130	130
8. *Methuselah*	187	67	187	187	16. *Reu*	32	132	132	130
9. *Lamech*	182	53	188	182	17. *Serug*	30	130	130	132
10. *Noah* (at the Flood)	600	600	600	600	18. *Nahor*	29	79	79	120
					19. *Terah* (Gen. xi. 32, xii. 4.)	130	130	130	130
* 165 is doubtless the correct reading. Total	1656	1307	2262	2256	So to *Abraham*	352	1002	1002	1053

The above, like all other tables compiled by theological computators to illustrate so-called "Biblical chronology," assumes the *numerals* of current printed exemplars to be correct; but, if we set to work, archæologically, to verify the original Hebrew, Greek, and Samaritan *manuscripts,* we find even this apparent uniformity to be a delusion — indeed, another orthodox figment. A few instances pleasingly exhibit this fact (347): —

"In one of the manuscripts collated by Dr. Kennicott, and which is marked in his Bible, codex clvii., this century [in the Hebrew generation of Jared] is omitted, and there is much probability that it was also omitted in the copies used by the eastern Jews. According to the testimony of Ismael Sciahinshia, an eastern writer, all these copies reckon only 1556 years from Adam to the flood, instead of 1656. . . . According to the numbers still existing in the vast majority of [Greek] manuscripts, Methuselah dies 14 years *after* the deluge, and had not the fifty-three, of the generation of Lamech, been changed to eighty-eight, he would have died 49 years after the deluge. . . . The deluge occurred, according to the Septuagint, in the year of the world 2242, and by adding up the generations previous to his, we shall find that he was born in the year 1287. He lived 969 years, and therefore died in 2256. But this is 14 *years after the deluge!* . . . And had they [the theologers] not, by a previous system of changes, added a century [in Greek *MSS.*] to all the generations, he would have died 249 years after it. . . . Origen appears to have been the first who gave notoriety to the contradiction; and for a long time, the fact greatly disturbed theologians. The reader will be hardly surprised to learn that in a subsequent age some manuscripts were *found* with the error *corrected.* . . . Some [Greek *MSS.*] make the generation of Adam 330 years; one makes it 240. Another gives 180 to Canaan, a third 170 to Jared, while others allow 177 or 180 to Methuselah. . . . One [Hebrew] manuscript, codex lvii. of Holmes, makes the age of Methuselah 947: three or four other authorities make the generation of Lamech 180: the two corrections conjoined, bring the death of Methuselah to the year of the deluge. We also find three other authorities making the generation of Methuselah 180 years; this connected with the 188 of Lamech, places the death of Methuselah *only one year* after the deluge, even allowing him full age. Another manuscript makes his generation 177 years, three other authorities give the number 165, while one manuscript makes his total age 965. . . . Dr. Kennicott has given readings of 320 Hebrew manuscripts of the book of Genesis. 97 of these have been collated throughout, 223 in part only. . . . One manuscript (codex clvii.) omits the hundred years in his [Jared's] generation; two others (codices ci. and clxxvi.) omit it in that of Methuselah; and one (codex xviii.) in that of Lamech. Codex clxxvi. makes the generation of Lamech 172 and his total age 772, and codex xviii. makes his total age 909. . . . We also find that, in three

(346) Rev. E. B. Elliott, A. M.: *Horæ Apocalypticæ;* London, 1846; iv. p. 254, note. Compare "Tables of the discrepancies of the three Texts with regard to the Ante-diluvian Patriarchs" in Wallace: *Dissertation on the True Age of the World;* London, 1844, pp. 14–16.

(347) Burke: *Ethnological Journal;* 1848; pp. 27, 28, 82, 83, 84, 87, 78–91.

or four manuscripts, some of the numbers of Methuselah are written over *erasures*. This, of course, looks suspicious. One manuscript (codex clv.) makes Enoch live after the birth of Methuselah 'five and sixty and three hundred years' [i. e., the old 365 *days* of an Egyptian vague year!], instead of 300 years simply."

Thus far Luke Burke in his studies of the *Hebrew* variations exhibited by Kennicott. (348) The annexed Table shows how he found matters in the *Greek* of Holmes. (349)

"TABLE III.

NAMES.	BEFORE GENERATION.				AFTER GENERATION.				TOTAL AGES.			
	1.	2.	3.	4.	1.	2.	3.	4.	1.	2.	3.	4.
ADAM	330	330 240 130	4 1 2	MSS. 31,121, Ald., Theop. p. 13. MS. 77 Slav., Arm. Ed.	700	705 800	1 3	MS. 135 Slav., Ostrog., 127	930	1200	1	Corrected in the margin to 930, 300 having been accidentally put for 30. MS. 18
SETH	205	132 805	1 1	MS. 127 Coptic	707	807	1	MS. 127	912	910 902 772	1 1 1	MS. 19. MS. 18. Arab. 2.
ENOS	190	180 140 95	1 1 1	MS. 65 MS. 75 MS. 127	715	705 916 800	1 4 1	MS. 135 " 14, 78, 130, 133* MS 127	905	915	1	MS. 79.
CAINAN	170	180	1	MS. 106	740	800	1	MS. 127	910			
MAHALALEEL	165	65	1	MS. 127	730	830	1	MS. 127	895	795	9	MS. 14, 25, 31, 38, 57, 73, 77, 78, 79.
JARED	162	170	1	MS. 75	800	...	...	...	962	847	1	MS. 127.
ENOCH	165	65	1	MS. X	200	...	...	...	365	465	1	MS. 71.
METHUSELAH	167	165 177 180 187	4 1 3 18 &c	MS. 106, 107, Compl., Georg. MS. 75! MS. 71, Slav., Theop. p. 133. MS. I, X, 15, 16, 55, 59, 64, 68, 83, 120, 121, 131, 135, 187, Ald., Alex., Chrysos. IV., Arm. Ed. and a few others.	802	782	32	MS. I., X., 14, 15, 20, 25, 55, 57, 59, 64, 68, 71, 73, 75, 77, 78, 79, 83, 121, 128, 130, 131, 133 135, Ald., Cat Nic., Arm. 1, Arm. Ed., Arab. 1, 2, Alex., Slav., & perhaps another examin'd by Vossius.	969	947 965	1 1	MS. 57. MS. 82.
LAMECH	188	180 182	3 2	MS. 75, 187, Chrysos. IV. Arab. 2. Chron. Orient.	565	595	1	Arab. 2	753	783 755 765 768 777	1 3 1 1 1	Arm. 1. MS. 19, 107, 107. MS. 25. Arab. 3. Arab. 2.

* In this case, nine hundred has been corrected by another hand into seven hundred. There are several minor remarks and explanations relative to this table, which we should have been glad to have afforded, were we not much pressed for time and space. These, however, would, after all, be of little interest to the general reader, and the learned reader will not need them.

. . . The first glance at this table will show the inquirer, that he has got into a region of various readings, very different from that presented to him by the Hebrew manuscripts. Instead of some *eight* or *nine* variations found in some *three hundred* manuscripts, he has about 118, found in a much smaller number of manuscripts! . . . Are we to say, then, that the Christian scribes were, in general, so wretchedly careless, that they made twenty errors where a Jew made but one? . . . These things, therefore, evince design, not accident. We find one variation followed by more than 32 authorities, another by 18, a third by 9. There are three which are each copied by four manuscripts, four which are copied by three each, and two which have each two manuscripts agreeing in them: thirty-one only are single variations, and some of them, at least, are as clearly intentional as any of the others. As to the variation which makes Methuselah live 782 years after the birth of Lamech, instead of 802, no one can doubt of its being intentional. 788 is the Hebrew date, and it was here copied from the Hebrew for the same reason that the Hebrew was previously invented, viz.: for the purpose of bringing the death of Methuselah within the antediluvian period, instead of fourteen years after it. . . . Codex LVII. has the total age

(348) *Vetus Testamentum Hebraicum, cum variis lectionibus*; folio, Oxon. 1776-'80.
(349) *Vetus Testamentum Græcum, cum variis lectionibus*; folio, Oxon. 1798-1827.

of Methuselah 947, while four authorities have his generation 165. . . . The whole number of variations in the case of Methuselah is 60; more than half the number in the entire Antediluvian Chronology. Every one of them but four, or at the utmost five, viz., those making the generation 165, and codex LXXXII. making the total age 965, have reference to the error in the age of Methuselah. This fact is of course significant; and at once reduces, to nearly one-half, the number of variations that can be supposed accidental. This number is easily reduced still farther. Codex Arabicus II. has all the Hebrew numbers, in the case of Lamech. The Chronicon Orientalis has the generation like the Hebrew, and, for anything we know to the contrary, may have the other periods in harmony with this generation. Codex CXXVII. has the Samaritan numbers in five instances. The Sclavonic version gives us both the Hebrew numbers in the case of Adam, the Armenian edition gives one of them, and the Ostrogoth version the other. Thus we have 13 more intentional variations, making the whole number, thus far, 73 out of 118. Nine manuscripts make the total age of Mahalaleel 795, instead of 895; four makè the generation of Adam 330 instead of 230; four others make the age of Enos after generation 915 instead of 715; and four make the generation of Lamech 180, instead of 188 or 182. Three make the total age of Lamech 755, while three others make it respectively 733, 765, and 768. These make 27 other cases in which the intention is apparent though less obviously than the former. So that we thus have 99 instances out of 118, which cannot be reasonably attributed to accident. And even of the remaining nineteen, there are not more than *two* that have any unequivocal indications of being accidental. The substitution of 300 for 30 in Codex XVIII., in the total age of Adam, is evidently accidental, as is the 805 for 205 in the Coptic version, of the generation of Seth. Accident may also have occasioned some of the other changes, but this is not probable. . . . When Origen, in the early part of the IIId century, began to collate these manuscripts and versions, he was confounded at the clashings which he discovered in them. Whole passages existed in some [Greek biblical MSS.] for which there was no counterpart in others, nor in the Hebrew, nor in the Samaritan. . . .

"The reader will here naturally ask, how is it that the commentators have managed to confront these hosts of difficulties, and yet avoid the inevitable inferences which a clear view of them discloses? The answer is simple. They never have fairly confronted them. They never have classified them, or analyzed them, in a manner likely to lead to the truth. They would not admit that any conclusion could be true which did not harmonize with their pre-conceived theory of the entire inspiration of every portion of the Scriptures — of every portion at least which they severally regarded as canonical. This with them was a settled point, from which they neither wished to recede, nor dared to recede. Their works therefore present us with little more than vain attempts to reconcile, to soften down, to slur over these contradictions.

"Thus, it is evident that this *antediluvian* chronology, as we now have it, is not the work of any one person, or of any one era. In its original form [not earlier than B. C. 130 to 420] it was not only contradictory to all human experience, and to the laws of organization, but also glaringly self-contradictory. It is plain, too, that it has been repeatedly altered, in various ages, and by various people, and that these alterations have been made in a perfectly arbitrary manner, and without any reference to facts or historical data bearing upon the subject. Who can say by whom, or when it was drawn up, or how many stages it has passed through previously to the changes we have spoken of? Is it not folly, then, to pretend to regulate history by a series of numbers thus tampered with, to say nothing of their scientific and historic impossibility?"

Folly! It is worse than folly: it is an absolute disregard of every principle of rectitude; an impudent mockery of educated reason; a perpetualized insult to honest understandings; and a perdurable dereliction, on the part of interested and self-conceited supernaturalists, of Almighty *truth*. Ignorance, abject ignorance, is the only plea through which future sustainers of genesiacal numerals can escape from the charge of knavery. Let imbecility impale itself, henceforward, on either horn of this dilemma for edification of the learned; and with the derisive jeers of men of science, who are now endeavoring to reconstruct a solid *chronology* out of the débris of universal and primeval humanity yet traceable, in their various centres of Creation, upon our planet's superficies.

The reader of Essay I. in the present work is aware of the conjectural hundreds of thousands of variants proceeding from what Kennicott, De Rossi, and the Rabbis, qualify as the "horrible state" of the *Manuscripts* of the Old Testament. He also may infer the historical metamorphoses of alphabets, and the alterations of *numbers* which, to suit different schools of theology, the Hebrew and Samaritan Texts, and Septuagint version, underwent between the third century before C. and the fourth century after. A pledge, too, has been incidentally made to him, that a future publication shall demonstrate why the "*ten* patriarchs," from A-DaM to NoaK*h*, were no more *human beings*, in the idea of their original writers, than are the ethno-geographical names catalogued in Xth *Genesis*. Abler hands, in another chapter [XI.] of this volume, have set forth what of geology and palæontology throws more or less light upon Types of Mankind.

Leaving the *Deluge*, its universality or its fabled reality, to professional reconcilers;(350) the chronological bearings of this hypothetical event compel us not to dodge, at the same time that it is far from our intention to dwell upon, its passing consideration. No *Hebraist* disputes that, according to the literal language of the Text, the flood was universal. To make the Hebrew Text read as if it spoke of a partial or local catastrophe may be very harmonizing, but it is false philology, and consequently looks very like an imposture.

"The waters *swelled up* (prevailed) infinitely over the earth; all the high mountains, beneath all the skies, were covered: fifteen cubits upward did the waters rise; the mountains were covered."(351)

The level of the flood was, therefore, 22½ *feet* above the Dhawalaghiri (28,074 feet) and over the Sorata (25,200 feet); according to Humboldt.(352) Equivalent to some *two miles* above the line of perpetual snow must, therefore, have been the level whereupon the Ark would have been frozen solid but for an universal thaw. This is what the Hebrew chronicler meant by KuL HaHeRIM, HaGiBuHIM — *all the high mountains;* even if Hindostan and America were as alien to his geography, as such an aqueous elevation is to the physicist.

"If there is any circumstance," declares Cuvier, "thoroughly established in geology, it is, that the crust of our globe has been subjeeted to a great and sudden revolution, the epoch of which cannot be dated much further back than *five or six thousand years ago;* that this revolution had buried all the countries which were before inhabited by men and by the other animals that are now best known."(353)

Science has found nothing to justify Cuvier's hypothesis, conceived in the infancy of geological studies; whether in *Egypt*, (354) in *Assyria*, (355) or on the *Mississippi:*(356) whilst, without delving into the wilderness of geological works for flat contradictions of this oft-quoted passage of the great Naturalist, here are three extracts by way of arrest of judgment: —

"Of the Mosaic Deluge I have no hesitation in saying, that it has never been proved to have produced a single existing appearance of any kind, and that it ought to be struck out of the list of geological causes." (357)

"There is, I think (says the President of the London Geological Society, 1831), one great negative fact now incontestably established; that the vast masses of Diluvial Gravel, scattered almost over the surface of the earth, *do not belong to one violent and transitory period.* . . . Our errors were, however, natural, and of the same kind which led many excellent observers of a former century to refer all secondary formations to the NOACHIAN DELUGE. Having been myself a believer, and, to the best of my power, a propagator of what I now regard as *philosophic heresy*, . . . I think it right, as one of my last acts before I quit this chair, thus publicly to read my recantation."

A later President of the same illustrious corps, 1834, uses similar language: —

"Some fourteen years ago I advanced an opinion . . . that the entire earth had . . . been covered by *one general but temporary deluge* . . . I also now read my recantation." (358)

Were it not for such denials of Cuvier's six-chiliad doctrine (to which hundreds might be added of the whole school of true geologists at the present day), then, it would be evident to archæologists that "geology" must be of necessity a *false science:* and for the following reason:—It has been shown [*supra*, p. 562], that the first chapter of the "book of Genesis" is an ancient cosmogenical *ode*, with a "chorus" like the plays of Grecian dramatists; — that its authorship, if entirely unknown, is not *Mosaic;* — that its age, the style being

(350) Such as, the Rev. Dr. PYE SMITH, the Rev. Dr. HITCHCOCK, or "The *Friend* of Moses."

(351) *Genesis;* vii. 18, 19; — CAHEN'S *Text;* i. p. 21.

(352) *Cosmos;* Otte's trans., 1850, i. p. 28, 31, 330–332.

(353) *Essay on the Theory of the Earth;* 1817; p. 171.

(354) GLIDDON; *Otia Ægyptiaca;* pp. 61–69.

(355) AINSWORTH: *Assyria, Babylonia, and Chaldæa;* London, 1838; pp. 101, 104–107.

(356) DOWLER: *Tableaux of New Orleans;* 1832; pp. 7–17.

(357) McCULLOCH: *System of Geology;* i. p. 445.

(358) Rev. Dr. J. PYE SMITH: *Relation*, &c.; 1841; pp. 138, 139, 141.

Elohistic and the writing *alphabetical*, cannot ascend even to the tenth century before C.; and that, being based upon the harmonic scale of 7 *notes*, in accordance with the erroneous planetary system of Chaldaic magianism (of 5 *planets*, and the *sun* and *moon*); it is an arbitrary human production, founded upon ignorance of the physical laws and phenomena of Nature — as this Nature is unfolded by science in the nineteenth century.

In consequence, did *geologists* pretend to arrange the dozen, or more, distinct creations manifested in the earth's crust through rocky stratifications and different fossil remains (divided from each other by immeasurable periods of interjected time), according to the "7 musical notes" of Genesis, they would perpetrate a caricature of God's works more gross, and less excusable, than that of COSMAS-*Indicopleustes*: at the same time that they would make parade of stolid ignorance of *philology* and biblical exegesis such as every Orientalist, versed in archæology, must laugh to scorn. On the other hand (whether practical "geology" be or be not a fiction), were a *philologist* at the present day to argue, that the writer of "Genesis i–ii. 3" possessed *more* knowledge between the fifth and tenth centuries before C., than Cosmas did in the sixth after that era, his logic would establish two things: 1st, his absolute ignorance of geology; 2d, of every principle of historical criticism.

Indifferent, ourselves, to the self-appropriation, by either side, of one or both of these branches of the alternative, we cannot leave the "Deluge" without one observation; the force of which theologers and geologists would do well to keep constantly in view. It is, that this genesiacal Flood is inseparable from NuK*h*'s *Ark*, or boat. Without the buoyant convenience of the latter, let ethnographers remember, the entire human race would have been drowned in the former.

We could quote a real historian, and living divine, who seriously speaks of Noah as "the great navigator." We have *seen* a wondrous plate of the "Ark,"(359) exhibiting the Noachic family pursuing their domestic and zoological avocations with the placidity of a Van Amburgh, and the luxuriousness of a Lucullus. We have read abundant descriptions of this diluvian packet-ship, in ecclesiastical and ponderous tomes, "usque ad nauseam." But, there is no work that does such pains-taking justice to the "Ark;" there is no man who has exhausted Noachian seamanship, antediluvian ship-building, cataclysmal proprieties, human and animal (from the "leopard *lying* down with the kid" in their berth, to the cheerful smartness of Ham the cabin-boy)—than Father Kircher,(360) almost two centuries ago. It is a shame that some great publisher does not reprint such a sterling good work, abounding in plates; as it might be a most useful field-manual to the orthodox geologist, and pleasing, at the same time, to children. Unable to do adequate honor to the Arkite researches of this Herculæan Jesuit, we must be content with the lucid description, in plain English, of the Rev. Dr. Lightfoot; who, living above two hundred years nearer to the Deluge than ourselves, no doubt knew considerably more than we do about the vessel that survived it. (361)

"The dimensions of the Arke were such, as that it had contained 450,000 square cubits within the walls of it, if it had risen in an exact square unto the top; but it sloping in the roofe, like the roofe of an house, till it came to be but a cubit broad in the ridge of it, did abate some good parcell of that summe, but how much is uncertain; should we allow 50,000 cubits in the abatement, yet will the space be sufficient enough of capacity, to receive all the creatures, and all their provisions that were laid in there. The building was three stories high, but of the staires that rose from story to story, the Text is silent; in every story were partitions, not so many, as to seclude one kinde of creature from another, for that was needlesse, there being no enmity between them, while they were there, and it would have been more troublesome to Noah to bring their provisions to them: but there were such partitions, as to divide betwixt beasts and their provisions in store: betwixt provisions and provisions, that by lying neer together might receive dammage. The doore was in the side of the lowest story, and so it was under water all the time of the flood; but God by so speciall a providence had shut them in, that it leaked not. In what story every kinde of creature had its lodging and habitation, is a matter undeterminable; how their excrements were conveyed out of the Arke, and water conveyed in, the Text hath con-

(359) YEATES: *Dissertation on the Antiquity, Origin, and Design of the principal Pyramids of Egypt*; London, 1833; pp. 9, 10, and pl. i.

(360) *De Arca Noë*; 1 vol. fol., Amsterdam, 1675.

(361) *The Harmony, Chronicle, and Order of the Old Testament*; London, 1647; ch. vi. pp. 8, 9.

cealed. All the creatures were so cicurated and of a tamed condition for this time, that they lived together, and dieted together without dissention: *The wolf dwelte with the lamb, and the leopard lay down with the kid, and the calf and the young lion together:* and Noah or any of his family might come among lions, dragons, serpents, and they had forgot the wildness and cruelty of their nature, and did not meddle with him."

Chronology, therefore, among men of science, possesses relation neither to the unknown epoch of the "Deluge," nor to that of the "Creation." These events, scientifically unseizable, are abandoned by positivists to theological tenacity.

Archæologists, in efforts to re-arrange the World's occurrences from the chaos into which ecclesiastical presumption had cast them, now pursue an altogether different process of inquiry. Beginning from *to-day*, as a fixed point in history if not in universal nature,(362) they retrograde, as closely as possible, year by year to the Christian era; said to be 1858 years backwards from the present year. From that assumed point, chronologers continue to retrocede, year by year, so long as history or monuments warrant such annual registration of events: but when, owing to absence of record or to confusion of accounts, the impossibility of identifying a given date for a given occurrence becomes manifest, they endeavor to define it approximately within a few years, more or less. In the ratio of their recession into the mists of antiquity, so does the possibility of fixing an approximate epoch diminish; and, therefore, it becomes necessary to group a given number of events into masses; which conventional masses become larger and less distinctly marked in proportion as they are remote from that era we call "the Christian."

The era of the miraculous birth of JESUS was the stand-point of chronologists; the pivot upon which every modern system turns. How minutely precise to the mathematician this era is, may be perceived, by archæologists, at a glance.

EPOCHS OF THE NATIVITY.

			Authorities	Year of Rome.	Year before C.
According to	3	*authorities*—	Tillemont, Mann, Priestley	747	7
"	4	"	Kepler, Capellus, Dodwell, Pagi	748	6
"	5	"	Chrysostom, Petavius, Prideaux, Playfair, Hales	749	5
"	2	"	Sulpitius Severus, Usher	750	4
"	8	"	Irenæus, Tertullian, Clemens Alex., Eusebius, Syncellus, Baronius, Calvisius, Vossius	751	3
"	7	"	Epiphanius, Jerome, Orosius, Bede, Salian, Sigonius, Scaliger	752	2
"	3	"	Alexander Dionysius, Luther, Labbæus	753	1
			The moment of the Nativity is, consequently, *zero*		0
					Year after C.
"	1	"	Herwart	754	1
"	1	"	Paul of Middleburgh	755	2
"	1	"	Lydiat	756	3

35 authorities, of the most orthodox schools, here differ among themselves *ten years* about the era of the grandest præternatural event in human annals; which event is itself dependent in epoch upon the implied accuracy of a date—*Anno Urbis Conditæ*, the "year of the building of Rome"—that, in his next pages, the Rev. Dr. Hales (363) shows to be fluctuating, according to *six* dates established by 34 chronologists, between the assumed year B. C. 753 and B. C. 627!

And this is what theologers term "chronology." In the American edition of Calmet,(364) the date of the Nativity appears thus (the reader being free to adopt, in a free country, whichever date he pleases)—the editor naively remarking, "It must, however, be borne in mind, that the particularity of the dates here assigned rests chiefly on mere conjecture":—

Year of World.	Before Christ.	Before A. D.	Year of Christ.
CALMET.	HALES.	CALMET.	CALMET.
4000	5	4	1

(362) HUMBOLDT: *Cosmos*; i. p. 178; note, on "The English Sunday"!

(363) *New Analysis of Chron.*; 1830; i. pp. 214, 217; GLIDDON: *Chapters*; 1843; p. 33; and *Otia*; 1849; p. 42.

(364) *Dictionary*; "Chronological Table;" 1832; pp. 947, 981.

However, avers the Rev. Dr. Horne,(365) "The true date of the birth of Christ is *four* years before the common æra, or A. D." This date we should not be unwilling to accept but for the Rev. Dr. Jarvis (366) — "The date being taken of December 25, by reckoning back thirty years from his baptism, we come to his birth, A. J. P. 4707, *six* years before the common æra." It would not be decorous in us to hold fast to such dogmatic extension by a Churchman who sacrilegiously derides a *mitre* — "Abp. Newcombe could say, 'Jesus was born, says Lardner, between the middle of August and the middle of November, A. U. C. 748 or 749. (Cred. I. 796, 9, 3d ed.) We will take the *mean* time, October 1.'!!!" The notes of admiration are the Rev. Dr. Jarvis's.

We have preferred quoting the latest authorities; but it need not be observed to the learned that this discussion has been revived periodically during the last ten centuries with no better result, than when agitated previously between the unbelieving Rabbis and the all-believing Fathers. *Ex. gr.*, John *of Spain* (367) sums up: —

"That there has been sought in what season of the year, in what month, and on what day our Saviour was born: some place this birth at the winter solstice; others, at the equinox of autumn or at the equinox of spring."

And again, Bossuet, one of the most enlightened men of his age, winds up his chronological investigations as follows: —

"Birth of Jesus, son of Joseph and Mary. — It is not agreed *as to the precise year* when he came into the world, but it is agreed that his *true birth precedes* by some years our vulgar era. Without disputing further upon the year of the birth of our Lord, it suffices that we know it happened in the *year* 4000 *of the world*." [!] (368).

If we inquire the *age* of Jesus at his death, Bossuet tells us, that — "According to Matthew, he was 33 years old; to Pagan legend, 21; to Luke, 39; to Bossuet, 40,"

"Common Christians," as the Rev. Dr. Hitchcock designates them (ubi supra), may start back in amazement at these results upon the *year* of the Savior's *birth*, which the first slashes of an archæologic scalpel have now laid bare. Mystified by childlike or fraudulent authorities, they may or may not be grateful for the truth; but their conscientiousness will hereafter whisper to their minds that it is safest, perhaps, to become more charitable towards men of science; whose unwearied struggles to arrive at *a* chronology are superinduced by acquaintance with these facts. In the meanwhile, readers of Strauss and Hennell know why the settlement of the *year* of Jesus's nativity is one of those things not to be looked for; because, as Scaliger wrote — "to determine the day of Christ's birth belongs to God alone, not to man."

To "uncommon Christians," whose effrontery has led them to accuse Egyptologists of dissensions as to the epoch of the first Pharaoh, Menes, (by no thorough hierologist dogmatically fixed) we have merely to advise their prior determination of the year of Christ's nativity, before they henceforward venture into Egyptian polemics wherein they themselves are the only parties liable to "get hurt."

In a recent hieroglyphical work, to which allusion will be briefly made in its natural department, the Royal Astronomer, Professor Airy, (369) through profound mathematical calculations, obtains a celestial conjunction which he designates "2005 B. C.; April 8th." "B. C." implies *before Christ*. Now, as no human being can determine the *year* of Christ's advent; and inasmuch as the foregoing table exhibits a difference of opinion oscillating between ten years at least; we would respectfully solicit the astronomical era upon which the learned Professor founds his minute coincidence. Is it upon the "*star* of the east"(370) seen by the *Magi?* Or does he take the unknown moment of time "C." to be *zero?* Among archæologists, to say "B. C.," merely implies before an epoch conjectural for one or more

(365) *Introd. to the Crit. Study and Knowledge of the Holy Scriptures;* 8th ed., London, 1839; iii. pp. 527, 535.

(366) *Chronol. Introd. to the Hist. of the Church;* London ed., 1844; Preface, p. vii., and pp. 535, 563.

(367) *Quad. Istor. del. Lit. Arm.;* Venezia, 1829.

(368) BOSSUET: *Discours sur l'Hist. Univ.;* and *Art de vérif. les Dates,* par les Bénédictins de Saint-Maur.

(369) *Horæ Ægyptiacæ;* London, 1851; pp. 216 217.

(370) *Matthew;* ii. 1, 9, 10; omitted by MARK; called an "angel" in *Luke* ii. 9–15; and unmentioned by JOHN. Vide STRAUSS: *Vie de Jesus;* 1839; i. pp. 254–292.

years; but, without some more mathematical indication of the *astronomical* date of the birth of Jesus, those Egyptian calculations made at the Royal Observatory must be pregnant with error; and, at present, seem as valueless to chronological science, as are the *hieroglyphic* malinterpretations that originated such a waste of official labor and of nationally-important time.

To us, however, the forms "B. C." and "A. D." are merely conventional. No astronomical certitude is implied by their use. This year, which is the LXXVIIth *of the Independence of these United States*, may be, for aught we know, "A. D. 1850" or "A. D. 1860;" although vulgarly termed "the year 1853." When we use the customary era, chronologically, it simply means *one thousand eight hundred and fifty-three years* backwards from the present day; and "B. C." signifies whatever number of years the necessities of illustration compel us to place *before* the 1853d year thus specified. We leave Astronomy to astronomers.

With this proviso constantly present, the reader will understand that the only ancient chronological era, positively fixed, is the *Nabonassarian* — "February 26, B. C. 747." All other dates in ancient history are to this subordinate; although, for ordinary purposes, save when phenomena in the heavens can be historically connected with human events passing on the earth, "B. C." is both usual and adequate to the requirements of archæological science; still more of ethnological, wherein precision of specific eras is less imperative.

Our object, in this Essay (III), is to lay before the reader a general view of the relative positions which *Egypt*, *China*, *Assyria*, *Judæa*, and *India*, now occupy, in the eye of the monumental chronologist, on the tableau of different human origins. Like every other science that of chronology is progressive: in the cases of Egyptian and Assyrian time-registry essentially so; for, at the present year, 1853, the former study is immature, the latter scarcely commenced. That of China must be accepted upon the faith (which there is not the slightest reason to impugn) of what Chinese historians who, having no *theological* motives for unfair curtailment or for preposterous extension, have rebuilt from the archæology of their own country. There is but one nation of the five of which the utmost limit can, nowadays, be absolutely determined, and that is the Judæan; whose chronicles, in lieu of the first place still claimed for them by ignorance, now occupy, among archæologists, a *fourth* place in universal history. For Greece, Rome, and more recent populations, according to the criteria of their own annals, we refer the reader to well-known histories.

It will be remembered that, in "Types of Mankind," chronology is only one element out of many; and that we here profess merely to present the *results* of those chronological laborers who are now reputed to be the most scientific, and consequently the most accurate.

CHRONOLOGY—EGYPTIAN.

"Un certain public, ce public qui tour à tour admet sans preuve ce qui est absurde, et rejette sans motif ce qui est certain, satisfait dans les deux cas, parce qu'il se donne le plaisir de trancher les questions en s'épargnant la peine de les examiner; ce public qui croit aux Osages quand ils viennent de Saint Malo, mais qui ne croit pas aux Chinois, quand ils viennent de Pékin; qui est fermement convaincu de l'existence de Pharamond, et n'est pas bien sûr que le latin et l'allemand puissent être de la même famille que le sanscrit; ce public gobe-mouche quand il faut douter, esprit fort quand il faut croire, hochait et hoche encore la tête au nom de CHAMPOLLION, trouvant plus commode et plus court de nier sa découverte que d'ouvrir sa *grammaire*." (371)

"Quant aux hommes éminens qui ont conquis une belle place dans la carrière des études égyptiennes, il ne peut être question ici d'analyser leurs livres: il suffit que l'on sache bien que tous ont marché franchement dans la voie ouverte par CHAMPOLLION, et que la science qui a dû sa première illustration aux Young, aux Champollion, aux Humboldt, aux Salvolini, aux Nestor l'Hôte, et dont la réalité a été proclamée sans rétinence par les Sylvestre de Sacy et les Arago, compte aujourd'hui pour adeptes fervens et convaincus, des hommes tels que MM. Letronne, Ampère, Biot, Mérimée, Prisse, E. Burnouf, Lepsius, Bunsen, Peyron, Gazzera, Barucchi, Gliddon, Leemans,—[Abeken, Birch, Böckh, Bonomi, Brugsch, Brunet de Presle, De Saulcy, De Rougé, Harris, Hincks, Kenrick, Lanci, Lenormant, Lesueur, Mariette, Maury, Morton, Nott, Osburn, Perring, Pickering, Raoul-Rochette, Sharpe, Ungarelli, Wilkinson,] &c.—On connait maintenant les amis et les ennemis du système de CHAMPOLLION." (372)

"In short, the little spring of pure water which first bubbled from the Rosetta Stone, has, in twenty-three years, now swoln into a mighty flood; overwhelming all opposition;

(371) AMPÈRE: *Recherches en Égypte et en Nubie*; 1st art.; Revue des Deux Mondes, Aug. 1846; pp. 390, 391;—see also, *Ibid.*: *Promenade en Amérique*; Rev. des D. Mondes, June, 1853, pp. 1225, 1226.

(372) DE SAULCY: *De l'Étude des Hiéroglyphes*; Rev. d. D. Mondes, June, 1846; p. 983.

sweeping aside, or carrying in its surges, those whose inclination would induce them to stem its force; and, at the present hour, we know more of positive Egyptian history and of the ancient inhabitants of Egypt, ages previously to the patriarch Abraham, than on many subjects we can assert of our acquaintance with England before Alfred the Great, or with France before Charlemagne!" (373)

The work last cited, accessible to every reader of English at an insignificant cost, renders explanations on the incipient steps of hierological discovery herein superfluous. As a synoptical report of the progress of Egyptian studies it is correct enough, for general purposes, to the close of the year 1841. Our present point of departure is A. D. 1822.

"With Dr. Young's key, and Champollion's alphabet contained in his letter to M. Dacier, a group of scientific Englishmen, headed by Henry Salt, and subsequently aided by A. C. Harris, commenced in Egypt itself, about 1822, the scrutiny and examination of all the monuments of antiquity existing, from the Sea-beach to Upper Nubia, from the Oases to the peninsula of Mount Sinai, and in every direction through the Eastern and Western Deserts. These gentlemen, mutually aiding and co-operating with each other, were enabled to take instant advantage of the true method of interpretation. Egypt was then all virgin ground. Every temple, every tomb, contained something unknown before; and which these gentlemen were the *first* to date, and to describe with accurate details. A more intensely interesting field never opened to the explorer — every step being a discovery. Nobly did these learned and indefatigable travellers pioneer the way, and mighty have been the results of their arduous labors. They procured lithographic presses from England; and, at their individual expense, for private circulation, Messrs. Felix, Burton, and Wilkinson printed (at Cairo—1826 to 1829) and circulated a mass of hieroglyphical tablets, legends, genealogical tables, texts mythological and historical, with other subjects, which, under the modest titles of "Notes," (374) "Excerpta," (375) and "Materia Hieroglyphica," (376) were disseminated to learned societies in Europe. Lord Prudhoe's distant excursions and correct memoranda rendered the collections of antiquities, with which he enriched England, extremely valuable; and his labors were the more appreciated, as his lordship's liberal mind and generous patronage of science were above any sordid motives of acquisitiveness. Mr. Hay's own accurate pencil, aided by various talented artists whom his princely fortune enabled him to employ, amassed an amount of drawings that rendered his portfolios the largest then in the world. The researches of all these gentlemen have been of incalculable value to the cause. They have preserved accurate data on subjects, (377) that the destroying hand of Mohammed Ali has since irrevocably obliterated; and as they all pursued science for itself, they deserve and enjoy a full measure of respect. The rumor of their successes reached Europe; and Champollion, with reason, apprehended that, if he delayed his visit to Egypt any longer, the individual labors of English travellers would render that visit as unprofitable as unnecessary. National jealousy was excited; and, to preserve her position as the patroness of Egyptian literature, France determined not to be anticipated.

"In 1828, the French government sent a commission, consisting of Champollion le Jeune, and four French artists, well supplied with every necessary outfit, to Egypt, in order that the master might, for his own and his country's honor, and at her expense, reap the harvest for which his hand had sown the seed. A similar design having suggested itself to another patron of arts and sciences, the Grand Duke of Tuscany, the celebrated archæologist and oriental scholar, Professor Ippolito Rosellini, of the University of Pisa, and four Italian artists under his direction, were appointed a commission to proceed to Egypt, with the same intent as the French mission. It was amicably arranged by the respective governments, and between the chiefs of each expedition, that their labors should be united; and, in consequence, the French and Tuscan missions were blended into one, and both reached Alexandria in the same vessel, and prosecuted their labors hand in hand from Memphis to the second Cataract. They returned in 1829.

"It was amicably arranged, between Champollion and Rosellini, that they were to combine their labors in the works that were to be issued; each, however, taking separate branches—Champollion undertaking the illustration of the "Historical Monuments," and the grammar of the hieroglyphic language of Egypt — to Rosellini was assigned the task of elucidating, by the "Civil Monuments," the manners and customs of this ancient people, and the formation of a hieroglyphical dictionary. Each set to work by 1830; but Champollion, finding his end approaching, hastened the completion of his grammar. Intense application had prostrated the fragile frame which enveloped one of the most gifted mental

(373) GLIDDON: *Chapters on Early Egyptian History*; New York, 1843; p. 10: 15th ed., Philad., 1850.

(374) FELIX: republished in Italian, at Pisa; but now out of circulation.

(375) JAMES HALLIBURTON: out of print, and extremely rare.

(376) WILKINSON: like the preceding.

(377) GLIDDON: *Appeal to the Antiquaries of Europe on the Destruction of the Monuments of Egypt*; 1841; London, Madden.

capacities ever vouchsafed to man. The government gave him, in the Collège de France, a professor's chair, created for him alone; and his address to his pupils, at the first and only occasion accorded to him by Providence, is a marvel of eloquence, sublimity of thought, and classical diction.

"He finished his grammar on his death-bed, and summoning his friends around him, delivered the autograph into their custody, with the injunction 'to preserve it carefully, for I hope it will be my *visiting card* to posterity.' A few weeks after, Champollion le Jeune was followed to the grave by the noblest men of France; and the wreath of 'Immortelles' hung over his sepulchre (at his native town, *Figeac*), symbolized the imperishable fame of the resuscitator of the earliest records mankind has hitherto possessed."

His posthumous works were put to press at the expense of the nation, nor is their entire publication as yet complete. Death removed Rosellini (1841) before the *Monumenti dell' Egitto e della Nubia* received his final touches: and his worthy Italian colleague, Ungarelli, also died (1846) previously to the termination of the latter's *Interpretatio Obeliscorum Urbis.*

We may now proceed with a brief historical sketch of the steps through which Egyptian Chronology has become the criterion whereby the annals of all antique nations are now measured; subjoining references sufficient for the educated inquirer to verify bibliographical accuracy.

When Fourier, the polytechnic philosopher, in that masterpiece of eloquent erudition — the *Preface* to the "Description de l'Egypte"—claimed a period of *twenty-five hundred years* before the Christian era, (378) for the monuments which he, and the corps of illustrious Savans of whom Jomard is the surviving patriarch, had beheld in the valley of the Nile, his intuitive grasp of the amount of time adequate to the construction of then-unnumbered piles as gigantic in their architecture as diversified in their sculptures, obtained but little favor with the scholars, and none with the public of Europe, from 1810 to 1830. As when the immortal Harvey announced his discovery of the circulation of the blood, no surgeon, over forty years of age, but died an unbeliever in the theory; so forty years after the utterance of this chronological estimate by Fourier, and notwithstanding the victorious labors of the hierologists, do we still encounter cultivated minds unwilling to accept, or incapable of comprehending, the general truth of his proposition.

Equally unpalatable was this scale of 2500 *years*, at the time of its publication, to the representatives of two distinct schools; whom, for convenience sake, we will designate as the *long* and the *short* chronologists. On the one hand Dupuis and those astronomers who had claimed as much as 17,000 years B. C. for the erection of the temple of Dendera, and on the other, the followers of the *Petavian* and *Usherian* computations of the chronological element in Scripture, coincided in its rejection; the former deeming it too restricted, the latter too extensive for their respective cosmogenical theories. And, in a controversy in which the first principles of historical criticism, and a common basis of debate were alike wanting; before Young had deciphered the first letter in the hieroglyphical name of *Ptolemy;* before Champollion-le-jeune's "Précis" broke the spell in which the antique writings of the Egyptians had been bound for fifteen centuries: and at a day when absolutely *nothing* was known of the respective ages of Nilotic remains; the dogmatical assertions of the latter were infinitely preferable to the hallucinations of the former.

On his death-bed, in 1830, Fourier was solaced by the glimpse which Champollion, then just returned from his triumphant mission to Egypt, afforded him of the probable accuracy of his prospective vision: but, before the founder of Egyptological science could arrange the enormous materials collected for his *chronological* edifice, the 4th of March, 1832, overtook Champollion on his own death-bed, in the act of bequeathing the manuscript of his immortal *Grammar*, as "my visiting-card to posterity." (379)

In the same year, Rosellini commenced the publication of the "Monumenti dell' Egitto

(378) CHAMPOLLION-FIGEAC: *Fourier et Napoleon — l'Égypte et les cent jours;* 1844; p. 61.

(379) *Grammaire Égyptienne;* 1835; Introduction. See also in CHAMPOLLION-FIGEAC (*Notice sur les Manuscrits autographes de Champollion le Jeune*, perdus en l'année, 1832, et retrouvés en 1840; Paris, 1842) the account of that wretched larceny which, while it accounts for the non-publication up to this hour of all the *Manuscripts* left by this indefatigable scholar, compels the historian to wipe his pen after writing the name—SALVOLINI. The example had, however, been previously set by the plagiarist of JOHN HUNTER's MSS.

e della Nubia;" in which, for the first time, an effort was made to embrace in one grand compendium all Egyptian documents in that day deciphered. Inheritor of the ideas, and associate in the labors of the great master, the Tuscan Professor's frame-work of chronology reflects Champollion's views on Pharaonic antiquity down to the close of 1830. The practical result of the erudite Italian's researches was the monumental restoration of the lost history of Egypt, back to the XVIIIth Dynasty, computed by him at B. C. 1822,—and the vindication of the general accuracy of Manetho, back to the XVIth dynasty, at B. C. 2272: (380) confirmed by Champollion-Figeac,(381) with many improvements and valuable suggestions; mainly drawn from "les papiers de mon Frère."

In 1835, Wilkinson's admirable work, "Topography of Thebes," presented a summary of the learned author's personal exploration of Egyptian monuments during some twelve years of travel in the valley of the Nile. The epoch of Menes, first Pharaoh of Egypt, was conjecturally assigned to the year B. C. 2201; but the accession of the XVIIIth dynasty placed at B. C. 1575, corroborated by the collation of hieroglyphical and Greek lists, evinced the critical author's appreciation of the solidity of Egypt's chronological edifice, and of Manethonian authority, at least up to the latter era.

We thus reach the year 1836; when B. C. 1822 as the *maximum*, and B. C. 1575 as the *minimum*, for the accession of Manetho's XVIIIth dynasty of Diospolitans, were already recognised by the world of science in general principle as established *facts:* and sixteen centuries of lost monumental history became resuscitated from the sepulchre of ages, through *hieroglyphical* researches that only commenced in A. D. 1822. (382)

But there had been, in Egypt, times *before!* there were still extant the *pyramids*, with the lengthy chain of tombs extending for above 20 miles along the Memphite necropolis, *unexplored;*—there were the "unplaced Kings" recorded in the "Materia Hieroglyphica" —the "Excerpta"—and the "Notes"—of Wilkinson, Burton, and Felix;—and there existed in the museums of Europe, as well as throughout the valley of the Nile, innumerable vestiges, recognised by every qualified student of Egyptology to belong to ages long anterior to the XVIIIth dynasty — immensely older than the year 1575—1822 B. C.; to say nothing of many biblical and classical texts that attested the necessity for more elbow-room in the chronology of the ancient Egyptians. Every one felt it: — every man who had *beheld* the storied ruins in Egypt itself asserted it, with more or less assurance according to the elasticity of the social atmosphere he breathed: — every hierologist *knew* it.

How was the conscientious discussion of these overwhelming questions avoided? Why were the countless monumental documents, that vindicated the claims of Manetho's first fourteen human dynasties to historical acceptance, left out of sight? Rosellini, while faithfully publishing all the materials in his possession, and throwing back pyramidal questions into the category of things anterior to the XVIth dynasty, having the fear of Petavius before his eyes, modestly declares —"Nè a me occorre indagare più addentro in *tanto bujo* di tempi."(383) Wilkinson, — in whose invaluable "Materia Hieroglyphica," among a host of "unplaced Kings," the names of *Shoopho*, *Shafra*, and *Menkera*, builders of the three great pyramids of Geezeh, had been published years before, and *two* of them at least read and identified,—Wilkinson, appalled perhaps at the authority of Usher, jumps at a bound, in his Plate I. of the "Dynasties of the Pharaohs," from MENaI, over SE-NEFER-KE-RA and RA-NEB-NAA, to RA-NUB-TER (which last he places in the XVth dynasty at B. C. 1830); omits every "unplaced King" published in his previous researches; ignores some *fifty Pharaohs* whose *monuments* prove they lived between Menes and the XVIIIth dynasty; and assigns only the year B. C. 2201 (!) to Menes, "for fear of *interfering* with the Deluge of Noah, which *is* 2348 B. C."

"I am aware," wrote, in 1835, the yet-unknighted Mr. Wilkinson, "that the era of Menes might be carried back to a much more remote period than the date I have assigned

(380) GLIDDON: *Chapters;* 1843; pp. 48, 49, and General Table, pp. 64, 65, 66.
(381) *Égypte Ancienne;* Univers Pittoresque, 1839.
(382) CHAMPOLLION: *Lettre à M. Dacier;* 1822.
(383) *Monumenti Storici;* 1832; vol. 1. p. 111

it; but as we have as yet no authority further than the uncertain accounts of Manetho's copyists to enable us to fix the time and the number of reigns intervening between his accession and that of Apappus, I have not placed him earlier, for fear of interfering with the date of the deluge of Noah, which *is* 2348 B. C." (384)

The inconsistencies inherent in this scheme of chronology were exposed in 1843; (385) nevertheless, in his most excellent later work, "Modern Egypt and Thebes," 1843, as well as in his "Hand-book," 1847, this erudite Egyptologist has left *chronological* disquisitions pretty much as he had defined them in 1835 — as if inquiry had been *stationary* in Europe during twelve years! — although, when treating *geologically* on the antiquity of the *Delta*, "il laisse percer le bout d'oreille" in the following scientific assertions: —

"We are led to the necessity of allowing an immeasurable time for the total formation of that space, which, to judge from the very little accumulation of its soil, and the small distance it has encroached on the sea, since the erection of the ancient cities within it, would require ages, and throw back its origin *far beyond the Deluge*, or even the *Mosaic era of the Creation*." (386)

In consequence, Sir J. G. Wilkinson granted a reprieve of some few years to poor Menes; for (1837) in the same "Manners and Customs," this Pharaoh's accession is placed at B. C. 2320; or only 28 years after the Flood!

It is sufficient, herein, to point out to the reader, that the year 1836 closed with a mighty stride, already accomplished, into the "darkness of Egypt;" through which a *mass of time*, exceeding *fifteen centuries* in duration, was irrevocably restored to the world's history. The mutilated annals of the oft-maligned Priest of Sebennytus were vindicated by an unanswerable appeal to monuments contemporaneous with the Pharaohs recorded by him, back to his XVIIIth Theban dynasty. More than one-half of the *twenty-five hundred* years claimed by Fourier, and Napoleon's "Institut d'Égypte," was thenceforward restored to positive history by the *Hierologists*.

The years 1837 to 1839 witnessed the munificent expenditures, and fulfilment of the grand conception, of a Vyse; the self-sacrificing exertions of a Perring, but for whose fortitude, enthusiasm, and engineering skill, small, indeed, would have been the scientific results accruing from such immense undertakings; and the archæological acumen of a Birch, in deciphering and assigning an historical place to the fragmentary legends disenterred among some 39 pyramidal mausolea (387) of the *Memphite* and *Arsinoïte* nomes. (388) Simultaneously with these successes, the *Tablet of Abydos*, that most precious register of the genealogy of the RAMESSIDES, found its way to the British Museum. (389)

Lenormant, (390) we believe, was the first to apply the new discoveries to *chronology*; and Nestor L'Hôte (391) to retread the Memphite necropolis, and verify some of the data obtained by the English explorers.

The combined result of these researches, in the year 1840, was the recognition of the great principle, that the *pyramids*, without exception, antedated the XVIIIth dynasty, already established between the fifteenth and the eighteenth centuries B. C.: — that a mass of "unplaced Kings," and a vast field of unopened tombs in the burial-ground of Memphis; together with a prodigious variety of lesser monuments, stretching from the peninsula of Sinai to the temples of *Samneh* and *Soleb* in Upper Nubia; still preserved authentic records coetaneous with the first *twelve dynasties* of MANETHO: and that, from out of the chaos, the

---

(384) *Topography of Thebes*; 1835, pp. 506 and 509.

(385) GLIDDON: *Chapters*; pp. 51, 52.

(386) *Manners and Customs*; 1837–'41; i. pp. 5–11; ii. pp. 105–121;—compare *Otia Ægyptiaca*; pp. 61–69.

(387) *Operations carried on at the Pyramids of Geezeh*, from 1837 to 1839.

(388) SHARPE: *Chronology and Geography of Ancient Egypt*; 1849; pl. 11, Map, *Ancient Egypt under Ant. Pius*.

(389) LEPSIUS: *Auswahl*; 1842; pl. 11; — BIRCH: *Gallery of Antiquities*; part ii. pl. 29, and pp. 66–71; — LETRONNE: *Table d'Abydos*, imprimée en caractères mobiles; Paris, 1845; pp. 24–36; — BUNSEN: *Egypt's Place*; 1848; pp. 44–51; — DE ROUGÉ: *Examen de l'Ouvrage de M. Bunsen*; 1847; pp. 16, 17, *Extrait des Annales de Philosophie chrétiennes*; and *Ibid.*: *Deuxième Lettre à M. Alfred Maury, sur le Sesostris de la XIIme Dynastie*; Revue Archéologique, 15 Oct. 1847; pp. 479, 480; — LESUEUR: *Chronologie des Rois d'Égypte*; ouvrage couronné; Paris, 1848; pp. 260–263; — PRISSE: *Notice sur la Salle des Ancêtres de Thoutmes III.*; Rev. Archéol.; Paris, 1845.

(390) *Eclaircissemens sur le Cercueil de Mycerinus*; Paris, 1839.

(391) *Lettres d'Égypte*: Paris, 1840.

IVth Manethonian dynasty, cotemporary with the building of the *Geezeh* group of pyramids, loomed like a meteor in the night of time.

Some perceptions were entertained, about those days, even in America, of the probable extent to which *monumental* researches would eventually carry the epoch of MENES. In 1845, Bunsen's era for this monarch was B. C. 3643; and in 1849, Lepsius's is B. C. 3893. Our "*Chapters*" (1843) assert, that "if 1000 more years could be shown admissible by Scripture, there is nothing in Egypt that would not be found to agree with the extension." It is a happy coincidence, exhibiting how different minds, in countries widely apart, reasoning upon similar data, arrive at conclusions nearly the same, that, if the above "1000 years" be added to our former conjectural and *minimum* estimate, printed *ten* years ago, of the date of MENES, noted at *about* B. C. 2750,(392) the sum B. C. 3750 falls, almost equidistantly, between the eras assigned to this primordial Pharaoh by two of the *three* highest hierological chronographers: — the third, it need scarcely be observed, being Mr. Birch; who, whilst tabulating Egyptian events in the recognised order of Manethonian *dynasties*, (393) has never yet put forth an arithmetical *system* of hieroglyphical chronology. As remarked by us (*Otia*, p. 45):—

"We are dealing, in events so inconceivably remote, with *stratified masses of time*, and not with supposititious calculations of the *exact* day, week, month, or year; in futile attempts to ascertain which so many learned investigators "ne font qu'un trou dans l'eau."

Our sketch of the progressive conquests over the past, commenced by Champollion in 1822, through which a pathway has been hewn, inch by inch, by the axes of the Hierologists, far into the briery jungle of Pharaonic antiquity, has reached the year 1843; and already Fourier's "*twenty-five hundred* years B. C." for the monuments of the Nile, even to the uninformed eye, began to wear the garb of probability — to the hieroglyphical student, who had *actually beheld with his own eyes* these monuments *in Egypt itself*, they had assumed in that year the aspect of certainty.

It is a remarkable fact, that with the exception of Wilkinson, whose chronological consistency has been indicated (*supra*), not one of those Egyptologists of whom the critical opinion is now authoritative, and who, at this day, yet aspires to the name of a *short*-chronologist (that is, one to whom the *Usherian deluge*, at B. C. 2348, is a bed of Procrustes), has ever studied Egyptian monuments *in Egypt!* Much allowance, therefore, should be made for living English scholars who still, like the ostrich, bury their heads in sand; surrounded as they are, essentially, by the "intellectual *flunkeyism*" for which this age, in England, is eminently celebrated among scientific men on the Continent and in the United States. The ponderous weight of brains, congealed in the "cast-iron moulds" of Oxford and Cambridge, presses upon British intelligence and education with the numbing power of an incubus. Among recent vindicators of the claims of Egypt to the *longest* chronology is Ferguson ("True Principles of Beauty in Art," &c., London, 1849), to whose crushing pamphlet we must refer admirers of the educational "standard of a by-gone and semi-barbarous age," upheld in "the Sister Universities;" with which standard the citizens of republican America, of course, need have nothing to do, physically, morally, or intellectually.(394)

The discovery made by Lepsius, in 1840 (not publicly known for some years later), that the *Tablet of Abydos*, between *Cartouche* No. 40 and No. 39, omits the XIIIth, XIVth, XVth, XVIth, and XVIIth Manethonian dynasties, thus *jumping over the entire Hyksos-period*, (395)

(392) I am happy to find that this (by myself long ago abandoned — *Otia*, pp. 37–42) scheme of the possible epoch of Menes, approximates so nearly to the date adopted by Nolan; who places, according to the "Old Chronicle," Menes (whom he takes to be Noah!) at B. C. 2673; or only *ten* years difference from "my reduction of the *Old Chronicle*, B. C. 2683," five years previously — (compare *Egyptian Chronology analysed*; London, 1848; pp. 133, 156, 212, and 399, with *Chapters*, p. 51). Still less does it differ from the point at which a "great authority, whose permission I have not asked to give his name," fixes (*astronomically* speaking) the era of Egypt's first Pharaoh: viz., B. C. 2714–'15 — the *very date* (B. C. 2715) to which I had reduced Manetho, in 1848. Compare *Literary Gazette*; London, 1849; pp. 485, 522, and 641; with *Chapters*; p. 51.) — G. R. G.

(393) "Relative Epochs of Mummies," in *Otia Ægyptiaca*; pp. 78–87; also, pp. 113–115.

(394) *Observations on the British Museum, National Gallery, and National Record Office*; London, 1849.

(395) BUNSEN: *Ægypten's Stelle*; 1845; ii. p. 277; and *Egypt's Place*; 1848; pp. 42, 49, 52. Compare HINCKS: *On the Egyptian Stele*; 1841; p. 68; and BARUCCHI: *Discorsi Critici sopra la Cronologia Egizia*; Torino, 1845; pp. 129–131.

had marked a new era in the chronological consideration to be awarded to some royal *genealogical* Tablets. This discovery was by far the most important feature of that day; but so varied and unforeseen were the victorious achievements effected, in the year 1843, by the Prussian Scientific Mission, among the *pyramids*, from Memphis to the Labyrinth; so completely have they revolutionized all preceding judgments upon Nilotic antiquity; that we must pause to indicate how they originated, and where they are to be found.

Chevalier Richard Lepsius, long celebrated as Corresponding Secretary of the *Institute of Archæological Correspondence* at Rome, directed his studies into Egyptology soon after the publication of a prize-essay, (396) that placed him in the front rank of linguistical scholarship in 1834. A *Lettre à M. le Prof. Hippolite Rosellini sur l'Alphabet Hiéroglyphique*, 1837, (397) next announced, to the world of science, that the loss of the illustrious Champollion had but momentarily arrested the onward march of his disciples. The return of Perring from Egypt after his indefatigable exploration of 39 pyramids, (398) rendered the fact generally known that, immense as had been his own successes, the necropolis of Memphis had, notwithstanding, scarcely begun to yield up its historical treasures. French and Tuscan national, with English private enterprise, had been rewarded, in the valley of the Nile, by victories over past time as noble as they were scientific. It remained for Frederic William IVth of Prussia to give full scope to the hitherto pent-up yearnings of Germany towards Egyptian discovery; and upon Lepsius, in 1842, naturally fell the mantles of his predecessors.

With eight coadjutors, the Chief of the Prussian Scientific Mission pitched his tents in the shadow of the great Pyramid on the 9th of November, 1842.

By May, 1843, he was enabled to announce that the Germans had gleaned the sites of "*thirty other pyramids*, entirely unknown to him (Mr. Perring), or to any preceding travellers. Of these, not a few are of very considerable extent, bearing evident traces of the mode in which they were raised, and surrounded by the ruins of temples, and extensive fields of tombs or burial-grounds. All these pyramids, without exception, belong to the *ancient kingdom* of Egypt *before* the irruption of the Hykshos, who invaded Lower Egypt about the year 2000 B. C., and the whole of them were erected (those at least between Abrorooàsh and Dashoor) by kings who reigned at Memphis. To the same period belong also the majority of the *effaced* tombs, of any importance, that surround them." (399)

After determination of the sites, and unfolding much of the history of "*sixty-seven* pyramids," sepulchres of ancient Egyptian sovereigns; together with "*one hundred and thirty* private tombs" of noble families, with these sovereigns coetaneous, back to the "*fourth thousand year* before Christ," the Prussians proceeded up the river; exploring every foot of ground, as far as *Soba* on the Blue Nile (*Bahr-el-Azrek*), and *Sennàr* to the 13th degree of N. latitude; returning to Thebes on the 2d November, 1844. While his able assistants prosecuted the necessary labors amid Theban ruins, Lepsius crossed the Red Sea and explored the Sinaic Peninsula; not only, thereby, rescuing from perdition hieroglyphical records of mining operations conducted between the IVth and the XIIth dynasty, 3400—2200 B. C., but also ascertaining that, if the *Gebel Serbàl* be not the Mount of MOSES, of which there is little doubt, (400) the peaks above the Convent of St. Catherine most assuredly are not. Revisiting Thebes, Lepsius left it with his party on the 16th May, 1845: and after examining the land of Goshen, much of Palestine, and touching at Smyrna and Constantinople, landed at Trieste on the 5th January, 1846: having spent above *thirty-six months* in unparalleled monumental researches on the river, alluvium, and deserts of the Nile.

The reader will now perceive that we are dealing in realities; that our Egyptian deductions are based upon actual and positive researches, made by the "primi inter pares" of

(396) *Palæographie als Mittel für die Sprachforschung zunüchst am Sanscrit nachgewiesen*; Berlin, 1835; 8vo.

(397) *Annali dell' Instituto di Corrispondenza Archeologica*; vol. ix.; Roma, 1837.

(398) VYSE: *The Pyramids from Actual Survey*; iiird vol.; 1841.

(399) LEPSIUS; *Ueber den Bau der Pyramiden*: Berlin Academy, August, 1843; pp. 2, 3; — see the order of announcement of these discoveries in GLIDDON: *Otia*; 1849; pp. 30–42.

(400) *Tour from Thebes to the Peninsula of Sinai, in March and April*, 1845; transl. COTTRELL; London, 1846. We possess the *German* edition; with its tinted *map*, without which LEPSIUS's certain discovery is not so evident to the general reader.

living Archæologists, previously qualified by lengthened discipline, and furnished by munificent governments with facilities as unexampled as unbounded. We subjoin a list of the works (401) since published by Lepsius, that have been carefully consulted in the preparation of "Types of Mankind;" and may mention that, while one of its authors sojourned at Berlin in May, 1849, both are in frequent epistolary communication, on the themes this work discusses, with the esteemed Chevalier himself.

Consequently, whether the deductions drawn by the authors of the present volume be right or wrong, the *facts* upon which these are grounded are vouched for by the highest authorities. No attention is bestowed, in "Types of Mankind," to the puerilities of the ephemeral tourist, to the twaddling inanities of the unlettered missionary, or to the Egyptian hallucinations of the theological rhapsodist. At the present day (without disparagement to the less-known literary resources of other cities on our continent), (402) a qualified student, in this year A. D. 1853, can sit down quietly at *Mobile*, Alabama; and the books contained in four private libraries will enlighten him, upon almost every point our work discusses, with smaller trouble and greater economy of time, labor, and money, than if he resided for *years*, without previous knowledge of these works, in the valley of the Nile: or, should such student prefer Philadelphia, there, at her Library, his bibliothecal aspirations can be satisfied.

How utterly hopeless it is for any man (apart from erudition) unsupported by enormous pecuniary means, to advance Egyptian sciences, at the present day, by a steam-boat excursion up the Nile, may be inferred from three facts. In 1844–5, Ampère, one of the living luminaries of archæological knowledge, was sent out by the French Government expressly to make discoveries. His "Recherches en Egypte et en Nubie" in literary excellence are unsurpassable; yet, withal, his predecessors had left him so little to do, without a protracted sojourn, that he refers to Lepsius for every novelty discoverable:—

"Je n'ai pas touché, sans un certain respect, ce livre *des Rois*, commencé par lui avant son voyage d'Egypte, et qui contient une collection de noms royaux plus complète qu'aucune autre ne peut l'être, et un ensemble de chronologie Égyptienne depuis l'ancien roi Ménès jusqu'à Septime Sevère. Cette série va plus loin encore, car M. Lepsius ne s'arrête pas à ce nom, le dernier qu'eussent trouvé écrit en hiéroglyphes Champollion et ses autres successeurs. M. Lepsius a été assez heureux pour découvrir, dans un petit temple de Thèbes où Champollion avait trouvé le nom d'Othon, les noms de *Galba*, de *Pescennius Niger*, et, ce qui est plus important, de l'empereur *Dèce*. Par cette découverte, M. Lepsius prolonge la série hiéroglyphique d'un demi-siècle au déla de Septime Sevère, où elle s'arrêtait jusqu'ici. *On a donc une suite de monumens et d'inscriptions qui s'étendent depuis* 2500 *avant Abraham jusqu'à* 250 *ans après Jesus Christ.* Il n'y a rien de semblable dans les annales humaines." (403)

Two years previously, Prisse d'Avennes had rescued the *Ancestral Chamber of Karnac*, the *Tablet of Ramses* XIV, (404) and other precious relics, from Turkish demolition. A residence of sixteen years in Egypt, of which about five in the Upper country among the monuments, had enabled this proficient Orientalist to fill his portfolios with every archæological item discovered, chiefly too by himself, between the departure of the French and Tuscan Scientific Commissions under Champollion and Rosellini, 1830, and the advent of the Prussians in 1842. So valuable were M. Prisse's self-sacrificing labors in Egyptology

(401) *Vorläufige Nachricht über die Expedition;* Berlin, 1849; — *Briefe aus Ægypten, Æthiopien, und der Halbinsel des Sinai;* Berlin, 1852; also, its excellent English translation, by Mr. KENNETH B. H. MACKENSIE: "Discoveries in Egypt," &c.; London, 1852; — *Einleitung zur Chronologie der Ægypter;* Berlin, 1848; vol. i.; — *Ueber der Ersten Ægytischen Götterkreis;* Berlin, 1851; — *Ueber den Apiskreis;* Leipzig, 1853; — *Ueber die Zwölfte Ægyptische Königsdynastie;* Berlin, 1853; — and, above all, the magnificent *Denkmäler aus Ægypten und Æthiopien;* Berlin, 1849; folio. Of this vast work, besides a series of the earlier ethnological plates kindly selected for him by Chev. LEPSIUS, and in his own possession, the writer has enjoyed the free use of two copies at Mobile, in the private libraries of Mr. A. STEIN and of the Rev. Dr. HAMILTON — to both of whom he here begs to reiterate his obligation — and of another in the Philadelphia Library. Altogether, he has seen the *plates* down to *Abth.* III., *Bl.* 172.

(402) I am speaking of public libraries. The private library of my honored friend, Mr. R. K. HAIGHT of New York, has been, from the commencement of my studies in 1842, the main source whence my individual facilities have been drawn.

(403) *Recherches en Égypte;* vii.; Thébes, 21 Jan. 1845; — *Revue des Deux Mondes;* 1842; p. 1085.

(404) *Salle des Ancêstres de Thoutmès III.;* Rev. Archéol.; 1845; pp. 1–23, tirage à part; — BIRCH: *Egyptian Inscription in the Bibliothèque Nationale;* Trans. R. Soc. Lit., new series, iv.; 1852.

deemed by Parisian science that, at national expense, he was appointed to continue the great folios of Champollion; (405) at the same time that his contributions to the *Revue Archéologique* are standard documents for posterity.

Last though not least, in Egypt itself resides a gentleman, affluent and influential, versed in many branches of ancient lore as thoroughly as 30 years of domicile have familiarized him with modern affairs, who never allows an opportunity of advancing archæological science to escape him; nor will any Egyptian student mistake our allusions to A. C. Harris. (406)

No clap-trap pretensions to acquaintance with hieroglyphical arcana recently made by theologers who speak not any continental tongue through which alone these subjects are accessible—no "ad captandum" figments of the possession of Oriental knowledge when men cannot spell a monosyllable written in the Hebrew alphabet — detract from the Memphite exhumations conducted at French ministerial expense by a Mariette; for whose enormous discoveries in the *Serapeum*, as yet confined to reports, we wait impatiently. 'T were well if, in view of the contemptuous silence with which Egyptologists treat their publications, some writers on these matters were to become *readers*.

Our part, however, is to indicate to the reader those sources upon which Egyptian chronology is dependent at the present day, in regard to the date of the first Pharaoh, Menes: a personage considered, in the subjoined works, to be historical; and neither connected with the mythical *Mestræans* invented by the Syncellus (407) in the seventh century after c.; nor, except nationally, with the MTsRIM (not *Mizraïm*) of the Hebrew Text, whom, in our examination of Xth Genesis, we have proved to be nothing more or less than the "Egyptians," inhabitants of MiZR, *Muss'r;* the Semitic name of "Merter," *Egypt* [*supra*, p. 494]: —

	Authorities.	*Dates of Menes.*
1839, Paris..........	LENORMANT: *Cercueil de Mycerinus*—	B. C.
	IVth Dyn. (p. 24) "Mycerinus, la date de 4136 avant J. C."	
	Add IIId " *Africanus* .... " 214 "	
	" IId " " .... " 302 "	
	" Ist " " .... " 263 "	
		4915
1840, Paris..........	CHAMPOLLION-FIGEAC: *L'Égypte Ancienne*..........	5867
1845, Berlin..........	BÖCKH: *Manetho und die Hundssternperiode*..........	5702
1845, Turin..........	BARUCCHI: *Discorsi Critici sopra la Cronologia Egizia*..........	4890
1845, Hamburg......	BUNSEN: *Ægyptens Stelle in der Weltgeschichte*..........	3643
1846, Paris..........	HENRY: *L'Égypte Pharaonique*..........	5303
1848, Paris..........	LESUEUR: *Chronologie des Rois d'Égypte*..........	5773
1849, Berlin..........	LEPSIUS: *Chronologie der Ægypter*..........	3893
1851, Dublin..........	HINCKS: *Turin Papyrus*..........	3895
1851, London..........	KENRICK: *Egypt under the Pharaohs*..........	3892
1854, Philadelphia..	PICKERING: *Geographical Distribution of Animals and Plants*..........	4400

The views of the authors of *Types of Mankind*, while with Humboldt, (408) for reasons to be given anon, they follow Lepsius, incline to the longer rather than to the shorter period. Ampère's opinion has been previously cited. The following is that of the first hierologist of France, Count Em. de Rougé, Conservator at the Louvre Museum: —

"Les efforts de M. de Bunsen seraient la meilleure preuve du contraire; après avoir, sans égard pour l'histoire et les monumens, supposé des *règnes constamment collatéraux*, trois dynasties à la fois et huit ou dix rois *simultanés* pendant la moitié des 12 premières dynasties, il n'en fixe pas moins le règne de *Ménès* à l'an 3643 av. J. C. L'obstiné fils de *Chanaan*, mutilé avec acharnement pendant 3 volumes, se relève enfin de ce lit de Procuste où l'avait étendu son critique impitoyable, et l'on s'apperçoit alors qu'il dépasse encore de plu-

(405) *Continuation des Monumens;* 100 plates; 1848; — *Papyrus Égyptien;* 1849.

(406) Mr. HARRIS's contributions, in the *Trans. of the R. Soc. of Literature*, the *Revue Archéologique*, and in the pages of several Egyptologists, are too numerous for specification here: but we may refer to his *papyrus*, "Fragments of an Oration against Demosthenes," London, 1848; also to the papyric fragments of "Books of Hom [illegible] *Athenæum*, 8 Sept. 1849), and of the "Grammarian Tryphon" (*Athenæum*, 7 Dec. 1850): while of the very important work — "Hieroglyphical Standards representing Places in Egypt supposed to be Nomes and Toparchies, collected by A. C. HARRIS," M. R. S. L., 1852 — his kindness allows us to acknowledge receipt.

(407) LETRONNE: in BIOT's *Année Vague des Égyptiens;* p. 25: — *supra*, p. 494.

(408) *Cosmos;* ii. pp. 114, 115, 124: — *supra*, p. 245.

sieurs siècles les mesures qu'on lui avait imposées au nom des calculs que la chronologie ordinaire avait fondés sur la *généalogie d'Abraham*." (409)

We moreover coincide entirely in the same author's doctrine, when, after indicating the various chances of miscalculation inherent in Egyptian no less than in all other *chronologies*, he declares: —

"These causes of error, which cross each other in every direction, make up a large part of uncertainty, for any chronological sum that it may be wished to draw from the sole addition of reigns, after a number of centuries at all considerable. The chances of inexactitude augment with the number of partial sums; and I have always thought that an uncertitude of more than 200 years was very admissible, in the ciphers that result from monumental dates combined with the lists of Manetho, when one remounts to the XVIIIth dynasty, after the expulsion of the shepherds." (410)

Nor need any doubt be entertained upon De Rougé's adoption of the most lengthy chronology, when he declares elsewhere — "Were we to accept the data most clearly preserved in Manetho, the XIIth dynasty must have preceded the Christian era by *thirty-four centuries*." (411)

We have already seen that, in England, the profoundest hieroglyphical scholar, Birch of the British Museum, tabulates Manethonian dynasties in their serial order, but without encumbering his monumental discoveries with any arithmetical *chronology*. Kenrick follows Lepsius. Hinck's former depression of the reign of Ramses II., in the XVIIIth dynasty, and of Thotmes III. to the year 1355 B. C., on the ground that Egyptian armies (born amidst solar calorics) avoided the heat of the weather, (412) was an argument too feeble to be seriously combated; but the matured judgment of this universal savant favors every scientifical extension demanded for Nilotic annals.

"A statement has been preserved, to which I am now inclined to attach more credit than I did formerly, that the Egyptians reckoned all the dynasties from Menes to Ochus as occupying 3555 years. If from this number we subtract 2291, which the Egyptians reckoned from Menes to the end of the XIIth dynasty, we have 1264 from the end of the XIIth dynasty to Ochus, or to 340 B. C. This would place the XIIth dynasty between the limits 1817 and 1604 B. C.; and I am disposed to accept these dates as the genuine Egyptian computation. Nor indeed do I see much reason to question their correctness."

Followers ourselves "of the German and French school," we pause not to debate the learned Irishman's deductions as to such an untenably modern date for the XIIth dynasty; but, adding his accepted 3555 years to the reign of Ochus, B. C. 340, we are gratified in finding that Dr. Hincks, (413) with several Germans and Frenchmen, places Menes at 3895 *years before* C.; and henceforward, therefore, can enrol, as we have already, his great name among the long chronologists.

On the opposite side, as representative of the shortest Egyptian computation, stands a gentleman, whose vast classical erudition, and keener criticism, we are always proud to acknowledge; and it is with pain that, having so often availed ourselves of his instructive pages, especially in regard to biblical history and exegesis, that, in Egyptian *chronology*, we must protest against the contracted system of a great Hellenist, Mr. Samuel Sharpe. With respectful deference we would, however, submit objections to his assumed dates for Osirtesen, whom he arbitrarily changes into an "*Amunmai Thor* I.;" (414) still more emphatically to his views upon Menes. Scientific criticism, to be practically useful, must be free; and pupils, often, of Mr. Sharpe in its application to the Greek *New Testament*, and to the theosophical notions of the Alexandria School, we feel persuaded that no writer of the day loves truth more than himself. We may therefore utter our mode of viewing it.

---

(409) *Examen de l'Ouvrage de M. Bunsen*; p. 82, Annales de Philosophie Chrétiennes, 1847.

(410) DE ROUGÉ: *Mémoire sur quelques Phenomènes Célestes*; Rev. Archéol., 183; p. 654; — Comp. *Otia*, p. 41.

(411) *Sur le Sesostris de la Douzième Dynastie*; Rev. Archéol., 1847; p. 482.

(412) Rev. Dr. HINCKS: *On the Age of the XVIIIth Dynasty*; Trans. R. Irish Acad., 1846; xxi. pp. [illegible]-9.

(413) *Observations of Dr. E. Hincks*, in WILKINSON'S "Hieratic Papyrus of Kings at Turin," 1851; pp. 57, 58.

(414) *History of Egypt*; new edition; London, 1846; pp. 7, 9, 10; — *Chronology and Geography of Ancient Egypt*; 1849; pp. 4, 14, pl. 2, figs. 25, 32.

The *contemporaneousness* of Egyptian dynasties (415) we have always repudiated; (416) but, until the appearance of Lepsius's "Book of Kings," when our assent may possibly be yielded (if *monuments* to us now unknown establish it), in respect to the Ist and IId, VIth and VIIth (VIIIth), Xth and XIth, XIIIth and XIVth, and XVth and XVIth, Manethonian dynasties, we should commit the same fallacy, so frequently blamed in others, if we spoke dogmatically on that point without the new documents of the Prussian Mission. There is no more foundation, however, for Mr. Sharpe's dynastic arrangement than were we to make *Canute's* invasion of England coeval with WILLIAM *the Conqueror* in the reign of JAMES I., under the synthronic sway of GEORGE III and the Prince Regent. It is a favorite hypothesis of his own; in which not an Egyptologist coincides. But for the exposure of a radical error in Mr. Sharpe's system—root of all his deviations from hierological practice—our knife must be applied to one of its many vital spots. In his immensely-valuable folio *plates*, (417) through inadvertency, he had read

 *nfr*, (418) the "lute," *théorbe*, in lieu of  *tt*, (419) the "blade of an oar,"

as the sculpture stands. Through misapprehension of the groups (in *line* 9 compared with *line* 2, of the same inscription), Mr. Sharpe then deemed that this malcopied sign "*nfr*" was the homophone of  *b*, (420) the "human leg;"

and, in consequence, he always reads "*nfr*" as if it were the latter articulation—"That the arrow-shaped character is rightly sounded B or V is proved by its admitting that sound in the above four names, as also in No. 160 and No. 165." (421) The extraordinary metamorphoses of well-known royal names which this misconception, founded upon a *mistake*, has occasioned, are too evident to the hierologist to require comment. Unfortunately, through such concatenation of fallacies, Mr. Sharpe (422) transmutes the *prenomen* of Queen AMENSeT, (423) and the *nomen* of this queen's husband AMENEMHA, (424) and the oval of MENKERA, (425) into a fabulously bisexual "Mychera-Amun Neitchori"—rolls up the IVth, VIth, and XVIIIth dynasties into one—and thus makes the 3d pyramid of Geezeh (B. C. 3300) *contemporary* with the majestic obelisk (B. C. 1600) in the temple of Karnac! It is as if one were to call EDWARD *the Confessor* the same *personage* as "VICTORIA and ALBERT;" and then to insist that the former's *tomb* in Westminster Abbey must be *coeval* with the equestrian statue of WELLINGTON at Hyde Park corner! (426)

Mr. Sharpe's restricted system of Egyptian chronology, for times anterior to THOTHMOSIS III. (placed by him in the 14th century B. C.), may now be considered as "non-avenu." But, while compelled to shatter its superstructures down to his XVIIIth dynasty, let no one impute to us lack of respect for the profound author of the "History of Egypt"—a work that (from *page* 30 to 592) ever has our warmest admiration. Contenders for the longest

(415) SHARPE: *Chronology;* pp. 14, 15.
(416) GLIDDON: *Chapters;* p. 57;—*Otia;* pp. 39, 45.
(417) SHARPE: *Inscriptions in British Museum;* pl. cxvi., line 9, and line 2.
(418) BUNSEN: *Eg. Pl.*, i. p. 587, No. 31;—CHAMPOLLION: *Dictionnaire;* p. 293, No. 338—"NOFRE."
(419) BUNSEN: No. 30;—CHAMPOLLION: p. 378, No. 459—"TOUW."
(420) BUNSEN: p. 558, B, 1;—CHAMPOLLION: p. 100, No. 60—"B."
(421) *Chronology;* p. 4.
(422) *Op. cit.;* p. 6, Nos. 60, 61, 60; and plate ii., figs. 60, 61, 62.
(423) ROSELLINI: *Cartouche* No. 103.
(424) *Ibid.; Cartouche* No. 103 *f.*
(425) BUNSEN: *Ægyptens Stelle;* iii., pl. i.—*Men-ke-u-ra.*
(426) It is a year ago since this was written, and so reluctant do I feel to contradict a respected fellow-labore[illegible] I should have suppressed these comments but for a "rifacimento" of the same doctrines reported in the London *Athenæum*, Nov. 19, 1853. "The third aim of the paper was to show that the 3d and 4th pyramids were both made by Queen Nitocris, who governed Egypt during the minority of Thotmosis the IIId. The name of King Mycera has been found in both of these pyramids; Mycera is the first name of Queen Nitocris [!], and it was probably the name used in Memphis for Thothmosis the IIId." &c.—(*Syro-Egyptian Soc.*, Nov. 8.)

human chronology ourselves, it is imperative upon us to carry the outworks of truly-erudite short-chronologists before storming their last English citadel: a facile exploit now to be performed.

> "The thistle that *was* in Lebanon
> Sent to the cedar that *was* in Lebanon
> Saying, 'Give thy daughter to my son to wife':
> And there passed by a wild beast that *was* in Lebanon,
> And trode down the thistle." (2 *Kings* xiv. 9.)

On the part of one of the authors of "Types of Mankind," old Nilotic associations—on that of the other, convictions of the scientific worthlessness of HORÆ ÆGYPTIACÆ,(427) have, for two years, restrained both of them from printed notice of this production: and, if now they conjoin to chant its requiem, the necessity is superinduced, on one hand, by a desire to vindicate Egyptology; on another, the deed has been fastened upon the writer individually by the incessant officiousness of theologers in the United States, in local obtrusions uncalled-for, and in appeals continual to the illusory authority of an adolescent scholar.

It has been already shown [*supra*, p, 670] how Mr. Wilkinson, in 1835, had obliterated, with a dash of his pen, all the "unplaced kings" he had previously published; (428) and had cut down the *era of* MENES to the year B. C. 2201, "for fear of *interfering* with the deluge." During twelve years, Sir Gardner Wilkinson compassionately refrained from diluvial interference; but, from 1837 (429) to 1847, (430) he made a retrocession of MENES, on a sliding scale, to the year B. C. 2320; thereby placing this unfortunate king amid the paludic miasmata (he was killed by a *hippopotamus*) consequent upon that grand catastrophe—only *twenty-eight years* after Archbishop Usher's cataclysm, with which the gallant Knight scrupled to interfere.

The consequence was, that, for twelve years, no hierologist thought it incumbent upon him to quote Wilkinson in matters of chronology; even if scientific justice toward the latter's innumerable Egyptian discoveries occasionally induced Egyptologists to cite a most erudite author notoriously chary of mentioning the labors of continental contemporaries. (431)

Solitude, however, in time becomes tiresome even to an anchorite. Between the years 1835 and 1847, the bound made by Egyptian studies was enormous. Lepsius, followed by the whole school of *Champollionists*, had discovered the XIIth *dynasty of Manetho;* (432) and the XVI—XVIIth dynastic arrangement of Rosellini, abandoned by every other scholar, survived, in 1847, through Wilkinson's *Hand-book* alone. It became desirable, therefore, to "wear ship" in the smoke of Cairo, and to reappear to windward on the other tack; just as if the gallant Knight had been sailing in line with *Manetho's* XIIth dynasty all the time! A "cat's paw" of breeze, nevertheless, was requisite for these nautical evolutions, and *Horæ Ægyptiacæ* kindly wafted it over seas to the London "Literary Gazette."

"And I think this conjecture," wrote the author of *Horæ*, (433) "strengthened by the fact, that Sir G. Wilkinson has found with the name of Phiops (Pepi) a king's name, which I believe he agrees with me in considering as that of Othoes, the first king of the VIth dynasty."—"And this explanation is most strikingly confirmed by a fact [known 14 years previously (434) to every reader of Rosellini!], of which some very remarkable instances are found in some of the unpublished papers of Sir Gardner Wilkinson, which he has kindly shown me, as well as in some of his published works; that in numerous sculptures

(427) *Horæ Ægyptiacæ*—"or the Chronology of Ancient Egypt *discovered* from Astronomical and Hieroglyphical records upon its Monuments; including many dates found in coeval inscriptions from the period of the building of the Great Pyramid to the times of the Persians: and Illustrations of the History of the first nineteen Dynasties, showing the order of their succession, from the Monuments." London, Murray, 8vo, 1851.

(428) *Materia Hieroglyphica;* Cairo, 1827–'32; *Supplement*, and *Text*, Malta.

(429) *Manners and Customs;* 1837; i. p. 41.

(430) *Hand-book for Travellers in Egypt;* 1847; p. 17.

(431) GLIDDON: *Chapters;* p. 11, *a*.

(432) BUNSEN: *Ægyptens Stelle;* 1845; i., Vorrede, pp. 18, 19; ii. pp. 271–362; iii. pl. 3.

(433) *Literary Gazette;* 1849; p. 486; "Cairo, May, 1849."

(434) Compare also LEPSIUS—"Culte fréquent en Nubie de Sesertusen III.". *Lettre*, 20 *Juin*, 1845; in Rev. Archéol., June, 1844, p. 208.

in Nubia, we find kings of the XVIIIth dynasty worshipping Sesertesen [Wilkinson always wrote "Osirtasen"] III. as a god." (435) — "I was unable to find it [*Hor-em-bai!*] during my last visit to Thebes, owing to its but once occurring, and to the great extent of the tomb; and I have to thank Sir Gardner Wilkinson in giving me a copy of it." (436) — "I must express my obligations to Sir Gardner Wilkinson, for his having greatly promoted these investigations, during his last visit to Egypt, *in discussing with me every point of importance* in the first four numbers (all I had then written), as well as for the kindness and liberality which he showed me in allowing me to examine and copy many of his unpublished transcripts from Egyptian monuments." (437)

These meritorious acknowledgments were due to the paternal solicitude with which the gallant Knight had watched at Cairo over *Horæ*. Nevertheless, expostulations were addressed from London to its author about the suppression of the names of so many other fellow-laborers; as well through private channels, as also hinted, in public session, before the "Syro-Egyptian Society." (438)

Years passed away. The 12 articles entitled *Horæ Ægyptiacæ*, originally published in the "Literary Gazette," having received unparalleled aid from the highest quarters, reappear, considerably altered, in a beautiful octavo.

We read first Sir J. Gardner Wilkinson's endorsement of *Horæ*: (439) —

"It is indeed the less necessary to enter into a detailed examination of the chronology, and the succession of the Pharaohs, as Mr. Stuart Poole's work on the subject will soon be published; and I have much pleasure in stating *how fully I agree with him* in the contemporaneousness of certain kings, and in the order of succession he gives to the early Pharaohs."

Secondly, we admire *Horæ's* re-endorsement of Sir Gardner Wilkinson: (440) —

"*I* have avoided, as much as possible, quoting or examining the works of others, *excepting* Sir Gardner Wilkinson. My object has been to explain what *I* learned from the monuments; not to combat the assertions of others. Sir Gardner Wilkinson stands in a position *different* from that of any others who have written on the subject; he has never written to support a chronological hypothesis ['in order not to interfere with the Deluge,' *supra*], and is entitled to the utmost confidence on account of his well-known accuracy, the many years which he has spent in the study of the monuments in Egypt, and the caution which he has shown in refraining from putting forth any complete system of Egyptian chronology: *I* am aware how greatly *I* disagree with all others who have written on this subject; but it is a sufficient consolation to me, since all differ, that it is little more to differ from *all others* than to differ from all of them but *one*." (441)

Thirdly, Sir Gardner Wilkinson again endorses *Horæ*: (442) —

"And the contemporaneousness of others [kings—*entirely arbitrary!*] have been very ingeniously and satisfactorily explained by Mr. Stuart Poole, in his *Horæ Egyptiacæ;* where he acknowledges that it was first suggested to him by Mr. Lane. That arrangement may be seen in the following table, which *he has obligingly communicated*, and which I have the more pleasure in inserting, as *I agree with him* in the contemporaneousness of the kings, and in the general mode of arranging those of the same line."

Fourthly, THE FRIEND OF MOSES endorses both: —

"So complete and satisfactory is the train of evidence adduced by Mr. Poole, that Sir J. G. Wilkinson, one of the most learned of living men, in all that relates to Egyptian archæology, has openly published in his last great work on the Architecture of Egypt, his entire concurrence in the views of Mr. Poole, and his conviction of the complete and satisfactory character of the evidence that gentleman has adduced from the monuments." (443)

Ever and anon, after reiterating this endorsement, the same FRIEND OF MOSES adds in Italics: —

"*Egypt, with all her splendid Monuments, is found a witness* [as much as and not less than Spitsbergen] *to the truth of the Bible, and to the correctness* ["credat Judæus Apella!"] *of the Mosaic chronology*. . . . These concessions of the Chevalier Bunsen prepare us to receive with greater confidence the statements of Mr. R. S. Poole, in his *Horæ Ægyptiacæ*, claiming to adduce proofs from the monuments themselves, that several of the dynasties which

(435) *Ibid.*; p. 552; "Cairo, June, 1849."
(436) *Ibid.*: p. 522.
(437) *Ibid.*; p. 910.
(438) London, 10th April, 1849; *Literary Gazette*, 28th April, 1849.
(439) *Horæ Ægyptiacæ*; Preface, p. 23 — citation from WILKINSON: *Architecture of Ancient Egypt*.
(440) *Horæ*; p. 23.
(441) *Horæ*; p. 23.
(442) *Hieratic Papyrus of Turin*; 1851; p. 29.
(443) "Mobile, Jan. 27, 1852" — *Southern Presbyterian*; Milledgeville, Ga., Feb. 19, 1852.

have been generally represented as successive were actually contemporaneous, as *e.g.* the twelfth and the fifth [!]; and that thus, the monumental history of Egypt covers not a period of duration beyond what may be readily reconciled with [poor Moses !] the Mosaic chronology as given in the Septuagint. A conclusion, to the accuracy of which, Sir J. G. Wilkinson has affixed the sanction of his great name in these matters." (444)

The Friend of Moses soon after becomes mystified: —

"I became acquainted with several gentlemen of distinction in the learned world. . . . Mr. R. S. Poole, a *bold* writer on Egyptian chronology." (445)

He next assures us: —

"I have carefully compared the copies taken by Champollion in *all these tombs and temples*, from the second Cataract to Thebes, and I have collated his hieroglyphics, *line by line* [this is the more miraculous, as it was performed between *Alexandria*, Nov. 12, and *Cairo*, Feb. 14—after going up the Nile, 1200 miles, to *Samneh;* and returning, 1050 miles, to Cairo !], and *character by character*, with the originals. . . . There is a magnificent error somewhere—though *I* am not prepared [!] to point out where; nor how precisely it may be detected and exposed. Of one thing *I* am satisfied — that Sir J. G. Wilkinson, and *my kind young friend*, Mr. R. S. Poole, of the British Museum, are much nearer the truth, in their chronology, than is Dr. Lepsius, or the Chevalier Bunsen." (446)

The scientific reader now comprehends our local situation, and will compassionately forgive the inhumanities which such every-day offences compel us finally to perform. "Le jeu ne vaut pas la chandelle;" else we would at once refute *Horæ Egyptiacæ*, page by page, and hieroglyphic by hieroglyphic; in the interpretation of which last the juvenile author (or Sir G. Wilkinson) has committed blunders as egregious as they are multiform — altogether unpardonable in the actual state of hierology. For the present, our criticisms shall be chiefly confined to the publication of "three fragments," upon the principles of a world-renowned master, Letronne. (447) They are from the highest Egyptologists in Europe; two of them in epistles to the authors; one already in print.

First Extract. (448)

"I have nothing to say about the book of Poole, if not that I regard it as a juvenile and sufficiently-pretentious essay, written without conscientiousness, and dangerous rather to the theologians than to science."

Second Extract. (449)

"Not one of its followers can read three lines of hieroglyphics correctly. The G. P. Y. (450) and G. P. M. (451) are only in the mind of the author. Examined by the microscope of philology, all vanishes into a few unimportant observations — for example;

, , is not "the first month"—"the first half month," of the *Great Panegyrical Year;* but merely

 = "monthly,"  = "half-monthly."

The consequence is that this expression does not fix the age of Chufu [builder of the great pyramid]. The "7th ," (452) on the base of the Karnac obelisk, refers to the seven *smat*, or *periods-months*, I believe that the obelisk was in the quarry. Hence the whole cyclical part is a delusion; and all the inferences are *nil*. The rest of the book is a string of hypotheses — where there are not actual misapprehensions."

Third Extract. (453)

"Mr. Poole is of the number of those young workmen who deserve that one should tell them the whole truth. Either he has not read what recent archæologists have written

(444) *The Friend of Moses;* New York, 1852; pp. 376, 377, 514.

(445) *Mobile Daily Advertiser*, Oct. 9, 1852 — "Correspondence — Paris, Sept. 14, 1852."

(446) *Mobile Daily Register*, April 1, 1853 — "Letter from Egypt — Cairo, Feb. 14, 1853."

(447) *Trois Fragments* — Mémoires et Documents publiés dans la Revue Archéol.; Paris, 1849; pp. 100–119.

(448) *Letter to Mr. Gliddon.*

(449) *Letter to Dr. Nott.*

(450) *Horæ;* p. 59 — "Great Panegyrical Year."

(451) *Do.;* p. 56 — "Great Panegyrical Month."

(452) *Do.;* p. 66.

(453) De Rougé: *Phénomènes Célestes;* Rev. Archéol., 15 Feb. 1853; pp. 664, 665; and *note*.

upon this subject, which would be inexcusable; or he has read them and does not cite them, which would be still more grave. I have not read the name of Lepsius a single time in his book, in respect to all these questions so lengthily treated in the *Introduction to Chronology* [Berlin, 1848–9]. . . . Not content with this discovery [viz., the imaginary Panegyrical Months] M. Poole thinks also to find other new cycles, with the dates which refer to them. I confess that it has been impossible for me to comprehend how, in the presence of pretensions so important, Mr. Poole has not deemed himself obliged to prove the truth of his allegations, by minutely analyzing the inscriptions which he alleges. Far from that, he contents himself with indicating them, and sometimes even without producing their text in his plates. One cannot lean upon an Egyptian inscription, as upon a passage of Titus Livius, without new explanation, and I will frankly say that I believe in none of the cycles and in none of the dates of Mr. Poole. . . . It is evident that in thus handling the ciphers, without controlling their signification and the manner in which they are introduced into the inscriptions, one may end in imagining all the periods that one wishes, and in giving them a certain appearance of truth to the eyes of persons who can discuss but the results. A work thus based must pass for *non-avenu*."

But, after all, *Horæ* has no "fear of interfering with the Deluge;" so the work becomes only another thorn in the side of orthodoxy. Mr. Wilkinson (1835, *supra*), devoutly following archbishop Usher and the margin of king *James's version*, says the date of the Flood "*is* 2348 B. C." In its author's first articles, *Horæ* had declared—

"The date of the accession of Menes, the first king of Egypt, is probably that of the commencement of the first great panegyrical year and first capital year. Eratosthenes and Josephus [say, modern *computators* on these ancient writers] place his accession somewhat later—namely, about 2300 years B. C., instead of 2715. The history of the 1st, 2d, 3d, 4th, and 5th dynasties [of the IV–Vth dynasties, Lepsius found the amplest details, while the author of *Horæ* dwelt only 15 miles off, at Cairo!] is but scantily furnished us by Manetho and the monuments, and the latter give us but one date [and that fabulous!], that of the commencement of what *I* have called the second great panegyrical year in the time of Suphis I., the builder of the great pyramid, and second king of Manetho's fourth dynasty, B. C. 2350." (454)

Horæ thus fixed the building of the great pyramid *two* years before Wilkinson's Deluge; and set Menes on the throne, in Egypt, 367 years before the same authority's catastrophe. But, it was promptly shown, that *Horæ*, in selecting the year B. C. 2715 for Menes, had merely stolen another man's thunder (455): wherefore, when its author came to reprint those twelve articles in an octavo volume, he so translated his hieroglyphics, astronomically, as to obtain *two* years' difference!—"The commencement of the great panegyrical year which preceded that of the Suphises, *I* have already shown to be in the year B. C. 2717" (456); and then he informs us that "the Septuagint chronology dates the *Dispersion* of Mankind about the year B. C. 2758; that is, about 41 years before the era of Menes"!

Computations upon the different copies of the LXX, every one of them as rotten as the MSS. themselves, cause the *Creation* to fluctuate between B. C. 5904, and B. C. 5054. (457) And the above sentence merely shows its penman's incompetency to discuss *Septuagint* questions. To the reader of our disquisition on Xth *Genesis* [PeLeG, *supra*, p. 545], the following specimens of *Horæ's* biblical knowledge will be amusing; as much as, to use its author's favorite adjective, the latter's credulity is "remarkable":—

"*I* therefore believe that the Vague year was instituted in the time of Noah; probably by Ham [!], not by Noah. . . . *I* have only to notice one other important epoch of Bible history—the dispersion of nations. The division [read "split"] of the earth is indicated as having occurred at the birth of Peleg [a "split"]; when we are told, (Gen. x, 25), 'unto Eber were born two sons; the name of the one (was) Peleg (or division); for in his days was the earth divided.' [*Vide supra*, what the *Hebrew* writer meant!] Now, it was a common custom of Hebrews to name their children from circumstances which occurred at their birth; and the custom of ancient Arabs was precisely the same, and has continued to the present day. We cannot reckon as exceptions to this the few cases where *God changed a name*, or imposed a new one; and in the latter case the old name was retained with the new one [!]. The *birth* of Peleg, according to Dr. Hales, happened B. C. 2754;

(454) *Art.* XII.; *Literary Gazette*, Dec. 15, 1849; p. 910;—compare *Art.* VII., p. 522.
(455) "By my reduction of 'Manetho'—2715" B. C.; Gliddon, *Chap.*, 1843, p. 51:—and *Hand-book*, 1849, p. 47.
(456) *Op. cit.*: p. 63, and p. 97.
(457) Riccioli: *Chronol. reformata*; p. 293.

but, calculated from *my* hate of the Exodus, B. C. 2758."(458) — "*I* say that the Pharaoh of the Exodus reigned undoubtedly not more than about one year; for, although *his being drowned in the Red Sea* is not expressly mentioned by MOSES, it is so mentioned in the 136th Psalm [what a clinching argument!], and *I* hold all the books of the Bible to be equally true."(459).

It is to be deplored that, after being promoted for his Hebraism to a post in the British Museum, "my kind young friend," as *the Friend of Moses* affectionately terms him, should have expunged these delightful samples of pious feeling from the republication of *Horæ* in its octavo form. So imbued, we fear, is he likely to become in that enlightened institution with self-immolating principles, that it would not surprise us to learn through newspapers that *Horæ* likewise—as SCALIGER says, "ut signatius loquar"—for the sake of Oriental literature were to turn *Mohammedan*.

No inclination remains to follow *Horæ's* farthing-rush-light any further. We leave the pupil for the teacher, when we here exhibit on the margin a table printed by WILKINSON in the pamphlet-text accompanying the latter's truly-valuable contribution to archæological science — *The fragments of the Hieratic Papyrus at Turin: containing the names of Egyptian Kings, with the Hieratic inscription at the back.*

Here is that "magnificent error" which the FRIEND OF MOSES could not discover by going to Egypt: —

"Respecting the construction of the table, he observes: 'The relative positions and the lengths of most of these dynasties are founded *upon some kind* of monumental authority. The rest *I* have placed within approximative extremes. There are several points of *exact* [!] contemporaneousness, as in the 2nd and 4th and 5th dynasties, again in the 5th and 15th, and in the 9th and 11th; and these, with other evidence *of the same nature*, enable us to adjust the general scheme of all the dynasties.'" (460)

Reader! Suppose a Chinese archæologist, with a little red button on his cap, were to come all the way from Pe-kin to America, and tell us that good old king EGBERT was a

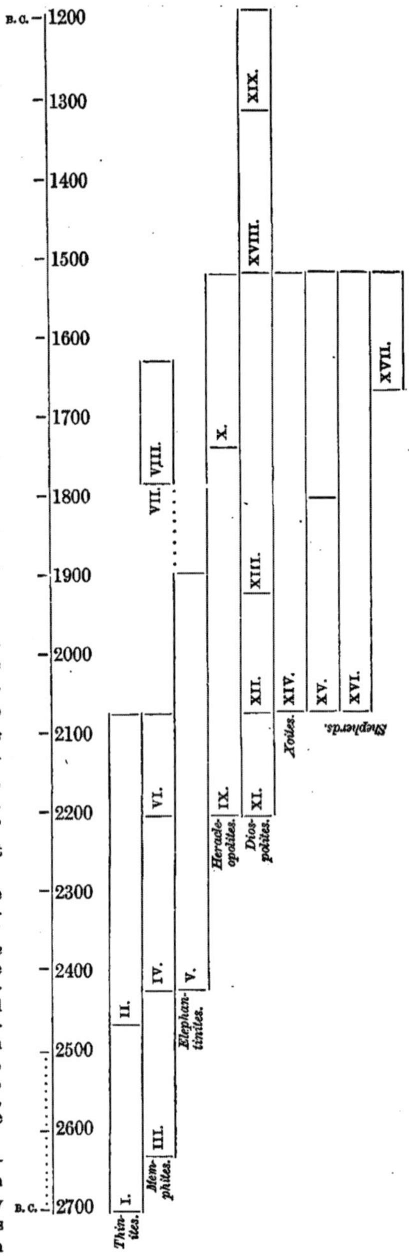

(458) *Art.* X.; *Lit. Gaz.*; p. 641. (459) *Art.* V.; *Lit. Gaz.*; p. 432. (460) *Hier. Papyr.*; pp. 30, 31, and *table*, p. 31.

mythe—that the consecutive dynasties of our common English father-land could fit no Hottentot's estimate of the chronology of John-Chinaman's sacred book, the *Chou-king;* unless, after rejecting Boudicea and Caractacus, we were to permit his reduction of *Danes, Saxons, Normans, Plantagenets, Lancastrians, Yorkites, Tudors, Stuarts, Orangites, Hanoverians,* &c.; together with all British, Scottish, and Irish, periods of anarchy; not forgetting Cromwell and the Commonwealth; into one century. Suppose that, after proving why every Anglo-Saxon had erroneously classified, as distinct, those personages, epochas, and historical events, which the "Tribunals of Literature" of China had pronounced to be identical, the said mandarin were to show us how beautifully the whole could be reduced, through electro-magnetic typography, into one line of a *table,* and expressed algebraically by an x, representing an infinitesimal fraction of a second of Creative time. What should we say to His Excellency "Uncle *Josh*"?

Now, whatever the American reader might be pleased to hint to such Chinese mandarin, would be uttered in demotic tongue with "brutale franchise" by old MANETHO (could his mummy arise) to Sir Gardner Wilkinson, at the first glance over the above table: where, in wilful disregard of Lenormant, Champollion, Böckh, Barucchi, Bunsen, Henry, Lesueur, Lepsius, Hincks, Kenrick, Pickering, Ampère, De Rougé, Birch, and of every hierologist past, present, and to come, the gallant Knight has made the IIId, IVth, VIth (VII), VIIIth Egyptian dynasties (consecutive in Manetho and, where mentioned, serial upon all monuments), *contemporaneous!*—has actually jammed *eleven* dynasties, VI, VII, VIII, IX, X, XI, XII, XIII, XIV, XV, XVI, into a space (2200 *a* 1700) of 500 years! And perpetrated, too, all these inexplicable vagaries with theological applause, when, by placing MENES (1st dynasty, *Thinites*) at 2700 B. C., he shows that valiant knighthood, in A. D. 1851, no longer creeps all over "for fear of *interfering* with the Deluge of Noah; which (*was*) 2348 B. C." before an aspirant to ecclesiastical patronage had won his gilded spurs.

We dismiss, therefore, *Horæ Ægyptiacæ* as beneath scientific notice, reserving to ourselves the privilege of a reviewer's criticism, whenever circumstances may demand its annihilation. With it we snap off the last published peg upon which short-chronology can suspend its clerical hat; because Mr. Sharpe's arrangement of Egyptian dynasties anterior to the XVIIIth has been respectfully disposed of. When other writers, with hieroglyphical handles to their patronymes, adventure into the rude arena of archæology as champions of *short*-chronography, may their armor be well tempered and their lances tough!

The list of *long*-chronologists, above given, comprehends the "preux chevaliers" of archæological science at this day. The *minimum* of their respective dates for MENES is B. C. 3643; the *maximum* approaches the 6th chiliad B. C. By each authority all biblical computations, *Hebrew, Samaritan,* and *Septuagint,* are thrown aside among the rubbish of the things that were.

"The sum of all the dynasties varies according to our present sources from 4685 to 5049 years; the number of kings from 300 to 350, and even 500. It is evidently impossible to found a chronology on such a basis, but Syncellus tells us that the number of generations included in the 30 dynasties was, according to Manetho, 113; and the whole number of years, 3555. This number falls much short of what the summation of the reigns would furnish according to any reading of the numbers, but is nearly the same as 113 generations would produce, at any average of 32 years each." (461)

Fifteen years ago, the learned ethnographer, De Brotonne, reasoning upon this very number, "3555 de Manethon," obtained B. C. 3901 as "le chiffre le moins élevé" for MENES. (462)

To neither of the present writers have these results been unknown:—

"On my return to Cairo [April, 1840, from a voyage with Mr. Harris to the second cataract], I devoted a twelvemonth's leisure to the verification of the solidity of the basis upon which hieroglyphical revelations had placed Egyptian *monumental chronology.* The result was a conviction as profound then, as subsequent researches,—echoed by the voice of universal erudition, and embodied in the works of a host of savans whose names gild the

(461) KENRICK: *Ancient Egypt under the Pharaohs:* 1850; ii. p. 93.
(462) *Filiations et Migrations:* i. p. 203.

brightest page illuminated by science in the XIXth century,—have since demonstrated its accuracy, of the utter impossibility of reconciling *Egyptian facts*, geological, topographical, ethnological, hieroglyphical, and historical, with Archbishop Usher's system of patriarchal *chronology*.

"A *manuscript* compilation, over which an old and valued colleague, M. Prisse, and myself wiled away at Cairo many delightful weeks in reciprocal exchanges of our several gleanings, under the title of "Analecta Hieroglyphica," condensed every *cartouche*, with references to most of the historical monuments, known to hierologists up to April, 1841; and, as many personal friends are aware, this manuscript is still a most important *ground-text* and manual to those who, like myself, are anxious to ascertain the stability of prior investigations, before hazarding the erection of a theoretical superstructure." (463)

What, then, is the present state of scientific opinion on the era of MENES? The reader has it before him in the list on p. 682; and, without perplexing himself with vain speculations founded upon ignorance of the stupendous materials transferred from Egypt to Berlin by the Prussian Mission, let him do as we do, await patiently for the publication, hourly due, of Lepsius's "Book of Kings." The authors may be pardoned when stating that, in books, manuscript-notes, and epistolary communications from Egypt, Italy, France, Germany, and England, they probably possess as much specific and detailed information here at Mobile, on Egyptian monumental chronology, as most men in the world, less a dozen European hierologists — with whom they are in agreeable accord. When, therefore, they put forward no dogmatical system of their own, but wait for the "Book of Kings," they act themselves in accordance with the counsel offered to fellow-inquirers. Should Lepsius's work reach their hands before the issue of the present volume, a synopsis of its *chronology* will be appended to our essay. We may also look forward to Biot, the scholarlike astronomer of France, for a profound investigation of the *astronomical* data, revealed by Egyptian monuments, in their relations to mundane chronology; (464) which will supersede any future recurrence to the cyclic reveries of such youthful star-gazers as *Horæ*.

Should, however, a qualified student desire to prepare himself for thorough mastery of Lepsius's "Book of Kings," he should commence with Rosellini's *Monumenti Storici;* and, that being fundamentally acquired, his next guide is Bunsen, *Ægyptens Stelle in der Weltgeschichte;* wherein most of the royal Egyptian names, discovered up to 1845, are compared with the classical lists, and in which the grand alteration produced by Lepsius's resuscitation of the XIIth dynasty (unknown to the lamented Pisan Professor, or, in 1847, to Wilkinson), is abundantly set forth. "There is no royal road to the mathematics," nor is there a straighter path to the comprehension of Egyptian *chronology* than the one we indicate; but, after these two works, the study of Lepsius, *Chronologie der Ægypter*, "Einleitung, 1849," becomes imperative.

Such reader will appreciate the general correctness of the following method of verifying, archæologically, the progressive layers in which Egyptian history stretches backwards from the Christian era, assumed at 1853 years ago; until the unknown-commencements of Nilotic humanity merge into an undated, but ante-alluvial, period of geology. (465)

We gladly borrow the first points of departure, in our journey from the Christian era backwards, from Sharpe (466): —

"The reigns of Ptolemy, of Darius, of Cambyses, and of Tirhakah are fixed by the Babylonian eclipses. Hophra and Shishank are fixed because they are mentioned in the Old Testament, since the length of the Jewish reigns, after Solomon, is well known, while those Jewish dates are themselves fixed by the earliest of the Babylonian eclipses in the reign of Tirhakah. Thus are fixed [by Mr. Sharpe] in the Table of Chronology the dynasties of Sais, Ethiopia, and Babastis. Petubastes lived in the first Olympiad; this fixes the dynasties of Tanis."

Thus, king by king, and event by event, we ascend with precision back to Alexander the Great, B. C. 332; and thence, through the XXXIst, XXXth, XXIXth, XXVIIIth, XXVIIth,

(463) GLIDDON: *Hand-book;* London, Madden, 1849; p. 40;—conf. NOTT: *Biblical and Physical History of Man:* 1849; pp. 69–86; — also *Chronology, Ancient and Scriptural:* South. Quart. Rev., Nov. 1850.

(464) DE ROUGÉ: *Rev. Archéol.*, Feb. 1853; pp. 656, 666.

(465) GLIDDON: *Otia;* pp. 61–69.

(466) *Chronology and Geography;* 1849; p. 13, and table, pp. 14, 15.

XXVIth, XXVth, XXIVth, XXIIId Egyptian consecutive dynasties, back to S*h*eS*h*oNK, Shishak, founder of the XXIId dynasty; who, conquering Jerusalem "in the Vth year of king Rehoboam," (467) as is hieroglyphically recorded in Karnac, (468) enables us to establish a perfect synchronism, between Egyptian and Judaic history at B. C. 971–3.

Prior to this date, Egyptian monuments never once refer to the *Hebrews*, throw not a glimmer of light upon *Jewish* annals; and with Sheshonk also ceases the possibility of fixing any Pharaoh, to him anterior, within 5 or 10 years. *Chronology*, year by year, stops in fact at B. C. 972; as well in Israelitish as in Nilotic chronicles: although the foundation of Solomon's *temple* cannot be far removed from B. C. 1000.

Leaving Hebrew computation to ascend along its own stream, innumerable Egyptian documents — *tablets, papyri, genealogical lists*, public and private, together with an astounding mass of collateral and circumstantial evidence, — carry us upward, through the XXIst, XXth, XIXth, and XVIIIth dynasties, reign by reign, and monument by monument, to RAMSES I. (Ramesu); whose epoch belongs to the ———— *century* 15th–16th B. C.

Here intervenes a period, though for a few years only, of anarchy; represented in the *Disk heresy*, and by sundry royal claimants; at the head of whom stands ATENRA-BAKHAN, or *Beχ-en-aten*; (469) called by Lepsius "Amenophis IV." But upward from his *father's* reign, Amenoph III, every king is known, with many events of their respective reigns, through hieroglyphical sculptures and papyri, back to the beginning of the XVIIth Theban dynasty, in the reign of AAHMES, *Amosis*, I; computed, by Lepsius, to be about the year 1671 B. C. At this point, which begins the "Restoration," or "New Empire," after the expulsion of the *Hyksos*, we lose the thread of *annual* chronology, for times anterior to the 17th century, before C.

We refrain from discussion of the *Hyksos*, or shepherd kings. (470) They are supposed to occupy the XVIth and XVth dynasties; and, according to Manetho, their duration covered 511 years of time. The XIVth dynasty has not been disentangled clearly from the mutilated lists; and the hieroglyphical records have not yet spoken intelligibly, although they are numerous. We pause for Lepsius; and in the meanwhile refer the reader for a summary of the monumental edifices of the Old and the New Empires to his published travels. (471) To us at present this "middle Empire" is chaos; but, even supposing the XIVth, XVth, and XVIth dynasties could, by a *short*-chronologist, be expunged from Egyptian records, it must be remembered, by *long*-chronologists, that the XVIIth dynasty stands erect in the 17th century B. C. We leave the "middle Empire's" duration to be adjusted along a sliding scale from *zero* upward; and next proceed to show that we possess above 1500 years of positive monuments, behind this "middle Empire," by which all *Septuagint* computations of the Deluge, at B. C. 3246, or 3146, or 3155, encounter a "reductio ad absurdum."

The mists begin to clear off as we commence ascending to the latest representatives of the "Old Empire" in the land of K*h*aM, *Ham*, *Chemmis*: viz., the Sebakhetps and Nepherhetps of the XIIIth dynasty (472): but, at the XIIth dynasty, the glories of the olden time blaze forth again effulgently; (473) thanks to Lepsius's investigations of the *Genealogical Papyrus of Turin*. (474)

---

(467) 1 *Kings* xiv. 25; 2 *Chron*. xii. 2.

(468) GLIDDON: *Chapters*; p. 9.

(469) PRISSE: *Legendes de Sckai*; Rev. Archéol., 1845; pp. 472–474; also his arrangement of these kings, in WILKINSON, *Hand-book*, p. 393; — LEPSIUS: *Götterkreis*; 1851; pp. 40–43; — DE ROUGÉ: *Lettre à M. Alfred Maury*; Rev. Archéol., 1849; 120–124.

(470) GLIDDON: *Otia*; pp. 44, 45.

(471) *Briefe aus Ægypten*; pp. 364–369.

(472) BIRCH, in *Otia Ægyptiaca*; p. 82; and his *Historical Tablet of Ramses II.*; 1852; p. 19; — DE ROUGÉ: *Rochers de Semné*; Rev. Archéol., 1848; pp. 312, 313.

(473) BUNSEN: *Ægyptèns Stelle*; ii. p. 271, *seq.*; — DE ROUGÉ: *Annales de Philosophie Chrétiennes*; xiv., xv., xvi.; and HINCKS: *Turin Book of Kings*; R. Soc. of Lit.; iii., part i., pp. 128–150; but considerably emended in WILKINSON'S *Papyrus of Kings*; 1850; "Observations of Dr. E. HINCKS"; p. 55: — DE ROUGÉ: *Le Sesostris de la Douzième Dynastie*; Rev. Archéol., 1847; pp. 481–489.

(474) *Auswahl*; Taf. iii., iv., v., vi.: — most superbly recopied by Sir J. G. Wilkinson: *Fragments of the Hieratic Papyrus at Turin*; 1851: but consult also the critical history of this document as displayed by CHAMPOLLION-FIGEAC (Rev. Archéol.), with the caveat that the luckless disposal of these fragments is due to SEYFARTH alone.

The hieroglyphical names of some of these kings may be consulted in Bunsen; but we borrow from Lepsius this table of the XIIth dynasty; which cannot become more than slightly modified in his "Book of Kings." (475)

"THE XIITH MANETHONIAN DYNASTY.

		According to Manetho.			*According to the Turin Papyrus.*	*Highest year on the Monuments.*
1. Amenemhe I alone..................	9 y'rs	9 Am. I	[Afr. 16	Eus. 16]	9 y'rs	
2. Sesurtesen I and Amenemhe I.	7 "					8. of Am. and Ses. I.
Sesurtesen I alone..................	35 "	46 Ses. I	[Afr. 46	Eus. 46]	45 "	44. of Ses. I=2 of Am. II.
Sesurtesen I and Amenemhe II	4 "					
3. Amenemhe II alone................	28 "	38 Am. II	[Afr. 38	Eus. 38]	3(7) "	35. Am. II=3. Ses II.
4. Sesurtesen II & Amenemhe II.	10 "					
Sesurtesen II alone.................	28 "	28 Ses. II	[Afr. 48	Eus. 48]	(2)9 "	11. — —
5. Sesurtesen III.........	38 "	38 Ses. III	[Afr. 8	Eus. 8]	3(7) "	26. — —
6. Amenemhe III alone	41 "	42 Am. III	[Afr. 8	Eus. 42]	4(1) "	43. — —
Amenemhe III & Amenemhe IV	1 "					
7. Amenemhe IV alone........	8 "	8 Am. IV	[Afr. 8		9 y'rs 3 m. 27 d.	6. — —
8. Ra-Sebeknefru.......................	4 "	4 Sebek.	[Afr. 4		3 " 10 " 24 "	
					Total 213 " 1 " 24 " "	

The XIIth dynasty ends, according to Lepsius, about B. C. 2124.

What relics are extant of XIth dynasty belong to the Enuantefs, (476) including perhaps Ra-nub-Cheper, discovered lately by Mr. Harris.

Little can here be related about the Xth, IXth, VIIIth, and VIIth dynasties, to be intelligible without a lengthy argument; but the duration of this last is felicitously suggested by Maury. (477) Solid as a rock, however, is the VIth dynasty; (478) so is the Vth on the *Turin Papyrus* and through the recovery of all its kings (but one?) from the tombs opened by the Prussian Commission at Memphis. (479) Of the IVth the vestiges surpass belief, to persons who have not opened the folio plates of Lepsius's *Denkmäler;* wherein the petroglyphs of these three dynasties, earliest and grandest relics of antique humanity, are now preserved for posterity, so long as the pyramids of *Geezeh* shall endure.

With the IIId dynasty Egyptian monuments cease. There is nothing extant of the IId, nor coeval with the Ist dynasty. Their existence is deduced from the high state of the arts, and the extensive knowledge possessed by the denizens of the Nile, as demonstrated by the *pyramids, sepulchres,* and *hieroglyphed records,* of the IVth dynasty, compared with the fragmentary catalogues of Manetho and Eratosthenes, and supported by Græco-Roman tradition.

MENES—Egypt's first Pharaoh—is recorded, in hieroglyphics carved, during the 14th century B. C. at the Theban Ramesium, by Ramses II. as his earliest ancestor; and, in hieratic, on the *Turin Papyrus*, a document written in the twelfth—fourteenth century B. C., "king MeN*ai*, of a firm life," is twice chronicled. (480)

By Lepsius, whose computations we adopt, Menes is estimated to have founded the Ist dynasty of *Thinites* about the year ———————————— B. C. 3893.

"There is nothing incredible in such an antiquity of the Egyptian monarchy." (481) Indeed, long before hieroglyphical discoveries had demonstrated its natural adaptation to all the circumstances of Egypt (when due allowance is made for *pre-Menaic* chiliads of years for alluvial existence), the researches of mathematicians had pointed to similar results.

"On supposing the 11340 years of Herodotus, taken for the Egyptian seasons of three months, we should have 2794 solar years, according to Freret, and 2835 years, according

(475) *Ueber die Zwölfte Ægyptische Königsdynastie;* 1853; p. 28.

(476) LEEMANS: *Lettre à Salvolini:* 1838; No. 22; — and *Lettre à M. De Witte:* Rev. Archéol., 1848, pp. 718–720; — BIRCH, in *Otia Ægyptiaca;* pp. 80, 81; and *Tablet of Ramses II.;* p. 18.

(477) *Chronologie des Dynasties Égyptiennes:* Rev. Archéol., 1851; pp. 166, 167.

(478) BUNSEN: *Ægyptens Stelle:* ii. p. 191, *seq.;* — MARIETTE: *Fragment du Papyrus Royal de Turin et la VIe Dynastie de Manéthon;* Rev. Archéol., 1849; pp. 306–315; — HINCKS: Trans. R. Soc. Lit., Mar. 12, 1846; p. 137; and "Observations" in WILKINSON'S *Papyrus;* pp. 53, 54.

(479) GLIDDON: *Otia;* p. 38. For all details see authorities in the preceding note.

(480) *Column I., fragment* 1, *lines* 11 and 12; Sir G. WILKINSON'S copy.

(481) KENRICK: *Op. cit.;* p. 110.

to Bailly. These finished at the reign of Sethos and with the war of Sennacherib, in the year 710 before J. C. Following this hypothesis, the commencement of Menes fell about the year 3504 B. C., according to Freret; and in 3545 B. C., according to Bailly." (482)

Having thus indicated to junior students of Egyptian chronology the order in which they should read the works of our common seniors in this technical speciality of science, we will now reverse the process, and exhibit, from MENES downward, the stratifications in which Time's hour-glass has marked, historically, the consecutive events witnessed, during above forty-three centuries, by the Egyptian "Type of Mankind" down to the 4th century after the Christian era; assumed at 1853 years ago.

It is a convenient plan to group several portions of Egypt's history into the following separate masses, like the primary, secondary, and tertiary formations of our earth's crust; and to view the dynasties, in those masses included, as if they were so many distinct strata contained in such formations. We thereby divest the subject of the perplexities and dubiousness of arithmetical chronology; because, the viril existence of Menes, as an historical entity, is no more dependent upon *ciphers*, than Owen's *Dinornis giganteus* (in palæontology) hangs upon a "B. C. 2320" of a Knight's, or upon a "B. C. 2348" of an Archbishop's diluvian phantasms.

I.—The ANTE-MONUMENTAL period. This of course is an utter *blank* in chronology. Science knows not where geology ends, nor when humanity begins; and the definitive, or artificial systems, current on the subject, are of modern adoption and spurious derivation.

At what era of the world's geological history the River *Nile*, the *Báhr-el-abiad* in particular, first descended from palustrine localities in Central Africa, along the successive levels of Nubian plateaux, through its Egyptian channel to the Mediterranean (beyond the indisputable fact that its descent took effect *after* the deposition of the so-termed DILUVIAL DRIFT upon the subjacent *limestone*) is a problem yet unsolved. But were proper investigations, such as those commenced in 1799 by Girard, (483) and cut short by European belligerent interference, entered upon, in the valley of the Nile itself, by competent geologists, the *alluvial* antiquity of the "Land of Khem" could be approximately reached. (484) The very rough estimates heretofore made by geologists yield a *minimum* of 7000 years for the depositions of the present alluvium by the river Nile. The *maximum* remains utterly indefinite; but, nevertheless, we are enabled to draw, from the data already known, the following among other deductions, of primary importance to Nilotic *chronology*:—

1st.—Previously to the advent of the "Sacred River" no deposition of *alluvium* having taken place upon the limestone, Egypt was uninhabitable by man.

2d.—Since the deposition of this alluvium, there has been no *Deluge*, in the literal Hebrew and genesiacal sense of the term, whether in Egypt, or in Asiatic and African countries to the Nile adjacent.

3d.—Humanity must have commenced in the valley of the Nile, under conditions such as exist at this day, *after* a sufficiency of alluvium had been deposited for the production of vegetable aliment, but at a time when the depth of this alluvium was at least twenty (fifty, or *more*, for aught we can assert to the contrary) feet below the level of the highest portion of the Nile's bed at this hour; but how much soil had been previously deposited — that is, what its *thickness* was over the limestone when humanity first developed itself in Egypt — it is yet impossible to define.

4th.—Many centuries (in number utterly unknown) must be allowed for the multiplication of a human Type *in Egypt*, from a handful of rovers to a mighty nation; and for the acquirement, by self-tuition, of arts and sciences adequate to the conception and execution of a pyramid: thus yielding us a *blank* amount of chronological interval: bounded on the one hand by the unknown depth and surface of the Nilotic alluvial,

(482) DE BROTONNE: *Filiations et Migrations;* i. p. 198, 199.
(483) *Description de l'Égypte:* tom. xx. p. 33, *seq.*
(484) GLIDDON: *Otia;* pp. 62–69; and "Geological Sections." For the *botanical* argument, vide PICKERING.

sufficient for the growth of human food, at the time of man's introduction; and on the other (after this nomad had been transmuted by time and circumstance into a farmer and then into a monument-building citizen) by the *pyramids* and *tombs* of the IVth Memphite dynasty; placed by Lepsius's discoveries in the thirty-fifth century B.C.

II.—The PYRAMIDAL period, or *Old* Empire.—Occupying, according to late scientific views, about fifteen centuries; probably beginning with Manetho's *first* dynasty (king OUENEPHIS); and ending with the XIIth or XIIIth, about twenty-two centuries prior to the Christian era. The XIIth dynasty is marked architecturally by the employment of *obelisks*.

III.—The period of the HYKSOS, or *Middle* Empire.—There being few *monuments* for this period extant, we are dependent, apart from Greek lists, upon the *Turin Papyrus*, and on the names chronicled long after on the "Chamber of Karnac" &c. Here is the *grand* difficulty in Egyptian chronology; it having been hitherto impossible to determine its duration; which is now generally considered to be far shorter than is estimated in Bunsen's "Ægyptens Stelle in der Weltgeschichte," and perhaps to embrace all *Scriptural* connexions with Egypt from Abraham to the *Exodus* inclusive; on every one of which the *hieroglyphics* are utterly silent. It includes, however, the XIVth, XVth, and XVIth dynasties.

IV.—The positive HISTORICAL period, or *New* Empire.—Commencing about 1600 to 1800 years B. C., with the *Restoration* (after the expulsion of the Hyksos tribes), under AAHMES, the founder of the XVIIth dynasty. It may be called the *Temple*-period; because, although temples existed in the Old Empire, all the grand sanctuaries standing at present upon the alluvia belong to the XVIIth dynasty downward.

Dated *hieroglyphical* records descend to the third century after Christ, with the name of the Emperor DECIUS: (485) but *demotic papyri* and *mummies* are extant as recent as the 4th century of the same era.(486) Greek inscriptions at Philæ corroborate Priscianus, who relates how, about A. D. 451, a treaty, between the Christian Emperor of Constantinople and the heathen Blemmyes, stipulated that—"every year, according to ancient customs, the Ethiopians were to take the statue of *Isis* from Philæ to Ethiopia;"(487) and a Grecian traveller bears witness, in an inscription, that he was once present at the temple when the goddess returned. In fact, history proves that *ISIS* was yet worshipped at Philæ, if not throughout Egypt, even in the year A. D. 486: and the pagan emblem of "eternal life," *Ankh*, continued still to be inscribed, in lieu of the Christian *cross*, over orthodox churches; as in the following instance discovered by the accurate Sir J. Gardner Wilkinson(488):—

"ΚΑΘΟ☥ΛΙΚΗ + ΕΚΚΛΗ☥CΙΑ"

Catho☥lic + Chu☥rch.

Finally, to enable the reader to classify, chronologically, the Egyptian data comprised in "Types of Mankind," a table is subjoined which the forthcoming "Book of Kings" will show to be in the main correct. It is made up, in part from the first volume of the *Chronologie der Ægypter*, and in part from Chevalier Lepsius's oral communications to the writer at Berlin, in May, 1849.(489) To it are added such excerpts of the Chevalier's subsequent epistolary correspondence with the authors as may give a general idea of his system, and a precise one of his scientific liberality.

---

(485) LEPSIUS: *Vorläufige Nachricht*, 1849; pp. 17, 29.
(486) BIRCH, in *Otia Ægyptiaca*, p. 87.
(487) LETRONNE: *Matériaux pour servir à l'Histoire du Christianisme.*
(488) LETRONNE: *Examen Archéologique*, "Croix Ansée Égyptienne," 1846; p. 23.
(489) GLIDDON: *Hand-book to the Nile:* London, Madden, 1849; pp. 20–2, 51.

MANETHO'S SYSTEM OF EGYPTIAN CHRONOLOGY, AS RESTORED BY LEPSIUS.

EPOCHAS anterior to MENES — Cyclic Periods: —

Divine dynasties:—	19 *gods* ...... reigned	13,870	Julian years	= 19 Sothic *demi*-periods.
	30 *demi-gods* "	3,650	"	= 30 *twelfths* of a Sothic-period.
		17,520	"	= 12 Sothic-periods of 1460 years.
Ante-historical dyn.:	10 *Manes*, Thinites,	350	"	— commencement of a *new* Sothic-period.

EPOCH OF MENES — commencement of *historical* period; *thirty* dynasties: —

Old Empire:—	1st dynasty — Accession of Menes	3893 B. C.
	Commencement of *monumental* period; third dynasty.	
	4th dynasty — Pyramids and tombs extant — began	3426 "
Subdivisions: —		
	5th dynasty — Began about	3100 "
	7th " "	2900 "
	10th " "	2500 "
	12th " Ends about	2124 "
	13th " "	2100 "
Invasion of the Hyksos — comprising the		
	14th, 15th, and 16th dynasties — from about B. C. 2101 to about	1590 "
New Empire — Restoration:—		
	17th dynasty — Began	1671 "
	30th " Ending on the *second* Persian Invasion	340 "
Conquest of Egypt by Alexander the Great		332 "
Ptolemaic dynasty began B. C. 323 — ends		44 "
Roman dominion began		30 "
Hieroglyphical records of the Emperor Decius		250 A. D.

Thus, from an indefinite period prior to the year B. C. 3893, down to 250 years after the Christian era, the hieroglyphical character is proved to have been in uninterrupted use: while, from the year B. C. 3893, modern hierology has determined the chronologic order of Egyptian dynasties, through present archæological re-construction of the Nile's monuments.

The Romans held Egypt from the 27th year B. C. until 395 A. D.; when the sons of Theodosius divided the Empire. Egypt lingered under the sovereignty of the Eastern Emperors until A. D. 640–1; when, subjected by AAMER-EBN-EL-AS, she became a province of OMAR's Saracenic caliphate. In the year A. D. 1517—*Hedjra* 953—her valley was over-run by the Ottoman hordes of SOOLTAN SELEEM; and has ever since been the spoil of the Turk:—

O! Egypte, Egypte! . . . Solæ supererunt fabulæ et æque incredibiles posteris . . . sola supererunt verba lapidibus incisa. Et inhabitabit Ægyptum Scythus aut (ANGLO-) *Indus, aut aliquis talis.*(490)

CHRONOLOGY—CHINESE.

> "The Philosopher said: SAN! (name of his disciple THSENG-TSEU) *my doctrine is simple and easy to be understood.* Thseng-tseu replied: 'that is certain.' The Philosopher having gone out, his disciples asked what their master had meant to say. Thseng-tseu responded: 'The doctrine of our master consists uniquely in possessing rectitude of heart, and in loving one's neighbor as oneself.'" (491)

Such were the ethics put forth in China by that "pure Sage" whom three hundred and seventy millions of humanity still commemorate, after the lapse of 2330 years, as the "most saintly, the most wise, and the most virtuous of human legislators:" this was Chinese "positive philosophy" in the VIth century before Christ; already at the *second* period of its historical development. (492)

About a century later, in a distinct Asiatic world, the school of EZRA at Jerusalem embodied a similar conception in the compilation termed *Deuteronomy*, or "secondary law:" (493)

---

(490) *Books of Hermes* — MERCURIUS TRISMEGISTUS's dialogue with *Asclepius*; — GLIDDON: *Appeal to the Antiquaries*: London, Madden, 1841, *passim*.

(491) The LUN-YU, or *The Philosophical Conversations*, of KHOUNG-TSEU (Confucius); ch. iv. v. 15; Livres Sacrés de l'Orient, p. 183.

(492) PAUTHIER: *Histoire de la Philosophie Chinoise*; Revue Indépendante, Aug. 1844; tirage à part, p. 9.

(493) N. B. My justification of this date is contained in the suppressed portions of our vol.; *supra*, pp. 626–7.

"But if any man hate his neighbor. &c. . . . then shall ye do unto him, as he had thought to have done unto his brother." (494) At an epoch approximate, this idea became simplified into a maxim: "Better is a neighbor that is near, than a brother far off:" (495) and it is still more concisely expressed in *Leviticus*: "Thou shalt love thy neighbor as thyself." (496)

During the same fifth century B. C., the simultaneousness of moral as well as of other developments among Types of Mankind radically distinct, and remote from each other's influences, encounters a parallelism in the beautiful dictum of a Grecian Isocrates — "Do unto others as ye would they should do unto you."

About three generations earlier there flourished in Persia the philosopher Zoroaster; some of whose elevated doctrines have reached our day, although through turgid Grecian, Jewish, and Persic streams. "*Gate* the 71st" of his *Sadder* contains the following:—

"Offer up thy grateful prayers to the Lord, the most just and pure ORMUZD, the supreme and adorable God, who thus declared to his prophet Zardusht (Zoroaster): '*Hold it not meet to do unto others what thou wouldst not have done to thyself:* do that unto the people which, when done to thyself, proves not disagreeable to thyself.'" (497)

Five hundred years afterwards, the writer of *Matthew* (498) reported — "Ye have heard that it was said: *Thou shalt love thy neighbor and hate thine enemy;* but I say unto you, love your enemies." The writer of *Luke* (499) considerably extends the idea in language and contextual circumstances — "And he answering said: '*Thou shalt love the Lord thy God* [Hebraicè, IeHOuaH ELoHeK] *with all thy heart, and with all thy soul, and with all thy strength, and with all thy mind, and thy neighbor as thyself:*" thus combining, into one discourse, two citations from the Old Testament (500) slightly varied; owing probably to the evangelists' habit of following the Greek LXX in lieu of the Hebrew Text.

But, among the more exalted of the Hebrew nation, in the schools of Babylon and Jerusalem, such pure ethics had been taught long previously. Thus (as our learned friend, Dr. J. J. Cohen of Baltimore, opportunely reminds us while writing):—

"Let us recall the celebrated reply made by the Pharisee Hillel to a pagan who came declaring to him that he was ready to embrace Judaism, if the Doctor could make known to him in a few words the *résumé* of all the law of Moses: — '*That which thou likest not* [done] *to thyself*,' said Hillel, '*do it not unto thy neighbor;* therein is all the law, the rest is nothing but the commentary upon it.'" (501)

These comparisons made, we can revert with more pleasure to China and to CONFUCIUS.

"The lessons of KHOUNG-TSEU were often less indirect. His moral [doctrine] is summed up in the following lines: 'Nothing more natural, nothing more simple, than the principles of that morality which I endeavor to inculcate in you through salutary maxims. . . . 1st.— It is *humanity;* which is to say, that universal charity amongst all of our species, without distinction.'"

Father Amiot, the great Sinicized Jesuit, commenting upon this passage, observed — "Because it is *humanity*, and that *humanity* is nothing else than *man* himself." Which Pauthier explains:—

"In Chinese, JIN TCHE: JIN YE: word for word; *humanitas quæ, homo quidem.* . . . To render comprehensible how much *humanity*, or benevolence, universal charity, was recommended by KHOUNG-TSEU, it suffices to say that the word which expresses it is repeated above a hundred times in one of his works, the *Lun-yu*. And it is pretended, with as much levity as ignorance, that this grand principle of *universal charity* for mankind had only been revealed to the world five hundred years after the Chinese philosopher, in a little corner of Asia! *Quelle pitié!*" (502)

We have deemed it expedient to preface an inquiry into the archæological bases of

---

(494) *Deuteronomy*, xix. 11, 19.

(495) *Proverbs*, xxvii. 10.

(496) *Leviticus*, xix. 18.

(497) *Dabistan*, i. 338: and see the same quotation in HYDE, *De Relig. Vet. Persarum*, p. 471.

(498) *Good Tidings*, v. 43. SHARPE'S *N. T.*, p. 9.

(499) *Good Tidings*, x. 27, 27 — *Ibid.*, p. 132.

(500) *Deuteronomy*, vi. 5, with *Leviticus*, xix. 18.

(501) MUNK: *Palestine;* p. 565; from Babylonian Talmud (*Shabbath*, ch. 2). *Ibid.: Réflexions* in Appendix to CAHEN'S *Bible;* 1833; iv. p. 20.

(502) *Chine;* pp. 146, 147, and note.

Chinese *chronology* with the above extracts. They will furnish at once to the reader a very different idea of the teachings of Confucius (five hundred years before any Greco-Judæan writers of the Gospels lived) than he can gather from Macao supercargoes, Hong-kong opium-smugglers, or Canton missionaries. Whatever practical developments the latter may diurnally give to the sublime principle of "universal charity;" whatever merit may be due to the first human being who enunciated this exalted sentiment; or whatever thorough knowledge of humanity's best and loftiest interests such sentiments may imply; all these ascriptions, history attests, equally belong to a Sinico-mongol, Confucius; who died B. C.479, or about 2332 years ago. [See his portrait; *supra*, Fig. 330, p. 449.]

Whether among the *Hong* merchants "universal charity" (and there are noble instances) be unexceptionably practised, any more than in *Wall* street, *Lombard* street, or in the *Place de la Bourse*, concerns us not. These commercial princes are taught to reverence its principles as much as the DORIAS or the MEDICIS of Christendom; and they are exposed to infinitely greater temptations toward its violation, than are those Chinese archæologists, who, scattered throughout the empire, pursue, at national expense, their historical studies of their own monuments; in lettered seclusion, but with every honorable recompense scholarship may aspire to. (503) For above twenty-three centuries, moreover, the 4th and 5th maxims of Khoung-tseu have been instilled into each generation of them from earliest infancy.

"It is *uprightness;* that is, that rectitude of spirit and of heart, which makes one seek for truth in everything and to desire it, without deceiving oneself or deceiving others: it is finally *sincerity* or *good faith;* which is to say, that frankness, that openness of heart, tempered by self-reliance, which excludes all feints and all disguising, as much in speech as in action."

That the moral influence of such principles has not perished, even through the transitory irruption of the present and expiring dynasty of *Mantchou* Tartars, is testified by Sir Henry Pottinger in the eulogiums pronounced by him, at London, upon the high Chinese diplomatists with whom he concluded the Treaty of 1844. Nor should Americans forget the excellent conduct which such principles have already exhibited among thousands of our Chinese fellow-citizens in the State of California.

We have not the slightest right to doubt, therefore, whatever reasonable account Chinese scholars may furnish us of their nation's indigenous history; of which, otherwise, not a syllable is known to us prior to the fourteenth century after Christ; and, where not irrational, such annals, from such sources, may be received in the more good faith, that the *Chinese* archéologue, having none of our hagiographers' motives for chronological curtailment or extension, cares nothing about "outside barbarians," their alien history or superstitions, and did not compose his national chronicles with a view to such foreigners' edification.

The day is evermore passed that modern science should strive to reduce Chinese chronology, for the mere whim of adapting it to the spurious computations on a Hebrew Text, and Samaritan, Septuagint, or Vulgate version; as was the case before *Egyptian* monumental annals were proved to ascend, at least, to the thirty-fifth century B. C. (504) And we shall presently show (sketched also in our table of *Alphabetical origins, supra*, p. 638), how the highest point claimed by Chinese historians, for their nation's antiquity, falls centuries below that which hierologists now insist upon for Egypt: so that, if *Egypt* and *Egyptians* were a civilized country and populous people in the thirty-fifth century, B. C., it would be preposterous not to feel assured that Sinico-mongols (indeed every human type of Mongolia) were already in existence, in and around China, their own centre of creation, during the same parallel ages. What is the objection to believing that China was populated, by her Mongolian autocthones, chiliads of years previously? Reader! "one blushes" redder than St. Jerome to mention, that, now-a-days, the acceptance of this fact is questioned by the Rev. Dr. *This*, or the Rev. Mr. *That:* neither of whom, perhaps, has ever studied Sinology — never even opened a Sinological work!

(503) *Chine;* pp. 194, 218, 228, 236, 248, 286, 308, 336, 352, 359, 388, 397, &c.: also, BIOT, *Sur la Constitution Politique de la Chine au 12ème siècle avant notre ère;* 1845; pp. 3, 9, &c.

(504) DE BROTONNE: *Filiations et Migrations des Peuples;* ii. pp. 1–43.

The reveries of Fortia D'Urban (505) are now superannuated; the monstrous extravaganzas of a Paravey are preserved as ceaseless sources of merriment. (506) To refute, either, seriously, would be sheer waste of time. The inundations of the river *Hoang-ho*, overcome by the engineer Yu, (507) lie parallel with the Egyptian XIIth dynasty; when, in the 23d century B. C., similar causes induced smaller constructions along the Nubian Nile: (508) and a reader of Pauthier will as soon associate those local dikings, buttresses, dams, and sluices, in China or Egypt, with Usher's universal Flood, as by anybody else the Noachian deluge might be proposed in explanation of the *levees* along our Louisianian Mississippi. It would be an equal outlay of labor to discuss Hales's views upon Chinese subjects; (509) after his Hebraical knowledge has been so repeatedly shaken throughout these pages: nor need we perplex the reader with other works whose authors, like ourselves, are not Sinologists; but who, in this respect unlike ourselves, do not seek for information at its only clear fountains.

It will be now plain that "Types of Mankind" recognizes for Chinese history none but Chinese historians. The chances of error lie uniquely in the channels through which its authors receive their accounts: and these, to our view, are completely guarded against when we accept Rémusat and Pauthier, as, above all Europeans at this day, qualified to be their interpreters. Furthermore, every relevant passage from the Jesuit missionaries is embraced within Pauthier's volumes.

Under the caption of *Mongolian Origin* and ideographic writings, we have displayed the argumentative process through which it becomes certain, that Europe knew naught about China, nor China aught about Europe, until the end of the 1st century after C.: but modern acquaintance with *Cathay* dates from the Venetian Marco Polo, who resided in China about A. D. 1275; followed by the first Jesuit missionary, Father Michæl Rogerius, who penetrated thither about A. D. 1581; and the second, Father Matthæus Riccius, in 1601. From that time, during more than a century, many accomplished Europeans *è Societate Jesu* flocked into the Celestial Empire; and to their vast labors are we indebted for complete reports upon China, derived by them from the highest scholastic and official sources of the realm — which narratives, now collated by Sinologists in Europe with the immense literary treasures accessible, in Chinese, to students at Paris and Rome, prove to have been conscientiously executed. No Europeans, before or since, have possessed such opportunities for acquiring thorough knowledge of everything Chinese as these lowly preachers of the Gospel. Indeed, the official report made, in 1692, by the "President of the Supreme Court of Rites" to the Emperor Khang-hi, and by him approved, alone suffices to show their powerful claims upon *Mantchou-Tartar* affections: —

"We have found that these Europeans have traversed vast seas, and have come from the extremities of the earth. . . . They have at present the supervision of astronomy and of the board of mathematics. They have applied themselves with great pains to making warlike machines, and to casting cannon; of which use has been made in the last civil troubles [that is, the missionary ordnance had been found effective in quelling *Chinese* revolts against the Tartar dynasty]. When sent to Nip-chou with our ambassadors [the reverend Fathers Pereyra and Gerbillon, *è Soc. Jesu,*] to treat about peace with the Muscovites, they caused those negotiations to succeed: in short, they have rendered great services to the [*Mantchou*] empire. . . . The doctrine which they teach is not bad, nor capable of seducing the [Chinese] people, or of causing any troubles. It is permitted to every body to go into the temples of the *Lamas*, of the *Ho-chang*, of the *Tao-ssé;* and it is forbidden to go into the churches of these Europeans, who do nothing contrary to the laws: this does not seem reasonable." (510)

The emperor himself had been previously instructed by the scientific Father Verbiest, "chief of the bureau of astronomers"; whose evangelical virtues comprised gnomonics,

(505) *Histoire Anté-diluvienne de la Chine.*

(506) *Documents sur le Déluge de Noë:* Paris, 1838.

(507) PAUTHIER: *Chine;* pp. 12–4; and his *Chou-king;* pp. 49–56.

(508) LEPSIUS: *Nachricht;* p. 11: — *Briefe aus Ægypten;* pp. 259, 260: — DE ROUGÉ: *Phénom. Célestes;* Rev. Archéol., Feb. 1853.

(509) *Analysis:* i. pp. 199–203.

(510) *Chine:* pp. 435, 440, 445–449.

geometry, land-surveying, and music. The reverend Fathers Bouvet, Regis, Jartoux, Fridelli, Cardoso, de Tartre, de Mailla, and Bonjour, at government expense, made official maps of the different provinces of China, after European methods; and, at the same time that such labors familiarized the whole of these Propagandic missionaries with Chinese literature, Fathers Amiot, Gaubil, and Du Halde, devoted their leisure more especially to minute study of Chinese archæology. In one word, the admiration avowed by the Jesuits for Chinese civilization on the one hand, and the influence which Chinese philosophy possessed over their intellects on the other, had led to such a fusion at Pe-kin, during the 17th century, that one is at a loss to decide whether the Chinese were becoming converts to spiritual Christianity, or whether the disciples of Loyola were adopting the materialistic "doctrine of the Lettered."

Unhappily for our desires to solve this curious problem, certain puritanic *Dominicans* arrived from Rome; and, Pandora-like, let loose fanatic ills heretofore preserved hermetically. It was they who started that everlasting question whether the Chinese word *chang-ti* be a synonyme for "God" or the "sky." Pig-tailed converts to Christianity *à la Jésuite* were incontinently bambooed by hog-tails *à la Dominicain;* for heretical notions upon an equivocal point by aliens indicated for Mongol salvatory "credo." Khoung-tseu's "universal charity" being interrupted by swinish brawls at which the writers of *Leviticus*(511) would have shuddered, policemen duly reported their real causes to mandarin magistracy: which reports, in official course, reached a new embodiment of the Sun upon earth, Young-tching. This unsophisticated Tartar at once relieved himself. and his successors for more than a century, of these foreign theologers, by shipment of a live cargo, including missionaries Jesuit and Dominican, consigned to Macao under judiciary "bill of lading," about the years A. D. 1721–'25.

It is to the *Jesuits*, nevertheless, that impartial science looks back, gratefully, for throwing the portals of Chinese history widely open to European Sinology: and it is especially to the late Rémusat, Klaproth, and Ed. Biot, as to MM. Stanislas Julien and Pauthier, that our generation owes the reappearance of Chinese studies on the continent, since the demise of the famed historian of the *Huns*, Deguignes. At Paris, the Chinese department of the Bibliothèque Impériale comprehends quantities stupendous of that country's literature.

Every element for our purposes being in consequence accessible, we proceed, Pauthier's works in hand, to sketch 1st, — the mode through which archæologists in China have definitely tabulated, in precise stratifications, the relative order of national events; and 2d, — to present a chronological table of Chinese dynasties, from such tabulations accruing.

It is as certain as any other fact in history (512) that about 1000 years B. C., parallel with the reign of Solomon, books existed in China with such titles as these: — "Laws of the administration of ancient kings;" and that recurrence was common to "ancient documents." It is also certain that arts and sciences continued to prosper down to the year 484 B. C., (513) when Confucius compiled the *Chou-king*, sacred book of the Chinese, from anterior documents. Literature was immensely diffused among the "Lettered" in China; when, B. C. 213, Chi-hoang-ti burned all the books which torture could extort, together with multitudes of their readers; (514) because the latter quoted the former against his imperial innovations. Nevertheless, this splendid miscreant served practical objects, not altogether indefensible, when he relieved the empire of its "old-fogiedom;" to judge by the withering oration of his prime-minister, Li-sse: —

"Prejudiced in favor of antiquity, of which they admire even the stupidities, they are full of disdain for every thing which is not exactly chalked after models that time has nearly effaced from the memory of man. Incessantly they have in their mouths, or at the tips of their pencils, the *three* Ho-ang [the Chinese august triad], and the *five* Ti [the Chinese pentateuch]."

Nearly 2000 years previously, disputes among religious sects in China had risen to such

(511) XI. 7.

(512) *Chine;* pp. 59, 194, 200.

(513) *Chou-king, Préface du Père Gaubil;* PAUTHIER'S "Liv. Sac. de l'Orient," Paris, 1843; pp. 1, 2.

(514) *Chine;* pp. 222-228.

an intolerable pitch, that the pious Emperor Mou-wang, about B. C. 950, records how Yao, in B. C. 2337, in order to suppress false prophecies, miracles, magic, and revelations, —

"Commanded the two Ministers of Astronomy and Religion to cut asunder all communication between 'sky' and earth; and thus (says Mou-wang) there was no more of what is called this *lifting-up* and *coming-down*."

And, so inveterate, in sporadic instances of the Chinese mind, was this childish reliance upon invisible powers, that fifteen centuries after the burning of the books, the Minister Tchang-kouei, about A. D. 1321, during a period of great physical calamities, pestilence, inundations, &c., felt it incumbent upon his office to include the subjoined remarks in a long and manly expostulation: —

"A prince must not think to govern his country save as the father of his subjects; and it is not through *Bonzes* [Budhist priests] that he must seek felicity. Ever since the *Bonzes*, the *Lamas*, and the *Tao-ssé*, make so many prayers and sacrifices to their idol, 'Heaven' has given constant signs of its indignation; and until such time as one sees the worship of Fo [Budha] abolished, and all these *priests* driven away, one must expect to be unhappy."

Such political necessities may palliate some of Chi-Hoang-ti's deeds; which obliterated so much of earlier literature extant down to the Chinese "era of the martyrs" for science, B. C. 213.

Upon accession of the famous *Han* dynasty, B. C. 202, a reaction in favor of letters immediately commenced; and from this period of "renaissance" downwards no nation upon earth possessed, till recently, annals comparable to the Chinese. About B. C. 176, the *Chou-king* of Khoung-tseu was recovered, partly, by taking down the recitations of a nonogenarian savant, Fou-cheng, who had been president of literature prior to the conflagration of libraries. Through this venerable scholar (who is to the Chinese what Ezra was to the Jews) and the fortuitous discovery, B. C. 140, of a copy of the *Chou-king* with other books in the ruined house of Confucius, the more important documents of Chinese antiquarian lore were restored.

European authors, who claim that we possess the plenary words if not the autograph of Moses, have doubted this account. We accept it, notwithstanding, in good faith; because neither the books themselves nor their transcribers pretend to supernaturalism in any shape; whilst the nature of the local researches subsequently undertaken renders nugatory such unwarrantable European objections.

"But the man who has thrown the grandest éclat over the reign of the Emperor Wou-ti, is Sse-ma-thsian, whom M. Abel Rémusat has called the *Herodotus of China*."(515) His portrait is given under our Fig. 331 [*supra*, p. 349]. About B. C. 104 he commenced his *Historical Memoirs;* which, in 130 books (extant in European libraries, and consulted by the Sinologists we quote), furnish a vast encyclopædia of Chinese annals, of every kind, from the reign of the old Hoang-ti, 2697 years before C., down to B. C. 140.

"Sse-ma-thsian made good use of all that remained of the *Classical Books;* of those of the *Ancestral Temple* of the Tcheou-dynasty; the *Secret Memoirs of the House of Stone*, and of the *Golden Coffer;* and of the registers called *Plates of Jasper*. It is added that he stript the *Liu-ling*, for what concerns the laws; the *Tactics of Han-sin*, for what regards military affairs; the *Tchang-tching*, for what relates to general literature; and the *Li-yi* for every thing that is relative to usages and ceremonies."

There are no further breaks in Chinese archæological labors down to our time; which researches, for care and magnitude, may challenge the universe. We mention, however, only the *Researches profound of the Monuments left by Savans*, published at royal expense, in 348 books, by Matouan-lin, in A. D. 1321; which covers history from the twenty-fourth century B. C. down to the twelfth after C. Copies exist in European libraries. After the death of Chi-Hoang-ti: —

"The tombs, the ruins of cities, the canals and rivers, saved some moneys, some bronze vases, some urns and other objects of his proscription. A certain number of these has been found since the fall of the Thsin-dynasty. They have been carefully collected and preserved in museums or in private cabinets; descriptions have been made

(515) *Chine;* pp. 246-248.

of them, accompanied by figured designs that faithfully reproduce them with their ancient inscriptions. The emperor Kien-loung, who reigned from A. D. 1736 to 1796, caused to be published, in 42 *Chinese folio volumes*, a description and engraving of all the antique vases deposited at the Imperial Museum. An exemplar of this magnificent work, which has no rival in Europe, being at the Bibliothèque Royale of Paris."

Pauthier has selected, out of 1444 *vases* of different species contained in these "Memoirs of the Antiquities of Occidental Purity," those beautiful specimens we behold, reduced in size, in his work.(516)

The earliest originals, now extant in China, go back in date to the *Chang*-dynasty, B. C. 1766:—an epoch when Abraham, according to Lepsius's computation of biblical chronology, was yet unborn. One more ancient inscription, upon a rock of Mount *Heng-chan*, yet remains to vindicate the engineering ability of Yu. It dates about the year B. C. 2278;(517) and is therefore parallel in age with the thousand records we possess of Egypt's XIIth dynasty. Its translation, given by Pauthier, disconnects it from any diluvial hypotheses; with which, moreover, no geologist or archæologist need distress himself further.

We trust the reader has now attained to our point of view, and perhaps perceives three things—1st, the historical meritoriousness of Chinese literature; 2d, the nature of the materials examined by Jesuits whose evangelical prepossessions were essentially hostile to the literature they laud; and 3d, that there are Sinologists living in the world competent to liberate historical truth from chances of error. We now proceed to lay before him a brief summary of Chinese time-registry; commending to his perusal the "Researches upon times anterior to those of which the *Chou-king* speaks, and upon Chinese mythology," by Father de Prémare, together with an old rule of Vico's.(518)

"We have heard Diodorus Siculus declare, in respect to the *pride of nations*, that these, 'whether they may have been Greek or barbarian, have pretended, each one, to have been the first to discover all the comforts of life, and to have preserved their own history since the commencement of the world.'" (519)

Greece, Rome, and Judæa, possess first their fabulous and then their semi-historical periods. Tradition alone pierces through the gloom of the latter, in the ratio of approximation to the several epochas at which given nations first began to chronicle their events. In later days, progressive science invests such fables and faintly-shadowed incidents of a nation's childhood with the garb of mythico-astronomical sanctity. Thus does the founder of chronology, Manetho, preface his historical dynasties with cycles of *Gods*, *Demigods*, and *Manes*; thus do the compilers of *Genesis* antecede Abraham with symbolical names of mythic patriarchs gifted with impossible longevity; and so do the Chinese place mythology before history. The sole difference being that neither did Manetho nor the *Chinese* archéologues ever believe their respective mythologies to be otherwise than unhistorical: at the same time that the whole of these antique systems represent that instinctive consciousness of nations who feel that an unrecorded national infancy must have preceded a recorded national adolescence.

Chinese Ante-historical Periods. (520)

Pan-kou — first symbolical man — followed by the *three* Hoang, viz.: —

1st.—Reign of the *Sky*.
2d.— " " *Earth*.
3d.— " " *Man*.

They are comprehended in a grand cyclic period of 129,600 years; composed of twelve parts called *conjunctions*, each of 10,800 years.

(516) *Chine*; p. 201; Plates 38–41.
(517) *Ibid.*; pp. 53–54.
(518) *Liv. Sac. de l'Orient*; pp. 13–42.
(519) Vico: *Scienza Nuova*; Principles, axiom iii.
(520) *Chine*; pp. 22–24; — *Livres Sacrés*, pp. 16, 19.

META-HISTORICAL PERIOD.

FOU-HI—first Emperor—estimated at.. B. C. 3468
Several of his descendants are named, with traditionary discoveries in arts affixed to each personage.

Fou-hi, however, is a collective name under which the Chinese figure many centuries of national existence coupled with progressive developments in civilization, marked by consecutive artistic inventions: just as the Hebrews ascribe all legislation to their noun of multitude, Moses. This traditionary and semi-mythical *first* Emperor stands parallel with the Egyptian IVth *dynasty*, during the thirty-fifth century B. C. The latter is positively historical: to reject the former, on the imaginary ground of recent mundane antiquity, is rendered futile by existing pyramids at Memphis. Fou-hi, Menes, and Abraham, to us appear equally historical, as human individuals who once lived; although of none of the three are contemporaneous monuments, carved by their respective people, now extant.

HISTORICAL PERIOD.

Chronological Table.—We condense into dynasties that chronology of *all the Sovereigns* who have reigned in China,(from B. C. 2637 down to A. D. 1821),which Father Amiot transmitted from Pe-kin to Paris in 1769; and which is printed "in extenso" at the end of Pauthier's *Chine*, after collation with the learned Jesuit's manuscript notes, and with parts of the 100 *volumes* of the Chinese chronographic work *Li-tai-ki-sse.*

The 61st year of the Chinese emperor Hoang-ti, corresponding to our B. C. 2637, falls, according to Lepsius's computation, within Egypt's "Old Empire," and between the VIIth and Xth dynasties of Manetho, in any case during the pyramidal period.

Ist	*Dynasty*	—1st King, HOANG-TI, "Yellow Emperor," 61st year	2637	B. C.
		Five successors down to YAO, B. C. 2337.		
	"	6th " YAO, 81st year	2277	"
	"	8th " CHUN, ...9th of his synthronism	2277	"
		[*Monuments* commence—"Inscription of YU," B. C. 2278.]		
IId	"	"Hia"—1st King, YU, 10th year of his synthronism	2205	"
	"	" 4th " TCHOUNG-KANG 5th year of his reign, *eclipse of the Sun*, B. C. 2155 (521)	2155	"
IIId	"	"Chang"	1783	"
		[Contemporary *vases* exist, dating from B. C. 1766.]		
IVth	"	"Tcheou"	1134	"
Vth	"	"Thsin" [whence the name of "China"]	255	"
VIth	"	"Han"	202	"
		King YOUAN-TI, of the "Wei," A. D. 292.		
VIIth	"	"Tçin"	265	A. D
VIIIth	"	"Northern Soung"	420	"
IXth	"	"Tsi"	479	"
Xth	"	"Liang"	502	"
XIth	"	"Tchin"	557	"
XIIth	"	"Souï"	581	"
XIIIth	"	"Thang"	618	"
		The *Five Little Dynasties.*		
XIVth	"	1st, "Posterior *Liang*"	907	"
XVth	"	2d, "Posterior *Thang*"	923	"
XVIth	"	3d, "Posterior *Tsin*"	936	"
XVIIth	"	4th, "Posterior *Han*"	947	"
XVIIIth	"	5th, "Posterior *Tcheou*"	951	"
XIXth	"	"Soung"	960	"
XXth	"	"*Kin*, simultaneously with *Soung*"	1123	"
XXIst	"	Commencement of "Youan," *Mongols*	1260	"
XXIId	"	*Mongols*	1295	"
XXIIId	"	"Ming"	1368	"
XXIVth	"	"Taï-thsing," *Mantchou*-Tartars	1616	"
		Now reigning—and down to	1821	"

24 *Dynasties*, whose consecutive rule covers *years* 4458.

(521) *Chine*, p. 58; and *Chou-king*, p. 47:—but, compare BIOT, *Syzigies*, 1848, for astronomical doubts.

Egyptian priests had told Herodotus, (522) that lengthened experience and observation of their own history enabled them to predicate the future through the cyclic recurrence of the past. In no chronicles do similar causes oftener reproduce similar events, through perpetual cycles, than the reader of Pauthier will recognize among the *Chinese.* No political acumen is required by historians to foretell the inevitable downfall of the present alien *Mantchou*-Tartar dynasty. Its doom is sealed; its knell is ringing. One fact will illustrate its Tartarian despotism, and explain the repugnance to prolongation of its hateful rule nurtured in the bosom of every true *Chinaman;* precisely paralleled by *Arab* hatred to the cognate Tartar-*Turks.*

In the same manner that the radical poverty of the Ottoman speech compels the Turk to draw all his polite terms from the *Persian,* his scientific from the *Arabic,* so, in China, the uncouth and slender vocabulary of the *Mantchou*-Tartars became enriched, after their conquest, with Chinese words of civilization. This gave offence to the Tartar emperor, Kien-loung; who, anxious to preserve the *Mantchou* idiom in its natural if barbaric "purity," appointed an Imperial Commission, to compose, from *Mantchou* radicals, 5000 *new words,* to stand in place of those which his courtiers had borrowed from the Chinese tongue. This new nomenclature, printed and proclaimed, was imposed upon all high government functionaries; who had thus to learn 5000 unknown words by heart, under severe penalties! Truly, as Champollion-Figeac remarks — "Il n'y a qu'un *Tartare* régnant sur des *Chinois* qui soit assez puissant pour introduire d'emblée et par ordonnance cinq mille mots dans une langue!" (523)

CHRONOLOGY—ASSYRIAN.

"The spider weaves his web in the palace of Cæsar;
The owl stands sentinel upon the watch-tower of Afrasiab!"
(FIRDOOSEE—*Shah Nameh.*)

THE eighteenth century, fecund precursor of those conquests in historical science that have immortalized the nineteenth, passed away, without permitting its contemporaries to illumine the gloom which, since the decline of the Alexandria School at the Christian era, for 2000 years had enveloped with equal obscurity the pyramids and temples of the Nile, the lightning-fused towers and crumbling brick mounds on the Euphrates and Tigris, or the rock-hewn sepulchres and thousand-pillared fanes of "lorn Persepolis."

In the year 1800, absolutely nothing was known about these huge colossi of the past beyond the fact of their existence!

A wondrous change has been wrought, by half a century of research, in historical knowledge: almost inconceivable when we reflect that, upon the Assyrian theme before us, modern science knew nothing in 1843 — only ten years ago. "Palpitants d'actualités," Lamartine would say, are these glorious discoveries — still damp from the press are the volumes that unfold them.

Antithesis serves to place past ignorance and present information in the strongest light. Persepolis and her arrow-headed inscriptions suffice by way of illustration.

The German Witte ascribed these ruins, not to human agency, but to an "eruption of the earth." De Rœsch deemed them the work of an antediluvian *Lamech,* "whose exploits are exhibited in these sculptures." Discarding *Homer's Iliad* in the sense vulgarly understood of its glowing heroics, De Rœsch believes Persia to be figured by Troy, Media by Europe, and Assyria by Asia. According to this logopœist, or compiler of invented facts, the Grecian siege of Ilium was but a war between Medes and Persians: and the cuneatic letters of Persepolis "record a series of kings from Cain to Lamech."

Chardin, in 1673, pronounced these remains to be about "4000 years old;" a limit too restricted for the astronomer Bailly: who attributes the foundation of Persepolis to the

(522) Aptly cited by HENRY, *L'Égypte Pharaonique,* ii. pp. 27, 28.
(523) *Paléographie Universelle;* 1841; Introduction, p. 48.

Persian hero, *Djemshid*, (524) whose fabulous because mythic epoch he fixed at 3209 B. C. To the same Iranian demigod are these edifices assigned by Sir W. Jones, estimating their age at about 800 years before Christ.

Semitic historians without exception, as Sheridan neatly observed, "draw upon memory for their wit, and upon imagination for their facts:" wherefore slim clews to a reality could be obtained through them. Like the libraries of Alexandria, of Jerusalem, of China, of Budhic Hindostan, and of Hebraical Christendom, those of ante-Mohammedan Persia perished, from similar fanatical causes, in Saracenic flames with the dynasty of Chosroes, about A. D. 637. Such fitful traditions as survived the wreck of Persic literature became invested (after Bédawee destructiveness had become altered into caliphate restorations) with the hyperbolic extravagancies of Eastern poetry and romance.

One immortal epic, Firdoosee's *Shah Nameh*, or "Book of Kings," composed in the eleventh century, purports, indeed, to cover 3600 years of his country's annals, from the taurokephalic Kaiomurs down to the Arab invasion. Persepolis, under its local name of *Istakhàr*, is mentioned in twenty-eight passages, and its existence is referred to as coeval with Kai-kobad; whose apochryphal era, under Sir W. Jones's hypothesis, falls about B. C. 610: but, neither from the "History of the early kings of Persia" by Mirkavend, in the fifteenth century, nor from the "Dabistàn," was archæological acumen able to disentangle a solitary thread indicative of the age, the builders, or the writings, of Persepolis.

As in Egypt the present *fellàh*, or peasant, ascribes the pyramids to "Pharaòon" (525) or Pharaoh — a name to him the synonyme for Satan — so in Persia, the illiterate native is content that an ancient edifice should be the work of Suleymàn; at once the archimagus of Oriental necromancy and the sage monarch of Israel: for at Murghàb, *Pasargadæ*, the mausoleum whence we have drawn the portrait of that great man [*supra*, p. 138, Fig. 43] whose sculptured epitaph is simply "I am Cyrus, the king, the Achæmenian," is called *Takhti Suleymàn*, or "Solomon's throne." Like Jephtha's, who was buried "in the *cities* of Gilead," (526) Solomon's tomb is shown at Shiràz and again on the road to Kashgàr! Nimrod is even still more ubiquitous.

Equally futile were attempts to rescue history applicable to Persia's monuments from the *Zend-Avesta* of Zoroastric attribution, or from the later *Boundehesh-Pehlvi:* sacred books containing the rituals and theosophy of the Guebres, or Persian expatriated ignicolists of Guzerat, now called Parsees. From Greek writers alone (Herodotus, Xenophon, Ctesias, &c.) were such elements of early Persian history derived as have stood the test of monumental investigation: but the science of the last century had ransacked all these sources without obtaining a glimmer of light as to the nature of Persepolitan wedge-shaped characters. Like the once-mysterious hieroglyphs of Egypt, as interpreted by Father Kircher, the inscriptions of Persia were supposed to veil occult and awful things, black arts of magic, or diabolic talismans. With naught to guide them but the more or less faithless copies printed by De la Valle, Le Brun, Kaemfer, and other old travellers, how could the opinion of a student be other than a conjecture more or less rational according to the mental calibre of each critic?

Thus, by Leibnitz and by Cuper, these inscriptions were reasonably conjectured to contain the letters and elements of "some very ancient writing." Lacroze, the great Coptologist, conceived them to be hieroglyphical inscriptions similar to those of Egypt (at that day undeciphered) and of China, which last are not "sacred sculptured characters" at all.

---

(524) DJEMSHID is the Persic, as SAMSON is the Hebrew, *Hercules.* The former we opine to be DJoM, the Egyptian *Hercules*, coupled with ShaDI, the *strong:* the latter is simply SheMS-on, the *Sun*, with its Arabian euphonizing suffix. *Hercules* is but HaR-GoL, "revolution of heat." Compare LANCI, *Paralipomeni;* and RAOUL-ROCHETTE, *Archéologie Comparée;* with DUPUIS in *Anthon's Class. Dic.*, "Hercules."

(525) "*Yà Pharaòon ebn Pharaòon*" is generally rendered "Thou Pharaoh son of a Pharaoh"! Why not "Thou *crocodile* son of a *crocodile*"? Conf. ROSENMULLERI *Instit. Ling. Arabicæ;* 1818; p. 211.

(526) Text. *Judges* xii. 7. The *sacrifice* of Jephtha's daughter is beautifully told by EURIPIDES; for *Iphigenia*, in its Greek sense of Ιφιγένεα, is only a "daughter of Jephtha."

Chardin opined them to be a "veritable writing like our own;" and Le Brun happily describes these ruins as covered with "ancient Persian characters."

In the face of sensible speculations on matters then entirely inexplicable, the intrepidity of ignorance is exemplified from a quarter whence it would have been least expected; viz., in Hyde's *History of the Religion of the Old Persians* (Oxon. 1760). Not only does he deny that these Persepolitan inscriptions are "old Persian writings," but the author backs assertion with professions of faith:—"I am of opinion that they are neither letters nor intended for letters; but a mere playful *jeu d'esprit* of the chief architect; who, to adorn the walls of Persepolis, imagined a trial of how many divers forms a single elementary stroke (the *wedge*) could be produced combined with itself"! This is as pitiable for such a scholar, as the unfortunate Seetzen's mistake, when he took the *sunken spaces* between each Himyaritic letter for the characters themselves. In the same manner, one of Hyde's contemporaries (the Abbé Tandeau, 1762) stoutly maintained that Egyptian "hieroglyphics were mere arbitrary signs, only employed to serve as ornaments to the edifices on which they were engraven, and that they were never invented to picture ideas."

These arrow-headed sculptures, like the still-unintelligible carvings on aboriginal monuments of Mexico, Central America, and Peru, seemed so enigmatical even to the great explorer of Babylon in 1816, that J. Claudius Rich disconsolately embodies the sum total of knowledge in these words:—

"Their real meaning, or that of the Persepolitan obeliscal character, and the still more complicated hieroglyphics of Egypt, however partially deciphered by the labors of the learned, will now, perhaps, never be fathomed, to their full extent, by the utmost ingenuity of man."

By strange coincidence (serving to add another example of the simultaneousness of discovery, at every age of human development), while Rich penned the above lament, Grotefend in Germany communicated to Heeren, 1815, those successful decipherings of Persepolitan cuneiform inscriptions he had commenced in 1802; which is the identical year of the arrival in England of that *Rosetta Stone;* whence, about 1816, Young's deduction of the letter L in the name "Ptolemy" originated those astounding revelations from Egyptian sculptures which are now so familiar in the archæological world as no longer to require notes of admiration.

Egyptologists, by rough and ready processes, have so completely vanquished opposition, that, at this day, disbelievers in Champollion confine their lugubrious chants to hearers illiterate and inarticulate: but, to judge by the pertinacity with which one, who is no mean scholar, (527) insists that Moses wrote—"The Tigris flows *to the east* of Assyria;" (528) and, therefore, that Botta and Layard have discovered Nineveh on the *wrong* side of the river—the battles of cuneiformists have only commenced! Happily, the Louvre boasts of an Orientalist (529) who can always quote to M. Hoefer the Muslim poet's mnemonic to St. Louis:—

"(O king of the Franks!) if thou preservest the hope of avenging thy defeat, if any temerarious design should bring thee back to our country, forget not that the house of Ebn-Lokmân, that served thee for a prison, is still ready to receive thee. Remember that the chains which thou hast worn, and the eunuch Sabêeh who guarded thee, are ever there and waiting for thee." (530)

Such was the picture on the obverse page of Assyrian archæology in the year 1843. Before contrasting which with its illuminated face in 1853, it is due to the memory of that master, whose teaching of the methods for deciphering the meaning of all antique records has been the true cause as well of Champollion's as of Grotefend's successes—and hence of the whole of our present Egyptian and Assyrian knowledge—to name Silvestre de Sacy.

---

(527) Hoefer: *La Chaldée, &c.*; 1852; p. 146.

(528) *Genesis;* ii. 14.

(529) De Longpérier: *Antiquités Assyriennes;* Rev. Archéol., 1850; pp. 429-432: who reads, most triumphantly, "Le Tigre coule *en avant vers* Assour."

(530) Michaud: *Hist. des Croisades;* iv. p. 274.

In that part of our work discussing *Alphabetic Origins*, the student will find a sufficiency of authorities cited to verify the accuracy of those results to which this volume is confined. Recapitulation here is needless: but, should ever such inquirer follow the developments of palæographical discovery, book by book, backwards from to-day, his bark will not ground until he reaches the year A. D. 1797, and touches the *Mémoire sur les antiquités de la Perse, et sur les médailles des Rois Sassanides*. Its author, De Sacy, is to palæography that which his colleague Cuvier is to palæontology: each being the inventor of the only true method of ratiocination in either science. From the former's Memoir we have borrowed many of the citations above presented; and, our remarks being but introductory to Assyrian chronology, a reference to the excellent compendium of Vaux (531) indicates the shortest road to summary annals of cuneiform investigation; no less than corroborates our assertion that *monumental* Assyria was a blank down to 1843.

Paul-Emile Botta (whose surname is dear to all American readers of his uncle's *Storia dell' Independenza*), appointed French Consul at Mosul in 1842, was the first to resuscitate *Nineveh* since her fall in B. C. 606. Proficient as an Orientalist and Eastern traveller, through residence in Syria, Egypt, Ethiopia, and Arabia, since 1829–30, none possessed higher qualifications for the task; yet, with rare modesty, he attributes his own discoveries (as Newton to an apple his finding the laws of gravitation) to an accident; viz., to a couple of bricks, brought to him by a Nestorian dyer, who unearthed them whilst digging a foundation for stoves and boilers on the mound of *Khorsabàd*. (532) But, these two forlorn bricks were impressed with arrow-heads — things which Botta's education at once permitted him to appreciate. Ten years have since elapsed. The Louvre proudly displays his sculptured deterrations — national typography splendidly perpetuates his unaffected narrative — and, those who weigh science by "dollars and cents" may sneer at legislative munificence on learning that France, in 1849, had already voted $150,000 to eternalize Botta's Assyrian deeds; without either forgetting an individual's future, or considering the balance of an account-current between a man and his country thereby stricken. His consulate is now at Jerusalem.

An intimate friend, and enthusiastic spectator of the French Consul's achievements, commenced operations where the latter relinquished them. Henry Austen Layard — of noble Huguenot extraction — born at Ceylon, and brought up at Florence, is essentially a man of the East. Leaving England in 1839, he reached Mosul, 1842, by way of Germany, Russia, Dalmatia, the Bosphorus, Asia Minor, Persia, and Kusistàn. His performances are familiar to all readers of *Nineveh and its Remains*, 1849; and *Babylon and Nineveh*, 2d Exped., 1853. The letters LL.D. and M.P., and the office of Under Secretary of Foreign Affairs, tell how a nation can reward living merit: at the same time that "Eastern questions" point to eventualities not less nationally important. The British Museum consecrates for science the innumerable exhumations of Layard.

Great as have been, however, the exploits of these discoverers, they must not dazzle our vision from beholding the less ostentatious if archæologically superior researches of Rawlinson and of Hincks; but for whom, the cuneiform records of Nineveh and Babylon might have yet remained sealed books: although, so closely followed have these savants been by a Löwenstern, a De Longpérier and a De Saulcy; so materially aided by Birch, Norris, and other skilful palæographers; that by grouping them all into a "Cuneiform School" the invidious task of assigning a place to any one is cheerfully avoided. Our inquiry simply is, what have they all done in Assyrian *chronology?*

Let it first be observed "en passant," that the long lists of Chaldæan, Arab, Assyrian, and Babylonish sovereigns, preserved by Ctesias, Ptolemy, and the Hebrews; (533) coupled with the pseudo-antiquity popularly assigned to the Xth *Chapter of Genesis;* had occasioned the most exaggerated notions, about 1844–50, of the epochas to which these sculptures of

(531) *Nineveh and Persepolis;* London, ed., 1852.

(532) *Lettres à M. Mohl;* Découvertes à Khorsabad, 1845, p. 2: — *Monument de Ninive*, chap. ii., p. 23.

(533) FRASER's excellent *Mesopotamia*, pp. 47–50; and CORY's *Ancient Fragments;* supply the classical authorities.

Assyria should be attributed. Nowhere was this sentimentality exhibited more strongly than at the British Museum. Ninevite bas-reliefs of the 7th century B. C. were reverenced by pious crowds who looked upon them as if their carving had actually been coeval with the "Tower of Babel"; at the same time that Egyptian relics of the IVth Memphite dynasty, belonging to the 4th chiliad before C., and those stupendous granites of the XVIIth–XVIIIth dynasties, positively dating in the 16th–13th centuries prior to the same era, were passed over in contemptuous silence; although displayed in gigantic halls, whilst Assyria (for want of room) lay in an underground cellar! And yet, withal, the only monumental proof of the existence of either BaBeL, or NINWE, 1500 years B. C., depended then, as it does now, upon Thotmes IIId's "Statistical Tablet" of Karnac! (534) Nor, excited by the magnificence of their monumental resurrections, can we be surprised that the two explorers somewhat participated, at that time, in the general feeling.

But, the habit of dispassionate comparison of art (upon itself alone) among sculptured antiquities of every period and region collected in European Museums, had instinctively led thorough archæologists to pronounce the word "modern," over every fragment brought to London and Paris from Nimroud or Khorsabàd; and this before a single Assyro-cuneatic inscription had been deciphered. First to undertake this thankless office was De Longpérier; (535) who proclaimed, to shocked orthodoxy, that nothing found or published of Assyrian bas-reliefs could possibly ascend beyond the 9th century; at the same time that Khorsabàd had then not yielded anything older than the 7th–8th century B. C.

Nevertheless, it was published —

"On the most moderate calculation, we may assign a date of 1100 or 1200 before Christ, to the erection of the most ancient [palace]; but the probability is, that it is much more ancient:" (536) and maintained — "There is no reason why we should not assign to Assyria the same remote antiquity we claim for Egypt" [B. C. 3500?].

Col. Rawlinson too, whilst conceding that "the whole structure of the Assyrian graphic system evidently betrays an Egyptian origin: first organized upon an Egyptian model," (537) formerly considered the *Obelisk of Nimroud* to date about the 12th–13th century B. C.

Now, this age for Assyrian monumental commencements harmonizes perfectly with Egyptian conquests and dominion over much of that country, during the XVIIth dynasty, 15th–16th centuries B. C. It is merely the archæological attribution of any sculptures, yet found and published, to such an epoch that we contest. We are the last to curtail any nation's chronography; but, misled so often by hypotheses, we cease to depend any further upon arithmetic where not supported by positively archæological stratifications. Lepsius, it seems to us, has fairly stated the possibilities of *Chaldaic chronology*; (538) and future researches by cuneiform scholars will doubtless determine the relative position of each historical stratum as firmly for Assyria as has been already done for Egypt.

With these provisoes, we may safely present a synopsis of the last chronological results put forth by Layard. Possessing all the resources at present attainable, and profoundly versed himself in Assyrian studies, his tabulation of the monumental series of reigns inspires full confidence, at the same time that his results accord naturally with the histories of adjacent countries and people. (539)

ANTE-MONUMENTAL PERIOD.

Into this category are cast the vague and semi-mythical traditions of Nimrod, Ninus, Belus, and their several lines; which, according to classical writers, may ascend to 1903 years before Alexander, equivalent to 2234 B. C. (540)

---

(534) BIRCH: *Op. cit.*; 1846; p. 37: — *Two Egyptian Cartouches found at Nimroud*; 1848; pp. 161–177: — GLIDDON: *Otia*; p 103. Vide also BIRCH, *Annals of Thotmes III.*; Archæologia, 1853, xxxv. p. 160.

(535) *Revue Archéologique*, Oct. 1847: — *Galerie Assyrienne*, Musée du Louvre, 1849; p. 16; — *Revue Archéol.* Oct. 1850.

(536) LAYARD: *Nineveh and its Remains*; Am. ed., 1849; pp. 176, 179, 185.

(537) *Commentary on the Cuneiform Inscriptions*, &c.; 1850; pp. 4, 7, 21, 71, 73, 74.

(538) *Chronologie der Ægypter*; i. pp. 6–12.

(539) *Babylon*; pp. 611–625: — already RAWLINSON extends Assyrian antiquity to the 14th century B. C.; *Jour. R. Asiat. Soc.*, 1853, p. xviii., note.

(540) LEPSIUS: i. p. 10.

Genealogical Period.

This class embraces those *Assyrian Kings*, of whose reigns no *contemporaneous* monuments have been discovered, but who are recorded in the pedigrees or archives of their successors: distinguishing Rawlinson's reading by R, and Hincks' by H.

King (conjectural reading).		*About* B. C.
I.	Derceto (R.)	1250
II.	Divanukha (R.), Divanurish (H.)	1200
III.	Anakbar-beth-hira (R.), Shimish-bal-Bithkhira (H.)	1130
IV.	Mardokempad? } (R.)	
V.	Mesessimordacus? } (R.)	—
VI.	Adrammelech I. (R.)	1000
VII.	Anaku Merodak (R.), Shimish Bar (H.)	960

Monumental Period.

VIII.	Sardanapalus I. (R.), Ashurakhbal (H.) — North-west Palace, Nimroud	930
IX.	Divanubara (R.), Divanubar (H.)—Obelisk; cotemporary with Jehu	900
X.	Shamas Adar (R.), Shamsiyav (H.)	870
XI.	Adrammelech II. (R.)	840
XII.	Baldasi? (H.)	—
XIII.	Ashurkish? (H.)	—
XIV.	? Pul, or Tiglath-Pileser	750
XV.	Sargon	722
XVI.	Sennacherib	703
XVII.	Essarhaddon	690
XVIII.	Sardanapalus III. (R.), Ashurakhbal (H.)	—
XIX.	(Son of preceding)	—
XX.	Shamishakhadon? (H.)	—
	Fall of Nineveh	606

The chronological approximations of our sketch hinge upon the name of Jehu, king of Israel, who, on the *Obelisk of Nimroud*, is made tributary to Divanubar; thus establishing a synchronism about the year 885 B. C.

Everything yet discovered on the site of *Babel* seems to belong to the reign of "Nabukudurruchur (i. e., *Nebuchadnezzar*), king of Babylon, son of Nabubaluchun, king of Babylon" — not earlier than about B. C. 604.

Time, the performer of so many marvels in archæology, will assuredly enable us soon to attain greater Assyrian precision; already foreshadowed through the pending excavations of M. Place, and the personal studies of M. Fulgence Fresnel and of Col. Rawlinson, on the sites of Mesopotamian antiquity.

CHRONOLOGY—HEBREW.

"For a thousand years in thy sight are but as yesterday when it is past."—(*Psalms* xc. 4.)

"One day is with the Lord [IeHOuaH] as a thousand years, and a thousand years as one day." (2 *Peter* iii. 8.)

It would be affectation if not duplicity, on the part of the authors of "Types of Mankind," after the variety of shocks which the plenary exactitude of Hebrew chronicles has received at their hands, not to place everything Israelitish on precisely the same human footing as has been assigned to the more ancient time-registers of Egypt and of China, and to the more solid restorations of Assyria.

The reader of our Essay I, in the present volume, can form his own estimate of the historical weight that Hebraical literature may possess hereafter in scientific ethnography.

Monumental history the Hebrews have none. Even their so-called "Tombs of kings," owing to the absence of *inscriptions*, have recently occasioned a discussion among such deep archæologists as De Saulcy, Quatremère, and Raoul-Rochette, (541) that shows upon how tremulous a foundation their attribution rests. The "arch" and massive basements of Jerusalem's temples (discovered by Catherwood, Arundale, and Bonomi, 1832–3) may

(541) *Revue Archéologique;* 1851–'52. Also, De Saulcy: *Journey round the Dead Sea;* 1853; ii. p. 131.

belong to Zerubbabel's or to Solomon's edifices; or, in part, to the anterior *Jebusites*, for anything by tourists imagined to the contrary. In the absence of monumental criteria, we are compelled to give the Hebrews but a *fourth* place in the world's history; at the same time that justice to a people whose strenuous efforts to preserve their records has encountered more terrible obstacles and more frequent effacements than any other nationality, demands the amplest recognition.

The numerous citations and tables with which the subject of chronology has been already ushered, spare us from recapitulation of the manifold instances whereby the Text contradicts the versions; the numerical designations of a given manuscript, those of another; and the modern computations of one individual, the estimates of almost every other individual; whensoever the date of any Jewish event, anterior to Solomon's semi-pagan temple, is the object sought after.

In fact, we may now realize with Lepsius, that the strictly-chronological element was wanting in the organism of Hebrew, as of other Semitish, minds; until MANETHO *the Sebennyte*, about B. C. 260, first established the principles of chronology through Egyptian indigenous records; and, by publishing his results, in Greek, for the instruction of the Alexandria School, first planted the idea of human "chronology" upon a scientific basis. All systems of computation (heretofore followed by Christendom) take their departure, historically, from Manetho.

It is deeply to be lamented, for the sake of education, that no qualified translator has yet honored Anglo-Saxon literature with an English version of Lepsius's "Introduction" to his *Chronology of the Egyptians;* of which the writers, through the Chevalier's complaisance, have possessed the *first-half* since December, 1848, and the second since May, 1849. Impossible, we fear, until such translation be accessible, is it to convey to the majority of our readers, the *entirely-new* principles of chronological investigation this wonderful grasp (of a mind at the pinnacle of the culture of our time) has condensed into 554 pages quarto. Erudition stands humbled at the aspect of this volume's conscientious and universal probity of citation: at the same time that its perspicacity of arrangement is such, that those who, like ourselves, possess no acquaintance with German, can track the footsteps of its author almost paragraph by paragraph. Through the kindness of many Allemanic friends, the writers have been enabled to annotate their copies of the *Chronologie der Ægypter* with marginal and other notes that justify whatever assertions they respectively make upon an authority otherwise to them Germanically concealed: and, in consequence, with reference to Rabbi Hillel and many of the facts subjoined, they may confidently refer the reader of "Types of Mankind" to Lepsius's compendium; (542) as a ground-text which the writers' comparative studies of works in other tongues, more or less familiar, have resulted in deeming the highest, in these peculiar branches, of our common generation. In any case, a German scholar can easily verify our desired accuracy by opening a *printed* book; four copies, at least, of which are now even at Mobile, Alabama.

We have said that Manetho is the founder of the science called "chronology." We mean that he is the first writer who developed through the Greek tongue, at his era the language of Occidental science, those methods of computation in vogue from very ancient times among the sacerdotal colleges of the Egyptians. He is the exponent, not the inventor of his country's system: Eratosthenes, Apollodorus, &c., are his successors; together with Josephus, Africanus, Eusebius, and the Syncellus; whose Judaico-christian theories have been the sources of that fabric of superstition heretofore reputed to inform us concerning the epoch of God's *Creation*.

No doubt remains any longer that, centuries prior to Manetho, the Egyptian priesthood did possess chronological registers; because, aside from inferences patent in his predecessor Herodotus's "Euterpe," we have before our eyes in the *Turin hieratic papyrus* (dating in the 12th–14th century B. C., or 1000 years before Manetho) the same system, often with the same numerals, of reigns of *Gods*, *Demi-Gods*, and *Men*, that this chronographer subsequently expounded to the Alexandrian schools. Alas! Manetho's mutilators, not his

(542) *Einleitung;* 1849; pp. 14–20, 359–404, 405–410.

own imaginary inaccuracies, are the cause of that confusion of personages and dates, from out of which modern archæology is now beginning, through hieroglyphical collations, to emerge.

Of course, *Chinese* computations are distinct: being the production of other lands, other races, other histories, other worlds of thought and action. So, likewise, may be the lost Chaldæan systems, of which fragments survive through scanty extracts of Sanconiatho and of Berosus; or, as we shall see, through the more recent Sanscrit astrologico-cyclic fables of the Hindoos: but, with the above exceptions, and (if you please) of Mexico and Peru, there is no system of what we call "chronology" but is historically posterior to Manetho, whose era stands at the middle of the 3d century B. C.

This is facile of comprehension to the reader of our Essay I. He therein perceives that the oldest computatory data based upon Judaic traditions are found in the Greek *Septuagint;* being itself a collection of translations manufactured at Alexandria after B. C. 250, and before B. C. 130; in which, Alexandrian Greek dialects and Alexandro-Egyptian "sothic periods" of 1460 years, betray a people, an age, and a fusion of philosophical notions, such as could have been produced, through natural causes, in no locality upon earth but Alexandria; and that too during Ptolemaic generations subsequent to Manetho.

The next in order is the Hebrew Text. Its canonical antiquity, in its oldest and last form, cannot reach up to Ezra in the 5th century, and descends unto the Maccabee princes in the 2d century B. C., *i. e.* after the writer of the book called "Daniel." But, our *Introductory* has effaced the validity of textual numeration in any Hebrew codex (no MSS. being 900 years old); because, while on the one hand its radically discordant numbers show that, when the *Septuagint* was translated, the original Hebrew exemplar in its patriarchal enumeration either did not then exist, or must have been identical with its copied Greek version; on the other, the *Hebrew square-letter* character, of this Text's present form, not having been invented until the 3*d century after* C., the chronological elements now in the Text must originate from manipulations made above 400 years after Manetho.

Thirdly, and lastly, there is the *Samaritan* Pentateuch. Its numerical system altogether departs, for patriarchal ages, from both the Septuagint and the Hebrew Text. The age of its compilation is utterly unknown; but the palæographic shape of its alphabetic letters bring such MSS. as exist now to an epoch below that of our Hebrew Text itself. Supposing the rumored estimate of one *Nabloosian* codex did make that unique copy attain to the 6th century after C., such fact would merely prove our view to be correct; but, in Europe, no *Samaritan* MS. is older than the 13th century. In consequence, we cannot accept, in scientific chronology, any more than Siracides, the modern hypotheses of that "stultus populus qui habitat in Sicimis."

These facts being posited, one can understand the apparatus and the efforts made upon them by the learned Rabbi Hillel, about the year 344 after C., to place *Jewish* chronology upon a scientific basis that it never possessed before his labors. He was acquainted with Grecian calendrical computations; probably with the cycles of Meton and Callippus, the mathematical formulæ of Theon of Alexandria, and with the chronography of Africanus, perpetuator of Manetho.

A quotation from Lepsius has been submitted on a preceding page. Another extract will illustrate his views(543): —

"But then it is very improbable that Hillel went to work in the manner that Ideler believes. 'Evidently,' says Ideler, 'he started from the then-still-generally used (by the Jews) *Seleucidan era*, viz.: the autumn of the year 312 B. C. Calculating backwards, his next epoch was the destruction of the second Temple. This epoch he fixed at only 112 years (before); thus counting more than 150 years too little, and making Nebuchadnezzar contemporary with Artaxerxes I. Going back to the Building of the first Temple, the Exodus, the Deluge and the Creation, partly according to the express dates of the Bible, partly according to his explanation of those dates, he found, as the epoch of the *Minjan Shtaroth* beginning of the year 3450 of the World.' So gross and inconsistent an error of 160 years in so modern a time was *impossible* to a *savant* of the 4th century. But there is not much difficulty in explaining it, if we suppose, that the Rabbis, after the great *hiatus* in Jewish literature

543) *Chronologie*—"Kritik der Quellen"; i. pp. 363, 364.

(which began with the conclusion of the Talmud, 500 A. D. to the 8th century,) did receive the few general points, which Hillel had connected with his universal calendar, from him, and that then, only then, they began to fill up their universal history of 5000 years according to the records of the Old Testament. Indeed, we find neither in the Talmud nor even in the ante-Talmudic writings,—ex. gr. in the *Seder Olam Rabba*, one of the most ancient of these writings—the whole chronological fillings up. This seems to have taken place in the 12th century; consequently at the epoch of a long-previously commenced scientifico-literary barbarism. From the Creation to the Deluge, and the Exodus, they had only to follow the numbers of the Pentateuch to attain the given date (A. M.) 2448 = 1314 (B. C.). But thenceforward they based themselves upon the convenient number of 480 years to the Building of the Temple (in the 1st Book of *Kings*), and according to this they arranged the chronology of the time of the Judges. By this, then, was the real link of chronology dislocated for 160–170 years, which occasioned the displacement of all the succeeding members. Only when arrived at the next fixed point, in the year (A. M.) 3450 = 312 (B. C.), was it found, that the chain of events, for the given space from the Building of the first to that of the second Temple, was much too long. The history of the second Temple, built under Darius Hystaspis, down to Alexander, from whom the Greek era took its name, shrunk then at once from 184 to 34 years. At first this created little sensation, but afterwards the difficulties becoming greater, they were removed by the simple means of adopting Darius II. and (Darius) III,, as one and the same person. In this manner alone can we explain the singular phenomenon of an entirely dislocated and mutilated chronology, which notwithstanding possesses two firm and only-sure points; and at the same time offers us the most important and probably most accurate determination of the epoch of the Exodus by a really learned chronologist."

It is from the original that the reader must gather, what our space and objects permit us not to transcribe, the citations, &c., through which the author establishes his view conclusively. To us the important facts are these—1st, that the Jews had made no attempts at scientific chronology prior to the 4th century after C.; nor did they complete such as their later schools adopt until the 12th.—2dly, that, through their childlike prepossessions, and owing to their superstitious notions that the era of "Creation" could be humanly attained, they ciphered out a fabulous number, equivalent to "B. C. 3762," for a divine act, which their ignorance of the phenomena of astronomical and geological unceasing progression, led them to imagine *instantaneous*—"Fiat lux!"—and 3dly, that, having blundered by 160–170 years, only between the *Exodus* and Solomon's temple, they sank deeper into the mud when, in efforts to account for their own imbecilities, they made one man of *two* Dariuses in order to rob the world's history (184 *minus* 34) of 150 years! And it is such wretched stuff as this rabbinical arithmetic which is to be set up, forsooth, against the *stone-books* of Egypt and Assyria, the records of China, the annals of Greece and Rome at the age of Alexander the Great, and every fact in terrestrial history! Well might Lesueur indite the passage above quoted—"Nous sommes, depuis dix-huits cents ans, dupes de la sotte vanité des Juifs:" and justifiably may archæological science hold cheaply the acumen of the whole series of those who, amid other conceits, have adopted 480 years between Solomon's temple and the *Exodus*.

Before examining which fact, it may be expedient that we should set forth our own point of view, founded upon the same principles hitherto pursued, viz., that our process is always retrogressive; ever starting from *to-day*, as the known, and going backwards, in all questions of human registration of events.

The *era of Nabonassar*, if astronomy be certainty, is a point fixed, by eclipses, &c., in the year B. C. 747. Thence, backwards to the "5th year of Rehoboam," when Jerusalem was plundered by the Egyptian Sheshonk (of which event the hieroglyphical register stands at Thebes), we have a positive synchronism *about* the years 971–3, "B. C.;" for, in ancient chronology, asserted precision to a year or so is next to imposition. Thence, taking Solomon with his "chariots dedicated to the sun," and his Masonico-zodiacal *Temple*, for granted, we accept the era "1000 years B. C.," as an assumed fixed point when that temple was already completed. We say "assumed," because Calmét's date for the completion of this edifice is B. C. 1000; whilst Hales's is B. C. 1020: and, rather than trouble ourselves with ascertaining which of these computations may be the least wrong, we would greatly prefer discussing whether Solomon ever built a *Temple* at all. Why, if for the second, or

Zerubbabel's Temple, we have to choose among 19 biblical chronologers, whose *maximum* is B. C. 741, and *minimum* 479—if, for a Jewish event of scarcely 2400 years ago, we cannot through Judaic books get nearer the truth, according to "chronological" arithmetic, than 262 years, up or down—how much nearer are we likely to get to another Jewish event (itself fraught with preternatural dilemmas), supposed to have happened somewhere about 2853 years ago, when the epoch of the building of the first Temple depends upon what computation we may elect to adopt out of 19 different orthodox authorities for the age of the second?

Thus much for the sake of furnishing our colleagues with practical means of rendering ecclesiastical opposers of "Types of Mankind," if not less supercilious, at least more malleable; whenever these may be pleased to obtrude Jewish "chronography"—or, as it is fashionably termed, "the received chronology"—into the rugged amphitheatre of Egyptian time-measurement.

Archæologically speaking (not "chronologically"), there is no material objection to such assumption as Solomon's *Temple* at (*circa*) B. C. 1000; a few years more or less. Under this historical view, apart from episodic circumstances (to be discussed hereafter), archæology may rationally concede that Hebrew tradition, through alphabetic facilities developed not much less than *three* centuries posterior, does really contain chronological elements back to about 2853 years ago—say to B. C. 1000.

We continue with Lepsius—

"The question is now whether we must give up, for lost, the number 480 (to which we cannot attach greater importance than to the numerous simple "*Arbaïndt*," or *forties* [40*s*], in the same parts of Israelitish history); and with it, also, every chronological helm for events anterior to the Exode? But such is not the case, because we find, in the [so-called] Mosaic writings themselves, a true chronological standard, by which we can compute [the chronological weight of] the views hitherto held, and confirm anew the truthfulness of Egyptian record. Such a standard I conceive to be the *Registers of generations*."

Allusion has been made, in other parts of this volume, to the Nos. 7, 12, 70 or 72, as mystic in original association; and how the latter always, the former two frequently, are unhistorical wherever found. To these numbers (of cabalistic employment since the days of Jeremiah), we may now add, as equally vague in Hebrew chronography, all the "*arbaïndt*" or "forties." By opening Cruden's *Concordance* the reader can see a list of above 50, out of many more instances, where the presence of "forty" renders the narrative, in this respect at least, unsafe. Here is a schedule of some that are positively apocryphal; especially when, through a conventional *No.* 40, an event, in itself præternatural, is rendered still more impossible by the numerals that accompany it.

APOCRYPHAL FORTIES.

Old Testament.

1. *Gen.* vii. 4............ "40 days and 40 nights."
2. *Exod.* xxiv. 18...... "40 days and 40 nights."
3. *Numb.* xiii. 25...... "40 days."
4. *Deut.* ix. 25........ "40 days."
5. *Josh.* v. 6............ "40 years."
6. *Jud.* iii. 11.......... "40 years."
7. 1 *Sam.* iv. 18....... "40 years."
8. 2 *Sam.* v. 4......... "40 years."
9. 1 *Kings* xix. 8...... "40 days and 40 nights."
10. 2 *Kings* xii. 1....... "40 years."
11. 1 *Chron.* xxvi. 31.. "40th year."
12. 2 *Chron.* xxiv. 1... "40 years."
13. *Ezra* ii. 24........... "40 and *two*."
14. *Nehem.* v. 15........ "40 shekels."
15. *Job* xlii. 16.......... "*hundred* and 40 years."
16. *Psalms* xcv. 10..... "40 years."
17. *Ezek.* iv. 6............ "40 days."
18. *Amos* ii. 10......... "40 years."
19. *Jon.* iii. 4.............. "40 days."

New Testament.

20. *Matt.* iv. 2.......... "40 days and 40 nights."
21. *Mark* i. 13........... "40 days."
22. *John* ii. 20........... "40 *six* years."
23. *Acts* i. 3................ "40 days."
24. *Heb.* iii. 9............ "40 years."
25. *Rev.* vii. 4, xiv. 1, 3 "*hundred* and 40 *four* thousand."

"It is evident from the narratives in the Pentateuch, as well as in other books of the Holy Scriptures, that in ancient times the number 40 was considered not merely as a round number, but even as one totally vague and undetermined, designating an uncertain quantity. The Israelites remained in the desert during 40 years; the judges, Athniel, Ehud (*Septuag.*), Debora and Gideon, governed each 40 years. The same did Eli, after the Philistines had ravaged the country during 40 years. The 40 days of the increasing and the 40 days of decreasing of the waters of the Deluge are well known. But one of the most striking instances of this use of the number 40 is 2 *Sam.* xv. 7, where, during the 40 years of David's reign it is said: 'And after 40 years it happened that Absalom went to the king and said, Let me go to Hebron, that I may fulfil the vow which I have made to Jehovah.'

"The Apocryphic books go still farther. According to them, Adam entered the Paradise when he was 40 days old—Eve 40 days later. Seth was carried away by angels at the age of 40 years, and was not seen during the same number of days. Joseph was 40 years old when Jacob came to Egypt; Moses had the same age when he went to Midian, where he remained during 40 years. The same use of this number is also made by the Phœnicians and Arabs. [See *Dissertatio Bredovii de Georgii Syncelli Chronographia* (second part of the edition of Bonn) Syncellus, p. 33, *seq.*] We must not forget hereby the *Arbaïnât* (the forties) in Arabian literature; a sort of books which relate none but stories of 40 years, or give a series of 40, or 4 times 40 traditions. They have a similar kind of books, which they call *Sebayât* (sevens). Their calendar has 40 rainy and 40 windy days. Also in their laws the numbers of 4, 40, 44, occur very often. In Syria the graves of Seth, Noah and Abel are still shown. They are built in the usual Arabian style. Their length is recorded to be 40 ells, and thus I have found them by my own measuring. This may also account for the tradition that the antediluvian men were 40 ells high, that is, not 'about 40 ells,' but '*very tall.*' Only afterwards was this expression so naively misunderstood. The Arabs give, in the conversational language, the same sense to *sittîn*, 60, and *mïeh*, 100. I have already observed, in an earlier writing [*Zwei Sprachergleichende Abhandlungen* (Two lectures upon the Analogy of Languages), Berlin, 1836, pp. 104, 139], that of all the Semitic numerical words, *arbă*, 4, is the sole one which has no connexion whatever with the Indo-Germanic, and seems rather to be derived from *rab*, רב, 'much,' ארבה, 'the locust.' This would account for its undetermined use.'(544)

The historical spuriousness of the numeral 40, in its application to human chronology, may be illustrated by another example out of many. It is said, "Israel walked 40 *years* in the wilderness,"(545) after the Exode. On which Cahen:—

"It is probable that this itinerary contains but the principal stations: they are in number 42. In the first year they count 14 stations; in the last, or 40th, they count 8 stations; thus the 20 other stations occupied 38 years (*Jar'hi*, in the name of Moses the preacher). According to the ingenious remark of St. Jerome, the number 40 seems to be consecrated to tribulation: the Hebrew people sojourned in Egypt 10 times 40 years; Moses, Elias, and Jesus, fasted 40 days; the Hebrew people remained 40 years in the desert; the prophet Ezekiel lay for 40 days on his right side. This accordance shows us that Goëthe had some reasons for conjecturing that the 40 years in the desert might very well possess no historical certitude." (546)

Again—"Thus, during these 40 years, notwithstanding the miserable life which the Israelites had led in the desert, maugre the plagues, the maladies, and the wars, there was but a diminution of 1820 Israelites and an augmentation of [just!] 1000 Levites. Such results exist not within the domain of natural things, and consequently possess nothing historical." . . . "Savage tribes sing of their petty quarrels, their conquests and their disasters, upon the lofty tone of, and even loftier tone than, the greatest nations. Thus the septs along the river Jordan had their poets, their national ballads; these songs, there, as everywhere else, have preceded history. We have just read extracts from these productions, perhaps the most ancient that have reached us. It is probable that to them were afterwards added some events of a date much later than the political existence of Moabites, Edomites, &c." (547)

Finally, speaking of the "40 years" in the Sinaic desert, Cahen observes:—

"One finds in the Pentateuch only those events that occurred during the first *two* and the last or *fortieth* year. The history of the intermediary 37 years is totally unknown to us." (548)

All theological conjectures about this unhistoric interval are merely conjectures theological; because the Jews used the expression "forty," as we do "a hundred," for a vague number of anything uncounted. To Lepsius's numerous illustrations of the utter impossibility that uneducated nations or individuals can possess any clear ideas about *dates* for circumstances that may have happened during their respective lifetimes, we might add two parallels—the first (or Oriental) is that, in Egypt, if you ask an intelligent but illiterate

(544) LEPSIUS: *Chronologie der Ægypter:* i. pp. 15, 16, note.
(545) *Josh.* v. 6.
(546) CAHEN: iv. p. 158; note on *Numb.* xxiii. 1.
(547) CAHEN: *Op. cit.;* p. 134; note on the *two* censuses in the Desert: and p. 124, on BILAM and BALAK.
(548) *Op. cit.;* p. 96.

native his age, he cannot express it by *years;* but replies, that his stature was about so high (holding out his hand at the elevation required), *fee ayàm en-Nussàra*— "in the days of the Christians;" alluding to Napoleon's conquest of Egypt, 1798–1802: or else tells you that he had not a white hair in his beard, *fee hurrèekut el-Qalâa,* "at the fire of the citadel" of Cairo, 1825. The second (or Occidental) is, that no *Indian,* or *Negro,* in the United States (save among the paucity that have been educated), can tell you his own age, by *years;* but the one dates either from such a time when "he and Col. —— shot that *bar;*" or the other from when he butted for cheeses against another negro-kephalus at such a local election.

This introduces a question upon which European biblical commentators, ignorant of living Oriental customs, have gone sadly astray. Whenever the number of personages, in a given Hebrew pedigree, has been found insufficient to occupy (that is, to fill up naturally, without improbable longevity), the length of time required to suit the chronological scale a given commentator may have elected to invent or follow, it has been incontinently assumed, that the Hebrew *numerals* were right; and that the anomaly proceeds from the accidental loss of one, or more, intermediary ancestors, in the genealogical list. Thus, says the learned Dr. Prichard, (549) adopting the suggestions of the great Michælis:—

"The result is that the difficulty which seems to have induced some of the ancients to alter the text requires a different explanation. It can only be solved, as it would seem, by allowing an *omission* of several generations in the genealogies of the Israelites. At present only two generations are interposed between Levi and Moses. It is probable that several are *omitted.*"

So again the Abbé Glaire, (550) in respect to the two genealogies of *Joseph:*—

"The first (method) is to suppose that these names (*Ochosias, Joas, Amasias*) were wanting in the genealogical tables the evangelist made use of; an hypothesis the more probable that the names of intermediary persons are often missing in many genealogies of the Old Testament. . . . Esdras, in his genealogy, omits seven of his ancestors, by jumping from Amarias to Achitob II, father of Sadoc II. . . . The genealogy of Saul, for a space of 800 years, names but seven persons. . . . From Mardocheus to Jemini or Benjamin, who lived 1200 years before, but four are named. . . . From Reuben to Beera, who was carried captive by Tiglath-pilesar, they give us but 12 generations to fill a space of more than 1000 years. In the genealogy of Judith, for a space nearly equal, there are but 16 generations. By fixing, as is commonly done, the generation at 33 years, one perceives that there are a good many degrees omitted in these genealogies. . . . Grotius, upon whose acquirements one may confide without difficulty, assumes that this happens frequently, as may be seen in genealogical trees. *Sæpe eodem temporis spatio familias inter se comparatas generationes habere unam aut alteram plures et pauciores; quod in omnibus stemmatibus videre est.* 'Veut-on un example d'une grande inégalité de générations dans les différentes branches d'une même souche? Scripture affords one very striking. The children of Jacob (*Numb.* i. 3) each formed a branch or tribe. When, a year after their issue from Egypt, Moses, by the order of GOD, caused the numbering of these tribes, there was found among them a prodigious inequality; but the most surprising is that which was beheld between the tribe of Levi and that of Judah: the latter comprised 74,000 males above the age of 20 years, and the former 22,300 counting (even) those above one month.'"

One would suppose, so naïvely does the Abbé accept all these *numerals* as historical, that he was actually present! But these violent statistics are susceptible of more rational solution. Such attempts at reconcilement have their unique origin in the uncritical ideas of eminent scholars upon the true ages of the composition of the fragments extant of Jerusalem literature; which the perusal of our *suppressed* pages might supersede: and similar weak explanations would not have been thought of by any Orientalist (Fresnel, Lane, or Layard, for instance) who had actually resided among Semitic populations. Lepsius (551) is the first, that we are aware of, to have placed the matter in its true light.

We know that unlettered Arabian Bédawees do preserve, for centuries, orally from father to son, their individual and clannish genealogies; and this too for an almost infinite number of generations. They even thus consecrate, legally, the pedigrees of their blood-

(549) *Researches;* 1847; v. p. 559.

(550) *Livres Saints Vengés;* ii. pp. 284–285, 201–202; quoted chiefly from BULLET: *Réponses Critiques.*

(551) *Op. cit.;* pp. 365, 366.

horses. (552) But, as for defining the *length of time* each tribe, man, or horse, may have lived, that the Bédawee has no means of doing beyond his own grandfather's lifetime; and for which he has no *annual* calendar. Thus, in ante-Mohammedan history, "the battle of Khazaz," fought by the *Mâadd* tribes under Koulayb-Waïl against the Yemenite confederacy, is the earliest stand-point of Arabian historical tradition; (553) but the era before *Islâm* — 250 — to which such battle is assigned, has been computed, *for* these wild children of the desert, by later and highly-cultivated Arab historians, and at best conjecturally.

It would be foolish to deny to the sedentary and somewhat educated Hebrews, of days anterior to the Captivity, equal faculties of preserving their own *genealogies*, that we recognize among cognate Semitish and still more barbarous tribes of Arabia: nor is there any reason to doubt the existence of *genealogical lists*, stretching backwards for many generations, from the days of Ezra. (554) These may even have ascended, ancestor by ancestor, to the times of Abraham. (555) But it was one thing to preserve, through saga, rythme, song, or oral legend, the *names* of predecessors in their natural order; and quite another to guess at the duration of these ancestors' respective lifetimes, or to infer, through traditionary events with any of the earlier ancestors coetaneous, the chronological remoteness of the age during which they lived, excepting approximately. In consequence, Lepsius (and we entirely agree with him) sustains, that the *genealogies* of the Hebrews are probably right; but that the chronological computations accompanying these lists are certainly wrong. Indeed, of this last fact there can be no doubt, when we remember that Rabbi Hillel, in the fourth century after Christ, was the first to regulate Jewish chronology by the verbal literalness of the Hebrew Text; independently of fabulous numeration such as that borrowed by Josephus from an Alexandrian Greek system adopted by the writers of the *Septuagint*. The manifest interpolation of an Egyptian "Sothic-period" of 1460–'61 years (so felicitously discovered Mr. Sharpe, *supra*, pp. 618, 619), obviates further necessity for recurrence to the spurious chronology of the Greek version.

These numerical estimates, we now see, are both modern and erroneous. But, to convince the reader of the fact; and to prove that the 480 years between the first Temple and the Exodus are erroneous; we copy Lepsius's synopsis, after remarking that, just as in all ancient pictures the artist gave colossal proportions to the figures of gods, or heroes, while the plebeian classes receive pigmaic stature, so among the antique Israelites, in their organic absence of "art," it was customary to assign to the royal line, or High-Priest pedigree, the attributes of longevity together with extensively-procreating capabilities; and to measure such exalted patricians by generations of 40 *years*; at the same time that to the vulgar herd were ascribed generations of only 30!

"I give here a Table of the principal genealogies, in which the Levitish generations follow in the same order as they are recorded in 1 *Chron.* chap. 7 (according to the LXX; in the Hebrew Text, ch. v. and vi.). These are preceded by the genealogical chain from Levi to Zadok according to Josephus, and also his list of the *High-Priests* from Aaron to Zadok. Lastly comes a genealogical table of Judah. Albeit I have excluded some other genealogies, *ex. gr.*, the three of Ephraim (*Numb.* xxvi. 35 — 1 *Chron.* viii. 20; xxi. 24–27), because they were in evident confusion and led to no result.

"The first column," says Lepsius, (556) "contains the patriarchs from Abraham to Amram; next, 12 leaders (chiefs) of the people, beginning with Moses, who seem to have been regarded as representatives of the 12 *generations* of 40 *years* each; and thus to have occasioned the calculation of 480 years [as the chronological interval between the *Temple* and the *Exode*]. Ewald and also Bertheau give another list—for the subject, in general, admits of no precision: albeit, for us, the recognition of the *division into* 12 *parts* of this period is important. But one, likewise, (VIII.) of the aforesaid genealogies (1 *Chron.* vii. 39–43) contains 12 *generations of one and the same family*. It might therefore be possible that this last list, and not the other, had originated the calculation of 480 years. This list has the peculiarity of beginning with Gersom, the *first-born* of Levi. But the most noble line of the Levites was that of the *High-Priests*, who descended from Aaron and Kahath (I.): this list, as well as that of Musi (IX.), contains only 11 *generations*. This may be the reason why the LXX count but 440 *years*."

---

(552) Layard: *Babylon:* pp. 220, 221, 250, 326–331.

(553) Fresnel: *Arabes avant l'Islamisme;* 1st Letter; 1836; p. 16.

(554) *Ezra;* ii. 59–62; *Nehem.* vii. 61–64.

(555) *Numb.* i. 5–18, 26.

(556) *Chronologie;* pp. 367–371.

THE JUDAIC LINEAGES

Generations from ABRAHAM to DAVID.	Years.	Plebeian generation.	Series of *High-Priests* to ZADOK. [Josephus, A. J., 5, 11, 5.]		ZADOK'S Parentage. [Josephus, A. J., 8, 1, 3].		I. AARON'S Generations. 1 *Chron.* vii. 1–9, 50–53; *Ezra* vii. 2–5.		II. Generations Gersom-LIBNI. 1 *Chron.* vii. 20, 21. (=VIII.)	III. Generations Kahat-AMINADAB 1 *Chron.* vii. 22–24. (=VI.)	
1. Abraham	100 *or*	30									
2. Isaac	100	30									
	200		—		—		|		—	—	
3. Jacob	100	30									
		90									
1. Levi	100	30			1. Levi		1. Levi		1. Levi	1. [Levi]	
2. Kahath	100	30			2. Kaathos		2. Kahath		2. Gersom	2. Kahath	
3. Amram	100	30			3. Amarames		3. Amram		3. LIBNI	3. AMINADAB	
	400	90									
1. Moses	40		1. Aaron	30	1. AARON	30	1. AARON	30	1. (Jahath)	1. Korah	30
2. Joshua	40		2. Eleazares	30	2. ELEAZARES	30	2. *Eleasar*	30	2. Simma	2. Assir	30
3. Othniel	40		3. Phineeses	30	3. PHINEESES	30	3. *Pinehas*	30	3. Joah	3. Elkana	30
4. Ehud	40		4. Abiezeres	30	4. Iosepos	30	4. *Abisua*	30	4. Iddo	4. Ebjassaph	30
5. Samgar	40		5. Bouki	30	5. Bokkias	30	5. *Buki*	30	5. Serah	5. Assir	30
6. Barak	40		6. Ozis	30	6. Iothamos	30	6. *Usi*	30	6. Jeathrai	6. Thahath	30
7. Gideon	40		7. Ilei	30	7. Maraïothos	30	7. Serahja	30	—	7. Uriel	30
8. Jephtha	40		8. (Phineeses)	30	8. Arophaios	30	8. Merajoth	30	—	8. Usija	30
9. Simson	40		9. Iokabes	30	9. Akitobos	30	9. Amarja	30	—	9. Saul	30
10. Eli	40		10. Akimelekos = Akias	30	10. Zadokos	30	10. Ahitub	30	—	10. [Jonathan]	30
11. Samuel, Saul	40		11. Abiatharos with Zadok	30			11. *Zadok*	30	—		
12. David	40										
	480			330		300		330			300

The practical result of which is, that *all* chronologers, by not perceiving the surplusage due to these absurd generations of 40 *years*, have assigned about 160–170 years too much between SOLOMON and MOSES; and *ergo*, the Exodus must descend from B. C. 1491, its date in the English version, to B. C. 1314–'22, *circa*.

After studying the above Table, the reader may perhaps perceive with us several things not generally known: —

1st. — That the whole of this Jewish chronology is unhistorical; because it is not based upon positive records of the number of years each personage lived, but it was fabricated, long after their times, by semi-scientific, semi-literary, computators; whose process was to assign impossible generations of 40 *years* to their country's pre-historic heroes; and then, having obtained a maximum-period in which the lives of such worthies were thereby inclosed, these modern computators (probably about the 3d century after C., when the Books were re-transcribed into the *square*-letter alphabet) apportioned to each hero, in the anew-manipulated Hebrew Text, those irreconcileable *numerals* that have come down to our time.

2d. — That, whether the *genealogical* catalogues be right or not, the chronology is a later intercalation.

FROM ABRAHAM TO DAVID.

IV. Generations Elkana-AMASAI. 1 *Chron.* vii. 25–28. (=VII.)		V. Generations Merari-MAHELI. 1 *Chron.* vii. 29, 30.		VI. HEMAN'S Parentage to JEZEHAR. 1 *Chron.* vii. 36–38. (=III,)		VII. [HEMAN'S Parentage] to AMASAI. 1 *Chron.* vii. 33–36. (=IV.)		VIII. ASSAPH'S Parentage to JAHATH. 1 *Chron.* vii. 39–43. (=II.)		IX. ETHAN'S Parentage to MUSI. 1 *Chron.* vii. 44–47.		DAVID'S Parentage to JUDAH. *Ruth* iv. 18; 1 *Chron.* ii. 4–13; *Matth.* i. 3–6; *Luke* iii. 32, 33.	
—		—		—		—		—		|		—	
1. [Levi]		1. Levi		1. Levi		1. [Levi]		1. Levi		1. Levi		1. Judah	
2. Elkana		2. Merari		2. Kahath		2. Elkana		2. Gersom		2. Merari			
3. AMASAI (and)		3. MAHELI		3. JEZEHAR		3. AMASAI		3. (JAHATH)		3. MUSI		2. Perez	
1. Ahimoth	30	1. Libni		1. Korah	30	1. Mahath	30	1. Simei	30	1. Maheli	30	1. Hezrom	30
2. Elkana	30	2. Simei		2. [Assir]	30	2. Elkana	30	2. Sima	30	2. Samer	30	2. Ram	30
3. Elk.Zophai	30	3. Usa		3. [Elkana]	30	3. Zuph	30	3. Ethan	30	3. Bani	30	3. Aminadab	39
4. Nahath	30	4. Simea		4. Ebjassaph	30	4. Thoah (Thohu)	30	4. Adaja	30	4. Amzi	30	4. Nahesson	30
5. Eliab	30	5. Hagija		5. Assir	39	5. Eliel (Elihu)	30	5. Serah	30	5. Hilkia	30	5. Salma	30
6. Joram	30	6. Asaja		6. Thahath	30	6. Jeroham	30	6. Ethni	30	6. Amazia	30	6. Boas	30
7. Elkana	30	——		7. Zephanja	30	7. Elkana	30	7. Malchija	30	7. Hasabja	30	7. Obed	30
8. Samuel	30	——		8. Asarja	30	8. Samuel	30	8. Baesaja	30	8. Maluch	30	8. Isai	30
9. Vasni	30	——		9. Joel	30	9. Joel	30	9. Michael	39	9. Abdi	30	9. DAVID	30
10. ——	30	——		10. [HEMAN]	30	10. HEMAN	30	10. Simea	30	10. Kisi	30		
								11. Berechja	30	11. ETHAN	30		
								12. ASSAPH	30				
	300				300		300		360		330		270

3d.— That, as said before, there are no recorded *dates* in the Jewish Scriptures that are trustworthy; that, it is we moderns who must make Hebrew chronology for the antique Jews — who, until Rabbi Hillel, had not thought of doing it themselves; — and that, in these restorations, we cease to tread upon historical ground so soon as we retrograde to Solomon's era, said to correspond to B. C. 1000. Beyond that cipher, Jewish chronology is all conjecture, within a few approximate limitations.

Moses, or the *Hebrews*, being unmentioned upon Egyptian monuments of the 12th–17th centuries B. C., and never alluded to by any extant writer who lived prior to the *Septuagint* translation at Alexandria (commencing in the 3d century B. C.), there are no extraneous aids, from sources alien to the Jewish books, through which any information, worthy of historical acceptance, can be gathered elsewhere about him or them.

With these emphatic reservations, we are quite willing to consider Lepsius's computative synchronisms as not merely the most scientific but the only probable. His estimates place the Jewish *Exodus* in the reign of Pharaoh Menephthes, of the XIXth dynasty, about the year 1318 B. C.; (557) or rather *between* the years 1314 and 1322 B. C.: if we have understood our authority correctly: (558) to which we add the following comparative view

(557) *Chronologie;* p. 379, compared with pp. 335–337. (558) Vide GLIDDON: *Hand-book;* 1849; p. 44.

of *dates* for the Mosaic Exodus, as computed by Usher from the *Hebrew Text*, and generally appended to the English translation authorized since the reign of king James, A. D. 1611; and by Hales from the *Greek Septuagint version*. The new synchronisms between Hebrew and Egyptian events, put forward by Lepsius, may assist the hierological student in authenticating monumental history through what are still called the *established* dates of Scripture. It will be remarked that, while Hales extends, Lepsius reduces the antiquity assigned to each Israelitish era by archbishop Usher.

BIBLICAL SYNCHRONISMS.

Epoch of	*Pharaonic Contemporaries.*	A. D. 1660. USHER.	A. D. 1830. HALES.	A. D. 1849. LEPSIUS.
ABRAHAM	AMUNOPH III. (*Memnon*)	B. C. 1920	2077	about 1500
JOSEPH	SETI I. (*Sethos*)	" 1706	1863	" 1460
MOSES	RAMSES II. (Jewish oppression	" 1491	1648	1394—1328
Exodus (B. C. 1322?)	MENEPTHA			1328—1309

Jewish computation by "forties" ceases so soon as we ascend beyond Moses; who was 40 *years* old when he fled from Egypt; 40 *years older* when, after dwelling with Jethro, he returned to liberate his people; and *oldest by* 40 more years when he died at the age of 120 — "but no man knoweth of his sepulchre *unto this day*."(559) Vico supplies a formulary:

I. — The *indefinite nature of the human mind* is the cause that man, plunged in ignorance, *makes of himself* the rule of the Universe.

It is from this truth that are derived the two human tendencies thus expressed: *Fama crescit eundo et minuit præsentia famam.* Fame has travelled, since the world's *Creation*, a very long road; and it is during the voyage that she has collected *opinions so magnificent*, and so exaggerated, upon *epochas* which to us are but imperfectly known. This disposition of the human intellect is indicated to us by Tacitus, in his 'Life of Agricola,' where he tells us: — *Omne ignotum pro magnifico est.*" (560)

From Moses backwards to Abraham, post-Christian Jewish computation assumed 100 years for each generation; but every dozen MSS. of the Text or versions differ; and the general principle followed seems to have been, to make generations the longer, in the ratio that the lifetime of a given hero was more and more distant from each Judæan writer's day. The model copied was a Grecian theogonic idea, because the Esdraic Jews proceeded by the *four Hesiodic ages;* considering their own period to be the *Iron;* the Davidic the *Brazen;* the Mosaic the *Silver;* and that from the Abrahamic to the Adamic, to have been the *Golden* age of Hebrew humanity. To Moses, in consequence, they assigned only 120 years of longevity; but his worthier antecedents had their holier lives extended along a sliding scale, of which the numbers 240, 480, and 960, are the simple arithmetical proportion: their divisor being "40."

Here, then, we have finally arrived at the great fact; which, in different or less outspoken words, all the scientific authors we have quoted are at this day agreed upon: viz.: that the *Jews knew not an atom more of* "Humanity's Origins" *than we do now;* and that, as they really had no human historical ancestor before Abraham (whose epoch floats between Lepsius's parallel at 1500, and Hales's at 2077, B. C.), there is no *chronology*, strictly so-called, in the Bible, anteriorly to the Mosaic age; itself vague for one or more generations.

This posited, we shall close further argument with a Table of *Hebrew Origins;* conformably to the same principles upon which we have already tabulated the distinct histories of Egypt, China, and Assyria. Each of these nationalities possesses its *historical*, *semi-historical*, and *mythical* times. And, inasmuch as it is conceded by every true historian that the Israelites (under the literary aspect in which they first present themselves to the gentile world), had been previously educated in *Chaldæa;* it will be interesting to place the ante-diluvian "patriarchs" of the preceptors alongside those of the pupils. Berosus, Philo Byblius, Julius Africanus, Alexander Polyhistor, Eusebius, and the Syncellus, have preserved for us transcripts of the original Chaldæan catalogues: the whole texts of which are accessible in Cory's *Ancient Fragments*, or in Bunsen. (561)

(559) *Deut.* xxxiv. 6. (560) VICO: *Scienza Nuova;* 1720; "Elemento 1mo." (561) *Egypt's Place;* i. pp. 704–719.

Mythological Periods.

Symbolical Ante-Diluvian Patriarchs.

Græco-Chaldæan Decade.			*Hebræo-Chaldæan Decade.*	*Phœnico-Chaldæan Decade.*	
1. Alorus..........	years	36,000	ADaM	Protogonos	1. = First-born.
2. Alaparus........	"	10,800	SeT*t*	Genos, Genea	2. = Genus, family.
3. Almelon.........	"	46,800	ANoS*h*	Phos, pur, phlox	3. = Fire, light, flame.
4. Ammenon......	"	43,200	KINaN	Cassios, Libanos	4. = Cassius, Libanus (*mount's*).
5. Amelegarus.....	"	64,800	MaHaLaLeL	Memrounos, ousoos	5. = Celsus, "par cœlo," wood.
6. Daonus..........	"	36,000	IRaD	Agrios, alieus	6. = Peasant, hunter, fisher.
7. Edoranchus....	"	64,800	K*h*eNUK	Chrusor, hephaistos, artifex, geinos	7. = { Vulcan, fire, artificer, earth-worker.
8. Amempsinus...	"	36,000	MeT*t*USeLaK*h*		
9. Otiartes..........	"	28,800	LaMeK	Agros, agroueros	8. = Rustic, agriculturist.
10. Xisuthrus......	"	64,800	NuK*h*	Amunos, magos	9. = Warrior, magician.
				Misor (Sydyc, Saduc)	10. = Egypt, and the "just" *king*, MELCHISEDEK.
	Years	432,000			

CHALDÆAN DELUGE.

1st *Note.* — The 36 *Decans* of the Zodiac, (562) multiplied by the 12 months of the year, give the mystic number 432. The "grand year" of Astronomy — or the time anciently supposed to be required for the sun, planets, and fixed stars, to return to the same celestial starting-point — was at first 25,000, then 36,000, and lastly 432,000 years; being the supposed duration of the *ten* Græco-Chaldæan generations. A *Deluge* terminated the cycle. (563)

2d *Note.* — The *Phœnico-Chaldæan* list, derived from SANCONIATHO, presents us with the Greek *translations*, not with the real names of its lost Oriental original. The Phœnicians had originally crossed from the Persian Gulf to the Mediterranean, and their intercourse with Chaldæa was incessant; while the two people spoke *Semitic* dialects. More saliently than the other two forms of the same theogony, this Phœnician stream exhibits the rationale of its "ex post facto" construction. According to it, we have the stages of *family, hunter, fisherman, artizan, husbandman, soldier, priest,* and *king,* through which antique humanity developed itself. A parallelism seems to be preserved in the offshoots of the Adamic stem in *Genesis,* where ABEL *the wandering shepherd* is hateful to CAIN *the sedentary peasant.*

Chaldaic Ethnological Division — [contained in Xth Genesis.]

Theoretical Post-Diluvian Commencements.

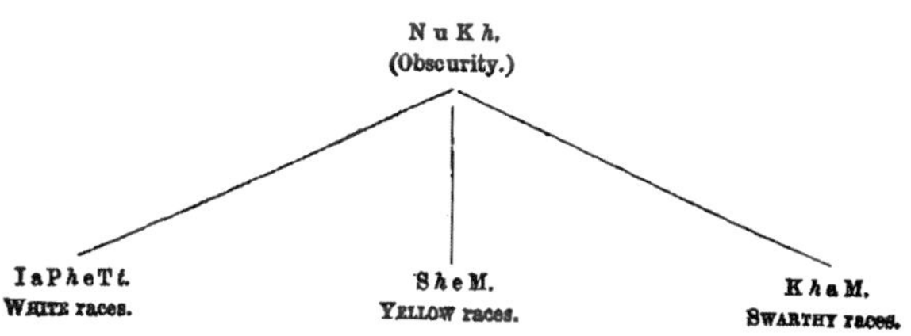

Babylonish Theory for Diversity of Tongues.

"City and Tower of B a B y L"-on = *confusion* = "B a B e L-babblings."

Hebrew Geographical Origins.

ARP*h*a-KaSD = ORFA-the-*Chaldæan* (District).
SaLaK*h* = SALACHA (City).
AĉBeR = the-*yonderer* (Tribe).
PeLeG = a-*split* (Earthquake?).

Earliest Legendary Ancestors.

RêU.
SeRUG.
NaK*h*UR.
T*t*eRaK*h*.

(562) LEPSIUS: *Chronologie;* i. pp 66–76.

(563) DE BROTONNE: *op. cit.;* pp. 234–246.

JUDAIC META-HISTORICAL PERIOD.

"Thou shalt no more be called AB-RaM (FATHER of the HIGH-land = *Aramæa*)—
Thy name shall be.............. AB-RaHaM" (FATHER of a MULTITUDE). (564)

Abrahamidæ.

ITsKhaK = "laughter."
IâKoB, surnamed ISRAEL.
(12 Signs of the Zodiac, 12 *Sons*, 12 Tribes of Israel.)
Levi.
Kohath.
Amram.
MOSES.

JUDAIC HISTORICAL PERIOD.

MOSES — assumed epoch .... 14th century B. C.

[Interval between *Exodus* and the *first Temple*, about 314–322 years.]

SOLOMON — (Chronological times begin) .... about B. C. 1000
First monumental synchronism, REHOBOAM and SHESHONK.................... " 971–3

[*Alphabetic-writing* does not begin until the 9th–8th century B. C.]

HILKIAH — "found a book of the Law" .... " 620
Jerusalem burnt, and *Captivity* commenced .... " 586

EZRA — *Second Temple* — "VIIth year of Artaxerxes" .... " 457
Esdraic School — "Renaissance" begins .... " 400

ALEXANDER — visits Jerusalem.................... " 332

Alexandria School:

MANETHO — the earliest known *chronologist*.................... " 260
Septuagint translations commence.................... " 250

ANTIOCHUS-*Epiphanes* — plunders Jerusalem, and burns the books .... " 164
DANIEL, the Satirist, wrote .... " 160

JUDAS, the Hammerer — restores the books.................... " 150
Maccabee coin-letters extant — SIMEON.................... " 142
Septuagint translations finished.................... " 130

SIRACIDES, *Canon* closes.................... " 130

(Roman dominion — B. C. 49.)

CHRISTIAN ERA.

BETWEEN B. C. 7 and A. D. 3; but *assumed at* 1853 *years ago.*

HEROD — decorates the *Third Temple* with pagan Hellenic architecture .... A. D. 15

Fall of Jerusalem:

TITUS razes the Temple to its foundations .... " 74

JOSEPHUS — receives the *Templar*-copy of the Hebrew Text, as a present from VESPASIAN at Rome, about .... " 75

(Earliest citation of "Gospels" — JUSTIN MARTYR, died about 166.)

Controversies between the *Fathers* and the *Rabbis* here commence.

The *Oriental* Jews transcribe the *Text* into the *square-letter* alphabet, during the 3d century after C.

HILLEL HANASSI — computes *Jewish chronology*.................... " 344
The *Masoretic points* begun by Rabbis of Tiberias .... " 506

Oldest Manuscripts of Greek LXX extant, 5th century after C.
Oldest Manuscripts of *Hebrew* Text extant, 10th century after C.
King James's English Version, printed A. D. 1611.

---

(564) *Genesis;* xvii. 5; — CAHEN: i. p. 42, note 5.

CHRONOLOGY—HINDOO.

"Originally this [Universe] was naught but SOUL: nothing else existed active [or passive]. HE had this thought—*I will create worlds*. It is thus that He created these [divers] worlds, the water, the light, the mortals, and the waters. This water is the [region] above the sky, (365) which the sky supports; the atmosphere contains the light; the earth is mortal; and the regions beneath are the *waters*."—(*Vedas*, "Aitarêya A'ran'ya"—PAUTHIER: *Liv. Sac.*, p. 318.)

Although, in our Table of *Alphabetical origins*, we have dealt as sternly with unhistorical Indian documents, as with the metaphysical fables of all other nations, it may be well to say a few passing words upon Hindoo *chronologies;* lest it be supposed that we are not prepared to reagitate that which, to us, is no longer a "vexata quæstio." Referring the reader to the citations from Wilson, Turnour, and Sykes, therein adduced, we repeat, that there is no connected chronology, to be settled archæologically by existing monuments, throughout the whole Peninsula of Hindostan, of a date anterior to the fifth century B. C.

That vast centre of creation swarmed with varied indigenous and exotic populations, from epochas coeval with the earliest historical nations; but, if any of these Indian philosophers ever composed a rigidly-chronological list of events, we have lost the record; or, what is more probable, the chronological element was wanting in the organism of Hindoo minds, until the latter received instruction (from Chaldæan magi scattered by Darius) through the Persians;—tuition greatly improved after contact with the Bactrian Greeks during the third century B. C.

In any case, the extract subjoined will show that the antiquarian dreams of Sir W. Jones and of Colebrooke are now fleeting away.

"Whether safe historic ground is to be found in India earlier than 1200 B. C., according to the chronicles of Kashmere (*Radjtarangini*, trad. par Troyer), is a question involved in obscurity; while Megasthenes (*Indica*, ed. Schwanbeck, 1846, p. 50) reckons for 153 kings of the dynasty of Magadha, from Manu to Kandragupta, from 60 to 64 centuries; and the astronomer Aryababhatta places the beginning of his chronology 3102 B. C. (Lassen, *Ind. Alterthumsk.*, bd. I., s. 473–505, 507, and 510)."

From Humboldt (566) we pass on to Prichard; whose Hindoo prepossessions of 1819 (567) have not only been nullified by Egyptian discoveries, but, with the learned ethnographer's usual candor, have become greatly modified by his own later reflections. (568) The inquirer can judge from the perusal of the passages referred to whether he can make out a fixed chronological idea, in India, prior to the age of *Budha* in the sixth century B. C.

Lepsius (569) contents his objects (confined to a general review of the world's chronological elements) by mentioning, that the Hindoo astronomical cycle *kali yuga* falls on the 18th Feb. 3102 B. C.; that the Cashmeerian king Gonarda I. is supposed to have reigned about B. C. 2448; and that king Vikramaditya's era is fixed at B. C. 58. But he also shows that the 4th–5th centuries B. C. comprise all we can depend upon, archæologically, in Hindoo history.

However, by opening the excellent work of De Brotonne, (570) the reader will easily perceive how the Chaldæan astrological cycle of 432,000 years became extended by later Brahmanical pundits to one, equally fabulous, of 4,320,000 years: and inasmuch as this fact merely invalidates *Sanscrit* hallucinations the more, we are fain to leave Hindoo chronology in the same "slough of despond" in which we found it.

Reader!—the task proposed to myself in the preparation of these three *supplementary* Essays here ends. It was assumed under the following circumstances:—

(565) This is the same cosmogony as that of COSMAS-Indicopleustes, herein-before described. Indeed, the notion was universal; and, in theography, is so still.

(566) *Cosmos;* transl. Otté; 1850; ii. p. 115.

(567) *Analysis of Mythology.*

(568) *Researches into the Physical History of Mankind;* 1844: iv. pp. 98–139.

(569) *Chronologie;* i. pp. 4–5.

(570) *Filiations;* i. pp. 238, 239, 414–433.

Within the past five years, various sectaries (momentarily suspending polemics amongst one another) had entered into a sort of tacit combination to assail those who, like Morton, Nott, Van Amringe, Agassiz, and others, were devoting themselves to anthropological researches. Each of the above-named gentlemen has successfully repelled the intrusions of dogmatism into his especial scientific domain.

In these literary "mêlées," it has so happened that my surname has been frequently made the target for indiscreet allusions on the part of certain *teologastri;* without any provocation having been given on my side, through a single personality, in the course of ten years' lectureship upon Oriental archæology in the United States. To treat such in any other manner than with silent indifference would have been unbecoming, as well as, at the moment of each offence, unavailing. I preferred abiding my own convenience; and, in the foregoing Part III., have indicated an easy method of carrying "the war into Africa."

I believe that, thereby, good service is done in the general cause of the advancement of knowledge, and in the special one of my favorite study, *Archæology*. Geologists, Naturalists, and Ethnologists (absorbed in the promotion of positive science through the discovery of new facts), have rarely devoted time adequate to the mastery of Hebraical literature; and, in consequence, they are continually laying themselves open to chagrin and defeat in the arena of theological wranglings. My former pursuits (in Muslim lands) were remote from Natural Science, and as they disqualify me from sharing the labors of its votaries, I have thought that a contribution like the present, to the biblical armory of scientific men, might be of utility; even if it should merely spare them the trouble of ransacking for authorities generally beyond the circumference of their higher sphere of research: at the same time that a work such as "Types of Mankind" would be deficient unless the Hebrew department of its themes were to some extent complete. To future publication [*supra*, pp. 626, 627], I reserve further analyses which, without these preliminary Essays, would be unintelligible to ordinary scriptural readers. Confident of her own strength, Archæology (let *one* of this science's thousand followers hint to her opponents) neither courts nor deprecates biblical or any other agitation, and will prosecute her investigations peaceably while she can, otherwise when she must.

Repeating the direct and manly language of Luke Burke — to whose conception of a real "Ethnological Journal" scientific minds will some day accord the homage that is its due:—

"For all our arguments, there is the ready answer that our statements directly contradict the express words of Scripture, and must therefore be false, however plausible they may appear. We may reply that the word of God cannot be in opposition to genuine history, any more than it can oppose any other truth, and that therefore the passages in question cannot be a portion of this word, or if so, that they cannot have hitherto been properly understood. But experience has abundantly proved that such answers as these give satisfaction to very few, until facts have become so numerous and unequivocal that further opposition is madness. In the meantime, a war of opinion rages, embittered by all the virulence of sectarian partisanship, and the credulous and simple-minded are taught to look upon the advocates of the new doctrines as the enemies of morality, religion, and the best interests of man. For ourselves, we have no ambition to appear in any such light, nor shall we quietly submit to be placed in such a position." (571)

And for myself — whilst thoroughly endorsing the sentiments of a valued friend and colleague — I cannot better express the feelings with which I close my individual portion of an undertaking that has occupied the thoughts and hands of some men not unknown in the world of science, than by applying to our antagonists the last words ever written by me at the dictation of him to whom, with being itself, I owe all that mind and heart still hold to be priceless after more than forty years' experience of a wanderer's life: —

"*La medicina diventa amara. Spero che sarà salutifera. Intanto, si prenderà.*"(572)

G. R. G.

(HOWARD'S — MOBILE BAY, 20th July, 1853.)

(571) "Critical Analysis of the Hebrew Chronology" — *Ethn. Jour.;* London; No. I., June, 1848; pp. 9, 10.

(572) JOHN GLIDDON, United States' Consul for Egypt (1832-'44): *Letter to H. Ex.* BOGHOS YOUSSOUF *Bey* — MOHAMMED ALI'S *Prime Minister* — "Cairo, li 5 Febbrajo, 1841."

APPENDIX I.

REFERENCES AND NOTES.

No. (of Notes, &c.)

1 Ethnological Journal, London, 1848; June 1, No. I.
2 Op. cit., pp. 1, 2. An excellent précis of the meaning and scientific attributes of "Ethnology" has long been published by the venerable Jomard, in Mengin, Histoire d'Égypte, 1839, iii. p. 403.
3 Nat. Hist. of Man, London, 1848. p. 6.
4 Varieties of Man, London, 1851.
5 North British Review, Aug., 1849.
6 Op. cit., p. 6.
7. Knox, Races of Man, Philadelphia ed., 1850.
8 Burke, op. cit., p. 30.
9 Researches, v. p. 564.
10 Jacquinot, Considerations générales sur l'Anthropologie (Voyage au Pole Sud), Zoologie, 1846, ii. p. 36.
11 Nott, Two Lectures on the Biblical and Physical Hist. of Man; New York, 1849, p. 64.
12 The Friend of Moses, New York, 1852; Preface viii, and Text, pp. 442, 446, 449-51, 492-7.
13 Briefe aus Ægypten und Æthiopien, Berlin, 1852, p. 35.
14 Genesis, vii., 19-23. We quote the Hebrew Text; referring the reader to Cahen, La Bible, Traduction Nouvelle, Paris, 1831; Tom. i. p. 21.
15 Cf. Jacquinot, op. cit., chap. i. From this remarkably scientific work we have borrowed freely in this chapter, and elsewhere.
16 We ought to mention that Dr. Pickering favored us with the sight of his pages while they were yet in "proofs."
17 Op. cit., pp. 161, 163.
18 Op. cit., p. 41.
19 Races of Men, pp. 75-99.
20 Des Races Humaines, p. 169.
21 Christian Examiner, Boston, July, 1850.
22 Nott, Two Lectures, 1849.
23 Researches, ii. p. 105.
24 Proceed. Acad. Nat. Sciences; Philadelphia, 10 Sept., 1850, p. 82—Additional Observations on Hybridity in Animals, "Reply to the Rev. John Bachman, D.D.," Charleston Medical Journal, 1850, p. 8.
25 Bodichon, Études sur l'Algérie, Alger, 1847, p. 135.
26 Jacquinot, op. cit., p. 173.
27 Wood-cut, fig. 1. L'Égypte Ancienne, 1840, Pl. I., and Champollion-le-Jeune's description in pp. 29-31.
28 Rosellini, Mon. dell'Egitto, M. R. clvii., clvi., ix., &c. Mon. Stor., iv. pp. 238-44; iii. pp. 1, 433, seq. Lepsius, Denkmäler, Abth. iii, Bl. 136.
29 See the discussion in Bishop Warburton's Divine Legation of Moses; and in Munk, Palestine, pp. 146-150.
30 Hennell, Origin of Christianity, 1845, pp. 8-21.
31 Amédée Thierry, Histoire des Gaulois, Paris, 1844.
32 Strabo, lib. iv. p. 176—Fr. ed.
33 Thierry, p. xxxv., Introd. W. de Humboldt held the same opinion.
34 Hist. de la Filiation et des Migrations des Peuples, Paris, 1837; i. pp. 294-336.
35 British Association for the advancement of Science, 1850; reported in London Literary Gazette.
36 Antiquités Celtiques Antédiluviennes.
37 Retzius, cited in Morton's MSS.
38 Schmerling, Recherches sur les Ossemens Fossiles, Liège, 1833, i. pp. 59-66: referred to in our Chapter XI.
39 Vide infra, Part II., pp. 469, 470.
40 Edwards, Des Caractères Physiologiques des Races Humaines, &c., Paris, 1839.
41 Op. cit., p. 22.
42 Paulmier, Aperçus généalogiques sur les descendants de Guillaume, Rev. Archéol., 1845, p. 794, seq.
43 Virey, Hist. Nat. du Genre Humain, Disc. Prélim., i. pp. 14, 15.
44 On the question of hair, consult the microscopic experiments of Mr. Peter A. Browne, in Proceed. Academy Natural Sciences, Philadelphia, Jan. and Feb., 1851; also Ibid., in Morton's Notes on Hybridity, second Letter to Editors "Charleston Med. Jour.," 1851, p. 6.
45 Wood-cut, fig. 2. Italie, Didot's Univers Pittoresque.
46. August, 1849; American ed.
47 Edwards, op. cit.
48 Wood-cut, fig. 3. Pouqueville, Grèce, Pl. 9.
49 Wood-cut, fig. 4. Op. cit., Pl. 84.
50 Wood-cut, fig. 5. Bunsen, Ægyptens Stelle, ii., frontispiece.
51 Wood-cut, fig. 6. Pouqueville, op. cit., Pl. 85.
52 Wood-cut, fig. 7. Rosellini, M.R., Pl. xx., fig. 66.
53 Wood-cut, fig. 8. Ibid., Pl. xxii, fig. 82. N.B. The profiles are reduced with exactitude; but we have altered the eyes from the Egyptian canon of art to ours.
54 Edwards, op. cit. Mr. Gliddon's two years' residence in various parts of

No. (of Notes, &c.)

Greece led him, he tells me, to observe the same fact: particularly among the Speziotes; whence also sprung Canaris, the bravest Greek Admiral of the Revolution. — J. C. N.

55 Études, pp. 153, seq.

56 Wood-cut, fig. 9. Crania Æg. p. 54; from Rosellini, M. R. 161; M. S. iv. 53, 62, 250. Compare Wilkinson, Manners and Cust., i. pl. 62, fig. 2, *a*, *b*; and p. 367; with Osburn, Testimony, p. 137.

57 Morton's inedited Letter to myself, "Philadelphia, 23 Nov. 1842." — G. R. G.

58 Layard, Babylon, 1853, pp. 144, 231. We attribute differences of physiognomy chiefly to the ethnographic inferiority of Assyrian artists.

59 Phys. Hist. 1841, iii. pp. 24–5.

60 Varieties of Man, 1851, pp. 551–2.

61 De Brotonne, Filiations et Migrationes des Peuples, Paris, 1837.

62 In order that we may not be suspected of considering Plato's ethical romance about the "Atalantic Isles" to be historical, we refer the reader to Martin, Études sur le Timée de Platon, cited hereinafter.

63 The Archæology and Pre-historic Annals of Scotland, Edinburgh, 1851, pp. 700–1.

64 Genesis xi. 31; xii. 1, 2, 5 — Cahen, i. p. 31.

65 Genesis xvii. 5; Ib., p. 42.

66 Genesis xvii. 15; — Lanci, Paralipomeni, 1845. Travellers have not only hunted for, but narrate how they have actually found the "double cave" they call Machphelah! (Vide report of Syro-Egypt. Soc., Nov. 8—in London Athenæum, Nov. 19, 1853; p. 1391.)

67 Genesis xxiv. 3, 4; — Cahen, pp. 65–6.

68 Genesis xli. 45; — Lanci, Paral., i. p. 26.

69 Genesis xxxviii. 2.

70 Exodus ii. 19.

71 Exodus ii. 21.

72 Exodus xii. 38;—Cahen, Text, ii. p. 50.

73 Leviticus xxiv. 10.

74 1 Kings xi. 1, 2.

75 Crania Æg., pl. xi. fig. 2; p. 47.

76 Birch, Criteria, in Otia, p. 84.

77 Layard, Babylon, p. 610.

78 History of the Jews.

79 The Asmonean, New York, 27 March, 1850, contains a confirmatory article on the Jews of Malabar, translated from the Parisian "Archives Iraelites."

80 Missionary Researches, p. 308.

81 Remarks on the Mats'Hafar Tomar, or "Book of the Letter," an Ethiopic Manuscript: Syro-Egypt. Soc., London, 1848.

82 Encyclopædia Britannica.

83 Phys. Hist., 1844, iv. pp. 82, 83.

84 Wood-cut, fig. 13—Dubeux, Tartarie.

85 Borrow, Gipsies in Spain.

86 Lest our positions should be questioned, we refer to Prichard for Continental instances, to Wilson for the Pre-Celtic in Scotland and Scandinavia, to Logan, Crawfurd, and Earl, for those among islanders of the Indian Archipelago.

87 Races of Men; vol. ix. U. S. Exploring Exped., 1848, p. 305.

88 Wood-cut, fig. 14—Layard, Babylon, pp. 152, 153.

89 Wood-cut, fig. 15—op. cit., pp. 582–584.

90 Wood-cut, fig 16—op. cit., p. 105.

91 Wood-cut, fig. 17—op. cit., p. 583.

92 Wood-cut, fig. 18—op. cit., p. 538.

93 Wood-cut, fig. 19—Wilkinson, Man. and Cust., i. p. 384, pl. 69, fig. 8.

94 Lepsius, Auswahl, Leipsig, 1840, "Canon der Proportionen"; — ibid., Briefe aus Ægypten, Berlin, 1852, pp. 105, 106; —and Birch, Gallery of Antiquities, Br. Museum, pl. 33, fig. 147.

95 Rev. Archéol., 1844, p. 213, seq.; 1847, p. 296, seq.:—Commentary on the Cuneiform Inscrip., 1850, pp. 4–7.

96 Wood-cut, fig. 20—Botta, Mon. de Ninive, pl. 36.

97 Wood-cut, fig. 21—ibid., pl. 68 bis.

98 Polyhym., lxxvii.; Bonomi, Nineveh, pp. 182, 301.

99 Wood-cuts, figs. 22, 23 — Botta, op. cit., pl. 14.

100 Wood-cut, fig. 24 — Lettres de M. Botta sur ses découvertes à Khorsabad, 1845, pl. xxii., and p. 28.

101 Essai de déchiffrement de l'Écriture Assyrienne, 1845, pp. 22–25.

102 De Longpérier, Galerie Assyrienne, 1850, p. 16; and Nos. 1, 12, 27, 33.

103 Gliddon, "Hist. Sketches of Egypt," No. 5, New York Sun, Jan. 14, 1850.

104 Wood-cut, fig. 25 — Botta, Mon. de Ninive, pl. 45.

105 Wood-cut, fig. 26 — Layard, Monuments of Nineveh, folio pl. 42.

106 Wood-cut, fig. 27—Layard, Babylon, pp. 150, 143–4.

107 2 Kings xviii.; Isaiah xxxvi.

108 Wood-cut, fig. 28—Layard, Babylon, pp. 617–9.

109 2 Kings xv. 19–21.

110 Wood-cut, fig. 29—Layard, op. cit., p. 361.

111 Vide infra, Part III., p. 714.

112 Deuteron. xxiii. 8, 9; Cahen, v. p. 99.

113 Egyptian Cartouches found at Nimroud, R. Soc. Lit., Jan. 1848, p. pp. 164–71

114 Mr. Birch's translation—Private letter to G. R. G.

115 Wood-cut, fig. 31 — Rosellini, M. R., pl. xii. fig. 46; — Conf. Bunsen, Ægyptens Stelle, iii. p. 133.

116 Bonomi, Nineveh and its Palaces, 1852, pp. 77, 78.

117 Babylon, pp. 153–9, 280–2, 630–1.

118 Egypt. Inscrip. in Bibliothèque Nationale, 1852, p. 17.

119 Wood-cut, fig. 32 — Layard, Babylon, p. 630: — Lepsius, Denkmäler, Abth. iii. Bl. 88.

120 Babylon, 623.

121 Birch, Stat. Tablet of Karnac, 1846, pp. 29, 37: — Gliddon, Otia Ægyptiaca, p. 103.

122 Birch, in Layard's Babylon, p. 630: — or Lepsius, Auswahl, Taf. xii. line 21.

123 Wood-cut, fig. 33—Rosellini, M. R., pl. i. fig. 2: — Conferre Lepsius, Denkmäler, Abth. iii. Bl. i., at Berlin. Lepsius (Letters, pp. 278, 381) calls her Amunoph's "mother, Aahmes-nufre-Ari"—"Amenophis I. and the black Queen Aahmes-nefruari." That she is painted black, as well as red, no one disputes; but did the Negro-black pigment ever accompany such osteological structure?

124 Crania Ægypt. p. 47.

No. (of Notes, &c.)

125 Wood-cuts, figs. 34, 35—Lepsius, Denkmäler, Altes Reich, Dyn. IV., Grab 75, Abth. ii. Bl. 8, 10.
126 Wood-cut, fig. 36—Bunsen, op. cit. ii. Frontispiece.
127 Wood-cut, fig. 37—Afrique Ancienne, Carthage, Univ. Pittor., from a coin.
128 Wood-cut, fig. 38—idem.
129 Wood-cut, fig. 39—Rosellini, M. R. pl. 157; M. S. iv. p. 237:—Osburn, Egypt's Testimony, pp. 114–6, fig. 1.
130 Wood-cut, fig. 40—M. R. 151, M. S. iv. p. 82:—Wilkinson, Man. and Cust. i. pl. 69, fig. 7:—Birch, Stat. Tablet, p. 34.
131 Wood-cut, fig. 41—M. R. 161, fig. 1; 159, fig. 3; M. S. iv. p. 120:—Morton, pl. xiv. fig. 20, p. 48.
132 Rawlinson, Persian Cuneiform Inscrip. of Behistun, 1847, p. 270.
133 Wood-cut, fig. 43—Vaux, Nineveh and Persepolis, 1851, pp. 350–1.
134 Letronne, Civilisation Égyptienne, 1845, pp. 30–43.
135 Rawlinson, op. cit. p. xxviii.
136 Wood-cut, fig. 44—Coste et Flandin, Perse Ancienne, pl. 18.
137 Rawlinson, op. cit. p. 323.
138 Wood-cut, fig. 45—Perse Ancienne, pl. 154.
139 De Sacy, Antiquités de la Perse, et médailles des rois Sassanides, Paris, 1793; pp. 12, 64; A, No. 3—recopied in Perse Ancienne.
140 Woodcut, fig. 46—Perse Ancienne, pl. 185
141 Perse Ancienne, pl. 49, bas-relief A.
142 Woodcut, fig. 47—Perse Ancienne, pl. 51, bas-relief D.
143 Layard, Monuments of Nineveh, 1849, folio plate; Nineveh and its Remains, ii. pp. 329–31:—well described by Bonomi, op. cit. pp. 287–95.
144 Wood-cut, fig. 50—Rosellini, M. R. pl. 103, and 87; M. S. iii. part 2, p. 157:—Morton, Crania Ægypt. p. 63.
145 Pauthier, Chine, pp. 417. 427, 429. According to Callery and Yvan (L'Insurrection en Chine, depuis son origine jusqu'à la prise de Nankin, Paris, 1853) the present Chinese insurgents let all their hair grow, as their ancestry did under the Mings, to distinguish themselves from the Tartar usurpers.
146 Lepsius, Chronologie, i. p. 379. Ibid., Discoveries, transl. Mackenzie, p. 381.
147 De Sola, Lindenthal, and Raphall; New Transl. of the Scriptures, London, pp. 46–7:—Genesis xi. 10–26.
148 Monumenti Storici, ii. p. 461, seq.
149 Apochrypha, xiv. 17.
150 Wood-cuts, figs. 44 to 71—Rosellini, Monumenti Reali, pl. i. to xxiii.; and Mon. Storici, ii., "Iconografia de' Faraoni." Our selections are arranged in accordance with the more recent improvements of Egyptian chronology.
151 Prisse, Suite des Monumens de Champollion, 1848, pl. x.:—but compare Lepsius, Denkmäler, Abth. iii. Bl. 100. Ibid., Ægyptischen Götterkreis, 1851, pp. 40–5. Ibid., Briefe aus Ægypten, 1852, pp. 89, 362.
152 Morton, Cr. Æg. p. 44, pl. xiv. 3; from Rosellini.
153 Colossus at Aboosimbel; M. R. pl. vi. fig. 22.
154 Chron. der Ægypter, i. pp. 321–2, 358, 379.
155 Notes upon an Inscription in the Bibliothèque Nationale of Paris, Trans. R. Soc. Lit. 1852, iv. pp. 16, 17, 21.
156 Gliddon, Chapters, p. 22; and Otia, p. 134.
157 Wood-cuts, fig. 71, bis—Rosellini, M. R. pl. 79.
158 Ibid., M. R. pl. clx. lxxx.; M. S. iii. pp. 2, 95, seq.; iv. pp. 245–9:—Morton, Cr. Æg. p. 55:—Osburn, Test., p. 121:—Birch, Tabl. of Karnac, pp. 14, 15–35.
159 Morton's inedited MSS.—Letter to Mr. Gliddon, entitled, "Reflections on Mr. G.'s Ethnological Charts," 1842; corrected by Dr. Morton's autographic notes, Philadelphia, 23d March, 1843. We shall refer to it as "Morton's MS. Letter."
160 Wood-cut, fig. 74—Rosellini, M. R. clvi. and lx; M. S. iii. pp. 1, 433, seq.; iv. pp. 228–44:—Lenormant, Cours d'Histoire Ancienne, 1838, pp. 322–36:—Champollion-le-Jeune, Lettr. d'Egypte, p. 250, seq.:—Champollion-Figeac, Ég. Anc. pp. 29–31, pl. i.;—Wilkinson, Topog. Thebes, 1835, pp. 106–7:—Man. and Cust. i. pp. 364, 371, pl. 62, No. 4, fig. *a*:—Mod. Egypt. ii. p. 105:—Osburn, Testimony, pp. 22–7, 114, 143:—Birch, Stat. Tab. Kar. p. 20.
161 Wood-cut, fig. 75—Lepsius, Denkmäler, Abth. iii. Bl. 136, fig. 37 *a*.
162 Woodcut, fig. 76—Rosellini, M. R. clxi. fig. 1; clix. fig. 3; M. S. iv. p. 150:—Morton, Cr. Æg. p. 48, pl. xiv. 20.
163 Denkmäler, Abth. iii. Bl. 136, fig. *d*.
164 Woodcut, fig. 78—Rosellini, M. R. clxi; M. S. iv. pp. 91, 251:—De Saulcy, Recherches, Inscrip. de Van, 1848, p. 26.
165 Wood-cut, fig. 80—Rosellini, M. R. lxix.; M. S. iii. part. 2, p. 29:—Birch, Gallery, pp. 93, 97, pl. 38:—Morton, p. 46, pl. xiv. 24. It is moulded in colors at the British Museum.
166 Wood-cut, fig. 81—M. R. cli.; M. S. iv. p. 82, seq.:—Wilkinson, M. and C. i. p. 384, pl. 69, fig. 7;—Osburn, p. 53;—Birch, Stat. Tab. p. 34.
167 Wood-cut, fig. 82—Rosellini, M. R. clix.:—Champollion-Figeac, pp. 208–9, pl. 62:—Hoskins, Ethiopia, p. 329, pl. i. ii.:—Morton, p. 41, pl. xiv. 22;—Wilkinson, M. and C. i. pl. iv. p. 379:—Birch, Gallery, p. 80; and Stat. Tab. p. 61:—Prisse, Salle des Ancêtres, Rev. Archéol. 1845, p. 11, and note. N. B. After this page was stereotyped, we received Mr. Birch's freshest paper (Annals of Thotmes III., 1853) wherein he assigns these KeFa to the Island of Cyprus. Vide infra, pp. 479–480, voce "KTtIM."
168 Wood-cut, fig. 83—Rosellini, M. R. clix; M. S. iii. p. 435; iv. p. 234:—Birch, Gallery, pp. 88–9, 97, pl. 38:—Stat. Tab. pp. 13–14.
169 Woodcuts, figs. 84, 85—Rosellini, M. C. xxii.:—Wilkinson, i. pl. iv.:—Champollion-Figeac, pp. 376–8:—Morton, p. 50; pl. xiv. 21:—Osburn, Testimony, p. 52:—Hoskins, Ethiopia, plates, part

No. (of Notes, &c.)

iii. first line, p. 332:—Birch, Stat. Tab., pp. 18-9: — Pickering, Races, p. 372; also, Geog. Distribution, 1854.

170 References as above.

171 Wood-cut, fig. 86—Rosellini, M. C., xlix; M. C., ii. pp. 254-70: — Wilkinson, M. and C., ii. p. 99: — Mod. Egypt, 1843, ii. p. 237:—Osburn, Antiquities, Relig. Tract Soc., 1841, pp. 220-1: — Keith, Demonstrations of Christianity:—Taylor, Illustrations of the Bible, 1838, pp. 79-84:—Kitto, Cyclopædia, i. pp. 353-4: —Morton, Cr. Æg., p. 47: — Lepsius, Denkmäler, Abth. iii. Bl. 40: compare ibid., Dyn. IV., Grab I., Abth. ii. Bl. 96 for "chin sprouts."

172 See references under Nos. 144, 145.

173 Wood-cut, fig. 88—Rosellini, M. R., lxiii.; M. S., iii. part ii. p. 12:—Morton, p. 48, pl. xiv. 19.

174 Wood-cut, fig. 89—Rosellini, M.R., clvii.; M. S., iv. p. 237; — Osburn, Test., pp. 114-6, plate, fig. 1.

175 Wood-cut, fig. 90—Lepsius, Denkmäler, Abth. iii. Bl. 116, fig. *a*.

176 Wood-cut, fig. 91 — Rosellini, M. R., lxxxiii; M. S., iii. part ii. p. 103: — Champollion-Figeac, pl. 79:—Morton's MS. letter.

177 Wood-cut, fig. 92 — Rosellini, M. R., cxlxxx. fig. 7; M. S., iv. pp. 91-4.

178 Wood-cut, fig. 93 — Rosellini, clviii; M. S., pp. 234, 239: — Birch, Gallery, pp. 89, 104:—Osburn, p. 27:—Morton, p. 46, pl. xiv. 23:—Layard, Babylon, pp. 142, 146, 628.

179 Lepsius, Denkmäler, Dyn. XIX. *a*, Abth. iii. Bl. 136; compared with Rosellini, M. R., pl. clv.; M. S., iv. pt. i. pp. 228-43. In common with Morton we were always at a loss to account for the presence of *two* white races in Rosellini's copy of this tableau. It turns out that an error of *coloring* on the part of the Tuscan artists was the unique cause of such perplexities; because they have tinted this figure *light flesh-color*, instead of tawny yellow.

180 Wood-cuts, figs. 97, 98—Rosellini, M. R., lxvii.; M. S., iii. part ii. p. 126:—Birch, Gallery, p. 99, pl. 38: — Osburn, pp. 77, 124.

181 Wood-cuts, figs. 99, 100 — Rosellini, M. R., clx.; M. S., iv. p. 235: — Champollion-Figeac, pp. 30-1, pl. i. fig. 4:—Osburn, pp. 114, 142-3.

182 Wood-cut, fig. 101 — Rosellini, M. R., cxliii. fig. 9.

183 Wood-cut, fig. 102 — Rosellini, M. R., cxliii. fig. 5.

184 Wood-cut, fig. 103 — Rosellini, M. R., cxliii. fig. 10.

185 Wood-cut, fig. 104 — Rosellini, M. R., cxliii. fig. 3.

186 Wood-cut, fig. 105 — Rosellini, M. R., cxliii. fig. 8.

187 Wood-cut, fig. 106 — Rosellini, M. R., lxv.; and Morton, p. 47. Compare with these heads, and with that one in M.R., cxliii. fig. 11; M. S., iv. p. 96 (also Wilkinson, M. and C., i. pp. 370-1; pl. 62, fig. 3, *a*, *b*, *c*:) what Layard (Babylon, p. 355) has written about the *Shairetana* of hieroglyphics contrasted with the *Sharutinian* in the cuneiform sculptures.

188 Researches, ii., chap. x., xi., pp. 193-205.

No. (of Notes, &c.)

189 Ibid., op. cit., p. 220. How is it possible that Dr. Prichard, in 1837, could have known nothing of the triumphant missions of France and Tuscany to Egypt of 1828-30—when all Europe rang with applause?

190 Appendix to first edition to the Natural History of Man, London, 1845, pp. 570-583; quoted in Dr. Patterson's Memoir of Morton, ubi supra.

191 Sopra i Popoli Stranieri introdotti nelle Rappresentanze Storiche de' Monumenti Egiziani — Annali dell' Instit. di Corr. Archeol., Roma, 1836, pp. 333-50.

192 Égypte Pharaonique, Paris, 1846, ii. pp. 352-4.

193 Prisse, Trans. R. Soc. Lit., 1841:—Gliddon, Appeal to the Antiquaries, London, 1841, p. 53:—Wilkinson, Materia Hieroglyphica, 1824, part ii. pl. 2; and Text, p. 118;—Top. of Thebes, 1835, p. 420, &c.:—Mod. Eg., 1843, ii. pp. 223-6:—Hand-book, 1857, pp. 306-7, 392-3: — Leemans, Lettre à M. Salvolini, 1840, pp. 149-51: — L'Hôte, Lettres, 1840, pp. 27, 93, 99, 131, 185, 198: —Perring, Trans. R. Soc. Lit.; followed by Morton, Cr. Æg., p. 54:— Hincks, On the Egyptian Stele, 1842, pp. 1, 18-9; Age of the XVIIIth Dynasty, 1843, p. 5:—Bunsen, Ægyptens Stelle, iii. p. 58. The Revue Archéologique contains the following—1845, Prisse, Legendes Royales, pp. 457-74; Lettre à M. Champollion-Figeac, p. 730; 1847, Antiquités Égyptiennes, pp. 693-723:—Leemans, Lettre à M. Witte, pp. 531-41:—1849, De Rougé, Lettre à M. A. Maury, pp. 120-3;—1851, Maury, Dynasties Égyptiennes, pp. 180-2: — Rosellini, Cartouches, Nos. 69, 69 bis: — For. Quart. Review, "Egyptian Hieroglyphics," Jan. 1842, p. 157: — Pauthier, Sinico-Ægypt., 1842, Frontispiece: — Prisse, Suite des Monumens, 1847, Preface:—Birch, Tablet of Ramses II., p. 24: — Ampère, Recherches, Rev. des Deux Mondes, 1846-7: — Lepsius, Ægyptischen Götterkreis, 1851, pp. 37-46: — Briefe, 1852, p. 368: — Denkmäler, iii. 111.

194 Denkmäler, Abth. iii. Bl. 111. Even Lepsius's copies slightly differ among themselves — compare Bl. 99 with 100, 103, and 109.

195 Crania Ægyptiaca, p. 54—from Perring's paper in Trans. R. Soc. Lit., London, 1843, i. p. 140.

196 Letters, transl. Mackenzie, p. 297. Conf. Denkmäler, Abth. iii. Bl. 113.

197 Rosellini, M. R., xv. fig. 63.

198 Lepsius, Auswahl; and Wilkinson's Turin Papyrus.

199 Wood-cut, fig. 110—Dyn. XII., Abth. ii. Bl. 141.

200 Wood-cut, fig. 108 — Rosellini, M. R., xxvi. xxvii. xxviii.; M. S., i. p. 189; iii. p. 48, seq.; M. C., i. p. 56: — Denkmäler, Altes Reich, Dyn. XII., Abth. ii. Bl. 31.

201 Stat. Tab. Karnac, p. 5.

202 Hist. Tab. of Ramses II., p. 28.

203 Letter to M. Humboldt, "Korusko, Nov. 20, 1843," London Athenæum, 2 March, 1844. Compare Briefe, 1852, p. 97-100.

No. (*of Notes, &c.*)

204 Discoveries in Egypt, Ethiopia, and the Peninsula of Sinai, in the years 1842–1845; London, 1852, pp. 108–10.
205 Denkmäler, Abth. ii. Bl. 123–33.
206 Geognostische Karte von Ægypten, Wien, 1842.
207 Wood-cut, fig. 111—Abth. ii. Bl. 107, Grab 2.
208 Wood-cut, fig. 112—Abth. ii. Bl. 109, Grab 2.
209 and 210 Wood-cuts, figs. 113, 114—Abth. ii. Bl. 73, Grab 26.
211 and 212 Wood-cuts, figs. 115, 116—Abth. ii. Bl. 10, "Pyr. v. Giseh," Grab 78.
213 Wood-cut, fig. 117—Abth. ii. Bl. 8, "Pyr. v. Giseh," Grab 75.
214 Woodcut, fig. 118—Abth. ii. Bl. 20, 22, "Pyr. v. Giseh," Grab 24; Briefe, pp. 36–8.
215 Wood-cut, fig. 119—Abth. ii. Bl. 2, "Wadi Maghara."
216 Abth. ii. Bl. 39 *f*; and Briefe, p. 336.
217 Researches, ii. p. 44. Where not referred to others, our citations are also taken from Prichard.
218 Beke, Journal. R. Geog. Soc., xvii.; and in Gliddon, Hand-book, 1849, pp. 26–33.
219 Ritter, Géog., transl. Buret, 1836, i.; and Jomard, Notes pour un Voyage dans l'Afrique Centrale, 1849, pp. 19–20.
220 This fact is established by D'Eichthal (Hist. et Origine des Foulahs), by Hodgson (Notes on the Sahara and Soudàn), by Perron (Transl. of Voyage du Cheykh Mohammed-el-Tounsy), by Jomard (Observations sur le Voyage au Darfour, &c.), and by Ritter, i. pp. 432–7.
221 Gliddon, Hand-book, p. 35.
222 Beke, Sections, in Map of Journey; Jour. R. Geog. Soc., xvii.
223 See all authorities in D'Eichthal.
224 Researches, ii. p. 97.
225 Op. cit., ii. p. 343.
226 Op. cit.
227 Prichard, ii. p. 129:—Beke, Jour. R. Geog. Soc.
228 Op. cit., ii. p. 132:—Harris, Highlands of Ethiopia, 1843:—Fresnel, Mém. sur le Waday, 1848:—Beke, Essay on the Sources of the Nile, 1848:—Origin of the Gallas, 1848:—Observations sur la communication supposée entre le Niger et le Nil, 1850:—Jomard, Sur la pente du Nil Supérieur, 1848.
229 Beke; and Newman; Trans. Philological Soc., London, 1843–5, i. and ii.
230 Larrey, Notice sur la conformation physique des Égyptiens; Descrip. de l'Égypte, ii.
231 Essai sur les Mœurs des habitants modernes de l'Égypte—id., ii. part 2, p. 361.
242 Prisse, Oriental Album, Madden, London, 1846, pl. 28, 29:—Pickering, Races, pl. xii. pp. 221–4.
233 Cherubini, Nubie, pp. 50, 51.
234 Gliddon, "Excursus on the Berbers," Otia, pp. 117–46.
235 "Et-Tullàk b'-et tellàteh," or "triple divorce."—G. R. G.
236 Cr. Æg., pp. 58–9: Gliddon, Otia, p. 119.
237 Tablet of Ramses II., 1852, p. 21.
238 Prichard, ii. p. 135.
239 Travels in Nubia, p. 439.
240 2 Chron. xii. 3.
241 Wiseman, Lectures, p. 136.

No. (*of Notes, &c.*)

242 Nott, Unity of the Human Race (Reply to "C."), Southern Quart. Rev., Jan. 1846, p. 24.
243 Champollion, L'Égypte sous les Pharaons, 1814, i. p. 255—"Coptic MS.":—Wilkinson, Mod. Eg. and Thebes, 1843, ii. p. 312—"Inscription of King Silco."
244 Tribus des Ababdeh et des Bicharis, Magazin Pittoresque, Paris, Nov. 1845, pp. 371–3.
245 Gliddon, Otia, pp. 134–5.
246 Compare Briefe aus Ægypten, pp. 220, 251, 263.
247 Gräberg de Hemso, Specchio geografico e statistico dell' Impero di Marocco, Genova, 1834, pp. 251–6.
248 Notes on Northern Africa, the Sahara, and Soudan, New York, 1844, pp. 22-32:—also, Daumas, "Les Tuareg du Saharah," Revue d'Orient, Paris, Fev. 1846, pp. 168–171.
250 A Series of Chapters on Early Egyptian History, Archæology, and other subjects connected with Hieroglyphical Literature; New York, 1843, p. 58. Conf. Jomard, Études sur l'Arabie, in Mengin's Hist. d'Égypte sous Mohammed Ali; vol. iii., Paris, 1839:—Champollion-Figeac, Égypte Ancienne, Paris, 1840, pp. 28, 34, 417:—Champollion, Grammaire Égyptienne, p. xix.
251 Burke's Ethnological Jour., London, 1848, pp. 367, 368; and Otia Ægyptiaca, 1849, pp. 77–79.
252 Pettigrew, Encyc. Ægyp., 1841, pp. 2, 3.
253 Filiations, &c., 1837, i. pp. 210–17.
254 Asie Moyenne, 1839, i. p. 155.
255 Voyage en Syrie, i. p. 75.
256 Réflexions sur l'Origine, &c., des Anciens Peuples, 1747, pp. 303, 383.
257 Herodotus, lib. ii. § 105.
258 Trans. R. Soc. Lit., iii. part i.; 1836, pp. 345–6.
259 Gen. xlii. 23, 30, 33.
260 Deut. xxiii. 7, 8.
261 Gen. xli. 50–2.
262 Crania Ægyp., pp. 28–9:—Young, Discoveries in Hieroglyphical Literature, 1823, p. 63, &c.:—Champollion-Figeac, Contrat de Ptolémaïs, p. 43:—and John Pickering, Egyptian Jurisprudence, Boston, 1840, p. 313.
263 Wood-cuts, figs. 121, 122—Champollion, Monumens, ii. pl. 160, fig. 3.
264 Wood-cut, fig. 123—Rosellini, M. C., pl. 133, fig. 3.
265 Wood-cut, fig. 125—Hoskins, Ethiopia, pl. xi.
266 Cailliaud, Meroë, pls. xvi–xx.
267 Wood-cut, fig. 126—Rosellini, M. C., pl. 133.
268 Champollion-Figeac, Égypte Anc., p. 356.
269 Wood-cut, fig. 128—Rosellini, M. C., pl. 97.
270 Wood-cuts, figs. 129, 130, 131, 132—ibid., M. C., 126.
271 Wood-cut, fig. 133—ibid., M. C., pl. 37.
272 Wood-cut, fig. 134—ibid., vol. i. pl. 4.
273 Wood-cut, fig. 135—ibid., M. C., pl. 86.
274 Wood-cut, fig. 136—ibid., M. C., pl. 41.
275 Wood-cut, fig. 137—ibid., M. C., pl. 29.
276 Wood-cuts, figs. 138, 139—ibid., M. C., pl. 132.
277 Morton, p. 37:—Trans. R. Soc. Lit., 1794, pl. 16, fig. 4:—Gliddon, Chs., p. 23.

No. (of Notes, &c.)

278 Rosellini, M. S., parte 1ma, ii. 1833, pp. 476–521; Portraits, M. R., pl. i.–vii.
279 Vide infra, p. 688, "Chronology."
280 These *drawings* were our "stamps"; lithographed, infra, pls. i.–iv.
281 Humboldt, Cosmos, French ed. 1846, i. pp. 430, 579: on which see Dr. Patterson's commentary, supra, "Memoir." The heretical author of Vestiges of Creation (first Amer. ed., New York, 1845, pp. 209–242), however inaccurate in other theories—and the very orthodox Guyot (Earth and Man, Boston, 1851, p. 253, seq.), however exact in other data—owing to similar philanthropic sentimentalities, also break down when they discuss the Natural History of mankind.
282 Vansleb, in Quatremère, Recherches sur la langue Copte.
283 Manetho, apud Syncell. Chron., p. 40:—Lepsius, "Lettre à M. le Prof. Hippolyte Rosellini," Annali dell' Institutò di CorrispondenzaArcheologica, Roma, ix. 1837, p. 18.
284 Kenrick, Ancient Egypt under Pharaohs, London, 1850, i. p. 99.
285 Op. cit., pp. 107–8.
286 Op. cit., p. 131.
287 Wood-cut, fig. 152—Rosellini, M. R., 155; M. S., iv. pp. 230, 241–2:—Osburn, Testimony, pp. 23–4.
288 Lepsius, Denkmäler, Abth. ii. Bl. 19.
289 Rosellini, M. R., 101, and 87.
290 Wilkinson, Man. and Cus., i. p. 285; iii. pp. 141, 346:—Henry, Égypte Pharaonique, ii. pp. 274–89:—Birch, Lettre à Letronne, Rev. Archéol.; and De Saulcy, Note, Rev. Archéol., 1847, p. 430.
291 Testimony, pp. 23–4.
292 Wood-cut, fig. 156—Rosell., M. R., pl. 96.
293 Wood-cut, fig. 157—ibid., M. C., pl. 13.
294 Wood-cut, fig. 158—ibid.
295 Wood-cuts, figs. 159, 160—Morton's MSS. for 2d ed. of Cr. Ægyp.
296 Wood-cut, fig. 161—ibid.
297 Ampère, Revue des Deux Mondes, Aug. 1846, p. 391.
298 Gliddon, Hand-book, pp. 20—22.
299 Denkm., Dyn. IV.–VI., Tombs at Berlin.
300 Crania Ægyptiaca, pp. 26, 27.
301 I was present in Dr. M's office when he opened it; and so vivid is my remembrance of the conversation its joint perusal superinduced, that, although I had never seen the letter from 1844 to this Sept. 1853, I sought for and found it among my deceased friend's papers.—G. R. G.
302 Pickering, Races of Men, 1848, p. 10.
303 Grammaire Égyptienne, Introd., p. xix.
304 Cosmos, ii. p. 147, French ed.
305 Jerem. xiii. 23:—Morton's notes for 2d ed. Crania Æg.; but vide infra, pp. 487–8.
306 Institutiones ad Fundamenta Linguæ Arabicæ, Lipsiæ, 1818, pp. 38–9.
307 Dubois, Voyage autour du Caucase, &c.; cited hereinafter.
308 Wood-cut, fig. 166—Rosellini, M. R., 142; M. S., iv. p. 292.
309 Wood-cut, fig. 167—Nubie, p. 8:—Ros., M. R., 85; M. S., iii. part ii. p. 114:—Osburn, Testimony, p. 32:—Champollion, Monuments, pl. xvi.
310 Wood-cuts, figs. 168–170—Rosellini, M. R., pl. lxxxv.

No. (of Notes, &c.)

311 Birch, Gallery, pp. 68, 86, 104:—Gliddon, Otia, p. 119.
312 Madden's Oriental Album, pl. 25; "Nubian Females, Kenoosee Tribe, Philæ."
313 Wood-cut, fig. 171 — Rosellini, M. R., 156, 160; M. S., iv. pp. 231, 250.
314 Wood-cut, fig. 172—Rosellini, M. R., 60; M. S., iii. part i. p. 407.
315 Wood-cut, fig. 173—Wilkinson, Man. and Cust., p. 404, No. 73.
316 Otia, pp. 147–8.
317 Nott, Bibl. and Phys. Hist., pp. 138–146:—Gliddon, Otia, p. 147. James Cam, 1480, was the first who sailed along Africa to a little beyond the river Congo. Hottentot tribes were altogether unknown until after the voyage of Bartholomew Diaz in A. D. 1486 (Churchill's Collection of Voyages).
318 Anthon, Class. Dict., voce "Hanno." We have re-examined Heeren (Reflections on the Ancient Nations of Africa, i., chaps. ii., v., vi.—particularly pp. 214–241), and can find nothing but *hypotheses* to support Carthaginian possession of *Negro* slaves. The account of Hanno's voyage, &c., is given (op. cit., pp. 492–501).
319 L'Arménie, la Perse, et la Mesopotamie, Paris, folio, 1842, pl. 113:—compare pl. 126.
320 Botta et Flandin, Mon. de Ninive, folio, 1847–50, pl. 88.
321 Virgile, Moretum, "The Salad," Nisard's ed., Paris, 1843, p. 463.
322 Wood-cuts, figs. 177, 178—Rosellini, M. R., xliv. bis, quater.
343 Abth. iii. Bl. 120.
324 Archæologia, xxxiv. pp. 18–22.
325 Compare Gliddon's assertions of the same fact in 1843, Chapters, pp. 47, 59; in 1849, Otia, pp. 78–81; and Hand-book, p. 35.
326 Hist. Tablet of Ramses II., London, 1852, pp. 1822.
327 Hincks, Hieroglyphical Alphabet, p. 16; pl. i. figs. 23, 26, 27:—Gliddon, Otia, p. 133.
328 Wood-cut, fig. 181—Mon. Civ., pl. xxii.
329 Travels, plate, part i. line 3.
330 Man. and Cust., i. pl. iv. line 3.
331 Egypte Ancienne, pl. 55.
332 Wood-cut, fig. 182—Rosellini, Hoskins, Wilkinson, and Champollion-Figeac, supra No. 331.
333 Races, 1848, p. 224—compare "Abyssinian," in plate xii.
334 Gallery, pp. 94, 97; pl. 38.
335 Topog. of Thebes, 1835, pp. 135, seq.:—Man. and Cust., i. pp. 58, 404; iii. 179:—Champollion, Monuments, pl. 158.
336 Gliddon, Otia, p. 148.
337 Gliddon's MS. Diary, "Thebes, February, 1840":—Wilk., Materia Hieroglyphica, "Amuntuonch":—Rosellini, Appendice, Oval No. 13:—Leemans, Lettre à Salvolini, p. 75. Compare Birch, Tablet of Ramses II., Tomb of Hui, p. 24.
338 Wood-cuts, figs. 183, 184—Denkmäler, "Neues Reich," Dyn. XVIII., Abth. iii. Bl. 117.—N. B. The children sometimes are *red*—see the same paternity exemplified in Hoskins, Ethiop., "Grand Procession," lowest line.

No. (of Notes, &c.)

339 As among the "wrestlers" at Benihassan (Cailleaud, Arts et Métiers, pl. 39): —the "wine-pressers" at Thebes (ibid. pl. 34)—and other scenes.
340 Wilkinson, Man. and Customs, ii. p. 265.
341 Chev. Lepsius's private letters to Morton and to Gliddon.—Vide Chapters, 15th ed., Peterson, Phila., 1850, p. 68.
342 Crania Ægyptiaca, p. 41.
343 Wood-cut, fig. 187—Hoskins, pl. x.
344 Wood-cut, fig. 188—ibid.
345 Hanbury and Waddington, Travels in Ethiopia, pl. xiv.—compare Cailleaud, Voyage à Meroë; and Hoskins, pl. xxix.
346 Syncell. Chronograph., p. 120, ed. Venet.
347 Crania Ægyptiaca, pp. 49-50:—Rosellini, M. S., ii. pp. 174, 238.
348 Wood-cut, fig. 193, Crania Ægyptiaca, pl. xii., fig. 7; and p. 18:—Catalogue, 1849, No. 823.
349 Letronne, Matériaux pour servir à l'histoire du Christianisme en Égypte.
350 Crania Ægyp. p. 44:—Champ. Mons., I., pl. 1; Rosellini, pl. xxv. (eye wanting) —Cherubini, Nubie, pl. 10. p. 33.
351 Gliddon's Otia, p. 144.
352 Lepsius, Denkmäler, Part II., pl. 136; *i*, lines 1 and 2.
353 Mémoire sur quelques Phénomènes Célestes; Revue Archéol., 1853, p. 674, note 34.
354 Arundale, Bonomi and Birch's Gallery of Antiquities, selected from Brit. Mus.—before cited.
355 Champ. Mons. I., pl. lxxi, lxxii; Rosellini, M. R., lxxv.
356 Crania Ægyptiaca, pp. 61-2: corrected by "standing," for "seated," in MSS. for 2d ed.
357 "Parable"—It is well known that the earlier colonists of Barbadoes, Montserrat, and some other W. Indian islands, were Irish exiles. Odd to relate, while a few of their Negro slaves actually speak *Gaelic*, many have acquired the "brogue!" An Hibernian, fresh from the green isle, arrived one day at the port of Bridgetown, and was hailed by two Negro boatmen who offered to take him ashore. Observing that their names were "Pat" and "Murphy," and that their brogue was uncommonly rich, the stranger (taking them to be Irishmen) asked—"and how long have ye been from the ould counthree?" Misunderstanding him, one of the darkies replied, "sex months, y're honor." "Sex months! . . . . . only sex months, and turned as black as me hat!! J—!!! what a climate! Row me back to the ship. I'm from Cork last—and I'll soon be from here!"

Every one laughs at the verdant ignorance which believed that a Celt could be transmuted by climate into a Negro in 6 months. All would smile at the notion of such a possibility within 6, or even 60 years. Most readers will hesitate over 600 years. Anatomy, history, and the monuments prove that 6000 years have never metamorphosed one type of man into another.

No. (of Notes, &c.)

358 Second Visit to the United States, Part II., p. 188.
359 Tableaux of New Orleans, 1852, pp. 8-17:—also, Dickeson and Brown, Cypress Timber of the Mississippi, 1848, p. 3.
360 Scottish Archæologists, Dr. Wilson tells me, have found similar indications of early human existence in the Shetland Isles; and he considers this criterion very valuable.—G. R. G.
361 Morton, Crania Americana, p. 260.
362 "Information respecting the History, Condition and Prospects of the Indian Tribes of the United States," vol. I.
363 As Morton happily wrote—"The works of giants and the stature of pigmies"—MSS. for 2d ed. Cr. Ægyp.
364 The Serpent Symbol, &c., in America, 1851, pp. 26-7.
365 Westminster Review—"The Greek of Homer a Living Language." So true is this, that one word will illustrate the fact: *e. g.*, *νερο* is now the name for *water* in ordinary Grecian parlance, just as it was in Homeric days, to the exclusion of *ὑδωρ* which belongs to the classical ages intervening.—G. R. G.
366 Christian Examiner, Boston, July, 1850, p. 31.
367 Trans. Am. Ethnol. Soc., II.
368 Bunsen, Life and Letters of B. S. Niebuhr, New York ed., 1852.
369 Connection between Science and Revealed Religion.
370 Ancient Monuments of the Mississippi Valley, 1848, p. 304.
371 Wilson, Archæology of Scotland.
372 Op. cit., p. 168.
373 Layard's Babylon abundantly establishes this fact; but vide infra, p. 427, figs. 263, 264.
374 Morton, Cr. Ægyp. pp. 5, 7, pl. i.
375 Wood-cut, fig. 200—Martin, Man and Monkeys, p. 298, "Bushman."
376 Wood-cuts, figs. 201, 202—Wilson's Archæology—vide infra, pp. 369-70.
377 Hamilton Smith, Natural History of the Human Species, Edinb. ed., 1848, p. 93.
378 Trans. Am. Ethnol. Soc., New York, i. p. 192.
379 Rev. Dr. John Bachman, of Charleston, S. C., in a book on the Unity of the Races, did raise a question as to the American origin of maize, but Humboldt, Parmentier, Linnæus, and the best botanists are against him.
380 Gallatin, Notes, op. cit., p. 57.
381 Chronologie der Ægypter, i. pp. 131-3.
382 Pauthier, Chine, p. 180.
383 Gallatin, p. 58.
384 Vetruvius, lib. vi., cap. 1.
385 Kaimes, Sketches of the History of Man, 2d ed., Edinb., 1778; i. pp. 50, 75-7.
386 Layard, 2d Exped. Babylon, pp. 531-2.
387 Morton was here somewhat misled by a hastily written passage in my Otia. (Burke's Ethnol. Journal, p. 310.)—G. R. G.
388 This is by far too high a date for "castes"—see further on, pp. 635-6.
389 Also, and more probably, Petubastes; but the hieroglyphics reveal nothing for or against either supposition.—G. R. G.
390 They came from the old Jewish burial-

No. (of Notes, &c.)

ground, behind Muss'r-el-Ateeka, on the desert toward Bussateen: and no Muslim is interred near a Jew.—G.R.G.

391 Travels in Kordofan, London, 1844.

392 Proceed. Acad. Nat. Sciences, Philada., September, 1850, p. 82.

393 Canidæ, i. p. 104.

394 Want of space alone prevents the apposite citation of the corroborative statements of M. Hombron, "De l'Homme dans ses rapports avec la Création;" Voyage au Pole Sud; Zoologie, i. pp. 80–92, 110–7.

395 This is what the Halicarnassian states—"I am surprised (for my narrative has from the commencement sought for digressions), that in the whole territory of Elis no *mules* are able to breed, though neither is the climate cold, nor is there any other visible cause. The Eleans themselves say, that *mules* do not breed with them in consequence of a curse; therefore, when the mares' breeding approaches, they lead them to the neighboring districts, and there put the he-asses with them until they are in foal; then they drive them home again." (Melpomene, iv. 30—"A new and Literal Version, from the Text of Baehr"—by Henry Cary, M. A., Oxford—London, 1849, p. 247.)

396 Columella, p. 135.

397 Ham. Smith—Nat. Hist. of the Equidæ, p. 154.

398 Leidy; in Proceed. Acad. Nat. Sciences, Phila., Sept., 1847.

399 Equidæ, p. 183.

400 Ibid., p. 120.

401 Morton's posthumous papers.

402 Ibid.—Replies to the Rev. J. Bachman, &c., 1850–51.

403 Buffon, Quadrupèdes, xxii. p. 400; xxx. p. 230.

404 Chevreul, in Journal des Savans, Juin, 1846; p. 357. It was my good fortune to have marked, for Dr. Morton, that passage in Chevreul's skilful paper which Dr. Bachman so queerly ascribed to "old and musty" authorities.—G. R. G.

405 Karl Ritter's Geography of Asia; viii. Division 1st.—pp. 655, 659. Compare Frazer, Mesopotamia and Assyria, pp. 366–7; for "Turkoman Camel."

406 Canidæ, p. 19.

407 Sonnini's Buffon, Quad. xxxiii. p. 321, supp.

408 Pennant's Arctic Zoology, i. p. 42.

409 Fauna Boreale-Americana, Mamm., p. 61.

410 First Voyage, Supp., p. 186.

411 Fauna, p. 65.

412 Idem, pp. 74, 79.

413 American Edition, p. 365.

414 Martin, Nat. Hist. of the Dog, p. 30.

415 Hamilton Smith, Canidæ, ii. p. 123.

416 Nat. Hist. of Paraguay, p. 151.

417 Rural Sports, p. 16.

418 Lyell, Principles, ch. 38.

419 Wood-cut, fig. 235—Champollion, Grammaire, pp. 51, 173; Dictionnaire, pp. 117, 127:—Bunsen, Egypt's Place, i. p. 514, figs. 248, 249:—Wilkinson M. and C., iii. p. 32:—Lepsius, Denkmäler, IVth, Vth, and VIth, dynasty, passim.

420 Wood-cut, fig. 237—Denkmäler, Abth. ii. Bl. 9.

421 Wood-cut, fig. 238—Denkmäler, Abth. ii. Bl. 96.

422 Wood-cut, fig. 239—Denkmäler, Abth. ii. Bl. 11:—See varieties in Cailleaud, Arts et Métiers des Anc, Eg., pl. 37.

423 Wood-cut, fig. 240—Denkmäler, Abth. ii. Bl. 20.

424 Wood-cut, fig. 241—Rosellini, M. C., xvii., fig. 3.

425 Wood-cut, fig. 242—Martin, Nat. Hist. of the Dog, p. 138.

426 Oriental Album, pl. 41.

427 Martin, op. cit., p. 53.

428 Wood-cut, fig. 243—Ibid., p. 50:—Denkmäler, Abth. ii. Bl. 132.

439 Wood-cut, fig. 244—Denkmäler, Abth. ii. Bl. 131.

430 Wood-cut, fig. 245—Rosellini, M. C., No. 5.

431 Wood-cut, fig. 246—Wilkinson, M. and C. iii. p. 13.

432 Wood-cut, fig. 247—Ibid., op. cit., p. 32.

433 Hoskins, Ethiopia, Plate i., line 3.

434 Bennett, Tower Menagerie, p. 83.

435 Wood-cut, fig. 248—Wilkinson, M. and C. iii. p. 12:—Lepsius, Denkmäler, ii. 131.

436 Wood-cut, fig. 249—Denkmäler, ii. 134.

437 The head resembles the skulls of Egyptian mummied-dogs now in the Academy, Philadelphia.

438 Wood-cut, fig. 250—Denkmäler, ii. 96.

439, and 440 Wood-cut, fig. 251—Layard, Babylon, p. 526:—Vaux, Nineveh, p. 198; discovered by Rawlinson. "Ctesias (says Photius in his Excerpta), in his description of India, speaks of the gigantic dogs of that country."—Indica, cap. 5; apud Heeren, Hist. Res.; London, 1846; i. p. 35.

441 Morton, Additional Observations on Hybridity, Oct., 1850, p. 26.

442 Lepsius, Denkmäler, Abth. ii. Bl. 131, and Passalacqua, Catalogue, 1826, pp. 231–3.

443 Zoologie, ii. p. 79:—Another, not less curious, arrived too late for us to use in our studies; viz: Courtet de l'Isle, "Tableau Ethnographique du Genre Humain," Paris, 1849. We shall revert to it elsewhere.

444 October, 1849:—Amer. Jour. of Med. Sciences, Jan., 1850.

445 Thoughts on the Original Unity of the Human Races, New York, 1830.

446 Zoologie, ii. p. 109.

447 Op. cit., p. 107.

448 Lyell, Principles, chap. xxxvii.

449 South. Quar. Rev., Charleston, S. C., Jan., 1846.

450 Second Visit to the United States, i. p. 105.

451 Hist. of Napoleon Buonaparte.

452 Notes to Azara's Quadrupeds, i. p. 24.

453 Amer. ed., No. ccciv, July, 1853. p. 55.

454 Genesis v. 4.

455 Études sur l'Algérie, p. 148.

456 Cahen's Hebrew Text, i. p. 8: Genesis ii. 20.

457 Layard, Babylon, p. 623.

458 Pauthier, Chine, p. 24:—Livres Sacrés de l'Orient, "Temps antérieures au Chou-king," p. 33.

459 De la Domestication du Llama et de la Vigogne; "Projêt d'une Ménagerie Nationale d'Acclimatation," 1848.

No. (of Notes, &c.)

460 The Black Man, "Comparative Anatomy and Psychology of the African Negro" —transl. Friedlander and Tomes, New York, 1853, pp. 11–12.
461 Crania Ægyptiaca, 1844. p. 1.
462 Observations on a Second Series of Ancient Egyptian Crania; Proceed. Acad. Nat. Sc., Phila., Oct. 1844, pp. 8–10.
463 Catalogue of Skulls, 3d ed., 1849: to which ought to be added those crania presented to him in 1851 by Mr. Gliddon; and, in 1851–2, the two shipments received from Mr. A. C. Harris of Alexandria, Egypt.
464 Cr. Ægyp., p. 3.
465 Gliddon's Otia, pp. 74–5, 80.
466 Ægyptens Stelle in der Weltgeschichte, ii. pp. 166–70.
467 Crania Ægyp., p. 19.
468 Observations, &c. Proceed. Acad. Nat. Sciences, Phila., Oct. 1844:—Lepsius, Briefe, p. 33.
469 Crania Ægypt., p. 20.
470 Exodus xii. 38; Cahen's Hebrew Text, ii. p. 50.
471 Champollion, L'Égypte sous les Pharaons, 1814, ii. p. 5. seq.: and Quatremère, Recherches sur la Langue et la Littérature des Coptes.
472 Abeken, Rapport à la Société Égyptienne du Kaire; in Bulletin de la Soc. de Géog., Paris, Sept., 1845; pp. 171–2.
473 Lepsius, Auswahl, pl. xx.; as well as in Briefe, pp. 105–6.
474 Cr. Ægyp., pl. ii. fig. 1.
475 Cr. Ægyp., pl. ii. fig. 2.
476 Cr. Ægyp., pl. ii. fig. 3.
477 Cr. Ægyp., pl. x. fig. 8.
478 Cr. Ægyp., pl. viii. fig. 1.
479 Cr. Ægyp., pl. xi. fig. 1
480 Cr. Ægyp., pl. x. fig. 1.
481 Cr. Ægyp., pl. x. fig. 4.
482 Cr. Ægyp., pl. x. fig. 5. Note to Woodcuts, figs. 263, 264; "Ancient Assyrian" (supra, pp. 426–7). After my remarks were stereotyped, I had the pleasure to receive another letter from Mr. J. B. Davis (dated, Shelton, Nov. 15, 1853), which affords the following, among other particulars, corroborative of the authenticity of this cranium:— * * "The skull is the veritable skull of an ancient Assyrian. It was found with the fragments of others, and a great many other bones and armor, in a chamber of the North-west palace at Nimroud, to which there was an entrance but no exit. This is marked in Mr. Layard's Nineveh, Vol. I., p. 62; Plan III., Chamber I. It was supposed to be the one to which the defenders of the palace had retreated. * * * * * The skull is undoubtedly allied to Morton's Pelasgic group, but, yet, I think possesses a distinct character which at once strikes my eye, as belonging to the people of the sculptures. The full, rounded, equable form like the ancient Greek, only decidedly larger and fuller, is striking."—J. C. N.
483 Égypte Ancienne, pl. 2. p. 261.
484 Gliddon, Appeal to the Antiquaries of Europe on the destruction of the Monuments of Egypt, 1841; pp. 125–129.
485 Proceed. Acad. Nat. Sciences, Philadel., Dec. 24, 1850. On the "leathern straps," cf. Birch in Gliddon's Otia, p. 85; and Osburn's paper on the Leed's Mummy, 1828, pp. 4, 33–4, pl. ii.
486 Promenade en Amérique, Revue des Deux Mondes, Juin, 1853.
487 Martin, Man and Monks., p. 298, fig. 233.
488 Op. cit., p. 298.
489 Prichard, Phys. Hist. i. p. 297.
490 Ibid., op. cit. p. 290. "Fulah" means "white:" Cf. Beecham, Ashantee, or the Gold Coast: p. 161, note.
491 Ibid., op. cit.; and Latham, Varieties of Man, p. 6.
492 Morton, Cr. Æg., pl. xii. fig. 7.
493 Virey, Histoire Naturelle du Genre Humain, i, p. 240; pl. 2: drawn in colors, on a folio scale, by Geoffroy and Cuvier, Mammiferès, 1829: i. pl. 1 and 2; and described in pp. 1–7.
494 Morton, Cr. Æg., p. 16.
495 Prichard, Researches, v. p. 3. Thus amply confirmed by Crawfurd—"There are 15 varieties of Oriental Negroes. * * * * There is no evidence, therefore, to justify the conclusion that the Oriental Negro, wherever found, is of one and the same race." (Edin. New Philos. Jour., 1853. p. 78.—"Negroes of the Ind. Archip.")
496 Churchill's Collection of Voyages, i.; "History of Navigation, supposed to have been written by the celebrated Locke." This information may be relied on, as it was furnished me by Dr. Charles Pickering.—G. R. G.
497 Anthropologie, p. 348.
498 Op. cit.; from "Voyage de l'Uranie."
499 Morton, Catalogue, 1849, No. 1327.
500 Prichard, Researches, i. p. 298, fig. 7.
501 Dumoutier, Atlas, pl. 35, fig. 6.
502 Ibid., pl. 37, fig. 2.
503 Martin, Man and Monkeys, p. 310, fig. 227.
504 Dumoutier, Atlas, pl. 36, fig. 4—"Van Diemen."
505 Prichard, Researches, i. p. 297, fig. 6.
506 Dumoutier, Atlas, pl. 36, fig. 2—"Van Diemen."
507 Op. cit., pl. 34.
508 Martin, Man and Monkeys, p. 312, fig. 229. There is nothing herein stated about the almost inconceivable animality of Papuans, Ahetas (Ajetas) or Negritos, Arruans, Al Foers, which the reader cannot find in a new work—"Ethnographical Library, Conducted by Edwin Norris, Esq., Vol. I. The Native Races of the Indian Archipelago, by George Windsor Earl," London, 1853.
509 Observations faites pendant le 2me voyage de Cook, p. 208.
510 Mœrenhout, ———, ii. p. 248; cited by D'Eichthal, "Races Océaniennes et Américaines," 1845.
511 Polynesian Researches, ii. p. 13.
512 Dumoutier, pl. 26, fig. 6—"Cavernes sepulchrales—Teneriffe."
513 Ibid., pl. 29, fig. 4—"Marquesas."
514 Ibid., pl. 30, fig. 4—"Caverne ossuaire—Taiti."
515 Ibid., pl. 31, fig. 4—"Sepultures abandonnées—Isle Vavao."

No. (of Notes, &c.)

516 Martin, Man and Monkeys, p. 310.
517 Dumoutier, pl. 32, fig. 2—"Isle Mawi."
518 Philadelphia, 2d ed., 1844; pp. 4, 5.
519 Mr. Strain's letter to Dr. Morton, "Rio Janeiro, 7th Decem., 1843"—Proceed. Acad. Nat. Sciences., Phila., Dec., 1844.
520 Putnam's American edition, New York, 1853, p. 36.
521 Ethnography and Archæology; American Journ. of Science and Art, ii. 2d series; New Haven, 1846; tirage à part, pp. 67, 117–9.
522 Crania Americana, p. 145.
523 Rivero and Tschudi (pp. 39–40) doubt the possession by Dr. Morton of crania of the royal Inca family: but the note of the translator (p. 41) may be passed over as inconsequent.
524 The Creole Negro; supra, No. 491.
525 Cr. Americana, p. 130; pl. xi. C.
526 Op. cit., p. 131; xi. D.
527 Peruvian Antiquities, pp. 39–40.
528 Cr. Americana, p. 152; pl. xvi.
529 Op. cit., p. 155; pl. xviii.
530 Op. cit., p. 166; pl. xxii.
531 Op. cit., p. 198; pl. xxxix.
532 Op. cit., p. 220; pl. lii.
533 Op. cit., p. 224; pl. lv.
534 Op. cit., p. 259.
535 Op. cit., p. 257.
536 Anthropologie, pp. 229–30, 232.
537 Martin, Man and Monkeys, p. 273.
538 Ibid., p. 273.
539 Chine, d'après les documents Chinois, p. 1.
540 Wood-cut, fig. 329—Paravey, Documents, &c., sur le Deluge de Noé, Paris. 1838, pp. 11, 56:—Pauthier, Chou-king, Part II., chap. i. p. 62; Part IV., chap. xxvii., p. 131:—Ibid., Chine, pp. 55–7.
541 Pauthier, Chine, pl. 22; pp. 120–1.
542 Ibid., pl. 51, fig. 4; pp. 246–8.
543 Ibid., pl. 12; pp. 57–8.
544 Ibid., pp. 472–4.
545 Révolutions des Peuples de l'Asie Moyenne, Paris, 1839; ii. p. 432.
546 Catalogue, 3d ed., 1849; Intro., pp. 1–2.
547 Nat. Hist. of Human Species; Edinb., 1848, p. 157.
548 Bremer, Homes of the New World, Am. ed., 1853, ii. pp. 162–3. [Note, 24 Jan., 1854. Let me confirm my colleague's accuracy by two additional extracts—1st, as regards crosses between American Indians and white men. All readers are aware with what gusto a superior civilization has been attributed to the Mandans; and how sundry instances of fair complexion, light hair and blue eyes, among individuals of that tribe, have also led to surmises that they might even be of Welsh descent! Major John Le Conte pointed out to me a solution in the fact that Lewis and Clark wintered among them with a party of 43 able-bodied men. As a specimen, read the following account of one orgie, on Saturday night, Jan. 5, 1805—"Unus nostrum sodalium multum alacrior et potentior juventute, hac nocte honorem quatuor maritorum custodivit." (Lewis and Clark, Travels to the source of the Missouri river; 1804–6; London ed., 1814; ch. vi., pp. 109–111.)—2d, As respects crosses between Negroes, Indians, and white persons, on the Panama Isthmus; a passage which was indicated to me by Mr. Conrad:—

"The character of the half-castes is, if possible, worse than that of the Negroes. These people have all the vices and none of the virtues of their parents. They are weak in body, and are more liable to disease than either the whites or other races. It seems that as long as pure blood is added to the half-castes proper, when they intermarry only with their own colour, they have many children, but these do not live to grow up; while in families of unmixed blood the offspring are fewer, but of longer lives. As the physical circumstances under which both are placed are the same, there must really be a specific distinction between the races, and their intermixture be considered as an infringement of the law of Nature."—Berthold Seemann, F.L.S.—Narrative of the Voyage of H. M. S. Herald, 1845–51: London, 1853, I., p. 302.—G. R. G.]
549 Martin, Man and Monkeys, p. 210, fig. 180.
550 Ibid.—fig. 181.
551 Ibid.—fig. 182.
552 Savage and Wyman, Troglodytes Gorillæ; Boston, Jour. of Nat. Hist., 1847, p. 27.
553 Martin, op. cit., p. 228.
554 Ibid., p. 280.
555 Ibid., p. 384.
556 Ibid., p. 223.
557 Prichard, Researches, i. p. 290, fig. 3.
558 Martin, op. cit., p. 367.
559 Virey, Hist. Nat., ii. p. 42.
560 Martin, op. cit., p. 254.
561–562 Wood-cuts, figs. 346, 348—Illustrated London News, 1851—"drawn by an English officer at the Cape."
563 Amaryllidaceæ, pp. 338, 339.
564 Races of Men, p. 12.
565 American Jour. of Science and Art, Vol. xxxviii., No. 2.
566 Anatomie comparée, tome ii.

PART II.

567 Geographiæ Sacræ Pars prior; Cadomi, fol., 1651—(Loganian Library, Phila.)
568 Spicilegium Geographiæ Hebræor. exteræ, post Bochart., vol. ii., 1769–80.
569 Gliddon, Otia, London, 1849, pp. 16, 124.
570 Rev. Dr. Eadie, Early Oriental History—Encyclopædia Metropolitana, London, 1852, p. 2.
571 Rev. Dr. Hales, Analysis of Chronology; 2d ed., 1830; Preface, p. 21, and i. p. 352.
572 Pauthier, Livres Sacrés de l'Orient, Paris, Intro., p. 1.
573 Cahen, La Bible, Traduction Nouvelle, Paris, 1831; i. pp. 26–8.
574 Avec un Atlas géographique, pittoresque, archéologique, géologique, &c.—"Ouvrage qui a remporté le prix de la Société de Géographie de Paris, en 1838;" Paris, 6 vol. Text, 8vo., 1839–43.

No. (of Notes, &c.)

575 Bulletins de l'Académie royale de Bruxelles, vi.; and Notions élémentaires de Statistique, Paris, 1840.

576 Voyage dans les steps d'Astrakhan et du Caucase; and Histoire Primitive des Peuples qui ont habité anciennement ces contrées.

577 GoMeR. Bochart, pp. 194–6. — Homer, Odyss. xi. 14.—Diodor., v. 32.—Herod., iv. 100.—Josephus, Antiq. i. 6.—Rawlinson, Commentary, 1850, p. 68.—Dubois; i. 61, iv. 321, 327, 350, 391; v. 22, 35, 44.

578 MaGUG. Bochart, pp. 212–19. — Rev. Moses Stuart, Interpretation of Prophecy, Andover, 1842, p. 123. — De Wette, transl., Parker, i. p. 95–7, &c. — Kur'àn, Ch. xviii., v. 93, 96; xxi. 95, &c. — Pauthier, Liv. Sac. de l'Orient, p. 495: Lane, Selections, p. 140.—Barthelemy, Anciennes Religions des Gaules; Rev. Archéol., 1851, p. 338, note.—Dubois, iv. 321, 345; 363–407.—Josephus, Ant., i. 6. — Hieronymus, Comm. in Ezek. xxxviii, 2. — Lenormant, Cours d'Hist. Ancien., Paris, 1837, p. 289.—Emelin, 1774, and Porter (Travels, ii. 520), 1819 — "wall of Gog and Magog at Derbend." — Anthon, Classic. Dict., 1843; voce "Asi," p. 218. "Scythic" is here used in the sense proposed by Rawlinson (Commentary, pp. 68, 75: and Cuneiform Inscriptions, 1847, pp. 20, 34–7,) and adopted by Norris, (Memoir on the Scythic Version of the Behistun inscription; Jour. R. Asiat. Soc., 1853; xv., Part 1, p. 2. — Sir W. Jones, 6th Discourse, on Persians; Asiatic Researches, 1799, ii. p. 64. — Gliddon, Otia, p. 124. — Westergaard, Median Species of Arrowheaded writing: Antiq. du Nord, 1844; pp. 273–8, 289.—Hincks, Persepolitan Writing, 1846, p. 18. — D'Omalius d'Halloy, Races Humaines, ou éléments d'ethnographie, 1845, "Ossètes," p. 79.

579 MeDI. Bochart, pp. 219–25.—Herod., vii. —De Saulcy, Recherches sur l'Écriture cunéiforme Assyrienne; Paris, 1848, p. 26. — Layard, Babylon, p. 628. — De Longpérier, Lettre à M. Löwenstern; Rev. Archéol., 1847, p. 505. — Rawlinson, Tablet of Behistun.—Birch, Tablet of Karnac, pp. 14–5. — Dubois, iv. 321, 339.

580 IUN. Bochart, pp. 174–6.—Aristophanes, In Acharnum; Act i., scene 3.—Homer., Iliad, xiii. 685.—Pausanias, Achaic., p. 397. — Herodotus, viii. 44. — Rosetta Stone, in Lepsius's Auswahl; or in Birch's Gallery, pp. 114–17, pl. 49: — also, Lenormant, Essai sur le Texte Grec, 1840; pp. 10, 11; lines No. 54; and p. 45.—Hincks (True date of the Rosetta Stone, Dublin, 1842, pp. 6, 8,) claims "March, 197, B. C.," as date of this decree; but a Letronne would first have determined the year of "C.:" vide infra, pp. 665–7. — Champollion, Grammaire Égyptienne, pp. 151, 175; Dict., p. 66. — "Ouinin," in conquests of Seti-Meneptha, and of Ramses II.—De Saulcy, Recherches, p. 26; Inscriptions trouvées à Khorsabad, Rev. Archéol., 1850, pp. 769–72. — Rawlinson, Behistùn, pp. 1, xxvii.—Layard, Babylon, p. 628. Pauthier's Manou, lib. x., v. 44. —Wilford, Asiatic Researches, 1799; iii. p. 358.—Sykes, Jour. R. Asiat. Soc., 1841., vol. vi.; Art. xiv. pp. 434–6. — "J. P. S." (in Kitto, Biblical Encyclopædia, ii., p. 393–400) omits any explanation of Tubal, Meshech, and Tiras, in his "sons of Japheth" (p. 397)! There are numerous similar oversights in Kitto, no less than in Robinson's Calmet. — Dubois, iv. 321. 334.

581 T*t*uBaL. Bochart, pp. 204–13. — Munk, Palestine, p. 420. — De Wette, ii. 366. seq. — Strabo, ii. 129. — Herod., vii. 78. Rawlinson, Commentary, pp. 63–4. — Layard, Babylon, p. 628. — Dubois, iv. 321, 388.

582 MeS*h*eK. Bochart, pp. 204–13.—Herod., iii., 94; vii. 78. — Rawlinson, Commentary, pp. 63–4.—Birch, Stat. Tablet of Karnac, pp. 14–5. — Hincks, Report of Syro-Ægyptian Soc., 1846.—Dubois, ii. 17; iv. 321, 336, 347.

583 T*t*IRaS. Bochart, p. 172–3. For hieroglyphical mention of "Thraces," in Egyptian conquests, see Champollion (Lettres) and Rosellini (MS., iv. 288); for classical, the "Inscrip. of Adulis" —Champollion-Figeac, Eg. Anc., p. 67. —Dubois, iv. 321, 324.

584 AS*h*KeNaZ. Bochart, pp. 196–8.—Pliny, iv. 24.—Kitto, ii. p. 397.—Rawlinson, Commentary, p. 46; "Nimroud Obelisk." — Ibid., London Lit. Gazette, Aug., 1851.—Dubois, iv. 321, 330, 391.

585 RIPaT*t*. Bochart, pp. 198–9. — Strabo, vii. 341. — Pliny, iv. 24. — Dubois, iv. 321, 330.

586 T*t*oGaRMaH. Bochart, pp. 200–4. — Moses Choren., Hist. of Arm., p. 24.— St. Martin, Mémoires sur l'Arménie, 1818; i. pp. 205, 271–8.—Strabo, xii. — Josephus, Ant., i. 1, 6. — Löwenstern, Lettre à M. de Saulcy, Rev. Archéol., 1849, p. 494. — Dubois, ii., p. 9; iv. pp. 332–3.—Jardot, Révolutions, ii. p. 6.

587 ALISaH. Bochart, pp. 176–8.—Homer, Il., ii. 617. — Grote, Hist. of Greece, i. p. 487.—Herod, i. § 146, &c.

588 Wood-cut, fig. 355—Layard, folio Monuments; and Babylon, pp. 343, 350.—De Longpérier, Rev. Archéol., 1844, pp. 224–5; 1847, p. 297. — Stuart, Crit. Hist. and Def., pp. 113, 114, 120. — De Wette, ii. pp. 452–6.—Cahen, Notes on Jonah, vol. xii.—"Berosiana," in Bunsen's Eg. Pl., i. pp. 704–19. — Munk, Palestine, pp. 451–2. — On "Sibylline verses" see Letronne, Examen Archéologique, Croix Ansée, 1846, pp. 33–4.

589 T*t*aRSIS. Acts, xxii. 3. — Lanci, Paralipomeni, i. pp. 150–5. — Gesenius, in Parker's De Wette, i. p. 455, note. — Munk, Pal., p. 29. — Gliddon, Otia, p. 50. — Pickering, Races, p. 373. — Pauthier, Sinico-Ægyptiaca, p. 10. — Bochart, pp. 188–94. — London Lit. Gaz., May, 1852.

590 KiT*t*IM. Bochart, pp. 178–83. — Birch, Ivory ornaments found at Nimroud, pp. 174–5; and Annals of Thotmes III., pp.

No. (of Notes, &c.)

157–60. — Boeckh, Corpus Inscrip. Græc., i. p. 523.—Ptolemy, lib. v. 14.—Josephus, Antiq., i. 6. 1.—Rev. Archéol., 1846, pp. 114–15; and 1847, p. 448.

591 DoDaNIM. Bochart, pp. 183–8. —Wiseman, Connection between Sci. and Rev. Rel., 1836: ii. pp. 168–9.—Champollion-Figeac, Dissert. s. l'Étymologie, p. 8. —Herod., ii., § 52.

592 Wood-cut, fig. 356.—Champollion, Grammaire, pp. 150, 151, 195, 407; Dictionnaire, p. 409.—Hincks, Hierog. Alphabet, p. 16; pl. i., figs. 23, 26, 27.

593 Letronne, Opinions cosmographiques des Pères de l'Église; Rev. des deux Mondes, 1837, pp. 601–33: and Récueil des Inscrip., ii. p. 37, seq. — Raoul-Rochette, Archéologie comparée, 1848; Part ii. p. 190, seq.—Lenormant, Cours d'Hist. Anc., p. 228.

594 KUS*h*. Bochart, p. 238, and 241.—Martin, Études sur le Timée de Platon, Paris, 1841; "Atlantide," i. p. 332.—Walton, Bibl. Polygl.; Proleg., xv. pp. 97–9.—De Wette, i. pp. 228–31.—Wells, Hist. Geog. of O. and N. Test., 1804, pp. 103–105. — Lanci, Paralip., ii. p. 45. Nott, Bibl. and Phys. Hist., p. 143.—Forster, Geog. of Arabia, 1844, i. pp. 26–7, 28, 29. — Burckhardt, Travels in Arab., ii. p. 385.—Rosellini, Monumenti Civili, ii. pp, 394–403.—Gliddon, Otia, p. 133.—Forster, op. cit., i. 14–6.—Letronne, Mém. et Docum., Rev. Archéol., 1849, p. 85. — Cahen, Bible, v.; avant propos, p. 13. — Quatremère, Recher., Coptes.—De Wette, i. pp. 202–6.—Peyron, Coptic Lexicon, voce Ethosh.—Parthey, Vocabularium Copticum, p. 549. Wilkinson, Topog. of Thebes, p. 487; Mod. Eg. and Theb., ii. p. 317.—Birch, Stat. Tabl. Karnac, p. 47. — Anthon, Class. Dict.; and Syst. of Anc. Geog.; voce "Asia."—Rémusat, in Pauthier's Chine, p. 259.—Kitto, Bibl. Cyclop., i. p. 238.

595 Volney, Recherches Nouvelles, Paris, 1822, iv. — Lenormant, Cours d'Hist. Anc., 1838, pp. 24, 129. — Jomard, Arabie; in Mengin, 1839, iii. p. 327–9, and passim. — Fresnel, "Histoire des Arabes avant l'Islanisme," in Jour. Asiat., "4me Lettre" Djeddah, Jan., 1838. — Sale's Introd. to the Kur'ân, Liv. Sac. d'Or., p. 467. — Lane, Selections, p. 17. — Forster, Geog., i. p. 20. — Gesenius, in De Wette, i. pp. 433–4. — Hyde, Hist. rel. veter. Persarum, p. 37.—Kitto, "Cush," i. p. 503.—Assemani, Bibliotheca Orientalis, iii., part 2, p. 568, seq. — Turner, "Himyarite Inscriptions," Trans. Amer. Ethnol. Soc., New York, 1845, art. iv.—Fresnel, Recherches sur les Inscrip. Himyariques, 1845; Jour. Asiatique, No. 11; also, Lettres, Feb., March, April, May, 1845. — Gesenius, Geschichte der Heb. Sprache und Schrift, 1815. — Forster, Geog. of Arabia, i. pp. 24–76, 94–102.

596 Syncellii "Chronographeion," p. 51. — Letronne, in Biot's Recherches sur l'Année vague des Égyptiens, 1831, pp. 25–7.—Biot, Mémoire sur divers points de l'Astron. Anc., 1846, p. 37.—Matter, Hist. de l'École d'Alexandrie, 1844; ii. pp. 190–1.—Barucchi, Discorsi Critici, Torino, 1844; pp. 14, 15. — Böckh, Manetho und die Hundstern-periode, Berlin, 1848; p. 40. — Bunsen, Ægyptens Stelle, 1845; i. pp. 256–63. — Raoul-Rochette, Jour. des Savans, 1846; pp. 141, 241–2. — Lepsius, Chron. der Ægypter, i. p. 446. — Kenrick, Egypt under the Pharaohs, 1851. — Maury, in Rev. Archéol., Juin, 1851; pp. 160–3.

597 MiT'sRIM. Grotefend's "Analyse de Sanconiathon," trad. Lebas, Paris, 1839; Introduction, pp. 79–85.—Champollion, L'Égypte sous les Pharaons, 1814; i. Chap. 2. — Parthey, Vocab. Copt., pp. 511–2.—Rawlinson, Behistun, 1846, pp. 1, 27.—Commentary, 1850, pp. 60–7.—De Saulcy, Rev. Archéol., 1850, pp. 768–9, 771; pl. 133, No. 19; and Recherches, Inscrip. de Van, 1848, p. 27. Nash, on the term Copt, and the name of Egypt; Burke's Ethnol. Jour., No. 11, 1849, p. 496. — Hincks, Hierog. Alph.; p. 28, pl. i. fig. 78. — Gliddon, Chapters, p. 41.—Rosellini, Mon. Stor., i. p. 58. — Portal, Symboles des Égyptiens, pp. 51, 73. — Lanci, Lettre à M. Prisse, 1847, pp. 99–103. — Lenormant, Cours, p. 233. — Birch, "Merter," in Annals of Thotmes III., p. 138; Eg. Inscrip. in Bibliothèque Nat., p. 12; also, on "Kam, the black country," as found in the Ritual, in Chæremon on Hieroglyphics, p. 11.—Bochart, p. 292.

598 P*h*UT. Bochart, pp. 333–9. — Gliddon, Otia, p. 127.—D'Eichthal, Foulahs, pp. 1, 8, 150. — Jerome, Commentary on Isaiah, lxvi. 19.—Ptolemy, lib. iii. 1.—Pliny, Hist. Nat., v.—Josephus, Antiq., i. 6, 2. — Gräberg de Hemso, Specchio, p. 291, seq. — Cervantes de Marmol, Descripcion general dé Africa, Grenada, 1573; i. fol. 31, seq. — Champollion, Dict., pp. 339–40. — D'Avezac, Afrique Anc., p. 31. — Lenormant, Cours, pp. 233–6. — Hengstenberg, Eg. and Books of Moses; transl. Robbins, p 211.—De Saulcy, Rev. Archéol., 1850, pp. 769, 772.—Birch, Eg. Inscrip., p. 13.

599 KNA*ă*N. Cahen, Genèse, i. p. 25. — Procopius, De bello Vandalico, ii. cap. 20.—St. Augustin, Expos. Epist. Rom.; cited in De Wette, i. p. 431. — Lanci, Bassorilievo Fenicio di Carpentrasso; Roma, 1824, p. 126. — Munk, Inscrip. Phœnicienne de Marseilles; Journal Asiat., 1847, pp. 473, 483, 526; and Palestine, pp. 87–8, 192. — Gesenius, Geschichte der Heb. Sprache, 1815, pp. 8, 9.—De Saulcy, Mém. sur une Inscrip. Phœnicienne, 1847, passim.—Josephus, Cont. Apion., i, 22. — Kitto, i. p. 823, "Hebrew Language."—Eusebius, Præpar. Evang., i. cap. 10. — Lenormant, Cours, p. 236.—Bochart, pp. 339–42.

600 ScBA. Volney, Recherches, iv. p. 232. —Josephus, Antiq. viii. 6. 5.—Ludolph. Hist. Æthiopica, ii. cap. 3. — Forster, Geog., i. p. 157, seq. — Wathen, Arts, Antiq. and Chron. of Egypt, 1842, pp. 69–70. — Hoskins, Ethiopia, p. 339 [not directly, I find, but inferentially. — G. R. G.]. — Fresnel, 4me Lettre, Jan.,

No. (of Notes, &c.)

1838, pp. 71–7; and Inscriptions Himyariques, pp. 34, 67–9. — Pauthier, Chine, pp. 94–100, notes.—D'Herbelôt, Bibliothèque Orientale, voce "Salomon," and "Thahamurath." — De Wette, ii. pp. 248–65.—Forster, Geog., i. pp. 33–8, and Maps. — Bochart, pp. 146–56.

601 KhUILaH. Bochart, pp. 161–3.—Forster, i. pp. 9, 38, 54.

602 SaBTtaH. Lenormant, Cours, pp. 237–8. — Strabo, xvi. p. 771, Fr. Transl. — Jomard, Arabie, pp. 373, 389–90. — Pliny, vi. 32. — Volney, iv. p. 232. — Fresnel, Inscrip. Himyar., pp. 51–2. — Forster, Geog., i. pp. 57–8. — Bochart, pp. 252–4.

603 RAáMaH. Volney, iv. p. 235.—Forster, i. pp. 59–76; ii. 223–7. — Fresnel, 4me et 5me Lettres, 1838.—Wellsted, Trav. in Arabia, 1838, ii. p. 430. — Burckhardt, Arabia, ii. p. 385. — Bochart, p. 247.

604 SaBTteKA. References as above, No. 603.

605 SseBA. Munk, Palestine, p. 438, on "Ezra." — De Wette, ii. pp. 47–8. — Forster, ii. pp. 323–4; and i. pp. 71–3. — Bochart, pp. 249–51.

606 DeDaN. Bochart, p. 248.—Forster, i. 38; and Maps. — Letronne, "Vénus Angérone," Mém. et Doc., Rev. Archéol., 1849, p. 277.—Glaire, Les Livres Saints vengés, Paris, 1845, passim. — Rev. Sidney Smith, Elementary Sketches of Moral Philos., New York ed., 1850; p. 254.—Strauss, Vie de Jesus, trad. Littré, Paris, 1839; Preface, p. 8.

607 NiMRoD. Vide W. W.'s profound articles "Scripture," and "Verse," in Kitto, ii. pp. 717, 910. — [For hallucinations on "Nimrod," see Anc. Univ. Hist., i. p. 275, seq.; Faber, Origin of Pagan Idolatry, and Bryant, Anc. Mythology, passim; Hales, Analysis of Chron., i. pp. 358–9, and ii.] "Nimrod, a Discourse on certain passages of History and Fable." London, 1829, printed for Richard Priestley. — Higgins, Anacalypsis, London, 1836, i. p. 6. — Wiseman, Lectures, i. p. 37.—Birch, Two Egypt. Cartouches, 1846, pp. 168–70.—Lepsius, Chron. der Ægyp., i. p. 223. — Bunsen, Ægyptens Stelle, iii. p. 133. — Sharpe, in Bonomi's Nineveh, 1852, pp. 69–78. —Rawlinson, Commentary, pp. 4, 6, 7, 22.—Layard, Babylon, pp. 33, 123.—De Saulcy, Dead Sea, ii. p 544.—D'Herbelôt, voce "Nimrod;" and Ouseley, Oriental Collections, ii. p. 375. — Josephus, Antiq. i. 4, 21.

608–609 De Sola, Lindenthal, and Raphall, Scriptures in Heb. and English; London, 1846; p. 40, notes. — Glaire, Liv. Sts. vengés, i. pp. 313–20.—Rawlinson, Commentary, p. 14: — Lanci, Paralipomeni, ii. parte 8va. — Gesenius, in De Wette, i. p. 435.—Meyer, Hebraïsches Wurzel-Wörterbuch; cited by Bunsen, Disc. on Ethnol., 1847, p. 273.—D'Olivet, Langue Hebraïque restituée, 1815; pp. 281, 343. — Bochart, 256–60.

610 Gliddon, MS. "Remarks on the Introduction of Camels and Dromedaries, for Army-Transportation, Carriage of Mails, and Military Field-service, into the States and Territories lying south and west of the Mississippi, between the Atlantic and Pacific coasts — presented to the War-department, Washington, Oct. 1851." As I intend to publish an entire account of this affair for public edification ere long, it is sufficient now to determine the very recent introduction of the Arabian camel into Africa by quoting Humboldt (Aspects of Nature, p. 71); Ritter (Das Kameel, in Asien, viii. pp. 755–9); Procopius (Bello Vandalico, i. 8; ii. 11); Corippus (iv. 598–9); and Bodichon, Études sur l'Algérie, pp. 62–3.—G. R. G.

611 LUDIM. Bochart, pp. 299–310. — Gräberg de Hemso, Marocco, pp. 69, 246, 251, seq.—Castiglione, Recherches sur les Berbères Atlantiques, Milan, 1846; pp. 89, 100–1.—Lacroix, Numidie, p. 4. — D'Avezac, Afrique Anc., p. 28. — Yanoski, L'Afrique Byzantine, pp. 93, 99. — Ebn-Khaledoon, "Fee ahbar el-Berber," 3d book: transl. Schulz, in Jour. Asiat., 1828; pp. 140–1.—Asiatic Miscellany, p. 148. — Marmol, op. cit., trad. Perrot, 1667, i. p. 68. — Leo Africanus (Hassan ebn Mohammed el Gharnàtee) Africæ Descriptione, 1556, p. 5. — Bertholet, Guanches, Mém. Soc. Ethnol., Paris, 1841; Part i., pp. 130–46. Agassiz, Diversity of Origin of Human Races; Christian Examiner, Boston, July, 1850, p. 16.—Dureau de la Malle, Carthage, pp. 1–3, 13. — Gibbon, Milman's, viii., pp. 227–8. — Bodichon, Études, pp. 32, 64, 103, 109. — Quatremère, 1st art. on Hitzig's Philistaer; Jour. des Savans, 1846, May; pp. 260, 266: — [That these views upon the "Ludim" are new, the reader can perceive by opening Munk (Palestine, p. 432); Lenormant (Cours, p. 244); Cahen (Genèse i. pp. 27, 184); Kitto (Cyclop., pp. 397–8); and all English commentators.]

612 AáNaMIM. Forster, i. pp. 56–9. — De Saulcy, Dead Sea, 1853; i. p. 64; ii. p. 837.—Birch, Hieratic Canon of Turin, p. 6. — Anthon, Class. Dict., p. 872. — Bochart, p. 322.

613 LeHaBIM. Bochart, p. 316. — Anthon, Anc. and Mod. Geog., pp. 708, 749.— D'Avezac, Afrique, pp. 4, 28, 64–9. — Champollion, Ég. s. l. Phar., ii. p. 363. — Parthey, Vocab. Copt., pp. 497, 530. — Gliddon, Otia, p. 131.

614 NiPhaiaTtuKhIM. Bochart, pp. 317–21. Otia, pp. 9, 16, 133, 136.—Nott, Bibl. and Phys. Hist., pp. 144–5.— Champollion, op. cit., i. p. 55; ii. pp. 5, 31, 144, seq. — Parthey, pp. 110, 506, 530. — Herod., ii., § 18.—Champollion, Lettres, p. 124; and the hieroglyphics in Gram., pp. 169, 363, 406; Dict., pp. 339, 341. — Peyron, Gram. Ling. Copticæ, pp. 30, 36–8. — Hengstenberg, p. 211; and Gliddon, Chapters, p. 41.—Lenormant, Cours, pp. 235, 244–5.—Brugsch, Scriptura Ægyptiorum Demotica, p 25.—De Saulcy, Lettre à M. Guigniaut, p. 18.— Lepsius, Lettre à M. Rosellini, p. 66.—

No. (of Notes, &c.)

Bunsen, Eg. Pl., i. pp. 285, 471.—Schulz's Ebn Khaledoon, p. 122.—Castiglione, Berbères, p. 104.—Quatremère, Mém. Geog. sur l'Égypte, i. p. 37; and in Jour. des Savans, 1846, p. 266.

615 P*h*eT*t*uRiSIM. Most of the above references here apply. These are special—Peyron, Papyr. Græc., Part ii. p. 27.—Parthey, pp. 56, 291, 500, 539.—Wilkinson, Mod. Eg. and Theb., ii. p. 137. D'Avezac, Afrique, p. 27.—Champ., Gram. pp. 98, 169, 327; Dict., p. 81.—De Hemso, p. 296, seq.—Lacroix, Numidie, p. 6.—Anthon, Anc. Geog., p. 749.—Quatremère, loc. cit., p. 266.

616 KS*h*iLuK*h*IM. Bochart, pp. 323-9.—De Sola, Genesis, p. 42.—Cahen, i. p. 27. Glaire and Franck's Bible, i. p. 50.—Munk, Palestine, pp. 82. 432.—Kitto, i. pp. 399, 388; ii. 398.—Hales, Analysis, i. p. 355.—Ritter, Vorhalle, p. 35, seq.—Morton, Cr. Æg., pp. 23-27, on "Herodotus."—Eadie, Early Orient. Hist.—Mignot, "3me Mém. sur les Phœniciens;" Acad. R. d. Inscrip., Paris, xxxiv. 1770, p. 146.—Marmol, 1ra parte, fol. 31.—Lepsius, Lettre. pp. 14, 18, 44: Pl. A, No. I, 12.—Birch, in Otia, p. 115.—De Longpérier, Rev. Archéol., 1850, p. 450.—Botta, Écrit. cunéiforme Assyr., pp. 6, 93, 192.—Rawlinson, Commentary, pp. 10-14.—De Hemso, p. 246.—Hitzig, Urgeschichte und Mythologie der Philistaer, 1845; reviewed by Quatremère, loc. cit, p. 266.—Koenig, apud Jomard, Récueil des Voyages, 1829; iv. p. 130, seq.—Hodgson, Sahara, pp. 33-5:—and, for "Oases," Wilkinson, Mod. Eg., ii. pp. 353-79.

617 P*h*iLiST*t*IM. Wilford, Asiat. Res.; iii. 1799, pp. 317-20, 322.—Hales, i. pp. 368, 380; after a disclaimer, p. 198.—[On "Col. Wilford," who is the cause of all those Hindostanic stupidities still current among English hagiographers, conf. Klaproth; in the Journal Asiat., Paris, xxv. p. 13, note; and Vans Kennedy, Hindu Mythology, London, 1831; Appendix A, pp. 406-22.] Champollion, Gram., p. 180.—Osburn, Testimony, pp. 137-41, 155.—Mignot, op. cit, p. 148, seq.—Quatremère (op. cit., pp. 258-69, 411-24, 497-510,) dispenses with more than reference to Kitto, ii. pp. 521-4.—Raoul-Rochette, Archéologie comparée, i. pp. 190-2. 373-4.—De Saulcy, Dead Sea, i. pp. 27-9. 55-6.

618 KaP*h*T*t*oRIM. Bochart, pp. 329-33.—Volney, iv. p. 229.—Quatremère, loc. cit.

619 T*s*IDoN. Bochart, p. 342.—Homer, Il. xxiii. 743; Odys., xv. 425.—Justin, lxviii. 3.—De Saulcy, Dead Sea, i. 52, 57-9.—Quatremère, on Mover's "Phönizier," op. cit., p. 503.—Gliddon, Otia, p. 136.—Eadie, Early Or. Hist., pp. 425-6.—Layard, Babylon, p. 627.

620 K*h*eT*t*. Bochart, p. 344-8, for this and the following names.—Lanci, Paralipomeni, i. pp. 13, 144.—Munk, Palestine, p. 78.—Birch, Archæologia, xxxv. 1853.—Layard, Babylon, pp. 142, 354, 633.

621 IBUSI. Osburn, Testimony, pp. 37-43, 123-5, 154.—Champollion, Lettres, pp. 76-7.—De Saulcy, Inscriptions de Van, p. 26.

622 AMoRI. On "Nephilim," cf. the Paralipomeni.—Talmud, apud Rabbi Ben-Ouziel; Cahen, iv. p. 107, note.—Gliddon, Otia, p. 137.—Rosellini, Mon. Stor., iii. part 1, pp. 368-70; iv. pp. 94, 237-9.—Birch, Gallery, part i. p. 86.—Hincks, Hierog. Alph., p. 13; pl. i. fig. 17.—Osburn, Test., 65, 128-9, 154.—Birch, Stat. Tab. Kar., pp. 20-3.—De Saulcy, Dead Sea, i. p. 347.

623 GiRGaSI. Munk, Palestine, pp. 69, 79.

624 K*h*UI. Hieronymus, Epist. ad Dardanum, 129.—Kitto, Cyclop., voce "Hivite."—Vico, Scienza Nuova, transl. Paris, 1844, p. 288.

625 A*â*RKI. Vaux, Nineveh, pp. 459, 468, 478.—Gliddon, Otia, pp. 137-8.—Anthon, Class. Dict., pp. 1049-53.

626 SINI. Otia, p. 130.—Munk, p. 78.—Osburn's error of "Sinim" for SIN-KAR (Test., p. 158, No. 30), was corrected by Birch, Stat. Tab. Kar., p. 37.

627 ARUaDI. Osburn, pp. 52, 58, 69, 80, 118, 156.—Vaux, Nineveh, pp. 459, 468, 478.—Layard, Babylon, p. 627.

628 T*s*iMRI. Otia, p. 137.—Bochart, p. 347.

629 K*h*aMaT*t*I. Rawlinson, in Vaux, p. 462, seq.—De Saulcy, Rev. Archéol., 1850, pp. 767-8.—Layard, Babylon, p. 627.—Osburn, pp. 98, 101, 142, 155.—"Vico, et ses Œuvres," Introd., p. 1.

630 A*â*ILaM. Ainsworth, Assyria, &c., pp. 108, 196-216.—Rawlinson, March from Zohàb to Khusistàn, 1836; R. Geog. Soc., ix. p. 47.—Dubeux, Perse, pp. 1, 9, 13, 31.—Frazer, Mesopotamia, p. 22.—Polybius, v. 44.—Strabo, xvi. p. 744.—Layard, Khuzistàn; R. Geog. Soc., xvi. pp. 61-84.—Tychsen, De Cuneatis Inscrip., 1798, pp. 10, 13.—Ouseley, Travels, 1819, p. 325.—Löwenstern, Rémarques; Rev. Archéol., 1850, pp. 687-723.—De Saulcy, Inscrip. trouvées à Khorsabad; Rev. Archéol., 1850, pp. 767-70.—Layard, Babylon, pp. 212, 353, 628.

631-632 ASUR. De Sola, Genesis, note, p. 41.—De Longpérier, Rev. Archéol., 1850, pp. 429-32.—Rich's Narrative of a Journey to Nineveh; London, 1839; Introd., note, p. xvii.—The Friend of Moses, New York, 1852; pp. 181, 185, 200, 215-6, 220.—Rawlinson, Commentary, pp. 26-7.—Birch, in Layard's Nineveh and its Remains, ii., p. 340, note.—Layard, Babylon, pp. 212, 530, 629.

633 ARP*h*a-KaSD. Kitto, Cyclop., i. p. 229; but see ii, p. 398.—Volney, iv. pp. 249-50.—Lenormant, Cours, p. 203.—Bochart, p. 83.—Michaelis, Spicileg. Geog. Heb., ii., p. 75.—Dubois, Caucase, iii. pp. 421, 434, 488; iv. p. 342-3.—St. Martin, Mémoires, i. p. 205.—Ritter, Asien, vii. p. 320, seq.—Ainsworth, Assyria, pp. 152-156; and "An Evening at Diarbekir," Ainsworth's Mag., 1843, iv. pp. 221-6.—Loftus, in Rev. Archéol., 1850, p. 126.—Layard, Babylon, p. 628.

634 LUD. Herod., i. 7; vii. 74.—Grote,

No. (of Notes, &c.)

Greece, i. pp. 127–30, 206, 320, 462, 618. — Raoul-Rochette, Archéologie Comparée, i. pp. 38, 206–227, 271–277, 284.—Champollion, Dict., p. 80.—Prisse, Salle des Ancêtres de Thotmes III., pp. 11–12. — Osburn, Test., pp. 27, 30, 44. — Tacitus, Annal. ii. 60, 4. — Birch, Annals of Thotmes III., pp. 158–60.

635 ARaM. Quatremère, Jour. des Sav., 1846, pp. 503–4. — Bochart, pp. 83–5.—Volney, iv. pp. 246–8. — Munk, Palestine, p. 435.—Champollion, Gram., pp. 500–1.—De Rougé, on Statue of Out'ahorsoun, Rev. Archéol., 7me Année, p. 15. — Judas, in op. cit., 1847, p. 622. — Layard, Babylon, p. 628.

636 ǎUTs. De Wette, ii. pp. 554–70.—Bochart, pp. 90, 91. — Forster, "Sinaic Inscriptions," 1851, pp. 12–68; compared with Kircher, Œdipus Ægyptiacus, Amsterdam, 1652; ii. pp. 103–13.—Hunt, Himyaric Inscriptions, 1848; pp. 46.—Fresnel, Recherches, p. 23. — See also the "Asmonean," New York, 1852, March and April.

637 KhUL. Bochart, pp. 91–2. — Grotius, Annot., lib. i. de V. R. C.

638 GeTteR. Bochart, pp. 92–3.—Pauthier, Liv. Sac. de l'Orient. p. 465; and Kasimirski's "Koran," xxv. 40, 41.—Lane, Selections, p. 12–15. — Volney, iv. pp. 235, 249.—Pliny, iv. 36.—Solinus, c. 23.

639 MaSh. De Wette, ii. pp. 253–316.—Bochart, pp. 93–4. Forster, Geog., i. p. 284–5.

640 SaLaKh. Bochart, pp. 100–4.

641 ěiBeR. Gliddon, Chapters, pp. 18, 19.—Lane, Modern Egyptians, Pref.—Gesenius, in De Wette, i. pp. 433–4.—Munk, Palestine, p. 102. — Lenormant, Cours, p. 203.—Fresnel, "Lettre à M. Mohl," Jour. Asiat., 1845, pp. 63–65.

642 PeLeG. "Hebrew Language;" see Gesenius, in De Wette, i. p. 459; and Bunsen, Eg. Pl., i. p. 270.—Athenæum Français, No. 1; Juillet, 1852, p. 7. — Lenormant, Cours, p. 214.

643 IoKTaN. Bochart, 109–12. — Fresnel, Arabes avant l'Islamisme, 1836, 1838.—Jomard, Arabie, in Mengin, iii. pp. 330, 346, 389–91. Forster, Geog., i. pp. 77–107.

644 ALMUDaD. Bochart, p. 112. — Volney, iv. p. 252. — Forster, i. pp. 107–11.

645 SeLePh. Same references.

646 KhaTsRaMUTt. Add to the above, — Plate, Province of Hadramaut, Syro-Eg. Soc., 1845, pp. 112–23; and Jomard, op. cit., p. 349.

647 IeRaKh. Bochart, 124–7. — Forster, i. p. 115, 137–43. — Fresnel, 4me Lettre, "Djeddah, Jan. 1838."

648 HaDURaM. Bochart, pp. 128–30.—Sale's Introd. to Koran, Liv. Sac. d'Or., pp. 465–8.—Pococke, Specimen Hist. Arabum. p. 41. —Volney, iv. p. 252.

649 AUZaL. Bochart, p. 130–4. — Rosenmüller, Bibl. Geog., iii. p. 171. — Lane, Selections, p. 3. — Volney, iv. p. 253. — Forster, i. p. 145–7.

650 DiKLeH. Bochart, pp. 134–9.—Forster, i. pp. 147–8.

651 ǎUBaL. References as above.

652 ABIMAL. Idem.

653 SeBA. Bochart, pp. 146–56.—Forster, i. pp. 154–7.

654 AUPhiR. Munk, Palestine, p. 294. — Volney, iv. pp. 255–76. — Bochart, pp. 156–61. — Michaelis, Quæstiones, No. 39. — Forster, i. pp. 165–71.

655 KhUILaH. } Same authorities.
656 IUBaB. }

---

657 Prichard, Researches, iii. p. 348.

658 Die Deutschen und die Nachbarstamme; Ibid.

659 Strauss, Vie de Jesus; Littré's transl., Paris, 1839; i. pp. 434, 436–7.

660 Oxlee, Letters to Archbishop of Cant., 2d series, London, 1845, p. 37.

661 Hennell, Origin of Christ., p. 299.

662 Vide Fresnel (Arabes avant l'Islamisme, 1836, p. 61), for a marvellous effort in Arabic by the Shèykh Abbas-el-Yamanèetee.

663 So read De Sola, Lindenthal, and Raphall, Genesis, p. 44.

664 Birch, Stat. Tabl. of Karnac, pp. 36–7. — Gliddon, Otia, p. 75.

665 Layard, Babylon, pp. 496, 506, 529, 543.

666 Lacour, Æloïm, i. pp. 115, 129, 144–6.

667 De Sola's Bible, Genesis, p. 44.

668 Josephus, Antiq. Jud., lib. x. 11, 7

669, 670 N. B. These numbers are inadvertently omitted.

671 Cahen, Genèse, i. p. 188.

672 Ethnological Journal, London, 1848, pp. 197–226.

673 Introd. to the Canon. Scrip. of the Old Test.; Parker's transl., Boston, 1843; ii. pp. 78–82.

674 Account of the worship of Priapus, at Isermia, Naples; London, 1786.

675 Stromata, v. § 42.

676 Apuleius, Metamorph.; apud R. P. Knight, Symbolical Language of Anc. Art, &c.; Soc. of Dilettanti, 1835.

677 Humboldt, Cosmos, III., pp. 122–6.

678 See remains of Orpheus, Hesiod, Aristophanes, Damascius, &c., in Cory's Ancient Fragments, pp. 291–300; and Gliddon, Otia, pp. 55–6, on "Ereb."

679 Civilisation Primitive, 1845, p. 45—"Quia non supplices humi Mutino procumbimus atque Tutuno, ad interitum res lapsas, atque ipsum dicitis mundum leges suas et constituta mutasse?" (Arnobius, lib. iv. p. 133.)

680 Sama Veda, Kena-Oupanishad; Pauthier, Liv. Sac., Introd. p. 18.

681 Academical Lectures, Boston, 1840; ii. pp. 18–30.

682 Cahen, Genèse, i. p. 5, note. — Munk, Palestine, pp. 423, 445.

683 Peri-Archon, lib. iv. c. 2; Huet, Origeniana, p. 167.

684 Homil. vii. in Levit. — Franck, Kabbale, p. 166.

685 Strom., iii. 42; Righellini, Franc-Maçonnérie, i. p. 33.

686 Recognit., x. 30; Ibid., Mosaïsme et Christianisme, iii. p. 499.

687 Ibid., i. p. 29.

688 De Gen. contr. Manichéos, i. 1; Ibid., Maçonnérie, i. p. 33.

689 Epist. ad Helvet., iii.; Lenormant, Cours, p. 122.

690 Cf. Mosheim, i. p. 186.

No. (of Notes, &c.)

691 Hist. of Egypt, p. 574.
692 Hist. de l'École d'Alexandrie, ii. p. 69, seq.; and Biot, Astronomie Ancienne, p. 87, seq.
693 Chron. der Ægypter, i. pp. 125–48.—De Rougé, Rev. Archéol., 1853. pp. 671–86.
694 Cosmas-Ægyptius, Alexandrinus, Indicopleustes, wrote under Justinian, about 535, A. D. His "Topographia Christiana" was printed from MSS. by Montfaucon, in the "Collectio Nova Patrum et Scriptorum Græcorum;" Paris, 1706; fol., Tom. II.—Montfaucon's Latin version, pp. 190–1; Pl. ii. fig. 2.
695 Præfatio in Cosmæ, p. 4: with extracts from St. Augustine, Lactantius, Chrysostom, Severianus, "Beda; multique alii, quos recensere supervacaneum esset."
696, 697, and 698 Franck, Kabbale, pp. 102, 136–7.
699 Montfaucon's translation.
700 Cahen, xv. p. 172.—Noyes's Job, pp. 71, 194, note 18.
701 Harwood, German Anti-Supernaturalism, London, 1841.

No. (of Notes, &c.)

702 Mankind in Europe during the XIIIth century.
703 Lanci, La Sagra Scrittura Illustrata; Roma, 1827; cap. ix. 5; xi. 7.—Ibid., Paralipomeni all'illustrazione della Sagra Scrittura; Parigi, 1845; "Aleph-tau," parts ii. iii. and viii.

P. S. 1st Feb., 1854. To-day's mail has brought me the first number (Jan. 1,) of a "New Series" of the *Ethnological Journal*, edited by Luke Burke, Esq. (John Chapman, publisher, London). I have only space to express my hearty satisfaction at the re-appearance of this much-needed vehicle for free and manly thought; and to state that my colleagues, Dr. J. C. Nott, Dr. Henry S. Patterson, and the Hon. E. Geo. Squier, while vouching with myself for the great erudition, clear intellect, and high moral worth of its editor, have no hesitation in recommending it as an exponent of, as well as an admirable medium for, the most advanced views in Ethnology.—G. R. G.

APPENDIX II.

ALPHABETICAL LIST OF SUBSCRIBERS TO TYPES OF MANKIND.

E. S. Adrich, M. D., San Francisco, Cala.
Prof. Louis Agassiz, Cambridge, Mass.
John G. Aikin, Esq., Mobile, Ala.
J. H. Alexander, Esq., Baltimore, Md.
Thomas S. Alexander, Esq., "
Chilton Allan, Esq., Lexington, Ky.
Mrs. S. G. Allan, Richmond, Va.
Hon. Philip Allen, Providence, R. I.
Philip Allen, Jr., Esq., "
S. Austin Allibone, Esq., Philadelphia, Pa.
Col. J. S. Allison, Lexington, Ky.
S. Ames, M. D., Montgomery, Ala.
Thomas C. Amory, Jr., Esq., Boston, Mass.
C. G. Anderson, Esq., New Orleans, La.
L. H. Anderson, M. D., Mobile, Ala.
S. H. Anderson, M. D., Sumterville, Ala.
Alfred A. Andrews, Esq., Boston, Mass.
C. G. Andrews, Esq., New Orleans, La.
Rich'd Angell, M. D., Huntsville, Ala.
Hon. H. B. Anthony, Providence, R. I.
Nathan Appleton, Esq., Boston, Mass.
Samuel Appleton, Esq., " (2 copies.)
Rob't B. Armistead, Esq., Mobile, Ala.
Capt. Jos. J. Armstrong, "
Hon. Samuel G. Arnold, Providence, R. I.
Richard D. Arnold, M. D., Savannah, Ga.
J. H. Ashbridge, Esq., New Orleans, La.
Athenæum Library, Philadelphia, Pa.
Washington L. Atlee, M. D. "
W. P. Aubrey, Esq., Mobile, Ala.
C. Auzé, Esq., himself and friends, Mobile, Ala. (22.)

Franklin Bache, M. D., Philadelphia, Pa.
G. Bailey, Esq., Charleston, S. C.
Munro Banister, M. D., Richmond, Va.
Geo. C. Barber, Esq., Philadelphia, Pa.
Milton Barlow, Esq., Lexington, Ky.
Edward Barnett, Esq., New Orleans, La.
Henry Barnewall, Esq., Mobile, Ala.
Godfrey Barnsley, Esq., New Orleans, La., (2 copies.)
Dr. Barry, U. S. N., Washington, D. C.
Hon. J. R. Bartlett, Providence, R. I.
E. H. Barton, M. D., New Orleans, La.
Judge Bates, San Francisco, Cala.
Hon. James A. Bayard, Wilmington, Del.
R. Bean, M. D., New Orleans, La.
C. Beard, M. D., "
E. Begouen, Esq., Mobile, Ala.
Isaac Bell, Esq., "
N. B. Benedict, M. D., New Orleans, La.
Henry C. Berrie, M. D., Philadelphia, Pa.
Thos. F. Betton, M. D., Germantown, Pa.
J. G. Bibby, Esq., New Orleans, La.
Clement C. Biddle, Esq., Philadelphia, Pa.
Henry J. Bigelow, M. D., Boston, Mass.
Samuel Birch, Esq., British Museum, London.
James Birney, Esq., Mobile, Ala.
Geo. S. Blanchard, Esq., for Merc. Lib., Boston, Mass.
Col. W. W. S. Bliss, U. S. A., New Orleans, La.
G. W. Blunt, Esq., New York.
Henry S. Boardman, Esq., Philadelphia, Pa.
Geo. Boldin, Esq., "
S. M. Bond, Esq., Savannah, Ga.
James Bordley, M. D., Baltimore, Md.
Henry I. Bowditch, M. D., Boston, Mass.
W. B. Bowman, Esq., Mansfield, O.
M. Boullemet, Bookseller, Mobile, Ala., (10 copies.)
Thos. J. Bouve, Esq., Boston, Mass.
Burwell Boykin, Esq., Mobile, Ala.
E. M. Boykin, M. D., Camden, S. C.
J. F. Boynton, Esq., Syracuse, N. Y.
A. P. Bradbury, Esq., Bangor, Me.
Charles F. Bradford, Esq., Roxbury, Mass.
Dr. Brierly, San Francisco, Cala.
M. Bright, Jr., Esq., Mobile, Ala.
Geo. Brinley, Esq., Hartford, Conn.
Jno. M. Broomal, Jr., Esq., Chester, Pa.
A. Brother, Esq., New Orleans, La.
Geo. L. Brown, Esq., Mobile, Ala.
N. H. Brown, Esq. "
Jno. Brown, Esq., "
Peter A. Browne, Esq., Philadelphia, Pa.
Jos. Bryan, Esq., Savannah, Ga.
George S. Bryant, M. D., Aberdeen, Mi.
G. S. Bryant, Newbern, Ala.
Jos. Brummel, Esq., Richmond, Va.
Sam. D. Buck, Bookseller, Hopkinsville, Ky., (10 cop.)
Thos. C. Buckley, Esq., N. Y.
W. Gaston Bullock, Esq., Savannah, Ga.
Capt. Owen Burns, Wilmington, N. C.
M. Burton, Esq., Richmond, Va.
W. M. Burwell, Esq., Lynchburg, Va.
Dr. Geo. Bush, New York.
W. A. Butters, Esq., Richmond, Va.
H. L. Byrd, M. D., Savannah, Ga.

D. J. Cain, M. D., Charleston, S. C.
James Campbell, Esq., Mobile, Ala.
Edwin Canter, M. D., New Orleans, La.
Geo. W. Carpenter, Esq., Germantown, Pa.
Jesse Carter, M. D., Mobile, Ala.
A. H. Cenas, M. D., New Orleans, La.
Paul Chaudron, Esq., Mobile, Ala., (15 copies.)
Chas. M. Cheves, Esq., Charleston, S. C.

Langdon Cheves, Jr., Esq., Charleston, S. C.
Julian J. Chisolm, M. D., "
Samuel Choppin, M. D., New Orleans, La.
N. T. Christian, Esq., Georgetown, Ga.
Rev. Dr. J. D. Choules, Newport, R. I.
Jno. C. Claiborne, Esq., New Orleans, La.
A. Clapp, M. D., New Albany, Ia.
W. R. Clapp, Esq., Philadelphia, Pa., (2 copies.)
Jas. M. Clark, Esq., Providence, R. I.
Major M. Lewis Clark, St. Louis, Mo., (2 copies.)
C. Cleaveland, Esq., Yazoo City, Miss.
J. Breckenridge Clemens, M. D., Easton, Pa.
G. B. B. Clitherall, Esq., Mobile, Ala.
Stephen Colwell, Esq., Philadelphia, Pa.
Col. M. I. Cohen, Baltimore, Md.
Octavus Cohen, Esq., Savannah, Ga.
Henry A. Coit, Esq., New York.
A. Comstock, Esq., "
A. Comstock, M. D., Philadelphia, Pa.
Timothy Conrad, Esq., "
Miss Anna S. Coolidge, Boston, Mass.
W. C. Cooper, Esq., Savannah, Ga.
—— Corbet, Esq., Brit. Legation, Washington, D. C.
W. W. Corcoran, Esq., Washington, D. C.
Chas. S. Coxe, Esq., Philadelphia, Pa.
Jno. C. Cresson, Esq., "
John Crickard, Esq., New Orleans, La.
Charles P. Curtis, Esq., Boston, Mass., (2 copies).
Thos. B. Curtis, Esq., "
Hermann Curtius, Esq., New Orleans, La.
Theod. Cuyler, Esq., Philadelphia, Pa.

Mrs. R. P. Dana, New York.
W. H. Dandridge, Esq., Gainesville, Ala.
Hon. John M. Daniel, Richmond, Va.
W. C. Daniell, M. D., Savannah, Ga.
John Darrington, Esq., Mobile, Ala.
Isaac Davenport, Esq., Richmond, Va.
Chas. Davis, Esq., New York.
Jos Barnard Davis, F. S. A., Shelton, England.
Major Geo. Deas, U. S. A., Mobile, Ala.
Henry Deas, Esq., "
W. C. Deas, Esq., "
Zach. Deas, Esq., "
G. P. Delaplaine, Esq., Madison, Wis.
A. B. Deloach, M. D., Livingston, Ala.
John Devereux, Esq., Raleigh, N. C.
Joseph Devilin, Esq., Mobile, Ala.
Rev. Henry M. Dexter, Boston, Mass.
Thos. Dexter, Esq., Mobile, Ala., (4 copies.)
Chas D. Dickey, Esq., "
Prof. S. Henry Dickson, Charleston, S. C.
L. Poulson Dobson, Esq., Philadelphia, Pa.
Geo. W. Dorr, Esq., New York.
Jas. Augustus Dorr, Esq., "
Geo. Douglass, Esq., Goshen Hill, S. C.
Sam'l R. Dubbs, Esq., Philadelphia, Pa.
B. F. Duncan, Esq., Jackson, Ala.
W. B. Duncan, Esq., New York.
Hon. James Dunlop, Pittburg, Pa.
E. Durand, Esq., Philadelphia, Pa.

A. M. Eastman, Esq., New York.
Chas. J. M. Eaton, Esq., Baltimore, Md.
Geo. N. Eaton, Esq., "
Jno. H. Ecky, Esq., Philadelphia, Pa.
Dr. Ege, San Francisco, Cala.
Jno. A. Elkinton, M.D., Philadelphia, Pa.
Albert T. Elliott, Esq., Providence, R. I.
W. N. Ellis, P. M., Lippican, Mass.
David F. Emery, Esq., West Newbury, Mass.
Moses H. Emery, Esq., Philadelphia, Pa.
Robert D. England, M. D., Mobile, Ala.
T. C. English, Esq., Mobile, Ala.
Richard Esterbrook, Esq., New Orleans, La., (2 cop.)
F. A. Eustis, Esq., Milton, Conn.
Alexander Everett, Esq., Mobile, Ala.
C. C. Everett, Esq., Brunswick, Me.
Hon. E. Everett, for Lib. State Dep., Washington.
Hon. Edward Everett, Boston, Mass.

John Fagan, Esq., Philadelphia, Pa.
Prof. J. E. Farman, Georgetown, Ky.
C. C. S. Farrar, Esq., New Orleans, La.
J. Farrell, M. D., "
Daniel Fearing, Esq., New York.
E. D. Fenner, M. D., New Orleans, La.
Chas. W. Fisher, Esq., Philadelphia, Pa.
Redwood Fisher, Esq., "
Dr. Fonerden, for Md. Hospital, Baltimore, Md.
E. G. Forshey, Esq., New Orleans, La.
Geo. Fort, M. D., Milledgeville, Ga.
B. W. Fosdick, Esq., Savannah, Ga.
Wm. B. Fosdick, Esq., Boston, Mass.
Hillary Foster, Esq., Mobile, Ala.
W. Parker Foulke, Esq., Philadelphia, Pa.
Prof. Jno. F. Frazer, "
J. B. Futch, Esq., New Orleans, La.

Charles Ganahl, M. D., Savannah, Ga.
P. C. Gaillard, M. D., Charleston, S. C.
A. Gaines, M. D., Mobile, Ala.
E. B. Gardette, M. D., Philadelphia, Pa.
James Gardiner, Esq., San Francisco, Cala.
John L. Gardiner, Esq., Boston, Mass.
J. R. Gardner, Esq., New Orleans, La.
L. M. Gaylord, M. D., Sodus, N. Y.
David Geiger, M. D., Charleston, S. C.
R. W. Gibbes, M. D., Columbia, S. C.
Mrs. M. A. E. Gibson, Richmond, Va.
Jno. Gibson, Esq., Mobile, Ala.
David Gilbert, M. D., Philadelphia, Pa.
Hon. Henry D. Gilpin, " (2 copies.)
Thomas Gilpin, Esq. "
F. E. Gordon, Esq., Mobile, Ala.
Theo. Gordon, Esq., "
W. M. Guilford, M. D., Lebanon, Pa.
Wm. Graddy, Esq., Georgetown, Ga.
Calvin Graddy, Esq., "
Edmund A. Grattan, Esq., H. B. M. Cons., Boston.
Jno. Gravely, Esq., Charleston, S. C.
Hon. John C. Gray, Boston, Mass.
Charles Green, Esq., Savannah, Ga.
A. J. Green, M. D., Columbia, S. C.
J. Green, M. D., Washington, D. C.
J. Green, Esq., for Merc. Lib. Co., Baltimore, Md.
D. S. Greenough, Esq., Boston, Mass.
W. W. Greenough, Esq., "
John Grigg, Esq., Philadelphia, Pa.
James Grignon, Esq., H. B. M. Cons., Portland, Me.
Edmund Grundy, Esq., Philadelphia, Pa.

John Haig, Esq., Mobile, Ala.
R. K. Haight, Esq., New York, (5 copies.)
Jno. S. Haines, Esq., Germantown, Pa.
C. S. Hale, Esq., Burlington, N. J.
Rev. A. O. Halsey, Richborough, Pa.
John Halsey, Esq., New York, (5 copies.)
Hon. J. H. Hammond, Charleston, S. C.
M. C. M. Hammond, Esq., "
P. T. Hammond, Lancaster, S. C.

C. F. Hampton, Esq., Columbia, S. C.
W. Hampton, Esq., "
W. Hampton, Jr., Esq., "
Geo. S. Harding, Esq., Savannah, Ga.
General Jos. Harlan, Philadelphia, Pa.
S. N. Harris, M. D., Savannah, Ga.
Jas. B. Harrison, Esq., Georgetown, Ga.
Samuel T. Harrison, Esq., Washington, D. C.
Thos. Willis Hartley, Esq., Philadelphia, Pa.
John Hastings, M. D., San Francisco, Cala.
Judge Hastings, "
Elias S. Hawley, Esq., Buffalo, N. Y.
W. G. Hay, Esq., Philadelphia, Pa.
Geo. Hayward, M. D., Boston, Mass.
E. H. Hazard, Esq., Providence, R. I.
Isaac P. Hazard, Esq, "
Thos. R. Hazard, Esq., "
Rev. G. W. Heacock, Buffalo, N. Y.
Dr. G. C. Hebbe, Washington, D. C.
Alfred Hennen, Esq., New Orleans, La.
Geo. M. Heroman, Bookseller, Baton Rouge, La. (4)
W. C. Henzey, Esq., Philadelphia, Pa.
T. Higham, Jr., Esq., S. C.
C. W. Hill, M. D., Mobile, Ala.
Geo. S. Hilliard, Esq., Boston, Mass.
W. L. Hodge, Esq., for Lib. Trs. Dep., Washington.
W. B. Hodgson, Esq., Savannah; Ga.
Judge Ogden Hoffman, San Francisco, Cala.
J. E. Holbrook, M. D., Charleston, S. C.
Geo. Holly, Esq., Mobile, Ala.
Prof. Francis S. Holmes, Charleston, S. C.
O. W. Holmes, M. D., Boston, Mass.
Thos. F. Hoppin, Esq., Providence, R. I., (2 copies.)
Daniel Horlbeck, Esq., Charleston, S. C.
Henry Horlbeck, Esq., "
Mrs. Lavinia E. A. Howard, Daphne, Mobile Bay, Ala.
Rev. Geo. Howe, D. D., Columbia, S. C.
Dudley Hubbard, Esq., Mobile, Ala.
Benj. F. Huddy, Esq., Philadelphia, Pa.
J. A. Huger, Esq. Charleston, S. C.
R. W. Hughes, Esq. Richmond, Va.
Thos. Hunt, M. D., New Orleans, La.
A. J. Huntington, Esq., "
Albert Hurd, Esq., Galesburg, Ill.
Henry J. Hyams, Esq., New Orleans, La.

Col. Irving, San Francisco, Cala.

Sam'l Jackson, M. D., Philadelphia, Pa.
Henry Jacobs, Esq., Providence, R. I.
Robert James, Esq., Mobile, Ala.
N. R. Jennings, Esq., New Orleans, La.
W. E. Jennings, Esq., Mobile, Ala.
Dr. J. C. Jennings, Bonn, Prussia.
Jas. P. Jervey, M. D., Charleston, S. C.
Gen. Thos. S. Jesup, U. S. A., Washington, D. C.
Gov. David Johnson, Limestone Springs, S. C.
W. E. Johnson, Esq., Camden, S. C.
T. A. Johnston, Esq., Livingston, Ala.
R. F. Johnstone, Esq., Detroit, Mich.
Allen C. Jones, Esq., Mobile, Ala., (2 copies.)
Edw'd E. Jones, Esq., Philadelphia, Pa.
James Jones, Esq., "
James Jones, M. D., New Orleans, La.
W. Cary Jones, Esq., San Francisco, Cala.
Wm. Jones, M. D., Mobile, Ala.
Wm. Jones, Jr., Esq., "
Messrs. Jordan & Bro., Philadelphia, Pa.
W. J. Joynes, Esq., Petersburg, Va.

Hon. J. P. Kennedy, for Lib. Navy Dep., Washington.
Hon. John P. Kennedy, Baltimore, Md.
James Kennedy, M. D., New York.
L. C. Kennedy, Esq., Charleston, S. C.
P. M. Kent, Esq., New Albany, Ind.
Edward M. Kern, Esq., Philadelphia, Pa.
Geo. Kern, Esq., "
Jno. Kern, Jr., Esq., "
Richard H. Kern, Esq., "
Elisha W. Keyes, Esq., Madison, Wis.
E. H. Kimbark, M. D., New York.
A. C. Kingsland, Esq., "
Robert L. Kirk, Esq., Mobile, Ala.
S. D. Kirk, Esq., Charleston, S. C.
James Kitchen, M. D., Philadelphia, Pa.
Jno. Kitchenmann, Esq., "
W. H. Klapp, M. D., "
Sam'l Kneeland, M. D., for Boston Soc. Nat. Hist.
S. Kneeland, Jr., M. D., Boston, Mass.
E. G. Knight & Co., Booksellers, Cleveland, O., (10 c.)
G. Kursheedt, Esq., New Orleans, La.

John De Lacey, M. D., Philadelphia, Pa.
John Lambert, Esq., "
I. A. Lapham, Esq., Milwaukie, Wis.
Prof. C. W. Lane, Milledgeville, Ga.
W. Langermann, Esq., San Francisco, Cala.
Henry Laurence, Esq., Yazoo City, Miss.
Hon. Abbott Lawrence, Boston, Mass.
James Lawrence, Esq., "
Wm. Beach Lawrence, Esq., Newport, R. I.
Jno. Laurence, Esq., Mt. Upton, Chenango Co., N. Y.
Edw'd Lawton, M. D., Boonville, Mo.
D. Leadbetter, Esq., Mobile, Ala.
Vr. Lecesne, Esq., "
Robert Lebby, M. D., Charleston, S. C.
Joseph Leidy, M. D., Philadelphia, Pa.
Col. Opt. H. Leja, Mobile, Ala.
J. C. Levy, Esq., Savannah, Ga.
S. Yates Levy, Esq., Savannah, Ga.
K. H. Lewis, Esq., Tarboro, N. C.
Levi Lewis, Spread Eagle, Pa.
Mifflin Lewis, Esq., Spread Eagle, Pa.
Richard H. Lewis, Esq., Mobile, Ala.
Saunders Lewis, Esq., Philadelphia, Pa.
Winslow Lewis, M. D. Boston, Mass.
Library of South Carolina College, Columbia, S. C.
Library Company of Easton, Pa.
Library of Young Men's Association, Buffalo, N. Y.
Jacob Little, Esq., New York.
Jack Littlejohn, Esq., Spartanburg, S. C.
Wm. Littlejohn, Esq., "
Chas. A. Locke, Esq., Boston, Mass.
J. L. Locke, Esq., Savannah, Ga.
Rev. S. K. Lothrop, D. D., Boston, Mass.
Robert Lovett, Jr., Esq., Philadelphia, Pa.
Andrew Low, Esq., Savannah, Ga.
Henry A. Lowe, Esq., Mobile, Ala., (2 copies.)
Francis C. Lowell, Esq., Boston, Mass., (5 copies.)
John A. Lowell, Esq., "
E. H. Ludlow, Esq., New York.
R. M. Lusher, Esq., New Orleans, La.

Rev. Geo. Macaulay, Milledgeville, Ga.
Wm. Mackay, Esq., Savannah, Ga.
Charles Magarge, Esq., Germantown, Pa.
Jas. Magee, Esq. New Orleans, La,
C. T. Mann, Esq., Yazoo City, Miss.
Peter Marcy, Esq., Mobile, Ala.
James B. Markham, Esq., Mobile, Ala.
J. H. Markland, Esq., Philadelphia, Pa.

Francis Markoe, Esq., Washington, D. C.
B. F. Marshall, Esq., Mobile, Ala.
Chas. H. Marshall, Esq., New York.
E. Mason, M. D., Wetumka, Ala.
C. H. Mastin, M. D., Mobile, Ala.
H. B. Mattison, Esq., Washington, D. C.
Joseph Mauran, M. D., Providence, R. I.
B. Mayer, Esq., for Md. Hist. Soc., Baltimore, Md.
W. E. Mayhew, Esq., Baltimore, Md.
Hon. Theo. H. McCaleb, New Orleans, La.
Jas. McClean, Esq., Philadelphia, Pa.
J. H. B. McClellan, M. D., "
Thos. McConnell, Esq., Mobile, Ala.
J. H. McCulloh, Esq., Baltimore, Md.
E. H. McDonald, Esq., Philadelphia, Pa.
T. F. McDow, M. D., Liberty Hill, S. C.
Wm. McGuigan, Esq., Philadelphia, Pa.
Messrs. McKee & Robertson, Hagerstown, Md.
P. B. McKelvey, M. D., New Orleans, La.
Andrew McLaughlin, Esq., Baltimore, Md.
Mrs. McPherson, Baltimore, Md.
M. Megonegal, Esq., Philadelphia, Pa., (2 copies.)
Charles D. Meigs, M. D., Philadelphia, Pa.
J. Aitken Meigs, M. D., "
J. Forsyth Meigs, M. D., "
Thos. Mellon, Esq., "
N. L. Merriweather, Esq., Montgomery, Ala., (5 cop.)
M. H. Messchert, Esq., Philadelphia, Pa.
John G. Michener, Esq., "
Francis T. Miles, M. D., Charleston, S. C.
Clark Mills, Esq., Washington, D. C.
Charles Millspaugh, M. D., Richmond, Va.
J. F. G. Mittag, Esq., Lancaster, S. C.
E. J. Mollet, Esq., New York,
James Moncreif, Esq., New York.
Cyrus C. Moore, M. D., Philadelphia, Pa.
Comm. E. W. Moore, Texan N., Washington, D. C.
S. Mordecai, Esq., Richmond, Va.
James W. Morgan, Esq., Lynchburg, Va.
Israel Morris, Esq., Philadelphia, Pa.
Jacob G. Morris, Esq., "
John S. Morris, Esq., Phœnixville, Pa.
T. H. Morris, Esq., Baltimore, Md.
B. M. Moss, M. D., New Orleans, La.
E. L. Moss, Esq., Philadelphia, Pa.
Valentine Mott, M. D., New York.
James Moultrie, M. D., Charleston, S. C.
John Munro, Esq., San Francisco, Cala.
Wm. M. Murray, Esq., Charleston, S. C.
G. A. Myers, Richmond, Va.

M. H. Nace, Esq., Richmond, Va.
T. C. Newbold, Esq., Philadelphia, Pa.
Thos. A. Newhall, Esq., Germantown, Pa.
H. Newman, Esq., Boston, Mass.
J. B. Newman, Esq., Washington, D. C.
Jos. Newton, Esq., Philadelphia, Pa.
New York Society Library, N. Y.
W. M. Nicholls, Esq., Chesterville, S. C.
B. M. Norman, Bookseller, New Orleans, La., (25 cop.)
Gustavus A. Nott, M. D., New Orleans, La.
James Nott, M. D. San Francisco, Cala.
Jno. R. Nunemacher, Esq., New Albany, Ind. (2 cop.)

Rob't W. Ogden, Esq., New Orleans, La.
J. W. Osgood, Esq., Saxonville, Mass.
J. W. Orr, Esq., New York, (5 copies.)
Rev. S. Oswald, York, Pa.

Edward Padelford, Esq., Savannah, Ga.
B. R. Palmer, M. D., Pittsburg, Pa.
John S. Palmer, M. D., Charleston, S. C.
Alexander Pantoleon, A. M. Smyrna, Turkey.
Comm. F. A. Parker, U. S. N., Philadelphia, Pa.
Henry T. Parker, Esq., Boston, Mass.
Capt. James Parker, Mobile, Ala.
Socrates Parker, Esq., Livingston, Ala,
S. Parkman, M. D., Boston, Mass.
Henry S. Patterson, M. D., Philadelphia, Pa.
Morris Patterson, Esq., "
Joseph Patterson, Esq., " (5 copies.)
Louis L. Pauly, Esq., "
Abraham Payne, Esq., Providence, R. I.
W. I. Peale, Esq., Philadelphia, Pa.
Miss Mary Pearsall, "
Davis Pearson, Esq., "
John Penington, Esq. "
Amos Pennebaker, M. D., "
J. A. Pennypacker, M. D., "
Granville J. Penn, Esq., Penn Castle, England.
I. Pennington, Esq., Baltimore, Md., (2 copies.)
Mrs. C. W. Pennock, Philadelphia, Pa.
J. W. Perard, Jr., Esq., New York.
Chas. T. Percival, M. D., Mobile, Ala.
O. H. Perry, Esq., for Vig. Lib. Assoc., Baltimore, Md.
Rob't E. Peterson, Esq., Philadelphia, Pa.
Jesse E. Peyton, Esq., "
Philadelphia Library Company, Philadelphia, Pa.
Jona. Phillips, Esq., Boston, Mass.
John Phillips, M. D., Bristol, Pa.
Hon. P. Phillips, Mobile, Ala.
Charles Pickering, M. D., Boston, Mass.
J. C. Pickett, Esq., Washington, D. C.
E. B. Pierson, M. D., Salem, Mass.
Henry L. Pierson, Esq., New York.
Hon. Albert Pike, Little Rock, Arkansas.
Wm. M. Pippen, Esq., Tarboro, N. C.
J. N. Platt, Esq., New York.
George Poe, Esq., Washington, D. C.
J. G. Poindexter, Esq., New Orleans, La.
Prof. F. A. Porcher, Charleston, S. C.
George Porteus, Esq., Mobile, Ala.
John Potts, Esq., Chihuahua, Mexico.
I. Pratt, M. D., Philadelphia, Pa.
Wm. Pratt, Esq., Baltimore, Md.
Wm. H. Pratt, Esq., Mobile, Ala.
J. H. Prentice, Esq., New York.
J. S. Preston, Columbia, S. C.
H. C. Price, Esq., Chester, Pa.
Isaac Pugh, Esq., Philadelphia, Pa.
Jno. M. Pugh, M. D., West Philadelphia, Pa.
G. P. Putnam & Co., Publishers, New York, (10 cop.)

B. Howard Rand, M. D., Philadelphia, Pa.
Jno. Randall, Esq., New York.
R. C. Randolph, M. D., Greensboro, Ala.
Edmund Ravenal, M. D., Charleston, S. C.
Edward Rawle, Esq., New Orleans, La.
Daniel T. Rea, Esq., Mobile, Ala.
J. B. Read, Esq., Savannah, Ga.
Wm. Reed, Esq., New Orleans, La.
J. J. Reese, M. D., Philadelphia, Pa.
John R. Reid, Esq., New Orleans, La.
D. Elliott Reynolds, M. D., New Orleans, La.
Col. James Rice, San Francisco, Cala.
W. Bordman Richards, Esq., Boston, Mass.
W. W. Richards, Esq., Philadelphia, Pa.
Maurice Richardson, Esq., Great Valley, Pa.
J. L. Riddell, M. D., New Orleans, La.
Mrs. G. W. Riggs, Baltimore, Md.
J. H. Riley & Co., Booksellers, Columbus, O., (5 cop.)
Thomas Ritchie, Esq., Washington, D. C.

Col. George Rivers, Providence, R. I
J. A. Roberts, Greensville, Pa.
W. Lea Roberts, Esq., New York.
F. M. Robertson, M. D., Charleston, S. C
John Blount Robertson, Esq., New Orleans, La.
Col. W. S. Rockwell, Milledgeville, Ga.
Prof. Henry D. Rogers, Boston, Mass.
Chas. H. Rogers, Valley Forge, Pa.
Hon. Molton J. Rogers, Philadelphia, Pa.
Jno. S. Rohrer, M. D., "
O. A. Roorback, Bookseller, New York, (16 copies.)
Wm. Ropes, Esq., Boston, Mass.
A. H. Rosenheim, Esq., Philadelphia, Pa.
James S. Rowe, Esq., Bangor, Me.
Samuel Ruffin, Esq., Mobile, Ala.
E. H. Rugbee, Esq., Providence, R. I.
James Rush, M. D., Philadelphia, Pa.
Mrs. Rush, "
John Russell, Bookseller, Charleston, S. C., (3 copies.)
Charles Ryan, Esq., Philadelphia, Pa.
Rev. Dr. Ryerson, Toronto, Canada, (2 copies.)

B. J. Sage, Esq., New Orleans, La.
Richard G. Sager, Esq., Mobile, Ala.
Hon. James Savage, Boston, Mass.
W. H. De Saussure, Charleston, S. C.
J. P. Scriven, M. D., Savannah, Ga.
Chas. Scott, Esq., Philadelphia, Pa.
John Scoville, Esq., Salisbury, Conn.
E. M. Seabrook, Esq., Charleston, S. C.
Hon. Benjamin Seaver, Boston, Mass.
P. T. Seibel, M. D., Savannah, Ga.
S. E. Sewall, Esq., Boston, Mass.
George C. Shattuck, Esq., Boston, Mass., (2 copies.)
Lemuel Shattuck, Esq., "
Quincy A. Shaw, Esq., "
Robert G. Shaw, Esq., " (2 copies.)
R. O. Shaw, M. D., Mobile, Ala.
W. W. Shearer, Esq., Livingston, Ala.
—— Shepherd, Esq., Cairo, Egypt.
John H. Sherard, Esq., Livingston, Ala.
W. Sherman, Esq., New York.
Nath. B. Shurtleff, M. D., Boston, Mass.
Origen Sibley, Esq., Mobile, Ala.
Hon. Chas. Sitgreaves, New Jersey.
H. N. Skinner, Esq., New York.
J. R. Slack & Co., Booksellers, Steubenville, O., (3 c.)
Jno. Sloan, M. D., New Albany, Ind.
A. A. Smets, Esq., Savannah, Ga.
F. Gurney Smith, Jr., M. D., Philadelphia, Pa.
Howard Smith, M. D., New Orleans, La.
Jacob Smith, Esq., Georgetown, Ga.
J. Broom Smith, Esq., San Francisco, Cala.
Jno. Jay Smith, Esq., Germantown Pa.
Joseph P. Smith, Esq., Philadelphia, Pa.
J. E. J. Smith, Esq., Georgetown, Ga.
John T. Smith, Esq., Livingston, Ala.
Samuel Smith, Esq., New York.
J. A. Spencer, Esq., Philadelphia, Pa.
Truman & Spofford, Booksellers, Cincinnati, O., (5 c.)
Hon. E. Geo. Squier, New York.
Wm. H. Squire, M. D., Germantown, Pa.
W. E. Stacke, Esq., New Orleans, La.
W. H. Stark, Esq., Mobile, Ala.
Albert Stein, Esq., Mobile, Ala.
Jacob Steiner, Esq., Philadelphia, Pa.
J. P. Steiner, Esq., "
Claudius C. Stewart, Esq., Florida.
Wm. Stevenson, Esq., Baltimore, Md.
D. D. Stewart, M. D., "
F. Stewart, Esq., Mobile, Ala.

Scott Stewart, M. D., Philadelphia, Pa.
Wm. Stewart, Esq., Hagerstown, Md., (2 copies.)
John Stoddard, Esq., Savannah, Ga.
Prof. I. M. Stone, Hanover, Ind.
Warren Stone, M. D., New Orleans, La.
Lt. Isaac G. Strain, U. S. N., Philadelphia, Pa.
Wm. Strickland, Bookseller, Mobile, Ala., (10 copies.)
Col. C. B. Strode, San Francisco, Cala., (10 copies.)
Hon. A. H. H. Stuart, for Lib. Dep. Int., Washington.
Albert Sumner, Esq., Newport, R. I.
Hon. Charles Sumner, Washington, D. C.
Chas. G. Swartz, Esq., Philadelphia, Pa.
Jos. Swift, Esq., "
Samuel Swett, Esq., Boston, Mass.
Mrs. T. A. Swett, "

T. A. Tankusley, Esq., Mobile, Ala.
Benjamin Tanner, Esq., Baltimore, Md.
Rev. S. K. Talmage, LL. D., Milledgeville, Ga.
Henry W. Taylor, Esq., Mobile, Ala.
Wm. Taylor, Esq., Richmond, Va.
J. K. Tefft, Esq., Savannah, Ga.
J. S. Teft, Bookseller, Houston, Texas, (10 copies.)
Carlisle Terry, M. D., Georgetown, Ga.
Charles L. Tew, Esq., New Orleans, La.
Richard H. Thomas, M. D., Baltimore, Md.
Edwin Thompson, Esq., Philadelphia, Pa.
John Thorne, Esq., Baltimore, Md.
Col. James J. Thornton, Mobile, Ala.
B. C. Ticknor, Esq., Mansfield, O.
Osmond Tiffany, Esq., Baltimore, Md.
Howard Tilden, Esq., Philadelphia, Pa.
J. Tisdale, Esq., Boston, Mass.
Dr. Toland, San Francisco, Cala.
Gen. Joseph Totten, U. S. A., Washington, D. C.
Henry Toulmin, Esq., Mobile, Ala.
Morton Toulmin, Esq., "
Elisha Townsend, Esq., Philadelphia, Pa.
Robert Trueman, Esq., Boston, Mass.
David H. Tucker, M. D., Richmond, Va.
J. W. Tucker, Esq., Spartanburg, S. C.
Wm. E. Tucker, Esq., Philadelphia, Pa.
Fred'k Tudor, Esq., Boston, Mass.
Alexander Turnbull, Esq., Baltimore, Md.
T. I. Turner, M. D., U. S. N., Philadelphia, Pa.
Prof. M. Tuomey, Tuscaloosa, Ala.
J. W. Tuthill, Esq., New Orleans, La.
J. A. Tyler, Esq., Boston, Mass.

J. E. Uhlhorn, Esq., New Orleans, La.

Aaron Vail, Esq., New York.
Jacob B. Vandever, Esq., Wilmington, Del.
Col. Henry Vaughan, Yazoo City, Mi.
W. S. Vaux, Esq., Philadelphia, Pa.
A. L. Vegus, Mobile, Ala.
Henry Vollmer, Esq., Philadelphia, Pa.

Henry Wadsworth, M. D., Philadelphia, Pa.
George H. Walker, Esq., New Orleans, La.
Isaac R. Walker, M. D., Spread Eagle, Pa.
Rev. J. B. Walker, Mansfield, O.
J. J. Walker, Esq., Philadelphia, Pa.
S. J. Walker, Esq., Mobile, Ala.
James P. Walker, Esq., Lowell, Mass.
John N. Walthall, Esq., Mobile, Ala.
J. J. V. Wanroy, Esq., "
J. C. Warren, M. D., Boston, Mass.
J. Mason Warren, M. D., "
Jas. S. Waters, Esq., Baltimore, Md.

Col. John G. Watmough, Germantown, Pa.
Thomas H. Webb, M. D., Providence, R. I.
Nicholas Weeks, Esq., Mobile, Ala.
A. J. Wedderburn, M. D., New Orleans, La.
Plowden C. J. Weston, Esq., Hagley, S. C.
T. M. Wetherill, Esq., Laurel Hill, La.
Wm. Wetherill, M. D., Philadelphia, Pa.
W. West, Esq., Philadelphia, Pa.
Chas. M. Wheatley, Esq., Phœnixville, Pa., (4 copies.)
Wm. Augustus White, Esq., N. York.
Benjamin A. White, M. D., Milledgeville, Ga.
Eli White, Esq., New York.
Hon. W. H. Witte, Philadelphia, Pa., (2 copies.)
Rev. R. S. Whitehall, New Orleans, La.
E. D. Whitehead, Esq., Havanna, Green Co., Ala.
W. C. Wilde, Esq., New Orleans, La.
Capt. Charles Wilkes, U. S. N., Washington, D. C
John Williams, Esq., Lancaster, S. C.
W. C. Williams, M. D., Philadelphia, Pa.
Hon. W. Thorne Williams, Savannah, Ga.
W. Williamson, M. D., Philadelphia, Pa.
A. P. Willis, Esq., New Orleans, La.
Chas. Wilson, Esq., Savannah, Ga.
T. McK. Wilson, Esq., Cannonsburg, Pa.
Rev. W. D. Wilson, D. D., Geneva, N. Y.
Hubbard Winslow, Esq., Boston, Mass.
John Wiltbank, M. D., Philadelphia, Pa.
Philip Winfree, Jr., Esq., New Orleans, La.
James W. Winter, Esq., New York.
C. J. Wister, Esq., Germantown, Pa.
James H. Witherspoon, Esq., Lancaster, S. C.
Thomas R. Wolfe, Esq., New Orleans, La.
Wm. B. Wolfe, Esq., Philadelphia, Pa.
A. Wolle, Esq., Bethlehem, Pa.
F. Wolgamuth, Esq., Philadelphia, Pa.
Messrs. Wood & Conner, Carlisle, Pa.
A. T. Wood, Esq., New Orleans, La.
George B. Wood, M. D., Philadelphia, Pa.
Rev. W. D. Wood, D. D., Geneva, N. Y.
Mrs. Woodbury, New York.
H. A. Wright, Esq., Madison, Wis.
Wm. Wright, M. D., Philadelphia, Pa.
Jacob Wyand, Esq., Philadelphia, Pa.
Wm. W. Wyatt, Esq., "
Messrs. Wylie, Mobley & Strait, Lancaster, S. C.
Samuel G. Wyman, Esq., Baltimore, Md.
Thomas K. Wynne, Esq., Richmond, Va.

Gregory Yale, Esq., San Francisco, Cala.
Jno. C. Yeager, Esq., Philadelphia, Pa.
Philip Yeiser, M. D., New Orleans, La.
Harry M. Young, Baltimore, Md.
J. A. Young, Esq., Camden, S. C.
John B. Young, Esq., Richmond, Va.

ADDITIONAL NAMES,

RECEIVED SINCE THE ABOVE LIST WAS MADE OUT.

G. W. Ball, Esq., Philadelphia, Pa.
A. Billings, Esq., Nashville, Tenn.
Beriah Brown, Esq., Madison, Wis.
Wm. H. Van Buren, M. D., New York.
Stacy B. Collins, Esq., "
John Le Conte, Esq., Philadelphia, Pa.
Jno. Le Conte, Jr., Esq., "
T. J. Crowen, Bookseller, New York, (2 copies.)
Gov. Nelson Dewey, Lancaster, Wis.
John Evans, Esq., West Haverford, Pa.
W. Wayne Evans, Esq., Paoli, Pa.
Felix B. Gaudet, Esq., Philadelphia, Pa.
A. T. Gray, Esq., Madison, Wis.
Prof. S. S. Haldeman, Columbia, Pa.
Charles H. Hall, Esq., Philadelphia, Pa.
E. H. Janssen, Esq., Madison, Wis.
Jno. McBride, M. D., Philadelphia, Pa.
B. Meyer, Esq., Baltimore, Md.
Joshua Moss, Esq., Birmingham, England, (2 copies.)
J. West Nevins, Esq., Philadelphia, Pa.
Jo. S. Pender, Esq., Tarboro, N. C.
Library of Pennsylvania Hospital, Philadelphia, Pa.
D. T. Pratt, Esq., Philadelphia, Pa.

THE END.